SOCIAL PSYCHOLOGY

third edition

SOCIAL PSYCHOLOGY

third edition

David Myers, Jackie Abell and Fabio Sani

Social Psychology, Third Edition
David Myers, Jackie Abell, Fabio Sani
ISBN-13 9781526847928
ISBN-10 1526847922

Published by McGraw Hill
338 Euston Road
London
NW1 3BH
Telephone: +44 (0) 203 429 3400
Website: www.mheducation.co.uk

British Library Cataloguing in Publication Data
A catalogue record for this book is available from the British Library

Library of Congress Cataloguing in Publication Data
The Library of Congress data for this book has been applied for from the Library of Congress

Portfolio Managers: Rosie Churchill and Isabel Berwick
Production Manager, EMEA: Ben King
Content Developer: Maggie du Randt

Typeset by SPi Global
Cover design by Adam Renvoize
Text design by Kamae Design

First edition published in 2010, and second edition published in 2014, by McGraw-Hill Education

ISBN-13 9781526847928
ISBN-10 1526847922
eISBN-13 9781526847935

Printed in Great Britain by Bell and Bain Ltd, Glasgow

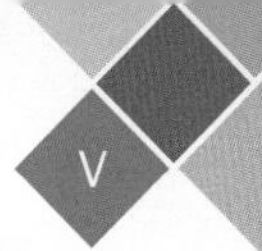

Brief Table of Contents

Detailed Table of Contents

Preface

Welcome to the third edition of our *Social Psychology,* European Edition textbook. We are excited to bring you a freshly revised and updated version of this key social psychology textbook.

To give a little background: Our first edition of this book was published in 2010. It was born out of the successful US edition of the Myers *Social Psychology* textbook. That book covers many of social psychology's key topics which appear in the European editions. The US version has many strengths. It is scientific in its coverage, compares and contrasts classic and contemporary social psychological theories, and yet manages to balance this with a writing style that is warm, humorous, and perhaps most importantly of all for students, is accessible. We have endeavoured to carry these strengths through to the European editions. The US version though, is targeted for a predominantly North American audience. Consequently this influences the tone, content and examples used in the book. The impact a researcher's own cultural background has on what they research and how they write about it is something we discuss in the European editions. Therefore, a textbook that covered social psychological topics, theories and real-world examples relevant to a primarily European and non-North American audience was deemed necessary. Hence, we published our initial European version of this Myers textbook in 2010. The second European edition was produced in 2014. It built upon the firm foundations laid down by the first edition (and the US textbook), but updated aspects of the structure and content in accordance with reviewers' feedback and current research. In particular, it strove to maintain pace with social psychological responses to an ever-changing social world, and presented in a style that students would feel facilitated their learning.

In the space of just a few years, our social world has changed considerably. Topics such as climate change, environmental sustainability, knife crime, terrorism, cyberbullying, and changing perceptions of sex and gender, to name just a few, have come to dominate the news headlines, politics and conversations. Furthermore, students' needs and expectations adapt in line with social change. The challenge for us as social psychologists is to evolve our discipline accordingly so that it remains relevant and contributes to the well-being of us all. And that includes our textbooks!

For this third edition we have implemented valuable reviewer feedback to create a social psychology textbook that is factually rigorous, yet an accessible, up-to-date and a compelling read. We have included real-world examples and in doing so we hope we have illustrated the relevance of social psychology to our everyday lives – including yours! There are up-to-date references to international research throughout to provide a global overview of the discipline. We have also sought to ensure the book covers key topics, theories and ideas that are reflected in undergraduate social psychology teaching curriculums. Details on specific changes to the pedagogy and content of this third edition, are described below.

Organization and Hallmark Features

The third edition has undergone a number of changes, following reviewer feedback. Particular attention has been paid to:

- Updating references to incorporate recent research into each chapter.
- Expanding the book's critical content. Critiques to social psychological theories, concepts and research and the assumptions upon which they rest, are presented. Critical questions have been updated and elaborated upon to invite students to critically evaluate the material presented.
- Key terms have been updated where necessary.
- Americanisms, including language, research and examples, which are unfamiliar and/or inappropriate for non-US readers have been removed and/or replaced with examples from within Europe and also more globally, to reach out to a more international readership.

- The book has increased its coverage of real-world examples which we hope are familiar to our readers. In doing so we seek to further illustrate the relevance of social psychology to contemporary daily life.
- Chapter 14: Biology, Culture and Gender has been revised in terms of focus, content and structure. 'Biology' has replaced the previous term 'Genes' (used in editions 1 and 2) in the title of this chapter to reflect the broader biological influence within social psychology. The focus of this chapter is to transcend the classic nature vs nurture debate in accounting for human behaviour, to discuss how biology and culture interact with each other to shape our lives. Classic and contemporary research on sex and gender is presented and discussed to illustrate the forces of biology and culture. Coverage of evolutionary psychology has been expanded throughout the book, but is particularly prevalent in this chapter to illustrate recent work in the area, and challenge hard boundaries between biological determinism and socialization.
- Chapter 15: Applied Social Psychology, has been reintroduced back into the textbook. This chapter appeared in the first edition, but was removed and placed on the website for the second edition. The chapter has since been revised and thoroughly updated with examples of applied social psychology in the areas of work, health and the environment. Social psychological interest and research has developed rapidly in these three areas in response to current-day concerns (such as workplace stress, mental health, environmental degradation and disasters), and we felt it was important to present this work as an integral part of the discipline.
- In the second edition of this book, we noted an emerging debate known as 'the replication crisis' in social psychology. This coverage has been expanded in the third edition to reflect the continuing debate, consider its implications for social psychology, and present recent attempts to overcome this crisis.
- This textbook has three authors. It also has reviewers and an editorial team who input material. Consequently trying to write with one voice can prove difficult! Each of us have our own writing style. In this third edition we have tried to ensure the book represents a more consistent single narrative voice, which guides students through the content. Links across chapters have also been made more explicit to assist with narrative coherence and consistency.

Research Close-Up: This feature has been altered slightly from the second edition. It still follows the layout of published journal articles but presents the material in a more accessible manner. The style of writing, length and detail are stripped back to take students to the main point of the work more easily. We have updated and/or replaced some of the cases to reflect important work on the chapter's topic. We have also added a Critical Reflections section to the end of each Research Close-Up. The purpose of this is to stimulate critical thinking about the research presented. What are its strengths and weaknesses? How might it have been improved?

Focus On: These remain a popular feature of this textbook and have been retained for this third edition. They have been updated in line with changes in the field, but have also been generally refreshed. The questions posed at the end of each Focus On have been revised, with new questions added to encourage further critical engagement with the topic.

Recommended Reading: This feature has also been retained for the third edition, and is divided into 'Classic' and 'Contemporary' readings so that pertinent developments in the subject over the years can easily be seen. Some of the recommended readings have been replaced with more current work, and additions have been made to the reading lists where it was felt this would be useful for students.

Critical Questions: These have been updated from the previous editions to prompt deeper, critical reflection on the issues raised.

Summing Up: The Summing Up sections have been carried through to this third edition, and appear at the end of each chapter. They have been revised in line with new content, to ensure accurate summarizing of each chapter's content. The summary remains broken up by section heading, making it easy to go back to sections that need reading through again.

Updates to the Third Edition

CHAPTER 1: INTRODUCING SOCIAL PSYCHOLOGY

- This chapter continues to offer the reader a historical background to the discipline we now call social psychology. We have added a little more in this chapter on some key figures, such as Immanuel Kant, to contextualize some of our key concepts and ways of thinking in social psychology further.
- The replication crisis in the discipline has gained further momentum since the second edition of this book. Therefore we have extended our coverage of this, both in this chapter and in Chapter 2. This incorporates more recent work on the replication crisis and debates on its impact on social psychology.
- References and research have been updated to showcase some of the most important and influential classic and contemporary work that shape the vision of social psychology, and improved the narrative.

CHAPTER 2: RESEARCH METHODS IN SOCIAL PSYCHOLOGY

- This chapter has been revised to extend our existing coverage on the replication crisis and include wider debates about the use of research methods in social psychology.
- References and research have been updated to expose some of the most recent social psychological work, and to highlight the diverse array of research methods we use.

CHAPTER 3: THE SELF

- This chapter has been updated to include more recent research on the self, throughout. We have also added more visuals and references to popular culture to aid with understanding the importance and relevance of social psychological work on the self to our everyday lives.
- As our social world changes with the growth of social media, social psychological research on the impact this has upon our sense of self also develops. In this chapter, we reflect this growth, noting some of the latest and diverse social psychological studies into the self.
- The chapter has been restructured to assist with narrative flow but the key areas outlined in the previous editions remain here (such as self-concept, self-esteem and impression management).

CHAPTER 4: SOCIAL BELIEFS AND JUDGEMENTS

- This chapter has been updated to reflect current and important cutting-edge research into social cognition as well as retaining classic theories and concepts.
- The critique of some classic theories and concepts (such as the self-fulfilling prophecy) has been expanded to show the progression in critical thinking in social psychology with new ways of looking at our modern technological world.
- We have extended the use of visuals to facilitate learning and understanding.
- The area of social neuroscience remains an important component of this chapter and we have refreshed this with current examples.
- We have included more applied examples to illustrate the real-world application of this area of social psychology, and have done so especially where the field becomes quite technical and challenging. This has been done to demonstrate the importance of this work and also assist with understanding the research carried out.
- The influence social media has upon our social beliefs and judgements has impacted more heavily on social psychology since the second edition of this book. Hence, we have offered more explanation and examples of research that focuses on this.
- Throughout the chapter, references and research have been updated in line with the changing face of social cognition work.

CHAPTER 5: ATTITUDES AND BEHAVIOUR

- We have updated this chapter to provide greater depth of some of the topics we covered in the previous editions of this book. We have also tried to ensure research and examples are more relevant to our reader.
- Studies into attitudes and behaviour have progressed since the second edition of this book. As such we have expanded critiques of classic studies such as that carried out by La Piere, and also more recent work such as implicit association tests.
- In this book we have also included social psychological research that focuses on the genetics of attitudes, which was previously absent from previous editions.
- We have also made clearer how our attitudes are subject to social influences with reference to recent work in the area.
- New Research Close-Up: Assessing Public Attitudes and Behaviour to Household Waste in Cameroon.

CHAPTER 6: PERSUASION

- This chapter remains strong in terms of its coverage, but it has been updated to include more recent research in the area and more visual content.

CHAPTER 7: CONFORMITY AND OBEDIENCE

- This chapter continues to offer comprehensive coverage of classic and contemporary social psychological research into conformity and obedience. Classic studies have been revisited in the context of new critiques. We have updated the contemporary research to give a flavour of current directions in this field, with particular emphasis on studies that consider the role social media plays in facilitating conformity and obedience.

CHAPTER 8: AGGRESSION

- This chapter has consistently provided an excellent review of social psychological work on aggression. We have added to this review with more material that examines the link between aggression and different forms of social media (e.g. video games) and evolutionary perspectives on aggression.
- We have also explored current work on techniques such as mindfulness, which seek to relieve aggression through self-awareness and control.
- New Research Close-Up: Can Self-Control and Mindfulness Help to Reduce Aggression?

CHAPTER 9: ATTRACTION AND INTIMACY

- Significant changes have been made to this chapter in terms of content and structure. This parallels shifts in research into attraction and intimacy that has become increasingly diverse and nuanced. How we define relationships and ourselves within them is fluid. This has brought challenges and opportunities for social psychologists working in this area.
- Research into a diverse range of relationships has been added to this chapter, including polyamory, being single, and cultural differences in what we understand a relationship to be.
- Evolutionary work on attraction and intimacy has been expanded to facilitate dialogue and debate into love, attraction and relationships.
- Coverage of the impact the Internet has on attraction and intimacy has been further developed, along with social psychological work with LGBT communities.
- In this chapter we explore a critique of social psychology which notes the continuing focus and prevalence of research into heterosexual relationships, and the implications this has for different kinds of relationships.

CHAPTER 10: HELPING

- Examples of real-world events crises and disasters which have prompted courageous acts of help, have been updated to reflect events familiar to the reader.
- Where appropriate, some American examples of helping behaviour have been replaced with instances from other countries to resonate better with our readers.
- The chapter now includes more diverse forms that helping behaviour can take, such as group-based helping and help substitution.

CHAPTER 11: SMALL GROUP PROCESSES

- This chapter now contains more examples of small group processes which will be familiar to non-American students.
- We have included more coverage on leadership and minority influence, and have linked this to Chapter 15 where the social psychology of the workplace is explored.
- Social psychological research into the occurrence and relevance of small group processes to online environments (such as MMPORGs, Internet chatrooms and virtual self-help groups) has been further elaborated upon.
- New Research Close-Up: The Frustrating Experience of Free-riders in Group Work.

CHAPTER 12: SOCIAL CATEGORIZATION AND SOCIAL IDENTITY

- We have included a new, large section on Social Identity and Health, which explores the ways in which the two topics are connected and influence each other.
- Expanded Social Identity and Help subsection, with a cross link to Chapter 10.
- New Research Close-Up: Laughing: The Influence of the Ingroup.

CHAPTER 13: PREJUDICE, INTERGROUP RELATIONS AND CONFLICT

- This chapter has been revised, with the topic of prejudice coming first, followed by intergroup conflict and then intergroup harmony. This has been done to create a more logical flow to the chapter, making it easier to understand prejudicial behaviours and conflicts and the methods that can be used to combat these. This has also facilitated more discussion of individual prejudice before moving on to a discussion of group prejudice.
- The Social Identity Theory and Self-Categorization Theory section in 'Understanding Prejudice' has been expanded to include 'basking in reflected glory' and 'cutting off reflected failure'.
- New coverage of the linguistic intergroup bias.
- New section on 'dual identities', covering the idea that minority group members may hold superordinate and subordinate identities.
- New Focus On: Is Prejudice All in our Heads?

CHAPTER 14: BIOLOGY, CULTURE AND GENDER

- This chapter has received a major overhaul in response to feedback regarding its coverage and structure. This is reflected in the new title, Biology, Culture and Gender, as we consider a broader range of biological and cultural explanations for behaviour.
- The emphasis on gender remains popular with students and reviewers, so this has been retained for the new edition. We adopt a biological and cultural lens to explore social psychological research into gender.

The aim is to transcend the nature vs nurture argument, and instead show how biology, culture and our social context are integrated in their impact on our understandings of sex and gender.

- Evolutionary explanations for behaviour and gender have received considerable expansion. Critiques of this approach have also been developed as we examine evolutionary paradoxes such as homosexuality and voluntary childlessness.
- New Research Close-Up: Don't Stand So Close to Me? The Influence of Sex and Gender on Interpersonal Distance.

We hope that you enjoy this third edition of our *Social Psychology* textbook, and that it proves to be a useful aid to your learning about social psychology and fuels your passion for the field. This book reflects real life, so it will at times make you smile and frown, and possibly even a little sad, depending on the subject matter. Above all, we hope it makes you think about the fascinating relationship we each have with the world around us and each other, and assists in developing a lifelong enthusiasm for social psychology. Any feedback that you may have on the third edition would be very welcome. We always listen in our continued endeavour to ensure this remains a comprehensive and relevant textbook that assists you in your studies. Happy reading!

Jackie Abell and Fabio Sani

About the Authors

Professor David Myers

Professor David Myers is the John Dirk Werkman Professor of Psychology at Hope College where he has taught for the past 30 years. David Myers' love of teaching psychology has been rewarded by students on many occasions with numerous "Outstanding Professor" awards. An award-winning researcher, Professor Myers received the Gordon Allport Prize from Division 9 of the American Psychological Association for his work on group polarization. His scientific articles have appeared in more than two dozen journals, including *Science*, *American Scientist*, *Psychological Bulletin*, and *Psychological Science*. He has served his discipline as consulting editor to the *Journal of Experimental Social Psychology* and the *Journal of Personality and Social Psychology*.

Dr. Jackie Abell

Dr. Jackie Abell is Associate Professor at the Research Centre for Agroecology, Water and Resilience, based at Coventry University, UK. Her current areas of research interest include the application of social psychology to wildlife conservation and environmental issues to facilitate resilience and sustainable development, place attachment and identity, social cohesion and inclusion. She is a member of the International Union for Conservation of Nature – Conservation Planning Specialist Group, and the African Lion Working Group. Jackie is also a Chartered Psychologist with the British Psychological Society and is currently an Associate Editor for the *British Journal of Social Psychology*, She publishes in a wide range of international scientific journals, spanning the natural, human and social sciences.

Professor Fabio Sani

Professor Fabio Sani holds a Chair in Social and Health Psychology at the University of Dundee. His general research interest concerns the mental and physical health implications of group processes, social identity and sense of belonging. He has been the leader of 'Health in Groups', a cross-national and longitudinal research project on the health implications of group life, funded by the UK-based Economic and Social Research Council. His scientific articles are regularly published in international journals such as *Personality and Social Psychology Bulletin*, *Depression and Anxiety*, *Annals of Behavioral Medicine*, and the *Journal of Experimental Social Psychology*. He has also co-authored *Experimental Design and Statistics for Psychology* (Blackwell, 2006), co-edited *The Development of the Social Self* (Psychology Press, 2004), and edited *Self-Continuity: Individual and Collective Perspectives* (Psychology Press, 2008). He has served his discipline as associate editor to the *European Journal of Social Psychology*.

Acknowledgements

Authors' acknowledgements

As you can imagine, writing a core textbook on a discipline as broad as social psychology, takes a lot of time, and even more patience! As such, we would like to thank colleagues and anonymous reviewers who suggested material and offered advice in revising the chapters, and also family and friends who supported us whilst we worked on the book. We would also like to extend our particular thanks to our editors, Rosie Churchill, Nina O'Reilly, Maggie du Randt, Ben King, and everyone at McGraw Hill for their continued enthusiasm, vision and critical engagement for the third edition of this textbook.

Jackie Abell is especially grateful to James and their young son Joshua, who were very patient with a partner and mummy who seemed tied to the laptop, at times, writing this book!

Fabio Sani is particularly grateful to his colleagues, peers and students in social, health and clinical psychology for stimulating discussions; and would like to extend special thanks to his wife, Lorella, and his son, Leonardo, for their support and patience during the project.

Publisher's acknowledgements

Our special thanks go to Lin Bailey at Southampton Solent University and Emma Vine at Sheffield Hallam University for their contributions to the book.

Our thanks go to the following reviewers for their comments at various stages in the text's development:

Chris Bale, University of Huddersfield
Hilary Tait, Edinburgh Napier University
Jason Tipples, Leeds Beckett University
Kai Jonas, Maastricht University
Steven Ludeke, University of Southern Denmark
Hermann Swart, Stellenbosch University
Gareth Hall, Aberystwyth University
Charlotte Pennington, University of the West of England
Kimberley Hill, University of Northampton

We would also like to thank all the reviewers who commented and advised on the first and second editions.

We would like to thank the following for their contributions to our digital support materials:

Steven Ludeke, University of Southern Denmark
Karlijn Massar, Maastricht University
Charlotte R. Pennington, University of the West of England
Fuschia Sirois, University of Sheffield

We would like to thank the following for permission to reprint images:

Alamy Images
Getty Images
Shutterstock

Every effort has been made to trace and acknowledge ownership of copyright and to clear permission for material reproduced in this book. The publishers will be pleased to make suitable arrangements to clear permission with any copyright holders whom it has not been possible to contact.

Guided Tour

Research close-up

Are Liars Easy to Detect?

Source: Rai, R., Mitchell, P., & Faelling, J. (2012). The illusi
or do people think that lies are easy to detect? *Psychologica*

Introduction

Have you ever felt self-conscious in a job interview? Have
might spot your anxiety or your 'creative' account of your pa

The illusion-of-transparency concept refers to the assumption
transparent to other people than they really are. We attribu
that they can read our thoughts. But does that also mean t
sought evidence for this 'illusion of transparency' from stude
think it would be spotted by the person they told it to? And w

Study 1

Method

Thirty British university students, (age range: 18–25 years
their real memories of four different events, and to make-up
were presented to the students in a standard template (see

Research Close-Up

Research Close-Up boxes introduce you to the format of real research in social psychology. Each box summarizes an important research paper, explaining the methods the authors used, the results they obtained and a discussion to help you think critically about the significance of the study.

Focus on

Are We Witnessing an Epidemic of Narcissism Among

It is fairly common to hear older people complaining about yo
as self-centred, arrogant and disrespectful, and are said to c
This popular view of younger people is echoed by the writin
science spectrum, particularly in North America. Over the las
Western societies in general, and the US in particular, have em
all attentions and preoccupations revolve around the self at the
solidarity and societal concerns. For instance, Putnam (2000)
communities and social networks, and Lane (2000) stressed
replacing appreciation of companionship. Similarly, Frank (199
enhance the self has led to a 'luxury fever', a tendency to con
is forcing people to spend more time at work while neglecting
to be living in an era of self-centredness or, as the sociologist
'culture of narcissism'.

But is this truly the case? Are we really witnessing a fast-gr
and egotism? The social psychologist Jean Twenge and
characterized the current climate as an 'epidemic of narcissism
agrees that cultural and pedagogic trends are largely respons
she blames American parents for wanting to make their childr

Focus On

These boxes focus on opposing viewpoints or controversial topics and research that are related to each chapter. They are supported by questions to help you think critically about the topic and challenge pre-conceptions.

To some extent – as Leary (2004) has n
preoccupations may be a curse, becc
We often find ourselves managing the
for others in our increasingly hectic
mental and physical well-being suffer
practices seek to prune, by quieting th
pleasures and redirecting it. The recent
tradition of '**mindfulness**' perhaps ref
us to stop and take notice of the wor
within it. Reconnecting with our emot
they are impacted upon by the busy w
social anxiety and even depression. S
Krause (2018) suggest that psychologis
to experience and appreciate the b
participants. Having a sense of self al
assess our present, and to plan our fut
our existence more miserable; on the c
control we have on our life.

Mindfulness based on Eastern meditation techniques, this approach focuses attention on experiencing the present moment

In this chapter, we explore all these a
concept is formed and organized, an
strategically present ourselves, pointin
as well as to its adaptive functions.

Key Terms

These are highlighted and defined in the margins. An ideal tool for last-minute revision or to check definitions as you read.

SUMMING UP: THE SELF

SPOTLIGHTS AND ILLUSIONS

- Concerned with the impression we make on others, we te
attention to us than they are (the spotlight effect).
- We also tend to believe that our emotions are more obvious t

SELF-CONCEPT: WHO AM I?

- Our sense of self helps organize our thoughts and actions. Wh
ourselves, we remember it well (the *self-reference effect*). *Sel*
schemas that guide our processing of self-relevant informat
of or dread.
- *Self-esteem* is the overall sense of self-worth we use to apprai
are determined by multiple influences, including the roles we
identities, how we perceive others appraising us, and our exp
- Cultures shape the self, too. Many people in individualistic
self. Others, often in collectivistic cultures, assume a more
explains, these contrasting ideas contribute to cultural differ
- Our self-knowledge is curiously flawed. We often do not kn
influences upon our behaviour are not conspicuous enough

Summing Up

Use this section at the end of the chapter to check your understanding of the core theories and concepts.

Critical Questions

1 How have social psychologists define
2 What implications does the definition
3 Are men more aggressive than wome
4 What are some of the causes social p
5 Under what circumstances do you thi
games, leads to aggressive behaviou
6 Can aggression ever be beneficial for
7 What can we do to reduce aggression

Critical Questions

Each chapter concludes with a set of questions that have been designed to help students critically reflect on the topics and discussions raised in the chapter.

Recommended Reading

Classic Works

Goffman, E. (1959). *The presentation of self in everyday lif*

Higgins, E. T. (1987). Self-discrepancy: A theory relating
319–340.

Lash, C. (1979). *The culture of narcissism: American life in*
& Company.

Contemporary Works

Dufner, M., Rauthmann, J. F., Czarna, A. Z., & Denissen, J.
in on the effect of narcissism on short-term mate appeal.
39, 870–882.

Leach, C. W., & Spears, R. (2008). 'A vengefulness of the
and schadenfreude toward successful out-groups. *Journa*
1383–1396.

Twenge, J. M., & Campbell, W. K. (2013). *The*
of entitlement. Atria.

Recommended Reading

Use the recommended reading section at the end of each chapter as a starting point for further research.

Transform learning with Connect®

Boost grades, stimulate engagement and deliver an amazing course

Connect® is an online platform that integrates the science of learning with award-winning adaptive technology, to offer students and teachers a more effective teaching and learning experience.

Connect increases my students' knowledge and has made my teaching more effective.

University of Birmingham Business School, UK

The Three Pillars of Connect®

Flexible and high quality content tailored to your course

Use a combination of your content with McGraw-Hill and OER resources to customise your course with the support of our dedicated academic and implementation consultants.

Detailed reporting and analytics

Monitor progress and improve efficiency with detailed Connect® reports. Students and teachers can use real-time performance measurement tools to monitor learning and focus on the gaps that require more attention.

Ease of set-up and continuous support

McGraw-Hill offers comprehensive service, support and training - face-to-face, online or over the phone, throughout every phase of working with us to ensure easy set-up and access to the platform.

Bring theory to life **within Connect®**

Students can **test and apply their knowledge** with our engaging excercises and activities within Connect®.

Discover the features on offer for your discipline on the next page!

Connect® for Psychology

We have a wide selection of activities on hand to help students gain valuable practice during their course. By applying what they have learned to real world scenarios, these exercises help test their knowledge and skills in preparation for their next steps in Psychology.

Application-Based Activities (ABAs)

Provide students with valuable practice, using problem solving skills to apply their knowledge to realistic scenarios. Students progress from understanding basic concepts to using their knowledge to analyse complex scenarios and solve problems.

Each activity has been created to align with higher order thinking skills, from Bloom's Taxonomy to ensure students are developing from simple memorisation, to concept application. They are also categorised by difficulty to cater to each student's abilities.

Interactivities

Engage students with content through experiential activities. Students develop critical thinking skills and apply the concepts they have learned in these game like activities.

Videos and Concept Clips

Promote engagement and student understanding, offering content in a fresh format and reinforcing key concepts. They help students break down key themes and difficult concepts in psychology by using easy-to-understand analogies, visual cues, and colorful animation.

Power of Process

Moving students toward advanced critical thinking skills, Power of Process offers a hands-on tool for reviewing and analysing journal articles. Students are able to develop essential academic skills, such as understanding, analysing and synthesizing.

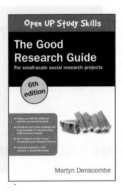

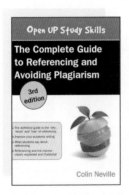

1 INTRODUCING SOCIAL PSYCHOLOGY

What is Social Psychology?

To begin a textbook on social psychology we need first to define what we mean by **social psychology**. So, what is it about?

social psychology the scientific study of how people think about, relate to, and influence one another, either interpersonally or within groups

Social psychology is interested in the way people think about and subjectively experience themselves and their social world, as well as in the way people influence and relate to one another in either interpersonal exchanges or group settings. More specifically, we can say that social psychology deals with both '*within skins*' issues (the 'thinking' and experiential aspect of our social existence, which includes self-concept, perceptions, emotions, motivation, values and attitudes) and '*between skins*' issues (the relational dimension of social life, which includes interaction, communication and mutual influence among individuals and groups). (See **Figure 1.1** for a schematic illustration of what social psychology is about).

Because it is interested in a vast and diverse range of phenomena, social psychology intersects with various other disciplines. Social psychologists share interests in common with sociologists, anthropologists, economists, historians, geographers, philosophers, linguists, neuroscientists and biologists. In addition, social psychological research and theory may have implications for other branches of psychology, including cognitive, organizational, personality, developmental, evolutionary, clinical, health, and biological psychology (see **Figure 1.1**).

The structure of this textbook is based around some of the main areas that social psychologists have studied and researched in order to understand human social behaviour.

Most of us are interested in social behaviour, or at least some aspects of it. You probably wouldn't be studying or reading about social psychology if you weren't interested. However, there are important differences between lay people and social psychologists' way of looking at people's social relationships and behaviour.

Social psychology is
the study of ...

Social thinking	Social influence	Social relations	Groups and identities
• The self • Social beliefs and judgements • Attitudes and behaviours	• Persuasion • Conformity and obedience	• Aggression • Attraction and intimacy • Helping	• Small group processes • Social categorization and social identity • Prejudice, intergroup relations, and conflict

FIGURE 1.1 Social psychology is. . .

You may have a hunch about why someone has behaved in the way they have in a particular set of circumstances, but social psychologists try to investigate *how* and *why* that behaviour has occurred. This requires established methods to collect evidence of the behaviour and systematically analyse it, comparing it to existing research and social psychological theory. Sometimes the conclusions reached by lay people and social psychologists are very different, which can make social psychological discoveries surprising and intriguing. But, of course, there are times when social psychology confirms what we already thought.

As we shall see throughout this textbook, how social psychologists go about studying these aspects of humans' social and cultural life are varied. They don't always agree. Yet, taken together, these studies offer us a comprehensive investigation of human social behaviour and food for thought as we develop our knowledge.

A Brief History of Social Psychology

To begin to understand how these diverse perspectives came to exist in their current form let us briefly explore the history of social psychology and some of its early influences (see **Table 1.1** for a summary).

At a first glance it can appear that social psychology is fairly modern. The first social psychology experiments were reported barely more than a century ago (1898), and the first social psychology texts did not appear until just before and after 1900, in France, Italy, the USA and Germany (Smith, 2005). In the 1930s social psychology took on its current form, and after the Second World War it emerged as the vibrant field it is today.

But an interest in social psychological issues has a much longer history than this.

In the eighteenth century, important contributions to social psychological theorizing were given by both European and North American scholars. For instance, the British philosopher David Hume wrote the *Treatise on Human Nature,* which dealt with passions or strong emotions, sympathy and the relation between self and others (Hume, 1739). He thought sympathy contributed to social conformity and is the basis of our attachment to society. In 1742 he also wrote an essay about the cause and content of national characters, stating that there are differences in frequencies of national traits. This was a forerunner for the classic work, *The Nature of Prejudice,* by the notable American social psychologist Gordon Allport (1954). Another British thinker, the economist Adam Smith, considered the formation of the 'self'. In his book *The Theory of Moral Sentiments* (Smith, 1759), he reasoned that the person we become is largely shaped by interactions with other people. Adam Smith used metaphors like the 'mirror' and the 'looking glass self', which were later adopted by Charles H. Cooley and George Herbert Mead, who made important theoretical contributions to how the self develops (see Chapter 3 for a more detailed description).

Social psychological theorizing was also evident in Germany in the eighteenth century. A recent article by Teymoori and Trappes (2017) for the British Psychological Society's flagship magazine, *The Psychologist,* reviews the influence of German philosopher Immanuel Kant on the discipline. Kant rejected the idea that the human mind merely reflects external reality. Instead he argued

TABLE 1.1 Summary of some prominent figures and their contribution to social psychology

Name	Dates	Country of origin	Examples of their contribution to social psychology
David Hume	1711–76	Scotland	'Of national characters' (1742) influenced later work on prejudice (such as Gordon Allport) that emphasizes trait explanations for behaviour
Adam Smith	1723–90	Scotland	*The Theory of Moral Sentiments* (1759) influenced some modern-day thinking on the self
Immanuel Kant	1724–1804	Germany	Theorizing on the mind influenced the subsequent rise of gestalt psychology
Johann Friedrich Herbart	1776–1841	Germany	Emphasizes the social aspects of the self. These ideas shaped the later development of *Völkerpsychologie* (mass psychology)
Auguste Comte	1798–1857	France	Argues that the methods used in the natural sciences could be used in the social sciences. The principle of positivism subsequently enters social psychology
Wilhelm Wundt	1832–1920	Germany	Develops *Völkerpsychologie.* Advocates the use of laboratories to study human mental processes. Known as the founding father of experimental psychology
Gustave Le Bon	1841–1931	France	*La psychologie des foules* (1895) influenced modern-day psychology of the crowd, intergroup relations and aggression
William James	1842–1910	USA	The founder of American psychology. Produces the book *Principles of Psychology* (1890). Around this time social psychology becomes a discipline in its own right
Emile Durkheim	1858–1917	France	Distinguishes between individual and collective thought. His ideas contributed to theorizing on language, social interactions and 'Social Representations Theory'
George Herbert Mead	1863–1931	USA	Lectures and publications on self and society influenced modern theorizing on language and communication
Edward Alsworth Ross	1866–1951	USA	Produces American textbook *Social Psychology* (1908)
William McDougall	1871–1938	England	Writes textbook *An Introduction to Social Psychology* (1908)
Kurt Lewin	1890–1947	Germany	Gestalt psychologist. His theorizing on prejudice, intergroup relations, leadership and decision making contributes to present-day social psychology
Floyd Allport	1890–1978	USA	Publishes social psychology textbook (1924), emphasizing individual processes in understanding human behaviour
Gordon Allport	1897–1967	USA	Focuses on the role of personality traits to understand social psychological topics such as prejudice

gestalt psychology a German school of psychology advocating a holistic theory of mind and brain, focusing on how these actively structure our perceptions and impressions. It emphasizes that one needs to look at the comprehensive situation to fully understand the human conscious experience, asserting 'the whole is more than the sum of its parts'

that the mind actively constructs external reality, including our perception of time and space. Kant concerned himself with psychological topics such as knowledge, feeling, the self, how people manipulate each other, the inclination for power, and characters of people. However, he maintained that the focus of our investigations should be the 'whole mind', and the way in which the person experiences the world. Even our experience of fundamental dimensions such as time and space is largely shaped by the functioning of the mind. We cannot escape the mind, and as such, we can never truly have an objective view of the world around us. Kant's 'holistic' ideas have heavily influenced modern-day psychology, and are particularly evident in **gestalt psychology**, which emphasizes how the mind constructs reality and perceptually orders the world (see **Figure 1.2** for an example). The social psychologist Kurt Lewin (1930s) took a gestaltic approach to the analysis of social interaction and group behaviour, which implied an examination of the whole situation rather than some isolated elements of it. Lewin's 'action research' tried to understand and tackle prejudice, and foster positive intergroup relations. His research remains influential in social psychology today.

FIGURE 1.2 Two faces or a vase? Gestalt psychologists have used visual illusions such as Rubin's Goblet to illustrate the point that the mind creatively constructs reality.

Johann Friedrich Herbart stressed the inextricable link between individual and society, by contending that the 'human being is nothing outside society'. Many believe that Herbart is the founder of social psychology as his ideas were taken up in Central Europe and later influenced social psychological work in England, the USA and the rest of the world, either directly or indirectly.

Herbart inspired German scholars who first formulated **Völkerpsychologie**, a German word for mass psychology or the psychology of the people, which was established in 1879. *Völkerpsychologie* is typically associated with the work of Wilhelm Wundt, who saw it as concerning 'those mental products which are created by a community of human life and are, therefore, inexplicable in terms merely of individual consciousness since they presuppose the reciprocal action of many' (Wundt, 1916, p. 3). However, Wundt did not dismiss individual mental functions as irrelevant, and advocated the use of laboratories to investigate perception, mental disorders and abnormal behaviour. As a consequence, he is often referred to as the 'father of experimental psychology'.

Völkerpsychologie sometimes called mass psychology, folk psychology or 'the psychology of the people'. It claims that people who belong to the same social group(s) tend to think in the same way, holding collective beliefs, norms and values

positivism an approach to science that claims true knowledge can be achieved only through sense perception and empirical investigation

Topics studied in social psychology today were also analysed by scholars in nineteenth-century France, for instance, by the philosopher Auguste Comte (1798–1857), who is regarded by many as one of the founding fathers of social psychology. He certainly had an influence on the methods social psychologists use to study behaviour. Comte is best known for his claim that social phenomena can be studied by the same methods as those used in natural science, since there are general laws existing in all sciences. The aim of the researchers, according to Comte, is to reveal these laws by 'positivistic' methods (**positivism**). As we shall see, this claim has gained increasing popularity over the years.

Towards the end of the nineteenth century the work of Gustave Le Bon, captured in his book *Psychologie des foules* (*The Crowd*) (Le Bon, 1895), had an enormous impact, and continues to do so in modern social psychology (see Chapter 13). Gordon Allport declared it 'Perhaps the most influential book ever written in social psychology' (Allport, 1954, p. 35). Émile Durkheim was another influential French social scientist in this period making important contributions to social psychology, noting a distinction between individual thought and collective thought. He suggested that collective thought was social ideas and values which exist independently of individuals but at the same time have great influence on individual ways of thinking. Durkheim's work shaped the later theorizing of Serge Moscovici who produced 'social representations theory', a flourishing field in European social psychology in recent years (see Chapter 4), which emphasizes the role of language and shared social understandings of the world in guiding our behaviour.

Johann Friedrich Herbart (1776–1841), thought by many to be the founding father of social psychology.

SOURCE: © Getty Images

Perhaps controversially, Norman Triplett (1898) is often credited with carrying out the first social psychology experiment provoked by his observation that people's behaviour is often facilitated by the presence of other people. He had noticed that cyclists rode their bikes quicker when

The presence of others can facilitate our behaviour. Athletes often produce their 'personal best' performance when competing against others.
SOURCE: © Seb Oliver/Image Source

racing someone else than they did when racing themselves against the clock. To test this he asked girls and boys aged 8–17 to wind in fishing rods. The 'experiment' had two conditions. In one condition the young people competed against one another. In the other condition, they wound in the rods as fast as they could alone, and against the clock. He found that in the first condition the fishing rods were wound up much quicker. So, the presence of others did seem to facilitate some behaviour. Despite disagreements concerning whether it was truly an experiment or not, this study is an important stepping stone in what became social psychology's fascination with laboratory experiments in its quest for facts about human social behaviour. It also became important in social psychology's sought-after status as a 'science'. In Chapter 2 we consider in more detail the principles and practices of experiments in our exploration of the many methods social psychologists use. Throughout this textbook we will examine many laboratory and field experiments and scientific studies of various aspects of human social behaviour.

Wilhelm Wundt (1832–1920), the father of experimental psychology.
SOURCE: © Bettmann/ Getty Images

In the second half of the nineteenth century social psychology was given its name and became a discipline in its own right. Ways of thinking about social relationships had emigrated to the USA and continents outside Europe, including colonies in Africa, Asia and Australia. Social psychology soon became a well-known discipline in many places in the world. Not least in the New World, in the United States of America.

William James is generally regarded as the founder of North American psychology and, in his renowned *Principles of Psychology* (James, 1890), he deals with what he calls the 'social self', meaning 'the recognition [a man] gets from his mates'. He went on to say that '*a man has as many social selves as there are individuals who recognize him* and carry an image of him in their mind' (James, 1890, vol. 1, pp. 293–294, emphasis in original).

William James (1842–1910), the founder of North American psychology.
SOURCE: © Hulton Archive/ Getty Images

George Herbert Mead also became a famous name in (sociological) social psychology, especially his analysis of the self (see Chapter 3). His works were published posthumously in the 1930s but he was formulating his ideas about social psychology at the turn of the nineteenth century. From 1901 he gave an annual course in social psychology at the University of Michigan. His lectures were later published under the title *Mind, Self and Society: From the Standpoint of a Social Behaviourist* (Mead, 1934). Mead was an original thinker combining Darwinism with other scientific issues including communication. This was one of his most important contributions to social psychology.

1908: A Crucial Year?

The year 1908 has been said to be crucial in social psychology since two textbooks with social psychology in the title were published. The two textbooks were both looking more backwards than forwards. In England, William McDougall's (1908) book, *An Introduction to Social Psychology*, was heavily influenced by evolutionary theory and the work of Charles Darwin. McDougall had the idea that instinctive dispositions were part of our evolutionary heritage and that these instincts made human social life possible. **Evolutionary psychology** remains a part of modern-day social psychology. The other book was Edward Alsworth Ross's (1908) *Social Psychology*. Ross was an American sociologist who had originally trained as an economist. Unlike McDougall, Ross did not take Darwinism as his point of departure but focused on the relationship between individuals and their group, discussing topics like social influence, crowds and control. His book was very successful on first publication and the issues presented in it are still relevant in social psychology.

evolutionary psychology a field of study that looks at the role of evolutionary processes and principles of natural selection in shaping cognition and behaviour

These two textbooks managed to put the name 'social psychology' more generally on the map. However, from our journey so far you can see that social psychology did not start in 1908; the phrase 'social psychology' had been used several times before by other scholars and social scientists.

At the time these two textbooks were published, social psychology became established in the USA. Social psychology in the USA became an empirical and even experimental social science. In fact by the 1940s and 1950s, the USA characterized much of social psychology. Large research centres were founded and developed for social psychological research.

However, a social psychology that was dominated by the USA reflected the history and ideological values of individualism which characterized the USA. Floyd Allport had published a famous textbook on social psychology in 1924 that focused more on the individual than on the social or the group. For Allport there was nothing about the group or social relations that couldn't be explained as a function of the individuals concerned.

'There is no psychology of groups which is not essentially and entirely a psychology of individuals.'
Allport (1924)

So, if we quickly summarize, the first 'social psychologists' were scholars engaged in analytical reflection, intellectual and logical thinking. However, from the eighteenth century there began a search for empirical methods to better understand the topic studied: man and social relationships. With the advance of the scientific method in the natural sciences, social psychology departed even further from its philosophical roots and became increasingly concerned with scientific empiricism in its quest for knowledge about human social behaviour. The extent to which this was achieved or desirable was, and still is, debatable. Perhaps, in the words of Bandawe (2010), 'Much of the history of social psychology has been considered intellectual self-interest at the expense of addressing real needs' (p. 34).

The 'Crisis' in Social Psychology

With its increasing emphasis on individual psychology some social psychologists became concerned that social psychology was beginning to lose its 'social' aspect. In the late 1960s and early 1970s, some serious questions were being asked about the direction of the discipline. In particular, there were concerns about over-reliance on experimental methods at the expense of more naturalistic approaches such as observation and interviewing, and about excessive emphasis on individuals *as individuals* rather than as parts of more complex social, historical, cultural and political contexts. Canadian psychologist Cathy Faye (2012) characterizes the 'crisis' in social psychology as a reflection of a lack of confidence in North

America's political and social systems during the 1960s and 70s, as well as the apparent failings of social psychology to engage with those systems and make positive changes.

Dissatisfied social psychologists – some American, but mostly European – came together in meetings and conferences to plan a new direction for a European social psychology. We see the fruits of this movement reflected in the abundance of European journals and conferences today. It emphasizes the study of human behaviour in terms of the individual but also their relationships with others, the social groups they belong to, and the cultural norms and ideological values that form their everyday social world. In other words, to understand human beings, we need different '**levels of explanation**'.

levels of explanation
human behaviour can be understood and interpreted at different levels: the personal, interpersonal, group and ideological

At the time of the crisis, two main figures were prominent in redirecting European social psychology. They were Henri Tajfel and Serge Moscovici. Both were committed to putting the 'social' back into social psychology. Tajfel used experiments to investigate how identity and behaviour are influenced by the social groups to which one belongs, in his social identity theory (see Chapters 12 and 13). Moscovici started with the exploration of the mechanisms that allow minorities to influence majorities, using laboratory experiments as method (see Chapter 11). Subsequently, he emphasized the importance of studying how everyday language shapes 'social representations' – that is, shared understandings of aspects of reality – encouraging the use of an array of non-experimental methods, such as the analysis of interview data and media communications (see Chapter 4). As we shall see, these theories remain influential in modern social psychology, particularly – although not only – in Europe.

It is important to consider that, while promoting a more 'social' and less individualistic social psychology, from a methodological perspective many representatives of this European movement did not object to the use of experimentation. In fact, experiments remained a major methodological approach among these social psychologists, to the extent that the first name of the association that they created was the European Association of *Experimental* Social Psychology. The word 'experimental' has been dropped only recently, following a far from unanimous decision.

Experiments (and other forms of investigations based on the collection of quantitative data) remain the predominant research methodology in North American social psychology, and a very important methodology in Europe and other continents. This may be due to various reasons, but the most important is probably that social psychologists are trained in psychology departments, where experimenting is traditionally considered the most rigorous method for the investigation of mental processes (see Chapter 2 for the specific features of the experimental approach to research). As a consequence, much of this book is based on findings produced by experiments and other quantitative approaches. Having said that, we report studies based on qualitative approaches (see Chapter 2 for a detailed discussion of this methodological perspective) when they have contributed to a better understanding of the phenomena and issues under scrutiny. As neither quantitative nor qualitative approaches offer a perfect method for studying the complexities of human social behaviour, Chapter 2 also considers some of those strengths and weaknesses.

Critical Social Psychology

The 'crisis' drew attention to the role of human values in social psychological research and the context of human social behaviour. These claims have led to the rise of **critical social psychology**. This movement has embraced the influence of **social constructionism** (e.g. Gergen, 1973, 1999), and to some extent includes forms of **discursive psychology**, **phenomenological psychology**, and the promotion of qualitative and non-experimental methods. The Qualitative Methods Section of the British Psychological Society is currently the largest section in terms of membership. Critical social psychology defines a diverse array of social psychologists dedicated to examining the social (and ideological) context in which human behaviour occurs and the role of the researcher in producing the knowledge s/he discovers, and promoting social psychology's role in social reform and change. For example, early discursive social psychology examined how racism and prejudice are embedded within discourse as speakers construct differences between race groups (e.g. Wetherell & Potter, 1992; also see Chapter 13 for more examples). More recently discursive social psychology has been used to explore a diverse range of topics, such as counselling (e.g. Lester et al., 2018) and couples therapy (e.g. O'Reilly et al., 2018), wealth and taxes (e.g. Carr et al., 2019), sex education in South African schools (Jearey-Graham & Macleod, 2017), sport (e.g. McGannon & Smith, 2015), learning disabilities (e.g. Jingree, 2017), parenting (e.g. Locke & Yarwood, 2017) and even revisiting classic social psychological experiments on obedience (Weatherall & Hollander, 2018; also see Chapter 7). Critical discourse analysts note that people are often not free to behave in any way they wish, but are positioned in relations of power to one another within a particular society. These power relationships require analytical attention (e.g. Parker, 1989, 2002). Phenomenological psychologists examine conscious experience of the social world and how this shapes our feelings and sense of self within it (e.g. Langdridge, 2007, 2008). For example, Kirkham et al., (2015) asked their participants, who suffer from chronic pain, to draw what their pain felt like. This, the authors argue, offers health professionals a real insight into the lived experiences of chronic pain sufferers.

critical social psychology a movement promoting a social psychology that (i) recognizes its own political, social, historical situatedness, and that of its researchers and participants, and that (ii) pursues social change and reform

social constructionism an approach to how our understanding of reality is formed and structured, which argues that all cognitive functions originate in social interaction, and must therefore be explained as products of social interactions

discursive psychology proposes a view of language as 'social action' as speakers construct the social world and their position within it through talk and text. It examines how cognitive entities and psychological phenomena are constructed in discourse

phenomenological psychology influenced by phenomenological philosophy, this form of psychology argues that understanding human psychology presupposes the study of subjective conscious experience, and the acknowledgment that, rather than being somehow separated from a supposedly 'external'world, we are fully immersed in the world.

Social Psychology and Human Values

Social psychologists' values penetrate their work in ways both obvious and subtle. What are these ways?

The crisis in social psychology flagged how human values shape research. Social psychology is less a collection of findings than a set of strategies for answering questions. In science, as in courts of law, personal opinions are inadmissible. When ideas are put on trial, evidence determines the verdict. But are social psychologists really that objective? Because they are human beings, don't their *values* – their personal convictions about what is desirable and how people ought to behave – seep into their work? If so, can social psychology really be scientific?

As we've already noted, the extent to which social psychology can be considered a science, and the usefulness of examining human social behaviour using experiments, is a matter of discussion. Martin and Sugarman (2009) outline the debate between the philosophers Charles Taylor and Thomas Kuhn. Taylor argues that because social psychology relies on human social beings (social psychologists) studying other human social beings, it cannot possibly produce objective knowledge that remains independent from the human beings who study it. This is a feature of social psychology that sets it apart from the natural sciences whose subject matter is not human. But not everyone agrees that this is peculiar to social psychology. Thomas Kuhn proposes that as all science involves human scientists, then none of it can ever be objective in a true sense as it all relies on a degree of human interpretation. However, this particular debate is academic for the present purposes. What matters is the concern over social psychology's claim to be a 'science', and to study human social behaviour using scientific principles and practices.

Obvious Ways Values Enter Psychology

Values enter the picture when social psychologists *choose research topics.* It was no accident that the study of prejudice flourished during the 1940s as fascism raged in Europe; that the 1950s, a time of look-alike fashions and intolerance of differing views, gave us studies of conformity; that the 1960s saw interest in aggression increase with riots and rising crime rates; that the feminist movement of the 1970s helped stimulate a wave of research on gender and sexism; that the 1980s offered a resurgence of attention to psychological aspects of the arms race; and that the 1990s and the early twenty-first century were marked by heightened interest in how people respond to diversity in culture, race and sexual orientation. Recently we have seen a surge in research that applies social psychology to matters of health, wealth, and the environment. Social psychology reflects contemporary society.

Values differ not only across time but also across cultures. People take pride in their nationalities. But this is not to the same degree in all nations and occurs in some historical periods more than in others. Social psychologists in Europe have been concerned about this phenomenon of belonging and pride in social groups, and as a result have given us major theories of 'social identity' and 'social categorization' (see Chapters 12 and 13). On the other hand, American social psychologists have typically focused more on individuals and independence – but also on how one person thinks about others, is influenced by them and relates to them (Fiske, 2004; Tajfel, 1981; Turner, 1984).

Values obviously enter the picture as the *object* of social psychological analysis. Social psychologists investigate how values form, why they change, and how they influence attitudes and actions. None of that, however, tells us which values are 'right'. But it can teach us to be tolerant towards many values, including those different from the ones at the top of our personal value hierarchy.

Modern-day social psychology reflects our social world.
SOURCE: © Shutterstock / milanzeremski

Not So Obvious Ways Values Enter Psychology

We less often recognize the subtler ways in which value commitments masquerade as objective truth. Consider the not-so-obvious ways values enter psychology.

'Science does not simply describe and explain nature; it is part of the interplay between nature and ourselves; it describes nature as exposed to our method of questioning.'

Heisenberg, 1958

The Subjective Aspects of Science

Scientists and philosophers now agree: science is not purely objective. Scientists do not simply read the book of nature. Rather, they interpret or construct nature and the social world, using their own mental categories. In our daily lives, too, we view the world through the lens of our preconceptions. Pause a moment: what do you see in **Figure 1.3**? Can you see a young girl or an old lady? Once your mind grasps the concept, it informs your interpretation of the picture – so much so that it becomes difficult *not* to see the one or the other.

FIGURE 1.3 What do you see?
SOURCE: ©Science History Images/ Alamy Stock Photo

This is the way our minds work. While reading these words, you have been unaware that you are also looking at your nose. Your mind blocks from awareness something that is there, if only you were predisposed to perceive it. This tendency to prejudge reality based on our expectations is a basic fact about the human mind.

Because scholars working in any given area often share a common viewpoint or come from the same **culture**, their assumptions may go unchallenged. What we take for granted – the shared beliefs, or our **social representations** (Moscovici, 1988) – are often our most important yet most unexamined convictions (see Chapter 4). Sometimes, however, someone from outside the camp will call attention to those assumptions. During the 1980s feminists and Marxists exposed some of social psychology's unexamined assumptions. Feminist critics called attention to subtle biases – for example, the political conservatism of some scientists who favoured a biological interpretation of gender differences in social behaviour (Unger, 1985). Some feminist critics have also challenged one of the most accepted traditions in social psychology, *the bystander effect,* for not taking into consideration the gender aspect of what initiated that tradition: the murder of Kitty Genovese (see Chapter 10). More recently, feminists have questioned psychology's implicit role in reproducing the sexist assumptions upon which societies are based, and which feminists seek to challenge (Rutherford et al., 2010). Marxist critics called attention to competitive, individualist biases – for example, the assumption that conformity is bad and that individual rewards are good. This critique has been expressed not only by Marxists. Today most social psychologists accept that conformity also reveals social identity and solidarity (Chapter 7). Marxists and feminists, of course, make their own assumptions, as critics of academic 'political correctness' are fond of noting.

culture the enduring behaviours, ideas, attitudes and traditions shared by a large group of people and transmitted from one generation to the next

social representations socially shared beliefs – widely held ideas and values, including our assumptions and cultural ideologies. Our social representations help us to make sense of our world

Psychological Concepts Contain Hidden Values

Implicit in our understanding that psychology is not objective is the realization that psychologists' own values may play an important part in the theories and judgements they support. They may talk as if they were stating facts, when they are really making *value judgements.* Here are some examples.

In Chapter 4 we see more ways in which our preconceptions guide our interpretations. As research in social psychology reminds us, what guides our behaviour is less the situation-as-it-is than the situation-as-we-construe-it.

Defining the Good Life

Values influence our idea of the best way to live our lives. The personality psychologist Abraham Maslow, for example, was known for his descriptions of 'self-actualized' people – people who, with their needs for survival, safety, belonging and self-esteem satisfied, go on to fulfil their human potential. Few readers noticed that Maslow himself, guided by his own values, selected the sample of self-actualized people he described. The resulting description of self-actualized personalities – as spontaneous, autonomous, mystical and so forth – reflected Maslow's personal values. Had he begun with someone else's heroes – say, Napoleon, Miriam Makeba, Nelson Mandela, Malala Yousofzai – his resulting description of self-actualization would have differed (Smith, 1978). This hierarchy of values also expresses the values of the Western individualistic culture in which it was formed. To develop in Western culture means to be more individualistic and independent, and to realize your personal self, rather than uphold collectivistic values or be able to create harmony with others. What characterizes well-functioning and modern humans in other cultures is sometimes the opposite: the ability to control and reduce your individuality in the name of harmony and solidarity.

Professional Advice

Tell me your problems? In offering advice, we display our personal and cultural values.
SOURCE: © Filimonov/Shutterstock

Psychological advice also reflects the advice-giver's personal values. When mental health professionals advise us how to get along with our spouse or our co-workers, when child-rearing experts tell us how to handle our children, and when some psychologists advocate living free of concern for others' expectations, they are expressing their own personal and cultural values. (In Western cultures, those values usually will be individualistic – encouraging what feels best for 'me'. Non-Western cultures more often encourage what's best for 'us'.) Many people, unaware of those hidden values, defer to the 'professional'. But professional psychologists cannot answer questions of ultimate moral obligation, of purpose and direction, and of life's meaning.

Forming Concepts

Hidden values even seep into psychology's research-based *concepts*. Pretend you have taken a personality test and the psychologist, after scoring your answers, announces: 'You scored high in self-esteem. You are low in anxiety. And you have exceptional ego-strength.' 'Ah,' you think, 'I suspected as much, but it feels good to know that.' Now another psychologist gives you a similar test. For some peculiar reason, this test asks some of the same questions. Afterwards, the psychologist informs you that you seem defensive, for you scored high in 'repressiveness'. 'How could this be?' you wonder. 'The other psychologist said such nice things about me.' It could be because all these labels describe the same set of responses (a tendency to say nice things about oneself and not to acknowledge problems). Shall we call it high self-esteem or defensiveness? The label reflects the judgement.

Labelling

Value judgements, then, are often hidden within our social psychological language – but that is also true of everyday language. Whether we label someone engaged in guerrilla warfare a 'terrorist' or a 'freedom fighter' depends on our view of the cause. Whether we view wartime civilian deaths as 'the loss of innocent lives' or as 'collateral damage' affects our acceptance of such. Whether we call public assistance 'welfare' or 'aid to the needy' reflects our political views. When 'they' exalt their country and people, it's ethnocentrism; that is, the belief that my ethnic group is better than others. Whether someone involved in an extramarital affair is practising 'open marriage' or 'adultery' depends on one's personal values and if we want to condemn or accept. We select concepts that justify the intention. Language is never neutral. 'Brainwashing' is social influence we do not approve of. 'Perversions' are sex acts we do not practise. Remarks about 'ambitious' men and 'aggressive' women convey a hidden message.

As these examples indicate, values lie hidden within the language and the concepts we use. They influence our cultural definitions of mental health, our psychological advice for living and our psychological scientific labels. Throughout this book we will call your attention to additional examples of hidden values. The point is never that the implicit values are necessarily bad. The point is that scientific interpretation, even at the level of labelling phenomena, is a human activity. It is therefore natural and inevitable that prior beliefs and values will influence what social psychologists think and write.

Should we dismiss science because it has its subjective side? Quite the contrary: the realization that human thinking always involves interpretation is precisely why we need researchers with varying biases to undertake scientific analysis. By constantly checking our beliefs against the facts, as best we know them, we check and restrain our biases. Systematic observation, empirical data and experimentation help us clean the lens through which we see our research object.

Social Psychology's Key Ideas

The historical journey of social psychology from its early philosophical beginnings to the present day reveals a diverse discipline, containing a wealth of knowledge and debate about human social behaviour and how we should study it. So, what are its big lessons – its overarching themes, debates and questions? In many academic fields, the results of tens of thousands of studies, the conclusions of thousands of investigators, and the insights of hundreds of theorists can be boiled down to a few central ideas. Biology offers us principles such as natural selection and adaptation. Sociology builds on concepts such as social structure and organization. Music harnesses our ideas of rhythm, melody and harmony.

What concepts are on social psychology's shortlist of key ideas? What are some of the crucial questions that social psychologists dedicate their time and resources to answering? What themes or fundamental principles will be worth remembering long after you have forgotten most of the details? Let us consider some of the candidates (see **Figure 1.4**).

We Construct our Social Reality

We humans have an irresistible urge to explain behaviour, to attribute it to some cause, and therefore to make it seem orderly, predictable and controllable. We may react differently to similar situations because we 'think' and 'feel' differently from one another. We may also describe and 'construct' that situation very differently.

The same event can be described and evaluated very differently by two people. They may not pay attention to the same features of that event, but actively select

Some key ideas in social psychology
1. We construct our social reality
2. Our social intuitions are powerful, sometimes perilous
3. Attitudes shape, and are shaped by, behaviour
Social thinking
4. There are social influences on behaviour
5. Dispositions shape behaviour
6. Behaviour is influenced by our social group memberships
Social influences
7. Social behaviour is also biological behaviour
8. Feelings and actions towards people are sometimes negative and sometimes positive
9. Behaviour is shaped by our intragroup and intergroup relations
Social relations
Social psychology's principles are applicable to everyday life
Applying social psychology

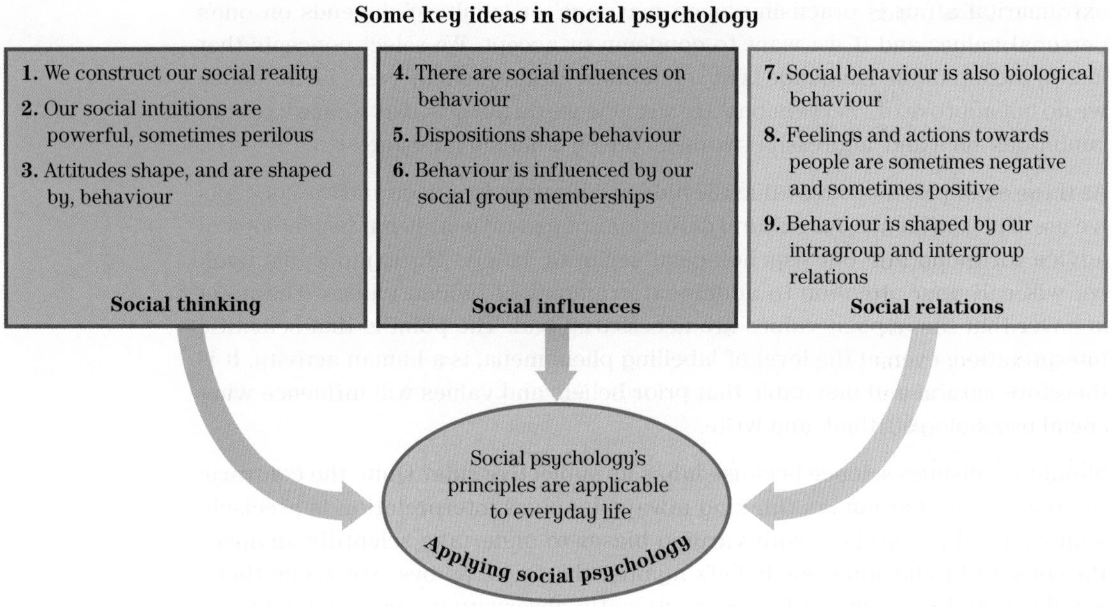

FIGURE 1.4 Some key ideas in social psychology

aspects to describe. Sometimes people see what they want to see, and they explain or evaluate an event in a way that is in accordance with their expectations, or serves us in some way. In this way we construct social events, people and social 'facts' so it suits our interests and what we want to perceive and convey to others.

Let us consider an example based on tragic circumstances. On 15 December 2012, 20-year-old Adam Lanza shot his mother and then walked into Sandy Hook Elementary School in the US where he continued his shooting spree with devastating and fatal consequences for the victims. Unsurprisingly, in the aftermath of the event distraught and bewildered politicians, media and the public questioned why this had happened and what could be done to prevent anything like this from ever happening again. Debates raged around issues of gun control, as well as mental health. Were tighter gun control laws needed? Did society need to rethink its care for the mentally ill? A few years later, psychologists Joslyn and Haider-Markel (2017) pondered whether owning a gun influenced the way you constructed and explained such events. Their survey suggests it does. Although both gun-owners and non-gun-owners agreed that the shooters should be blamed for the tragic murders, the gun-owners then blamed the shooters' behaviour on poor parenting and popular culture. In contrast, the non-gun-owners laid blame with the availability of guns and poor gun-control laws. Whereas the non-gun-owners felt optimistic that society could take non-violent action to prevent future shootings, the gun-owners were less enthusiastic. The conclusion: we grasp reality in a subjective way. We create it through the lens of our own interests, values, expectations and beliefs. *Cognitive social psychologists*, for example, have examined how the demands and limits of our mental abilities (such as the need to categorize) result in biases that influence how we construct the world around us. In constructing it in particular ways, we also simplify it.

We discuss the process by which we produce the world around us in Chapter 4 and Chapter 12.

Our beliefs about ourselves also matter. Do we have an optimistic outlook on life? Do we see ourselves as in control of things? Do we view ourselves as relatively inferior or superior to others? Our answers influence our emotions and actions. Of course, the way we view ourselves is influenced by the context of our culture and the society in which we are socialized. We internalize a culture's beliefs and values and they form part of our own. Much of the time we are unaware of this influence and often assume that the way we see ourselves and others is how others see them too. We consider this in some detail in Chapter 3, where we examine the self. This is an accusation that has been levelled at social psychology. As we've noted earlier in this chapter, cultural values enter social psychological research in subtle and obvious ways. The explanations social psychologists have arrived at to explain human social behaviour may reflect the social and cultural context of the theorist.

Social Intuitions are Powerful but can be Perilous!

Our instant intuitions shape our fears (is flying dangerous?), impressions (can I trust him?) and relationships (does she like me?). Intuitions influence governments in times of crisis, gamblers at the roulette table, jurors in their assessments of guilt, employers when interviewing prospective employees. We rely on our intuitions in our everyday lives.

This intuition is our everyday wisdom in making decisions and judgements. Writing for the journal *Nature*, Simon Gachter (Schot et al., 2016) suggests evidence is needed for the intuitions upon which British people voted for or against remaining in the European Union, so that we can understand their behaviour better. What hunches did they take about topics such as immigration, poverty, employment and identity to the polling station which ultimately resulted in Brexit? As well as it being a powerful aspect of our decisions, social intuitions can also be perilous. For example, Wohl and his team (2017) explored the rise of social casino gaming (SCG) amongst adolescents in Canada, where losses and rewards are virtual, and the link from SCGs to land-based monetary gambling, where those losses and wins are real. They found that one of the key attractions of SCGs is the algorithms used, which inflate the chances of the player to win. Fuelled by this apparent 'skill' for gambling, players are led into thinking they're better at it than they really are. Buoyed up by their new-found confidence in their gambling skills the player shifts from virtual to monetary-gambling to reap the real rewards, but unfortunately more likely, the very real losses.

Even our intuitions about ourselves often err. We intuitively trust our memories more than we should. We misread our own minds; in experiments we deny being affected by things that do influence us. We mispredict our own feelings – how bad we'll feel a year from now if we lose our job or our romance breaks up, if we fail our examinations, and how good we'll feel a year from now if we win the lottery. And we often mispredict our own future.

By reminding us of intuition's gifts and alerting us to its pitfalls, social psychologists aim to fortify our thinking. In most situations, 'fast and frugal' snap judgements serve us well enough. But in others, where accuracy matters – as when needing to fear the right things and spend our resources accordingly – we had best restrain our impulsive intuitions with critical thinking. So our intuitions are powerful resources in navigating us through our daily lives, but they carry an element of danger and can be perilous. We explore beliefs and judgements in more detail in Chapter 4.

Social Influences Shape our Behaviour

We are, as Aristotle long ago observed, social animals. We speak and think in words and ways we learned from others (such as parents and friends), and from the society and culture into which we're socialized. Parents and guardians are sometimes considered to be the 'agents of culture' as they shape our psychological functions in accordance with social norms, values and ways of thinking. Part of the socialization process is to be an integrated and valuable member of a society. Some of the norms and values we share with other members of our culture, while others are individual to us. We long to connect, to belong and to be thought well of. Throughout this textbook we present examples of how a sense of 'we-ness' and membership of a social group shapes our behaviour, thinking and our sense of self.

As social creatures, we respond to our immediate contexts. Sometimes the power of a social situation leads us to act in ways that depart from beliefs, values and behaviour in other situations. Indeed, powerful situations sometimes overwhelm good intentions, inducing people to agree with falsehoods or comply with cruelty. For example, behaviourist theory which dominated social psychology in the 1950s, concerned itself precisely with the role of the situation in eliciting social behaviour (Skinner, 1963). **Behaviourism** considers how behaviour is related to reinforcement and positive and negative outcomes. We may engage in aggressive behaviour if we are positively reinforced and receive positive outcomes from others (e.g. enhanced reputation and status) for doing so (see Chapter 8). We have to wonder what situational factors played a role in eliciting certain negative behaviours throughout our history. For example, between 1948 and 1993 in South Africa, racial segregation based on white-minority superiority was enshrined in law. The system, named Apartheid, geographically, socially, culturally and psychologically separated black and white people. It was widely accepted by many white Europeans, particularly those living in South Africa. The colonialism in Africa was not questioned at the time by many in Europe. Under Nazi influence, many decent-seeming people supported the Nazi regime. But, of course, other situations can elicit great generosity and compassion. In August 2017, monsoon flooding claimed the lives of 1,200 people across Nepal, India and Bangladesh, and disrupted the lives of millions. As the catastrophic event unfolded across global newsrooms and social media, the disaster was met with offers of help and aid from people all over the world.

behaviourism a school of psychology that emphasizes the effects of learning, reinforcement and situational factors on the facilitation or inhibition of behaviour. The theory claims psychology should be a study of observable behaviour, since thoughts, motives and feelings are unavailable for research

More generally, our cultures help define the situation in which we find ourselves, and guide behaviour. For example:

- whether you define social justice as equality (everyone receives the same) or as equity (those who earn more receive more) depends on whether your ideology has been shaped more by socialism or capitalism
- whether you tend to be expressive or reserved, casual or formal, hinges partly on your culture
- whether you focus primarily on yourself – your personal needs, desire and morality – or on your family, clan and communal groups depends on how much you are a product of Western individualism.

Social psychologist Hazel Markus (2005) sums it up: 'People are above all, malleable.' Said differently, we do not just adapt to our culture and society, but we actively engage in forming it.

Genetic Heritage and Individual Dispositions Influence Behaviour

Our genetic heritage and individual dispositions affect and create our individual psychological functions and behaviour. We are not passive tumbleweeds merely blown this way and that by the social and cultural winds. Our values and attitudes acquired during socialization will influence behaviour. For example, our political attitudes influence voting behaviour. Our attitudes to smoking influence our susceptibility to peer pressure to smoke. Our attitudes towards the poor influence our willingness to help. As we see in Chapter 5, our attitudes also follow our behaviour, which leads us to believe in those things we have committed ourselves to, or suffered for. Temperament and personality dispositions also affect behaviour. Facing the same situation, different people may react differently. Whilst one person responds to an argument with aggression, another simply walks away. Emerging from years of political imprisonment, one person exudes bitterness. Another, such as South Africa's Nelson Mandela, seeks reconciliation and unity with former enemies.

We discuss more about the individual differences in aggression in Chapter 8 and how biology, circumstances and environment influence aggressive behaviour.

Behaviour is Shaped by Intragroup and Intergroup Relations

The way we define and experience ourselves is not always in terms of our individual and unique characteristics. In many contexts the self is defined and experienced in terms of group membership ('I am African'; 'I am a woman'; 'I am a socialist'; 'I am a student'). The groups and social categories to which we belong and which define who we are, are at the basis of many of our behaviours. We may drink heavily in order to feel accepted by a group of friends that matter to us; we can make an effort to attend a given lecture even though we dread the idea, because this is what a committed student is expected to do; we may go on strike to defend the rights of our professional category; and so on. What is more, when we are acutely aware of being part of a group, we are likely to make an effort to be cooperative and supportive with other members of our group. Furthermore, if our group is competing with another for scarce resources, we may develop forms of bias and prejudice toward the members of the other group.

Social psychologists have always been interested in collective behaviour, and have produced important findings and insight about a number of processes both within and between groups. As we discover in Chapters 11, 12 and 13, some of the most celebrated studies in the history of modern social psychology have concerned group related phenomena.

Social Psychological Processes are Biologically Rooted

Since the end of the twentieth century, there has been an ever-growing focus on behaviour's biological foundations. The 1990s was introduced as the 'decade of the brain' and it was heavily researched for its role in guiding behaviour. With the development of imaging techniques such as computed axial tomography (CAT), magnetic resonance imaging (MRI), and nuclear magnetic resonance imaging (NMRI) our understanding of the structure and functions of the brain has advanced rapidly. With these imaging techniques we can consider in detail the localization of neuropsychological functions and processes.

If every psychological event (every thought, every emotion and every behaviour) is simultaneously a biological event, then we can also examine the neurobiology that underlies social behaviour. What brain areas enable our experiences of love and contempt, helping and aggression, perception and belief? How do brain, mind and behaviour function together as one co-ordinated system? What does the timing of brain events reveal about how we process information? Such questions are asked by those in **social neuroscience** (e.g. Cacioppo & Cacioppo, 2013; Heatherton et al., 2004; Ochsner & Lieberman, 2001). For example, social neuroscience has observed that mirror neurons, located in the premotor cortex, become active when a person watches someone perform an action and when that person then performs the action for him/herself. Interestingly, the more expert s/he is at the action, the stronger the activation in the brain (e.g. Calvo-Merino et al., 2005; Fiske & Taylor, 2007; Marshall, 2014).

social neuroscience seeks to understand how physiology, in particular the brain, influences behaviour

But to know where something is processed in the brain does not tell us why it happens. With an ever-increasing focus on the brain, the relationship between mind, brain and the social world becomes a topic for discussion and research. The forces of biology and the social act on each other. But how they are related remains a scientific and social psychological challenge. *Evolutionary psychologists* argue our inherited human nature predisposes us to behave in ways that helped our ancestors survive and reproduce. We carry the genes of those whose traits enabled them to survive and reproduce (whose children did the same). Evolutionary psychologists ask how natural selection might predispose our actions and reactions when dating and mating, hurting and hating, caring and sharing. For example, Conway et al.'s (2015) study of UK online daters found that as heterosexual men age, they prefer younger and younger women. Conversely, heterosexual women are more attracted to older men as they increase with age themselves. Homosexual men and women have broader age tolerances for a potential partner than their heterosexual counterparts. Evolutionary psychology suggests this is because younger women represent better fertility prospects for ageing heterosexual men, and older men indicate more financial security and stability for younger heterosexual women. Without these reproductive concerns, the homosexual sample are less constrained by age preferences for a partner (see Chapter 14 for more on evolutionary psychology).

Chapter 9 discusses how women look for a mate who can protect and provide for them, while men's decisions are based on a potential mate's nurturing abilities to care for their potential offspring.

Social neuroscientists do not reduce complex social behaviours, such as helping and hurting, to simple neural or molecular mechanisms. Their point is this: to understand social behaviour, we must consider both under-the-skin (biological) and between-skins (social) influences. Mind and body are one grand system. Stress hormones affect how we feel and act. We are bio-psycho-social organisms. We reflect the interplay of our biological, psychological and social influences. And this is why today's psychologists study behaviour from these different levels of analysis.

Social Psychology's Principles are Applicable in Everyday Life

Social psychology has the potential to illuminate your life, to make visible the subtle influences that guide your thinking and acting. And, as we will see, it offers many ideas about how to know ourselves better, how to win friends and influence people, how to transform closed fists into open arms.

Scholars are also applying social psychological insights. Principles of social thinking, social influence and social relations have implications for human health and well-being, for war and peace, for performance and relationships in organizations and the workplace, and for the encouragement of behaviours that will enable an environmentally sustainable human future.

As but one perspective on human existence, psychological science does not seek to engage life's ultimate questions: what is the meaning of human life? What should be our purpose? What is our ultimate destiny? But social psychology does give us a method for asking and answering some exceedingly interesting and important questions. *Social psychology is all about life – your life: your beliefs, your attitudes, your relationships.*

SUMMING UP: INTRODUCING SOCIAL PSYCHOLOGY

WHAT IS SOCIAL PSYCHOLOGY?

- Social psychology is the scientific study of how people think about, influence and relate to one another.
- Social psychology's central themes concern (1) how we think about the self, others, and social issues (social thinking), (2) what shapes people's minds and behaviour (social influence), (3) the mechanisms underlying aggression, intimacy and helping (social relations), and (4) processes within and between groups (people in groups).

A BRIEF HISTORY OF SOCIAL PSYCHOLOGY

- Social psychological topics and issues have been debated in Europe for centuries by philosophers and other scholars and thinkers, long before social psychology became a discipline in its own right. Much of this early thought formed the basis for present-day social psychology.
- Its history of debates about the underlying assumptions and methods social psychologists use to examine human social behaviour remains a feature of modern-day social psychology, giving us a rich and diverse discipline.

SOCIAL PSYCHOLOGY AND HUMAN VALUES

- Social psychologists' values penetrate their work in obvious ways, such as their choice of research topics and the types of people who are attracted to various fields of study.
- They also do this in more subtle ways, such as their hidden assumptions when forming concepts, choosing labels and giving advice.
- This penetration of values into science is not a reason to fault social psychology or any other science. That human thinking is seldom dispassionate is precisely why we need systematic observation and experimentation if we are to check our cherished ideas against reality.

SOCIAL PSYCHOLOGY'S KEY IDEAS

- Social psychology's central themes concern (1) how we construct and construe our social worlds, (2) how our everyday thinking, habits and social intuitions guide and sometimes deceive us, (3) how our psychological functions are shaped by biology, temperament, culture and other people, and (4) how social psychology's principles apply to our everyday lives and to various other fields of study.

Critical Questions

1. What do you think are the most important lessons modern social psychology has learned from its historical beginnings?
2. Should social psychology try to model itself on the harder sciences (e.g., physics, biology)?
3. Social psychology is to some extent driven by current social concerns and problems. What modern-day examples can you think of that have received recent social psychological attention?
4. What role do you think social psychology should play in wider society?

Recommended Reading

Farr, R. M. (1996). *The roots of modern social psychology.* Blackwell.

Greenwood, J. (2004). *The disappearance of the social in American social psychology.* Cambridge University Press.

Jahoda, G. (2007). *A history of social psychology: From the eighteenth-century enlightenment to the Second World War.* Cambridge University Press.

Rizzoli, V., Castro, P., Tuzzi, A., & Contarello, A. (2019). Probing the history of social psychology, exploring diversity and views of the social: Publication trends in the *European Journal of Social Psychology* from 1971 to 2016. *European Journal of Social Psychology, 49*(4), 671–687. https://doi.org.libezproxy.open.ac.uk/10.1002/ejsp.2528

2 RESEARCH METHODS IN SOCIAL PSYCHOLOGY

'The application of philosophical ideas to social research must not lose touch with the practices and aims of social researchers.'
Alan Bryman, 1988

Research methods are extremely important. To find something out about human behaviour we need to examine it. But this isn't always terribly easy. Human beings are complex. How do we decide which aspects of behaviour to focus on? How should we collect evidence of that behaviour? How should we then interpret and evaluate it? What is the status of the knowledge we discover? Have we revealed universal and stable 'facts' about human beings, or have we discovered socially and historically contingent 'facts', which are prone to change? Does social psychology differ from common sense? Social psychologists have developed a variety of methods for the study of human behaviour, and this chapter considers what these are.

I Knew it All Along: Is Social Psychology Simply Common Sense?

Social psychology can produce findings that surprise us. Yet, there are those other times when social psychology simply seems to confirm what we already know. So does social psychology provide new insights into the human condition? Or does it only describe the obvious?

In Chapter 1, our historical journey into social psychology alerted us to the fact that social behaviour has been a topic for discussion and scrutiny by scholars and thinkers for centuries. But, it is also a topic that everyday human beings feel they know something about. After all, it's *our* social behaviour that is the focus of interest. So does that mean social psychology is just common sense in fancy words? Do we need a rigorous study of human beings' social behaviour at all if, in fact, we knew it all along? Some research on the matter has shown that for some members of the public, social psychology appears to be little more than common-sense (Lilienfeld, 2012).

Of course, one problem with common sense is that we invoke it after we know the facts. Events are far more 'obvious' and predictable in hindsight than beforehand. In everyday life we often do not expect something to happen until it does. *Then* we suddenly see clearly the forces that brought about the event and feel unsurprised. After the recession in the world economy from the end of 2008, it seemed obvious that economists and political commentators (and social psychologists?) should have anticipated the crisis in the financial sector due to rotten loan financing and extreme profit in the financial sector of the economy. Should another global financial crisis occur, will we retrospectively claim 'I-knew-it-all-along'?

hindsight bias the tendency to exaggerate, after learning an outcome, one's ability to have foreseen how something turned out. Also known as the 'I-knew-it-all-along' phenomenon

If this **hindsight bias** (also called the *I-knew-it-all-along phenomenon*) is pervasive, you may now be feeling that you already knew about this phenomenon. Indeed, almost any conceivable result of a social psychological study can seem like common sense – *after* you know the result.

You can demonstrate the phenomenon yourself. Take a group of people and tell half of them one psychological finding and the other half the opposite result. For example, tell half as follows:

Social psychologists have found that, whether choosing friends or falling in love, we are most attracted to people whose traits are different from our own. There seems to be wisdom in the old saying 'Opposites attract'.

Tell the other half:

Social psychologists have found that, whether choosing friends or falling in love, we are most attracted to people whose traits are similar to our own. There seems to be wisdom in the old saying 'Birds of a feather flock together'.

The beauty of hindsight! Did we anticipate the global recession?

SOURCE: © goir/Shutterstock

Ask the people first to explain the result. Then ask them to say whether it is 'surprising' or 'not surprising'. Virtually all will find a good explanation for whichever result they were given and will say it is 'not surprising'.

Indeed, we can draw on our stockpile of proverbs to make almost any result seem to make sense. If a social psychologist reports that separation intensifies romantic attraction, the public responds that everybody knows that 'absence makes the heart grow fonder'. Should it turn out that separation *weakens* attraction, the public will say, 'out of sight, out of mind'.

Let's consider a scientific study of a topic that attracts some vigorous debate. Menec and Weiner (2000) were interested in people's opinions on genetic screening for disorders prior to deciding whether to have children. Their participants read a short statement in which a woman refused genetic testing. Some of these participants then read that the woman went on to have a child with a genetic disorder. The rest of the participants were told a child with no genetic disorder was born. When participants were asked to judge the probability of the woman having a child with a genetic disorder, those who read she had done so 'knew-it-all-along'. Furthermore, they tended to blame the woman for the outcome based on her refusal to have the genetic screening test.

The I-knew-it-all-along phenomenon can have unfortunate consequences. It is conducive to arrogance – an overestimation of our own intellectual powers. Moreover, because outcomes seem as if they should have been foreseeable, we are more likely to blame decision makers for what are in retrospect 'obvious' bad choices than to praise them for good choices, which also seem 'obvious'.

Likewise, we sometimes blame ourselves for 'stupid mistakes' – perhaps for not having handled a person or a situation better. Looking back, we see how we should have handled it. 'I should have known how busy I would be at the term's end and started that paper earlier.' But sometimes we are too hard on ourselves. We forget that what is obvious to us *now* was not nearly so obvious at the time.

What do we conclude – that common sense is usually wrong? Sometimes it is. At other times, conventional wisdom is right – or it falls on both sides of an issue: does happiness come from knowing the truth or preserving illusions? From being with others or living in peaceful solitude? Opinions are numerous and commonplace; no matter what we find, there will be someone who foresaw it. But which of the many competing ideas best fit reality? And what is actually the 'reality', if it is constructed? Research can specify the circumstances under which a common-sense truism is valid, but never reach absolute truth.

'Everything important has been said before.'
Philosopher Alfred North Whitehead (1861–1947)

The point is not that common sense is predictably wrong. Rather, common sense usually is right – *after the fact.* We therefore easily deceive ourselves into thinking that we know and knew more than we do and did. And that is precisely why we need science to help us sift reality from illusion and genuine predictions from easy hindsight. There are other causes as well, however, why research is necessary if we want to understand and explain human behaviour and relationships.

Approaches to Doing Research

Although there are several methods and techniques that can be used to investigate social psychological phenomena, it is possible to distinguish between two general approaches: the quantitative and the qualitative approach. These approaches differ practically in the ways in which they collect and analyse data about people and the world around them. However, they can also differ in terms of the way the knowledge that they produce is eventually evaluated. For instance, can we consider our findings like universal truths? Or should we see them as only applying to specific situational, cultural and historical settings? Typically, the quantitative approach would endorse the former, and the qualitative approach would align with the latter view. That means that these two approaches may differ in their **epistemology**. Social psychologists often have a predilection for either one or the other, although many researchers are perfectly happy to use both.

epistemology the study of knowledge and the underlying status we give it. For example, is the knowledge we obtain about human behaviour a 'fact' or a 'version'?

Quantitative Social Psychology

Social psychologists adopting a **quantitative research** approach see the social psychological world in terms of **variables**. For quantitative researchers things such as gender and nationality, but also anxiety, self-esteem, life satisfaction, physical attraction to one's partner, empathy, academic performance, attachment to a social group, attitude toward immigrants, commitment to work, willingness to help a person in a crisis, motivation to achieve a goal, and so on are first and foremost variables. That means that a variable may concern any conceivable characteristic – demographics, feelings, cognitions, behaviours – that can vary in some way. Self-esteem may vary from being very low to very high, commitment to work may range from being tenuous to very strong, and so on. People are stable on some variables (for example nationality tends to remain the same across the lifespan), but may easily change over time on other variables (one may be unsatisfied with life when young but become increasingly more satisfied while ageing) and across situations (one may feel anxious in the company of strangers but totally at ease with close friends).

quantitative research approach to research aimed at studying the relationships between variables. Variables are expressed numerically, and their relationships are explored via statistical analyses

variable a thing that can vary in quantity and quality. Of particular relevance to social psychology are variables such as self-esteem, aggression, attraction, etc. Their level will vary from person to person, situation to situation

Quantitative social psychologists are interested in studying the interplay between variables. For example, they may want to discover whether, in general, students who perform well have greater self-esteem than students whose performance is not so good. Or they could decide to investigate whether a relaxed leadership style leads to greater group productivity than an authoritarian style. Obviously, social psychologists can also consider physical variables (e.g., temperature in a room, level of noise, etc.) in their research, insofar as these may impact upon social psychological phenomena. For instance, does heat make people more aggressive? Does noise facilitate cohesion in a football crowd?

In order to conduct these sorts of investigation, researchers need to *measure* the variables under scrutiny. For instance, self-esteem may be measured by using a set of questions that will produce a total score ranging from 0 (total lack of self-esteem) to 10 (very high self-esteem), and mathematical performance could be expressed in terms of number of problems in a test that have been resolved. Subsequently, researchers must perform some statistical calculations – which may have various degrees of complexity – aimed at establishing whether and how strongly the variables are linked to one another. The term quantitative approach derives from the fact that variables and their connections are expressed numerically, that is, in terms of *quantities*.

Qualitative Social Psychology

Social psychologists adopting a **qualitative research** approach tend to be more sceptical about reducing people's social psychological life into discrete, neatly identified variables. Representing psychological states and experiences numerically does not say much about what people's true states and experiences really are like. For instance, what do people really mean when they say that, on a 7-point scale where 1 = not at all satisfied and 7 = totally satisfied, their satisfaction with life equals 5? People's inner life is much more complex and textured than that. Also, qualitative social psychologists often feel uncomfortable with the idea that human social psychology can be understood by studying people in artificial situations such as the laboratory experiment – which is what many quantitative psychologists do. The real situations that people have to face in everyday life cannot easily be reproduced in the lab.

qualitative research approach to research based on the interpretation of qualitative data, not statistical analysis of numerical data (contrasted with quantitative research)

As a result, qualitative methods try to capture the richness and complexity of human psychology. This may involve, for example, studying the meanings attached to specific experiences (e.g., being the target of prejudice, living with a chronic illness, participating in a rally). The data used for these studies may involve texts obtained via the transcription of recorded interviews (that tend to be in-depth and unstructured) or field-notes taken by the researcher during specific events. Normally, the researcher will try to collect the data in contexts and/or ways that are as natural as possible. In general, qualitative researchers are happy to accept the idea that their findings concern socially contingent phenomena, rather than 'stable', universal facts. In other words, these social psychologists believe that, while laws of nature are fixed (e.g., protons will always be positively charged), human social behaviour depends on a whole array of things, such as the immediate context in which it occurs and broader cultural values. Gergen (1973) makes the point that while the natural scientist receives no argument from his or her subject about the findings s/he produces, the social psychologist has no such luxury. Our subjects talk back. And, as we've seen, can dismiss our findings as common sense (remember the hindsight bias and the I-knew-it-all-along phenomenon) or untrue. Gergen argues that the better able a theory is to predict human behaviour the more likely it is the population will then change its behaviour to invalidate it. Human beings react to revelations about their own behaviour.

Some General Observations on the Two Approaches

Are the two approaches to research irreconcilable? Well, not necessarily. They may be so for social psychologists who believe that these approaches stem from completely different conceptions of what human psychology and its study are about (i.e. different epistemologies). In particular, some qualitative researchers actively resist quantitative methods in the belief that they are not the appropriate way to research human beings. These debates over method reflect those considered in Chapter 1 concerning *if*, and *to what extent*, social psychology is a 'science' capable of producing objective 'facts' about human beings and their social behaviour. Some social psychologists, however, are more flexible, and are happy to use whatever method appears to be ideal and suitable for the specific research question at stake. This attitude has produced an increasing body of mixed-methods research in social psychology. That is, there are researchers who like to run projects involving both quantitative and qualitative methodologies.

In the next section we will discuss in some detail what each type of approach to research involves in practice. To anticipate briefly we can say that, at the broadest level, the main features of the quantitative approach are a high degree of control exerted by the researcher on the research setting, the rigorous measurement of behaviour, and an analysis of **data** based on statistical procedures. On the contrary, the main characteristics of the qualitative approach are the use of more naturalistic (often real-world) research settings, the observation of spontaneous behaviour and the facilitation of subjective experience unconstrained by rigid protocols, and the interpretative analysis of behaviours and language in terms of their intrinsic meaning. Most of what you will learn about social psychological methods will come from your reading of the next chapters as we consider specific topics in social psychology. Here we will glimpse behind the scenes so you can get some insight into how social psychologists do their research, and this should help in appreciating and evaluating the studies considered throughout the rest of this textbook.

data notes, information, registered observations, statistical measurements or responses, collected together for scientific analysis or interpretation, and then to inform knowledge

We summarize the main differences between quantitative and qualitative research methodologies in **Table 2.1**.

TABLE 2.1 Some of the main differences between quantitative and qualitative approach to research

Quantitative approach	Qualitative approach
Pursue the systematic measurement of phenomena, often in controlled laboratory settings	Focus on the interpretation of phenomena as emerged in naturalistic, unconstrained situations
Make predictions about the outcome of research	Are open to new, surprising and previously unthought-of findings
Aim at establishing general laws and principles about types of phenomena	Aim at providing a thorough description and understanding of the specific phenomena under investigation

Quantitative Research

Social psychologists conducting quantitative research tend to adhere to a standard process involving a number of stages. All investigations start with a **research question**. For instance, do young people who have low self-esteem tend to engage in risky behaviour (such as smoking and alcohol consumption) more than those with high self-esteem? Do people who feel lonely spend more time on social media? Do people with many friends feel happier than more solitary people? It is to address questions such as these that social psychologists undertake research.

research question a question that guides the focus of current research

But how are research questions generated? A research question may stem from existing **theory** in social psychology. Theories consist of a set of assumptions and propositions that organize findings from previous research into a coherent story. However, theories also contribute to the generation of new research questions to be investigated. For instance, suppose that there exists a theory stating that people find uncertainty aversive. Then suppose that, according to such a theory, when people facing an uncertain situation experience anxiety they, as a consequence, become especially dependent on significant others such as a friend or spouse. Now, you might decide that this is a plausible and convincing theory but that at the same time, there are aspects that the theory overlooks. For instance, you may wonder whether people facing uncertainty may also become more prone to join groups holding firm and clear views on reality, and decide that this is a worthwhile research question to be addressed.

theory an interrelated set of principles that guide what should be studied, and explain and predict the observed relationship between variables

A specific research question may also be triggered by events currently going on in the world. In Chapter 1, we consider how many of social psychology's studies are driven by world events and concerns. For example, there is a recent spurt in social psychological work on climate change and the sustainability of the planet as a response to contemporary concerns (Kazdin, 2009) (see Chapter 15 for social psychological work on this), as well as the impacts of online gaming, dating and gambling on young people (e.g. Whitty & Young, 2016).

Finally, the decision to address a certain question may be based on your everyday experience and life. You might want to understand the reasons underlying some of your behaviours. For instance, you may have observed that when you play a competitive game and believe you will lose, you tend to do things that will actually increase the probabilities of being defeated, such as using a bad racket in a tennis game. You may therefore wonder why you behave that way and whether this is a common phenomenon.

Blaming your equipment is a phenomenon known as 'self-handicapping'; Chapter 3 discusses this in more detail

Once a research question has been established, social psychologists formulate a **hypothesis**. This means that, when asking a research question, social psychologists normally have an answer in mind. For instance, you could hypothesize that the reason people may handicap themselves when playing a competitive game is to have a ready-made excuse for defeat, thereby protecting self-esteem. The important feature of hypotheses is that of being testable. It has to be possible to test a hypothesis in order to see if it is correct. Like research questions, hypotheses are often derived from theories. What is more, when a hypothesis is based on a theory, testing the hypothesis implies testing the theory too (Sani & Todman, 2006). If the hypothesis is proved incorrect, then some aspects of the theory may need revision, or the theory may even be rejected altogether. If, on the other hand, the hypothesis is confirmed, the theory will increase its credibility. That will not imply, however, that the theory is true once and for all, but rather that for the time being the theory cannot be said to be false. This general approach to research derives from the work of a philosopher of science, Karl Popper. In a widely acclaimed book titled *Conjectures and Refutations* (Popper, 1963), he contended that the objective of scientific research should be that of disproving, rather than proving, theories. A theory can be considered a plausible account of the phenomenon at stake as long as researchers fail to disprove the theory. Building on this idea, philosophers and researchers taking a positivistic stance believe that, to be considered 'scientific', a theory must be *falsifiable*.

hypothesis a testable proposition that describes a relationship that may exist between variables

It's good for our self-esteem to maintain our social relationships
SOURCE: © Uber Images/Shutterstock

Once a testable hypothesis has been formulated, social psychologists must decide which specific method they want to use. In general, the chosen method depends on the nature of the hypothesis. If this is concerned with the association (or **correlation**) between variables, the researcher will likely opt for a survey study. But if the hypothesis concerns the possibility that changes in one variable cause changes in another variable, then the researcher will be more likely to conduct an experiment.

Correlational Research: Exploring Associations

correlational research
the study of naturally occurring relationships among variables

longitudinal study
research that involves repeat testing, questioning and/or observations of participants over a long or short period of time.

Today's psychologists relate personal and social factors to human health. In a **longitudinal study** that lasted 13 years, Wagner et al. (2015) looked at changing self-esteem in 462 adults, aged between 70 and 103 years, all resident in Berlin. Their interest was whether our self-esteem takes a nose-dive as we get older. As we approach the end of our lives, does our self-esteem suffer? Furthermore, how might our health, social and personal factors be associated with feelings of self-esteem late in life? Drawing on a range of data obtained from surveys as well as physician records they found that self-esteem remained relatively stable until individuals reached their late 80s and early 90s, where it started to decline. However, this decline was minor and seemed to be associated with feelings of loneliness and social exclusion, poor health and disability, and weakened ability to control their own behaviour. Participants who remained healthy, socially networked, and felt in control over their behaviour, enjoyed very little decline in self-esteem in their final years of life.

The research conducted by Wagner and colleagues made use of some information that they did not need to produce themselves because it was already available. However, they, like many researchers also had to devise ways of producing the rest of the information they needed. To obtain data that allow assessing the degree of association between variables, researchers commonly design a questionnaire and ask people to complete it. The questionnaire will obviously include items tapping upon the variables of interest. For instance, if you decided to investigate the relationship between social status and health by means of a questionnaire, your questionnaire should include questions aimed at measuring one's social status (e.g., employment, educational attainments, salary earned) as well as questions that are able to produce a measure of the respondent's health status (e.g., whether they suffer from a chronic illness, whether they are under medication, number of working days missed because of illness, etc.). Questionnaires can be administered in various ways, for instance by telephone, online or more simply by handing respondents a pencil and a paper copy of the questionnaire.

When designing a questionnaire we must take into consideration five important aspects.

1 **Nature of sample.** Is it important that the sample is representative of a given population? It might not. But if it is important then we must ensure that we use an appropriate sampling strategy (see **Table 2.2**).

2 **Order of questions.** The order in which we ask questions may produce biased responses. For instance, people's support for civil unions of gays and lesbians rises if they are first asked their opinion of gay marriage, compared with which civil unions apparently seem a more moderate alternative (Moore, 2004). Therefore, we need to give careful consideration to the way we order the questions.

3 **Response options.** Consider the dramatic effects the response options can have on the answers you receive. Participants will usually diligently try to fit the answer into one of your response options – but does it actually fit? Have you provided enough response options to capture all possible answers? If you haven't your participant's chosen response option might not accurately reflect their answer.

4 **Wording of questions.** The precise wording of questions may also influence answers. For example, one poll found that most people favour cutting 'foreign aid' and *increasing* spending 'to help hungry people in other nations' (Simon, 1996). How questions are asked in a questionnaire is a very delicate matter. Subtle changes in the tone of a question can have marked effects (Krosnick & Schuman, 1988; Robinson & Leonard, 2018). Even when people say they feel strongly about an issue, a question's form and wording may affect their answer.

5 **Validity and reliability of measures.** Questionnaire items are used to measure variables. For these measures to produce meaningful results, they must be valid and reliable. For instance, suppose we measure 'academic self-esteem' using the following two items: 'I regard myself as a competent student', 'I have good studying skills'. What we need to ensure in this case is that the items (i) are valid indicators of the construct they are meant to assess, that is self-esteem (validity issue), and that (ii) they jointly contribute to measure self-esteem and would produce the same results under similar conditions (reliability issue).

TABLE 2.2 Sampling strategies in correlational research

Type of sampling strategy	Main features
Random sampling	Where everyone in the population under study has an equal chance of being represented in the sample
Systematic sampling	Where members are drawn from a population at fixed intervals (e.g. every fifth person)
Stratified sampling	Aims to ensure all features of a population are represented in the sample
Cluster sampling	When the population is organized into groups (or clusters) and some 'clusters' feature in the sample
Opportunity/convenience sampling	A pragmatic form of sampling, where those who form the sample are those we have the best access to – or are the most 'convenient' (e.g. due to limited time and resources)
Snowball sampling	When the researcher 'snowballs' further participants from one respondent (e.g. their family and friends)
Theoretical/principled/ purposive sampling	When participants are chosen for inclusion in research on 'principled' reasons for their inclusion. Does not seek representativeness

Association and Causation

Correlations are often the basis of one of the most irresistible thinking error made by both amateur and professional social psychologists: when two factors such as self-esteem and academic achievement go together, it is terribly tempting to

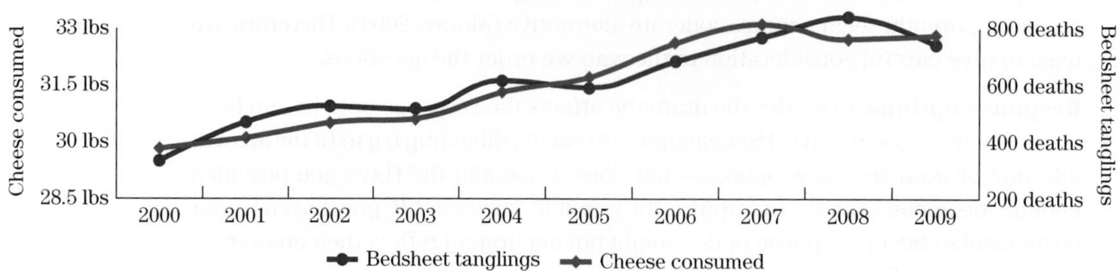

FIGURE 2.1 Caution: Correlation does not necessarily mean causation!

SOURCE: http://www.tylervigen.com/spurious-correlations

conclude that one is causing the other. High self-esteem, we might presume, leads to high academic achievement. But might it be the other way around? Could it be that academic achievement promotes self-esteem? Associations indicate a relationship, but to establish what *causes* what is not straightforward. In other words, research that detects associations cannot necessarily tell us whether changing one variable (such as self-esteem) will *cause* changes in another (such as academic achievement). The association–causation confusion is behind much muddled thinking in popular psychology.

correlational research the study of naturally occurring relationships among variables

The investigation of these associations in social psychology is called **correlational research**. Let's return to this very real correlation – between self-esteem and academic achievement. Children with high self-esteem tend also to have high academic achievement. (As with any correlation, we can also state this the other way around: high achievers tend to have high self-esteem.) Why do you suppose that is (**Figure 2.2**)?

Some people believe a 'healthy self-concept' contributes to achievement. Thus, boosting a child's self-image may also boost school achievement. But when

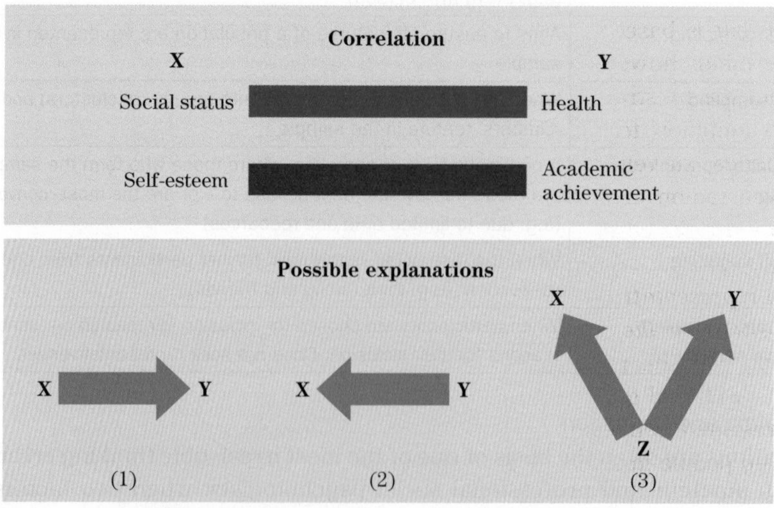

FIGURE 2.2 Correlation and causations

two variables correlate, any combination of three explanations is possible. Either one may cause the other, or both may be affected by an underlying 'third factor'. For instance, we could say that the correlation between self-esteem and academic achievement are both affected by IQ or perhaps self-efficacy. It is not surprising, therefore, that alternative accounts of the association between self-esteem and academic achievement among children have been proposed.

negative correlation when one variable increases as the other decreases

positive correlation when two variables both increase, or both decrease

One way of quantifying correlations is by using the coefficient known as Pearson's *r,* which is a measure of the degree of relationship between two variables. Scores on this coefficient may range from –1.0 (as one variable score goes up, the other goes down) through 0 to +1.0 (scores on the two variables rise and fall together). So for example, scores on self-esteem and depression tests have a **negative correlation** (about –0.6). Identical twins' intelligence scores have a **positive correlation** (above +0.8). The great strength of correlational research is that it tends to occur in real-world settings where we can examine factors such as race, gender and social status (variables that we cannot manipulate in the laboratory). **Figure 2.3** is a graph representation of a positive correlation presented between revision and higher exam results, and a negative correlation presented between flu jabs and the number of people with the flu. As shown, the positive correlation suggests that those who spend more time revising are more likely to perform better on exams and for the negative correlation, if the number of people who get flu jabs increases, there is higher immunity and the prevalence of the flu decreases.

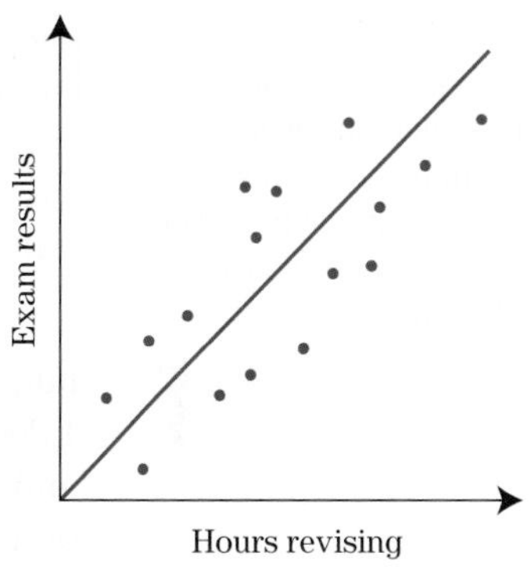
Exam results
Hours revising
Positive correlation
• People who do more revision get higher exam results.
• Revising increases success.

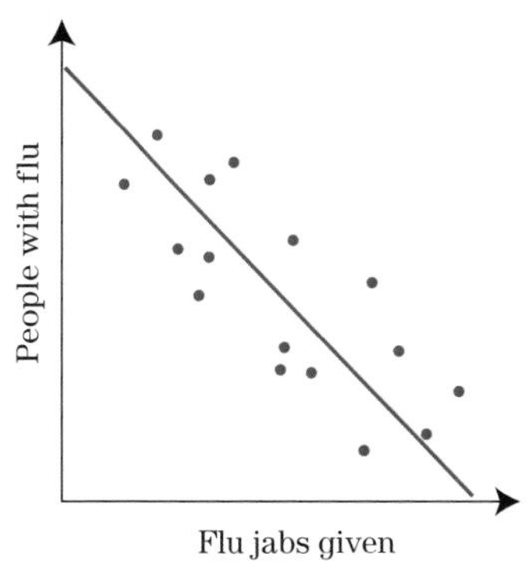
People with flu
Flu jabs given
Negative correlation
• When more jabs are given the number of people with flu falls.
• Flu jabs prevent flu.

FIGURE 2.3 Examples of a positive correlation and a negative correlation

SOURCE: https://scienceaid.net/psychology/approaches/representing.html

Advanced correlational research and techniques can *suggest* cause–effect relations. *Time-lagged* correlations reveal the *sequence* of events (for example, by indicating whether changed achievements more often precede or follow changed self-esteem). A third variable, such as IQ or self-efficacy, may have an influence on the apparent association of self-esteem and academic achievement. Third variables like these, sometimes called **'confounding' variables**, can be removed using statistical techniques to see if the association between self-esteem and academic achievement still survives.

A study that is based on a questionnaire is often called a *survey study.* Bear in mind, however, that survey studies are very often employed to gather fairly straightforward descriptive information about people, with no ambition to assess correlations between complex dimensions. For instance, surveys may be used to assess the percentage of people in a given region or country who intend to vote for a specific political candidate. In this case, researchers want to make predictions about what could be expected to happen in a whole population. Therefore they may obtain a *representative* group by taking a **random sample** – *one in which every person in the population being studied has an equal chance of inclusion.* With this procedure any subgroup of people – blondes, joggers, liberals – will tend to be represented in the survey to the extent that they are represented in the total population. It is an amazing fact that whether we survey people in a city or in a whole country, 1,200 randomly selected participants will enable us to be 95 per cent confident of describing the entire population with an error margin of 3 percentage points or fewer. Imagine a confounding variables in an experiment, these are uncontrolled variables that interact with the independent variable, which affect the outcome of the research. The researcher can then not determine which variable (or which combination of variables) is responsible for the observed results

random sample survey procedure in which every person in the population being studied has an equal chance of inclusion

TABLE 2.3 Recognizing correlational and experimental research

	Can participants be randomly assigned to condition?	Independent variable	Dependent variable
Are early-maturing children more confident?	No ⟶ Correlational		
Do students learn more in online or classroom courses?	Yes ⟶ Experimental	Take class online or in classroom	Learning
Do school grades predict vocational success?	No ⟶ Correlational		
Does playing violent video games increase aggressiveness?	Yes ⟶ Experimental	Play violent or non-violent game	Aggressiveness
Do people find comedy funnier when alone or with others?	(you answer)		
Do higher-income people have higher self-esteem?	(you answer)		

huge jar filled with beans, 50 per cent red and 50 per cent white. Randomly sample 1,200 of these, and you will be 95 per cent certain to draw out between 47 per cent and 53 per cent red beans – regardless of whether the jar contains 10,000 beans or 100 million beans. If we think of the red beans as supporters of one political candidate and the white beans as supporters of the other candidate, we can understand why, since 1950, the Gallup polls taken just before national political elections have diverged from election results by an average of less than 2 per cent. As a few drops of blood can speak for the whole body, so can a random sample speak for a population.

Experimental Research: Searching for Cause and Effect

The difficulty of discerning cause and effect among naturally correlated events prompts many social psychologists to create laboratory simulations of everyday processes whenever this is feasible and ethical.

Control: Manipulating Variables

Social psychologists experiment by constructing social situations that simulate important features of our daily lives. By manipulating the value of just one or two variables at a time – called **independent variables** – the experimenter pinpoints their influence on another variable – called the **dependent variable**. The experiment enables the social psychologist to discover principles of social thinking, social influence and social relations (the following chapters offer many research-based insights, a few of which will be highlighted in 'Research Close-Up' boxes that describe a sample study in depth).

independent variables the experimental factors that a researcher manipulates

dependent variable the variable expected to be dependent on the manipulation or change in the independent variable(s)

To illustrate the laboratory experiment, let's consider a very current topic: the impact social media has on our sense of well-being.

Correlational and Experimental Studies of Social Media on Well-Being

Tromholt (2016) cites a range of correlational studies that have shown an association between Facebook use, depression and poor life satisfaction. Can we therefore confidently state that using Facebook *causes* poor well-being? To find out, Trombolt devised an experiment. He recruited 1,300 Danish participants to take part. They were mostly women (86%), and across the sample had an average age of 34 years, used Facebook for approximately one hour every day, and had an average of 350 friends on Facebook. Participants were randomly assigned to either an **experimental condition** or a **control condition**. In the experimental condition participants were not allowed to go on Facebook for an entire week, whilst in the control condition participants continued to use Facebook as they usually would. Whether or not participants could use Facebook constituted the independent variable, that is the variable whose levels were predefined (manipulated) by the researcher. Prior to taking part in the experiment, participants had been asked to complete questionnaires about their satisfaction with their lives, and also their emotions. On the last day of the 7 days of testing, they were given these questionnaires again. The responses to these questionnaires formed the dependent variable. Would taking a break from Facebook change participants' life satisfaction and depression scores? By comparing the experimental condition participants' scores with those of the control condition participants, after 7 days of no Facebook use (experimental) or normal Facebook use (control), Tromholt found the experimental group reported higher levels of life satisfaction and positive emotions than the control group. Furthermore, the experimental group's scores had significantly increased from their pre-test questionnaire scores, prior to quitting Facebook. Tromholt also noticed that bigger increases in positive life satisfaction and emotions were experienced by those individuals in the experimental condition who were normally heavy Facebook users. The study concludes that not only are the correlational studies indicating causal relationships, but that Facebook use is having an adverse effect on our well-being.

Do social media platforms have an adverse affect on our well-being?

SOURCE: © Rawpixel.com/Shutterstock

experimental condition the condition in which the independent variable is presented to measure its effect on the performance (dependent variable) on participants in this condition

control condition the condition where the independent variable is absent and the data generated from this condition is used to compare with the experimental condition

So far we have seen that the logic of experimentation is simple: by creating and controlling a miniature reality, we can vary one factor and then another and discover how those factors, separately or in combination, affect people. Now let's go a little deeper and see how an experiment is done.

Every social psychological experiment has two essential ingredients. We have just considered one – *control*. We manipulate one or more independent variables while trying to hold everything else constant. The other ingredient is *random assignment*. Recall that in Tromholt's study he randomly assigned his participants to either the control or the experimental condition. Why did he do that?

Random Assignment: The Great Equalizer

Recall that we were reluctant, on the basis of a correlation, to assume that Facebook use *caused* poor well-being. A survey researcher might measure and remove other factors that might be responsible for the association and see if the correlations survive. But one can never control for all the factors that might distinguish individual Facebook users and their sense of well-being. Maybe Facebook users differ in education, culture, intelligence, health – or in dozens of ways the researcher hasn't considered.

random assignment the process of assigning participants to the conditions of an experiment such that all persons have the same chance of being in a given condition

In one fell swoop, **random assignment** (not to be confused with the concept of random *sampling* in surveys) eliminates all such extraneous factors. With random assignment, each person has an equal chance of being in the experimental condition (Facebook use stopped) or the control condition (Facebook use continues as normal). Thus, the people in both groups would, in every conceivable way – family status, intelligence, education, health, culture – average about the same. Highly intelligent people, for example, are equally likely to appear in both groups. Because random assignment creates equivalent groups, any later difference in well-being between the two groups will almost surely have something to do with the only way they differ – whether or not they took a break from Facebook for 7 days (**Figure 2.4**).

experimental research studies that seek to understand cause–effect relationships by manipulating one or more factors (independent variables) while controlling others (holding them constant)

ecological validity the extent to which findings observed in a study reflect what actually occurs in natural settings. Psychological laboratory research has been criticized for its low ecological validity

confounding variables in an experiment, these are uncontrolled variables that interact with the independent variable, which affect the outcome of the research. The researcher can then not determine which variable (or which combination of variables) is responsible for the observed results

Quasi-Experiments

Sometimes social psychological research cannot be conducted in a laboratory, yet the principles of **experimental research** are still required. In these circumstances researchers may adopt a quasi-experiment design. There are two basic types.

Natural Experiments

These are experiments in which the researcher does not directly manipulate the independent variable (IV). This may be for practical reasons or for research reasons. For example, you might want to see how long male shoppers spend in the supermarket shopping for groceries as compared to female shoppers. You cannot directly control the IV (gender), but you can match the number of respondents in each group (e.g. 20 male shoppers and 20 female shoppers), and you can still measure the effect the IV has on the dependent variable (amount of time shopping). There are some strengths in doing research in this way. As they do not rely on any intervention from the researcher, they have high **ecological validity**. However, there are some limitations also. As they occur in a natural setting you have no control over other variables (**confounding variables**). For example, we don't know if our sample are doing their weekly shop or just a daily shop. We can't control if they meet people they know in the supermarket and start talking to them.

Field Experiments

Unlike natural experiments, field experiments do offer the researcher the opportunity to control the IV, but they take place 'in the field'. This means the researcher has

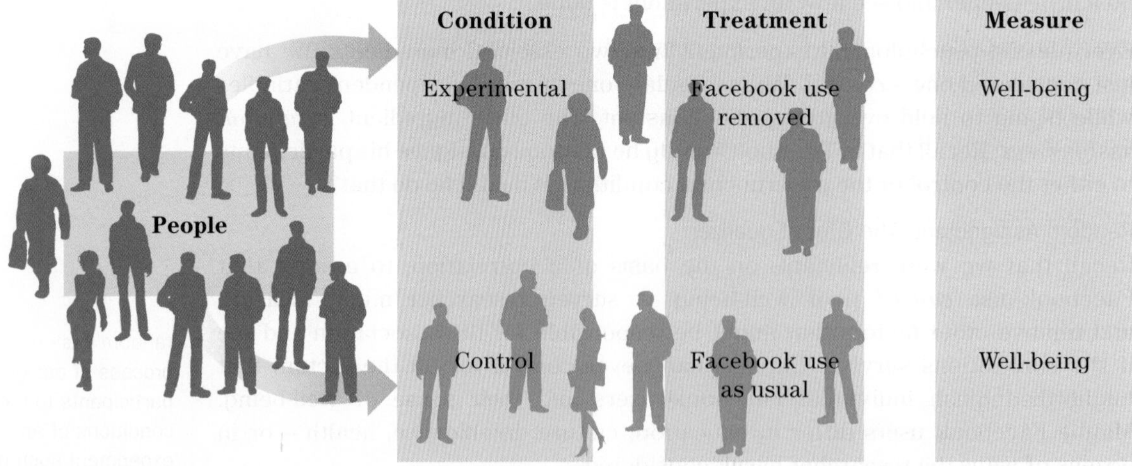

FIGURE 2.4 Random assignment Experiments randomly assign people either to a condition that receives the experimental treatment or to a control condition that does not. This gives the researcher confidence that any later difference is somehow caused by the treatment.

directly intervened with the research in some way. For example, a researcher might want to see if women are more helpful than men in a particular situation. To test this, the researcher might conduct the field experiment in a busy shopping centre and 'drop' bags of shopping in front of men and women to see if they help him or her to pick them up. Will women be more likely than men to go chasing after the researcher's fallen apples and oranges as they roll across the precinct floor? These kinds of experiments have their advantages. As they take place in a natural environment (in the field) they have high ecological validity. However, they also have their problems. Taken out of the confines of the laboratory, the researcher has much less control over the experiment and cannot foresee all the confounding variables. For example, whether a shopper helps may not be due to their gender but whether they are capable of helping (e.g. what if s/he has an unobservable back problem?).

Both of our examples here are of an 'observation study', which we consider in more detail later in this chapter.

Generalizing from Laboratory to Life

As the growing research on social media and well-being illustrates, social psychology mixes everyday experience with experimental designs. Hunches gained from everyday experience often inspire experiments, which deepens our understanding of our experience.

This interplay appears in the Facebook experiment. What people saw in everyday life suggested correlational research, which led to experimental research. Social media platforms, health authorities and government policy makers, those with the power to make changes, are now aware of the results. The effects one finds in the laboratory have been mirrored by effects in the field.

We need to be cautious, however, in generalizing from laboratory to life. Although the laboratory uncovers basic dynamics of human existence, it is still a simplified, controlled reality. It tells us what effect to expect of variable *X*, all other things being equal – which in real life they never are! And it seems we have good reason to be cautious. Psychologists often conduct field studies to demonstrate the generalizability of a finding from the laboratory. But how successful are they? Mitchell (2012) reviewed the results of 217 comparable laboratory and field studies. If they're comparable the results should correlate with each other. He found that not only were some of these lab to field studies not comparable at all, but sometimes the direction of results changed! Furthermore, as you will see, the participants in many experiments are university students. Although that may help you identify with them, college students are hardly a random sample of all humanity. Would we get similar results with people of different ages, educational levels and cultures? That is always an open question.

Nevertheless, we can distinguish between the *content* of people's thinking and acting (their attitudes, for example) and the *process* by which they think and act (for example, *how* attitudes affect actions and vice versa). The content varies more from culture to culture than does the process. People from various cultures may hold different opinions yet form them in similar ways.

Although our behaviours may differ, we are influenced by the same social forces. Beneath our surface diversity, we are more alike than different.

The Importance of Replication

A key aspect of quantitative research is that it should be replicable. As behaviours and parts of the social world are defined, isolated and measured, this level of rigorous standardization and control means that the study and its findings should be repeatable across time and space. If indeed we have found a truth about human behaviour as a result of an experiment, that truth should be revealed in any subsequent repeat of that experiment time and time again. However, in a study by Nosek et al. (2015), it was shown that this might not be easy to achieve. His attempt to replicate the findings of 100 published social psychological experiments resulted in only a third to a half of them producing results that matched those obtained in the original published study. Nosek's written report on this stirred a concern that was already gathering momentum in social psychology. In 2011, the work of Daryl Bem had already led social psychologists to suspect that the gold standard of the experiment as the revealer of universal truths, might not be as golden as we hoped (see Focus On).

Focus on

Daryl Bem and the Replication Crisis in Social Psychology

A prominent North American social psychologist, Daryl Bem, conducted a very unusual study. He recruited a sample of students and showed them 48 words, one at a time, asking them to visualize the referent of each word (e.g. if the word was *tree,* they were to visualize a tree). Then, students were given a (surprise) free recall test that involved typing all the words they could recall in any order. Subsequently participants were instructed to scan the full list of 48 words and click on 6 specific words that the computer had randomly selected, as a way to practise. The list of 48 words was then re-scrambled and the task of clicking on the 6 words was repeated. This specific task was performed a total of four times. Data analysis produced some bewildering results. In the recall task, students were more likely to write those words that were subsequently used in the practice task. Basically, students appeared to know in advance which words they would eventually practise. This provided evidence that a well-known psychological phenomenon – the effect of practice on recall – had been time-reversed. In sum, Bem seemed to have demonstrated the existence of precognition and psychic power! This study, together with eight other similar studies, was included in a paper titled 'Feeling the Future' published in the prestigious *Journal of Personality and Social Psychology* (Bem, 2011).

Needless to say, the paper was received with a great deal of scepticism, which has grown even stronger after two independent research teams failed to replicate Bem's findings (Galak et al., 2012; Ritchie et al., 2012). As well as casting serious doubts on the veracity of the phenomenon allegedly proved by Bem, these failed attempts at replicating his findings started the debate about the validity of the results that are regularly published in social psychology journals. To what extent can we trust those results? Are the processes and phenomena reported by social psychologists real or just fiction?

Questions

1 Why do you think that many social psychology studies fail to replicate?

2 Can you think of any other initiative, beyond those mentioned above, that could contribute to increase our confidence in published results?

3 How confident can we be in social psychology research findings?

For sure, the problem is not specific to social psychology. For instance, epidemiologist John Ioannidis, currently at the Stanford School of Medicine, claimed that most published research findings in medicine are false (Ioannidis, 2005). In line with that, Glem Begley, vice president of research at Amgen, a prominent bio-technology firm based in California, admitted that they are often unable to reproduce findings published by researchers in bio-medical journals (Naik, 2011).

Many scientists, including social psychologists, are now insisting that authors of studies that produce interesting results should make an effort to reproduce these results, especially if they are surprising and counter-intuitive, before publishing them. This would prevent non-existing effects and processes from being published in journals and from being accepted by many as established *facts*. This sounds like a simple recipe, but there is a problem: Researchers are often in a hurry to publish for career reasons, and so they are unwilling to spend time conducting replications after some interesting results have been obtained. But then, shouldn't researchers at least try to replicate their results after their first set of studies have been published? Or indeed, shouldn't researchers try to replicate published studies more generally, regardless of who the author of the original article was? The consensus is that, ideally, they definitely should! The problem in this case is that there are no incentives to do so. Attempts to replicate previously published studies are generally not welcome by academic journals. This is especially the case when an attempt at replication fails to reproduce the original results, because journals prefer to publish studies with *positive* results, that is, studies that successfully demonstrate the hypothesized existence of processes, mechanisms and phenomena. Daniele Fanelli (2011), a social scientist based at Edinburgh University, found that the proportion of positive results published in scientific journals is on the rise, and this is especially the case with psychology and psychiatry journals (see **Figure 2.5**).

Some argue that, actually, scientists are already sending replication studies to journals, as testified by the fact that many published studies actually replicate previous studies using different methods (e.g., different ways of measuring the variables under scrutiny, different participants, etc.). But although *conceptual replications* – as psychologists like to call these types of replications – are important because they show the generalizability of the results (Nussbaum, 2012), many researchers still believe that what is needed is *direct replications,* that is, exact copies of the studies to be replicated. Christian Montag (2018), a researcher in molecular and genetic psychology, suggests that more cross-cultural studies involving international samples would help produce globally valid findings. Brian Nosek, a social psychologist from the University of Virginia, put it plainly: 'To show that "A" is true you don't do "B". You do "A" again' (cited in Yong, 2012). One of the reasons for preferring direct over conceptual

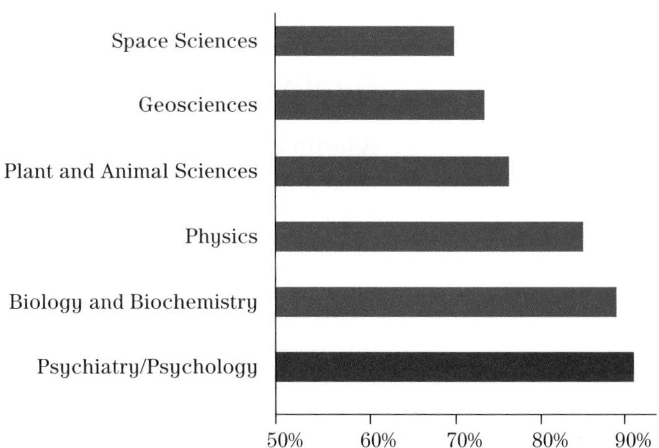

FIGURE 2.5 Percentage of published studies reporting positive findings (i.e. those that support the tested hypotheses) across disciplines.
SOURCE: Data from Fanelli (2011).

replications is that, as demonstrated by Simmons et al. (2011), flexibility in the way we try to reproduce previous studies enhances the chances of confirming the existence of the phenomenon.

The necessity of conducting direct replications and finding out what is true and what is actually not true has recently prompted interesting initiatives among psychologists. The prestigious journal *Perspectives in Psychological Science* is now publishing 'registered replication reports'. These are replications of important psychology experiments based on shared and vetted protocols that are commented upon by the authors of the original studies. Also, Brian Nosek has launched the *reproducibility project,* where a group of psychologists will replicate a large number of papers recently published in some selected journals, including the *Journal of Personality and Social Psychology.* To encourage early-career social psychology researchers to address the replication problem, Everett and Earp (2015) recommend that PhD students should be required to produce a replication of at least one key finding from their thesis before they graduate.

But does social psychology really have a replication crisis? No, argues Gilbert et al. (2016). Revisiting Brian Nosek's attempt to reproduce the findings of 100 published social psychological studies, Gilbert pointed to alterations that Nosek and his team had made when repeating the experiments. These alterations included changes in procedures for administering the experiment, different populations of people being tested (e.g. Americans rather than Italians), smaller sample sizes than those used in the original, and so on. Gilbert found that when all of this had been taken into account, the experiments were in fact, replicable. He concluded 'There is no evidence of a replication crisis in social psychology'. Whether there is, or there isn't an issue with replication in social psychology, the bottom line remains that it is something we should aim for in quantitative work.

In sum, while we may legitimately worry that some psychological phenomena we assume to be true may actually not be so, it is encouraging to see that psychologists, including social psychologists, have boldly started a process of self-correction. Hopefully, in the future we will feel more confident in the results produced by our research community.

Qualitative Research

As with quantitative research, social psychologists taking a qualitative approach start with a research question they wish to address. However, such a research question does not concern the interplay between variables and is not meant to produce hypotheses to be tested. Instead, the question is framed in a way that allows a free exploration of the issue at stake, with no specific expectations about what is to be found. For instance, a qualitative researcher could ask: 'How do foreign students experience their first year at university?' or 'How do European people define happiness?' This type of question implies a focus on the meaning of experiences and the understanding of situations and issues. The findings of qualitative research can be interpreted as representing 'facts' (or testimony) about human experience (essentialist), or as 'socially constructed' (or versions). This takes us back to our earlier mention of **epistemology**. Most qualitative research is open to either interpretation. While essentialist interpretations try to

epistemology the study of knowledge and the underlying status we give it. For example, is the knowledge we obtain about human behaviour a 'fact' or a 'version'?

reveal psychological properties of people (e.g. emotions, memory, personality), social constructionists regard what people say and/or do as embedded within the context of its production. The concerns over accuracy of data (sometimes the honesty of the participant in relaying their experiences) which trouble the essentialist are not a concern to the social constructionist. For the social constructionist, what is of interest is 'why this version now?'

Qualitative research differs from quantitative research in other important ways. First of all, sampling is typically not as random as that found in quantitative studies, but is purposive (sometimes called 'principled' or 'theoretical' sampling – see **Table 2.1**). As the concern is not necessarily with generalization but with people's experiences, samples do not always need to be representative. Indeed, a study may involve only one person (a case study), chosen because s/he is interesting in some way. People can be selected for inclusion in a qualitative study for all kinds of reasons. They may typify what we've already seen and heard among our sample. For example, in a sample of left-wing voters perhaps we've noticed that they all explain homelessness as the fault of the government. We may seek more left-wing voters to warrant this further, or we might try to find someone who may say something different. What might a right-wing voter say about homelessness? Or a liberal voter? So participants are selected for inclusion in a study for *principled* reasons.

Another important difference between qualitative and quantitative research concerns the role of the researcher. While quantitative researchers see themselves as interchangeable and almost like neutral elements that are external to the phenomena that are investigated, qualitative researchers see themselves as enmeshed in what they are studying. They are fully aware that by virtue of being present, they may change, alter or influence in some way the behaviour of research participants. So, qualitative researchers feel compelled to reflect on their role in the research process and make this clear in the analysis. This is usually referred to as '**reflexivity**' and denotes the influence of the researcher, as well as the immediate and wider social context, upon the research process.

reflexivity to recognize the role of the researcher in the production of the research findings

Collecting Data in Qualitative Research

Qualitative researchers have a vast array of methods that they can use, some of which may be similar to the methods used by quantitative researchers. **Interviewing** is perhaps the most commonly used method. The researcher may follow a schedule, but this is unlikely to include structured questions, that is, questions to be answered with pre-formatted response options. Interviews used by qualitative researchers tend to have minimal structure. The researcher may either have some fairly open questions to ask, to which the participant will give personal and usually lengthy responses, or opt for a conversational approach where the only constraint is to adhere to the research question. (See **Table 2.4** for the different styles of interviewing.)

interviewing a strategy to obtain qualitative data based on talking with and asking questions of research participants; questions may be asked either directly or indirectly, and responses are given in an open format

Researchers normally record the interviews and transcribe them either partially or fully, so that the text can be carefully analysed and interpreted. However, interviewing does not need to be done on an individual basis. In fact, some research questions are better investigated with small groups of people, known as **focus groups**. When running a focus group, the role of the researcher is to facilitate the discussion of the topic under investigation (i.e. act as moderator). Focus groups have typically been used in market research, but can be used to investigate all sorts of issues, including health education and promotion (Stopher, 2012).

focus group a strategy to obtain qualitative data based on a small group discussion about the issue of interest facilitated by the researcher

TABLE 2.4 Different styles of interviewing

Type of interview	Main features of interview	Limitations of interview style
Structured	Fixed questions asked in the same order. These are typically answered using a predefined set of response options. Because response options tend to correspond to quantities, this type of interview is more commonly used in a quantitative approach	Can lack validity as the questions may not reflect participants' experiences or understandings
Semi-structured	Contains key questions to maintain relevance. Flexible order in which questions are phrased and presented during interview to suit the experiences of the participant. Can build good rapport with interviewee. Useful for studying sensitive topics and issues	Lacks reliability. Poor researcher control for directing what is discussed in the interview and how it is discussed
Conversational/ unstructured	Contains key topic(s). Very flexible wording and presentation of questions. Participant-driven to capture their experience and understanding of the phenomena under investigation. Can build good rapport with interviewee. Useful for studying sensitive topics and issues	Very poor reliability. Researcher has very little control over the interview. Interview may not reflect interests or concerns of the research

Qualitative researchers may also use observational methods. This will often involve the direct participation of the researcher in the event or situation studied, in which case we talk of **participant observation**. By using direct involvement and full immersion in the context examined, the researcher tries to see the world through the eyes of the individuals and groups being studied. This is meant to provide the researcher with deep knowledge and understanding.

participant observation a research strategy in which the researcher spends time in close contact with the people studied (tribe, group, community, team) for a prolonged period of time in order to gain a deep understanding of their perspectives and practices

Other ways of obtaining data for qualitative research include the recording of naturally occurring conversations (e.g. interactions between a doctor and patient), and the collection of texts available from various sources including newspaper articles, diaries, letters, political transcripts, pamphlets, leaflets, booklets and the Internet (e.g. forums, blogs, dating sites).

Qualitative Data Analysis

The aim of qualitative data analysis is to capture 'meaning'. This requires researchers to carefully code data and discern themes, patterns and deviances present within their sample. Researchers have developed particular ways of doing this. Let's consider some of the main traditions of qualitative analysis.

Grounded Theory

Grounded theory (GT) was founded by Glaser and Strauss (1967), who developed the technique to challenge the grand theories that imposed a priori ways of collecting and analysing data. Working as sociologists involved in research with hospital patients, they had become frustrated with research techniques that understood their experiences in relation to pre-existing grand theories. These are outlined in their earlier work *Awareness of Dying* (Glaser & Strauss, 1965). So, in grounded theory, rather than beginning by developing a hypothesis or research question based on existing research and theory, data collection is the first step. From the data collected, concepts are developed and from these concepts categories are formed, which, using the **method of constant comparison**, are the basis for the creation of a theory. 'In discovering theory, one generates conceptual categories or their properties from evidence, then the evidence from which the category emerged is used to illustrate the concept' (Glaser and Strauss, 1967, p. 23).

method of constant comparison a technique whereby the researcher compares categories of responses to establish similarities and differences in meaning

Grounded theory does not aim for the 'truth' but seeks to develop a theory which accounts for every single piece of data, to explain what's going on in the data.

So it remains humble in its claims. It doesn't seek to generalize this theory beyond the data, thus resulting in another 'grand theory'. However, researchers may check their findings against similar studies for the validity and robustness of their claims. In a way GT resembles what many researchers do when retrospectively formulating new hypotheses to fit the data. However, in GT the researcher does not claim to have formulated the hypotheses in advance since this is not allowed (Glaser and Strauss, 1967).

Grounded theory can be used on most kinds of data. Field-notes can come from informal interviews, lectures, seminars, expert group meetings, newspaper articles, Internet mail lists, even television shows, conversations with friends, etc. It is even possible, and sometimes a good idea, for a researcher with much knowledge in the studied area to interview him/herself, treating that interview like any other data, coding and comparing it to other data and generating concepts from it.

Discourse Analysis

Discourse analysis (DA) has a long history in the social sciences, but is typically credited with being brought into social psychology by Jonathan Potter and Margaret Wetherell. Their book, *Discourse and Social Psychology: Beyond Attitudes and Behaviour* (Potter & Wetherell, 1987), applies the principles of DA to social psychological phenomena. Discourse analysts argue that 'talk' and 'text' should be the principal concerns of social psychology. Potter (1996) argues that language is not simply a mirror neutrally reflecting how we see the world and ourselves but is the construction yard in which social (and psychological) life is constructed (see also Edwards, 1997; Edwards & Potter, 2005). In other words, through language we create the world around us and our position within it, and in a way that is appropriate at the time. Discourse analysis typically studies language obtained from interviews, focus groups, natural conversations and forms of text (such as diaries, online forums, and newspaper articles). For example, people's responses to questions asked in interviews or questionnaires, or their thoughts, feelings, memories and experiences reported in a focus group or interview, or even written down in a diary, should be evaluated, interpreted and put into the context in which they were produced before it is possible to conclude what is actually being communicated. The analytical tool of DA is the '*interpretative repertoire*', which is used to refer to the linguistic resources people have available to them in understanding aspects of their social world.

A good example of findings produced through a discourse analytic method is research conducted by Burke and Goodman (2012). They were interested in how people discussed asylum seekers on Facebook online forums. Selecting six such forums where people openly discussed their attitudes to asylum-seeking, their discourse analysis of what was posted identified three interpretative repertoires.

1 Support for asylum seekers – this repertoire accused those who opposed asylum seekers of being uneducated racists and Nazis. They were dismissed as 'pathetic' and 'ridiculous' with reference to their spelling mistakes to evidence their stupidity. For example, one pro-asylum seeker posts: 'My seven year old foreign students over here in Hungary make fewer spelling and grammar mistakes. So CONGRATULATIONS one and all. I must remember to pack my swastika and jackboots next time I am visit England, or they might not let me in at Heathrow.'

2 Opposition to asylum seekers – this repertoire concerned the accusations of being racist and a Nazi by pro asylum-seekers, as a strategy to shut down a reasonable debate about asylum-seeking. For example, from one annoyed poster: 'why dont we actually organize a protest march to the gates of Buckingham Pallace. thousands of people marching through london would make the government sit up and listen. but we would more than likely be labled as BNP skin heads that where rioting by the biasted BBC who would not be able to ever hold a non bias discussion if they wanted to.'

3 Opposition to asylum-seekers and support for Hitler – this repertoire portrayed asylum-seekers in very derogatory terms. Regarded as social deviants and sexual deviants, asylum-seekers were blamed for stealing 'our' jobs. For example, posts included: 'Whos sick ov asylum seekers? Bring back Hitlers gas chambers. There nothing but rapists anyhow. Whos sick ov asylum seekers? (sic) init mate, all fukin rapists & thives!!!'

Burke and Goodman concluded that these interpretative repertoires offer important insights into how support and opposition to asylum-seekers are understood. They recommend that a more effective strategy for bridging support for asylum-seekers is to develop a repertoire that focuses on the harsh realities they face in their own country and the host one. Simply accusing those who oppose asylum-seekers as racists and Nazis is not going to win any support nor change any hearts and minds.

Some discourse analysts (sometimes called critical discourse analysts) have argued that the form of DA presented by Potter and Wetherell tends to assume people are free to use language in whatever way they choose (e.g. Parker, 1992). They point out that this isn't always the case. They are influenced by the work of the philosopher Michel Foucault, who emphasized the role of power in shaping language (e.g. Wodak, 2009;Wodak & Meyer, 2009). Foucault remarked that people are positioned in society in relations of power to one another. The most powerful make decisions about what is appropriate social behaviour, what can be said and what can't. Throughout history, ruling governments and leaders have decreed homosexuality as deviant and even an illness. This has shaped how sexuality is talked about and people's own behaviour. It has defined what can be said and what cannot. The point is that we are not always free to construct the world in precisely the way we'd like.

Discourse analysis has become widespread and popular among social psychologists, especially in Europe and Australia. For example, studies of prejudice or racism often benefit from a more detailed analysis of the language in which they are produced, warranted and justified as acceptable or deviant ways of seeing the world (see Chapter 13 for more detailed studies).

Interpretative Phenomenological Analysis

Interpretative phenomenological analysis (IPA) is based on the philosophy of phenomenology. Phenomenologists emphasize the inextricable relationship between the mind and the outside world (sometimes referred to as 'lifeworld'). They consider how our conscious experience of being-in-the-world is constituted by our feelings, embodiment, relationships, and sense of time and space, with the outside world. Founded by Jonathan Smith, IPA adopts an idiographic approach to focus on the subjective conscious experience of individuals. Drawing on data obtained from interviews or focus groups, and written texts including social media, letters and reports, IPA encourages the researcher to obtain as much description and knowledge of the participant's lifeworld as possible. In analysing the data, IPA engages with the meaning conveyed by participants in their described experiences. It tries to identify themes that occur and reoccur in the description of the participant, and if appropriate group or team, and organize the themes hierarchically. Does the participant prioritize the importance of some things over others? The production of a summary of themes for each participant then enables the researcher to look for comparisons in data obtained from other individual participants. Are any experiences common across all the data?

Michel Foucault (1926–84).
SOURCE: © INTERFOTO/Alamy

Let's return to the topic of social media. Kasket (2012) takes an IPA approach to study the fascinating, if mournful, topic of memorial Facebook groups. These are 'in-memory' pages dedicated to someone who was on Facebook and is now deceased. Kasket's interest is in people's experiences of engaging with these pages and the role a social media site such as Facebook can play in coping with bereavement. Kasket collected 943 Facebook posts made to five 'in-memorial' groups, dedicated to adolescents who had died in car crashes. She also conducted in-depth interviews with three people who had engaged with these sites. Kasket organized the data into four themes. The first theme was Modes of Address which denoted the Facebook user's relationship with the deceased. Whilst a few didn't know the person at all, most adopted a mode of address that was informal and chatty, appropriate for chatting to a friend. The second theme was Beliefs about Communication. This concerned whether the deceased was thought to be in receipt of communication with the Facebook user, and acting as a guide to the living in some form (e.g. a bright star in the sky). Thirdly, Facebook offered posters the Experience of Continuing the Bond, meaning they could continue to update the deceased on their news. The final theme was Nature and Function of Facebook, which illustrates the role this virtual platform can play in facilitating support, coping and management of grief amongst an identifiable community. As Kasket points out, with rapid changes in our technological landscape, sites such as Facebook will perform greater roles in bereavement management, offering users a different kind of interaction with the deceased than if they simply visited the graveyard. Unlike our earlier encounter with an experiment revealing some rather negative causal relationships between individuals generally, and Facebook, here the IPA study shows a richer, deeper and more positive picture of the individuals' engagement with the social media platform.

Research Ethics

Researchers often walk a tightrope in designing experiments and research that will be involving yet ethical. To believe that you are hurting someone, or to be subjected to strong social pressure, may be temporarily uncomfortable. Even the simple fact of being deceived about the real purpose of a study – which is what happens to participants in a substantial number of cases – may be an unpleasant experience. Such research raises the age-old question of whether the ends justify the means. Do the insights gained justify deceiving and sometimes distressing people?

Clearly, since social psychological research usually involves human beings, we have to be extra careful in how we treat them. That means that, however we conduct research, whatever methods we use, they all raise ethical issues. University ethics committees review social psychological research to ensure that it will treat people humanely.

To provide social psychologists, and psychologists more generally, in ethical practices, codes of conduct have become ingrained within the psychological professional bodies that represent the discipline. The American Psychological Association devised the first ethical guidelines for research in 1972. These were revised in 2002 and other psychological professional bodies representing the discipline in other countries followed suit. For example within the UK, psychologists are guided by the British Psychological Society's code of ethics, centred on four principles: Respect, Competence, Responsibility and Integrity. The values that social psychologists should consider in relation to each of these principles is laid out in **Table 2.5**.

As you can see, adherence to ethics is not simply a matter of being nice to our participants! It is an issue all psychologists have to take seriously when engaging in research and practice. If we reflect back on some of the classic social psychological studies, especially experiments, we appreciate why ethics has become such an integral part of the discipline. The scientific findings may not justify the research done to arrive at them! Ethical principles and codes of conduct developed by the British Psychological Society, American Psychological Association and the

TABLE 2.5 British Psychological Society's Ethical Guidelines for what psychologists should consider when conducting research

Principle	Value
Respect	- privacy and confidentiality - respect - communities and their shared values - impacts on broader environments - power issues - consent - self-determination - compassionate care
Competence	- possession of appropriate skills and care - recognize limits of competence and refer to another professional when necessary - advances in evidence base - maintain technical and practical skills - matters of professional ethics and decision-making - take mitigating actions when required - caution in making knowledge-claims
Integrity	- honesty, openness and candour - accurate, unbiased representation - fairness - avoidance of exploitation and conflicts of interest - maintain personal and professional boundaries - address misconduct
Responsibility	- professional accountability - responsible use of knowledge and skills - respect for welfare of humans, non-humans and living world - potentially competitive duties

Canadian Psychological Association amongst others, are rigorous, updated regularly and mandate investigators to do the following:

- Tell potential participants enough about the experiment to enable their **informed consent**. This is usually written consent but can be verbal in some cases. Under normal circumstances, our participants should give their consent to taking part in our research in the full knowledge of what it is about. They should also be aware of what you plan to do with your research findings. So will you publish it and if so, where? Who will you disseminate it to? Where will it be stored? How secure will it be?

informed consent an ethical principle requiring that research participants be told enough to enable them to choose whether they wish to participate

- Be truthful. Use **deception** only if essential and justified by a significant purpose and not 'about aspects that would affect their willingness to participate'. However, in some experiments we need participants to be a little naive about the true nature of what it is about. Telling participants we're recruiting them for an experiment that looks at how sexist they are, for example, might well cause those participants to change their behaviour so as not to appear sexist. Full knowledge would affect their behaviour and render the experiment meaningless. In these cases we tell participants as much as we possibly can about the study without negatively impacting upon the research's potential to reveal authentic behaviour.

deception in research, an effect by which participants are misinformed or misled about the study's methods and purposes

- Protect participants (and bystanders, if any) from harm and significant discomfort. This concerns not exposing participants to physical or psychological harm. Protecting participants from physical harm is usually relatively easy. Protecting our participants from psychological harm is more difficult to assess. We can deliberately avoid sensitive topics which we think might distress people, but sometimes even giving participants a word memory task can cause distress if they feel they're performing badly. It is the duty of the social psychologist to foresee and minimize the possibility of harm as much as possible and where it may have inadvertently occurred, to offer help and support, even if this means referring an individual to another professional.
- Treat information about the individual participants confidentially. Social psychological research can obtain a range of private information from people, such as their name, their sexual orientation, their health, their behaviour, and so on. It is essential that the social psychologist treats all such information as confidential, removes any features of the data that would render an individual identifiable to anyone beyond the researcher, and anonymizes the individual. Once that data has been used for the research purposes set out at the start, it should be destroyed.
- **Debrief** participants. Fully explain the study or experiment afterwards, including any deception. This of course carries the risk of upsetting participants who discover they've been 'fooled' in some way. Debriefing therefore should be done carefully and sensitively, and delivered in such a way that your participants feel they have made an important contribution to the discipline of social psychology and their own dignity and self-respect remains intact. The only exception to this rule is when the feedback would be unavoidably distressing, such as by making participants realize they have been stupid or cruel. In such cases the debrief should be as detailed as possible without causing undue distress. The experimenter should be sufficiently informative

Debrief in social psychology, the post-experimental explanation of a study to its participants. Debriefing usually discloses any deception and often questions participants regarding their understandings and feelings *and* considerate that people leave feeling at least as good about themselves as when they came in. Or, in other words, people should leave your research unaffected by it. Better yet, the participants should be compensated by having learned something.

SUMMING UP: RESEARCH METHODS IN SOCIAL PSYCHOLOGY

I KNEW IT ALL ALONG: IS SOCIAL PSYCHOLOGY SIMPLY COMMON SENSE?

- Social psychology is criticized for being trivial because it documents things that seem obvious.
- Systematic research methods, however, reveal that 'outcomes' are more 'obvious' after the facts are known.
- This hindsight bias (the 'I-knew-it-all-along' phenomenon) often makes people overconfident about the validity of their judgements and predictions.

APPROACHES TO DOING RESEARCH

- There are two broad approaches to doing research in social psychology: the quantitative and the qualitative approach.
- Researchers using a quantitative approach focus on the relationship between variables. With this aim in mind, the researcher will set up studies where the variables of interest can be measured, and then he/she will perform statistical analysis on the data.
- Researchers adopting a qualitative approach are interested in the experiential dimension of social psychological phenomena. Data are normally collected in naturalistic (not artificial) settings, and the data analysis focuses on the interpretation of meanings.

QUANTITATIVE RESEARCH

- Quantitative researchers start by formulating a research question and deriving testable hypotheses. Then, the researcher must decide upon a method to be used for hypothesis testing, with correlational and experimental methods being the two common procedures.
- Correlational methods are used to explore the relationship between variables, such as between amount of education and amount of income. Knowing two things are related is valuable information, and represent what often happens in and between humans: the variables interact and there is a multicausality in real life.
- The experimental method is based on the construction of a miniature reality that is under the control of the experimenter. We randomly assign participants to an experimental condition, which receives the experimental treatment, or to a control condition, which does not. We can then attribute any resulting difference between the two conditions to the independent variable. This is the essence of experimentation in social psychology.
- Quasi-experimental designs offer less (or no) control than laboratory designs over variables, but are also concerned with relationships between variables.
- The replication crisis has highlighted the importance of ensuring social psychological experiments produce results that reoccur over time and space, before making any truth claims about human behaviour.

QUALITATIVE RESEARCH

- Qualitative methods of data collection and analysis seek to consider social behaviour in the context in which it occurs, and focus on how people construct, understand and give meaning to their own experience of the social world.

- In qualitative research, data can be collected using a number of strategies, the most common being interviewing, focus groups and participant observation.
- The analysis of qualitative data can be conducted in accordance with different traditions. Three important traditions are grounded theory, discourse analysis and interpretative phenomenological analysis. (1) Grounded theorists use the data in order to create a theory about the phenomena under scrutiny. (2) Discourse analysts are interested in the way people actively construe the world through language. (3) Researchers using interpretative phenomenological analysis are interested in finding out how a person will experience and frame facts or life such as marriage or illness.

RESEARCH ETHICS

- In doing research, social psychologists sometimes stage situations that engage people's emotions, or observe them in their everyday lives. In doing so, they are obliged to follow professional ethical guidelines, such as obtaining people's informed consent, protecting them from harm, and fully disclosing afterwards any temporary deceptions.

Critical Questions

1. Does social psychology really differ from common sense? If so, how?
2. In your opinion, are the two general approaches to doing research in social psychology radically different, or are they complementary?
3. Do you think that establishing cause–effect relationships between psychological variables is more important than establishing a correlation? What is the difference between correlation and causation?
4. How strict should researchers be concerning ethical issues? Might exaggerated concerns limit researchers' ability to make progress?

Recommended Reading

Howitt, D., & Cramer, D. (2016). *Research methods in psychology*. Pearson Education.

3 THE SELF

"There are three things extremely hard, Steel, a Diamond, and to know one's self."
Benjamin Franklin

self a complex web of psychological entities (e.g., cognitions, emotions) and processes (e.g., monitoring, evaluating) concerning one's own person

At the centre of our worlds, more fundamental for us than anything else, is our **self**. As we journey through our daily lives, our sense of self engages with the world. We have more information about our self than anybody else has. We know our self better than we know any other person and than any other person knows our self. Or perhaps not? Sometimes we doubt. We start thinking 'Who am I really?' In the play *Peer Gynt* Henrik Ibsen tells the story of a man searching for his real self, but he does not find it. It is like peeling an onion: you can take away layer after layer but there is no hard substance there at the end. Similarly, we may be unsure about our own value. Sometimes we may feel fairly happy about ourselves, while other times we are unsatisfied, we feel insecure. This links to our preoccupations for the impression we make on others. We may wonder whether we are behaving appropriately, whether others like or despise our conduct. In sum, we cannot escape thinking about who we are, how much we are worth, how we should behave, and what others think of us. We cannot escape ourselves!

To some extent – as Leary (2004) has noted – our self-centredness and egocentric preoccupations may be a curse, becoming an impediment to a satisfying life. We often find ourselves managing the various 'selves' we feel we must perform for others in our increasingly hectic and complicated lives, and in return our mental and physical well-being suffers. This is what some forms of meditation practices seek to prune, by quieting the self, reducing its attachments to material pleasures and redirecting it. The recent surge of interest in the Eastern meditation tradition of '**mindfulness**' perhaps reflects this. Practising mindfulness requires us to stop and take notice of the world around us, and reflect upon our place within it. Reconnecting with our emotions, thoughts and self, and noticing how they are impacted upon by the busy world around us, can help in tackling stress, social anxiety and even depression. Stanley, Edwards, Ibinarriaga-Soltero, and Krause (2018) suggest that psychologists themselves should practise mindfulness to experience and appreciate the benefits it can bring to their clients and participants. Having a sense of self allows us to take our past into account, to assess our present, and to plan our future. In this respect the self does not make our existence more miserable; on the contrary, it can improve it by enhancing the control we have on our life.

Mindfulness based on Eastern meditation techniques, this approach focuses attention on experiencing the present moment

In this chapter, we explore all these aspects of the self. We discuss how the self-concept is formed and organized, and how we perceive, evaluate, protect and strategically present ourselves, pointing to the burden that the self may represent, as well as to its adaptive functions.

Spotlights and Illusions

Humans, especially those raised and living in Western cultures, tend to overestimate their conspicuousness. This **spotlight effect** means that we tend to see ourselves at centre stage, and so intuitively overestimate the extent to which others' attention is aimed at us.

spotlight effect the belief that others are paying more attention to one's appearance and behaviour than they really are

Have you ever got to the checkout of a supermarket, laden with goods in your basket, only to discover you've forgotten your wallet? Did you feel embarrassed? Have you been too embarrassed to buy condoms, super-strength deodorant, hair-loss cream or verucca remover, despite needing them? If so, you're not alone.

Feeling embarrassed in these kinds of situations is one of the negative aspects of the spotlight effect. We might feel everyone is looking at us, judging us, and possibly laughing at us! Lau-Gesk and Drolet (2008) explored the spotlight effect by comparing people identified as having High Public Self-Consciousness (HPUBSC) with those considered to have Low Public Self-Consciousness (LPUBSC). People with HPUBSC get embarrassed easily. They feel the spotlight effect intensely. Acutely aware of what they believe other people are thinking about them, they regulate their social behaviour accordingly. Highly sensitive to negative evaluation from others they will do anything to avoid social embarrassment. Lau-Gesk and Drolet discovered this influenced the shopping behaviour of those with HPUBSC. In their study, they found participants who are HPUBSC were less likely to buy embarrassing items such as an anti-flatulence product than those participants who were LPUBSC. Although we might feel mortified about buying such products, thankfully fewer people notice than we presume. We often suffer an **illusion of transparency**. If we're happy and we know it, then our face will surely show it. If we're embarrassed and we know it, then others, we presume, will notice. Actually, probably not. We can be more opaque than we realize. (See Research Close-Up: Are Liars Easy to Detect?.)

illusion of transparency the illusion that our concealed emotions leak out and can be easily read by others

We also overestimate the visibility of our social blunders and public mental slips. When we trigger the library alarm or are the only guest who shows up for the dinner without a gift for the host, we may be mortified. But research shows that what we agonize over, others may hardly notice and soon forget (Savitsky et al., 2001).

The spotlight effect and the related illusion of transparency are only two of many examples of the interplay between our sense of self and our social worlds. Here are more examples:

- *Social surroundings affect our self-awareness.* As members of a specific culture, race, gender or social class, we may notice how we differ and how others are reacting to our difference. Being a white European in a rural village in Africa, a wealthy person walking through a deprived suburb of a large city, or a woman being exceptionally invited to visit a men-only golf club in Scotland, would certainly raise self-consciousness!
- *Self-concern motivates our social behaviour.* In the hope of making a positive impression, we agonize about our appearance. (In fact, as we will see, even if our clothes and little imperfections are noticed less than we suppose, one's overall attractiveness does have effects.) Like shrewd politicians, we also monitor others' behaviour and expectations, and adjust our behaviour accordingly.
- *Social relationships help define our self.* In our varied relationships, we have varying selves, note Andersen and Chen (2002). We may be one self with Mum, another with friends and then another with teachers. How we think of ourselves is linked to whom we are in relationship with at the moment. This is even more typical for interdependent and collectivistic cultures where people are more engaged in creating harmony and balance in a group of people. To be a mature person in such cultures means to know how to fit in and change yourself accordingly.

Bad hair day? Fewer people notice our flaws than we think.

SOURCE: © Lars A. Niki

'No topic is more interesting to people than people. For most people, moreover, the most interesting person is the self.'

Baumeister (1999)

Research close-up

Are Liars Easy to Detect?

Source: Rai, R., Mitchell, P., & Faelling, J. (2012). The illusion-of-transparency: Are people egocentric or do people think that lies are easy to detect? *Psychological Studies, 57* (1), 58–66.

Introduction

Have you ever felt self-conscious in a job interview? Have you been concerned that the interviewer might spot your anxiety or your 'creative' account of your past experience and qualifications?

The illusion-of-transparency concept refers to the assumption that our thoughts and emotions are more transparent to other people than they really are. We attribute others with the power of mind-reading, that they can read our thoughts. But does that also mean they can see through our lies? This study sought evidence for this 'illusion of transparency' from students who were asked to tell a lie. Did they think it would be spotted by the person they told it to? And was it?

Study 1

Method

Thirty British university students, (age range: 18–25 years), were individually asked to write down their real memories of four different events, and to make-up one memory of a fifth event. The events were presented to the students in a standard template (see **Figure 3.1**). The five events were: (1) *an evening's activities in the last 2 weeks;* (2) *a journey taken within the last 6 months;* (3) *a childhood memory;* (4) *a recent shopping trip;* and (5) *a holiday.* The students were then placed into six groups of five people and taken to a room. Each group were then told that there would be five rounds. In each round, they were to tell the rest of their group one of their memories. In each round, one of the participants would be telling a lie (the made-up event) and the others would be telling the truth. Their job was to identify the liar for each round. Each participant was asked to write down the answer to three questions after each round: (1) *Which participant do you think is lying?,* (2) *How many people do you think will think you are the liar?* and (3) *How many people do you think will correctly identify who the liar is?*

Example of the holiday template

Once I went on holiday to __________. The holiday was around [time of year] __________. The holiday lasted for __________.
The weather was very __________. On holiday I [*insert activity/ something you saw or did*] __________

FIGURE 3.1 Template from the study
SOURCE: Rai et al. (2012)

Results

When telling the made-up event (i.e. lying), the liars thought that others would think and correctly identify them as the liar. They reported that 54 per cent of the group would think they were the liar. However, when the students were recalling a true event, they thought only 28 per cent of the group would think they were the liar. All of the students thought detecting the liar would be easier than it actually was.

So, it seems we are not only victims of this illusion-of-transparency, but we're also a little egocentric. Assuming others can read our minds, our truths and our lies, we see the world from our own point of view.

►

However, might there be something about the group dynamics which influences our judgements? What if someone appears a bit shifty, despite telling the truth? Also listening to five memories before making a judgement about the fake one relies heavily on **episodic memory**. Might this have affected the results? A further study was conducted to find out.

episodic memory refers to our memory for autobiographical events, including times, places and emotions experienced

Study 2

Method

Twenty-six students studying at a British university (age range 18–22 years) were asked to individually complete 20 statements (see **Figure 3.1**). Ten of these statements were to be true, and ten false. Students were then paired up, and told to read each statement out loud to their partner. As each statement was read out, the partner had to answer whether they thought it was true or false, and on a scale of 0–100 how doubtful they were of the truth being said (with 0 = definitely telling the truth, 100 = definitely lying). The speaker was also asked to rate on a scale of 0–100, how much they thought the listener would doubt the truth of what they were being told.

Results

Both speaker and listener expressed more doubt over the truthfulness of a statement when it was a lie.

Discussion

Generally speaking, people think that lies are easier to detect than they actually are. The illusion-of-transparency seems to prevail. When we lie, we overestimate the ability of other people to read our minds and spot the untruths. However, perhaps something about how accomplished the liar is at telling lies has some influence. In experiment 2, acutely aware of being asked to tell a lie to one other person, did the student give something away? How plausible was the lie they told? A stumbling delivery might sow seeds of doubt in the mind of the listener as well as the speaker's confidence in having successfully pulled the wool over their listener's eyes. Might we have a smoother delivery to a friend, a member of our family, a potential employer? Interpretation of the results needs to be done with caution.

Critical Reflections

The authors themselves note that we should exercise caution when reaching conclusions on the basis of their results. Indeed, there are things to be cautious about here.

Of the 26 participants, 8 sets of results had to be excluded as the scales had been completed incorrectly. With so few participants left whose data could be analysed, it's a limitation for trying to generalize these results beyond the experiment.

ecological validity the extent to which findings observed in a study reflect what actually occurs in natural settings. Psychological laboratory research has been criticized for its low ecological validity

We can question the **ecological validity** of studies such as this. How reflective are they of the real-world situations we might find ourselves in when we might lie? How representative are university students of the general population when it comes to detecting liars? And how many people do we need to test in a study to be confident about the findings?

So are we able to detect lies? Perhaps.

Self-concept: Who Am I?

What determines the concept we have of ourselves? And how accurately do we actually know ourselves?

As a unique and complex creature, you have many ways to complete the sentence 'I am _____.' (What five answers might you give?) Taken together, your answers define your **self-concept**.

self-concept a person's answers to the question 'Who am I?'

This simple but effective way to elicit one's self-concept – known as the Twenty Statements Test (TST) – was developed by Manfred Kuhn, one of the founders of the Iowa School of Social Psychology, and his collaborator Thomas McPartland (Kuhn & McPartland, 1954).

Self-knowledge

'Know thyself', admonished an Ancient Greek oracle. We certainly try. We readily form beliefs about ourselves, and we don't hesitate to explain why we feel and act as we do. According to Mead (1934), self-knowledge comes mainly from feedback we receive from other people. We may rely either on what particular individuals have to say about us, or on the picture offered by a combination of other people (what Mead called the 'generalized other'). And feeling like we know our 'self' can have positive repercussions for how we feel about the world around us. In their study, Schlegel et al. (2011) noted how those of us who feel we really know our true self find more meaning in life and report higher levels of self-esteem than those who struggle to 'know thyself'. But how well do we actually know ourselves?

'There is one thing, and only one in the whole universe which we know more about than we could learn from external observation' noted Lewis (1952, pp. 18–19). 'That one thing is [ourselves]. We have, so to speak, inside information; we are in the know.' Indeed. Yet sometimes we *think* we know, but our inside information is wrong. Or to put it in a less dramatic way: my understanding and perception of myself is different from how other people understand and perceive me. That is the unavoidable conclusion of some fascinating research.

Self-schemas

We tend to think of ourselves as separate from the places and other people we encounter. We imagine our 'self' as a physically and psychologically bounded entity, distinct from the world around us. As a child, we learn the impact of 'cause-and-effect', noticing that the 'self' can have an effect upon the world. As our sense of self develops, so does our sense of 'not-self'. Who I am becomes defined in relation to who I am not.

Psychologists have explored the concept of self using a range of approaches. One of the most prevalent is that which focuses on how we understand and represent the self cognitively. From this approach, the elements of your self-concept are your **self-schemas** (Fiske & Taylor, 2013; Markus & Wurf, 1987). *Schemas* are mental templates by which we organize our world, which obviously includes ourselves. Our self-schemas – our perceiving ourselves as athletic, overweight, intelligent, or whatever – powerfully affect how we see, remember and evaluate other people and ourselves. If athleticism is central to your self-concept then you will tend to notice others' bodies and skills. You will quickly

self-schemas beliefs about self that organize and guide the processing of self-relevant information recall sports-related experiences. And you will welcome information that is consistent with your self-schema (Kihlstrom & Cantor, 1984).

We discuss schemes and their role in guiding us around the social world in more detail in Chapter 4.

Self-reference

The self-concept has implications for information processing and memory. Consider the phenomenon known as the **self-reference effect**: when information is relevant to our self-concepts, *we process it quickly and remember it well* (Higgins & Bargh, 1987; Kuiper & Rogers, 1979; Symons & Johnson, 1997). Nicholas Kuiper's ground-breaking studies in the 1970s and 1980s asked students to rate adjectives (e.g. 'energetic', 'prudent') to describe themselves and other people. For the self-referent task, adjectives independently assessed as being extremely like or unlike the self had significantly faster rating times than adjectives only moderately self-descriptive. This has been called the 'inverted-U Rating Time effect' (Kuiper, 1981).

self-reference effect the tendency to process efficiently and remember well information related to oneself

Do you find it easier to remember some of your friends' birthdays than others? Are those the ones that are closest to your own birthday? If so, you're not alone. That's what Kesebir and Oishi (2010) found. In their study, participants remembered the birthdays of friends much better when the date was close to their own birthday. Furthermore, this effect isn't just found for our friends. Participants also remembered the made-up birthdays of fictitious people more easily when the date was close to their own birthday. And this effect was found to be stronger for men than it was for women. So the self-reference effect aids memory. When we think about something in relation to ourselves, we remember it better.

The self-reference effect illustrates a basic fact of life, at least in Western cultures: our own self is the centre of gravity of our world. Not only do people tend to see themselves on centre stage, overestimating the extent to which they are noticed by others (see the spotlight effect in this chapter), but when judging someone else's performance or behaviour we often spontaneously compare it with our own (Dunning & Hayes, 1996). And if, while talking to one person, we overhear our name spoken by another in the room, our auditory radar instantly shifts our attention. If the self-reference effect is an expression of focusing on the personal self we would expect it to occur less in collectivistic cultures, where people do not want to stand out and be exceptional, than in individualistic cultures.

But of course, many of us belong to more than one culture. And those cultures may uphold very different values. So how does this impinge upon our sense of self? Brannon et al. (2015) explored the self-schemas of African Americans. They wondered how being embedded within both American culture and African American culture, impacted upon the self. They found that when their participants were primed with mainstream American culture, their self-schemas reflected independent values such as personal achievement and ambition. However, when primed with African American culture, those self-schemas shifted into ones that reflected more cooperative interdependent values. Brannon and her team suggest that African Americans experience a 'double consciousness' of self as they are situated within two very different cultures. Interestingly, this study also incorporated African American culture into their studies. African American content such as films and literature were integrated into the course, as were culturally relevant ceremonies and holidays (e.g. Black History Month). The researchers found that as a result African American students performed much better academically than they had done previously. So when our environment is aligned with our sense of self, we may feel more self-assured, secure and therefore perform much better.

Predicting our Behaviour and Feelings

People err when predicting their behaviour. If asked whether they would hesitate to help a victim if several other people were present, people overwhelmingly deny their vulnerability to such influences. But as we will see, experiments have shown that many of us are vulnerable.

People also frequently err when predicting the fate of their relationships. Dating couples tend to predict the longevity of their relationships through rose-tinted glasses. Their friends and family often know better, report MacDonald and Ross (1997) from studies with University of Waterloo students. In fact, the people who know you can probably predict your behaviour in a variety of situations better than you can – for example, how nervous and chatty you will be when meeting someone new (Kenny, 1994). How can you improve your self-predictions? The best advice is to consider your past behaviour in similar situations (Osberg & Shrauger, 1986, 1990). To predict your future, consider your past.

In Chapter 7 you can read about yawning as something contagious. Generally humans have a tendency to react with congruent facial expressions when looking at an emotional face. This phenomenon is called *facial mimicry*. It appears to be an automatic and unconscious reaction, without awareness or conscious control, and it cannot be completely suppressed (Dimberg et al., 2002). Our 'self' therefore accomplishes activities with consequences for our relationship to others without being able to fully control it.

Many of life's big decisions involve predicting our future feelings. Would marrying this person lead to lifelong contentment? Would entering this profession make for satisfying work? Would going on this holiday produce a happy experience? Or would the likelier results be divorce, job burnout and holiday disappointment?

Sometimes we know how we will feel – if we fail that examination, win that big game or soothe our tensions with a half-hour jog. We know what exhilarates us and what makes us anxious or bored. Other times we may mispredict our responses. Asked how they would feel if asked sexually harassing questions on a job interview, most women studied by Woodzicka and LaFrance (2001) said they would feel angry. When actually asked such questions, however, women more often experienced fear.

Moreover, we are especially prone to impact bias after *negative* events. When people being tested for HIV predict how they will feel five weeks after getting the results, they expect to be feeling misery over bad news and elation over good news. Yet, five weeks later, the bad news recipients are less distraught and the good news recipients are less elated than they anticipated (Sieff et al., 1999). Impact bias is important, say Wilson and Gilbert (2005), because people's 'affective forecasts' – their predictions of their future emotions – influence their decisions. If people overestimate the intensity and the duration of the pleasure they will gain from purchasing a new car or undergoing cosmetic surgery, then they may make ill-advised investments in that new Mercedes or extreme makeover.

Research close-up

An Illusion of Conscious Will

Source: Wegner, D. M., Sparrow, B., & Winerman, L. (2004). Vicarious agency: Experiencing control over the movements of others. *Journal of Personality and Social Psychology, 86*, 838–848.

Introduction

In everyday life, we routinely will actions, such as raising our hand. We will an act. It happens. And, witnessing the sequence, we understandably infer that we caused it. Sometimes though, we experience what psychologist Daniel Wegner (2002) calls an 'illusion of conscious will'. People whose hand is jointly controlling a computer mouse will perceive that they caused it to stop on a square that actually was predetermined by their partner (an experimenter's accomplice). Could people also be induced to sense themselves raising someone else's hand?

Method

In one condition of the experiment participants watched themselves in a mirror while another behind them placed their hands where the participants' hands would normally appear (see **Figure 3.2**). The participants knew those arms weren't their own; they didn't perceive the arms as looking or feeling like their own. Then, participants were requested hand movements, such as 'make the A-OK sign'. That enabled the participant to anticipate the observed hand movements. There was also a baseline condition, in which the same hand movements occurred without any instruction (and thus no mental anticipation).

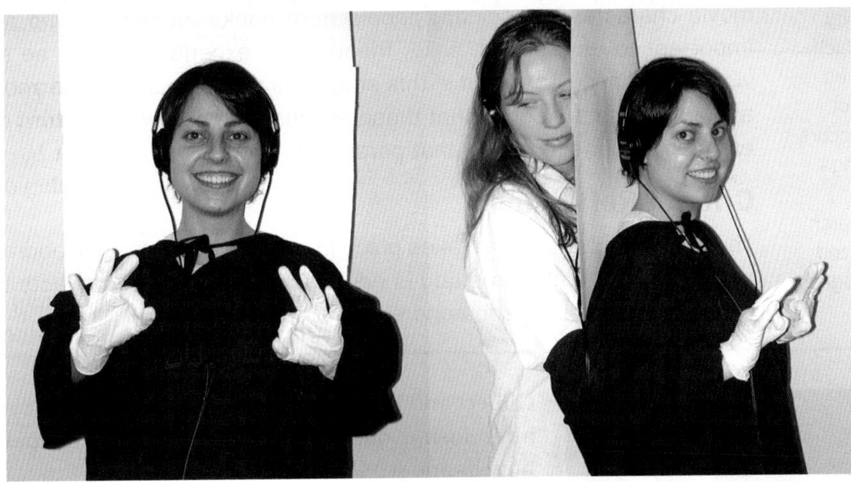

FIGURE 3.2 Vicarious agency. The photo at left shows a participant seen as she would have seen herself in the mirror. The photo at right shows the participant and a research assistant.
SOURCE: Wegner et al. (2004), reprinted with permission.

Results

When participants could anticipate the hand movement, they reported feeling some degree of control, as if they were willing the hands to move (**Figure 3.3**). In the baseline condition, however, participants felt little sense of control. It was when the participants visualized an action and it promptly happened that they felt some responsibility.

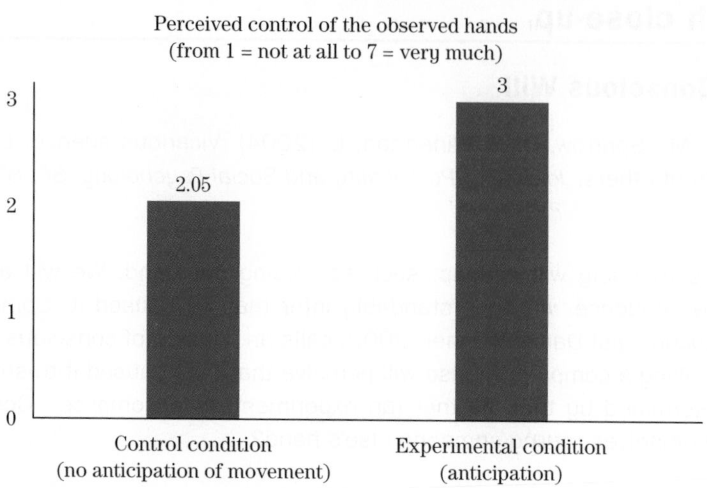

FIGURE 3.3 An illusion of willpower
When watching themselves in a mirror and witnessing a simulation of their own hand movements, people who anticipated the movement felt increased control over it.

Discussion

This study shows that when our thoughts are consistent with someone else's action, we may feel that we have caused the action. These findings relate to our ability to empathize with other people's actions in our daily life. We often experience an empathic extension of self to movie characters, imaginary people from books, or people who are close and important to us (spouse, child, friend). This experience might be a form of the vicarious agency observed in this study: our ability to anticipate another person's actions prompts a sense that those actions are ours, which in turn enhances our emotional connection with that person.

ecological validity the extent to which findings observed in a study reflect what actually occurs in natural settings. Psychological laboratory research has been criticized for its low ecological validity

Critical Reflections

The study described here takes place in a carefully controlled laboratory. To what extent do you think this study is **ecologically valid**–that it reflects the real-world illusion of controlling someone else's actions?

Predicting behaviour, even one's own, is no easy matter, which may be why this visitor goes to a fortune teller in hope of help.

SOURCE: © Photographee.eu/Shutterstock

Gilbert and Wilson invite us to imagine how we might feel a year after losing our non-dominant hands. Compared with today, how happy would you be?

Thinking about that, you perhaps focused on what the calamity would mean: no clapping, no shoe tying, no competitive tennis, no speedy keyboarding. Although it is likely that you would forever regret the loss, your general happiness some time after the event would be influenced by 'two things: (a) the event, and (b) everything else' (Gilbert & Wilson, 2000). In focusing on the negative event, we discount the importance of everything else that contributes to happiness and so over-predict our enduring misery. 'Nothing that you focus on will make as much difference as you think,' concur researchers Schkade and Kahneman (1998).

The Wisdom and Illusions of Self-analysis

To a striking extent, then, our intuitions are often wrong about what has influenced us and what we will feel and do. But let's not overstate the case. When the causes of our behaviour are conspicuous and the correct explanation fits our intuition, our self-perceptions will be accurate (Dunning, 2005). When the causes of behaviour are obvious to an observer, they are usually obvious to us as well.

As Chapter 4 explores further, we are unaware of much that goes on in our minds. Perception and memory studies show that we are more aware of the *results* of our thinking than of its process. For example, we experience the results of our mind's unconscious workings when we set a mental clock to record the passage of time or to awaken us at an appointed hour, or when we somehow achieve a spontaneous creative insight after a problem has unconsciously 'incubated'. Similarly, creative scientists and artists often cannot report the thought processes that produced their insights, although they have superb knowledge of the results.

Possible Selves

As we've begun to hint at in the earlier sections, the self-concept does not just concern who we think we are in the present but also who we think we might become in the future – the **possible selves**. Hazel Markus and her colleagues (Inglehart et al., 1989; Markus & Nurius, 1986) note that the possible selves include the visions of the self we dream of becoming – the helping self, the wise self, the passionately loved and loving self. They also include the self we fear becoming – the underemployed self, the unloved self, the academically failed self. Such possible selves motivate us with a vision of the life we long for.

possible selves images of what we dream of or dread becoming in the future

Our vision of who we *could* be can have important life-changing consequences. Writing from the field of forensic psychology, Meek (2011) looked at the role possible selves play in the rehabilitation of imprisoned young fathers, aged 18–21 years, in England. Meek asked these young men to describe who they hoped to be, who they expected to be, and who they feared they would be, upon being released from prison. They feared re-offending and returning to prison. However, they hoped and expected to be good parents, to achieve good things, obtain secure employment, and lead a life away from crime. Meek suggests that rehabilitation programmes for offenders in prison might benefit enormously from focusing on possible selves, such as being a parent, to motivate positive behaviour and create a sense of self post-prison.

Self-discrepancy Theory

Our various self-perceptions may not be consistent with one another, thereby creating discrepancies that may produce psychological discomfort. This idea is elaborated by Higgins (1987) in his self-discrepancy theory. This theory identifies three types of self-representation:

1. the *actual* self, regarding features that people believe they possess;
2. the *ideal* self, which includes characteristics that people wish or hope to possess; and
3. the *ought* self, concerning attributes that people believe they have a responsibility to possess.

The theory postulates that a discrepancy between the actual and the ideal self leads to dejection-related emotions (disappointment, dissatisfaction, sadness), and that a discrepancy between the actual and ought self generates agitation-related emotions (fear, threat, restlessness). Because of the negative mental states deriving from self-discrepancies, people strive to match their actual self with both their ideal and their ought self. In their study of self-discrepancies amongst university students, Barnett et al. (2017) discovered some interesting associations, which mirrored Higgins' theory. They found that with an increasing discrepancy between their actual self and their ideal self, students felt increasing sadness. However, as the actual and ideal self became more aligned, students reported feelings of joviality, self-assurance and surprise. Guilt and shame were the emotions commonly reported with discrepancy between the ought self and the actual self. Interestingly, Bizman and Yinon (2002) extended self-discrepancy theory to social identity (one's sense of self derived from membership in a social group). These authors studied a sample of Israelis and found that a discrepancy between actual and ideal Israeli identity produced dejection-related emotions while a discrepancy between actual and ought Israeli identity prompted agitation-related emotions.

It should be kept in mind, however, that a motivation to maintain a sense of consistency between different self-perceptions may be more marked in Western than in Eastern cultures. In fact, in East Asian cultures people tend to accept inconsistency and even antagonism in their self. They also accept that sometimes there will be differences between their aspirations and their actual behaviours.

The Self and its Brain

Of course, much of our sense of self comes from the sensory information we process. We have a physical, or biological, sense of self. If I ask you to point to where your sense of self resides within your body, where would you point? Limanowski and Hect (2011) found that most adults point to an area between our ears and eyes. We may not know it, but we are pointing at a location in our brain where sensory information is processed. Researchers in the field of social cognitive neuroscience (Lieberman, 2007) investigate the brain activity that underlies different aspects of the self. To start with they have asked themselves where our constant sense of being oneself arises. Some studies suggest an important role for the right hemisphere. Put yours to sleep (with an anaesthetic to your right carotid artery) and you likely will have trouble recognizing your own face. One patient with right hemisphere damage failed to recognize that he owned and was controlling his left hand (Decety & Sommerville, 2003). The 'medial prefrontal cortex', a neuron path located in the cleft between your brain hemispheres just behind your eyes, seemingly helps stitch together your sense of self. It becomes more active when you think about yourself (Zimmer, 2005). Consistent with that, studies have found that thinking about our own personality traits leads to greater activation of the medial prefrontal cortex, but also the medial parietal cortex, than thinking about someone else's personality characteristics (D'Argenbeau et al., 2005; Kjaer et al. 2002).

Intriguingly, social cognitive neuroscientists have also observed significant activations of the medial prefrontal cortex when people think about the personality traits and mental states of their mother (Ruby & Decety, 2004), a close friend (Ochsner et al., 2005), or someone considered as similar to self (Mitchell et al., 2005). The fact that thinking about oneself and thinking about others who are somehow associated with oneself activate similar areas of the brain, suggests that others may be experienced as in some way enmeshed with oneself.

The Social Construction of the Self

Researchers taking a constructionist perspective to the self, such as Gergen (1994, 2001; Gallagher and Gergen, 2011), Kitayama (2000), or Wetherell and Maybin (1996), contend that considering self-conceptions as enclosed and private, as residing in one's own head, gives an incomplete and misleading description of the human self. My thoughts and feelings about myself may seem to be locked inside my head, to be properties of my mind, but actually they are part of an always changing, fluid, dynamic system of social relationships in which I am involved. 'Who I am' is not just in my mind but it is recounted in the stories I tell other people, the diaries I may write, and the letters I exchange. People who listen to us and read what we write form ideas about us, and relate to us on the basis of their own version of who we are, which in turn impacts upon our sense of self. As a consequence, the self is better described as *distributed* rather than localized, as embedded into a web of social relationships rather than as an entity under the skull (Bruner, 1990). This perspective also emphasizes that the self finds expression in our daily social encounters and interactions, which should be seen as *joint actions* within which the self emerges (Shotter, 1993). For example, Beames (2005) explored how the sense of self for young British adults, aged 17–25 years, was shaped by an expedition to Ghana. As the young people experienced new cultures, objects, traditions, ways of thinking, and interacted with new people, Beames reports how their mental resilience, attitudes towards people and society, and overall sense of self, were transformed by the trip. Clearly, if the self emerges in conversations and interactions, then it is largely contextual rather than singular and unitary.

The Social Self

The self-concept has become a major social psychological focus because it helps organize our thinking and guide our social behaviour. But what determines our self-concepts? Our sense of self is heavily influenced by our environment and experiences. These contribute to the shaping of our self-concept. Culture and social experience play, according to George Herbert Mead and many social psychologists today, a very important part (e.g. Heine, 2005 et al., 2002; Rattan, 2011; Sullivan et al., 2014). Among these influences are the following:

- the roles we play
- the social identities we form
- the comparisons we make with others
- our successes and failures
- how other people judge us
- our wider cultural values and beliefs

The Roles We Play

When we take on a new role – student, parent, salesperson – we initially feel self-conscious. Gradually, however, what begins as play-acting in the theatre of life is absorbed into our sense of self. For example, while playing our roles we may support something we haven't really thought much about. Having made a pitch on behalf of our organization, we then justify our words by believing more strongly in it. Role playing becomes reality (see Chapter 5).

Social Identity

social identity one's sense of self and identity based on membership in social groups

Following the pioneering work of Henri Tajfel (1981), social psychologists make a distinction between a personal and a **social identity**. Personal identity concerns our unique, idiosyncratic attributes, such as being hardworking (or laid back), and extrovert (or introvert). Social identity is the sense of who we are, derived from our membership in groups and collectives of various sorts. Being female, Iranian, Muslim, British-Asian, a psychology student, socialist, a teacher, or a Real Madrid supporter are all aspects that may confer on one's social identity; that is, an identity that is shared in common with other people. The extent to which we are aware of any specific social identity depends, however, on the nature of the context. For instance, when we're part of a small group surrounded by a larger group, we are often conscious of our social identity; when our social group is the majority, we think less about it. As a solo female in a group of men, or as a solo Indian in a group of Europeans, we are more conscious of our unique social identity or belongingness (Oakes et al., 1994).

Chapter 12 discusses Tajfel's work and the distinction between personal and social identity in more detail.

Social Comparisons

social comparison evaluating one's abilities and opinions by comparing oneself with others

People are generally eager to compare themselves with other individuals. By engaging in **social comparisons** (Festinger, 1954), people try to establish if they are richer, smarter, or taller than others. As we explore throughout this book, comparing ourselves with others has a huge impact on how we think and act. Others around us help to define the standard by which we define ourselves as rich or poor, intelligent, tall or short: we compare ourselves with them and consider how we differ. Social comparison explains why students tend to have a higher academic self-concept if they attend a school with few exceptionally capable students (Marsh et al., 2000), and how that self-concept can be threatened when a student who excelled in an average high school goes on to an academically selective university. The 'big fish' is no longer in a small pond.

Much of life revolves around social comparisons. We feel handsome when others seem plain, smart when others seem dull, caring when others seem callous. When we witness a peer's performance, we cannot resist implicitly comparing ourselves (Gilbert et al., 1995). In a competitive society we may, therefore, privately take some pleasure in a peer's failure, especially when it happens to someone we envy and when we don't feel vulnerable to such misfortune ourselves. Colyn and Gordon (2013) found that their participants experienced pleasure in an envied friend's misfortune, especially when that misfortune negatively affected their physical attractiveness and was the same sex as the participant. This is a phenomenon known as **schadenfreude**. But social comparison does not just concern our personal identity, but also the in-groups that are part of our social identity. That is, people may compare their in-group with relevant out-groups in order to ascertain the status and prestige of the in-group (Tajfel, 1981). Intriguingly, taking pleasure at the misfortunes of others may imply taking malicious pleasure at the suffering of another group which we normally compare to our own group. Group schadenfreude has been studied in detail by Russell Spears and Colin Wayne Leach (Spears & Leach, 2004; Leach & Spears, 2009). These social psychologists have found that the strong drive for the experience of schadenfreude is the pain of in-group inferiority and the anger based on this pain (Leach & Spears, 2008).

schadenfreude to take pleasure in somebody else's misfortune

Social comparisons can also diminish our satisfaction. When we experience an increase in affluence, status or achievement, we 'compare upwards' – we raise the standards by which we evaluate our attainments. When climbing the ladder of success, we tend to look up, not down; we compare ourselves with others doing even better (Gerber et al., 2018). When feeling low about our selves, we often protect our shaky self-concept by comparing downwards. **Downwards Comparison Theory** (Wills, 1981) describes this process. For example, Lew et al. (2007) found that when women with low body satisfaction were presented with pictures of attractive and thin women, they compared themselves favourably against them on non-appearance dimensions such as intelligence. Focusing and comparing downwards can buffer against anxiety and low self-esteem.

downwards comparison theory when our self-esteem is threatened we compare downwards to restore it

Success and Failure

Self-concept is fed not only by our roles, our social identity and our comparisons, but also by our daily experiences. To undertake challenging yet realistic tasks and to succeed is to feel more competent. After mastering the physical skills needed to repel a sexual assault, women feel less vulnerable, less anxious and more in control (Ozer & Bandura, 1990). In India, Mary Kom founded the country's first ever Fight Club for women teaching self-defence techniques to women. Her initiative began after being a victim of sexual assault. Unbeknownst to her attacker, Kom (or 'Magnificent Mary' as she is known to her fans!) was the bronze winner of the 2012 Olympics for female boxing. Her attacker hadn't expected such a petite woman to be an Olympic boxer. He was left on the ground, bleeding, with a broken nose. Whilst Kom's classes cannot stop widespread sexual assaults, they can empower women to repel them and perhaps change a few ideas about gender along the way (Rumbelow, 2014). Feeling competent also has benefits in the classroom. After experiencing academic success, students develop higher appraisals of their academic ability, which often stimulate them to work harder and achieve more (Felson, 1984; Marsh & Young, 1997).

The success-feeds-self-esteem principle has led several research psychologists to question efforts to boost achievement by raising self-esteem with positive messages ('You are somebody! You're special!'). Self-esteem comes not so much from telling children how wonderful they are – which according to Twenge (2006) has actually damaged a generation of young Americans – but from hard-earned achievements. Feelings follow reality.

Low self-esteem does sometimes cause problems. But, as we will see, critics argue that it's at least as true the other way around: problems and failures can cause low self-esteem.

Self and Culture

Let's return to the 20 statements test we mentioned at the beginning of this chapter. How did you complete the 'I am _____' statement on page 54? Did you give information about your personal traits, such as 'I am honest', 'I am tall' or 'I am outgoing'? Or did you also describe your social identity, such as 'I am a Pisces', 'I am European' or 'I am a Muslim'?

For some people, especially those in industrialized Western cultures, **individualism or independence** prevails. Identity is pretty much self-contained. Adolescence is a time of separating from parents, becoming self-reliant and defining one's personal, *independent self*. Uprooted and placed in a foreign land, one's identity – as a unique individual with particular abilities, traits, values and dreams – would remain intact.

individualism or independence a cultural orientation where the individual is more important than the group. People in such cultures commonly give priority to one's own goals over group goals, and define one's identity in terms of personal attributes rather than group identifications (compare to collectivism)

The psychology of Western cultures assumes that your life will be enriched by defining your possible selves and believing in your power of personal control. Western literature, from the *Iliad* to *Pride & Prejudice,* celebrates the self-reliant individual. Movie plots feature heroes such as Wonder Woman and the Avengers who buck the establishment. Popular television series adapted from literature such as *Game of Thrones* chart the rise and fall of good over evil, bravery over cowardice, personal struggle over adversity. Songs have proclaimed 'Love Myself' and 'Born this Way', which are about loving oneself. Individualism flourishes when people experience affluence, mobility, urbanism and mass media (Hamamura, 2011; Kashima & Kashima, 2003; Ogihara, 2017)

collectivism a cultural orientation where the group is more important than the individual. People in such cultures commonly give priority to the goals of their group and define their identity accordingly (the opposite of individualism)

interdependent self construing one's identity in relation to others

Many cultures native to Asia, Africa, and Central and South America place a greater value on **collectivism**. They nurture what Kitayama and Markus (1995) call the **interdependent self**. People are more self-critical and have less need for positive individual self-regard (Heine et al., 1999). Malaysians, Indians, Japanese and traditional Kenyans such as the Maasai, for example, are much more likely than Australians, Americans and the British to complete the 'I am' statement with their group identities (Kanagawa et al., 2001; Ma & Schoeneman, 1997). When speaking, people using the languages of collectivist countries say 'I' less often (Kashima & Kashima, 1998, 2003). A person might say 'Went to the cinema' rather than 'I went to the cinema.'

However, researchers should resist the temptation to oversimplify the picture. As a matter of fact, most cultures have a combination of individualism and collectivism qualities. A categorization of cultures as either individualistic or collectivistic fails to reflect the cultural diversity in most modern societies, for instance in Europe (Lu, 2003; Lu & Yang, 2006). There are individualist Chinese and collectivist Americans, and most of us sometimes behave communally, sometimes individualistically. Cultures can also change over time and many seem to be growing more individualistic. For example, Chinese citizens under 25 are more likely than those over 25 to agree with individualistic statements such as 'make a name for yourself' and 'live a life that suits your tastes' (Arora, 2005). In their review of 51 years worth of individualistic practices and values across 78 countries including China, Japan and the US, Santos et al. (2017) discovered that individualism is on the rise with socio-economic development. This has found expression in practices as wide-ranging as responses to climate change and employment, to what name you give your child.

FIGURE 3.4 Asian and Western thinking. When shown an underwater scene, Asians often describe the environment and the relationships among the fish. Americans attend more to a single big fish.
SOURCE: © Photo 24/Getty Images

In his book *The Geography of Thought,* social psychologist Richard Nisbett (2003) proposes that interdependence is not only evident in social relations but is also apparent in ways of thinking. For example, consider: which two – of a panda, a monkey and a banana – go together? Perhaps a monkey and a panda, because they both fit the category 'animal'? Asians more often than North Americans see relationships: monkey eats banana. When shown an animated underwater scene (Figure 3.4), Japanese participants spontaneously recalled 60 per cent more background features than American participants, and they spoke of more relationships (the frog beside the plant). Americans, as confirmed in a follow-up eye-tracking study, attend more to the focal object, such as a single big fish, and attend less to the surroundings (Chua et al., 2005a; Nisbett, 2003). These results have been duplicated in studies examining activation in different areas of the brain (Goh et al., 2007; Lewis et al., 2008), leading to the conclusion that a person's socio-cultural context is likely to shape the neural mechanisms that underlie cognition (Han & Northoff, 2008). Nisbett and Masuda (2003) conclude from such studies that East Asians think more holistically – perceiving and thinking about objects and people in relationship to one another and to their environment.

With an interdependent self, one has a greater sense of belonging. Uprooted and cut off from family, colleagues and loyal friends, interdependent people would lose the social connections that define who they are. As **Figure 3.5** and **Table 3.1** suggest, the interdependent self is embedded in group memberships. Conversation is less direct and more polite (Holtgraves, 1997). The goal of social life is not so much to enhance one's individual self as to harmonize with and support one's communities. For example, in Korea, people place less value on expressing their uniqueness and more on tradition and shared practices (Choi & Choi, 2002, and **Figure 3.6**). Korean advertisements tend to feature people together; they seldom highlight personal choice or freedom (Markus, 2001).

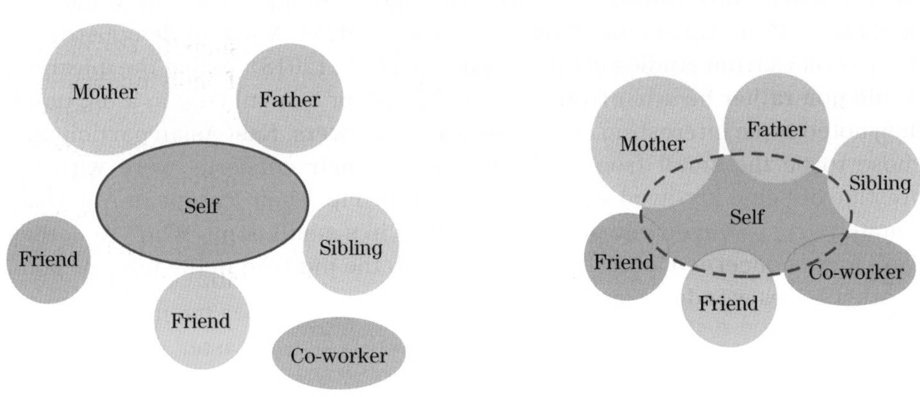

FIGURE 3.5 Self-construal as independent or interdependent
The independent self acknowledges relationships with others, but the interdependent self is more deeply embedded in others (Markus & Kitayama, 1991).

TABLE 3.1 Self-concept: independent or interdependent?

	Independent	Interdependent
Identity is	Personal, defined by individual traits and goals	Social, defined by connections with others
What matters	Me – personal achievement and fulfilment; my rights and liberties	We – group goals and solidarity; our social responsibilities and relationships
Disapproves of	Conformity	Egotism
Illustrative motto	'To thine own self be true'	'No one is an island'
Cultures that support	Individualistic Western	Collectivistic Asian and 'Third World'

FIGURE 3.6 Which pen would you choose?

In their study, Kim and Markus (1999) invited people to choose one of the pens (**Figure 3.6**) – 77 per cent of Americans but only 31 per cent of Asians chose the uncommon colour (regardless of whether it was purple, as here, or green). This result illustrates differing cultural preferences for uniqueness and conformity, noted Kim and Markus.

Self-esteem is influenced by cultural context too. Tafarodi et al. (2011) note that the Japanese typically report lower self-esteem than Canadians. But as they point out, how we define self-esteem is tied up with cultural norms and values. For instance, in collectivist cultures self-esteem correlates closely with 'what others think of me and my group'. For those in individualistic cultures, self-esteem is more personal and less relational and contextual. Threaten our *personal* identity and we'll feel angrier and gloomier than when someone threatens our collective identity (Gaertner et al., 1999). Unlike the Japanese, who persist more on tasks when they are failing (not wanting to fall short of others' expectations), people in individualistic countries persist more when succeeding, because success elevates self-esteem (Heine et al., 2001). Western individualists like to make comparisons with others that boost their self-esteem. Asian collectivists make comparisons (often upwards, with those doing better) in ways that facilitate self-improvement (White & Lehman, 2005). A useful demonstration of this comes from studies conducted by Wu et al., (2018). Asked the question: Would you rather be a big frog in a small pond, or a small frog in a big pond, they noted some interesting culture-informed answers. East Asian participants chose to be the small frog in the big pond. Their concerns were with the prestige of being involved with a high-status group. Their European-American counterparts however, chose to be a big frog in a small pond. Why? Well, they were more concerned with their image. Being the big frog in the inferior pond of others does wonders for your self-esteem!

Self-esteem

People desire self-esteem, which they are motivated to enhance. But inflated self-esteem also has a dark side.

self-esteem a person's overall negative or positive self-evaluation or sense of self-worth

Is **self-esteem** – our overall self-evaluation – the sum of all our self-schemas and possible selves? If we see ourselves as attractive, athletic, clever and destined to be rich and loved, will we have high self-esteem? Crocker and Wolfe (2001) think we will when we feel good about the domains (looks, abilities or whatever) important to our self-esteem. 'One person may have self-esteem that is highly contingent on doing well in school and being physically attractive, whereas another may have self-esteem that is contingent on being loved by God and adhering to moral standards.' Thus, the first person will feel high self-esteem when made to feel clever and good looking, the second person when made to feel moral.

But Brown and Dutton (1994) argue that this 'bottom-up' view of self-esteem is not the whole story. The causal arrow, they believe, also goes the other way. People who value themselves in a general way – those with high self-esteem – are more likely to value their looks, abilities and so forth.

Specific self-perceptions do have some influence, however. If you think you are good at maths, you will be more likely to do well at maths. Although general self-esteem does not predict academic performance very well, academic self-concept – whether you think you are good in school – does predict performance (Marsh & O'Mara, 2008). Of course, each causes the other: Doing well at maths makes you think you are good at maths, which then motivates you to do even better. So if you want to encourage someone (or yourself!), it's better if your praise is specific ('you are good at maths') instead of general ('you are great') and if your kind words reflect true abilities and performance ('you really improved on your last test') rather than unrealistic optimism ('you can do anything'). Feedback is best when it is true and specific (Swann et al., 2006).

Self-esteem Motivation

Tesser (1988) reported that a 'self-esteem maintenance' motive predicts a variety of interesting findings, even friction among brothers and sisters. Do you have a sibling of the same gender who is close to you in age? If so, people probably compared the two of you as you grew up. Tesser presumes that people's perceiving one of you as more capable than the other will motivate the less able one to act in ways that maintain self-esteem. (Tesser thinks the threat to self-esteem is greatest for an older child with a highly capable younger sibling.) Men with a brother with markedly different ability typically recall not getting along well with him; men with a similarly able brother are more likely to recall very little friction. Interestingly, Polizzi and her team (2016) found that having a sibling enhances the self-esteem of children suffering from asthma. Our siblings can provide valuable assistance in providing a supportive environment which contributes to our self-esteem.

Self-esteem threats occur among friends whose success can be more threatening than that of strangers (Zuckerman & Jost, 2001). And it can occur among married partners, too. Although shared interests are healthy, *identical* career goals may produce tension or jealousy (Clark & Bennett, 1992). When a partner outperforms us in a domain important to both our identities, we may reduce the threat by affirming our relationship, saying, 'My capable partner, with whom I'm very close, is part of who I am' (Lockwood et al., 2004). Our sense of 'one-ness' within loving relationships means our self-esteem can be tied to our partner's. For example, Wagner et al. (2018) found that older Australian wives within heterosexual marriages experienced declines in self-esteem if their husbands' self-esteem lowered. However, this didn't happen the other way around: the husband's self-esteem was not affected by any change in his wife's. Culture also plays a significant role in our feelings of self-esteem. Tahir (2012) found that married women in Pakistan displayed higher levels of self-esteem than unmarried women. Self-esteem was not found to be affected by personal levels of income, education, whether women worked or not, or their age. Tahir points out that in Pakistan self-esteem is tied to satisfaction in interdependent relationships and perceived ability to care for our family and friends. Holding down a well-paid career might actually lead to increased levels of anxiety in Pakistani women, if they cannot dedicate sufficient time to nurturing these relationships.

What underlies the motive to maintain or enhance self-esteem? Leary (1998, 2003) believes that our self-esteem feelings are like a fuel gauge. Relationships enable

Serena and Venus Williams are sisters and are also professional tennis players. Among sibling relationships, the threat to self-esteem is greatest for an older child with a highly capable younger brother or sister.

SOURCE: ©Ellen McKnight/Alamy Stock Photo

surviving and thriving. Thus, the self-esteem gauge alerts us to threatened social rejection, motivating us to act with greater sensitivity to others' expectations. Studies confirm that social rejection lowers our self-esteem and makes us more eager for approval. Spurned or jilted, we feel unattractive or inadequate. Like a blinking dashboard light, this pain can motivate action – self-improvement and a search for acceptance and inclusion elsewhere (also see Chapter 9).

The 'Dark Side' of Self-esteem

Does low self-esteem lead to greater aggression, anti-social behaviour and delinquency? Although researchers have tried to address this important issue for decades, they haven't reached agreement (Boulton et al., 2010; Ostrowsky, 2010). Some researchers have produced evidence confirming the hypothesis and found that low self-esteem is associated with higher levels of aggression (Bushman et al., 2009; Donnellan et al., 2005b). Research is revealing with sufficient clarity that people finding their favourable self-esteem threatened often react by putting others down, sometimes with violence. A recent example comes from an investigative study carried out by McVie (2010) for the Scottish Government, which reports on the rising number of knife crimes in Scotland. The surge in knife crime violence amongst young people across the United Kingdom has attracted widespread media and academic attention. McVie observes similarities in the profiles of those young people involved, including poor parental supervision, a history of truancy and drug and alcohol abuse. She also cites the role of low self-esteem exemplified in rates of self-harming behaviour and depression as a causal factor. Inflicting violence on others may, temporarily, raise self-esteem. A youth who develops a big ego, which then is threatened or deflated by social rejection, is potentially dangerous. In one experiment, Heatherton and Vohs (2000) measured the self-esteem of undergraduate men. They then threatened those in the experimental condition with a failure experience on an aptitude test. In response to the failure, only high-self-esteem men became considerably more antagonistic (**Figure 3.7**).

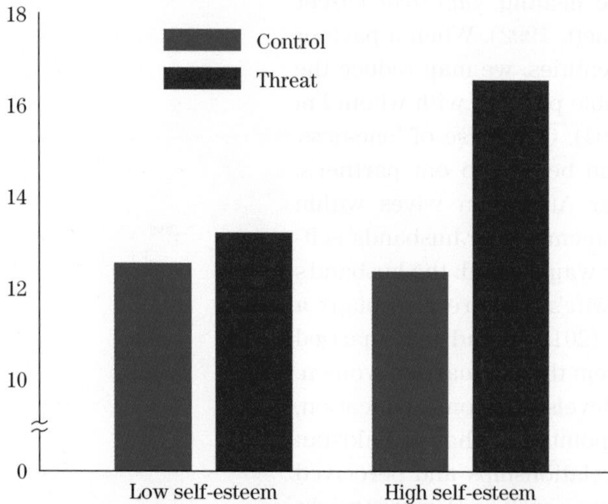

FIGURE 3.7 When big egos are challenged When feeling threatened, only high-self-esteem people became significantly more antagonistic – arrogant, rude and unfriendly.

SOURCE: Heatherton and Vohs (2000).

In another study, Bushman and Baumeister (1998) had 540 undergraduate volunteers write a paragraph, in response to which another supposed student gave them either praise ('great essay!') or stinging criticism ('one of the worst essays I have read!'). Then each essay writer played a reaction time game against his or her evaluator. When the evaluator would lose, the writer could assault him or her with noise of any intensity and for any duration. After receiving criticism, the writers with the biggest egos – those who had agreed with 'narcissistic' statements such as 'I am more capable than other people' – were 'exceptionally aggressive'. They delivered three times the auditory torture of those with normal self-esteem. Wounded pride can motivate retaliation. A more recent study has found that students with high self-esteem receiving poor feedback from a professor were more likely to evaluate the professor using aggressive language such as 'hope that I never find you!', than students with lower self-esteem (Vaillancourt, 2012).

So perhaps self-esteem is not so good for us. 'The enthusiastic claims of the self-esteem movement mostly range from fantasy to hogwash,' says Baumeister (1996). High-self-esteem people, he reports, are more likely to be obnoxious, to interrupt, and to talk at people rather than with them (in contrast to the more shy, modest, self-effacing folks with low self-esteem). He concludes: 'I'm sorry to say, my recommendation is this: Forget about self-esteem and concentrate more on self-control and self-discipline' (Baumeister, 2005a).

Machiavellianism manipulative behaviour aimed at obtaining an advantage for the self, without any moral concern and regard for the dignity of others. The term derives from the name of the Italian Renaissance writer Niccolò Machiavelli, who described this behaviour in the work The Prince

Self-love

Sometimes people become extremely focused on themselves and even start to love themselves more than anybody else. This egocentric loving attitude has got a particular name: *narcissism*, used by Greek writers and philosophers thousands of years ago. According to Ancient Greek mythology, a young man named Narcissus wandered the countryside in search of love. Thirsty from his travels, he stopped to drink from a pool of water where he became entranced by his own reflection. This self-love and self-preoccupation eventually caused Narcissus to die of thirst as he could not disturb the image of himself.

Narcissism is an uncontrolled, compulsive self-love. Narcissists have an overwhelming desire to be admired, and have an unrealistic highly exaggerated sense of their own importance. Narcissus has given name to a psychiatric disorder characterized by a pervasive pattern of grandiosity (in fantasy or behaviour), need for admiration, lack of empathy, excessive self-love and selfishness, disregard for others and the use of people for one's self gain, according to the DSM-V definition. Studies indicate that narcissists maintain low views of others, express mistrust, hostility and **Machiavellianism** (Sedikides et al., 2004). Researchers have recently defined the 'digital narcissist', obsessed with their own mirror-image they share photographs and videos of themselves across a wide-range of social media (Jin & Ryu, 2018). We would expect that high self-esteem is typical for narcissists, that self-esteem and narcissism are positively correlated, and that this has an impact on psychological health. And indeed this is what has been demonstrated (e.g. Sedikides et al., 2004).

Is the selfie an expression of narcissism?
SOURCE: © Eugenio Marongiu/Shutterstock

Certainly the goals of most narcissistic actions serve to bolster high self-esteem. Narcissism and high self-esteem, though, are not synonymous. Narcissists and individuals with high self-esteem both hold favourable self-views and may even see themselves as better than average. However, the distinction between the two rests on their differing interpersonal implications. Narcissism is a detriment to interpersonal relationships because narcissists feel a strong sense of superiority and entitlement. When their high personal opinions are challenged or questioned, narcissists tend to respond aggressively towards the specific individuals

Narcissus by Caravaggio.
SOURCE: © INTERFOTO/Alamy

Secure positive self-esteem is based on feeling good about who you are.
SOURCE: © pixelheadphoto digitalskillet/Shutterstock

providing the threat (Bushman & Baumeister, 1998). The self-serving bias offers some explanation why narcissists engage in such behaviour (e.g. Sedikides et al., 2004). High self-esteem, on the other hand, is beneficial to interpersonal relationships as it confers confidence (not egotism) necessary for forming successful communal bonds (Campbell et al., 2002).

In their study of bullying behaviour, Fanti and Henrich (2015) report that bullies are typically individuals with low self-esteem and high narcissism. Those with 'genuine self-esteem' – who feel secure self-worth without seeking to be the centre of attention or being angered by criticism – are more often found defending the victims of bullying. When we feel securely good about ourselves, we are less defensive (Epstein & Feist, 1988; Jordan et al., 2003). We are also less thin-skinned and judgemental – less likely to inflate those who like us and berate those who don't (Baumgardner et al., 1989).

Secure self-esteem – one rooted more in feeling good about who one is than in grades, looks, money or others' approval – is conducive to long-term well-being (Kernis, 2003; Schimel et al., 2001). Crocker (2002) and her colleagues (Crocker & Knight, 2005; Crocker & Luhtanen, 2003; Crocker & Park, 2004) confirmed this in studies with students. Those whose self-worth was most fragile – most contingent on external sources – experienced more stress, anger, relationship problems, drug and alcohol use, and eating disorders than did those whose worth was rooted more in internal sources, such as personal virtues.

Self-serving Bias

As we process self-relevant information, a potent bias intrudes. We readily excuse our failures, accept credit for our successes, and in many ways see ourselves as better than average. Such self-enhancing perceptions enable most people to enjoy the bright side of high self-esteem, while occasionally suffering the dark side.

One of social psychology's most provocative yet firmly established conclusions concerns the potency of **self-serving bias**, which influences how we account for our behaviour and that of other people (also see Chapter 4).

self-serving bias the tendency to perceive oneself favourably

Explaining Positive and Negative Events

Many dozens of experiments have found that people accept credit when told they have succeeded. They attribute the success to their ability and effort, but they attribute failure to external factors such as bad luck or the problem's inherent 'impossibility' (Campbell & Sedikides, 1999). Similarly, in explaining their victories, athletes commonly credit themselves, but they attribute losses to something else: bad breaks, bad referee calls, or the other team's super effort or dirty play (Grove et al., 1991; Lalonde, 1992; Mullen & Riordan, 1988). This phenomenon of **self-serving attributions** (attributing positive outcomes to oneself and negative outcomes to something else) is one of the most potent of human biases (Mezulis et al., 2004).

self-serving attributions a form of self-serving bias; the tendency to attribute positive outcomes to oneself and negative outcomes to other factors

Can We All Be Better than Average?

Self-serving bias appears when people compare themselves with others. There are cultural differences, however, and in Eastern cultures there has been a tradition for being modest and not standing out. The sixth-century BC Chinese philosopher Lao-tzu expressed this attitude when he stated that 'at no time in the world will a man who is sane over-reach himself, over-spend himself, overrate himself'. In the West most people see themselves as better than the average person on *subjective* and *socially desirable* dimensions. Compared with people in general, most people see themselves as more ethical, more competent at their job, friendlier, more intelligent, better looking, less prejudiced, healthier, and even more insightful and less biased in their self-assessments. A meta-analysis of 266 studies conducted by Mezulis and her colleagues (2004) confirmed the existence of a substantial cross-cultural variation in self-serving bias, with Asians displaying much smaller biases than Westerners.

The French social psychologist, Jean-Paul Codol, found evidence of self-serving bias in group life. He conducted a large number of experiments demonstrating that an individual group member considers him/herself as being more respectful of group norms and values than the average member (Codol, 1975). Lee and Waite (2005) observed a marital version of self-serving bias, in a study involving 265 US heterosexual married couples with children. Husbands estimated they did 42 per cent of the housework, while the wives estimated their husbands did 33 per cent. When researchers tracked actual housework (by sampling participants' activity at random times using beepers), they found husbands actually carrying 39 per cent of the domestic workload. This contrasts with Goldberg et al. (2012) who compared the division of domestic chores between heterosexual, gay and lesbian adoptive parents. Same-sex couples displayed a much more even distribution of domestic chores than their heterosexual counterparts and discrepancies were associated with differences in paid working hours. As Goldberg suggests, perhaps one reason for this are the lessened constraints on same-sex couples to adhere to gendered roles for perceivably feminine and masculine tasks.

People display one other ironic bias: they see themselves as freer from bias than most people (Ehrlinger et al., 2005; Pronin et al., 2002). Indeed, people even see themselves as less vulnerable to self-serving bias. They will admit to some bias in the abstract, and they see others as biased. But when asked about specific traits and behaviours, such as when rating their own ethics or likability, they judge their self-assessments as untainted.

Unrealistic Optimism

Neil Weinstein (1980, 1982) at Rutgers University developed the idea of unrealistic optimism about future life events. Optimism predisposes a positive approach to life and many of us have this ability to look towards a happy and successful future. Partly because of their relative pessimism about others' fates, students perceive themselves as far more likely than their classmates to get a good job, draw a good salary and own a home. They also see themselves as far *less* likely to experience negative events, such as developing a drinking problem, having a heart attack before age 40, or being fired (Shepperd, 2003).

Those who cheerfully shun seat belts, deny the effects of smoking and stumble into ill-fated relationships remind us that blind optimism, like pride, may go before a fall.

When gambling, optimists more than pessimists persist even when piling up losses (Gibson & Sanbonmatsu, 2004). Clarke et al., (2000) report the prevalence of the unrealistic optimism bias amongst women with respect to detecting, curing and surviving breast cancer, and for men in relation to prostate cancer. In this context, unrealistic optimism might hamper early proaction. If those who deal in the stock market or in real estate perceive their business intuition superior to that of their competitors, they too, may be in for disappointment. Even the seventeenth-century economist Adam Smith, a defender of human economic rationality, foresaw that people would overestimate their chances of gain. This 'absurd presumption in their own good fortune', he said, arises from 'the overweening conceit, which the greater part of men have of their own abilities' (Spiegel, 1971, p. 243).

Optimism definitely beats pessimism in promoting self-efficacy, health and well-being (Armor & Taylor, 1996; Segerstrom, 2001). Being natural optimists, most people believe they will be happier with their lives in the future – a belief that surely helps create happiness in the present (Robinson & Ryff, 1999).

defensive pessimism the adaptive value of anticipating problems and harnessing one's anxiety to motivate effective action

Yet a dash of realism – or what Norem (2000) calls **defensive pessimism** – can reduce anxiety by anticipating problems and motivating effective coping. Students who are overconfident tend to under-prepare, whereas their equally able but less confident peers study harder and get higher grades (Goodhart, 1986; Norem & Cantor, 1986; Showers & Ruben, 1987). Lim (2009) found very high levels of defensive pessimism amongst Singaporean university students. This pessimism motivated students to perform better and achieve mastery. Lim notes how Chinese culture, which emphasizes not bringing shame upon the family, compels students to avoid failure at any cost. We shall return to defensive pessimism when we consider how self-handicapping might further alleviate our anxieties about poor performance. There is a power to negative as well as positive thinking. The moral: success in school and beyond requires enough optimism to sustain hope and enough pessimism to motivate concern.

False Consensus and Uniqueness

We have a curious tendency to enhance our self-images by overestimating or underestimating the extent to which others think and act as we do. On matters of *opinion,* we find support for our positions by overestimating the extent to which others agree – a phenomenon called the **false consensus effect** (Krueger & Clement, 1994; Marks & Miller, 1987; Mullen & Goethals, 1990).

false consensus effect the tendency to overestimate the commonality of one's opinions and one's undesirable or unsuccessful behaviours

When we behave badly or fail in a task, we reassure ourselves by thinking that such lapses are common. If we cheat on our income taxes, or smoke, we are likely to overestimate the number of other people who do likewise. If we feel sexual desire towards another, we may overestimate the other's reciprocal desire. Four studies illustrate this.

1. People who sneak a shower during a shower ban believe (more than non-bathers) that lots of others are doing the same (Monin & Norton, 2003).
2. Those thirsty after hard exercise imagine that lost hikers would become more bothered by thirst than by hunger. That's what 88 per cent of thirsty post-exercisers guessed in a study by Van Boven and Lowenstein (2003), compared with 57 per cent of people who were about to exercise.

3 As people's own lives change, they see the world changing. Protective new parents come to see the world as a more dangerous place. People who go on a diet judge food ads to be more prevalent (Eibach et al., 2003).

4 Athletes with a history of drug-abuse overestimate the prevalence of drug use in sport (Dunn et al., 2011).

'Everybody says I'm plastic from head to toe. Can't stand next to a radiator or I'll melt. I had [breast] implants, but so has every single person in LA.'
Actress Pamela Lee Anderson (quoted by Talbert, 1997)

'We don't see things as they are,' says the Talmud. 'We see things as we are.'

Dawes (1990) proposes that this false consensus may occur because we generalize from a limited sample, which prominently includes ourselves. Lacking other information why not 'project' ourselves; why not impute our own knowledge to others and use our responses as a clue to their likely responses? Most people are in the majority; so when people assume they are in the majority they are usually right. Also, we're more likely to spend time with people who share our attitudes and behaviours and, consequently, to judge the world from the people we know.

On matters of *ability* or when we behave well or successfully, however, a **false uniqueness effect** more often occurs (Goethals et al., 1991). We serve our self-image by seeing our talents and moral behaviours as relatively unusual. For example, those who use marijuana but use seat belts will *overestimate* (false consensus) the number of other marijuana users and *underestimate* (false uniqueness) the number of other seat belt users (Suls et al., 1988). Thus, we may see our failings as relatively normal and our virtues as relatively exceptional.

false uniqueness effect the tendency to underestimate the commonality of one's abilities and one's desirable or successful behaviour

To sum up, self-serving bias appears as self-serving attributions, self-congratulatory comparisons, illusory optimism, and false consensus for one's failings (**Figure 3.8**).

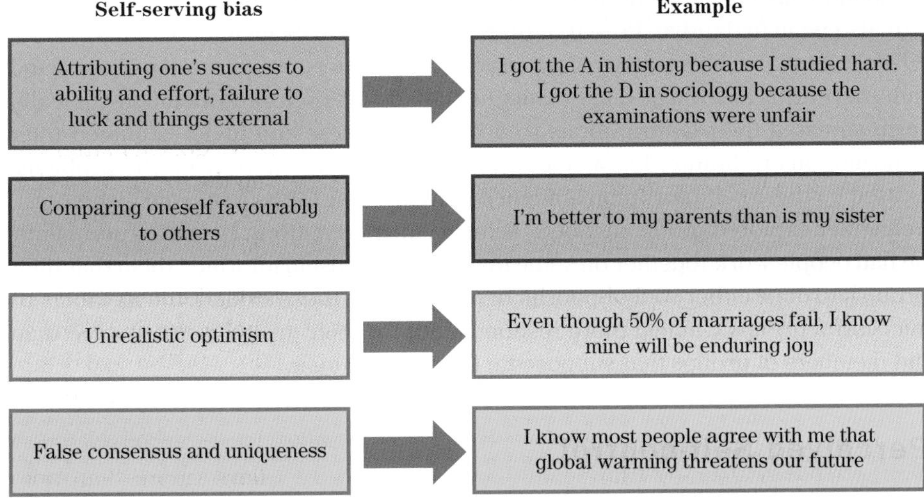

FIGURE 3.8 How self-serving bias works

Reflections on Self-esteem and Self-serving Bias

If you are like some readers, by now you are finding the self-serving bias either depressing or contrary to your own occasional feelings of inadequacy. Even the people who exhibit the self-serving bias may feel inferior – to specific individuals, especially those who are a step or two higher on the ladder of success, attractiveness or skill. Moreover, not everyone operates with a self-serving bias. Some people *do* suffer from low self-esteem. Positive self-esteem does have some benefits.

The Self-serving Bias as Adaptive

Self-esteem has its dark side but also its bright side. When good things happen, high more than low-self-esteem people tend to savour and sustain the good feelings (Wood et al., 2003). 'Believing one has more talents and positive qualities than one's peers allows one to feel good about oneself and to enter the stressful circumstances of daily life with the resources conferred by a positive sense of self,' note Taylor et al., (2003). Self-serving bias and its accompanying excuses also help protect people from depression (Snyder & Higgins, 1988; Taylor et al., 2003). Non-depressed people usually exhibit self-serving bias. They excuse their failures on laboratory tasks or perceive themselves as being more in control than they are. Depressed people's self-appraisals and their appraisals of how others really view them are not inflated.

Terror management theory proposes a basic psychological conflict resulting from having a desire to live but realizing that death is inevitable; TMT is discussed in more detail in Chapter 13.

In their 'terror management theory', Greenberg et al., (1997) propose another reason why positive self-esteem is adaptive: it buffers anxiety, including anxiety related to our certain death. In childhood we learn that when we meet the standards taught us by our parents, we are loved and protected; when we don't, love and protection may be withdrawn. We therefore come to associate viewing ourselves as good with feeling secure. Greenberg and colleagues argue that positive self-esteem even protects us from feeling terror over our eventual and inevitable death. Their research shows that reminding people of their mortality (say, by writing a short essay on dying) motivates them to affirm their self-worth. When facing such threats, self-esteem buffers anxiety.

The Self-serving Bias as Maladaptive

Although self-serving pride may help protect us from feeling sad and useless it can also be maladaptive. Research by Schlenker (1976; Schlenker & Miller, 1977a, 1977b) has shown how self-serving perceptions can poison a group. As a rock band guitarist during his college days, Schlenker noted that 'rock band members typically overestimated their contributions to a group's success and underestimated their contributions to failure. I saw many good bands disintegrate from the problems caused by these self-glorifying tendencies'. In his later life as a social psychologist, Schlenker explored group members' self-serving perceptions. In nine experiments, he had people work together on some task. He then falsely informed them that their group had done either well or poorly. In every one of those studies, the members of successful groups claimed more responsibility for their group's performance than did members of groups that supposedly failed at the task.

Perceived Self-control

Several lines of research point to the significance of our perceived self-control. What concepts emerge from this research?

So far we have considered what a self-concept is, how it develops, how well (or poorly) we know ourselves and our self-serving biases. Now let's see why our self-concepts matter, by viewing the self in action.

The self's capacity for action has limits, note Baumeister et al. (2000; Muraven et al., 1998). For instance:

- People who exert self-control – by forcing themselves to eat radishes rather than chocolates, or by suppressing forbidden thoughts – subsequently quit faster when given unresolvable puzzles.
- People who have tried to control their emotional responses to an upsetting movie exhibit decreased physical stamina.
- People who have spent their willpower on tasks such as controlling their emotions during an upsetting film become more aggressive and more likely to fight with their partners (DeWall et al., 2007; Finkel & Campbell, 2001). They also become less restrained in their sexual thoughts and behaviours. In one study students who depleted their willpower by focusing their attention on a difficult task were later, when asked to express a comfortable level of intimacy with their partner, more likely to make out and even remove some clothing (Gailliot & Baumeister, 2007).

Effortful self-control depletes our limited willpower reserves. Our brain (especially in the prefrontal areas of the frontal lobe) consumes available blood sugar when engaged in self-control (Gailliot, 2008). Self-control therefore operates similarly to muscular strength, conclude Baumeister and Exline (2000): both are weaker after exertion, replenished with rest, and strengthened by exercise.

Although the self's energy can be temporarily depleted, our self-concept does influence our behaviour (Graziano et al., 1997). Given challenging tasks, people who imagine themselves as hardworking and successful outperform those who imagine themselves as failures (Ruvolo & Markus, 1992). Envision your positive possibilities and you become more likely to plan and enact a successful strategy. Stanford psychologist Albert Bandura (1997, 2000) captured the power of positive thinking in his research and theorizing about **self-efficacy** (how competent we feel on a task). Believing in our own competence and effectiveness pays dividends (Bandura et al., 1999; Maddux & Gosselin, 2003). Children and adults with strong feelings of self-efficacy are more persistent, less anxious and less depressed. They also live healthier lives and are more academically successful.

self-efficacy one's sense of competence and ability to handle different situations, and produce an intended result: distinguished from self-esteem, which is one's sense of self-worth. A bombardier, for instance, might feel high self-efficacy and low self-esteem

However, as we have seen earlier in this chapter, anticipating possible negative outcomes (negative thinking) may help very anxious people coping with situations that present the possibility for failure and threat to self-esteem.

Locus of Control

'I have no social life,' complained a 40-something single man to student therapist Jerry Phares. At Phares's urging, the patient went to a dance, where several women danced with him. 'I was just lucky,' he later reported. 'It would never happen again.' When Phares reported this to his mentor, Julian Rotter, it crystallized an idea he had been forming. In Rotter's experiments and in his clinical practice, some people seemed to persistently 'feel that what happens to them is governed by external forces of one kind or another, while others feel that what happens to them is governed largely by their own efforts and skills' (quoted by Hunt, 1993, p. 334).

TABLE 3.2 The extent to which people perceive outcomes as internally controllable by their own efforts and actions, or as externally controlled by chance or outside forces

a		b
In the long run, people get the respect they deserve in this world	or	Unfortunately, people's worth passes unrecognized no matter how hard they try
What happens to me is my own doing	or	Sometimes I feel that I don't have enough control over the situation
The average person can have an influence in government decisions	or	This world is run by the few in power and there is not much the little guy can do about it

locus of control a person's belief about who or what is responsible for what happens. Can either be internal (I control my life) or external (the environment, a higher power or other people control my life)

What do you think about your own life? Are you more often in charge of your destiny, or a victim of circumstance? Rotter called this dimension **locus of control**. With Phares, he developed 29 paired statements to measure a person's locus of control. Imagine yourself taking this test (**Table 3.2**). Which do you more strongly believe? If your answers to these questions (from Rotter, 1973) were mostly 'a', you probably believe you control your own destiny (*internal* locus of control). If your answers were mostly 'b', you probably feel chance or outside forces determine your fate (*external* locus of control). Those who see themselves as *internally* controlled are more likely to do well in school, successfully stop smoking, wear seat belts, deal with marital problems directly, save money, adopt new technologies, and delay instant gratification to achieve long-term goals (Abay et al., 2017; Cobb-Clark et al., 2016; Findley & Cooper, 1983; Lefcourt, 1982).

How much control we feel is related to how we explain setbacks. Perhaps you have known students who view themselves as victims – who blame poor grades on things beyond their control, such as their feelings of stupidity or their 'poor' teachers, texts or tests. If such students are coached to adopt a more hopeful attitude – to believe that effort, good study habits and self-discipline can make a difference – their academic performance tends to go up (Hasbrouck, 2017).

Learned Helplessness Versus Self-determination

learned helplessness the hopelessness and resignation learned when a human or an animal perceives no control over repeated bad events; this commonly leads to depressive symptoms

The benefits of feelings of control also appear in animal research. Dogs confined in a cage and taught that they cannot escape shocks will learn a sense of helplessness. Later, these dogs cower passively in other situations when they *could* escape punishment. Dogs that learn personal control (by successfully escaping their first shocks) adapt easily to a new situation. Researcher Martin Seligman (1975, 1991) noted similarities to this **learned helplessness** in human situations. Depressed or oppressed people for example, become passive because they believe their efforts have no effect. Helpless dogs and depressed people both suffer paralysis of the will, passive resignation, even motionless apathy (**Figure 3.9**).

On the other hand, people benefit by training their self-control 'muscles'. That is the conclusion of studies by Oaten and Cheng (2006). For example, students who

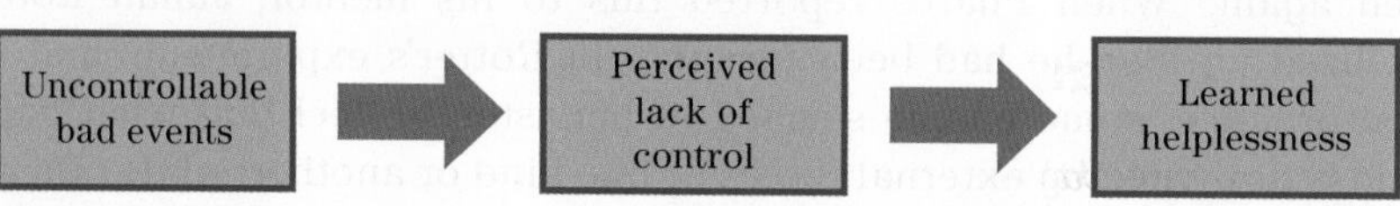

FIGURE 3.9 Learned helplessness
When animals and people experience uncontrollable bad events, they learn to feel helpless and resigned.

were engaged in practising self-control by daily exercise, regular study and time management became more capable of self-control in other settings, both in the laboratory and when taking exams. Learning to exercise self-control from early childhood can reap benefits throughout your life. Moffitt and colleagues (2011) followed 1,000 children from their birth until they reached the age of 32 years. They found that having self-control in childhood predicted a range of benefits in later years, including financial and physical health and reduced likelihood of criminality and substance abuse (tobacco, alcohol, cannabis). Furthermore, being able to exercise self-control trumps intelligence and social class as a predictor for these benefits. Conversely those children who exhibited low self-control in childhood experienced worse health, wealth, criminality and substance abuse outcomes than their more self-controlled counterparts.

The Costs of Excess Choice

Can there ever be too much of a good thing such as freedom and self-determination? Swarthmore College psychologist Barry Schwartz (2000, 2004) contends that individualistic modern cultures indeed have 'an excess of freedom', causing decreased life satisfaction and increased clinical depression. Too many choices can lead to paralysis, or what Schwartz calls 'the tyranny of freedom'. After choosing from among 30 kinds of jams or chocolates, people express less satisfaction with their choices than those choosing from among six options (Iyengar & Lepper, 2000). With more choice comes information overload and more opportunities for regret. Another study, conducted by Gilbert and Ebert (2002), has revealed that people are more satisfied with irrevocable choices (such as those made in 'all purchases final' sale) than with reversible ones (as when allowing refunds or exchanges). This is somewhat ironic, given that people like and will pay for the freedom to reverse their choices. The fact is that, as noted by Gilbert and Ebert, that same freedom 'can inhibit the psychological processes that manufacture satisfaction'.

Hsee and Hastie (2006) illustrate how choice may enhance regret. Give employees a free trip to either Paris or Hawaii and they will be happy. But give them a choice between the two and they may be less happy. People who choose Paris may regret that it lacks the warmth and the ocean. Those who choose Hawaii may regret the lack of great museums.

It is important to note, however, that whether or not any negative psychological consequence of having too much choice will occur may depend on the extent to which 'too much choice' increases the complexity of the choice. Greifeneder et al. (2010) found that consumers who had to choose from a vast array of products felt dissatisfied when the products were differentiated by many attributes, but not when the differences concerned a small number of attributes. For instance, participants who had to choose the one coloured pen they liked best from a set of six different pens, felt more satisfied with their choice when the pens differed only by colour than when they differed on a number of additional attributes such as design, pen width and duration of use.

Impression Management

Humans seem motivated not only to perceive themselves in self-enhancing ways but also to present themselves favourably to others. We engage in 'impression management'.

Perhaps you have wondered: are self-enhancing expressions always sincere? Do people have the same feelings privately as they express publicly? Or are they just putting on a positive face even while living with self-doubt?

False Modesty

There is indeed evidence that people sometimes present a different self than they feel. The clearest example, however, is not false pride but false modesty. Perhaps you have by now recalled times when someone was not self-praising but self-disparaging. Such put-downs can be subtly self-serving, for often they elicit reassurance. 'I felt like a fool' may trigger a friend to say 'You did fine!'

There is another reason people disparage themselves and praise others. Understating one's own ability serves to reduce performance pressure and lower the baseline for evaluating performance (Gibson & Sachau, 2000). Think of the coaches who, before the big game, extol the opponent's strength and point out weaknesses that their own team 'needs to work on'. Is the coach utterly sincere? When exalting their opponents, coaches convey an image of modesty and good sportsmanship, and set the stage for a favourable evaluation no matter what the outcome. A win becomes a praiseworthy achievement, a loss attributable to the opponent's 'great defence'. Modesty, said the seventeenth-century philosopher Francis Bacon, is but one of the 'arts of ostentation'.

Pomerantz (1978) was the first researcher to study how people respond to compliments in everyday conversation. She found that people experienced something of a dilemma when they were complimented. On the one hand they did not want to reject the compliment, but on the other they did not want to look immodest.

Let us consider some of her examples of displays of modesty to overcome this dilemma:

For example:
R: You're a good rower, Honey
I: These are very easy to row. Very light
(Pomerantz, 1978, p. 102)

Here the recipient deflects the praise by pointing out the type of boat she is (easily) rowing.

Gould et al., (1977) found that, in a laboratory contest, their students similarly aggrandized their anticipated opponent, but only when the assessment was made publicly. Anonymously, they credited their future opponent with much less ability.

False modesty appears in people's autobiographical accounts of their achievements. At awards ceremonies, recipients of honours graciously thank others for their support. Does such sharing of credit contradict the common finding that people readily attribute success to their own effort and competence?

To find out, Baumeister and Ilko (1995) invited students to write a description of 'an important success experience'. They asked some students to sign their names and to anticipate reading their story to others; these students often acknowledged the help or emotional support they had received. Those who wrote anonymously rarely made such mentions; rather, they portrayed themselves achieving their successes on their own. To Baumeister and Ilko, these results suggest 'shallow gratitude' – superficial gratitude that *appears* humble, whereas 'in the privacy of their own minds' the students credited themselves.

Shallow gratitude may surface when we outperform others around us and feel uneasy about other people's feelings towards us. If we think our success will make others feel envious or resentful – a phenomenon that Exline and Lobel (1999) call 'the perils of out-performance' – we may downplay our achievements and display gratitude. For super-achievers, modest self-presentations come naturally.

Self-handicapping

You may recall our earlier discussion of the defence-mechanism defensive pessimism and how this can help alleviate our anxieties by lowering expectations. Well, sometimes people deliberately sabotage their chances for success by creating impediments that make success less likely (**self-handicapping**), hence also lowering expectations. Far from being deliberately self-destructive, such behaviours typically have a self-protective aim (Arkin et al., 1986; Baumeister & Scher, 1988; Rhodewalt, 1987): 'I'm really not a failure – I would have done well except for this problem.'

self-handicapping protecting one's self-image with behaviours that create a handy excuse for later failure

In their extensive review of published work on self-handicapping within academic contexts, Schwinger et al. (2014) distinguish between two types of self-handicapping: behavioural and claimed. Behavioural self-handicapping refers to actively acquiring an obstacle to performance, such as not spending enough time revising, drinking too much alcohol and so on. Claimed self-handicapping describes the 'stated' presence of barriers such as anxiety and depression. Schwinger et al., note that behavioural self-handicapping is considered the more credible in terms of its relationship to actual performance.

But why would people handicap themselves with self-defeating behaviour? Recall that we eagerly protect our self-images by attributing failures to external factors. Can you see why, *fearing failure*, people might handicap themselves by partying half the night before a job interview or playing computer games instead of studying before a big examination? When self-image is tied up with performance, it can be more self-deflating to try hard and fail than to procrastinate and have a ready excuse. If we fail while handicapped in some way, we can cling to a sense of competence; if we succeed under such conditions it can only boost our self-image. Handicaps protect both self-esteem and public image by allowing us to attribute failures to something temporary or external ('I was feeling sick'; 'I was out too late the night before') rather than to lack of talent or ability. However, as Akin (2012) found, self-handicapping can also be related to stress, exhaustion, feelings of low self-competence and depersonalization. Self-handicapping can be a destructive behaviour which diminishes our psychological energy and sense of self.

'With no attempt there can be no failure; with no failure no humiliation.'
(James, 1890)

Berglas and Jones (1978) were the first to confirm this analysis of *self-handicapping*. One experiment was announced as concerning 'drugs and intellectual performance'. Imagine yourself in the position of their Duke University participants. You guess answers to some difficult aptitude questions and then are told, 'Yours was one of the best scores seen to date!' Feeling incredibly lucky, you are then offered a choice between two drugs before answering more of these items. One drug will aid intellectual performance and the other will inhibit it. Which drug do you want? Most students wanted the drug that would supposedly disrupt their thinking, thus providing a handy excuse for anticipated poorer performance.

Self-presentation

Erving Goffman, a sociologist and social psychologist born in Canada, collected the material for his book *The Presentation of Self in Everyday Life* on the Shetland Islands in the North Sea, in 1950 (Goffman, 1959). His account of social life was based on a symbolic interactionist perspective (see Chapter 1), and was modelled on the theatre. Goffman saw people as actors, executing different performances in front of various audiences. He also claimed that when in public (front stage), people strive to comply with societal norms and expectations. When not in public (behind stage), these social rules do not need to be followed.

self-presentation the act of expressing oneself and behaving in ways designed to create a favourable impression or an impression that corresponds to one's ideals

Goffman pioneered the study of **self-presentation**, which refers to our wanting to present a desired image both to an external audience (other people) and to an internal audience (ourselves). We work at managing the impressions we create. We excuse, justify or apologize as necessary to shore up our self-esteem and verify our self-images (Schlenker & Weigold, 1992). In familiar situations, this happens without conscious effort. In unfamiliar situations, perhaps at a party with people we would like to impress or in conversation with someone we have romantic interest in, we are acutely self-conscious of the impressions we are creating and we are therefore less modest than when among friends who know us well (Leary et al., 1994; Tice et al., 1995).

But of course not all of our interactions are face to face. Online social networking (OSN) sites such as Instagram and Facebook provide a new and sometimes intense venue for self-presentation. They are, says communications professor Joseph Walther, 'like impression management on steroids' (cited in Rosenbloom, 2008). Within the virtual environment we can create our self; choosing which aspects to present to the public and which to conceal. Consequently users make careful decisions about which pictures, activities and interests to present and promote in their profiles. Some even think about how their friends will affect the impression they make on others; one study found that those with more attractive friends were perceived as more attractive themselves (Walther et al., 2008).

Do people use OSN sites to portray idealized versions of themselves, or do people consider OSN sites just as an extended social context for the expression of the actual self? Researchers disagree on this (Back et al., 2010). Proponents of the *idealized virtual-identity hypothesis* believe that people use the internet to display idealized selves that do not match actual personality characteristics (Manago et al., 2008). On the contrary, some researchers endorse an *extended real-life hypothesis*, according to which the personal information that people include on OSN sites mirrors their real thoughts, feelings, interests and physical appearance (Vazire & Gosling, 2004). Although the question is still open, a study conducted by Back and his colleagues in which the two hypotheses were compared indicates that the *extended real-life hypothesis* might be a better account of the way in which people tend to use OSN sites. These researchers assessed both the actual and ideal personality of 236 OSN users from either the US or Germany, and then compared these with personality ratings made by some external judges, based on the information about participants that was available on OSN sites. It was found that observers' impressions of participants matched participants' actual, but not ideal, personality. Nonetheless, there is no doubt that, as proposed by McKenna and Bargh (2000), the internet offers a 'blank slate, the individual is then free to construct him or herself in any number of ways' (p. 63). Aren't people really capitalizing on this opportunity to present a different self? It seems that people may do so, but not necessarily in order to present a faked, more desirable self, but rather to present their 'true', most genuine self. Some theorists point out that in face-to-face interactions, who we present ourselves to be is limited by the roles we fulfil, who our friends and family believe us to be, and sometimes because aspects of our 'true self' are controversial (e.g. Bargh et al., 2002; McKenna & Bargh, 2000). So there are aspects of our self which we consider important, which we would like recognized, but which we are not comfortable with expressing. This has received empirical support. For example, in a series of experiments, Bargh et al. (2002) found that New York students were not only more aware of their true selves in online interactions with strangers, but were also more likely to present them online than face to face. We consider the influence of the internet and computer-mediated interaction on our friendships and romantic relationships in more detail in Chapter 9.

After losing to some younger rivals, tennis great Martina Navratilova confessed that she was 'afraid to play my best . . . I was scared to find out if they could beat me when I'm playing my best because if they can, then I am finished' (Frankel & Snyder, 1987).

SOURCE: ©Jo Crebbin/ Alamy Stock Photo

Are there particular sorts of people who are more likely to use social media for self-presentation purposes? Probably, you will not be surprised to hear that people high in narcissistic traits thrive on Facebook, tallying up more friends and choosing more attractive pictures of themselves. Davenport et al., (2014) noted that college students high in narcissism were keen tweeters on Twitter.

Eager to acquire followers, narcissists become avid tweeters to generate self-interest. Buffardi and Campbell (2008) believe that narcissists are particularly willing to join online communities for two reasons. First, 'narcissists function well in the context of shallow (as opposed to emotionally deep and committed) relationships' (p. 1304). Second, by creating their own web pages narcissists get a perfect opportunity to present themselves in a self-promoting fashion.

For some people, conscious self-presentation is a way of life. They continually monitor their own behaviour and note how others react, then adjust their social performance to gain a desired effect. Those who score high on a scale of **self-monitoring** tendency (who, for example, agree that 'I tend to be what people expect me to be') act like social chameleons – they adjust their behaviour in response to external situations (Gangestad & Snyder, 2000; Snyder, 1987). Having attuned their behaviour to the situation, they are more likely to espouse attitudes they don't really hold (Zanna & Olson, 1982). Being conscious of others, they are less likely to act on their own attitudes. As Leary (2007) observed, the self they know often differs from the self they show.

self-monitoring letting situational cues guide the way one presents oneself in social situations, and adjusting one's performance to create the desired impression, rather than acting on own needs or values

Those who score low in self-monitoring care less about what others think. They are more internally guided and thus more likely to talk and act as they feel and believe (McCann & Hancock, 1983). For example, if asked to list their thoughts about gay couples, they simply express what they think, regardless of the attitudes of their anticipated audience (Klein et al., 2004). As you might imagine, someone who is extremely low in self-monitoring could come across as an insensitive boor, whereas extremely high self-monitoring could result in dishonest behaviour worthy of a con artist. Most of us fall somewhere between those two extremes.

Presenting oneself in ways that create a desired impression is a delicate balancing act. People want to be seen as able but also as modest and honest (Carlston & Shovar, 1983). In most social situations, modesty creates a good impression. Hence the false modesty phenomenon: we often display lower self-esteem than we privately feel (Miller & Schlenker, 1985). But when we have obviously done extremely well, the insincerity of a disclaimer ('I did well, but it's no big deal') may be evident. To make good impressions – as modest yet competent – requires social skill.

Self-presented modesty is greatest in cultures that value self-restraint and self-improvement, such as those of China and Japan (Heine, 2005; Mezulis et al., 2004). Japanese children learn to share credit for success and to accept responsibility for failures. 'When I fail, it's my fault, not my group's' is a typical Japanese attitude (Anderson, 1999).

Loss of Self

Throughout this chapter we have focused on having an acute awareness of self. We have also noted its relationship to the brain. Our memories form an important part of the self. But what happens to the sense of self if those memories fade, or even disappear? The Alzheimer's Association report a worldwide increase in the degenerative condition dementia. Dementia is a general term used to define damage to brain cells causing a decline in mental ability, which disrupts everyday life. Globally, 50 million people were diagnosed with dementia in 2018, and this figure is expected to rise to 152 million by 2050. In their comprehensive review of the psychological literature on dementia, Caddell and Clare (2010) report a variety of methods and findings on how, and if, dementia impacts upon a person's sense of self. Put simply, it depends on how you define and measure the self. If the self is located squarely within the brain and tied to autobiographical memory, then yes, dementia will have a big impact. Take a more social constructionist view and locate the self within our culture and our relationships with others, and the impact is different. The sense of self might not be so much lost as changed.

Changes to our sense of 'self' can highlight some taken-for-granted assumptions, as Fernandez and Bliss (2016) point out from their studies of schizophrenia. Schizophrenia is a mental disorder which, amongst other things, disrupts our sense of self. Delusions, thought insertions, hearing voices, and acting on impulses which we don't feel are our own, characterize some of the many distressing symptoms of this condition. Ordinarily, our sense of self is tied up with not only being the bearer, or host, for conscious and physical states (thoughts, feelings, emotions, motor movements) but also our ownership of them. However, for many schizophrenics it is possible to be conscious of these states, but not feel ownership of them.

Fernández and Bliss offer some intriguing examples from clinical patients, for example:

> '. . .*I began to realize that the houses I was passing were sending messages to me: Look closely. You are special. You are especially bad. Look closely and you shall find. There are many things you must see. See. See. I didn't hear these words as literal sounds, as though the houses were talking and I were hearing them; instead, the words just came into my head – they were ideas I was having. Yet I instinctively knew they were not my ideas. They belonged to the houses, and the houses had put them in my head.*'
>
> (2016, p. 616)

Fernández and Bliss conclude that what we take for granted with respect to the self, might not be so inevitable. Aspects of the self can change, dissociate and become located outside the physical body.

In Asian countries, self-presentation is restrained. Children learn to share credit for success with other group members.

SOURCE: © Indeed/Getty Images

Focus on

Are We Witnessing an Epidemic of Narcissism Among Younger Generations?

It is fairly common to hear older people complaining about younger generations, which are depicted as self-centred, arrogant and disrespectful, and are said to dismiss traditions and good old habits. This popular view of younger people is echoed by the writings of scholars from across the social science spectrum, particularly in North America. Over the last two or three decades – it is argued – Western societies in general, and the US in particular, have embraced an individualistic ethos, whereby all attentions and preoccupations revolve around the self at the expense of civic engagement, empathy, solidarity and societal concerns. For instance, Putnam (2000) lamented the gradual disintegration of communities and social networks, and Lane (2000) stressed how a focus on individual success is replacing appreciation of companionship. Similarly, Frank (1999) argued that our obsessive desire to enhance the self has led to a 'luxury fever', a tendency to consume self-promoting luxury goods that is forcing people to spend more time at work while neglecting family and friends. In sum, we are said to be living in an era of self-centredness or, as the sociologist Christopher Lash (1979) foresaw, in a 'culture of narcissism'.

But is this truly the case? Are we really witnessing a fast-growing tendency toward self-absorption and egotism? The social psychologist Jean Twenge and her colleagues believe so, and have characterized the current climate as an 'epidemic of narcissism' (Twenge & Campbell, 2009). Twenge agrees that cultural and pedagogic trends are largely responsible for such an epidemic. In particular, she blames American parents for wanting to make their children feel 'special' regardless of their real skills and abilities. In order to put this thesis under test, Twenge et al., (2008) decided to investigate changes in levels of narcissism among different generations of college students in the US. These researchers amassed 85 studies conducted between 1982 and 2006, in which the degree of narcissism

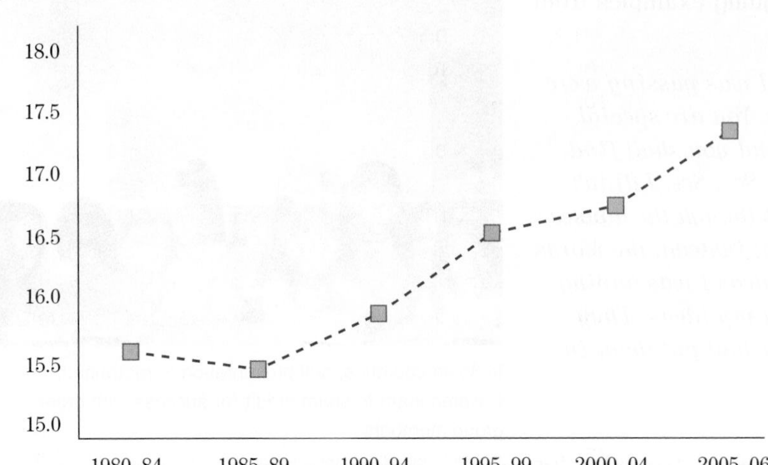

FIGURE 3.10 American college students' scores on narcissism by time period

SOURCE: Adapted from Twenge et al. (2008, p. 883).

of over 16,000 college students had been assessed using the Narcissistic Personality Inventory (NPI). The NPI is based on 40 forced-choice dyads. For each dyad the person taking the test may choose either a narcissistic response (e.g., 'I really like to be the centre of attention') or a non-narcissistic response ('It makes me uncomfortable to be the centre of attention'). Each narcissistic response counts as 1 in the overall score, which therefore may range between 0 and 40. The analysis of these data revealed that more recent generations have higher levels of narcissism. More precisely, NPI scores have gradually increased over the years, moving from an initial average score of 15.06 in 1982 to an average score of 17.29 in 2006 (see **Figure 3.10**).

Twenge considers these results as consistent with cultural trends and indicators. For instance, the lyrics of the more popular songs are more individualistic than ever (DeWall et al., 2011), the rates for plastic surgery are constantly increasing (Twenge & Campbell, 2009), and being rich and famous is increasingly judged as important in polls. According to Twenge, these are all signs that people want to feel special, they want to stand out rather than fit in.

Some researchers, however, believe that the claims made by researchers like Twenge are grossly exaggerated, and that there is no epidemic of narcissism in contemporary society. For instance, Arnett (2010) contends that rather than selfish, younger people are self-focused as they need to explore their identities and options for future life. Arnett also thinks that, rather than grandiose, younger people are optimistic because their dreams have not yet been tested by the reality of adult life. Along similar lines, Roberts et al. (2010) re-analysed the data previously used by Twenge using alternative statistical procedures and did not find significant generational changes in narcissism. What they found, instead, was evidence that every generation of younger people is more narcissistic than their elders. But perhaps the sharpest attack on Twenge's thesis comes from US-based social psychologists Kali Trzesniewski and Brent Donnellan (2009, 2010). First, these authors stress the fact that Twenge's data stem from college students, whose characteristics cannot be generalized to the whole American youth. In addition, Trzesniewski and Donnellan noted that the trend for increasing narcissism in Twenge's data is much more pronounced for women than for men. Therefore, rather than unveiling a general epidemic of narcissism, Twenge's results might simply indicate that the last generation of women have become more assertive and confident than previous generations. Finally, Trzesniewski and Donnellan question the relevance of the increase in narcissism found by Twenge. Is a change of slightly more than 2 scale points on the NPI a meaningful change? Does it have any practical implications? They suspect that such change should not be of concern, and that it does not justify an alarm about today's youth. On the other hand, Twenge and Campbell believe that a change of 2 points on the NPI deserves to be taken seriously (Twenge & Campbell, 2010). If the average level of narcissism has increased even by a small amount, they argue, then there must be many more young people than before having extreme scores on NPI. Having thousands more people out there with a very strong sense of entitlement and low empathy – Twenge and Campbell believe – may have noticeably negative consequences for society.

The debate is still open and heated. More data and studies, and perhaps new analyses of existing data are required to resolve it. It certainly is an issue that deserves attention. If the epidemic of narcissism was found to be a myth, it would be important to acknowledge that younger generations are not more self-absorbed than previous ones, and to avoid fuelling a negative stereotype of today's young people. On the other hand, if the epidemic of narcissism was confirmed, then the negative consequences of our contemporary culture and ethos should be taken very seriously by politicians, intellectuals and general public alike.

Questions

1. Can you see any evidence of an epidemic of narcissism in the country where you live? If so, how worrying do you think that is?
2. Would you agree that younger people, regardless of their generation, tend to be more self-centred than older people? If so, why do you think that is the case?
3. Do you think our engagement with social media platforms such as Facebook, Twitter and Instagram are fostering a more narcissistic society?

SUMMING UP: THE SELF

SPOTLIGHTS AND ILLUSIONS

- Concerned with the impression we make on others, we tend to believe that others are paying more attention to us than they are (the spotlight effect).
- We also tend to believe that our emotions are more obvious than they are (the illusion of transparency).

SELF-CONCEPT: WHO AM I?

- Our sense of self helps organize our thoughts and actions. When we process information with reference to ourselves, we remember it well (the *self-reference effect*). *Self-concept* consists of two elements: the *self-schemas* that guide our processing of self-relevant information, and the possible selves that we dream of or dread.
- *Self-esteem* is the overall sense of self-worth we use to appraise our traits and abilities. Our self-concepts are determined by multiple influences, including the roles we play, the comparisons we make, our social identities, how we perceive others appraising us, and our experiences of success and failure.
- Cultures shape the self, too. Many people in individualistic Western cultures assume an independent self. Others, often in collectivistic cultures, assume a more interdependent self. As Chapter 14 further explains, these contrasting ideas contribute to cultural differences in social behaviour.
- Our self-knowledge is curiously flawed. We often do not know why we behave the way we do. When influences upon our behaviour are not conspicuous enough for any observer to see, we, too, can miss them. The unconscious, implicit processes that control our behaviour may differ from our conscious, explicit explanations of it. We also tend to mispredict our emotions.

SELF-ESTEEM

- Self-esteem motivation influences our cognitive processes: facing failure, high-self-esteem people sustain their self-worth by perceiving other people as failing too, and by exaggerating their superiority over others.
- Although high self-esteem is generally more beneficial than low, researchers have found that a variety of social offenders tend towards *higher*-than-average self-esteem. Someone with a big ego, which then is threatened or deflated by social rejection, is potentially aggressive.

SELF-SERVING BIAS

- Such perceptions arise partly from a motive to maintain and enhance self-esteem, a motive that protects people from depression but contributes to misjudgement and group conflict.
- Self-serving bias can be adaptive in that it allows us to savour the good things that happen in our lives. When bad things happen, however, self-serving bias can have the maladaptive effect of causing us to blame others or feel cheated out of something we 'deserved'.
- Research has consistently found that many people exhibit a *self-serving bias*. In experiments and everyday life, we often take credit for our successes while blaming failures on the situation. In addition, people often rate themselves as better than average on subjective, desirable traits and abilities, and can exhibit unrealistic optimism about their futures. Also, we overestimate the commonality of our opinions and foibles (*false consensus*) while underestimating the commonality of our abilities and virtues (*false uniqueness*).

PERCEIVED SELF-CONTROL

- Several lines of research show the benefits of a sense of *self-efficacy* and feelings of control. People who believe in their own competence and effectiveness, and who have an *internal locus of control*, cope better and achieve more than others.
- *Learned helplessness* often occurs when attempts to improve a situation have proven fruitless; *self-determination*, in contrast, is bolstered by experiences of successfully exercising control and improving one's situation.
- When people are given too many choices, they may be less satisfied with what they have than when offered a smaller range of choices.

IMPRESSION MANAGEMENT

- As social beings, we adjust our words and actions to suit our audiences. To varying degrees, we note our performance and adjust it to create the impressions we desire.
- Such tactics explain examples of false modesty, in which people put themselves down, extol future competitors, or publicly credit others when privately they credit themselves.
- Sometimes people will even self-handicap with self-defeating behaviours that protect self-esteem by providing excuses for failure.
- Self-presentation refers to our wanting to present a favourable image both to an external audience (other people) and to an internal audience (ourselves). Many people these days make use of online social networking sites for self-presentation purposes. With regard to an external audience, those who score high on a scale of self-monitoring adjust their behaviour to each situation, whereas those low in self-monitoring may do so little adjusting that they seem insensitive.
- Our sense of self might be lost or changed as a consequence of an accident or condition such as dementia.

Critical Questions

1. To what extent, in your opinion, does one's sense of self depend on culture?
2. Should we help people with low self-esteem to increase their self-esteem?
3. How would you rate your self-knowledge in terms of accuracy?
4. Do you think narcissistic people are more attractive than non-narcissistic ones? If so, why?
5. Is conscious self-monitoring a good or a bad thing?

Recommended Reading

Classic Works

Goffman, E. (1959). *The presentation of self in everyday life.* Penguin Books.

Higgins, E. T. (1987). Self-discrepancy: A theory relating self and affect. *Psychological Review, 94,* 319–340.

Lash, C. (1979). *The culture of narcissism: American life in an age of diminishing expectations.* Norton & Company.

Contemporary Works

Dufner, M., Rauthmann, J. F., Czarna, A. Z., & Denissen, J. J. A. (2013). Are narcissists sexy? Zeroing in on the effect of narcissism on short-term mate appeal. *Personality and Social Psychology Bulletin, 39,* 870–882.

Leach, C. W., & Spears, R. (2008). 'A vengefulness of the impotent': The pain of in-group inferiority and schadenfreude toward successful out-groups. *Journal of Personality and Social Psychology, 95,* 1383–1396.

Twenge, J. M., & Campbell, W. K. (2013). *The narcissism epidemic: Living in the age of entitlement.* Atria.

4 SOCIAL BELIEFS AND JUDGEMENTS

'Most of the mistakes in thinking are inadequacies of perception rather than mistakes of logic.'
Edward De Bono

On 28 September 2018, an earthquake followed by a tsunami struck Indonesia's capital, Palu, killing over 2,000 people and leaving many more badly injured, homeless and possessionless. You may have witnessed the devastation through the media as witnesses reported and downloaded videos and accounts of the scene across many media platforms. This earthquake was not the first for Indonesia. In fact it wasn't even the first in 2018 for Indonesia. Between April and December 2018, they suffered nine earthquakes, affecting more than two million people across the country. Indonesia is made up of a series of islands, some of which are volcanic. As the tectonic plates move, the volcanoes erupt, and quakes and tsunamis follow. Whilst we might be able to explain the cause of the earthquake based on physical geography, people always ask 'Could this have been avoided?' Should scientists have predicted it much earlier? Were rescue operations too slow? Earthquakes often expose poor building standards that cannot withstand volcanic activity. Modern buildings such as houses, schools and hospitals crumble in the wake of a quake. Were the engineers and builders incompetent or non-compliant with regulations for structures in an earthquake zone? Ultimately who is to blame for the destruction and devastation that ensues? Our history tells a story about tsunamis, earthquakes, droughts, flooding and other natural disasters that occur across the globe. From the 1920 Haiyuan Earthquake in China, the 2004 earthquake and tsunami in the Indian Ocean, to Cyclone Idai that devastated lives across Zimbabwe, Mozambique and Malawi in 2019, addressing social beliefs and judgements is important. Even the most physical of events quickly become sociopolitical issues to be made sense of. And how we understand, explain and evaluate events such as these, has profound real-world consequences.

Such social beliefs emerge as we:

- *perceive* and recall events through the filters of our own culturally influenced assumptions
- *judge* events, informed by our intuition, by implicit rules that guide our snap judgements, and by our moods
- *explain* events by attributing them to the situation or to the person
- therefore *expect* certain events, which sometimes helps bring them about.

This chapter explores how we perceive, judge and explain our social worlds, and how – and how much – our expectations influence others. Because this chapter is about social thinking and thought processes involved in social judgements, the focus is broadly on social cognition and therefore on experimental social psychology. Other perspectives, such as the psychodynamic approach and social learning are not included in the scope of the chapter. However, we would still encourage you to also consider alternative explanations and influences with regard to how we perceive, judge and make sense of our social world.

Perceiving Our Social World

Striking research reveals the extent to which our assumptions and prejudgements guide our perceptions, interpretations and recall.

Chapter 1 notes an important fact: that our cultural preconceptions guide how we perceive and interpret information.

Let us consider some provocative experiments. The first group of experiments examines how *pre*dispositions and *pre*judgements affect how we perceive and interpret information. The second group plants a judgement in people's minds *after* they have been given information to see how after-the-fact ideas bias recall. The overarching point: *we respond not to reality as it is but to reality as we construe it.*

Priming

Even before we attend to the world around us, unattended stimuli can subtly predispose how we will interpret and recall events. Imagine yourself, during an experiment, wearing earphones and concentrating on ambiguous spoken sentences such as 'We stood by the bank'. When a pertinent word (*river* or *money*) is simultaneously sent to your other ear, you do not consciously hear it. Yet the word 'primes' your interpretation of the sentence (Baars & McGovern, 1996).

Our memory system is a web of associations, and **priming** is the awakening or activating of certain associations. Priming experiments reveal how one thought, even without awareness, can influence another thought, or even an action. What is out of sight may not be completely out of mind. An electric shock that is too slight to be felt may increase the perceived intensity of a later shock. A subliminal colour name facilitates speedier identification when the colour appears on the computer screen, whereas an unseen wrong name delays colour identification (Epley et al., 1999; Merikle et al., 2001). In each case, an invisible image or word primes a response to a later task.

priming activating particular associations in memory

In a fascinating study conducted in Japan, Kimura and her colleagues (2009) looked at implicit gender-associations with food. As part of their study they noted that certain foods in Japan have a gender-stereotype. So for example cake is feminine, whereas barbecued meat is masculine. In the experiment, participants were individually seated at a laptop to watch a presentation. Their task was to indicate whether a forename that was displayed on the screen was male or female, using keys on the keyboard. However, before each forename was displayed, an image of a stereotypically feminine or masculine food item was flashed onto the screen for 200 milliseconds. Kimura wanted to know, would they be quicker to identify the gender of the forename (e.g. female) if a congruent gendered food item (e.g. cake) was flashed immediately before it than if an incongruent food item (e.g. steak) was presented? Indeed they were faster. Her Japanese participants seemed to adhere to the stereotype that 'you are what you eat', and for women that was sweet but also low-fat foods. For men, it was high-fat meat and rice. As the research team point out, such associations need taking into account when we seek to change eating behaviours.

We are what we eat? Stereotypes around food can influence what we eat.

SOURCE: © Rodrigo A Torres/Glow Images

Often our thinking and acting are primed by events of which we are unaware. Holland et al. (2005) observed that Dutch students unknowingly exposed to the scent of an all-purpose cleaner were quicker to identify cleaning-related words. In follow-up experiments, other students exposed to a cleaning scent recalled more cleaning-related activities when describing their day's activities and even kept their desk cleaner while eating a crumbly cookie. Moreover, all these effects occurred without the participants' conscious awareness of the scent and its influence.

Priming experiments have their counterparts in everyday life.

- Watching a scary movie alone at home can prime our thinking, by activating emotions that, without our realizing it, cause us to interpret creaking door noises as a ghost!
- Depressed moods, as this chapter explains later, prime negative associations. But put people in a *good* mood and suddenly their past seems more wonderful, their future brighter.
- Watching violence primes people to interpret ambiguous actions (being pushed by a passer-by) and words ('punch') as aggressive.
- For many psychology students, reading about psychological disorders primes how they interpret their own anxieties and gloomy moods. Reading about disease symptoms similarly primes medical students to worry about their congestion, fever or headache.

Categorical Thinking

Priming effects can lead us to perceive people as members of social groups. Categorical thinking describes this process of perceiving a person in terms of cues that indicate their social group membership. Interestingly, theorists have found that group stereotypes can be triggered simply through the presence of a category-relevant feature. This certainly has its uses. Such a mechanism certainly saves us a lot of time and effort working out who someone is. As Macrae and Martin (2007, p. 793) state, 'categorical thinking economises the process of person understanding'. However, while this might have benefits, it comes with costs such as negative stereotyping, discrimination and prejudice simply on the basis of a visual feature. Macrae and Martin found that simply perceiving the visual cue of long or short hair caused the activation of sex stereotypes (i.e. if long hair was primed then the person was assumed to be female). Seiter and Hatch (2005) discovered that men and women with tattoos were considered less competent, sociable, and credible than people without a tattoo. Tattoos are typically associated with prisoners, broken homes, and vulnerability. However, as cultural behaviour changes so do our associations. Martin and Dula (2010) report the rise in popularity of tattoos in the Western world across many sections of society. They suggest that perhaps this will shift negative perceptions of tattoo-wearers, especially by those who hold some form of power over us, such as jurors, employers, and teachers. The fact that most of the young people they studied had tattoos on parts of the body that could be easily covered, suggests we're not quite there yet. Tattoos still evoke negative associations. This categorical thinking influences how we perceive, judge and behave towards people. We consider this again in Chapter 12 where we examine how categorical thinking shapes the identities we ascribe to ourselves and other people, and in Chapter 13 to see how perceptions of social group membership and stereotypes can lead to discrimination and prejudice.

> The way we categorize within our social world has implications for stereotyping, the production of prejudice and discriminatory behaviour. See Chapter 13 for an overview of prejudice.

However, we need to be a little cautious here. It isn't simply the case that we will always engage in stereotypical categorical thinking.

Macrae and Bodenhausen (2000), and Castelli et al. (2004) have suggested that stereotyping occurs when:

- it is relevant to the perceiver's information-processing goals
- the perceiver holds prejudiced beliefs about such groups
- the perceiver has sufficient attentional resources to engage in this kind of information processing
- the cues are easy to process and are presented to the perceiver for a period of time.

More recently, in their meta-analysis of 39 published experimental psychological studies on stereotype priming, spanning 20 years worth of research, Kidder et al. (2018) found some interesting discrepancies in how they were carried out. Their analysis noted that the differences between the various studies' methods for measuring stereotypical thinking might account for the results obtained. For example differences in the stereotype being investigated, whether 'primes' were repeated in a study, what the prime was (e.g. image and/or word) and the amount of time participants had between being presented with the prime (e.g. long hair) and giving a response ('female'), all had an impact on whether stereotypical thinking was discovered, and if so, how strongly it occurred. They conclude that whilst we do indulge in stereotypical thinking, how psychologists capture and measure it has an impact on the evidence we obtain and publish.

We make assumptions about people on the basis of their physical appearance. How might categorical thinking influence your perceptions and behaviour?

SOURCE: © hurricanehank/Shutterstock

Studies of how implanted ideas and images can prime our interpretations and recall illustrate one of this book's take-home lessons from twenty-first-century social psychology: *much of our social information processing is automatic*. It is unintentional, out of sight and without awareness.

Perceiving and Interpreting Events

Despite some startling and often confirmed biases and logical flaws in how we perceive and understand one another, we're mostly accurate (Jussim, 2005). The better we know people, the more accurately we feel we can read their minds and feelings. But on occasion our prejudgements err. The effects of prejudgements and expectations are standard fare for psychology's introductory course. Note the optical illusion in Chapter 1. Or consider this phrase:

A

BIRD

IN THE

THE HAND

Did you notice anything wrong with it? There is more to perception than meets the eye. The same is true of social perception. As social perceptions are very much in the eye of the beholder, even a simple stimulus may strike two people quite differently. Saying Germany's Angela Merkel was 'an OK President of the European Council' may sound like a put-down to one of her ardent admirers and like praise to someone who regards her with contempt. When social information is subject to multiple interpretations, preconceptions matter (Bodenhausen, 2005).

Two studies conducted by Liberman et al. (2011) reveal just how powerful preconceptions can be. They focus on the increased provision of diversity training across the Western world by companies, educational establishments, governments and so on. Such training is put in place to heighten awareness of cultural differences and promote communication and equality across increasingly diverse workforces. However, as Liberman and his team point out, little has been done to examine how effective these programmes are. In particular, does it matter who delivers the training? How might our preconceptions of the diversity trainer impact upon our engagement with the training? Well, quite a lot it would appear. Liberman and colleagues found that white diversity trainers were considered less effective, were less likely to be hired, and resulted in less knowledge transfer than black diversity trainers. Participants assumed the white trainers, regardless of whether they were male or female, would have no experience of minority issues, whereas the black trainer would. Furthermore, even if the white trainer explained their own experiences of being victim to diversity issues, it did not help matters. For this job preconceptions about race matter. The research team note that these preconceptions, even before a training programme begins, perhaps ironically, has implications for the employment of diversity trainers and engagement with the training.

'There is no subject about which people are less objective than objectivity', noted one media commentator (Poniewozik, 2003). Indeed, people's perceptions of bias can be used to assess their attitudes (Saucier & Miller, 2003). Tell me where you see bias, and you will signal your attitudes.

Researchers have manipulated people's preconceptions – with astonishing effects upon their interpretations and recollections.

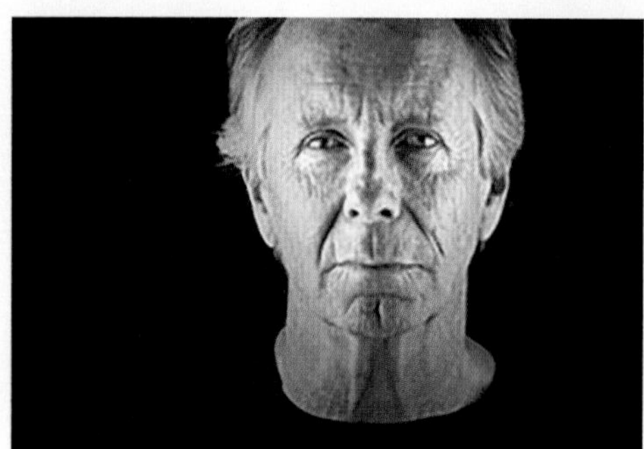

FIGURE 4.1 Judge for yourself: is this person's expression cruel or kind? If told he was a leader of the anti-Nazi movement, would your reading of this face differ?

SOURCE: ©JPagetRFphotos/Alamy Stock Photo

In a classic study, Rothbart and Birrell (1977) had university students assess the facial expression of a man. Those told he was a Gestapo leader responsible for barbaric medical experiments on concentration camp inmates during the Second World War intuitively judged his expression as cruel. Those told he was a leader in the anti-Nazi underground movement whose courage saved thousands of Jewish lives judged his facial expression as warm and kind.

Film-makers can control people's perceptions of emotion by manipulating the setting in which they see a face. They call this the 'Kulechov effect', after a Russian film director who would skilfully guide viewers' inferences by manipulating their assumptions. Kulechov demonstrated the phenomenon by creating three short films that presented identical footage of the face of an actor with a neutral expression after viewers had first been shown one of three different scenes: a dead woman, a dish of soup or a girl playing. As a result, in the first film the actor seemed sad, in the second thoughtful and in the third happy.

Construal processes also colour others' perceptions of us. When we say something good or bad about another, people spontaneously tend to associate that trait with us, report Mae et al. (1999; Carlston & Skowronski, 2005) – a phenomenon they call *spontaneous trait inference*. If we go around talking about others being gossipy, people may then unconsciously associate 'gossip' with us. Describe someone as sensitive, loving and compassionate, and you may seem more so. There is, it appears, intuitive wisdom in the childhood taunt, 'I'm rubber, you're glue; what you say bounces off me and sticks to you.'

The bottom line: we view our social worlds through the spectacles of our beliefs, attitudes and values. These are shaped by the normative framework of the culture, society and community in which we live. That is one reason our beliefs are so important: they shape our interpretation of everything else.

Belief Perseverance

Imagine a grandparent who decides, during an evening with a crying infant, that bottle-feeding produces colicky babies. If the infant turns out to be suffering a high fever, will the sitter nevertheless persist in believing that bottle-feeding causes colic? To find out, Lee Ross, Craig Anderson and their colleagues planted a falsehood in people's minds and then tried to discredit it.

Their research was one of the first to reveal that it is surprisingly difficult to demolish a falsehood, once the person conjures up a rationale for it. Each experiment first *implanted a belief*, either by proclaiming it to be true or by showing the participants some anecdotal evidence. Then the participants were asked to *explain why* it is true. Finally, the researchers totally *discredited* the initial information by telling the participants the truth: the information was manufactured for the experiment, and half the participants in the experiment had received opposite information. Nevertheless, the new belief survived about 75 per cent intact. Therefore, only a quarter of the implanted belief was lost when the researchers discredited it. This is presumably because the participants still retained their invented explanations for the belief. This phenomenon, called **belief perseverance**, shows that beliefs can grow their own legs and survive the discrediting of the evidence that inspired them.

belief perseverance
persistence of one's initial conceptions, as when the basis for one's belief is discredited but an explanation of why the belief might be true survives

In a classic example of belief perseverance, Anderson et al. (1980) asked participants to decide whether individuals who take risks make good or bad firefighters. One group considered a risk-prone person who was a successful firefighter and a cautious person who was an unsuccessful one. The other group considered cases suggesting the opposite conclusion. After forming their theory that risk-prone people make better or worse firefighters, the participants wrote explanations for it – for example, that risk-prone people are brave or that cautious people have fewer accidents. Once each explanation was formed, it could exist independently of the information that initially created the belief. When that information was discredited, the participants still held their self-generated explanations and therefore continued to believe that risk-prone people really do make better or worse firefighters.

Experiments like this one suggest that the more we examine our theories and explain how they *might* be true, the more closed we become to information that challenges our beliefs. Once we consider why an accused person might be guilty, why an offending stranger acts that way, or why a favoured stock might rise in value, our explanations may survive challenging evidence to the contrary (Davies, 1997; Guenther & Alicke, 2008; Jelalian & Miller, 1984).

The evidence is compelling: our beliefs and expectations powerfully affect how we mentally construct events. Usually, we benefit from our preconceptions, just as scientists benefit from creating theories that guide them in noticing and interpreting events. But the benefits sometimes entail a cost: we become prisoners of our own thought patterns. Thus, the supposed Martian 'canals' that twentieth-century astronomers delighted in spotting turned out to be the product of intelligent life – an intelligence on Earth's side of the telescope. Germans, who widely believed that the introduction of the euro currency led to increased prices, overestimated such price increases when comparing actual restaurant menus – the prior menu with German mark prices and a new one with euro prices (Traut-Mattausch et al., 2004). We might wonder to what extent the UK's referendum decision to leave the European Union would be a relatively simple process to carry out, is a consequence of preconceptions. As an old Chinese proverb says, 'Two-thirds of what we see is behind our eyes.'

Belief perseverance may have important consequences, as Lewandowsky et al. (2005) discovered when they explored implanted and discredited information about the Iraq war that began in 2003. As the war unfolded, the Western media reported and repeated several claims – for example, that Iraqi forces executed coalition prisoners of war – that later were shown to be false and were retracted. Alas, having accepted the information, which fitted their pre-existing assumptions, Americans tended to retain the belief (unlike Germans and Australians, who tended to be more predisposed to question the war's rationale).

Is there a remedy for belief perseverance? There is: *explain the opposite*. There is some social psychological evidence to show that presenting the opposite view or position can lead us to let go of those beliefs we've steadfastly clung on to (Lord et al., 1984; Ross et al., 1975). Let's consider a recent example. We've probably all seen and heard stories and evidence that has discredited some of our favourite celebrities from the worlds of sport and entertainment. But does this negative information have an impact on our former positive beliefs about them? Bui (2014) decided to investigate. Imagine you're one of the 201 participants in this study. You're asked to name a famous living person you admire. Then you're asked to note what they're famous for. Now here's the crucial bit: why might other people not like them? Where did this negative information about this famous person come from? By asking these questions Bui nudges you into thinking about any bad conduct your celebrity might have displayed. Has this changed your beliefs about the celebrity? Well, possibly. Bui found that his participants' *feelings* about their chosen celebrity did not change regardless of what the negative information was or where it came from. However, their *beliefs* changed when the source of the information was the result of being caught by the media (e.g. in a photograph) or the behaviour had been publicly displayed by the celebrity. Family and friends' reports of reasons to dislike a celebrity had no impact on the participants' beliefs or feelings. Explaining the opposite can diminish our beliefs but not necessarily our feelings, and it matters where this disconfirming information comes from.

'No one denies that new evidence can change people's beliefs. Children do eventually renounce their belief in Santa Claus. Our contention is simply that such changes generally occur slowly, and that more compelling evidence is often required to alter a belief than to create it.'

Ross and Lepper (1980)

Constructing Memories of Ourselves and Our Worlds

Do you agree or disagree with the following statement?

> Memory can be likened to a storage chest in the brain into which we deposit material and from which we can withdraw it later if needed. Occasionally, something is lost from the 'chest', and then we say we have forgotten.

About 85 per cent of college students said they agreed (Lamal, 1979). As one magazine advertisement put it: 'Science has proven the accumulated experience of a lifetime is preserved perfectly in your mind.'

Actually, psychological research has proved the opposite. Our memories are not exact copies of experiences that remain on deposit in a memory bank. Rather, we construct memories at the time of withdrawal, as well as when we store experiences. Like a palaeontologist inferring the appearance of a dinosaur from bone fragments, we reconstruct our distant past by using our current feelings and expectations to combine information fragments. Thus, we can easily (though unconsciously) revise our memories to suit our current knowledge. But there has to be something stored in the memory to be used when constructing what happened.

When an experimenter or a therapist manipulates people's presumptions about their past, a sizeable percentage of people will construct false memories. Asked to imagine vividly a made-up childhood experience in which they ran, tripped, fell and stuck their hand through a window, or knocked over a punch bowl at a wedding, about a quarter will later recall the fictitious event as something that actually happened (Loftus & Bernstein, 2005). In its search for truth, the mind sometimes constructs a falsehood.

In experiments involving more than 20,000 people, Loftus (2003) and her collaborators have explored our mind's tendency to construct memories. In the typical experiment, people witness an event, receive misleading information about it (or not), and then take a memory test. The repeated finding is the **misinformation effect**. People incorporate the misinformation into their memories: they recall a give way sign as a stop sign, hammers as screwdrivers, *Vogue* magazine as *Grazia*, Dr Henderson as Dr Davidson, breakfast cereal as eggs, and a clean-shaven man as a fellow with a moustache. However, of greater concern, analyses of hundreds of cases in which patients were led to falsely believe that they were abducted by aliens or molested in satanic rituals reveal that suggestion is a key factor in these beliefs. This shows that suggested misinformation may even produce false memories of supposed child sexual abuse, argues Loftus. These false memories can have severe consequences for the individual. And, as Roediger and Garcia (2007) discovered in their study of eyewitness memory, we become more susceptible to misinformation effects as we get older.

misinformation effect incorporating 'misinformation' into one's memory of the event, after witnessing an event and receiving misleading information about it

Furthermore, suggestion has important implications for criminal investigations that rely on memory in order to track down a perpetrator or work out a motive.

Eyewitness testimony remains an important part of a criminal investigation (Brewer & Wells, 2011). Suspects and witnesses who are subject to suggestive police interviews can confuse suggestions made in the interview for memories of the actual event. So merely imagining the occurrence of the suggested event can lead to the development of false memories for the event (e.g. Garry et al., 1996; Lindsay et al., 2004). Drivdahl et al. (2009) observed that when participants were asked to emotionally elaborate on a suggested event, it not only increased false memories for the event having actually happened, but also false beliefs in its authenticity.

More recently researchers have examined the role of social media platforms such as Facebook, in fuelling misinformation effects. Zollo and Quattrociocchi (2018) consider what they call the 'digital wildfires' caused by the rapid spreading of false and misleading information and rumours online. Without qualified expertise to debunk such misinformation, people can be subjected to mass confrontation of incorrect information which then impinges on their views, perceptions and memories for actual events.

The Island of Ireland Peace Park, Belgium. Reconstructing national memories.
SOURCE: ©Maurice Savage/Alamy Stock Photo

Researchers have also used qualitative methods to focus on the content of constructed memories as they occur in language. Edwards and Middleton (1987) argue that memories are better understood as rhetorical strategies that produce a version of an event that is appropriate for the context in which it is produced. This sidelines an analysis of whether memories are an accurate representation of what happened, and instead looks at why and how they are created in language and for what purposes. For example, Poulter (2018) considers the role the Island of Ireland Peace Park, established in 1998 in Belgium, plays in reconstructing a harmonious national memory of the First World War. As Poulter observes, British, Irish and Unionists (Northern Ireland) have very different memories of the war. For the Irish, a national memory of serving alongside Great Britain does not fit well with a political agenda to be separate from it. Consequently, it was erased from collective memory. For Unionists within Northern Ireland, it was seen as further evidence of Ireland's service to the British Crown, and together with the British is celebrated as a glorious and necessary war. Poulter analyses the texts that are displayed in the Peace Park. These texts re-tell the history of the war in a way that emphasizes the suffering of all groups involved, the deaths, and the losses. The Park constructs a memory of the First World War that is acceptable to all parties, unites them, which everyone can visit to grieve and lament the atrocities of war.

Memories are not only constructed through words but also images. In their qualitative study of Finnish history, Hakokongäs and Sakki (2016) looked at how Finland's collective history is portrayed in a series of official images, depicting a particular culture, politics and significant wars. The authors reflect on how this produces a national memory which is a positive and coherent, if not fully accurate nor comprehensive, account of who the Finnish are.

In this kind of research memory is not studied as an accurate reflection of what actually happened, but is considered a *version* of what happened, rhetorically designed to attend to the demands of the context in which it is produced.

Reconstructing our Past Attitudes

The construction of positive memories brightens our recollections of the past. Mitchell and Thompson (1994) and Mitchell et al. (1997) report that people often exhibit *rosy retrospection* – they recall mildly pleasant events more favourably than they experienced them. College students on a three-week bike trip, older adults on a guided tour of Austria, and undergraduates on vacation all reported enjoying their experiences as they were having them. But they later recalled such experiences even more fondly, minimizing the unpleasant or boring aspects and remembering the high points.

McFarland and Ross (1985) found that, as our relationships change, we also revise our recollections of other people. They had university students rate their steady dating partners. Two months later, they rated them again. Students who were more in love than ever had a tendency to recall love at first sight. Those who had broken up were more likely to recall having recognized the partner as somewhat selfish and bad-tempered.

Holmberg and Holmes (1994) discovered the phenomenon also operating among 373 newlywed couples, most of whom reported being very happy. When resurveyed two years later, those whose marriages had soured recalled that things had always been bad. The results are 'frightening', say Holmberg and Holmes. 'Such biases can lead to a dangerous downward spiral. The worse your current view of your partner is, the worse your memories are, which only further confirms your negative attitudes.'

It's not that we are totally unaware of how we used to feel, just that when memories are hazy, current feelings guide our recall. Parents of every generation bemoan the values of the next generation, partly because they misrecall their youthful values as being closer to their current values. And teens of every generation recall their parents as – depending on their current mood – wonderful or woeful (Bornstein et al., 1991).

Reconstructing our Past Behaviour

As Bernstein et al., (2011) discovered, the hindsight bias affects us all, from as young as 3 years old to 95 years old. The hindsight bias involves memory revision, which can include our own histories. Blank et al., (2003) showed this when inviting University of Leipzig students, after a surprising German election outcome, to recall their voting predictions from two months previously. The students misrecalled their predictions as closer to the actual results.

How long is an elephant pregnant for? This is one of a series of questions that Pohl et al. (2010) asked 9-year-old and 12-year-old children, and adults. In their intriguing study, these three age groups were given two questionnaires containing 50 identical items presented in the same order. Participants were asked to complete the first questionnaire. Thirty minutes later they were asked to recall their answers for the second questionnaire. This second questionnaire contained correct answers to some of the questions. So for our elephant example, 21 months was presented to the participant. Instructed not to allow the correct answer to influence their memory for the original answer, children and adults were asked to recall their previous answer. Did they? Well, not really! Pohl and his colleagues found that all three age groups exhibited the hindsight bias for the questions where the correct answer had been presented to them. Regardless of whether they were nine years old, 12 years old, or adults, they falsely recalled their original answer as being closer to the correct answer than it actually was.

Sometimes our present view is that we've improved – in which case we may misrecall our past as more unlike the present than it actually was. This tendency resolves a puzzling pair of consistent findings: those who participate in psychotherapy and self-improvement programmes for weight control, anti-smoking and exercise show only modest improvement on average. Yet they often claim considerable benefit (Myers, 2004). Having expended so much time, effort and money on self-improvement, people may think, 'I may not be perfect now, but I was worse before; this did me a lot of good.' We all selectively notice, interpret and recall events in ways that sustain our ideas. Our social judgements are a mix of observation and expectation, reason and passion.

So far we have seen that there can be many influences on our perceptions and also that perceiving our social world can become distorted. This has a knock-on effect on our social judgements too. These judgements can also occur very quickly as we will see when we turn to a consideration of social judgements in the following section.

Judging Our Social World

As we have already noted, our cognitive mechanisms are efficient and adaptive, yet occasionally error-prone. Usually they serve us well. But sometimes clinicians misjudge patients, employers misjudge employees, people of one race misjudge people of another, and spouses misjudge their partners. The results can be misdiagnoses, workplace stress, prejudices and divorces. So, how – and how well – do we make intuitive social judgements?

By drawing on advances in cognitive psychology – in how people perceive, represent and remember events – social psychologists have shed welcome light on how we form judgements. Let us look at what that research reveals of the marvels and mistakes of our social intuition.

Intuitive Judgements

What are our powers of intuition – of immediately knowing something without reasoning or analysis? Advocates of 'intuitive management' believe we should tune in to our hunches. When judging others we should plug in to the non-logical aspects of our 'right brain'. When hiring, firing and investing, we should listen to our premonitions. In making judgements, we should follow the example of *Star Wars'* Luke Skywalker by switching off our computer guidance systems and trusting the force within.

Are the intuitionists right that important information is immediately available apart from our conscious analysis? Or are the sceptics correct in saying that intuition is 'our knowing we are right, whether we are or not'?

Priming research suggests that the unconscious indeed controls much of our behaviour. As Bargh and Chartrand (1999) explain, 'Most of a person's everyday life is determined not by their conscious intentions and deliberate choices but by mental processes that are put into motion by features of the environment and that operate outside of conscious awareness and guidance.' When the light turns red, we react and hit the brake before consciously deciding to do so. Indeed, reflect Macrae and Johnston (1998), 'to be able to do just about anything at all (e.g., driving, dating, dancing), action initiation needs to be decoupled from the inefficient (i.e., slow, serial, resource consuming) workings of the conscious mind, otherwise inaction inevitably would prevail'.

However, a word of caution is perhaps needed here. Although conscious decisions are slower than automatic processes this does not mean that they are less important. They characterize human beings. Behaviour that has become automated has previously been deliberate and conscious. For example, if you are a driver, you once consciously thought through all the steps of driving, but now it is a fairly automatic process. Riding a bike involved learning to ride, yet once this is accomplished not much conscious thought is needed to balance the bike and to cycle.

The Powers of Intuition

'The heart has its reasons which reason does not know,' observed seventeenth-century philosopher-mathematician Blaise Pascal. Three centuries later, scientists have proved Pascal correct. We know more than we know we know. Studies of our unconscious information processing confirm our limited access to what's going on in our minds (Bargh & Morsella, 2008; Bargh et al., 2012; Greenwald et al., 2003a; Greenwald & Banaji, 1995; Perkins et al., 2008; Strack & Deutsch, 2004). Our thinking is partly **controlled processing** (reflective, deliberate and conscious) and – more than psychologists once supposed – partly **automatic processing** (impulsive, effortless and without our awareness). Automatic, intuitive thinking occurs not 'on-screen' but off-screen, out of sight, where reason does not go. But we should remember that humans are not born with some preferred knowledge or behaviour. What is automatic today has been acquired and learned by conscious training.

controlled processing
mental activities that require conscious, deliberate and reflective thinking

automatic processing
mental activities happening with little or no conscious awareness. This is both effortless and habitual

Social judgements have a profound influence upon our behaviour. So can what we already know influence our social judgements and bring about automatic behaviour change? Researchers argue that for these automatic processes to occur we need to be able to activate pre-existing knowledge (Amodio & Ratner, 2011; Bertram & Bodenhausen, 2005). To test whether the presence of situational cues will bring about automatic behaviour change, Bargh et al. (1996b) primed participants with the task of unscrambling scrambled sentences. There were three conditions. Either the scrambled sentences contained rude words or polite words or neutral words. Participants were then told to approach the experimenter to ask what their next task would be. However, the experimenters had set up a fake situation where the experimenter was supposedly engaged in conversation and did not acknowledge the presence of the participant. If you were in this situation would you think the experimenter was rude? Would you interrupt the experimenter and if so how long do you think you would wait before interrupting? In the study, 60 per cent of those who had taken part in the rude words condition interrupted within 10 minutes while less than 40 per cent of participants in the neutral condition interrupted during this time and less than 20 per cent interrupted if they were in the polite condition. The researchers argue that the participants' behaviour was driven by the environmental stimuli – rude words or polite words – and that this was preconscious and automatic. Because we need to have some idea about what is rude and polite and what these mean we need to draw on what we have already learned – what we already know. Therefore, Bargh et al. (1996b) also point out the implications of implicit rather than explicit cognition with regard to making judgements and stereotyping. After two further experiments were carried out that activated stereotypes automatically, Bargh et al. (1996b) argued that this indicates people can behave in negative ways towards stereotyped groups without even realizing it! This clearly shows that we know more than we know we know and it also demonstrates the more negative implication of our automatic behaviour.

Amodio and Ratner (2011) propose that there are different memory systems for different patterns of learning and behaviour. Exploring memory systems can help us to understand more about the processes involved in making social judgements that appear to be intuitive. Spunt and Lieberman (2013) argue for a dual process model of the brain system: one process when we automatically identify a person's behaviour and one process when we make judgements about a person's behaviour. Spunt and Lieberman propose that when we are making judgements these are controlled rather than spontaneous because we are 'weighing up' the causes of someone's behaviour in an effort to understand this behaviour. They also argue that it would be impossible to function in the social world if all our social cognition was controlled. Imagine how huge the effort would be for making sense of people and engaging in social interactions if it was all down to conscious awareness and control.

Amodio and Ratner's (2011) and Spunt and Lieberman's (2013) work is within social neuroscience. Social neuroscience is a fast growing discipline in social psychology. What appears to be intuitive may actually involve complex processing and social neuroscience can explore this further.

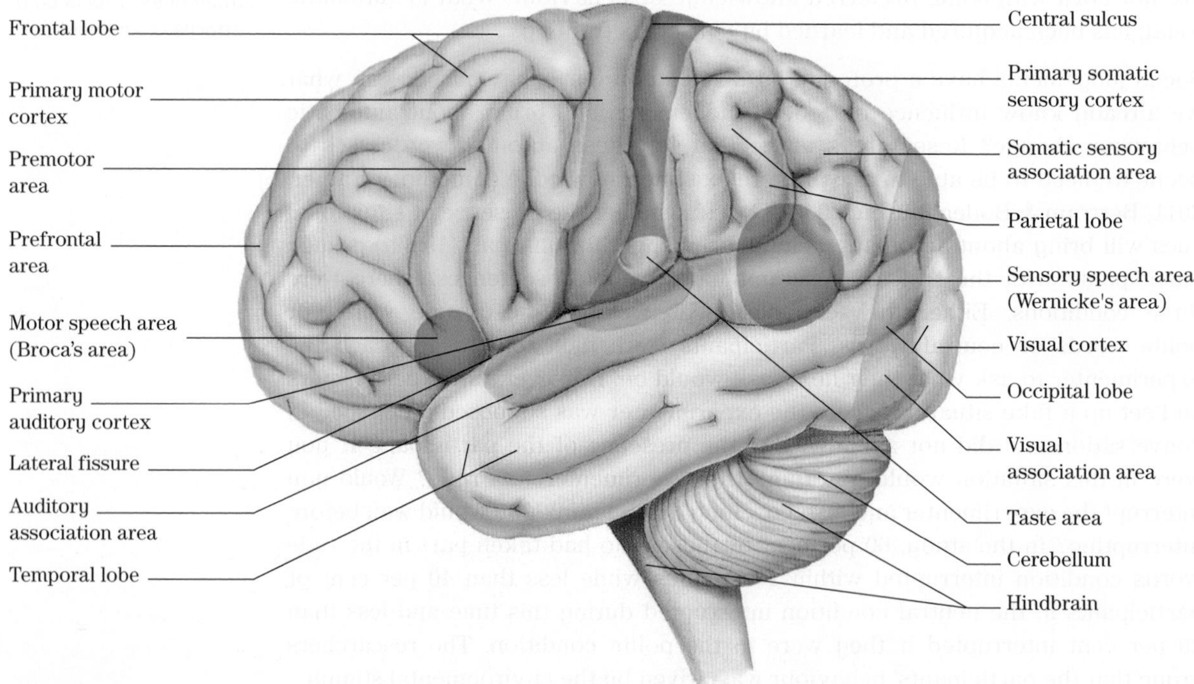

Basic anatomy of the brain.
SOURCE: ©McGraw-Hill Education

Social neuroscientists argue that our biology helps shape our social environments. As outlined in Chapter 1, social neuroscience is concerned with understanding the structure and functions of the brain that underlie our behaviour and enable our emotional experiences and how we process information. This discipline is therefore making important contributions in furthering our understanding of how we make social judgements.

Social neuroscience brings together multi-levels of analysis and is concerned with the biological, psychological and the social. Cacioppo et al. (2010), and Cacioppo and Berntson (1992) argue that research in social psychology and social neuroscience is important in two main ways: to investigate how neurochemical events influence social processes and to investigate how social processes influence neurochemical events. They therefore argue that social psychological theories should also consider physiological factors and mechanisms.

Three methods of neuroimaging are frequently used in social neuroscience. Functional magnetic resonance imaging (fMRI) and event-related potentials (ERPs) are both non-invasive methods that provide images of brain activity. ERPs are derived from averages of EEG activity in response to certain stimuli (Cacioppo et al., 1994). Both are correlational techniques. fMRI provides exploration of brain regions that are active when engaged in specific mental operations and ERPs provide exploration of rapid changes in brain activity. The third method, transcranial magnetic stimulation (TMS), stimulates brain cells and allows exploration into what causes particular brain regions to become activated for specific mental operations.

The networks in the brain region that are involved in making social judgements may not function in the same way for everybody. Neuroimaging has also been applied to understanding impairments in social judgements of people diagnosed with schizophrenia or with autistic spectrum disorders (ASD). For example, Hall et al. (2010) used fMRI to investigate the neural systems activated when people make social decisions. They found that there is a common network of brain regions activated when people without any history of psychiatric disorders make social judgements about approachability or intelligence based on faces. They propose that it is the dysfunction of this network that could contribute to a broad range of deficits in social functioning seen in people diagnosed with schizophrenia and ASD. Later in the chapter we consider how social neuroscience can help us further understand the way we explain our social world.

Social Schema Theory

We consider the concept of 'schemas' in Chapter 3 where we discuss how people understand their sense of 'self'. Schema is a construct social psychologists use to illustrate how we store information about the world, people, roles and how to behave in particular situations. Schemas serve many functions including guiding our memory, predicting what will happen, informing us how to behave appropriately and enabling us to work out what to do when it's not obvious from a situation. Fiske and Taylor (1991) define the four main schema types that we have as follows:

1. Self schemas – the most complex. This is the information we hold about ourselves in terms of our traits, our values, our mannerisms and so on. They define 'who I am'. See also Chapter 3 for more detail on the implications they have for presentations of our 'self' and our sense of well-being.

2 Person schemas – these include personality traits so we can categorize people when we first meet them on the basis of their perceived personality, and specific traits related to a particular person (e.g. your mother or your best friend).

3 Role schemas – these contain information about what behaviour and norms to expect of someone holding a particular role in society (e.g. doctor, mother, politician, lecturer).

4 Event schemas – these hold information about appropriate behaviour for events (e.g. going to a football match, attending a funeral).

Before a schema is activated and made available, we must first categorize the event, person or object appropriately. This is largely an automatic process. Rosch (1975) argued that we hold prototypes for each category so we can compare new instances to see if it belongs there. So imagine visiting a Michelin star fine-dining restaurant for the first time. We need to make use of our event schemas to work out how to behave appropriately. Is this an example of the category 'restaurant', or is it something else? To make such a judgement you compare it against a prototype of restaurant (which may be a specific instance or an amalgamation of several instances). This will then inform you how to behave in Le Gavroche. Should you leave a tip? Will someone clear the table for you when you've finished your meal? In Chapter 12 we discuss the role of prototypicality in categorization processes in more detail.

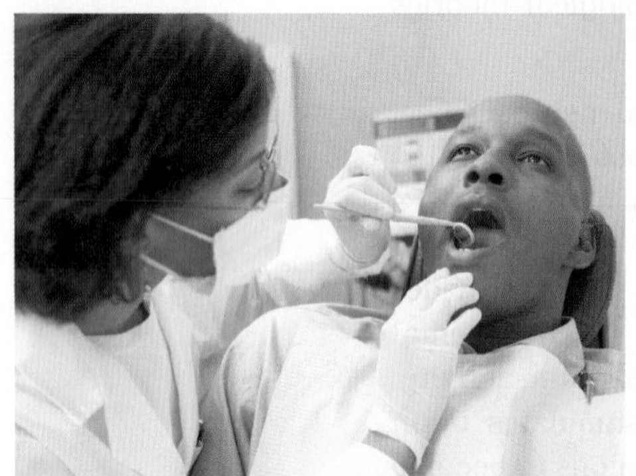

Our knowledge of the role of the dentist (role schema) and the event of a visit to the dentist (event schema) help us to anticipate what will happen and how we should behave. Without this knowledge a trip to the dentist would prove very confusing!
SOURCE: © Kris Timken/Blend Images LLC

Clearly schemas serve many advantageous functions. They enable us to categorize a complex social world quickly and efficiently, guiding us around it. However, as we shall see, they can malfunction!

The Limits of Intuition

We have seen how automatic, intuitive thinking can 'make us smart' (Gigerenzer & Todd, 1999) or at least process information faster and repeatedly. Loftus and Klinger (1992) nevertheless speak for other cognitive scientists in having doubts about the brilliance of intuition. They report 'a general consensus that the unconscious may not be as smart as previously believed'.

Social psychologists have explored not only our error-prone hindsight judgements but also our capacity for illusion – for perceptual misinterpretations, fantasies and constructed beliefs. If we return to social schema theory, we can imagine the problems if we select the wrong schema in a particular situation. Imagine a young employee, someone who walks in to his regular place of work and alights upon a young woman he's never seen before. He may assume this is an office assistant and ask her to do some photocopying for him. Now suppose it turns out this woman is actually his new manager! Suddenly his behaviour is inappropriate. As we categorize people, events and objects in order to work out how to behave towards them these can lead to stereotypical judgements. Such generalizations may not be accurate, and may lead to inappropriate behaviour.

Should you tip the waiter? Our schemas help guide our actions.
SOURCE: © Image Source

While schemas have become established within social psychology as the fundamental processes involved in social thought and attitude, Landau et al. (2010) propose that people use schemas to structure their social environment in a straightforward way but use conceptual metaphors to make sense of the world. Conceptual metaphors are unique cognitive mechanisms that shape social thought and attitudes. They liken social concepts to superficially dissimilar things and rely on taken-for-granted shared knowledge. For example, we know what somebody means if they describe a person as 'shallow' but the literal meaning of this word is actually quite different. Therefore, conceptual metaphors complement the schema view in social psychology through the way people use them to infer personal attributes and also to interpret and evaluate abstract social concepts. We will next consider how we encode information about people and make judgements about them.

In the following section on social encoding we will consider the seminal work of Asch (1946) concerning person perception and see how the words warm or cold were highly influential in creating an image of a person when added to a list of personal character traits. This gives an indication of conceptual metaphors in action because warm and cold can describe physical properties but when applied to configuring a person they take on particular meanings and facilitate images of particular persons and in turn are involved in forming attitudes towards them.

Social Encoding

Social encoding occurs within social cognition. Higgins and Bargh (1987) refer to social cognition as 'the knowing of people'. Social cognition refers to the way we perceive our social world and also our beliefs about people, their behaviour and the causes of social events.

social encoding the process of getting social information into memory. It comprises initially attending to and perceiving social information, understanding it and making connections with information already in memory. Our previous social experiences are a very important part of the process

Social encoding involves how we think about ourselves and other people. It is about how we select, interpret, remember and use social information to make judgements and decisions. Processing of the social world involves:

- Preattentive analysis – the unconscious and automatic taking in of information
- Focusing of attention – identifying, and categorizing information
- Comprehension – giving meaning to information
- Elaborative reasoning – linking information together and elaborating information.

Social information is ambiguous so when we encode information about a person, relevant person-related information is activated which helps us to make sense of the new information. Encoding and interpretation of a person or person's behaviour are in part a function of easily accessible mental representations and stereotypes, especially if aspects of the person or their behaviour are salient. This means that if these particular aspects are distinctive and different they will stand out and capture the attention of the person encoding the information. This also means that we remember a more clear and consistent impression of salient people and salient behaviour. If, for example, somebody was talking loudly on their mobile phone in a library and everyone else was quietly choosing books and reading, this behaviour would stand out for being different as well as for not fitting in with expectations. If you witnessed this behaviour you might find yourself making immediate judgements about the type of person the mobile phone user is. When people memorize information about a person based on their behaviour at the same time as they encode this information they base personality judgements by drawing on the most memorable aspects of this behaviour.

When we meet someone at a party and spend time talking with them, how do we decide what we think of our new acquaintance? Are we seeing them through the way we perceive their personality traits to be or are we thinking about them in a much more holistic way and forming an impression of their whole personality?

In a study that has deservedly become a classic within social psychology, Asch (1946) argues that people appear to configure impressions of people holistically rather than simply as a collection of various independent traits. Asch's (1946) configural model is a model of person perception that argues that central traits have a stronger influence on configuring an impression of others than peripheral traits. Asch noted that the process of person perception appears to happen so fast it seems to be automatic. He also noted that once we have formed an impression of a person this impression appears to be long lasting and difficult to change.

Asch (1946) recruited psychology undergraduates for his study of person perception. A series of 10 experiments were conducted. In one experiment two different groups of participants were read identical lists of traits except for the inclusion of one different word for each group. For example, both groups were read the following list: intelligent—skilful—industrious—determined—practical—cautious but Group A's list had the word warm within their list of characteristics and Group B had the word cold within their list. Cold and warm are central traits while the other words on the list were peripheral traits. Participants were then asked to describe the impression they had formed of the person based on their list of traits and were able to give quite detailed descriptions of an overall type of person from lists of traits. They were then asked to select from a list of pairs of characteristics the characteristic that most agreed with the impression they had formed.

Here are some examples of the pairs of traits Asch used for the experiment. Most of the pairs Asch constructed were opposites:

Shrewd—wise

Irritable—good-natured

Sociable—unsociable

Unreliable—reliable

Persistent—unstable

Imaginative—hard-headed

Participants in Group A – the warm condition – were more positive about the person they described and selected the more positive characteristic from the list of paired characteristics whereas Group B – the cold condition – were not as positive as Group A about the person they described and selected the more negative characteristic from the list of pairs. Just changing one word in a list of characteristics led participants to form very different overall impressions. Therefore, the characteristics warm and cold as central traits had a greater influence on the way people form impressions of others than the peripheral traits intelligent, skilful, industrious, determined, practical and cautious. Asch (1946) also proposed that the value of a particular trait can change. For example, a trait seen as central in one person may not be seen as a central trait in another person. This may be involved with the way in which people configure an overall impression of a person. However, the way we conceive people as a whole was not explored fully. Asch addressed this further by seeing what would happen if participants were given traits that did not fit with each other (Asch & Zukier, 1984). If these contradictory traits provided obstacles to configuring an overall impression of a person, the way participants attempted to overcome this would indicate the processes involved when configuring a person as unified.

Asch and Zukier compiled a list of pairs that also included some pairs of non-contradictory characteristics. Psychology students were asked to describe a person after being given a pair of characteristics selected from the list. For example:

Sociable—lonely

Cheerful—gloomy

Warm—humorous

Shy—courageous

Strict—kind

Do you think a person is a unified whole or a multiplicity of characteristics? Can we only be one thing but not another – that is, have certain characteristics without their opposites? Furthermore, are we consistent as a person or are we a multiplicity of malleable characteristics?

Asch and Zukier (1984) found that the processes participants engaged in seemed to be an attempt to reconcile inconsistencies in order to configure the person as a whole. When participants were given pairs of contradictory traits, one of the traits would become dominant and this was usually the positive one. Participants also described the less dominant trait as temporary and also dependent on the context. This meant that focusing on the positive trait as dominant was less complicated when describing a person. For example, with the pair sociable—lonely it was easier to attribute loneliness to a temporary situation when configuring the person as sociable. Yet when loneliness was conceived of as the dominant trait, this was interpreted more deeply, such as imagining the person puts on a façade to hide their loneliness. It appears that we do a lot of cognitive work when we organize and put into order the way we configure a coherent image of a person and, as Asch and Zukier showed, this can all be on very little initial information too. They argue that we strive for unity when configuring an image of a person so we do more than try to resolve discrepancies; we try to assimilate these inconsistencies within a comprehensive image.

Further studies have also shown that if people are primed with particular traits before they encode information about a target person this will affect how people judge the target person. However, Lerouge and Smeesters (2008) found that when people are primed with behavioural traits after encoding particular aspects of behavioural information, this can lead to assimilating an image of a person and making a social judgement post-encoding. This suggests that the initial social encoding is malleable in certain conditions and also that new trait information works together with already encoded person information to construct a unified image of that person.

How much difference do you think it makes in studies that investigate the social encoding of traits when the traits themselves have been selected by the researchers?

Higgins and McCann (1984) propose that the way we encode social information is 'context-driven' and this process also interacts with personal goals, person perception and interpersonal communication. They point out that interpersonal communication provides a situation where social encoding frequently occurs and that the way we perceive that other people in the social context view a person will influence our own judgement of that person. This influence will be higher the more we are motivated to make a favourable impression upon these others. This is an important consideration in experimental studies on social encoding. In everyday situations we are influenced by others around us. We also have differences in motivation depending on individual differences and the context. A criticism of social encoding studies is the way they tend to rely on giving participants lists of words and verbal/written descriptions. Fieldler et al. (2005) argue that picture presentations, especially moving pictures such as film clips, can evoke behaviour information far more than verbal descriptions. Actually seeing behaviour enhances relevance and external validity as well as facilitates rich inferences.

It is not just behaviour that facilitates the way in which we encode information about a person. Physical appearance is also very important and is perhaps the first thing that we notice. Engell et al. (2007) found that judgements about a person's trustworthiness were extremely rapid when looking at faces. The researchers used fMIR to investigate this and propose that the amygdala automatically categorizes faces in terms of facial features that are commonly perceived as signifying untrustworthiness. Furthermore, the extent to which a person is perceived as physically attractive can have a profound effect on our social judgements. Back in 1972, Dion et al. argued that there is a 'What is beautiful is good' stereotype. In their study American students were told that they were taking part in a study on person perception accuracy. The photographs used for this study had been rated in a previous study for varying levels of physical attractiveness. The participants assumed that the physically attractive people in the photographs were more likely to be successful and happy and were more likely to possess socially desirable personalities. The 'What is beautiful is good' stereotype was supported by Lemay et al. (2010) who found that participants attributed more positive interpersonal traits and qualities to images of people they considered as attractive, than those they deemed less attractive. These studies indicate that with no other knowledge about a person except their physical appearance, people make all kinds of assumptions about the type of person someone is and even make assumptions about their future life.

Overconfidence

So far we have seen that our cognitive systems process a vast amount of information efficiently and automatically. But our efficiency has a trade-off; as we interpret our experiences and construct memories, our automatic intuitions sometimes err. Usually, we are unaware of our flaws. The 'intellectual conceit' evident in judgements of past knowledge ('I knew it all along') extends to estimates of current knowledge and predictions of future behaviour. Although we know we've messed up in the past, we have more positive expectations for our future performance in meeting deadlines, managing relationships, following an exercise routine and so forth.

To explore this **overconfidence phenomenon**, Kahneman and Tversky (1979) gave people factual questions and asked them to fill in the blanks, as in the following: 'I feel 98 percent certain that the air distance between New Delhi and Beijing is more than _____ miles but less than _____ miles.' Most individuals were overconfident: about 30 per cent of the time the correct answers lay outside the range they felt 98 per cent confident about.

overconfidence phenomenon the tendency to be more confident than correct – to overestimate the accuracy of one's beliefs

The air distance between New Delhi and Beijing is 2,500 miles.

To find out whether overconfidence extends to social judgements, Dunning et al. (1990) created a little game show. They asked students to guess a stranger's answers to a series of questions, such as 'Would you prepare for a difficult exam alone or with others?' and 'Would you rate your lecture notes as neat or messy?' Knowing the type of question but not the actual questions, the participants first interviewed their target person about background, hobbies, academic interests, aspirations, astrological sign – anything they thought might be helpful. Then, while the targets privately answered 20 of the two-choice questions, the interviewers predicted their target's answers and rated their own confidence in the predictions.

The interviewers guessed right 63 per cent of the time, beating chance by 13 per cent. But, on average, they *felt* 75 per cent sure of their predictions. When guessing their own room-mates' responses, they were 68 per cent correct and 78 per cent confident. Moreover, the most confident people were most likely to be overconfident. People also are markedly overconfident when judging whether someone is telling the truth or when estimating things such as the sexual history of their dating partner or the activity preferences of their room-mates (DePaulo et al., 1997; Swann & Gill, 1997).

Interestingly, brain imaging studies have revealed that confidence in the recollection of a memory is located in different places of the brain depending on whether it was a real event or an illusory one. Kim and Cabeza (2007) found that while high confidence for real events was indicated by brain activity in the medial temporal lobe, high confidence for false memory was reflected in brain activity in the frontoparietal regions.

Ironically, a raft of studies shows that incompetence feeds overconfidence (e.g. Burson et al., 2006; Kelemen et al., 2007; Moore & Healy, 2008). It takes competence to recognize what competence is, note Kruger and Dunning (1999). Students who score at the bottom on tests of grammar, humour and logic are most prone to overestimating their gifts at such. Those who don't know what good logic or grammar is are often unaware that they lack it. If you make a list of all the words you can form out of the letters in 'psychology', you may feel brilliant – but then stupid when a friend starts naming the ones you missed. Caputo and Dunning (2005) re-created this phenomenon in experiments, confirming that our ignorance of our ignorance sustains our self-confidence. Follow-up studies indicate that this 'ignorance of one's incompetence' occurs mostly on relatively easy-seeming tasks, such as forming words out of 'psychology'. On really hard tasks, poor performers more often appreciate their lack of skill (Burson et al., 2006).

Are people better at predicting their own *behaviour*? To find out, Vallone et al. (1990) had college students predict in September whether they would drop a course, declare a major, elect to live off campus next year, and so forth. Although the students felt, on average, 84 per cent sure of those self-predictions, they were wrong nearly twice as often as they expected to be. Even when feeling 100 per cent sure of their predictions, they erred 15 per cent of the time.

Overconfidence: is there a downside to being too confident?

SOURCE: ©ronstik/Alamy Stock Photo

In estimating their chances of success on a task, such as a major examination, people's confidence runs highest when removed in time from the moment of truth. By examination day, the possibility of failure looms larger and confidence typically drops (Gilovich et al., 1993; Shepperd et al., 2005). Buehler et al. (1994, 2002; Buehler & Griffin, 2003) report that most students also confidently underestimate how long it will take them to complete papers and other major assignments.

What produces overconfidence? Why doesn't experience lead us to a more realistic self-appraisal? For one thing, people tend to recall their mistaken judgements as times when they were *almost* right. Tetlock (1998, 1999) observed this after inviting various academic and government experts to project – from their viewpoint in the late 1980s – the future governance of the Soviet Union, South Africa and Canada. Five years later communism collapsed, South Africa had become a multiracial democracy, and Canada's French-speaking minority had not seceded. Experts who had felt more than 80 per cent confident were right in predicting these turns of events less than 40 per cent of the time. Yet, reflecting on their judgements, those who erred believed they were still basically right. I was 'almost right', said many. 'The hardliners almost succeeded in their coup attempt against Gorbachev.' 'The Quebecois separatists almost won the secessionist referendum.' 'But for the coincidence of de Klerk and Mandela, there would have been a lot bloodier transition to black majority rule in South Africa.' Among political experts – and stock market forecasters, mental health workers and sports prognosticators – overconfidence is hard to dislodge.

'When you know a thing, to hold that you know it; and when you do not know a thing, to allow that you do not know it; this is knowledge.'

Confucius, *Analects*

Confirmation Bias

People also tend not to seek information that might disprove what they believe. Wason (1960) demonstrated this, as you can, by giving participants a sequence of three numbers – 2, 4, 6 – that conformed to a rule he had in mind. (The rule was simply *any three ascending numbers.*) To enable the participants to discover the rule, Wason invited each person to generate additional sets of three numbers. Each time, Wason told the person whether or not the set conformed to his rule. As soon as participants were sure they had discovered the rule, they were to stop and announce it.

The result? Seldom right but never in doubt: 23 of the 29 participants convinced themselves of a wrong rule. They typically formed some erroneous belief about the rule (for example, counting by twos) and then searched for *confirming* evidence (for example, by testing 8, 10, 12) rather than attempting to *disconfirm* their hunches. We are eager to verify our beliefs but less inclined to seek evidence that might disprove them, a phenomenon called the **confirmation bias** (Nickerson, 1998).

confirmation bias a tendency to search for information that confirms one's preconceptions, rather than considering opposing information

The confirmation bias helps explain why our self-images are so remarkably stable. In experiments at the University of Texas at Austin, Swann and Read (1981; Swann et al., 1992a, 1992b) discovered that students seek, elicit and recall feedback that confirms their beliefs about themselves. People seek out friends and spouses who bolster their own self-views – even if they think poorly of themselves (Swann et al., 1991, 2003).

The confirmation bias has some profound relevance in disciplines beyond psychology. For example, writing from the field of biomechanics, Balsamo et al. (2018) report the effects of this bias on the adoption and perceived effect of medical aids. In their experiment, students who were asked to wear a cutting-edge computerized knee-brace thought that it was preferable to a more traditional one. The reality? Both knee-braces were identical off-the-shelf ones. The researchers had simply put some superficial accessories on the 'computerized' one, including an LED light, a USB port, and silver paint. Unsurprisingly, the researchers found no difference in how the students walked with either brace. In receipt of this information, the students still preferred the computerized one. The students expected the computerized brace to function better, and as such reported that it did. So it seems the impact of our cognitive biases can have some serious implications for our take-up of medical interventions such as orthopaedic devices. Balsamo and her team recommend that where possible patients receiving them should trial them blind to avoid the consequences of the confirmation bias.

Remedies for Overconfidence

What lessons can we draw from research on overconfidence? One lesson is to be wary of other people's dogmatic statements. Even when people are sure they are right, they may be wrong. Confidence and competence need not coincide.

Three techniques have successfully reduced the overconfidence bias. One is prompt feedback (Lichtenstein & Fischhoff, 1980). In everyday life, weather forecasters and those who set the odds in horse racing both receive clear, daily feedback. And experts in both groups do quite well at estimating their probable accuracy (Fischhoff, 1982).

To reduce 'planning fallacy' overconfidence, people can be asked to 'unpack' a task – to break it down into its subcomponents – and estimate the time required for each. Kruger and Evans (2004) report that doing so leads to more realistic estimates of completion time. When people think about why an idea *might* be true, it begins to seem true. Thus, a third way to reduce overconfidence is to get people to think of one good reason why their judgements might be wrong; that is, force them to consider disconfirming information (Koriat et al., 1980), in the same way Karl Popper (see Chapter 2) is arguing for falsification rather than verification of theories. Managers might foster more realistic judgements by insisting that all proposals and recommendations include reasons why they might *not* work.

Still, we should be careful not to undermine people's reasonable self-confidence or to destroy their decisiveness. In times when their wisdom is needed, those lacking self-confidence may shrink from speaking up or making tough decisions. Overconfidence can cost us, but realistic self-confidence is adaptive.

Heuristics: Mental Shortcuts

People interpret others' behaviour by making inferences based on other people's intentions, thoughts and personality. Social inference can involve two processes: top-down, which relies on stored information in memory such as schemas and stereotypes; and bottom-up which relies on specific events. With precious little time to process so much information, our cognitive system is fast and frugal. It specializes in mental shortcuts. With remarkable ease, we form impressions, make judgements and invent explanations. We do so by using **heuristics** – simple, efficient and fast thinking strategies. In some situations, however, haste makes error. When we make errors in social judgements these are often prone to biases.

heuristic a thinking strategy and problem-solving method that enables quick and easy judgements and search procedures

The Representativeness Heuristic

The representative heuristic is a cognitive shortcut that we use to place people into categories based on deciding that they resemble this category through having the relevant traits or characteristics. Categorization requires knowing a good deal of information and also requires a lot of information processing to do this effectively. Unfortunately when we do this with people we tend to take a shortcut based on very little information about the person or people and this is where errors can occur. For example, errors can occur when we ignore base rates when making cognitive shortcuts to categorize people. A base rate is factual information about people and categories. So rather than weighing up and considering factual information when making a social categorical decision, we ignore this to make our assumptions as quickly as possible.

Imagine you're a participant in Lonsdale and North's (2012) musical study. You are told that:

> Beth is a 14-year-old white girl from an average income family household. She is of below average intelligence, an extrovert and relatively open-minded, but can be somewhat disorganized and lazy. Beth is also known to hold no particular political beliefs.

Which of the following musical styles do you think she is likely to enjoy most: Heavy Metal, Classical, Chart Pop, Jazz?

In Lonsdale and North's study, 150 psychology students were given some basic details about 10 fictitious people, one of which included Beth. Their task was to decide which of four possible musical styles s/he was likely to enjoy the most. Did you choose Chart Pop? The researchers found that if their participants were given the personal description with or without a portrait photograph, most thought she was a Chart Pop fan. Those given just a portrait photograph thought she was either a Classical or Chart Pop fan. Put simply, judgements were made on the basis of how representative the fictitious person was thought to be of people who like particular styles of music.

To judge something by intuitively comparing it to our mental representation of a category is to use the **representativeness heuristic**. Representativeness (typicalness) usually is a reasonable guide to reality. But, there are times when this short-cut proves to be unreliable. Consider Linda, who is 31, single, outspoken and very bright. She has a degree in philosophy. As a student she was deeply concerned with discrimination and other social issues, and she participated in anti-nuclear demonstrations. Based on that description, would you say it is more likely that:

representativeness heuristic the tendency to presume, sometimes despite contrary odds, that someone or something belongs to a particular group if resembling (representing) a typical member

1 Linda is a bank teller
2 Linda is a bank teller and active in the feminist movement.

Most people think *2* is more likely, partly because Linda better *represents* their image of feminists (Mellers et al., 2001). But ask yourself: is there a better chance that Linda is *both* a bank teller *and* a feminist than that she's a bank teller (whether feminist or not)? As Tversky and Kahneman (1983) remind us, the conjunction of two events cannot be more likely than either one of the events alone.

The Availability Heuristic

The availability heuristic is a cognitive shortcut based on whatever information is most readily available. This can be from what we already 'know' and on what is going on around us at the time and how we interpret all this. It is therefore rather a 'lazy' way to make inferences and judgements and is also open to errors. When we use the availability heuristic we draw on whatever comes to mind so we are likely to ignore important information.

We use heuristics to quickly make social inferences. As outlined above heuristics can be prone to biases but they can sometimes be accurate and efficient. This can give the impression that they rely on intuition. However, one of the problems is the way we rely on schemas to make inferences. Schemas can have quite powerful influences on our judgements and can also lead us to pay attention to misleading information.

If examples are readily *available* in our memory then we presume that other such examples are commonplace. Usually this is true, so we are often well served by the **availability heuristic** (**Table 4.1**). However, this heuristic can still fail us from time-to-time.

availability heuristic a rule of thumb that judges the likelihood of things based on their availability in memory. If something comes readily to mind, we presume it to be commonplace

TABLE 4.1 Fast and frugal heuristics

Heuristic	Definition	Example	But may lead to
Representativeness	Snap judgements of whether someone or something fits a category	Deciding that Carlos is a librarian rather than a trucker because he better represents one's image of librarians	Discounting other important information
Availability	Quick judgements of the likelihood of events (how available in memory)	Estimating teenager violence after reports of knife crime	Overweighting vivid instances and, for example, fearing the wrong things

The publicizing of lottery winners, pools winners, or even the audible sound of coins falling into the payout tray of a fruit machine indicating a 'win', can lead people to think that wins are commonplace, encouraging gambling behaviour (Fortune et al., 2012; Griffiths, 1994). Vivid, easy-to-imagine events, such as shark attacks or diseases with easy-to-picture symptoms, may likewise seem more likely to occur than harder-to-picture events (Dunn et al., 2011). Likewise events which we cannot bring to mind easily, such as loss of biodiversity and global warming may be dismissed as untrue or rare unless people experience first-hand dead wildlife and bouts of warm weather (Borick & Rabe, 2010; Guéguen, 2012). The more absorbed and 'transported' the reader ('I could easily picture the events'), the more the story affects the reader's later beliefs (Diekman et al., 2000).

Our use of the availability heuristic highlights a basic principle of social thinking: people are slow to deduce particular instances from a general truth, but they are remarkably quick to infer general truth from a vivid instance. No wonder that South Africans, after a series of headline-grabbing gangland robberies and slayings, estimated that violent crime had almost doubled between 1998 and 2004, when actually it had decreased substantially (Wines, 2005). Writing for *The Guardian* newspaper in the UK, Gayle and Younge (2017) lament the media coverage of knife-crime which portrays young black people as the perpetrators. This does not reflect the reality, and gives rise to misguided fear and distrust of sections of society.

The availability heuristic explains why powerful anecdotes can nevertheless be more compelling than statistical information and why perceived risk is therefore often badly out of joint with real risks (Allison et al., 1992). As news footage of aeroplane crashes is a readily available memory for most of us we often suppose we are more at risk travelling in commercial airplanes than in cars. A plane crash in Bishoftu, Ethiopia (on 10 March 2019) resulted in the death of all 157 people on board. However, travelling by aeroplane remains one of the safest forms of travel. For most air travellers, the most dangerous part of the journey is the drive to the airport.

By now it is clear that our naive statistical intuitions, and our resulting fears, are driven not by calculation and reason but by emotions attuned to the availability heuristic. After this book is published, there is likely to be another dramatic natural or terrorist event, which will again propel our fears, vigilance and resources in a new direction. Terrorists, aided by the media, may again achieve their objective of capturing our attention, draining our resources and distracting us from the mundane, undramatic, insidious risks that, over time, devastate lives, such as the rotavirus that each day claims the equivalent of four 747 aeroplanes filled with children (Glass, 2004). But then again, dramatic events can also serve to awaken us to real risks.

Counterfactual Thinking

Easily imagined (cognitively available) events also influence our experiences of guilt, regret, frustration and relief. If our team loses (or wins) a big game by one point, we can easily imagine how the game might have gone the other way, and thus we feel greater regret (or relief). Imagining worse alternatives helps us feel better. Imagining better alternatives, and pondering what we might do differently next time, helps us prepare to do better in the future (Smallman et al., 2018).

In Olympic competition, athletes' emotions after an event reflect mostly how they did relative to expectations, but also, in one analysis, **counterfactual thinking** – *mentally simulating what might have been* (McGraw et al., 2005; Medvec et al., 1995). Bronze medallists (for whom an easily imagined alternative was finishing without a medal) exhibited more joy than silver medallists (who could more easily imagine having won the gold). Similarly, the higher a student's score within a grade category (such as B+), the *worse* they feel (Medvec & Savitsky, 1997). The B+ student who misses an A– by a point feels worse than the B+ student who actually did worse and just made a B+ by a point.

counterfactual thinking imagining alternative scenarios and outcomes that might have happened, but did not

Such counterfactual thinking occurs when we can easily picture an alternative outcome as in the following examples:

- If we barely miss a plane or a bus, we imagine making it *if only* we had left at our usual time, taken our usual route, not paused to talk.
- If we miss our connection by a half hour or after taking our usual route, it is harder to simulate a different outcome, so we feel less frustration.
- If we change an examination answer, then get it wrong, we will inevitably think 'If only . . .' and will vow next time to trust our immediate intuition – although, contrary to student lore, answer changes are more often from incorrect to correct (Kruger et al., 2005).
- The team or the political candidate that barely loses will simulate over and over how they could have won (Sanna et al., 2003).

Counterfactual thinking underlies our feelings of luck. When we have barely escaped a bad event – avoiding defeat with a last-minute goal or standing nearest a falling icicle – we easily imagine a negative counterfactual (losing, being hit) and therefore feel 'good luck' (Teigen et al., 1999). 'Bad luck', on the other hand, refers to bad events that did happen but easily might not have.

The more significant the event, the more intense the counterfactual thinking (Roese & Hur, 1997). Bereaved people who have lost a spouse or a child in a vehicle accident, or a child to sudden infant death syndrome, commonly report replaying and undoing the event (Davis et al., 1995, 1996). Broomhall et al. (2017) report the link between counterfactual thinking and depression. We slip into a cycle of ruminating on what could have been and compare it with the sometimes tragic reality.

Across Asian and Western cultures most people, however, live with less regret over things done than over things they failed to do. In 2017 the journalist Emma Freud asked the question 'What is your biggest regret?' on Twitter. She received over 300 tweets in response. Most reported regret about things people had failed to do. They ranged from 'Not flying on Concorde to New York with Lionel Richie. He wanted to take me for dinner. I was working', to 'Not calling my Dad the night before he suffered a fatal heart attack, just because I had only lost ½lb and I didn't want him to be disappointed'.

Anchoring and Adjustment

When people make an inference, they often begin from a starting point – an anchor (Tversky & Kahneman, 1974). The **anchoring and adjustment** heuristic is a cognitive shortcut influenced by initial knowledge and information. This provides

anchoring and adjustment when inferences are based on an initial starting point (standard) and adjusted accordingly a starting point to make inferences and judgements and we use these initial impressions as an anchor. We tend to stick with our initial impression but may make adjustments based on later information. Therefore, this later information would not make much change to our (anchored) initial impression.

We can think of everyday examples of this. In negotiating the value of a house, the initial figure given serves as an anchor for further discussion. When negotiating the price of a car, the price on the windscreen serves as the starting point for debate. How far we stray from this anchor is called 'adjustment'. Janiszewski and Uy (2008) give us a further anecdotal example. If you are asked 'Is the freezing point of water 0°C? and then 'What is the freezing point of vodka?', the initial 0°C serves as the anchor for your judgement. You know 0°C is the freezing point for water therefore it can't be the same for vodka (which is actually around –26.95°C). Yet, this figure of 0°C serves as a diagnostic tool for adjusting downwards in your educated guess at the answer. The influence and real effects of anchoring and adjustment have also been demonstrated in the medical field. Michie et al. (2005) found that medical patients respond very differently to how medical information is presented. If an illness is described as of 'moderate risk' then while patient response might be more positive, the seriousness with which they treat it may be inadequate in terms of seeking sufficient help. They may adjust their perception away from the dangers of the illness and not regard medical intervention and lifestyle changes as necessary. If, on the other hand, an illness is presented as reducing life expectancy to 60 per cent, it will be treated much more seriously and encourage less adjustment away from the original diagnosis. Michie et al. (2005) found that medical patients respond very differently to how medical information is presented. If an illness is described as of 'moderate risk' then while patient response might be more positive, the seriousness with which they treat it may be inadequate in terms of seeking sufficient help. They may adjust their perception away from the dangers of the illness and not regard medical intervention and lifestyle changes as necessary. If, on the other hand, an illness is presented as reducing life expectancy to 60 per cent, it will be treated much more seriously and encourage less adjustment away from the original diagnosis.

How far we adjust from the anchor depends on how much confidence we have in the anchor. If we perceive the asking price for a house to be a fair reflection of its value we will probably adjust downwards only slightly. If we feel it is a trick to get us to pay more than its value, we will adjust much more severely downwards.

We make social inferences through using different types of heuristics but do we use different social inferences at the same time? Studies have shown that multiple social inferences can occur simultaneously and automatically about other people's traits and social situations based on their behaviour. Fieldler et al.'s (2005) found that multiple simultaneous inferences regarding traits of different target persons were evident using complex ambiguous film clips as an experimental stimulus. In Todd et al.'s (2011) study, participants activated both trait and situational inferences about a person's behaviour within similar times despite reporting no intention or awareness of this. Even when researchers manipulated the goal for inference – and participants deliberately pursued a trait inference or deliberately pursued a situational inference, they still activated both inferences at the same time and reported they were not aware of doing this.

Our social inferences may also have different levels of importance as they occur. Malle and Holbrook (2012) propose that there is a hierarchy of social inferences. They argue that even though making inferences can occur simultaneously, researchers often study inferences one at a time. They claim that by studying inferences one at a time we don't know how inferences relate to each other or if one inference is more important than another. Malle and Holbrook (2012) investigated the speed of forming inferences. They also investigated whether inferences occur simultaneously and whether some inferences have greater priority. They found that inferences about intentionality and desire had greater priority because both were more likely to be inferred and were formed quicker than inferences about belief and personality. The slowest and least likely to be inferred from these four inferences was personality. Therefore, a hierarchy was demonstrated and the most important inferences in this hierarchy were formed more quickly.

It is interesting that personality inferences were at the bottom of this hierarchy. As already discussed, many studies investigate how we make judgements about a person and form an overall image of that person. However, Malle and Holbrook (2012) point out that these studies have investigated person perception using traits. The researchers included sentences about people's behaviours and also video clips of people's behaviours in naturalistic settings. They argue that asking participants to infer traits from stimuli designed especially to bring to mind certain traits in tightly controlled experimental conditions will increase people's tendency to make personality inferences. However, they propose that this is less likely in a more naturalistic context such as those used in their study. This is an important consideration because it is in everyday settings that we encounter people's behaviours and make inferences about them. It suggests that there may be a lot of other information in everyday contexts influencing our thinking about personality.

Illusory Thinking

Another influence on everyday thinking is our search for order in random events, a tendency that can lead us down all sorts of wrong paths.

Illusory Correlation

It's easy to see a correlation where none exists. When we expect to find significant relationships, we easily associate random events, perceiving an **illusory correlation**. In a landmark study Ward and Jenkins (1965) showed people the results of a hypothetical 50-day cloud-seeding experiment. Cloud seeding is where clouds are sprayed with chemicals in the attempt to induce rain. They told participants which of the 50 days the clouds had been seeded and which days it rained. That information was nothing more than a random mix of results: sometimes it rained after seeding; sometimes it didn't. Participants nevertheless became convinced – in conformity with their ideas about the effects of cloud seeding – that they really had observed a relationship between cloud seeding and rain. Of course this can have real-world consequences. In February 2019 the UK Government reported figures that revealed Black people were nine times more likely to be stopped and searched by the British police force, than White people, between 2017 and 2018. Risen et al. (2007) have observed how the occurrence of a behaviour displayed by a rarely encountered group is quickly attributed to the entire group, forming a group stereotype. They call this the 'one-shot illusory correlation'. In their comprehensive review of psychological research into illusory

illusory correlation
perception of a relationship where none exists or perception of a stronger relationship than actually exists

correlations, Wiemer and Pauli (2016) observed that one of the most prevalent is the fear of animals based on expected negative outcomes (e.g. they'll harm me).

Other experiments confirm that people easily misperceive random events as confirming their beliefs (Zhao et al., 2014). If we believe a correlation exists, we are more likely to notice and recall confirming instances (recall our earlier discussion of the confirmation bias). If we believe that premonitions correlate with events, we notice and remember the joint occurrence of the premonition and the event's later occurrence. Have you ever read your daily horoscope and seen a relationship between the zodiac forecast and the events of that day? This phenomenon is sometimes referred to as the 'Barnum Effect', named after Phineas Taylor Barnum who was a master of inventing hoaxes, circuses and museums. We seldom notice or remember all the times events do not coincide. We dismiss those occurrences which do not fit the pattern. If, after we think about a friend, the friend calls us, we notice and remember that coincidence. We don't notice all the times we think of a friend without any ensuing call or receive a call from a friend about whom we've not been thinking.

Illusion of Control

illusion of control perception of uncontrollable events as subject to one's control or as more controllable than they are

Our tendency to perceive random events as related feeds an **illusion of control** – the idea that *chance events are subject to our influence.* This keeps gamblers going and makes the rest of us do all sorts of unlikely things.

Gambling

Gambling behaviour, and in particular gambling addiction has received quite a lot of attention from social psychologists. With a rise in the availability of online gambling sites, coupled with a rise in people using them, psychologists have become increasingly concerned with: Why do some people gamble? Is there a profile of a typical gambler? And, is there a difference between those who gamble on land, and those who gamble online? Whilst there are many answers to these questions (for example, see Canale et al., 2016; McCormack & Griffiths, 2012) the illusion of control seems to be an important part of this behaviour. Langer (1977) demonstrated the illusion of control with experiments on gambling, as people expect a rate of success more than random chance would predict. Compared with those given an assigned lottery number, people who chose their own number demanded four times as much money when asked if they would sell their ticket. When playing a game of chance against an awkward and nervous person, they bet significantly more than when playing against a dapper, confident opponent. Throwing the dice or spinning the wheel increases people's confidence (Wohl & Enzle, 2002).

Observations of real-life gamblers confirm these experimental findings. The specialist features on a fruit machine ('nudge', 'hold') may lead regular fruit machine gamblers to believe more skill is involved than there actually is, encouraging continuous play as s/he becomes familiar with the machine and develops their 'skills' (Griffiths, 1994). The gambling industry thrives on gamblers' illusions.

Stock traders also like the 'feeling of empowerment' that comes from being able to choose and control their own stock trades, as if their being in control can enable them to outperform the market average. One advertisement declared that online investing 'is about control'. Alas, the illusion of control breeds overconfidence, and frequent losses after stock market trading costs are subtracted (Barber & Odean, 2001).

Research close-up

Heuristics and Illusions of Control in Slot Machine Gamblers

Source: Parke, J., Griffiths, M. D., & Parke, A. (2007). Positive thinking among slot machine gamblers: A case of maladaptive coping? *International Journal of Mental Health Addiction, 5,* 39–52.

Introduction

People engage in particular cognitive processes to compensate for a negative emotional state. An exaggerated sense of optimism and overestimating personal control has also been found to be key responses to extremely bad news (Taylor, 1983, 1989; Taylor & Brown, 1988). Gambling carries a high risk towards negative emotional states because regular gamblers lose money regularly. Therefore, regular gamblers engage in certain cognitive strategies to avoid the negative emotions of losing money. According to Wagenaar (1988), gamblers selectively use a variety of heuristics and cognitive biases and hence gamblers are motivated by their way of reasoning, not some personality defect. Regular gamblers appear to engage in an 'illusion of control'. The present study aims to investigate the strategies that gamblers use to evoke positive thinking to compensate and reduce negative emotions from experiencing a loss.

Method

Eighty-seven regular slot machine gamblers in the UK aged between 12 and 64 years took part in 104-item semi-structured interview schedules. These were administered in places they frequent to use slot machines. Recruiting participants and administering the interview schedules to them in their natural environments aimed to aid the ecological validity of the study. The interview schedule investigated motivation, demographic information, physiological experiences, thought processes, emotions, personality and the existence of other potentially addictive behaviours. The questionnaire yielded qualitative data from the semi-structured questions as this enabled participants to express their view. In addition, the questionnaire used a 10-point scale labelled at the endpoints – Never (1) and Always (10). Thus, participants had 10 options to choose when reporting how much they agreed or disagreed with a statement. Seven areas were assessed: leisure time availability; risk taking; responsibility; negative affect; environmental preferences; competitiveness; enterprise. The qualitative data was categorized into nine types of positive thinking.

Results

The nine types of positive thinking by gamblers were categorized as: *Comparative thinking; Prophylactic thinking; Biased frequency thinking; Chasing validation; Responsibility avoidance; Prioritization: Resourcefulness; Thoughtfulness; Fear reduction.* The findings indicated that regular slot machine gamblers use cognitive biases to sustain their gambling and to alleviate feelings of guilt when they inevitably lose. For example, Comparative thinking consisted of at least two comparative evaluations. One was thinking that at least the money was spent with the chance of winning some money in comparison to other ways of spending money. Another was comparing gambling more favourably than other types of addiction such as drinking alcohol/drug use and smoking. Prophylactic thinking consisted of perceiving large losses of money as a way to prevent gambling in the future. Chasing validation involves thinking that persistence in trying to win back losses is rewarded in the long run. Fear reduction assumed personal improvement and increases in self-esteem as a result of risk taking ability.

Discussion

The results demonstrate the way in which gamblers seek to reduce negative feelings caused by guilt by attributing anger, frustration and feeling cheated to a third party such as the machine manufacturers.

Persistence and imagining one has control are usually seen as psychologically healthy. However, positive thinking strategies are maladaptive in the context of gambling. Within the context of gambling, believing that one will win eventually is an example of the representative bias where information that is contradictory to winning is ignored and illusory thinking is engaged in. The cognitive mechanisms used by gamblers assist in compensating them from feelings of loss and guilt and constrain gamblers from accepting that gambling has a negative impact on their life, therefore preventing the gambler from stopping his or her gambling behaviour. Future research should investigate which type of gambler uses which type of positive thinking and whether or not they employ a number of these thinking styles.

Critical Reflections

Attempting to capture and measure people's feelings about gambling is a complex task. In this study the researchers sought to increase the ecological validity of their work by interviewing gamblers whilst they were gambling, but were also mindful to control certain elements of the study. Let's think about the type of gambling being studied here – slot machines. How representative is this of gambling per se? Is this equivalent to gambling at the roulette wheel, bingo, horse-racing, and the lottery? We can also reflect on the participants. The study involved children as young as 12 years old. What ethical issues might come into play here? Should permission be obtained from their parents/guardians, and if so how might this affect the child and the study? Finally, let's consider the methods used for data collection. Participants were interviewed and given questionnaires whilst in the slot machine arcade. Bearing in mind some of these participants were acting illegally (gambling under the age of 18 years), how might the environment they were in, influence the responses? Given an opportunity to reflect on the questions asked, away from the arcade, might we get different responses?

The illusion of control has also been linked with dangerous driving behaviour such as speeding, tailgating and driving under the influence of drugs or alcohol. Confident in our superior driving abilities and that we have full control over our vehicles we falsely believe we can successfully avoid an accident (Hammond & Horswill, 2002; Stephens & Ohtsuka, 2014).

Regression Towards the Average

Tversky and Kahneman (1974) noted another way by which an illusion of control may arise: we fail to recognize the statistical phenomenon of **regression towards the average**. Because examination scores fluctuate partly by chance, most students who get extremely high scores on an examination will get lower scores on the next examination. Because their first score is at the ceiling, their second score is more likely to fall back ('regress') towards their own average than to push the ceiling even higher. That is why a student who does consistently good work, even if never the best, will sometimes end a course at the top of the class. Conversely, the lowest-scoring students on the first examination are likely to improve. If those who scored lowest go for tutoring after the first examination, the tutors are likely to feel effective when the student improves, even if the tutoring had no effect.

regression towards the average the statistical tendency for extreme scores or extreme behaviour to return towards one's average

Indeed, when things reach a low point, we will try anything, and whatever we try – going to a psychotherapist, starting a new diet and exercise plan, reading a self-help book – is more likely to be followed by improvement than by further deterioration. Sometimes we recognize that events are not likely to continue at an unusually good or bad extreme. Experience has taught us that when everything is going great, something will go wrong, and that when life is dealing us terrible blows, we can usually look forward to things getting better. Often, though, we fail to recognize this regression effect. We puzzle at why Formula 1's rookie of the year often has a more ordinary second year – did he become overconfident? Self-conscious? We forget that exceptional performance tends to regress towards normality.

Regression to the average can have some benefits. As Verkooijen et al. (2015) discovered, it can be used to encourage healthy eating and discourage some of our more unhealthy eating habits. In their studies, students were asked to keep a record of their consumption of fruit or unhealthy snacks over a period of 3 days. These students were then told how much their consumption of these food items deviated from the average of all participants' consumption. They were then asked to continue the record of their eating habits after receiving this information. The result? Those previously eating below the average amount of fruit, increased their intake. Those eating more unhealthy snacks than the reported average, reduced their consumption. Okay, so far, so good. However, those eating above the average amount of fruit, reduced their intake. So it seems that we moderate our behaviour positively or negatively, towards the average, to fit in with others who we identify with in some way.

Table 4.2 provides examples of biases, heuristics and illusions along with strategies and definitions.

TABLE 4.2 A summary of biases, heuristics and illusions

Strategy	Examples	Definition
Bias: when our assumptions and prejudgements guide our perceptions and interpretations of the social world	Priming	The activation of learned or experienced associations in memory
	Belief perseverance	The persistence of one's initial conceptions
	Misinformation effect	The incorporation of false information into memory, guided by assumed relevance and appropriateness
	Intuition	When past learning and repeated experience cause us to process information automatically
	Overconfidence	To overestimate the accuracy of one's beliefs, memory or account of some aspect of social reality
	Confirmation bias	To search for information that confirms one's preconceptions (and ignore disconfirming information)
Heuristics: thinking strategies that enable quick and efficient judgements	Representative heuristic	The tendency to assume something is an instance of a group or category based on its perceived similarity to typical members
	Availability heuristic	The assumption that what comes to mind most easily is more commonplace
	Recognition heuristic	To assume that what is easily recognized is important
	Anchoring and adjustment	When inferences are guided by an initial starting point and adjusted accordingly
	Counterfactual thinking	Imagining counter scenarios and outcomes that didn't actually happen
Illusory thinking: to search for order in otherwise random events	Illusory correlations	The perception that a relationship exists between things where one doesn't exist
	Illusion of control	The perception that uncontrollable events are under one's own control

Moods and Judgements

Social judgement involves efficient, though fallible, information processing. It also involves our feelings: our moods infuse our judgements. We are not cool computing machines; we are emotional creatures. The extent to which feeling infuses cognition appears in new studies comparing happy and sad individuals (Myers, 1993). Unhappy people – especially those bereaved or depressed – tend to be more self-focused and brooding. A depressed mood motivates intense thinking – a search for information that makes one's environment more understandable and controllable (Andrews & Thomson, 2009).

Regression to the average. When we are at an extremely low point, anything we try will often seem effective. 'Maybe a yoga class will improve my life.' Events seldom continue at an abnormal low.
SOURCE: © Jose Luis Pelaez Inc/Blend Images LLC

Happy people, by contrast, are more trusting, more loving, more responsive. If people are made temporarily happy by receiving a small gift while shopping, they will report, a few moments later on an unrelated survey, that their cars and television sets are working beautifully – better, if you took their word for it, than those belonging to folks who replied after not receiving gifts. Qiu and Yeung (2008) report that being happy (or sad) even influences what products we buy.

Our moods can colour how we judge our worlds partly by bringing to mind past experiences associated with the mood. In a bad mood, we have more depressing thoughts. Mood-related thoughts may distract us from complex thinking about something else. Thus, when emotionally aroused – when angry or even in a very good mood – we become more likely to make snap judgements and evaluate others based on stereotypes (Bodenhausen et al., 1994; Paulhus & Lim, 1994).

Now that we have considered ways that people make social judgements about people and situations, we next turn to the way we understand our social world in order to attempt to explain it.

Explaining Our Social World

People make it their business to explain other people, and social psychologists make it their business to explain people's explanations. So, how do people explain others' behaviour? Attribution theory suggests some answers.

Our judgements of people depend on how we explain their behaviour. Depending on our explanation, we may judge killing as murder, manslaughter, self-defence or heroism. Depending on our explanation, we may view a homeless person as lacking initiative or as victimized by job and welfare cutbacks. Depending on our explanation, we may interpret someone's friendly behaviour as genuine warmth or as ingratiation. To some extent we are all lay psychologists, constructing theories to explain people's behaviour and the world around us. How we explain something has real-world consequences.

Attributing Causality: to the Person or the Situation

We endlessly analyse and discuss why things happen as they do, and formulate plausible theories (Hilton, 2007). In particular we tend to explain why things happen in terms of internal attributions, which place the cause within the individual (e.g. the personality, traits or dispositions) and external explanations, which locate the reason in the environment.

So as an employer, if worker productivity declines, do we assume the workers are getting lazier? Or has their workplace become less efficient? A teacher trying to work out why a young boy hits his classmates wonders if he has a hostile personality or is responding to relentless teasing?

Where we locate cause can lead to some dubious explanations and real-world challenges. Musher-Eizenman et al. (2004) found that preschool children exhibited some very negative attitudes towards obese figures. The reason? They assumed the cause was internal to the person, such as they're lazy, and therefore obesity was controllable. Haider-Markel and Joslyn (2008) discovered their participants reported more supportive feelings about same-sex marriage and gay rights when they situated the cause for homosexuality beyond the person's control, that is, in their genes. If it was considered a lifestyle choice, and therefore an act of free will, support was diminished.

How we attribute cause indicates the likelihood of us helping.

SOURCE: © Halfpoint/Shutterstock

Spouses in unhappy relationships typically offer distress-maintaining internal explanations for negative acts ('she was late because she doesn't care about me'). Happy couples more often externalize ('she was late because of heavy traffic'). With positive partner behaviour, their explanations similarly work either to maintain distress ('he brought me flowers because he wants sex') or to enhance the relationship ('he brought me flowers to show he loves me') (Hewstone & Fincham, 1996; Weiner, 1995).

Abbey (1987, 1991) and Abbey et al. (1998) have repeatedly found that heterosexual men are more likely than women to attribute a woman's friendliness to mild sexual interest. That misreading of warmth as a sexual come-on – an example of **misattribution** – can contribute to behaviour that women regard as sexual harassment (Johnson et al., 1991; Pryor et al., 1997; Saal et al., 1989). Furthermore, Larsen and Fitzgerald (2011) noted that women who reported sexual harassment were more likely to develop post-traumatic stress disorder if they blamed themselves or their harasser for the incident.

misattribution
mistakenly attributing a behaviour to the wrong source

Some research suggests men and women have quite different attributional styles. For example, Assouline et al. (2006) found that gifted female students tended to account for success in some subjects, such as mathematics and science, using external attributions (e.g. I worked hard), whereas boys tended to use internal attributions (I am smart). In a study done by Smirles (2004), male and female students read an account of an employer who sexually harasses an employee. She found that if participants didn't know the gender of the victim, men tended to hold the victim more responsible, whereas women thought the perpetrator was more accountable. Smirles suggests this occurs because these women were displaying defensive attribution. They minimized blame towards those people they most readily identified with.

Taking action to combat loneliness
SOURCE: © Shutterstock / Diego Cervo

Misattributions often characterize a tricky relationship between parent and adolescent. Caught in an argument, parent and adolescent misattribute thoughts, feelings and intentions to one another, which fuels the battle. In their study of parent-adolescent arguments, Sillars et al. (2010) found that parents tended to assume the thoughts and behaviours of their adolescent were more negative and avoidant than they actually were. Likewise, the adolescents over-attributed intentions of control to their parents. No wonder, these arguments can rapidly escalate!

How we attribute cause for our own behaviour can actually have an effect on our psychological well-being. Sadly, loneliness is a condition that affects many of us, and increasingly so as we age. Newall and colleagues (2009) tracked how lonely 1,243 older adults (72 years +) felt over a period of 5 years. They also tracked their social activities and participation in social and community events. They found that those adults who believed they had control over feeling lonely by putting in the effort to mix with others, engaged in more social activities and events than those who believed they had little or no control over loneliness. Furthermore, over the course of the 5 years, those who socialized more reported lower feelings of loneliness. Those who felt it was outside their control, remained lonely.

Attribution Theory

attribution theory the theory of how people explain others' behaviour; for example, by attributing it either to internal dispositions (enduring traits, motives and attitudes) or to external situations

dispositional attribution attributing behaviour to the person's disposition and traits

situational attribution attributing behaviour to the environment

Attribution theory was developed to examine these patterns of internal and external explanations, and why they occur. The theory arose out of three theoretical foundations:

1 Heider's (1958) 'theory of naive psychology'
2 Jones and Davis's (1965) 'theory of correspondent inference'
3 Kelley's (1973) 'covariation model'.

The early pioneer of attribution theory, Fritz Heider (1958), formed his 'theory of naive psychology' to account for how people explain everyday events. Heider noted that we tend to assume people's behaviour is not random, but is motivated and intentional. While sometimes we will attribute someone's behaviour to *internal* causes (**dispositional attribution**), at other times it will be explained as having an external cause (**situational attribution**). Some people are more inclined to attribute behaviour to stable personality; others tend more to prefer to attribute behaviour to situations (Bastian & Haslam, 2006; Robins et al., 2004). However, Heider maintained that, on the whole, people have a preference for applying internal attributions, as personality characteristics tend to be regarded as stable and therefore predictable. But Heider's conclusions tend to come from experiences and studies in individualistic cultures, where people tend to focus on the individual and their own responsibility for their behaviour. In collective or interdependent cultures people in general seem to pay more attention to the context and the situation when explaining behaviour.

Inferring Traits

Jones and Davis (1965) noted that we often infer that other people's actions are indicative of their intentions and dispositions. If I observe Rick making a sarcastic comment to Linda, I infer that Rick is a hostile person. Jones and Davis's 'theory of correspondent inferences' specified the conditions under which people infer traits. For example, normal or expected behaviour tells us less about the person than does unusual behaviour. If Samantha is sarcastic in a job interview, where a person would normally be pleasant, that tells us more about Samantha than if she is sarcastic with her siblings.

To what should we attribute a student's sleepiness? To lack of sleep? To boredom? Whether we make internal or external attributions depends on whether we notice him consistently sleeping in this and other classes, and on whether other students react as he does to this particular class.
SOURCE: © Lorena Fernandez/Shutterstock

In experiments it has been found that the ease with which we infer traits is remarkable. In Uleman's (1989) experiment students were given statements to remember, such as 'The librarian carries the old woman's groceries across the street.' The students would instantly, unintentionally and unconsciously infer a trait. When later they were helped to recall the sentence, the most valuable clue word was not 'books' (to cue librarian) or 'bags' (to cue groceries) but 'helpful' – the inferred trait that we suspect you, too, spontaneously attributed to the librarian.

Although Heider had noted people's preference for internal attributions, it was the work of Edward Jones with Keith Davis (1965), and later Harold Kelley (1973), that aimed to explain how we choose between internal and external explanations for behaviour.

Common-sense Attributions

Jones and Davis (1965) suggested that we use five different sources of information to judge whether a behaviour should be given an internal or external explanation. These are as follows:

1. Was it freely chosen behaviour or prescribed by someone else? If it was freely chosen then we are likely to give an internal attribution.
2. Was the behaviour unusual? If so, then we are likely to give an internal explanation.
3. Was it socially desirable behaviour? Socially desirable behaviour actually tells us very little about a person as they are simply behaving as they should. So when behaviour is socially deviant, then we are likely to give an internal explanation for it.
4. Does it serve the interests of the person doing the behaviour (i.e. is it hedonistic)? If so, then we are likely to give an internal explanation.
5. Does it have a high impact on us personally? If so, then an internal explanation is likely.

As Heider, Jones and Davis claim, we have a preference for internal attributions as they make people appear more predictable to us, owing to stable traits and dispositions. However, as we shall see later in this chapter, it is important to note that these theories have some drawbacks.

So far our reading of the foundations of attribution theory has focused on intentional behaviour. But what about those behaviours that are not intentional? This has been examined in later reformulations of attribution theory.

The attribution theorist Harold Kelley (1973) described how we use information about 'consistency', 'distinctiveness' and 'consensus', often called CCD information (**Figure 4.2**). When explaining why Edgar is having trouble with his computer, most people use information concerning *consistency* (Is Edgar usually unable to get his computer to work?), *distinctiveness* (Does Edgar have trouble with other computers, or only this one?) and *consensus* (Do other people have similar problems with this make of computer?). If we learn that Edgar alone consistently has trouble with this and other computers, we likely will attribute the troubles to Edgar, not to defects in this computer. Note how this allows us to take into account unintentional behaviour by making a judgement based on consistency of behaviour across time and space.

Three factors – consistency, distinctiveness and consensus – influence whether we attribute someone's behaviour to internal or external causes. Try creating your own examples, such as: if Mary and many others criticize Steve (with consensus), and if Mary isn't critical of others (high distinctiveness), then we make an external attribution (it's something about Steve). If Mary alone (low consensus) criticizes Steve, and if she criticizes many other people too (low distinctiveness), then we are drawn to an internal attribution (it's something about Mary).

Consistency: How consistent is the person's behaviour in this situation?
Distinctiveness: How specific is the person's behaviour to this particular situation?
Consensus: To what extent do others in this situation behave similarly?

Carter and Murphy (2017) drew upon Kelley's covariation theory to examine prejudices towards Black people by Whites living in the US. They found that exposing White people to many examples of discrimination against Blacks in the UK, changed their perceptions. As they witnessed the consistency, distinctiveness and consensus around what happened in these situations, to multiple Black people, White participants changed their original perception of Black people as unjustified complainers to people with a legitimate reason for complaint in an anti-Black US environment.

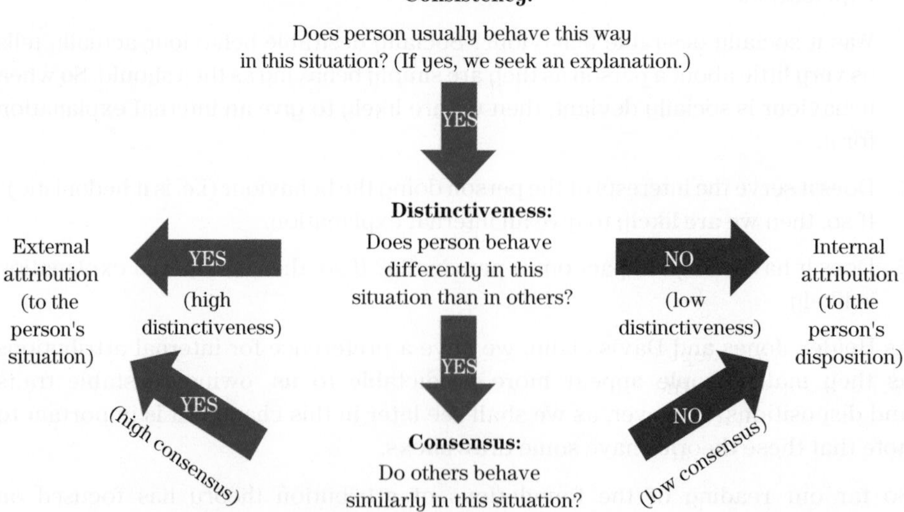

FIGURE 4.2 Harold Kelley's theory of attributions

So our common-sense psychology often explains behaviour logically. But Kelley also found that people often discount a contributing cause of behaviour if other plausible causes are already known. If we can specify one or two sufficient reasons a student might have done poorly on an exam, we often ignore or discount alternative possibilities (McClure, 1998).

As well as making attributions about others we make attributions about ourselves. This is a way to understand ourselves. As we shall see later, perceived self-knowledge also appears to be highly influential to our attributions about others. **Self-perception theory** (Bem, 1972) proposes that self-knowledge comes about through making self-attributions. Thus, we observe our own behaviour, examine our thoughts and feelings and attribute these to the type of person we think we are by making assumptions about ourselves. Weiner's (1986) attributional theory proposes that the attributions made for our experiences of success and failure are based on three areas: locus (can be internal or external), stability (whether the internal or external cause is stable or changes over time) and controllability (the extent to which something is under the individual's control). This theory includes an emotional aspect. Positive or negative emotions are experienced depending on whether the individual has succeeded or failed and in turn individuals make attributions about success or failure which then produce more specific emotions. This theory brings us onto the next self-attribution theory – Schachter's 2-factor emotion theory. This theory proposes that the experience of emotion depends on attributions made about those feelings. According to Schachter (1964) emotions have two distinct components (or factors): a physiological component which leads to arousal and a cognitive component which labels the arousal and establishes the emotion that is being experienced. Taken together, we therefore make attributions to understand the type of person we are, our abilities and our feelings. When we make self-attributions these tend to lead to the idea that we are fairly stable and consistent and this occurs when we make attributions about others.

self-perception theory proposes that attitudes are inferred from observations of one's own behaviour

Self-perception theory is discussed further in Chapter 5 in relation to our own attitudes and behaviours and how we view ourselves.

Even though people sometimes behave in ways that are inconsistent and unpredictable, we form very stable impressions of what people are like. This is despite encountering new information which might not fit with our initial impressions. To illustrate, let's consider a classic study by Croker et al. (1983). They begin with the observation that people sometimes behave in ways that surprise us. The lecturer we think is quiet and shy, turns out to also be the singer in a band. The fellow student we believe is notoriously mean with money, offers to pay for our lunch. Surprised? Yes. But does this impact on our impressions of this person? The researchers wanted to find out. To investigate, their 99 participants were shown 17 slides in total. Twelve slides contained information that related to the friendliness of a target person, called John. For some participants, John was portrayed as a dispositionally friendly person. For others, the 12 slides described John as an unintelligent man. The slideshow also included four slides that depicted very neutral behaviour – such as going shopping. Importantly within the slideshow, the eighth slide (the target slide) described a behaviour that was either congruent with being friendly or unintelligent – for example 'He gave up his seat on the subway to an elderly man' or 'John was late for his flight because he couldn't find the departure gate' – or was incongruent with John as a friendly or unintelligent man – for example, 'He cut in line in front of three people at the bank' or 'He won a prize for his senior essay from the English department'. Participants were then asked to recall as many of John's behaviours as they could. The researchers were really interested in whether they remembered the eighth slide. Croker and her team discovered that participants were more likely to remember the eighth slide if it portrayed incongruent behaviour to their overall impression of John, and if that incongruent behaviour was attributed to their disposition. So for example, if John had been depicted as friendly, but the eighth slide described John not giving up his seat for the elderly man because he didn't care, it was well remembered by participants. However, if the incongruent behaviour was attributed to a situational cause, it was no more likely to be recalled than any of the other behaviours on the rest of the slides. So for example, if John's behaviour at the bank was the result of just having been paged about an emergency, it made no impact on the participants' overall impression of John. Croker et al. (1983) propose this indicates that recall is related to impression formation in certain situations such as when people infer or are told that behaviour reflects a person's dispositional character rather than situational pressures. If people are told a person's behaviour occurs because of their disposition and this behaviour does not fit with initial information about that person, then this dissimilar behaviour will be recalled and it will influence overall impression formation. It also seems that we are drawn to internal explanations of behaviour rather than situational explanations. However, as we shall see in the next section, this can often lead to errors of judgement.

Neuroscience has made important contributions to exploring social beliefs about causal attributions. For example, a study in Germany used fMRI to explore self-attributions and external attributions for social events. Seidel et al. (2010) found that different regions of the brain are more active when participants are attributing blame towards the self for a social event than when they are attributing external blame for the social event. The right temporaparietal junction (TPJ) is activated for self-attributions. Seidel et al. (2010) propose that this contributes to evidence that the right TPJ is involved with self-representation and agency and this region has a fundamental role in shaping the self-concept. Attributing external blame for a social event revealed activation in the left region of the TPJ. This region could be where we differentiate between self and others. The fMRI scan also revealed that the activations for self-attributions were clustered with quicker reaction times but the activations for external attributions were more extended. The researchers suggest that this indicates self-attributions may be automatic whereas external attributions require more work.

The Fundamental Attribution Error

fundamental attribution error the tendency for observers to underestimate situational influences and overestimate dispositional influences upon others' behaviour. (Also called correspondence bias, because we so often see behaviour as corresponding to a disposition)

One of social psychology's most important lessons concerns the influence of our social environment. At any moment, our internal state, and therefore what we say and do, depends on the situation as well as on what we bring to the situation.

What theories of attribution agree on is that people in individualistic cultures have a preference for internal explanations for behaviour. When explaining someone's behaviour, we in the West often underestimate the impact of the situation and overestimate the extent to which it reflects the individual's traits and attitudes.

This discounting of the situation, dubbed by Ross (1977) the **fundamental attribution error**, appears in many experiments. In the first such study, Jones and Harris (1967) had university students read debaters' speeches supporting or attacking Cuba's leader, Fidel Castro. When told that the debater chose which position to take, the students logically enough assumed it reflected the person's own attitude. But what happened when the students were told that the debate coach had assigned the position? People who are merely feigning a position write more forceful statements than you'd expect. Thus, even knowing that the debater had been told to take a pro-Castro position did not prevent students from inferring that the debater in fact had some pro-Castro leanings (**Figure 4.3**).

The error is so irresistible that even when people know they are *causing* someone else's behaviour, they still underestimate external influences. If individuals dictate an opinion that someone else must then express, they still tend to see the person as actually holding that opinion (Gilbert & Jones, 1986). If people are asked to be either self-enhancing or self-deprecating during an interview, they are very aware of why they are acting so. But they are *un*aware of their effect on another person. If Juan acts modestly, his naive partner Bob is likely to exhibit modesty as well. Juan will easily understand his own behaviour, but he will think that poor Bob suffers low self-esteem (Baumeister & Scher, 1988). In short, we tend to presume that others *are* the way they act. Observing Cinderella cowering in her oppressive home, people (ignoring the situation) infer that she is meek; dancing with her at the ball, the prince sees a suave and glamorous person.

When viewing a movie actor playing a 'good-guy' or a 'bad-guy' role, we find it difficult to escape the illusion that the scripted behaviour reflects an inner disposition. Perhaps that is why Leonard Nimoy, who played Mr Spock in the original *Star Trek,* titled one of his books *I Am Not Spock.*

SOURCE: © Frazer Harrison/Getty Images

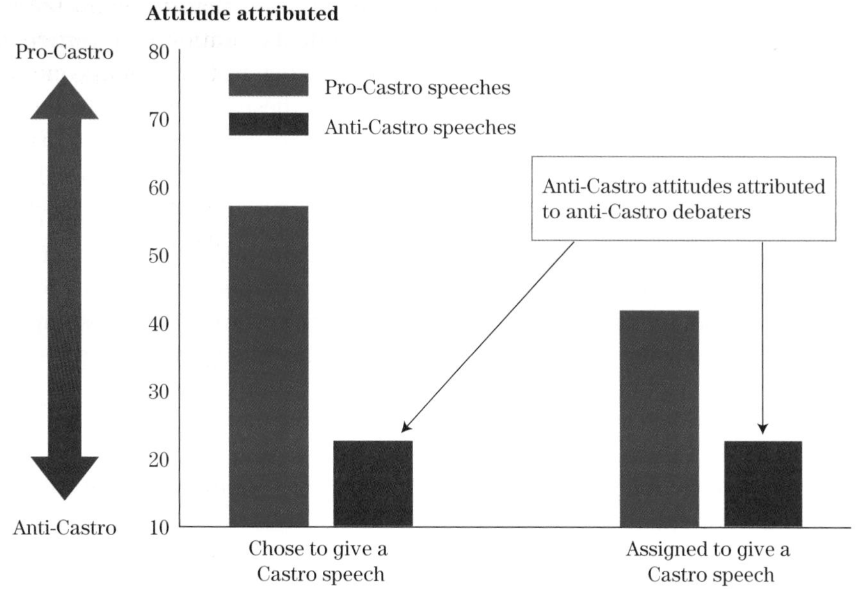

FIGURE 4.3 The fundamental attribution error

When people read a debate speech supporting or attacking Fidel Castro, they attributed corresponding attitudes to the speechwriter, even when the debate coach assigned the writer's position.

SOURCE: Data from Jones and Harris (1967).

The discounting of social constraints was evident in an experiment by Ross et al. (1977). The experiment re-created Ross's first-hand experience of moving from graduate student to professor. His doctoral oral examination had proved a humbling experience as his apparently brilliant professors quizzed him on topics they specialized in. Six months later, Dr Ross was himself an examiner, now able to ask penetrating questions on *his* favourite topics. Ross's hapless student later confessed to feeling exactly as Ross had done a half-year before – dissatisfied with his ignorance and impressed with the apparent brilliance of the examiners.

In the experiment, with Teresa Amabile and Julia Steinmetz, Ross set up a simulated quiz game. He randomly assigned some Stanford University students to play the role of questioner, some to play the role of contestant, and others to observe. The researchers invited the questioners to make up difficult questions that would demonstrate their wealth of knowledge. Any one of us can imagine such questions using one's own domain of competence: 'Where is Bainbridge Island?' 'How did Mary, Queen of Scots, die?' 'Which has the longer coastline, Europe or Africa?' If even those few questions have you feeling a little uninformed, then you will appreciate the results of this experiment.*

Everyone had to know that the questioner would have the advantage. Yet both contestants and observers (but not the questioners) came to the erroneous conclusion that the questioners *really were* more knowledgeable than the contestants (**Figure 4.4**). Follow-up research shows that these misimpressions are hardly a reflection of low social intelligence. If anything, intelligent and socially competent people are *more* likely to make the attribution error and the correspondence bias (Block & Funder, 1986).

In real life, those with social power usually initiate and control conversations, which often leads underlings to overestimate their knowledge and intelligence. Medical doctors, for example, are often presumed to be experts on all sorts of questions unrelated to medicine. Similarly, students often overestimate the brilliance of their teachers. (As in the experiment, teachers are questioners on subjects of their special expertise.) When some of these students later become teachers, they are usually amazed to discover that teachers are not so brilliant after all.

Psychology is not immune from the fundamental attribution error either. Gilibert and Banovic (2009) report that the fundamental attribution error is embedded within clinical psychology training. This prompts students into seeking out internal explanations for psychological disorders, and is based on assumptions that the client has some control over their symptoms. The medical field has also been subject to an examination of fundamental attribution errors running through its practices. Crumlish and Kelly (2009) report on how medical professionals can over-simplify the cause of medical problems, by locating it squarely within the person. As such, treatment fails to recognize the more complex picture that may be behind the condition.

---

* Bainbridge Island is across Puget Sound from Seattle. Mary was ordered to be beheaded by her cousin Queen Elizabeth I. Although the African continent is more than double the area of Europe, Europe's coastline is longer. (It is more convoluted, with lots of harbours and inlets, a geographical fact that contributed to its role in the history of maritime trade.)

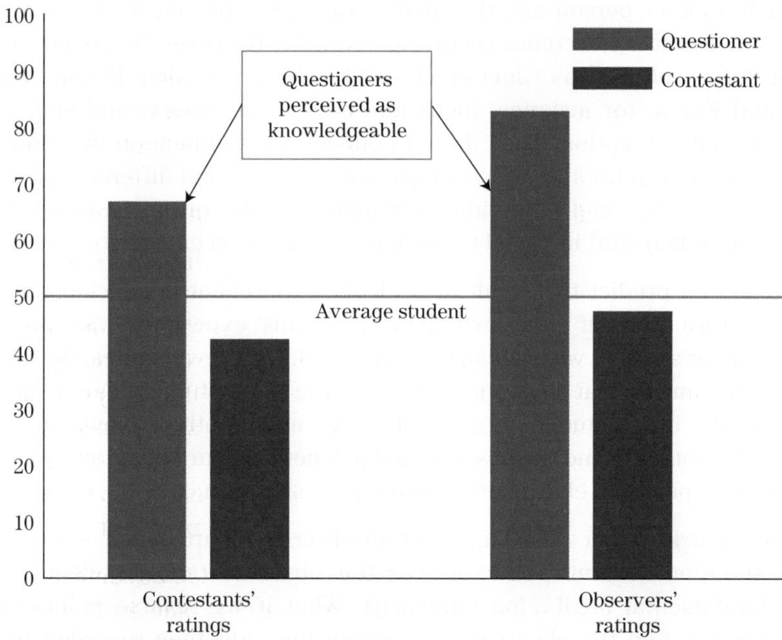

FIGURE 4.4 Rating of general knowledge
Both contestants and observers of a simulated quiz game assumed that a person who had been randomly assigned the role of questioner was far more knowledgeable than the contestant. Actually the assigned roles of questioner and contestant simply made the questioner seem more knowledgeable. The failure to appreciate this illustrates the fundamental attribution error.

SOURCE: Data from Ross et al. (1977).

To illustrate the fundamental attribution error, most of us need look no further than our own experiences. Determined to make some new friends, Ann plasters a smile on her face and anxiously plunges into a party. Everyone else seems quite relaxed and happy as they laugh and talk with one another. Ann wonders to herself, 'Why is everyone always so at ease in groups like this while I'm feeling shy and tense?' Actually, everyone else is feeling nervous, too, and making the same attribution error in assuming that Ann and the others *are* as they *appear* – confidently convivial.

Why Do We Make the Attribution Error?

So far we have seen a bias in the way we, and especially people in the Western individualistic cultures, explain other people's behaviour: we often ignore powerful situational determinants. However, this is not true when attributing cause for our own behaviour. As Nisbett et al. (1973) observed in an early study on the attribution error, when participants are asked to describe their friends' behaviour they tick the dispositional items provided on a checklist. However, when asked to describe their own behaviour, they tick the situational items. So why do we tend to underestimate the situational determinants of others' behaviour but not of our own? Some of the explanations are outlined below.

Perspective and Situational Awareness

Actor–Observer Difference Attribution theorists point out that we observe others from a different perspective than we observe ourselves (Jones, 1976; Jones &

Nisbett, 1971). When we act, the *environment* commands our attention. When we watch another person act, that *person* occupies the centre of our attention and the environment becomes relatively invisible. However, this is not the case in East Asian cultures, as Chua et al. (2005b) have revealed. People in Japan, China and Korea, for instance, focus and notice the context and environment in their visual perception. They do not concentrate so much on the 'figure', but pay much more attention to the 'background'. This cultural difference, due to the importance of the single individual compared to the group or collective and the corresponding shift in visual focus, has an impact on causal attribution.

See if you can predict the result of a clever experiment conducted by Storms (1973). Picture yourself as a participant in Storms' experiment. You are seated facing another student, with whom you are to talk for a few minutes. Beside you is a television camera that shares your view of the other student. Facing you from alongside the other student are an observer and another television camera. Afterwards, both you and the observer judge whether your behaviour was caused more by your personal characteristics or by the situation.

Question: Which of you – participant or observer – will attribute less importance to the situation? Storms found it was the observer (another demonstration of the fundamental attribution tendency). What if we reverse points of view by having you and the observer each watch the videotape recorded from the other's perspective? (You now view yourself, and the observer views what you were seeing while you were being videotaped.) This reverses the attributions: the observer now attributes your behaviour mostly to the situation you faced, and you now attribute it to your person. *Remembering* an experience from an observer's perspective – by 'seeing' oneself from the outside – has the same effect (Frank & Gilovich, 1989).

However, before we get excited into thinking we've fully understood why the fundamental attribution error occurs, a few words of caution are required. From his analysis of 173 studies, Malle (2006) concludes that the actor–observer difference is often minimal. In fact, it only really works in a laboratory when the focus is on a single behaviour. But of course, real-life isn't like that. People typically exhibit empathy when they observe someone after explaining their own behaviour in the same situation. It's when one person misbehaves while another observes that the two will offer strikingly different attributions. In later work, Malle (2008) points out that the results of Storms' camera-studies were not replicated in five further experiments between 1975 and 1985. Furthermore, he argues that the actor-observer effect only tells us where actors and observers locate explanations for a single behaviour, not how. And when we look at how explanations are formed, they do not neatly fall into either the internal or external dichotomy. As Malle suggests, whether we believe our own or someone else's often complex behaviour is intentional or not, also needs to be factored in.

The Camera Perspective Bias In some experiments, people have viewed a videotape of a suspect confessing during a police interview. If they viewed the confession through a camera focused on the suspect, they perceived the confession as genuine. If they viewed it through a camera focused on the detective, they perceived it as more coerced (Lassiter & Irvine, 1986; Lassiter et al., 2005). The camera perspective influences people's guilt judgements even when the judge instructed them not to allow it to (Lassiter et al., 2002).

More recently, Ware et al. (2008) used eye-tracking technology to see how visual attention contributes to this bias. As the camera is positioned to focus on either the suspect or interrogator, visual attention is also shifted. Whilst our attention might not be fixed like this in our everyday lives, research like this does have important implications for criminal investigations and trials that use camera recordings.

In law courts, most confession videotapes focus on the confessor. As we might expect, noted Lassiter and Dudley (1991), such tapes yield a nearly 100 per cent conviction rate when played by prosecutors. Aware of this research, reports Lassiter, New Zealand has made it a national policy that police interrogations be filmed with equal focus on the officer and the suspect, such as by filming them with side profiles of both.

The camera never lies. Or does it? What we see can influence how we judge.

SOURCE: © J.R. Bale / Alamy

The False Consensus Effect (McArthur, 1972) If we think back to Kelley's CCD model of attribution, we'll recall that a feature we attend to when deciding how to attribute cause to someone's behaviour is consensus – that is, what other people would do in a similar situation. However, when assuming what the 'consensus' is, we tend to assume everyone behaves as we (and our friends and acquaintances) do! Recall in Chapter 3 that we noted that people tend to assume they are just like everyone else. We typically assume our behaviour is 'typical', or 'normal'. People seek people who are similar to themselves, so deviances from our consensus are regarded as 'atypical'. For example, Mannarini et al. (2015) considered the views of 1,785 people based in an area of Turin, earmarked for the implementation of a high-speed railway (HSR) through the Susa Valley. They discovered that all participants, regardless of whether they were opposed to the HSR or in support of it, believed that most people held the same opinion as they did. Clearly, they can't all be right! This false consensus effect was particularly pronounced for those opposing the HSR on the grounds that they thought it was a threat to the location.

The Self-serving Bias Often people make attributions that are designed to enhance their own image in the eyes of others and themselves. This means we deny our failures and take credit for our successes. As Augoustinos et al. (2006) have noticed, athletes often give internal explanations for winning an event (e.g. level of fitness, being 'in the zone'), but blame their failures on external circumstances (e.g. weather, being pushed by another athlete). And parents are not exempt either! Verrastro and her team (2016) found that parents evaluate themselves as better at parenting than their partner, and especially more so than their exes! The attributions we make to self and others can serve to protect, enhance and justify our selves.

Self-serving attributions also raise our image in the eyes of others; see Chapter 3 for further discussion of this.

Self-knowledge It may simply be the case that, because we know ourselves better than we know anyone else, we are able to make more external attributions for our negative behaviour than for other people's. If I omit to say 'Thank you' to the host of a party, it isn't because I'm rude but because the host was unpleasant. I know that I am, by and large, a nice person. However, if someone else doesn't say thank you to the host, without such knowledge of their usual behaviour, I may make an internal attribution of their being a hostile and ungrateful person by nature.

Perspectives Change with Time As the once-visible person recedes in their memory, observers often give more and more credit to the situation. The day after a presidential election, Burger and Pavelich (1994) asked voters why the election turned out as it did. Most attributed the outcome to the candidates' personal traits and positions (the winner from the incumbent party was likeable). When they asked other voters the same question a year later, only a third attributed the verdict to the candidates. More people now credited circumstances, such as the country's good mood and the robust economy.

Self-awareness Circumstances can also shift our perspective on ourselves. Seeing ourselves on television redirects our attention to ourselves. Seeing ourselves in a mirror, hearing our tape-recorded voices, having our pictures taken, or filling out biographical questionnaires, similarly focuses our attention inwards, making us *self*-conscious instead of *situation*-conscious. Looking back on ill-fated relationships that once seemed like the unsinkable *Titanic*, people can more easily see the icebergs (Berscheid, 1999).

self-awareness a self-conscious state in which attention focuses on oneself. It makes people more sensitive to their own attitudes and dispositions

Robert Wicklund, Shelley Duval and their collaborators have explored the effects of **self-awareness** (Duval & Wicklund, 1972; Silvia & Duval, 2001). When our attention focuses upon ourselves, we often attribute responsibility to ourselves. In an important study Fenigstein and Carver (1978) demonstrated this by having students imagine themselves in hypothetical situations. Some students were made self-aware by thinking they were hearing their own heartbeats while pondering the situation. Compared with those who thought they were just hearing extraneous noises, the self-aware students saw themselves as more responsible for the imagined outcome.

Some people are typically quite self-conscious. In experiments, people who report themselves as privately self-conscious (who agree with statements such as 'I'm generally attentive to my inner feelings') behave similarly to people whose attention has been self-focused with a mirror (Carver & Scheier, 1978). Thus, people whose attention focuses on themselves – either briefly during an experiment or because they are self-conscious persons – view themselves more as observers typically do; they attribute their behaviour more to internal factors and less to the situation.

All these experiments point to a reason for the attribution error: *we find causes where we look for them.* To see this in your own experience, consider: would you say your social psychology tutor is a quiet or a talkative person?

Our guess is you inferred that he or she is fairly outgoing. But consider: your attention focuses on your tutor while he or she behaves in a public context that demands speaking. The tutor also observes their own behaviour in many different situations – in the classroom, in meetings, at home. 'Me talkative?' your tutor might say. 'Well, it all depends on the situation. When I'm in class or with good friends, I'm rather outgoing. But at conventions and in unfamiliar situations I feel and act rather shy.' Because we are acutely aware of how our behaviour varies with the situation, we see ourselves as more variable than other people (Vazire & Carlson, 2010; Vazire & Wilson, 2012), for example, 'Nigel is uptight, Fiona is relaxed. With me it varies.'

The Just World Hypothesis Lerner (1980) claims that we tend to hold a common-sense belief that 'people get what they deserve'. This is a general notion that we live in a 'just' world where good things happen to good people, and bad things happen to the bad. This can mean that we assume people are responsible for their own misfortunes. This can lead to such things as blaming poverty on laziness, rape as a woman's own fault, the depressed for wallowing in self-pity, and so on. In their study of televised discussions between the unemployed living on state benefits and politicians, Goodman and Carr (2017) examine how the just world hypothesis is used by politicians to lay blame for poverty at the feet of the poor rather than society. What is worrying about such hypotheses is that victims can falsely believe they are responsible for their misfortunes. To consider yourself to be personally responsible can be a way of regaining control of the problem. The idea that negative things happen to people in a random fashion, subject to the whims of a complex social world, renders that world as uncontrollable, unpredictable and a very disorientating place to be.

The just world hypothesis seems to have a powerful influence on the judgements we make about others but do we all draw on this belief in the same way and across all contexts? Lerner and Miller (1978) argue that individuals may adopt cognitive strategies such as blaming victims for their misfortune and derogation towards them in order to minimize the injustices they perceive are happening to others. They reviewed a number of studies that investigated the just world hypothesis and argue that the just world hypothesis is far from a simple process. Lerner and Miller (1978) propose that people's concern over injustices depends on a number of factors. For example, it depends on whether upsetting events are close to home. If people directly witness an event such as a car accident or if they were survivors of a disaster such as the earthquake outlined at the beginning of the chapter, they will have a much greater need to explain and make sense of what has happened. In these close-to-home situations, people will be far more likely to believe in a just world and blame the victims for what happened to them.

Empathy is another factor that can have an impact on people's belief in a just world. How much empathy people feel for victims also has an influence on victim derogation and whether we blame people for their misfortunes. We are far less likely to blame a victim we empathize with and we see this as reducing the likelihood that we would be blamed if we found ourselves in the same situation. Lerner and Miller (1978) also note that individual differences are involved with the belief in a just world. They argue that this is evident from the way not all participants in experiments investigating the just world hypothesis blame the victim. Wolfradt and Dalbert (2003) investigated the relationship between individual differences and the belief in a just world. They found that those who endorsed the belief in a just world also valued security and conformity and were conscientious. In addition, those with an internal locus of control appear to have higher beliefs in a just world than those with an external locus of control. It would seem that people who believe that they have control over their own lives tend to blame the victim more than people who believe that the external world influences our fate. Furnham (2003) points out that this is a challenging notion to social psychology because the locus of self-control is conceived as a psychologically healthy individual difference variable making it difficult to reconcile with victim derogation and blame because these behaviours can have detrimental consequences.

The threat to an individual's belief in a just world may be increased if the victim shares a common identity with the observer and may also be affected by how much the observer endorses the belief in a just world. Correia et al. (2012) found that high believers in a just world are more likely to engage in victim derogation and blame an innocent victim who shares a common identity with them, than an innocent victim who they do not identify with. If the observers are low believers in a just world, the degree of victim derogation is not affected by whether observers identify with the innocent victim or not. Correia et al. (2012) propose that when a victim shares a common identity with an observer, the observer perceives a threat of interchangeability with the victim so attempts to create as much distance from the victim as possible. This threat becomes more apparent when the observer has a high belief in a just world because this belief also becomes threatened. Individuals believe that the same misfortune will not happen to them because they are different in certain ways to the victim. This restores their belief in a just world by blaming and devaluing the victim without threatening their own identity.

The just world hypothesis is highly influential in social psychology and can be applied to understanding a range of issues such as prejudice and the extent that people are likely to help others. However, to date studies investigating individuals' belief in a just world tend to use correlations which cannot determine cause and effect and often use questionnaires with scales for participants to complete in response to artificial situations. Ethically, artificial situations must be used in studies that investigate individuals' responses to victims as real victims should not be created in studies! Nevertheless, the just world hypothesis provides a way to further our understanding of victim derogation and victim blaming over a range of important real-life issues. For example, the just world hypothesis has been applied to traumatic events such as understanding people's judgements about rape victims and perpetrators (Strömwall et al., 2013). Many studies have been conducted to understand judgements on people with different diseases such as AIDs (Furnham, 2003). The just world hypothesis has also been applied to understanding stigmatization such as stigma towards eating disorders (Ebneter et al., 2011) and discrimination such as gender discrimination in the workplace (Bastounis & Minibas-Poussard, 2012).

Cultural Differences

But how 'fundamental' is the fundamental attribution error? Many researchers have noted its absence in non-Western cultures. You may have read about the experiences of Hazel Markus and Shinobu Kitayama (outlined in Chapter 3), who observed cultural differences in understandings and explanations for self-behaviour. Markus and Kitayama (1991) argue that the fundamental attribution error exists only in cultures where this is an independent understanding of 'the self'. As children grow up in Western culture, they learn to explain behaviour in terms of the other's personal characteristics (Rholes et al., 1990; Ross, 1981).

So cultures influence how we attribute cause and the attribution error (Ickes, 1980; Krull et al., 1999; Watson, 1982). In the West, it is believed that you get what you deserve and deserve what you get. Yet people in Eastern Asian cultures are somewhat more sensitive to the importance of situations. Thus, when aware of the social context, they are less inclined to assume that others' behaviour corresponds to their traits (Choi et al., 1999; Farwell & Weiner, 2000; Masuda & Kitayama, 2004).

Some languages promote external attributions. Instead of 'I was late', Spanish idiom allows one to say, 'The clock caused me to be late.' In collectivist cultures, people less often perceive others in terms of personal dispositions (Lee et al., 1996; Zebrowitz-McArthur, 1988). They are less likely to spontaneously interpret a behaviour as reflecting an inner trait (Newman, 1993).

The Not-So-Fundamental Attribution Error?

As we've discovered so far in this chapter, the fundamental error is perhaps not as universal as we once thought. It is, to some extent a cultural concept. However, a raft of evidence suggests it is a fairly robust phenomenon within Western culture. Or is it?

Gawronski (2004) suggests that there may be more problems with the fundamental attribution error than just its cultural roots. He reviews a range of psychological work that shows the conditions under which the fundamental attribution error does not occur. These include when the observer is highly motivated to process all available information before arriving at an explanation for the events they witness. And this is assuming they can see all possible contributing factors. As researchers have pointed out, situational and environmental aspects are typically less salient than dispositional ones. Furthermore, where the fundamental attribution error is observed, the rather special conditions under which it is typically measured can elicit exactly the response it is looking for. How long does this effect last beyond the experiment? This does leave a question regarding the **ecological validity** of these findings.

ecological validity the extent to which findings observed in a study reflect what actually occurs in natural settings. Psychological laboratory research has been criticized for its low ecological validity

So, on the one hand the fundamental attribution error is *fundamental* because it colours our explanations in basic and important ways. This *dispositional attribution* ascribes behaviour to the person's disposition and traits. That said, many social psychologists now refer to this concept as the **correspondence bias**, acknowledging that the 'fundamental' attribution error, may not be that fundamental (Gawronski, 2004; Gilbert & Malone, 1995).

correspondence bias the tendency to explain behaviour according to stable personality traits and dispositions

Intergroup Attribution

As we noted earlier in this chapter we often perceive people as members of social groups (e.g. students, Spaniards, nurses, Muslims) and may therefore explain their behaviour in accordance with what we know and feel about that group. This includes our fellow ingroup members (e.g. other students) as well as outgroup members. As we discuss in Chapters 12 and 13, people feel affiliated or as though they psychologically belong to various social groups, and often behave according to what is expected of a group member. So explanations for behaviours do not just occur at an individual level, but also at an intragroup (within group) and intergroup (between groups) level.

To explain a social group's behaviour we make inferences about that social group and classify the group. Ames (2004) proposes that when we make inferences about social groups these inferences rely on both the self – individual differences in social projection – and on stereotypes – prevalence of stereotyping. Social projection is a simple heuristic and occurs when people project their attitudes onto another group. This means that people will greatly estimate that attributes they see in themselves are also present in members of a particular group. Social projection can therefore be related to wanting to be liked as well as having our attributes validated by others.

Ames (2004) also proposes that the more a person perceives themselves to be similar to a particular group, the less they will stereotype this group. Instead, they will project their own attributes and values onto the group, estimating that the group also shares a high level of the same attributes and values as them. However, the opposite will happen if a person perceives themselves to be dissimilar to a group. They will then search their memory for stereotyped information to make sense of a dissimilar group. The implications of perceived similarity are important because getting people to focus on similarities with another social group can contribute towards reducing stereotyping, especially as Ames (2004) found that perceived similarity wasn't related to actual similarity. It is simply the thinking that one is similar to a social group that reduces stereotyping regardless of how similar a person really is to this group.

As mentioned at the beginning of this chapter, classifying people into social groups is a fundamental part of stereotyping and forms a process of social categorization. We categorize people into social groups and then judge them on the basis of how similar we perceive them to be to us. This process is therefore based on our self-knowledge. Stereotyping is a powerful influence towards making attributions about people's behaviour and is involved with how different we perceive social groups from ourselves. DiDonato et al. (2011) suggest that self-knowledge is highly important within the process of social categorization and that social categorization has an effect on social projection. They also propose that social categorization occurs at a fairly early stage when forming social inferences. In their study, social projection was high for ingroups (groups participants perceived themselves belonging to) and low for outgroups (groups that participants did not perceive themselves to belong to). Social projection towards a mixed ingroup/outgroup was lower than towards an ingroup and higher than towards an outgroup. DiDonato et al. (2011) observed that self-judgements related to ingroup judgements were formed faster. They argue that this suggests people project self-judgements to the ingroup rather than drawing on perceived inferences about the ingroup to make self-judgements. Most people have a positive self-image and most strongly project this positive image to ingroups rather than outgroups. The more that is known about a person's self-image the easier it is to understand how they make attributions about social groups.

These attributions follow very similar patterns to those we considered at an individual level. Intergroup attributions are often characterized by self-serving biases and ethnocentrism. We give internal explanations for 'our' group's positive behaviour, and explain away our negative behaviour by pointing to situational factors. On the contrary, we explain 'their' positive behaviour as having an external cause, but regard their negative behaviour as driven by the internal characteristics of members of that group. 'How predictable!' you may exclaim, when members of another group behave badly. Pettigrew (1979) termed this the '**ultimate attribution error**'. We see examples of this in our everyday lives. If our favourite football team wins, it's because it is made up of very good players. If it loses, the referee was biased and the pitch was in a poor condition. If our rival team wins, it got lucky, or perhaps it cheated. If it lost, it's because we know its players are not very good and have a bad attitude. Of course examples of the ultimate attribution error can be much more serious than this. We only need to pick up a newspaper to see how a rise in crime may be attributed to the criminal tendencies of an incoming national, racial or ethnic group. This has been demonstrated many times in empirical work. For example, in Ruback and Singh's (2007) study, they drew upon

ultimate attribution error a bias in which positive actions of one's own group are perceived as normative, and negative acts are seen as unusual or exceptional. Conversely, negative actions carried out by a member of an outgroup are seen as normative for that group, and positive acts are regarded as unusual a history of Muslim–Hindu riots that had accounted for many deaths in five states of India. In an experimental design, they asked Muslim and Hindu participants to read descriptions of riots that had been instigated by either Muslims or Hindus. The task of the participant was to attribute blame for the deaths that occurred as a result. What they found was ingroup bias. Blame for the riots was placed upon the opposite group from the participant (so if the participant was Hindu the blame was placed upon Muslims) and their perceptions of that group became even more negative than previously. Such attributions serve to reinforce stereotypes held at the time about particular groups. They also enable 'us' to compare ourselves favourably in comparison to 'them'. As we explore in Chapters 12 and 13, we belong to social groups to the extent that they give us positive self-esteem. To maintain this we engage in a process of social comparison in which 'we' are better than 'them'.

A growing number of studies investigate how we make attributions about others through social neuroscience. These judgements may occur, for example, when we are weighing up another person in terms of personality traits, mental states and behavioural dispositions (Cacioppo & Decety, 2011). As we have seen, the decisions we make about people we don't really know in terms of personality and behaviour involve judgements related to person perception and person categorization and can lead to attributions influenced by stereotyping. But what processes are involved in accessing stereotypical knowledge?

Quadflieg and Macrae (2011) have reviewed recent social neuroscience studies exploring stereotyping and point out that fMRI data indicate that the retrieval of stereotypic knowledge activates brain regions such as the medial prefrontal cortex, the posterior cingulated and the anterior temporal lobe. The important thing about these brain regions is that they are all considered to be involved in social cognition. However, Quadflieg and Macrae (2011) argue that it is possible stereotypic person knowledge is more widely distributed across brain regions because we draw on different aspects of the person when forming stereotypes. For example, stereotyping a person's behaviour may be involved in an action stereotype, which is activated in different regions in the left hemisphere of the brain known to be involved with action knowledge. On the other hand, stereotyping a person's appearance is activated in regions of the brain known to be involved with visual knowledge such as the ventral occipital and the temporal region.

Can social neuroscience contribute to reducing stereotyping? A study in Australia using undergraduate students explored this in relation to implicit gender stereotypes (Wong et al., 2012). Participants were assigned to either an inhibitory repetitive transcranial magnetic stimulation (rTMS) of the anterior temporal lobe (ANL) or a pretend stimulation of the ANL. Both groups took part in a gender implicit association test (IAT). IATs are designed to measure prejudice that people either try to hide or may be unaware of, so in this study the researchers were measuring gender stereotyping that participants may either try to hide or gender stereotyping they may be unaware of. Wong et al. (2012) found that there was a reduction in the IAT scores for implicit gender stereotyping in those participants who had received rTMS to the ANL. Manipulating this brain region and reducing the IAT scores also provides evidence that the ANL region of the brain is involved with some aspect of stereotypical processes. This has important implications for understanding the neural networks in the ANL that are involved in implicit stereotypes and prejudice. That said, some interesting challenges have been made about the results generated from IATs, which we consider in Chapter 5. Berntson and Cacioppo (2000) point out that social neuroscience can show how people may hold both prejudiced and non-prejudiced beliefs. Looking at prejudice in this two-sided way suggests that people may believe that they do not hold prejudiced views but they may act in a discriminatory manner because this discriminatory behaviour may be unintentional. This can have considerable contributions towards our understanding of the processes involved in prejudice. On the other hand, it may also point towards prejudice being an inevitable attitude.

Studies in social neuroscience are often criticized for lacking ecological validity. Quadflieg and Macrae (2011) argue that social neuroscience is no less ecologically valid than traditional social cognitive studies. Participants do very similar tasks to those in many traditional social psychology experiments, such as investigations into social judgements. Quadflieg and Macrae also defend the use of brain scanners and say in everyday life people do lie down in darkened rooms at times. They also point out that neuroscience is a fairly new discipline and has a great deal of scope for development; exploring general rules of brain function can enable specific psychological constructs to be further explored and redefined. Neuroscientists argue that a main strength of this discipline and its contribution to social psychology is the way that multi-levels of analysis are explored without reducing the exploration to brain mechanisms alone. However, see the Focus On Box at the end of this chapter to consider these arguments further.

While Quadflieg and Macrae argue that social neuroscience is no less ecologically valid than social cognitive studies, this not only leaves open to question how ecologically valid social cognitive studies are but brings into question how 'social' they are. Social attributions occur in everyday life within rich social environments and appear to be influenced by the people around us. Our attributions are also highly influenced by our personal experiences and our personal histories as well as our cultural experiences. Therefore, it is important to emphasize here that how attributions are made depends on the relations that exist at that time between groups in a particular cultural, social, political and historical context. They are shaped by the cultural and societal norms that we live by.

Communicating Our Social World: Social Representations Theory and a Thinking Society

Some social psychologists have argued that cognitive theories of social beliefs and judgements have underplayed the importance of social factors in shaping these processes. This was a particular concern of social psychologist Serge Moscovici. He felt social psychology had offered theories about processes within the individual's mind (e.g. schemas, illusory correlations, attribution processes) without really exploring how they got there. You may recall his criticism of experimental social psychology, which he claimed had become 'asocial' (see Chapters 1 and 2). His primary aim, therefore, was to reintroduce a 'social' focus into the discipline by emphasizing how society, ideology and cultural norms shaped how we perceive, think about and judge our social world. In other words he wanted to stress the importance of language in communicating social reality, as people discuss their ideas, values and beliefs with each other in everyday life.

Research close-up

Can the Way We Retrieve Information from Memory Affect How We Judge Other People?

Source: Bertram, G., & Bodenhausen, G. V. (2005). Accessibility effects on implicit social cognition: The role of knowledge activation and retrieval experiences. *Journal of Personality and Social Psychology, 89*, 672–685.

Introduction

Techniques to measure implicit attitudes, stereotypes, self-esteem and self-concept have made a considerable contribution to social cognition (e.g. De Houwer, 2003; Nosek & Banaji, 2001). These techniques use indirect measurements to measure psychological attributes such as the attitudes and beliefs we are either not aware of or try to conceal. Therefore the tests used are also designed to minimize the tendency for individuals to conceal their underlying attitudes. Techniques often investigate implicit measures through the speed of responses when individuals make connections to concepts or sort them into categories and also by examining the strength of an individual's automatic associations between a concept and an attribute. The experiment in the present study aims to investigate the different influences of an individual's knowledge activation and subjective experiences of retrieval on implicit measures of gender stereotyping.

Method

Participants were 48 female and 22 male undergraduates in America. They were randomly assigned to four conditions in a between-subjects design. There was an 'easy' or 'difficult' condition for a retrieval task and there was a *stimulus* compatibility condition and a *response* compatibility condition for a priming task. For the retrieval task, participants were asked to generate lists of counter-stereotypical women. In the 'easy' condition participants were asked to provide a list of three women who were 'strong'; in the 'difficult' condition participants were asked to generate a list of ten women who were 'strong'. It may be that if participants feel that they struggle to identify counter-stereotypical women (i.e. identify ten women who were 'strong') they may implicitly believe that they hold stereotypical views of women. Immediately afterwards participants performed a priming task. Early in this task the word 'Male' or 'Female' appeared on a computer screen for 15 milliseconds. After this, letter sequences from a set of stereotypically female target words such as dainty or fragile, and from stereotypically male target words such as powerful or assertive, and letter sequences from non-words, appeared on the screen. Participants in the stimulus compatibility condition were asked to make a lexical decision about whether the letter sequences made up words or non-words. Participants in the response compatibility condition were asked to think about whether the letter sequences made them think about strength or weakness. In the response compatibility condition participants were additionally told that they might see non-words included in the letter sequences but to respond to these with their first inclinations anyway. Participants therefore took part in one of four combinations: 'easy' plus *stimulus* compatibility; 'difficult' plus *stimulus* compatibility; 'easy' plus *response* compatibility; or 'difficult' plus *response* compatibility. The quantitative data was analysed by a between-subjects ANOVA.

Results

Participants in the stimulus compatibility condition (where they had to identify gender stereotypical words that had missing letters) showed a lower level of implicit gender stereotyping if they had been in the 'difficult' condition (where they had to try to generate a high number of counter-stereotypical women). In contrast to this, participants in the response compatibility condition (where they had to evaluate whether the target word sequences made them think about strength or weakness) showed a higher level of implicit gender stereotyping if they had been in the 'difficult' condition.

Discussion

The results demonstrate higher implicit gender stereotyping when participants are asked to make evaluative judgements. This effect appears to be from the nature of the two tasks (evaluative judgements in the response compatibility task or lexical decisions in the stimulus compatibility task) because the initial task (the difference in generating lists of low or high numbers of counter-stereotypical women – 'easy' or 'difficult') did not have an overall influence on these results. The findings suggest that implicit attitudes based on evaluative judgements are influenced by the ease of retrieving relevant information from memory. However, implicit attitudes that are based on making lexical decisions are influenced by direct knowledge activation in associated memory. When more effort is put into retrieval such as making decisions by activating knowledge, the influence upon attitudes is not as great as when retrieval of information is easier. By investigating the underlying mechanisms of implicit gender stereotyping the present study goes beyond demonstrating the influence of externally provided context stimuli on implicit measures. Furthermore, the findings from the present study may indicate that subjective experiences and feelings translate into overt responses and may not just influence responses in response compatibility tasks but may also influence spontaneous responses in social interactions. In contrast, implicit measures in the stimulus compatibility task may represent a conceptual cognitive component rather than represent subjective feelings. Overall, the present study demonstrates that the way information is retrieved from memory influences different types of implicit measures. Future research could investigate the underlying mechanisms of other kinds of context effects to not only gain an understanding of the influence of different contexts but to also develop an understanding of implicit measures in general.

Critical Reflections

This is quite a complex study into implicit gender stereotyping. The researchers adopt the implicit association test (IAT) framework to try and examine these stereotypes without the participants' knowledge. Criticisms of this method for eliciting stereotypes are discussed in Chapter 5. However, with respect to the current study, to what extent do you think this method successfully manages to study gender stereotypes without the participants knowledge? Are there any **demand characteristics** that might give the game away? And if a participant does figure out what the study is testing, how might their responses be influenced? Critics of IATs have argued that these are not tests of stereotyping as it occurs in the real world, but are tests of familiarity or semantic associations between two or more stimuli.

demand characteristics occur when participants interpret what the expected findings of a study are based on implicit cues, such as the presence of certain objects, or the researchers' manner, and alters their behaviour to fit with those expectations

As we live as members of a collective, Moscovici reasoned that this must influence how we see the world. We are a 'thinking society' capable of shaping society as we share and discuss our thoughts and ideas with one another.

The sociologist Emile Durkheim had already defined collective social thought – that is, those thoughts that are shared by members of a group (e.g. common sense, traditions, legends, myths, and so on). Moscovici redefined these as 'social representations', which are the knowledge, images, thoughts and ideas members of a collectivity share and communicate with one another through language.

For example, in Western society there is a social representation that people are autonomous agents, responsible for their own actions, which goes some way to explaining why we see the fundamental attribution error occur in such societies.

But where do these social representations come from? Moscovici thought people turn the unfamiliar into the familiar through two processes.

1 *Anchoring:* we compare the unfamiliar with our existing stock of knowledge and anchor it onto what we already know. So, by giving something a name we are not only able to now recognize it, but we also give it meaning. This reveals something about our society, culture, and group norms and values. We can view it positively or negatively. Treat it as normative or deviant.

2 *Objectification:* the process in which an unfamiliar idea, notion or image is transformed into a concrete object. Consider Freud's concept of 'neurosis'. What do you see when you think of the concept? Is it represented in a concrete image of a person?

Moscovici was particularly interested in the popularization of scientific concepts by the mass media, noting how they become shared social representations that we discuss in our everyday lives. This gives us a population of amateur scientists. The television phenomenon of *Big Brother* turned many people into lay psychologists as they analyse the behaviour of the housemates. Thanks to the mass media, ordinary people can have a discussion about the greenhouse effect, give relationship advice, and even diagnose medical conditions and suggest treatment. We hold social representations about scientific issues through communicating our perceptions and judgements about them in our talking and thinking society.

More recently Thi et al. (2008) have considered how people with HIV and AIDS are evaluated in Ho Chi Minh City in Vietnam (with over 260,000 people suffering from HIV). Focus groups conducted with people who have HIV and/or AIDS, revealed how social representations present in the media and everyday understandings of the condition include misperceptions about how it is contracted (e.g. through casual contact) and how people should be treated. The representation of HIV and AIDS as a 'social evil' means people with the condition are perceived as socially deviant, and are marginalized and discriminated against in all areas of their lives.

Studying Social Representations

Are people who live in the countryside less likely to suffer ill health than those who live in the city? In a classic study Herzlich (1973) set out to examine the social representations that people in France held of health and illness, in terms of how to explain them. Using open-ended interviews with 80 middle-class Parisians, Herzlich concluded that there exists a social representation that city life is responsible for illness. Those who live in the city were perceived to be unhealthy on the basis of poor diet, contaminated water, stress and pollution. City life was thought to be responsible for heart attacks, cancer and fatigue. On the other hand, those who live in the country were thought to be much healthier. Indeed it was believed that a move to the country could improve your health! The countryside was associated with a slower pace of life, clean water, fresh food and clean air. So being ill or healthy was not attributed to the individual, but to the environment in which they lived.

When it comes to explaining people's behaviour in our social world, we use attributions and these can be prone to error. However, as we have seen, culture

Is living in the countryside really better for your health than living in the city?
SOURCE: © jiuquanyyl/123RF

makes an important difference to our attributions, especially the fundamental attribution error. So we need to carefully consider the social when thinking about how we explain people's behaviour. Social representation theory does take more account of the social and incorporates the values held in a particular culture, the common sense beliefs and norms. In the final section, we turn to how important our social beliefs are.

Expectations of Our Social World

Having considered how we explain and judge others – efficiently, adaptively, but sometimes erroneously – we conclude this chapter by pondering the effects of our social judgements. Do our social beliefs matter? Do they change reality?

Our social beliefs and judgements do matter. They influence how we feel and act, and by so doing may help generate their own reality. When our ideas lead us to act in ways that produce their apparent confirmation, they have become what sociologist Merton (1948) termed **self-fulfilling prophecies** – beliefs that lead to their own fulfilment. For example, faced with the possibility of the UK leaving the European Union, manufacturers and suppliers within the country have begun stockpiling food, from bread to crisps. In November 2018, *The Guardian* newspaper reported that the situation had got so bad, Britain was fast running out of space to store it all (O'Carroll, 2018).

self-fulfilling prophecy occurs when people's expectations lead to the occurrence of the expected behaviour or outcome. A girl or a teacher's belief that girls are never good at sciences could thus lead to its own fulfilment

In his well-known studies of *experimenter bias,* Rosenthal (1985) found that research participants sometimes live up to what they believe experimenters expect of them. In one study, experimenters asked individuals to judge the success of people in various photographs. The experimenters read the same instructions to all their participants and showed them the same photos. Nevertheless, experimenters who expected their participants to see the photographed people as successful obtained higher ratings than did those who expected their participants to see the people as failures. Even more startling – and controversial – are reports that teachers' beliefs about their students similarly serve as self-fulfilling prophecies. If a teacher believes a student is good at mathematics, will the student do well in the class? Let's examine this.

Teacher Expectations and Student Performance

Teachers do have higher expectations for some students than for others. Perhaps you have detected this after having a brother or sister precede you in school, or after receiving a label such as 'gifted' or 'learning disabled', or after being tracked with 'high-ability' or 'average-ability' students. Perhaps conversation in the staff room sent your reputation ahead of you. Or perhaps your new teacher scrutinized your school file or discovered your family's social status. It is clear that teachers' evaluations correlate with student achievement: teachers think well of students who do well. That's mostly because teachers accurately perceive their students' abilities and achievements (Jussim, 2005).

Could we test this 'teacher-expectations effect' experimentally? Weaver et al. (2016) conducted an experiment in which 'coaches' were provided with false information about the players they were instructed to train. They were told players were either great or not-so-great. Would this affect the coaching, and in turn, the ability of the players? Well, yes it did. The coaches gave more opportunities to shoot to the 'great' players, and far less to the not-so-great. In return, although the information about their playing ability was false, the researchers reported that the players fulfilled their coaches' expectations of them. Those labelled great successfully landed more shots than those labelled not-so-great. Spurred on by their coaches' confidence in them, and taking advantage of those extra opportunities, the 'great' achieved more.

However, let's consider another example. Suppose we gave a teacher the impression that Dana, Sally, Todd and Manuel – four randomly selected students – are unusually capable. Will the teacher give special treatment to these four and elicit superior performance from them? In a famous classic experiment, Rosenthal and Jacobson (1968) reported precisely that. Randomly selected children in a San Francisco elementary school who were said (on the basis of a fictitious test) to be on the verge of a dramatic intellectual spurt did then spurt ahead in IQ score.

That dramatic result seemed to suggest that the school problems of 'disadvantaged' children might reflect their teachers' low expectations. The findings were soon publicized in the national media as well as in many college textbooks in psychology and education. However, further analysis – which was not as highly publicized – revealed the teacher-expectations effect to be not as powerful and reliable as this initial study had led many people to believe (Spitz, 1999). By Rosenthal's own count, in only about 4 in 10 of the nearly 500 published experiments did expectations significantly affect performance (Rosenthal, 1991, 2002). Low expectations do not doom a capable child, nor do high expectations magically transform a slow learner into a valedictorian. As Jussim (2017; Jussim & Harber, 2005) points out, where self-fulfilling prophecies have been found, the effect has been quite small. Furthermore, they do not seem to last over time and they tend to affect stigmatized groups the most (see Riley & Ungerleider's 2012 work on teacher expectations of Aboriginal students in Canada, and Sorhagen's 2013 work on academic expectations of children from disadvantaged backgrounds). In teacher-student studies the effects seen might simply reflect the teacher's rather accurate perception of the student's ability rather than any self-fulfilling prophecy at work. So perhaps human nature is not quite as pliable as these studies might suggest.

But, despite these words of caution about attempts to study this phenomenon, the evidence is that self-fulfilling prophecies do occur. How are such expectations transmitted? Rosenthal and other investigators report that teachers look, smile and nod more at 'high-potential students'. Teachers also may teach more to their 'gifted' students, set higher goals for them, call on them more, and give them more time to answer (Rist, 2000).

In one study, Babad et al. (1991) videotaped teachers talking to, or about, unseen students for whom they held high or low expectations. A random 10-second clip of either the teacher's voice or the teacher's face was enough to tell viewers – both children and adults – whether this was a good or a poor student and how much the teacher liked the student. (You read that right: 10 seconds.) Although teachers may think they can conceal their feelings and behave impartially towards the class, students are acutely sensitive to teachers' facial expressions and body movements (**Figure 4.5**).

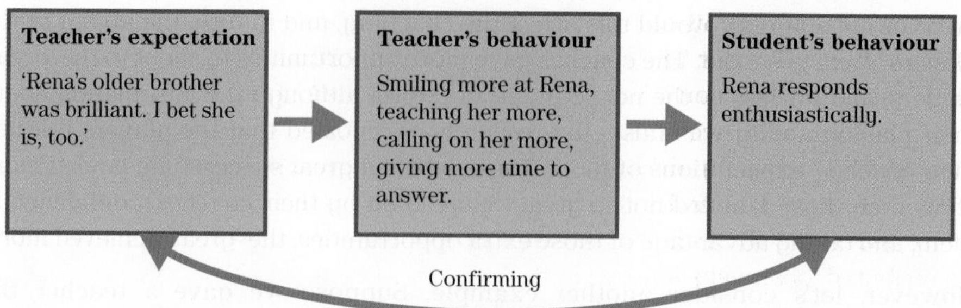

FIGURE 4.5 Self-fulfilling prophecies
Teacher expectations can become self-fulfilling prophecies. But, for the most part, teachers' expectations accurately reflect reality (Jussim & Harber, 2005).

Reading the experiments on teacher expectations makes us wonder about the effect of *students'* expectations upon their teachers. You no doubt begin many of your courses having heard 'Professor Smith is interesting' and 'Professor Jones is a bore'. Feldman and Prohaska (1979; Feldman & Theiss, 1982) found that such expectations can affect both student and teacher. Students in a learning experiment who expected to be taught by an excellent teacher perceived their teacher (who was unaware of their expectations) as more competent and interesting than did students with low expectations. Furthermore, the students actually learned more. In a follow-up experiment, Feldman and Prohaska videotaped teachers and had observers rate their performances. Teachers were judged most capable when assigned a student who non-verbally conveyed positive expectations.

To see whether such effects might also occur in actual classrooms, a research team led by David Jamieson (Jamieson et al., 1987) experimented with four high school classes taught by a newly transferred teacher. During individual interviews, they told students in two of the classes that both other students and the research team rated the teacher very highly. Compared with the control classes, the students given positive expectations paid better attention during class. At the end of the teaching unit, they also got better grades and rated the teacher as clearer in her teaching. The attitudes that a class has towards its teacher are as important, it seems, as the teacher's attitude towards the students.

Getting from Others What We Expect

So the expectations of experimenters and teachers, though usually reasonably accurate assessments, occasionally act as self-fulfilling prophecies. How widespread are self-fulfilling prophecies? Do we get from others what we expect of them? Studies show that self-fulfilling prophecies also operate in work settings (with managers who have high or low expectations), in law courts (as judges instruct juries), in simulated police contexts (as interrogators with guilty or innocent expectations interrogate and pressure suspects), and in sport (where athletes expect doping to occur) (Kassin et al., 2003; Moston et al., 2015; Rosenthal, 2003).

Do self-fulfilling prophecies colour our personal relationships? There are times when negative expectations of someone lead us to be extra nice to that person, which induces him or her to be nice in return – thus *dis*confirming our expectations. But a more common finding in studies of social interaction is that, yes, we do to some extent get what we expect (Olson et al., 1996).

Do our social media relationships enhance our lives?
SOURCE: © View Apart/Shutterstock

To what extent do you consider your 'friends' on Facebook or 'followers' on Twitter to reflect real and close relationships? How much time do you invest in these relationships? Do these relationships enhance your life? Your online expectations are almost certainly driving your online behaviour. Clark and Green (2018) found that those participants in their study who believed that their online relationships were 'real' and contributed positively to their lives, were willing to disclose personal information and offer social support to an unknown online 'friend' or 'follower'. They were keen to put in the effort to build a close relationship, which they felt would be successful. Those who felt these relationships were less positively impactful on their lives, were much more reserved in their online interactions, and success was not expected. If you expect your online social relationships to be beneficial for you, they will be.

So, do intimate relationships prosper when partners idealize each other? Are positive illusions of the other's virtues self-fulfilling? Or are they more often self-defeating, by creating high expectations that can't be met? Among university dating couples followed by Murray et al. (1996a, 2000), positive ideals of one's partner were good omens. Idealization helped buffer conflict, bolster satisfaction, and turn self-perceived frogs into princes or princesses. When someone loves and admires us, it helps us become more the person he or she imagines us to be.

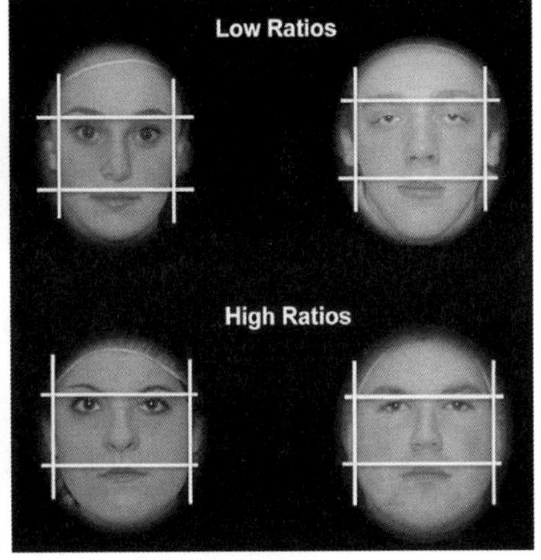

Who do you trust? Self-fulfilling prophecies might mean we get what we expect.
SOURCE: Geniole et al. (2015)

Would you trust a man with a face that displayed a large width-to-height-ratio (fWHR)? Research conducted in evolutionary social psychology suggests many of us don't. But with good reason? From a biological and evolutionary point of view, having a larger fWHR is an indicator of high levels of testosterone. Testosterone is associated with aggression. In evolutionary terms, high baseline levels of testosterone coupled with high levels of aggressive behaviour can be beneficial. Survival of the fittest involves competition for resources and mates, so aggression might be very useful. But, it comes at a social cost. Highly aggressive individuals can also be regarded as selfish, individualistic and untrustworthy. But are these unattractive characteristics driven by fWHRs and those high levels of testosterone? Might men with large fWHRs simply be living up to other people's expectations of them? That's exactly what Haselhuhn et al. (2013) discovered. In a series of studies they found that observers treated men with large fWHRs as if they were selfish, aggressive, untrustworthy. This in turn elicited those behaviours from the observers themselves, as well as the men. In other words, expectations of men with large fWHRs were fulfilled not only by the men but also those they interacted with. The point is an interesting one. Whilst biology might be responsible for some behaviour, social processes are also involved.

Several experiments conducted by Snyder (1984) show how, once formed, erroneous beliefs about the social world can induce others to confirm those behavioural confirmation a type of self-fulfilling prophecy whereby people's social expectations lead them to behave in ways that cause others to confirm their expectations

beliefs, a phenomenon called **behavioural confirmation**. In a now-classic study, Snyder et al. (1977) had men students talk on the telephone with women they thought (from having been shown a picture) were either attractive or unattractive. Analysis of just the women's comments during the conversations revealed that the supposedly attractive women spoke more warmly than the supposedly unattractive women. The men's erroneous beliefs had become a self-fulfilling prophecy by leading them to act in a way that influenced the women to fulfil the men's stereotype that beautiful people are desirable people.

Behavioural confirmation also occurs as people interact with partners holding mistaken beliefs. People who are believed lonely behave less sociably (Rotenberg et al., 2002). Men who are believed sexist behave less favourably towards women (Pinel, 2002).

Imagine yourself as one of the 60 young men or 60 young women in an experiment by Ridge and Reber (2002). Each man is to interview one of the women to assess her suitability for a teaching assistant position. Before doing so, he is told either that she feels attracted to him (based on his answers to a biographical questionnaire) or not attracted. The result was behavioural confirmation: applicants believed to feel an attraction exhibited more flirtatiousness (and without being aware of doing so). Ridge and Reber believe that this process may be one of the roots of sexual harassment. If a woman's behaviour seems to confirm a man's beliefs, he may then escalate his overtures until they become sufficiently overt for the woman to recognize and interpret them as inappropriate or harassing.

Behavioural confirmation. The image above shows English fans in France for a football match for Euro 2016. When England football fans came to France for the 1998 World Cup, they were expected to live up to their reputation as aggressive 'hooligans' (e.g. Stott et al., 2001). Local French youth and police, expecting hooligan behaviour, reportedly displayed hostility towards the English, who retaliated, thus confirming the expectation (Klein & Snyder, 2003).

SOURCE: ©Vanya Bovajo/StockimoNews/Alamy Stock Photo

Expectations influence children's behaviour and achievements too. Englund et al. (2004) looked at the influence parents expectations and behaviours had upon their children. The participants were from low-income families. The research found positive relationships between parents' levels of education, involvement with their child's school, expectations for their children, and parenting style, with their child's IQ and achievement in school. The researchers conclude that early parenting style has a profound effect on children's academic abilities and achievements.

Told that someone we are about to meet is intelligent and attractive, we may come away impressed with just how intelligent and attractive he or she is. These experiments help us understand how social beliefs, such as stereotypes about people with disabilities or about people of a particular race or sex, may be self-confirming. How others treat us reflects how we and others have treated them.

As with every social phenomenon, the tendency to confirm others' expectations has its limits. Expectations often predict behaviour simply because they are accurate (Jussim, 2005).

'The more he treated her as though she were really very nice, the more Lotty expanded and became really very nice, and the more he, affected in his turn, became really very nice himself; so that they went round and round, not in a vicious but in a highly virtuous circle.'

Elizabeth von Arnim, *The Enchanted April*, 1922

Conclusions

Social psychology studies reveal that our information-processing powers are impressive for their efficiency and adaptiveness ('in apprehension how like a god!' exclaimed Shakespeare's Hamlet), yet vulnerable to predictable errors and misjudgements ('headpiece filled with straw', said T. S. Eliot). How we perceive, judge and explain our social experiences is guided by the norms and values that exist within society. What practical lessons, and what insights into human nature, can we take home from this research?

We have reviewed some reasons why people sometimes come to believe what may be untrue. We cannot easily dismiss these studies; most of their participants were intelligent people, often students at leading universities. Moreover, these predictable distortions and biases occurred even when payment for right answers motivated people to think optimally. As one researcher concluded, the illusions 'have a persistent quality not unlike that of perceptual illusions' (Slovic, 1972).

Research in cognitive social psychology thus mirrors the mixed review given humanity in literature, philosophy and religion. Many research psychologists have spent lifetimes exploring the awesome capacities of the human mind. We are intelligent enough to have cracked our own genetic code, to have invented talking computers, to have sent people to the moon.

However, before we get too carried away with ourselves, let's remember that the mind's premium on efficient judgement makes our intuition more vulnerable to misjudgement than we suspect. With remarkable ease, we form and sustain false beliefs. Led by our preconceptions, overconfident, persuaded by vivid anecdotes, and perceiving correlations and control even where none may exist, we construct our social beliefs and then influence others to confirm them. 'The naked intellect', observed novelist Madeleine L'Engle (1973), 'is an extraordinarily inaccurate instrument'.

But have these studies just been intellectual tricks played on hapless participants, thus making them look worse than they are? Nisbett and Ross (1980) contended that, if anything, they overestimate our intuitive powers. The experiments usually present people with clear evidence and warn them that their reasoning ability is being tested.

Often our everyday failings are inconsequential, but not always so. False impressions, interpretations and beliefs can produce serious consequences. Even small biases can have profound social effects when we are making important social judgements: why are so many people homeless? Unhappy? Homicidal? Does my friend love me or my money? Cognitive biases even creep into sophisticated scientific thinking.

Is this too cynical? Martin and Erber (2005) invite us to imagine that an intelligent being swooped down just for a moment and begged for information that would help it understand the human species. When you hand it this social psychology text, the alien says 'thank you' and zooms back off into space. After resolving your remorse over giving up this book, how would you feel about having offered social psychology's analysis? Krueger and Funder (2004a, 2004b) wouldn't feel too good. Social psychology's preoccupation with human foibles needs balancing with 'a more positive view of human nature', they argue.

Fellow social psychologist Lee Jussim (2005) agrees, adding, 'Despite the oft-demonstrated existence of a slew of logical flaws and systematic biases in lay judgement and social perception, such as the fundamental attribution error, false consensus, over-reliance on imperfect heuristics, self-serving biases, etc., people's perceptions of one another are surprisingly (though rarely perfectly) accurate.' The elegant analyses of the imperfections of our thinking are themselves a tribute to human wisdom. Were one to argue that all human thought is illusory, the assertion would be self-refuting, for it, too, would be but an illusion. It would be logically equivalent to contending 'All generalizations are false, including this one.'

Nobel laureate psychologist Herbert Simon (1957) was among the modern researchers who first described the bounds of human reason. Simon contends that to cope with reality, we simplify it. Consider the complexity of a chess game: the number of possible games is greater than the number of particles in the universe. How do we cope? We adopt some simplifying rules – heuristics. These heuristics sometimes lead us to defeat. But they do enable us to make efficient snap judgements.

Focus on

How Do We Know if We are Poor Judges of Social Reality or Highly Efficient at These Judgements?

Are human beings inaccurate judges of social reality? The research on heuristics, biases and mental shortcuts suggests that we are. However, Gigerenzer and Goldstein (1996; Goldstein & Gigerenzer, 2002) argue that these cognitive processes are not 'errors' but are illustrations of our creative and complex human mind. With the cognitive revolution of the 1960s in psychology computers were used to model the human brain. This led to a rethinking of the mind, and what they call 'the mind as computer'. But whereas the computer could perform calculations and solve problems perfectly every time, the human brain was fallible. But are people really deficient thinkers? Or is this a sign of our intelligence? Gigerenzer and Goldstein invite their reader to consider the recognition heuristic as an example. The recognition heuristic proposes that if one of two objects is recognized then it can be inferred that the recognized object is of higher value. They now ask their reader to imagine three Parisian sisters who are told they will take a test on the 100 largest German cities. The test will comprise pairs of cities, and they must decide which is the larger. Before the test the older sister studies the cities of Germany so she can find out the 100 largest ones. She will recognize all the cities presented in the test. The middle sister has heard of some of the cities of Germany and will recognize about half of those presented in the test. The youngest sister has never heard of any of the cities in Germany, nor has she done any studying. So who will perform the best? The eldest sister relies on her knowledge and gets more than half of them correct. The youngest sister can only guess throughout the test. The middle sister does the best. Why? She's the only one using the recognition heuristic. She recognizes half of the cities and assumes that the reason she's heard of them is because they're large. So she chooses them. She doesn't have to sort through all the cities, like the eldest sister does, nor does she have to completely guess, like the youngest sister.

As Gigerenzer and Goldstein observe, we learn to associate recognition with quality, power and importance. To be able to recognize important things has distinct advantages for us. It enables us to distinguish things that will be of benefit to us, from those that are of no value or may even be harmful. So far from being deficient processors of social reality, the use of heuristics is 'a capacity that evolution has shaped over millions of years that allows organisms to benefit from their own ignorance' (Goldstein & Gigerenzer, 2002, p. 88). As they conclude, in a complex social world, heuristics may be evidence of the unique intelligence of human beings to exploit information to make creative, accurate and efficient judgements. But to what extent can this research be applied to our ability to use quick judgements about others? And how do we know if we are efficient at social judgements or poor judges of social reality?

Harris and Fiske (2006) propose that social neuroscience is ideal for studying the efficiency and spontaneity of social judgements. We have seen in this chapter the contribution social neuroscience is making towards understanding activities in our brains when we are making inferences and making sense of social information. This approach assumes that brain mechanisms and structures guide our judgements and shape the way we behave. Social neuroscientists propose that studying brain activity can aid our understanding about how we make apparently spontaneous judgements such as through the use of heuristics and inferences. Todorov et al. (2006) argue that research in social neuroscience demonstrates that person inferences are highly efficient and that this has significant consequences for our social judgements and behaviour. Cacioppo and Berntson (1992) see exploring the brain as a gateway to the mind.

Gigerenzer and Goldstein refer to the human mind as a computer, not just able to efficiently distinguish important information in our social world but also able to think logically and scientifically. This distinction between efficient logical scientific thinking and faulty irrational thinking has been established in the social cognition studies on inferences and attributions outlined in this chapter. However, critical social psychologists such as Gough et al. (2013) argue that the human mind is not completely 'scientific' or 'logical'. Furthermore, they argue methods of research within social cognition treat individuals and their minds as objects separate from the social environment to be investigated in carefully controlled experimental conditions. Not only this, they also argue that social neuroscience tends to reduce people to the effects of psychobiological processes. Taken together, the concern to critical social psychologists is just how 'social' are both social neuroscience and social cognition? How much can studies in social neuroscience and social cognition tell us about people's everyday experiences in understanding our social world and how we view ourselves and others? Not only this, what can these studies tell us about where we get our ideas of reality in the first place?

Methods adopted within social cognition and social neuroscience aim to tightly control variables in order to carefully measure the ways people make social judgements. Social phenomena in the form of lists of words or lists of specific traits contrived by the researchers are typically used in these experimental tasks and cognitive processes or brain activities are inferred from the results. Increasingly photographs are used in experimental tasks such as implicit association tests (IAT) and film clips are used depicting people's behaviour. These are closer to everyday situations but still not the same as experiencing real everyday situations and may not enable us to fully understand how and why people make social judgements in their real-life social situations.

Research within social neuroscience and social cognition often aims to address social issues such as stereotyping and prejudice by seeking to understand how we form these judgements and engage in negative behaviour towards certain others. Therefore, whether we efficiently make social inferences or are prone to make errors of judgement through cognitive shortcuts can lead to crucial assumptions about the way individuals engage in negative judgements and behaviour towards others. Critical social psychologists are particularly concerned with the way that social cognition and social neuroscience make assumptions that these types of thinking and the ensuing behaviour are innate processes that are not only universal but are also inevitable. From the point of view of social cognition, the individual is a contained information processor who will engage in stereotyping as the most efficient way to make sense of their self and others even though the stereotypes may have very little to do with an accurate picture of those who are stereotyped. This can appear to paint a gloomy deterministic picture rather than addressing how stereotyping and prejudice may be reduced. To explore how prejudice may be reduced, critical social psychologists look to how people draw on cultural values and the taken-for-granted ways of talking about people in their society to make assumptions about others. Some critical social psychologists explore how these taken-for granted ideas about people become constructed, reinforced and maintained through language. (See 'The Language of Prejudice' in Chapter 13.)

A key criticism by critical social psychologists of social neuroscience and research into social cognition is that these approaches fail to take account of a person's personal history or their experiences within their social environment and culture. As pointed out earlier in this chapter, a person's culture has a considerable influence upon their social judgements and understanding their social world. Furthermore we cannot assume that everyone in the same culture has the same social experiences.

Questions

1 How far do you think people's social judgements are influenced by their individual characteristics, cognitions and brain mechanisms?

2 What other factors could be involved in the way people make social judgements in real-life situations and in experimental tasks?

3 Discuss the 'social' in social neuroscience and social cognition.

SUMMING UP: SOCIAL BELIEFS AND JUDGEMENTS

PERCEIVING OUR SOCIAL WORLD

- Our preconceptions strongly influence how we interpret and remember events. In a phenomenon called *priming,* people's prejudgements have striking effects on how they perceive and interpret information.
- Experiments have planted judgements or false ideas in people's minds *after* they have been given information. These experiments reveal that as *before-the-fact judgements* bias our perceptions and interpretations, so *after-the-fact judgements* bias our recall.
- *Belief perseverance* is the phenomenon in which people cling to their initial beliefs and the reasons why a belief might be true, even when the basis for the belief is discredited.
- Far from being a repository for facts about the past, our memories are actually formed when we construct them in language, and are subject to strong influence by the attitudes and feelings we hold at the time, and the demands of the context in which they are produced.

JUDGING OUR SOCIAL WORLD

- We have an enormous capacity for automatic, efficient, intuitive thinking. We quickly assimilate information to judge types of persons. Our cognitive efficiency, though generally adaptive, comes at the price of occasional error. Since we are generally unaware of those errors entering our thinking, it is useful to identify ways in which we form and sustain false beliefs.

- First, we often overestimate our judgements. This *overconfidence phenomenon* stems partly from the much greater ease with which we can imagine why we might be right than why we might be wrong. Moreover, people are much more likely to search for information that can confirm their beliefs than for information that can disconfirm them.
- Second, when given compelling anecdotes or even useless information, we often ignore useful base-rate information. This is partly due to the later ease of recall of vivid information (the *availability heuristic*).
- Third, we are often swayed by illusions of correlation and personal control. It is tempting to perceive correlations where none exists (*illusory correlation*), and to think we can predict or control chance events (the *illusion of control*).
- Finally, moods infuse judgements. Good and bad moods trigger memories of experiences associated with those moods. Moods colour our interpretations of current experiences. And, by distracting us, moods can also influence how deeply or superficially we think when making judgements.

EXPLAINING OUR SOCIAL WORLD

- Attribution theory involves how we explain people's behaviour.
- Although we usually make reasonable attributions, we often commit the *fundamental attribution error* (also called *correspondence bias*) when explaining other people's behaviour. This is more common in Western, individualistic cultures than in Eastern interdependent or collective cultures. We attribute their behaviour so much to their inner traits and attitudes that we discount situational constraints, even when those are obvious. Social categorization and stereotyping also influence our attributions. We expect people from certain social groups to behave in particular ways and this is based on very little actual information about them, therefore prone to error. We make this attribution error partly because when we watch someone act, that *person* is the focus of our attention and the situation is relatively invisible. When *we* act, our attention is usually on what we are reacting to – the situation is more visible.
- Social representations are the common-sense beliefs, values, theories and norms we hold about social phenomena. They are communicated and shared between people and are discussed by a 'thinking society' that shapes how we experience the world around us.

EXPECTATIONS OF OUR SOCIAL WORLD

- Our beliefs sometimes take on lives of their own. Usually, our beliefs about others have a basis in reality. But studies of experimenter bias and teacher expectations show that an erroneous belief that certain people are unusually capable (or incapable) can lead teachers and researchers to give those people special treatment. This may elicit superior (or inferior) performance and, therefore, seem to confirm an assumption that is actually false.
- Similarly, in everyday life we often get *behavioural confirmation* of what we expect.

CONCLUSIONS

- Research on social beliefs and judgements reveals how we form and sustain beliefs that usually serve us well but sometimes lead us astray. A balanced social psychology will therefore appreciate both the powers and the perils of social thinking.

Critical Questions

1. What cognitive biases have social psychologists identified in how we perceive, understand and evaluate the world around us? Think further about what may influence these biases.
2. When might it be useful to use mental shortcuts?
3. Are these biases a symptom of flaws in human thinking, or evidence of our intelligence? And how 'social' are these biases?
4. Under what conditions is the fundamental attribution error likely to occur?
5. How 'fundamental' is the fundamental attribution error?
6. To what extent does social representation theory offer a more 'social' view of how we perceive, understand and evaluate the world around us?

Recommended Reading

Here are some recommended classic and contemporary readings on social judgements and how they have been understood and investigated in social psychology.

Classic Papers

Kraut, R. E., & Lewis, S. H. (1982). Person perception and self-awareness: Knowledge of influences on one's own judgments. *Journal of Personality and Social Psychology, 42,* 448–460.

Kulik, J. A. (1983). Confirmatory attributions and the perpetuation of social beliefs. *Journal of Personality and Social Psychology, 44,* 1171–1181.

Lerner, M. J., & Miller, D. T. (1978). Just world research and the attribution process: Looking back and ahead. *Psychological Bulletin, 85,* 1030–1051.

Contemporary Papers

Blanchard-Fields, F., Hertzog, C., & Horhotta, M. (2012). Violate my beliefs? Then you're to blame! Belief content as an explanation for causal attribution biases. *Psychology and Aging, 27,* 324–337.

Browman, A. S., Destin, M., Carswell, K. L., & Svoboda, R. C. (2017). Perceptions of socioeconomic mobility influence academic persistence among low socioeconomic status students. *Journal of Experimental Social Psychology, 72* (C), 45–52.

Timmermans, A., Boer, C., & Werf, H. (2016). An investigation of the relationship between teachers' expectations and teachers' perceptions of student attributes. *Social Psychology of Education, 19* (2), 217–240.

5 ATTITUDES AND BEHAVIOUR

"Better contraceptives will control population only if people will use them."
B. F. Skinner, Beyond Freedom and Dignity, 1971

Back in 1935, Gordon Allport declared 'attitudes' as social psychology's 'most distinctive and indispensable concept'. Indeed, attitudes may answer the question 'Why do people do what they do?' Philosophers, theologians and educators have long speculated about the connections between attitude and action, character and conduct, private word and public deed. Underlying much teaching, counselling and child rearing is an assumption that our private beliefs and feelings determine our public behaviour. So if we want to change someone's behaviour, we need to change their attitudes. This goes some way to explaining why our attitudes are under so much exploitation from the mass media, advertisers, politicians, policy-makers, and so on. We often see, for example, media coverage of Parliament or presidential elections in most countries, and witness the direct appeals to the population's attitudes by politicians in order to win votes.

Although there are lots of different ways of defining attitudes, social psychologists are agreed that they involve evaluations (McGuire, 1985; Zanna & Rempel, 1988). These can be evaluations of anything. Darwin, religion, chocolate, exercise, Spain, war, the Internet, even the virtues of green tea! When social psychologists talk about someone's attitude, they refer to beliefs and feelings related to a person, object or an event. Taken together, favourable or unfavourable evaluative reactions towards something – often rooted in beliefs and exhibited in feelings, and inclinations to act – define a person's **attitude** (Eagly & Chaiken, 2005). A person may have a negative attitude towards coffee, a neutral attitude towards the European Union and a positive attitude towards their next-door neighbour. Attitudes provide an efficient way to size up the world. When we have to respond quickly to something, the way we feel about it can guide how we react. For example, a person who *believes* a particular ethnic group is lazy and aggressive may *feel* dislike for such people and therefore tend to *act* in a discriminatory manner. Yale University researchers proposed the ABC model of attitudes to define these three kinds of responses someone can have towards an 'attitude-object' (such as coffee, fox-hunters or green tea). These are affective emotional responses, behavioural responses (verbal and non-verbal) and cognitive responses (our knowledge and beliefs). Or in other words, the ABC model proposes that attitudes are made up of feeling (A), doing (B) and thinking (C).

attitude a favourable or unfavourable evaluative reaction towards something or someone, rooted in one's beliefs, and exhibited in one's feelings and inclinations to act

These three components of attitudes are thought to be responsible for our overall evaluation of an attitude-object. Social psychologists have sought to measure each of these components in assessing their contribution to an overall attitude. Affect can be measured physiologically (e.g. heart rate) or through self-report: 'Tell me how you feel about X.' Behaviour can be investigated through observations, or asking people to self-report on their past and present behaviour and their future intentions. Cognition requires information from the participant about their knowledge, beliefs and perceptions of whatever the attitude-object is being studied. But are all three always involved in the formation of an attitude? Do they all equally contribute? Consider Hood and Shook's (2013) finding that women's attitudes towards, and intentions to use, condoms was related to feelings (A) and beliefs (C) about them, but less so to past behaviour (B). The women in their study often expressed negative feelings about using them but had very positive beliefs and knowledge about why they should be used. The authors recommend that information such as this can aid researchers and health practitioners in encouraging people to practise safe sex. Hence, an attitude may contain a mix of these components to a greater or lesser degree.

This ABC-model has a fairly long history in social psychology, having been around since the 1960s. It is not without its critics. This model contains within it some underlying assumptions about the nature of attitudes and their role. First, this model assumes that attitudes are enduring across time and space. As we shall see later in this chapter, not all social psychologists agree. Many argue that attitudes are constructed in the moment and are tailored for a specific context (see 'Attitudes as Social Actions'). Second, this model assumes that attitudes are linked to behaviour. But are they? As we shall see throughout this chapter, this is a major point of debate. If, and to what extent, attitudes are linked to behaviour is an argument that has exercised social psychologists for decades!

Where do these attitudes reside? Some social psychologists consider attitudes to be underlying cognitive entities within individuals that are fairly stable and enduring features of people. So, the reason why people tend to behave consistently is in some part due to their underlying stable and consistent attitudes. However, attitudes are also a part of our everyday interactions with other people. We offer our attitudes about various aspects of the world, and we listen to other people's. On the one hand they seem to have a cognitive aspect to them and on the other they also have a communicative component as we express and discuss our attitudes about things with one another in our everyday lives.

Our attitudes position and label us within the societies and communities where we live. If you hold negative attitudes towards eating meat, you may be labelled a vegetarian, which not only affects your own behaviour but also how other people evaluate and behave towards you. Attitudes define cultural and societal ideologies. Attitudes also explain our behaviour towards certain people and objects. If we hold negative attitudes about the poor (see the 'just world hypothesis' in Chapter 4) this might explain why we do not give money to people who beg on the streets. There appears to be a link between attitude and behaviour.

In the beginning, social psychologists agreed: to know people's attitudes is to predict their actions. As demonstrated by the Nazi genocide, extreme attitudes can produce extreme behaviour. But some scepticism on the link had already been cast. The American sociologist Richard LaPiere (1934) demonstrated that attitudes do not necessarily predict behaviour. In a famous study, LaPiere travelled with a Chinese couple along the US west coast, staying overnight at guest houses and campsites. It is important to bear in mind that this study took place at a time when there was much anti-Chinese feeling throughout the USA. Despite this, only once were the Chinese couple denied accommodation during their travels. But when LaPiere later wrote to all the guest houses and campsites asking if they would accept Chinese guests, over 90 per cent said 'No'. So here we seem to have a difference in behaviour and attitudes towards the Chinese couple. Why? Perhaps the respectable middle-class Chinese couple simply didn't fit the stereotype the guest-house and campsite managers held of Chinese people. Or maybe the relationship between attitudes and behaviour is more complex. Or, as we shall see later in this chapter, perhaps we have good reason to doubt the findings of this study?

Further problems with the attitude–behaviour relationship were found by Leon Festinger. In 1964 Festinger concluded that the evidence showed that *changing* people's attitudes hardly affects their behaviour at all. Rather, Festinger believed the attitude–behaviour relation works the other way around. As Robert Abelson

(1972) put it, we are 'very well trained and very good at finding reasons for what we do, but not very good at doing what we find reasons for'.

The topic of attitudes is a rich and complex one in social psychology. In this chapter we will consider both cognitive and communicative understandings of attitude, and explore this complex interplay of attitudes and behaviour.

Organization of Attitudes

mere-exposure effect the tendency for novel stimuli to be liked more or rated more positively after the rater has been repeatedly exposed to them

classical conditioning a learned response which results from the repeated pairing of a neutral stimulus with a conditioned stimulus

demand characteristics occur when participants interpret what the expected findings of a study are based on implicit cues, such as the presence of certain objects, or the researchers' manner, and alters their behaviour to fit with those expectations

instrumental learning when behaviour is modified on the basis of consequences

Formation of Attitudes

How are our attitudes formed? Where do we get them from? Social psychologists have offered some explanations.

The behavioural approach (or behaviourism) proposes that most attitudes are the result of direct experience with an object. Whether that experience is positive or negative will influence the formation of our attitudes towards it. A disastrous experience at the hairdresser as a child may well give you negative attitudes towards hairdressers for the rest of your life. Zajonc (1968) suggested that simply being repeatedly presented with an object, or what he terms '**mere exposure**', would invoke and influence an evaluation of it (see Chapter 9 on how exposure makes something more attractive). And as Addison and Thorpe (2004) discovered, people who had direct positive experiences with those who are mentally ill formed positive attitudes to mental illness.

Within the behaviourist approach **classical conditioning** has also been suggested as an explanation for the formation of attitudes. This occurs when an attitude object is regularly paired with another stimulus that can be positive or negative. The presentation of an object in a pleasant environment increases our positive attitudes towards that object. For example, the child who is given crisps on a visit to the dentist may well form more positive attitudes about dentists as a consequence. The attitude object (the dentist) has been paired with a positive stimulus (crisps). Early empirical evidence for this comes from Janis et al. (1965) who found that those participants who read a message while drinking a pleasant soft drink found it much more persuasive than those who did not. But are we seeing the formation of an attitude in these studies, or is it simply participants correctly guessing what the experimenter wants to hear? After all, it isn't too difficult to work out the hypothesis of the study. The **demand characteristics** of the experiment might well have given the game away!

A paper by Greenwald et al. (1998), listed in the Recommended Reading for this chapter, outlines their thoughts on implicit measures of attitudes.

Do you live in an environmentally sustainable way? Our attitudes towards climate change go some way to predicting our actions.

SOURCE: ©Jan Martin Will/Shutterstock

Instrumental learning (sometimes called operant conditioning) suggests that positive or negative consequences that follow behaviour will inform positive or negative attitudes towards it. Many parents have told their children that if they behave in the doctor's waiting room, they will receive some sweets afterwards. This form of learning can have a large influence on children's attitudes. Recent neuroscience work has demonstrated that instrumental learning can be accomplished subconsciously. For example, Pessigli and his colleagues (2008) note the ability of pro-gamblers to subconsciously associate winning with behavioural cues from their opponents: 'the gamblers tell'. The player isn't consciously aware of what it is that she perceives about the opponent, but is able to subconsciously detect the likelihood of winning. Pessiglione and colleagues report that even when participants are consciously unaware that instrumental learning is taking place, activity occurs in a specific area of the brain (ventral striatum) which demonstrates it is. This activity corresponds to participants when performing well on a task which requires subconscious instrumental learning to obtain rewards. In other words, participants have learned to associate consciously undetectable cues with rewards, but they don't know how they've done it. Advances in neuroscience now allow us to see where this subconscious learning has taken place. Both classical conditioning and instrumental learning focus on the role of positive and negative enforcers in forming attitudes towards an object.

Parental and peer influence are also responsible for the formation of some of our attitudes. Mähöen et al. (2011) considered the development of attitudes to other ethnic groups among young people aged 13–16 years. They found that for girls, their family's positive attitudes to other ethnic groups is sufficient to ensure they are also favourable. However, for boys, family influence is not enough. Boys also require direct positive personal experience with members of other ethnic groups. That said, for both boys and girls, family influence outweighs peer influence in the formation of attitudes.

From *social learning theory*, the concept of **modelling** describes the acquisition of behaviour through direct observation of other people (models) performing it and the subsequent positive or negative consequences (Bandura, 1973). Observing good consequences may well dispose us to form positive attitudes towards an object or behaviour. So attitudes are often formed on observations of behaviour rather than what we are told they should be. The instruction, 'Do as I say, not as I do' is familiar to many of us, yet we may focus on actions rather than words.

modelling the acquisition of behaviour on the basis of observing that of others (models)

We base our attitudes on those of other people when it is unclear what they objectively should be. Engaging in a process of *social comparison*, we check the legitimacy of our views. Festinger (1954) argues that we tend to compare ourselves to other people we consider to be similar to ourselves in some way. O'Fallon and Butterfield (2012) note how this tendency can lead to unethical attitudes in the workplace. If our colleagues are perceived to be adopting unethical attitudes in order to get ahead, we are likely to join them. Sharing attitudes with colleagues, no matter how dubious they may be, gives the individual a shared sense of identity with their fellow workmates as well as a means of getting ahead.

We consider social learning theory and the role of modelling in Chapter 8 on aggression; this concept is important when considering if aggression is a learned social behaviour rather than an innate one.

Bem's 'self-perception theory' (see also Chapters 3 and 4 for more detail on this theory) suggests that actually, when it comes to forming attitudes, we perhaps don't put much thought into it at all. Instead we look at our own behaviour and from that deduce what our attitudes must be. We will consider self-perception theory in more detail later in this chapter.

Cognitive theories emphasize the role of cognitive development in the formation of attitudes. As we acquire experience of objects in the social world we develop attitudes about them. These attitudes require something of a balancing act as we build more and more associative connections between them. For example, Heider's (1946) **balance theory** considers the objects that are cognitively represented within the mind of the individual. Balance theory proposes that individuals are motivated to maintain balance between all the attitudes held about these various

balance theory proposes that people will avoid having contradicting attitudes and evaluations of one object. If such inconsistency occurs, people are likely to adjust this objects. We have a preference for agreement or accordance. In the absence of information to the contrary we tend to assume people see the world in the same way we do. Heider's theory suggests that because we have a preference to maintain balance in our attitudes, we will do whatever costs least effort to retain it.

This issue of cognitive consistency is the cornerstone of Festinger's *Theory of Cognitive Dissonance* (1957), which asserts that people are motivated to keep their attitudes, beliefs and behaviour consistent. When they get out of line, people will reduce feelings of dissonance by changing their attitudes, beliefs or behaviour or may even justify having them to rationalize the discrepancy. We will return to this theory later in this chapter when we discuss the link between attitudes and behaviour.

Genetic influences on attitudes have also been reported within social psychology. It seems that our biology might also explain individual differences in attitudes. But to what extent? Twin studies have typically been used to examine the impact of biology and environment upon attitudes. This research has traditionally compared identical with non-identical twins, and those raised together with those raised apart, to try and tease out genetic and social influences on our attitudes. In their substantial review of published evidence on biological and environmental influences on human differences, Bouchard and McGue (2003) conclude that genetics plays a heavier role than the environment in influencing a range of human psychological traits, including attitudes. This is a finding shared across many subsequent studies that seek to establish the genetic contribution made to our attitudes. For example, Smith and his team (2012) report on the heritability of political attitudes. They suggest that whilst social influences on attitudes cannot be dismissed, neither can the greater contribution of biology. Likewise, Spotts and colleagues (2004) found that genetics plays a more significant part in forming twin Swedish women's attitudes towards marriage.

However, whilst we might debate the relative importance of biology over environment in forming attitudes, what we cannot ignore is the complex relationship between them, which makes pinpointing the exact extent tricky. Let's briefly note the findings of a study by Hatemi et al. (2015) on attitudes towards divorce to illustrate this point. These researchers found that whilst genetic heritability was a significant influence on attitudes towards divorce, it was the experience of getting divorced that was the biggest influencer on attitudes, especially for women. So in this example, it is the environment that exerts the strongest force over the attitude. And indeed, there is a wealth of evidence that shows when it comes to the formation of some attitudes, it is the environment that matters most. In another study, Eaves et al. (2008) found that genetics only accounted for a very small contribution to young people's (aged 11–18 years) attitudes towards religion. Here, parenting style and the family environment had more influence over young people than familial genetic material. Perhaps the take-home message here is that teasing biology and the environment apart to study their relative contribution to attitudes in a scientific way is complex, but clearly biology and environment both matter in forming our attitudes. In Chapter 14, we discuss the relationship between biology and environment in more detail.

Function of Attitudes

Attitudes of course, also have functions. They 'do' things. Perhaps most importantly, they immediately provide us with information about how to respond to an attitude-object. In Chapter 4, we discuss how human beings have developed a range of cognitive strategies to help them navigate their way around a complex world. Having attitudes about things focuses our attention, enabling us to filter out unnecessary or unimportant features of our environment. They also aid our memory, free up cognitive space to deal with other things, help us make decisions, and categorize the world in meaningful ways. For example, knowing that we have positive or negative attitudes towards fox-hunting helps us work out how to respond when confronted by a fox-hunting parade that goes through our village. Some researchers have proposed that the main function of attitudes also includes serving our psychological needs. The work of Daniel Katz has been at the forefront of developing a functional approach to the study of attitudes. Katz (1960) suggests attitudes have four main functions:

1. A knowledge function – they provide a sense of structure and order, helping us to explain and understand the world based on our knowledge of objects and our evaluations of them.
2. An instrumental function – they allow us to maximize our chances of receiving rewards and minimizing the likelihood of negative outcomes due to our evaluation of objects as 'good' or 'bad'. We will change our attitudes if it is likely to result in favourable rewards.
3. An ego defensive function – they protect threats to our sense of self by projecting insecurities about our self onto others. Attitudes can serve as a defence mechanism against anxiety.
4. A value-expressive function – they allow us to express and reinforce our sense of self and identity by displaying those attitudes we consider important.

Katz (1960) maintains that attitudes may serve one or more of these functions at any one time. Which ones they will fulfil depends upon the context in which it is presented. Katz further suggests that we will change our attitudes towards something when they no longer serve our psychological needs. So it isn't so much our perception of the attitude-object which changes, but our psychological requirements.

Social psychological work has tended to focus upon the structure of attitudes rather than their content and function. But, thankfully, there have been some attempts to empirically demonstrate Katz's functional approach. Vollum and Buffington-Vollum (2010) observed that people's support for the death penalty served a value-expressive function. It enabled those individuals to portray a particular self-image to the world, which is so important that she or he will hold on to that attitude even when presented with information that points out some of the problems of having a death penalty. Grewal et al. (2000) advise that understanding the value-expressive functions of attitudes can assist commercial companies in targeting products at consumers. Owning products helps people achieve a particular identity and status, therefore they have positive attitudes towards them. Knowing what identity someone wants to achieve can help in targeting a particular product at them.

Attitudes can also help or hinder us in coping during times of trouble. Van Zoonen and her research team (2016) revealed that amongst a sample of sub-clinical depressed participants, those who held positive attitudes towards professional health-care were much more likely to use it and feel in control of their psychological condition. Those with less favourable attitudes tended to cope without professional help, felt less in control, and relied more heavily on self-help. Indeed, it seems that once formed, attitudes are extremely resistant to change, as Lines (2005) found out when changes were proposed within the workplace. Employees expressed resistance to the changes based on their positive attitudes about their current working practices and structure. Change was perceived as a threat to jobs, regardless of any reassurance otherwise.

Attitude theorists have revised Katz's original functions, adding to the list. Herek (1987) identifies an *experiential schematic* function based on experience and stereotypes that help guide our reactions to objects. For example, Griffiths and Pedersen (2009) found that experience helped explain positive reactions to Muslim and indigenous Australians by residents in Perth. Those who had negative reactions towards these groups lacked direct positive experiences and instead were influenced by stereotypes. Similar findings are reported by Khan and Pedersen (2010) who observed the importance of value-expressive and experiential-schematic functions of attitudes in accepting Black African immigrants to Australia, and *indirect experiential schematic* (reliance on stereotypes) in rejecting them.

So it seems that attitudes only change when they no longer serve their function. It is important to remember that attitudes not only perform a function for the individual that holds them, but also social functions in establishing meaning in social interaction. We shall consider these social aspects of attitudes more closely later in this chapter.

Measuring Attitudes

So far we've noted the complex definitions, organization and functions of attitudes. We've already begun to see some of the problems in trying to capture them. They are organized in complex associative networks and are prone to change depending on the context in which they are produced. There are some attitudes we're not even consciously aware of. How can the social psychologist begin to measure them, if at all?

One of the earliest methods for studying attitudes was to simply ask people what they were. The *case method* asks people what their, or their friends', attitudes are towards something. These kinds of studies can require participants to verbally describe the attitudes (sometimes called the informal case method) or to write them down essay style (formal case method). For example, Bogardus (1925) asked Americans to outline their attitudes to Filipinos in this way. However, as early as the 1930s, the limitations of this approach were reported. Droba (1932) pointed out that while case studies provide us with some understanding of the development and depth of someone's attitudes, such descriptions cannot easily be subject to any kind of statistical analyses. Consequently, while different methods have been put forward, many social psychologists agree that the best way to study attitudes is quantitatively.

People, for example these climate change protesters, often display their attitudes publicly to express their sense of self-identity.
SOURCE: ©Gasper Butina/Shutterstock

Droba outlines some of the historical development of quantitative measures for studying attitudes in social psychology. For example, the *method of absolute ranking* requires participants to read a statement such as: 'Jews will try to get the best of a bargain even if they have to cheat to do so', and then indicate their attitude by choosing one of five options: 'All', 'Most', 'Many', 'Few', 'No'. Quick to administer but they have drawbacks, some of which may already be apparent to you. Firstly, participants are given very few choices to reflect their attitude. Secondly, how can we be sure that the choices have the same meaning for everyone who takes the test? What one participant takes 'Most' to mean, may be very different from another's definition. Thirdly, how do we know the distance between 'All' and 'Most' is equivalent to that between 'Most' and 'Many'? The alternative *method of relative ranking* requires participants to rank either attitude-objects in order of preference (e.g. nationalities) or attitude statements about an object. However, once again we have the problem of analysing such responses. How do we know that what one participant has ranked as number 1 (e.g. the French) is equivalent to someone else's number 1 rank? Does this reflect the same positive attitude in strength and intensity? The *graphic rating scale* is the indication of an attitude along a line. There are steps plotted along the line which may be represented by words, statements or numbers. Somewhere along the line the participant notes his or her attitude towards some object or idea. These could be completed to reflect the participant's own attitude or those of friends and family. The *method of paired comparisons,* first used by Thurstone (1928b), as shown in **Figure 5.1**, presented participants with a pair of words or statements, from which they must choose which one of the pair best reflected their attitude. Thurstone used this method to measure attitudes to different nationalities and races. None of these methods are perfect but acknowledgement of their limitations as well as their virtues has shaped modern-day social psychological use of attitude scales. It is from these early attempts to quantitatively measure attitudes that different attitude scales have been developed.

Let's consider some of the types of attitude scales currently used in social psychology.

The Thurstone Scale

Developed by Thurstone (1928a) it comprises a questionnaire containing 22 independent statements about a particular issue. The participant was asked to rate their feelings towards each of the items on a scale of 1–11, indicating whether they had favourable or unfavourable feelings towards it. This method of measuring attitudes was based on a one-component model of feelings towards an object. Those items that reflected a positive attitude were given higher numerical scores than those that were negative. The statements could then be statistically analysed.

A more recent example comes from Guffey et al. (2007) who used the Thurstone scale to examine attitudes towards the police by serving police officers and police agencies. On a scale of 1–11, participants rated how favourable each of the 27 statements presented to them was in evaluating police officers – 1 reflected extremely unfavourable, and 11 extremely favourable. The statements included: 'He/She possesses excellent judgement' and 'He/She possesses excellent moral character'.

The Likert Scale

This bipolar scaling method was developed to simplify the Thurstone questionnaire in terms of scoring. Likert (1932) produced a scale that contained statements

Method of Absolute Ranking
Choose the response which best reflects your attitude to the following statement:

'Jews will try to get the best of a bargain even if they have to cheat to do so'

All

Most

Many

Few

No

(from Droba, D.D. (1932). Methods for measuring attitudes. Psychological Bulletin, *29(5), 309–323.)*

Method of Relative Ranking
Arrange the following list of occupations in order of their social standing according to your own judgment:

Banker

Carpenter

Engineer

Clergyman

Professor

Factory Manager

Insurance Agent

Machinist

Man of Leisure

Soldier

(from Anderson, W.A. (1927). The occupational attitudes and choices of a group of college men, Part I. Social Forces, *6(2), 278–283.)*

Graphic Rating Scale
Indicate using an 'X', your own general political attitude:

Radicalism / Liberalism / Conservatism / Reactionaryism /

(from Rice, S.A. (1926). Differential changes of political preference under campaign stimulation. Journal of Abnormal and Social Psychology, *21(3), 297–303.)*

Method of Paired Comparisons
Underline the one nationality of the pair, that would you rather associate with:
Japanese – Italian

(from Thurstone, L.L. (1928). An experimental study of nationality preferences. Journal of General Psychology, *1, 405–425.)*

FIGURE 5.1 Early methods for measuring attitudes

(similar to the Thurstone scale); for example, 'A university education makes people more selfish', but this scale allowed for five response categories:

1 = Strongly disagree

2 = Disagree

3 = Neither disagree or agree

4 = Agree

5 = Strongly agree

For each item the participant ticks which numbered response best reflects their attitude to the statement presented. On completion of the scale the participant's scores are calculated and used as a measure of his or her attitudes towards a particular issue. In developing the attitude measurement instrument the researcher

Research close-up

Development and Validation of a Scale Measuring Attitudes toward Non-Drinkers

Source: *Regan, D., & Morrison, T. G. (2011).* Development and validation of a scale measuring attitudes toward non-drinkers. *Substance Use & Misuse, 46,* 580–590.

Introduction

Is binge-drinking a way of fitting in? Do we engage in excessive alcohol consumption to avoid the social embarrassment of being a non-alcohol drinker? This research was conducted in Ireland, a country that has one of the highest rates of binge-drinking in Europe. Social Identity Theory (SIT) proposes that individuals are motivated to identify with groups that they feel they belong to, and to evaluate those groups positively. In countries such as Ireland, where drinking alcohol is the 'norm', might non-drinkers constitute an outgroup that many people are motivated to avoid being identified with? Is this expressed in the form of negative attitudes towards non-drinkers, and excessive consumption of alcohol?

Method

Three studies aimed to find out whether attitudes towards non-drinkers motivated the quantity and frequency of alcohol consumption and binge-drinking. Whilst the first study tested the robustness of the Regan Attitudes towards Non-Drinkers Scale (RANDS), studies 2 and 3 assessed how well it predicted drinking behaviour. The RANDS contains 74 items such as: 'I would not see there being a problem socially, with myself being a non-drinker' and 'I would hate to be a non-drinker'.

In study 2, 148 undergraduate students of a university in Western Ireland, between the ages of 19 and 21 took part. They were given two questionnaires. The first asked them to estimate the amount of alcohol they drank, and how frequently they engaged in binge-drinking. The second was the RANDS. RANDS is an 11-item scale about attitudes towards non-drinkers. Attitudes are assessed using a 5-point Likert scale, where a high score indicates negative attitudes to non-drinkers.

In study 3, 236 individuals comprising students and non-students, with an age range of 17–63, took part. They were given six questionnaires. As in study 1, they were given a measure of the quantity and frequency of their alcohol consumption, and the RANDS. In addition they were also given a 5-point Likert scale to measure their *sensation-seeking behaviour,* with a high score denoting high levels of this behaviour. Participants were also given a 5-point Likert scale to measure their *fear of being negatively evaluated.* A high score denoted a greater fear of being negatively evaluated. They were also tested for their *need to belong.* This 5-point scale was scored such that a high score denoted high need to fit in with others. Finally, participants were given a *social-desirability* scale to check they were giving answers that reflected their actual behaviour and attitudes rather than reporting socially desirable ones.

Results

In both studies 2 and 3, attitudes on RANDS predicted the amount of alcohol participants consumed and the frequency with which they indulged in binge-drinking. The more negative their attitudes towards non-drinkers, the more likely they were to drink alcohol.

In study 3, participants under the age of 21 years reported higher quantities and frequencies of drinking alcohol than older participants. This younger age group also indicated a stronger need to belong, greater levels of sensation-seeking behaviour, and higher negative attitudes towards non-drinkers than those participants over the age of 21 years. However, scores on RANDS show no relationship with those on the fear of negative evaluation scale. For those over the age of 21 years, scores on RANDS correlate with sensation-seeking behaviour (but not for those under 21 years old). So, for the older age group, the more you engage in sensation-seeking behaviour, the more negative your attitudes are towards non-drinkers.

Discussion

Those people who express negative attitudes towards non-drinkers (as identified on RANDS) consume more alcohol, engage in binge-drinking, and have a stronger need to belong. However, attitudes towards non-drinkers are not related to a fear of negative evaluation, and for those under 21 years of age, it doesn't have any relationship with sensation-seeking either.

So it seems peer pressure and the desire to identify positively with 'normative' behaviour can involve excessive alcohol-drinking to avoid the risk of social exclusion as a non-drinker. Group boundaries between drinkers (normative) and non-drinkers (deviant) are marked in terms of behaviour (alcohol consumption) and attitudes. However, the authors note that their study concerned predominantly university students, so further research is needed into attitudes towards non-drinkers from a broader population.

Critical Reflections

The authors themselves note a limitation of this study with respect to the sample being university students. Whilst this study might tell us something about students, we might reasonably ask what does it reveal about the wider population? However, this is arguably not the only limitation of this study. These three studies asked students to self-report on their drinking behaviour, as well as their attitudes. We might wonder if there is any discrepancy between what people *say* they do and think and what they *actually* do and think. Can you think of any other ways in which we could study alcohol drinking behaviour and attitudes to non-drinkers?

What you will also see at the start of this paper is the assumption that drinking alcohol in Ireland is the 'norm'. Might you want to question this assumption? And if so, how would you do this?

Finally, we can ask questions about the **reliability** and **validity** of this study. How replicable do you think this study is, across time and space? Do you think you would get the same results? And to what extent do you think this study captures the link between attitudes and drinking behaviour?

reliability refers to the consistency of a psychological study or experiment to produce the same results over time and space

validity is the extent to which a psychological study or experiment measures what it sets out to measure ensures that all the statements used are good indicators of attitudes (i.e. they provoke scores of 1–2 or 4–5), and any ambiguous ones, or those that simply do not provoke an attitude (regularly getting a score of 3), are removed (a process sometimes referred to as 'item analysis'). The Likert scale remains a very popular measuring tool for attitudes in social psychology. For example, Long et al. (2012) examined predominantly female students' attitudes towards sex-workers, using the Hostility Towards Women Likert scale as part of their investigation. This scale includes 10 statements such as 'Sex workers are unattractive' and 'Sex workers are responsible for sexually transmitted infections'. Participants rate on a scale of 1–7 how much they disagree (1 – strongly disagree) or agree (7 – strongly agree) with each item. They found that those who held more hostile attitudes towards women held negative stereotypical attitudes towards sex-workers.

Osgood's Semantic Differential Scale

Unlike Thurstone and Likert scales, Charles Osgood's semantic differential scale does not use statements, but instead asks participants to rate their feelings on a topic on a bipolar scale of opposing adjectives. For example:

Government's policy on tackling economic recession								
Good	1	2	3	4	5	6	7	Bad
Strong								Weak
Nice								Evil
Informed								Misguided

On a series of seven points (with a midway point) ranging from one adjective to its opposing other, the participant rates their feelings about the issue in question. Osgood makes the case that attitudes contain emotional meaning (connotative) reflected in our use of adjectives to describe how we feel about something (e.g. good/bad, nice/evil). Osgood proposed that there are essentially three evaluative dimensions which people use in attitudes: activity, evaluation and potency.

Cazáres (2010) used the Osgood semantic differential scale to examine psychology students' attitudes towards the use of technology in their classes. The scale consisted of 28 bipolar adjectives (i.e. Necessary – Not Necessary) presented on a scale of 1–7. What she discovered was that attitudes towards the use of technology in the classroom did not predict proficiency at using it.

The development of attitude scales has proved popular. They are extremely quick to construct and convenient to administer and score. But, they do suffer from some problems such as restricting people's responses to a narrow range of options and inducing what is sometimes called **acquiescence biases** (just saying yes/agreeing to everything!). One obvious problem with attitude scales such as these is that of **social desirability**. Might people be simply giving us socially desirable attitude expressions rather than their true attitudes? If so, how accurate can our measures be? As we shall see, this becomes an issue when trying to study people's prejudicial attitudes. Will someone self-report that they hold prejudiced attitudes to old people, homosexuals, women? Unlikely. We also know that people are often unaware of their attitudes. They hold implicit attitudes. How can they inform us about attitudes of which they are unaware?

acquiescence bias occurs when participants consistently respond 'yes' to all items in a questionnaire, regardless of what's being asked

social desirability refers to the tendency of participants to respond in a way that will be viewed favourably by others, including the researcher

The quantitative measures outlined so far rely on people being able to self-report on their attitudes accurately, which as we've noted can be problematic for several reasons. There are some ways around this. One way is to use *symbolic attitude measures*. These present statements that are more subtle in their approach. Consider this example from a questionnaire to look at Australians' attitudes to refugees (Schweitzer et al., 2007): 'The quality of social services available to Australians has remained the same despite refugees coming to Australia.' The researchers found that using this subtle approach revealed some worrying prejudices towards refugees in over half the sample. These prejudices related to perceived threats to Australians' welfare and resources (realistic threats), as well as cultural values (symbolic threats). But there are problems here too. Whilst this may ensure a less monitored response, it may also rely on knowledge rather than attitudes towards refugees. Another way is to obtain physiological measures of attitudes, such as heart rate, skin resistance, pupil dilation. These are not usually under our conscious control and can be measured without the participant realizing it is their attitudes that are being studied. For example, Walla et al. (2011) note some interesting physiological differences in their participants when shown 20 brand names flashed on a screen for 5 seconds. They had to rate on a scale of 1–5 how likely they would be to buy a product carrying this brand name. They found that for those brand names they liked, participants had reduced eye blinks, and decreased heart-rate and electrical skin conductance, than when they saw brands they didn't like. The authors suggest this is a physiological indication of the emotional component of attitudes held about these particular brands. However, the problem with these kinds of measures is that it is difficult to relate a physiological response to an attitude (Cacioppo & Petty, 1981). Physiological responses happen in response to all kinds of environmental features (e.g. the heating, the lighting, the presence of someone in the room). Can we be sure it's in response to the attitude we're interested in?

Another method that's been used is observational techniques. These are really only useful when the person being observed is unaware that they are the subject of an observation. Awareness of being observed can lead to changes in behaviour, which may reflect social desirability responses (as in self-reports). Watching people can tell us a lot about their attitudes. You may have witnessed the non-verbal behaviour of a group of friends sitting down for a meal. Who they choose to sit next to, and who they avoid, tells us a lot about their attitudes towards certain people. Bogardus' **social distance scale** (1925) has been developed and used in social psychology to study attitudes towards ethnic and racial groups. We are more likely to share our personal space with those people we like, than those we do not. To illustrate this empirically Dogra and colleagues (2012) used the social distance scale to examine the attitudes of Nigerian children towards people with mental illness. They found that these children held very negative attitudes towards people who are mentally ill. These negative attitudes were reflected in maintenance of social and physical distance from the mentally ill. They didn't socialise with those they considered of poor mental health and actively avoided sharing physical space with these individuals.

social distance scale measures people's willingness to have close social contact with people from diverse social groups

Another way to get around the problems associated with measures of explicitly expressed attitudes is to measure those attitudes we hold unconsciously. Greenwald et al. (1998), wanted to study implicit attitudes and the influence they have on behaviour. To do so, they developed the **implicit association test (IAT)**. The most prevalent IATs study race bias (see Chapter 13 on prejudice) measuring associations between the presentation of black faces and negative words. IATs have even been used to measure racial bias in young children (Dunham et al., 2014). They are also adopted as a method in the study of other kinds of prejudices such as ageism (e.g. Hummert et al., 2002), sexism (Rudman & Glick, 2008), facial disfigurement (Stock et al., 2013; Stone & Wright, 2012), obesity (Waller et al., 2012) and even cybersex addiction (Snagowski et al., 2015). More recently, they've been used to predict people's intentions to buy electric cars (Bennett & Vijaygopal, 2018). IATs have become increasingly popular as they appear to avoid the tricky problems faced by explicit measures such as faking responses in attending to concerns with social desirability.

implicit association test (IAT) an implicit method of measuring attitudes based on automatic associations that exist between objects and concepts

What happens in an IAT? Well, here's a standard example of an IAT design. Participants are faced with four sets of stimuli comprising two types of attitude objects (e.g. old people and young people), and two types of words based on 'valence' (attractiveness and aversiveness). During the test, the participant is presented with pairs of the attitude object (e.g. a picture of a young face) with a valence word (e.g. attractive). The task of the respondent is simply to decide as quickly as they can whether the valence word is Good or Bad, indicating their decision by pressing a computer response key. If we associate some things together (e.g. young people as attractive) we should be very quick to recognize that the valence word is Good. However, if the attitude object is paired with a valence word we wouldn't normally associate them with (e.g. a young face and the word 'slow') we should be much slower to recognize that this is a Bad word. To give a research example, Brand et al. (2011) measured athletes' attitudes towards illegal doping using an IAT. Athletes were given words to indicate two types of attitude object: those relating to illegal doping substances (e.g. 'peptide hormones', 'amphetamines') and those relating to tea (e.g. 'herbal', 'hibiscus flowers'). These words were then paired with valence words (e.g. 'joy', 'agony'). The speed at which they recognized the valence word as Good or Bad was measured. What Brand found was that his athletes were much quicker to recognize Bad words when they were paired with doping substances than when paired with tea words. His conclusion? Athletes, thankfully, hold negative attitudes towards doping substances.

Champions of IAT tests argue that the tests rely solely on automatic processes and as participants have no conscious control over them, they are robust tests of attitudes. But IATs have come under scrutiny from other researchers. One criticism concerns the **construct validity** of these tests. Are they actually a measure of attitudes, or of something else? Eric Siegel (Siegel et al., 2012) is sceptical. He argues there is a lack of consistency on these tests by individuals over time. The context in which these tests take place seems to have some effect on people's responses. Rather than attending fully to the stimulus material provided in the test, participants may find themselves responding to cues in the environment in which the test takes place, be that the physical environment and/or the researcher conducting the experiment, which affects how quickly they respond to the IAT. Siegel also suggests that these tests may be a measure of processing speed rather than attitudes. You may simply be very quick to respond to these kinds of tasks. If we compare younger people with older people we may find older people are slower to respond. Is this because they hold different attitudes or because their

construct validity the extent to which a study or test actually measures the construct it set out to measure processing speed is slower? In their review of IAT studies conducted with children, Rae and Olson (2018) note the range of mixed evidence for the reliability and validity of such tests ranging from strong to none at all! The researchers report that how the IAT is designed and administered and the lag-time between test and replication of the test (test-retest) can have an impact on how reliable the IAT is. They also point to research that suggests that whilst IATs are reliable measures for some attitudes, such as race, they are poor for others, such as attitudes about the self. The evidence is also mixed for IATs, **predictive validity**. For example, what children score on an IAT may not be a terribly accurate predictor for future behaviour. Similarly, developmental changes within the individual may account for differing results obtained on an IAT by that individual over time. These criticisms are not limited to IAT studies with children. They have also been levelled at studies with adult participants. Many critics of IATs have pointed to the rather big leap that is required to assume that how quickly you respond to images flashed on a screen predicts how you think about and interact with someone of a different race, or weight, or age, or religion, and so on (for further detail on this critique see Oswald et al., 2013, 2015).

predictive validity the extent to which the results obtained on an experiment or study predict results obtained on a different but related measure

In 2008 the American Psychological Association published a debate titled, IAT: Fad or Fabulous? (Azar, 2008), outlining criticisms and strengths of IATs. Its conclusion is that the debate over the usefulness of implicit association tests is by no means resolved. Like all attitude tests, it has its limitations and virtues. The conclusions we arrive at from an attitude test, including IATs, can have real-world implications if we take them seriously. So perhaps a way forward is the one proposed by Greenwald et al. (2009): that we should use both explicit and implicit attitude measures and acknowledge those limitations and virtues.

Observing people's seating arrangements and non-verbal behaviour can sometimes offer some interesting insights into their attitudes towards each other.

SOURCE: ©Purestock/SuperStock

As we move to consider the relationship between attitudes and behaviour, we shall come across many empirical examples of studies using various methods for measuring attitudes (and behaviour). On our journey we can ponder their relative strengths and weaknesses in providing social psychologists with an understanding of the nature and expression of attitudes and their role in the performance of behaviour.

How Well Do our Attitudes Predict our Behaviour?

To what extent, and under what conditions, do the attitudes of the heart drive our outward actions? Why were social psychologists at first surprised by a seemingly small connection between attitudes and actions?

A blow to the supposed power of attitudes came when social psychologist Allan Wicker (1969) reviewed several dozen research studies covering a wide variety of people, attitudes and behaviours. Wicker offered a shocking conclusion: people's expressed attitudes hardly predicted their varying behaviours.

- Student attitudes towards cheating bore little relation to the likelihood of their actually cheating.

- Attitudes towards the church were only modestly linked with church attendance on any given Sunday.
- Self-described racial attitudes provided little clue to behaviours in actual situations.

An example of the disjuncture between attitudes and actions is what Daniel Batson and his colleagues (1997a, 2002; Batson & Thompson, 2001) call 'moral hypocrisy' (appearing moral while avoiding the costs of being so). Their classic studies presented people with an appealing task (where the participant could earn raffle tickets towards a cash prize) and a dull task with no positive consequences. The participants had to assign themselves to one of the tasks and a supposed second participant to the other. Only 1 in 20 believed that assigning the positive task to themselves was the more moral thing to do, yet 80 per cent did so. In follow-up experiments on moral hypocrisy, participants were given coins they could flip privately if they wished. Even if they chose to flip, 90 per cent assigned themselves to the positive task! (Was that because they could specify the consequences of heads and tails after the coin toss?) In yet another experiment, Batson put a sticker on each side of the coin, indicating what the flip outcome would signify. Still, 24 of 28 people who made the toss assigned themselves to the positive task. When morality and greed were put on a collision course, greed won.

If people don't walk the same line that they talk, it is little wonder that attempts to change behaviour by changing attitudes often fail. Warnings about the dangers of smoking affect only minimally those who already smoke if used as the only means. Increasing public awareness of the desensitizing and brutalizing effects of television violence has stimulated many people to voice a desire for less violent programming – yet programmes that depict violent murder remain as popular as ever. Sex education programmes have often influenced *attitudes* towards abstinence and condom use without affecting long-term abstinence and condom use *behaviours*. Aikman et al. (2006) discovered that having positive attitudes towards healthy foods did not predict eating them. Rather, taste and having eaten food in the past was a better predictor of current eating habits. Healthcare professionals tasked with advising smokers on the negative effects of smoking are often smokers themselves (La Torre et al., 2014). We are, it seems, a population of hypocrites.

All in all, the developing picture of what controls behaviour emphasized external social influences, such as others' behaviour and expectations, and played down internal factors, such as attitudes and personality. The original thesis that attitudes determine actions was countered during the 1960s by the antithesis that attitudes determine virtually nothing.

So it seems that what people *say* often differs from what they *do*. This has resulted in social psychologists seeking to find out why.

When Attitudes Predict Behaviour

The reason why our behaviour and our expressed attitudes differ is that both are subject to other influences. Back in the 1980s, one social psychologist counted 40 factors that complicate their relationship (Triandis, 1982; see also Kraus, 1995). But if we could just neutralize the other influences on behaviour – make all other things equal – might attitudes accurately predict behaviours?

When Social Influences on What We Say Are Minimal

Unlike a physician measuring heart rate, social psychologists never get a direct reading on attitudes. Rather, we measure *expressed* attitudes. Like other behaviours, expressions are subject to outside influences. Sometimes, for example, we say what we think others want to hear.

Today's social psychologists have research tools at their disposal for minimizing social influences, such as social desirability, on people's attitude reports. One method offers a 'bogus pipeline' to the heart. It wires people to a fake lie detector, which the participants are told is real. In one study that used the bogus pipeline technique, students admitted less acceptance of someone who has AIDS once hooked up than what they had suggested prior to this (Grover & Miller, 2012). No wonder people who are first persuaded that lie detectors work may then admit the truth – in which case, the lie detector has worked! (Note the irony of deceiving people to elicit their truthfulness.)

When Other Influences on Behaviour Are Minimal

On any occasion, it is not only our inner attitudes that guide us but also the situation we face. Social influences can be enormous – enormous enough to induce people to violate their deepest convictions. So, would *averaging* many occasions enable us to detect more clearly the impact of our attitudes?

Let's consider a research example to illustrate this. People's general attitude towards politics is a poor predictor of whether they will vote in a particular political election. Going to the poll station to vote that day may be impeded by bad weather, illness, or a dislike for all candidates. However, political attitudes predict quite well voting behaviour over time (Fishbein & Ajzen, 2011; Kahle & Berman, 1979). The findings define a *principle of aggregation:* the effects of an attitude become more apparent when we look at a person's aggregate or average behaviour rather than at isolated acts. We also need to take into account if people actually can engage in the behaviour they have an attitude towards. For example, someone may have very positive attitudes towards vigorous exercise yet not be able to engage in such exercise for health reasons.

When Attitudes Specific to the Behaviour Are Examined

Ajzen and Fishbein (1977, 2005; Fishbein & Ajzen, 2011) suggest that when the measured attitude is a general one – say, an attitude towards Asians – and the behaviour is very specific – say, a decision whether to help a particular Asian in a particular situation – we should not expect a close correspondence between words and actions. Indeed, report Fishbein and Ajzen, in 26 out of 27 such research studies, attitudes did not predict behaviour. But self-reported attitudes did predict self-reports of behaviour in all 26 studies they could find in which the measured attitude was directly pertinent to the situation. Thus, attitudes towards the general concept of 'health fitness' poorly predict specific exercise and dietary practices, but an individual's attitudes about the costs and benefits of jogging are a fairly strong predictor of whether he or she jogs regularly. Ajzen and Fishbein's **theory of reasoned action (TRA)** offers us a model for explaining the relationship between attitude and behaviour.

theory of reasoned action (TRA) that a person's intended behaviour is contingent upon their attitude about that behaviour and subjective norms

The Theory of Reasoned Action

To predict behavioural intention we need to know four things about a person:

1. their expectation of important or significant others – i.e. how they will view your behaviour (subjective norms)
2. their attitudes towards the behaviour (positive or negative)
3. their behavioural intention
4. their actual behaviour.

What is immediately striking about this approach is that it goes beyond simply a consideration of attitude and behaviour. It also includes an understanding of subjective norms (what other people think about the behaviour) and intentions for behaviour. This theory has received much empirical support. Four dozen experimental tests confirm that inducing new intentions induces new behaviour (Webb & Sheeran, 2006).

However, this theory has one quite serious limitation. It can only be applied to those behaviours we have conscious control of (volitional control). What about those behaviours we have less, or no, control of? How can those be understood in relation to attitudes?

The Theory of Planned Behaviour

Acknowledging this limitation, Ajzen revisited the theory to include an additional element, that of 'perceived behavioural control'. This new element refers to how much control someone believes they have in doing a behaviour. Ajzen thought this was probably a crucial part in working out whether they would perform it or not. So the renamed **theory of planned behaviour (TPB)** now accounted for those behaviours we have less control of (see **Figure 5.2**).

theory of planned behaviour (TPB) as TRA, but with the addition that people's behaviour is shaped by their confidence in being able to perform it, or having it under their control

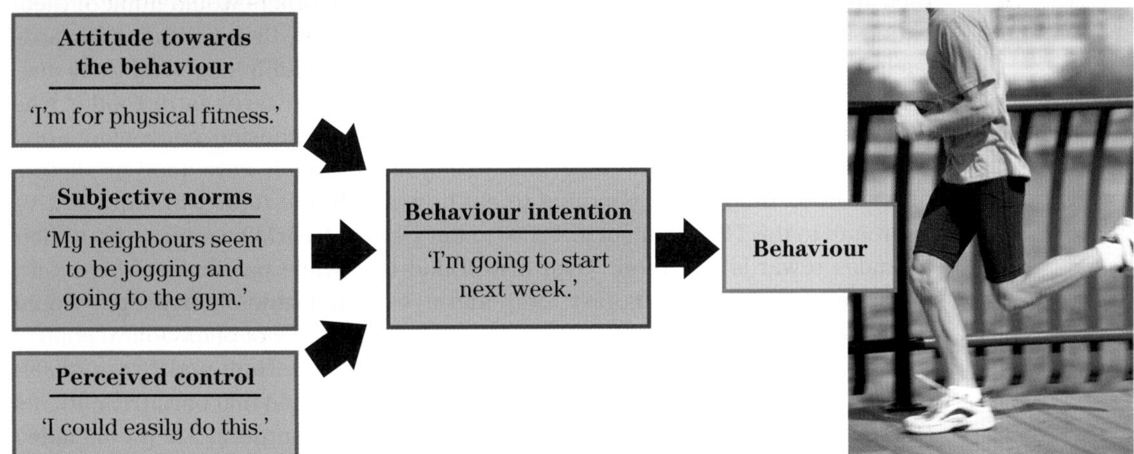

FIGURE 5.2 The theory of planned behaviour

Icek Ajzen, working with Martin Fishbein, has shown that one's (a) attitudes, (b) perceived social norms, and (c) feelings of control together determine one's intentions, which guide behaviour.

Compared with their general attitudes towards a healthy lifestyle, people's specific attitudes regarding jogging predict their jogging behaviour much better.

SOURCE: ©Tom Grill/Getty Images

The theory of planned behaviour has received a lot of empirical support. For example, Smith et al. (2008) found that men are less likely to seek psychological help (or therapy) than women. Using the TPB the authors found that men hold negative attitudes about psychological help, being worried how they will be viewed by others and society if they seek such services. Cha et al. (2008) discovered that the TPB could explain gender differences in condom use among Korean students. While peer norms (i.e. what significant others will think) were important for men in predicting condom use, it wasn't important for women. The authors suggest this reflects a cultural norm which dictates that men can discuss sexual activities with others but for women this is taboo. Wood and Griffiths (2004) used the TPB to explain the relationship between young people's attitudes to gambling and playing the National Lottery and scratchcards in the UK. They revealed a range of factors to explain why young people engage in such behaviour, including the positive reinforcement of gambling from parents, friends and society, and that it is often not recognized as gambling. Of particular interest is the role of perceived behavioural control in this study. Wood and Griffiths found that when they asked participants about the likelihood of winning, many participants thought they had a good chance of doing so. There's a belief they can control the odds of winning (see the **illusion of control** noted in Chapters 4 and 15). The authors themselves point to the **availability heuristic** we also mention in Chapters 4 and 15, which suggests that in the absence of detailed information, people make assumptions on the basis of the limited information they do have. Exposed to the publicity given to winners, gamblers do indeed believe it could be them.

illusion of control perception of uncontrollable events as subject to one's control or as more controllable than they are

availability heuristic a rule of thumb that judges the likelihood of things based on their availability in memory. If something comes readily to mind, we presume it to be commonplace

The TPB has been extensively applied to health research to investigate the relationship between attitudes and healthy eating behaviour. In the Netherlands, De Bruijn et al. (2008) noted that the TPB is a good predictor of the amount of saturated fat an adult consumes. Their Dutch participants were asked how often they ate food high in saturated fat, what they believed others would think of them eating such food, what kinds of food they usually eat, their attitudes towards such food, and how much control they believed they had in choosing their diet. While their participants often held negative attitudes towards fatty food it was their perceived lack of control over their diet (e.g. choosing convenient food due to a busy lifestyle) and their past eating habits which were good predictors of what food they would continue to eat now and in the future. In a qualitative approach to the TPB, Dunn et al. (2008) interviewed Australian adults about their attitudes towards fast food. They also found that while participants held very negative attitudes towards fast food, and even noted how other people would think badly of them for eating it, it was their perceived lack of behavioural control over their diet that led to the consumption of fast food. Hunt and Gross (2009) compared the TRA and the TPB on predicting the likelihood that bariatric patients (the extremely obese) would engage in exercise post-surgery. They concluded that perceived behavioural control, embedded within the TPB, was the single best indicator of intentions to exercise and self-reports of doing so.

So we can see that the relationship between attitudes and behaviour is complicated by a range of other factors.

In some research work, the TPB has been modified slightly to include 'identity'. One example comes from Giles et al. (2004). They incorporated the TPB to predict whether students at the University of Ulster would give blood when the blood donation service arrived. The basis of their prediction rested on the basis of the answers the students had given on a questionnaire prior to the arrival of the blood donation service. On that questionnaire, students were asked about their attitudes towards blood donation, what other people would think if they donated blood and their ability to give blood. In addition to this, the researchers also included an item about their self-identity (e.g. 'To give blood is an important part of who I am'). When they analysed the data in relation to who actually donated blood, they found a correlation between having blood donation as part of one's self-identity and donating.

Further elaboration on the relationship between identity and caring about what others think is offered by social identity theorists. They report a body of evidence that reveals we only seem to care about the opinions of those we share a social identity with (our fellow ingroup members). If we briefly return to the study by Giles and her team (2004), the decision to give blood will be impacted upon by what they believe their fellow students will think of that act (ingroup members). Social identity theorists refer to this social pressure as **subjective norms**, which are formed around the expectations of fellow group members (Hogg & Smith, 2007) (see Chapter 12 for a detailed account of social identity theory).

subjective norms the exertion of social pressure based on the perception and expectations of important others, such as fellow ingroup members, that guide our actions

Although the TPB has received considerable empirical support, and is very popular in applied areas such as health research, it has been subject to some criticism. Fazio and Olson (2003) think that the theory requires too specific a definition of the attitude for it to be linked to behaviour. As they suggest, discovering the attitude towards 'eating chocolate on the counter within the next two minutes' leads to subsequently eating it, would not be very surprising. Perhaps in its efforts to pin down the detailed relationship between specific attitude and specific behaviour, the TPB has lost sight of relating more general enduring attitudes to behaviour? Fazio and Olson's biggest criticism though, of the TPB, is that it only considers intentional behaviour. The TPB tends to assume that we cogitate and deliberate over whether we want to, can do, and what others will think about us if we do behave in a particular way. Considering the automaticity of attitudes in helping us to navigate our way around our environment, it seems likely then that we often just behave accordingly but thoughtlessly. We do not always ruminate over our behaviour before we do it. We don't worry what our parents will think, whether the behaviour fits in with our image of ourselves, or whether we can actually succeed. Behaviour can be spontaneous rather than carefully thought through.

So far we have seen two conditions under which attitudes will predict behaviour:

1 when we minimize other influences upon our attitude statements and on our behaviour, and

2 when the attitude is specifically relevant to the observed behaviour.

There is a third condition: an attitude predicts behaviour better when the attitude is potent.

When Attitudes Are Potent

Much of our behaviour is automatic. We act out familiar cultural scripts without reflecting on what we're doing. We respond to people we meet in the hall with an automatic 'Hi'. We answer the restaurant cashier's question 'How was your meal?' by saying, 'Fine', even if we found it tasteless.

Such mindlessness is adaptive. It frees our minds to work on other things. For habitual behaviours – seat belt use, coffee consumption, class attendance – conscious intentions hardly are activated. As the philosopher Alfred North Whitehead (1911) argued, 'Civilization advances by extending the number of operations which we can perform without thinking about them.' However, we need to exercise some caution here, as mindlessness can also be maladaptive. Let's consider an example that might be, unfortunately, familiar to many of us! In their study of Dutch students, Verhoeven et al. (2014) showed that engagement with habitual activities such as watching television, triggered snacking on unhealthy foods such as cookies and crisps. It was only when students were made aware of their eating habits, that snacking behaviours were curbed.

In novel situations, where our behaviour is less automatic, attitudes become more potent. Lacking a script, we think before we act. If we are prompted to think about our attitudes before acting, our behaviour might be guided in our own best interests. Consider an example from Zimbabwe; a country with one of the highest rates of HIV in the world. Young women are most affected due to inequality in relationships where the right to decline sex or insist on condom use is frowned upon (AVERT, 2017). In 2001, Schatz and Dzvimbo encouraged 3,429 high school students in Zimbabwe to reflect on their attitudes towards a variety of sex-related topics such as marriage, gender, sexual practices and culture. What they found was that cultural gender-role expectations guided attitudes towards these sex-related topics. For women, this included a lack of empowerment to control one's own sexual behaviour (see Chapter 14 for more discussion on gender roles), despite the desire to do so. These students were also asked to review current sex education provision, noting which seemed appropriate and which did not. The researchers make the point that young people's attitudes to sex are important and that they should be empowered to contribute to sex education and health programmes to ensure that what they provide speaks directly to their young audience. In doing so, current health-care and educational interventions which are trying to address the HIV and AIDS epidemic in the country and create greater equality between men and women, will become more effective in achieving their aims. In 2017, new cases of HIV dropped for the first time in Zimbabwe since the initial outbreak. This has been attributed, in part, to more effective education programmes that focus on attitudes to create behaviour change (AVERT, 2017). Our attitudes become potent *if* we think about them.

'Thinking is easy, acting difficult, and to put one's thoughts into action, the most difficult thing in the world'.

Goethe, 1749–1832

Social psychologists have established that self-conscious people usually are in touch with their attitudes (Carver, 2003; Duval & Wicklund, 1972; Miller & Grush, 1986). This chimes with what some researchers have termed our 'inner speech' that informs and guides us with respect to who we are, what we like and don't like, how we'll act and so on (Morin, 2017; Morin & Everett, 1990). Rather conveniently, this suggests that another way to induce people to focus on their attitudes is to *make them self-aware*, perhaps by having them act in front of a mirror (Carver & Scheier, 1981). Maybe you, too, can recall suddenly being acutely aware of yourself upon entering a room with a large mirror. Other researchers have found similar results: making people self-aware in this way promotes consistency between attitudes and actions (Backåberg et al., 2015; Silvia & Philips, 2012; Winston & Gervis, 2006).

Research close-up

Assessing Public Attitudes and Behaviour to Household Waste in Cameroon

Source: Mbeng, L. O., Probert, J., Phillips, P. S., & Fairweather, R. (2009). Assessing public attitudes and behaviour to household waste management in Cameroon to drive strategy development: A Q methodological approach. *Sustainability, 1*(3), 556–572.

Introduction

Doula is the capital of Cameroon, with over 2 million residents. This number is rapidly growing at a rate of 5 per cent per year. As such, household waste management is a pressing issue as numbers increase. Social scientists recognize the importance of changing attitudes and behaviours to waste management globally. In particular, attention needs to be paid to developing countries, such as Cameroon, where the infrastructure may not be there to deal with these issues at a municipal level. Therefore, individuals need to take responsibility for their waste. This study examined participants' attitudes and behaviours about waste management in Doula.

Method

Thirty participants based in Doula, aged 22–64 years, were recruited for the study; 18 were male and 12 female. They were **theoretically sampled** chosen for their differing socio-economic, demographic and geographical backgrounds to try and capture heterogeneity within the sample. Participants were given 50 opinion statements, covering waste management themes of: best practice, pro-environmental behaviour, environmental and health impacts, market for recyclates, recycling and reuse, waste prevention and minimization, incentives, public participation and acceptability. They were asked to rate their agreement or disagreement with each statement, on a scale from –5 to +5. Examples are:

theoretical sampling also known as purposive sampling, this defines a sampling method where participants are recruited on the basis of their characteristics which are of interest to the study

- 'I re-use plastic bags when I can.'
- 'I know how to compost household waste.'
- 'I think second-hand goods are better.'
- 'I think a community composting scheme is a necessity.'

After completing this exercise, participants were interviewed about their views on household waste and its management.

Results

A statistical analysis (Principal Components Analysis) of participants' responses to the 50 statements revealed 4 main factors, or themes, running through them. Each factor was explained in more depth using the interview data. These factors are:

1. **Environmentally Concerned Information Seeker:** This factor describes a majority view that people in Cameroon wish to behave in a more environmentally friendly way. However, there is a need for more information on how to change behaviour. For example, one respondent states: 'Cameroonians are prepared to go "green" but need assistance with regards to advocacy, capacity building, information and education (formal and informal).'
2. **Pragmatist:** In Cameroon there is a gender and age bias with respect to environmental concerns and practices. The analysis and interviews revealed that women do most of the composting and

express the highest levels of concern regarding environmental and hazardous waste. Young people also express high levels of concern, noting a moral responsibility for engaging in environmentally friendly behaviours such as composting. However, these attitudes do not necessarily translate into behaviours for this group. Instead, they request a more transparent relationship between private and public agencies to implement change.

3. **The Concerned Consumer:** This defines a concern with over-consumption and unnecessary waste for some respondents. Recycling and minimizing consumption are considered good things to do and are a matter of personal responsibility but wider waste management needs to be tackled at a public level.
4. **Inactive Composter:** This theme notes that composting and recycling are considered time-consuming activities and the benefits are unknown. Consequently, some participants do not do any. Municipal authorities need to get involved in educating people about the benefits of waste management.

Discussion

To summarize, different people have different views on waste management and their own, and the municipal authorities, responsibility for it. When designing and implementing waste management policies and awareness campaigns, these perceptions need to be taken into account so that groups can be more effectively targeted for behaviour change. Attitudes will only translate into behaviours when barriers, such as gender, education, and technology are overcome.

Critical Reflections

This is a mixed-methods (quantitative and qualitative) study into people's attitudes and self-reported behaviours about waste management in Cameroon. Let's reflect on what the researchers set out to do and the methods they used to do it. To process and analyse their participants' responses to the 50-item questionnaire, the researchers used Principal Components Analysis (PCA). It is helpful if researchers can convey clearly to their reader how processing and analysing of the data has been done. This means that anyone reading the paper should be able to *replicate* the methods used. If you have a look at the original paper, one criticism that can be made is the lack of clarity on how PCA was carried out. Additionally, when you interview participants you should clearly describe to your reader how the data generated from them is processed and analysed. Again, not much is said about this. Nor is it clear how the results of the PCA and the findings from the interviews were integrated. Instead the focus is on the findings. Critical evaluation of research is not just about what was done, but also how it is communicated. If we turn our attention to evaluate what was done in this study, to what extent do you think the researchers successfully captured their respondents' attitudes and behaviours? The research relies on overt self-reports of both. Do you think there could be any other influences on the responses participants gave, which were not accounted for by the study? In other words, how well does this study tick the '**ecologically valid**' box? And to what extent can we generalize from this work? How might you address these concerns in a follow-up study?

ecological validity the extent to which findings observed in a study reflect what actually occurs in natural settings. Psychological laboratory research has been criticized for its low ecological validity

When Does our Behaviour Affect our Attitudes?

If social psychology has taught us anything it is that we are likely not only to think ourselves into a way of acting but also to act ourselves into a way of thinking. What evidence supports that assertion?

Now we turn to the more startling idea that behaviour determines attitudes. It's true that we sometimes stand up for what we believe. But it's also true that we come to believe in what we stand up for. Social psychological theories inspired much of the research that underlies that conclusion.

Role Playing

The word **role** is borrowed from the theatre and, as in the theatre, refers to actions expected of those who occupy a particular social position. In Chapter 3 we consider how the roles we perform shape our sense of self. When enacting new social roles, we may at first feel fake, and perhaps experience what has been termed **imposter syndrome**. But with time, our sense of unease may lessen as we adjust into the new role.

role a set of norms that defines how people in a given social position ought to behave

imposter syndrome defines a fear of being exposed as a fraud based on perceived self-incompetency

Think of a time when you stepped into some new role – perhaps your first days on a job or at university. That first week on campus, for example, you may have been supersensitive to your new social situation and tried valiantly to act mature, competent and as though you belonged there. At such times you may have felt self-conscious. The behaviour felt forced. You observed your new speech and actions because they weren't natural to you. However, with time and repeated experiences of your new role as a university student or employee, talking the talk and walking the walk feel more natural as they become part of your everyday reality.

Role-playing has been widely used in educational contexts. Zamboanga et al. (2016) found that role-playing exercises for students assisted with awareness about the challenges people face as they try to settle into a culture different from their own. As a consequence, students seem to become more empathetic towards people who have switched cultures (for some further recent and interesting examples see Kilgour et al., 2015; Shapiro & Leopold, 2012; Westrup & Planader, 2013). Video-gaming has also been used to examine the use of role-play in changing prejudicial attitudes. In their study on attitudes towards Palestinians and Israelis, Alhabash and Wise (2012) asked their US participants to complete an attitude questionnaire about people from Palestine and Israel. The researchers note that in the US, attitudes are generally more favourable towards Israel than Palestine. Participants were invited to play the video-game Peacemaker, in which they were randomly assigned to either the role of the Palestine President or the Israeli Prime Minister. Peacemaker is a game based on the Israeli–Palestinian conflict. The aim of the game is conveniently reflected in the title: be the peacemaker. Alhabash and Wise found no change in attitudes towards Israelis for those who played the Israeli Prime Minister. However, those participants who played the role of the Palestinian President displayed more positive explicit attitudes to Palestinians generally and more negative explicit attitudes to Israelis, after playing the game than they had held previously. That said, whilst their explicit attitudes changed, a test of their implicit attitudes using an implicit association test (IAT) showed no change. Moreover as the researchers themselves recognize, what we do not know is how long term these explicit attitude changes are.

Role-playing has proven to be an effective tool in changing attitudes as well as behaviours.

SOURCE: ©alexkorobov2019/Shutterstock

When Saying Becomes Believing

Tory Higgins and his colleagues (Echterhoff & Higgins, 2017; Echterhoff et al., 2013; Higgins & McCann, 1984; Higgins &

Rholes, 1978) have illustrated how saying becomes believing – or what they call the SIB (saying-is-believing) effect. For example, in one study they had university students read a personality description of someone and then summarize it for someone else, who was believed either to like or to dislike that person. The students wrote a more positive description when the recipient liked the person. Having said positive things, they also then liked the person more themselves. Asked to recall what they had read, they remembered the description as more positive than it was. In another study, they found that it doesn't matter how many people are in the audience listening to the message. The communicator will still tailor the message to suit that audience, which then influences the communicator's memory of it (Hausmann et al., 2008). In short, people tend to adjust their messages to their listeners, and, having done so, believe the altered message.

Evil and Moral Acts

The attitudes-follow-behaviour principle works with immoral acts as well. Evil sometimes results from gradually escalating commitments. A trifling evil act can whittle down one's moral sensitivity, making it easier to perform a worse act. To paraphrase La Rochefoucauld's *Maxims* (1665), it is not as difficult to find a person who has never succumbed to a given temptation as to find a person who has succumbed only once. After telling a 'white lie' and thinking, 'Well, that wasn't so bad', the person may go on to tell a bigger lie.

In Chapters 7 and 13 we consider a field experiment conducted by Philip Zimbardo, that provides a classic demonstration of how behaving can influence attitudes, and how both are shaped by the situation an individual finds him or herself in. In his Stanford Prison Experiment, participants randomly assigned to the role of prisoners or guards not only behaved according to these roles, but also formed consistent attitudes. Behaving as the situation required, acts and attitudes rapidly became increasingly extreme with demonstrations of brutality by the guards towards the prisoners. Zimbardo later termed this the 'Lucifer Effect' (2007) to describe what happens when the social situation overwhelms someone, causing a shift in behaviour from good to evil.

Another way in which evil acts influence attitudes is the paradoxical fact that we tend not only to hurt those we dislike but also to dislike those we hurt. Several studies (Berscheid et al., 1968; Davis & Jones, 1960; Glass, 1964) found that harming an innocent victim – by uttering hurtful comments or delivering electric shocks – typically leads aggressors to disparage their victims, thus helping them justify their cruel behaviour. This is especially so when we are coaxed into it, not coerced. When we agree to a deed voluntarily, we take more responsibility for it.

The phenomenon appears in wartime. Prisoner-of-war camp guards would sometimes display good manners to captives in their first days on the job, but not for long. Soldiers ordered to kill may initially react with revulsion to the point of sickness over their act. But not for long (Waller, 2002). Often they will denigrate their enemies with dehumanizing nicknames.

Attitudes also follow behaviour in peacetime. A group that holds another in slavery is likely to come to perceive the slaves as having traits that justify their oppression. Prison staff who participate in executions experience 'moral disengagement' by coming to believe (more strongly than do other prison staff) that their victims deserve their fate (Osofsky et al., 2005). Actions and attitudes feed each other, sometimes to the point of moral numbness. The more one harms another and adjusts one's attitudes, the easier harm-doing becomes. Conscience is corroded.

Evil acts shape the self, but so, thankfully, do moral acts. Our character is reflected in what we do when we think no one is looking. Researchers have tested character by giving children temptations when it seems no one is watching. Consider what happens when children resist the temptation. In a dramatic experiment, Freedman (1965) introduced elementary school children to an enticing battery-controlled robot, instructing them not to play with it while he was out of the room. Freedman used a severe threat with half the children and a mild threat with the others. Both were sufficient to deter the children.

Several weeks later a different researcher, with no apparent relation to the earlier events, left each child to play in the same room with the same toys. Of the 18 children who had been given the severe threat, 14 now freely played with the robot; but two-thirds of those who had been given the mild deterrent still resisted playing with it. Apparently, the deterrent was strong enough to elicit the desired behaviour yet mild enough to leave them with a sense of choice. Having earlier chosen consciously *not* to play with the toy, the mildly deterred children apparently internalized their decisions. Moral action, especially when chosen rather than coerced, affects moral thinking.

A memorial to the victims of the 1994 Rwandan genocide. Such cruel acts tend to breed even crueller and more hate-filled attitudes.

SOURCE: ©karenfoleyphotography/Shutterstock

Moreover, positive behaviour fosters liking for the person. Doing a favour for an experimenter or another participant, or tutoring a student, usually increases liking of the person helped (Blanchard & Cook, 1976). It is a lesson worth remembering: if you wish to love someone more, act as if you do.

Why Does our Behaviour Affect our Attitudes?

What theories help explain the attitudes-follow-behaviour phenomenon?

We have seen that several streams of evidence merge to indicate that our behaviour can influence our attitudes. Social psychological theories investigate *why* action affects attitude. *Cognitive dissonance theory* assumes that to reduce discomfort, we justify our actions to ourselves. *Self-presentation theory* assumes that for strategic reasons we express attitudes that make us appear consistent. *Self-perception theory* assumes that our actions are self-revealing (when uncertain about our feelings or beliefs, we look to our behaviour, much as anyone else would). Let's examine each.

Presenting Consistency

In Western cultures especially, appearing inconsistent is undesirable. To avoid seeming so, we express attitudes that match our actions. To appear consistent, we may pretend or 'fake' those attitudes. Even if that means displaying a little insincerity or hypocrisy, it can pay off in managing the impression of consistency we are displaying. Two theories explain how people manage a concern with consistency.

Self-justification: Cognitive Dissonance

One theory is that our attitudes change because we are motivated to maintain consistency among our cognitions. That is the implication of Festinger's (1957) **cognitive dissonance** theory. John Bargh argues Festinger's theory could be considered the 'opening salvo of the cognitive revolution in social psychology' (2018, p. 60). The theory is simple, but its range of application is enormous, making 'cognitive dissonance' part of our everyday vocabulary. It assumes that we feel tension, or a lack of harmony ('dissonance'), when two simultaneously accessible thoughts or beliefs ('cognitions') are psychologically inconsistent – as when we decide to say or do something we have mixed feelings about. Furthermore, the greater the discrepancy between the attitude and the behaviour, the greater the feeling of discomfort. Cooper (2007) neatly sums this up when he states Festinger's theory has 'magnitude'. Festinger argued that to reduce this unpleasant arousal, we often adjust our thinking. This simple idea underlines a theory that has been dominant in attitude and behaviour research for over 60 years.

cognitive dissonance tension that arises when one is simultaneously aware of two inconsistent cognitions. For example, dissonance may occur when we realize that we have, with little justification, acted contrary to our attitudes. This inconsistency is unpleasant, and people use different methods to combat the dissonance. Concept coined by Leon Festinger (1957)

Dissonance theory pertains mostly to discrepancies between behaviour and attitudes. We are aware of both. Thus, if we sense some inconsistency, perhaps some hypocrisy, we feel pressure for change. That helps explain why, in a Spanish survey of nursing and physiotherapy students, those who smoke disagree with non-smokers that health professionals should be a role-model for others, and that smoking is as damaging to health as it is claimed. Smokers were also less supportive of laws that reduce tobacco consumption than non-smokers (Pericas et al., 2009). In a rather sobering study, Glatz et al. (2012) found that parents confronted with their intoxicated adolescents on a regular basis, shifted their previously strict attitudes opposed to underage drinking to a more lenient approach.

Cognitive dissonance theory offers an explanation for self-persuasion, and it offers several surprising predictions.

Insufficient Justification

Imagine you are a participant in an experiment staged by Festinger and his student, J. Merrill Carlsmith (Festinger & Carlsmith, 1959). For an hour, you are required to perform dull tasks, such as turning wooden handles again and again. After you finish, the experimenter (Carlsmith) explains that the study concerns how expectations affect performance. The next participant, waiting outside, must be led to expect an *interesting* experiment. The seemingly upset experimenter explains that the assistant who usually creates this expectation couldn't make this session. They ask if, instead, you could convince the next participant that this study is interesting. You agree and tell the next participant (who is actually the experimenter's accomplice) what a fascinating study this is to take part in. Finally, someone else who is studying how people react to experiments asks you to complete a questionnaire that asks how much you actually enjoyed the experience.

Now for the prediction: under which condition are you most likely to believe your little lie and say that the experiment was indeed interesting? When paid $1 for fibbing, as some of the participants were? Or when paid a then-lavish $20, as others were? Contrary to the common notion that big rewards produce big effects, Festinger and Carlsmith made a surprising prediction: those paid just $1 would be most likely to adjust their attitudes to their actions. Having **insufficient justification** for their actions, they would experience more discomfort (dissonance) and thus be

insufficient justification effect reduction of dissonance by internally justifying one's behaviour when external justification is 'insufficient'

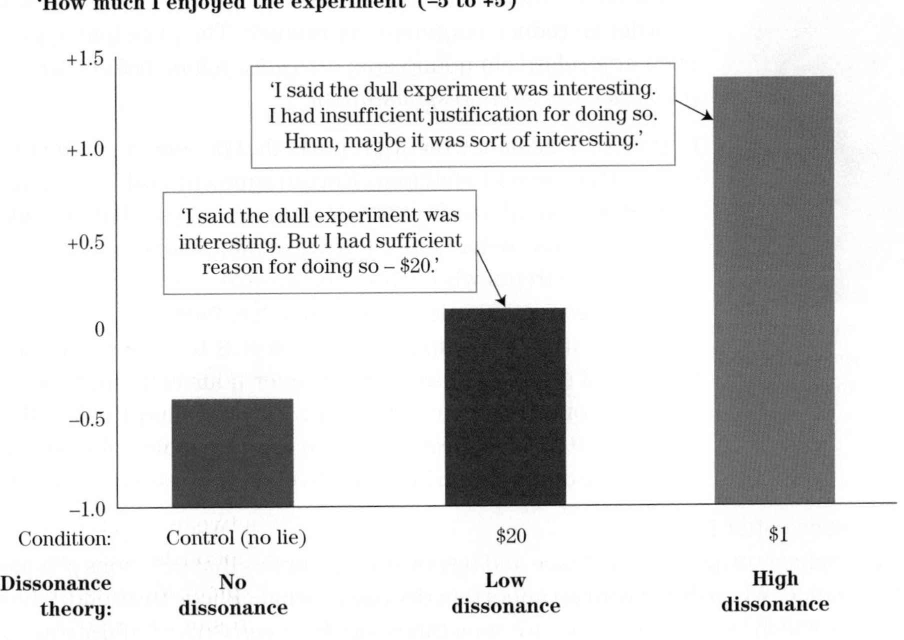
'How much I enjoyed the experiment' (–5 to +5)
+1.5
+1.0
+0.5
0
–0.5
–1.0
'I said the dull experiment was interesting. I had insufficient justification for doing so. Hmm, maybe it was sort of interesting.'
'I said the dull experiment was interesting. But I had sufficient reason for doing so – $20.'
Condition:
Control (no lie)
$20
$1
Dissonance theory:
No dissonance
Low dissonance
High dissonance

FIGURE 5.3 Insufficient justification
Dissonance theory predicts that when our actions are not fully explained by external rewards or coercion, we will experience dissonance, which we can reduce by believing in what we have done.
SOURCE: Data from Festinger and Carlsmith (1959).

more motivated to believe in what they had done. Those paid $20 had sufficient justification for what they had done and hence should have experienced less dissonance. As **Figure 5.3** shows, the results fit this intriguing prediction.*

The effect has also been recorded in children as young as six years of age. Benozio and Diesendruck (2015) compared children of 3–4 years of age with children 5–6 years old on this phenomenon. All children were asked to engage in tasks in order to obtain a reward: stickers. Some of the tasks involved much effort whilst others required very little. Some of the stickers were what the children found to be attractive (e.g. Spongebob Squarepants figures), whilst others were less so (e.g. plant stickers). Children were given the option of distributing their hard-won, or easily-won, stickers to a stranger. The researchers discovered that the 4 year olds distributed the attractive stickers fairly evenly regardless of how much effort was put into obtaining them. The unattractive stickers, however, were quickly discarded by the four year olds, despite how much effort they'd put into winning them. In contrast, the six year olds distributed less stickers, attractive and unattractive ones, when more effort had been put into obtaining them. The researchers concluded that whilst the four year olds reduced dissonance behaviourally (by distributing or discarding the stickers), the six year olds were able to suppress this immediate behavioural response and re-evaluate the stickers based on the effort they had put into winning them. This signals an important

* There is a seldom reported final aspect of this 1950s experiment. Imagine yourself finally back with the experimenter, who is truthfully explaining the whole study. Not only do you learn that you've been duped, but also the experimenter asks for the $20 back. Do you comply? Festinger and Carlsmith note that all their Stanford student participants willingly reached into their pockets and gave back the money. This is a foretaste of some quite amazing observations on compliance and conformity discussed in Chapter 7. As we will see, when the social situation makes clear demands, people usually respond accordingly.

Dissonance theory suggests that parents should aim to elicit desired behaviour non-coercively, thus motivating children to internalize the appropriate attitudes.

SOURCE: ©Eric Audras/SuperStock

cognitive development, where children are able to self-regulate in order to reduce cognitive dissonance. The principle applies, even at a relatively young age: *attitudes follow behaviours for which we feel some responsibility.*

Cognitive dissonance theory reports that people are unlikely to internalize forced behaviour. Encouragement and inducement should be enough to elicit the desired action (so that attitudes may follow the behaviour). For example, Madjar et al. (2016) found that parents who gently encouraged their children to do their homework in order to self-improve, facilitated the child's self-motivation to complete it. This seems to be a much more successful strategy than standing over your child and forcing them to complete their homework, or punishing them if they don't. But it also suggests that managers, teachers and parents should use only enough incentive to elicit the desired behaviour.

Dissonance after Decisions

The emphasis on perceived choice and responsibility implies that decisions produce dissonance. When faced with an important decision – what college to attend, whom to date, which job to accept – we are sometimes torn between two equally attractive alternatives. Perhaps you can recall a time when, having committed yourself, you became painfully aware of dissonant cognitions – the desirable features of what you had rejected and the undesirable features of what you had chosen. If you decided to live on campus or in a student town, you may have realized you were giving up the spaciousness and freedom of an apartment in favour of cramped, noisy student halls. If you elected to live off campus in non-student accommodation, you may have realized that your decision meant physical separation from campus and friends, and having to cook and clean for yourself.

After making important decisions, we usually reduce dissonance by upgrading the chosen alternative and downgrading the unchosen option. In the first published dissonance experiment, Brehm (1956) asked women to rate eight products, such as a toaster, a radio and a hairdryer. Brehm then showed the women two objects they had rated closely and told them they could have whichever they chose. Later, when re-rating the eight objects, the women increased their evaluations of the item they had chosen and decreased their evaluations of the rejected item. It seems that after we have made our choices, we become more committed to them.

Festinger notes that it matters whether we feel coerced into acting in a particular way. If we feel as though we've been forced into acting in a way that is inconsistent with our attitudes we are much less likely to shift our attitudes to match the behaviour than if we feel we've acted with freedom of choice.

With simple decisions, this deciding-becomes-believing effect can breed overconfidence (Blanton et al., 2001): 'What I've decided must be right.' The effect can occur very quickly. In an early study on this phenomenon Knox and Inkster (1968) found that racetrack betters who had just put down their money felt more optimistic about their bets than did those who were about to bet. In the few moments that intervened between standing in line and walking away from the betting window, nothing had changed – except the decisive action and the person's feelings about it.

Once made, decisions grow their own self-justifying legs of support. Often, these new legs are strong enough that when one leg is pulled away – perhaps the original one – the decision does not collapse.

Dissonance and Group Identity

Recent research in social psychology has suggested that the groups to which we psychologically belong and feel attached also have an influence on how we deal with feelings of cognitive dissonance. Social groups, such as being a university student, guide our behaviour and often also our broader moral, social and political values. However, if those groups adopt behaviour or attitudes that differ from those we personally believe, then we should experience feelings of dissonance. In such circumstances, Festinger predicts we should feel motivated to reduce such dissonance.

Glasford et al. (2008) wondered how American citizens would respond when confronted with ingroup values about basic health care that conflicted with their own. To find out, they first established how strongly each participant identified with the national ingroup (American) and what their personal beliefs were towards health care. Some of the participants were then presented with a scenario in which health care was strongly endorsed by America, and others given a report in which American values were opposed to basic health care. The most discomfort was felt by those participants who strongly identified with the national ingroup (American) and held strong personal beliefs about basic health care, and were presented with a scenario which described America as being against basic health care for its citizens. When participants were later asked how much they identified with the national group, their levels of identification had reduced. A strategy for dealing with their discomfort was to distance themselves from the national group. But could dissonance motivate them to change the group itself? In a follow-up study participants were given one of two scenarios in which the USA was seen to be upholding the value of self-reliance, or flouting it. Again the researchers found that the most discomfort was experienced by those participants who strongly identified with the national ingroup, held positive values for self-reliance and had read a scenario in which their national ingroup had flouted this value. However, this time participants were also asked about their willingness to actively engage in changing the values of the group. They found that those who had displayed the most discomfort were also those who were most willing to engage in behaviour to redress the group's value of self-reliance.

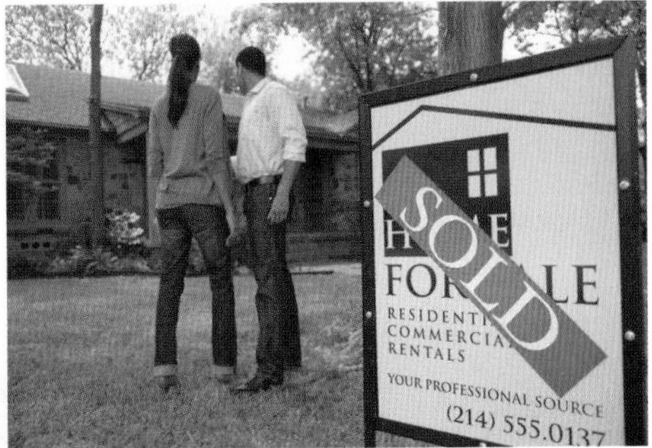

Big decisions can produce big dissonance when one later ponders the negative aspects of what is chosen and the positive aspects of what was not chosen.

SOURCE: ©Blend Images/Alamy Stock Photo

What Glasford and his colleagues had observed was that group identity had an influence on feelings of cognitive dissonance experienced by people, and also influenced their strategies for reducing it – either by psychologically distancing themselves from the group or attempting to change the behaviour of the group. This has some important real-world implications. When a group behaves in a way that differs from the values of individual members (e.g. in the case of displays of extreme prejudice), what may happen is that those more tolerant members leave and the bias within the group continues. But, on the other hand there are times when a group member may try to tackle the group norms.

However, before we get swept away by this wealth of evidence on the effects of dissonance, it's worth drawing breath for a quick word of caution here. We should be aware that the motivation to reduce feelings of dissonance may be a Western phenomenon. In parts of East Asia, to experience contradictions within oneself is what makes you human and it actually is not desirable to resolve them (e.g. Heine & Lehman, 1997; Hoshino-Browne et al., 2004). So while the research tells us something extremely interesting about behaviour in certain cultures, it would be a folly to generalize this as a feature of human beings per se.

Self-perception

Although dissonance theory has inspired much research, an even simpler theory also explains its phenomena. Consider how we make inferences about other people's attitudes. We see how a person acts in a particular situation, and then we attribute the behaviour either to the person's traits and attitudes or to environmental forces (we consider these tenets of attribution theory in Chapter 4) (**Figure 5.4**).

self-perception theory
the theory that when we are unsure of our attitudes, we infer them much as would someone observing us, by looking at our behaviour and the circumstances under which it occurs

Self-perception theory (proposed by Bem, 1972) assumes that we make similar inferences when we observe our own behaviour. When our attitudes are weak or ambiguous, we are in the position of someone observing us from the outside. Hearing myself talk informs me of my attitudes; seeing my actions provides clues to how strong my beliefs are. This is especially so when I can't easily attribute my behaviour to external constraints. The acts we freely commit are self-revealing.

The pioneering psychologist William James (see Chapter 1) proposed a similar explanation for emotion a century ago. We infer our emotions, he suggested, by observing our bodies and our behaviours. A stimulus, such as a growling bear, confronts a woman in the forest. She tenses, her heartbeat increases, adrenaline flows and she runs away. Observing all this, she then experiences fear.

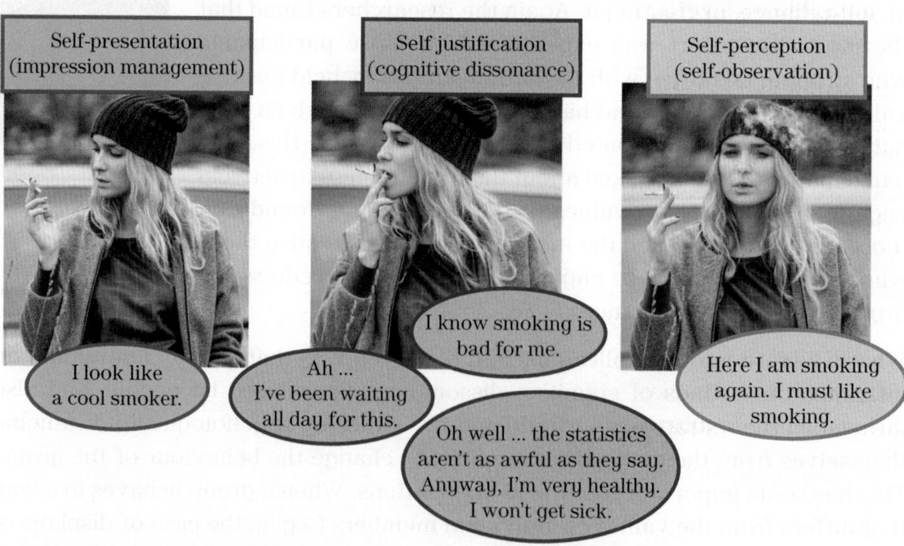

FIGURE 5.4 Attitudes follow behaviour
SOURCE: ©ANTON DOTSENKO/123RF

When James's brother, Henry, died, he was deeply depressed but persuaded himself to act as if life were manageable; it soon became so.

'Self-knowledge is best learned, not by contemplation, but action.'
Goethe, 1749–1832

Do people who observe themselves agreeing to a small request indeed come to perceive themselves as the helpful sort of person who responds positively to requests for help? Yes, report Burger and Caldwell (2003). Behaviour can modify self-concept.

Self-presentation: Expressions and Attitude

When Laird (1974, 1984) induced college students to frown while attaching electrodes to their faces – 'contract these muscles', 'pull your brows together' – they reported feeling angry. Those induced to make a smiling face felt happier and found cartoons more humorous. Those induced to repeatedly practise happy (versus sad or angry) expressions may recall more happy memories and find the happy mood lingering (Schnall & Laird, 2003). Viewing one's expressions in a mirror magnifies the self-perception effect (Kleinke et al., 1998).

Even your gait can affect how you feel. When you get up from reading this chapter, walk for a minute taking short, shuffling steps, with eyes downcast. It's a great way to feel depressed. 'Sit all day in a moping posture, sigh, and reply to everything with a dismal voice, and your melancholy lingers,' noted James (1890, p. 463). Want to feel better? Walk for a minute taking long strides with your arms swinging and your eyes straight ahead.

Our facial expressions also influence our attitudes. In an experiment by Wells and Petty (1980) University of Alberta students tested headphone sets by making either vertical or horizontal head movements while listening to a radio editorial. Who most agreed with the editorial? Those who had been nodding their heads up and down. Why? Wells and Petty surmised that positive thoughts are compatible with vertical nodding and incompatible with horizontal motion within Western cultures.

Interestingly it is not just our own facial expressions that influences our attitudes, but also the expressions of others. As Van Kleef et al. (2015) discovered in a series of experiments, we read the facial expressions of others as emotional clues about how we should feel about something. When their participants were confronted with someone who was visibly happy about an event (e.g. the introduction of kite-surfing into the Olympic Games) participants developed positive attitudes about this too. Confronted by someone who was angry over something (e.g. Greenpeace thought to be wasting money on high salaries), the participants shared their own negative attitudes. The authors make an important point: if emotions can be authentically and visibly conveyed by the advertiser, the teacher, the lawyer, the politician, then attitudes can be manipulated accordingly.

This can also occur the other way around: attitudes can influence our facial expressions. Social psychologists have observed that we tend to engage in facial mimicry when we want to connect with someone in some way (Lakin & Chartrand, 2003). Furthermore, this mimicry is done unconsciously. We visibly mirror their emotional state to create a harmonious bond. As Likowski et al. (2008)

found out, this mimicry goes further than our faces. In their study, participants were introduced to computer-generated avatars. The avatars' characters were described using positive, negative or neutral traits. Participants believed their task was to consider which characters would be suitable for inclusion into a video-game. The facial expression of the avatars was experimentally manipulated to be either smiling, neutral or unhappy. Likowski and the team measured the facial expressions of their participants as they saw each avatar. They found that if the avatar had been described as a positive character, participants mimicked their facial expressions. If the avatar was happy, so was the participant. If sad, the participant also expressed sadness. However, if the avatar had been described as a negative character, the participant's own facial expressions did not mimic the avatar. In short, participants developed attitudes very quickly about the avatars, which influenced their behaviour: facial mimicry.

Overjustification and Intrinsic Motivations

Recall the insufficient justification effect – the smallest incentive that will get people to do something is often the most effective in getting them to like the activity and keep on doing it. Cognitive dissonance theory offers one explanation for this: when external inducements are insufficient to justify our behaviour, we reduce dissonance by justifying the behaviour internally.

Self-perception theory offers a different explanation: people explain their behaviour by noting the conditions under which it occurs. Imagine hearing someone proclaim the wisdom of an increase in tuition fees, after being paid to do so. Surely the statement would seem less sincere than if you thought the person was expressing those opinions for no pay. Perhaps we make similar inferences when observing ourselves. We observe our uncoerced action and infer our attitude.

Contrary to the notion that rewards always increase motivation, self-perception theory suggests that unnecessary rewards can have a hidden cost. Rewarding people for doing what they already enjoy may lead them to attribute their action to the reward, thus undermining their self-perception that they do it because they like it. Experiments by Deci and Ryan (1991, 1997) at the University of Rochester, by Lepper and Greene (1979) at Stanford, and by Boggiano and her colleagues (Boggiano & Ruble, 1985; Boggiano et al., 1987) at the University of Colorado have confirmed this **overjustification effect**. More recently Warneken and Tomasello (2014) observed the overjustification effect in children as young as 20 months old. Although intrinsically willing to provide help without reward, these same toddlers became much more reluctant to help once they'd received a material reward for doing so. Pay people for playing with puzzles, and they will later play with the puzzles less than those who play for no pay. Promise children a reward for doing what they intrinsically enjoy (for example, playing with Magic Markers), and you will turn their play into work (**Figure 5.5**).

overjustification effect *the result of bribing people to do what they already like doing; they may then see their actions as externally controlled rather than intrinsically appealing*

The role of intrinsic motivation has been examined in relation to the development of pro-environmentally friendly attitudes and behaviour. Markowitz and Shariff (2012) argue that if we try to force people to change their everyday practices using a mix of coercion and extrinsic rewards, we may diminish their sense of moral responsibility for the environment. Similarly, Di Falco and Sharma (2018) found that intrinsic motivations are key to shifting attitudes and behaviours about climate change in the Fiji Islands. Furthermore, motivations to adapt behaviours towards environmental

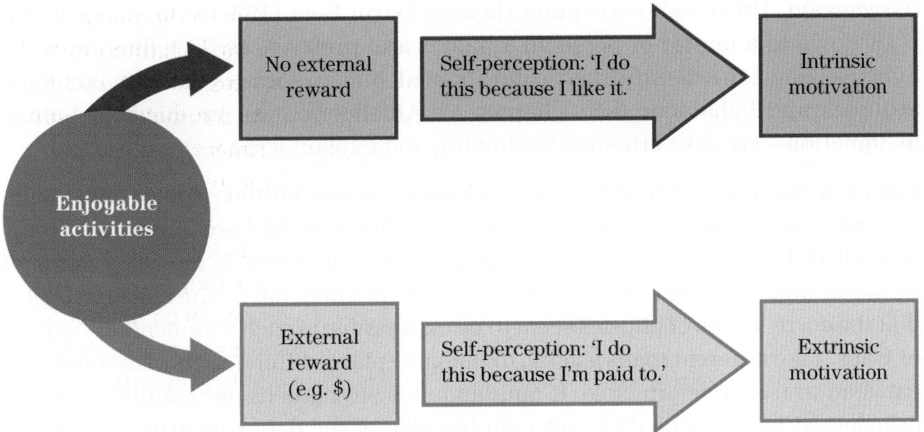

FIGURE 5.5 Intrinsic and extrinsic motivation
When people do something they enjoy, without reward or coercion, they attribute their behaviour to their love of the activity. External rewards undermine intrinsic motivation by leading people to attribute their behaviour to the incentive.

sustainability can be diminished when green incentives, such as economic rewards, are introduced. See Chapter 15 for further discussion about social psychology's contribution to environmentally sustainable attitudes and behaviour.

That said, an unanticipated reward does not necessarily diminish intrinsic interest if people can still attribute their actions to their own motivation (Aknin et al., 2018; Tang & Hall, 1995). And if compliments for a good job make us feel more competent and successful, this can actually increase our intrinsic motivation. When rightly administered, rewards may also boost creativity (Eisenberger & Rhoades, 2001; Eisenberger & Shanock, 2003).

The overjustification effect occurs when someone offers an unnecessary reward beforehand in an obvious effort to control behaviour. What matters is what a reward implies: rewards and praise that inform people of their achievements – that make them feel, 'I'm very good at this' – boost intrinsic motivation. Rewards that seek to control people and lead them to believe it was the reward that caused their effort – 'I did it for the money' – diminish the intrinsic appeal of an enjoyable task.

A group of friends laughing together, showing facial mimicry.
SOURCE: ©antonioguillem/123RF

Comparing the Theories

We have seen one explanation of why our actions might only *seem* to affect our attitudes (self-presentation theory). And we have seen two explanations of why our actions genuinely affect our attitudes: (1) the dissonance-theory assumption that we justify our behaviour to reduce our internal discomfort; and (2) the self-perception-theory assumption that we observe our behaviour and make reasonable inferences about our attitudes, much as we observe other people and infer *their* attitudes.

The last two explanations seem to contradict each other. Which is right? It's difficult to find a definitive test. In most instances they make the same predictions, and we can bend each theory to accommodate most of the findings we have considered

(Greenwald, 1975). Self-perception theorist Daryl Bem (1972) even suggested it boils down to a matter of personal loyalties and preferences. This illustrates the human element in scientific theorizing about all human social behaviour, including attitudes and behaviour (see Chapter 1). All theories are products of human imagination – creative attempts to simplify and explain what we've observed.

It is not unusual in science to find that a principle, such as 'attitudes follow behaviour', is predictable from more than one theory. Physicist Richard Feynman (1967) marvelled that 'one of the amazing characteristics of nature' is the 'wide range of beautiful ways' in which we can describe it: 'I do not understand the reason why it is that the correct laws of physics seem to be expressible in such a tremendous variety of ways.' Like different roads leading to the same place, different sets of assumptions can lead to the same principle. If anything, this strengthens our confidence in the principle. It becomes credible not only because of the data supporting it but also because it rests on more than one theoretical pillar.

Dissonance as Arousal

On one key point, strong support has emerged for dissonance theory. Recall that dissonance is, by definition, an aroused state of uncomfortable tension. To reduce that tension, we supposedly change our attitudes. Self-perception theory says nothing about tension being aroused when our actions and attitudes are not in harmony. It assumes merely that when our attitudes are weak to begin with, we will use our behaviour and its circumstances as a clue to those attitudes.

Are conditions that supposedly produce dissonance (for example, making decisions or acting contrary to one's attitudes) uncomfortably arousing? Clearly yes, providing that the behaviour has unwanted consequences for which the person feels responsible (Cooper, 2007). If, in the privacy of your closet, you say something you don't believe, dissonance will be minimal. It will be much greater if there are unpleasant results – if someone hears and believes you, if the statement causes harm and the negative effects are irrevocable, and if the person harmed is someone you like. Bargh (2018) argues that dissonance is essentially about social consistency. It is when we are publicly seen to be inconsistent with our attitudes and behaviours that we feel uncomfortable. Moreover, some researchers have suggested that arousal is detectable as increased perspiration, heart rate and neural activity (Cacioppo & Petty, 1986; Croyle & Cooper, 1983; Izuma et al., 2010; Losch & Cacioppo, 1990).

self-affirmation theory a theory that (a) people often experience a self-image threat, after engaging in an undesirable behaviour; and (b) they can compensate by affirming another aspect of the self. Threaten people's self-concept in one domain, and they will compensate either by refocusing or by doing good deeds in some other domain

But why is inconsistency so arousing? Because, suggests Steele's (1988) **self-affirmation theory**, we are motivated to portray ourselves as competent, truthful and stable. Inconsistency threatens our sense of personal competence and goodness. Justifying our actions and decisions is therefore *self-affirming;* it protects and supports our sense of integrity and self-worth (Lannin et al., 2013).

So dissonance conditions arouse tension, especially when they threaten positive feelings of self-worth. But is this arousal necessary for the attitudes-follow-behaviour effect? Steele et al. (1981) believe the answer is yes. Writing from the field of medicine Ayres and colleagues (2014) agree. In their UK study, injecting heroin users were interviewed about their habit practices and their desire to take part in an opioid substitution intervention programme. On a random basis some were offered treatment the same day, others were not. Interestingly, Ayres et al. found that users who were not offered the treatment the same day became highly motivated to seek treatment independently. Moreover, a 3-month follow-up found that more than half of those participants were continuing with their treatment. The researchers suggest that having been put into a position of high dissonance by taking part in the study, but not offered treatment, these drug-users shifted not only their behaviours but also their attitudes towards their drug-use to reduce feelings of dissonance.

Self-perceiving When Not Self-contradicting

Dissonance procedures are uncomfortably arousing. That makes for self-persuasion after acting contrary to one's attitudes. But dissonance theory cannot explain attitude changes that occur without dissonance. Dissonance theory also does not explain the overjustification effect, since being paid to do what you like to do should not arouse great tension. And what about situations where the action does not contradict any attitude – when, for example, people are induced to smile or grimace? Here, too, there should be no dissonance. As we have seen, for these cases, self-perception theory has a ready explanation.

In short, it appears that dissonance theory explains what happens when we act contrary to clearly defined attitudes: we feel tension, so we adjust our attitudes to reduce it. Dissonance theory, then, explains attitude change in Western cultures. In situations where our attitudes are not well formed, self-perception theory explains attitude *formation*. As we act and reflect, we develop more readily accessible attitudes to guide our future behaviour.

Attitudes as Social Actions

So far we have considered the complex relationship between attitudes and behaviour. What this work has illustrated is that how these attitudes are expressed and their relationship to behaviour is dependent on the context. It is this dependency on the context that has led some social psychologists to question whether attitudes have any cognitive basis at all.

In their landmark book *Discourse and Social Psychology: Beyond Attitudes and Behaviour,* Potter and Wetherell (1987) boldly questioned some of the claims and assumptions made by social psychologists in their hunt for attitudes.

These included the following:

- *Attitudes as cognitive entities:* Potter and Wetherell argued that if attitudes do have a stable cognitive component then they should be more consistent than they actually are. However, attitudes tend to be highly variable and often contradictory. The same person can express different attitudes about an event, person, object or idea over the course of a single conversation. So rather than thinking of attitudes as cognitive evaluations located somewhere in the head, that exist pre-communication, Potter and Wetherell argue they are produced during communication. Or as social psychologist Billig (1989) puts it in a key paper on the topic, attitudes are a form of argumentative thinking done in dialogue with others. They change as the dialogue progresses.
- *Attitudes predict behaviour:* if attitudes are produced in language as we interact with other people, Potter and Wetherell propose that attitudes don't lead to behaviour, but actually *are* the behaviour (or social action). Indeed, if you think about it we use attitudes all the time to perform social actions (for example justifying, blaming, excusing, explaining).

- *Attitudes can be measured quantitatively:* as we have seen, attitudes are often measured using rating scales (such as Likert scales), which require participants to rate their attitude towards something on a pre-labelled scale. Potter and Wetherell warn that this data shouldn't be relied upon too heavily or treated as accurate reflections of cognitive processes. When confronted with a rating scale, the participant gives attitudes that best fit the current context (e.g. what they think the researcher wants, the labels on the rating scale, or monitoring their self-presentation).
- *Attitudes are formed towards predefined objects in the environment:* Potter and Wetherell suggest that what we have attitudes about is a rhetorical construction. How we describe a person, an event, an object or idea is something we do in language. So in evaluating something, we produce the thing we evaluate about. Or in other words we don't only produce the attitude about an object, but we produce the attitude-object itself.

These arguments become a little clearer when we consider some examples.

On 24 July 2014, Norwegian authorities issued a security alert warning of a possible imminent terror attack by an extreme Islamist group based in Syria. Of interest to researcher Joel Rasmussen (2015) was how this was communicated and responded to on Twitter. In his analysis of the Tweets that followed, he examined three themes that developed during the discussion that followed. The first concerned how Twitterers evaluated the authorities, communication of the threat to the public. Whilst some praised the authorities' swift reactions, noting how safe they felt as a result, others were critical, arguing that no real information had been given and as such they felt very unsafe. The second noted the authorities' advice that people should be 'vigilant'. Twitterers responded with humour (e.g. *'Now it would have been good to sleep, but PST asks everyone to be awake. #pst #terror #terrorthreat'*), praise, or criticism for the vagueness of the advice. Finally, blaming of ethnic minority groups was explored, with most tweeters keen to distance themselves from this. Rasmussen argues that focusing on the language used in the Tweets highlights how the thing to be evaluated (the terrorist threat and how the authorities communicate this to the public) is subject to discussion and argumentation in terms of how it is defined and understood. Attitudes are constructed online, quite literally in this case!

See Chapter 13 for further discussion on the use of disclaimers and prejudice; disclaimers and an expression of cultural tolerance can inoculate against the prejudice which follows.

The topic of attitudes provokes debates and tensions in social psychology about how we should define and study them, and what we consider their role to be in the prediction of behaviour. Despite these ongoing debates, what social psychologists do agree on is that attitudes are important evaluations and that they are sensitive to the context in which they are produced.

Focus on

Do Attitudes to Conservation and the Environment Predict Protective Behaviours towards Wildlife?

The accelerated global loss in biodiversity has led to increased social scientific study of the psychological, cultural and social factors that contribute to it (Bekoff & Bexell, 2010). What are the barriers that prevent people from engaging in pro-environmental behaviours? Under what conditions will we act in environmentally sustainable ways that could ensure a future for us all? What role do our attitudes towards other animals and the environment play in conservation behaviour?

Dunlap and Van Liere (1978) devised the New Environmental Paradigm (NEP) Scale to measure environmental attitudes. Since its original development, the NEP has been revised and adapted, and become the world's most used measure of environmental attitudes. For example, it has been used to show that individuals who engaged in outdoor activities as a child have more pro-environmental attitudes in later life (Ewert et al., 2005). The NEP has also been used to explore whether pro-environmental attitudes predict pro-environmental behaviours (for example, Poortinga et al., 2004). However, as Poortinga et al. (2004) discovered, and many other researchers besides, a simple mapping of environmental attitudes onto environmental-friendly behaviours is fraught with difficulties. There are many different kinds of pro-environmental behaviours, some of which we can choose to do (e.g. recycle glass), but some which may simply not be possible for us to do (e.g. buy an eco-friendly car), despite our pro-environmental attitudes.

Dunlap (2008) points out that the NEP was never intended as a predictor of specific pro-environmental behaviours, and other factors may need to be considered. The NEP may not be applicable beyond the Western cultural context in which it was developed. The 'anti-environmental' attitudes it measures (e.g. 'Plants and animals exist primarily to be used by humans') may not translate as necessarily negative cross-culturally, and can, as we shall see, under certain conditions, facilitate conservation behaviour.

Scanlon and Kull (2009) wanted to know how well attitudes predicted conservation behaviours amongst poor southern African communities, where conservation may be a luxury they can ill afford. People will only act in environmentally sustainable ways, and conserve wildlife, if there are benefits and incentives for doing so. Scanlon and Kull focused their efforts specifically on the Torra Conservancy in northwest Namibia, a community-based natural resource management (CBNRM) initiative. Here, Conservancy residents benefit from protecting wildlife in terms of employment (eco-tourism), meat (sustainable hunting), and selling crafts. As a result attitudes and behaviours towards conserving wildlife have changed rapidly. From a series of interviews and attitude scales, Scanlon and Kull proposed a three-way relationship between attitudes, benefits and behaviours (**Figure 5.6**).

The researchers discovered that 80 per cent of Conservancy members had positive attitudes towards the environment and conservation when they were in receipt of benefits (e.g. 'Now that I have received benefits, I support conservation because I can see that it brings me benefits like money and meat'). These benefits also fostered conservation behaviours ('We get the benefits because we protect the wildlife and don't hunt anymore'). However, Scanlon and Kull thought that although attitudes do influence behaviour, it was the conservation behaviour that was most influential in shaping attitudes ('Through my involvement I have learned about conservation and now I'm much more interested in conservation'). Remember Leon Festinger's Cognitive Dissonance

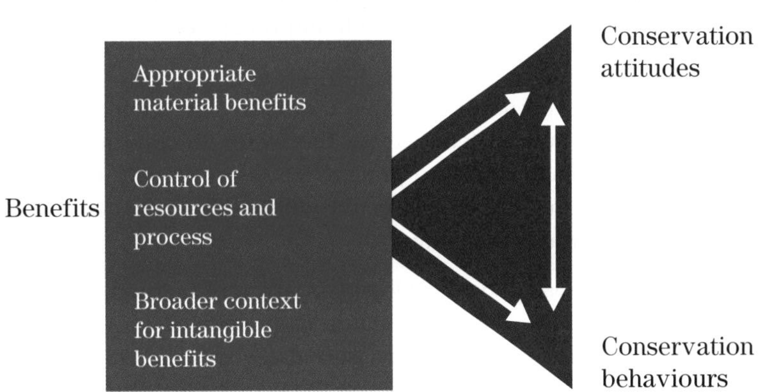

FIGURE 5.6 The framework for understanding the relationship between benefits, attitudes and behaviours to conservation

Theory? Festinger claimed that the stronger influence was behaviour over attitudes rather than the other way around. Importantly, what Scanlon and Kull found by mixing qualitative (interviews) with quantitative (attitude scales), was that the conditions under which attitudes and behaviours are linked is complex and mediated, in this case, by appropriate benefits (such as meat and employment) to this community.

So, general attitude measures, like the NEP, can be problematic once we try to apply them beyond the context in which they were devised. What we might consider to be a positive or negative attitude, might not be recognized as such cross-culturally. Furthermore, the link between attitudes and behaviour is not as clear-cut as we might hope.

The debate continues about the importance of measuring attitudes and the usefulness of developing attitude scales such as the NEP, in understanding if and when people behave in particular ways.

Questions

1 To what extent do you think negative attitudes towards the environment lead to disengagement with environmentally responsible behaviours?

2 Would incentives encourage people to adopt more environmentally sustainable behaviours, and if so, what might these be?

3 How useful are attitude scales in exploring people's evaluations and behaviours towards the environment?

4 Are attitudes just 'all talk'?

SUMMING UP: ATTITUDES AND BEHAVIOUR

ORGANIZATION OF ATTITUDES

- Social psychologists have offered various explanations for how attitudes are formed. These include direct experience with objects and living things, classical and operant conditioning, parental and peer influence and modelling.
- Attitudes are useful as they enable us to 'do' certain things. They have particular functions such as providing us with knowledge about the world, facilitating us to receive positive outcomes and avoid negative ones, enabling us to protect our sense of self, and expressing and reinforcing our sense of identity. Our attitudes can help us through a crisis but they can also hinder us, depending on what our attitudes are towards something.
- Social psychologists have developed an array of methods for measuring people's attitudes. These have included case studies and rating scales. The most well-known attitudes scales in social psychology include those by Thurstone, Likert and Osgood. These explicit measures of attitudes have been subject to criticism as participants may express those attitudes which are socially desirable rather than those they actually hold.
- More subtle and implicit measures of attitudes have recently been developed to avoid social desirability biases which can hamper explicit measures such as rating scales. These have included the implicit association test (IAT) and rely on reaction times rather than explicit declarations of attitudes. However, IATs have also been criticized for their validity. The extent to which they measure attitudes, rather than processing speed, has been questioned.

HOW WELL DO OUR ATTITUDES PREDICT OUR BEHAVIOUR?

- How do our inner attitudes (evaluative reactions towards some object or person, often rooted in beliefs) relate to our external behaviour? Although popular wisdom stresses the impact of attitudes on behaviour, in fact, attitudes are often poor predictors of behaviours. Moreover, changing people's attitudes typically fails to produce much change in their behaviour. These findings sent social psychologists scurrying to find out why we so often fail to play the game we talk.
- Our expressions of attitudes and our behaviours are each subject to many influences. Our attitudes will predict our behaviour (1) if these 'other influences' are minimized, (2) if the attitude corresponds very closely to the predicted behaviour (as in voting studies), and (3) if the attitude is potent (because something reminds us of it, or because we acquired it by direct experience). Thus there is, under these conditions, a connection between what we think and feel and what we do.

WHEN DOES OUR BEHAVIOUR AFFECT OUR ATTITUDES?

The attitude–action relation also works in the reverse direction: we are likely not only to think ourselves into action but also to act ourselves into a way of thinking. When we act, we amplify the idea underlying what we have done, especially when we feel responsible for it. Many streams of evidence converge on this principle. The actions prescribed by social roles mould the attitudes of the role players.

- Similarly, what we say or write can strongly influence attitudes that we subsequently hold.
- Actions also affect our moral attitudes: that which we have done, even if it is evil, we tend to justify as right.

WHY DOES OUR BEHAVIOUR AFFECT OUR ATTITUDES?

- Three competing theories explain why our actions affect our attitude reports. *Self-presentation theory* assumes that people, especially those who self-monitor their behaviour hoping to create good impressions, will adapt their attitude reports to appear consistent with their actions. The available evidence confirms that people do adjust their attitude statements out of concern for what other people will think. But it also shows that some genuine attitude change occurs.
- Two theories propose that our actions trigger genuine attitude change. *Dissonance theory* explains this attitude change by assuming that we feel tension after acting contrary to our attitudes or making difficult decisions. To reduce that arousal, we internally justify our behaviour. Dissonance theory further proposes that the less external justification we have for our undesirable actions, the more we feel responsible for them, and thus the more dissonance arises and the more attitudes change.
- *Self-perception theory* assumes that when our attitudes are weak, we simply observe our behaviour and its circumstances, then infer our attitudes. One interesting implication of self-perception theory is the 'overjustification effect': rewarding people to do what they like doing anyway can turn their pleasure into drudgery (if the reward leads them to attribute their behaviour to the reward).
- Evidence supports predictions from both theories, suggesting that each describes what happens under certain conditions.

ATTITUDES AS SOCIAL ACTIONS

- Some social psychologists (usually discursive) have argued that attitudes do not predict behaviour, but *are* a form of social action.
- They suggest that attitudes are constructed in interaction between people, and are shaped according to the context in which they are produced. This means attitudes can be highly variable.

- They also argue that what we have attitudes about (attitude–objects) do not pre-exist the evaluation but are themselves constructed in language as part of that evaluation.
- Discursive psychologists argue that we should study attitudes qualitatively and examine how they are formed, and what they are used for, in language.

Critical Questions

1. What definitions have social psychologists offered to describe 'attitudes'?
2. Do IATs offer a truer reflection of people's attitudes than other methods?
3. How well can attitudes predict behaviour?
4. What social psychological theories have been proposed to explain attitude change?
5. Where do attitudes reside?
6. Are attitudes just talk?

Recommended Reading

Here are some recommended classic and contemporary readings on attitudes and how they have been understood and measured in social psychology.

Classic Papers

Bem, D. J. (1972). Self-perception theory. *Advances in Experimental Social Psychology, 6*, 1–62.

Festinger, L. (1964). Behavioral support for opinion change. *Public Opinion Quarterly, 28*(3), 404–417.

Katz, D. (1960). The functional approach to the study of attitudes. *Public Opinion Quarterly, 24*(2), 163–204.

Contemporary Papers

Bargh, J. A. (2018). It was social consistency that mattered all along. *Psychological Inquiry, 29*(2), 60–62.

Fazio, R. H., & Olson, M. A. (2003). Implicit measures in social cognition research: Their meaning and use. *Annual Review of Psychology, 54*(1), 297–327.

Greenwald, A., McGhee, D. E., & Schwartz, J. L. K. (1998). Measuring individual differences in implicit cognition: The implicit association test. *Journal of Personality and Social Psychology, 74*(6), 1464–1480.

Poobalan, A. S., Aucott, L. S., Clarke, A., Smith, W., & Cairns, S. (2012). Physical activity attitudes, intentions and behaviours among 18–25 year olds: A mixed methods study. *BMC Public Health, 12*(1), 640–649.

6 PERSUASION

'Character may almost be called the most effective means of persuasion.'
Aristotle, Rhetoric

The Ancient Greek philosopher Aristotle (384–322 BC) wrote extensively on the art of persuasion. In his classic work *Rhetoric,* he stated that persuasion involves the manipulation of the audience's mind through emotion or reasoned argument. But, when rhetoric is coupled with scientific certainty ('logic') and reasoned informed debate ('dialect') people can be persuaded and educated on the basis of knowledge rather than emotion. As history teaches us, when it's achieved, the consequences of successful persuasion can range from revolution to catastrophy.

Joseph Goebbels, Germany's Minister for National Enlightenment and Propaganda from 1933 to 1945, certainly understood the power of persuasion. Given control of publications, radio programmes, motion pictures and the arts, he undertook to persuade Germans to accept Nazi ideology in general and anti-Semitism in particular. His colleague Julius Streicher published a weekly anti-Semitic newspaper, *Der Stürmer,* which boasted a circulation of 500,000 and was the only paper read cover to cover by Adolf Hitler. Streicher also published anti-Semitic children's books and, with Goebbels, spoke at the mass rallies that became part of the Nazi propaganda machine. Hitler himself, however, hardly mentioned the Jews from the moment he took power in 1933 until the outbreak of the war (Koonz, 2003, from Reicher et al., 2008; also see Chapter 7). In his propaganda speeches Hitler focused on the virtues of (ethnic) Germans as moral, pure, selfless and loyal. Hitler pledged to defend these qualities and promised to create a new society in which they could flourish (Reicher et al., 2008). This was a propaganda most Germans acknowledged even if they did not want to be anti-Semitic, anti-homosexual or against the mentally challenged. The Nazis persuaded many Germans by emphasizing ingroup virtue, and paved the way for outgroup hatred towards the groups that blocked the realization of the Third Reich.

How effective were Goebbels, Streicher and other Nazi propagandists? Did they, as the Allies alleged at Streicher's Nuremberg trial, 'inject poison into the minds of millions and millions' (Bytwerk, 1976)?

Most Germans were not persuaded to express raging hatred for the Jews. But some were. Others became sympathetic to measures such as firing Jewish university professors, boycotting Jewish-owned businesses and, eventually, sending Jews to concentration camps. Most other Germans became either sufficiently uncertain or sufficiently intimidated to condone the regime's massive genocidal programme, or at least to allow it to happen. Without the complicity of millions of people, there would have been no Holocaust (Goldhagen, 1996).

persuasion the process by which a message induces change in beliefs, attitudes or behaviours

The powers of **persuasion** were partly apparent in what a Pew (2003) survey called the 'rift between Americans and Western Europeans' over the Iraq war. Surveys shortly before the war revealed that Americans favoured military action against Iraq by about two to one, while Europeans were opposing it by the same margin (Burkholder, 2003; Moore, 2003; Pew, 2003). Once the war began, Americans' support for the war rose, for a time, to more than three to one (Newport et al., 2003). Except for Israel, people surveyed in all other countries were opposed to the attack.

The huge rift between Americans and the citizens of other countries is partly a sign of persuasion at work. What persuaded most Americans to favour the war? What persuaded most people elsewhere to oppose it?

Attitudes were being shaped, at least in part, by persuasive messages in the US media that led half of Americans to believe that Saddam Hussein was directly involved in the 9/11 attacks and four in five to falsely believe that weapons of mass destruction would be found (Duffy, 2003; Newport et al., 2003). Sociologist James Davison Hunter (2002) notes that culture-shaping usually occurs top-down, as cultural elites control the dissemination of information and ideas. Thus, Americans, and people elsewhere, learned about and watched two different wars (della Cava, 2003; Friedman, 2003a; Goldsmith, 2003; Krugman, 2003; Tomorrow, 2003). Depending on the country where you lived and the media available to you, you may have heard about 'America's liberation of Iraq' or 'America's invasion of Iraq'.

In the view of many Americans, the other nations' media combined a pervasive anti-American bias with a blindness to the threat posed by Saddam. To many people elsewhere, the 'embedded' American media were biased in favour of the military. Regardless of where bias lay or whose perspective was better informed, this much seems clear: depending on where they lived, people were given (and discussed and believed) somewhat differing information. So the written and spoken word, and the cultural and societal context of norms and values upon which they are based, are a crucial component in understanding persuasion. Moreover, persuasion really matters.

Persuasive forces have been harnessed to promote healthier living. Thanks partly to health-promotion campaigns, smoking among UK adults dropped from 45 per cent of the population in 1974, to just under 15 per cent in 2017 (NHS, 2018). Surveys also show that there has been a decline in the number of adults aged 16+ years, who drank alcohol in the last week from 64.2 per cent in 2005 to 56.9 per cent in 2016. This might not look like much of a drop at first glance but this actually equates to 29 million people, and represents the lowest drinking levels in the UK since the survey began (General Lifestyle Survey, ONS, 2017). More than at any time in recent decades, health-and safety-conscious educated adults are shunning cigarettes and beer. So in contemporary society we see 'rhetoric', 'logic' and 'dialect' combine, influencing the way we conduct our everyday lives.

As these examples show, efforts to persuade are sometimes diabolical, sometimes controversial and sometimes beneficial. Persuasion is neither inherently good nor bad. It is a message's purpose, form and content that elicits judgements of good or bad. The bad we call 'propaganda'. The good we call 'education' or 'information'. Education is less coercive than propaganda. Yet generally we call it 'education' when we believe it, 'propaganda' when we don't (Lumsden et al., 1980). In 2001, the Netherlands became the first country to legalize same-sex marriage. On 1 January 2019, Austria became the latest country of European jurisdiction to decriminalize same-sex marriage. It was the 17th European country to do so (Pew Research Center, 2019). Support for gay rights and gay civil unions or marriage has significantly increased across Europe and some states of the US (Chamie & Mirkin, 2011). Some people view such attitude changes as reflecting 'education', others as reflecting 'propaganda'. Our opinions have to come from somewhere. Persuasion – whether it be education or propaganda – is, therefore, inevitable. Indeed, persuasion is everywhere – at the heart of politics, marketing, courtship, parenting, negotiation, religion and courtroom decision making.

However, persuasion doesn't just describe the practices of these large-scale campaigns designed to influence our attitudes and opinions about wars, healthy living and political policies, but is part of our everyday lives – what we might call '**mundane persuasion**'. When we engage in dialogue with one another we are

mundane persuasion we are involved in acts of persuasion in our everyday lives involved in rhetorical discourse, whether it be explaining events that happened in a nightclub or on holiday, or justifying our actions towards a friend. We are trying to persuade someone else of our version of events. In Chapter 5, we turned our attention towards some social psychologists (such as discursive psychologists) who have argued that persuasion is part and parcel of our everyday attitudes and our daily lives. So the kinds of questions about persuasion and rhetoric that the Ancient Greek philosophers sought to address are the same as those social psychologists are still trying to answer today. The act of persuasion crosses time and space.

However, social psychologists differ in how they study the act of persuasion. Experimental social psychologists seek to understand what leads to effective, long-lasting attitude change. What factors affect persuasion? And how, as persuaders, can we most effectively 'educate' others? Other, more discursive social psychologists have focused primarily on language to examine how messages are put together in rhetorical ways that present versions of social reality as 'facts', either on a grand scale or at a mundane level. In all cases, the 'art' of persuasion has become a 'science' of identifying how and what works. To begin to consider these things, it's useful to distinguish between the 'form' and 'content' of a message in understanding how they achieve influence.

'A fanatic is one who can't change his mind and won't change the subject.'
Winston Churchill, 1954

In his landmark book *Arguing and Thinking*, Billig (1996) argues that social psychologists tend to study persuasion in the way some geologists study erosion – by observing the effects of various factors in brief, controlled experiments. The effects are small and are most potent on weak attitudes that don't touch our values. Yet they enable us to understand how, given enough time, such factors could produce big effects. However, such experiments have frequently focused on the 'form' of a message – what aspects of its style, structure and delivery can be noted as being 'successful' in persuading an audience. There have been fewer experimental studies of the 'content' of messages in ensuring persuasive influence. What we shall consider here are some of the general features of persuasion that have been suggested in social psychology, using experiments. That said, persuasion is inextricably linked to local and broader social context (for example our cultural ideology, social networks, the narrative course of a conversation, societal norms and values) and as this varies across time and space, from individual to individual, group to group, it is impossible to provide an abstract generalizable list of factors of persuasion as you will always come across the exception to the rule (Billig, 1996). What 'works' in one case may not work in another. When examining the factors of persuasion that have been confirmed in experimentation, we should also bear in mind that these should be understood as 'working' within a specific social context at a particular time.

So we approach this topic with a caveat: social psychology does not always fully understand or is not able to explain all forms of persuasion. This chapter does not aim to suggest otherwise. That said, social psychology has made some extremely useful inroads into understanding and explaining some aspects of the phenomenon. To begin, let's first consider the main cognitive routes to persuasion that have been identified using controlled experiments.

What Paths Lead to Persuasion?

What two paths lead to influence? What type of cognitive processing does each involve – and with what effects?

One of the earliest and most comprehensive contributions to the social psychology of persuasion came from the work of Yale professor Carl Hovland in his attempts to understand the effectiveness of propaganda. While serving as chief psychologist for the US War Department during the Second World War, Hovland et al. (1949) helped the war effort by studying persuasion. Hoping to boost soldier morale, Hovland and his colleagues systematically studied the effects of training films and historical documentaries on new recruits' attitudes towards the war. Back at Yale after the war, they continued studying what makes a message persuasive. Their research found varied factors related to the communicator, the content of the message, the channel of communication and the audience. They summarized the goal of their research as the study of 'the formula of who says what to whom with what effect' (Hovland et al., 1953, p. 12).

Hovland's work resulted in a categorization of factors that characterized successful persuasion. To elicit action from someone, a persuasive message must clear several hurdles, i.e. that person's willingness to pay attention to it, to comprehend it, to believe it, remember it, behave accordingly, and finally to act. Any factors that clear the hurdles in the persuasion process increase the likelihood of persuasion. For example, if an attractive source increases your attention to a message, then the message should have a better chance of persuading you. The Yale group's approach to studying persuasion provides us with a good understanding of *when* persuasion is likely to occur.

Researchers at Ohio State University then suggested that people's thoughts in response to persuasive messages also matter. If a message is clear but unconvincing, then you will easily counter-argue the message and won't be persuaded. If the message offers convincing arguments, then your thoughts will be more favourable and you will most likely be persuaded. This 'cognitive response' approach helps us understand why persuasion occurs more in some situations than in others.

The Central Route

Petty and Cacioppo (1986; Petty & Wegener, 1999) and Eagly and Chaiken (1993, 1998) theorized that persuasion is likely to occur via one of two routes. Petty and Cacioppo developed the *Elaboration-likelihood model* of persuasion (ELM), which proposes that when people are motivated and able to think about an issue, they are likely to engage with the content of a message and as such take the **central route to persuasion** – focusing on the arguments. If those arguments are strong and compelling, persuasion is likely. People scrutinize the information embedded within a message and relate it to the information they already have stored in memory about an issue. They evaluate and may modify their existing attitudes about the issue accordingly (see Chapter 5). If the message offers only weak arguments, thoughtful people will notice that the arguments aren't very compelling and will counter-argue.

central route to persuasion occurs when after careful consideration of the content of a message people find the argument persuasive (the opposite of the peripheral route to persuasion)

The Peripheral Route

But sometimes the strength of the arguments doesn't matter. It's the form that counts. Petty and Cacioppo suggest that this happens when people do not think too much about an issue. So if we're distracted, uninvolved, or just plain busy, we may not take the time to reflect on the message's content. Rather than noticing whether the arguments are particularly compelling, we might follow the **peripheral route to persuasion** – focusing on cues that trigger acceptance without much thinking. So an attractively packaged message will be better received than one that has compelling arguments. In these situations, easily understood familiar statements are more persuasive than novel statements with the same meaning.

peripheral route to persuasion occurs when people are influenced by incidental cues (such as the speaker's attractiveness) and, due to this, find the argument persuasive, rather than by careful consideration of the argument's validity (the opposite of the central route to persuasion)

If we consider central and peripheral routes to persuasion, Billig (1996) argues that what we have here are 'the two competing demands of experience: one whispers seductively that people can be fooled and the other warns that the audience can argue back. For any given situation, orators must use their Judgement to decide between these two voices of theirs' (p. 109). Smart advertisers adapt advertisements to their consumers' thinking. They do so for good reason, given how much of consumer behaviour – such as one's spontaneous decision, while shopping, to pick up some ice cream of a particular brand – is made unthinkingly (Dijksterhuis et al., 2005). It must be worth their while because in 2015, $590 billion was spent globally on advertising (Cacioppo et al., 2018). Playing music and wafting the aroma of vanilla under the noses of your customers in a fashion retail store can increase the amount of time they spend in there and their purchasing of items (Morrison et al., 2011). Billboards and television commercials – media that consumers are able to take in for only brief amounts of time – therefore, use the peripheral route, by using visual images as peripheral cues. Instead of providing arguments in favour of smoking, cigarette advertisements associate the product with images of beauty and pleasure. So do soft-drink advertisements that promote 'the real thing' with images of youth, vitality and happy polar bears. On the other hand, magazine computer advertisements (which interested, logical consumers may pore over for some time) seldom feature movie stars or great athletes. Instead they offer customers information on competitive features and prices. Government campaigns that ask us to recycle our rubbish and decrease our dependence on plastic carrier bags may well decide to engage their audience with the central arguments on the virtues of greener ways of living.

Different Routes for Different Purposes

The ultimate goal of the advertiser, the politician, and even the teacher, is not just to have people pay attention to the message and move on. Typically, the goal also involves some sort of behaviour change (buying a product, loving one's neighbour, or studying more effectively). Are the two routes to persuasion equally likely to fulfil that goal? Petty et al. (1995) note how central route processing can lead to more enduring change than does the peripheral route. When people are thinking carefully and mentally elaborating on issues, they rely not just on the strength of persuasive appeals but on their own thoughts in response as well. It's not so much the arguments that are persuasive as the way they get people thinking. And when people think deeply rather than superficially, any changed attitude will more likely persist, resist attack and influence behaviour (Petty & Krosnick, 1995; Verplanken, 1991).

Thus, the central route is more likely to lead to attitude and behaviour changes that 'stick', whereas the peripheral route may lead merely to superficial and temporary attitude change (Bhattacherjee & Sanford, 2006). As sex educators know, changing attitudes is easier than changing behaviour. Studies assessing the effectiveness of abstinence education find some increase in attitudes supporting abstinence but little long-term impact on sexual behaviour (Hauser, 2005). Likewise, HIV-prevention education tends to have more effect on attitudes towards condoms than on condom use (Albarracin et al., 2003). In both cases, changing behaviour as well as attitudes seems to require people actively processing and rehearsing their own convictions.

None of us has the time to thoughtfully analyse all issues. Often we take the peripheral route, by using simple rule-of-thumb heuristics, such as 'trust the experts' or 'long messages are credible'.

Chaiken (1980) developed the 'heuristic-systematic model' (HSM) to describe the differences between heuristic processing and systematic processing. It has much in common with the ELM. Both were developed in the 1980s, and both propose that there are different persuasion processes which can occur depending on the situation. However, the HSM distinguishes between systematic processing and heuristic processing. Whereas systematic processing involves a thorough cognitive engagement with the arguments within a message (similar to the central processing of ELM), heuristic processing is a way of dealing with information quickly taking mental short-cuts (not too dissimilar from the peripheral processing of ELM). We all make snap judgements using such heuristics: if a speaker is articulate and appealing, has apparently good motives, and has several arguments (or, better, if the different arguments come from different sources), we usually take the easy peripheral route and accept the message without much thought (**Figure 6.1**).

In Chapter 4 we discuss the role of heuristics in social thinking and judgements. Snap judgements based on heuristics are common in everyday life.

Where this confidence comes from may be in part down to our social networks and what attitudes already exist among the people around us. Our social networks are made up of the people with whom we have personal and professional relationships. Levitan and Visser (2007) have found that the amount of variability there is in the attitudes of your social network affects how likely you are to be persuaded and which route to persuasion you are likely to take. In their study of 353 US participants who favoured capital punishment, those who came from attitudinally diverse social networks were much more likely to be persuaded against it than those from fairly homogenous social networks. Furthermore, they were persuaded by the presentation of strong arguments rather than weak ones, therefore using the central (or systematic) methods for processing the information. Those participants from more attitudinally homogeneous networks did not distinguish between strong and weak arguments and were much more resistant to persuasion. Levitan and Visser argue that when we are surrounded by like-minded people, we are not motivated to change our attitudes and beliefs about things. Indeed, to do so might risk ridicule and even ostracism within the social network or ingroup. However, when we are within diverse social networks we are motivated to examine information carefully, working out our own attitudes.

Of course our social networks are not just those people we see face-to-face. Interest in our online social networks and their role in persuasion has increased, as has our use of online platforms (Bernhardt et al., 2012). This interest has not just

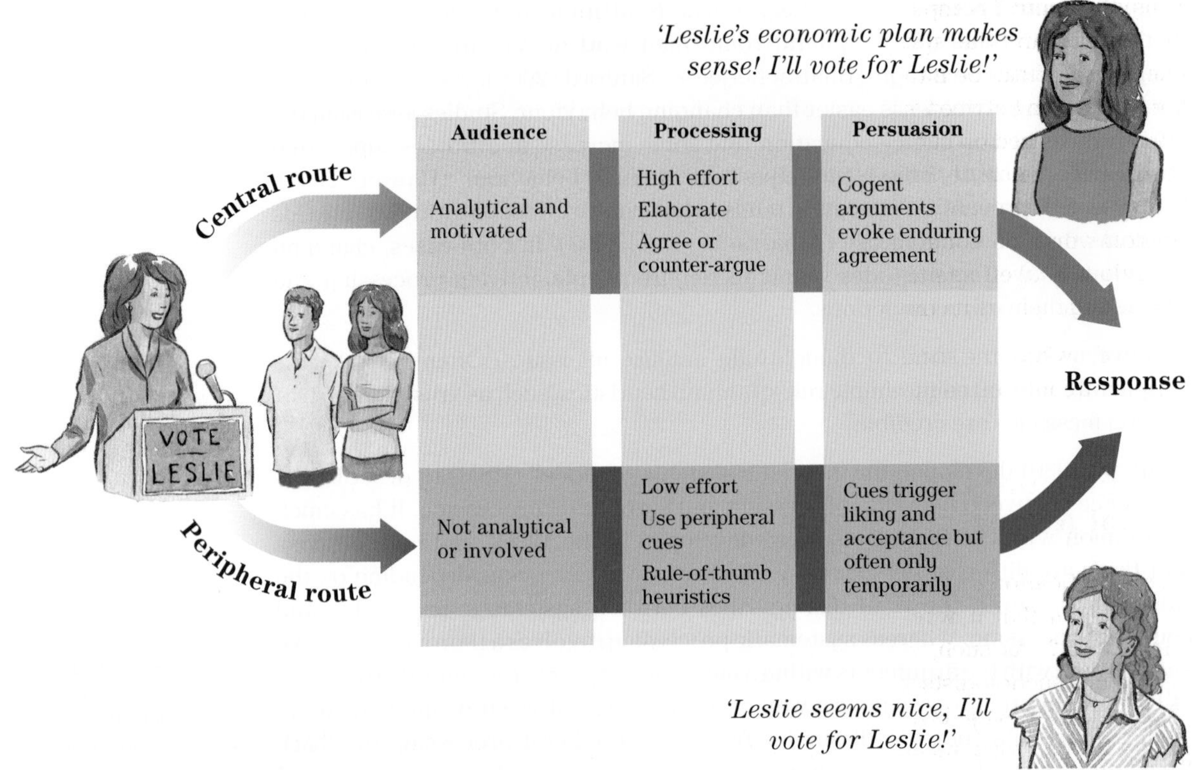

FIGURE 6.1 The central and peripheral routes to persuasion
Computer advertisements typically take the central route, by assuming their audience wants to systematically compare features and prices. Soft-drink advertisements usually take the peripheral route, by merely associating their product with glamour, pleasure and good moods. Political election campaigns typically use both routes, to appeal to all audiences. Central route processing more often produces enduring attitude change.

come from social psychologists but also, perhaps predictably, the advertiser, the politician, the media, and indeed anyone with a stake in persuading us to buy, vote, act, agree, or believe in whatever they are marketing online. This has resulted in a growing body of research that ranges from the effective targeting of online viral advertisements to social networks (e.g. De Gregorio & Sung, 2010; Subramani & Rajagopalan, 2003; Miller & Lammas, 2010), to job-seeking (e.g. Chiang & Suen, 2015), to the influence our online 'friends' have over us (e.g. Svensson, 2011). One revelation of this research is that electronic word-of-mouth (e-WOM) is more influential than an advertisement (Trusov et al., 2009). An insightful example comes from work conducted in Iran that focused on how people make decisions about purchasing a car. Reza Jalilvand and Samiei (2011) found that e-WOM has a huge impact on a car's brand image and also a customer's intention to buy the car. It is important to us to read other people's reviews of the product as they become an important factor in our decision to buy, or not. Whether our social networks are online or offline, the point remains: they matter when it comes to persuasion.

Just One Route to Persuasion?

Some social psychologists have been critical of these two route models of persuasion, and have suggested that really there's just one route to persuasion.

Kruglanski and Thompson (1999) argue that the 'central' and 'peripheral' routes of the ELM, and the 'systematic' and 'heuristic' paths of the HSM, are really just one path, and can be integrated into a *unimodel* of persuasion. They propose that the distinction between 'central' processing of a message's content, and peripheral processing based on cues, is actually a feature of the information presented rather than a description of the persuasion process we go through. In other words, they are all types of persuasive evidence. Kruglanski and Thompson suggest that, in the real world, messages contain a variety of content and cues in order to achieve their rhetorical effects. Both the content and the cues of the message are working to persuade you of its truth.

However, whatever social psychologists consider to be the route of persuasion, they are all interested in how messages convince you of their truth.

The Elements of Persuasion and their Relationship to Social Norms

The classification of the elements of persuasion developed partly from Laswell's (1948) claim that it was about 'Who says what in what channel to whom with what effect?' As such, among the primary ingredients of persuasion explored by social psychologists are these four: (1) the communicator; (2) the message; (3) how the message is communicated; and (4) the audience. In other words, who says what by what means to whom? Using experimental methods some social psychologists have examined how each of these factors affects the likelihood that we will take either the central or the peripheral route to persuasion, as well as their overall success in achieving influence. As we have already seen, some of this experimental work acknowledges the role of the situation and the broader social context in which the individual is embedded in the effectiveness of social influence. Using qualitative methods some social psychologists have sought to investigate this relationship between persuasion and social context. So, in this section we will consider the four main elements from a range of experimental and qualitative studies and ideas (see Figure 6.6 for a summary of these four elements).

Who Says? The Communicator

'It is simplicity that makes the uneducated more effective than the educated when addressing popular audiences.'

Aristotle, *Rhetoric*

Social psychologists have found that the way in which an audience receives a message will depend not just on 'what' is said, but also on 'who' says it. In other words, it is not just the content that counts but also the characteristics of the communicator. What then, makes one communicator more persuasive than another?

Credibility

Many of us would find a statement about the benefits of exercise more believable if it came from the European Non-Governmental Sports Organization (ENGSO) rather than from a tabloid newspaper. But the effects of source **credibility** (perceived expertise and trustworthiness) diminish quite quickly. If a credible person's message is persuasive, its impact may fade as its source is forgotten or dissociated from the message. Meanwhile, the impact of a non-credible person

credibility believability; a credible communicator is perceived as both expert and trustworthy may correspondingly increase over time if people remember the message better than the reason for discounting it (Pratkanis et al., 1988).

However, of course what, or who, is perceived as a credible source depends on the context in which it is presented.

Perceived Expertise

How does one become an authoritative 'expert'? One way is to begin by saying things the audience agrees with, which makes one seem smart. Another is to be introduced as someone who is *knowledgeable* on the topic.

The findings from experiments can tell us a lot about how people respond to sources they consider to be 'experts'. However, producing a credible source in terms of expertise relies on shared cultural understandings that some individuals, or categories of people, are experts in some social contexts. The sociologist Harvey Sacks (1992) explains that within each culture there is shared knowledge and understandings about the roles people occupy and the social categories to which they belong. These categories carry with them implicit knowledge about what such people know (category entitlements) and how they 'ought' to behave in accordance with their category membership (category bound activities). For example, we 'know' dentists are experts with respect to certain kinds of knowledge (health and medicine) and we have a shared understanding of how they 'ought' to behave. There are clear limits to their expertise. As we share this knowledge people can populate their accounts of social life with references to such 'experts' rhetorically bolstering the persuasiveness of the message they are trying to convey.

Jason Clark and his research collaborators point out that we tend to scrutinize messages more when they are delivered by an expert than by a non-expert. We give them greater cognitive attention. Consequently, research evidence has suggested that the effectiveness of an expert depends on whether the expert is arguing from a position that we agree with, or one we do not (Clark et al., 2012). When an expert tries to convince us about something for which we are already convinced, we do not really scrutinize what they say. When you're preaching to the converted, it doesn't matter who's doing the preaching. But when the message is one we do not already agree with, this is when an expert might prove more effective. A credible expert and message can force us to engage with the message at a deeper level than previously, and shift our attitudes from an unfavourable stance to a favourable one.

The expressive hands of Donald Trump: Speaker confidence can be expressed non-verbally as well as verbally.

SOURCE: ©mark reinstein/Alamy Stock Photo

Another way to appear credible is to communicate *confidence*. In their book which teaches the principles of influential communication, Lewis and Mills (2012), state that confidence is something an influential speaker must convey in the first 10 seconds of meeting an audience. First impressions, they argue, really do matter. That confidence must not only be communicated through what you say but also through your non-verbal behaviour, such as posture, eye contact, facial expressions, gestures and movement and use of space. Hall et al. (2016) studied the style Donald Trump adopted during his rallies for the US presidency. His deliberately comedic political style exuded confidence through not only what he said (see also Quam & Ryshina-Pankova, 2016), but also his use of space and gesture, which won him supporters even when he made claims many found offensive.

Perceived Trustworthiness

Speech style also affects a speaker's apparent trustworthiness. It is fairly well documented in social psychology that when someone looks us straight in the eye, we deem them more trustworthy than if they avert their gaze (e.g. Wyland & Forgas, 2010). However, this knowledge can facilitate the 'savvy liar' into misleading a courtroom jury about his or her innocence (Rand, 2000).

Trustworthiness is also higher if the audience believes the communicator is *not trying to persuade* them. In an early experimental version of what later became the 'hidden camera' method of television advertising, Walster and Festinger (1962) had some undergraduates eavesdrop on graduate students' conversations. (What they actually heard was a recording.) When the conversational topic was relevant to the eavesdroppers (having to do with campus regulations), the speakers had more influence if the listeners presumed the speakers were unaware of the eavesdropping. After all, if people think no one is listening, why would they be less than fully honest?

As millions of us now surf the Internet looking for advice and guidance, how do we know what information to trust? This was exactly the question that Briggs et al. (2002) asked. Firstly, they found that people trust an online source of information when it appears as though the source is credible, knowledgeable and impartial. Secondly, people need to feel the information is personal to them. Finally, people tend to trust websites that offer the advice they expected. In a study of how women in England choose and use online health advice about hormone replacement therapy (HRT), Sillience et al. (2007) noticed how women began the selection process by sifting through sites simply on the basis of their appearance. Websites that were attractive to the user were then examined for the quality and credibility of their information. However, the researchers are quick to point out the limited role the Internet has in shaping behaviour. We don't blindly follow. While it influences our decisions, the women in Sillience's study still tested it against advice from friends and family, and fundamentally trusted their own doctor as the prime source of help and advice. As we noted earlier in this chapter, our social networks matter.

We also perceive as sincere those who *argue against their own self-interest.* Eagly et al. (1978) presented students with a speech attacking a company's pollution of a river. When they said the speech was given by a political candidate with a business background or to an audience of company supporters, it seemed unbiased and was persuasive. When the same anti-business speech was supposedly given to environmentalists by a pro-environment politician, listeners could attribute the politician's arguments to personal bias or to the audience.

Discursive social psychologists have termed this the '**dilemma of stake and interest**' (Edwards, 1997; Potter, 1996). This means that if people are seen to have an 'axe to grind' in presenting a particular message, or having a personal interest or motivation in persuading people, they may not be regarded as trustworthy or credible. The canvassing politician seeking your vote, who tries to convince you that your taxes will not be raised should they be elected into power, is likely to be accused of having an interest in the version they present of

dilemma of stake and interest the management of self-interest in language their intended policies, and may not be believed. The man accused of assault in a bar-room brawl, who later tries to convince a jury that he was not responsible, can have his protestations dismissed on the grounds of 'Well, you would say that, wouldn't you!' In a classic research example, Gilbert and Mulkay (1984) found that when biochemists were asked to account for the trustworthiness of their scientific findings they emphasized the objectivity of science, the data-driven nature of the findings, free from human intervention. They called this an 'empiricist repertoire': one that managed their own stake in their findings to present accurate and trustworthy results. However, when asked to explain how other biochemists had achieved contradictory results to their own, they switched to a 'contingent repertoire', which emphasized how personal motives can drive scientific research contaminating the accuracy of the findings. So, to present your case as that of a disinterested and unmotivated communicator is often a very real concern in persuading people of the credibility and the trustworthiness of you and the message you convey.

In an early study on this, Miller et al. (1976) found that trustworthiness and credibility also increase when people *talk fast*. People who listened to tape-recorded messages rated fast speakers (about 190 words per minute) as more objective, intelligent and knowledgeable than slow speakers (about 110 words per minute). They also found the more rapid speakers more persuasive. More recently, Guyer et al. (2019) found that not only does fast speech increase confidence and persuasiveness of a speaker, but so does falling intonation and lowered pitch.

Some television advertisements are obviously created to make the communicator appear both expert and trustworthy. A drug company may peddle its pain reliever using a speaker in a white laboratory coat, who declares confidently that most doctors recommend their key ingredient (which is merely aspirin). Given such peripheral cues, people who don't care enough to analyse the evidence may automatically infer that the product is special without questioning the expertise of the speaker in the white coat. Other advertisements seem not to use the credibility principle. It's not primarily for his expertise in coffee that Nestlé paid George Clooney millions of dollars to appear in its advertisements!

Attractiveness and Liking

Many of us might deny that endorsements by star athletes and entertainers affect us. We know that stars are seldom knowledgeable about the products they endorse. Besides, we know the intent is to persuade us; we don't just accidentally eavesdrop on Kim Kardashian discussing clothes or fragrances. Such advertisements are based on another characteristic of an effective communicator: **attractiveness**.

attractiveness having qualities that are pleasing or appealing to others. Also refers to a person being physically attractive or sexually alluring

We're more likely to respond to those we like, a phenomenon well known to those organizing charitable solicitations, door-to-door sales and tupperware parties. Marketing experts have discovered an attractive presenter for an unattractive product can persuade the public to buy the product (Praxmarer & Rossiter, 2011). Even a mere fleeting conversation with someone is enough to increase our liking for that person and be more responsive to their influence (Burger et al., 2001). Our liking may open us up to the communicator's arguments (central route persuasion), or it may trigger positive associations when we see the product later (peripheral route persuasion). As with credibility, the liking-begets-persuasion principle suggests applications (see **Table 6.1**).

TABLE 6.1 Six persuasion principles

Principle	Application
Authority: People defer to credible experts	Establish your expertise; identify problems you have solved and people you have served
Liking: People respond more affirmatively to those they like	Win friends and influence people. Create bonds based on similar interests, praise freely
Social proof: People allow the example of others to validate how to think, feel and act	Use 'peer power' – have respected others lead the way
Reciprocity: People feel obliged to repay in kind what they've received	Be generous with your time and resources. What goes around, comes around
Consistency: People tend to honour their public commitments	Have others write or voice their intentions. Don't say 'Please do this by . . .'. Instead, elicit a 'yes' by asking
Scarcity: People prize what's scarce	Highlight genuinely exclusive information or opportunities

SOURCE: In his book *Influence: Science and practice*, persuasion researcher Robert Cialdini (2001) illustrates six principles that underlie human relationships and human influence. (This chapter describes the first two.)

Research suggests that we tend to find people we consider to be attractive as trustworthy, clever and popular (Langlois et al., 2000). Attractiveness varies in several ways. *Physical appeal* is one. Some studies have found that we will allow ourselves to be persuaded by someone we find physically attractive even when s/he is direct about wanting to change our behaviour in some way (e.g. Messner et al., 2008). Women who use their physical attractiveness to obtain a favour from a male stranger are generally successful at it (Davies et al., 2008).

Similarity is another. As Chapter 9 emphasizes, we tend to like people who are like us. We also are influenced by them, a fact that has been harnessed by a successful anti-smoking campaign that features youth appealing to other youth through advertisements that challenge the tobacco industry about its destructiveness and its marketing practices (Krisberg, 2004). People who *act* as we do, subtly mimicking our postures, are likewise more influential. This similarity effect even extends to our names. Howard and Kerin (2011) discovered that participants exposed to advertised products with brand names similar to their own name, were more favourably disposed to them than when the same product was given a generic name. So cranberry juice branded as V. Zack (participant's first name initial and full surname) was considered to be more desirable and beneficial than the same cranberry juice that was given a name dissimilar from their own. Why? Howard and Kerin suggest that the presence of a familiar name causes participants to engage in a more elaborate cognitive assessment of the product. And, we like things that are like us!

Arpan (2002) found that her participants were more likely to accept a fictitious report of a crisis involving an explosion in a paper factory, spilling toxic debris into the environment, as credible and convincing when the report came from someone they identified as being from the same ethnic group as themselves. As a general rule, people respond better to a message that comes from someone in their group. As we outline in Chapters 12 and 13, social identity theory and self-categorization theory would explain this as illustrative of ingroup favouritism. People discriminate in favour of their own group at the expense of

Often our desire to fit in and be accepted by our peers influences our behaviour.

SOURCE: ©Matrix Reloaded/Shutterstock

other perceptually relevant outgroups. As such, we are much more likely to be persuaded by someone we consider one of 'us' on some socially relevant dimension, than someone we consider one of 'them'.

Similarity can also be achieved through the content of a message. In an examination of the BBC *Panorama* interview the late Princess Diana gave in November 1997, Abell and Stokoe (2001) analysed how she presented herself as occupying roles that the audience could readily identify with. Referring to herself as a 'mother', 'wife' and 'woman', Diana presented herself as someone who understood the pressures everyday people were under to fulfil. Beneath the title and the nice palace she was just an ordinary woman trying to deal with the same issues they do. Drawing on her ordinariness, Diana detailed the cause of her depression, eating disorders, self-harming behaviour and her love affairs. As a princess, she may not have won the sympathy of her audience for her behaviour. As an ordinary woman, juggling the roles of wife and mother, experiencing the stresses of everyday life, as well as those of royal duties, she achieved an increase in popularity among her 21.1 million audience and a nation, who felt they understood.

But is similarity more important than credibility? Well it seems to depend on the situation as the answer is sometimes yes and sometimes no! We increasingly rely on the Internet to buy things we want or need. Clothes, groceries, gifts, and even houses and cars. Reichelt et al. (2014) wondered what matters more, credibility or similarity, when car retailers try to entice customers to purchase their cars over the Internet? They asked 839 people in Germany who had bought a car in the last 18 months over the Internet, what had worked in securing their custom. They found that when it came to searching out new information (such as the car's spec, safety features, etc.), then the perceived credibility and trustworthiness of the car retailer was key. This is what the researchers refer to as the *utilitarian function* of eWOM. However, potential customers were also keen to see what people similar to themselves had bought, found useful, and recommended. Reichelt and his colleagues concluded that online reviews written by previous buyers, as well as the car retailer's attempts to identify with their customer, perform a *social function* of eWOM. So when it comes to marketing products on the Internet, credibility matters to get your potential customer to read your website, but perceived similarity to the customer is what keeps them there and prompts a sale.

Perhaps when the choice concerns matters of personal value, taste or way of life, *similar* communicators have the most influence. But on judgements of fact – for example, does Sydney have less rainfall than London? – confirmation of belief by a *dissimilar* but trustworthy person provides a more independent and informed judgement.

What Is Said? The Message Content

It matters not only who says something but also *what* that person says. If you were to help organize an appeal to get people to vote for school taxes or to give money to world hunger relief, you might wonder how to concoct a recipe for central route persuasion. Common sense could lead you to either side of these questions:

- Is a purely logical message more persuasive – or one that arouses emotion?
- Will you get more opinion change by advocating a position only slightly discrepant from the listeners' existing opinions or by advocating an extreme point of view?
- Should the message express your side only, or should it acknowledge and refute the opposing views?
- If people are to present both sides – say, in successive talks at a community meeting or in a political debate – is there an advantage to going first or last?

Let's take these questions one at a time.

Reason versus Emotion

Remember at the start of this chapter we noted Aristotle's distinction between rhetoric (manipulation of the emotions), logic (scientific certainty) and dialect (reasoned debate). Suppose you were campaigning in support of world hunger relief. Which of these might you best rely on to convey your message? Would you best itemize your arguments and cite an array of impressive statistics? Or would you be more effective presenting an emotional approach – perhaps the compelling story of one starving child? Of course, an argument can be both reasonable and emotional. You can marry rhetoric, dialect and logic. Still, which is *more* influential – reason or emotion? Was Shakespeare's Lysander right: 'The will of man is by his reason sway'd'? Or was Lord Chesterfield's advice wiser: 'Address yourself generally to the senses, to the heart, and to the weaknesses of mankind, but rarely to their reason'?

The answer: it depends on the audience. Consider the following example. McKay-Nesbitt et al. (2011) found that younger adults (18–36 years) recalled negative emotional messages better than rational ones, and considered them to be more persuasive. However, older adults (48–89 years) showed the same levels of recall for rational and emotional messages. But, these older adults preferred rational and positive emotional messages and found them to be more persuasive than negative ones. Age seems to matter in how we receive persuasive rational and emotional messages.

Thoughtful, involved audiences often travel the central route; they are more responsive to reasoned arguments. Uninterested audiences more often travel the peripheral route; they are more affected by how much they like the communicator (Chaiken, 1980; Petty et al., 1981).

The Effect of Good Feelings

Messages also become more persuasive through association with good feelings. In classic social psychological research, Janis and colleagues (Janis et al., 1965; Dabbs & Janis, 1965) found that students were more convinced by persuasive messages if they were allowed to enjoy peanuts and Pepsi while reading the messages (**Figure 6.2**).

Good feelings often enhance persuasion, partly by enhancing positive thinking – if people are motivated to think – and partly by linking good feelings with the message (Gardner, 2004; Owolabi, 2009; Petty et al., 1993). As noted in Chapter 4, in

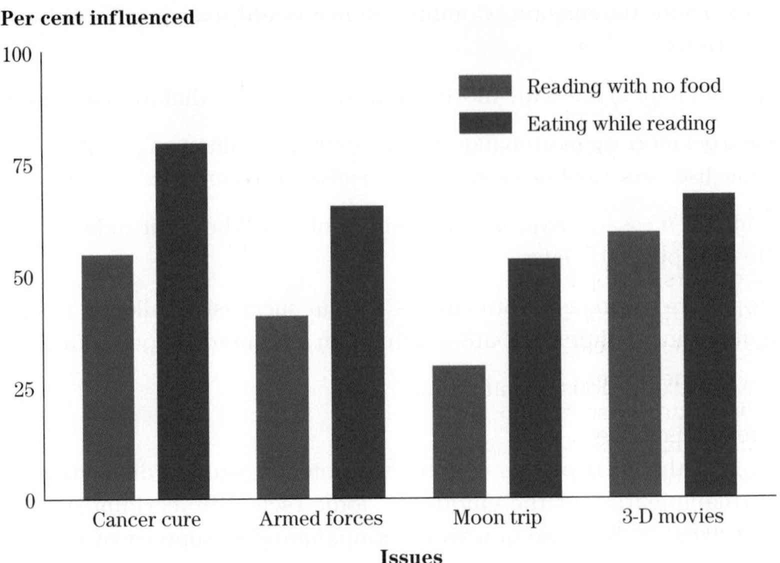

FIGURE 6.2 People who snacked as they read were more persuaded than those who read without snacking

SOURCE: Data from Janis et al. (1965).

a good mood, people view the world through rose-tinted glasses. But they also make faster, more impulsive decisions; they rely more on peripheral cues (Bodenhausen, 1993; Braverman, 2005; Schwarz et al., 1991). Unhappy people ruminate more before reacting, so they are less easily swayed by weak arguments. Thus, if you can't make a strong case, you might want to put your audience in a good mood and hope they'll feel good about your message without thinking too much about it.

Feeling 'right' about a message is a key part in achieving persuasion. Cesario and Higgins (2008) argue that the effect of non-verbal behaviour in making a recipient of a message feel right are extremely important in persuasion. In their study of 90 US students, they found that those who were 'promotion-focused' were persuaded by a message that was delivered by an animated and eager schoolteacher, advocating a new after-school assistance programme for children. Those who were identified as 'prevention-focused' were more persuaded when the teacher delivered the information in a cautious manner. Cesario and Higgins conclude that for a message to be persuasive the non-verbal cues must match the orientations of the participant such that the message 'feels right'.

Therefore, the style and manners of your lecturer in social psychology will not be assessed in the same way by all students. Some prefer to be entertained, to have a teacher who makes jokes and performs like an actor. Other students appreciate the presentation of complex theories and research results in a factual manner. Some enjoy lectures presenting subjective viewpoints, while others dislike those who do not present material in an objective manner. The saying 'you can please some of the people some of the time, but never all of the people all of the time', would seem to be very appropriate here!

The Effect of Arousing Fear

The use of fear as a persuasion technique has been documented in social psychology since the 1950s (Shen, 2016). Messages can be very effective when they evoke negative emotions. When one is trying to persuade people to brush their teeth more often, get a tetanus shot or drive carefully, a fear-arousing message can be potent (Mongeau, 2013). Dodge (2006) has noted how the police may persuade young informants to provide information about the criminal activities of their peers and social networks using a variety of incentives (e.g. money, promises of leniency), but also by instilling fear. But how much fear should you arouse? Should you evoke just a little fear, lest people become so frightened that they tune out your painful message? Or should you try to really terrify them? Early experiments by Leventhal (1970) and his collaborators and by Ronald Rogers and his collaborators (Robberson & Rogers, 1988) show that, often, the more frightened people are, the more they respond. And indeed recent research seems to agree. For example, women who are exposed to Flemish crime dramas are more fearful of becoming a victim of sexual violence in real life, than those women who are not (Custers & van den Bulck, 2013). Cauberghe et al. (2009) found that evoking fear in a sample of 18- to 28-year-old Belgian young people, fostered anti-speeding attitudes and behavioural intentions.

Fear-arousing communications have been used to increase people's detection behaviours, such as getting mammograms, doing breast or testicular self-examinations, and checking for signs of skin cancer. Banks, Salovey and their colleagues (1995) had women aged 40–66 who had never had a mammogram view an educational video on mammography. Of those who received a positively framed message that getting a mammogram can save your life through early detection), only half got a mammogram within the next 12 months. For those who received a fear-framed message (not getting a mammogram can cost you your life), two-thirds got a mammogram within 12 months. Another example comes from sunny Australia where sunbathing remains a popular past-time amongst young people, despite knowing the health risks. How do you curb this behaviour? Instil fear, suggests Lo Presti et al. (2014). In their study, ten young people aged 20–30 years old, were interviewed about their sunbathing habits. During the course of the interview they were shown a photo-aged photograph of themselves, displaying the ageing effects sunbathing had on their faces. The results were horrifying. 'It's a big shock . . . the photo just looks horrible', remarks one participant. 'Seeing this photo makes me want to change my behaviour', states another (p. 457). Participants reported that in future they would be using sunscreen and fake tan!

However, caution has been advised with respect to how much fear we instil into people. Jones and Owen (2006) found that producing too much fear about breast cancer in young Australian women increases perceived susceptibility beyond realistic levels. Furthermore, excessive fear can lessen intentions to go for a mammogram once they reach the target age for screening. So we need to be careful about how much fear we arouse within people.

That said, used at the right levels and for the right audience, it can be a very effective strategy to convince people to act in their own best interests. To have one's fears aroused is to become more intensely interested in information about a disease and the ways to prevent it (Das et al., 2003; Ruiter et al., 2001). For example, De Wit et al. (2008) have found that how fear and risk are presented to someone affects how they will respond to it. In their study of men who have sex with other men, the risk of contracting the Hepatitis B virus was presented to them in the form of either narrative evidence, statistics, a mere assertion of increased risk, or no risk information was given. Their results showed that when the risk was

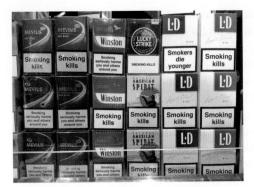

Fear is often used in healthcare warnings to persuade us to take better care of ourselves and our families.

SOURCE: ©TY Lim/Shutterstock

presented to the men as a narrative of evidence, they were much more likely to respond with the intention to have a vaccination against the virus. It seems that fear-framed messages work better when trying to prevent a bad outcome (such as cancer) than when trying to promote a good outcome (such as fitness) (Lee & Aaker, 2004).

Playing on fear won't always make a message more potent, though. For example, it has been found that fear arousal in promoting driver safety has little effect on actual behaviour (Lewis et al., 2007). Also, the person being targeted might not be in a position to change their behaviour. Maree (2010) notes that cervical cancer is the most common cancer amongst South African women. However, a campaign to promote condom use, no matter how fear-arousing it might be, is not going to work where women are not empowered to insist on their use. Huq and Chowdhury (2010) made similar conclusions amongst sex-workers in Bangladesh, where insisting on condoms could result in being beaten and losing clients.

Discrepancy

Some social psychologists propose that disagreement produces discomfort, and discomfort prompts people to change their opinions. This is central to Cognitive Dissonance Theory which we discuss in Chapter 5. So perhaps greater disagreement will produce more change under some circumstances. Based on the concepts of cognitive consistency and cognitive dissonance *social judgement theory* (SJT) (Sherif et al., 1965) proposes that how persuasive a person finds a message depends on how they evaluate the position or conclusions of that message. Does it fall within their own range of views and beliefs? The latitude of acceptance concerns all those attitudes that someone would find acceptable, whereas the latitude of rejection covers those they would find unacceptable. The latitude of non-commitment defines those attitudes that someone has no feelings about either way. Hence, for a message to be persuasive it should fall within the latitude of acceptance, or possibly non-commitment for it to work (Darity, 2008; Park et al., 2007). The influence of SJT has been particularly highlighted in clinical research when prescribing treatment for mental disorders (e.g. Smith et al., 2003) and campaigns to reduce binge-drinking among university students (e.g. Smith et al., 2006).

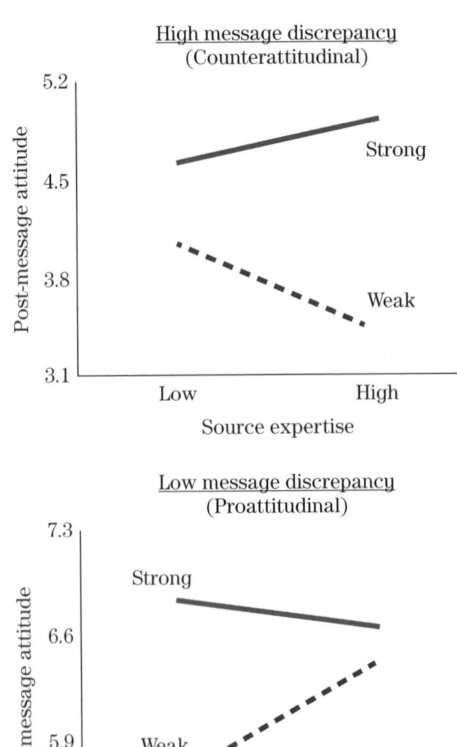

FIGURE 6.3 Discrepancy interacts with communicator credibility

Only a highly credible communicator maintains effectiveness when arguing an extreme position.

SOURCE: Clark et al. (2012).

But, this isn't to say messages which are discrepant from the receiver's own beliefs and values are necessarily doomed. Clark et al. (2012) report that a *credible source* – one hard to discount – elicits the most opinion change when advocating a position *greatly discrepant* from the recipient's. Thus, as **Figure 6.3** shows, discrepancy and credibility *interact:* the effect of a large versus small discrepancy depends on whether the communicator is credible.

Deeply involved people tend to accept only a narrow range of views. To them, a moderately discrepant message may seem foolishly radical, especially if the message argues an opposing view rather than being a more extreme version of a view with which they already agree (Ahluwalia, 2000; Pallak et al., 1972; Petty & Cacioppo, 1979).

One-sided versus Two-sided Appeals

Persuaders face another practical issue: how to deal with opposing arguments. Common sense offers no clear answer. Acknowledging the opposing arguments might confuse the audience and weaken the case. On the other hand, a message might seem fairer and be more disarming if it recognizes the opposition's arguments.

Werner et al. (2002) showed the disarming power of a simple two-sided message in experimental messages that promoted aluminium-can recycling. Signs added to wastebaskets in a university classroom building said, for example, 'No Aluminum Cans Please!!!!! Use the Recycler Located on the First Floor, Near the Entrance'. When a final persuasive message acknowledged and responded to the main counterargument – 'It May Be Inconvenient. But It Is Important!!!!!!!!!!' – recycling reached 80 per cent (double the rate before any message, and more than in other message conditions).

After Germany's defeat in the Second World War, the US Army did not want soldiers to relax and think that the still-ongoing war with Japan would become easy. Social psychologist Carl Hovland (whom we mentioned earlier in this chapter) and his colleagues (Hovland et al., 1949) in the Army's Information and Education Division designed two radio broadcasts arguing that the war in the Pacific would last at least two more years. One broadcast was one-sided; it did not acknowledge the existence of contradictory arguments, such as the advantage of fighting only one enemy instead of two. The other broadcast was two-sided; it mentioned and responded to the opposing arguments. As **Figure 6.4** illustrates, the effectiveness of the message depended on the listener. A one-sided appeal was most effective with those who already agreed. An appeal that acknowledged opposing arguments worked better with those who disagreed.

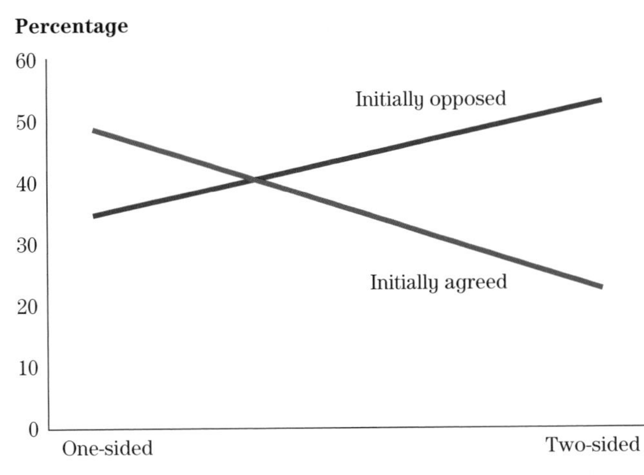

FIGURE 6.4 The interaction of initial opinion with one- versus two-sidedness
After Germany's defeat in the Second World War, American soldiers sceptical of a message suggesting Japan's strength were more persuaded by a two-sided communication. Soldiers initially agreeing with the message were strengthened more by a one-sided message.
SOURCE: Data from Hovland et al. (1949).

Experiments also reveal that a two-sided presentation is more persuasive and enduring if people are (or will be) aware of opposing arguments (Jones & Brehm, 1970; Lumsdaine & Janis, 1953). In the field of marketing psychology, Pizzutti et al. (2016) point out the usefulness of two-sided messages when persuading customers to buy a product. Acknowledging the product's negatives as well as its positives can lead the customer to regard the salesperson as truthful and worthy of taking advice from. So 'those jeans are a good fit, but they need ironing', might mean we purchase the jeans as we respect the opinion of the salesperson. However, if you were told 'this laptop has fantastic processing speed but poor battery life', would you buy it? Probably not. If the salesperson disregards an attribute that a customer considers important the intention to buy decreases. On the whole, bearing in mind this word of caution, a two-sided message works best. Apparently, a one-sided message stimulates an informed audience to think of counter-arguments and to view the communicator as biased. Thus, a political candidate speaking to a politically informed group would indeed be wise to respond to the opposition. So, *if your audience will be exposed to opposing views, offer a two-sided appeal.*

Primacy versus Recency

People often pay more attention to what comes first. Then again, people remember recent things better. So how might we seek to persuade someone? Speak first or last?

primacy effect other things being equal, information presented first usually has the most influence

The **primacy effect**: information presented early is most persuasive. First impressions are important. For example, can you sense a difference between these two descriptions?

- John is intelligent, industrious, impulsive, critical, stubborn and envious.
- John is envious, stubborn, critical, impulsive, industrious and intelligent.

When Asch (1946) gave these sentences to college students, those who read the adjectives in the intelligent-to-envious order rated the person more positively than did those given the envious-to-intelligent order. The earlier information seemed to colour their interpretation of the later information, producing the primacy effect.

A similar effect occurs in experiments where people succeed on a guessing task 50 per cent of the time. Those whose successes come early seem more capable than those whose successes come after early failures (Jones et al., 1968; Langer & Roth, 1975; McAndrew, 1981). A curious primacy effect also appears in political polls and in primary election voting: candidates benefit from being listed first on the ballot (Moore, 2004). Brunel and Nelson (2003) also reported primacy effects when men and women were presented with two advertisements asking them to give money to a cancer charity. When asked to write down their thoughts about the adverts, the first one was scrutinized much more carefully than the second one and consequently was the more persuasive.

recency effect information presented last sometimes has the most influence. Recency effects are less common than primacy effects

What about the opposite possibility? Would our better memory of the most recent information we've received ever create a **recency effect**? We know from our experience (as well as from memory experiments) that today's events can temporarily outweigh significant past events. Research on the positioning of television advertisements during a commercial break in programming concludes that we remember those shown towards the end of the break better than those shown at the start (Duncan & Murdock, 2000; Tse & Lee, 2001). Carlsson and Russo (2001) found that in a mock trial, participants thought the affadavit they read last, in a series of six, influenced their overall verdict more than the previous five did. So by virtue of us being able to recall information presented to us most recently, recency effects can operate to sway our opinions and actions.

Forgetting creates the recency effect (1) when enough time separates the two messages *and* (2) when the audience commits itself soon after the second message. When the two messages are back to back, followed by a time gap, it is the primacy effect that usually occurs (**Figure 6.5**). This is especially so when the first message stimulates thinking.

How Is It Said? The Channel of Communication

For persuasion to occur, there must be communication. And for communication to occur, there must be a **channel of communication**: a face-to-face appeal, a written sign or document, a television or radio advertisement.

channel of communication the way the message is delivered – whether face to face, in writing, on film or in some other way

Common-sense psychology places faith in the power of written words. How do we try to get people out to a campus event? We post notices. How do we get drivers to slow down and keep their eyes on the road? We put 'Drive Carefully' messages on billboards. How do we discourage students from dropping litter on campus? We post anti-litter messages on campus bulletin boards and in mailboxes.

Active Experience or Passive Reception?

Those of us who speak publicly, as teachers or persuaders, become so enamoured of our spoken words that we are tempted to overestimate their power. Ask college students what aspect of their college experience has been most valuable or what they remember from their first year, and few, sad to say, recall the brilliant lectures that we remember giving!

In an example of early work, Crawford (1974) and his associates tested the impact of the spoken word by going to the homes of people from 12 churches shortly before and after they heard sermons opposing racial bigotry and injustice. When asked during the second interview whether they had heard or read anything about racial prejudice or discrimination since the previous interview, only 10 per cent recalled the sermons spontaneously. When the remaining 90 per cent were asked directly whether their priest had 'talked about prejudice or discrimination in the last couple of weeks', more than 30 per cent denied hearing such a sermon. The end result: the sermons left racial attitudes unaffected.

When you stop to think about it, an effective preacher has many hurdles to surmount. As Figure 6.1 showed, a persuasive speaker must deliver a message that not only gets attention but also is understandable, convincing, memorable and compelling. A carefully thought-out appeal must consider each of those steps in the persuasion process.

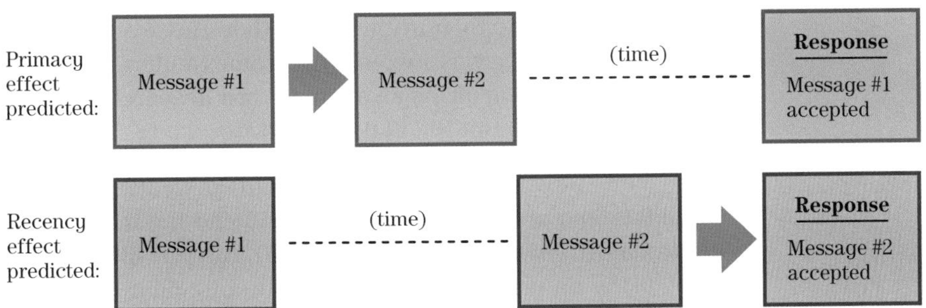

FIGURE 6.5 Primacy effect versus recency effect
When two persuasive messages are back to back and the audience then responds at some later time, the first message has the advantage (primacy effect). When the two messages are separated in time and the audience responds soon after the second message, the second message has the advantage (recency effect).

Let's consider another example. Researchers have invested their energies into finding effective persuasion strategies that motivate people to act in a more environmentally responsible way (also see Chapter 15 for more on this). As tourism opens up into protected areas, and more of us visit these spectacular places, increased litter becomes a problem for the resident wildlife and the habitat (Thompson et al., 2004). In response, anti-litter campaigns have been developed aimed at tackling this problem. But do they work? Studies suggest that written slogans such as 'Please do not litter' do not change people's actions. They are still prone to not completely tidy away the rubbish created by their picnic, nor stop to pick up a discarded bottle spotted lying on a track. However, a more targeted appeal such as 'Please put your rubbish in the bin' and 'If not you, who?', are much more effective at causing behavioural change (Roggenbuck, 1992; Brown et al., 2010). Appealing directly to social and personal norms is an effective persuasive strategy.

sleeper effect when a highly persuasive message is paired with a discounting, or low-credibility cue, leading to increased persuasiveness of the message over time

The aptly named **sleeper effect** describes how a message can become more persuasive over time when paired with information that discredits its validity (Hovland et al., 1949). For example, imagine you are given a vivid and informative leaflet about the degraded state of the environment that asks you to use eco-friendly household products, such as washing powder. Initially you may find the message extremely persuasive and resolve to act accordingly. Unfortunately, over time this persuasive influence decays and we continue to purchase our usual non-environmentally friendly brands. However, suppose that message about the state of the environment is sponsored by a well-known eco-friendly brand of washing powder. Their name is visible on the leaflet. Now we might be suspicious. Is the state of the environment really that bad, or is this company simply trying to sell us more of their product? Our attitude towards the environment and the need to use certain products may be unchanged. However, what experiments have shown is that over time that message becomes persuasive. In fact we may see a delayed attitude change towards the topic (environmental degradation), and even a trip to the shops to buy the product. Why? There have been two main hypotheses put forward (Kumkale & Albarracín, 2004). The first suggests we simply forget the discounting information, so all we remember is the leaflet about the state of the environment, and forget about the company that sponsored it. The second suggests that rather than forgetting the discounting information, we simply dissociate it from the message. We can recall both the message (the environment is in a terrible state) and the product (eco washing powder) but we do not associate them with one another. However, evidence for the sleeper effect is mixed, with some studies finding no proof that it exists at all. As an example, see Research Close-Up: I Know this Brand, But Did I Like the Ad?

Advertising power. Alcohol advertising campaigns have correlated with increases in underage drinking among adolescents (Jones & Magee, 2011; Siegfried et al., 2014).

SOURCE: ©Image Source/Alamy Stock Photo

With such power, can the media help a wealthy political candidate buy an election? Those who spend the most usually get the most votes (Open Secrets, 2005). Advertising exposure helps make an unfamiliar candidate into a familiar one. As we discuss in Chapter 9 on attraction, mere exposure to unfamiliar stimuli breeds liking. Moreover, *mere repetition* can make things believable. People rate trivial statements such as 'Mercury has a higher boiling point than copper' as more truthful if they read and rated them a week before.

As political manipulators know, believable lies can displace hard truths. Repeated clichés can cover complex realities. Even repeatedly saying that a consumer claim ('Shark cartilage is good for arthritis') is *false* can, when the discounting is presented amid other true and false claims, lead older adults later to misremember it as *true* (Skurnik et al., 2005). As they forget the discounting, their lingering familiarity with the claim can make it seem believable.

Mere repetition of a statement also serves to increase its fluency – the ease with which it spills off our tongue – which increases believability (McGlone & Tofighbakhsh, 2000). Moons et al. (2009) found that regardless of whether a message was weak or strong, mere repetition increased its persuasiveness to participants. Other factors, such as rhyming, also increase fluency and believability. 'Haste makes waste' may say essentially the same thing as 'rushing causes mistakes', but it seems more true. Whatever makes for fluency (familiarity, rhyming) also makes for credibility.

The persuasive techniques of **foot-in-the-door**, **door-in-the-face**, and **low-balling** cause behavioural changes which then lead to shifts in attitudes. These are discussed in relation to the persuasive power of cults later in this chapter.

foot-in-the-door phenomenon manipulation technique in which getting people to first agree to a small request increases the chances that they will later comply with a larger request

door-in-the-face technique manipulation technique for gaining concession in which after requesting something large (expecting that it will be turned down) the same requester counter-offers with a more reasonable request

low-balling when a previously attractive offer is changed upon acceptance to a less attractive one

Because passively received appeals are sometimes effective and sometimes not, can we specify in advance the topics on which a persuasive appeal will be successful? There is a simple rule: persuasion *decreases* as the significance and familiarity of the issue *increase*. On minor issues, such as which brand of aspirin to buy, it's easy to demonstrate the media's power. On more familiar and important issues, such as attitudes about a lengthy and controversial war, persuading people is like trying to push a piano uphill. It is not impossible, but one shove won't do it.

As we see in Chapter 5, 'Attitudes and Behaviour', active experience also strengthens attitudes. When we act, we amplify the idea behind what we've done, especially when we feel responsible. What is more, attitudes more often endure and influence our behaviour when rooted in our own experience. Compared with attitudes formed passively, experience-based attitudes are more confident, more stable and less vulnerable to attack. These principles are evident in many studies which show that the most effective HIV-prevention interventions not only give people information but also give them behavioural training, such as by practising assertiveness in refusing sex and using protection (Albarracin et al., 2005).

Personal versus Media Influence

Persuasion studies often demonstrate that the major influence on us is not the media but our contact with people. Modern selling strategies seek to harness the power of word-of-mouth personal influence through 'viral marketing', 'creating a buzz' and 'seeding' sales (Walker, 2004). The Harry Potter series of books was not expected to be a best seller (*Harry Potter and the Philosopher's Stone* had a first printing of 500 copies) until kids talking to other kids made it so.

'You do realize, you will never make a fortune out of writing children's books?'
J. K. Rowling's literary agent before release of *Harry Potter and the Philosopher's Stone*

In their book *World Class Communication*, Scudder et al. (2012) note that even in the age of social media, there is no substitute for the important role public speaking has for persuaders such as world leaders and CEOs to communicate with those they seek to influence. Having face-to-face contact with people can

Research close-up

I Know this Brand, But Did I Like The Ad?

Source: *Pashupati, K. (2003).* 'I know this brand, but did I like the ad?' An investigation of the familiarity-based sleeper effect. *Psychology and Marketing, 20*(11), 1017–1043.

Introduction

Existing research suggests that there are certain factors that increase the influence of an advertisement. We have better recall for advertisements that have emotional content than we do for advertisements that are neutral. But how long does this recall last? Can we increase its retention in memory, and if we do, will this make the advertisement more persuasive? Repeated exposure to an advertisement can also aid recall for it and increase its influential power. But is it possible to repeat something too much? Can influence turn to boredom? Does it enhance or diminish our evaluation of it?

Research also suggests that how we evaluate the advertisement will influence our attitudes towards the brand being promoted. However, the familiarity-brand-sleeper effect predicts that those advertisements that evoke strong positive or negative evaluations will result in positive attitudes towards the brand after a delay (see the sleeper effect earlier in the chapter). Put simply, this effect predicts that emotive advertisements (good and bad) are better recalled than neutral ones. Furthermore, we are good at recalling familiar brands and we tend to like them more than unfamiliar ones. So, even after a delay, we should be able to remember the brand quite well. A memorable advertisement (positive or negative) and a memorable brand (familiar, positively evaluated) should result in delayed positive evaluation of the brand. Advertisements that are neutral will be quickly forgotten, as will the brand they promoted.

Based on existing research, seven hypotheses were generated to examine the extent to which each of these factors matters in the persuasiveness of advertisements. The hypotheses were as follows:

H1: Affective (positive and negative) advertisements will be recalled better than neutral advertisements, both immediately after exposure and 7 days later.

H2: Regardless of content, recall for all advertisements will diminish after 7 days. However, there will be a greater decline in recall for the neutral advertisements than the positive and negative affective ones.

H3: Advertisements that are negatively evaluated will result in the most negative attitudes towards the brand. Those advertisements that are evaluated the most positive will lead to the most positive attitudes towards the brand. Those advertisements evaluated as neutral will result in intermediate evaluations of the brand.

H4: Advertisements evaluated positively or negatively will lead to positive evaluations of the brand after a 7-day delay (sleeper effect).

H5: Repeated exposure to advertisements will result in more positive evaluations of the advertisement, regardless of its content, than advertisements just seen once.

H6: Repeated exposure to an advertisement, regardless of content, will result in more positive evaluations of the brand, than for advertisements just seen once.

H7: Participants will have better recall for advertisements seen three times, than those seen once.

Method

Participants

A total of 211 undergraduate students were recruited, of which 87 were male and 124 were female. Age range was 17–53 years, with a mean age of 24 years.

Stimuli

The advertisements were TV commercials shown during a 30-minute documentary programme. To mimic real life as much as possible, the target advert was embedded amongst eight filler advertisements.

Independent Variables

Advertisement type: Three types to evoke positive (Instant Chicken), negative (Potato Chips) or neutral (Bread) evaluations of the advertisement.

Repetition of the advertisement: Participants either saw the target advertisement once, or three times.

Delay: Participants were either tested immediately after seeing the advert, or seven days later.

Dependent Variables

Participants were asked a series of questions in relation to the hypotheses.

Attitude to Brand – assessed on a 7-point Likert scale (1 = very negative, 7 = very positive), participants were asked to rate how favourable they were to the brand being advertised.

Purchase Intention – assessed on a bipolar scale (e.g. likely – unlikely, probably – improbably), participants were asked if they would intend buying the product if they were in the market for one. (See Chapter 5 for discussion on Likert and bipolar attitudinal scales.)

Advertisement Recall – participants were asked to recall what brand was advertised. This was divided into an Aided condition (presented with a list of brand names and asked to indicate which they had seen), and Unaided condition (simply list the brand names you remember seeing).

Procedure

Participants were asked if they would like to take part in a study on TV viewing habits and purchasing behaviour. Upon acquiring consent, they were then led to the testing room. They watched the TV programme, including the advertisements. Which target advert they saw depended on the condition they were in (positive, negative or neutral). Participants either saw the target advert once, or three times during the course of their TV viewing. Participants in the delay condition were thanked and asked to return in 7 days' time, whereupon they would be given the dependent measures. Participants in the immediate response condition were then given a post-test questionnaire that consisted of a recall test (aided or unaided) for the adverts and brands seen during the testing phase, and the Attitude to Brand and Purchase Intention scales. They were also asked for evaluations of each commercial for the target advertisement as a manipulation check to ensure that those adverts considered to be positive (Instant Chicken), negative (Potato Chips) and neutral (Bread) by the experimenters were also rated this way by the participants. This was done on a 7-point Likert scale (1 = very negative, 7 = very positive).

Results

The manipulation check showed that participants did rate the adverts in the same way as the experimenters. The Potato Chip advert was considered most negative (Mean 3.35), the Bread advert was evaluated more positively (3.90), and the Instant Chicken advertisement was considered the most positive (5.31).

To test H1, the percentage of accurate overall recall for the adverts (aided and unaided, immediate and after 7 days) was calculated. The highest overall recall was for the negative advert (Potato Chips) (unaided 60.9 per cent, unaided 92.6 per cent). The next highest recall was for the neutral advert (Bread) (unaided 51 per cent, aided 80 per cent). The lowest recall was for the positive advertisement (Instant Chicken) (unaided 35.3 per cent, aided 56.4 per cent). So H1 was partially rejected as the neutral advert produced higher recall than the positive advertisement.

H2 predicted that those advertisements that were positively and negatively evaluated (Chicken, Potato Chips) would be better remembered after 7 days than the neutral advertisement (Bread). The negative advert had the highest level of recall (63 per cent), the positive had the lowest (25.8 per cent) and the neutral had an intermediate recall rate (37 per cent). So H2 is partially supported as while the negative advert had the highest level of recall after 7 days, the positive one had the lowest.

H3 and H4 both took into account the sleeper-effect. For the no-delay group, negative attitudes towards the advertisement resulted in negative attitudes towards the brand (mean score 3.85). Likewise, advertisements that were evaluated as neutral produced slightly higher evaluations of the product (4.30), and positive adverts gave rise to the most positively evaluated products (4.39). H3 was therefore supported. However, consistent with the sleeper-effect, H4 predicted that these results would be somewhat different for the 7-day delay group. For this group, both the positive and negatively evaluated advertisements should produce more positive evaluations of the product than the neutral advertisement. This was not the case. Although the negative advertisement produced a more positive evaluation of the product after the 7-day delay than the no-delay group (mean = 4.08), the evaluations of the products from the positive and neutrally evaluated advertisements remained the same as the no-delay group. See **Table 6.2**.

A *t*-test revealed no significant differences in scores between the Delay (immediate, 7-day) groups in Product Attitude scores according to advertisement type (positive, negative, neutral).

H5, H6 and H7 concerned the effects of repetition on brand evaluation. H5 predicted that participants who were exposed to the target advertisement three times would be more positive towards it than those who had only seen it once. H6 predicted that this repetition effect would also lead to more positive evaluation of the brand being advertised. Both of these hypotheses were supported. An inspection of the means shows that evaluations of the advertisement and the product were more positive when participants saw them three times, regardless of the type of advert (positive, negative, neutral). See **Table 6.3**.

Despite this increase in means for positive evaluation when exposed to an advertisement three times, this increase was only statistically significant when the advertisement was a negative one (Potato Chips).

TABLE 6.2 Mean attitude towards brand scores by ad type and delay condition

	Attitude to product	
Ad type	**No delay**	**7-day delay**
Negative	3.85	4.08
Neutral	4.30	4.31
Positive	4.39	4.27

TABLE 6.3 Mean attitude scores to advertisement and product according to repetition

	Advertisement		Product	
Ad type	**Single exposure**	**Three exposures**	**Single exposure**	**Three exposures**
All ads	3.60	4.40	3.89	4.34
Negative	2.83	3.83	3.55	4.36
Neutral	3.36	4.23	4.18	4.35
Positive	4.99	5.65	4.22	4.28

H7 predicted that the advertisement would be better recalled when seen three times than when seen only once. This was supported as 69 per cent of participants who saw the advertisement three times, recalled it. This compares with only 38.2 per cent of participants who recalled an advertisement when only seen once.

Discussion

This study only offers partial support for some of the experimental hypotheses. It seems we recall negative advertisements better than positive or neutral ones (H1, H2). However, this does not lead to increased liking over time for the product being advertised as no support was found for the sleeper-effect (H3, H4). Repetition increases positive evaluations of advertisements and brands regardless of the type of advert (H5, H6). However, this is only statistically significant for negative advertisements. So perhaps being exposed to a negative advert means we become more tolerant of it over time. We also remember better those advertisements we see more often.

Critical Reflections

Overall, this study failed to find support for the sleeper-effect. However, there are some criticisms that could be made of the study. The TV commercials may not have been extreme enough in terms of their positive and negative content. Furthermore, there was only one example of each type of advertisement. Could more examples have produced different results? The sample consisted of undergraduate students. Might a more heterogeneous population have behaved in a different way? The study also did not check how familiar participants were with each of the brands being advertised. Any effect brand familiarity may have upon evaluations of it, needs to be investigated. Trying to pin down the factors which make advertisements persuasive and encourage us to buy products, is extremely complex.

prove crucial in swaying opinions and actions (also see Kalla & Broockman, 2018). In the context of healthcare, Anker et al. (2013) found that the granting of organ donation from families of the deceased was more likely if the organ donor coordinator made personal contact and expressed sympathy for their loss.

Do you recognize the potency of personal influence in your own experience? Many college students say in retrospect that they have learned more from their friends and other students than from contact with books or professors. Indeed the amount of research on peer-learning has exploded in recent times, as we increasingly recognize the persuasive power of our friends. For example, Nelwati et al. (2018) found peer-learning was crucial in the development of undergraduate nursing students towards professional registration. In an interview study, Werner and Dickson (2018) discovered that German Bundesliga elite football players thought that their peers were key sources of information and advice. Peers could offer help with a range of things including handling the pressure of playing at an elite level, dealing with fans, playing tactics, and learning about different cultures.

And it seems we aren't just persuaded by our peers and family about how the world is. We are also influenced by our environment. The controversial **broken window theory** (Wilson & Kelling, 1982) has been adopted by police and social scientists, to explain how certain features in an environment, such as noisy neighbours, graffiti, gangs and derelict buildings, can lead to high crime rates in the area. Proponents of this theory argue that visible cues of apparent disorder create norms for crime. Consequently, it has been argued that one way to tackle crime is

broken window theory states that visible displays of disorder set norms for crime and anti-social behaviour to tidy up an area and bring it in visible order. See the Research Close-Up, Adult Residents' Perceptions of Neighbourhood Safety, for an empirical example of how well broken window theory explains perceptions of crime amongst older adults.

Media Influence

Although face-to-face influence is usually greater than media influence, we should not underestimate the media's power. Those who personally influence our opinions must get their ideas from some source, and often their sources are the media. In a qualitative study of the language of televised political press conferences surrounding the meeting of the former Chinese President Jiang Zemin and the US president George W. Bush, Bhatia (2008) observes how what might appear a spontaneous discussion and airing of views is actually a carefully controlled piece of discourse. Bhatia notes how the media's influence over their discussion enables two ideologically opposed speakers to disguise their fundamental differences and appear to be in mutual agreement. The media becomes a powerful tool for persuading its audience that political similarity exists.

two-step flow of communication the process by which media influence often occurs through opinion leaders, who in turn influence others

In an early study about persuasion and how it works, Katz (1957) observed that many of the media's effects operate in a **two-step flow of communication**: from media to opinion leaders to the rank and file. In any large group, it is these *opinion leaders* and trendsetters – 'the influentials' – that marketers and politicians seek to woo (Keller & Berry, 2003). Opinion leaders are individuals perceived as experts. They may include talk show hosts and editorial columnists; doctors, teachers and scientists; and people in all walks of life who have made it their business to absorb information and to inform their friends and family. If I want to evaluate computer equipment, I defer to the opinions of my sons, who get many of their ideas from the printed page. Sell them and you will sell me.

The two-step flow model reminds us that media, both online and offline, influences penetrate the culture in subtle ways. Even if the media had little direct effect on people's attitudes, they could still have a big indirect effect. Those children who grow up without watching television or access to the Internet do not grow up beyond media influence. Unless they live as hermits, they will join in media-imitative play on the school ground. They will ask their parents for the media-related toys their friends have. They will beg or demand to watch their friends' favourite programmes, play on the computer, and may do so when an opportunity arises. Parents can just say no, but they cannot switch off media influence.

To Whom Is It Said? The Audience

As we see in Chapter 7, people's traits often don't predict their responses to social influence. A particular trait may enhance one step in the persuasion process (Figure 6.1) but work against another. Let's also consider two characteristics of those who receive a message: age and thoughtfulness.

How Old Are They?

People tend to have different social and political attitudes depending on their age. Social psychologists give two explanations for the difference, and these explanations seem to contradict each other. One is a *life-cycle explanation:* attitudes change (for example, become more conservative) as people grow older (Sears, 1981). The other is a *generational explanation:* attitudes do *not* change;

older people largely hold on to the attitudes they adopted when they were young (Glenn, 1980). Because these attitudes are different from those being adopted by young people today as society's norms and values change, a generation gap develops. There are differences between *cohorts* (those born in the same decade, for example) and not only differences due to age.

Well, they can't both be right! Unfortunately, the evidence offers no clear and consistent answer (Visser & Krosnick, 1998; Wang & Chen, 2006).

The teens and early twenties are important formative years. Attitudes are changeable during that time and the attitudes formed then tend to stabilize through middle adulthood. Young people might therefore be advised to choose their social influences – the groups they join, the media they imbibe, the roles they adopt – carefully. This has led to some very valuable yet distressing research. For example, some researchers have focused on online sexual exploitation of young people. Gámez-Guadix et al. (2018) asked 2,731 adolescents in Spain, aged between 12 and 15 years, about their online experiences. They explained their findings in the context of Cialdini's (2009) six strategies for social persuasion. Adult abusers would seek *recipriocity* from their victims, for example asking for favours in return for gifts. *Commitment* and *consistency* also featured as abusers extracted prior commitments from the young person who then felt compelled to be consistent and honour the commitment (the theory of **cognitive dissonance** is useful here – see also Chapter 5). Once the foot was in the door, the adult's requests intensified. Their *authority* over the young person was made explicit as they portrayed themselves as their guide and mentor, someone they could trust. The young people were given *social validation* for their behaviour as they were told others had also done this and it was nothing to be worried about. The abuser stressed the exclusive and secret nature of their online relationship, noting its *scarcity* and specialness. Finally, the adult would make efforts to identify with their victim in order to bolster their *likability*.

cognitive dissonance
tension that arises when one is simultaneously aware of two inconsistent cognitions. For example, dissonance may occur when we realize that we have, with little justification, acted contrary to our attitudes. This inconsistency is unpleasant, and people use different methods to combat the dissonance. Concept coined by Leon Festinger (1957)

Research close-up

Adult Residents' Perceptions of Neighbourhood Safety

Source: *Pitner, R. O., Yu, M., & Brown, E. (2011).* Exploring the dynamics of middle-aged and older adult residents' perceptions of neighborhood safety. *Journal of Gerontological Social Work, 54,* 511–527.

Introduction

Generally speaking, we all prefer to live in places where we feel safe. Middle-aged and older adults especially value this in their neighbourhood. It is important not only for well-being and happiness, but also retaining our independence and ability to remain in our own home as we get older. So what factors can make people feel unsafe in their neighbourhoods? What leads to feelings of vulnerability?

The broken window hypothesis states that we feel unsafe when there are visible cues of disorder in the environment. These include apparent physical incivilities (e.g. derelict buildings, graffiti) and social incivilities (noisy neighbours, sex-workers on the street). Broken window theory goes even further than this and argues that features such as these in our neighbourhoods directly contribute to a high crime rate as seemingly appropriate norms for crime and disorder emerge as a consequence.

Others have pointed towards community cohesion and attachment to an area in explaining why we may feel unsafe. Collective efficacy describes high levels of community cohesion, offering a safe (and monitored) environment for people to live. Where this doesn't exist, people may feel isolated and vulnerable. There is a lack of vigilance in ensuring the safety of residents.

This current study tested four hypotheses to see which of these theories best explains middle-aged and older adults' perceptions of crime in their neighbourhood:

H1 Community care and vigilance is a predictor of middle-aged and older adults' perceptions of neighbourhood crime.

H2 Perceptions of physical and social incivilities is the main predictor of perceptions of neighbourhood crime.

H3 The actual level of crime (as measured by police reports) predicts fears of safety, and this differs depending on whether they are crimes against the person or property.

H4 Actual incivilities are the strongest predictor of perceptions of crime.

Method

Eighty-five participants took part, of which 81 per cent were women and 19 per cent were men. Of this sample, 37 per cent were White residents, 63 per cent were African-American. Their average age was 61.4 years. There were 49 per cent middle-aged adults, aged 40–64, and 51 per cent older adults, aged 65 and above. They came from a large urban city in a Midwestern area in the US, which was divided into 9 police districts. A stratified sampling procedure was used to recruit participants from each of the 9 districts. They had lived in their neighbourhoods for a mean length of 19.7 years.

Participants were sent a postal survey to complete, which they returned, or were telephoned to complete it. Police crime data for all 9 districts was collected.

Participants completed a 22-item survey. The survey asked questions about their safety concerns in their neighbourhood (2 questions: e.g. 'How safe is your neighbourhood for children?'), their perception of community cohesion and vigilance (6 questions: e.g. 'My neighbourhood feels like a community'), physical incivilities (6 questions: e.g. the presence of graffiti), social incivilities (4 questions: e.g. the presence of nuisance neighbours). All items were rated on a 5-point Likert scale (1 = strongly disagree, 5 = strongly agree). They were also asked demographic questions (race, gender, annual income, length of residency).

The data were analysed using chi-square and independent *t*-tests, to see whether demographic variables (e.g. gender), perceived crime variables (incivilities, neighbourhood cohesion) and safety concerns, differed between middle-aged and older adults. Univariate analyses and correlations were conducted to assess the extent to which the crime variables (community cohesion, incivilities) and demographic variables (e.g. gender) predicted safety concerns.

Results

Ninety-six per cent of participants reported at least one example of incivility that made their neighbourhood feel less safe. Middle-aged participants noted more social incivilities than older adults. Middle-aged adults lived in areas with a higher crime rate than older adults ($t = 2.96$, $p = 0.004$). No other differences were found between the two age groups.

Feelings of neighbourhood safety were associated with perceptions of physical and social incivilities, low levels of community cohesion and vigilance, and actual high crime rates against the person and property. The strongest predictor of feelings of neighbourhood safety were perceptions of physical incivility ($t = 10$, $p = 0.002$). Actual crimes against property were the next highest predictor ($t = 7.33$, $p = 0.008$), and then community cohesion and vigilance ($t = 5.38$, $p = 0.023$).

Discussion

Support was found for H1, H3 and H4. Community care and vigiliance does predict feeling unsafe in a neighbourhood. Furthermore, actual crime rates against property was also a strong predictor of feeling unsafe. So the visibility of derelict buildings and graffiti matter in how safe people felt in their homes. H2 was only partially supported as it was only physical incivilities (and not social incivilities) that featured in people's concerns about safety in their neighbourhoods.

From this research it can be concluded that a sense of community, and taking pride in maintaining the physical aspects of it, really matter in making a place feel safe. Social incivilities, such as neighbours arguing in the street, do not affect how safe these people feel in their residential areas. So while the theory that community cohesion and attachment really matter in perceptions of neighbourhood safety, the broken window theory is only partially supported in this study.

Critical Reflections

This study has some limitations, which are worth pondering. These include response biases (who comes forward to take part), perceptions of safety and incivilities, the use of self-report measures (how accurate are they?), and a small sample size from just nine areas. All of these issues could contribute to results that are not as valid or representative as might be hoped. But, are there still valuable lessons to be learned from these results? If work such as this leads councils, police forces and residents to improve safety in their neighbourhoods, motivates the formation of community groups to repair visible displays of disorder (such as cleaning up graffiti) and instils a sense of pride and attachment to a place, then this can arguably make a lot of difference to increasing perceptions and actual safety.

Adolescent and early-adult experiences are formative partly because they make deep and lasting impressions. We may therefore expect that today's young adults will include events such as the invasion of Iraq, the deposing of Robert Mugabe in Zimbabwe, the 9/11 terrorist attacks on the US, the global recession, and the rise of social media as memorable turning points.

That is not to say that older adults are inflexible. Much of the persuasion research with respect to older people has focused on healthcare. For example, Cryer et al. (2002) looked at attitudes to, and uptake of, hip protectors for older adults living in residential homes. Crucial to this process was addressing participants' concerns such as the ease of fitting them, comfort, how to keep them clean and cost. Helping people to overcome these barriers contributes to the adoption of positive attitudes towards wearing them, and actually wearing them. Albouy and Decaudin (2018) found that participants (aged 55–70 years) were more likely to be persuaded by a charity advert requesting a monetary donation than younger people (aged 18–25 years) when the content was highly emotive. The researchers reason that older people have more self-efficacy – they are more motivated and capable of reducing anxiety caused by the advertisement through donating – than younger people.

What Are They Thinking?

The crucial aspect of central route persuasion is not the message but the responses it evokes in a person's mind. Our minds are not sponges that soak up whatever pours over them. If the message summons favourable thoughts, it persuades us. If it provokes us to think of contrary arguments, we remain unpersuaded.

Forewarned Is Forearmed – If You Care Enough to Counter-argue

What circumstances breed counter-argument? One is knowing that someone is going to try to persuade you. If you had to tell your family that you wanted to drop out of school, you would probably anticipate their pleading with you to stay. So you might develop a list of arguments to counter every conceivable argument they might make and in making your case adopt what Potter (1996) calls '**defensive rhetoric**'. This style of language is designed to resist and undermine potential counter-arguments. '**Offensive rhetoric**' is adopted when a speaker or writer attacks an alternative account to their own.

defensive rhetoric when a speaker or writer develops arguments to counter being undermined by other points

offensive rhetoric when a speaker or writer attacks an alternative account to their own

Janssen et al. (2010) found that forewarned is indeed forearmed, and a powerful resistor to persuasion. Resisting someone's efforts to persuade you requires some rather effortful self-control. However, when we're tired and exhausted, those resources are depleted. That makes us a prime target for persuasion. It is far easier to just say 'yes'. However, in a series of studies Janssen and her team discovered that even if you first exhaust your participants by asking them to retype a densely typed out passage from a statistics book, they still resist being persuaded to volunteer for a cleaning-up campaign if they had been forewarned about it. In law courts, too, defence attorneys sometimes forewarn juries about prosecution evidence to come. With mock juries, such 'stealing thunder' neutralizes its impact (Dolnik et al., 2003).

Distraction Disarms Counter-arguing

Verbal persuasion is also enhanced by distracting people with something that attracts their attention just enough to inhibit counter-arguing (Fennis et al., 2004; Fransen et al., 2014). Political advertisements often use this technique. The words promote the candidate, and the visual images keep us occupied so we don't analyse the words. Sometimes, though, distraction precludes our processing an advertisement. That perhaps helps explain why advertisements viewed during violent or sexual television programmes are sometimes unremembered and ineffective (Bushman, 2005; Bushman & Bonacci, 2002).

Uninvolved Audiences Use Peripheral Cues

Recall the two routes to persuasion – the central route of systematic thinking and the peripheral route of heuristic cues. Like a road that winds through a small town, the central route has starts and stops as the mind analyses arguments and formulates responses. Like the freeway that bypasses the town, the peripheral route speeds people to their destination. Analytical people – those with a high **need for cognition** – enjoy thinking carefully and prefer central routes (Cacioppo et al., 1996; Maio & Haddock, 2007). People who like to conserve their mental resources – those with a low need for cognition – are quicker to respond to peripheral cues such as the communicator's attractiveness and the pleasantness of the surroundings.

need for cognition the motivation to think and analyse. Assessed by agreement with items such as 'The notion of thinking abstractly is appealing to me' and disagreement with items such as 'I only think as hard as I have to'

Many experiments have explored ways to stimulate people's thinking:

- by using rhetorical questions
- by presenting *multiple speakers* (for example, having each of three speakers give one argument instead of one speaker giving three)

- by making people *feel responsible* for evaluating or passing along the message, by using *relaxed postures* rather than standing ones
- by *repeating* the message
- by getting people's *undistracted attention.*

The consistent finding with each of these techniques: stimulating thinking makes strong messages more persuasive and (because of counter-arguing) weak messages less persuasive.

'We send the EU £350 million a week.' A bold statement on a London bus helped Conservative Politician Boris Johnson to persuade the British public to vote to leave the European Union, in the 2016 EU Referendum.

SOURCE: ©Christopher Furlong/Getty Images

The theory also has practical implications. Effective communicators care not only about their images and their messages but also about how their audience is likely to react. The best teachers tend to get students to think actively. They ask rhetorical questions, provide intriguing examples, and challenge students with difficult problems. All these techniques are likely to foster a process that moves information through the central route to persuasion. In classes where the instruction is less engaging, you can provide your own central processing. If you think about the material and elaborate on the arguments, you are likely to do better on the course.

Extreme Persuasion: How Do Cults Indoctrinate?

What persuasion and group influence principles are harnessed by new religious movements ('cults')?

On 22 March 1997, Marshall Herff Applewhite and 37 of his disciples decided the time had come to shed their bodies – mere 'containers' – and be whisked up to a UFO (unidentified flying object) trailing the Hale-Bopp Comet, en route to Heaven's Gate. So they put themselves to sleep by mixing phenobarbital into pudding or apple sauce, washing it down with vodka, and then fixing plastic bags over their heads so they would suffocate in their slumber. On that same day, a cottage in the French Canadian village of St Casimir exploded in an inferno, consuming five people – the latest of 74 members of the Order of the Solar Temple to have committed suicide in Canada, Switzerland and France. All were hoping to be transported to the star Sirius, nine light years away.

The question on many minds: what persuades people to join these gangs? Shall we attribute their strange behaviours to strange personalities? Or do their experiences illustrate the common dynamics of social influence and persuasion? As we shall see, everyday strategies of persuasion are used. But social psychology cannot explain everything about the influence of cults. Their powers of persuasion go beyond the everyday.

Bear two things in mind. First, this is hindsight analysis. It uses persuasion principles as categories for explaining, after the fact, a troubling social phenomenon. Second, explaining *why* people believe something says nothing about the *truth* of their beliefs. That is a logically separate issue. A psychology of religion might tell us *why* a theist believes in God and an atheist disbelieves, but it cannot tell us who is right. Explaining either belief does nothing to change its validity.

What is perceived to be a 'cult' changes with time and place. Broadly speaking a cult is a group of people who share beliefs and practices that operate outside the mainstream way of doing things. Of course, what is considered to be 'mainstream' is different from culture to culture, society to society, and across time. In recent decades, several **cults** have been defined – which some social scientists prefer to call **new religious movements** – and have gained much publicity: Opus Dei, Zhushen Jiao (Religion of the primary deity), Order of the Solar Temple, Aum Shinrikyo, Jim Jones's People's Temple, Charles Manson's Manson Family, and Marshall Applewhite's Heaven's Gate.

cult (also called new religious movement) a group typically characterized by (1) distinctive ritual and beliefs related to its devotion to a god or a person, (2) isolation from the surrounding 'evil' culture, and (3) a charismatic leader. (A sect, by contrast, is a spinoff from a major religion)

Sun Myung Moon's mixture of Christianity, anti-communism and glorification of Moon himself as a new messiah attracted a worldwide following. In response to Moon's declaration, 'What I wish must be your wish', many people committed themselves and their incomes to the Unification Church.

In 1978 in Guyana, 914 disciples of Jim Jones, who had followed him there from San Francisco, shocked the world when they died by following his order to down a suicidal grape drink laced with tranquillizers, painkillers and a lethal dose of cyanide.

On 20 March 1995, Aum Shinrikyo, a Japanese cult founded in the 1980s and led by Shoko Asahara carried out a nerve gas attack on a Tokyo subway, killing 13 people and injuring thousands of others. Ashara believes himself to be the Saviour of the world. The attack seems to have been an attempt to bring an apocalypse, in which only his followers would be spared. The cult has thousands of followers, particularly in Russia and Japan (Alfred, 2015).

Having been fired from two music teaching jobs for affairs with students, Marshall Applewhite sought sexless devotion by castration, as had 7 of the other 17 Heaven's Gate men who died with him (Chua-Eoan, 1997; Gardner, 1997). While in a psychiatric hospital in 1971, Applewhite had linked up with nurse and astrology dabbler Bonnie Lu Nettles, who gave the intense and charismatic Applewhite a cosmological vision of a route to 'the next level'. Preaching with passion, he persuaded his followers to renounce families, sex, drugs and personal money with promises of a spaceship voyage to salvation.

How could these things happen? What persuaded these people to give such total allegiance? Shall we make dispositional explanations – by blaming the victims? Shall we dismiss them as gullible or unbalanced? Or can familiar principles of conformity, compliance, dissonance, persuasion and group influence explain their behaviour to some extent – putting them on common ground with the rest of us who in our own ways are shaped by such forces?

Attitudes Follow Behaviour

As we explored in Chapter 5 people usually internalize commitments made voluntarily, publicly and repeatedly. Cult leaders seem to know this.

Compliance Breeds Acceptance

New converts soon learn that membership is no trivial matter. They are quickly made active members of the team. Behavioural rituals, public recruitment and fund-raising strengthen the initiates' identities as members. As those in social psychological experiments come to believe in what they bear witness to, so a cult's initiates become committed advocates. The greater the personal commitment, the more the need to justify it.

The Foot-in-the-door Phenomenon

How are people induced to make a commitment to such a drastic life change? Seldom by an abrupt, conscious decision. Rather, the recruitment strategy exploits the **foot-in-the-door phenomenon** (Fern et al., 1986). This works simply on the principle that if someone can be persuaded to comply with a small request, then they can be persuaded by increasingly larger requests. Unification Church recruiters, for example, would invite people to a dinner and then to a weekend of warm fellowship and discussions of philosophies of life. At the weekend retreat, they would encourage the attenders to join them in songs, activities and discussion. Potential converts were then urged to sign up for longer training retreats. The pattern in cults is for the activities to become gradually more arduous, culminating in having recruits solicit contributions and attempt to convert others.

foot-in-the-door phenomenon
manipulation technique in which getting people to first agree to a small request increases the chances that they will later comply with a larger request

Benavides et al. (2016) report that gangs often target vulnerable individuals who feel on the outskirts of mainstream society. Feeling lonely, angry and powerless, a cult or gang can offer friendship, retribution, empowerment and wealth through criminalized activities. Sure enough, with time the individual becomes more and more embedded within the cult or gang.

Once into the cult, converts find that monetary offerings are at first voluntary, then mandatory. Jim Jones eventually inaugurated a required contribution of 10 per cent of income, which soon increased to 25 per cent. Finally, he ordered members to turn over to him everything they owned. Workloads also became progressively more demanding. Former cult member Grace Stoen recalls the gradual progress:

> *Nothing was ever done drastically. That's how Jim Jones got away with so much. You slowly gave up things and slowly had to put up with more, but it was always done very gradually. It was amazing, because you would sit up sometimes and say, wow, I really have given up a lot. I really am putting up with a lot. But he did it so slowly that you figured, I've made it this far, what the hell is the difference?*
>
> (Conway & Siegelman, 1979, p. 236)

The Door-in-the-face Technique

The **door-in-the-face** technique (DITF) has been used to great effect in persuading people to a request they had previously rejected (Cialdini et al., 1975). This rather risky strategy involves asking someone to comply with a very large request that will almost certainly be refused. On receiving the almost inevitable rejection, a second less demanding request is then made. In the context of the large request, this second one doesn't seem so bad. The theory goes that this second request therefore has a much better chance of being accepted in this context than if it was presented on its own. So you get what you wanted all along. And there's a lot of evidence to show that the strategy does indeed work. For example, Guéguen et al. (2011) found that if a server asked customers if they wanted tea or coffee immediately after offering them dessert (which they declined), they tended to say yes. If the server left a 3-minute gap between asking for dessert orders and tea/coffee orders, both requests were typically declined. This strategy can be, and has been, used in many areas of social life such as health, charity, retail and hapless researchers trying to encourage people to take part in their studies!

door-in-the-face technique (DITF)
facilitating the likelihood of a second less-demanding request being accepted by presenting a more demanding request first

The door-in-the-face technique is also of interest in considering helping, in Chapter 11. Research indicates that more people agree to help when the door-in-the-face technique is employed.

Low-balling

low-balling when a previously attractive offer is changed upon acceptance to a less attractive one

Low-balling works by getting someone to agree to an attractive, often cheap, deal, and then raising the charge for it. You may recognize this technique in the pitch of various financial sellers as they try to entice customers to accept their offers. Advertisements for cheap insurance sometimes offer to insure your car or home for a very cheap price. Attracted by the offer you give them a call. During the course of the phone call you may be told why it will be a bit more expensive to insure your car or home. Having already committed yourself to the idea of taking up their insurance, you find yourself agreeing to the newer, more expensive, deal. You reason that it will be more convenient to accept the offer here and now rather than chase around more insurance companies. But why do we allow this low-balling technique to work? In Chapter 5 we noted how people like to maintain consistency in their attitudes and behaviour. Having already formed a positive attitude towards the insurance company, you now behave accordingly and accept the offer.

A classic social psychological demonstration of this strategy comes from Cialdini et al. (1978), who invited students to take part in a study. On receiving a 'Yes' response, they were then told the study would begin at 7 a.m. and could withdraw if they now chose, owing to the unsociable hour. Almost all the students turned up for the study. Compare this with the students who were told the early starting time of the study at the time they were asked to take part. Only 24 per cent agreed.

Persuasive Elements

We can also analyse cult persuasion using the factors discussed in this chapter (and summarized in **Figure 6.6**): *who* (the communicator) said *what* (the message) to *whom* (the audience)?

The Communicator

Successful cults typically have a charismatic leader – someone who attracts and directs the members. In an essay on the plethora of high-school gangs in the Yogykarta region of Indonesia, Kadir (2012) explains how schoolboys are especially vulnerable to a charismatic gang leader, when family and state support systems have broken down. The charismatic leader can meet their psychological needs, but typically at a price.

We also know a credible communicator is someone the audience perceives as expert and trustworthy – for example, as 'Father' Moon.

Jim Jones used 'psychic readings' to establish his credibility. Newcomers were asked to identify themselves as they entered the church before services. Then one

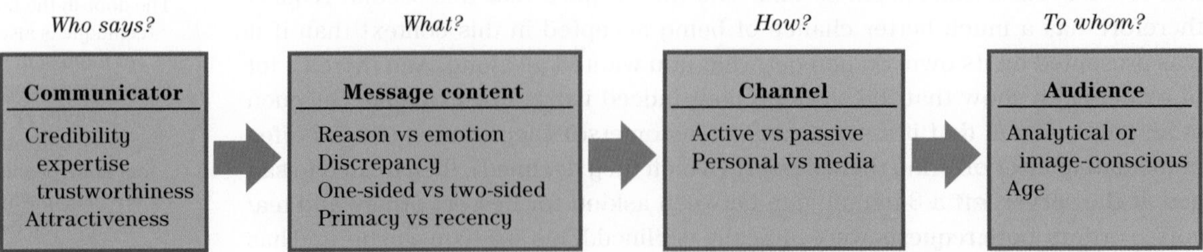

FIGURE 6.6 Variables known to affect the impact of persuasive communications
In real life, these variables may interact; the effect of one may depend on the level of another.

of his aides would quickly call the person's home and say, 'Hi. We're doing a survey, and we'd like to ask you some questions.' During the service, one ex-member recalled, Jones would call out the person's name and say:

Have you ever seen me before? Well, you live in such and such a place, your phone number is such and such, and in your living room you've got this, that, and the other, and on your sofa you've got such and such a pillow . . . Now do you remember me ever being in your house?
(Conway & Siegelman, 1979, p. 234)

As we've already seen, trust is an important part of persuasion. Trust, therefore, is also an important factor in joining a gang or cult. Exploring the dynamics of gang life in London, Densley et al. (2014) report they are often comprised of individuals who are low in *trust propensity,* which means there's a general distrust in people. Therefore, the gang or the cult and its leader fulfils an important role in providing individuals with others they can trust. Interestingly, the researchers also found that individuals high in **social dominance** tend to occupy the middle ranking positions in the gang or cult. In Chapter 13 we explore social dominance theory more closely, but here it's suffice to say that individuals strong in social dominance are defiantly individualistic with a preference for hierarchical competitive structures and intergroup aggression in order to assert their own interests. As Densley and colleagues suggest, those at the very top of those cults and gangs perhaps realize that to achieve your own personal interests, you need to rely on your fellow members and work as a team, and as such are lower in social dominance than those who occupy the middle.

social dominance orientation a motivation to have one's group dominate other social groups

The Message

The vivid, emotional messages and the warmth and acceptance with which the group showers lonely or depressed people can be strikingly appealing: trust the master, join the family; we have the answer, the 'one way'. The message echoes through channels as varied as lectures, small-group discussions and direct social pressure.

The Audience

Recruits are often young people under 25, still at that comparatively open age before attitudes and values stabilize. Some, such as the followers of Jim Jones, are less educated people who like the simplicity of the message and find it difficult to counter-argue. Lack of education and aspirations has been understood as a factor in the UK in the recruitment of young working-class men at football grounds into right-wing political groups and hooligan gangs, and has received much social psychological attention (Best, 2010; Frosdick & Marsh, 2005; Burke & Sunley, 1998; Hopkins & Treadwell, 2014). But most are educated, middle-class people who, taken by the ideals, overlook the contradictions in those who profess selflessness and practise greed, who pretend concern and behave indifferently.

Most of those who have carried out suicide bombings in the Middle East (and other places such as Bali, Madrid and London) were, likewise, young men at the transition between adolescence and adult maturity. Like cult recruits, they come under the influence of authoritative, sometimes religiously orientated communicators who indoctrinate them into seeing themselves as 'living martyrs' whose fleeting moment of self-destruction will be their portal into bliss and heroism. To help ensure their overcoming the will to survive, each candidate makes public commitments – creating a will, writing goodbye letters, making a farewell video – that create a psychological point of no return (Kruglanski & Golec de Zavala, 2005). All this typically transpires in the relative isolation of small cells, with group influences that fan hatred for the enemy.

Group Effects

Cults also illustrate the next chapter's theme: the power of a group to shape members' views and behaviour. The cult typically separates members from their previous social support systems and isolates them with other cultists. There may then occur what Stark and Bainbridge (1980) call a 'social implosion': external ties weaken until the group collapses inwards socially, each person engaging only with other group members. Cut off from families and former friends, they lose access to counter-arguments. The group now offers collective identity and defines reality. Because the cult frowns on or punishes disagreements, the apparent consensus helps eliminate any lingering doubts. Moreover, stress and emotional arousal narrow attention, making people 'more susceptible to poorly supported arguments, social pressure, and the temptation to derogate nongroup members' (Baron, 2000).

Marshall Applewhite and Bonnie Nettles at first formed their own group of two, reinforcing each other's aberrant thinking – a phenomenon that psychiatrists call *folie à deux* (French for 'insanity of two'). As others joined them, the group's social isolation facilitated more peculiar thinking. As Internet conspiracy theory discussion groups illustrate (Heaven's Gate was skilled in Internet recruiting), virtual groups can likewise foster paranoia.

These techniques – increasing behavioural commitments, persuasion and group isolation – do not, however, have unlimited power. The Unification Church has successfully recruited fewer than 1 in 10 people who attend its workshops and is dogged by controversy (Cowan & Bromley, 2015). Most who joined Heaven's Gate had left before that fateful day. David Koresh ruled with a mix of persuasion, intimidation and violence. As Jim Jones made his demands more extreme, he, too, increasingly had to control people with intimidation. He used threats of harm to those who fled the community, beatings for non-compliance, and drugs to neutralize disagreeable members. By the end, he was as much an arm-twister as a mind-bender.

Some of these cult influence techniques bear similarities to techniques used by more benign, widely accepted groups. Buddhist and Catholic monasteries, for example, have cloistered adherents with their kindred spirits. And fraternity and sorority members have reported that the initial 'love bombing' of potential cult recruits is not unlike their own 'rush' period. Members lavish prospective pledges with attention and make them feel special. During the pledge period, new members are somewhat isolated, cut off from old friends who did not pledge. They spend time studying the history and rules of their new group. They suffer and commit time on its behalf. They are expected to comply with all its demands. The result is usually a committed new member.

Groupthink is explained further in Chapter 10 where we consider small group influence.

Group processes similar but not identical to what has been demonstrated above in cults, have also been found in the most respected layers of society – for instance, the Masonic Lodge. The secret meetings and rituals going on in this kind of brotherhood among the wealthiest and most influential people in society, create unity and protect members from other influences and counter-arguments. Even in the highest political circles, among the members of the President's Administration or the Prime Minister's government, there are examples of cohesive ingroup processes where the desire for concurrence between group members overrides realistic appraisals. This phenomenon is called 'groupthink'.

A constructive use of persuasion is in counselling and psychotherapy, which social-counselling psychologist Stanley Strong views 'as a branch of applied social psychology' (1978, p. 101). Like Strong, psychiatrist, Jerome Frank (1974, 1982) recognized years ago that it takes persuasion to change self-defeating attitudes and behaviours. Frank noted that the psychotherapy setting, like cults and zealous self-help groups, provides (1) a supportive, confiding social relationship, (2) an offer of expertise and hope, (3) a special rationale or myth that explains one's difficulties and offers a new perspective, and (4) a set of rituals and learning experiences that promises a new sense of peace and happiness.

Military training creates cohesion and commitment through some of the same tactics used by leaders of new religious movements, fraternities and therapeutic communities.
SOURCE: ©munktcu/123RF

These examples of fraternities, sororities, self-help groups and psychotherapy help to illustrate three concluding observations. First, if we attribute new religious movements to the leader's mystical force or to the followers' peculiar weaknesses, we may delude ourselves into thinking we are immune to social control techniques. In truth, our own groups – and countless political leaders, educators and other persuaders – successfully use many of these same tactics on us. Between education and indoctrination, enlightenment and propaganda, conversion and coercion, therapy and mind control, there is but a blurry line.

Second, the fact that Jim Jones and other cult leaders abused the power of persuasion does not mean persuasion is intrinsically bad. Nuclear power enables us to light up homes or wipe out cities. Sexual power enables us to express and celebrate committed love or exploit people for selfish gratification. Similarly, persuasive power enables us to enlighten or deceive, to promote health or to sell addictive drugs, to advance peace or stir up hatred. Knowing that these powers can be harnessed for evil purposes should alert us, as scientists and citizens, to guard against their immoral use. But the powers themselves are neither inherently evil nor inherently good; it is how we use them that determines whether their effect is destructive or constructive. Condemning persuasion because of deceit is like condemning eating because of gluttony.

Third, persuasion pervades our everyday lives. Whenever we interact with one another we are involved in some degree of persuasion through our language. We are persuading someone to accept our version of events, our portrayal of someone's behaviour, or perhaps just how we think things ought to be. Persuasion is not simply the weapon of the cult leader or the advertiser, it is a fundamental aspect of our social interactions with others.

How Can Persuasion Be Resisted?

How might we prepare people to resist unwanted persuasion?

Martial arts trainers devote as much time to teaching defensive blocks, deflections and parries as they do to teaching attack. 'On the social influence battlefield,' note Sagarin et al. (2002), researchers have focused more on persuasive attack than on defence. It is easier to accept persuasive messages than to doubt them. To *understand* an assertion (say, that lead pencils are a health hazard) is to *believe* it – at least temporarily, until one actively undoes the initial, automatic acceptance. If a distracting event prevents the undoing, the acceptance lingers.

Still, blessed with logic, information and motivation, we do resist falsehoods. If the credible-seeming repair person's uniform and the doctor's title have intimidated us into unthinking agreement, we can rethink our habitual responses to authority. We can seek more information before committing time or money. We can question what we don't understand.

Strengthening Personal Commitment

Chapter 7 presents another way to resist: before encountering others' judgements, make a public commitment to your position. Having stood up for your convictions, you will become less susceptible (or, should we say, less 'open') to what others have to say. As we see in the Asch experiment (Chapter 7), when participants were invited to declare which of the lines matched each other before anyone else, they gave the correct answer. When asked if they would like to change their mind having heard the confederates give a consistently incorrect answer, the participants rarely did so. So prior personal and public commitment to a position reduces the effectiveness of persuasion.

Confident Beliefs

The self-validation hypothesis proposes that the confidence we have in our own beliefs is subject to many different factors. The more confidence we have in what we believe, the less likely our attitudes are to change. Confidence can be increased by simply nodding your head when voicing your beliefs about something (Brinol & Petty, 2003), or by reminding yourself of a time when your beliefs helped you achieve a desired goal (Petty et al., 2002), or even writing them down (Brinol & Petty, 2003). As we have seen in this chapter, strong arguments tend to be more persuasive than weaker ones. The likelihood of having our beliefs and attitudes changed by strong arguments is higher. However, Brinol and Petty (2003) found that even when confronted by strong arguments, participants who shook their head to indicate their rejection of them were much less likely to accept the argument or consider it to be credible.

Challenging Beliefs

How might we stimulate people to commit themselves? From his classic experiments, Kiesler (1971) offered one possible way: mildly attack their position using *offensive rhetoric*. Kiesler found that when committed people were attacked strongly enough to cause them to react, but not so strongly as to overwhelm them, they became even more committed. Kiesler explained: 'When you attack committed people and your attack is of inadequate strength, you drive them to even more extreme behaviours in defense of their previous commitment' (p. 88). Perhaps you can recall a time when that happened in an argument, as those involved escalated their *defensive rhetoric*, committing themselves to increasingly extreme positions.

Developing Counter-arguments

There is a second reason a mild attack might build resistance. Like inoculations against disease, even weak arguments will prompt counter-arguments, which are then available for a stronger attack. McGuire (1964) documented this in a series of experiments. McGuire wondered: Could we inoculate people against persuasion much as we inoculate them against a virus? Is there such a thing as **attitude inoculation**? Could we take people raised in a 'germ-free ideological environment' – people who hold some unquestioned belief – and stimulate their mental defences? And would subjecting them to a small dose of belief-threatening material inoculate them against later persuasion?

attitude inoculation exposing people to weak attacks upon their attitudes so that when stronger attacks come, they will have refutations available

That is what McGuire did. First, he found some cultural truisms, such as 'It's a good idea to brush your teeth after every meal if at all possible'. He then showed that people were vulnerable to a powerful, credible assault upon those truisms (for example, prestigious authorities were said to have discovered that too much tooth-brushing can damage one's gums). If, however, before having their belief attacked, they were 'immunized' by first receiving a small challenge to their belief, *and* if they read or wrote an essay in refutation of this mild attack, then they were better able to resist the powerful attack.

Cialdini et al. (2003) agree that appropriate counter-arguments are a great way to resist persuasion, but wondered how to bring them to mind in response to an opponent's ads, especially when the opponent (like most political incumbents) has a huge spending advantage. The answer, they suggest, is a 'poison parasite' defence – one that combines a poison (strong counter-arguments) with a parasite (retrieval cues that bring those arguments to mind when seeing the opponent's advertisements). In their studies, participants who viewed a familiar political ad were least persuaded by it when they had earlier seen counter-arguments overlaid on a replica of the advertisement. Seeing the advertisement again thus also brought to mind the puncturing counter-arguments. Anti-smoking ads have effectively done this, for example by re-creating a 'Marlboro Man' commercial set in the rugged outdoors but now showing a coughing, decrepit cowboy.

Real-life Applications: Inoculation Programmes

Could attitude inoculation work outside the laboratory by preparing people to resist unwanted persuasion? Applied research on gangs offers encouraging answers.

Inoculating Children against Peer Pressure to Join a Gang

As we've seen already in this chapter, young people can be particularly vulnerable to persuasive attempts to recruit them into a gang or cult. Could we inoculate against this? Well, according to some researchers it is certainly worth a try. Concerned by the rising numbers of boys and young girls joining gangs, Breen and Matusitz (2008) propose an inoculation programme to help address the problem. They note that despite a range of anti-gang programmes implemented at local and national levels, they have failed to adequately tackle the lure of gang-recruitment. They advise that ahead of implementing any intervention programmes, young people watch a 5–10 minute inoculation video. Two important aspects of inoculation are the perception of *threat* and *refutational preemption*. Or to put this another way: the content of inoculation videos helps the audience to produce counter-arguments against joining. So an inoculation video could incorporate both threat and refutational preemption, by focusing on the loss of personal attitudinal freedom, the negative health implications of joining a gang, and the negative views significant others have on gangs. Moreover, such videos should be periodically reinforced with further inoculation materials. This, they note, can be done relatively inexpensively within a school context.

Inoculation programmes apply other persuasion principles, too. They use attractive peers to communicate information. They trigger the students' own cognitive processing ('Here's something you might want to think about'). They get the students to make a public commitment (by announcing it, along with their reasoning, to their classmates).

Inoculating Children against the Influence of Advertising

In their international study looking at advertising targeted at children in Australia, Asia, North and South America and Western Europe, Kelly et al. (2010) found a worrying trend. Foods that were unhealthy but which children would find very attractive (such as chocolate and sweets) were televised at children's peak television viewing times. These persuasive commercials have previously been linked to surges in childhood obesity in countries such as the UK (Livingstone, 2005).

In England, the 2004 National Health Service survey of 9,715 children aged 11–15 reported an increase in the consumption of alcopops by girls, and beer, cider and lager by boys. Most alarmingly they found that 45 per cent of 15 year olds surveyed reported having consumed an alcoholic drink within the last week. In 2006, the Advertising Standards Agency banned a series of alcopop advertisements on the grounds that they were too attractive to adolescents and young people, contributing to national trends in binge and underage drinking.

Advertisers know how to persuade children into wanting their products.
SOURCE: ©Morrowind/Shutterstock

It is perhaps no surprise, then, that parents resent it when advertisers market products to children, then place them on lower store shelves where kids will see them, pick them up, and nag and whine until wearing the parent down (sometimes referred to as "pester power"). For that reason, urges the 'Mothers' Code for Advertisers', there should be no advertising in schools, no targeting children under 8, no product placements in movies and programmes targeting children and adolescents, and no advertisements directed at children and adolescents 'that promote an ethic of selfishness and a focus on instant gratification' (Motherhood Project, 2001).

On the other side are the commercial interests. Commercial companies claim that advertisements allow parents to teach their children consumer skills and, more importantly, finance children's television programmes. Since 2002, the digital platform MediaSmart (https://mediasmart.uk.com/) has been in place as an intervention in the UK, created and delivered by the advertisers themselves. It states its aims are to ensure children aged 7–16 years are 'critical consumers' of the media, and to educate children, parents and advertisers about responsible marketing to young audiences. Its supporters applaud the initiative of the commercial industry for accepting responsibility for how it markets persuasive messages to children, and providing those children with educational tools to evaluate and critique those persuasive messages. Its opponents claim it exists to preempt any attempt by the government to enforce tighter control over the industry, or to hinder the possibility that advertising to young children is abolished (O'Sullivan, 2007).

Children, it seems, are an advertiser's dream: gullible, vulnerable and an easy sell. Armed with this data, citizens' groups have campaigned against the advertisers of such products.

Implications of Attitude Inoculation

The best way to build resistance to brainwashing probably isn't stronger indoctrination into one's current beliefs. If parents are worried that their children might become members of a cult, they might better teach their children about the various cults and prepare them to counter persuasive appeals.

For the same reason, religious educators should be wary of creating a 'germfree ideological environment' in their churches and schools. An attack, if refuted, is more likely to solidify one's position than to undermine it, particularly if the threatening material can be examined with like-minded others (Visser & Mirabile, 2004). Cults apply this principle by forewarning members of how families and friends will attack the cult's beliefs. When the expected challenge comes, the member is armed with counter-arguments.

Another implication is that, for the persuader, an ineffective appeal can be worse than none. Can you see why? Those who reject an appeal are inoculated against further appeals. Consider an older but revealing experiment in which Darley and Cooper (1972) invited students to write essays advocating a strict dress code. Because that was against the students' own positions and the essays were to be published, all chose *not* to write the essay – even those offered money to do so. After turning down the money, they became even more extreme and confident in their anti-dress-code opinions. Having made an overt decision against the dress code, they became even more resistant to it. Those who have rejected initial appeals to quit smoking may likewise become immune to further appeals. Ineffective persuasion, by stimulating the listener's defences, may be counterproductive. It may 'harden the heart' against later appeals.

Focus on

The Lucifer Effect: Bad Apples or Bad Barrels?

In Philip Zimbardo's classic Stanford Prison experiment (see Chapter 5) we see how attitudes can shift to match the roles we carry out. In the case of the Stanford prison study, when asked to act as prisoner or guard, participants not only behaved accordingly but internalized those roles, with shocking consequences for their acts towards one another. So shocking, the study was abandoned after only a few days as the guards' brutality towards the prisoners intensified. And it wasn't only the prisoners and guards who found their behaviour affected by the situation they were in. Zimbardo notes his own complicity in colluding with the guards, covering up the extent of deterioration in the prisoner-guard relationship, so as not to upset the prisoners' families. Zimbardo called this the Lucifer Effect. It explains how good people can become evil. Key to this effect is the power of the situation. Morality breaks down, as vulnerable humans allow the situation to overwhelm them. Norms of what is appropriate behaviour in that situation arise, and people adhere to them. It isn't simply a few bad apples turning the rest rotten, but a situation that turns everyone bad. Don't look at the apples, warns Zimbardo, look at the barrel which turned them bad. We might want to lay the blame at the door of a few dysfunctional people, states Zimbardo, but actually it's the situation they're in which requires analysis. The fundamental attribution error (Chapter 4) might hold a clue as to why there is a tendency to blame a few 'evil' people, rather than look to the context which everyone is in.

This effect could be used to explain what persuades people to evil acts throughout history – genocide, holocausts, suicide bombers, the Abu Ghraib atrocities in Iraq. However, it begs a question about responsibility. If the situation is to blame, to what extent should people be held responsible for their actions?

For further discussion of Zimbardo's work, see the Research Close-Up: The Psychology of Tyranny in Chapter 13.

Questions

1. To what extent can we hold people responsible for their actions?
2. Do you think Zimbardo's account of why good people turn evil is correct?
3. Social psychologists have tended to focus on when persuasion is a negative force. When might it be a force for good?

SUMMING UP: PERSUASION

WHAT PATHS LEAD TO PERSUASION?

- Sometimes persuasion occurs as people focus on arguments and respond with favourable thoughts. Such systematic, or 'central route', persuasion occurs when people are naturally analytical or involved in the issue.
- When issues don't engage systematic thinking, persuasion may occur through a faster, 'peripheral route', as people use heuristics or incidental cues to make snap judgements.
- Central route persuasion, being more thoughtful and less superficial, is more durable and more likely to influence behaviour.
- Unimodels of persuasion propose that there is just one route to persuasion, but messages contain a variety of kinds of persuasive evidence in convincing their readers/hearers of their truth.
- Whether we are convinced may be subject to wider social factors such as the attitudes and beliefs of people within our social networks.

THE ELEMENTS OF PERSUASION AND THEIR RELATIONSHIP TO SOCIAL NORMS

- What makes persuasion effective? Researchers have explored four factors: the communicator (who says it), the message (what is said), the channel (how it is said) and the audience (to whom it is said).
- Credible communicators have the best success in persuading. People who speak unhesitatingly, who talk fast and who look listeners straight in the eye seem more credible. So are people who argue against their own self-interest and manage their 'dilemma of stake or interest'. An attractive communicator also is effective on matters of taste and personal values.
- The message itself persuades; associating it with good feelings makes it more convincing. People often make quicker, less reflective judgements while in good moods. Fear-arousing messages can also be effective, especially if the recipients can take protective action.
- How discrepant a message should be from an audience's existing opinions depends on the communicator's credibility. And whether a one- or two-sided message is more persuasive depends on whether the audience

already agrees with the message, is unaware of opposing arguments and is unlikely later to consider the opposition.

- When two sides of an issue are included, the primacy effect results in the first message being more persuasive. If a time gap separates the presentations, the result is likely to be a recency effect in which the second message prevails.
- Another important consideration is how the message is communicated. Usually, face-to-face appeals work best. Print media can be effective for complex messages. And the mass media can be effective when the issue is minor or unfamiliar, using rhetorical strategies for persuasion.
- Finally, it matters who receives the message. The age of the audience makes a difference: young people's attitudes are arguably more subject to change. What does the audience think while receiving a message? Do they think favourable thoughts? Do they counter-argue? Were they forewarned?

EXTREME PERSUASION: HOW DO CULTS INDOCTRINATE?

The successes of religious cults provide an opportunity to see powerful persuasion processes at work. It appears that their success has resulted from four general techniques:

- eliciting behavioural commitments (described in Chapter 4)
- applying principles of effective persuasion (this chapter)
- isolating members in like-minded groups (discussed in Chapter 10)
- forming a collective identity which group members conform to (see Chapters 12 and 13).

HOW CAN PERSUASION BE RESISTED?

- How do people resist persuasion? A *prior public commitment* to one's own position, stimulated perhaps by a mild attack on the position, breeds resistance to later persuasion.
- A mild attack can also serve as an *inoculation*, stimulating one to develop counter-arguments that will then be available if and when a strong attack comes.
- This implies, paradoxically, that one way to strengthen existing attitudes is to challenge them, though the challenge must not be so strong as to overwhelm them.

Critical Questions

1 What are the main aspects of persuasion that social psychologists have identified and studied?
2 Are some people more likely to be persuaded than others?
3 How can social psychology help to understand why some people join gangs and cults?
4 What strategies can we use to resist persuasion?
5 Should we always try to resist being persuaded?
6 With the sharp rise in the use of digital media, in what ways could social psychology further investigate the persuasiveness of the messages communicated?

Recommended Reading

Classic Readings

Billig, M. (1987). *Arguing and thinking: A rhetorical approach to social psychology.* Cambridge University Press.

Cialdini, R. (2001). *Influence: Science and practice.* Allyn & Bacon.

Hovland, C. I., Janis, I. L., & Kelley, H. H. (1953). *Communication and persuasion: Psychological studies of opinion change.* Yale University Press.

Petty, R. E., & Cacioppo, J. T. (1986). *Communication and persuasion: Central and peripheral routes to persuasion.* Springer-Verlag.

Contemporary Readings

Briscoe, C., & Aboud, F. (2012). Behaviour change communication targeting four health behaviours in developing countries: A review of change techniques. *Social Science & Medicine, 75*(4), 612–621.

Clark, J. K., Wegener, D. T., Habashi, M. M., & Evans, A. T. (2012). Source expertise and persuasion: The effects of perceived opposition or support on message scrutiny. *Personality and Social Psychology Bulletin, 38*(1), 90–100.

Keren, G., & Schul, Y. (2009). Two is not always better than one: a critical evaluation of two-system theories. *Perspectives on Psychological Science, 4*(6), 533–550.

Zimbardo, P. G. (2007). *The Lucifer effect: Understanding how good people turn evil.* Random House.

7 CONFORMITY AND OBEDIENCE

It is striking how often those involved in the greatest brutality are those who expend great efforts to extol ingroup virtue.
Reicher et al. (2008)

You have surely experienced the phenomenon: as a controversial speaker or music concert finishes, the adoring fans near the front leap to their feet, applauding. The approving folks just behind them follow their example and join the standing ovation. Now the wave of people standing reaches people who, unprompted, would merely be giving polite applause from their comfortable seats. Seated among them, part of you wants to stay seated. But as the wave of standing people sweeps by, will you alone stay seated? It's not easy, being a minority of one. Unless you heartily dislike what you've just heard, you will probably rise to your feet, at least briefly.

Such scenes of conformity raise this chapter's questions:

- Why, given the diversity of individuals in large groups, do they so often behave as social clones?
- Under what circumstances do people conform?
- Are certain people more likely than others to conform?
- Who resists the pressure to conform?
- Is conformity as bad as the image of a docile 'herd' implies? Should we instead be describing their 'group solidarity', 'interdependence' and 'social sensitivity'?

What Is Conformity?

Let us take the last question first. Is conformity good or bad? That is a question that has no scientific answer. Assuming the values most of us share, we can say that conformity is at times bad (when it leads someone to drive drunk or to join in racist behaviour due to peer pressure), at times good (when it inhibits people from cutting into a theatre queue), and at times inconsequential (when it disposes men to wear a tie).

In Western individualistic cultures, where submitting to peer pressure is not admired, the word 'conformity' tends to carry a negative value judgement. How would you feel if you overheard someone describing you as a 'real conformist'? We suspect you would feel hurt. Hence, North American and European social psychologists, reflecting their individualistic cultures, give social influence negative labels (conformity, submission, compliance) rather than positive ones (communal sensitivity, responsiveness, co-operative team play).

In Japan, going along with others is a sign not of weakness but of tolerance, self-control and maturity. It is an important marker of connectedness with others (Güngör et al., 2014).

The moral: we choose labels to suit our values and judgements. Labels both describe and evaluate, and they are inescapable. We cannot discuss the topics of this chapter without labels. So let us be clear on the meanings of the following labels: conformity, obedience, compliance, acceptance.

Conformity is not just acting as other people act; it is also being affected by how they act. It is acting or thinking differently from the way you would act and think if you were alone. Thus, **conformity** is a change in behaviour or belief to accord with others or be affected by others against one's own beliefs. When, as part of a crowd, you rise to cheer a game-winning goal, are you conforming? When, along with millions of others, you drink milk or coffee, are you conforming? When you and

conformity a change in behaviour or belief as the result of real or imagined group pressure other people agree that women look better with longer hair than with crewcuts, are you conforming? Maybe, maybe not. The key is whether your behaviour and beliefs would be the same apart from the group. Would you rise to cheer the goal if you were the only fan in the stands?

Conformity has to do with implicit social influence. Sometimes we conform to an expectation or a request without really believing in what we are doing. We put on the tie or the dress, though we dislike doing so. Or we find it unpleasant not to agree with the majority. This insincere, outward conformity is **compliance**. We comply primarily to reap a reward or avoid a punishment.

compliance conformity that involves publicly acting in accord with an implied or explicit request even if privately disagreeing

If our compliant behaviour is a result of explicit social influence, for instance an explicit command, we call it **obedience**.

obedience acting in accord with a direct order or command

Sometimes we genuinely believe in what the group has persuaded us to do. We may join millions of others in exercising because we all have been told that exercise is healthy and we accept that as true. This sincere, inward conformity is called **acceptance**. Acceptance sometimes follows compliance; we may come to inwardly believe something we initially questioned. As Chapter 5 emphasizes, attitudes follow behaviour. Unless we feel no responsibility for our behaviour, we usually become sympathetic to what we have stood up for.

acceptance conformity that involves both acting and believing in accord with social pressure

What are the Classic Conformity and Obedience Studies?

How have social psychologists studied conformity in the laboratory and beyond it? What do their findings reveal about the potency of social forces, the power of the situation and in particular the nature of evil?

Experimental researchers who study conformity and obedience construct miniature social worlds – laboratory micro-cultures that simplify and simulate important features of everyday social influence. Other researchers study conformity using the method of naturalistic observation and even analyse historical events. Some of the laboratory studies revealed such startling findings that they have been widely replicated and widely reported by other researchers, earning them the name of 'classic' experiments. We will consider three studies, each of which provides a method for studying conformity – and plenty of food for thought.

Sherif's Studies of Norm Formation

The first of the three classics bridges Chapter 14's focus on culture's power to create and perpetuate norms and this chapter's focus on conformity. Sherif (1935, 1937) wondered whether it was possible to observe the emergence of a social norm in the laboratory. Like biologists seeking to isolate a virus so they can then experiment with it, Sherif wanted to isolate and then experiment with norm formation.

As a participant in one of Sherif's studies, you might have found yourself seated in a dark room. Fifteen feet in front of you a pinpoint of light appears. At first, nothing happens. Then for a few seconds it moves erratically and finally disappears. Now you must guess how far it moved. The dark room gives you no way to judge distance, so you offer an uncertain '6 inches'. The experimenter repeats the procedure. This time you say, '10 inches'. With further repetitions, your estimates continue to average about 8 inches.

The next day you return to the darkened room, joined by two other participants who had the same experience the day before. When the light goes off for the first time, the other two people offer their best guesses from the day before. 'One inch,' says one. 'Two inches,' says the other. A bit taken aback, you nevertheless say, 'Six inches.' With successive repetitions of this group experience, both on this day and for the next two days, will your responses change? The Columbia University men whom Sherif tested changed their estimates markedly. As **Figure 7.1** illustrates, a group norm typically emerged. In actual fact the norm was completely arbitrary, with no correspondence to reality. Why? The light never moved! Sherif had taken advantage of an optical illusion called the **autokinetic phenomenon**.

autokinetic phenomenon self (auto) motion (kinetic). The apparent movement of a stationary point of light in the dark

Sherif and others have used this technique to answer questions about people's suggestibility. When people were retested alone a year later, would their estimates again diverge or would they continue to follow the group norm? Remarkably, they continued to support the group norm (Rohrer et al., 1954). (Does that suggest compliance or acceptance?)

Struck by culture's seeming power to perpetuate false beliefs, Jacobs and Campbell (1961) studied the transmission of false beliefs in their laboratory. Using the autokinetic phenomenon, they had a confederate give an inflated estimate of how far the light moved. The confederate then left the experiment and was replaced by another real participant. The newcomer conformed to the inflated estimate, and the inflated illusion persisted (although diminishing) in successive exchange of single participants, at least for five generations. These people had become 'unwitting conspirators in perpetuating a cultural fraud'. The lesson of these experiments: our views of reality are not ours alone.

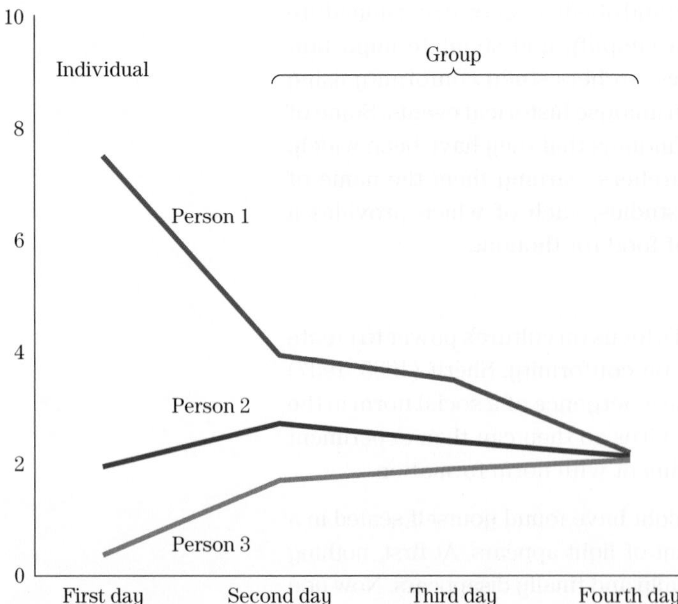

FIGURE 7.1 A sample group from Sherif's study of norm formation
Three individuals converge as they give repeated estimates of the apparent movement of a point of light.
SOURCE: Data from Sherif and Sherif (1969, p. 209)

In everyday life the results of suggestibility are sometimes amusing. One person coughs, laughs or yawns, and others are soon doing the same. (See Research Close-Up: Contagious Yawning.) Comedy-show laugh tracks capitalize on our suggestibility. Laugh tracks work especially well when we presume that the laughing audience is people like us – 'recorded here at La Trobe University' in one study by Platow et al. (2005) – rather than a group that's unlike us (see Chapter 12 for more on this study). Just being around happy people can help us feel happier, a phenomenon that Totterdell et al. (1998) call 'mood linkage'. In their studies of British nurses and accountants, people within the same work groups tended to share up and down moods.

'Why doth one man's yawning make another yawn?'
Robert Burton, *Anatomy of Melancholy*, 1621

Another form of social contagion is what Chartrand and Bargh (1999) call 'the chameleon effect'. Picture yourself in one of their experiments, working alongside a confederate who occasionally either rubbed her face or shook her foot. Would you – like their participants – be more likely to rub your face when with a face-rubbing person and shake your foot when with a foot-shaking person? If so, it would quite likely be an automatic behaviour done without any conscious intention to conform. And, because our behaviour influences our attitudes and emotions, it would incline you to feel what the other feels (Neumann & Strack, 2000). An experiment in the Netherlands by Van Baaren and his colleagues (2004) indicates that your mimicry would also incline the other to like you and be helpful to you and to others. People become more likely to help pick up dropped pens for someone whose behaviour has mimicked their own. Being mimicked seems to enhance social bonds, which even leads to actions like donating more money to a charity.

Fashion is another example of conformity and common norm formation, even if we vehemently deny we are victims of the trends set by others. We may confidently declare that we do not follow trends in clothing, hairstyles and the kind of coffee we prefer simply because everybody else does. We may be convinced that we are following our own taste, our personal aesthetic preferences and what kind of coffee we personally like, even if five years later when the fashions have changed, we dress differently and drink another kind of coffee. Similarly, how many students would you expect to order a glass of lemonade when the rest of the regular gang is ordering a beer? There are specific norms to follow and conform to as a student as well, and that is of course not necessarily a bad thing. It lubricates social relations and improves feelings of togetherness.

Suggestibility and social influence are not always harmless. Hijackings, UFO (unidentified flying object) sightings, and even suicides tend to come in waves. Shortly after the 1774 publication of *The Sorrows of Young Werther,* Johann Wolfgang von Goethe's first novel, young European men started dressing in yellow trousers and blue jackets, as had Goethe's protagonist, a young man named Werther. Although the fashion epidemic triggered by the book was amusing, another apparent effect was less amusing and led to the book being banned in several areas. In the novel, Werther commits suicide with a pistol after being rejected by the woman whose heart he failed to win; after the book's publication, reports began accumulating of young men imitating Werther's desperate act.

Two centuries later, sociologist David Phillips confirmed such imitative suicidal behaviour and described it as 'the Werther effect'. Phillips and his colleagues (Phillips, 1985; Phillips et al., 1989) discovered that suicides, as well as fatal automobile accidents and private airplane crashes (which sometimes disguise suicides), increase after a highly publicized suicide. For example, following Marilyn Monroe's suicide on 6 August 1962, there were 200 more August suicides in the USA than normal. Moreover, the increase happens only in places where the suicide story is publicized. The more publicity, the greater the increase in later fatalities. More recently, there has been debate surrounding the possible existence and influence of a controversial online game called 'Blue Whale'. In 2015, troubled Russian teenager Rina Palenkova, posted a selfie declaring her intention to commit suicide on Russia's largest social network, Vkontake. A spate of apparently copy-cat teen suicides in the immediate aftermath of Palenkova's death sparked social media interest and the story went viral. The young people

Research close-up

Contagious Yawning

Source: *Provine, R. (2005). Yawning.* American Scientist, *93, 532–539.*

Introduction

Yawning is a behaviour common to most vertebrates. Yawning appears to be a primal activity and can even be seen in babies in the womb (around week 12 of pregnancy). This research is interested in when we yawn and the potential social aspect of such a behaviour.

Yawning can be described as a 'fixed action pattern' that lasts about 6 seconds, with a long inward breath and shorter climactic (and pleasurable) exhalation. It often comes in bouts, with just over a minute between yawns. And it is equally common among men and women. Even patients who are totally paralysed and unable to move their body voluntarily may yawn normally, indicating that this is automatic behaviour.

In addition to the apparently physiological reasons behind yawning, we also appear to yawn as a social response to seeing others yawn. In later work, this has led to this phenomenon being termed the 'Doomsday Yawn' (Provine, 2012) because of its inevitability! This socially contagious aspect of yawning has only been evidenced in human beings and chimpanzees. Hence it seems that contagious yawning has evolved in species with higher-order levels of cognitive processing to deliver some benefits. A series of experiments was conducted to determine how common contagious yawning is, using video footage of a man yawning as a stimulus.

Method

Participants were divided into two conditions. In the experimental condition, the participants were shown a 5-minute video of 30 repetitions of a man yawning. In the control condition, the video was of a man smiling. The experiment was also carried out with alterations to the experimental condition that altered the yawning video stimulus, masking part of the face, changing the video from colour to black and white, as well as using still images of yawns. To see what parts of the yawning face were most potent, viewers watched a whole face, a face with the mouth masked, a mouth with the face masked, or (as a control condition) a non-yawning smiling face.

Four groups of 30 people each were invited to watch 5-minute videotapes of a smiling adult, or a yawning adult, parts of whose face were masked for two of the groups. The researchers looked to see if the participants would yawn or smile in response to watching the videos.

Results

In the yawning condition, 55 per cent of viewers yawned, as compared to only 21 per cent of those viewing a video of smiles. The changes in the presentation of the video – changing the colour or altering the position of the picture – did not alter the participants' yawning responses. The results support the argument that a yawning face acts as a stimulus that activates a yawn's fixed action pattern, even if the yawn is presented in black and white, upside down, or as a mid-yawn still image.

Discussion

These experiments show that we are triggered to yawn when we see someone else yawning, even if we only see a yawning mouth, or the rest of the yawning face without the mouth. The discovery of brain 'mirror neurons' – neurons that rehearse or mimic witnessed actions – suggests a biological mechanism that explains why our yawns so often mirror others' yawns. This goes some way to explaining why contagious yawning is peculiar to species with higher-order cognitive processes; human beings and chimpanzees. These 'mirror neurons' could explain why we seem to find ourselves mimicking the actions of others, so when other people smile at us, we are very likely to smile back. This is probably why people around us who are happy and smiling seem to make us smile more, and so lift our own mood. Their cheerfulness seems to make us cheerful.

Thus, covering your mouth when yawning probably won't suppress yawn contagion. This totally unconscious response to others is an example of a neurologically programmed social behaviour. Thus, the unconsciously controlled human behaviour opens the discussion of human behaviour to a much wider scope of study.

It is suggested that contagious yawning serves a social function for those social species capable of doing it. It has evolved as a way of signalling empathy, which is important for maintaining and strengthening social bonds (for more recent work on this see Franzen et al., 2018). Whilst different cultures have different norms about how yawning should be expressed (e.g. covering your mouth when you yawn), 'Yawning is a reminder that ancient and unconscious behavior lurks beneath the veneer of culture, rationality and language, continuing to influence our lives' (p. 539).

Just thinking about yawning usually produces yawns – a phenomenon you may have noticed while reading this box. Influenced by the yawning your brain believes you are tired.

Critical Reflections

The original paper is a comment on studies Provine has conducted on yawning and smiling, rather than an experimental report on the work. Consequently it does not contain the finer details regarding methods, data and calculation of results we would expect from a scientific report.

Provine acknowledges that his work, despite being substantial in scope, does not offer a 'Grand Unified Theory of Yawning' (p. 539). This is appropriate as there are arguably some gaps in this work which need addressing.

Provine notes that contagious yawning transcends culture. Whether this is true or not requires evidencing with cross-cultural research. Furthermore, if yawning serves an important social function in species which rely on social bonds for their existence, why hasn't this spread to other behaviours such as smiling? In Provine's study smiling was shown to be considerably less contagious than yawning. However, you might imagine that smiling would be at least as equally important for maintaining social bonds as yawning. So what's so special about yawning?

Interestingly, more recent work has found evidence for contagious yawning in other social species including domestic dogs (Silva et al., 2012), sheep (Yonezawa et al., 2016), and rats (Moyaho et al., 2014). This suggests that contagious yawning has evolved to assist with social bonds in some species, but perhaps does throw some doubt on the suggestion that higher-order cognitive processes are required to engage in unconscious contagious yawning. Alternatively, perhaps some species have more complex cognitions than previously thought?

who died shared some similarities with Rina. They were from Russia; some were from the same town as Rina. They were members of the same, or similar, online groups as Rina. And perhaps most disturbing of all, they had all included images of Rina and blue whales in social media posts prior to their death. Panic ensued about the existence of the Blue Whale game thought to be responsible, who was behind it, and the apparent spreading of more copy-cat teen suicides beyond

Russia. It is unclear whether the game actually exists, but it is attributed with targeting and recruiting vulnerable children and young people into a series of dares, ending in their eventual suicide. If true, it uses social media peer pressure to achieve devastating consequences for the young players.

Phillips reports that teenagers are most susceptible, a finding that would help explain the occasional clusters of teen copycat suicides. In a baffling set of cases, Bridgend – a small community in Wales – has seen at least 24 suicides of young people between 2007 and 2012, far above the expected number of suicides. There was a lot of speculation about why there were so many cases in such a small area. One of the things raised as possibly being part of the cause was the use of social media. It was speculated that the suicide victims' social media activity was a contribution to the trend, as well as tribute sites set up after each case where people left messages of remembrance and support. However, the police looked into this and they stated that although some of the people who committed suicide knew each other, they could find no concrete link between them all. The police also asked the media to stop reporting on suicides in the town to stop it potentially influencing other young people. For some further opinion on this case, see Cadwalladr (2009).

Asch's Studies of Group Pressure

Participants in Sherif's darkened-room autokinetic experiments faced an ambiguous reality. Consider a less ambiguous perceptual problem faced by a young boy named Solomon Asch (1907–96). While attending the traditional Jewish Seder at Passover, Asch recalled:

> I asked my uncle, who was sitting next to me, why the door was being opened. He replied, 'The prophet Elijah visits this evening every Jewish home and takes a sip of wine from the cup reserved for him.'
>
> I was amazed at this news and repeated, 'Does he really come? Does he really take a sip?'
>
> My uncle said, 'If you watch very closely, when the door is opened you will see – you watch the cup – you will see that the wine will go down a little.'
>
> And that's what happened. My eyes were riveted upon the cup of wine. I was determined to see whether there would be a change. And to me it seemed . . . that indeed something was happening at the rim of the cup, and the wine did go down a little.
>
> (Aron & Aron, 1989, p. 27)

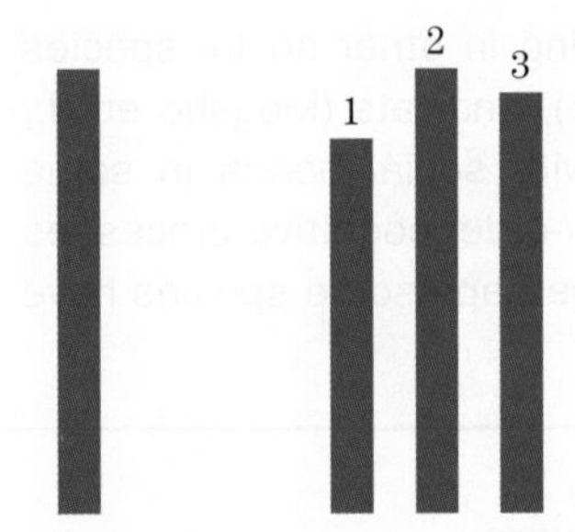

FIGURE 7.2 Sample comparison from Solomon Asch's conformity procedure. The participants judged which of three comparison lines matched the standard

Years later as a social psychologist, Asch re-created his boyhood experience in his laboratory. Imagine yourself as one of Asch's volunteer participants. In **Figure 7.2** you can easily see that line 2 matches the standard line. So it's no surprise when the five people responding before you all say, 'Line 2'.

In the second trial of the experiment, the answer seems just as obvious and the group give the correct answer. But the third trial startles you. Although the correct answer seems just as clear-cut, the first person in your group gives a wrong answer. When the second person gives the same wrong answer, you sit up in your chair and stare at the cards. The third person agrees with the first two. Your jaw drops; you start to perspire. 'What is this?' you ask yourself. 'Are they blind? Or am I?' The fourth and fifth people agree with the others. Then the experimenter looks at you. Now you are experiencing an epistemological dilemma: 'What is true? Is it what my peers tell me or what my eyes tell me?'

Dozens of college students experienced that conflict as participants in Asch's experiments. Those in a control condition who answered alone were correct more than 99 per cent of the time. Asch wondered: if several others (confederates coached by the experimenter) gave identical wrong answers, would people declare what they would otherwise have denied? Although some people never conformed, three-quarters did so in at least one trial. All told, 37 per cent of the responses were conforming (or should we say '*trusting* of others'). Of course, that means 63 per cent of the time people did *not* conform. The experiments show that most people 'tell the truth even when others do not', note Hodges and Geyer (2006). Despite the independence shown by many of his participants, Asch's (1955) feelings about the conformity were as clear as the correct answers to his questions: 'That reasonably intelligent and well-meaning young people are willing to call white black is a matter of concern. It raises questions about our ways of education and about the values that guide our conduct' (p. 54).

The Sherif and Asch results are startling because they involved no obvious pressure to conform – there were no rewards for 'team play', no punishments for individuality. The Sherif and Asch experiments are also interesting because they show how quickly people will change their answers in the face of conflicting information from others. In the Sherif experiment the ambiguity of the autokinetic effect seems to provide a task that you might easily reassess your answer on. Without anything to measure the movement against, maybe you are wrong and it really *did* move that far. In the Asch experiment, the task is far less ambiguous and the difference in the lengths of lines is much clearer; you are more in a position to give an answer that you *know* is wrong in order to agree with others. These experiments replicate the day-to-day social influence that leads us to agree with others or go along with other people to appear socially acceptable or compliant. It is often much easier to agree with others in public, just for a quiet life and to avoid conflict.

Asch's experiments are also influential from a group perspective and are further considered in Chapters 11 and 12.

If people are that conforming in response to such minimal pressure, how compliant will they be if they are directly coerced? Could someone force the average American or European citizen to perform cruel acts? We would have guessed not: their humane, democratic, individualistic values would make them resist such pressure. Besides, the easy verbal pronouncements of those experiments are a giant step away from actually harming someone; you and I would never yield to coercion to hurt another. Or would we? History tells us otherwise. In Africa, Asia and Australia, American and European people have performed cruel acts against others often without being ordered or forced to. Think about the treatment of Native Americans and First Nations people in North America. Or the British killing of the Australian aborigines and the destruction of the cultures in the Pacific. Or the Nazis' treatment of Jews, Gypsies, homosexuals and disabled people during the Second World War, and the European and Israeli treatment of the Palestinian refugees for more than 60 years.

Social psychologist Stanley Milgram wondered if direct coercion and compliance to perform cruel acts could be reproduced in the laboratory. His work about obedience to authority started and was funded in the USA at a time when conformity was regarded exclusively as a 'bad thing' as it came on the back of the Second World War. The Western world was horrified by the obedience and its consequences in the Third Reich. To conform (to a Nazi regime and propaganda) was regarded as antithetical to Western values of individualism (although there's a conundrum here about how if everyone conforms to individualism this is an act of conformity in itself!). Governments and people in general wanted to know what caused it so they could prevent it. The topics of obedience, authoritarianism and 'mass psychology' were studied extensively by social researchers, psychologists and psychiatrists after the Second World War. In Germany the social psychoanalyst Wilhelm Reich wrote about the mass psychology of fascism, and in the USA German and American sociologists, social psychologists and psychoanalysts under the lead of Theodor Adorno published in 1950 the influential book *The Authoritarian Personality* (referred to in Chapter 13). These and many other research programmes and studies illustrate how social psychology is 'situated' in the times. Conformity was regarded as a bad thing after the Second World War and Stanley Milgram has been the most influential social psychologist in carrying this spirit of obedience as something evil into science and examining it in the laboratory.

Milgram's Studies of Obedience

Milgram (1965, 1974) tested what happens when the demands of authority clash with the demands of conscience. These have become social psychology's most famous and controversial laboratory studies. 'Perhaps more than any other empirical contributions in the history of social science', notes Ross (1988), 'they have become part of our society's shared intellectual legacy – that small body of historical incidents, biblical parables, and classic literature that serious thinkers feel free to draw on when they debate about human nature or contemplate human history'. Although you may therefore recall a mention of this research in a prior course, let's go backstage and examine the studies in depth. Although the studies take place in a laboratory, Milgram's empirical work is more properly described as a series of demonstrations, rather than as an experiment (Burger, 2009). For those interested in the fascinating personal history that shaped Milgram's work, it is worth reading the paper by Russell (2011) which outlines much of this influence.

Here is the scene staged by Milgram, a creative artist who wrote stories and stage plays: two men come to Yale University's psychology laboratory to participate in a study of learning and memory. A stern experimenter in a laboratory coat explains that this is a pioneering study of the effect of punishment on learning. The experiment requires one of them to teach a list of word pairs to the other and to punish errors by delivering shocks of increasing intensity. To assign the roles, they draw slips out of a hat. One of the men (a mild-mannered, 47-year-old accountant who is actually the experimenter's confederate) says that his slip says 'learner' and is ushered into an adjacent room. The other man (a volunteer who has come in response to a newspaper advertisement) is assigned to the role of 'teacher'. He takes a mild sample shock and then looks on as the experimenter straps the learner into a chair and attaches an electrode to his wrist.

Teacher and experimenter then return to the main room (see **Figure 7.3**), where the teacher takes his place before a 'shock generator' with switches ranging from 15 to 450 volts in 15-volt increments. The switches are labelled 'Slight Shock', 'Very Strong Shock', 'Danger: Severe Shock', and so forth. Under the 435- and 450-volt switches appears 'XXX'. The experimenter tells the teacher to 'move one level higher on the shock generator' each time the learner gives a wrong answer. With each flick of a switch, lights flash, relay switches click and an electric buzz sounds.

If the participant complies with the experimenter's requests, he hears the learner grunt at 75, 90 and 105 volts. At 120 volts the learner shouts that the shocks are painful. And at 150 volts he cries out, 'Experimenter, get me out of here! I won't be in the experiment any more! I refuse to go on!' By 270 volts his protests have become screams of agony, and he continues to insist to be let out. At 300 and 315 volts, he screams his refusal to answer. After 330 volts he falls silent (**Table 7.1, overleaf**). In answer to the teacher's inquiries and pleas to end the experiment, the experimenter states that the non-responses should be treated as wrong answers. To keep the participant going, he uses four verbal prods:

Prod 1: Please continue (or Please go on).
Prod 2: The experiment requires that you continue.
Prod 3: It is absolutely essential that you continue.
Prod 4: You have no other choice; you must go on.

How far would you go? Milgram described the experiment to 110 psychiatrists, college students and middle-class adults. People in all three groups guessed that they would disobey by about 135 volts; none expected to go beyond 300 volts. Recognizing that self-estimates may reflect self-serving bias, Milgram asked them how far they thought *other* people would go. Virtually no one expected

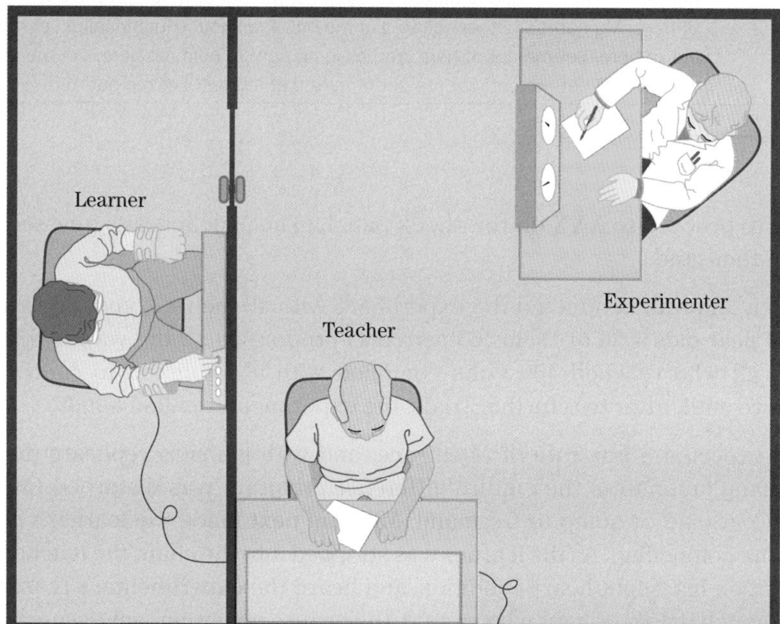

FIGURE 7.3 Milgram's obedience experiment
SOURCE: Milgram (1974).

TABLE 7.1 The learner's schedule of protests in Milgram's 'heart disturbance' experiments

75 volts	Ugh!
90 volts	Ugh!
105 volts	Ugh! (Louder)
120 volts	Ugh! Hey, this really hurts.
135 volts	Ugh!!
150 volts	Ugh!!! Experimenter! That's all. Get me out of here. I told you I had heart trouble.
	My heart's starting to bother me now. Get me out of here, please. My heart's starting to bother me. I refuse to go on. Let me out
165 volts	Ugh! Let me out! (Shouting)
180 volts	Ugh! I can't stand the pain. Let me out of here! (Shouting)
195 volts	Ugh! Let me out of here. Let me out of here. My heart's bothering me. Let me out of here! You have no right to keep me here! Let me out! Let me out of here! Let me out!
	Let me out of here! My heart's bothering me. Let me out! Let me out!
210 volts	Ugh! Experimenter! Get me out of here. I've had enough. I won't be in the experiment any more.
225 volts	Ugh!
240 volts	Ugh!
255 volts	Ugh! Get me out of here.
270 volts	(Agonized scream) Let me out of here. Let me out of here. Let me out of here. Let me out. Do you hear? Let me out of here.
285 volts	(Agonized scream)
300 volts	(Agonized scream) I absolutely refuse to answer any more. Get me out of here. You can't hold me here. Get me out. Get me out of here.
315 volts	(Intensely agonized scream) I told you I refuse to answer. I'm no longer part of this experiment.
330 volts	(Intense and prolonged agonized scream) Let me out of here. Let me out of here. My heart's bothering me. Let me out, I tell you. (Hysterically) Let me out of here. Let me out of here. You have no right to hold me here. Let me out! Let me out! Let me out! Let me out of here! Let me out! Let me out!

SOURCE: From Milgram (1974, pp. 56–57)

anyone to proceed to XXX on the shock panel. (The psychiatrists guessed about one in a thousand.)

But when Milgram conducted the experiment with 40 men – a vocational mix of 20 to 50 year olds – 26 of them (65 per cent) progressed all the way to 450 volts. In fact, all who reached 450 volts complied with a command to *continue* the procedure until, after two further trials, the experimenter called a halt.

Having expected a low rate of obedience, and with plans to replicate the study in Germany and assess the culture difference, Milgram was disturbed (Milgram, 2000). So instead of going to Germany, Milgram next made the learner's protests even more compelling. As the learner was strapped into the chair, the teacher heard him mention his 'slight heart condition' and heard the experimenter's reassurance that 'although the shocks may be painful, they cause no permanent tissue damage'. The learner's anguished protests were to little avail; of 40 new men in this experiment, 25 (63 per cent) fully complied with the experimenter's demands (**Figure 7.4, overleaf**).

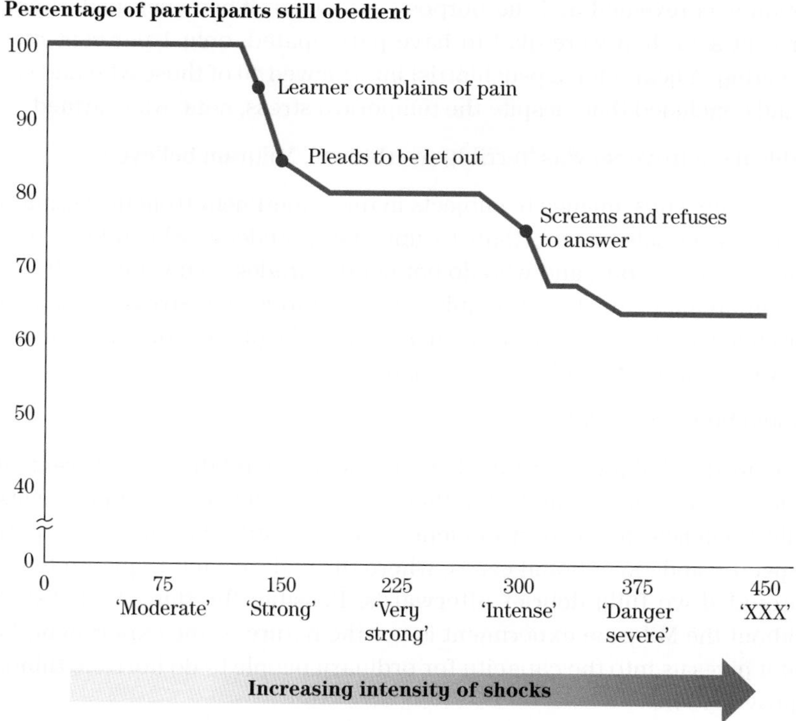

FIGURE 7.4 The Milgram obedience experiment

Percentage of participants complying despite the learner's cries of protest and failure to respond.

SOURCE: Adapted from Milgram (1965)

The Ethics of Milgram's Experiments

The obedience of the participants disturbed Milgram. The procedures he used disturbed many social psychologists and has consequently shaped ethical procedures for modern-day psychology research (Baumrind, 2013; Tolich, 2014). The 'learner' in these experiments actually received no shock (he disengaged himself from the electric chair and turned on a tape recorder that delivered the protests). Nevertheless, some critics said that Milgram did to his participants what they presumed they were doing to their victims: he stressed them against their will. Indeed, many of the 'teachers' did experience agony. They sweated, trembled, stuttered, bit their lips, groaned, or even broke into uncontrollable nervous laughter. A *New York Times* reviewer complained that the cruelty inflicted by the experiments 'upon their unwitting subjects is surpassed only by the cruelty that they elicit from them' (Marcus, 1974).

Critics also argued that the participants' self-concepts may have been altered. One participant's wife told him, 'You can call yourself Eichmann' (referring to Nazi death camp administrator Adolf Eichmann). CBS television depicted the results and the controversy in a two-hour dramatization. 'A world of evil so terrifying no one dares penetrate its secret. Until Now!' declared a *TV Guide* advertisement for the programme (Elms, 1995).

In his own defence, Milgram pointed to the important lessons taught by his nearly two dozen studies with a diverse sample of more than 1,000 participants. He also reminded critics of the support he received from the participants after the deception was revealed and the purpose explained. When surveyed afterwards, 84 per cent said they were glad to have participated; only 1 per cent regretted volunteering. A year later, a psychiatrist interviewed 40 of those who had suffered most and concluded that, despite the temporary stress, none was harmed.

The ethical controversy was 'terribly overblown', Milgram believed:

> There is less consequence to subjects in this experiment from the standpoint of effects on self-esteem, than to university students who take ordinary course examinations, and who do not get the grades they want. . . . It seems that [in giving exams] we are quite prepared to accept stress, tension, and consequences for self-esteem. But in regard to the process of generating new knowledge, how little tolerance we show.
>
> (quoted by Blass, 1996)

If we consider Milgram's original experiments in relation to current ethical guidelines, it can be argued that there was nothing in the experiments that actually breaches the current guidelines. We are still able to use deception in very specific and exceptional cases, where the ends are felt to justify the means and provided we fully debrief afterwards. Possibly the thing that disturbs us most about the Milgram experiment is not the nature of the experiment, but the insight it gives us into the capacity for ordinary people to do horrible things with little provocation.

What Breeds Obedience?

Milgram did more than reveal the extent to which people will obey an authority; he also examined the conditions that breed obedience. When he varied the conditions, compliance ranged from 0 to 93 per cent fully obedient. Four factors that determined obedience were (1) the victim's distance, (2) the authority's closeness and legitimacy, (3) whether or not the authority was part of a respected institution, and (4) the liberating effects of a disobedient fellow participant.

The Victim's Distance

Milgram's participants acted with greatest obedience and least compassion when the 'learners' could not be seen (and could not see them). When the victim was remote and the 'teachers' heard no complaints, nearly all obeyed calmly to the end.

That situation minimized the learner's influence relative to the experimenter's. But what if we made the learner's pleas and the experimenter's instructions more equally visible? When the learner was in the same room, 'only' 40 per cent obeyed to 450 volts. Full compliance dropped to a still-astonishing 30 per cent when teachers were required to force the learner's hand into contact with a shock plate.

In everyday life, too, it is easiest to abuse someone who is distant or depersonalized. People who might never be cruel to someone in person may be downright nasty when posting comments aimed at anonymous people on Internet discussion boards. The fairly recent phenomenon of Internet trolls has led to some fascinating research and insights into how anonymity facilitates online abuse (for example see Klempka & Stimson, 2014). Throughout history, executioners have often depersonalized those being executed by placing hoods over their heads. The ethics of war allow one to bomb a helpless village from 40,000 feet but not to shoot an equally helpless villager or a wedding party when watching it close.

As the Holocaust began, some Germans, under orders, used machine guns or rifles to kill men, women and children standing before them. But others could not bring themselves to do so, and some who did were left shaken by the experience of face-to-face killing. That led Heinrich Himmler, the Nazi 'architect of genocide', to devise a killing, more 'humane' for the executioners, one that would visually separate the killers and their victims and was highly 'efficient'. The solution was the construction of concrete gas chambers, where the killers would not see or hear the human consequences of their horror (Russell & Gregory, 2005).

On the positive side, people act most compassionately towards those who are personalized and need care. That is why appeals for the disabled, for the hungry or for animal rights are nearly always personalized with a compelling photograph or description (e.g. Bartsch & Kloß, 2019; Chang & Lee, 2009).

Closeness and Legitimacy of the Authority

The physical presence of the experimenter also affected obedience. When Milgram's experimenter gave the commands by telephone, full obedience dropped to 21 per cent (although many lied and said they were obeying). Other studies confirm that when the one making the command is physically close, compliance increases (see Haslam et al., 2014 for an excellent review of all 23 conditions of Milgram's experiments).

The authority, however, must be perceived as legitimate. In another twist on the basic experiment, the experimenter received a rigged telephone call that required him to leave the laboratory. He said that since the equipment recorded data automatically, the 'teacher' should just go ahead. After the experimenter left, another person, who had been assigned a clerical role (actually a second confederate), assumed command. The clerk 'decided' that the shock should be increased one level for each wrong answer and instructed the teacher accordingly. Now 80 per cent of the teachers refused to comply fully. The confederate, feigning disgust at this defiance, sat down in front of the shock generator and tried to take over the teacher's role. At that point most of the defiant participants protested. Some tried to unplug the generator. One large man lifted the zealous confederate from his chair and threw him across the room. This rebellion against an illegitimate authority contrasted sharply with the deferential politeness usually shown the experimenter.

It also contrasts with the behaviour of hospital nurses who in one classic study were called by an unknown physician and ordered to administer an obvious drug overdose (Hofling et al., 1966). The researchers told one group of nurses and nursing students about the experiment and asked how they would react. Nearly all said they would not have followed the order. One said she would have replied, 'I'm sorry, sir, but I am not authorized to give any medication without a written order, especially one so large over the usual dose and one that I'm unfamiliar with. If it were possible, I would be glad to do it, but this is against hospital policy and my own ethical standards.' Nevertheless, when 22 other nurses were actually given the phoned-in overdose order, all but one obeyed without delay (until being intercepted on their way to the patient). More recently, researchers from the nursing profession have exposed this apparent tension between the need for nurses to act as autonomous professionals, and the demands of hospital policy that require them to be obedient to procedure (Bail et al., 2009). As social psychologists we need to recognize the push and pull forces that underlie (non)conformity.

Institutional Authority

If the prestige of the authority is that important, then perhaps the institutional prestige of Yale University legitimized the Milgram experiment commands. In post-experimental interviews, many participants said that had it not been for Yale's reputation, they would not have obeyed. To see whether that was true, Milgram moved the experiment to less prestigious Bridgeport, Connecticut. He set himself up in a modest commercial building as the 'Research Associates of Bridgeport'. When the 'learner-has-a-heart-condition' experiment was run with the same personnel, what percentage of the men do you suppose fully obeyed? Although the obedience rate (48 per cent) was still remarkably high, it was significantly lower than the 65 per cent rate at Yale.

In 1962, Orne carried out a series of experiments looking at the demand characteristics of laboratory experiments. He argued that asking participants to act 'normally' in such an artificial setting simply didn't work, participants are driven by demand characteristics, wanting to give the experimenter what they think they want. As an example, participants were given unrealistically huge tasks to complete; one was a maths task, asking participants to add two numbers – there were 244 of these on each page, and participants were given a stack of 2,000 pages. Once the participants were given the task and the instructions, they were told that the experimenter had to leave but that they would return 'eventually'. One participant carried on for so long that after over five hours the experimenter gave up and stopped them. Participants were given tasks that were clearly pointless and repetitive, yet they continued them for hours at a time. Orne's position is that the very 'scientific' nature of laboratory experiments is one of the flaws, that they lack ecological validity. We might do things in a laboratory experiment that we would never do in our everyday lives.

In everyday life, too, authorities backed by institutions wield social power. Ornstein (1991) tells of a psychiatrist friend who was called to the edge of a cliff above San Mateo, California, where one of his patients, Alfred, was threatening to jump. When the psychiatrist's reasoned reassurance failed to dislodge Alfred, the psychiatrist could only hope that a police crisis expert would soon arrive.

Although no expert came, another police officer, unaware of the drama, happened onto the scene, took out his power bullhorn, and yelled at the assembled cliffside group: 'Who's the ass who left that Pontiac station wagon double-parked out there in the middle of the road? I almost hit it. Move it *now,* whoever you are.' Hearing the message, Alfred obediently got down at once, moved the car, and then without a word got into the police cruiser for a trip to the nearby hospital.

Agentic State Theory

The evidence is solidly supportive of Milgram's view that the power of authority, rather than aggressive tendencies, was the primary determinant of the punishing behaviour in his studies. Milgram (1974) argued that obedience involves denial of responsibility of one's actions and a willingness to hand it over to authority. A person comes to view him or herself as an instrument for carrying out another person's wishes, and therefore no longer sees him or herself as responsible for their own actions. Milgram referred to this process as a shift from a state of autonomy to an *agentic state*. The evidence is not very supportive, however, since the theory cannot explain the different levels of obedience obtained in variants of the baseline study (varying from 65 per cent when participants only hear the reactions of the 'learner' to 30 per cent where they have to force his hand down onto an 'electric contact plate' and down to 10 per cent where there is a dissenting confederate teacher). Film and transcript of the studies also show that, far from becoming morally disengaged and passive, participants were profoundly troubled by what they were doing and initiated long debates about the justification for continuing the study. Subsequent studies do not find a relationship between the amount of responsibility attributed to the experimenter and levels of obedience. In short, the '*agentic state*' theory does not give the complete explanation (Blass, 2004). Our tendency to be obedient in specific situations has a more complex causality than people giving up their autonomy.

Reflections on the Classic Studies

The common response to Milgram's results is to note their counterparts in recent history: the 'I was only following orders' defences of Adolf Eichmann in Nazi Germany; of American Lieutenant William Calley, who in 1968 directed the unprovoked slaughter of hundreds of Vietnamese in the village of My Lai; the American soldiers, among them Lynndie England, who humiliated Islamic war-prisoners in Abu Ghraib prison and British soldiers who did the same in Basra; and of the 'ethnic cleansing' occurring in Iraq, Rwanda, Bosnia and Kosovo. In legal terms the 'I was only following orders' is known as the defence of 'superior orders', and can be used to diminish responsibility for one's own actions (Gibson et al., 2018).

Adolf Eichmann on trial for his role in the Holocaust. Eichmann famously claimed "I was only following orders". Does Milgram's experiments expose the ordinary monster in us all?

SOURCE: ©PICTORIAL Press Ltd/Alamy Stock Photo

Soldiers were trained to obey superiors even if the orders were illegal and would result in atrocities. Thus, one participant in the My Lai massacre recalled:

> [Lieutenant Calley] told me to start shooting. So I started shooting, I poured about four clips into the group. . . . They were begging and saying, 'No, no.' And the mothers were hugging their children and . . . . Well, we kept right on firing. They was waving their arms and begging.
> (Congressional Record, 1969)

The Structural Atrocities

These examples of humiliation and atrocities focus on individuals as perpetrators. But sometimes a whole system or society is responsible for the misdeeds, killings and maltreatment of the enemies of the state. The slaughter becomes natural and the rule rather than the exception. Some social structures have an inbuilt injustice. The people in power and their followers have their benefits and protect the status quo by any means. Apartheid in South Africa was such a system for more than a hundred years. The atrocities could not be personified, the social structure was the main perpetrator and many white South Africans looked at themselves as good patriots when they killed and humiliated black enemies. The apartheid system developed gradually over many years. In the second half of the eighteenth century, the colonists – mainly of Dutch, German and French stock – had begun to lose their sense of identification with Europe and looked at themselves as the masters and owners of South Africa, including the black people. The separation of the blacks and whites (the apartheid system) became official government ideology from 1948 when the Nationalist Party gained power. The 1950s brought more and more repressive laws against black South Africans, which naturally created growing resistance. This set the stage for the even more polarized 1960s, when the suppression, violence and cruelty towards the black South Africans increased.

Many white South Africans were born and socialized into a society where hostility towards the black majority was looked upon as natural and necessary, and many conformed and participated in the cruelties during the apartheid period. One of the most high profile of these was Eugene de Kock, nicknamed 'Prime Evil', apartheid's chief murderer. He was later sentenced to 212 years for crimes against humanity. However, Pumla Goboda-Madikizela, a black female psychologist at the University of Cape Town, tried to understand the person behind these crimes and claimed to find a human being worthy of pardon and freedom. She published a remarkable book about her conversations with de Kock, entitled, *A Human Being Died that Night: A South African Story of Forgiveness* (Goboda-Madikizela, 2003). Her conclusion was that even the Prime Evil is a human being and was a victim of conformity to a suppressing and cruel system more than a man of absolute malignity.

The 'safe' scientific contexts of the obedience experiments differ from the real-world contexts. Moreover, much of the mockery and brutality of war and genocide goes beyond obedience (Miller, 2004). Some of those who implemented the Holocaust were 'willing executioners' who hardly needed to be commanded to kill (Goldhagen, 1996). Many of them were proud to participate in the new Third Reich by being obedient and trustworthy. Few were aggressive or emotional and unable to control their temper when they dealt with the victims of the Nazi ideology. They conformed to the vision of building a new Germany – a new 'magnificent World', and as such, believed that all those considered unworthy or unfit for this ideal had to be exterminated. See Focus On: The Ordinary Monster.

The obedience studies differ from the conformity experiments in the strength of the social pressure: obedience is explicitly commanded. Without the coercion, people did not act cruelly. Yet both the Asch and the Milgram experiments share certain commonalities. They showed how compliance can take precedence over moral sense. They did more than teach an academic lesson; they sensitized us to moral conflicts in our own lives. And they illustrated and affirmed some familiar social psychological principles: the link between behaviour and attitudes, the power of the situation, and the strength of the fundamental attribution error.

Step by Step towards Insensibility

In Chapter 5 we noted that attitudes fail to determine behaviour when external influences override inner convictions. These experiments vividly illustrate that principle. When responding alone, Asch's participants nearly always gave the correct answer. It was another matter when they stood alone against a group.

In the obedience experiments, a powerful social pressure (the experimenter's commands) overcame a weaker one (the remote victim's pleas). Torn between the pleas of the victim and the orders of the experimenter, between the desire to avoid doing harm and the desire to be a good participant, a surprising number of people chose to obey.

Why were the participants unable to disengage themselves? Imagine yourself as the teacher in yet another version of Milgram's experiment (one he never conducted). Assume that when the learner gives the first wrong answer, the experimenter asks you to zap him with 330 volts. After flicking the switch, you hear the learner scream, complain of a heart disturbance and plead for mercy. Do you continue?

We think not. Recall the step-by-step entrapment of the **foot-in-the-door** phenomenon (Chapter 6) as we compare this hypothetical experiment to what Milgram's participants experienced. Their first commitment was mild – 15 volts – and it elicited no protest. By the time they delivered 75 volts and heard the learner's first groan, they already had complied five times, and the next request was to deliver only slightly more. By the time they delivered 330 volts, the participants had complied 22 times and reduced some of their dissonance. They were therefore in a different psychological state from that of someone beginning the experiment at that point. This method of gradually increasing shocks, starting from something harmless and moving slowly towards more and more severe punishment, is sometimes overlooked as an important contribution to obedience. Milgram has been criticized for not taking this aspect of sequentialization into account in his obedience experiments. Burger (2009) has made a comment on this in his replication of Milgram's demonstration of obedience (see the section, 'Milgram's Studies of Obedience' above). If people are obedient to authority per se, then surely Milgram could have started at, for example, 330 volts and people would have delivered the fatal electric shock. But he didn't. Instead he crept along an incremental sequence of shocks in order to get the effect by the help of the foot-in-the-door phenomenon.

foot-in-the-door phenomenon
manipulation technique in which getting people to first agree to a small request increases the chances that they will later comply with a larger request

So it is in our everyday lives: the drift towards evil usually comes in small increments, without any conscious intent to do evil.

Blame-the-Victim

As we saw in Chapter 5, external behaviour, attitudes and internal disposition can feed each other, sometimes in an escalating spiral. Thus:

> Many subjects harshly devalue the victim as a consequence of acting against him. Such comments as, 'He was so stupid and stubborn he deserved to get shocked,' were common. Once having acted against the victim, these subjects found it necessary to view him as an unworthy individual, whose punishment was made inevitable by his own deficiencies of intellect and character.
>
> (Milgram, 1974, p. 10)

During the early 1970s, Greece's military junta used this 'blame-the-victim' process to train torturers (Haritos-Fatouros, 1988, 2012; Staub, 1989, 2003). The military selected candidates based on their respect for and submission to authority. But such tendencies alone do not a torturer make. Thus, they would first assign the trainee to guard prisoners, then to participate in arrest squads, then to hit prisoners, then to observe torture, and only then to practise it. Step by step, an obedient but otherwise decent person evolved into an agent of cruelty. Compliance bred acceptance.

As a Holocaust survivor, University of Massachusetts social psychologist Ervin Staub knows too well the forces that can transform citizens into agents of death. From his study of human genocide across the world, Staub (2003) shows where gradually increasing aggression can lead. Too often criticism produces contempt, which licenses cruelty, which, when justified, leads to brutality, then killing, then systematic killing. Evolving attitudes both follow and justify actions. Staub's disturbing conclusion: 'Human beings have the capacity to come to experience killing other people as nothing extraordinary' (1989, p. 13).

But individuals and groups also have capacity for heroism. During the Nazi Holocaust, Oskar Schindler's rescue of over 1,000 Jews resulted in the Booker Prize winning novel *Schindler's Ark* (1982) by Thomas Keneally, and the blockbuster multi-award winning film *Schindler's List* (1994). Other acts of heroism have not aspired to the dizzy heights of Hollywood but are no less impressive. The French village of Le Chambon sheltered 5,000 Jews and other refugees destined for deportation to Germany. The villagers were mostly Protestants whose own authorities, their pastors, had taught them to 'resist whenever our adversaries will demand of us obedience contrary to the orders of the Gospel' (Rochat, 1993; Rochat & Modigliani, 1995). Ordered to divulge the locations of sheltered Jews, the head pastor modelled disobedience: 'I don't know of Jews, I only know of human beings'. Without knowing how terrible the war would be, the resisters, beginning in 1940, made an initial commitment and then – supported by their beliefs, by their own authorities and by one another – remained defiant until the village's liberation in 1944. Here and elsewhere, the ultimate response to Nazi occupation came early. Initial helping heightened commitment, leading to more helping. Even within the concentration camps there was resistance and Langbein (1994) makes the point that resistance was only possible at a collective level. Those who were most effective in fighting back (and in surviving) were those that had most solidarity and most cohesion: the communists among the political prisoners, the Zionists among the Jews, the Russians and the Spaniards among nations.

Sometimes social psychologists have given the impression that groups or crowds necessarily lead to destructive and antisocial behaviour (Le Bon, 1895). We discuss the social psychology of crowds further in Chapter 13. Reicher and his colleagues reject such a view and give historical examples of self-sacrifice on behalf of others:

> It is certainly true, for example, that, in the Soviet Union, many millions were imprisoned or starved simply for being designated a 'kulak' or a member of some other pathologized category. But it is equally true that, without collective solidarity, this and other dictatorships would not have been toppled. The Romanian revolution, for instance, began in Timisoara where large crowds challenged Ceausescu's notorious Securitate police force. Many demonstrators were killed. Still, the numbers of demonstrators grew . . . the fate of the Romanian people was more important than life itself.
>
> (Reicher et al., 2008)

The Power of the Social Context

In Chapter 14 we explore the very important role that culture and context take in influencing our lives. Although we like to think of ourselves as entirely independent in our thinking and actions, we are influenced by external factors. The situational forces that influence us are very powerful. Where we are, who we are with, what we are doing and the social context we are in make a huge impact on our behaviour. To feel this for yourself, imagine violating some minor norms: standing up in the middle of a class; singing out loud in a restaurant; playing golf in a suit. In trying to break with social norms and constraints, we suddenly realize how strong they are.

Milgram's experiments also offer a lesson about evil. According to what we see in horror movies and suspense novels, evil results from a few bad apples, a few depraved killers. In real life we similarly think of Hitler's extermination of Jews, and the more recent acts of terrorism attributed to Al Qaeda and ISIS. Evil also results from social forces, from heat, humidity and disease that help make a whole barrel of apples go bad (see the Lucifer Effect noted in Chapter 6). The American military police, whose abuse of Iraqi prisoners at Abu Ghraib prison horrified the world, were under stress, taunted by many of those they had come to 'save', angered by comrades' deaths, overdue to return home and under lax supervision – an evil situation that produced evil behaviour (Fiske et al., 2004). Situations can induce ordinary people to capitulate to cruelty.

Social psychologist Stephen Gibson has obtained exceptional permission and access to previously unpublished recordings of the Milgram study from Stanley Milgram's surviving family. Their content has proved revealing and has contributed to the claim that Milgram's experiments do not show a psychological shift in participants towards obedience to authority. Rather, they show the power of the social context that is language. In a body of social psychological work Gibson (2013, 2014, 2019; Gibson et al., 2018) adopts a discursive analysis of the post-experiment interviews Milgram conducted (see Chapter 2 for more on discursive psychology and the social constructionist view of language). These are important transcripts as they are the 'evidence' upon which Milgram based his claim that people who carried out electric shocks to the highest levels psychologically experienced loss of responsibility because an authority figure (the teacher) was commanding they delivered them. However, a closer look at the transcripts shows something a little different. Firstly, the 'teacher' did not 'command' his participants to administer electric shocks, but rather requested them to do so (e.g. 'Please continue') (Gibson, 2019). Secondly, participants were taken-to-task and held accountable by Milgram for their actions (Gibson et al., 2018). If you were in such a position, what would you do? You might well blame the person who asked you to deliver the shocks. This is exactly what Milgram's participants did. Feeling somewhat guilty, they blamed someone else, the teacher. The point Gibson makes is what status we give to those denials of responsibility. Is it that the participants *psychologically* lost a sense of responsibility due to an experimenter (authority) requesting (rather than commanding) they deliver the shocks, or is it more likely that their response is not a reflection of their actual psychological state, but rather a rhetorical one when confronted about their actions? The most powerful social context of all might be the interaction that took place between Milgram and his participants post-experiment. Taking the participants' explanations as accurate reflections of their psychological state led Milgram to the conclusion that obedience to authority was the result of a psychological shift based on loss of sense of self and responsibility. However, blaming authority might simply be a rhetorical strategy to explain away responsibility in the context of confrontation.

The Fundamental Attribution Error

Why do the results of these classic experiments so often startle people? Is it because we expect people to act in accord with their dispositions? The **fundamental attribution error** is the tendency to interpret others' actions as expressing their dispositions rather than the situation they are in (see Chapter 4). It doesn't surprise

fundamental attribution error the tendency for observers to underestimate situational influences and overestimate dispositional influences upon others' behaviour. (Also called correspondence bias, because we so often see behaviour as corresponding to a disposition) us when a surly person is nasty, but we expect those with pleasant dispositions to be kind. Bad people, we assume, do bad things; good people do good things.

The 'senseless' 9/11 horror was perpetrated, we heard over and over again in the media, by 'madmen', by 'evil cowards', by 'demonic monsters'. Today, some still hold these opinions, but we now also know that the perpetrators did have their own logic for the attacks on the USA. The aim was not only to kill innocent people (though by creating 'terror' in this way, Al Qaeda drew attention to its cause), but also to attack the symbols (the World Trade Center and the Pentagon) of Western capitalist society, which is itself seen by some as an unfair, immoral and repressive system, responsible for widespread human suffering all over the world. The man behind the bombing of the MEN Arena in the city of Manchester, UK, on 22 May 2017, was revealed to be an otherwise ordinary 22-year-old resident Salman Ramadan Abedi. During a pop concert featuring Ariana Grande at the MEN, Abedi walked into the arena and set off a bomb. Twenty-three people died and 139 were wounded, many of them children, in the attack. It seems that Abedi acted alone but was connected to Islamic extremist groups. To conquer the enemy it is always a good idea to try to understand their motives and ways of thinking, as opposed to demonizing them as mad monsters without any human qualities. If we know why people behave in the way they do, then we can argue against their thinking rather than just react senselessly to their behaviour.

In Chapter 6 we examine how 'cults' are defined and indoctrinate their followers, sometimes with tragic consequences for the indoctrinated as well as those they hurt.

When you read about Milgram's experiments, what impressions did you form of the obedient participants? Cruelty, we presume, is inflicted by the cruel at heart.

It is tempting to assume that Eichmann and the Auschwitz death camp commanders were uncivilized monsters. Indeed, their evil was fuelled by virulent anti-Semitism. And the social situation alone does not explain why, in the same neighbourhood or death camp, some personalities displayed vicious cruelty and others heroic kindness. Still, the commanders would not have stood out to us as monsters. After a hard day's work, they would relax by listening to Beethoven and Schubert. Of the 14 men who formulated the Final Solution leading to the Nazi Holocaust, 8 had European university doctorates (Patterson, 1996). Like most other Nazis, Eichmann himself was outwardly indistinguishable from common people with ordinary jobs (Arendt, 1963; Zillmer et al., 1995). Mohamed Atta, the leader of the 9/11 attacks, reportedly had been a 'good boy' and an excellent student from a healthy family. Zacarias Moussaoui, the would-be twentieth 9/11 attacker, had been very polite when applying for flight lessons and buying knives. He called women 'ma'am'. The pilot of the second plane to hit the World Trade Center was said to be an amiable, 'laid-back' fellow, much like the 'intelligent, friendly, and "very courteous"' pilot of the plane that dove into the Pentagon. Osama Bin Laden also has a reputation for being a warm and caring person, paying much attention to those suffering from an unjust world. Salman Ramadan Abedi was a 22-year-old ex-college and university student, born in Manchester and a Manchester United supporter. If these men had lived next door to us, they would hardly have fitted our image of evil monsters. They were 'unexceptional' people (McDermott, 2005).

> 'I would say, on the basis of having observed a thousand people . . . that if a system of death camps were set up in the United States of the sort we had seen in Nazi Germany, one would be able to find sufficient personnel for those camps in any medium-sized American town.'
>
> Stanley Milgram, on CBS's *60 Minutes*, 1979

As Milgram (1974, p. 6) noted, 'The most fundamental lesson of our study is that ordinary people, simply doing their jobs, and without any particular hostility on their part, can become agents in a terrible destructive process.' Under the sway of evil forces, even nice people are sometimes corrupted as they construct moral rationalizations for immoral behaviour (Tsang, 2002). So it is that ordinary soldiers may, in the end, follow orders to shoot defenceless civilians; admired political leaders may lead their citizens into ill-fated wars; ordinary employees may follow instructions to produce and distribute harmful, degrading products; and ordinary group members may heed commands to brutally haze initiates.

So, does a situational analysis of harm-doing exonerate harm-doers? Does it absolve them of responsibility? In laypeople's minds, the answer is to some extent yes, notes Miller (2006). But the psychologists who study the roots of evil insist otherwise. To explain is not to excuse. To understand is not to forgive. You can forgive someone whose behaviour you don't understand, and you can understand someone whom you do not forgive. Moreover, adds Waller (2002), 'When we understand the ordinariness of extraordinary evil, we will be less surprised by evil, less likely to be unwitting contributors to evil, and perhaps better equipped to forestall evil.'

Social psychologists from the University of St Andrews and the University of Exeter in England have re-examined the historical and psychological case for 'the banality of evil' – the idea that people commit extreme acts of inhumanity in a state where they lack awareness or control over what they are doing. Reicher et al. (2008) argue that those who commit great wrongs, for instance genocides, knowingly choose to act as they do because they believe that what they are doing is right. The British social psychologists present a five-step social identity model explaining why inhumane acts against other groups can come to be celebrated as right.

Banality of Evil or Celebration of Virtue?

After the Second World War many people were left asking the question of how apparently normal, ordinary people could do such terrible things. Once the men and women who were responsible for the Holocaust were captured, these people did not look evil, they were just like everyone else. Hannah Arendt coined the phrase 'banality of evil' in her book on the trial of Eichmann. She was struck by his unassuming appearance, so counter to the assumption that the people who took part in the Holocaust must have been monsters (see Focus On: The Ordinary Monster at the end of the chapter for more on this). The idea of 'the banality of evil' explanation was fuelled by many studies in social psychology, according to Reicher et al. (2008). Sherif (1966) created hostility between ordinary friends simply by dividing them into two competing groups, and made nice boys into wicked, disturbed and vicious individuals (see Chapter 13). The conformity studies by Asch (1952) are also remembered by most people as illustrations of how group processes can lead innocent people into wrongdoing.

Milgram's 'obedience' studies are also directly associated with the 'banality of evil' perspective, conducted when Eichmann's trial was in progress. According to Reicher and his colleagues, Milgram demonstrated that ordinary Americans, no less than ordinary Germans, are capable of cruelty through unthinking conformity. People simply focus on how well they can serve an authority. The ordinary person who shocked a stranger did so out of a sense of obligation, not from any peculiarly aggressive tendencies (Milgram, 1974, pp. 23, 24).

We will revisit Zimbardo's study in Chapter 13 when we examine intergroup relationships and prejudice.

Zimbardo's Stanford Prison Experiment (SPE) also explains nasty and abusive behaviour in terms of conformity to roles. The situation alone is sufficient to produce immoral acts since the role players lose the ability to make moral choices. The prison guard's aggression was 'emitted simply as a "natural" consequence of being in the uniform of a "guard" and asserting the power inherent in that role' (Haney et al., 1973, p. 12).

Reicher et al. (2008), who re-examined the classical social psychological studies and the 'banality of evil' explanation, did not accept that inhumanity is thoughtless. Rather, people *believe* that what they are doing is right. They manage to make a virtue out of evil. The purpose of Reicher and his colleagues' attempt is to understand from a social identity approach how this is made possible.

First, the issues are to do with collective phenomena and collective identities. Genocides are perpetrated against others not because of what they have done but because of the groups they belong to. Second, there is nothing inherent about ingroup processes that tends to be either ill or good. The same underlying psychological processes can lead to both good and evil acts. Third, there are five steps in the definition of social identities that allow for acts of extreme inhumanity. These are: (1) the creation of a cohesive ingroup through shared social identification; (2) the exclusion of specific populations from the ingroup; (3) the constitution of the outgroup as a danger to the existence of the ingroup; (4) the representation of the ingroup as uniquely virtuous; and (5) the celebration of outgroup annihilation as the defence of (ingroup) virtue. Let's consider each of these in more detail.

- *Step 1: The creation of a cohesive ingroup through shared social identification.* The definition of the ingroup is *as* crucial, if not *more* crucial, than definitions of outgroups in generating hatred. The very notion of 'them' is contingent upon how we determine the criteria that define 'us'. One cannot understand how people can do ill in the name of their group unless one also acknowledges the good that they derive from group membership. According to the social identity tradition, and to self-categorization theory in particular, a shared sense of category membership (i.e. of social identity) is the psychological basis of group action. It is only to the extent that we think of ourselves as Catholics, Fascists, Germans, or whatever, that we can act together as Catholics, Fascists or Germans. Groups, especially cohesive and powerful collectivities, are essential to our social presence and our social being. That is why people are so attached to and so passionate about their group memberships. That is why they can kill and are even prepared to die for their group.
- *Step 2: Exclusion – placing targets outside the ingroup.* How we define ingroup and outgroups or the category boundaries is critical between 'us' and 'them'. It is impossible to explain the appeal of Nazism without understanding how it was presented as a *moral* project – a project of cleansing and renewal in a world of decay and chaos. Above all, it was about rediscovering community and solidarity: creating bonds to others and putting service above self. As Goebbels put it: 'What is the first Commandment of every National Socialist? . . . Love Germany above all else and your ethnic comrade [*Volksgenosse*] as yourself' (quoted in Koonz, 2003, p. 7). The German ingroup is defined in an exclusive way that excludes Jewish people, Gypsies and others. All the love and support and

service are reserved for the ethnic ingroup, and the ethnic outgroup can have no hope of their solidarity (Reicher et al., 2008).

- *Step 3: Threat – the outgroup represents a danger to the existence of the ingroup.* There are many groups who are not 'us', but this fact does not necessarily make them 'against us'. The problems come when the problems in the ingroup are seen as the fault of outgroups: their stupidity, their aggressiveness, their deviousness, or whatever. It becomes possible to see the destruction of the outgroup as an act of self-defence rather than an act of aggression. However, although self-defence may be a legitimate act and one that makes aggression something that is acceptable to the ingroup (and even to wider communities beyond the group), it is still not sufficient to make attacks on others into something noble and something to be celebrated. For this to be possible, one further step is needed.
- *Step 4: Virtue – representing the ingroup as (uniquely) good.* Despite Hitler's candid anti-Semitism in *Mein Kampf,* Claudia Koonz notes that, from the moment he took power in 1933 until the outbreak of war, he hardly ever made mention of Jews. Instead, he devoted his efforts to extolling the distinctive virtues of (ethnic) Germans. The German *Volk,* he argued, were moral and pure and selfless and loyal. They were humble and they were just and they were devout. His watchword was, 'Cleanliness everywhere, cleanliness of our Government, cleanliness in public life, and also this cleanliness in our culture' (quoted in Koonz, 2003, p. 22). When 'we' are held to be virtuous, the more serious the outgroup threat becomes and the more it becomes acceptable to 'defend ourselves' by eliminating this outgroup threat – even if this means eliminating the outgroup itself.
- *Step 5: Celebration – eulogizing inhumanity as the defence of virtue.* Once all the pieces are in place, it becomes easy to see how genocide can be made something to celebrate. Where 'they' are defined as not being one of 'us' but as being against 'us', and where we create a view of the world in which we represent good and they represent evil, extreme violence towards other groups is possible.

It is frightening to think how easily we could be persuaded to abandon our ethical and moral objection to harming others. If we look at conflicts like Rwanda, Libya or Myanmar, we can see the group identities shifting to allow for the attempted destruction of the outgroup. The people who carried out crimes against humanity in these conflicts were as ordinary as the German war criminals were; they had come to think that they were defending the honour or purity of their ingroup.

Infrahumanization

This tacitly held belief that one's ingroup is more human than the outgroup is also called *infrahumanization,* a term proposed by the Belgian Jacques-Philippe Leyens and colleagues at Université Catholique de Louvain (UCL). Infrahumanization arises when people view their ingroup and outgroup as essentially different and accordingly reserve the 'human essence' for the ingroup and deny it to outgroups. It has been studied by looking at what kind of emotions people believe ingroup and outgroup members possess (Leyens et al., 2000). In a series of studies Leyens and colleagues showed that people attribute uniquely human emotions (e.g. love, regret, nostalgia) to the ingroup, but not the outgroup, reflecting the tacit belief that they are less human than the ingroup. Interestingly, although the ingroup regards the outgroup negatively, potential negative traits of the ingroup may be treated as evidence of human nature. They are, after all, 'only human'. Thus, the trait being judged is not viewed objectively, but subjectively, in the context of the group membership (Koval et al., 2012).

Evidence of infrahumanization can be seen in conflicts, including the Nazi treatment of the Jews – describing them as 'rats', and the description of Hutus as 'cockroaches' during the Rwandan genocide (Haslam, 2019). Clearly, by reducing the outgroup to less than human, it becomes easier to justify treating them in a less than human manner (Haslam & Loughnan, 2014; Lammers & Stapel, 2011). It is, after all, easier to justify killing a cockroach than a human. Haslam et al. (2011) analysed animal metaphors used in dehumanization of outgroups. In their analysis they found that the most offensive metaphors were those of disliked animals, such as rats or snakes. These metaphors appear not to carry the meaning that the outgroup are actually rats or snakes, but that they provoke moral disgust. The metaphors that most dehumanize the outgroup were metaphors such as dog or ape. These were found to be more dehumanizing, equating the outgroup with the animal metaphor.

Infrahumanization can have practical consequences, such as unwillingness to offer help at a time of crisis. Studying helping in the aftermath of Hurricane Katrina, which devastated New Orleans in the USA in 2005, Cuddy et al. (2007) found that people were less likely to help people they perceived to be members of an outgroup. How helping behaviour is influenced by our membership of social groups will be considered in more detail in Chapter 11.

If infrahumanization impacts how we view outgroup members and their behaviour, this has implications for judgement of our own behaviour. As already mentioned, we are more likely to judge our own transgressions as evidence of 'being human', although those of the outgroup are more likely to be judged as reinforcement of their negativity and failure. By forgiving our own transgressions of social and moral codes, while condemning the transgressions of others, we are viewing these social and moral codes through a lens of our own bias.

Laboratory and Everyday Life

Finally, a comment on the laboratory studies used in conformity research (see synopsis, **Table 7.2**): conformity situations in the laboratory differ from those in everyday life. How often are we asked to judge line lengths or administer shock?

TABLE 7.2 Summary of classic studies

Topic	Researcher	Method	Real-life example
Norm formation	Sherif	Assessing suggestibility regarding seeming movement of light	Interpreting events differently after hearing from others; appreciating a tasty food that others love
Conformity	Asch	Agreement with others' obviously wrong perceptual judgements	Doing as others do; fads such as tattoos
Obedience	Milgram	Complying with commands to shock another	Soldiers or employees following questionable orders

Research close-up

Judging Our Own and Others' Misdeeds*

Source: *Lammers, J., Stapel, D.A., & Galinksy, A.D. (2010). Power increases hypocrisy: Moralizing in reasoning, immorality in behaviour.* Psychological Science, *21(5), 737–744.*

Introduction

'Power corrupts' is a statement you might be familiar with. In particular, it has been argued that power corrupts the moral compass of those who are powerful. History is littered with politicians and world leaders who preached virtues such as honesty and family values, yet had extra-marital affairs. In modern times there are regularly stories in the news about politicians who abuse their position of power, yet condemn the actions of others. Financial institutions have requested multibillion dollar loans to support their organizations from bankruptcy, whilst awarding themselves massive bonuses (Kanagaretnam et al., 2008). This hypocrisy is infuriating! If they are telling us how to behave and demand conformity, why don't they follow their own guidance? This study set out to investigate if there is a link between power and moral hypocrisy. The hypothesis is that the powerful are less likely to practise what they preach and be moral hypocrites than the powerless.

Experiment 1

Method

Sixty-one Dutch students (47 male, 14 female, mean age = 19.3 years) were randomly assigned to two conditions – high power and low power. Participants had a sense of power induced using an experiential power prime. An experiential power prime uses experiences that participants have had that made them feel either more powerful or less powerful. In the high power condition participants were asked to recall a high power experience, for example winning a prize in sport. In the low power condition participants were asked to recall an experience where they felt non-powerful, such as getting a really bad mark in an exam. Participants were placed in private cubicles to complete the tasks in the experiment.

Next came the opportunity to cheat! Half of the participants in both conditions were told that they would be financially compensated for their participation. Their financial reward would be determined by lottery and the more lottery tickets they had, the better chance they had of winning a larger amount. They were provided with a pair of 10-sided dice to determine their number of lottery tickets. The participants were told that they should roll the dice once and the numbers that they rolled would be multiplied together to give the number of lottery tickets that they would receive. They rolled the dice in private without the researcher watching. They were then asked what numbers they rolled, without the researcher verifying it. This procedure provided the participants ample opportunity to cheat and increase their number of lottery tickets. As the range of numbers they could get was theoretically between 0 and 99, the mean number of tickets should have been 50. If the recorded mean was significantly higher than this it would show that participants had cheated in reporting the results of their dice rolls. In the ANOVA this is the 'behaviour' condition.

The other half of the participants were not involved in the lottery, but were asked to judge whether it is morally acceptable to exaggerate travelling expenses, using a 9-point Likert scale. This is the 'judgement' condition of the ANOVA.

*In September 2011, Diederik Stapel was suspended from his professorship duties, after it was suspected that he used fake data for his research publications. In October 2011 the Levelt Committee was entrusted with investigating the extent of Stapel's fraud. The article on which this Research Close-Up is based has been cleared by the Levelt Committee, as their investigation has found no evidence of fraudulent data or practice. See: http://pss.sagepub.com/content/23/7/828

Results

The data were analysed on a 2 (power: high vs. low) × 2 (behaviour vs. judgement) analysis of variance. A significant interaction was found between the participant's decision (to cheat, or how to judge the morality of exaggerating travel expenses): $F(1, 57) = 7.33$, $p = .009$, $\eta_p^2 = .12$. For those participants who 'judged' whether exaggerating travel expenses was morally acceptable, those in the high-power condition were stricter in their judgement of cheating than low power participants: $t(57) = 1.78$, $p = .08$. However, when we turn to the cheating 'behaviour' of the high power participants, they claimed a larger number of lottery tickets than the low power participants: $t(57) = 2.09$, $p = .04$.

While this finding is interesting, there is the potential flaw that the measures of honesty and hypocrisy are different. Cheating and judging whether exaggerating travel expenses is immoral, are arguably quite different things! For example, if you score quite low on an honesty scale, then act in a dishonest way, your behaviour wouldn't be hypocritical. However, if you were to score highly on an honesty scale, and then you were dishonest, this would be hypocritical. To address this flaw, three further experiments were carried out.

Experiments 2, 3 and 4

Method

A total of 172 different Dutch students were again randomly assigned to high or low power conditions. In experiment 2, 42 participants were primed for their power status by placing them in a simulated bureaucratic environment with some in prime ministerial roles and others in civil servant roles. The 88 participants in experiment 3 used the same experience recall power priming as in experiment 1. In experiment 4, 42 participants were given a power priming word search (Chen et al., 2001). In all experiments, participants were also assigned to one of two conditions; either they were judging themselves, or they were judging the behaviour of others.

Participants in the experiments were presented with a variety of moral dilemmas; in experiment 2 they were given one about speeding offences, in experiment 3 it was tax evasion, and in experiment 4 they were presented with one about keeping apparently stolen property. Participants judging the behaviour of others were given gender neutral names of hypothetical others such as Chris, Kim, and Renee. They were asked how acceptable it would be for that hypothetical person to engage in the described behaviour. In the other condition, participants were asked how acceptable it would be if they themselves engaged in the described behaviour.

Results

The data in these experiments were analysed using a *t* test. All three experiments showed the same results in the same direction as were found in Study 1: the powerful were more likely to engage in moral hypocrisy than the powerless. In all three experiments, the interaction between the power of the participant and the target of that participant's judgement was found to be significant. In experiment 2 the interaction was marginally significant: $F(1, 38) = 3.53$, $p = .068$, $\eta_p^2 = .09$, and significant in both experiment 3, $F(1, 68) = 9.05$, $p = .004$, $\eta_p^2 = .12$, and experiment 4, $F(1, 70) = 8.16$, $p = .007$, $\eta_p^2 = .18$. Participants in the high-power condition were more likely to show moral hypocrisy, regardless of the offence being committed (speeding, tax evasion, or keeping stolen property) than participants in the low power condition. Furthermore, those participants in the low-power condition were more likely to be lenient in judging others' immorality than their own: $F(1, 86) = 5.99$, $p = .02$, $\eta_p^2 = .08$. On the other hand, participants in the high-power position imposed stricter views on the moral transgressions of others ($F(1, 81) = 16.81$, $p < .001$, $\eta_p^2 = .17$) than their own transgressions ($F(1, 85) = 6.24$, $p = .01$, $\eta_p^2 = .07$).

Discussion

In all the experiments, only the participants in the powerful condition showed moral hypocrisy. Indeed, it seems that the powerless were more likely to be lenient in judging others' behaviour in comparison with their own. This is referred to as '*hypercrisy*': being overly critical of one's own actions.

These experiments highlight some fascinating aspects of the way that power imbalances in societies allow the misbehaviour of the powerful while maintaining the conformity of the powerless to the social norms of that society. It certainly implies that those with less power are more likely to self-police, while those in power are more likely to justify their own transgressions of the social code. In other words 'the powerless collaborate in reproducing social inequality' (p. 743). The powerful impose social rules on the powerless, but are themselves more likely to break their own rules. Conformity is not maintained by the knowledge or fear of the law's reach but instead by the apparent acceptance of social inequality, and the individual's belief in their own power status.

Critical Reflections

This is an interesting set of experiments that offer some food for thought with respect to perceptions of power and conformity. The researchers themselves note a limitation of experiment 1; this being the possible conflation of honesty and hypocrisy. The following experiments attempt to redress this flaw.

There are other critical points we might want to raise with respect to these experiments. In terms of methodology all four studies are laboratory-style experimental attempts to measure power and hypocrisy. The participants are all students, and the situations are hypothetical. **Ecological validity** is a concern. To what extent do these studies recreate the real-life experience of powerful (and non-powerful) people? Yet the results across the four experiments are consistent and arguably chime with our assumptions about the powerful: they don't conform and they are moral hypocrites. But might this confirmation of the results we anticipated be a problem, both for the researchers and the participants? Could the concept of **confirmation bias** be applicable here?

ecological validity the extent to which findings observed in a study reflect what actually occurs in natural settings. Psychological laboratory research has been criticized for its low ecological validity

confirmation bias a tendency to search for information that confirms one's preconceptions, rather than considering opposing information

Fromm (1973) argued that the Milgram experiments, and others like them, are flawed. The very nature of the experimental model leads the participants into a specific set of responses. He stated 'I do not think that this experiment permits a conclusion with regard to most situations in real life. The psychologist was not only an authority to whom one owes obedience but as a representative of science and on one of the most prestigious institutions of higher education in the United States' (1973, p. 74). By creating an experiment of conformity in the laboratory, the experience of conformity is removed from the real world and placed in the artificiality of the research lab, with its unfamiliar equipment and personnel. But as combustion is similar for a burning match and a forest fire, so we assume that psychological processes in the laboratory and in everyday life are similar (Milgram, 1974). We must be careful in generalizing from the simplicity of a burning match to the complexity of a forest fire, yet experiments on burning matches can give us insights into combustion that we cannot gain by observing forest fires. So, too, the social psychological laboratory studies offer insights into behaviour not readily revealed in everyday life. The situation is unique, but so is every social situation. By testing with a variety of unique tasks, and by repeating the studies in different times and places, researchers probe for the common principles that lie beneath the surface diversity.

The classic demonstrations of core items in social psychology have answered some questions but raised others: (1) sometimes people conform or obey; sometimes they do not. *When* do they conform or obey? (2) *Why* do people conform or obey? Why don't they ignore the group and 'to their own selves be true'? (3) Is there a type of *person* who is likely to conform or obey? In the next section we will take these questions one at a time.

What Predicts Conformity?

Some situations trigger much conformity, others little conformity. If you wanted to produce maximum conformity, what conditions would you choose?

Social psychologists wondered: if even Asch's non-coercive, unambiguous situation could elicit a 37 per cent conformity rate, would other settings produce even more? Researchers soon discovered that conformity did grow if the judgements were difficult or if the participants felt incompetent. The more insecure we are about our judgements, the more influenced we are by others.

Group attributes also matter. Conformity is highest when the group has three or more people and is unanimous, cohesive and high in status. Conformity is also highest when the response is public and made without prior commitment. Let's look at each of these conditions.

Group Size

In laboratory experiments, a small group can have a large effect. Asch and other researchers found that three to five people will elicit much more conformity than just one or two. Increasing the number of people beyond five yields diminishing returns (Gerard et al., 1968; Rosenberg, 1961). In a field experiment, Milgram et al. (1969) had 1, 2, 3, 5, 10 or 15 people pause on a busy New York City sidewalk and look up. As **Figure 7.5** shows, the percentage of passers-by who also looked up increased as the number looking up increased. However, the effect of increasing the number of persons looking up slowed down considerably in this study when the crowd had reached five people. Researchers have suggested that whether the

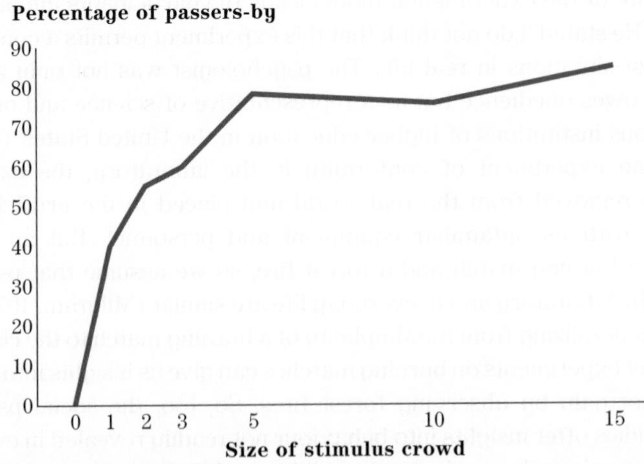

FIGURE 7.5 Group size and conformity

The percentage of passers-by who imitated a group looking upwards increased as group size increased to five persons.

SOURCE: Data from Milgram et al. (1969).

growth in conformity with group size is linear or not depends on the type of task (Campbell & Fairey, 1989; Claidière et al., 2012; Rosander & Eriksson, 2012).

The influence of a minority on the responses of a majority was first demonstrated in laboratory studies on colour perception tasks carried out in France in the 1960s (Moscovici et al., 1969). Serge Moscovici and his colleagues identified three main determinants of a minority being able to influence a majority: consistency, self-confidence and defection (Moscovici, 1985). Mucchi-Faina and Pagliaro (2008) observed how the presence of a minority produces ambivalence among the majority. Presented with a minority who consistently argue a counter position, the members of the majority group start to experience ambivalence or dissonance as unpleasant (as discussed in Chapter 5). Accepting the views of the minority can reduce the uncomfortable feeling. Moscovici (1985) believed that it was the power of consistency and persistency of minority members that caused a majority to rethink their ideas and be influenced. Consistency and persistence convey self-confidence, and Nemeth and Wachtler (1974) reported that any behaviour by a minority that communicates self-confidence – taking the head seat at the table, for instance – tends to raise self-doubts among the majority.

Minority influence and the way that the minority can sway the majority to change their way of thinking links closely to persuasion (see Chapter 6). The Clark (1995) study shows what features are required for the minority to be influential; these have similar characteristics to how persuasive a message is in persuasion studies.

Unanimity

Recent studies have shown the impact of unanimity on children as young as 3 years (e.g. Schmidt et al., 2016). It has also confirmed the power of unanimity when the group is virtual, not physical. For example, Rosander and Eriksson (2012) found that when an individual was confronted with an online group providing a consistent but incorrect answer to questions (e.g. In which city would you find Hollywood?), the individual would most likely conform to the group's incorrect answer (e.g. San Franscisco).

But imagine yourself in a conformity experiment in which all but one of the people responding before you give the same wrong answer. Would the example of this one non-conforming confederate be as liberating as it was for the individuals in Milgram's obedience experiment? Several classic experiments reveal that someone who punctures a group's unanimity deflates its social power (Allen & Levine, 1969;

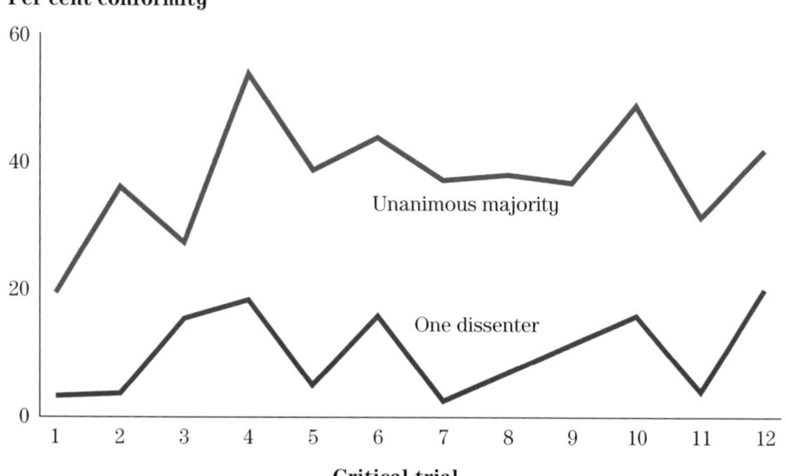

FIGURE 7.6 The effect of unanimity on conformity

When someone giving correct answers punctures the group's unanimity, individuals conform only one-fourth as often.

SOURCE: Asch (1955).

Asch, 1955; Morris & Miller, 1975). As **Figure 7.6** illustrates, people will usually voice their own convictions if just one other person has also differed from the majority. The participants in such experiments often later say they felt warm towards and close to their non-conforming ally. Yet they deny that the ally influenced them: 'I would have answered just the same if he weren't there.'

It is easier to stand up for something if you can find someone else to stand up with you. This finding has been replicated in more contemporary studies on conformity. Farmer et al. (2018) document the power of unanimity in their work on conformity. They found that a lone individual's views on climate change could be influenced in discussion with an online group who denied its occurrence – especially when someone in that group was considered to be an 'expert' on the topic. However, if just one member of that group broke the consensus and claimed that climate change was indeed occurring, conformity of the lone individual to the group's position was drastically reduced. Similarly, Schmidt et al. (2016) found that young children's conformity to a group's social norms weakened in the presence of a dissenter.

The impact of unanimity upon an individual's likelihood to be influenced by a group has been found to be mediated by its size. Mojtahedi et al. (2018) consider the real-world example of co-witness eye-testimony. Police officers investigating a crime scene often have to rely on witnesses to work out what happened, why, and who is to blame. Imagine you are a witness to a fight in a bar involving two men. When asked by the police for your account of what happened, you might depend on your memory or perception to explain what you saw. But our memories and our senses are not infallible, and can be influenced post-event by another source: co-witnesses. Witnesses to a criminal event will almost certainly discuss what they've experienced with each other. Here is fertile ground for misinformation to arise as they try to make sense of what just occurred. In Mojtahedi's study, participants were asked to watch CCTV footage of two men having a fight in a bar. In groups, they were asked to discuss what had happened and to state which man had delivered the first punch. Unknown to the real participants, the other members of their group were confederates of the researchers, with instructions to deliberately attribute the first punch to the wrong man. The researchers varied the size of the group of confederates from one to five. When the number of co-witnesses (confederates of the study) constituted a group size of between three and five members, the real participants conformed to their false account of who delivered the first punch. However, if the group of confederates was only one or two members, the participant was less likely to be influenced by them. The researchers conclude that whilst unanimity is an important feature of social influence, it is mediated by the group size. The individual looks to others for information. Confronted with a sizeable majority who consistently provide inaccurate information, the individual questions their own memory and perception of what happened. Perhaps their eyes did deceive them! We will return to why people conform later in this chapter. But for now, we note the warning that comes out of this research: a criminal investigation that is supported by a consistent story of events by a large number of co-witnesses, should be treated with caution.

Social Impact Theory

Conformity does not occur simply because we slavishly seek to copy others. Instead, there appear to be specific factors that are required for the environment to be ideal for conformity to occur. Latané (1981) devised Social Impact Theory, a mathematical theory of social influence. Latané expresses this as Influence = f(SIN). This means that the amount of influence that an individual experiences is a result of the combination of the strengths of the sources of influence (S), the immediacy or proximity of these sources (I), and the number of sources of influence (N). This combination is not the factors added together, but instead these factors are multiplied together to produce their influence.

Latané suggests that it is the nature of the people who potentially have influence over us that has a large effect on the influence they exert. Those who are most likely to influence us tend to have a higher status, such as age or socio-economic, and prior relationship with, or future power over, us. Therefore *who* influences us is as important as the *number* of people who are influencing us. We are more likely to be influenced by those who are important to us – who we admire or value – than those whose opinion is of low importance to us. Think about how much easier it is not to conform to a group if we are away from it than when we are in it. So when we are with a group and they are doing something that we may not want to go along with, if that group is something we want to be a part of, we are more likely to go along with them. It also explains how people in a position of power or status can have a disproportionate influence over us, persuading us to conform even when it is against our own norms.

Pedersen et al. (2008) carried out a study into the perceived drinking norms of American college students. They investigated how individuals respond in different contexts when asked about their drinking behaviours and attitudes, as well as the drinking behaviours and attitudes of relevant groups to the individual. These groups include the fraternities and sororities that are so important in American universities. Participants were questioned in both isolated online conditions as well as with their salient group. Pedersen et al. found that individual drinking behaviour and group specific behaviours differ when assessed in individual conditions as opposed to being in a group of peers of the salient group. The participants' perception of the group's drinking behaviour and attitudes were significantly higher in the group condition than the individual condition.

What this study highlights is that the context of self-report studies has an influence on the participants' response. They suggest that this may be because participants in groups have other members to refer to in devising their own answers, whereas in the individualized condition, they consider only their own behaviour. The discrepancy between responses from the same participant in different conditions seems to support Latané's theory that immediacy and strength are significant factors in social influence.

We will see in Chapter 9 on attraction that we tend to like others who are similar to ourselves. We discussed in Chapter 6 that people are persuaded by others they consider to be similar to themselves (either on an individual or group basis). So, as we might expect, people tend to align their opinions with members of their 'we' group. For example, they express more favourable opinions towards a piece of music after observing the liking of someone akin to themselves. And they express more negative opinions when the music is liked by someone unlike themselves (Hilmert et al., 2006).

Status

As you might suspect, higher-status people tend to have more impact (Dino et al., 2009; Driskell & Mullen, 1990). Junior group members – even junior social psychologists – acknowledge more conformity to their group than do senior group members (Jetten et al., 2006). Milgram (1974) reported that in his obedience experiments, people of lower status accepted the experimenter's commands more readily than people of higher status. After delivering 450 volts, a 37-year-old welder turned to the higher-status experimenter and deferentially asked, 'Where do we go from here, Professor?' (p. 46). Another participant, a divinity school professor who disobeyed at 150 volts, said 'I don't understand why the experiment is placed above this person's life' and plied the experimenter with questions about 'the ethics of this thing' (p. 48). The effect of status on conformity has also been found in more recent research on social influence amongst virtual online groups. Dino et al. (2009) found that low status users of online forums (defined as those who posted less than 30 messages) were more likely to conform to requests than high status members (defined as those who posted more than 200 messages).

Public Response

One of the first questions researchers sought to answer was this: would people conform more in their public responses than in their private opinions? Or would they wobble more in their private opinions but be unwilling to conform publicly, lest they appear wishy-washy? The answer is now clear: in experiments, people conform more when they must respond in front of others rather than writing their answers privately (Cialdini & Goldstein, 2004; Sowden et al., 2018). Asch's participants, after hearing others respond, were less influenced by group pressure if they could write answers that only the experimenter would see. It is much easier to stand up for what we believe in the privacy of the voting booth than before a group.

No Prior Commitment

People almost never back down. Once having made a public commitment, they stick to it. At most, they will change their judgements in later situations (Cialdini & Goldstein, 2004; Saltzstein & Sandberg, 1979). We may therefore expect that judges of ski-jumping or gymnastic competitions, for example, will seldom change their ratings after seeing the other judges' ratings, although they might adjust their later performance ratings.

Prior commitments restrain persuasion, too. Making a public commitment makes people hesitant to back down. Smart persuaders know this. Salespeople ask questions that prompt us to make statements for, rather than against, what they are marketing. Environmentalists ask people to commit themselves to recycling, energy conservation or bus riding – and find that behaviour then changes more than when environmental appeals are heard without inviting a commitment (Barata et al., 2017; Boo & Park, 2013; Katzev & Wang, 1994).

Why Conform?

Why do we generally like to tune in to 'our' group? There are three possibilities: a person may fit in and follow the group (a) to create a harmonious and pleasant atmosphere, (b) to be accepted and avoid rejection, or (c) because others are an important source of information. The first solution is frequent in collectivistic or interdependent cultures. Individuals in these cultures seek compromise to create harmony. They are more interested in understanding the other than promoting themselves and do not stick to their own but to the group. Deutsch and Gerard (1955) studied why Westerners bow to the group in individualistic cultures and named the two possibilities **normative influence** and **informational influence**.

normative influence conformity based on a person's desire to fulfil others' expectations, often to gain acceptance

informational influence conformity occurring when people accept evidence about reality provided by other people

Normative influence is 'going along with the crowd' to avoid rejection, to stay in people's good grace, or to gain their approval. Studies in the laboratory and in everyday life in the West have revealed that groups often reject those who consistently deviate (Miller & Anderson, 1979; Packer, 2008; Schachter, 1951). This is especially so when dissent is not just 'within the family' but when one's group is engaged with another group (Matheson et al., 2003). It is socially permissible for members of a parliament or of Congress to disagree with their country's war plans during the internal debate before a war. But once the conflict has begun, everyone is expected to 'support our troops'. In some Eastern, collectivistic and hierarchical cultures it is more common to agree even during the planning and accept the 'wise leader's' decisions.

As most of us know, social rejection is painful; when we deviate from group norms, we often pay an emotional price. Sometimes the high price of deviation compels people to support what they do not believe in, or at least to suppress their disagreement. Fearing a court martial for disobedience, some of the soldiers at My Lai participated in the massacre. Normative influence leads to compliance especially for people who have recently seen others ridiculed, or who are seeking to climb a status ladder (Beersma & van Kleef, 2011; Hollander, 1958; Janes & Olson, 2000). Informational influence, on the other hand, leads people to privately accept others' influence. When reality is ambiguous, as it was for participants in the autokinetic situation, other people can be a valuable source of information. The individual may reason, 'I can't tell how far the light is moving. But this guy seems to know.'

Evolutionary psychologists have argued that conformity, and non-conformity, have an adaptive function based on the situation in which we find ourselves in. Sometimes we need to conform for information and/or acceptance. But, the act of not conforming and exerting our uniqueness has its benefits! Griskevicius et al. (2006) illustrate this flexibility in a study that focuses on the benefits (non) conformity had for self-protection and the desire to attract a potential mate. They invite us to think about what prey animals do when they are faced with a predator. They move closer together (the herding instinct) and mimic each other's behaviour to avoid standing out from the crowd (self-protection). However, when faced with a potential mate, non-human animals, and humans, want to stand out from the crowd and display their uniqueness (mate-attraction).

In a series of experiments Griskevicius et al., (2006) sought to illustrate these evolutionary adaptations of (non)conformity in humans. Would inducing a mind-set of self-protection (in the context of imagined threat) and a mating mind-set (in the context of attractive others) produce different (non)conformity responses? In one study, 237 psychology undergraduate students were brought to the lab in same-sex groups of 3–6 people. Each participant was asked to privately rate how interesting they found a series of artistic images to be, on a **Likert scale**. A third of the participants were then asked to read a 850-word scenario in which a sense of fear was induced. They were to imagine they were in a house alone at night, and an intruder is heard in their bedroom (the self-protection scenario). Another third of the participants were also asked to read an 850-word scenario to prompt a

Likert scale typically used in attitudinal research, this is a rating scale consisting of a number of items (or statements) against which participants rate how they feel about them. The scale typically has a neutral midpoint (e.g. neither agree or disagree)

sense of romantic attraction. In this hypothetical situation, participants imagined being on a date with someone they found attractive, which ended in a passionate kiss (the mate-attraction scenario). The rest of the participants read an 850-word scenario which was designed to be neutral, not invoking either fear or attraction (the neutral scenario). All participants were then told they would be randomly assigned to a small same-sex group of four participants and they would publicly give their ratings of the artistic images they had seen earlier, using an online chat forum. Unbeknownst to the participants, the other four members of the groups did not exist. Moreover, their ratings of the images were 'staged'. Hence the other four ratings might all be presented as highly positive for an image, or highly negative. Similar to Asch's experiment, the real participant gave their rating of the images last in the group. Would the real participant move their earlier rating to conform to that of the group? What the researchers discovered was that those participants who had previously been primed with the self-protection scenario conformed to the group. They shifted their previous private rating of the images to match the groups. However, things were a little different for those participants who had read the mate-protection scenario prior to the public rating of images. For the male participants, it mattered whether the group's rating of the images had been positive or negative. If it was positive, then men conformed to the group, more-so than those men in the neutral-scenario. If negative, then men resisted group conformity more than those men in the neutral-scenario did. Primed with the mate-attraction mindset and keen to distinguish themselves from a negative group, nonconformity was the preferred course of action. For women primed with the mate-attraction mindset, they conformed more to the group when the images had been rated positively in the public group, than those women in the neutral-scenario condition. If the image had been rated negative, it had no effect on their judgements. They conformed no more and no less than those female participants who had previously read the neutral scenario. Griskevicius and his colleagues present the findings as evidence for an evolutionary basis to conformity. Social influence, they suggest, is related to social motives. Faced with threat, we display a herding instinct, and conform to the group. Faced with the possibility of a romantic mate, men compete with one another for individual status and attention, whereas women focus on upholding the status of the group (women) vis-à-vis men. We discuss the topics of sex, gender and evolutionary psychology, further in Chapter 14.

In many Eastern and more interdependent cultures the reason for changing attitudes due to others' opinion is also a result of dialectical, holistic and more complex thinking. Everything can be seen in different and even opposite ways, and from different angles, and most things contain opposite and different qualities at the same time: good and bad, cold and warm. The cloud can look like a camel or a whale, depending on the context and the person perceiving. The truth is not absolute, and the person seeing a cloud as something other than what I see, may be right. I may have to adjust my own perception. Two opposing standpoints may both be true, and by compromise an in-between or even a contradictory standpoint for everything can always be found. This is a typical Eastern way of thinking, far from the either–or thinking in the West where it is a virtue to hold attitudes and opinions independent of the context and the group you are communicating with. To change attitudes due to social pressure has many negative connotations in the West: indecisiveness – 'a wind vane', a weak ego, non-integration. To be an 'integrated' person in the West means not to be contradictory, incongruous, inconsistent or able to change depending on the context. The Western concept of the **independent self** embraces autonomy from the group, agency and internal consistency, In the East these are not preferable abilities or traits, and they are not encouraged during socialization. The opposite, to fall in with the other, is looked upon as more mature for a human being.

independent self a typically Western view of the 'self' that encapsulates independence, autonomy, and personal agency

Concern for *social image* produces *normative influence*. The desire to be *correct* produces *informational influence*. In day-to-day life, normative and informational influence often occur together.

Conformity experiments have sometimes isolated either normative or informational influence. Conformity is greater when people respond publicly before a group; this surely reflects normative influence (because people receive the same information whether they respond publicly or privately). On the other hand, conformity is greater when participants feel incompetent, when the task is difficult, and when the individuals care about being right – all signs of informational influence.

In many Eastern cultures the concern for the image (not 'losing face') and to do the right thing has a long tradition founded in philosophy and education. To find and accept their place in a hierarchy and obey the rulers – the father in the family and the eldest son among the siblings – has been natural for East Asian people for centuries. The right to govern, however, is not absolute but dependent on the moral qualities of the ruler (the Mandate of Heaven). This way of thinking and relating to each other was introduced in China 2500 years ago by Confucius (551–479 BC). His teachings gained pre-eminence and since then China has been a hierarchical family-orientated and interdependent society.

Culture

Cultural background also influences why people conform and prefer to agree in a group, and how obedient they are towards authorities. In some Eastern, collectivistic cultures, not to fit in to the group is looked upon as childish and as a sign of being unable to behave as a responsible grown-up. To seek harmony, compromise and balance in relationships is considered more mature.

An example is the traditional Chinese culture, which exhibits the very essence of Confucian collectivism and **interdependent selves**, emphasizing the precedence of social relationships and group welfare over individual needs and desires. As a result, behaviours, relative to the actions of people in the West, are more likely to strongly reflect social norms and obligations. Personal desires are still a determinant of behaviour, but play a secondary role. Co-operation and harmony in the group are given priority over individual interests. Effort and contribution are directed towards the collective good rather than towards personal benefits and self-recognition (Cinirella & Green, 2007; Matsumoto & Juang, 2016; Triandis et al., 1988).

interdependent self construing one's identity in relation to others

See Chapter 3 for more on social psychological understandings and research on the self.

In a classic replication of Asch's conformity experiment, in several countries, Whittaker and Meade (1967) found similar conformity rates in most – 31 per cent in Lebanon, 32 per cent in Hong Kong, 34 per cent in Brazil – but 51 per cent among the Bantu of Zimbabwe, a tribe with strong sanctions for non-conformity. A later analysis by Bond and Smith (1996) of 133 studies in 17 countries showed how cultural values influence conformity. Compared with people in individualistic countries, those in collectivist countries (where harmony is prized and connections help define the self) are more responsive to others' influence. However, fast forward another decade and we find evidence that whilst these cultural differences remain pretty robust in face-to-face Asch-type conformity experiments, they disappear in computer-mediated communication scenarios. In their study of university students from a range of collectivist and individualist cultural backgrounds, but based in the UK, Cinnirella and Green (2007) found significant differences according to culture when an Asch-type study was conducted face to face with these participants. However, when the study was moved online and participants couldn't see one another, conformity between the two cultures did not significantly differ. Why? Cinirella and Green suggest that it is the elimination of non-verbal visual cues in online scenarios that is important. The Asch study is about public compliance, not private conversion, to the group's view. In a face-to-face encounter, those normative pressures are at work. We fear rejection from the group and therefore publicly comply. However, if we cannot see the group, then those normative pressures are reduced. Participants cannot see any visual cues that reveal the identity of the other group members, including their culture. Consequently there is little to no information about their group norms and values. That means our desire to belong and to avoid rejection, may be diminished. It is more difficult to identify with a group we cannot see. This idea of group identity and the desire to belong is something we will consider in Chapter 13.

Confucius (551–479 BC) was a Chinese thinker and social philosopher, whose teachings have deeply influenced Chinese, Korean, Japanese, Taiwanese and Vietnamese thought and life. His philosophy emphasized personal and governmental morality, correctness of social relationships, justice and sincerity.

SOURCE: ©Gautier Willaume/ Shutterstock

Milgram (1961) conducted a cross-cultural study of conformity in Norway and France prior to his obedience research. Volunteers were asked to judge which of two sounds lasted longer. The participants wore headphones and heard the two tones followed by the judgement of five other people who always agreed but on just over half the trials gave an incorrect answer. In actual fact these other judges' responses were taped and only the one volunteer and the experimenter were present in the laboratory. Quite consistently, the Norwegians conformed more to the 'group' judgements (62 per cent of the time) than the French (50 per cent of the time) in the basic experiment. Overall, 12 per cent of Norwegian volunteers conformed completely to the group, but only 1 per cent of French volunteers; 25 per cent of the Norwegians showed 'strong independence', compared with 41 per cent of the French. Milgram suggests a relationship between these results and the 'highly cohesive' Norwegian society, orientated towards social responsibility and group identification, versus the politically unstable, low-consensus French society, with a 'tradition of dissent and critical argument'. That is to say that conformity is not necessarily something negative or bad, but is an expression of national unity and cultural cohesion.

However, cultures, values and norms may change over time. Replications of Asch's experiment with university students in Britain, Canada, Japan and the USA sometimes trigger less conformity than Asch observed (Lalancette & Standing, 1990; Larsen, 1974, 1990; Mori et al., 2014; Nicholson et al., 1985; Perrin & Spencer, 1981; Takano & Sogon, 2008). Conformity and obedience are universal phenomena, yet the prevalence varies across cultures and eras depending on cultural norms and values – as well as the situation.

The influence and importance of cultural norms on conformity are also revealed in subcultures and small groups. In a qualitative study based on interviews with adolescent children from 11 to 14 years old in Northern Ireland, Barbara J. Stewart-Knox of the University of Ulster and her co-workers (Stewart-Knox et al., 2005) demonstrated how starting to smoke could be explained by conformity to group norms. They found that starting smoking rarely occurred as a result of direct peer pressure, but it did happen as adolescents sought to fit in with the group, conforming to its norms and values.

The findings are consistent with social identity theory and self-categorization theory in that smoking activity appears to provide a means through which to visibly display membership of a social group.

Who Conforms?

Conformity varies not only with situations and cultures but also with people. How much so? And in what social contexts do personality traits shine through?

Are some people generally more susceptible (or should we say, more open and sensible) to social influence? Among your friends, can you identify some who are 'conformists' and others who are 'independent' and even egoistic? In their search for the conformer, researchers have focused on personality and social roles.

Personality

During the late 1960s and 1970s, researchers observed only weak connections between personal characteristics and social behaviours such as conformity (Mischel, 1968). In contrast to the demonstrable power of situational factors, personality scores were poor predictors of individuals' behaviour. If you wanted to know how conforming or aggressive or helpful someone was going to be, it seemed you were better off knowing about the situation than the person's psychological test scores. As Milgram (1974) concluded: 'I am certain that there is a complex personality basis to obedience and disobedience. But I know we have not found it' (p. 205). One reason could be that Milgram's obedience experiments created 'strong' situations; their clear-cut demands made it difficult for personality differences to operate since personality predicts behaviour better when social influences are weak.

Personality effects loom larger when we note people's differing reactions to the same situation, as when one person reacts with terror and another with delight to a roller-coaster ride.
SOURCE: ©Jacob Lund/Shutterstock

Even so, Milgram's participants differed widely in how obedient they were, and there is good reason to suspect that sometimes his participants' hostility, respect for authority and concern for meeting expectations affected their obedience (Blass, 1990, 1991; Gibson, 2013, 2017; Reicher & Haslam, 2011, 2014).

Individuals differ. An Army report on the Abu Ghraib prison abuse praised three men who, despite threats of ridicule and court martial, stood apart from their comrades (O'Connor, 2004). Lieutenant David Sutton terminated one incident and alerted his commanders. 'I don't want to judge, but yes, I witnessed something inappropriate and I reported it,' said Sutton. Navy dog handler William Kimbro resisted 'significant pressure' to participate in 'improper interrogations'. And Specialist Joseph Darby blew the whistle, giving military police the evidence that raised the alarm.

Darby, called a 'rat' by some, received death threats for his dissent and was given military protection. But, back home, his mother joined others in applauding: 'Honey, I'm so proud of you because you did the good thing and good always triumphs over evil, and the truth will always set you free' (ABC News, 2004).

It is interesting how the pendulum of professional opinion swings. Without discounting the undeniable power of the social forces recognized in the 1960s and 1970s, the pendulum has swung back towards an appreciation of individual personality and its genetic predispositions. Personality researchers are clarifying and reaffirming the connection between who we are and what we do, and most social psychologists agree with pioneering theorist Kurt Lewin's (1936) dictum: 'Every psychological event depends upon the state of the person and at the same time on the environment, although their relative importance is different in different cases' (p. 12) – socialization and situation.

Group Identity

We've already touched on the idea that people conform to the group because they want to belong, and are keen to avoid rejection. This is something the classic conformity researchers, like Asch and Milgram, recognized, and which social psychologists have elaborated upon to understand 'who' conforms (and why).

social identity theory a theory accredited to Tajfel and Turner, which is based on the assumption that people belong to social groups and derive a social identity from these groups. According to the theory we derive much of our self-esteem from our social identity, and when social identity is not satisfactory we may pursue a number of strategies to improve it

outgroup 'them' – a group that people perceive as distinctively different from or apart from their ingroup

referent informational influence social identity theorists subsume both normative and informational influence into this one term. Referring to our ingroup as a valid source of information satisfies both our desire to be correct and part of the group

Reicher and Haslam (2011) take a **social identity theoretical perspective** (SIT). We discuss this particular theory, which was founded by Henri Tajfel in Chapter 12 (also see Chapter 1 for more on Tajfel). For now, let's consider some of SIT's basic assumptions: our behaviour and sense of self is guided by the norms and values of the groups to which we psychologically belong. Furthermore, we enhance this social identity through favourable comparisons with other relevant social groups to which we do not belong (known as **outgroups**). Reicher and Haslam suggest that what happens in these classic studies of conformity is the emergence of a social (or group) identity. We identify with the confederates in Asch's study: we unwittingly believe they are participants just like us. Hence they are to be trusted and taken seriously. Consequently, there must be something wrong with my own judgement. Social identity theorists call this **referent informational influence**. We want to be correct and we trust our fellow ingroup members as valid sources of information.

Haslam et al.'s (2015) examination of the interaction between the experimenter and participants during Milgram's studies reveals the development of a sense of 'us' pursued by both experimenter and participant: scientific explorers of human behaviour. Participants report being 'proud' to take part in a scientific study. In Milgram's work obedience levels escalated when the experimenter is in close proximity to the participant, conducts the study in a prestigious lab wearing a lab-coat, and requests him or her to continue with the electric shocks. Obedience drops when the experimenter isn't present, and when the study takes place in an unscientific non-prestigious venue. In those moments, our guide for behaviour comes from those we identify with.

This social identity explanation for social influence and conformity shifts its explanation from within the individual (a feature of their personality) to social forces. The members of a group to which we belong – or aspire to belong – are sources of information about the group's norms, which constitute the correct view of the world. Therefore these members exert their influence upon us. Furthermore, the more a group member is seen as representative of the group (i.e. as a group **prototype**), the greater the influence this group member will exert on us.

prototype a social category member who is believed to possess the typical features of the social category

Would People Still Obey Today?

Perhaps you have wondered if people are as obedient today as they were in the 1960s when Milgram conducted his studies? You are not the only one. Many students learning about Milgram's (1963, 1965, 1974) obedience studies often ask whether similar results would be found today. Some people have argued that individuals these days are more aware of the dangers of blindly following authority than they were in the early 1960s and therefore the obedience rates are lower. The Hungarian social psychologist Thomas Blass performed a meta-analysis on the results of studies up to the year 2000. He found that the percentage of participants who are prepared to inflict fatal voltages remains remarkably constant, 61–66 per cent, regardless of time or place, and he found no evidence for a change in obedience over time (Blass, 2004).

Jerry Burger of Santa Clara University also wondered, and conducted a partial replication of Milgram's studies (Burger, 2009). As you hopefully have grasped by now, the obedience studies are arguably the most well-known social psychological research inside and outside the field. They are mentioned in most introductory textbooks in psychology, and references to the studies continue to appear in popular media, including movies and songs (Blass, 2004). Jerry Burger therefore had to select his respondents more carefully than in the 1960s. He had to be sure that the participants did not know anything about the study. When he did so he found obedience rates in the USA only slightly lower than those Milgram found 45 years earlier (Burger, 2009).

Due to critics of the ethical standards of Milgram's original study, the detailed procedure had to be changed in consecutive studies. In Burger's study the participants were stopped when giving a 150-volt shock and the percentage who would have given a 450-volt shock was calculated using probability measures. This could have had some impact on the results. But we have to conclude that there has been no dramatic change in people's willingness to harm another person if the situation makes it difficult to refuse, and if an authority gives orders and apparently takes the responsibility. The obedience studies therefore are a dramatic demonstration of how individuals typically underestimate the power of situational forces when explaining a person's behaviour.

Conformity as Entertainment?

'The Milgram studies are great drama as well as great science', write Reicher and Haslam (2011, p. 163). Although the ethics of the Milgram experiment make it difficult to replicate in the laboratory, there have been some interesting replications of conformity studies made as television programmes. In 2006 Derren Brown replicated the Milgram experiment in a larger experiment for Channel 4, billed as 'The Heist'. This scenario was that of a motivational seminar and documentary with 13 participants. He attempted to select and persuade four people to carry out an armed robbery, stealing £100,000. During the process of selecting participants to carry this out, there was a replication of the Milgram experiment, with the participants carrying out the same role as the 'teacher' in the original experiment.

The results of the replications reflected Milgram's original results, with over half of participants continuing to administer shocks to the 'learner' up to 450 volts.

In 2010 a French-Swiss documentary *Le Jeu de la Mort* replicated the Milgram experiment in the guise of a reality/game show format. Participants were given €40 and told that they would not win any money from the game as it was only a pilot. Again, the majority of participants continued up to 450 volts, with only 16 of 80 refusing to go all the way!

Gender Differences in Conformity?

Milgram relied almost exclusively on male participants in his obedience studies. The one exception was a replication of the basic procedure in which women were used as participants. The women complied fully with the experimenter's commands 65 per cent of the time, a rate identical with men as participants. Blass (2000) found no evidence of a gender difference in eight out of nine conceptual replications of Milgram's studies he reviewed. Also in Burger's recent study there was little difference in obedience rates between men and women (Burger, 2009). He did not find any effect for education, age or ethnicity either. The situation created in the laboratory seems to dilute all precaution. We examine the historical interest in seeking out sex and gender differences in social psychological studies further in Chapter 14.

The state of affairs today seems to be the same and Milgram's conclusion in his article from 1974 deserves to be repeated:

> I set up a simple experiment at Yale University to test how much pain an ordinary citizen would inflict on another person simply because he was ordered to by an experimental scientist. Stark authority was pitted against the subjects' strongest moral imperatives against hurting others, and, with the subjects' ears ringing with the screams of the victims, authority won more often than not. The extreme willingness of adults to go to almost any lengths on the command of an authority constitutes the chief finding of the study and the fact most urgently demanding explanation.
>
> (Milgram, 1974)

As we can learn from this quote, Milgram's obedience study was about harming another human being if ordered to.

Research close-up

A Virtual Replication of Milgram's Obedience Study

Source: *Slater, M., Antley, M., Davison, A., Swapp, D., Guger, C., Barker, C., Pistrang, N., & Sanchez-Vives, M. V. (2006). A virtual reprise of the Stanley Milgram experiment. PLoS ONE, 1(1), e39. https://doi.org/10.1371/journal.pone.0000039 (open access).*

Introduction

It is increasingly difficult to replicate the Milgram obedience experiments, given the serious ethical implications of the original study. While carrying out a study on a live participant would be ethically problematic, there are other ways of replicating the study, particularly with the use of virtual reality. By using virtual reality, the participant can be involved in an experiment that allows for conditions that would not be available in real life. This study created a virtual reality version of the Milgram study. The main aim was not to test for obedience, but to measure if participants would respond in an emotional and psychological manner to a virtual person, as if they were responding to a real person. Studies have shown that participants respond to virtual environments in a realistic way (Bailenson & Yee, 2006). This suggests that the use of virtual reality may enable the study of potentially problematic psychological scenarios. In the current study participants were required to give 'electric shocks' to a virtual woman character. All participants knew that the subject of the experiment was not a real human being, but did this knowledge eliminate the discomfort by hurting another human being?

Method

Thirty-four participants were recruited from the staff and students of University College London. They were divided into two groups: (1) Visual Condition (VC) where the virtual woman was visible ($n = 23$); and (2) Hidden Condition (HC) where the virtual woman was not visible for the participants ($n = 11$). The volunteers in the VC condition could see the virtual woman (see **Figure 7.7**). As you can see, the virtual woman had a quite realistic face; she could move her eyes and had facial expressions; she visibly breathed, spoke and appeared to respond with pain to the 'electric shocks'. She also seemed to be aware of the presence of the participant by gazing at him or her, and even protesting ('I don't want to continue – don't listen to him!'). Participants in the HC condition interacted only with text.

The procedure of the 'learning experiment' was the same as the original Milgram experiment, with 32 sets of 5 word learning trials. The participant was placed in front of an 'electric shock machine', and was instructed that they were to increase the voltage and shock the learner every time that she gave an incorrect answer.

In addition to the standard experiment, the participants in both conditions were given the Autonomic Perceptions Questionnaire (APQ) that had 24 questions designed to give a subjective measure of the participants' self-awareness of physiological indicators of stress. They were also monitored for their electrodermal activity (EDA), recording the participants' sympathetic arousal. EDA measures reactions that are beyond our control, our biological reactions to our environment. In stressful situations, our heart rate increases and we sweat more. The EDA measures several physiological responses, the skin conductance level (SCL), the skin conductance response (SCR), the heart rate and heart rate variability. These are symptoms of our sympathetic arousal and by measuring them we can see how stressed we are in a more objective way than giving a verbal report of how stressed we feel, for example on a scale of 1 to 10. Using both the APQ and EDA monitoring, the stress of shocking the virtual woman was measured both subjectively and objectively.

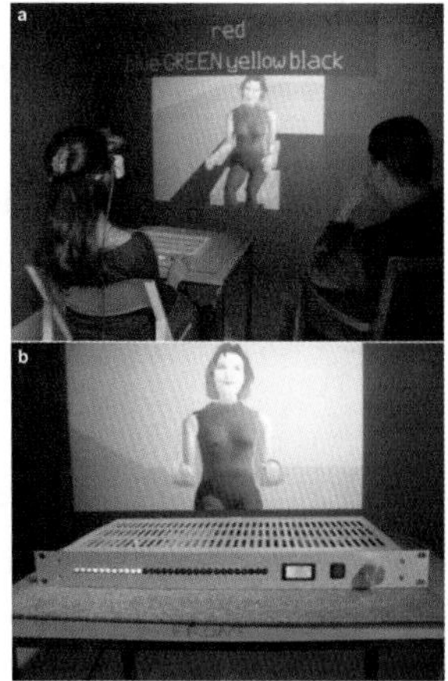

FIGURE 7.7 The virtual woman who was the victim in the study

Results

Participants who could not see the female character were more likely to administer shocks of maximum voltage than those who could see her.

The various data-gathering measures were analysed separately to determine the stress that participants felt giving shocks to the virtual woman in both the visual and hidden conditions. The APQ scores showed that the median stress score after the experiment had been raised from the score before the experiment; in the visual conditions, this rise was significant, but not for the hidden condition.

Analysing the data from the EDA, it was found that all of the factors measured were significant in showing increased stress for the visual condition, where participants could see the virtual woman, in comparison to the hidden condition, where the participants could not.

Discussion

The findings of this experiment reflect the findings of the original Milgram experiment. As the results show that stress is significantly higher for the participants who could see the virtual woman, it appears that the emotional brain of the human volunteers didn't quite get the message that this was only virtual reality.

In this study, participants were displaying obedience. They were willing to put up with their own discomfort for the sake of honouring their agreement to be a participant in the experiment. Similar arguments have been made in relation to the original experiments by Milgram.

The line of research opened up by Milgram stopped 40 years ago due to ethical concerns, especially the problem of major deception. But with advances in technology, virtual environments can provide an alternative methodology for pursuing laboratory-based experimental research even in an extreme social situation. The problem of major deception was avoided in this study since every participant knew for certain that the victim was a virtual character. The virtual environment studies could therefore open a new door to direct empirical studies of obedience in extreme social situations.

Critical Reflections

Although no pain was inflicted, the participants were still stressed by the situation, and certainly more so when they interacted directly with a visible victim rather than only through a text interface with a hidden victim. If virtual reality became so realistic as to be indistinguishable from reality, then its use in such experiments may raise the same ethical questions as Milgram's work did.

This study certainly seems to offer robust confirmation of Milgram's findings. However, bearing in mind recent critiques of why people conform in these experiments, an interesting addition to this study would be interviews with the participants to provide some qualitative insight into why they behaved in the way they did.

Do We Ever Want to Be Different?

Will people ever actively resist social pressure? When compelled to do A, will they instead do Z? What would motivate such anticonformity?

This chapter emphasizes the power of social forces. It is therefore fitting that we conclude by again reminding ourselves of the power of the person. We are not just billiard balls moving where pushed. We may act according to social and private values, independently of the immediate situational forces that push upon us. Knowing that someone is trying to coerce us may even prompt us to react in the *opposite* direction.

Reactance

Individuals in Western cultures value personal freedom, independence and self-efficacy. This is reflected in their sense of an independent self. When social pressure becomes so blatant that it threatens their sense of freedom, they often rebel. Think of Romeo and Juliet, whose love was intensified by their families' opposition. Or think of children asserting their freedom and independence by doing the opposite of what their parents ask. Shrewd parents therefore offer their children choices instead of commands: 'It's time to clean up: do you want a bath or a shower?' In Eastern, interdependent cultures individual freedom is traditionally not looked upon as the ultimate or even a very important goal, and children therefore listen to and obey their parents and even other adults to a higher degree. The **interdependent self** emphasizes the importance of relationships with others in the forming of self.

interdependent self construing one's identity in relation to others

The theory of psychological **reactance** – that people in the independent West act to protect their sense of freedom – is supported by experiments showing that attempts to restrict a person's freedom often produce an anticonformity 'boomerang effect' (Brehm & Brehm, 1981; Goldsmith et al., 2005; Nail et al., 2000).

reactance a motive to protect or restore one's sense of freedom. Reactance arises when someone threatens our freedom of action

Asserting Uniqueness

People feel uncomfortable when they appear too different from others. But in individualist Western cultures they also feel uncomfortable when they appear exactly like everyone else. It appears that our identity is bound up with how we view ourselves as either confirming the majority, or as being unique and therefore non-conformist. Landmark experiments by Snyder and Fromkin (1980) show that people feel better when they see themselves as moderately unique. Moreover, they act in ways that will assert their individuality. In one experiment, Snyder and Fromkin (1980) led Purdue University students to believe that their '10 most important attitudes' were either distinct from or nearly identical to the attitudes of 10,000 other students. When they next participated in a conformity experiment, those deprived of their feeling of uniqueness were the ones most likely to assert their individuality by non-conformity.

Sometimes the desire to be unique may mean that we may be actively not conforming to the majority group, but instead we are conforming to the minority non-conformist group. If you look at groups like youth sub-cultures you can see that while these people stand out in a group of majority conformists, when they are within their own sub-culture they are very much conforming to their own group's non-conformist position.

For those of us in Western cultures, our distinctiveness is central to our identity and independent self (Vignoles et al., 2000). This is not the case in all cultures. In the traditional interdependent cultures in the East people do not like to push themselves forward or to be unique and different. They are more modest in groups and do not have the urge to be something extraordinary, but rather try to fit in and create a balance between each other where everybody can contribute with strengths and weaknesses.

People in industrialized Western cultures are more likely to demonstrate an independent self, defining their identity in terms of their personal attributes rather than part of their social groups (see Chapter 3).

In the West, seeing oneself as unique is central to people's happiness (Demir et al., 2013; Koydemir et al., 2014). Uniqueness also appears in people's 'spontaneous self-concepts'. In some classic studies William McGuire and his colleagues (McGuire & Padawer-Singer, 1978; McGuire et al., 1979) report that when children are invited to 'tell us about yourself', they are most likely to mention their distinctive attributes. Foreign-born children are more likely than others to mention their birthplace. Redheads are more likely than black- and brown-haired children to volunteer their hair colour.

Asserting our uniqueness. Though not wishing to be greatly deviant, most of us express our distinctiveness through our personal styles and dress.

SOURCE: ©woodpencil/Shutterstock

When the people of two cultures are nearly identical, they still will notice their differences, however small. Even trivial distinctions may provoke scorn and conflict. Jonathan Swift satirized the phenomenon in *Gulliver's Travels* with the story of the Little-Endians' war against the Big-Endians. Their difference: the Little-Endians preferred to break their eggs on the small end, the Big-Endians on the large end. On a world scale, the differences may not seem great between Serbs and Croatians, Hutus and Tutsis, or Catholic and Protestant Northern Irish, and even between the Christians, the Muslims and the Jews. They all believe in the same God, though He has different 'faces'. But anyone who reads the news knows that these small differences mean big conflicts (Rothbart & Taylor, 1992). Rivalry is often most intense when the other group closely resembles you.

Focus On

The Ordinary Monster

One of the phenomena in the twentieth century that has caused a flurry of research and comments is why so many supported the Nazi movement. How was the Nazi Holocaust possible? What kind of situation was created that made it feasible for so many Europeans to take part in the extermination of Jews, Gypsies, homosexuals, and people with mental disabilities and disorders? We have already discussed the phenomena of obedience and conformity, and in Chapter 14 we consider Adorno et al.'s (1950) survey on anti-Semitism, ethnocentrism and racism trying to reveal some other mechanisms behind victimization and discrimination.

But there are other explanations, and three social psychologists from the University of St Andrews in Scotland and the University of Exeter in England have questioned the most influential explanation given for the participation in the Nazi Holocaust: Milgram's 'The obedience to authority' study. While Milgram studied the phenomenon in the laboratory there have been numerous books and papers analysing what happened in real life. Hannah Arendt, who wrote a book about Adolf Eichmann, an organizer of the Holocaust, tries to understand how Eichmann could be so barbarous. She wrote her book after her presence at the Eichmann trial in Jerusalem. There is a picture from the trial which also has become famous and embodies our understanding of the Holocaust participants; a picture of Eichmann, an ordinary man, somewhat slight and balding. He did not look like a monster able to do monstrous acts. His very ordinariness was profoundly shocking. Hannah Arendt caught and immortalized it in her book *Eichmann in Jerusalem* (Arendt, 1963/1994). According to Arendt, Eichmann looked like a typical bureaucrat, carrying out orders, making things work, doing his job efficiently. The fact that the job involved mass murder seemed almost incidental. The message to be drawn from this was: 'the lesson of the fearsome, word-and-thought defying *banality of evil*' (1963/1994, p. 252, emphasis in original). The term 'banality of evil', although it occurs only in the last sentence of her 250-page book, has become an explanatory concept also for many social psychologists dealing with evil-doing and monstrous behaviour: everybody will obey if the situation demands it since people lack awareness or control over what they are doing.

However, Reicher et al. (2008) reject this explanation. From a social identity approach (see Chapter 12 for further discussion of this theory) they re-examined the historical and psychological case for '*the banality of evil*', and suggested it consisted of three core elements.

The first was that Eichmann and his ilk did not represent a 'psychological type' distinct from the rest of us. The second was that Arendt suggested that the acts of Nazis arose out of commonplace motives that most people share: the desire to be valued and accepted by others, to do one's job well, to advance in one's career, and not simply because we *wanted* to conform or obey. These two arguments constitute the idea that 'anyone can do it'. This view is bolstered by a wealth of recent research arguing that the killers could be described as 'ordinary men'. Arendt's third argument deals with the psychological processes that permit ordinary men (and they almost always are men) to commit mass slaughter. They become obsessed with doing their jobs and how well they fulfil the demands put upon them. As Arendt puts it, Eichmann 'had no motives at all. He *merely,* to put the matter colloquially, "*never realized what he was doing*"' (Arendt, 1994, p. 287, emphasis added).

The concept of 'banality of evil' is further challenged by Cesarani (2004) who suggested that, as Arendt had only attended part of Eichmann's trial, specifically his own defence period, she gathered only a very carefully presented version of Eichmann. Eichmann had able defence lawyers who sought to present him as a mild-mannered man, not a sadistic monster. Cesarani argues that Arendt's representation of Eichmann as 'merely thoughtless' shows that she was taken in by his self-presentation. Acts of genocide, such as those of the Holocaust, as well as in many conflicts since then, do not occur in a social and political vacuum. The reduction of the outgroup to 'sub-human' is an important step on the way to justifying the destruction of them, as well as maintaining the superiority of ourselves as ingroup.

Reicher et al. (2008) sought to show that the picture of Eichmann as a man obeying and not knowing what he did has misled researchers by taking them down the wrong path when seeking to understand the psychology of genocide. They argue that killing does not derive from inattention. Rather, killing becomes acceptable (or 'natural') only when it can be celebrated as *the right thing to do.*

Another lesson is that the way we define ourselves may often be more relevant to genocide than the way we define others. It is our social identity and the protection of our values that counts, not our lack of awareness and desire to conform and be obedient in a particular situation. These phenomena are further dealt with in Chapters 13 and 14.

What is notable in Reicher et al.'s critique of both the Milgram study and the concept of '*the banality of evil*' is that it brings into question the idea that we are blindly obedient. Instead, we do obey, but only within specific limits. We need to identify ourselves and those we obey, as being within our specific ingroup. This raises questions about conformity and obedience; we are not blind or thoughtless in our conformity, we have agency and choice. Our context influences us, but we also have other factors that must be in play in order for us to conform. It is too simple to view the Milgram experiments and assume that they provide a comprehensive answer to the question of why people obey.

Questions

1. To what extent do you think conformity explains crimes against humanity?
2. Do you think experimental studies on conformity sufficiently replicate the basis on which evil acts can occur?
3. Can we ever understand conformity in such extreme situations as crimes against humanity without understanding the wider socio-political context they occur in?
4. What impact do you think the development of online communication has on conformity?

SUMMING UP: CONFORMITY AND OBEDIENCE

WHAT IS CONFORMITY?

- *Conformity* – changing one's behaviour or belief as a result of group pressure – comes in two forms. *Compliance* is outwardly going along with the group while inwardly disagreeing. *Acceptance* is believing as well as acting in accord with social pressure.

WHAT ARE THE CLASSIC CONFORMITY AND OBEDIENCE STUDIES?

Three classic sets of studies illustrate how researchers have studied conformity.

- Muzafer Sherif observed that others' judgements influenced people's estimates of the movement of a point of light that actually did not move. Norms for 'proper' answers emerged and survived both over long periods of time and through succeeding generations of research participants.
- Solomon Asch had people listen to others' judgements of which three comparison lines was equal to a standard line and then make the same judgement themselves. When the others unanimously gave a wrong answer, the participants conformed 37 per cent of the time.
- Stanley Milgram's obedience studies elicited an extreme form of compliance. Under optimum conditions – a legitimate, close-at-hand commander, a remote victim and no one else to exemplify disobedience – 65 per cent of his adult male participants fully obeyed instructions to deliver what were supposedly traumatizing electric shocks to a screaming innocent victim in an adjacent room.
- These classic laboratory studies expose the potency of several phenomena. Behaviour and attitudes are mutually reinforcing, enabling a small act of evil to foster the attitude that leads to a bigger evil act. The power of the situation is seen when good people, faced with dire circumstances, commit reprehensible acts (although dire situations may produce heroism in others). The fundamental attribution error leads us to think that evil is committed by people who are bad and that good is done by good people, and to discount situational forces and social categorization that induce people to conform to falsehoods or capitulate to cruelty.

WHAT PREDICTS CONFORMITY?

- Using conformity testing procedures, experimenters have explored the circumstances that produce conformity. Certain situations appear to be especially powerful. For example, conformity is affected by the characteristics of the group: People conform most when three or more people, or groups, model the behaviour or belief.
- Conformity is reduced if the modelled behaviour or belief is not unanimous.
- Conformity is enhanced by group cohesion.
- The higher the status of those modelling the behaviour or belief, the greater likelihood of conformity.
- People also conform most when their responses are public (in the presence of the group).
- A prior commitment to a certain behaviour or belief increases the likelihood that a person will stick with that commitment rather than conform.

WHY CONFORM?

- *Normative influence* results from a person's desire for acceptance: we want to be liked. The tendency to conform more when responding publicly reflects normative influence.
- *Informational influence* results from others' providing evidence about reality. The tendency to conform more on difficult decision-making tasks reflects informational influence: we want to be right.
- *Cultural influence* results from norms and values acquired during socialization. In some cultures it is more important to fit in, seek harmony and adjust to others.

WHO CONFORMS?

- The question 'Who conforms?' has produced few definitive answers. Global personality scores are poor predictors of specific acts of conformity but better predictors of average conformity. Trait effects are strongest in 'weak' situations where social forces do not overwhelm individual differences.
- Although conformity and obedience are universal, different cultures socialize people to be more or less socially responsive, independent or interdependent.
- Recent replications of classic conformity and obedience studies have shown that people do still allow themselves to be influenced in these kinds of situations.

DO WE EVER WANT TO BE DIFFERENT?

- Social psychology's emphasis on the power of social pressure must be joined by a complementary emphasis on the power of the person. We are not puppets. When social coercion becomes blatant, people often experience *reactance* – a motivation to defy the coercion in order to maintain their sense of freedom.
- We are not comfortable being too different from a group, but neither do we want to appear the same as everyone else. Most people, especially in the West, act in ways that preserve their sense of uniqueness and individuality.

Critical Questions

1. What is meant by 'the copycat suicide phenomenon'? Are we seeing higher numbers of suicide because the rate has increased or because we are looking for them?
2. Is the Milgram experiment disturbing because of the ethics involved or because of what it reveals about the capacity of ordinary people to inflict harm?
3. Can the classic conformity studies of Asch, Sherif and Milgram be applied to real-life situations? Try to give an example for each study as well as thinking about the limitations for these studies in real-life study.
4. Define and provide examples of both normative influence and informational influence.
5. 'Without conformity, there would be social chaos'. Do you agree? Why or why not?

Recommended Reading

Classic Papers

Asch, S. E. (1955). Opinions and social pressure. *Scientific American,* November, pp. 31–35.

Milgram, S. (1974). *Obedience to authority: An experimental view.* Harper & Row.

Sherif, M. (1935). A study of some social factors in perception. *Archives of Psychology,* 187.

Contemporary Studies

Lammers, J., & Stapel, D. A. (2011). Power increases dehumanization. *Group Processes and Intergroup Relations, 14,* 1–14.

Pedersen, E. R., LaBrie, J. W., & Lac, A. (2008). Assessment of perceived and actual alcohol norms in varying contexts: Exploring social impact theory among college students. *Addictive Behaviours, 33,* 552–564.

Reicher, S. D., Haslam, S. A., & Smith, J. R. (2012). Working toward the experimenter: Reconceptualizing obedience within the Milgram paradigm as identification-based followership. *Perspectives on Psychological Science,* **7,** 315–324.

Russell, N. J. C. (2011). Milgram's obedience to authority experiments: Origins and early evolution. *British Journal of Social Psychology, 50*(1), 140–162.

8 AGGRESSION

What do we mean by the term 'aggression'? Broadly speaking, aggression defines behaviour that is destructive in some way, causing harm or injury. This can be towards other people, but may also include damage to inanimate objects (e.g. furniture or property), or animals. Of course, some examples of aggressive behaviour are very easily recognized when they accompany intentional violence towards others (e.g. in the time of war). However, not all aggression is so obvious. Aggression can take other more subtle forms such as the verbal aggression displayed in an argument, the occurrence of bullying in the school or workplace, a scuffle in the street, an offensive text message or email, or Internet trolling, and as such may be witnessed in our everyday lives.

We may be tempted into believing that today's world is more aggressive than it used to be. Gun crime, knife crime, terrorism, and murder rates all dominate our daily news headlines. We are only ever a few clicks away from seeing aggression portrayed through social media. However, perhaps it's not that today's societies are more aggressive, but that we simply have better access to viewing examples of it. For example, the United Nations Global Study for Homicide (2019) reports a drop in homicide rates in Europe (of 63 per cent since 2002) and Asia (of 36 per cent since 1990). Yet in America homicide rates remain high, accounting for 37 per cent of intentional homicide deaths globally. Aggression has many faces, and how social psychologists define it has implications for what they treat as evidence of it, how they measure it, explain it, and the solutions offered for reducing or preventing it. In this chapter we consider some empirical studies, theories and influences on aggression, and examine the diverse range of definitions and methodologies for studying this phenomenon.

In doing so we ask four more-specific questions:

1 Is aggression biologically predisposed, or do we learn it?

2 What circumstances prompt hostile outbursts?

3 Do the media, including social media, influence and facilitate aggression?

4 How might we reduce aggression?

First, let's clarify what we mean by the term 'aggression'.

What Is Aggression?

The lack of consistency in defining aggression in everyday language is reflected in social psychology. How aggression is defined often depends on the theoretical perspective and the methods used. If we define aggression in its most direct form, as physical acts, then we collect evidence of physical behaviour. But if we define aggression in a more indirect form, perhaps as a subtle feature of language (e.g. spreading malicious gossip), then we would attend to what people say and perhaps how they say it. Some social psychologists have settled on a compromised definition of aggression as physical or verbal behaviour intended to cause harm, and this has been reflected in many Social Psychology textbooks. This definition excludes unintentional harm such as collisions in the street, or the accidental spilling of a hot drink onto someone else; it also excludes actions that may involve pain as an unavoidable side effect of helping someone, such as dental treatments or – in the extreme – assisted suicide. It does include kicks and slaps, threats and insults, even gossip or snide 'digs'; and decisions, during experiments, about how much to hurt someone, such as how much of an electric shock to impose. It also includes destroying property, lying and other behaviour whose aim is to cause mental or physical hurt. However, even this compromise of 'intentional' aggression is not without its problems. Not all aggression is intentional. Some aggressive acts are caused accidentally, with no intention to cause harm. For example, over-exuberance at a music concert can result in harm to others if we accidentally hit or push them as we express our excitement. Accidentally knocking over a cyclist whilst driving a car is another example. Unintentional aggression can also describe behaviour that harms others, but the individual causing that harm cannot be held responsible for that action. For example, children and adults with ADHD (Attention Deficit/Hyperactivity Disorder) may behave aggressively as a consequence of their disorder rather than intention to harm someone (Nigg, 2003).

The use of direct and indirect aggression can characterize bullying behaviour. For example, consider the substantial body of work carried out by Dan Olweus on bullying behaviour in schools (see the following for a flavour of this work: 1978, 1991, 1993b, 2001a; Olweus & Limber, 2010a) that has revealed some of the devastating consequences of being bullied, including depression, anxiety, isolation and thoughts of suicide. Olweus defines bullying as negative behaviour that happens to a victim 'repeatedly and over time' (1993a, p. 9) involving acts of direct physical aggression and indirect aggression. Such acts can be directly aggressive (such as hitting) and indirectly aggressive (such as social exclusion). From his 1993b study of Norwegian schoolchildren he found that boys tended to conduct most of the bullying. As we shall see in this chapter, this finding is consistent with a lot of aggression research that suggests men are more aggressive than women. In a global survey of homicide rates, the UN (2019) reports that 90 per cent of all homicides are conducted by men. Biology, and the presence of hormones such as testosterone and cortisol, is a major contributing factor. But, as we shall also see in this chapter, it is possible to learn aggressive behaviour, which is a feature of bullying recognized in Olweus's work. He notes the biological basis for bullying (including personality and physical strength of individuals), but also the environment's role in fostering and facilitating bullying behaviour (such as the school's rules around discipline and bullying and their enforcement, and the behaviour of adults). Olweus's work on bullying led to the development of the Olweus Bullying Prevention Program (OBPP), which has so far been rolled out to schools in Norway and the US to tackle bullying (Olweus & Limber, 2010b). The OBPP is founded on four principles:

1. Parents, carers and teachers should show a positive interest in the child.
2. Parents, carers and teachers should set clear boundaries regarding acceptable and unacceptable behaviour.
3. Parents, carers and teachers should consistently deliver negative, but non-physical, consequences for the breaking of those boundaries.
4. Parents, carers and teachers should act as positive figures of authority and role models for children.

These foundations of the OBPP emphasize the social environment of the school in preventing bullying behaviour.

Thus, given the role of social environment, women are as capable as men of aggression (Denson et al., 2018). This raises issues surrounding the definition and methods used for capturing aggressive behaviour for the social psychologist. Owens et al. (2000a, 2000b) found from their interviews and focus groups with Australian teenage girls, that they use fairly subtle and indirect ways to bully other girls. This bullying can take the form of excluding girls from peer groups. Girls seem to value friendship groups more than boys, so excluding girls from their friends can be a very effective method of bullying. Teenage girls also report using other strategies such as verbal bullying (e.g. spreading malicious gossip), and non-verbal bullying (e.g. hostile staring), which can leave their marginalized victims feeling miserable. These indirect forms of aggression can be more difficult for the social psychologist to capture. Consequently how we define aggression may boil down to what we can see, capture and analyse.

Some Theories of Aggression

In analysing the causes of aggression, social psychologists have broadly focused on three main explanations: (1) aggression is the result of a biologically based aggressive drive; (2) aggression is a response to frustration; and (3) aggressive behaviour is learned. Here we shall focus on some key theories in social psychology, which have taken these explanations as their starting point for understanding aggression. Those theories outlined here are not exhaustive of social psychology's engagement with aggression (there are many others!), but they do offer some important insights for the discipline.

Aggression as a Biological Phenomenon

Philosophers have debated whether our human nature is fundamentally that of a benign, contented, 'noble savage' or that of a brute. The first view, argued by the eighteenth-century French philosopher Jean-Jacques Rousseau (1712–78), blames society, not human nature, for social evils. His famous quote, 'Man is born free but everywhere he is in chains' (1762, reprinted 2016, p. 23), summarizes his opinion that the natural state of man was good, but it was society that corrupted him. On the other hand, the second idea, associated with the English philosopher Thomas Hobbes (1588–1679), credits society for restraining the human brute. In the twentieth century, the 'brutish' view – that aggressive drive is inborn and thus inevitable – was argued by Sigmund Freud in Vienna and Konrad Lorenz in Germany. Freud (1856–1939) was the founding father of **psychoanalysis**, whereas Lorenz (1903–1989) was an **ethologist**.

psychoanalysis the study of the unconscious mind

ethology the scientific study of natural animal behaviour, which is understood to have an evolutionary function

Instinct Theory

Freud speculated that human aggression springs from a self-destructive impulse. It redirects towards others the energy of a primitive death urge (the 'death instinct', sometimes called Thanatos in post-Freudian theory). Lorenz, an animal behaviour expert, saw aggression as adaptive rather than self-destructive. The two agreed that aggressive energy is instinctual (unlearned and universal), that is, causes **instinctive behaviour**. If not discharged, it supposedly builds up until it explodes or until an appropriate stimulus 'releases' it, like a mouse releasing a mousetrap.

instinctive behaviour an innate, unlearned behaviour pattern exhibited by all members of a species

The idea that aggression is an instinct collapsed as the list of supposed human instincts grew to include nearly every conceivable human behaviour. Nearly 6,000 supposed instincts were enumerated in one 1924 survey of social science books (Barash, 1979). The social scientists had tried to *explain* social behaviour by *naming* it. It is tempting to play this rather circular explaining-by-naming game: 'Why do sheep stay together?' 'Because of their herd instinct.' 'How do you know they have a herd instinct?' 'Just look at them: they're always together!'

Instinct theory also fails to account for the variations in aggressiveness from person to person, culture to culture and across time and space. How would a shared human instinct for aggression explain the difference between the peaceful Iroquois before White invaders came and the hostile Iroquois after the invasion (Hornstein, 1976)? Although aggression may be biologically influenced, the human propensity to aggress does not qualify as instinctive behaviour.

Evolutionary Psychology

Our distant ancestors nevertheless sometimes found aggression adaptive, according to evolutionary psychologists David Buss and Todd Shackelford (1997). Aggressive behaviour was a strategy for gaining resources, defending against attack, intimidating or eliminating male rivals for females, and deterring mates from sexual infidelity. In some preindustrial societies, being a good warrior made for higher status and reproductive opportunities (Roach, 1998). The adaptive value of aggression, Buss and Shackelford believe, helps explain the relatively high levels of male–male aggression across human history: 'This does not imply. . . that men have an "aggression instinct" in the sense of some pent-up energy that must be released. Rather, men have learned from their successful ancestors psychological mechanisms' (p. 613) that improve their odds of contributing their genes to future generations.

More recent evolutionary psychology research has revisited the assumption that it is only men who appear to use aggression as an adaptive response to securing a mate and defending themselves. Campbell (2013) reports that female aggression can be a common feature in deprived neighbourhoods with poor social cohesion, and amongst women and girls with absent fathers. She notes that for women, being perceived as aggressive and willing to physically fight, can be beneficial in avoiding victimization in a 'tough' neighbourhood. Under these circumstances, aggression not only serves as a mechanism for protection of self and others, it can be an attractive facet of 'femininity' portraying resilience, loyalty and strength. Furthermore, it can be an important weapon in intrasexual competition for desirable men. That said, the costs associated with aggression have more severe consequences for women than men, argues Campbell. A physical fight can cause injury and death. The centrality of women to reproduction and the survival of children, means they remain less willing, and less likely, to engage in physical aggression. Campbell also reports some neuropsychological evidence which suggests men and women differ in how the **amygdala** responds to threat. Women show higher amygdala activity in the context of threat than men do. But, it seems that women are more able to exert prefrontal corticol control over it. For evolutionary psychologists then, aggression has both a biological and a social basis – each influencing the other in the display, or not, of aggression.

We discuss evolutionary psychology further with respect to biology, culture and gender in Chapter 14.

amygdala most humans have two amygdala, located on either side of the brain. They arguably form part of the limbic system and play a crucial role in our survival system. They enable us to identify and regulate emotions, assist in storing memories, and facilitate our libido

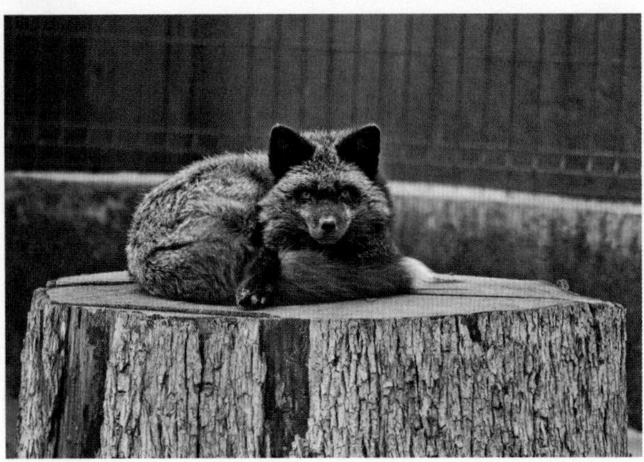

The silver fox study examines genetic breeding for tameness and aggression.

SOURCE: ©Barbosul/Shutterstock

Genetic Influences

Heredity influences the neural system's sensitivity to aggressive cues. For example, animals can be bred for aggressiveness. Sometimes this is done for practical purposes (the breeding of fighting cocks or dogs). Sometimes breeding is done for research. Since 1959, at the Institute of Cytology and Genetics (ICG) of the Russian Academy of Sciences, scientists have been selectively breeding silver foxes for tameness and aggression (Trut et al., 2009). Through careful selection, they have bred a population of silver foxes for their displays of tame and friendly behaviour, and another population for their aggressive behaviour. Fifty generations later, genetic testing conducted on 12 foxes bred from the 'tame' sample, and 12 from the 'aggressive' sample, shows gene alteration as a result of selective breeding. (Wang et al., 2018). Tameness and aggression could be genetically 'bred into' silver foxes.

Chapter 14 discusses the impact of genes on our behaviour more holistically as well as in relation to gender differences.

Our temperaments – how intense and reactive we are – are partly brought with us into the world, influenced by our sympathetic nervous system's reactivity (Atherton et al., 2017; Robins et al., 2002; Rothbart, 2011). A person's temperament, observed in infancy, usually endures (Cote et al., 2007). A child who is non-aggressive at age 8 will very likely still be a non-aggressive person at age 48 (Huesmann et al., 2003). But it is not easy to say if this is due to genetic inheritance or social learning or socialization, or to tease these two things apart.

Long-term studies following several hundred New Zealand children reveal that a recipe for aggressive behaviour combines a gene, called monoamine oxidase-A (MAOA), that alters the neurotransmitter balance with childhood maltreatment (Caspi et al., 2002; Moffitt et al., 2003). Caspi and colleagues found that 12 per cent of males in their study had low levels of MAOA and had been subjected to abuse as children between the ages of 3 and 11 years old. Of this group, 85 per cent of them had engaged in antisocial behaviour, which in some cases led to convictions for violent conduct. Consequently, MAOA has been termed the 'warrior gene' (Gibbons, 2004) due to the effect it seems to have upon behaviour. The warrior gene has also been used successfully as a form of mitigating circumstances in murder convictions. In Italy, Abdelmalek Bayout, who confessed to murdering Walter Perez, had his sentence reduced on the grounds of having low levels of MAOA (Levitt, 2013). However, genes alone do not explain aggressive behaviour. Nature and nurture interact. McDermott et al. (2009) found that participants with low activity of MAOA would be aggressive to opponents in an experimental study, but only when they had been severely provoked. So it appears that biology interacts with the environment in producing aggressive responses.

Biochemical Influences

Blood chemistry also influences neural sensitivity to aggressive stimulation.

Alcohol and Drugs

Both laboratory experiments and police data indicate that drugs and alcohol unleash aggression when people are provoked (Gan et al., 2015; Hammersley, 2011; Hoaken & Stewart, 2003; Hoaken et al., 2012; Taylor & Chermack, 1993; Testa, 2002; Wells et al., 2005).

Alcohol and aggressive behaviour. Laboratory experiments and police data indicate that alcohol unleashes aggression when people are provoked.

SOURCE: ©Dusan Petkovic/Shutterstock

> *In experiments, when asked to think back on relationship conflicts, intoxicated people administer stronger shocks and feel angrier than do sober people.*
>
> (MacDonald et al., 2000)

For example, in Scotland, the Scottish Crime and Justice Survey conducted in 2017/18 reports that 46 per cent of violent crime in the country is alcohol related (Scottish Government, 2019). Furthermore, between 2007 and 2017, 47 per cent of prisoners in Scotland accused of murder were under the influence of alcohol and/or drugs at the time of the offence (Scottish Government, 2017).

However, there is a question about the direction of causality here. In a study of young people aged 11–15 years in the west of Scotland, Young et al. (2007) found that antisocial behaviour can predict long-term alcohol (mis)use. The **susceptibility hypothesis** suggests that people who are already engaging in antisocial behaviour, or who are likely to do so, are much more 'susceptible' to abuse alcohol in the short or long term. So here we have an example where the causal order is reversed (antisocial behaviour causing alcohol misuse). But, whatever the direction of the relationship between alcohol and aggression, what is clear is that alcohol enhances aggressiveness by lowering people's self-awareness and their thresholds for antisocial behaviour (Bartholow & Heinz, 2006; Ito et al., 1996).

susceptibility hypothesis when features of someone's environment make him/her more susceptible to particular kinds of behaviour as a consequence

In their review of a decade's worth of research into the relationship between drugs, alcohol and aggression, Tomlinson et al. (2016) conclude that 'the drug most highly associated with physical, psychological, verbal, and sexual aggression is also the most readily and legally available (and sold by governments for profit) – alcohol' (p. 24). The researchers are left in no doubt that alcohol causes aggression. The relationship between aggression and other drugs, such as heroin, cannabis and opiods, is currently under-researched. The research which does exist and is reviewed by Tomlinson and her team suggests drugs such as these are linked to aggression, but the relationship is less straightforward and is mediated by personality and environmental factors, more so than alcohol.

Testosterone

Hormonal influences appear to be much stronger in lower animals than in humans. But human aggressiveness does appear to correlate to some extent with the male sex hormone, testosterone (Book et al., 2001).

Among the normal range of teen boys and adult men, those with high testosterone levels have been found to be prone to delinquency, hard drug use and aggressive responses to provocation (Archer, 1991; Dabbs & Morris, 1990; Herbert, 2015). After handling a gun, people's testosterone levels rise, and the more their testosterone rises the more aggression they will impose on another (Klinesmith et al., 2006). Geniole and his colleagues (2011) discovered that higher testosterone levels were associated with reactive aggression in men. Interestingly, Cote et al. (2013) found that sleep deprivation lowered testosterone levels and reactive aggression in men. Research has also focused on prenatal exposure to testosterone *in utero*, which affects the developing fetal brain (Ellis, 2005). Fetal exposure to high levels of testosterone via the mother's bloodstream has been associated with high levels of aggression and risk-taking behaviour in the child after its born, especially when the child is male (Ellis, 2011).

But we need to be careful here. Taken at face value this would lead us to the assumption that men must be more aggressive than women. As we shall see later in this chapter, this is not always the case. One reason to be cautious is the lack of research conducted on women and aggression (Denson et al., 2018). Another is that as we discuss in Chapter 2: correlation does not mean causation. As we've already seen, other factors are involved in whether this biological state translates into an aggressive behavioural one (Coccaro, 2017; Herbert, 2015; Turanovic et al., 2017). Winning a rugby match might cause a brief increase in testosterone levels among the players. Does this mean they will then behave aggressively? Most probably not.

Serotonin

Low levels of serotonin have been linked to heightened aggression (Birger et al., 2003; de Almeida et al., 2005; Yanowitch & Coccaro, 2011).

Those studies which propose a link between aggression and serotonin include the dietary manipulation of tryptophan, which is an amino acid used in the production of serotonin. In one study by Moeller and his team (1996) participants were put on a low tryptophan diet for 24 hours to reduce the levels of serotonin produced. These participants were also asked to take part in a maths task that involved being provoked by a researcher. What the researchers discovered was that aggressive responses started to increase from 5 hours of being on the diet.

Studies such as these directly manipulate serotonin levels through diet. Yet these studies show us that our environment may interact with our biology. For example, those individuals who find themselves of low social status often have low levels of serotonin (Manuck et al., 2004). So is it the biology that determines the risky behaviour, or the social standing? Most probably, it's an interaction of both.

Neural Influences

Exerting self-control in a situation where we feel angry can be extremely difficult. And, as neuroimaging studies show, it can be more difficult for some people than others.

reactive aggression an aggressive response to being provoked

Reactive aggression defines a response to being provoked. We may want to respond to being threatened, frustrated or angry at someone's actions or a set of circumstances. Perhaps you've been insulted, tricked, embarrassed or put in a dangerous position. How do you react?

Denson and his colleagues (2012) outline 'I-Theory', which states that there are three processes behind aggression: instigation (being provoked), impellance (dispositional and situational factors which prepare you for an aggressive response) and inhibition (self-control). So your ability to avoid an aggressive reaction is based on the relative strength of your self-control (inhibition) over provocation (instigation) and impellance (preparedness to be aggressive). And it seems that processes within the brain have some influence over our ability to exercise self-control. Prefrontal cortex regions are involved in regulating our emotions and help us to maintain self-control. Damage to these regions is often linked to violent behaviour. But they can be temporarily impeded too by alcohol consumption (as we'll see later in this chapter) and depletion from feeling overwhelmed. The good news is that practice makes perfect, as we control our urge to react aggressively to provocation. Another tastier method of controlling our aggressive urges seems to be consuming sugar, which has been shown to improve those neural processes involved in self-control (Denson et al., 2010).

But not all aggression is reactive. **Instrumental aggression** defines behaviour that is aggressive in order to acquire a desired reward. For example, a son who murders his father for the inheritance would be an act of instrumental aggression. Instrumental aggression requires a lack of empathy with the victim. Research suggests that this lack of empathy is related to poor functioning of the amygdala. This is particularly evident in psychopathic populations, where personality is characterized by a lack of guilt for their actions. Reidy et al. (2011) report examples of studies which have shown instrumental aggressive acts are much more likely to be conducted by psychopaths than non-psychopaths. It seems the amygdala, responsible for feelings of empathy and shame, plays a key role in instrumental aggression.

instrumental aggression
a behaviour which requires aggression in order to obtain a desired (often material) reward

The Interaction of Biology and Behaviour

It is important to remember that the traffic between hormonal influences, brain structure, alcohol, drugs and behaviour flows both ways. Testosterone, for example, may facilitate dominance and aggressiveness, but dominating or defeating behaviour also boosts testosterone levels (Mazur & Booth, 1998). After a World Cup football match or a big basketball game between arch-rivals, testosterone levels rise in the winning fans and fall in the losing fans (Bernhardt et al., 1998). That, plus celebration-related drinking, probably explains the finding of Cardiff University researchers that fans of *winning* rather than losing football and rugby teams commit more post-game assaults (Sivarajasingam et al., 2005). The more athletic competitions women enter, the more their levels of testosterone and cortisol rise (Edwards & Casto, 2013). As Denson et al. (2013) discovered, women with high levels of testosterone and cortisol reacted much more aggressively when insulted than women who had average or low levels of these hormones.

So, instinctive, genetic, neural and biochemical influences may predispose some people to react aggressively to conflict and provocation. But perhaps we need to be careful in interpreting these data, and not to assume that such features are solely responsible for aggressive behaviour.

Many of the tried and tested methods for treating and changing deviant behaviour do not involve biological intervention but concern adjustment of people's social environment and ways of thinking about themselves. Cognitive behavioural therapy (CBT) tackles the way in which people think about themselves, others and the world at large in order to alter their cognition and behaviour. So a complex array of factors is involved, and we need to think about 'what' we define as aggression and what we treat as evidence of it.

Some early social psychological theories of the causes of aggression focused on particular types: those aggressive acts which occurred as a result of frustration, and those that occurred as a consequence of relative deprivation. Let's consider each of these in turn.

Aggression as a Response to Frustration

frustration-aggression theory the theory that frustration triggers a readiness to aggress

frustration the blocking of goal-directed behaviour

One of the first psychological theories of aggression, **frustration-aggression theory**, argues 'Frustration always leads to some form of aggression' (Dollard et al., 1939). **Frustration** is anything that blocks our attaining a goal. In an important study, Barker et al. (1941) found that young children who were shown a room full of attractive toys but prevented from playing with them displayed much more aggressive behaviour towards those toys, compared to other children who had been allowed to play with them immediately, when finally allowed to enter the room.

displacement the redirection of aggression to a target other than the source of the frustration. Generally, the new target is a safer or more socially acceptable target

When Rupert Brown and his colleagues (2001) surveyed British ferry passengers heading to France, they found much higher than normal aggressive attitudes on a day when French fishing boats blockaded the port, preventing their travel. Blocked from obtaining their goal, the passengers became more likely (in responding to various vignettes) to agree with an insult towards a French person who had spilled coffee. In her classic study of queue-jumpers, Harris (1974) found that when people were pushed in front of in a supermarket queue, the closer they were to the checkout when the incident occurred was related to the level of aggression they displayed. The nearer they were to the goal, the more intense the expression of aggression displayed became.

As **Figure 8.1** suggests, the aggressive energy need not explode directly against its source. We learn to inhibit direct retaliation, especially when others might disapprove or punish; instead, we *displace* our hostilities to safer targets. **Displacement** occurs in an old anecdote about a man who, humiliated by his boss, berates his wife, who yells at their son, who kicks the dog, which bites the mail-carrier (who goes home and berates his wife . . .). In experiments and in real life, displaced aggression is most likely when the target shares some similarity to the instigator and does some minor irritating act that unleashes the displaced aggression (Marcus-Newhall et al., 2000; Miller et al., 2003; Pedersen et al., 2000). When a person is harbouring anger from a prior provocation, even a trivial offence – one that would normally produce no response – they may elicit an explosive overreaction (as you may realize if

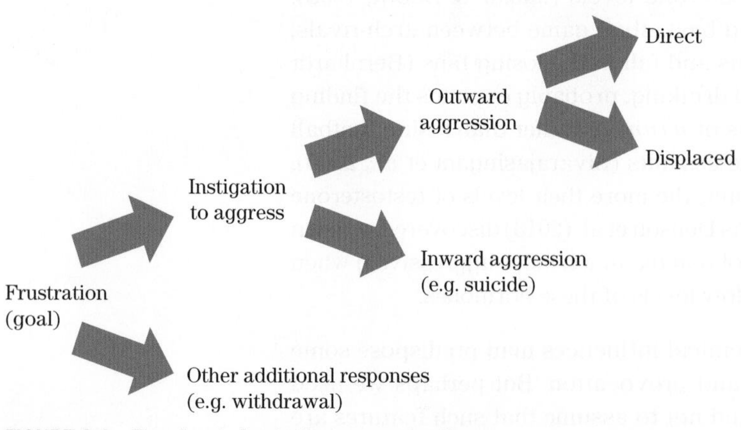

FIGURE 8.1 The classic frustration-aggression theory
Frustration creates a motive to aggress. Fear of punishment or disapproval for aggressing against the source of frustration may cause the aggressive drive to be displaced against some other target or even redirected against oneself.
SOURCE: Based on Dollard et al. (1939); Miller (1941)

you have ever yelled at your room-mate after losing money in a malfunctioning vending machine).

However, it is important to remember that frustration as well as aggression is culture dependent. In some cultures people do not have the same individual expectations as most people have in other cultures and they therefore do not feel frustrated for not reaching the individual goals. This also reduces the consequences of frustration and the prevalence of aggression.

A different approach to the aggression-frustration model is based in the work of Zillman (1979) and his **excitation-transfer model**. Zillman suggests that when we are physiologically aroused from a particular event or situation, this state of arousal does not simply disappear but can have effects on other situations we find ourselves in. Under such conditions a person may transfer feelings of frustration to a different situation and act aggressively.

excitation-transfer model when a state of physiological arousal is transferred from one situation to another, resulting in heightened expressive behaviour

relative deprivation the perception that one is less well off than others with whom one compares oneself

Various commentators have observed that the intense American anger over 9/11 contributed to the eagerness to attack Iraq. Americans were looking for an outlet for their rage and found one in an evil tyrant, Saddam Hussein, who was once their ally. 'The "real reason" for this war', noted Friedman (2003b), 'was that after 9/11 America needed to hit someone in the Arab-Muslim world. . . We hit Saddam for one simple reason: because we could, and because he deserved it, and because he was right in the heart of that world.' One of the war's advocates, Vice-President Richard Cheney (2003), seemed to concur. When asked why most others in the world disagreed with America's launching war, he replied, 'They didn't experience 9/11.'

Frustration-Aggression Theory Revised

Berkowitz (1978, 1989) realized that the original theory overstated the frustration-aggression connection, so he revised it. Berkowitz theorized that frustration produces *anger*, an emotional readiness to aggress. Anger arises when someone who frustrates us could have chosen to act otherwise (Berkowitz, 2012). A frustrated person is especially likely to lash out when aggressive cues pull the cork, releasing bottled-up anger (**Figure 8.2**). Sometimes the cork will blow without such cues. But, as we will see, cues associated with aggression amplify aggression.

Frustrated with the referee's decision, these players aggressively appeal for him to change it.

SOURCE: ©Oleksandr Osipov/Shutterstock

Relative Deprivation

Frustration is often compounded when we compare ourselves with others. Such feelings are called **relative deprivation**. This term was coined as a result of a classic study conducted by Stouffer et al. (1949). They looked at job satisfaction in a sample of US soldiers and found that surprisingly, it correlated negatively with the chances of these soldiers being promoted. Why? Well, the authors argued that how satisfied we feel depends on whether reality aligns with our expectations. Those soldiers who did not

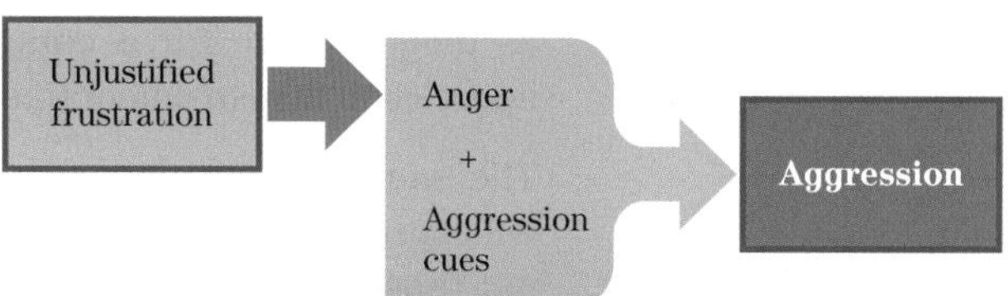

FIGURE 8.2 A simplified synopsis of Leonard Berkowitz's revised frustration-aggression theory

expect to be promoted, were more satisfied in their job than those soldiers who did. In the absence of an objective benchmark against which to assess our abilities and expectations, we look to other sources for information. Consequently one source of information comes from social comparisons with others; in this case, other soldiers. Feeling you are doing a better job than someone else, but not being rewarded for it with a promotion, will mean an unsatisfied soldier.

egoistic relative deprivation the sense of frustration an individual might feel when they feel deprived in comparison to others

fraternal relative deprivation the sense of frustration experienced by group members when they consider their group is being unfairly treated with respect to other groups

Theorists working in this area distinguish between egoistic and fraternal relative deprivation (Runciman, 1966; Schmitt et al., 2010). Whereas **egoistic relative deprivation** refers to the sense of frustration an individual might feel when they feel deprived in comparison to others, **fraternal relative deprivation** is frustration experienced by group members when they consider their group is being unfairly treated with respect to other groups. Fraternal relative deprivation goes some way to explaining why East Germans revolted against their communist regime: they had a higher standard of living than some Western European countries, but a frustratingly lower one than their West German neighbours (Baron et al., 1992).

One possible source of such frustration today is the affluence depicted in television programmes and commercials. In cultures where television is a universal appliance, it helps turn absolute deprivation (lacking what others have) into relative deprivation (feeling deprived). Yang et al. (2008) analysed the effects of US television and its displays of affluence and consumption, upon South Korean and Indian people in their study. They found that it fostered feelings of relative deprivation for both the Korean and the Indian participants. They felt dissatisfied with what they have in comparison to what US people have.

But of course, to claim that all aggression is simply the result of frustration and/or relative deprivation is simply untrue. So social psychologists have examined other causes and explanations for aggressive behaviour.

Aggression as Learned Social Behaviour

Theories of aggression based on instinct and frustration assume that aggression arises from hostile urges which erupt from within the individual, which naturally 'push' aggression out into the social world from forces within. However, some social psychologists contend that the source of aggression may be located within the social world.

The Rewards of Aggression

By experience and by observing others, we learn that aggression often pays. People can learn the rewards of aggression. A child whose aggressive acts successfully intimidate other children is likely to become increasingly aggressive (Patterson et al., 1967). Aggression can be a positive emotion felt by athletes as they prepare for a competitive sporting event (Bali, 2015). In these cases, aggression is instrumental in achieving certain rewards.

The same is true of terrorist acts, which enable powerless people to garner widespread attention. 'The primary targets of suicide-bombing attacks are not those who are injured but those who are made to witness it through media coverage,' note Marsden and Attia (2005). Terrorism's purpose is, with the help of media amplification, to terrorize. Deprived of what Margaret Thatcher called 'the oxygen of publicity', terrorism would surely diminish, concluded Rubin (1986). It is like the 1970s' incidents of naked spectators 'streaking' onto football fields for a few seconds of television exposure. Once the networks decided to ignore the incidents, the phenomenon ended.

Observational Learning

Bandura (1997) proposed a **social learning theory** of aggression. He believes that we learn aggression not only by experiencing its rewards but also by observing others. As with many social behaviours, we acquire aggression by watching others act and noting the consequences.

social learning theory
Bandura's theory that we learn social behaviour by observing and imitating others, and then by selfregulating our own behaviour accordingly

See Chapter 5 for more on social learing theory.

In one of Bandura's experiments (Bandura et al., 1961) a pre-school child is put to work on an interesting art activity. An adult is in another part of the room, where there are Tinker Toys, a mallet and a big, inflated, Bobo doll. After a minute of working with the Tinker Toys, the adult gets up and for almost 10 minutes attacks the inflated doll. She pounds it with the mallet, kicks it and throws it, while yelling, 'Sock him in the nose . . . Knock him down . . . Kick him'.

After observing this outburst, the child is taken to a different room with many very attractive toys. But after 2 minutes the experimenter interrupts, saying these are her best toys and she must 'save them for the other children'. The frustrated child now goes into yet another room with various toys designed for aggressive and non-aggressive play, two of which are a Bobo doll and a mallet.

Children who were not exposed to the aggressive adult model did not display any aggressive play or talk. Although frustrated, they nevertheless played calmly. However, those who had observed the aggressive adult were more likely to pick up the mallet and lash out at the doll. Watching the adult's aggressive behaviour lowered their inhibitions. Furthermore, the children often reproduced the model's specific acts and said her words. Observing aggressive behaviour had both lowered their inhibitions and taught them ways to aggress. Bandura argued that modelling this behaviour was enough for a child to acquire and perform aggressive behaviour.

In a later study Bandura tested whether the consequences of aggressive actions had any effect on children's modelling behaviour. He found that if children witnessed the adult being punished as a consequence of their negative actions towards the Bobo doll, the children did not mimic their actions. However, if they saw the adult rewarded, then their behaviour was re-enacted by the child towards the doll.

Since Bandura's studies there have been some questions raised over his claims. One relatively early and insightful critique of Bandura comes from Hayes et al. (1980). They replicated Bandura's study, and examined the levels of aggression children displayed to a free-moving Bobo doll as compared to one with limited movement. They found that when the Bobo doll was free-moving, providing the child with a lot of visual stimulation, this produced and maintained high levels of aggression. Drewes (2008) reviews some further concerns that surround Bandura's studies, including the observation that Bobo dolls are 'meant to be hit', so it's unclear to what degree these are demonstrations of aggression. She also asks if behaviours that are allowed in a study are fair reflections of acts of aggression that occur in real life. That said, Drewes does not dispute that

Bandura's work gives us some of the strongest evidence about how aggressive behaviour is acquired and performed.

Bandura (1979) believes that everyday life exposes us to three main aggressive models: the family, one's subculture and, as we will see, the mass media. And mass media, which in our modern world includes social media.

In Bandura's famous experiment, children exposed to an adult's aggression against a Bobo doll became likely to reproduce the observed aggression.

SOURCE: ImageZoo/Alamy Stock Photo

Family

The role the family plays in the acquisition, maintenance and extinguishing of aggressive behaviour in children has been well documented within the research. While many children engage in physical aggression between the ages of 1 and 3 years, its subsequent decline is attributed to prosocial parenting and socialization by peers and teachers into non-violent ways of behaving. Andreas and Watson (2009) suggest that it is when children believe aggression is a justifiable and valuable tool in social interactions that they develop the habit of aggression. However, optimal family environments which exhibit low conflict and high levels of cohesion can reduce aggression in children. Borge et al. (2004) found aggression was more common in children looked after at home in 'high-risk' families than those in daycare. She concluded that high physical aggression in children was associated with low maternal education, high number of siblings, low socio-economic status and very poor family functioning.

Sadly, not all family environments are havens of peace. Physically aggressive children often have had physically punitive parents, who disciplined them with screaming, slapping and beating (Lei et al., 2018; McDowell & Parke, 2009; Patterson et al., 1982). These parents are likely to have parents who were themselves physically punitive (Bandura & Walters, 1959; Straus & Gelles, 1980). In English et al.'s (2009) study with a non-clinical US sample, they found that children's outcomes were better when they came from homes that had never experienced domestic violence, neglect or maltreatment. But they also observed that much of the aggression reported was verbal rather than physical.

The presence of a violent parent or guardian within the family has received particular attention from psychologists. Ireland and Smith (2009) reported a relationship between violent partner and homes during adolescence and adolescent conduct problems. The absence of a parent or guardian has also been studied for its role in aggression (e.g. Ängarne-Lindberg, 2009). Uphold-Carrier and Utz (2012) document the mental well-being of children and adults who experienced their parents going through a divorce. This **longitudinal study** conducted between 1995 and 2006, found that children and adults had a greater chance of being diagnosed with depression than children and adults whose parents had not divorced. The point raised by these studies is not that children from single-parent homes are doomed to become delinquent, dysfunctional or violent but, rather, nurtured by a caring parent or guardian and extended family, most children thrive.

longitudinal study research that involves repeat testing, questioning and/or observations of participants over a long or short period of time

It is often thought that deprived neighbourhoods can be a harmful place for children and adolescents to grow up in. Yet, Odgers et al. (2009) found quite the reverse. In deprived neighbourhoods with high social cohension and a willingness to intervene in family situations where it was thought to be for the greater good, these local communities with 'collective efficacy' were capable of reducing youth aggression and protecting children.

In fact it would seem that a complex array of factors inside and outside the family contribute to aggression in children. What this array of diverse research does alert us to is how difficult it is to produce simple cause-and-effect relationships to explain the role of the family in aggression. As Margolin et al. (2009) observed from their longitudinal study of children and adolescents, different forms of violence tend to co-occur within the lifetime of an individual. These can include marital aggression, parent–child abuse and community violence. To understand aggression and violence we need to look further than just the family, and to the broader social context in which it occurs.

Culture

The social environment outside the home also provides models and societal norms. In communities where 'macho' images are admired, aggression is readily transmitted to new generations. The violent subculture of teenage gangs, for instance, provides its junior members with aggressive models. Among Chicago adolescents who are otherwise equally at risk for violence, those who have observed gun violence are at doubled risk for violent behaviour (Bingenheimer et al., 2005). The phenomenon of 'happy slapping' began in the UK in 2004, but quickly spread to other European countries including Ireland, Sweden and Spain. Happy slapping describes physical assault which is usually carried out by young people on an unsuspecting victim. The event is recorded on a mobile phone and then uploaded onto social media and shared. This seems to give those involved a sense of social connection with one another, as well as a sense of identity. Social media, unfortunately in this case, provides the platform which facilitates and perpetuates the phenomenon as young people model the behaviour and others copy (Ching et al., 2011).

Tajfel (1974) pointed out that explanations of aggression must also consider the broader cultural context in which the individual is placed. For example, McGuckin and Lewis (2003, 2008) have found that the prevalence of bullying in schools in Northern Ireland, where violent conflict between political and religious groups has been rife, is much higher than incidences found in Wales, England, Scotland and Ireland. In China and Japan, where the crime rates are low, children are thought not to be aggressive from an early age. Aggressiveness is looked upon as childish and a sign of being immature. In East Asian interdependent cultures the feeling of shame is also important in contributing to the low crime rates. To violate the law is to bring shame on oneself and the whole family, and to be caught means that the family is 'losing face'. These cultural norms reduce offending in East Asian shame cultures.

In their study of homophobic aggression, Vincent et al. (2011) note cultural influence in the development of heterosexual masculinity. Culture brings with it traditional expectations about how men 'ought' to behave, think and feel, and what the values and norms of men 'should' be. These cultural influences may underlie antigay aggression. Feeling insecure in one's own heterosexual masculine identity, or what Vincent and his colleagues call 'masculine gender-role stress', can express itself in antigay anger and aggression. It is the fear of being excluded from heterosexual groups and mainstream values that may motivate some reportedly straight men to be aggressive towards gay men, as an explicit reaffirmation of their heterosexual masculine identity.

Stanley Schachter's (1959) two-factor theory of emotion suggests that emotions, such as anger and frustration, are rooted in the physiology of the individual but also in how people interpret the situation and what is considered to be culturally appropriate behaviour. For example, Vandello and Cohen (2003) note how the cultural scripts in Brazil surrounding matters of 'honour' mean that under certain circumstances domestic violence is an acceptable way of punishing female infidelity and restoring a male's honour. Mosquera et al. (2002) found differences in responses of Spanish and Dutch participants when confronted with threats and insults. Whereas Dutch participants became angered when the insults were directed towards their autonomy and individual achievements, Spanish participants displayed anger when their family honour was challenged. The researchers argue that these different patterns of responses mark the contrasting significance of concepts of individualism (in the Netherlands) and honour (in Spain) provoking aggression when they are challenged or undermined. So, there are cultural scripts that influence what is regarded as an appropriate emotion to have under certain circumstances and what is an acceptable expression of it.

But when will aggressive responses actually occur? Bandura (1979) contended that aggressive acts are motivated by a variety of aversive experiences – frustration, pain, insults (**Figure 8.3**). Such experiences arouse us emotionally. But whether we act aggressively depends on the consequences we anticipate. Aggression is most likely when we are aroused, and it seems safe, appropriate and rewarding to aggress.

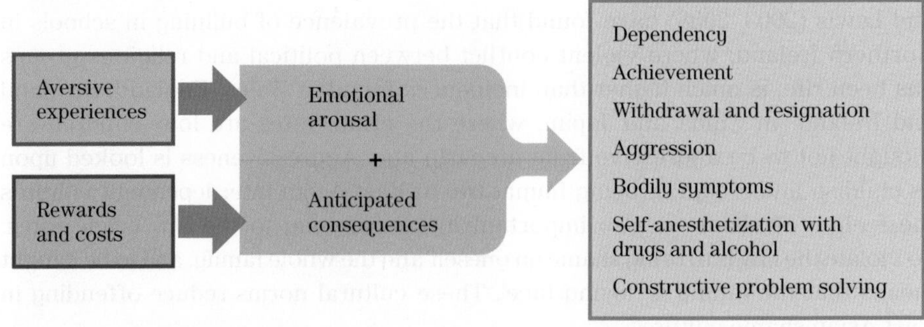

FIGURE 8.3 The social learning view of aggression

The emotional arousal stemming from an aversive experience motivates aggression. Whether aggression or some other response actually occurs depends on what consequences we have learned to expect.

SOURCE: Based on Bandura (1979, 1997).

Some Influences on Aggression

Under what conditions do we become aggressive? Here we examine some specific influences: aversive incidents, arousal, the media, hate and collective identity.

Aversive Incidents

Recipes for aggression often include some type of unpleasant experience: pain, uncomfortable heat, an attack or overcrowding.

Pain

Researcher Nathan Azrin (1967) was doing experiments with laboratory rats in a cage wired to deliver electric shocks to the animals' feet. Azrin wanted to know if switching off the shocks would reinforce two rats' positive interactions with each other. He planned to turn on the shock and then, once the rats approached each other, cut off the pain. To his great surprise, the experiment proved impossible. As soon as the rats felt pain, they attacked each other, before the experimenter could switch off the shock. The greater the shock (and pain) the more violent the attack. Of course today's ethical guidelines restrict researchers' use of painful stimuli.

Pain heightens aggressiveness in humans, too. Many of us can recall such a reaction after stubbing a toe or suffering a headache. Leonard Berkowitz and his associates demonstrated this by having students hold one hand in either lukewarm water or painfully cold water. Those whose hands were submerged in the cold water reported feeling more irritable and more annoyed, and they were more willing to blast another person with unpleasant noise. In view of such results, Berkowitz (1983, 1989, 1998, 2003) proposed that aversive stimulation rather than frustration is the basic trigger of hostile aggression. Frustration is certainly one important type of unpleasantness. But any aversive event, whether a dashed expectation, a personal insult or physical pain, can incite an emotional outburst. Even the torment of a depressed state increases the likelihood of hostile, aggressive behaviour.

Heat

People have theorized for centuries about the effect of climate on human action. Hippocrates (c. 460–377 BC) compared the civilized Greece of his day with the savagery in the region further north (what is now Germany and Switzerland) and decided that northern Europe's harsh climate was to blame. More than a millennium later, the English attributed their 'superior' culture to England's ideal climate. French thinkers proclaimed the same for France. Because climate remains relatively steady while cultural traits change over time, the climate theory of culture obviously has limited validity.

Pain attack. Frustrated after losing the first two rounds of his 1997 heavyweight championship fight with Evander Holyfield, and feeling pain from an accidental head butt, Mike Tyson reacts by biting off part of Holyfield's ear.
SOURCE: JEFF HAYNES/Getty Images

Temporary climate variations can, however, affect behaviour. Offensive odours, cigarette smoke and air pollution have all been linked with aggressive behaviour (for example, see Kristiansson et al., 2015). But the most studied environmental irritant is heat. Anderson (2001) reviews research conducted on the link between heat and aggression, and concludes that when the temperature is hot, so are our tempers! Feeling too hot can increase feelings of hostility and aggression. Anderson goes beyond the temperature in the room to consider the global temperature. As we experience climate change and the world becomes a warmer pace to live, there may well be a rise in violent crimes as a result.

Road rage has been found to be more likely in humid conditions.

SOURCE: ©StunningArt/Shutterstock

People certainly could be more irritable in hot, sticky weather. And in the laboratory, hot temperatures do increase arousal and hostile thoughts and feelings (DeWall & Bushman, 2009). There may be other contributing factors, though. Maybe hot summer evenings drive people into the streets. There, other group influence factors may well take over as group interactions increase. Then again, maybe there comes a point where stifling heat actually suppresses violence (Bell, 2005; Bushman et al., 2005b, 2005c; Cohn & Rotton, 2005).

Attacks

Being attacked or insulted by another is especially conducive to aggression. The **reciprocity principle** means we tend to react to a direct attack, which can of course lead to an escalation of violence. And there is some neuropsychological evidence to suggest that retaliatory aggression may offer a short-term reward. Chester and DeWall (2015) conducted an experiment which provoked their participants, but also used neuroimaging to see what was going on in their brains at the time of provocation. To provoke them, they engaged the participants in a fictitious competition with a fictitious opponent, and blasted the participant with a loud noise when they lost. As the event was rigged, participants seemed to 'lose' rather a lot and were subjected to a lot of annoying noise! They found increased activity in an area of the brain associated with reward (the nucles accumbens). The researchers concluded that the reason why we might engage in retaliation after being attacked is because it gives us a hedonic reward. We get a neural 'high' urging us to retaliate. However, we do have the capacity to control this urge and not retaliate.

reciprocity principle asserts that we should treat like with like. So responses to a positive action should be positive, whereas those to a negative action should be negative

So far we have seen that various aversive stimulations can arouse anger. Do other types of arousal, such as those that accompany exercise or sexual excitement, have a similar effect? Imagine that Lourdes, having just finished a stimulating short run, comes home to discover that her date for the evening has called and left word that he has made other plans. Will Lourdes more likely explode in fury after her run than if she discovered the same message after awakening from a nap? Or, since she has just exercised, will her aggressive tendencies be exorcised? To discover the answer, consider how we interpret and label our bodily states.

In a famous experiment, Schachter and Singer (1962) found we can experience an aroused bodily state in different ways. They aroused University of Minnesota men by injecting adrenaline. The drug produced body flushing, heart palpitation and more rapid breathing. When forewarned that the drug would produce those effects, the men felt little emotion, even when waiting with either a hostile or a euphoric person. Of course, they could readily attribute their bodily sensations to the drug. Schachter and Singer led another group of men to believe the drug produced no such side effects. Then they, too, were placed in the company of a hostile or a euphoric person. How did they feel and act? They were angered when with the hostile person, amused when with the person who was euphoric. The principle seemed to be: *a given state of bodily arousal feeds one emotion or another, depending on how the person interprets and labels the arousal.*

Returning to our example of Lourdes, although common sense might lead us to assume that Lourdes's run would have drained her aggressive tensions, enabling her to accept bad news calmly, studies show that *arousal feeds emotions.*

Sexual arousal and other forms of arousal, such as anger, can therefore amplify one another (Zillmann, 1989b). Love is never so passionate as after a fight or a fright. In the laboratory, erotic stimuli are more arousing to people who have just been frightened. Similarly, the arousal of a roller-coaster ride may spill over into romantic feeling for one's partner.

Research close-up

Harassment Online

Source: *Workman, M. (2010). A behaviourist perspective on corporate harassment online: Validation of a theoretical model of psychological motives.* Computers and Security, *29, 831–839.*

Introduction

Why do some people take to insulting and abusing others online? The phenomenon known as 'trolling' is receiving social psychological attention as its occurrence increases with the rise in our Internet use. So what motivates such cyber aggression? Perpetrators do not just abuse individuals, but also victimize companies. Cyber harassment can be dismissed as irritating, but at its worst can lead to considerable distress and in some cases suicide of their targeted victim. Corporate companies and their employees can be the targets of abuse, but also their employees can be the perpetrators. So what advice can be offered to businesses to prevent their employees from engaging in it?

This research draws on the findings of the Honeynet Project (2004), which identified six motives underlying individual attacks on computer systems. These included a need for entertainment, status-seeking, to promote a cause or ideology, a need for social acceptance, uncontrollable impulses and economic motives. Could motives such as these be behind cyber-attacks on individuals and corporations? The following six hypotheses were developed to predict who is likely to engage in trolling behaviour.

H1: People who are self-indulgent will be more likely to commit cyber harassment than people who are less self-indulgent.

H2: People who are more narcissistic will be more likely to commit cyber harassment than people who are less narcissistic.

H3: People who are more idealistic will be more likely to commit cyber harassment than people who are less idealistic.

H4: People who have a greater need for acceptance will be more likely to commit cyber harassment than people who have less need for acceptance.

H5: People who are less emotionally stable will be more likely to commit cyber harassment than people who are more emotionally stable.

H6: People who are more exploitative will be more likely to commit cyber harassment than people who are less exploitative.

Method

Of the 112 surveys given out to randomly sampled college students (mean age = 24 years), 54 were returned completed. The surveys consisted of a personality questionnaire to measure the characteristics of self-indulgence, narcissism, idealism, need for social acceptance, emotional stability and exploitation. This was a 7-point Likert scale that asked people how much they agreed with statements such as, 'My values are more important to me than offending people' (measure of idealism) and 'I seek to come out ahead no matter what' (a measure of exploitation). Participants were also asked whether they had ever written critical comments or something negative about people and companies on social media, which they knew was not true.

Results

A structured equation model was carried out. This provided correlations on the different personality measures (such as narcissism and self-indulgence) and having engaged in cyber harassment.

Statistical significance was found for all six hypotheses, and in the direction predicted by the research.

H1: People who are more self-indulgent are more likely to commit cyber harassment than people who are less self-indulgent ($\beta = -.55$, $p < .01$).

H2: People who are more narcissistic are more likely to commit cyber harassment than those who are less narcissistic ($\beta = -.33$, $p < .05$).

H3: People who are idealistic are more likely to commit cyber harassment than those who are less narcissistic ($\beta = -.25$, $p < .05$).

H4: People who have a greater need for acceptance are more likely to commit cyber harassment than those who have less need for acceptance ($\beta = -.46$, $p < .01$).

H5: People who are less emotionally stable are more likely to commit cyber harassment than those who are more emotionally stable ($\beta = -.27$, $p < .05$)

H6: People who are more exploitative are more likely to commit cyber harassment than people who are less exploitative ($\beta = .40$, $p < .01$).

Discussion

People who are more self-indulgent, narcissistic, idealistic, have high need for acceptance, emotionally unstable, and exploitative in their relationships with others are more likely to attack people and companies via social media, than those who are not strong on these personality characteristics.

So, what can companies do to discourage and prevent employees from getting involved in trolling, and protect themselves from becoming the victim of one? On a practical level companies can take out legal protection against incidences such as these happening. Software can be purchased that can trawl the Internet to detect any negative comments that have been posted up about a company. However, there are also things you can do to tackle perpetrators. These include ignoring the attacker in the hope that this will extinguish the behaviour. From a behaviourist perspective, this lack of reinforcement may be enough to stop the negative behaviour being continued. Alternatively, a company may wish to try and reason with an attacker to help him/her see the consequences of their behaviour. Finally, a company can punish the attacker either through corporate measures (such as dismissal) or via legal channels.

Critical Reflections

There are some limitations with this study. The truthfulness of participants' accounts may be compromised considering the sensitive and undesirable nature of the topic. The sample is also small in number (54) and young in age. This makes generalization to the wider population difficult. Moreover, these motives may not on their own explain trolling behaviour. There may be other attitudes involved, such as those about the legal system and fairness, which moderate trolling behaviour. We also have some potential discrepancy between individuals about what constitutes negative and critical comments. Furthermore, a study such as this does not consider any social factors involved in cyber-harassment including the context in which it is done. It assumes cyber-harassment is done by individuals.

Perhaps personality characteristics go some way to explaining cyber-harassment and targeted attacks on individuals and companies, but arguably other more social factors are involved.

A frustrating, hot or insulting situation heightens arousal. When it does, the arousal, combined with hostile thoughts and feelings, may form a recipe for aggressive behaviour (**Figure 8.4**).

Aggression Cues: the Influence of the Environment

As we noted when considering the frustration-aggression hypothesis, violence is more likely when aggressive cues in the environment release pent-up anger. Berkowitz (1968, 1981, 1995) and others have found that the sight of a weapon is such a cue. In one experiment, children who had just played with toy guns became more willing to knock down another child's blocks. In another classic study, angered University of Wisconsin men gave more electric shocks to their tormenter when a rifle and a revolver (supposedly left over from a previous experiment) were nearby than when badminton rackets had been left behind (Berkowitz & LePage, 1967). What's within sight is within mind. This is especially so when a weapon is perceived as an instrument of violence rather than a recreational item. So the labels and evaluative meanings we give people and objects influence our behaviour. For hunters, for example, seeing a hunting rifle does not prime aggressive thoughts, though it does for non-hunters (Bartholow et al., 2004). More recently, research has demonstrated that playing violent video games leads to aggressive thoughts and actions (Anderson et al., 2010; Bösche, 2010; Krahé & Busching, 2013). We will return to this later in the chapter.

Berkowitz notes how in the USA, a country with some 200 million privately owned guns, half of all murders are committed with handguns, and that handguns in homes are far more likely to kill household members than intruders. 'Guns not only permit violence,' he reported, 'they can stimulate it as well. The finger pulls the trigger, but the trigger may also be pulling the finger.' Perhaps this is echoed in the UK Government statistics which show a 6 per cent rise in knife crime between 2017 and 2018.

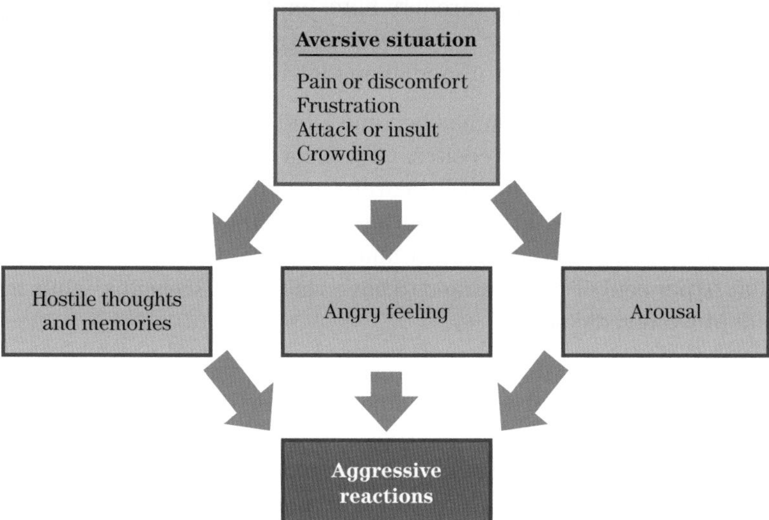

FIGURE 8.4 Elements of hostile aggression
An aversive situation can trigger aggression by provoking hostile cognitions, hostile feelings and arousal. These reactions make us more likely to perceive harmful intent and to react aggressively.
SOURCE: Simplified from Anderson et al. (1995).

Between 1995 and 2005, the UK saw a 30 per cent rise in the number of people admitted to hospital as a result of being attacked with a knife or other sharp object (Maxwell et al., 2007). Official UK statistics report increases in young people, especially teenage boys, carrying knives (Hern, Glazebrook, & Beckett, 2005). However, once again we need to be careful about correlation not necessarily meaning causation. Some writers have argued that a 'fear culture' is created by the government and media. In the UK this 'fear culture' has been described as a dramatizing of knife-crime culture to promote new policies on tough policing, whilst sidelining the causes of youth crime (Squires, 2009). Hence, the cues in the environment may not simply be the presence of the gun or the knife, but can extend to the social context in which we live.

Media Influences: Pornography and Sexual Violence

As we've already seen, Bandura makes the claim that the mass media is an influential model for aggressive behaviour. Berkowitz's study, and the work of Schachter, illustrates how we may take cues from the environment in interpreting states of arousal, and express our behaviour in a way that seems appropriate.

Sadly, aggression in the form of violent crime seems to be on the rise. As the numbers of arrests for violent crime have increased across Europe and the USA since the 1960s, we may attribute some of this to better techniques of detection, but we might also wonder what has prompted such increases in aggressive behaviour. What social forces caused the mushrooming violence? Might the answer partially lie in the media's increasing modelling of unrestrained sexuality and violence, such that these acts become acceptable, and the individual becomes desensitized to their effects?

Increased rates of criminal violence, including sexual coercion, coincided with the increased availability of violent and sexual material in the media that started during the 'sexual revolution' of the 1960s. Is the historical correlation a coincidence? To find out, researchers have explored the social consequences of pornography (which *Webster's* defines as erotic depictions intended to excite sexual arousal) and the effects of modelling violence in movies and on television.

In many countries pornography has become a big business thanks to the billions a year spent on subscription websites, as well as television channels, phone sex hotlines and magazines (National Research Council, 2002; Rich, 2001; Schlosser, 2003). Gender differences in the reported use of Internet sex sites have been widely suggested. In a survey of 1845 Chinese college students, Hong et al. (2007) found that 10 per cent of men claimed to have visited sex websites, while less than 1 per cent of women did so.

Social psychological research on pornography has focused mostly on depictions of sexual violence. A typical sexually violent episode finds a man forcing himself upon a woman. She at first resists and tries to fight off her attacker. Gradually she becomes sexually aroused, and her resistance melts. By the end she is in ecstasy, pleading for more. We have all viewed or read non-pornographic versions of this sequence: she resists, he persists. Dashing man grabs and forcibly kisses protesting woman. Within moments, the arms that were pushing him away are clutching him tight, her resistance overwhelmed by her unleashed passion. In *Gone with the Wind*, Scarlett O'Hara is carried to bed protesting and kicking, and wakes up singing.

Social psychologists report that viewing such fictional scenes of a man overpowering and arousing a woman can distort one's perceptions of how women actually respond to sexual coercion and increase men's aggression against women, at least in laboratory settings.

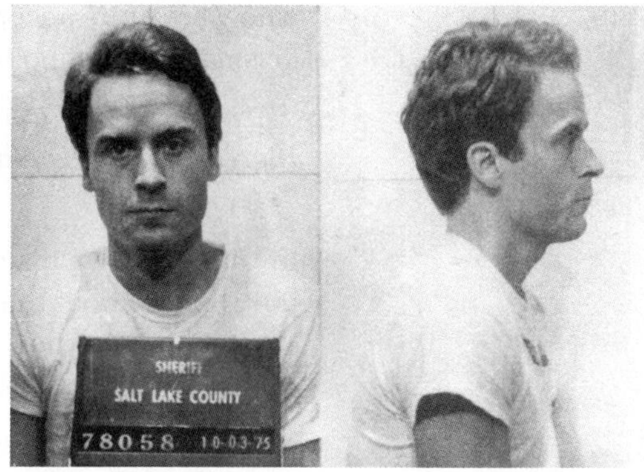

Did Ted Bundy's (1989) comments on the eve of his execution for a series of rape-murders acknowledge pornography's toll or make it a handy excuse? 'The most damaging kinds of pornography [involve] sexual violence. Like an addiction, you keep craving something that is harder, harder, something which, which gives you a greater sense of excitement. Until you reach a point where the pornography only goes so far, you reach that jumping off point where you begin to wonder if maybe actually doing it would give you that which is beyond just reading it or looking at it.'

SOURCE: ©GL Archive/Alamy Stock Photo

Distorted Perceptions of Sexual Reality

In 2006 Tarana Burke coined the term 'me too' to highlight the occurrence of sexual harassment experienced by women. In October 2017, the actress Alyssa Milano took the campaign to another level, She brought the #metoo campaign to the world via social media, encouraging women to open up about their experiences, and in doing so highlighted the global prevalence of sexual harassment, usually by men against women. That campaign was not without criticism. Some thought it unfairly depicted sexual harassment as something men do to women and demonized them. In their study of acceptance of the #metoo campaign, Kunst et al. (2019) discovered that men were more likely to regard it as harmful rather than helpful. However, this study also found greater levels of hostile sexism and acceptance of the rape myth by men than women. In a rather alarming survey, the Fawcett Society report (Fawcett Society, 2017) shows that in the UK, 38 per cent of men and 34 per cent of women believe a woman wearing a short skirt, who is drunk, and out late at night, is partly or fully to blame for being sexually assaulted.

So where does the 'rape myth' – that some women would welcome sexual assault – come from? Does viewing sexual violence reinforce the myth that 'no doesn't really mean no'? To find out, Kahlor and Eastin (2011) surveyed over 2,000 men and women in the US about their television viewing habits and asked them to complete a Rape Myth questionnaire. Their results show that television consumption is associated with rape myth acceptance. The researchers argue that US television transmits cultural norms where sexual violence against women is acceptable. This supports what Gerbner and Gross (1976) called the **cultivation hypothesis**. This predicts that television consumption is associated with the belief that it reflects reality. The more television you watch, the more you believe it accurately portrays the real world. And this arguably extends to video games which portray sexual violence against women. Fox and Potocki (2016) found a positive relationship between playing these kinds of video games, sexism, and rape myth acceptance. The more you play, the more you accept sexual violence against women.

cultivation hypothesis the belief that television consumption is associated with the belief it reflects the real-world

Other studies confirm that exposure to pornography increases acceptance of the rape myth (Oddone-Paolucci et al., 2000; Seabrook et al., 2019). For example, Wei et al. (2010) asked 1,688 Taiwanese young people aged 14–21 years about their Internet habits, in particular their pornography viewing habits. Just under half of the sample admitted to viewing pornographic material on the Internet. They were also given questionnaires which included attitudes and behaviours regarding sexual attraction, and also a rape myth questionnaire. The researchers found that those participants who viewed the most pornographic material were also the ones who were more accepting of permissible sexual attitudes and behaviours (such as kissing and holding hands) but also more accepting of the rape myth.

'Pornography that portrays sexual aggression as pleasurable for the victim increases the acceptance of the use of coercion in sexual relations.'
(Koop, 1987)

In Chapter 2 we discuss the ecological validity such experiments have. What do they tell us about the real world? The extent to which these can be translated into explanations of how and why sexual violence occurs remains a topic of debate within social psychology.

Aggression against Women: Femicide

The World Health Organization (WHO) states that: 'Femicide is generally understood to involve the intentional murder of women because they are women, but broader definitions include any killings of women or girls' (WHO, 2012). This definition includes honor killings, where women are murdered for deviating from cultural norms and values (e.g. becoming pregnant outside of marriage) and have brought shame upon the family. According to the United Nations, 87,000 women were intentionally killed in 2017. Of that number, 50,000 were murdered by their partner or a family member (UNODC, 2018). In their review of femicides in Australia in 2014, Cullen et al. (2018) concluded that women were most vulnerable in their own home and from their own partner. The UN report concludes that: 'women continue to bear the heaviest burden of lethal victimization as a result of gender stereotypes and inequality' (p. 11).

What factors lead to such fatal aggression towards women? In a review of femicide of Ethiopian immigrant women resident in Israel and existing international research into the topic, Edlestein (2018) suggests three triggers: sexual jealousy, willingness of the woman to leave her partner, and formal complaints she made about the abuse. Edelstein emphasizes the importance of understanding the social context in which a woman is killed as well as the characteristics of her self and her murderer. In line with research conducted on femicide in Western countries, Edelstein found that some of the features common to the men responsible were unemployment, low-status, and poor social integration (e.g. see Freysteinsdóttir's, 2018, work on femicide in Iceland). However, as Ethiopian immigrant women, and therefore a minority group within Israel, other sociocultural factors come into play here. Edelstein found that these women were often more successful in integrating into Israeli social life than their male partner. They had become **acculturated**. They were not only exposed to values which challenged their traditional gender roles, such as women going out to work to earn and achieving financial independence, and the unacceptability of

acculturated the process of adapting to another culture

TABLE 8.1 The number of men and women affected by homicide, worldwide

Although women and girls account for a far smaller share of total homicides than men, they bear by far the greatest burden of intimate partner/family-related homicide, and intimate partner homicide.

	Total Homicide	Intimate partner/ family-related homicide	Intimate partner/ homicide
Men	80%	36%	18%
Women	20%	64%	82%

SOURCE: UNODC (2018)

partner violence, but they were adapting to them. These women had come from a patriarchal culture in Ethiopia, to a multicultural, vibrant, and very modern Israel. More than half of the Ethiopian women who had been killed, had been willing to leave their partners. Some had formally reported the abuse they were experiencing from their partners. Hence, they had transgressed the norms and values of the patriarchal culture they had come from. Similar findings are apparent in Tosun Altınöz et al.'s (2018) study of the rising trend in femicide in Turkey. There, migration was the main factor behind femicide. Men reported the reason for killing women as being about honour and exerting dominance over their female partner. Edelstein (2018) makes the important point that when we try to understand aggression towards women the characteristics of the perpetrator and the victim cannot be disentangled from the sociocultural context in which it occurred.

Media Influences: Television

We have seen that watching an aggressive model attack a Bobo doll can unleash children's aggressive urges and teach them new ways to aggress. And we have seen that, after viewing movies depicting sexual violence, many angry men will act more violently towards women. Does everyday television viewing have any similar effects?

Although very recent data are scarce (funding for media monitoring waned after the early 1990s), these facts about television watching remain: today, in much of the industrialized world, nearly all households (99.2 per cent in Australia, for example) have a television set, more than those that have telephones (Trewin, 2001). With MTV in 140 countries and CNN spanning the globe, television is creating a global culture (Aksoy & Robins, 2002; Gundersen, 2001).

How much violence is depicted on television varies from survey to survey. Perhaps what is more important is not how much violence is portrayed, but what its effects are on our behaviour. For example, does prime-time crime stimulate the behaviour it depicts? Or, as viewers vicariously participate in aggressive acts, do the shows drain off aggressive energy? The latter idea, a variation on the **catharsis** hypothesis, maintains that watching violent drama enables people to release their pent-up hostilities. For example, Feshbach and Singer (1971) in their classic study of 9- to 15-year-old boys from underprivileged backgrounds and boarding schools, found that those who observed a diet of aggressive television displayed fewer acts of hostility (e.g. arguments and fights) than those who had watched non-aggressive programmes such as comedy shows. Defenders of the media cite this theory frequently and remind us that violence pre-dates television. However, more recently Anderson et al. (2003) found that listening to songs with aggressive lyrics led to an increase in violent thoughts. This research refutes the catharsis hypothesis. The researchers suggest that there is little reason to imagine why listening to violent songs is any different to watching violent television, in their effects on aggressive behaviour. In his review of experimental studies on television violence, violent video games and aggressive behaviour, Gentile (2013) concludes that the vast majority of it does not find support for the catharsis hypothesis. In fact, most of it finds that viewing television violence and playing violent video games increases aggressive behaviour. He argues: 'We do not become less likely to learn something by practicing it, reading it, or seeing it one more time. Every repetition increases learning' (p. 506).

catharsis emotional cleansing. In psychodynamic theory this is the process of expressing repressed emotions, so these no longer cause neurotic problems

'One of television's great contributions is that it brought murder back into the home where it belongs. Seeing a murder on television can be good therapy. It can help work off one's antagonisms.'
Alfred Hitchcock

Television's Effects on Behaviour

Correlating Television Viewing and Behaviour

Early social psychological research investigating the effects of television violence on behaviour typically adopted correlational designs. A trailblazer for this work is Eron (1963), who conducted a well-known longitudinal study (sometimes referred to as the Rip Van Winkle Study) into the television viewing habits of 875 third graders (8–9 years old) based in New York. The design was simple. Children were asked to rate their three favourite television shows. The amount of violence considered to be present within these shows and how long the child spent watching them, was assessed by the child's parents and was then correlated with indicators of the children's aggressive behaviour. Eron concluded that the more antisocial their favourite television programmes were, the more antisocial the child was. A decade later, Eron et al. (1972) followed up 427 of his original sample of children. They were now teenagers (Grade 13). Interestingly Eron and his colleagues found that the watching violent television correlated with aggression in boys, but not girls. In fact the boys had become more aggressive as they had got older, and their appetite for aggressive television had increased. This study and others like it have become indicative of a now large social psychological field of work on the subject that tends to conclude: the more violent the content of the child's television viewing, the more aggressive the child (Anderson et al., 2015; Bushman & Huesmann, 2006; Gentile et al., 2011).

However, considering Eron's studies, we can reasonably question this conclusion. Firstly, Eron's measure of how aggressive a child was, was taken from reports by peers and teachers. Moreover, the amount of television a child watched and its violent content was assessed by the child's parents. There are some issues with this. As we noted at the start of this chapter, how we define 'aggression' varies both within academia and outside of it, and it has implications for how we measure it. Hence, parents' and peers' definitions of what constitutes an aggressive act on the part of the child being studied becomes a crucial yet highly subjective part of the experiment. This brings into question the **validity** of the study. Secondly, Eron offered a very reasonable explanation as to why girls display less aggression than boys, and did not report watching violent television programmes. They were fulfilling a gender stereotype of what girls should and should not do, in US society at the time. Being aggressive is not what girls did. However, this has implications for Eron's study. As we've already discussed in this chapter, how girls display aggression can be more indirect and subtle than boys (e.g. bad-mouthing someone). So there's a chance it gets missed by observers (parents and peers), or it gets dismissed as 'not really being aggression'. If Eron isn't expecting the girls to be aggressive, then probably neither are those reporting on their behaviour. Consequently there is a danger that girls' aggression goes under-reported, and arguably boys' aggression may be over-reported. In an attempt to stop indirect aggression from being empirically overlooked Coyne and Archer (2004) examined its presence and effect. They found that in a content-analytic study of over 200 hours of television programmes watched by British adolescents,

validity is the extent to which a psychological study or experiment measures what it sets out to measure

92 per cent of these programmes contained indirect aggression. Moreover, the indirect aggressor was most likely to be an attractive female who was rewarded in some way for her actions. They discovered that, of 347 British female teenagers studied, those who engaged in indirect aggression were more likely to watch television that contained indirect aggressive acts than their non-aggressive counterparts.

However, in these correlational studies, the cause–effect relation could also work in the opposite direction. Maybe aggressive children prefer aggressive programmes. Or maybe some underlying third factor, such as lower intelligence, predisposes some children to prefer both aggressive programmes and aggressive behaviour. This is what researchers have sometimes called the 'third hidden factor'. As we emphasize throughout this book, correlation does not mean causation.

Researchers have developed ways to test the 'hidden third factor' explanation by statistically pulling out the influence of some of these possible factors (Ferguson & Savage, 2012). For example, back in the 1970s Belson (1978; Muson, 1978) studied 1,565 London boys. Compared with those who watched little violence, those who watched a great deal (especially realistic rather than cartoon violence) admitted to 50 per cent more violent acts during the preceding 6 months (for example, vandalizing a public telephone). In addition, Belson also examined 22 likely third factors, such as family size. The 'heavy violence' and 'light violence' viewers still differed after the researchers equated them with respect to potential third factors. So Belson surmised that the heavy viewers were indeed more violent *because* of their television exposure.

More recently, Miller et al. (2012) studied the affect exposure to television violence had on young children aged 3–5 years. But they also studied a range of other 'hidden third' factors which might be related to aggressive behaviour. This included demographic information on the child and their family, such as age, ethnicity, parents' occupation, and household income. It also measured the children's exposure to community violence and disorder, exposure to domestic violence between their mother and her intimate partner, any physical aggression directed at the children (such as slapping), and any aggression the children had shown towards their siblings, and maternal depression. In their study of 213 children and their mothers, 150 of these children had at least one sibling. Miller and her team found that the amount of television violence the children watched was related to the aggressive behaviour they displayed towards their siblings. This was the case even when all other factors were removed from the analysis. However, maternal depression was also related to aggressive behaviour. Furthermore, those children who had been exposed to physical aggression from their father *and* had witnessed community violence were also more likely to be aggressive than those children who had not. Taken separately, community violence, physical aggression from a parent, and domestic violence between the mother and her intimate partner, were not related to aggression.

This research might seem conclusive, but we need to be cautious about over-interpreting the results. As criminologist Joanne Savage point outs in a series of reviews of the existing literature, there is no clear relationship between TV violence and criminal behaviour. Furthermore, trying to capture whether television violence causes aggression, including criminal behaviour, is fraught with methodological challenges which arguably prevent any firm conclusions (2004, 2008; Savage & Yancey, 2008; Ferguson & Savage, 2012).

Television Viewing Experiments

The Bobo doll experiments by Bandura and Walters (1963) sometimes had young children view the adult pounding the inflated doll on film instead of observing it live – with much the same effect. Then Berkowitz and Geen (1966) found that angered college students who viewed a violent film acted more aggressively than did similarly angered students who viewed non-aggressive films. These laboratory experiments, coupled with growing public concern, seemed to confirm that viewing violence amplifies aggression (C. A. Anderson et al., 2003).

For example, research teams led by Ross Parke (1977) in the USA and Jacques Leyens (1975) in Belgium showed institutionalized American and Belgian delinquent boys a series of either aggressive or non-aggressive commercial films. Their consistent finding: 'Exposure to movie violence . . . led to an increase in viewer aggression.' Compared with the week preceding the film series, physical attacks increased sharply in cottages where boys were viewing violent films. Zillmann and Weaver (1999) similarly exposed men and women, on four consecutive days, to violent or non-violent feature films. When participating in a different project on the fifth day, those exposed to the violent films were more hostile to the research assistant. Likewise, Linder and Gentile (2009) found that teachers reported higher levels of aggression in students who had watched televised physical and verbal aggression than those who had not. Furthermore, they found that the television industry's age-based rating system for the coding of material was not a valid reflection of its aggressive content.

The aggression provoked in these experiments is not assault and battery; it is more on the scale of a shove in the lunch queue, a cruel comment, a threatening gesture. Nevertheless, the convergence of evidence is striking. All in all, conclude researchers Bushman and Anderson (2001), violence viewing's effect on aggression surpasses the effect of passive smoking on lung cancer, calcium intake on bone mass, and homework on academic achievement. As with smoking and cancer, not everyone shows the effect – other factors matter as well. Media executives have discounted the evidence. But the evidence is now 'overwhelming', say Bushman and Anderson: 'Exposure to media violence causes significant increases in aggression.' The research base is large, the methods diverse and the overall findings consistent (C. A. Anderson et al., 2003): 'Our in-depth review . . . reveals unequivocal evidence that exposure to media violence can increase the likelihood of aggressive and violent behaviour in both immediate and long-term contexts.'

Why Does Television Viewing Affect Behaviour?

Given the convergence of correlational and experimental evidence, researchers have explored *why* viewing violence has this effect. Consider three possibilities:

1 Arousal. This possibility suggests that it is not the violent content that causes social violence but the *arousal* it produces. As we noted earlier, arousal tends to spill over: one type of arousal energizes other behaviours.

2 Disinhibition. This possibility suggests that watching television violence frequently legitimizes it. It becomes normal. Viewing violence primes the viewer for aggressive behaviour by activating violence-related thoughts. In Bandura's experiment, the adult's punching of the Bobo doll seemed to make those outbursts legitimate and to lower the children's inhibitions.

3 Imitation. Media portrayals also evoke imitation. The children in Bandura's experiments re-enacted the specific behaviours they had witnessed. The commercial television industry is hard-pressed to dispute that television leads viewers to imitate what they have seen: its advertisers model consumption. Are media executives right, however, to argue that television merely holds a mirror to a violent society?

But there is good news here, too. If the ways of relating and problem solving modelled on television do trigger imitation, especially among young viewers, then television modelling of **prosocial behaviour** should be socially beneficial.

prosocial behaviour positive, constructive, helpful social behaviour; the opposite of antisocial behaviour

Television's Effects on Thinking

We have focused on television's effect on behaviour, but researchers have also examined the cognitive effects of viewing violence: does prolonged viewing desensitize us to cruelty? Does it give us mental scripts for how to act? Does it distort our perceptions of reality? Does it prime aggressive thoughts?

Desensitization

Repeat an emotion-arousing stimulus, such as an obscene word, over and over and the emotional response will 'extinguish'. After witnessing thousands of acts of cruelty, there is good reason to expect a similar emotional numbing (Bushman & Anderson, 2009; Ng-Mak et al., 2004). Cline et al. (1973) observed when they measured the physiological arousal of 121 Utah boys who watched a brutal boxing match that compared with boys who watched little television, the responses of those who watched habitually were more a shrug than a concern.

Of course, these boys might differ in ways other than television viewing. But in experiments on the effects of viewing sexual violence, similar desensitization – a sort of psychic numbness – occurs among young men who view 'slasher' films. Moreover, classic experiments by Drabman and Thomas (1974, 1975, 1976) confirmed that such viewing breeds a more blasé reaction when later viewing a brawl or observing two children fighting. In one survey of 5,456 middle-school students, exposure to movies with brutality was widespread (Sargent et al., 2002). Two-thirds had seen *Scream*. Teenagers 'appear to have become considerably more desensitized to graphic depictions of violence and sex than their parents were at their age', concludes Gallup researcher Mazzuca (2002).

However, it isn't just exposure to violent movies children experience, but in some parts of the world, it is also civil conflict and war. Tarabah and her colleagues (2016) examined whether exposure to violence, both from the television and as a result of war, had desensitized children in Lebanon. A total of 219 children from schools in Beirut, aged 8–12 years were randomly recruited to obtain a representative sample of children in the area. The children were asked to complete three questionnaires. The first asked them about their exposure to television violence. The second asked about their exposure to real-world conflict and war in Lebanon (in particular the Israeli-Lebanese war of 2006). The third asked them about their attitudes towards violence. This third questionnaire was a measure of desensitization to violence. What the researchers found makes for sobering reading. Most of these children had witnessed horrific violence on the streets of Lebanon as a result of war. And many, especially the older children, were regularly watching violent films on the television. High exposure to real-world violence and television violence did indeed 'cognitively and emotionally'

(p. 15) desensitize these children towards violence more generally. They were more accepting of it. Tarabah and her team warn that such desensitization has implications for the likelihood of these children engaging in violent behaviour, as they become somewhat immune to social and psychological forces which would otherwise restrain them.

The desensitizing effect of violent television and video games has received support from the neurosciences. Bartholow et al. (2006) show how watching violent video games leads to decreased brain activity in an area which should be highly activated when exposed to violence, and which is a motivator to avoid it. They argue that this neurological dampening down of activity, can have serious implications for individuals' aggressive behaviour.

Social Scripts and Social Representations

When we find ourselves in new situations, uncertain how to act, we rely on **social scripts** ('schemas'), or what Serge Moscovici termed 'social representations' (see Chapter 4) – which are culturally provided mental instructions for how to act. These are acquired through experience of the social world and in interactions with others. In the case of television viewing of so many action films, youngsters may acquire a script that is played when they face real-life conflicts. Challenged, they may 'act like a man' by intimidating or eliminating the threat. Likewise, after viewing multiple sexual innuendos and acts in most prime-time television hours – mostly involving impulsive or short-term relationships – youths may acquire sexual scripts they later enact in real-life relationships (Kunkel et al., 2001; Sapolsky & Tabarlet, 1991). Thus, the more sexual content that adolescents view (even when controlling for other predictors of early sexual activity), the more likely they are to perceive their peers as sexually active, to develop sexually permissive attitudes, and to experience early intercourse (Escobar-Chaves et al., 2005; Martino et al., 2005).

social scripts culturally provided mental instructions for how to act in various situations

Cognitive Priming

Some evidence also reveals that watching violent videos primes networks of aggressive-related ideas (Bushman, 1998; Kirsh et al., 2005). After viewing violence, people offer more hostile explanations for others' behaviour (was the shove intentional?). They interpret spoken homonyms with the more aggressive meaning (interpreting 'punch' as a hit rather than a drink). And they recognize aggressive words more quickly. That, argues Berkowitz (1984) is why we should be alert to the effects that watching televised violence can have on behaviour. Violent media content triggers networks of aggressive thoughts, feelings and ideas, which can then translate into aggressive action.

A recent demonstration of the priming effect comes from the work of Coyne et al. (2012). They asked their participants to watch a movie. Unknown to the participants, they had been randomly assigned to one of three conditions. Either they watched a movie containing physical aggression, relational aggression, or no aggression at all. Relational aggression refers to indirect aggression, where an individual's social relationships are targeted through acts such as spreading malicious gossip about that individual, and socially excluding them from a friendship group. After watching the movie, participants completed the emotional Stroop test. You may be familiar with original versions of the **Stroop test**. In this version, aggressive and non-aggressive words as well as emotion words (negative, positive and neutral) are presented to the

Stroop test a test which measures how long it takes a participant to state the colour a word is presented in, where the word is either congruent with the colour, or incongruent. For example, the word 'pink' presented in a pink colour should elicit a quick response (pink). However the word 'pink' presented in the colour blue, will probably elicit a slower response (blue) participant in a variety of colours. The participant is asked to state the colour the word is presented in, not the word itself. It is thought that the longer the participant takes to produce the name of the colour, the more they are processing the word (which is then inhibiting the colour response). What Coyne and her team discovered was that those participants who had watched the physical aggression or relational aggression video were slower to report the colour of negative emotion and aggressive words on the emotional Stroop test than those participants who had viewed the no-aggression video. Why? Well it is argued that for these participants, a network of thoughts, feelings and acts associated with violence had been primed by the video. So when faced with these negative emotional and aggressive words in the Stroop task, they were processing the word in detail.

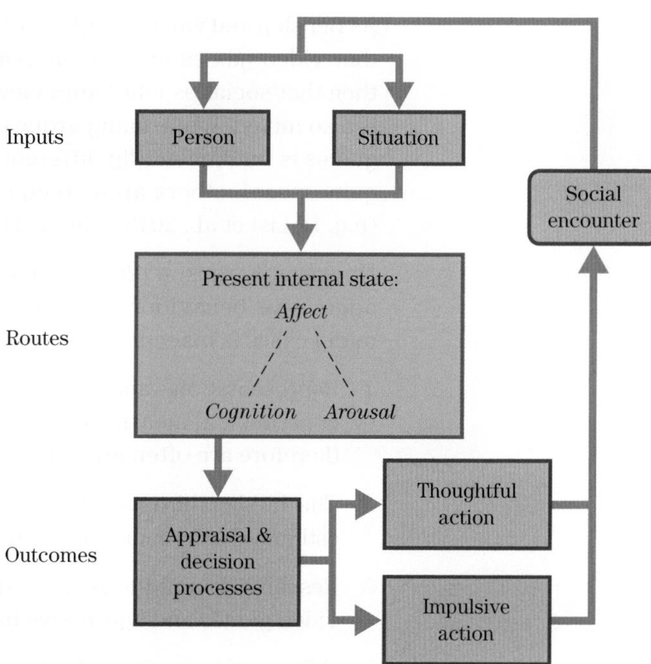

FIGURE 8.5 General Aggression Model
SOURCE: Anderson and Bushman (2002)

Coyne et al. (2012) interpret their results as offering support for the General Aggression Model (GAM), which was founded by Anderson and Bushman (2002). This model represents an attempt to unify the various theories of aggression, including the work of Bandura, Berkowitz, and Zillman. It also tries to incorporate personal and situational explanations for aggression including personality, sex, attitudes, frustration, pain, heat, alcohol and other drugs, aggressive cues in the environment. GAM also incorporates cognitive processes into its unifying model, such as mood, emotion and memory. In doing so, the GAM recognizes that all of these factors contribute in some way to explaining and predicting aggressive behaviour, but also recognizes that none of them can fully explain aggressive behaviour on their own.

Perhaps television's biggest effect relates not to its quality but to its quantity. Television annually replaces in people's lives a thousand or more hours of other activities. If, like most others, you have spent a thousand-plus hours per year watching television, think how you might have used that time if there were no television. What difference would that have made in who you are today? In seeking to explain the post-1960 decline in civic activities and organizational memberships, Putnam (2000) reported that every added hour a day spent watching television competes with civic participation. Television steals time from club meetings, volunteering, congregational activities and political engagement.

Media Influences: Video Games

Researchers have shifted their attention to video games, which have exploded in popularity and are exploding with increasing brutality. Since the first video game in 1972, we have moved from electronic ping-pong to splatter games (Anderson, 2004; Gentile & Anderson, 2003). Today's mass-murder simulators are not obscure games.

As Bensley and van Eenwyk (2001) have observed, society's attitudes on the impact that video games have on individuals is mixed. It perhaps shouldn't surprise us then that social psychology's view of their potential harm or educational benefits is also mixed. While many argue the kind of aggression displayed in playing video games is fundamentally different to that shown in real life (as no one gets hurt in gamespace), others argue they can foster violent thoughts, feelings and actions (e.g. DeLisi et al., 2013; Sherry, 2001).

However, Ferguson (2010) argues that the link between violent video games and aggressive behaviour has been exaggerated within the scientific arena, and in many cases is inaccurate. He suggests several reasons for this. These are:

1 Representations and definitions of 'aggression' in the video game and in the experimental measures do not reflect real-world acts of aggression. The studies therefore are often invalid.

2 The 'hidden third variable' (such as sex, history of violence, etc.) is often underestimated in accounting for aggressive behaviour.

3 Researchers only look at, and cite, work which shows a link between violent video games and aggressive behaviour. Work which disputes this, is ignored.

4 Editors of journals prefer to publish work which shows a relationship between video-game violence and aggression.

5 Many of the effect sizes in the experimental studies, whilst statistically significant, are also very small.

6 Aggression is always assumed to be undesirable, but it can have adaptive advantages (as noted by evolutionary psychologists).

7 Measures of aggression vary widely from study to study, meaning there is no standardized measure of it.

8 There is no robust evidence that playing violent video games causes violent crimes.

9 What is considered to be 'evidence' of a causal relationship between video-game playing and aggressive behaviour is exaggerated, and often inaccurate.

Ferguson argues that more intellectual attention needs to be paid to the positive aspects of violent video games. These include their role in increasing visuospatial capacity. He cites a range of research that notes how playing video games has been shown to enhance players' cognitive processes such as scanning the environment for relevant information, selection of relevant material, the ability to mentally manipulate and rotate objects in space and time, memory, and attention. Ferguson also states that the expansion of online video games to facilitate multiple players from all over the world, to play the same game together, and connect with each other, delivers an important social function of video games. He also suggests violent video games could be used as an educational platform to promote prosocial messages. However, whilst educational research shows that there are many benefits from video games, some researchers remain unconvinced. Gentile and Anderson (2003, p. 146) argue that 'video games are excellent teaching tools', but 'If health video games can successfully teach health behaviours, and flight simulator video games can teach people how to fly, then what should we expect violent murder-simulating games to teach?'

Effects of the Games Children Play

'There is absolutely no evidence, none, that playing a violent game leads to aggressive behaviour', contended Doug Lowenstein (2000), president of the Interactive Digital Software Association. Gentile and Anderson (2003) nevertheless offer some reasons why violent game playing *might* have a more toxic effect than watching violent television. With game playing, players:

- identify with, and play the role of, a violent character
- actively rehearse violence, not just passively watch it
- engage in the whole sequence of enacting violence – selecting victims, acquiring weapons and ammunition, stalking the victim, aiming the weapon, pulling the trigger
- are engaged with continual violence and threats of attack
- repeat violent behaviours over and over
- are rewarded for effective aggression.

For such reasons, military organizations often prepare soldiers to fire in combat (which many in the Second World War reportedly were hesitant to do) by engaging them with attack-simulation games. Craig Anderson (2003, 2004; Anderson et al., 2004) offers statistical digests of three dozen available studies that reveal five consistent effects. Playing violent video games, more than playing non-violent games:

1. *increases arousal.* Heart rate and blood pressure rise.
2. *increases aggressive thinking.* For example, Bushman and Anderson (2002) found that after playing games such as *Duke Nukem* and *Mortal Kombat,* university students became more likely to guess that a man whose car was just rear-ended would respond aggressively, by using abusive language, kicking out a window or starting a fight.
3. *increases aggressive feelings.* Frustration levels rise, as does expressed hostility.
4. *increases aggressive behaviours.* After violent game play, children and youth play more aggressively with their peers, get into more arguments with their teachers, and participate in more fights. The effect occurs inside and outside the laboratory, across self-reports, teacher reports and parent reports, and for reasons illustrated in **Figure 8.6** (overleaf). Is this merely because naturally hostile kids are drawn to such games? No, even when controlling for personality and temperament, exposure to video-game violence desensitizes people to cruelty and increases aggressive behaviour (Fraser et al., 2012). Moreover, observed Gentile et al. (2004) from a study of young adolescents, even among those who scored low in hostility, the percentage of heavy violent gamers who got into fights was ten times the 4 per cent involved in fights among their non-gaming counterparts. And after they start playing the violent games, previously non-hostile kids become more likely to have fights. Playing violent video games has a negative impact on our ability to empathize with others, and this lack of empathy may be responsible for behaviours such as cyber-bullying (Ang & Goh, 2010) and vandalism (Carrasco et al., 2006).

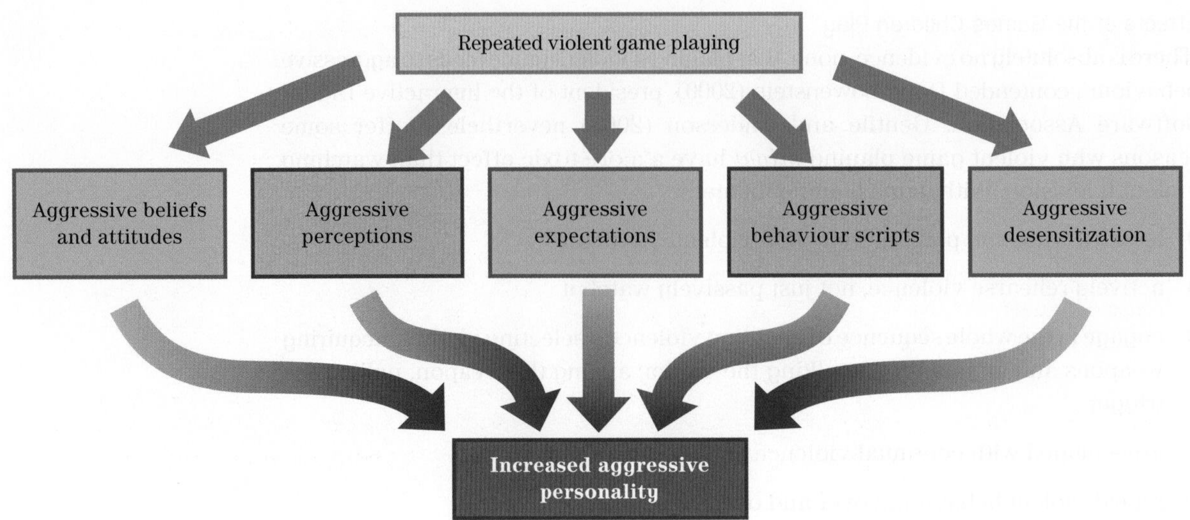

FIGURE 8.6 Violent video-game influences on aggressive tendencies

SOURCE: Adapted from Bushman & Anderson (2002).

5 *decreases prosocial behaviours.* After violent video-game playing, people become slower to help a person whimpering in the hallway outside and slower to offer help to peers. On a later monetary decision-making task, they become more likely to exploit rather than to trust and co-operate with a partner (Sheese & Graziano, 2005). They also, as revealed by decreased brain activity associated with emotion, become desensitized to violence (Bartholow et al., 2006).

Moreover, the more violent the games played, the bigger the effects. Video games *have* become more violent, which helps explain why newer studies find the biggest effects. Although much remains to be learned, these studies indicate that, contrary to the catharsis hypothesis, practising violence breeds rather than releases violence.

Anderson (2003, 2004) therefore encourages parents to discover what their kids are ingesting and to ensure that their media diet, at least in their own home, is healthy. Parents may not be able to control what their child watches, plays and eats in someone else's home. Nor can they control the media's effect on their children's peer culture. But parents can oversee consumption in their own home and provide increased time for alternative activities. Networking with other parents can build a child-friendly neighbourhood. And schools can help by providing media awareness education.

However, we may need to question whether what's being observed reflects real aggression or 'play' aggression. Griffiths (1997) found that while partaking in violent video games increases aggression in young children, it had no effect on teenagers. The discrepancy in these figures may reflect either that video games do not have the same effect on older children as they do on younger children, or that what is being defined as evidence of aggressive behaviour is present only in the younger sample. Interestingly, research suggests that violent video games do have an effect on older children and adults, but on lowering prosocial behaviour rather than directly heightening aggression. In their study of 780 young adults (mean age

19.60 years), Fraser et al. (2012) found that playing violent video games lowers empathy levels, which results in decreased prosocial behaviour towards strangers. So although displays of aggression may be absent from studies with older children and adults, what is more apparent are reductions in helping behaviour.

Gender and Aggression

The research on bullying alerts us to something of a stereotype within common sense and social psychological understandings of aggression: that men are more aggressive than women. On the face of it, this might seem to be a sensible assumption as official crime statistics repeatedly show that men are much more likely to appear as perpetrators of aggressive crimes.

Observation of aggression can heighten aggression; the same can be said for helping with prosocial models promoting altruism. See Chapter 11 for further discussion of prosocial behaviour, specifically helping.

Within social psychology, it is often assumed that women are not as aggressive as men for socio-biological reasons. First, there is the argument that claims men are more aggressive than women due to the presence of higher testosterone levels. We noted earlier in this chapter the link between hormones and violent behaviour in human beings, and men in particular. The second argument is evolutionary, documenting that women nurture their young. Conversely it is the role of men to protect women and their children from threats, which may mean using aggression to do so. Reinforcing these socio-biological arguments are processes of socialization into specific gender roles, such that while young boys might be rewarded for behaving aggressively, young girls may be punished.

However, there have been some studies that have examined the onset of physical aggression in girls. In a 15-year longitudinal study of 6- to 12-year-old girls, Fontaine et al. (2008) found that those with high levels of hyperactivity and high physical aggression were also more likely to report nicotine addiction, low educational attainment, physical aggression in intimate relationships, and early pregnancy. Fontaine concludes that targeted intensive prevention programmes would be useful in tackling these problems.

White and Kowalski (1994) make the point that aggressive women tend to be seen as social deviants and even mentally ill. Media attention on 'ladettes' has pointed to this stigmatization of women who do not present normative gender-role behaviour. Reidy et al. (2009) found that hyper-masculine men were more likely to be aggressive towards women who violated feminine gender-role behaviour.

White and Kowalski consider crime statistics that report a difference in men and women as perpetrators of aggressive crimes. They note a number of factors that might account for this, including the following.

- Willingness of a victim to report a crime. Men who are subject to domestic violence from their female partners may be less willing to report the crime for fear of being stigmatized.
- The act must be regarded as being 'serious' for it to be reported. This may be less likely where women are the perpetrators.
- Women may be treated much more leniently by the criminal justice system than men, and as such may not show up in the official crime statistics.

In a culture where the norm, or the stereotype, is of the 'unaggressive woman', recognizing aggressive behaviour may prove tricky. As men are predominantly used in social psychology studies of aggression, White and Kowalski argue that the definition and understanding of 'what' aggression is comes from a male perspective. They suggest that if researchers examine female aggression in situations that are congruent with their gender role, such as family settings, and extend the definition of aggression to include non-physical acts as well as just physical ones, then the evidence points to women being as, if not more, aggressive than men under such circumstances.

As well as the difficulties in defining aggression, we also have the problem of collecting evidence. If we rely on a method of collecting self-reports, which many of these studies do, then what we might be seeing are differences between men and women in terms of what *they* define as aggression rather than accurate reflections of its occurrence. In Tinkler and Jackson's (2007) study of 'ladettes' in the media, they consider how aggression is defined in particular ways to stigmatize young women. This is interesting when you consider Muncer et al.'s (2001) report that, for the young women themselves, there is no correlation between holding laddish attitudes and engaging in aggressive behaviour.

The point? There is no simple explanation or definition of aggression. Nor is there any simple way of collecting evidence of it. As we've seen throughout this chapter, there is a tendency to study examples of aggression which can be easily identified and measured in some way. This can mean an over-reliance on evidence of physical violence to represent aggression. We noted at the start of this chapter that aggression comes in many guises, but this complexity is arguably not reflected in social psychological studies of the topic. Indeed, it might be the attempt to simplify the behaviour that is partly responsible for the generalization that women are not as aggressive as men. Is this true? In Chapter 14 we discuss the relationship between gender and behaviour in terms of biological influences and cultural socialization.

Collective Identity

Behaviour is seldom random and is often organized around a shared sense of social identity which provides the group with norms about what is, and what is not, appropriate behaviour. Youths sharing antisocial tendencies and lacking close family bonds and expectations of academic success may find social identity in a gang (Staub, 1996). Members give themselves over to the group, often feeling a satisfying oneness with the others.

Social identity theory argues that crowds will be violent to the extent that violent actions are consistent with the group's identity. Where this does turn into acts of aggression they do not occur randomly but are aimed at very specific targets who represent a meaningful outgroup.

Hate crimes can occur when someone is attacked on the basis of being a member of a group. We have already seen in this chapter that individuals identified as members of a minority group, such as homosexuals, may be the victims of verbal and physical aggression. Often this is because these people represent deviance away from cultural norms and values. Prejudice towards the group they represent underlies these attacks. Stotzer and Hossellman (2012) consider how the increased presence of US students from ethnic and racial minority groups in higher education can lead to greater harmony between them, or aggravate tensions between them leading to heightened prevalence of hate crime on university campuses. On the one hand, increased contact between students of different racial and ethnic groups can lead to racial tolerance. We discuss Gordon Allport's 'contact hypothesis' in Chapter 13, which suggests that when certain optimal conditions are in place (most notably equal status of all groups), increasing contact between groups can lead to reduced prejudice. On the other, increased contact can intensify racial and ethnic tensions leading to the occurrence of hate crimes. Stotzer and Hossellman note that which way things go partly depends on the communication of values from the academic institution to its students, but also the values of the students themselves and how the white majority perceive the legitimacy of ethnic diversity in higher education.

In Chapters 5 and 13 we consider how behavioural expectations shape perception. There we have examples from the extensive research on football hooligans that has shown how the presence and perception of the police, opposing fans, and their actions, influences the levels of aggression displayed by the supporters (Drury et al., 2003; Reicher et al., 2004; Stott et al., 2001). Where opposing team supporters are perceived to be engaging in illegitimate acts of violence towards the ingroup, that group will respond by asserting its own identity in 'legitimate' violent ways towards the outgroup. We discuss these ideas in more detail in Chapter 13 when we consider intergroup relations.

The twentieth-century massacres that claimed over 150 million lives were 'not the sums of individual actions', notes Zajonc (2000). '*Genocide is not the plural of homicide.*' Massacres are *social* phenomena fed by 'moral imperatives' – a collective mentality (including images, rhetoric and ideology) that mobilizes a group or a culture for extraordinary actions. The massacres of Rwanda's Tutsis, of Europe's Jews and of America's native population were collective phenomena requiring widespread support, organization and participation. Before launching the genocidal initiative, Rwanda's Hutu government and business leaders bought and distributed 2 million machetes.

Aggression studies provide an apt opportunity to ask how well social psychology's laboratory findings generalize to everyday life. Do the circumstances that trigger someone to deliver electric shocks or allocate hot sauce really tell us anything about the circumstances that trigger verbal abuse or a punch in the face? Anderson and Bushman (1997; Bushman & Anderson, 1998) note that social psychologists have studied aggression in both the laboratory and everyday worlds, and the findings are strikingly consistent. In *both* contexts, increased aggression is predicted by the following:

- male actors
- aggressive or Type A personalities
- alcohol use
- violence viewing
- anonymity
- provocation
- the presence of weapons
- group interaction.

The laboratory allows us to test and revise theories under controlled conditions. Real-world events inspire ideas and provide the venue for applying our theories. Aggression research illustrates how the interplay between studies in the controlled laboratory and the complex real world advances psychology's contribution to human welfare. Hunches gained from everyday experience inspire theories, which stimulate laboratory research, which then deepens our understanding and our ability to apply psychology to real problems.

Can Aggression Be Reduced?

We have examined instinct, frustration-aggression and social learning theories of aggression, and we have scrutinized biological and social influences on aggression. How, then, can we reduce aggression?

Importantly, it depends on what level of aggression we are dealing with. Theory and research suggest that aggression can be tackled at the level of the individual, the group and society. For example, we can try to implement measures to control alcohol abuse, improve relationships within families, educate people about the effects of war and genocide, and enable groups in society to learn about one another, thus promoting shared understanding. For example, the role of society in educating young people has been highlighted in Sally Black and Alice Hausman's study of gun-carrying behaviour among adolescents (2008). They suggest that, 'Primary prevention starts by producing meaningful roles and economic opportunities for youth in inner cities and providing culturally competent prevention education. Generally, adolescents need safe opportunities for independence and the resources to build identity' (p. 606). However, all of these measures are complex to implement due to the multifaceted nature of aggression, but that is not to say we shouldn't try. There are some key factors that have been outlined in this chapter that are worth bearing in mind.

Catharsis?

We have considered the idea that television violence might offer a 'cathartic' experience, meaning children feel drained of any aggressive desires as a result of vicariously watching it carried out. However as we've also seen, this hypothesis has been disputed.

Research close-up

Can Self-Control and Mindfulness Help to Reduce Aggression?

Source: Meier, B. P., & Wilkowski, B. M. (2013). Reducing the tendency to aggress: Insights from social and personality psychology. *Social and Personality Psychology Compass, 7*(6), 343-354.

Introduction

Social psychology has offered much in the way of explaining the causes of aggressive behaviour, but considerably less on how to reduce it. This paper reviews a range of ways social psychologists have noted for reducing aggression, and incorporates them into the General Aggression Model (GAM). It is argued that understanding the cause of aggression is fundamental to figuring out its mitigation.

The GAM reports three stages of aggression: inputs, routes, and outcomes. Inputs include situational variables (such as heat or provocation, or exposure to television violence), personal variables (such as personality traits and sex). The routes concern people's internal states, such as mood or emotion cognitions (e.g. aggressive thinking), and arousal (e.g. physical arousal such as increased heart rate). The inputs and routes can then affect individuals' decisions about whether to act aggressively or not (the outcome). They influence how we interpret the situation.

Social and Personality Factors for Reducing Aggression

Aggression can be reduced if we can mitigate against the inputs and routes of aggression. Self-control over the routes of aggression is crucial here, for example controlling our thoughts and mood. Research shows that those higher in self-control tend to be less aggressive than those with low self-control. Being resilient against situational factors (inputs) which might otherwise lead us towards aggression is also important. Having pro-social traits (e.g. agreeableness), putting ourselves into pro-social situations (e.g. helping others) and past experiences of pro-social behaviour mitigates against aggressive behaviour. Pro-sociality impacts upon inputs and routes to aggression, reducing the likelihood of an aggressive outcome. Appraisal processes also matter. We are more likely to behave aggressively if we respond instantly. For example, imagine you are pushed in the supermarket queue. Your immediate appraisal of the situation will probably be negative and may well result in an aggressive reaction (e.g. push them back). However, if we take some time to stand back and reappraise the situation, we might avoid an aggressive outcome. Perhaps the shove was accidental or unavoidable. Perhaps an aggressive response is inappropriate. Perhaps in the grand scheme of things, a shove in the supermarket queue isn't that big a deal! For example, individuals high in mindfulness are capable of reflecting on their immediate feelings and thoughts, and controlling the urge to act on them. They allow their feelings to gradually disappear. They are taking a non-defensive and non-personal view of the situation. This ability to avoid a knee-jerk reaction to a situation, and to take time to reappraise it, can reduce an aggressive outcome and an escalation of events.

Summary and Conclusion

Social psychologists now need to dedicate more time to the practicalities of reducing aggression. Using a model of understanding why aggression occurs, such as the all-encompassing GAM, is a useful starting-point for working through aggression reduction strategies at the many levels in which it occurs. Whilst we can not, and should not, aim to eradicate all aggression (as aggression can be adaptive), we should certainly try to reduce it such that our societies are happier, healthier, co-operative, and more productive.

Critical Reflections

This is a review paper that certainly offers plenty of food for thought on how we might reduce aggression. Rather than producing an empirical study, it offers a reflection on the many factors identified in social psychology which can cause aggression, cites relevant published work on the area, and explores how GAM can assist in working out how and where to nip aggression in the bud! Acknowledgement that there is no silver bullet for stopping aggression is actually quite useful. The search for the 'one size fits all' solution is over. Instead we have to focus on the level at which aggression occurs (individual, group, society), how it is being defined. and the various factors that have given rise to the possibility of an aggressive outcome. Then we can think about the solution. That said, there is perhaps one nagging omission from this work, which is how GAM operates at the group level. What if a group is involved in an aggressive encounter, how might GAM help in mitigating against it? Although it is not terribly well spelled out in this paper, we turn to this topic in Chapter 13.

The concept of catharsis is usually credited to Western thinking, especially to the Ancient Greek philosopher Aristotle. Although Aristotle actually said nothing about aggression, he did argue that we can purge emotions by experiencing them, and that viewing the classic tragedies therefore enabled a catharsis (purging) of pity and fear. To have an emotion excited, he believed, is to have that emotion released (Butcher, 1951). The catharsis hypothesis has been extended to include the emotional release supposedly obtained not only by observing drama but also through our recalling and reliving past events, through our expressing emotions, and through our actions.

Assuming that aggressive action or fantasy drains pent-up aggression, some therapists and group leaders have encouraged people to ventilate suppressed aggression by acting it out – by whopping one another with foam bats or beating a bed with a tennis racket while screaming. If led to believe that catharsis effectively vents emotions, people will react more aggressively to an insult as a way to improve their mood (Bushman et al., 2001). Some psychologists, believing that catharsis is therapeutic, advise parents to encourage children's release of emotional tension through aggressive play. Actually, though, notes researcher Brad Bushman (2002), 'Venting to reduce anger is like using gasoline to put out a fire'.

The near consensus among social psychologists is that – contrary to what Freud, Lorenz and their followers supposed – viewing or participating in violence fails to produce catharsis. In laboratory tests of catharsis, Bushman (2002) invited angered participants to hit a punching bag while either ruminating about the person who angered them or thinking about becoming physically fit. A third group did not hit the punching bag. Then, when given a chance to administer loud blasts of noise to the person who angered them, people in the punching bag plus rumination condition felt angrier and were most aggressive. Moreover, doing nothing at all more effectively reduced aggression than did 'letting off steam' by hitting the bag.

In some real-life experiments, too, aggressing has led to heightened aggression. In a classic study, Ebbesen et al. (1975) interviewed 100 engineers and technicians shortly after they were angered by layoff notices. Some were asked questions that gave them an opportunity to express hostility against their employer or supervisors – for example, 'What instances can you think of where the company has not been fair with you?' Afterwards, they answered a questionnaire assessing attitudes towards the company and the supervisors. Did the previous opportunity to 'vent' or 'drain' off their hostility reduce it? On the contrary, their hostility increased. Expressing hostility bred more hostility.

'He who gives way to violent gestures will increase his rage.'

Charles Darwin, *The Expression of Emotion in Man and Animals,* 1872

As we note in analysing Stanley Milgram's obedience experiments (see Chapter 7), little aggressive acts can breed their own justification. People derogate their victims, rationalizing further aggression.

Retaliation may, in the short run, reduce tension and even provide pleasure (Ramirez et al., 2005). But in the long run it fuels more negative feelings. Should we therefore bottle up anger and aggressive urges? Silent sulking is hardly more effective, because it allows us to continue reciting our grievances as we conduct conversations in our head. Bushman et al. (2005a) experimented with the toxic effect of such rumination. After being provoked by an obnoxious experimenter with insults such as 'Can't you follow directions? Speak louder!' half were given a distraction (by being asked to write an essay about their campus landscape) and half were induced to ruminate (by writing an essay about their experiences as a research participant). Next, they were mildly insulted by a supposed fellow participant (actually a confederate), to whom they responded by prescribing a hot sauce dose this person would have to consume. The distracted participants, their anger now abated, prescribed only a mild dose, but the still-seething ruminators displaced their aggressive urge and prescribed twice as much.

Fortunately, there are non-aggressive ways to express our feelings and to inform others how their behaviour affects us. Across cultures, those who reframe accusatory 'you' messages as 'I' messages – 'I feel angry about what you said' or 'I get irritated when you leave dirty dishes' – communicate their feelings in a way that better enables the other person to make a positive response (Kubany et al., 1995). We can be assertive without being aggressive.

A Social Learning Approach

If aggressive behaviour is learned, then there is hope for its control. Aversive experiences such as frustrated expectations and personal attacks predispose hostile aggression. So it is wise to refrain from planting false, unreachable expectations in people's minds. Anticipated rewards and costs influence instrumental aggression. This suggests that we should reward co-operative, non-aggressive behaviour.

In experiments, children become less aggressive when caregivers ignore their aggressive behaviour and reinforce their non-aggressive behaviour (Hamblin et al., 1969). Punishing the aggressor is less consistently effective. Threatened punishment deters aggression only under ideal conditions when the punishment is strong, prompt and sure; when it is combined with reward for the desired behaviour; and when the recipient is not angry (Baron & Richardson, 2007).

Physical punishment can also have negative side effects. Punishment is aversive stimulation; it models the behaviour it seeks to prevent. And it is coercive (recall that we seldom internalize actions coerced with strong external justifications). These are reasons why violent teenagers and child-abusing parents so often come from homes where discipline took the form of harsh physical punishment.

To foster a gentler world, we could model and reward sensitivity and co-operation from an early age, perhaps by training parents how to discipline without violence. Training programmes encourage parents to reinforce desirable behaviours and to frame statements positively ('When you finish cleaning your room, you can go play', rather than, 'If you don't clean your room, you're grounded'). One 'aggression-replacement programme' has reduced re-arrest rates of juvenile offenders and gang members by teaching the youths and their parents communication skills, training them to control anger, and raising their level of moral reasoning (Goldstein et al., 1998).

If observing aggressive models lowers inhibitions and elicits imitation, then we might also reduce brutal, dehumanizing portrayals in films and on television – steps comparable to those already taken to reduce racist and sexist portrayals. We can also inoculate children against the effects of media violence. For example, Stanford University used 18 classroom lessons to persuade children to simply reduce their television watching and video-game playing (Robinson et al., 2001). They reduced their television viewing by a third – and the children's aggressive behaviour at school dropped 25 per cent compared with children in a control school.

Aggressive stimuli also trigger aggression. This suggests reducing the availability of weapons such as handguns and knives. However, the research remains mixed as to whether doing so decreases these crimes (Moorhouse & Wanner, 2006).

Suggestions such as these can help us minimize aggression, but we should be aware that this isn't as simple as flicking a magic wand. It is a sad irony that although today we understand human aggression better than ever before, humanity's inhumanity endures. Nevertheless, cultures can change.

Focus on

Teaching Them a Lesson: Motivations for Driver Aggression

Road rage is increasing in those countries where we rely heavily on vehicles to take us from A to B. Many of us have been subject at some point to actions such as someone honking their horn at us, sharply swerving in front of the car you're in, making obscene hand gestures, or driving far too close to the rear of the car. Statistics show that the majority of drivers in the UK, US and Australia have been on the receiving end of these behaviours. We're a little less willing to admit that we've been the person doing these behaviours to other motorists, however. But why does road rage happen? Are we stressed out? Are other drivers so bad that they deserve these actions? Do we enjoy the danger? Do we think we're invincible once we're behind the wheel of a car? Is it mostly young men who get road rage? All of these factors, and more besides, have been found to play a role in explaining road rage (Lennon & Watson, 2011). However, what is less clear is, do people who commit road rage intend on harming the recipient of their aggressive behaviour?

In their qualitative study of motorists, Alexia Lennon and Barry Watson found they explained their mildly aggressive acts (such as horn-honking and light-flashing) as points of information to let another driver know they were driving badly. The potential negative impact upon the other driver was denied or mitigated. So whilst these motorists recognized their behaviour as mildly aggressive, there was no intention to actually harm the other motorist. However, if the motorist perceived other drivers as intending to inflict harm, then they regarded their subsequent actions towards them as 'justified retaliation'. These people needed to be 'taught a lesson'. What Lennon and Watson found was that despite aggression being a socially undesirable behaviour, motorists were fairly open about admitting to it when they felt their actions had been deserved. However, many drivers downplayed the potential consequences of their actions. The aggression may be seen as justified, but the intention to cause harm is denied.

The distinction between intentional and unintentional aggression may not be quite so clear-cut. As we can see from this example, aggressors may admit their behaviour but deny the intent. Does this make the act any more palatable? Is it still aggression?

Questions

1 Who should define what counts as aggressive behaviour? The social psychologist? The person who commits the act?

2 Should we treat unintentional aggression with the same seriousness as intentional aggression?

3 If you were to design a study into aggression, what behaviours would you focus on? How would you collect evidence of them and analyse them?

4 How might you attempt to prevent driver aggression?

SUMMING UP: AGGRESSION

WHAT IS AGGRESSION?

- Aggression has been defined in various ways by social psychologists. Broadly speaking its definition can include direct and/or indirect physical and verbal acts. It can refer to intentional and/or unintentional behaviour.
- How we define aggression has implications for what we treat as evidence of it and the conclusions we reach about its presence in human society.

SOME THEORIES OF AGGRESSION

We have considered three broad theories of aggression.

- The *instinct* view, most commonly associated with Sigmund Freud and Konrad Lorenz, contended that aggressive energy will accumulate from within, like water accumulating behind a dam. Although the available evidence offers little support for that view, aggression is biologically influenced by heredity, blood chemistry and the brain.
- According to the second view, *frustration* causes anger and hostility. Given aggressive cues in the environment may provoke aggression. Frustration stems not from deprivation itself but from the gap between expectations and achievements.
- The *social learning* view presents aggression as learned behaviour. By experience and by observing others' success, we sometimes learn that aggression pays. Social learning enables family, cultural and subcultural influences on aggression, as well as media influences (which we will discuss in the next section). In some cultures children are taught not to be aggressive since it is an immature reaction.

SOME INFLUENCES ON AGGRESSION

- Many factors exert influence on aggression. One factor is aversive experiences, which include not only frustrations but also discomfort, pain and personal attacks, both physical and verbal.
- Arousal from almost any source, even physical exercise or sexual stimulation, can be transformed into anger.
- Aggression cues in the environment, such as the presence of a gun, increase the likelihood of aggressive behaviour.
- Viewing violence (1) breeds a modest increase in *aggressive behaviour,* especially in people who are provoked, and (2) *desensitizes* viewers to aggression and alters their *perceptions* of reality. These two findings parallel the results of research on the effects of viewing violent pornography, which can increase men's aggression against women and distort their perceptions of women's responses to sexual coercion.
- Television permeates the daily life of millions of people and portrays considerable violence. Correlational and experimental studies converge on the conclusion that heavy exposure to televised violence correlates with aggressive behaviour.
- Repeatedly playing violent video games may increase aggressive thinking, feelings and behaviour even more than television or movies do, as the experience involves much more active participation than those other media.
- A special kind of aggression is committed by groups. Circumstances that provoke individuals may also provoke groups. By diffusing responsibility and polarizing actions, group situations amplify aggressive reactions.

CAN AGGRESSION BE REDUCED?

- How can we minimize aggression? Contrary to the catharsis hypothesis, expressing aggression by catharsis tends to breed further aggression, not reduce it.

- Focusing on the causes of aggression, as exemplified in GAM, can offer direction in mitigating against it.
- The social learning approach suggests controlling aggression by counteracting the factors that provoke it: by reducing aversive stimulation, by rewarding and modelling non-aggression, and by eliciting reactions incompatible with aggression.

Critical Questions

1. How have social psychologists defined aggression?
2. What implications does the definition of aggression have for research on its occurrence?
3. Are men more aggressive than women?
4. What are some of the causes social psychologists have identified for aggression?
5. Under what circumstances do you think exposure to television violence and playing violent video games, leads to aggressive behaviour?
6. Can aggression ever be beneficial for us?
7. What can we do to reduce aggression?

Recommended Reading

Below are some recommended classic and contemporary readings within social psychology on aggression.

Classic Books and Papers

Bandura, A., Ross, D., & Ross, S.A. (1961). Transmission of aggression through imitation of aggressive models. *Journal of Abnormal and Social Psychology, 63,* 575–582.

Berkowitz, L. (1989). Frustration-aggression hypothesis: Examination and reformulation. *Psychological Bulletin, 106*(1), 59–73.

Dollard, J., Doob, L., Miller, N., Mowrer, O. & Sears, R. (1939). *Frustration and aggression.* Yale University Press.

Zillmann, D., & Bryant, J. (1974). Effect of residual excitation on the emotional response to provocation and delayed aggressive behavior. *Journal of Personality and Social Psychology, 30*(6), 782–791.

Contemporary Papers

Anderson, C. A., & Bushman, B. J. (2002). Human aggression. *Annual Review of Psychology, 53,* 27-51.

Denson, T. F., O'Dean, S. M., Blake, K. R., & Beames, J. R. (2018). Aggression in women: Behavior, brain and hormones. *Frontiers in Behavioral Neuroscience,* May 2. https://doi.org/10.3389/fnbeh.2018.00081

Gentile, D. A., Coyne, S., & Walsh, D. A. (2011). Media violence, physical aggression, and relational aggression in school age children: A short-term longitudinal study. *Aggressive Behavior, 37*(2), 193–206.

Workman, M. (2010). A behaviourist perspective on corporate harassment online: Validation of a theoretical model of psychological motives. *Computers & Security, 29,* 831–839.

Yang, H., Ramasubramanian, S., & Oliver, M. B. (2008). Cultivation effects on quality of life indicators: Exploring the effects of American television consumption on feelings of relative deprivation in South Korea and India. *Journal of Broadcasting & Electronic Media, 52*(2), 247–267.

9 ATTRACTION AND INTIMACY

'Love cures people – both the ones who give it and the ones who receive it.'
Psychiatrist Karl Meninger, 1893–1990

Our lifelong dependence on one another puts relationships at the core of our existence. We cannot survive as individuals without relationships with others, and we cannot survive as a species without procreation with other human beings. Social relationships, to care and be cared for are essential to human life. Aristotle called humans 'social animals'. Indeed, we have what today's social psychologists call a **need to belong** – to connect with others in close relationships.

need to belong a motivation to bond with others in relationships that provide ongoing, positive interactions

Interconnection, attachment and intimate relationships are, however, not only instruments for survival; they result in great pleasure and have important qualities in themselves, by making people feel happier, more able, and improving health and well-being. Consider the following:

- For our ancestors, mutual attachments enabled group survival. When hunting game or erecting shelter, ten hands were better than two. Today we still experience the benefits of working together and sharing.
- For children and their caregivers, social attachments make life easier and more pleasant, and enhance survival. If separated from each other, caregiver and toddler may both panic until reunited in a tight embrace.
- Feeling accepted and belonging to a primary group, such as a family, makes us stronger, more safe and relaxed. This is especially true of Eastern cultures where family ties are still very strong and parents and offspring prove a particular attraction, love and responsibility towards each other.
- For university students, relationships consume much of life. How much of your waking life is spent talking with people? One sampling of 10,000 tape recordings of half-minute slices of students' waking hours (using belt-worn recorders) found them talking to someone 28 per cent of the time – and that doesn't count the time they spent listening to someone (Mehl & Pennebaker, 2003).
- For people everywhere, actual and hoped-for close relationships can dominate thinking and emotions. Finding a supportive soul mate in whom we can confide, we feel accepted and prized. Falling in love, we feel irrepressible joy. Even seemingly dismissive people relish being accepted (Carvallo & Gabriel, 2006).
- Exiled, imprisoned or in solitary confinement, people ache for their own people and places. Rejected, we are at risk of sadness and depression (Nolan et al., 2003). Time goes more slowly and life seems less meaningful (Twenge et al., 2003).
- For the jilted, the widowed and the sojourner in a strange place, the loss of social bonds triggers pain, loneliness or withdrawal. Losing a soul-mate relationship, adults feel jealous, distraught or bereaved, as well as more mindful of death and the fragility of life.
- Reminders of death in turn heighten our need to belong, to be with others and hold close those we love (Mikulincer et al., 2003; Wisman & Koole, 2003). The shocking death of a classmate, a co-worker or a family member brings people together, their differences no longer mattering.

We are, indeed, social animals. When we do belong – when we feel supported by close, intimate relationships – we tend to be healthier and happier. In this chapter we'll explore how social psychologists have theorized and researched not only how we form intimate relationships with other people, but the principles behind attraction.

What Leads to Friendship and Attraction?

What factors nurture liking and loving? Let's start with those that help initiate attraction: proximity, physical attractiveness, similarity and feeling liked.

What predisposes one person to like, or to love, another? Few questions about human nature arouse greater interest. The ways affections flourish and fade form the stuff and fluff of soap operas, popular music, novels, and much of our everyday conversation.

So much has been written about liking and loving that almost every conceivable explanation – and its opposite – has already been proposed. For most people – and for you – what factors nurture liking and loving?

- Does absence make the heart grow fonder? Or is someone who is out of sight also out of mind?
- Do opposites attract? Or do we prefer those who are similar to ourselves?
- How much do good looks matter?
- What has fostered your close relationships?

Where Do You Find your Partner?

Going to university not only helps you to get an interesting career after years of improving your knowledge, it also sets you in a circle of friends and acquaintances among whom may be your life partner. Or do you have to go somewhere else to meet the right one? What about evening classes, holiday locations, beaches, hotels, gyms, swimming, walking and climbing? Perhaps you'll meet him or her at the theatre, opera, at an art exhibition, a music festival, even a funeral or birthday celebration. You can meet someone who is right for you everywhere of course, and often accidentally, without even planning for it.

Though it may seem trivial to those pondering the mysterious origins of romantic love and friendships, sociologists long ago found that proximity predicts liking (Bossard, 1932; Burr, 1973; Clarke, 1952; McPherson et al., 2001). This has been termed the **proximity principle**. According to this theory, we tend to develop friendships and close relationships with those people we have regular interaction with as a result of our paths frequently crossing (e.g. in the workplace). When the role of proximity was investigated in 1950 by Festinger and his team, it was understood as 'physical' proximity. Individuals who lived in the same building were highly likely to become friends, as a result of regular physical social contact. This may reflect your own initial friendships at university. Your friends were possibly those in the same student house as you or were members of the same class as you. However, in today's society, we understand proximity in broader terms than simply physical geography. Proximity is about regular contact which can be established over the phone, over email, using FaceTime or other social media platforms. As contemporary social psychologists now argue, the Internet can be an important mechanism for facilitating accessibility between individuals (Amichai-Hamburger et al., 2008).

proximity principle geographical nearness. Proximity (more precisely, 'functional distance') powerfully predicts liking

Close relationships with friends and family contribute to health and happiness.

SOURCE: ©anatoliy_gleb/Shutterstock

Due to increased migration, the Internet, travelling and moving around, most people in Western societies do not live in the same place all their life. They change universities, jobs and home. So the possibility of meeting somebody living far away when travelling to another country or around the world (which many students do), and making friends and falling in love with somebody who represents different and even mysterious qualities, is more prevalent than before. The increasing use of the Internet has challenged traditional social psychological theories' assumptions about the importance of proximity in forming and maintaining relationships. Accessibility is more important than geography. We do not have to choose the girl next door or the boy on the farm across the valley. The importance of physical proximity for relationships remains important but other factors are becoming more influential.

Interaction and the Anticipation of Interaction

More significant than geographical distance is therefore functional distance and interaction – how often people's paths cross. We frequently become friends with those who are in the same study groups or who use the same recreation areas as us, or who are members of the same online groups as us. Interaction enables people to explore their similarities, to sense one another's liking, and to perceive themselves as a social unit (McKenna et al., 2002; Peter et al., 2005).

And not only does proximity enable people to discover commonalities and exchange rewards, but also merely *anticipating* interaction boosts liking. In a classic study, Darley and Berscheid (1967) discovered this when they gave female students ambiguous information about two other women, one of whom they expected to talk with intimately. Asked how much they liked each one, the women preferred the person they expected to meet.

The phenomenon is adaptive. Anticipatory liking – expecting that someone will be pleasant and compatible – increases the chance of forming a rewarding relationship (Klein & Kunda, 1992; Montoya & Horton, 2014). It's a good thing that we are biased to like those we often see, for our lives are filled with relationships with people whom we may not have chosen but with whom we need to have continuing interactions – room-mates, siblings, grandparents, teachers, classmates, co-workers. Liking such people is surely conducive to better relationships with them, which in turn makes for happier, more productive living.

mere-exposure effect the tendency for novel stimuli to be liked more or rated more positively after the rater has been repeatedly exposed to them

Mere Exposure

Proximity leads to liking not only because it enables interaction and anticipatory liking but also for another reason: more than 200 studies reveal that, contrary to an old proverb, familiarity does not breed contempt. Rather, it fosters liking. The social psychologist Robert B. Zajonc made important contributions to the mere exposure effect more than 40 years ago. In 1968 he conducted three studies showing that the more people were exposed to all sorts of stimuli, the more they liked them. This effect even occurs in animals and birds (Zajonc et al., 1973). In 2004 he concluded that the **mere-exposure effect** is 'a robust phenomenon. These effects are valid across cultures, species, and diverse stimulus domains' (Zajonc, 2004).

Feeling close to those close by. People often become attached to, and sometimes fall in love with, familiar co-workers and co-students.
SOURCE: ©V.S.Anandhakrishna/Shutterstock

Do the supposed Turkish words *nansoma, saricik* and *afworbu* mean something better or something worse than the words *iktitaf, biwojni* and *kadirga*? Students tested by Zajonc (1968, 1970) preferred whichever of these words they had seen most frequently. The more times they had seen a meaningless word or a Chinese ideograph, the more likely they were to say it meant something good (**Figure 9.1**).

Consider: what are your favourite letters of the alphabet? People of differing nationalities, languages, and ages prefer the letters that frequently appear in their own languages and especially in their own names. This has been called the Name-Letter-Effect (NLE) and was first discovered by Josef Nuttin (1984, see also Hoorens et al., 1990; Hoorens & Nuttin, 1993; Kitayama & Karasawa, 1997; Nuttin, 1987). French students rate capital W, the least frequent letter in French, as their least favourite letter. Japanese students prefer not only letters from their names but also numbers corresponding to their birth dates. This 'name-letter and birthday-number effect' reflects more than mere exposure, however. It is also tied up with our sense of self-esteem. We are, as French writer Milan Kundera terms it 'ridiculously proud of it' (1990). The sense of pride and esteem tied up in our own name 'spills' out onto others who share it. We're great so they must be too! (Garner, 2005; Jones et al., 2002; Pelham, 2003).

The mere-exposure effect violates the common-sense prediction of boredom – *decreased* interest – regarding repeatedly beautiful scenery, heard music or tasted foods (Kahneman & Snell, 1992). Unless the repetitions are incessant ('Even the best song becomes tiresome if heard too often', says a Korean proverb), familiarity usually doesn't breed contempt, it increases liking (Green, 2007; Hansen & Wänke, 2009; Zebrowitz & Montepare, 2008). When completed in 1889, the Eiffel Tower in Paris was mocked as grotesque (Harrison, 1977). Today it is the beloved symbol

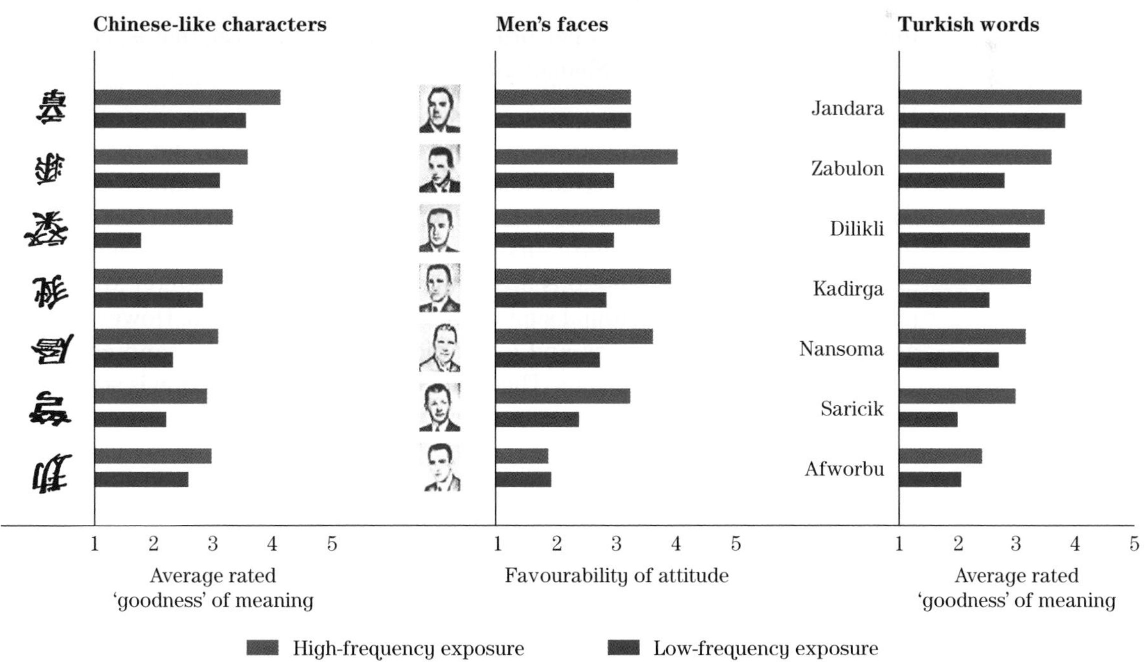

FIGURE 9.1 The mere-exposure effect

Students rated stimuli – a sample of which is shown here – more positively after being shown them repeatedly.

SOURCE: Zajonc (1968).

Leonardo Da Vinci's *Mona Lisa*. A pretty face or just a familiar one?

SOURCE: ©muratart/Shutterstock

of Paris. At its premiere in 1913, Stravinsky's *Rite of Spring* was vehemently condemned by critics and the public alike; today it is a classic admired the world over.

So, do visitors to the Louvre in Paris really adore the *Mona Lisa* for the artistry it displays, or are they simply delighted to find a familiar face? It might be both: to know her is to like her. Harmon-Jones and Allen (2001) explored this phenomenon experimentally. When they showed people a woman's face, their cheek (smiling) muscle typically became more active with repeated viewings. Mere exposure breeds pleasant feelings.

Zajonc and his co-workers William Kunst-Wilson and Richard Moreland reported that even exposure without awareness leads to liking (Kunst-Wilson & Zajonc, 1980; Moreland & Zajonc, 1977; Wilson, 1979). Joachim Hansen and Michaela Wänke at the University of Basel have more recently confirmed that repeated exposure affects attitude formation independently of conscious recognition, stressing the role of unconscious familiarity (Hansen & Wänke, 2009). In fact, mere exposure has, according to Bornstein and D'Agostino (1992), an even stronger effect when people receive stimuli without awareness. In one experiment, women students using headphones listened in one ear to a prose passage. They also repeated the words out loud and compared them with a written version to check for errors. Meanwhile, brief, novel melodies played in the other ear. This procedure focused attention on the verbal material and away from the tunes. Later, when the women heard the tunes interspersed among similar ones not previously played, they did not recognize them. Nevertheless, they *liked best* the tunes they had previously heard (Bornstein & D'Agostino, 1992). But, not everybody agrees with the findings of Bornstein and Agostino. Newell and Shanks (2007) found in their study of faces that a mere-exposure effect was found only when recognition performance was at a high level, that is, conscious or 'supraliminal' (Newell & Shanks, 2007).

Note that conscious judgements about the stimuli in Zajonc's experiments provided fewer clues to what people had heard or seen than did their instant feelings. You can probably recall immediately and intuitively liking or disliking something or someone without consciously knowing why. Zajonc (1980) argues that *emotions are often more instantaneous than thinking*. Zajonc's rather astonishing idea – that emotions are semi-independent of thinking ('affect may precede cognition') – has found support in recent brain research. However, there are also emotional reactions and evaluations tied to cognition and conscious evaluation of sense impressions. The immediate emotional reaction is sometimes overruled by later reflections and cognitions. The mere-exposure effect has 'enormous adaptive significance', notes Zajonc (1998). It is a 'hardwired' phenomenon that predisposes our attractions and attachments. It helps us to categorize things and people as either familiar and safe, or unfamiliar and possibly dangerous. The mere-exposure effect colours our evaluations of others: we like familiar people (Reis et al., 2011). It works the other way around, too: people we like (for example, smiling rather than unsmiling strangers) seem more familiar (Garcia-Marques et al., 2004). Mere exposure to something or somebody breeds liking since we are less afraid or suspicious towards things with which we are familiar. It also reduces stereotyping since we see individual traits and distinctiveness more.

The phenomenon's negative side is our wariness of the unfamiliar – which may explain the automatic, unconscious prejudice people often feel when confronting those who are different (as we see in Chapter 13). Fearful or prejudicial feelings are not always expressions of stereotyped beliefs; sometimes the beliefs arise later as justifications for intuitive feelings. Or they are enforced by a combination of emotions and cognitions of the unfamiliar. For example, increased familiarity with faces of a different race from our own increases liking for them (Zebrowitz & Montepare, 2008). So mere exposure can also reduce prejudice.

We even like ourselves better when we are the way we're used to seeing ourselves. In a delightful classic experiment, Mita et al. (1977) photographed women students and later showed each one her actual picture along with a mirror image of it. Asked which picture they liked better, most preferred the mirror image – the image they were used to seeing. (No wonder our photographs never look quite right.) When close friends of the women were shown the same two pictures, they preferred the true picture – the image *they* were used to seeing.

Advertisers and politicians exploit this phenomenon. When people have no strong feelings about a product or a candidate, repetition alone can increase sales or votes (Johnson et al., 2016; Loewenstein et al., 2011). After endless repetition of a commercial, shoppers often have an unthinking, automatic, favourable response to the product. If candidates are relatively unknown, those with the most media exposure usually win (Van Aelst et al., 2008; Patterson, 1980; Schaffner et al., 1981). Political strategists who understand the mere-exposure effect have replaced reasoned argument with brief advertisements that hammer home a candidate's picture, name and sound-bite message.

In Chapter 6 we look at peripheral routes to persuasion and when they are effective.

Online Dating

As a place for meeting romantic partners, the Internet has become a major environment since the 1990s. From tiny beginnings, online dating has become a huge source for contacting people and chatting with them. You might be looking on a broad basis on sites like PlentyOfFish or Tinder, or on apparently 'scientifically selecting' sites like eHarmony, or EliteSingles for the highly educated. Equally, you

The mere-exposure effect. If she is like most of us, German Chancellor Angela Merkel may prefer her familiar mirror-image (left), which she sees each morning while brushing her teeth, to her actual image (right).
SOURCE: ©360b/Shutterstock

might be more interested in more niche dating sites such as Bristlr for those who have a beard and those who want to stroke one, or perhaps Sizzl, which is for those who are serious about their bacon! You can be matched with your perfect partner on the basis of how you like your bacon. Whatever your preferences, it is claimed that online dating sites have revolutionized the way that we now find our romantic partners, and that they offer a way to meet far more people than we would in our normal day-to-day lives. Indeed, Valkenburg and Peter (2007) found that almost half of their sample of single Dutch participants had visited an online dating site. They also discovered that how much you earn or what your job is, does not predict the likelihood of you using online dating sites. That said, online dating sites seemed to be used most regularly by those aged 40 years and above, and divorcees. This is a time of life where various constraints, such as children, a busy career, a recent divorce, can make it difficult to meet a potential partner in the 'traditional' ways. The Internet offers a service that makes singles easily available and accessible.

Many online dating sites use mathematical algorithms to match us against compatible people and this apparently weeds out the people that we don't share anything in common with (Finkel et al., 2012). Dating sites are also useful for those people who may not have access to the groups that they find attractive, or who would otherwise have problems finding a romantic partner. For individuals in small communities online dating opens a much wider range of potential partners. McKenna et al. (2002) report that the Internet has provided a safer environment in which people who are socially anxious and lonely can form relationships, revealing aspects of themselves they would find difficult to articulate in face-to-face interactions. However, Valkenburg and Peter (2007) found that it was their gregarious Dutch participants with little dating anxiety who used online dating sites the most. For them, the Internet offered yet another avenue for them to create relationship possibilities.

Within social psychology there has been an explosion of research on 'who' uses online dating sites, 'why' they use them, and what happens as a consequence of doing so. For example, Whitty (2008) looked at how men and women present themselves on a dating website. She found that the importance of physical appearance was more of a live issue for women than it was for men, and that women were also more likely to list their personal interests. Perhaps the finding that users should pay particular heed to is that both men and women admitted to stretching the truth when constructing online identity in an attempt to attract a mate! Gibbs et al. (2011) lend support to this finding but also mitigate some of this stretching of the truth as a consequence of not revealing too much accurate information about the self due to fear of being the victim of fraud, stalking, or deception, as well as trying to stand out among the millions of others also appealing for a partner. But of course there are no guarantees that a relationship that works well online will also work well offline. As the real and virtual worlds meet, our illusions can be shattered. In a study, Guadagno et al. (2011) found that male participants were more likely to be deceptive in their self-presentation in online dating than female participants. Also, men are more likely to lie about their social or economic status, while women are more likely to lie about their weight (Hitsch et al., 2010). This seems to reflect evolutionary psychology's claims about people's understanding of sexual mate selection: that men seek women who are physically attractive and fertile, while women seek men who are resource rich. We will return to these heterosexual assumptions later in this chapter.

There is a smaller body of research into how gay men and lesbians use online dating sites. One of the most comprehensive European surveys comes from Potârc et al. (2015) who studied the online profiles of 24,598 gay men and lesbians who had posted onto eDarling, a European dating site. The participants were resident in Austria, France, Germany, Italy, Netherlands, Spain, Sweden and Switzerland. Their profiles were examined for personal information (e.g. number of children, previous marriages, occupation) and what they were looking for in a partner. The researchers noted a series of findings including:

- Gay men and lesbian women who reported having two or more children portrayed themselves as uninterested in monogamy and/or a long-term relationship. It seems the burden of raising children affects both gay men and lesbians in the same way.
- Lesbians who were divorced displayed quite strict criteria for a long-term partner and emphasized monogamy.
- Lesbians who had never married perceived few benefits of entering a long-term relationship and/or monogamy, and therefore did not pursue them.
- Gay men and lesbians who were resident in countries where gay marriage was legal at the time of the study (e.g. Sweden, the Netherlands) were keen to find a long-term partner in a monogamous relationship.

Physical Attractiveness

'We should look to the mind, and not to the outward appearances.'
Aesop, Fables

Good looks are a great asset, even if it is sometimes socially unacceptable to admit it.

Upon meeting someone for the first time, usually the first piece of information we receive about them is what they look like. Hence it is no surprise that physical attractiveness should be important to us. Heterosexual speed-daters cite physical attractiveness as the first thing that attracts them to a potential partner (Luo & Zhang, 2009). Moreover a substantial body of social psychological research confirms that people value physical attractiveness in their potential partners (for example, see Buss, 2016; Gangestad & Scheyd, 2005; Singh, 2004), regardless of their sexual orientation (Swami & Tovee, 2006).

The methodological innovation of **implicit measures** (see Chapters 5 and 13) has been useful for research on attraction, love and preferences. Results from surveys and experimental studies are often biased by **social desirability**. When asked in a survey, college students rated the romantic attractiveness of opposite-sex peers as equal, regardless of the presence or absence of a physical disability. However, using the *implicit association test* revealed a clear preference for physical health over physical disabilities. The discrepancy between the explicit attractiveness ratings and the implicit attitudes towards physical disabilities suggests that the former were biased by social desirability (Rojahn et al., 2008).

As we shall see, evolutionary psychology has greatly influenced our understanding of why physical attraction is so important.

implicit measures
implicit measures aim to assess attitudes that respondents may not be willing to report directly, or of which they may not even be aware

social desirability
refers to the tendency of participants to respond in a way that will be viewed favourably by others, including the researcher

Attractiveness and Dating

Evolutionary psychologists suggest that we tend to be attracted to those we consider physically attractive as this is an honest indicator of the quality of their genes, their health, their fertility, and how good a partner they will be for us (Buss, 2016). So whether we like it or not, a young woman's and a young man's physical attractiveness is a good predictor of how popular she and he is (Barber, 1995; Toma & Hancock, 2010). On dating websites, people consider physical attractiveness a key aspect of choosing a potential partner (Ellison et al., 2006; Walther, 2007). In their study of feminists and non-feminists who were either heterosexual or lesbian, Swami and Tovee (2006) discovered that Body Mass Index (BMI) was an important factor in deciding whether a woman was attractive or not. Interestingly, they also found that lesbians found women with a higher BMI more attractive than heterosexual women did, regardless of whether they identified as a feminist or not. One possible explanation for this finding is that this preference for heavier built women is a rejection of society's value for thin women, and the pressures women feel in conforming to this ideal. However, the point remains that physical appearance is an important factor in the dating game.

Our attractiveness can be displayed online through photographs and written descriptions of our physical appearance. The importance we place on physical attractiveness has a bearing on how accurately we present our physical characteristics online. Toma and Hancock (2010) have shown that people who are not considered conventionally physically attractive are more likely to manipulate their photographs and written descriptions, to reinvent their attractiveness. However, while those lucky enough to be considered physically attractive are less likely to manipulate photographs of themselves, they are keen to display as many photographs of themselves as possible to showcase their attractiveness. Also, it seems women were a little more concerned with displaying a physically attractive self than men were. However, men were more critical judges of 'beauty'. Toma and Hancock argue that even in the online arena, evolutionary theories of attraction, dating and mating apply. As we shall discover later in this chapter, evolutionary psychologists claim there are good reasons why women and men might differ in the value they place on physical attractiveness.

Much of this research on physical attractiveness has focused on young men and women. But what happens as our body ages? Is physical attraction still such an important feature of attraction and dating? There is no doubt, notes Vares (2009) that in most cultures, youth equates with beauty. The ageing body is perceived to be less physically attractive and less desirable. Yet the chances of us entering new relationships as we enter middle and older age, are increasingly likely as we live longer (Thorpe et al., 2014). In their interviews with Australian heterosexual women aged 55–72 years, Thorpe and her team discovered that all women regarded the ageing body as less attractive. However, those in stable long-term relationships often regarded it as unimportant. Consider this example from their study (2014, p. 160):

Anke: And I'm very lucky that the man I married loves me dearly and he doesn't care, he still thinks I'm the best looking female in the world.
Rachel: That's great
Anke: And that's great after 50 years of marriage, yeah. So no I don't like this bit myself [stomach], but I don't dwell on it. (Anke, 71).

In relationships such as Anke's, sexual intimacy is maintained through love and affection rather than striving to achieve what culture considers a beautiful body to be. However, for women entering new relationships, physical appearance is more of a concern. Even their partner's acceptance of their ageing body did not diminish women's concerns about revealing their ageing body.

What studies like Thorpe et al.'s reveal is that cultural assumptions about 'what' is considered physically attractive permeates our thinking throughout our lives. However, what they also show is that an ageing body can be considered as attractive and sexually desirable, but it is intimacy and love that are the foundations of a relationship.

The Matching Phenomenon

Originally put forward by Walster et al. (1966), the matching hypothesis proposes that when we are looking for a romantic partner or friend, we tend to look for someone whose level of physical attractiveness, social status, and so on, matches our own. In other, somewhat unromantic terms, we consider whether their market value matches our own. Several studies have found a strong correspondence between the rated physical attractiveness of husbands and wives, of dating partners, and even of those within particular fraternities (Buss, 2016; Buss & Shackelford, 2008).

'If you would marry wisely, marry your equal.'
Ovid, 43 BC–AD 17

Experiments seem to confirm this **matching phenomenon**. When choosing whom to approach, knowing the other is free to say yes or no, people often approach someone whose attractiveness roughly matches (or not too greatly exceeds) their own (Berscheid et al., 1971; Luo & Khlonen, 2005; Watson et al., 2004). They seek out someone who seems desirable, but are mindful of the limits of their own desirability.

matching phenomenon
the tendency for men and women to choose as partners those who are a 'good match' in attractiveness and other traits

Some researchers have pointed out that whilst the matching hypothesis seems robust, experiments have tended to focus on physical attractiveness and have not looked at real-world cases of selecting romantic partners and friends (Shaw Taylor et al., 2011). Think of happy couples who are not equally physically attractive. In such cases, the less attractive person often has other qualities with whom they are well-matched to their partner. Each partner brings assets to the social marketplace, and the value of the respective asset creates an equitable match. On the basis of their findings from a series of studies regarding online dating, Shaw Taylor et al. (2011) conclude that partners are chosen on the basis of their market value, as assessed by the individual advertising for a mate and those seeking one. And that market value is not based solely on physical attractiveness.

The term **assortative mating** has been put forward by some researchers to explain how couples pair up on the basis of shared social characteristics. In their study of newlyweds, Watson et al. (2004) found that couples were strongly matched for age, religious and political views, moderately matched for education and verbal intelligence, but only slightly matched for personality, emotionality and attachment. Friendships are also usually the result of a good match – especially our best friend. Friends are typically matched on physical attractiveness and social characteristics such as education, values and social status (Fehr, 1996;

assortative mating
the tendency for people to form relationships with those similar to themselves in social characteristics such as education, political and religious views, and social class.

Angelina Jolie and Brad Pitt (divorced in 2019): perfectly matched on their physical attractiveness and financial value, but not so perfectly matched on other aspects of their lives.

SOURCE: ©Twocoms/Shutterstock

Fehr & Harasymchuk, 2017). Friends who see the world in the same way we do are important allies and sources of support throughout our lives. Evolutionary psychologists further argue that because men place such a high value on physical attractiveness, this can encourage women to have same-sex friends who are more-or-less matched with them on this characteristic. According to this perspective, if female friends are more or less attractive than each other, this means they can't compete in the mating stakes and it could affect the likelihood of men approaching them. Therefore, the friendship will be tainted by feelings of rivalry and jealousy (Bleske-Rechek & Lighthall, 2010).

Research on the matching phenomenon and assortative mating within same-sex couples has been scarce, but is now starting to develop (Bartova et al., 2017). Existing work shows that same-sex couples, especially male-male, tend to be less closely matched on social characteristics than different-sex couples (Schwartz & Graf, 2009; Verbakel & Kalmijn, 2014). In particular, same-sex couples have been found to be less closely matched than opposite-sex couples on age and education (Andersson et al., 2006).

In dating advertisements, we might be tempted to think that heterosexual men typically offer wealth or status and seek youth and attractiveness, whereas women more often do the reverse: 'Attractive, bright woman, 26, slender, seeks warm, professional male.' But is this backed up by research?

Strasberg and Holty (2003) placed four 'female seeking male' advertisements on two large Internet bulletin boards which specialized in such advertisements, to study which ones received most responses. The most popular advertisement was the one in which the woman described herself as 'financially independent, successful [and] ambitious', producing over 50 per cent more responses than the next most popular advertisement, one in which the woman described herself as 'lovely . . . very attractive and slim'. Physical appearance might be of high value to men and women when choosing a mate, but heterosexual men don't seem to rely on it when deciding whether to answer a personal advertisement.

Some research suggests that what women want and offer seems to differ by sexual orientation. One study found that bisexual women offered the most physical descriptors and also requested more physical attributes in personal ads than lesbians and heterosexual women (Smith & Stillman, 2002). However, a more recent study of online dating ads found that homosexual men and women were more likely to include physical characteristics than their heterosexual counterparts, but less likely to include information regarding their personality or lifestyle (Morgan et al., 2010). Furthermore, in this study, homosexual men and women were more likely to request a short-term or casual relationship than heterosexuals.

The Physical-attractiveness Stereotype

Research has also found that we assume that beautiful people possess certain desirable traits. Other things being equal, we guess beautiful people are happier, sexually warmer, and more outgoing, intelligent and successful – though not more honest or concerned for others (Feingold, 1992b; Jackson et al., 1995; Langlois et al., 2000). Upon perceiving physical attractiveness, we experience positive emotional reactions, which have been identified neurologically. Seeing an attractive face causes heightened activity in the reward centres (medial orbitofrontal cortex) of our brain, and we become keen to establish close relationships with such people (Lemay et al., 2010).

Research suggests a **physical-attractiveness stereotype** meaning that what is beautiful is good. For example, Gurung and Vespia (2007) wondered if the appearance of instructors influenced students' evaluation of them as well as their grades and learning. It did. They found in a study with 861 undergraduate students that likeable, good-looking and well-dressed teachers had students who said they learned more, had higher grades and liked the class better.

physical-attractiveness stereotype the presumption that physically attractive people possess other socially desirable traits as well: what is beautiful is good

First Impressions

To say that attractiveness is important, other things being equal, is not to say that physical appearance always outranks other qualities. Some people more than others judge people by their looks (Livingston, 2001). Moreover, attractiveness probably most affects first impressions.

Zebrowitz and Montepare have reviewed studies on first impressions to see if there is a tendency to generalize what someone is like from a quick glance at their physical appearance. It seems there is. Even if we are warned not to form impressions about people's abilities and qualities based on their looks, we often still do just that (Zebrowitz & Montepare, 2008).

Though interviewers may deny it, attractiveness and grooming affect first impressions in job interviews, especially when the post involves contact with the public (Tsai et al., 2012). This helps explain why attractive people and tall people tend to have more prestigious jobs and make more money (Andreoni & Petrie, 2008; Engemann & Owyang, 2003; Hamermesh, 2011; Persico et al., 2004). Online profile photographs of attractive men lead to more favourable perceptions of their written text, than if the text is seen without the photograph (Brand et al., 2012). Sports professionals who are considered physically attractive earn more money than their less attractive counterparts through sponsorship and advertisement contracts (Berri et al., 2011). However, as Andreoni and Petrie (2008) illustrate from a series of experiments, the rewards of beauty may only be offered in the absence of evidence that disconfirms the 'beauty is good' stereotype. If the performance of an attractive individual is seen to be somewhat under par, then benefits are quickly removed and redistributed to those who are less attractive but perform better.

Research has shown that people tend to look longer at attractive than at unattractive faces (Sui & Liu, 2009). But, people should not be too stunningly beautiful, at least not women. When the effect of advertising using highly physically attractive models on male and female adolescents was investigated, the findings suggested that these highly attractive models were less effective (persuasive) than those models who were 'normally' attractive (Tsai & Chang, 2007).

The speed with which first impressions form, and their influence on thinking and attitudes, helps explain why pretty prospers. Even a .013-second exposure – too brief to discern a face – is enough to enable people to guess a face's attractiveness

(Olson & Marshuetz, 2005). Moreover, when categorizing subsequent words as either good or bad, an attractive face predisposes people to categorize good words faster. Pretty is perceived promptly and primes positive processing.

Is the 'Beautiful Is Good' Stereotype Accurate?

Do beautiful people have desirable traits? There is some truth to the stereotype. Attractive children and young adults are somewhat more relaxed, outgoing, enjoy better psychological well-being, and are more socially polished (Feingold, 1992b; Gupta et al., 2016; Langlois et al., 2000).

Any differences between attractive and unattractive people may result from self-fulfilling prophecies (Hebl & King, 2004). Attractive people are valued and favoured, and so many develop more social self-confidence (see Chapter 3). By that analysis, what's crucial to your social skill is not how you look but how people treat you and how you feel about yourself – whether you accept yourself, like yourself and feel comfortable with yourself.

If we look at this from an evolutionary lens, we can see how the 'beauty is good' stereotype might be more valid than we think. For evolutionary psychologists, being physically attractive is of high intrinsic value. Others invest in physically attractive people as means of developing relationships with them, ideally sexual relationships. Evolutionary psychologists Satoshi Kanazawa and Jody Kovar contend that beautiful people are more intelligent. How do they come to this conclusion? Well, they argue that: (1) men who are more intelligent are more likely to attain higher status than men who are less intelligent; (2) higher-status men are more likely to mate with more beautiful women than lower-status men; (3) intelligence is heritable; and (4) beauty is heritable (Kanazawa & Kovar, 2004). However this kind of 'logical truth' is not easy to verify empirically (e.g. Dupré, 2008; Wallace, 2013).

Who Is Attractive?

We have described attractiveness as if it were an objective quality like height, which some people have more of, some less. Strictly speaking, attractiveness is whatever the people of any given place and time find attractive. This, of course, varies. The beauty standards by which Miss World is judged hardly apply even to the whole planet. People in various places and times have pierced noses, lengthened necks, dyed hair, painted skin, gorged themselves to become voluptuous, starved to become thin, and bound themselves with leather corsets to make their breasts seem small – or used silicone and padded bras to make them seem big. For cultures with scarce resources and for poor or hungry people, plumpness seems attractive; for cultures and individuals with abundant resources, beauty more often equals slimness (Nelson & Morrison, 2005). In Europe, the use of size-zero models has proved controversial in promoting a particular image of beauty. But for all that, researchers have shown that whilst we may have some cultural, religious, sexual orientation, and age variations in what we consider to be attractive, we have universal agreement in what is considered to be beautiful. Moreover, we agree that an attractive individual is preferable to us as a sexual partner than an unattractive individual (Maestripieri et al., 2017).

Generally speaking, research has agreed that the universal standard for an attractive face are the three components of: bilateral symmetry (where both sides of the face match one another) sexual dimorphism (where 'feminine' and

Standards of beauty differ from culture to culture. Yet some people are considered attractive throughout most of the world.

SOURCE: (1) ©AJR_photo/Shutterstock; (2) ©evgenii mitroshin/Shutterstock; (3) ©Shooting Star Studio/Shutterstock; (4) ©Mamasuba/Shutterstock

'masculine' traits are clearly differentiated and emphasized), and averageness (achieves the average standard of facial features for that particular sex and age). Furthermore, evolutionary psychologists have argued that this standard is the result of biological processes, and specifically sexual selection, rather than cultural ones. Cultures tend to agree on which faces they find most attractive, and children show a preference for an attractive face that meets these three criteria long before they have been embedded within cultural preferences (Rhodes, 2006). So beauty is not in the eye of the beholder, but is hard-wired into our biological hard-drive. But why do we find sexual dimorphism, averageness and bilateral symmetry so attractive? Evolutionary psychologists believe they have the answer.

Evolution and Attraction

Psychologists working from the evolutionary perspective often explain the heterosexual human preference for attractive partners in terms of reproductive strategy. If we return to universally accepted attractive facial features – asymmetry, averageness, and sexual dimorphism – evolutionary psychologists offer an explanation that is based on sexual selection to enhance reproduction. All three of these features can be considered honest indicators of an individual being in good physical health and, therefore, fertility. Having average facial features has been associated with heightened resistance to disease and developmental stability (Rhodes, 2006). For example, having an average nose is the optimal shape for breathing. Similarly, symmetry is also associated with good health. Asymmetry often occurs as a result of some physical challenge such as inbreeding, mental retardation, or premature birth. Furthermore, sexual dimorphism, which occurs at puberty, is also a sign of fertility, but perhaps also good health. Testosterone, which causes facial hair, brow ridges, and prominence of the jaw in men, is also a stress to the immune system. Hence men with excessive testosterone, as evidenced through their facial features, may also be very fit and healthy men who can carry the cost of such high levels of the hormone. Excessive levels of oestrogen, as evidenced through full lips, small chin and nose, and large eyes, might also be an indicator of a woman's physical fitness as well as her fertility. Oestrogen is also, arguably, a stress on the immune system (Highfield, 2005; Rhodes et al., 2003; Rhodes, 2006).

This preference for facial features has received considerable empirical attention. Anthony Little at the University of Stirling has conducted a body of work on the evolutionary aspects of attraction. Together with colleagues at the University of Aberdeen and McMaster University in Canada, he examined preferences for symmetry, masculinity and femininity in features, using computer-manipulated

In Chapter 14 we discuss evolutionary psychology's explanation of homosexual attraction.

faces. Both males and females preferred symmetric faces more when judging the opposite sex than when judging same-sex faces. Women preferred more masculine male faces than men did and also showed stronger preference for femininity in female faces than men reported. This actually reveals that women are more concerned with female femininity than are men (Little et al., 2008).

Evolutionary psychologists have also explored men's and women's responses to other cues to reproductive success. Judging from glamour models and beauty pageant winners, men everywhere have felt most attracted to women whose waists are 30 per cent narrower than their hips – a shape associated with peak sexual fertility (Singh, 1993; Singh & Young, 1995; Streeter & McBurney, 2003). Circumstances that reduce a woman's fertility – malnutrition, pregnancy, menopause – also change her shape. But peak fertility does not say too much about ability to take care of, and raise, children. This waist and hip proportion seems more adequate for selecting a prestigious partner than an able mother.

According to evolutionary psychologists, when judging males as potential marriage partners, women also prefer a male waist-to-hip ratio suggesting health and vigour, and during ovulation they show heightened preference for men with masculinized features (Gangestad et al., 2004; Macrae et al., 2002). This makes evolutionary sense, notes Diamond (1996): a muscular hunk was more likely than a scrawny fellow to gather food, build houses and defeat rivals. But today's women prefer men with high incomes even more (Singh & Young, 1995). It seems that what is attractive is in the eye of the beholder, and the norms of a culture.

Much of the data used in studies of the female waist-to-hip ratio is problematic, coming from very small and non-representative samples. In one classic study, the body measurements used were from the Miss America contest winners between 1927 and 1987 (Bivans, 1991), and another, Playboy centrefolds (Garner et al., 1980). These were presented as historically evidenced 'proof' of the evolutionary psychology theory of female waist-to-hip ratio.

In most industrialized cultures today the beauty business is big and growing. In the USA, for example, the number of women aged between 19 and 34 years receiving botox, has risen by 41 per cent since 2011, and buttock augmentation has risen by 61 per cent in the last 5 years (ASAPS, 2018). The global market for cosmetic surgery services (surgical and non-surgical) was $26.3 billion in 2016, a figure that is forecast to rise 5.9 per cent year on year (Grand View Research, 2017). This rise in cosmetic procedures doesn't just reflect women's desire to achieve a particular physical appearance, but also men's. Increasingly men are visiting cosmetic practitioners for a 'daddy do-over' which can include botox, nose-reshaping, eyelid surgery and liposuction (ASPS, 2019). Within African countries, such as Ghana, Nigeria and South Africa, and Asian countries including India and Japan, the exposure to Western ideals of beauty has arguably led to the demand for cosmetic procedures such as skin whitening to achieve it (Calogero et al., 2007; Li et al., 2008; Okoro, 2014; Yan & Bissell, 2014).

In her 1995 book *Reshaping the Female Body*, Kathy Davis at Utrecht University reports her research on the increasing use of cosmetic surgery in the Netherlands. She argues that cosmetic surgery cannot be understood as a matter of individual choice; nor is it an artefact of consumer culture which, in principle, affects us all.

Rather, the shift to cosmetic surgery has to be understood in the context of how gender and power are exercised in modern Western culture. Cosmetic surgery belongs to a broad regime of technologies, practices and discourses, which define the female body as deficient and in need of constant transformation (Davis, 2002).

Evolution, then, predisposes women to favour male traits that signify an ability to provide and protect resources. That, Buss (2016) believes, explains why the males he studied in 37 cultures – from Australia to Zambia – preferred youthful female characteristics that signify reproductive capacity. It perhaps also explains why physically attractive females tend to marry high-status males, and why men compete with such determination to display status by achieving fame and fortune.

However, both 'beauty' and 'high status' could also be explained by social norms. There is no logic, for example, that a slim beautiful woman is more fertile or more able to give birth and raise a child, than a less attractive physically strong woman with lots of muscles who is able to lift 80 kg. In screening potential mates, report Norman Li and his fellow evolutionary psychologists (2002), men require a modicum of physical attractiveness, women require status and resources, and both welcome kindness and intelligence. But again, this could be a product of social norms in terms of what is considered to be desirable.

The Attractiveness of Those We Love

We perceive attractive people as likeable, but we also perceive likeable people as attractive. The beautiful-is-good stereotype also works the other way round: information about somebody's personality influences the perceptions of their physical attributes and beauty (Kniffin & Wilson, 2004). Some personality characteristics are more important than others. Sampo Paunonen (2006) informed students about the intelligence, independence and honesty of a person shown on a picture and asked the students to rate him or her on several physical characteristics. The person described as honest was seen as being in better health and as having a face that looked more kind, attractive and even feminine. It is not easy to accept that a nice and honest person is ugly or that a beautiful person is bad. We prefer consistency and try to get rid of cognitive and emotional dissonance (see Chapter 5).

Perhaps you can recall individuals who, as you grew to like them, became more attractive. Their physical imperfections were no longer so noticeable. Discovering someone's similarities to us also makes the person seem more attractive (Morry, 2005).

Similarity versus Complementarity

As people get to know one another more factors influence whether an acquaintance develops into friendship.

Do Birds of a Feather Flock Together?

You may have heard the saying: birds of a feather flock together. This refers to an assumption that individuals who are similar to one another tend to form close relationships with one another. However, you may have also heard another saying: opposites attract. This refers to an assumption that people tend to be attracted to, and form close relationships with, individuals who are very different from them. Well, both sayings cannot be right, can they? Let's explore the research to find out.

Likeness Begets Liking

When others think as we do, we not only appreciate their attitudes but also make positive inferences about their character (Montoya & Horton, 2004). Social psychological studies have found that the more similar someone's attitudes are to your own, the more likeable you will find the person (Morry, 2004, 2005). Likeness produces liking not only for college students but also for children and the elderly, and for people of various occupations (Graziano & Bruce, 2008). There are some cultural and gender differences documented. For example, Schug et al. (2009) found that the preference for similarity between friends is higher in the West than in East Asian countries. Selfhout et al. (2007) found from their study of 267 Dutch adolescents that similarity in general played a larger role in mutual best friendships between girls than between boys.

Whether there is love at first sight or if love develops more gradually also seems to matter: in a sample of 137 married or cohabiting couples, it was found that partners who fell in love at first sight became romantically involved more quickly, and showed more dissimilar personalities with regard to levels of extraversion, emotional stability and autonomy (Barelds & Barelds-Dijkstra, 2007).

The likeness-leads-to-liking effect has been tested in real-life situations by noting who comes to like whom.

- Have you noticed that when someone nods their head as you do and echoes your thoughts, you feel a certain rapport and liking? That's a common experience, report van Baaren et al. (2003a, 2003b), and one result is higher tips for Dutch restaurant servers who mimic their customers by merely repeating their order. Natural mimicry increases rapport, note Lakin and Chartrand (2003), and desire for rapport increases mimicry.
- In a study of 63 female Canadian adolescents, it was found that they had a more favourable rating of their friends when they perceived similarity on autonomy, prosociality and caregiving (Linden-Andersen et al., 2009).
- University students in the Netherlands rated their perceived similarity with friends during the acquaintanceship process in a naturalistic setting. The undergraduates' personality data were also gathered. While perceived similarity in personality was associated with more friendship, actual similarity in personality was not. What counts is in the eye of the beholder (Selfhout et al., 2009).
- When Buston and Emlen (2003) surveyed nearly 1,000 college-age people, they found that the desire for similar mates far outweighed the desire for beautiful mates. Attractive people sought attractive mates. Wealthy people wanted mates with money. Family-orientated people desired family-orientated mates.
- Studies of newlyweds reveal that similar attitudes and values help bring couples together and predict their satisfaction (Luo & Klohnen, 2005). That reality is the basis of one psychologist-founded online dating site, which claims to match singles using the similarities that mark happy couples (Carter & Snow, 2004; Warren, 2005).

So similarity breeds content. Birds of a feather *do* seem to flock together.

That said, where this research has focused on romantic relationships, it has been on heterosexual romantic relationships. What about other kinds of romantic relationships such as same-sex ones? Research on the principles that characterize opposite-sex romantic relationships remains scarce (Femlee et al., 2010). The literature that does exist suggests that what brings same-sex couples together is similar to the same processes that occur for opposite-sex relationships: physical attraction, admired personal characteristics such as agreeableness and intelligence, sharing space, and similarity to one another in terms of shared values, beliefs and attitudes (Kurdek, 2005; Peplau & Fingerhut, 2007).

Dissimilarity Breeds Dislike

We have a bias – the false consensus bias (see Chapter 4) – towards assuming that others share our attitudes. When we discover that someone has dissimilar attitudes, we may dislike the person. If those dissimilar attitudes pertain to our strong moral convictions, we dislike and distance ourselves from them all the more (Skitka et al., 2005).

In general, dissimilar attitudes depress liking more than similar attitudes enhance it (Singh & Teoh, 1999; Singh & Ho, 2000). Within their own groups, where they expect similarity, people find it especially hard to like someone with dissimilar views (Chen & Kenrick, 2002). That perhaps explains why dating partners and room-mates become more similar over time in their emotional responses to events and in their attitudes (C. Anderson et al., 2003; Davis & Rusbult, 2001). 'Attitude alignment' helps promote and sustain close relationships, a phenomenon that can lead partners to overestimate their attitude similarities (Kenny & Acitelli, 2001; Murray et al., 2002).

Whether people perceive those of another race as similar or dissimilar influences their racial attitudes. Wherever one group of people regards another as 'other' – as creatures who speak differently, live differently, think differently – the potential for conflict is high (see Chapter 13 for more on this). McGlothlin and Killen (2005) highlight the positive impact that contact between races and ethnicities has on children's perceptions of similarity and liking for children of a different race to them. Multi-ethnic and multi-racial schools are an important facilitator for this process.

'Cultural racism' persists, argues social psychologist James Jones (1988, 2003, 2004), because cultural differences are a fact of life. Black culture tends to be present orientated, spontaneously expressive, spiritual and emotionally driven. White culture tends to be more future orientated, materialistic and achievement driven. Rather than trying to eliminate such differences, says Jones, we might better appreciate what they 'contribute to the cultural fabric of a multicultural society'. There are situations in which expressiveness is advantageous and situations in which future orientation is advantageous. Each culture has much to learn from the other. In most Western European countries, where migration and differing birthrates make for growing diversity, educating people to respect and enjoy those who differ is a major challenge. Given increasing cultural diversity and given our natural wariness of differences, this may in fact be the major social challenge of our time.

See Chapters 12 and 13 for further discussion of inter- and intra-group relations and the conflict that results in relation to attitudes, perceptions and behaviours.

Do Opposites Attract?

Are we not also attracted to people who in some ways *differ* from ourselves, in ways that complement our own characteristics?

Sociologist Robert Winch (1958) reasoned that the needs of an outgoing and domineering person would naturally complement those of someone who is shy and submissive. The logic seems compelling, and most of us can think of couples who view their differences as complementary. However, this has not been verified by empirical research. In fact the research is fairly conclusive: as a general rule, opposites do not attract (Aron et al., 2006).

complementarity the popularly supposed tendency, in a relationship between two people, for each to complete what is missing in the other

That said, there may be some exceptions. Some **complementarity** may evolve as a relationship progresses (even a relationship between identical twins). The motivational and cognitive self-expansion model of close relationships (Aron et al., 2001, 2013) proposes that there are some contexts in which opposites do attract, and it might be beneficial for them to do so. When a potential partner has different yet complementary resources, ideas, attitudes, and identity to one self, that can be advantageous for both parties. By working as a team (or as an 'extension of one's self'), they can achieve goals they wouldn't have been able to do so on their own.

Self-esteem and Attraction

Walster (1965) wondered if another's approval is especially rewarding after we have been deprived of approval, much as eating is most rewarding when we're hungry. To test that idea, she gave some female students either very favourable or very unfavourable analyses of their personalities, affirming some and wounding others. Then she asked them to evaluate several people, including an attractive male confederate who just before the experiment had struck up a warm conversation with each woman and had asked each for a date. (Not one turned him down.) Which women do you suppose most liked the man? It was those whose self-esteem had been temporarily shattered and who were presumably hungry for social approval. (After this experiment Walster spent almost an hour talking with each woman and explaining the experiment. She reports that, in the end, none remained disturbed by the temporary ego blow or the broken date.)

This helps explain why people sometimes fall passionately in love on the rebound, after an ego-bruising rejection. Unfortunately, however, low-self-esteem individuals tend to underestimate how much their partner appreciates them. They also have less generous views of their partner and therefore feel less happy with the relationship (Murray et al., 2000). If you feel down about yourself, you are likely to feel pessimistic about your relationships. Feel good about yourself and you're more likely to feel confident of your dating partner or spouse's regard.

Gaining Another's Esteem

If approval that comes after disapproval is powerfully rewarding, then would we most like someone who liked us after initially disliking us? Or would we most like someone who liked us from the start (and therefore gave us more total approval)? Ray is in a small discussion class with his room-mate's cousin, Sophia. After the first week of classes, Ray learns via his 'pipeline' that Sophia thinks him rather shallow. As the semester progresses, he learns that Sophia's opinion of him is steadily rising; gradually she comes to view him as bright, thoughtful and charming. Would Ray like Sophia more if she had thought well of him from the beginning? If Ray is simply counting the number of approving comments he receives, then the answer will be yes. But if, after her initial disapproval, Sophia's rewards become more potent, Ray then might like her better than if she had been consistently affirming.

To see which is more often true, Aronson and Linder (1965) captured the essence of Ray's experience in a clever experiment. They 'allowed' 80 female students to overhear a sequence of evaluations of themselves by another woman. Some women heard consistently positive things about themselves, some consistently negative. Others heard evaluations that changed either from negative to positive (like Sophia's evaluations of Ray) or from positive to negative. In this and other experiments, the target person was especially well-liked when the individual experienced a gain in the other's esteem, especially when the gain occurred gradually and reversed the earlier criticism (Mettee & Aronson, 1974; Clore et al., 1975). Perhaps Sophia's nice words have more credibility coming after her not-so-nice words. Or perhaps after being withheld, they are especially gratifying.

It seems we tend to like others who grow to like us (the loss–gain hypothesis) and really dislike those who initially like us and then cool off on us (the gain–loss hypothesis). Sharma and Kaur (1996) found that the loss–gain liking sequence was associated more closely to interpersonal attraction than the gain–loss hypothesis. They also revealed that the most powerful determinant of interpersonal attraction is an indication that one is liked; and the best-liked person is often the one whose comments are initially negative but become increasingly positive.

Aronson and Linder (1965) speculated that constant approval can lose value. If someone regularly compliments their partner's appearance, these compliments will carry far less impact than the one time they instead criticized their looks. A loved one you've doted on is hard to reward but easy to hurt. This suggests that an open, honest relationship – one where people enjoy one another's esteem and acceptance yet are honest – is more likely to offer continuing rewards than one dulled by the suppression of unpleasant emotions, one in which people try only, as Carnegie (1998) advised, to 'lavish praise'.

Someone who really loves us will be honest with us but will also tend to see us through rose-tinted glasses. When Murray and her co-workers (1996b; Murray & Holmes, 1997) studied dating and married couples, they found that the happiest (and those who became happier with time) were those who idealized each other, who even saw their partners more positively than their partners saw themselves. When we're in love, we're biased to find those we love not only physically attractive but socially attractive as well. Moreover, the most satisfied married couples tend to approach problems without immediately criticizing their partners and finding fault (Karney & Bradbury, 1997). Honesty has its place in a good relationship, but so does a presumption of the other's basic goodness.

Evaluative Conditioning

Why do we like or prefer something at all? People often have little insight into the reasons behind their preferences and even why they like a particular activity.

Empirical evidence suggests that the majority of likes and dislikes are learned rather than innate, as the mere-exposure phenomenon illustrates. However, the nature of the underlying mechanism and processes behind the development of likes and dislikes has been relatively neglected. Sara Thomas at the University of Southampton in England, and Jan De Houwer and Frank Baeyens at the University of Leuven in Belgium have investigated this topic and in their research they have evaluative conditioning how we can come to like or dislike something through an association with something we already like or dislike

related the acquisition of liking through associative learning or conditioning. This is commonly referred to as **evaluative conditioning** (EC). We like those we associate with good feelings. Conditioning creates positive feelings towards things and people linked with other stimuli we already regard as positive, pleasant or beautiful (Byrne & Clore,1970; Lott & Lott, 1974; De Houwer et al., 2001). When, after a strenuous week, we relax in front of a fire, enjoying good food, drink and music, we are likely to feel a special warmth towards those around us. We are not likely to take a liking to someone we meet while suffering a splitting headache.

Evaluative conditioning effects have been obtained using a large variety of stimuli and procedures. In the classic so-called 'luncheon technique', participants were initially asked to rate a range of stimulus materials including music, photographs, paintings and political slogans (Staats & Staats, 1958). Next, participants were presented with the photographs a second time, either in the context of a positive stimulation or while exposed to unpleasant odours. The researchers found that the photographs paired with the pleasant experience were subsequently rated more positively than those associated with the aversive odours. It has also been demonstrated that nonsense words paired with either positive or negative words acquired the same affective value of the word with which they were paired.

The EC research has also contributed to understanding how preferences and liking can be changed. Merely presenting a stimulus in isolation appears to have little effect on the acquired valence of that stimulus. To change preferences, it seems to be more effective to pair the stimulus with another stimulus of the opposite valence (De Houwer et al., 2001). If you want to like a person who does not turn you on you should invite her or him to join you in something you already are fond of. In the landmark work of Hatfield et al. (1978) they offer a practical tip based on these research studies: 'Romantic dinners, trips to the theatre, evenings at home together, and vacations never stop being important . . . If your relationship is to survive, it's important that you *both* continue to associate your relationship with good things.'

This simple theory of attraction – we like those who reward us and those we associate with rewards – helps us understand why people everywhere feel attracted to those who are warm, trustworthy and responsive (Cottrell et al., 2007; Fletcher et al., 1999). The reward theory also helps explain some of the influences on attraction.

- *Proximity* is rewarding. It costs less time and effort to receive friendship's benefits with someone who lives or works close by, or who we have easy access to (such as in online relationships).
- We like *attractive* people because we perceive that they offer other desirable traits and because we benefit by associating with them.
- If others have *similar* opinions, we feel rewarded because we presume that they like us in return. Moreover, those who share our views help validate them. We especially like people if we have successfully converted them to our way of thinking.
- We like to be liked and love to be loved. Thus, liking is usually *mutual.* We like those who like us.

What Is Love?

What do we mean by the word 'love'? Can passionate love endure? If not, what can replace it?

Loving is more complex than liking and thus more difficult to measure, more perplexing to study. People yearn for it, live for it, die for it. Yet only in the last couple of decades has loving become a serious topic in social psychology.

Most attraction researchers have studied what is most easily studied – responses during brief encounters between strangers. The influences on our initial liking of another – proximity, attractiveness, similarity, being liked, and other rewarding traits – also influence our long-term, close relationships (Hendrick & Hendrick, 2008). The impressions that dating couples quickly form of each other therefore provide a clue to their long-term future (Berg & McQuinn, 1986; Morry et al., 2011; Urbaniak & Kilmann, 2006). Even if first impressions are important, long-term loving is not merely an intensification of initial liking. To understand why couples stay together, social psychologists study not only the attraction experienced during first encounters but also enduring, close relationships.

Passionate Love

The first step in scientifically studying romantic love, as in studying any variable, is to decide how to define and measure it. We have ways to measure aggression, altruism, prejudice and liking – but how do we measure love?

Psychologist Robert Sternberg (1998, 2004, 2006) views love as a triangle consisting of three components: passion, intimacy and commitment (**Figure 9.2**). Drawing from ancient philosophy and literature, sociologist John Alan Lee (1998) suggests romantic love stems from twelfth-century France and is a consequence of a capitalistic society. He concludes that love has become a consumer good in postmodern society. However, not everybody agrees. Elaine Hatfield and Richard Rapson (2006) argue that passionate love has always existed between humans.

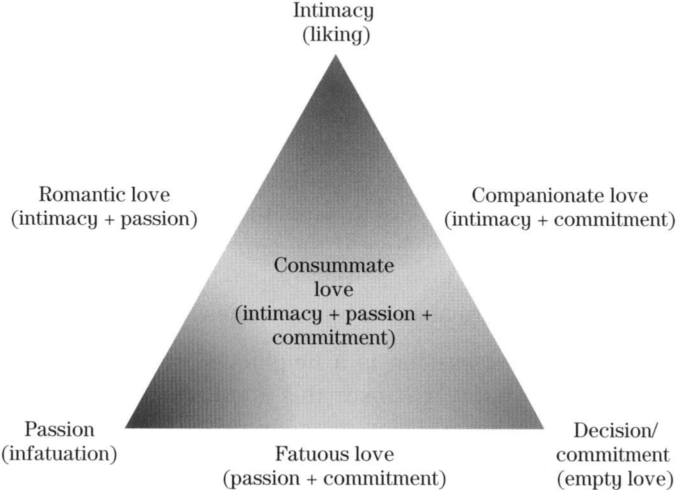

FIGURE 9.2 Sternberg's (1988) conception of kinds of loving as combinations of three basic components of love

But, culture has a profound impact on how people experience love, and on the way they think, feel and behave in romantic settings. According to Hatfield and her colleagues, people's love lives are written in their cultural and personal history, as well as in their genes (Hatfield et al., 2007).

positive psychology the study of the strengths and virtues of individuals founded on the belief that people want to cultivate what is best within themselves, and to enhance their experiences of love, work and play

Studies of love and relationships have become an important part of **positive psychology** (Hendrick & Hendrick, 2009). This branch of psychology focuses on a pleasant, good and meaningful life. It examines the 'life of enjoyment', studying how people experience the positive feelings that are part of normal and healthy living (e.g. relationships and romantic love). It also studies the extraordinary 'flow', which can be juxtaposed with falling in love, the feeling of being optimally engaged with somebody or something.

Some elements are common to all loving relationships: mutual understanding, giving and receiving support, enjoying the loved one's company. Some elements are distinctive. If we experience passionate love, we express it physically, we expect the relationship to be exclusive and we are intensely fascinated with our partner.

passionate love a form of love characterized by intense love and longing for the other. Passionate lovers are absorbed in each other, feel ecstatic at attaining their partner's love, and are disconsolate on losing it

Passionate love is emotional, exciting, intense. Hatfield (1988) defined it as 'a state of intense longing for union with another' (p. 193). If reciprocated, one feels fulfilled and joyous; if not, one feels empty or despairing. Passionate love therefore contributes to positive as well as negative emotions (Kim & Hatfield, 2004). Like other forms of emotional excitement, passionate love involves a roller-coaster of elation and gloom, tingling exhilaration and dejected misery.

Social Neuroscience and Passionate Love

Passionate love may seem to many people to be an ephemeral concept, so difficult to force into being or pin down and describe. Yet there are clearly some neurological processes in action when we are in love, and as technology has developed, we have developed a clearer picture of the processes involved (Hatfield et al., 2012).

To explain passionate love, Hatfield and Rapson (2009, 2011) notes that a given state of arousal can be steered into any of several emotions, depending on how we attribute the arousal. An emotion involves both body and mind – both arousal and the way we interpret and label that arousal. Imagine yourself with pounding heart and trembling hands: are you experiencing fear, anxiety, joy? Physiologically, one emotion is quite similar to another. You may therefore experience the arousal as joy if you are in a euphoric situation, anxiety if your environment is hostile and passionate love if the situation is romantic. In this view, passionate love is the psychological experience of being biologically aroused by someone we find attractive.

Researchers report that sustained eye contact, nodding and smiling are indicators of passionate love.

SOURCE: ©Nektarstock/Shutterstock

If indeed passion is a heightened state that's labelled 'love', then whatever causes this state should intensify feelings of love. In several classic experiments, heterosexual college men aroused sexually by reading or viewing erotic materials had a heightened response to a woman – for example, by scoring much higher on a love scale when describing their girlfriend (Carducci et al., 1978; Dermer & Pyszczynski, 1978; Stephan et al., 1971). Proponents of the **two-factor theory of emotion** (see Chapter 8), developed by Schachter and Singer (1962), argue that when the men who had been aroused responded to a woman, they easily misattributed some of their own arousal as due to her.

two-factor theory of emotion Schachter's theory that the perception of our emotions is based on two different cues: our evaluation of the environment tells us which emotion we are experiencing, while the intensity of the psychological arousal tells us how strong our emotion is

According to this theory, being aroused by *any* source should intensify passionate feelings – providing the mind is free to attribute some of the arousal to a romantic stimulus.

Scary movies, roller-coaster rides and physical exercise have the same effect, especially to those we find attractive (Foster et al., 1998; Meston & Frohlich, 2003). Those who do exciting things together often report the best relationships. And after doing an arousing rather than a mundane laboratory task (roughly the equivalent of a three-legged race on their hands and knees), couples also reported higher satisfaction with their overall relationship (Aron et al., 2000). Adrenaline makes the heart grow fonder. As this suggests, passionate love is a biological as well as a psychological phenomenon.

Social neuroscience is a growing field that seeks to use neuroscience research techniques to examine the social aspects of human life. Cacioppo and Ortigue (2011) describe social neuroscience as being a move on from cognitive neuroscience. They say that if cognitive neuroscience regards the human brain as a computer, social neuroscience regards it more as a computer connected to the Internet. They argue that our brain function and structure do not exist in isolation from our social selves, but are instead closely interconnected with it. By imaging the brain of people in love, we can gain a far wider understanding of how passionate love influences us through our cognitive mechanisms.

Research by social psychologist Arthur Aron and his colleagues (2005) indicates that passionate love engages dopamine-rich brain areas associated with reward. MRI scans from young adults who are intensely in love reveal areas, such as the caudate nucleus, which become more active when gazing at the loved one's photograph (but not when gazing at the photograph of another acquaintance) (Aron et al., 2005). This is a good example of a general social psychological idea: mind states influence brain states. As we see in Chapter 14, psychological functions, emotions and cognitions have an impact on the activity in the brain. The structure of the brain is not hardware, but software, changing with emotional and cognitive input.

Bartels and Zeki (2000, 2004) carried out fMRI studies on people who described themselves as 'truly, deeply, and madly in love'. The researchers gave 19 participants two colour photographs as stimulus, one of the person that they loved as the research stimuli and one of a friend as a control measure. When looking at the picture of their beloved, the imaging results from all the participants showed increased brain activity associated with euphoria-inducing drugs. This seems to explain the 'blissed-out' feeling of being passionately in love.

So if love makes our brains react with such euphoria, what happens when our relationships break down? Fisher (2004) conducted fMRI studies on people who had been rejected in love and were still feeling heartbroken. In these studies the areas of the brain associated with anxiety, pain and attempts to control anger were activated. This supports our understanding of relationship breakdown as painful and psychologically distressing. Just as the overwhelming feelings of falling in love are beyond our control, it would seem that the misery of being rejected is also outside our control.

Variations in Love: Culture and Gender

There is always a temptation to assume that most others share our feelings and ideas. We assume, for example, that love is a precondition for marriage. Most cultures – 89 per cent in one analysis of 166 cultures – do have a concept of romantic love, as reflected in flirtation or couples running off together (Jankowiak & Fischer, 1992). A monogamous marriage is the most common kind of romantic partnership globally (Lieberman & Hatfield, 2006). Whilst being in love is something we all experience, whether it is a prerequisite for marriage is where we differ. We often take for granted that we have to love before we marry or cohabit. But this is not a universal way of thinking. In many cultures outside of Europe and North America, such as China, India or Japan, the parents or another family member make suggestions and sometimes even the decision on who their children should marry. Marriage may be organized for reasons other than love. This can include economics and family status. Sometimes it is better not to prioritize passionate love. Research has shown that love may be the luxury for those who can afford it (Hatfield & Rapson, 2008). Individuals in affluent societies, regardless of where they are located in the world, typically regard love as an important prerequisite for marriage. For those in less affluent societies, the purpose of marriage may be for economic reasons rather than love. In cultures that practise arranged marriages, love tends to follow rather than to precede marriage (Epstein et al., 2013; Regan et al., 2012). Research has shown that individuals in arranged marriages experience just as much satisfaction, well-being and love as those in love marriages (Myers et al., 2005).

Companionate Love

companionate love an affectionate relationship, where one is dedicated and devoted to the partner and his or her happiness (commonly contrasted with passionate love)

Although passionate love burns hot, it inevitably simmers down. If a close relationship is to endure, it will settle to a steadier but still warm afterglow that Hatfield calls **companionate love**.

Unlike the wild emotions of passionate love, companionate love is lower key; it's a deep, affectionate attachment. It activates different parts of the brain (Aron et al., 2005). And it is just as real. Nisa, a !Kung San woman of the African Kalahari Desert, explains: 'When two people are first together, their hearts are on fire and their passion is very great. After a while, the fire cools and that's how it stays. They continue to love each other, but it's in a different way – warm and dependable' (Shostak, 1981).

It won't surprise those who know the rock song 'Addicted to Love' to find out that the flow and ebb of romantic love follows the pattern of addictions to coffee, alcohol and other drugs. At first, a drug gives a big kick, perhaps a high. With repetition, opponent emotions gain strength and tolerance develops. An amount that once was highly stimulating no longer gives a thrill. Stopping the substance, however, does not return you to where you started. Rather, it triggers withdrawal symptoms such as malaise and depression. The same often happens in love. The passionate high is fated to become lukewarm. The no-longer-romantic relationship becomes taken for granted – until it ends. Then the jilted lover, the widower, the divorcé, are surprised at how empty life now seems without the person they long ago stopped feeling passionately attached to. Having focused on what was not working, they stopped noticing what was (Carlson & Hatfield, 1992).

Unlike passionate love, companionate love can last a lifetime.

SOURCE: ©Lucigerma/Shutterstock

'When two people are under the influence of the most violent, most insane, most delusive, and most transient of passions, they are required to swear that they will remain in that excited, abnormal, and exhausting condition continuously until death do them part.'

George Bernard Shaw, *'Getting Married'*, 1908

The cooling of intense romantic love often triggers a period of disillusion, especially among those who regard that feeling of romantic love as essential both for a marriage and for its continuation. However, in its place emotional attachment and commitment take centre stage. For example, a study on older African Americans' romantic relationships reports that they exhibit three love styles: friendship (Storge), logical (Pragma) and selfless love (Agape) (Gupta et al., 2015). It is the quality of the emotional commitment and ability to care for another person that is most important in these relationships. Some research has shown that compared with North Americans, Asians tend to focus less on personal feelings and more on the practical aspects of social attachments (Dion & Dion, 1988; Sprecher et al., 1994b; Sprecher & Toro-Morn, 2002). Thus, they are less vulnerable to disillusionment. Asians are also less prone to the self-focused individualism that in the long run can undermine a relationship and lead to divorce (Dion & Dion, 1991, 1996; Triandis et al., 1988). They also feel more obliged to stay married and it is considered shameful to divorce. Therefore the divorce rate in most Asian countries is much lower than in the West. But the rate of divorce is increasing in Asia partly due to the strong cultural influence from the West. Korea, Japan, China and Taiwan have seen dramatic rises in their divorce rates. In a thorough review of these trends and suggested explanations for them, Huang (2005) offers the following:

1. Changing cultural norms and rapid economic growth. Individuals' focus has shifted towards the acquirement of wealth and career, and away from marriage and stable close relationships that has characterized Asian societies.
2. More educational and career opportunities are available to Asian women. This not only gives women economic independence, but also the power to leave unacceptable and abusive marriages.
3. Lack of social control over marriage. Families have less power over a couple's marriage and are less likely to keep them together.
4. It is easier to get divorced in Asian countries.
5. The rise of individualism. Asian marriages have become about the union of two people rather than the traditional view of two families. Personal desires now override collective ones, with each individual in the marriage striving to meet their own economic and social interests.
6. The rise of love marriages and the decline of arranged marriages. Asians now marry for love. Influences from Western media have changed the way Asian people think about relationships, and have arguably acquired an unrealistic and rather over-romanticized concept of love.

However some researchers have argued that romantic love needn't necessarily simmer down in a long-term relationship. Without the obsessiveness of early love, it can shape relationships throughout our life-course, in terms of positive well-being, good mental health, sexual satisfaction, and intense love (Acevedo & Aron, 2009).

Some research has challenged the stereotype that sex becomes less important and relevant to our relationships as we get older. For example, Gott and Hinchcliffe (2003) interviewed and measured the attitudes of older people aged 50–92 towards the importance of sex in their relationships. They found that sex only became unimportant for single individuals and for those the researchers call 'sexually retired' due to widowhood and/or poor health. They point out that the 'sexually retired' are more likely to be older people, typically in their 80s and 90s. But they warn against an assumption here. It isn't because of age that sex becomes unimportant but because the barriers to having sex are more likely to appear later in life, such as poor health. For the rest of their sample, sex remained an important part of their relationships. Sex, however, did not feature outside of these relationships.

Polyamory

Not all relationships are monogamous. Conley and Moors (2014) outline three different kinds of consensual non-monogamy (CNM). These are:

1. Polyamory – where all individuals involved agree on intimate relationships with one another. Love may be involved.
2. Swinging – usually couples who agree on sexual relationships with other couples. Love is not involved.
3. Open relationships – typically restricted to sexual relationships with individuals outside of a romantic partnership. Love is not involved.

These kinds of relationships challenge not only our traditional understanding of romantic relationships, but also how social psychology has theorized and empirically studied the field of attraction and intimacy in Western cultures. Perhaps controversially, Conley and Moors (2014) argue that switching from a monogamous to a polyamorous relationship can be beneficial for the two individuals involved. They note our typically Western conceptions of a monogamous relationship place a considerable burden on the people involved. Upon entering a monogamous relationship it is assumed that sexual attraction will not wane and that one individual can provide all our emotional and sexual needs. However, a polyamorous relationship can provide individuals with greater social networks, improve communication, and lead to better distribution and management of household duties such as childcare and housework among everyone involved. As we will see later in this chapter, the concept of equity can become a platform for argument within monogamous relationships when one partner feels the distribution of household tasks is unfair. Hence, argue Conley and Moors, polyamory can breathe some air into an otherwise stale relationship. Indeed some research has shown that polyamorous individuals experience more intimacy in their relationships than monogamous individuals do (Morrison et al., 2011). And interestingly, some research has shown that whilst people's perceptions of swinging and open relationships tend to be negative, the idea of polyamory is received more favourably (Matsick et al., 2013). Why? Well, it seems we're not too keen on relationships that are held together just on the basis of sexual attraction. We are much more accepting of relationships that involve love and emotional attachment.

This rapidly developing field into polyamorous relationships has also challenged social psychology's previous understandings and assumptions of gender and sexual identity. Research in this field has demonstrated the de-coupling of gender from sexual identity. Consequently sexual identities are considered to be more fluid. They are not determined by our gender, but by the relationships we happen to be involved in at the time (Diamond, 2003). In their study of polyamorous and monogamous couples, Manley et al. (2015) discovered polyamorous couples reported a much more fluid understanding of sexual identity and orientation. Whilst monogamous couples were more likely to identify as gay or heterosexual, polyamorous couples resisted these polarized categories and instead reported shifting sexual identities over time, depending on partners and relationships.

What Enables Close Relationships?

What factors influence the ups and downs of our close relationships? Let's consider commitment and some factors associated with it: attachment styles, equity and self-disclosure. We will also look at the role of apology and forgiveness in resolving relationship problems.

Commitment

Commitment can be defined as the intention to maintain a relationship as well as feelings of psychological attachment to the other (Rusbult et al., 1998). It may seem reasonable to expect that if a person cares about someone they would automatically commit to a relationship with that person. However, this would be a far too simplistic model of human relationships. We know that some people stay in apparently unsatisfactory relationships, as well as others who leave satisfactory relationships for another relationship. Caryl Rusbult's (1980; Rusbult et al., 1998) Investment Model (IM) of relationships puts forward a more nuanced approach to relationships and commitment and why some couples stay together and others split. The Investment Model is based on Kelley and Thibault's (1978) interdependence theory, positing that people are generally motivated to maximize the rewards of a relationship while at the same time minimizing the cost of that relationship. IM states that the more satisfied you are with a relationship the more you are desirous of maintaining it, and that increased satisfaction also reflects an increase in relationship rewards and a decrease in relationship costs. Support for this model has been found to some extent for same-sex couples, although additional obstacles such as societal prejudice and the lack of shared assets such as property and children, cause extra stress on commitment within these relationships (Beals et al., 2002). However, the recent legalization of marriage in many countries may ease these extra stressors on same-sex couples. Commitment not only is affected by the positive outcomes of the current relationship and the negative outcomes of the alternative to being in that relationship, but also reflects the amount of investment the individual has put into the relationship (Le & Agnew, 2003). Therefore, the more a couple have invested to make a relationship work, the more likely they are to maintain that relationship. As the commitment factors interact, they predict the likely outcome of the relationship (**Figure 9.3**).

The investment in our relationships can be extrinsic or intrinsic. Extrinsic relationship investments are things like the family home or children that a couple have together. These represent a physical or financial tie to the other person that would make leaving them more difficult and complicated. Where extrinsic investments exist in a relationship, the partners are less likely to leave the relationship. Intrinsic relationship investment represents things like the time and emotional effort that the partners put into the relationship. Rusbult states that both the extrinsic and intrinsic investments are non-portable, and that if the person leaves the relationship they cannot take these with them in that form – they are exclusive to that relationship. So although some ties, such as children, may continue once the relationship is over, the format of those ties is altered by the break-up – so the children may see much less of one parent after their parents separate than they did while their parents were still together.

In studies examining heterosexual, gay and lesbian relationships using IM it was found that commitment and investment predicted relationship satisfaction and durability (Kurdek, 1991, 1994, 1995, 2004, 2006, 2008).

Commitment in relationships, maintaining the stability and supportive nature of the couple, allows the people involved greater overall satisfaction. As well as commitment, other factors affect the level of satisfaction in a relationship. Factors such as: the feeling of 'belonging' that we share with our partner (Baumeister & Leary, 1995); the gratitude we have for them (Kubacka et al., 2011); the sharing of emotional burdens and the intimacy we enjoy (Wieselquist et al., 1999), all come together as investments in the relationship and its continuance. By investing in the relationship it becomes more valuable and stable for both parties.

Attachment

The relationships and attachments we have to other people vary from the distant and formal to the very close and intimate. We start our lives being attached to our parents and our immediate family. We learn from necessity to relate to other people, and we find pleasure in this. For the rest of our lives most of us strive to be attached and integrated, to be accepted and appreciated by others. The family attachment plays a particular role in most people's lives. We never forget the intimate and caring relationship to our closest family and we carry this experience

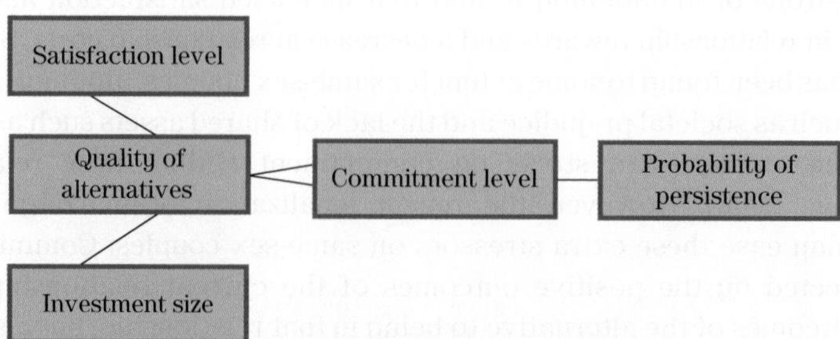

FIGURE 9.3 The investment model of commitment processes

SOURCE: Rusbult et al. (1998).

with us for the rest of our lives. In some cultures the interdependence on the family is stronger than in other cultures. In traditional Eastern cultures there are very close connections between grandparents, parents and offspring. They often live in the same house, share everything, and have a practical and emotional interrelationship. In modern Western civilization the generations do not relate in the same manner. The immediate family consists of parent(s) and children up to about 20 years of age. Then the children leave the parents and establish their own family. But the influence from the parents never disappears. The experience and longing for close connections to other people has been acquired from a very early age.

Our infant dependency strengthens our human bonds. Soon after birth we exhibit various social responses – love, fear, anger. But the first and greatest of these is love. As babies, we almost immediately prefer familiar faces and voices. We coo and smile when our caregivers give us attention.

Deprived of familiar attachments, sometimes under conditions of extreme neglect, children may become withdrawn, frightened, silent. After studying the mental health of homeless children for the World Health Organization, the renowned British psychiatrist John Bowlby (1980, p. 442) reflected: 'Intimate attachments to other human beings are the hub around which a person's life revolves . . . From these intimate attachments [people draw] strength and enjoyment of life.'

Researchers have compared the nature of attachment and love in various close relationships – between parents and children, between friends, and between spouses or lovers (Antonucci et al., 2004; Caron et al., 2012; Maxwell, 1985). Some elements are common to all loving attachments: mutual understanding, giving and receiving support, valuing and enjoying being with the loved one. Passionate love is, however, spiced with some added features: physical affection, an expectation of exclusiveness and an intense fascination with the loved one.

Attachment Styles

John Bowlby declared that the attachments young children develop with their caregiver(s) are the foundation for their later emotional development, and 'The propensity to make strong emotional bonds to particular individuals [is] a basic component of human nature' (1988). In a body of classic studies most infants and adults exhibit **secure attachment** (Baldwin et al., 1996; Bowlby, 1980, 1999; Jones & Cunningham, 1996; Mickelson et al., 1997). When infants in the USA and the Western world are placed in a strange situation (usually a laboratory playroom), they play comfortably in their mother's presence, happily exploring this strange environment. If she leaves, they become distressed; when she returns, they run to her, hold her, then relax and return to exploring and playing (Ainsworth, 1973, 1979). This trusting attachment style, many researchers believe, forms a working model of intimacy – a blueprint for one's adult intimate relationships, in which underlying trust sustains relationships through times of conflict (Ehrenberg et al., 2012; Miller & Rempel, 2004).

secure attachment
attachments rooted in trust and marked by intimacy

Bartholomew and Horowitz (1991) proposed an influential attachment model that classifies people's attachment styles according to their images of self (positive or negative) and of others (positive or negative). Secure people have a positive image of both self and others (**Figure 9.4**, overleaf). They sense their own worth and lovability, and expect that others will accept and respond to their love.

		Image of self	
		Positive	Negative
Image of others	Positive	Secure	Preoccupied
	Negative	Dismissing	Fearful

FIGURE 9.4 Attachment styles
Bartholomew and Horowitz (1991) proposed four distinct attachment styles based on a person's ideas of self and of others.

preoccupied attachment attachments marked by a sense of one's own unworthiness and anxiety, ambivalence and possessiveness

People with the **preoccupied attachment** style (also called *anxious-ambivalent*) have positive expectations of others but a sense of their own unworthiness. In the strange situation, anxious-ambivalent infants are more likely to cling tightly to their mother. If she leaves, they cry; when she returns, they may be indifferent or hostile. As adults, anxious-ambivalent individuals are less trusting, and therefore more possessive and jealous. They may break up repeatedly with the same person. When discussing conflicts, they get emotional and often angry (Cassidy, 2000; Simpson et al., 1996). By contrast, friends who support each other's freedom and acknowledge each other's perspectives usually have a satisfying relationship (Deci et al., 2006).

dismissing attachment an avoidant relationship style marked by distrust of others

fearful attachment an avoidant relationship style marked by fear of rejection

People with negative views of others exhibit either the **dismissing** or the **fearful attachment** style; the two styles share the characteristic of *avoidance.* Although internally aroused, avoidant infants reveal little distress during separation or clinging upon reunion. As adults, avoidant people tend to be less invested in relationships and more likely to leave them. They also are more likely to engage in one-night stands of sex without love. Examples of the two styles might be 'I want to keep my options open' (dismissing) and 'I am uncomfortable getting close to others' (fearful).

Some researchers attribute these varying attachment styles, which have been studied across 62 cultures (Schmitt et al., 2004), to parental responsiveness and social inheritance. Hazan and colleagues (2004) sum up the idea: 'Early attachment experiences form the basis of *internal working models* or characteristic ways of thinking about relationships.' Thus, sensitive, responsive mothers – mothers who engender a sense of basic trust in the world's reliability – typically have securely attached infants, observed Ainsworth (1979) and Erikson (1963). In fact, one study of 100 Israeli grandmother–daughter–granddaughter threesomes found intergenerational consistency of attachment styles (Besser & Priel, 2005).

An interesting development in the discussion of attachment styles and adult relationships is that it appears that adult relationships echo the child–caregiver relationship of childhood. Feeney and Van Vleet (2010) argue that attachment security has an influence on the exploratory behaviour of the adult; those who feel secure and supported in their relationship have a foundation for exploring new ideas and goals, safe in the knowledge that they have a strong relationship to support them through both success and failure. Also, a degree of dependence on the other partner in the relationship allows for greater self-confidence and autonomy.

Attachment, especially to caregivers, is a powerful survival impulse.

SOURCE: ©SUKJAI PHOTO/Shutterstock

Attachment style seems to have an influence on how we deal with threats to our relationship. Birnbaum et al. (2010) state that sexual intimacy is commonly used as a means of repairing a relationship, returning to the intimacy of our close attachment. They found that avoidantly attached individuals were the most likely to avoid intimacy with their partner, showing less desire and using distancing strategies in the face of relationship threats. Anxiously attached individuals were (unsurprisingly) the most anxious, and were the least likely to have hedonistic motivations in relation to intimacy.

The style of caregiving by the other partner seems to have an effect on the person. In a longitudinal study of newly married couples, Feeney and Thrush (2010) found that partners who were intrusive and interfered in their spouses' lives in the first year of marriage had a clear impact. A year after marriage, for those with intrusive spouses, women showed less exploration and autonomy, and men had lower self-esteem and self-efficacy. What is important is that we consider not just the attachment style of the individual, but also the caregiving style they exhibit.

Today most researchers agree that fathers and other caregivers are just as important as mothers (e.g. Day et al., 2005; Lewis & Lamb, 2006). And youths who have experienced nurturant and involved parenting tend later to have warm and supportive relationships with their romantic partners (Conger et al., 2000). Other researchers believe attachment styles may reflect inherited temperament (Harris, 1998). Teens who are prone to anger and anxiety tend to have, as young adults, more fragile relationships (Donnellan et al., 2005a). For better or for worse, early attachment styles do seem to lay a foundation for future relationships.

Friends with Benefits

The number of people (and not the least students) who engage in one-night stands of sex without love has become more prevalent. It seems, however, to be more of a fashionable lifestyle in some subcultures than a result of a particular attachment style in childhood.

'Friends with benefits' (FWB) is a phrase expressing sex in a non-romantic friendship where the benefit of the relationship is primarily sexual. Perhaps unsurprisingly, perceptions of people who engage in FWB relationships tend to be more negative towards women who participate than men (Weaver et al., 2011). Analysis of survey data from over 1,000 undergraduates at a large university in the USA revealed that over half reported experience in a FWB relationship. Those engaged in FWB were characterized as non-romantic hedonists who have a pragmatic view of relationships (Puentes et al., 2008). They were more likely to be males, and women and men differed significantly in their understanding of the FWB relationship. Women tended to view the relationship as more involved and emotional, with the emphasis on friends, while men tended to view the relationship as more casual with an emphasis on benefits (sexual pleasure) (Lehmiller et al., 2011; McGinty et al., 2007).

We might wonder whether these kinds of sexual relationships have any negative impact upon the well-being of those who partake in them. Psychological studies of people who have FWB relationships, show they have no worse health and mental well-being outcomes than individuals who are in more traditional style romantic relationships (Eisenberg et al., 2009; Garcia et al., 2014).

Perhaps one reason for this is that the 'friends with benefits' participants are under no illusion that they are with their one true love (indeed they reject such a notion) and they make it clear that they are cashing in on their friendships by adding sex. Erlandsson et al. (2012) make reference to the 'invisible contract' that underlines FWB relationships. This contract makes it clear to both partners that the relationship is undemanding, 'off-the-record', based on trust, and both partners remain independent of each other. That said, research shows that whilst some of these relationships can transition into a romantic relationship that goes beyond friendship, those that fail to do so risk feelings of jealousy and exploitation creeping into the agreement. Consider this extract from an interview conducted with a Swedish adolescent:

After a while I fell in love with him. . .but he never fell in love with me. . .I became very jealous and sad, felt very bad. . .he was pretty mean actually because he kept having sex with me even though he knew I was in love and felt bad (Girl, 18). (Erlandsson et al., 2012, p. 51).

Research suggests that those who do enter into FWB, and especially heterosexual women, tend to hope of transforming the relationship into a romantic one (Lehmiller et al., 2011; Mongeau et al., 2013). While some may argue that adding sex to a friendship may strengthen the friendship, others suggest that it complicates the friendship and compromises its stability.

Equity

equity a condition in which the outcomes people receive from a relationship are proportional to what they contribute to it. Note: Equitable outcomes needn't always be equal outcomes

If each partner pursues his or her personal desires willy-nilly, the relationship will die. Therefore, our society teaches us to exchange rewards by what Hatfield et al. (1978) have called an **equity** principle of attraction: what you and your partner get out of a relationship should be proportional to what you each put into it. If two people receive equal outcomes, they should contribute equally; otherwise one or the other will feel it is unfair. If both feel their outcomes correspond to the assets and efforts each contributes, then both perceive equity.

Long-term Equity

Is it crass to suppose that friendship and love are rooted in an equitable exchange of rewards? Don't we sometimes give in response to a loved one's need, without expecting any sort of return? Indeed, those involved in an equitable, long-term relationship are unconcerned with short-term equity. Clark and Mills (1979, 1993; Clark, 1984, 1986) argued that people even take pains to *avoid* calculating any exchange benefits. When we help a good friend, we do not want instant repayment. If someone invites us for dinner, we wait before reciprocating, lest the person attribute the motive for our return invitation to be merely paying off a social debt. True friends tune in to one another's needs even when reciprocation is impossible (Clark et al., 1986, 1989). More recent research has confirmed this, and also noted that the rewards we receive from relationships are not necessarily material ones (Cropanzano et al., 2007; Cropanzano & Mitchell, 2005; Mitchell et al., 2012).

Perceived Equity and Satisfaction

Those in an equitable relationship are more content (Bippus et al., 2008; Burgess & Houston, 2013; Canary & Stafford, 2001; Sprecher, 2001). Those who perceive their relationship as inequitable feel discomfort: the one who has the better deal may feel guilty and the one who senses a raw deal may feel strong irritation. (Given the self-serving bias – in heterosexual marriages most husbands perceive themselves as contributing more housework than their wives credit them for – the person who is 'overbenefited' is less sensitive to the inequity.)

Researchers have found that in heterosexual relationships women tend to do more housework and childcare than men, even if they are in full-time employment. What is really interesting is that this unequal division of domestic labour may not be seen as unfair by the couple themselves. Rather, to take on certain household tasks (or not!) may reflect what society expects of the gender roles in the distribution of domestic labour (see also Chapter 14). This may go some way to explaining why same-sex marriages are often considered to be fairer in terms of the division of labour, as they disrupt these norms about who does what around the house (Quam et al., 2012; Schechory & Ziv, 2007). As Dixon and Wetherell (2004) found out from their research with couples, what is 'fair' in a relationship is a matter of moral evaluations that are culturally contingent. The 'normalizing' of these unfair arrangements is apparent in people's everyday language. During the honeymoon and empty-nest stages, spouses are more likely to perceive equity and to feel satisfaction with their marriages (Feeney et al., 1994). When both partners freely give and receive, and make decisions together, the odds of sustained, satisfying love are good.

Perceived inequity triggers marital distress, agree Grote and Clark (2001) from their tracking of married couples over time. But they also report that the traffic between inequity and distress runs both ways: marital distress exacerbates the perception of unfairness (**Figure 9.5**).

self-disclosure revealing intimate aspects of oneself to others

social penetration theory states that closeness between people develops as a result of gradual self-disclosure

Self-disclosure

Deep, companionate relationships are intimate. They enable us to be known as we truly are and to feel accepted. We discover this experience in a good marriage or a close friendship – a relationship where trust displaces anxiety and where we are free to open ourselves without fear of losing the other's affection (Rempel et al., 2001). Such relationships are characterized by what Sidney Jourard called **self-disclosure** (Derlega et al., 1993). As a relationship grows, self-disclosing partners reveal more and more of themselves to each other; their knowledge of each other penetrates to deeper and deeper levels. Altman and Taylor (1973) developed **social penetration theory** to explain how over time relationships move to deeper levels of intimacy in terms of breadth and depth of self-disclosure.

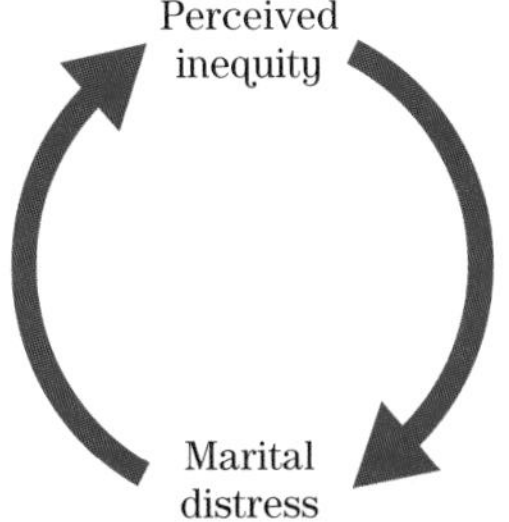

FIGURE 9.5 Perceived inequities trigger marital distress, which fosters the perception of inequities
SOURCE: Adapted from Grote and Clark (2001).

Research studies find that most of us enjoy this intimacy. We feel pleased when a normally reserved person says that something about us 'made me feel like opening up' and shares confidential information (Greene et al., 2006). It's gratifying to be singled out for another's disclosure. Not only do we like those who disclose, we also disclose to those whom we like. And after disclosing to them, we like them more.

Experiments have probed both the *causes* and the *effects* of self-disclosure. When are people most willing to disclose intimate information concerning 'what you like and don't like about yourself' or 'what you're most ashamed and most proud of?' And what effects do such revelations have on those who reveal and receive them?

disclosure reciprocity
the tendency for one person's intimacy of self-disclosure to match that of a conversational partner

The most reliable finding is the **disclosure reciprocity** effect: disclosure begets disclosure (Finkenauer et al., 2004; Sprecher & Hendrick, 2004; Villanueva, 2017). We reveal more to those who have been open with us. Recent research on disclosure reciprocity has focused on our online communications. It has been found, for example, that we often reveal more on computer-mediated-communication than face-to-face (Barak & Gluck-Ofri, 2007; Jiang et al., 2013). But intimacy is seldom instant. Appropriate intimacy progresses like a dance: I reveal a little, you reveal a little – but not too much. You then reveal more, and I reciprocate.

Some people – most of them women – are especially skilled 'openers'; they easily elicit intimate disclosures from others, even from those who normally don't reveal very much of themselves (Drescher & Schultheiss, 2016; Miller et al., 1983; Pegalis et al., 1994; Shaffer et al., 1996). They may also express interest by uttering supportive phrases while their conversational partner is speaking. They are what psychologist Carl Rogers (1980) called 'growth-promoting' listeners – people who are genuine in revealing their own feelings, who are accepting of others' feelings, and who are empathic, sensitive, reflective listeners.

What are the effects of such self-disclosure? Humanistic psychologist Sidney Jourard (1964) argued that dropping our masks, letting ourselves be known as we are, nurtures love. He presumed that it is gratifying to open up to another and then to receive the trust another implies by being open with us.

Children in a family also need openness and sincerity from parents. Self-disclosure is important in parent–child interaction and has an impact on how adolescents develop, according to research by Håkan Stattin and Margaret Kerr at Örebro University, Sweden. The parent who most actively seeks information about the child may not in fact be the one who is best informed. Being informed may rest on the child being forthcoming rather than on the parent actively seeking information (Fletcher et al., 2004a). When researchers have considered both child self-disclosure and elicitation by parents in having knowledge of the child's whereabouts and companions, child-disclosure was far more predictive of accurate knowledge than parental control or solicitation (Stattin & Kerr, 2000).

Child self-disclosure appears to be important in predicting child outcomes as well, with those disclosing more showing less delinquency and depression, fewer deviant peer connections, and better school performance (Kerr & Stattin, 2000; Stattin & Kerr, 2000).

Your behaviour on the Internet versus face-to-face contact can differ due to the security of anonymity; a wider discussion of individual behaviour and differences between virtual and physical behaviour can be found in Chapter 3.

As we have seen a little earlier in this section, sometimes self-disclosure is easier on the Internet where you do not meet people face to face. You can reveal things about yourself in a fairly anonymous situation. The people that you are revealing your inner secrets to may not even know your name. Researchers have found that the process of self-disclosure is much quicker in online relationships as the environment is a much safer one to reveal private aspects of our selves (e.g. Whitty, 2008). For example, Chiou and Wan (2006) found that adolescent boys in Taiwan were more likely to self-disclose about their sexual behaviour and concerns than adolescent girls were. This possibility of self-disclosure has been used in therapy and psychological counselling on the Internet. Those using these services sometimes find it easier or more convenient to talk about their problems and situations where nobody is watching them face to face. When you open up in cyberspace you have more control. You can stop whenever you feel like it, and turn off your computer.

Research close-up

Does Love Mean Never Having to Say You're Sorry?

Source: Schumann, K. (2012). Does love mean never having to say you're sorry? Associations between relationship satisfaction, perceived apology sincerity, and forgiveness. *Journal of Social and Personal Relationships, 29*(7), 997–1010.

Introduction

Researchers have often stated that apologies can heal relationships that are damaged and can be used in the resolution of conflict (Gibney et al., 2008; Lazare, 2004). An apology can increase a person's likelihood of forgiving the transgressor. This study argues that many studies of forgiveness have used hypothetical examples or apologies for minor offences against strangers. In order to gain a more 'real-world' understanding of forgiveness it is important to examine real relationships and forgiveness, rather than artificially created scenarios that have no real emotional context for the participants. Allemand et al. (2007) suggest that people in romantic relationships with high levels of satisfaction are more likely to forgive their partner for transgressions. However, what remains to be examined is the connection between apology and forgiveness in romantic relationships. Some apologies are more likely to evoke forgiveness. Certainly, the sincerity of an apology is important in forgiveness – the more sincere the apology is judged, the more likely a person is to forgive (Risen & Gilovich, 2007). This study sets out to examine cohabiting partners and determine if apologies were more strongly associated with forgiveness among participants who rate their relationship as high satisfaction than those who rate their relationship as low satisfaction, as well as the effects of the sincerity of the apology on the forgiveness by the other partner.

Method

A total of 120 participants (60 male and 60 female) were recruited. All were in some form of cohabiting romantic relationship. The mean relationship length was 4.93 years (sd = 2.89 years). Participants were asked to complete a four-item measure of relationship satisfaction, and the four items were combined to create a reliable satisfaction score.

Participants were then given a username and password and were asked to complete an online diary every night for seven consecutive nights. Participants were asked to keep their diary entry confidential, even from their partner. Each time they logged into their diary they were asked to report anything their partner had done that day to them that they felt was negative. They were then asked how severe they felt that transgression was, if they had forgiven their partner, and to what extent the issue was resolved. They were also asked if there had been an apology. For those participants who said there had been an apology, they were asked how sincere they felt the apology to be, and to report the apology verbatim. Apologies and transgression were coded into groups for quantitative analysis.

Results

Overall, the relationship satisfaction of the participants was reported as high. Of the 120 participants, the overall completion of the diary was high, with the average completion being 6.67 of the 7 days;

104 participants reported at least one transgression over the 7 days, and the mean number of transgressions for these participants was 2.23 over the week. Participants received an apology in 30.84 per cent of cases. The apologies given included some frequent elements, the most frequent element was remorse, and this was in 91.86 per cent of the reported apologies. The other elements that occurred in the apologies were an explanation (36.05 per cent), and acceptance of responsibility (27.91 per cent), admission of wrongdoing (6.98 per cent), an offer of reparation (5.81 per cent), forbearance or patience (5.82 per cent) and acknowledgement of harm (1.16 per cent). Interestingly, none of the apologies included a request for forgiveness. Participants' relationship satisfaction was strongly correlated with forgiveness. Also, one's willingness to forgive one's partner's transgression depended on the interplay between relationship satisfaction and whether or not there was an apology. Specifically participants' ratings of apology, forgiveness and the resolution of the dispute were highly correlated ($r = .71$, $p < .001$). The level of satisfaction in the relationship was also positively associated with forgiveness (parameter estimate = .35 (SE = .13), $t(79.49) = 2.74$, $p = .008$).

Discussion

These results support the idea that an apology is important in resolving conflicts in romantic relationships. But more interestingly, it seems that it is the state of the relationship as well as the presence of an apology, and the level of satisfaction felt, that is an indicator for forgiveness.

Interestingly, when there was no apology given, participants who reported high relationship satisfaction were more likely to forgive their partner than participants with low satisfaction even when they had received an apology. What also emerges from the analysis is that participants who felt more satisfied in their relationship were more likely to report the apology as sincere. This seems to indicate that disputes in highly satisfying relationship are more likely to be resolved, making them more secure. However, disputes in less satisfying relationships are less likely to be resolved, making those relationships less stable. This would explain why couples who are involved in mutually satisfying, happy relationships seem to be able to cope with problems that occur and maintain their relationship, while those in less stable relationships seem to have serious problems over things that other couples cope with.

Critical Reflections

In this study the mean level of relationship satisfaction was reported as high. This does bring into question what the results would be with a mean level of satisfaction that was lower. Also, the reporting took place every evening, giving participants a chance to cool off from the initial hurt or anger at the transgression. It would therefore be interesting to have a reporting method that allowed participants to give their feelings closer to the event. All participants in this study were heterosexual. Researchers on attraction, intimacy and close relationships acknowledge that social psychological research on other kinds of relationships, such as same-sex couples, is scarce. Hence, this study could offer an opportunity to have gay or lesbian participants included in order to be more representative of wider romantic relationships.

Forgiveness

As happy and fulfilling as relationships can be, there are almost inevitably going to be problems. Arguments, hurting the other's feelings, and betrayal can all cause bumps in the road of a relationship. In order to maintain the relationship, we need to forgive the other. While this is easy to say, it can be more difficult to do.

When our partner hurts us, whether purposively or not, in order for the relationship to be maintained and continue, we need to forgive them. Apologizing is important. We are far more likely to forgive someone who apologizes to us than if they don't. Relationships in which transgressions are apologized for, and where forgiveness takes place are likely to be more satisfactory than those where the apology/forgiveness process is not present (Hannon et al., 2010).

Being Single

As many societies place a high value on being in a close romantic relationship and marriage, it is unsurprising that those of us who find ourselves single, without a partner, can feel on the margins of society and something of a social failure. At a time with high divorce rates and falling marriage rates, being single is not an uncommon experience. In their interview study of young single women (aged 20–48 years), Sandfield and Percy (2003) found that they treated their single status as both problematic and temporary. In their qualitative study of single women, Reynolds and Wetherell (2003) noted that they can find themselves in a dilemma. On the one hand, single women can consider themselves a social failure. They have not met society's standards of a successful partnership. However, on the other hand, as a single woman they have achieved independence and exercised personal choice and self-actualization. It is perhaps notable that the research literature on single men is somewhat more scant!

Another reason for having a single status is because an individual is asexual. The social psychological research into asexuality offers some interesting challenges to how we traditionally understand notions of attraction, sex, love and relationships. How asexuality is defined seems to depend on who is doing the defining. The biological understanding of the word defines asexuality as sexual disinterest in everyone (Storms, 1980). Being asexual is often regarded as a consequence of a medical condition requiring treatment rather than a choice (Scherrer, 2008). However, academics, including social psychologists, have argued that these definitions and assumptions about asexuality are far too narrow (Bogaert, 2006). Consequently the term asexual has been expanded to incorporate the various facets of asexuality, including sexual behaviour, attraction, love and self-definition. Bogaert (2006) claims that asexuality is a sexual orientation (just like homosexuality or bisexuality) and some support for this is found in qualitative work conducted with asexual people. For example, in her interviews with individuals who self-identify as asexual, Scherrer (2008) discovered that they could describe their asexuality as an essential and unchangeable part of their biological make-up, hence lacking sexual desire for someone else, or constructed as a choice. As a choice, individuals can flip between being asexual, bisexual, homosexual and so on, depending on their chosen relationship at the time. We can see links here with constructions of self and identity explored in Chapter 3. Furthermore, some asexuals distinguish between romantic and sexual attraction, noting that it is perfectly possible to feel one without the other. An asexual person may have romantic non-sexual relationships. Or no relationships at all. Asexual people then, are varied in their definition of the term, their application of this identity to themselves, and their behaviour. Chasin (2011) states that we should not treat asexual people as a homogenous group, and categorizing asexuality as a sexual orientation unfortunately risks doing so.

How Do Relationships End?

Often love dies. What factors predict marital dissolution? How do couples typically detach or renew their relationships?

People are divorcing more often all over the world. The differences in divorce rates between countries, however, are huge and culturally dependent. Enduring relationships are rooted in enduring love and satisfaction, but also in inattention to possible alternative partners, fear of the termination cost, and a sense of moral obligation. As we have seen previously in this chapter, divorce rates are on the rise, particularly in those countries where exposure to Western values has also increased.

When relationships suffer, those without better alternatives or who feel invested in a relationship (through time, energy, mutual friends, possessions and, perhaps, children) will seek alternatives to exiting the relationship. Returning to the Investment Model (IM) previously discussed in this chapter, Rusbult et al. (1986, 1987, 1998) have explored three ways of coping with a failing relationship (**Table 9.1**). Some people exhibit *loyalty* – by waiting for conditions to improve. The problems are too painful to confront and the risks of separation are too great, so the loyal partner perseveres, hoping the good old days will return. Others (especially men) exhibit *neglect;* they ignore the partner and allow the relationship to deteriorate. With painful dissatisfactions ignored, an insidious emotional uncoupling ensues as the partners talk less and begin redefining their lives without each other. Still others will *voice* their concerns and take active steps to improve the relationship by discussing problems, seeking advice and attempting to change.

It's not distress and arguments that predict divorce in heterosexual marriages, add Huston and colleagues (2001) from their following of newlyweds through time. Rather, it's coldness, disillusionment and hopelessness that predict a dim marital future. This is especially so, observed Swann et al. (2003, 2006), when inhibited men are coupled with critical women.

Why do some relationships flourish while others fail? While it is difficult to be exact, some of the aspects of commitment we looked at earlier in the chapter seem to be important. In addition, there seem to be other factors at play as well. Deci and Ryan (1985; Ryan & Deci, 2000) devised the self-determination theory, in which the autonomy of the individual is central to understanding how people approach the resolution of conflict in relationships, and thus their continuance. Autonomy refers to the sense of control the individual has over their actions,

TABLE 9.1 Responses to relationship distress

	Passive	Active
Constructive	*Loyalty: Await improvement*	*Voice: Seek to improve relationships*
Destructive	*Neglect: Ignore the partner*	*Exit: End the relationship*

SOURCE: Rusbult et al. (1986, 1987, 1998, 2001).

behaviours or choices. They found that people who show autonomy in their romantic relationships and who are autonomously invested in those relationships will be less defensive in their response to relationship conflict. These people are likely to remain more satisfied in the relationship. So people who are in satisfying relationships where they have a sense of control over the relationship will tend to be open to resolving conflicts in that relationship. Knee et al. (2005) argue that the autonomy of one partner may help the other partner to feel unconditionally supported. This unconditional support is then related to a less-defensive response by the partners to conflict within the relationship, making it more likely that conflicts will be resolved and the relationship will continue.

There are also individual differences to threats to the romantic relationship. Murray et al. (2006) discussed how risk regulation theory examines the interaction of self-esteem and the security the individual feels in their relationship. Risk regulation theory states that those with low self-esteem often have high levels of anxiety about how much their partner loves and accepts them. In the face of threats to their relationship, even if that threat is very minor, they will tend to react with exaggerated self-protection, and distance themselves from their partner. As a result, this can often be a self-fulfilling prophecy, with the partner of the person with low self-esteem eventually withdrawing from the relationship in which their partner has distanced themselves from them in reaction to a threat. One strategy that can address this is the use of self-affirmation strategies to increase the self-esteem. By increasing the individual's self-esteem this should help to stop them from distancing themselves from their partner when a threat to a relationship occurs. This should then reduce the distancing which can lead to the break-up of the relationship (Jaremka et al., 2011).

Successful couples have learned, sometimes aided by communication training, to restrain the poisonous put-downs and gut-level reactions, to fight fairly (by stating feelings without insulting), and to depersonalize conflict with comments such as 'I know it's not your fault' (Notarius & Markman, 1993; Yovetich & Rusbult, 1994).

By enacting and expressing love, researcher Robert Sternberg (1988) believes the passion of initial romance can evolve into enduring love:

'Living happily ever after' need not be a myth, but if it is to be a reality, the happiness must be based upon different configurations of mutual feelings at various times in a relationship. Couples who expect their passion to last forever, or their intimacy to remain unchallenged, are in for disappointment . . . We must constantly work at understanding, building, and rebuilding our loving relationships. Relationships are constructions, and they decay over time if they are not maintained and improved. We cannot expect a relationship simply to take care of itself, any more than we can expect that of a building. Rather, we must take responsibility for making our relationships the best they can be.'

What is evident is that in order for relationships to flourish there must be commitment, investment and effort from both parties. The greater the effort, the more rewarding the relationship ultimately is.

Focus on

Sexuality and Attraction: Are there Real Differences?

Much of the research in the area of sexual mate attraction is still focused solely on heterosexual couples. This leaves an important question open: is there a difference in the role of physical attraction for people who are gay and lesbian in contrast to people who are heterosexual? Do gay men and lesbian women have different priorities around physical attraction from their heterosexual counterparts? Some perspectives on sexual mate selection don't seem to have answers to the question of what do people who find the same sex attractive find attractive about them. The evolutionary perspective focuses on heterosexual attraction, and views the attraction traits as evidence of their theory of biological imperative; the core goal of reproduction in heterosexual relationships. If attraction isn't heterosexual, do the traits valued by heterosexual individuals have the same desirability?

Lippa (2007) analysed data from a BBC Internet survey that attracted 119,733 male and 98,462 female participants from around the world, looking at the traits that they found attractive in a partner. Participants were asked to list the three traits that they found most important from a list of 23. Lippa found that there were predictable results for heterosexual men and women, with men valuing intelligence, good looks and humour as the most important and women valuing humour, intelligence and honesty as the most important traits in a mate. Interestingly, the traits that gay and lesbian participants identified were closely matched to their heterosexual counterparts, although the overall results for gay men did place slightly more emphasis on physical attractiveness than for heterosexual men. Lippa argues that the patterns of trait attractiveness are more of a function of your desired partners' gender than your own.

Ha et al. (2012) carried out a study examining partner preference in heterosexual male and female, gay and lesbian participants. Participants were shown hypothetical profiles of the gender that they were attracted to. These profiles included details of the person's status and ambition. The participants were also asked to complete self-reported ratings of the traits that they found most important in the desirability of a mate. They found that it was the heterosexual men that valued physical attractiveness the most, followed by homosexual men. Heterosexual women valued physical attractiveness slightly less than gay men, and homosexual women valued physical attractiveness least of all. In terms of status, heterosexual women rated social status as most important, followed by homosexual men, then heterosexual men, with lesbian women placing the lowest importance on status in a potential partner.

These studies seem to indicate that, while there are some differences between sexualities, the things that we find attractive are very similar, and that instead of looking at this question in terms of what do particular sexualities find attractive, it has more to do with the gender of the person we find attractive than our own gender. The major flaw of any study that examines what we find attractive is that the nuances and individualities of our own desires are lost in the mass of data. Human desire is complex and often surprising; just look around at the people you know, sometimes the people we would least predict as a couple come together in mutual desire.

Questions

1 How could the evolutionary perspective on sexual mate selection explain non-heterosexual desire?

2 If research shows that men and women both value similar traits in sexual mate selection, how useful is it to examine human desire divided by gender?

3 Current research on attraction, intimacy and close relationships is dominated by work on **romantic dyads**. Are there other kinds of romantic relationships which you think social psychology has ignored, and which you think might offer challenges to our current view of how relationships begin, endure, and sometimes fail?

romantic dyad a romantic relationship involving two people

SUMMING UP: ATTRACTION AND INTIMACY

WHAT LEADS TO FRIENDSHIP AND ATTRACTION?

- The best predictor of whether any two people are friends is their proximity or availability to each other. These are conducive to repeated exposure and interaction, which enables us to discover similarities and to feel each other's liking.
- In our modern world, the Internet has expanded proximity and availability of potential partners beyond geographical constraints. Online dating has become increasingly popular in our search for sexual and romantic relationships.
- An important determinant of initial attraction is physical attractiveness. Research consistently shows that we tend to prefer physically attractive people. Evolutionary psychologists argue that for each sex, attractiveness is an indicator of the ability to reproduce. As we get older, physical attractiveness remains important but not as important as affection and commitment in relationships.
- There are cultural ideals about what is considered to be physically attractive. However, we are increasingly reaching consensus on preferences for particular facial features and body shapes as Western culture permeates other cultures. The global rise in cosmetic procedures, for example, is an example of this influence.
- In everyday life, however, people often choose someone whose attractiveness roughly matches their own (or who, if less attractive, has other compensating qualities). This is known as the matching phenomenon and assortative mating.
- Positive attributions about attractive people define a physical-attractiveness stereotype – an assumption that what is beautiful is good.
- Liking is greatly aided by similarity of attitudes, beliefs and values. Likeness leads to liking; opposites rarely attract although complementarity does sometimes define a relationship.
- We are conditioned to like somebody or something placed in a context we already enjoy.

WHAT IS LOVE?

- Researchers have characterized love as having components of friendship, passion and uncommitted game playing.
- Passionate love is experienced as a bewildering confusion of ecstasy and anxiety, elation and pain. The two-factor theory of emotion suggests that in a romantic context, arousal from any source, even painful experiences, can be steered into passion.
- Social neuroscientists document the role of reward centres in the brain which are aroused as a consequence of passionate love.
- There are cultural differences in whether love is a prerequisite for marriage. Some researchers have suggested that love is a basis for marriage in those cultures, typically Western ones, that can afford it. For many non-Western cultures, arranged marriages are the norm, based on economic and social foundations.

- In the best of relationships, the initial passionate high settles to a steadier, more affectionate relationship called companionate love.
- Divorce is on the increase in many cultures. It has become particularly prevalent in societies where the empowerment of women has seen them gain greater access to resources, challenge relationship abuse, and secure financial independence. This has given women greater freedom in choosing whether to remain in a marriage or not.
- Social psychological research on polyamory has increased, as gender and sexual identities become more fluid. Polyamory offers interesting challenges to traditional understandings of romantic and sexual relationships, and the role of individuals within them.

WHAT ENABLES CLOSE RELATIONSHIPS?

- From infancy to old age, attachments are central to human life. Secure attachments, as in an enduring marriage or partnership, mark happy lives.
- Companionate love is most likely to endure when both partners feel the partnership is equitable, with both perceiving themselves receiving from the relationship in proportion to what they contribute to it.
- One reward of companionate love is the opportunity for intimate self-disclosure, a state achieved gradually as each partner reciprocates the other's increasing openness.
- More recently, social psychologists have investigated the trend for 'friends with benefits'. These relationships involve an invisible contract that places their foundations on sex and friendship, and not romance nor love. Some research has found men and women differ in their expectations from these relationships.
- Many individuals choose to remain single. Previously, people with this status have risked being stigmatized as being deficient in some way. Particularly in Western cultures, being single is now understood as an empowered choice.
- Asexuality is defined as a lack of sexual desire or attraction to any other person. This does not necessarily rule out romantic relationships with others. This can be understood as a result of a medical condition, an essential aspect of someone's biological make-up, or a conscious choice. Researchers debate whether asexuality is a sexual orientation.

HOW DO RELATIONSHIPS END?

- Often love does not endure and researchers have discerned predictors of marital dissolution. One predictor is an individualistic culture that values feelings over commitment; other factors include the couple's age, education, values and similarity.
- Researchers are also identifying the process through which couples either detach or rebuild their relationships. And they are identifying the positive and non-defensive communication styles that mark healthy, stable marriages.

Critical Questions

1. Why do we like things associated with ourselves?
2. How does online dating differ from the more traditional spaces for meeting a partner? If we start to use online dating more to find a partner, will this have an impact on the scope of people we are exposed to?

3 Critically evaluate the concept that beauty is a good predictor of character.

4 What challenges do polyamory and asexuality offer more traditional understandings of gender, sex and relationships?

5 Social psychological research into lesbian, gay, bisexual and transgender (LGBT) relationships remains scant and has been slow to develop. Why do you think this is?

6 What challenges do you think LGBT relationships pose for evolutionary psychology?

7 What can we learn from cross-cultural studies about attraction, intimacy and relationships?

Recommended Reading

Classic Papers

Berscheid, E., & Hatfield, E. (1969). *Interpersonal attraction* (pp. 46-51). Addison-Wesley.

Buss, D. M. (1989). Sex differences in human mate preferences: Evolutionary hypotheses tested in 37 cultures. *Brain and Behavioural Sciences, 12*, 1–49.

Sternberg, R. J., & Grajek, S. (1984). The nature of love. *Journal of Personality and Social Psychology, 47*(2), 312–329.

Storms, M. D. (1980). Theories of sexual orientation. *Journal of Personality and Social Psychology, 38*(5), 783–792.

Contemporary papers

Buss, D. (2016). *The evolution of desire: Strategies of human mating.* Basic Books.

Castro, F. N., & de Araujo Lopes, F. (2011). Romantic preferences in Brazilian undergraduate students: From the short term to the long term. *Journal of Sex Research, 48*(5), 479–485.

Conley, T. D., & Moors, A. C. (2014). More oxygen please! How polyamorous relationship strategies might oxygenate marriage. *Psychological Inquiry, 25*(1), 56–63.

Finkel, E. J., Eastwick, P. W., Karney, B. R., Reis, H. T., & Sprecher, S. (2012). Online dating: A critical analysis from the perspective of psychological science. *Psychological Science in the Public Interest, 13*(1), 3–66.

10 HELPING

'Man is by nature a social animal.'
Horace Mann, 1796–1859

The statue of Buddha at Wat Mahathat, Sukhothai (Thailand). The teachings of Buddhism are based on compassion and helping.
SOURCE: ©Dibrova/iStock

The De Long expedition, with their boat *Jeannette,* searched in vain from 1879 to 1881 for the Swedish polar explorer Nordenskjöld and his boat *Vega. Jeanette* became trapped in the ice in the Arctic Sea and, after one year, she went down in the ice and was abandoned by De Long and his crew. They had to walk across the ice towards Siberia and civilization. One of the crew, a Dane called Eriksen, got frostbitten legs and could not walk. They faced a dilemma. Should they leave him on the ice and hasten towards food and shelter, or should they reduce their speed, risking their own lives, but try to save Eriksen? The group of polar explorers chose the second option. Many of them, including Eriksen, did not survive. This situation has been a dilemma for many explorers and polar expeditions. De Long and his crew had demonstrated altruistic behaviour (De Long, 1883).

During the very busy rush hour on 22 July 2013, an unidentified woman estimated to be in her 30s, fell into the 20-cm gap between the train and the platform edge, at JR Minami-Urawa Station, Japan. Trapped underneath the train, over 40 fellow passengers teamed up to lift the 32 tonne train to allow the woman to crawl out and back onto the platform safely (Molloy, 2013). Less dramatic acts of comforting, caring and compassion abound every day. Without asking anything in return, people offer directions, donate money, give blood, volunteer time.

- Why, and when, will people help?
- Who will help?
- What can be done to lessen indifference and increase helping?

These are this chapter's primary questions.

We focus primarily on how and why individuals react towards others in need of help more than on how societies support those in need. Some cultures and societies emphasize helping more than others, by redistributing wealth and resources by their infrastructure (for example, taxation to pay for national healthcare). The welfare states in Europe practise what could be called 'prosocial politics'. Collectivistic cultures also offer help, but this tends to be done through family solidarity.

Altruism and Helping

altruism a motive to increase another's welfare without conscious regard for one's self-interests

Altruism is selfishness in reverse. An altruistic person is concerned and helpful even when no benefits are offered or expected in return. Most religions encourage altruism through stories of selfless acts. In Christianity, the well-known parable of the Good Samaritan conveys compassion for a stranger in distress. In Islam, the narration from the Prophet Muhammad 'None of you truly believes until he loves for his brother what he loves for himself' is a depiction of altruism, and one of the five pillars of Islam is *zakat* or almsgiving. Important principles of Buddhism include *Sila,* which requires people to treat others as they would prefer to be treated themselves, and *Dãna,* which loosely translates as 'generosity'. Buddha also proclaimed 'right action' (or altruism) as one of the eight steps on the path to enlightenment. The neopagan religion Wicca, has teachings in morality which are based on the Wiccan Rede, stating 'an it harm none, do what ye will'. Put simply, you are free to act as you wish, but you must take responsibility for your own actions and the consequences they have for others.

There are many examples of altruism outside of religion. On 29 November 2019, convicted and released Islamic terrorist Usman Khan, carried out a knife attack on innocent members of the public on London Bridge, in the UK. Wearing a fake suicide-bomb vest, Khan struck out randomly at passers-by, fatally stabbing two and injuring others. Risking their lives to stop him, members of the public directly tackled Khan, bringing him to the ground and disarming him before the police arrived and shot him dead. With little regard for their own lives in that moment, these 'have-a-go-heroes' effectively curtailed a vicious attack on the lives of others.

Why Do We Help?

To study helping acts, social psychologists identify circumstances in which people perform such deeds. Before looking at what the research reveals, let's consider what might motivate helping.

Social Exchange and Social Norms

Suppose the blood donation service turns up at your university campus and you're asked to participate. Might you not weigh the *costs* of donating (needle prick, time, fatigue) against those of not donating (guilt, disapproval)? Might you not also weigh the *benefits* of donating (feeling good about helping someone, free refreshments) against those of not donating (saving the time, discomfort and anxiety)? According to social-exchange theory – supported by studies of blood donors by Piliavin (2003) and Piliavin et al. (1982) – such subtle calculations precede decisions to help or not. This pro and contra calculation characterizes adults' decision making generally, not just with regard to helpful actions or deeds.

Several theories of helping agree that, in the long run, helping behaviour benefits the giver as well as the receiver. Most cultures do not only exchange material goods and money but also social goods – love, services, information, status (Fisek & Hysom, 2008; Foa & Foa, 1975). **Social-exchange theory** does not declare that we *consciously* monitor costs and rewards of every single social transaction, but that such considerations influence our behaviour.

social-exchange theory
the theory that human interactions are most accurately described as social transactions between people, where people exchange rewards and costs

Rewards

Rewards that motivate helping may be external or internal. When businesses donate money to improve their corporate image or when someone offers another a ride hoping to receive appreciation or friendship, the reward is external (e.g. Meijer et al., 2006). We give to get. Thus, we are most eager to help someone attractive to us, someone whose approval we desire (Krebs, 1970). External rewards from somebody else tell us that they appreciate our helpful behaviour. This acknowledgement is important for our status and reputation and we are eager to please. Helping is used as a tool for achieving something, such as honour, respect or money. External rewards could, however, reduce spontaneous motivation to help – altruistic behaviour.

Warneken and Tomasello (2008) found helping behaviour among infants 20 months of age. They concluded that external rewards undermine altruistic tendencies, 'even the earliest helping behaviours of young children are intrinsically motivated and socialization practices involving extrinsic rewards can undermine this tendency' (Warneken & Tomasello, 2008).

If helping is used as a tool for achieving money, could money be used to get help? And what kind of help would that be? Felix Oberholzer-Gee wondered if people would be more willing to allow an apparently busy and harassed stranger to jump the queue if they offered money as compensation. He found that money does encourage helping behaviour, but the exchange of favours is no ordinary market transaction. Money does not reliably trigger greater assistance on every occasion. Once helpers understand that a stranger wilfully employs incentives to encourage assistance, these incentives prove ineffective (Oberholzer-Gee, 2007).

Rewards may also be internal and personal when they increase our sense of self-worth. Nearly all blood donors in Jane Piliavin's research agreed that giving blood 'makes you feel good about yourself' and 'gives you a feeling of self-satisfaction'. Indeed, 'Give blood', advises an old Red Cross poster. 'All you'll feel is good'. This helps explain why people far from home will do kindnesses to strangers whom they will never see again.

The positive effect of helping on feelings of self-worth is one explanation for why so many people feel good after doing good. One month-long study of 85 couples found that giving emotional support to one's partner was positive for the giver; giving support boosted the giver's mood (Gleason et al., 2003). Schwartz et al. (2009) report that teenagers who engage in altruistic behaviours experience better mental health and have lower mortality rates than non-altruistic adults. They also found that altruism was positively associated with health for females and with well-being for both young males and females. Piliavin (2003) and Andersen (1998) point to dozens of studies showing that youth engaged in community service projects, school-based 'service learning' or tutoring children, develop social skills and positive social values. They are at markedly less risk for delinquency and school dropout, and are more likely to become engaged citizens. Volunteering likewise benefits the morale and even the health of adults (Wilson et al., 2008). Those who do good tend to do well.

This cost–benefit analysis can seem demeaning. In defence of the theory, however, is it not a credit to humanity that helping can be inherently rewarding, that much of our behaviour is not antisocial but 'prosocial', that we can find fulfilment in the giving of love? How much worse if we gained pleasure only by serving ourselves.

'Men do not value a good deed unless it brings a reward.'
Ovid, *Epistulae ex Ponto*

'True,' some readers may reply. 'Still, reward theories imply that a helpful act is never truly altruistic – that we merely call it "altruistic" when its rewards are inconspicuous. If we help the screaming woman so we can gain social approval, relieve our distress, prevent guilt or boost our self-image, is it really altruistic?'

egoism a motive (supposedly underlying all behaviour) to increase one's own welfare. The opposite of altruism, which aims to increase another's welfare

This has been hotly debated for a long time and concerns to some extent how we define altruism. Most social psychologists today will say that helping behaviour makes the helper feel good, but this is not the only motivation. **Egoism** – the idea that self-interest motivates all behaviour – has fallen into disrepute. By focusing on rewards within the individual it ignores the social aspects of a person – that they might actually want to help others.

Internal Rewards

The benefits of helping include internal self-rewards. Near someone in distress, we may feel distress. You feel hurt when innocent people are beaten or seen starving. You take care of your dog when it needs help because you feel bad leaving it alone. A woman's scream outside your window arouses and distresses you. If you cannot reduce your arousal by interpreting the scream as a playful shriek, then you may investigate or give aid, thereby reducing your distress (Paciello et al., 2012). In some early work by the well-known altruism researcher Dennis Krebs (1975), he found that male students whose physiological responses and self-reports revealed the most arousal in response to another's distress also gave the most help to the person. Also Stocks et al. (2009) found that higher rates of helping were observed among empathically aroused participants. The main reason, however, was not egoistical, to reduce one's own distress, but to help somebody else 'as empathy evokes an altruistic motive to reduce the victim's suffering rather than an egoistic aversive-arousal motive'.

Guilt

Distress is not the only negative emotion we act to reduce. Throughout recorded history, guilt has been a painful emotion, so painful that we will act in ways that avoid guilt feelings (Miller, 2010). Cultures and institutions, for instance the church, have institutionalized ways to relieve guilt: animal and human sacrifices, offerings of grain and money, penitent behaviour, confession, denial. In ancient Israel, the sins of the people were periodically laid on a 'scapegoat' animal that was then led into the wilderness to carry away the people's guilt. In more contemporary times charities have learned how to evoke our feelings of guilt, as they exhibit images of the homeless, the hungry, and the lonely, to increase the chances of us donating money (and sometimes our time) to relieve these guilty feelings (Chang, 2014).

Research close-up

Young Children Are Intrinsically Motivated to See Others Helped

Source: *Hepach, R., Vaish, A., & Tomasello, M. (2012).* Young children are intrinsically motivated to see others helped. *Psychological Science, 23*(9), 967–972.

Introduction

Psychological research has shown that young children, from about 12 months old, start to help others. By the time they are 2 years old, they will offer help to someone else at a cost to themselves. But why? Where does this intrinsic motivation to help come from? Is it because the infant benefits in some way, or is it because even at a young age humans can be motivated by a genuine desire to help someone in need? This study set out to investigate. The measure was a physiological one: pupil dilation. The pupil of the eye is connected to our sympathetic arousal system. In other words, when we feel sympathy for someone, it should be reflected in pupil dilation. This study tested whether the sight of seeing someone needing help induced sympathetic arousal in young children, and whether it was reduced only if the child themselves helped, or if it could also be reduced by watching someone else offer help.

Method

The 36 participants were 2 year olds, of which 18 were boys and 18 girls. A construction resembling a 'house' was placed in the lab, and each child in turn was placed on their parent's lap, seated facing the window of the house. At the window was a monitor screen. Every child watched a short video of an adult putting a toy cuddly dolphin to bed. During this stage, the child's pupil diameter was measured using an eye-tracking device. Children were then randomly assigned to one of three conditions.

Condition 1 was a 'help' condition. Children in this condition were carried away from the window and allowed to move freely inside the house for 15 seconds. In the house was the adult they had seen in the video, putting the toy dolphin to bed. Children were then carried back to the window and their pupil diameter was measured once again.

These children were then shown two further videos at the window. One video was of the adult reaching for the final can to complete a stacking tower. The other video showed an adult reaching for a crayon to complete a drawing. After each video, the child was carried into the house, allowed to move freely within 2 metres of the adult seen in the video, and given the opportunity to retrieve the object (crayon and can) the adult had been reaching for in the video, and hand it to the adult personally. Ten out of 12 children did so on both trials. The diameter of their pupil was re-measured once the child was carried back to the seat in front of the window.

Condition 2 was a 'no-help' condition. This followed the same procedure as for the 'help' condition, with one fundamental difference. The child was not allowed to retrieve the object for the adult. S/he was held back by the parent, and not allowed to move freely once inside the house between each viewing of the video. The diameter of their pupil was measured at each stage.

Condition 3 was a 'third-person-help' condition. This was almost identical to condition 2, but as the child was held back from helping the adult, a second experimenter retrieved the object for them, and handed it back to the adult. As in conditions 1 and 2, a measure of their pupil was taken at each stage.

Results

A one-way analysis of variance revealed that the size of the children's pupil dilation in condition 2 (no help) was significantly larger than in conditions 1 (help) and 3 (third person helps). There was no significant difference in pupil size between conditions 1 and 3.

Discussion

This physiological measure, pupil dilation, offers support for the idea that helping behaviour in young children is motivated by genuine concern for others. The enlarged pupil dilation in the no-help condition indicates higher levels of sympathetic arousal than in conditions 1 and 3. In this condition, the adult has not been helped, either by the infant or someone else. Their eyes indicate continued concern for the adult. However, in conditions 1 and 3, the adult has been helped, either directly or indirectly. As such, concern wanes. It doesn't matter who helps, as long as someone does. This suggests that 'young children are aroused when they see other people in need and are motivated to see them helped'.

Critical Reflections

Conducting research with very young children can be challenging as they typically do not do whatever the researcher wants them to do! Hence, designing such studies is often a compromise between what the researcher wants to do, and what a young child can reasonably do. It is difficult to imagine how we might study helping behaviour in young children. This research does it indirectly by focusing on a very specific indicator of helping behaviour: pupil dilation. Whilst this is arguably a good way of obtaining some measure of helping behaviour in a young sample, how confidently can we conclude that this physiological measure reflects a child's concern for an adult and a willingness to help? It is extremely difficult to measure young children's concern for others, and their motivations to help. This study offers one solution, but are there others we might want to include?

Picture yourself as a participant in a classic experiment conducted with university students by McMillen and Austin (1971). You and another student, each seeking to earn credit towards a course requirement, arrive for the experiment. Soon after, a confederate enters, portraying himself as a previous participant looking for a lost book. He strikes up a conversation in which he mentions that the experiment involves taking a multiple-choice test, for which most of the correct answers are 'B'. After the accomplice departs, the experimenter arrives, explains the experiment, and then asks, 'Have either of you been in this experiment before or heard anything about it?'

Prejudice in all forms (individual and group) is covered in Chapter 13 with intergroup relations and conflict.

Would you lie? The behaviour of those who have gone before you in this experiment – 100 per cent of whom told the little lie – suggests that you would. After you have taken the test (without receiving any feedback on it), the experimenter says: 'You are free to leave. However, if you have some spare time, I could use your help in scoring some questionnaires.' Assuming you have told the lie, do you think you would now be more willing to volunteer some time? Judging from the results, the answer again is yes. On average, those who had not been induced to lie volunteered only 2 minutes of time. Those who had lied were apparently eager to redeem their self-image; on average they offered a whopping 63 minutes.

Guilt seems to go some way to explaining people's motives to volunteer to help others. In their landmark paper on why people volunteer, Clary and Snyder (1999) identify guilt as one of six motives behind volunteering behaviour. Giving one's time and energy to help others can alleviate feelings of guilt over being more fortunate than others or to simply escape from your own problems by focusing on somebody else's. Abell (2012) found that feeling guilty over what humankind has done to other animals is important to volunteers in conservation organizations who work to protect those species humans have brought to the brink of extinction. A stain on our human identity can motivate helping behaviour and a positive volunteer identity.

Our eagerness to do good after doing bad reflects our need to reduce *private* guilt and restore a shaken self-image. It also reflects our desire to reclaim a positive *public* image. Corporate companies who have fallen foul of the public with bad behaviour are typically keen to restore their tarnished image. When the BP oil-rig, Deepwater Horizon, exploded leaking oil into the Gulf of Mexico, the environmental and ecological damage was vast and highly publicized (Muralidharan et al., 2011). Pope Francis had to publicly apologize when he was caught slapping a woman's hands away, when she reached out to him during the pilgrimage to the Vatican on New Year's Eve (Giuffrida, 2020). And when the actor Hugh Grant was arrested for 'lewd behaviour' with a known prostitute, the previously favourable public opinion towards him turned into something decidedly unfavourable (Benoit, 1997). In these high-profile examples, eagerness to do good after doing bad was reflected in their public engagements following these events. Corporate companies took advantage of the media, and especially social media, to repair the damage, apologize and take corrective action. Hugh Grant took advantage of a host of television interviews to apologize, explain, repair the damage, and take corrective action. In all cases reducing a private sense of guilt is tied up with taking action to repair the damage, and being publicly seen to be doing so (Van Norel et al., 2014). And in all cases, the damage has, arguably, been repaired.

All in all, guilt leads to much good. By motivating people to confess, apologize, help and avoid repeated harm, it boosts sensitivity and sustains close relationships.

Exceptions to the Feel Bad–Do Good Scenario

Among well-socialized adults, should we always expect to find the 'feel bad–do good' phenomenon? No. In Chapter 8 we see that one negative mood, anger, produces anything but compassion. Another exception is profound grief. We can imagine that people who suffer the loss of a spouse or a child, whether through death or separation, undergo a period of intense self-preoccupation and are not motivated to help others. However, with the passing of time after a period of bereavement, people are keen to re-establish meaning and purpose to their lives. Helping others is one way to do this (Gillies & Neimeyer, 2006). Roman (2006) tells of a person who helps her workmates deal with the death of a valued colleague while simultaneously struggling with her own personal feelings of loss.

Feel Good, Do Good

Happy people are helpful people. This effect occurs with both children and adults, regardless of whether the good mood comes from a success, from thinking happy thoughts, or from any of several other positive experiences. The *World Happiness Report 2019* documents the positive relationships between happiness and prosocial behaviour (Aknin et al., 2019). Evolutionary psychologists offer an explanation as to why this is the case. Helping others serves **adaptive goals**. Helping our families, friends, work colleagues and so on enhances and secures our own well-being, survival and chances of success (Schulkin, 2011).

adaptive goals goals which, when mastered, help an individual in the long term

Novels, drama and fictional literature often deal with the theme of how love and success make people generous and positive towards others, and the opposite: how misery and unfair treatment breed negative feelings and behaviour. In research on happiness and helpfulness this phenomenon is studied more systematically, with the aim of trying to explain what most people experience in their everyday life. Here is an example.

In Opole, Poland, Dolinski and Nawrat (1998) found that a positive mood of relief can dramatically boost helping. Imagine yourself as one of their unwitting subjects. After illegally parking your car for a few moments, you return to discover what looks like a ticket under your windshield wiper, where parking tickets are placed. However, when you pick up the apparent ticket, you are much relieved to discover it is only an advertisement. Moments later, a university student approaches you and asks you to spend 15 minutes answering questions – to 'help me complete my MA thesis'. Would your positive, relieved mood make you more likely to help? Indeed, 62 per cent of people whose fear had just turned to relief agreed willingly. That was nearly double the number who did so when no ticket-like paper was left or when it was left on the car door (not the usual place for a ticket).

Helping softens a bad mood and sustains a good mood (Grant & Sonnentag, 2010). In a good mood – after being given a gift or while feeling the warm glow of success – people are more likely to have positive thoughts and associations with being helpful. Positive thinkers are likely to be positive actors.

Feel Emotionally Confused, Do Good

In a more recent follow-up study, Nawrat and Dolinski (2007) adopted a similar strategy to see if students, deliberately misled about their grades, would be

Neighbours talk and eat around a table at a street party.

SOURCE: ©Shutterstock/Monkey Business Images

willing volunteers at a charity street party. Teachers, who acted as confederates of the experimenters, pretended to have got students' grades on a piece of coursework mixed up. Unbeknownst to the students, they had been entered into one of four experimental conditions or a control condition. In the control condition, the teacher simply gave them their results. In the positive-only and negative-only conditions, the teacher gave them either a high (positive) grade, or a low (negative) grade. The teacher then apologized for having made a mistake, and returned to confirm the high or low grade. In the see-saw conditions, students were either given a high grade or a low grade. After making the apology, the teacher than returned within 2 minutes, with a grade that was opposite to what they had initially received. So those given a high grade, had it replaced with a low one, and those with a low grade saw it replaced with a high one. Having the final grade confirmed all students were asked if they would volunteer for the street party. Interestingly, the researchers found that it was those students who had been in one of the see-saw conditions that were more likely to volunteer. Regardless of whether the students went from joy to disappointment, or disappointment to joy, it was this quick shift in emotions that led to greater compliance to a request to help. However, in the days following the experiment and before the street party, the majority of the see-saw students who had volunteered to help at the street party, either withdrew their help completely, or reduced the amount of time they could offer to help. Why? It seems that once the emotional confusion was over, and the students could rationally think about their actions, their decision to help was revoked or reduced. Hence sometimes our offers of help may occur at a time of emotional confusion, when we may be acting mindlessly, or irrationally.

Helping Norms

Often we help others not because we have calculated consciously that such behaviour is in our self-interest but because of a subtler form of self-interest: because something tells us we *ought* to. We ought to help a new neighbour move in. We ought to return the wallet we found. We ought to take notes for a fellow student who is ill. Norms, the *oughts* of our lives, are the non-written rules for social behaviour. These norms are often unconscious. They are perceived as natural, or *habitus;* a set of acquired patterns of thought, behaviour and taste (Bourdieu, 1977). There are also norms for helping behaviour, which inform us of what is expected of us if we experience somebody in need of help. But do these helping norms exist cross-culturally? Yes, note Philpot et al. (2019). In their review of CCTV footage taken from cities in the United Kingdom (Lancaster), South Africa (Cape Town) and the Netherlands (Amsterdam), they found that in the majority of cases of public conflict, people intervene to offer help and assistance. Norms of helping *prescribe* proper behaviour. They release more or less automatic behaviour. We think it is natural to act in the way the norms prescribe. We do not need any additional arguments. Researchers who study helping behaviour have classified two social norms that motivate altruism: the **reciprocity norm** and the **social-responsibility norm**.

reciprocity norm an expectation that people will help, not hurt, those who have helped them

social-responsibility norm an expectation that people will help those needing help

The Reciprocity Norm

Sociologist Alvin Gouldner (1960) contended that one universal moral code is a **reciprocity norm**: *to those who help us, we should return help, not harm.* Gouldner believed this norm is as universal as the incest taboo and starts at an early age. Young children seem to reciprocate prosocial behaviour spontaneously. Friends reciprocate gifts more frequently than non-friends, suggesting that friendship affects the amount of reciprocity expressed (Fujisawa et al., 2008). We 'invest' in others and expect dividends. Politicians know that the one who gives a favour can later expect a favour. Mail surveys and solicitations sometimes include a little gift of money or personalized address labels, assuming some people will reciprocate the favour. The reciprocity norm even applies in marriage. At times, one may give more than one receives, but in the long run the exchange should balance out. In all such interactions, to receive without giving in return violates the reciprocity norm. This reminds us of the social-exchange theory mentioned earlier: that the reciprocity norm is based on expected exchange and the social benefits of helping behaviour.

reciprocity norm an expectation that people will help, not hurt, those who have helped them

The reciprocity norm reminds us to balance giving and receiving in social relations. But reciprocity is not the only social norm influencing helping behaviour. You have probably experienced helping somebody who cannot give anything back. The social-reciprocity norm is not expected to be fulfilled, for instance, when offering charity for the homeless, or giving money to starving people on other continents. People in developed and wealthy countries often want to help those who are victims of natural disasters. Consider, for example, the wave of international aid following the tsunami disaster in September 2018, which killed and injured thousands of people in the Central Sulawesi province of Indonesia. In the first 24 hours of the appeal, £6 million was raised, and over £30 million within 6 months (Disasters Emergency Committee, 2018). Those who helped the victims by giving money did not expect anything back. It was 'natural', a social responsibility, to help fellow-beings hit by an environmental catastrophe.

The Social-responsibility Norm

With people who clearly are dependent and unable to reciprocate, such as children, the severely impoverished and those with disabilities, another social norm motivates our helping. The **social-responsibility norm** is the belief that people should help those who need help, without regard to future exchanges (Berkowitz, 1972; Schwartz, 1975). It is instilled into us from an early age, and informs many youth education and development programs (Siu et al., 2012). The norm motivates people to retrieve a dropped book for a person on crutches, for example. The social responsibility norm is fulfilled in different ways, and at different levels, in different countries and cultures. In the welfare states in Europe, for instance in the Nordic countries, people pay higher taxes so everybody can have free health services as well as free education, and a pension. This perhaps explains why these countries are often rated highly on World Happiness Reports. Between 2016 and 2018, Finland, Denmark and Norway occupied the three top spots in the World Happiness rankings (Helliwell et al., 2019). With their basic needs taken care of by paying a high rate of tax (28 per cent), there is arguably a lot to be happy about! A redistribution of wealth and income is accepted because of the social responsibility norm. And the norm is nurtured by welfare politics.

social-responsibility norm an expectation that people will help those needing help

Cultural values can also impact on our motivations to volunteer our time to help others. Grönlund et al. (2011) report the motivations for volunteering in 9,612 students across 13 different countries; Belgium, Canada, China, Croatia, Finland, India, Israel, Japan, Korea, the Netherlands, New Zealand, the UK and the US. They found that students from countries that score high in individualism (Belgium, Canada, Netherlands, New Zealand, UK, USA), were more likely to report their reasons for volunteering as a way of developing their résumé/CV, than those who came from countries who score much lower (China, Croatia, Finland, India, Israel, Japan, Korea). Furthermore, those students who came from countries that score highest on egalitarianism (i.e. the belief that it is important to help others) (Finland, the Netherlands), were more likely to report altruistic motives for volunteering than the students from other countries. Grönlund et al. (2011) conclude that what we 'ought' to do is apparent in our cultural norms. In traditionally collectivistic cultures, such as China, traditional cultural norms obligate people to take care of their family members and others close to them, but not to care to the same degree about people not belonging to their *guanxi,* or close social network (Chen & Silverstein, 2000). The Chinese philosopher Confucius (551–479 BC) is responsible for social norms focusing on the family and the obligation (the norm) for everybody to support their kin (see Chapter 7 for discussion of how these norms shape conformity and compliance in these cultures). Parents taking care of their offspring when their children need support could expect to be looked after by their children when they are in need of care. However, as Chen and Silverstein (2000) note, cultural and political change in China has seen traditional norms, such as this one, eroded. Consequently, ageing parents can no longer take it for granted that their children will look after them in their older age. This in turn has implications for the country's care system.

In Western countries, people tend to help those they feel deserve to be helped. If they are victims of circumstance, such as natural disaster, then they deserve generosity. If they seem to have created their own problems (by laziness, immorality or lack of foresight, for example), then, the norm suggests, they don't deserve help. Responses are thus closely tied to *attributions.* If we attribute the need to an uncontrollable predicament, we help. If we attribute the need to the person's choices, fairness does not require us to help; we say it's the person's own fault. Weiner (1980, 2006) linked attribution theory to decisions to help. He proposed that when we feel anger towards someone for their plight, because we believe it is their own fault, we are unlikely to help. However, if we feel pity, because we do not believe it is their own fault, we will help. This view has received mixed empirical support, and in particular has been challenged for being culturally (Western) biased. As we saw in Chapter 4, the way we attribute cause to people's behaviour and events and respond, is culturally influenced. For example, Badahdah (2005) looked at the willingness of men from Saudi Arabia to help a friend with AIDS. Using a vignette study, Arabic men either read a scenario in which their fictional friend had been infected with the AIDS virus accidentally as a result of a blood transfusion (uncontrollable) with contaminated blood, or as a result of unprotected sex (controllable). Men who read that their friend had been diagnosed with AIDS as a result of a controllable cause (sex) expressed much more anger and less pity than those men who were told their friend had contracted AIDS as a result of an uncontrollable cause (blood transfusion). But would feeling angry mean refusing help? No. In this study it didn't matter what the cause of the AIDS virus was. What mattered was that it was their friend in trouble and needed help. Help was therefore offered. What this study shows, argues Badahdah, is that in Arabic cultures (unlike Western cultures), the norms of brotherhood, alliances and friendship mean mutual aid, regardless of whether you're angry with your friend or not.

The key, say Rudolph et al. (2004) from their review of more than three dozen pertinent studies, is whether your attributions evoke sympathy, which in turn motivates helping (see **Figure 10.1**).

As we will see later in this chapter, knowing the victim or regarding him or her as belonging to your ingroup matters. Kogut and Ritov (2007) at the Hebrew University in Israel reviewed research that shows people are more willing to help strangers when the victims are identified. In their own studies they found that only when the victims are perceived as belonging to their own ingroup, willingness to help a single identified individual is greater than willingness to help a group of individuals.

Gender and Receiving Help

There has been much social psychology research into sex and gender differences, and how these differences manifest themselves in our behaviour, including our helping behaviour. In Chapter 14 we discuss the challenges and insights current understandings of sex and gender pose for the discipline as a whole. For now though, we will focus on research that has examined differences between men and women in their likelihood of helping and being helped.

For example, in some classic research, Eagly and Crowley (1986) located 35 studies conducted in Western countries that compared help received by male or female victims. Virtually all the studies involved short-term encounters with strangers in need – the very situations, as Eagly and Crowley note, in which people expect males to be chivalrous.

Let's quickly outline some of the work they reviewed. Interestingly, they found that women offered help equally to males and females, whereas men offered more help when the persons in need were females. Several studies in the 1970s found that women with car trouble (for example, with a flat tyre) got many more offers of help than men did (Penner et al., 1973; Pomazal & Clore, 1973; West et al., 1975). Similarly, solo female hitchhikers received far more offers of help than solo males or couples (Pomazal & Clore, 1973; Snyder et al., 1974). Since men dominate the crime statistics, with at least nine men for each woman in prison, most people are

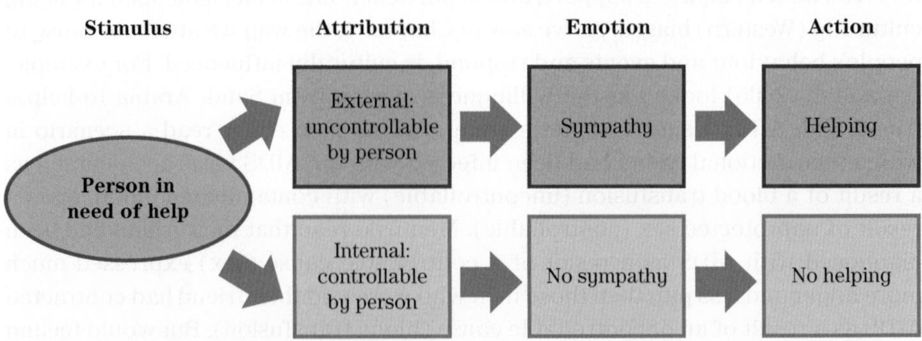

FIGURE 10.1 Attributions and helping

In this model, proposed by German researcher Udo Rudolph and colleagues (2004), helping is mediated by people's explanations of the predicament and their resulting degree of sympathy.

more afraid of helping a male than a female hitchhiker. Eagly and Crowley (1986) propose **social role theory** to explain these gender differences. In most societies, women are socialized into compassionate and nurturing beings, responsible for the care of others. Men are socialized into being dominant and assertive. However, men are also socialized into being the protectors of women.

social role theory proposes that differences between the genders is due to social conditioning and cultural values, rather than biological sex

Of course, men's chivalry towards lone women may be motivated by something other than pure altruism. As Barclay (2010) suggests, appearing altruistic may make up for a less than attractive physical appearance in men. Unsurprisingly, the research reviewed by Eagly and Crowley (1986) finds that men more frequently helped attractive than unattractive women (Mims et al., 1975; Stroufe et al., 1977; West & Brown, 1975).

We discussed in Chapter 9 evolutionary psychology explanations for what men and women find attractive, and how other factors can compensate when physical appearance is considered to be not terribly attractive.

More recent research has found that women not only receive more offers of help in certain situations but also seek more help (Addis & Mahalik, 2003). They are twice as likely to seek medical and psychiatric help. They are the majority of callers to radio counselling programmes and clients of college counselling centres. They more often welcome help from friends.

In a recent study on workplace mobbing, Mulder et al. (2014) considered whether gender, among other characteristics, mattered in the decision to offer help or not. Their study concerns the phenomenon of workplace mobbing. Workplace mobbing describes the dreadful situation in which an employee is systematically bullied at work, and seems incapable of defending him/herself. This bullying is usually psychological and can include acts such as verbal abuse, being excluded from social events, and deliberate acts of being set up to fail by their colleagues.

We discussed bullying in more detail in Chapter 8.

Mulder et al. (2014) suggest that decisions about whether to intervene depend on a few factors. These include the risk of also being stigmatized along with the colleague you're trying to help, characteristics of the helper and how accountable the victim is thought to be for being mobbed (did they deserve it?). In their vignette study with Dutch participants, Mulder and team discovered that men often assume victims of mobbing are responsible for it, that is, they get what they deserve. However, this does not necessarily mean they don't have sympathy for the victim. Indeed having sympathy for the victim is the catalyst for helping. But why help? If we return to the social role theory proposed by Eagly and Crowley (1986), (see also Eagly et al., 2000) we get an explanation. Men are socialized into being dominant, agentic, and responsible for their own actions. Consequently male helpers may identify and empathize with someone who is responsible for their own downfall. It could, under different circumstances, happen to them. For women, feeling anger towards a victim believed to be responsible for being bullied, means a decrease in feelings of sympathy and therefore less likelihood of offering help. But if a victim is considered to be undeserving of their victimization women will feel more sympathy than men, and will offer help.

Why does he help her? Social psychologists have debated and explored sex and gender differences in helping behaviour.

SOURCE: ©Inshyna/Shutterstock

Social psychological research on gender differences in helping offers a broad range of findings, often contradictory. In Chapter 14 we discuss more fully the challenge of searching for sex and gender differences in social psychology.

Evolutionary Explanations

We have hinted at evolutionary explanations for helping in this chapter. We discuss evolutionary psychology and the impact it has on social psychology in Chapters 1 and 14. Evolutionary psychology contends that the essence of life is gene survival. Our genes drive us in adaptive ways that have maximized their chance of survival (Schmitt & Pilcher, 2004). When our ancestors died, their genes lived on, predisposing us to behave in ways that will spread them into the future.

But how do genes influence helping behaviour? We know that more than 90 per cent of human genes are similar in all individuals. We also have very similar genes to some animals, for instance monkeys and mice. Only a very small proportion of our genes are specific or unique to us, not shared with other people. And why should we be so interested to maximize the chance of survival for just these few specific genes and not the rest? It would in some way be more rational from a genetic point of view to secure the survival of most human genes by helping all humans.

How do we detect the people in which copies of our genes occur most abundantly? One clue lies in physical similarities. Some physical characteristics are gene dependent, for instance the colour of the eyes and the hair. If we are particularly interested in the survival of our individual genes then we would take more care of people with the same colour of hair to us. But this is not the case. We do not discriminate between who we help in this way. Our desire to help someone does not depend on our shared physical attributes but on our shared *social characteristics.*

Consider: if we did focus only on the genes in our own biological family, then parents should not treat adopted children in the same caring and helping way as they treat their biological children. But this is not the case. Adopted children are cared for and supported in the same way as biological children. The social norms for taking care of and protecting children and other vulnerable groups are more important in human societies than genetic or biological forces. The sociobiologist E. O. Wilson (1978) stated that kin selection was 'the enemy of civilization'. If we only helped those we share genes with, human society would be in disarray.

As suggested by the title of Richard Dawkins' (1976) popular book *The Selfish Gene,* evolutionary psychology offers a humbling human image. Genes that predispose individuals to self-sacrifice in the interests of strangers' welfare would not survive in the evolutionary competition. Genetic selfishness should, however, predispose us towards two specific types of selfless or even self-sacrificial helping: kin protection and reciprocity. But this is not often the reason why we support strangers in need of help. We are taught by social norms and attitudes in society, acquired during socialization in a culture to do so. As Bowles (2012) argues, it is perhaps the bloody and violent history that humans have endured, which has led to the evolution of altruistic norms.

When the *Titanic* sank, 70 per cent of the females and 20 per cent of the males survived. The chances of survival were 2.5 times better for a first than a third-class passenger. Yet, thanks to gender norms for altruism, the survival odds were better for third-class passengers who were women (47 per cent) than for first-class passengers who were men (31 per cent).

SOURCE: ©chrisdorney/Shutterstock

Kin Protection

One form of self-sacrifice that *would* increase gene survival is devotion to one's biological children. Parents who put their children's welfare ahead of their own are more likely to pass their genes on than parents who neglect their biological children. As evolutionary psychologist David Barash (1979, p. 153) wrote, 'Genes help themselves by being nice to themselves, even if they are enclosed in different bodies'. Genetic egoism (at the biological level) fosters parental altruism (at the psychological level). Although evolution favours self-sacrifice for one's children, children have less at stake in the survival of their parents' genes. Thus, according to the theory, parents will generally be more devoted to their children than their children are to them.

And this is possibly the case in Western industrialized societies but not necessarily so in other cultures and societies. In traditional East Asian cultures with interdependent self-appraisal and where the influence from Confucius is still prevalent, such as China, Japan and Malaysia, children both love and feel obliged to take care of their parents, as well as their ancestors (Park & Muller, 2014). **Filial piety** is a social norm bred for many centuries in these cultures. It is an acknowledgement of the costs parents make to raise their children. Furthermore, in these cultures filial piety extends to the deceased, in recognition of and respect for ancestors. To help and support the parents when they are old is something natural in the same way as parents taking care of their adopted or biological children.

Filial piety a child's acknowledgement of the cost borne by their parents in raising them, and repaid in terms of reciprocal care for those parents. The term can also extend to outward displays of respect for deceased ancestors

Some evolutionary psychologists note that kin selection predisposes ethnic ingroup favouritism – the root of countless historical and contemporary conflicts. Wilson (1978, p. 167) noted that kin selection is 'the enemy of civilization. If human beings are to a large extent guided . . . to favour their own relatives and tribe, only a limited amount of global harmony is possible'.

Many societies are experiencing globalization. More than ever we are forging a global social identity, argues Buchan et al. (2011), which comes with an increase in social and geographical mobility. Our families may not be on our doorstep, they can be hundreds or thousands of miles away. Our communities are now more diverse and comprised of people we are unrelated to. Some researchers have argued this process has facilitated helping behaviour towards people outside of our family groups, and towards racial, religious and ethnic groups different to our own (Buchan et al., 2009, 2011; De et al., 2015; Li et al., 2019). This process can aid a 'harmonious society' and global harmony.

Reciprocity

Genetic self-interest, and self-interest in general, also predicts reciprocity. An organism helps another, biologist Robert Trivers (1971, 2006) argues, because it expects help in return. The giver expects later to be the getter, whereas failure to reciprocate gets punished. As we have already mentioned, Gouldner (1960) termed this the '**reciprocity norm**' – which states that we should help those who help us.

reciprocity norm an expectation that people will help, not hurt, those who have helped them

However, if individual self-interest inevitably wins in genetic competition, then why will we help strangers? Why will we help those whose limited resources or abilities preclude their reciprocating? Trivers' answer to this conundrum is reciprocal altruism. The basis of human society is sociality and reciprocity as evolved as a mechanism for ensuring cooperation. This has also been termed direct reciprocity, as it involves an individual giving help to another on the basis that this person being helped will help the helper at some point in the future. Or in other words, 'I'll scratch your back if you scratch mine' (Nowak & Sigmund, 2005).

But sometimes we offer help to those we know will never be able to return it. Therefore, there are explanations other than Trivers' reciprocal altruism theory to explain our willingness to help strangers. One answer, initially favoured by Darwin, is group selection. This theory suggests that prosocial cooperative genes evolve in human societies as this aids our survival. Whilst a selfish individual might win out over an altruistic one, groups of mutually supportive altruists outlast groups of non-altruists (Krebs, 1998; McAndrew, 2002; Pfeiffer et al., 2005; Sober & Wilson, 1998).

Campbell (1975a, 1975b) offered another basis for unreciprocated altruism: human societies evolved norms that serve as brakes on the biological bias towards self-interest. Dawkins (1976) offered a similar conclusion: 'Let us try to *teach* generosity and altruism, because we are born selfish. Let us understand what our selfish genes are up to, because we may then at least have the chance to upset their designs, something no other species has ever aspired to' (p. 3). This is what humans have been doing all the time, reflecting over their biological forces and tuning them to social norms and conscious behaviour.

Genuine Altruism

Are life-saving heroes, everyday blood donors and Red Cross volunteers ever motivated by an ultimate goal of selfless concern for others? Or is their ultimate goal solely some form of self-benefit, such as gaining a reward, avoiding punishment and guilt or relieving distress? Or in other words, is genuine altruism possible?

Psychologist Daniel Batson (2001; Batson & Powell, 2003) theorizes that our willingness to help is influenced by both self-serving and selfless considerations (**Figure 10.2**). Distress over someone's suffering motivates us to relieve our upset,

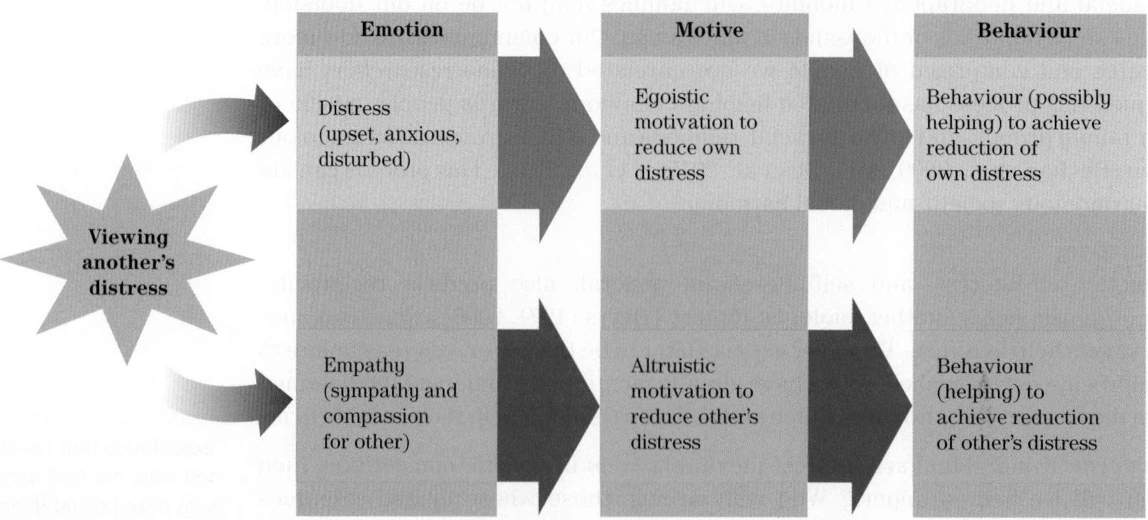

FIGURE 10.2 Egoistic and altruistic routes to helping
Viewing another's distress can evoke a mixture of self-focused distress and other-focused empathy. Researchers agree that distress triggers egoistic motives. But they debate whether empathy can trigger a pure altruistic motive.
SOURCE: Adapted from Batson et al. (1987).

either by escaping the distressing situation or by helping. But especially when we feel securely attached to someone, report both Batson and a team of attachment researchers led by Mario Mikulincer (2005), we also feel **empathy**. We feel empathy for those with whom we identify. In September 1997 millions of people who never came within miles of England's Princess Diana (but who felt as if they knew her after hundreds of tabloid stories and magazine cover articles) wept for her and her motherless sons – but shed no tears for the nearly 1 million faceless Rwandans who have been murdered or died in squalid refugee camps since 1994. This illustrates how the mass media shapes or at least contributes to our empathy and reaction towards human suffering. The way human suffering is presented and how massive the information is has an impact on our feelings; to watch people becoming sad (e.g. in the wake of Princess Diana's death) may make me sad. Even if I did not know Diana personally, I take part in the grief since so many others do. We smile when others smile at us and we feel sad when others show sadness.

empathy the capacity of sharing or vicariously experiencing other people's feelings

The degree of empathy we feel can vary depending on the situation and culture in which it is felt. Empathy can therefore also be seen to be a result of socialization or learned behaviour. The babies who cry when they hear another baby crying could be imitating the crying, but this does not mean that they are displaying empathy for the other baby. Caring may be a 'natural' trait, but for whom we care or feel empathy will depend on the social situation. Empathy can be developed by teaching infants to be helpful and interested in other people – to try to understand the other people's motives, emotions and their particular situation.

Often distress and empathy together motivate responses to a crisis. However, recent research shows that empathy and help occur when the victims of a crisis are not thought to be responsible for it. In a series of experimental studies, Zagefka et al. (2011) found that more monetary donations were offered when the disaster was considered to be the result of natural events rather than caused by the victims themselves. The **attribution** of cause is important in feeling empathy and willingness to help.

attribution theory the theory of how people explain others' behaviour; for example, by attributing it either to internal dispositions (enduring traits, motives and attitudes) or to external situations

To separate egoistic distress reduction from empathy-based altruism, Daniel Batson's research group conducted studies that aroused feelings of empathy. Then the researchers noted whether the aroused people would reduce their own distress by escaping the situation or whether they would go out of their way to aid the person. The results were consistent: with their empathy aroused, people usually helped.

In one of these experiments, Batson et al. (1981) had female students observe a young woman suffering while she supposedly received electric shocks. During a pause in the experiment, the obviously upset victim explained to the experimenter that a childhood fall against an electric fence left her acutely sensitive to shocks. The experimenter suggested that perhaps the observer (the actual participant in this experiment) might trade places and take the remaining shocks for her. Previously, half of these actual participants had been led to believe the suffering person was a kindred spirit on matters of values and interests (thus arousing their empathy). Some also were led to believe that their part in the experiment was completed, so that in any case they were done observing the woman's suffering. Nevertheless, their empathy aroused, virtually all willingly offered to substitute for the victim.

Is this genuine altruism? Schaller and Cialdini (1988) doubted it. Feeling empathy for a sufferer makes one sad, they noted. In one of their experiments, they led people to believe that their sadness was going to be relieved by a different sort of mood-boosting experience – listening to a comedy tape. Under such conditions, people who felt empathy were not especially helpful. Schaller and Cialdini concluded that if we feel empathy but know that something else will make us feel better, we aren't so likely to help. Everyone agrees that some helpful acts are either obviously egoistic (done to gain external rewards or avoid punishment) or subtly egoistic (done to gain internal rewards or relieve inner distress). But is there a third type of helpfulness – a genuine altruism that aims simply to increase another's welfare (producing happiness for oneself merely as a by-product)? Is empathy-based helping a source of such altruism?

Some findings suggest that genuine altruism really does exist: with their empathy aroused, people will help even when they believe no one will know about their helping. Their concern continues until someone *has* been helped (Fehr & Fischbacher, 2003; Gantt & Burton, 2013; Gintis, 2000, 2003). If their efforts to help are unsuccessful, they feel bad even if the failure is not their fault (Batson & Weeks, 1996).

'The measure of our character is what we would do if we were never found out.'
Paraphrased from Thomas Macaulay

After 25 such studies testing egoism versus altruistic empathy in Western populations, Batson (2001; Batson et al., 1999) concluded that sometimes people do focus on others' welfare, not on their own. He argues that 'In this world of growing numbers and shrinking resources, self-interest is a powerful and dangerous threat to the common good. It can lead us to grab for ourselves even when giving rather than grabbing – if others give as well – would bring more benefit to all, including ourselves' (1999, p. 14). Altruism is, he suggests, part of human nature. He argues that in some ways all human behaviour is part of the human nature, but this 'nature' has to be bred and developed. Altruism is therefore nothing against nature, but it has to be stimulated in order to be practised. It will not automatically show itself in all circumstances. That empathy also is part of human nature, says Batson, raises the hope – confirmed by research – that inducing empathy might improve attitudes towards stigmatized people – people with AIDS, the homeless, the mentally ill, the imprisoned and other minorities (see Focus On: The Benefit – and the Costs – of Empathy-induced Altruism).

When Will We Help?

What circumstances prompt people to help, or not to help? How and why is helping influenced by the number and behaviour of other bystanders? By the context? By mood states? By traits and values?

On 13 March 1964, 28-year-old bar manager Kitty Genovese was set upon by a knife-wielding attacker as she returned from work to her Queens, New York, apartment house at 3 a.m. Her screams of terror and pleas for help – 'Oh my God, he stabbed me! Please help me! Please help me!' – aroused some of her neighbours (38 of them, according to an initial *New York Times* report, though the number was later disputed). Some came to their windows and caught fleeting glimpses of a couple quarrelling and also a woman lying in the street. Some saw the attacker leave the scene, but did not see him return. They therefore did not witness when Kitty was killed. According to the article in the *New York Times* none of the witnesses called the police. This has also been disputed and the police have been criticized for not taking the early phone calls seriously enough. Rachel Manning at University of the West of England, and Mark Levine and Alan Collins at Lancaster University argue that the Kitty Genovese case has became an iconic event in the history of helping research, and that the way it is presented in the literature is not supported by the available evidence. Using archive material, the authors show that there is no evidence for the presence of 38 witnesses, or that witnesses observed the murder, or that witnesses remained inactive (Manning et al., 2007). They also suggest that the story itself has become a modern parable, the telling of which has served to limit the scope of inquiry into emergency helping.

What is documented is that Kitty Genovese was murdered that night in New York and many neighbours heard her screaming. Irrespective of the details of what actually happened, the event initiated new theories in helping behaviour and paved the way for one of the most robust phenomena in social psychology – Latané and Darley's (1970) **bystander effect**, the finding that individuals are more likely to help when alone than when in the company of others because of a diffusion of responsibility.

bystander effect the finding that the presence of several bystanders makes it less likely that people will provide help. This tendency is often explained by disseminated responsibility and social comparison

The questions raised by some social psychologists after the case was published on 27 March 1964 on page 1 of the *New York Times* were: why had Genovese's neighbours not come to her aid? Were they callous? Indifferent? Apathetic? If so, there are many people like them.

- 1965 in Brooklyn, 17-year-old Andrew Mormille was knifed in the stomach as he rode the subway home to Manhattan. After his attackers left the car, 11 other riders watched the young man bleed to death.
- On 7 September 2006 Eugene Obiora, a young man from Nigeria, visited a Social Office in Trondheim, Norway, to ask for money to celebrate his son's birthday. He had a discussion with the social officers and refused to leave until he was attended to. The social officers called the police. Obiora was handcuffed, kicked and dragged along the floor and the staircase. He died during the apprehension by the police using a fatal grip of the neck. Several people watched and listened to Obiora screaming and roaring: 'They kill me, they kill me.' Nobody intervened.
- On 18 April 2010 Hugo Alfredo Tale-Yax, a homeless Guatemalan immigrant bled to death on a sidewalk in New York, as pedestrians walked by. He had been stabbed whilst saving a woman from being attacked by the man carrying a knife. One passerby even took a photograph of him with his phone. Despite dozens walking past him, no-one came to his aid for an hour and a half. By then it was too late. Tale-Yax had died.

Bystander inaction. What influences our interpretations of a scene such as this, and our decisions to help or not to help?
SOURCE: ©Abd. Halim Hadi/ Shutterstock

What is shocking is not that in these cases some people failed to help, but that in each of these groups (of 38, 11, hundreds and thousands) almost 100 per cent of those involved failed to respond. Why? In the same or similar situations, would you or I react as they did?

Social psychologists were curious and concerned about bystanders' lack of involvement during events such as Kitty Genovese's murder. So they undertook experiments to identify when people will help in an emergency. Then they broadened the question to: who is likely to help in non-emergencies – by such deeds as giving money, donating blood or contributing time? Let's examine these experiments by looking first at the *circumstances* that enhance helpfulness and then at the characteristics of the *people* who help.

Number of Bystanders

Bystander passivity during emergencies has prompted social commentators to lament people's 'alienation', 'apathy', 'indifference' and 'unconscious sadistic impulses'. By attributing the non-intervention to the bystanders' dispositions, we can reassure ourselves that, as caring people, we would have helped. But were the bystanders such inhuman characters?

Latané and Darley (1970) were unconvinced. They staged ingenious emergencies and found that a single situational factor – the presence of other bystanders – greatly decreased intervention. By 1980 they had conducted four dozen studies that compared help given by bystanders who perceived themselves to be either alone or with others. In about 90 per cent of those comparisons, involving nearly 6,000 people, lone bystanders were more likely to help (Latané & Nida, 1981).

Sometimes the victim was actually less likely to get help when many people were around. When Latané and Dabbs (1975) and 145 collaborators 'accidentally' dropped coins or pencils during 1,497 elevator rides, they were helped 40 per cent of the time when one other person was on the elevator and less than 20 per cent of the time when there were six passengers.

This effect has not just been observed in adults, but also children as young as 5 years of age. Plotner et al. (2015) observed that 5-year-old children were less likely to help someone when others were also present who could potentially offer assistance. However, if the child was the only witness to someone needing help, they provided it. The researchers conclude that behind this behaviour is a diffusion of responsibility when others are present. We shall consider the effect this has on helping behaviour a little later in this section.

This bystander effect is also apparent in online encounters. In online communication, people are more likely to respond helpfully to a request (such as from someone seeking the link to the campus library) if they believe they alone (and not several others as well) have received it (Blair et al., 2005). Palasinski (2012) found that whether you thought you were being monitored also had an effect on the likelihood of offering help. In his study of cyberbystanders who witnessed a mock incident of sexual abuse against a minor in a chatroom, the likelihood of the participant intervening to help was reduced not only when more cyberbystanders were present, but also when they thought the chatroom was under surveillance.

There is some interesting research that took place in the bars of Amsterdam that suggests the consumption of alcohol reverses this bystander effect. Van Bommel et al. (2016) found that individuals who had consumed alcohol were much quicker to offer help to someone to pick up items they'd dropped, than their sober counterparts, regardless of how many bystanders there were. Why? Well, while the problems of the excessive drinking of alcohol are clearly established, its force as a 'social lubricant' and disinhibition of normal social behaviour, argue Van Bommel et al. (2016), mean imbibing alcohol can facilitate help in circumstances that would ordinarily inhibit that help. Furthermore, as alcohol causes selective attention (or what has been termed 'alcohol myopia', or beer-goggles!), it focuses perception on the person needing help rather than the bystanders. And noticing the need for help is key to offering it.

In more typical sober circumstances we can ask why do bystanders sometimes inhibit helping? Darley and Latané (1968) surmised that as the number of bystanders increases, any given bystander is less likely to *notice* the incident, less likely to *interpret* the incident as a problem or an emergency, and less likely to *assume responsibility* for taking action (**Figure 10.3**).

Noticing

Twenty minutes after Eleanor Bradley has fallen and broken her leg on a crowded city pavement, you come along. Your eyes are on the backs of the pedestrians in front of you (it is bad manners to stare at those you pass) and your private thoughts are on the day's events. Would you therefore be less likely to notice the injured woman than if the pavement were virtually deserted?

To find out, Latané and Darley (1968) had male students fill out a questionnaire in a room, either by themselves or with two strangers. While they were working (and being observed through a one-way mirror), there was a staged emergency: smoke poured into the room through a wall vent. Solitary students, who often glanced idly about the room while working, noticed the smoke almost immediately – usually in less than 5 seconds. Those in groups kept their eyes on their work. It typically took them about 20 seconds to notice the smoke.

Interpreting

Once we notice an ambiguous event, we must interpret it. Put yourself in the room filling with smoke. Though worried, you don't want to embarrass yourself by appearing flustered. You glance at the others. They look calm, indifferent. Assuming everything must be OK, you shrug it off and go back to work. Then one of the others notices the smoke and, noting your apparent unconcern, reacts similarly. This is yet another example of informational influence (Chapter 7). Each person uses others' behaviour as clues to reality. Such misinterpretations

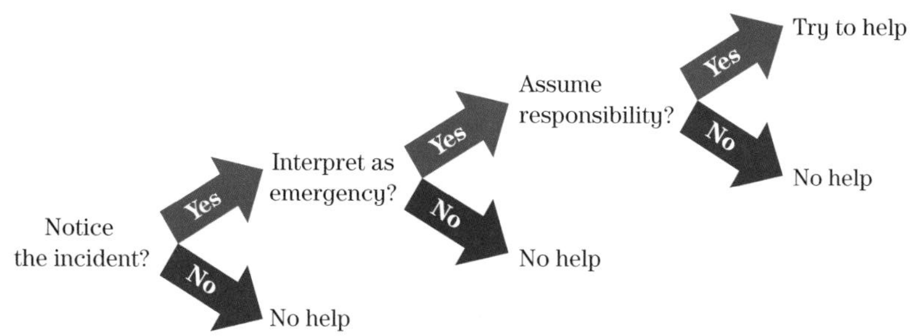

FIGURE 10.3 Darley and Latané's decision tree
Only one path up the tree leads to helping. At each fork of the path, the presence of other bystanders may divert a person down a branch towards not helping.
SOURCE: Adapted from Darley and Latané (1968).

can contribute to a delayed response to actual fires in offices, restaurants and other multiple-occupancy settings. In recent times we have seen the catastrophic effects of delayed responses and misinformation. On 14 June 2017, a 24-storey residential block known as Grenfell Tower caught fire. It spread rapidly up the tower, causing many people to lose their lives, and many more to be injured. Unsure of what to do and whose advice to follow, some residents tried to flee the building while others obeyed the building's safety regulations and the advice of the emergency services which was to 'stay put' in their apartment. A cataclysmic-mix of ambiguity, misinformation and poor building health and safety standards led to one of the worst tragedies experienced in the UK in recent times (MacLeod, 2018).

illusion of transparency the illusion that our concealed emotions leak out and can be easily read by others

Misinterpretations are fed by what Gilovich et al. (1998) call an **illusion of transparency** – a tendency to overestimate others' ability to 'read' our internal states. (See the Research Close-Up on the Illusion of Conscious Will in Chapter 3.) In their studies, people facing an emergency presumed their concern was more visible than it was. More than we usually suppose, our concern or alarm is opaque. Keenly aware of our emotions, we presume they leak out and that others see right through us. Sometimes others do read our emotions, but often we keep our cool quite effectively. The result is what in Chapter 11 is called 'pluralistic ignorance' – ignorance that others are thinking and feeling what we are. In emergencies, each person may think, 'I'm very concerned', but perceive others as calm – 'so maybe it's not an emergency'.

So it happened in Latané and Darley's (1968) experiment. When those working alone noticed the smoke, they usually hesitated a moment, then got up, walked over to the vent, felt, sniffed and waved at the smoke, hesitated again, and then went to report it. In dramatic contrast, those in groups of three did not move. Among the 24 men in eight groups, only one person reported the smoke within the first four minutes (**Figure 10.4**). By the end of the six-minute experiment, the smoke was so thick it was obscuring the men's vision and they were rubbing their eyes and coughing. Still, in only three of the eight groups did even a single person leave to report the problem.

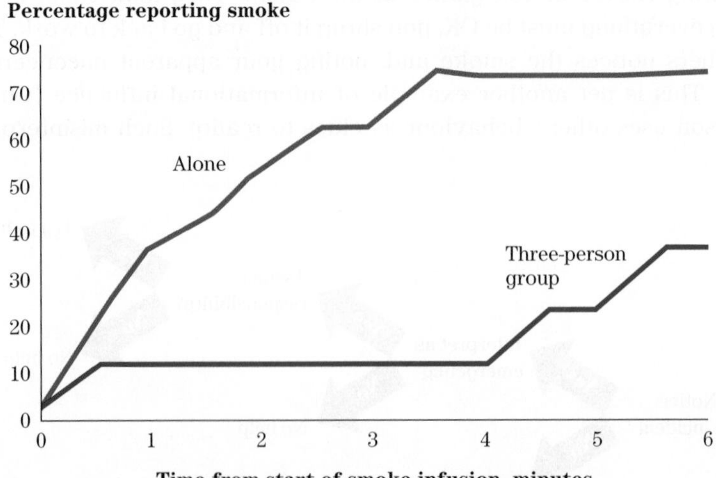

FIGURE 10.4 The smoke-filled-room experiment

Smoke pouring into the testing room was much more likely to be reported by individuals working alone than by three-person groups.

SOURCE: Data from Latané and Darley (1968).

Equally interesting, the group's passivity affected its members' interpretations. What caused the smoke? 'A leak in the air conditioning'. 'Chemistry labs in the building'. 'Steam pipes'. 'Truth gas'. Not one said, 'Fire'. The group members, by serving as non-responsive models, influenced one another's interpretation of the situation.

Interpretations matter. Is this man locked out of his car or is he a burglar? Our answer affects how we respond.

SOURCE: ©DedMityay/Shutterstock

That experimental dilemma parallels real-life dilemmas we all face. Are the shrieks outside merely playful antics or the desperate screams of someone being assaulted? Is the boys' scuffling a friendly tussle or a vicious fight? Is the person slumped in the doorway sleeping, high on drugs or seriously ill, perhaps in a diabetic coma? In their work on intimate partner violence, Weitzman and her colleagues (2017) note that fear of misinterpreting the situation can be a significant barrier against others intervening to help, especially when the victim is an acquaintance rather than a close friend or family member.

Unlike the smoke-filled-room experiment, these everyday situations involve another in desperate need. To see if the same *bystander effect* occurs in such situations, Latané and Rodin (1969) staged a well-known classic experiment around a woman in distress. A female researcher set male students to work on a questionnaire and then left through a curtained doorway to work in an adjacent office. Four minutes later she could be heard (from a tape recorder) climbing on a chair to reach some papers. This was followed by a scream and a loud crash as the chair collapsed and she fell to the floor. 'Oh, my God, my foot . . . I . . . I . . . can't move it,' she sobbed. 'Oh . . . my ankle . . . I . . . can't get this . . . thing . . . off me.' Only after 2 minutes of moaning did she manage to make it out of her office door.

Seventy per cent of those who were alone when they overheard the 'accident' came into the room or called out to offer help. Among pairs of strangers confronting the emergency, only 40 per cent of the time did either person offer help. Those who did nothing apparently interpreted the situation as a non-emergency. 'A mild sprain,' said some. 'I didn't want to embarrass her,' explained others. This again demonstrates the bystander effect. As the number of people known to be aware of an emergency increases, any given person becomes less likely to help. For the victim, there is no safety in numbers.

Assuming Responsibility

Failing to notice and misinterpretation are not the bystander effect's only causes. Sometimes an emergency is obvious. Those who saw and heard Kitty Genovese's pleas for help correctly interpreted what was happening. But the lights and silhouetted figures in neighbouring windows told them that others were also watching. That diffused the responsibility for action. As we saw a little earlier, social psychological research reports this phenomena in children as young as 5 years old, as well as adults (Plötner et al., 2015).

It is, however, not only the number of people that counts in assuming responsibility, but also the status and profession of those concerned. If those involved are expected to solve problems and give support then the bystanders are more reluctant to intervene even if there are not so many of them (see Fischer et al., 2011). That was the case when Eugene Obiora died under arrest. Nobody wanted to stop the police, and most people believed they knew how to handle a person without risking his life. The threshold for intervention is higher in a situation when you expect that the authorities will make the right decisions and handle people in the right way. People believe in experts and authority, and do not want to protest, but be in some way obedient (as we discussed in Chapter 7). To criticize the police for handling a person in a life-threatening manner is not what most people will do, especially if you can see no one else protesting.

Thankfully very few of us have observed a murder, but all of us have at times been slower to react to a need when others were present. Passing a stranded motorist on a busy highway, we are less likely to offer help than on a country road. To explore bystander inaction in clear emergencies, Darley and Latané (1968) simulated the Genovese drama. They placed people in separate rooms from which the participants would hear a victim crying for help. To create that situation, Darley and Latané asked students to discuss their problems with university life over a laboratory intercom. The researchers told the students that to guarantee their anonymity, no one would be visible, nor would the experimenter eavesdrop. During the ensuing discussion, when the experimenter turned his microphone on, the participants heard one person lapse into a seizure. With increasing intensity and speech difficulty, he pleaded for someone to help.

Of those led to believe there were no other listeners, 85 per cent left their room to seek help. Of those who believed four others also overheard the victim, only 31 per cent went for help. Were those who didn't respond apathetic and indifferent? When the experimenter came in to end the experiment, most immediately expressed concern. Many had trembling hands and sweating palms. They believed an emergency had occurred but were undecided whether to act.

After the smoke-filled room, the woman-in-distress and the seizure experiments, Latané and Darley asked the participants whether the presence of others had influenced them. We know the others had a dramatic effect. Yet the participants almost invariably denied the influence. They typically replied, 'I was aware of the others, but I would have reacted just the same if they weren't there.' That response reinforces a familiar point: *we often do not know why we do what we do.*

Living in a busy urban place can result in 'compassion fatigue' and 'sensory overload' from encountering so many people. This can restrain helping behaviour in large cities across the world (Yousif & Korte, 1995). Fatigue and overload help explain what happened when Levine and colleagues (1994) approached several thousand people in 36 US cities, dropping an unnoticed pen, asking for change, simulating a blind person needing help at a corner, and so forth. The bigger and more densely populated the city, the less likely people were to help. Levine (2001, 2003) found that willingness to help strangers also varies with culture and nationality (**Figure 10.5**). People in economically advanced countries tended to offer *less* help to strangers, and those in cultures marked by amiable and agreeable *simpat'a* (in Spanish) or *simpático* (in Portuguese) were *more* helpful. And many Europeans are more helpful than the US citizens of New York. Reysen and Levine (2014) note that it is purchasing power that predicts helpfulness. So perhaps reduced helping is related to extreme individualism, with an increased focus on yourself and not on others.

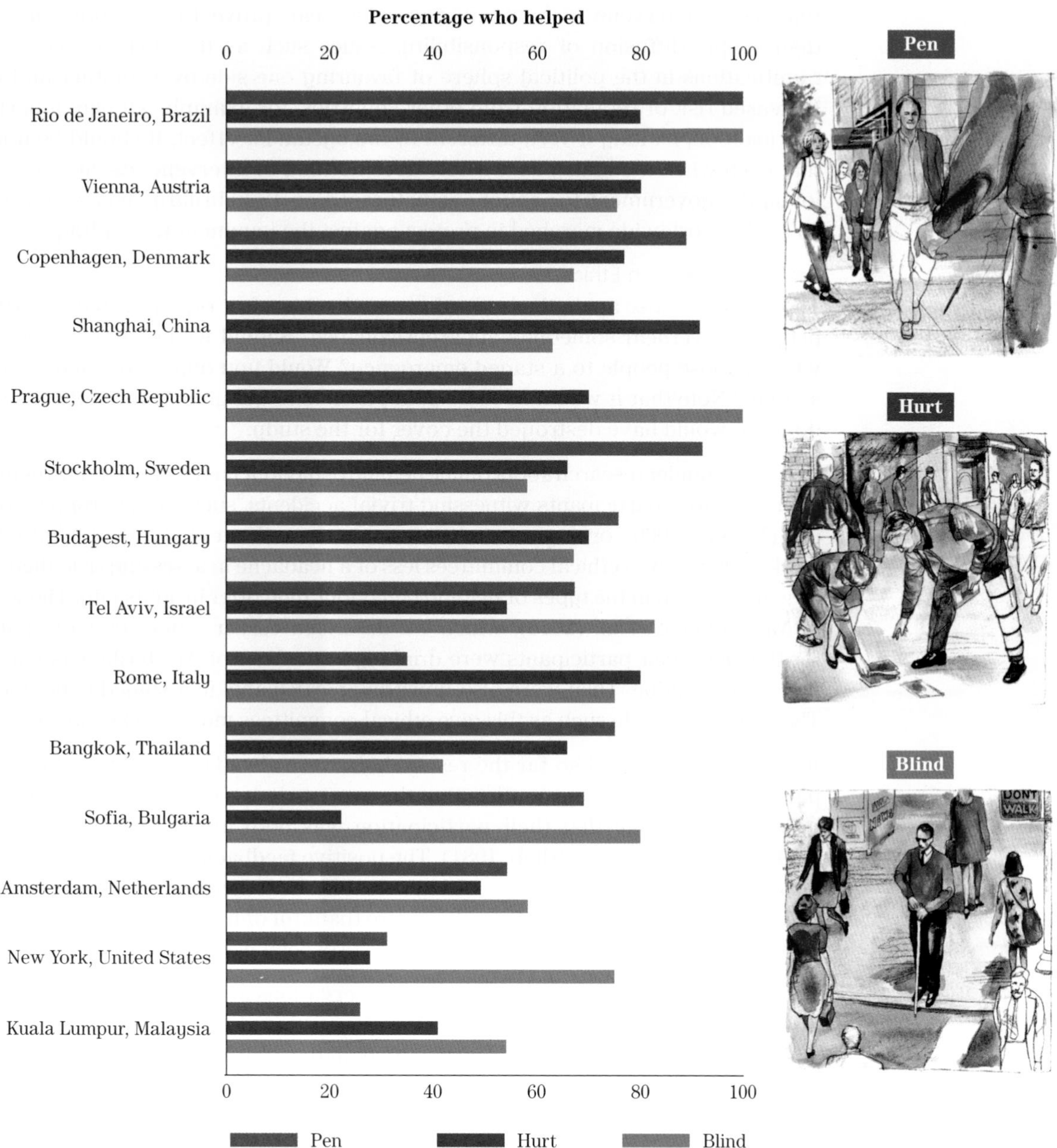

FIGURE 10.5 A world of difference in helping strangers

To compare helping in different cities and cultures, Robert Levine and his collaborators would 'accidentally' drop a pen, drop magazines while limping with an apparently injured leg, or feign blindness when approaching a crossing as the light turned green. Those dropping a pen in Rio were, for example, four times more likely to be helped than those doing so in New York City or Kuala Lumpur. (This is a sample of data from 14 countries.)

SOURCE: Adapted from Levine (2003).

Nations, too, have often been bystanders to catastrophes, even to genocide. As 800,000 people were murdered in Rwanda, between April and July 1994, most nations in the world stood by. And since February 2003, we have stood by again during the human slaughter in Sudan's Darfur region. This inaction by political regimes to intervene in humanitarian crises can prove to be more complex than simple diffusion of responsibility. Issues such as the financial cost, the ramifications in the political sphere of favouring one side over another and the increased risk of retaliation from other countries, for example, all play a part in this inaction, making it very different to the bystander effect. It should be noted that even when a country as a whole does nothing to intervene, its citizens may lobby the government for action, as witnessed on 15 February 2003, when over 600 cities worldwide marched in protest against the imminent war in Iraq.

Revisiting Research Ethics

These studies raise again the issue of research ethics. Is it right to force unwitting people to overhear someone's apparent collapse? Should we create experiments which expose people to a staged emergency? Would you object to being in such a study? Note that it would have been impossible to get your 'informed consent'; doing so would have destroyed the cover for the study.

Recent bystander research about online helping behaviour has often adopted a gentler approach, with participants witnessing trivial accidents, such as the dropping of a pen (Markey, 2000), or requests to locate somewhere (Blair et al., 2005). Whilst this work perhaps gives ethical committees less of a headache in assessing risk, they are arguably limited in the types of helping behaviour they offer insights into. The work of Van Bommel et al. (2016), which we described earlier, offers us more pause for thought. Their participants were drinking in the bars of Amsterdam as part of their usual routine. They were also unwitting participants in a staged experiment. The ethics of a study such as this give ethical committees more of a headache!

In the studies outlined so far the researchers were always careful to debrief the participants. Researchers confirm that the overwhelming majority of participants in such studies say that their participation was both instructive and ethically justified (Schwartz & Gottlieb, 1981). The positive feedback from the participants also tells us that people learn something valuable about themselves in these studies. Unaware of this tendency before, they were thankful of having the opportunity to correct themselves and to behave in a more prosocial way in the future.

But some social psychologists have deep reservations about the use of deception in research. Elms and Baumrind (2007) argued that deception is justified only when the benefits of research clearly outweigh the ethical costs of deception.

Remember that the social psychologist has a twofold ethical obligation: to protect the participants and to reveal hidden mechanisms explaining human behaviour. Such discoveries can alert us to unwanted influences and show us how we might exert positive influences. The ethical principle seems to be: after protecting participants' welfare, social psychologists fulfil their responsibility to society by doing such research.

Discussion of 'liking' in all forms can be found in Chapter 9, where we focus particularly on attraction and intimacy and how they come about.

Similarity

Because similarity is conducive to liking, and liking is conducive to helping, we are more empathic and helpful towards those *similar* to us (Miller et al., 2001). The similarity bias applies to both dress and beliefs and in general to those who share our social identity, our fellow ingroup members. The tendency to help ingroup members was revealed in the minimal group paradigm which we discuss in Chapter 12. (See also Research Close-Up: Identity and Emergency Intervention.)

No face is more familiar than one's own. That explains why, when DeBruine (2002) made university students play an interactive game with a supposed other player, they were more trusting and generous when the other person's pictured face had some features of their own face morphed into it (**Figure 10.6**). In me I trust. Even just sharing a birthday, a first name or a fingerprint pattern leads people to respond more to a request for help (Burger et al., 2004). The question, however, is how big this effect actually is. Even if there are differences in helping behaviour depending on similarity and ingroup feeling, this does not mean that we always help those more similar to ourselves or that we never help others. The situation and the context also play an important role in helping, and the complex and contextual real-life situation is something of a challenge to replicate in an experiment.

Cultural Context and Social Similarity

Darley and Latané's perspective and interpretation of Kitty's murder and how people reacted to it has recently been challenged by social psychologists in Europe and Canada. Sometimes a particular viewpoint or explanation of empirical facts dominates thinking. Few question the interpretation. The over-reliance upon Darley and Latané for many years as the only way to understand the lack of help given to Kitty inhibited other explanations, perspectives and interpretations. This happens in all sciences. People get accustomed to an obvious interpretation. This was the situation before Frances Cherry, a social psychologist at Carleton University in Canada and researchers at the Centre for Conflict and Social Solidarity in Lancaster, England, started to look at the Kitty Genovese case through new lenses. In a body of work by Mark Levine, Rachel Manning and colleagues (Levine, 1999; Levine et al., 2005; Manning et al., 2007, 2008; Levine, 2012) has argued that traditional explanations of Kitty's case are hampered by focusing on the physical presence of others rather than analysing the social meanings inherent in the (non) intervention. We will consider this work in more detail a little later in this chapter.

When Frances Cherry wrote her book in the mid-1990s many social psychologists in Europe were interested in the social and historical context as something crucial to understanding bystander behaviour. Some were also becoming more critical

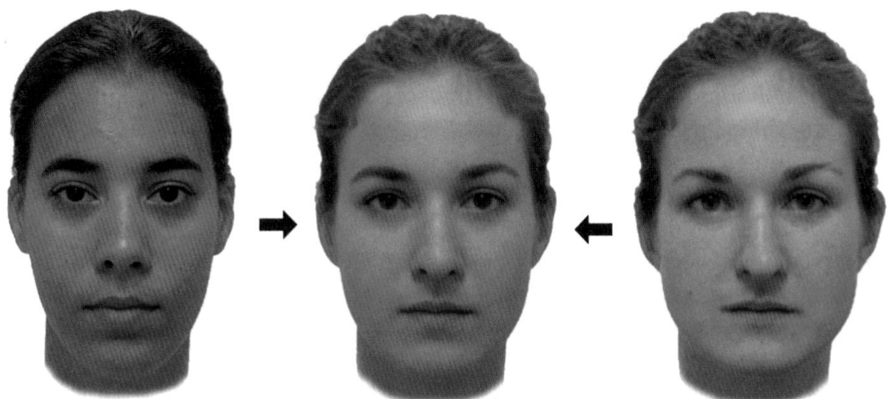

FIGURE 10.6 Similarity breeds co-operation. DeBruine (2002) morphed participants' faces (left) with strangers' faces (right) to make the composite centre face – towards whom the participants were more generous than towards the stranger

towards the experimental method as a suitable method to reveal the complex impact from history and culture, from time and place (see also Chapters 1 and 2).

Frances Cherry wanted to focus on the social context surrounding Kitty's murder and the fact she was a black woman, raped and killed by a black man. She argued that Darley and Latané's interpretation stripped the case of vital aspects of the social and cultural context that help us to understand the bystanders' responses to it. She also argued that 'in 1964 we lived in a world that did not recognize . . . the widespread abuse of women' (Cherry, 1995).

The most important means of understanding the reaction to Kitty's murder, in terms of gender and sexual relations, has been removed from Darley and Latané's view and replaced by general, acultural and quantifiable variables such as the number of bystanders. The bystanders' responses are, however, according to Cherry, 'thoroughly suffused with societal assumptions, norms and values' (Burr, 2006).

This does not mean that experiments are unable to take into consideration sociocultural variables. There are actually fairly early experiments showing that gender relation is a vital factor in cases like Kitty's. Borofsky et al. (1971), using simulated attacks, found that men were less likely to intervene in an attack by a man on a woman, and Shotland and Straw (1976) showed that intervention was less likely when the attacker and victim were perceived to be a couple.

Frances Cherry considers the lack of attention to matters of race and gender in bystander research probably has something to do with attitudes in the USA in the 1960s, towards women and black people. Cherry herself admits that she found the 'diffusion of responsibility' theory plausible as a student and that as she later developed her feminist awareness the alternative interpretation for what had happened in Kitty's case became possible for her. This tells us something about how scientific theories and explanations to some degree are products of their time and place, and seldom last 'for all time' (Burr, 2006).

Perceived Social Similarity

Levine et al. (2005) represent another perspective on Kitty's murder and the bystander phenomenon. In line with the social identity approach (see Chapter 12 for an overview), these British social psychologists focus on the importance of ingroup similarity and self-categorization to understand the bystander phenomenon and helping behaviour more generally. That is, rather than pointing towards individual and interpersonal factors, these researchers emphasize the degree to which bystander and victim share a common identity. The categorization of others as members of the ingroup leads to perception of similarity, cohesion and an increased feeling of responsibility for the welfare of others. As a consequence – and as demonstrated by the experiments conducted by Levine and his colleagues reported in the Research Close-Up – a sense of 'we-ness' with the victim increases the likelihood of intervention (Dovidio et al., 1991). (See Research Close-Up: Identity and Emergency Intervention.)

We shouldn't, however, rule out the possibility that people may help those they consider to be different from themselves in some way. In experimental studies, Van Leeuwen and Täuber (2011) have found that people who are members of low status groups (based upon poor performance in a general knowledge quiz) offer to help those in a high status group. Why? Well, the researchers suggest that by offering help the low status group can show that it does have something valuable to offer a higher status group. By doing so they increase their positive reputation in their own eyes and those of the outgroup.

The British bystander explanation represents an alternative theoretical explanation of why we do help and why we do not help others. Whether the person in need of help does or does not belong to 'my' group constitutes a crucial factor: I will be more willing to help a person if I perceive him or her as a member of my own group.

In sum, according to this perspective helping behaviour is based more on how I socially categorize myself and others than on my genetic make-up. In many ways the social identity approach to helping behaviour contrasts with the explanations given by evolutionary psychologists. It is not the genes that count, but whether I have something social in common with the people in need of help.

Research close-up

Identity and Emergency Intervention

Source: *Levine, M., Prosser, A., Evans, D., & Reicher, S. (2005).* Identity and emergency intervention: How social group membership and inclusiveness of group boundaries shape helping behavior. *Personality and Social Psychology Bulletin, 31*(4), 443–453.

Introduction

Social psychologists have invested a lot of work into understanding when and why people offer help in times of an emergency. Likeness breeds liking, and liking elicits helping. So, do people offer more help to others who display similarities to themselves? And do they refuse help to those they do not like? To explore the similarity–helping relationship, this study explores the behaviour of some Lancaster University, UK students who had previously identified themselves as fans of the nearby Manchester United football team. The success of this team has led to bitter rivalries between the fans of Manchester United and other football teams. One of the more notable rivalries is between supporters of Manchester United and those of Liverpool FC, a team that enjoyed huge success in the 1980s. Geographically close (just 30 miles apart), these teams have a long history of hostility towards one another. But, would a Manchester United supporter help a Liverpool fan if s/he was in trouble? Taking their cue from Darley and Batson's (1973) famous Good Samaritan experiment, this paper sought to find out.

Study 1

Method

Forty-five male Lancaster University students took part, aged between 18 and 21 years. Each participant was given two questionnaires. The first asked them about the football team they supported and why they did so. The second questionnaire required participants to answer on a 5-point scale, the extent to which they identified with fellow supporters of their team.

The researchers then directed each newly arrived participant to the laboratory in an adjacent building. Participants were told this was to watch a video about their team, supporters and crowd behaviour at football matches. En route, a confederate jogger – wearing a shirt from either Manchester United or rival Liverpool, or a plain shirt – seemingly slipped on a grass bank just in front of them, grasped his ankle, and groaned in apparent pain. This confederate did not ask for help, and did not make any eye contact with the participant. The participant was covertly observed.

A measure was taken of the degree of help (if any) the participant offered the confederate. The 5-point scale was taken from Darley and Batson's (1973) Good Samaritan experiment.

A score of 1 was given to a participant who did not notice that the confederate needed help.

A score of 2 was given if the participant did notice help was required but failed to offer any.

A score of 3 was given if the participant asked the confederate if he needed help.

A score of 4 was given if the confederate asked the participant if he needed help and then offered some.

Finally, a score of 5 was awarded if the participant helped the confederate by remaining with him, and escorting him out of the experimental context.

Results

Table 10.1 shows that more help was given to victims when they were in a Manchester United football shirt, than when in a plain or Liverpool shirt. A chi-square was conducted on this categorical data, to test if there was an association between type of shirt (Manchester United, Liverpool, Plain) and helping behaviour (No Help, Help). The result was statistically significant: χ^2 (2, N = 35) = 12.07, p = .0024. There is an association between type of football shirt and helping behaviour.

TABLE 10.1 Frequencies of helping by football shirt condition

	Manchester United	Plain	Liverpool
No Help	1	8	7
Help	12	4	3

As **Figure 10.7** shows, the Manchester fans routinely paused to offer help to their fellow Manchester supporter but usually did not offer such help to an apparent Liverpool supporter.

Study 2

Method

In this second study, the aim was to see what would happen if Manchester United fans were reminded of the identity they share with Liverpool supporters – that of being football fans who were positive ambassadors for the sport. The study was repeated with 32 male self-identified Manchester United football fans, but with one difference: before participants witnessed the jogger's fall, they were told that the study concerned the positive aspects of being a football fan. Given that only a small minority of fans are troublemakers, this research aimed to explore what fans get out of their love for 'the beautiful game'. Now a jogger wearing a football club shirt, whether for Manchester or

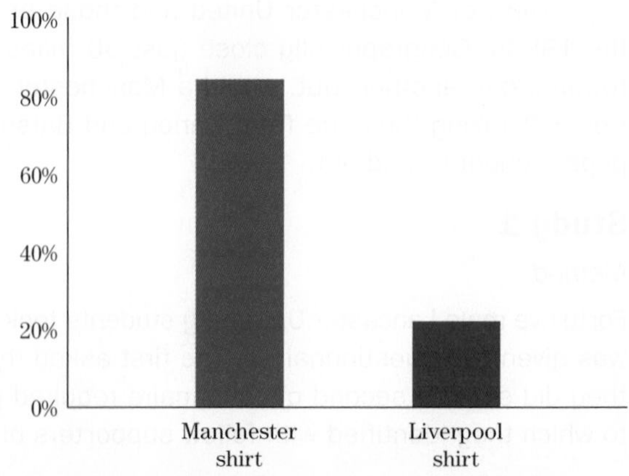

FIGURE 10.7 Percentage of Manchester United fans who helped victim wearing Manchester or Liverpool shirt

Liverpool, became one of 'us fans'. Would this make a difference to the results?

Results

As **Figure 10.8** shows, the grimacing jogger was helped regardless of which team he supported – and more so than if wearing a plain shirt.

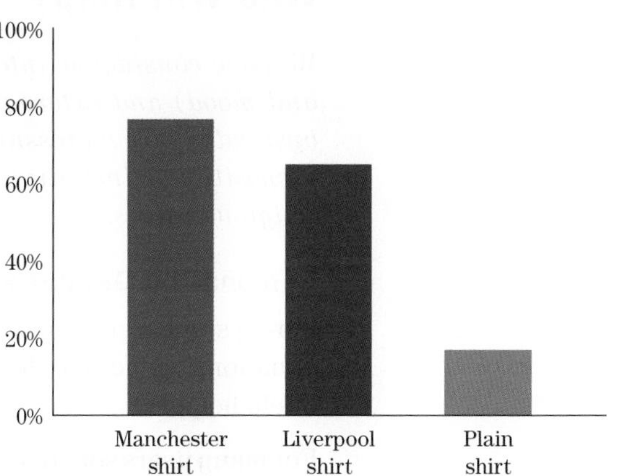

FIGURE 10.8 Common fan identity condition: percentage of Manchester United fans who helped victim wearing Manchester, Liverpool or plain shirt

Table 10.2 shows that more help was offered to both Manchester United and Liverpool football fans than to the victim wearing a plain shirt. A chi-square to test whether there is a significant association of football shirt (Manchester United, Plain, Liverpool) and helping behaviour (No Help, Help) was significant: χ^2 (2, N = 29) = 7.33, p = .25. Overall, type of shirt is associated with helping behaviour. Of particular interest is that more help was offered to Manchester United and Liverpool supporters, when participants were reminded of their common football supporter identity, than to plain-shirted supporters.

TABLE 10.2 Frequencies for helping by shirt condition

	Manchester United	Plain	Liverpool
No help	2	7	3
Help	8	2	7

Discussion

The principle in the two studies is the same: people are predisposed to help their fellow group members, whether those are defined more narrowly (as 'us Manchester fans') or more inclusively (as 'us football fans'). Hence, if even rival fans can be persuaded to help one another simply by thinking about what unites them, then surely other antagonists can as well. One way to increase people's willingness to help others is to promote social identities that are inclusive rather than exclusive. By re-categorizing we create new allies belonging to our ingroup.

Critical Reflections

This is a creative and insightful piece of research, which offers some food for thought with respect to facilitating a more cooperative society. Of course we have to be somewhat cautious whenever we seek to apply findings from studies such as these to the wider population. Often the sample sizes are quite small, as in the current case. Moreover, as all the participants in these two studies were 18–21 and male, we do not know if there might be any age or gender differences in this study. As is common with many studies in the field of prosocial behaviour, a stooge is involved to deceive the participants into believing an accident has occurred requiring their help. We noted some of the ethical concerns about studies like this one earlier in this chapter. That aside, can we be confident that all participants were suitably fooled by the confederate? Would you be fooled? And even if you were, might you be tempted to go along with the study anyway, perhaps with some clue as to what it was about? It is almost certainly impossible to design the perfect study, but work like this gives us some important insights into helping behaviour.

Who Will Help?

We have considered internal influences on the decision to help (such as guilt and mood) and external influences as well (such as social norms, number of bystanders, time pressures and similarity). We also need to consider the helpers' dispositions, including, for example, their personality traits, empathy and religious values.

Personality, Gender and Age

Surely some traits must distinguish the Mother Teresa types. Faced with identical situations, some people will respond helpfully, others won't bother. Who are the likely helpers?

For many years social psychologists were unable to discover a single characteristic that predicted helping with anything close to the predictive power of the situation, guilt and mood factors. Modest relationships were found between helping and certain variables, such as a need for social approval. Also personal empathy has a strong influence on helping behaviour, as we've already seen. But, by and large, the personality tests were unable to identify the helpers. Studies of rescuers of Jews in Nazi Europe reveal mixed conclusions. In one of the earliest attempts to identify personality traits, Oliner and Oliner (1988) interviewed many rescuers of Jews, and reported common traits among those who helped, including compassion, concern and care for others and social responsibility (Carlo et al., 2009). However, others have argued that it was the context that clearly influenced willingness to help as there was no evidence of a definable set of altruistic personality traits (Darley, 1992).

> *'There are . . . reasons why personality should be rather unimportant in determining people's reactions to the emergency. For one thing, the situational forces affecting a person's decision are so strong.'*
> Latané and Darley (1970, p. 115)

If that has a familiar ring, it could be from a similar conclusion by conformity researchers (Chapter 7): conformity and obedience, too, seemed more influenced by the situation than by measurable personality traits. Perhaps, though, as we discuss in Chapter 3, who we are does affect what we do.

However, technological advances have helped to provide insight into the physiological make-up of altruists. In some fascinating work into the brains of people who help, Haas et al. (2015) report that people who are identified as warm and altruistic on personality scales are able to correctly recognize the emotional states of others. Furthermore, using an MRI scan, they show increased activation in the temporoparietal junction (TPJ) (responsible for integrating external and internal information, and processes such as **Theory of Mind**) and medial prefrontal cortex (responsible for executive functioning of our thoughts and decision-making processes) of their brains. Both of these areas of the brain play an important role in empathy.

theory of mind the ability to attribute mental states to others and oneself. To be able to see the world from someone else's point of view

Some people are reliably more helpful. Those high in positive emotionality, empathy and self-efficacy are most likely to be concerned and helpful (Bierhoff et al., 1991; Bierhoff, 2002; Bierhoff & Rohmann, 2004; Eisenberg et al., 1991; Haas et al., 2015; Krueger et al., 2001). Perhaps you have the intuitive feeling that women are more helpful than men are. You are partly right in your conclusion. In their interviews with women home-based care volunteers, Naidu et al. (2012) found that responsibility in caring for others had become 'feminized'. It seems being a 'mother' instills the necessary characteristics and aspirations of volunteering to look after people. The women's accounts included personal histories of looking after others and commitment to being of service. But this is not a rule without exception. Many studies have compared the helpfulness of male and female individuals. In some classic work, after analysing 172 studies with 50,000 respondents Eagly and Crowley (1986) reported that when faced with potentially dangerous situations in which strangers need help (such as with a flat tyre or a fall in a subway), men more often help. In other situations, such as volunteering to help with an experiment or spend time with children with developmental disabilities, to volunteer with the Peace Corps and Doctors of the World (Becker & Eagly, 2004), women are slightly more likely to help. They also have been as likely as, or more likely than, men to risk death as Holocaust rescuers and to donate a kidney. Thus, the gender difference interacts with (depends on) the situation or the context.

We discuss the social psychological exploration for gender differences in Chapter 14.

Felix Warneken and Michael Tomasello studied how children as young as 18 months of age (pre-linguistic or just-linguistic) quite readily help others to achieve their goals even when the child self receives no immediate benefit and the person helped is a stranger. This behaviour requires both an understanding of others' goals and an altruistic motivation to help, and it seems that altruism can develop very early in humans (Warneken & Tomasello, 2006).

René Bekkers at Utrecht University made a random sample survey of altruistic behaviour in the Netherlands. Only 5.7 per cent donated the money they had received from taking part in the survey to a charity or an unknown person in need. Nearly 95 per cent of the respondents kept the money themselves (Bekkers, 2007). In line with other survey research on giving, generosity increased with age, education, income, trust and prosocial value orientation. Theurer and Wister (2010) suggest that altruism in older people, who may have retired from full-time employment, is based on having high social capital (feelings of belonging to, and engagement with, a community).

Religious Faith

A question of much interest to some researchers is whether the religious are more helpful than the non-religious. Or in other words, does religious faith make you altruistic? The answer is mixed with research confirming results in both directions.

In an excellent review of some of the most recent work in this area, Nguyen and Wodon (2018) report work that both confirms and denies the relationship. Against the hypothesis is the work of Decety et al. (2015), who reports that children from Christian and Muslim backgrounds are less helpful than their non-religious counterparts. On the other hand, Forbes and Zampelli (2014), and Kim and Joon Jang (2017) report increased volunteering behaviour among the religious as compared to the non-religious. However, priming your religious identity can hinder helping behaviour. Parra Osorio et al. (2016) observed that when religious identity was primed in their Ghanaian participants they were less likely to help those from another religion. This echoes the work we considered earlier in this chapter by Mark Levine and other British social psychologists who focus on the group identity aspect of helping behaviour.

Nguyen and Wodon (2018) are critical of how data is generated to explore any relationship between religion and helping behaviour, and where most of this work has been focused. Much of the data concerns small sample sizes, is generated in experiments, considers different kinds of helping, and is predominantly based in the US. It is perhaps then, hardly surprising we see mixed evidence!

In an attempt to pin down a more substantial answer to the question, whether the religious are more helpful than the non-religious, Nguyen and Wodon (2018) look at the Gallup Poll on religiosity and helping behaviour data (see **Figure 10.9** for an example). This survey is conducted in more than 140 countries, and has 1,000 individuals in each country. The Gallup survey offers some interesting results, revealing the complexity of the relationship under investigation. For example, while Muslims and Christians report helping strangers frequently, they are less likely to donate money or volunteer. However, Muslims are more likely to donate money to charitable causes than Christians. That said, we should bear in mind that the responses being analysed concern participants' behaviour over a month, rather than a year which, as Nguyen and Wodon (2018) note, is problematic. Consider the charitable giving that is very much part of Christian tradition. Had the survey asked the question in December, their results may look very different!

The Gallup survey is subject to further criticism. Some of the questions to determine religious faith are simplistic ('Is religion an important part of your daily life?'), and it only considers helping behaviour over the last month. The helping behaviours considered in the past month are also quite narrow: having donated money to a charity; having volunteered time to a charitable organization; and helping a stranger in the past month. Furthermore, most participants suggested that religious faith was important in their lives. Perhaps a different question might generate different responses? We cannot conclusively attribute the helping behaviours to the direct influence of religiosity, or claim that religion makes people more helpful.

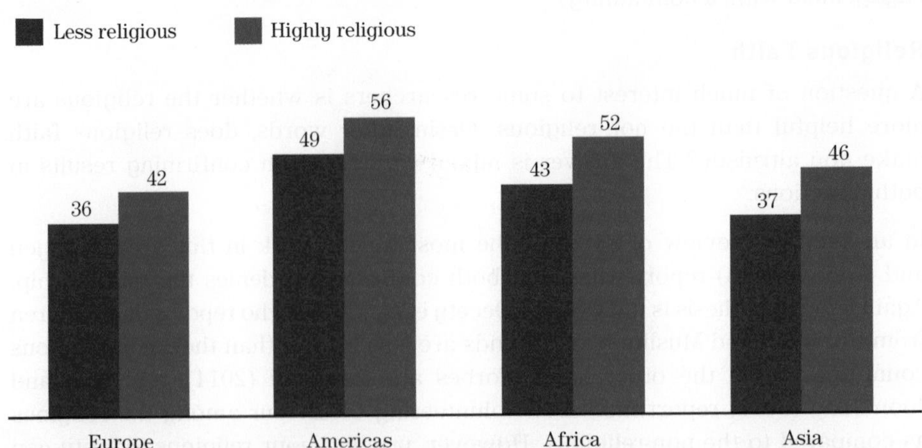

FIGURE 10.9 Percentage of less religious and highly religious people reporting that they helped a stranger or someone they didn't know who needed help in the past month

SOURCE: Pelham and Crabtree (2008).

Although far from perfect, this survey does stray beyond the US to give us a more global picture of helping behaviour and religious faith.

Perhaps the differences captured here occur because inherently helpful people are more attracted to religion. The World Gallup also reveals that poor people give more to those in need than wealthy people (Pelham & Crabtree, 2008).

Among Muslims it is common to support the poor with money collected during the Friday prayer in the Mosque, and many Muslims are much concerned about helping 'brothers' in need, that is, those having the same faith, even if they are not rich themselves.

But to have a religious faith is definitely not a guarantee of being a helpful or nice person (Duriez, 2004). Under some historical circumstances religion has been far from promoting prosocial behaviour. The slogan 'Gott mit uns', or 'God with Us', has been used more than once in history to justify misdeed and evil. A religious belief does not guarantee prosociality. The function of religion also depends on the context.

How Can We Increase Helping?

To increase individual helping, can we reverse the factors that inhibit helping? Or can we teach norms of helping and socialize people to see themselves as helpful?

As social scientists, our goal is to understand human behaviour, thus also suggesting ways to improve it. So, how might we apply research-based understanding to increase helping? To make society more fair and equal, to redistribute wealth and income so the differences between the rich and poor diminish is one option. To establish a welfare state financed by taxes is, for instance, a measure that supports the poor without giving them the impression that they are inferior. At an individual level, one way to promote altruism is to reverse those factors that inhibit it. Given that hurried, preoccupied people focusing on themselves are less likely to help, can we think of ways to slow people down and turn their attention outwards, towards fellow human beings all over the world? If the presence of others diminishes each bystander's sense of responsibility, how can we enhance responsibility?

Reduce Ambiguity, Increase Responsibility

If Darley and Latané's decision tree (see **Figure 10.3**) describes the dilemmas bystanders face, then prompting people to interpret an incident correctly and to assume responsibility should increase their involvement. Leonard Bickman and his colleague (Bickman, 1975, 1979; Bickman & Green, 1977) tested that presumption in a series of landmark experiments on crime reporting. In each, they staged a shoplifting incident in a supermarket or bookstore. In some of the stores, they placed signs aimed at sensitizing bystanders to shoplifting and informing them how to report it. The researchers found that the signs had little effect. In other cases, witnesses heard a bystander interpret the incident: 'Say, look at her. She's shoplifting. She put that into her purse.' (The bystander then left to look for a lost child.) Still others heard this person add: 'We saw it. We should report it. It's our responsibility.' Both comments substantially boosted reporting of the crime.

It is this acceptance of responsibility that becomes key in bystander intervention. Contemplate, for example, a study undertaken by Story and Forsyth (2008) that explores helping behaviour at the community level. The researchers note the rise in urbanization which threatens the environmental features of local communities. An increase in urban development can have dramatic consequences for the ability of the land to effectively drain rainfall. However, often urbanization goes ahead unopposed by the local community. Regardless of proenvironmental attitudes, residents remain bystanders. But, this changes when the residents are not only fully aware of the implications of environmental watersheds but also consider it to be an emergency and their responsibility to protect the land. Under these circumstances residents become environmentally engaged, participating in a series of activities to prevent the conversion of local land for urban purposes.

Take, for example, John Bird's launch of the *Big Issue* magazine, in London in 1991. The idea behind it is that the homeless themselves sell the magazine on the streets of the UK as a means of generating income for themselves. Hence it is not a handout to the faceless homeless but a way for the public to support someone they have come to know in their area, who is homeless. It has proved popular as a hand up rather than a hand out. Hibbert et al. (2002) asked people in Scotland what they thought of the initiative. One respondent said: 'the point to me was instead of giving a beggar 50p, you gave a guy 50p for selling you a magazine, that was the point of it.' Hibbert et al. (2002) conclude that the reasons people buy the magazine is not just for a quality product, nor to help the homeless. It is to support a particular person they've come to know. Hence reducing ambiguity about where charitable donations go, and increasing the homeless's responsibility for generating their own legitimate income, has proved a successful strategy in fostering help in the form of purchasing the *Big Issue* magazine. It is now sold across four continents including Japan, the UK, Australia, and Kenya. A personal approach makes one feel less anonymous, more responsible.

In some fascinating and insightful early work, Solomon and Solomon (1978; Solomon et al., 1981) explored ways to reduce anonymity. They found that bystanders who had identified themselves to one another – by name, age, and so forth – were more likely to offer aid to a sick person than were anonymous bystanders. Similarly, when a female experimenter caught the eye of another shopper and gave her a warm smile before stepping into an elevator, that shopper was far more likely than other shoppers to offer help when the experimenter later said, 'Damn. I've left my glasses. Can anyone tell me what floor the umbrellas are on?' Even a trivial momentary conversation with someone dramatically increased the person's later helpfulness.

Personal treatment makes bystanders more self-aware and therefore more attuned to their own altruistic ideals. By contrast, 'deindividuated' people are less responsible. Thus, circumstances that promote self-awareness – name tags, being watched and evaluated, undisrupted quiet – should also increase helping.

Guilt and Concern for Self-Image

Earlier we noted that people who feel guilty will act to reduce guilt and restore their self-worth. Some classic social psychology studies have demonstrated how heightening people's awareness of their transgressions can increase their desire to help. A Reed College research team led by Richard Katzev (1978) is one example. When visitors to the Portland Art Museum disobeyed a 'Please do not touch' sign, experimenters reprimanded some of them: 'Please don't touch the objects. If everyone touches them, they will deteriorate.' Likewise, when visitors to the Portland Zoo fed unauthorized food to the bears, some of them were admonished with, 'Hey, don't feed unauthorized food to the animals. Don't you know it could hurt them?' In both cases, 58 per cent of the now guilt-laden individuals shortly thereafter offered help to another experimenter who had 'accidentally' dropped something. Of those not reprimanded, only one-third helped. Guilt-laden people are helpful people.

Cialdini and Schroeder (1976) offered another practical way to trigger concern for self-image: ask for a contribution so small that it's hard to say no without feeling like a Scrooge. Cialdini (1995) discovered this when a United Way canvasser came to his door. As she solicited his contribution, he was mentally preparing his refusal – until she said magic words that demolished his financial excuse: 'Even a penny will help.' 'I had been neatly finessed into compliance,' recalled Cialdini. 'And there was another interesting feature of our exchange as well. When I stopped coughing (I really had choked on my attempted rejection), I gave her not the penny she had mentioned but the amount I usually allot to legitimate charity solicitors. At that, she thanked me, smiled innocently, and moved on.'

But of course, concerns about our self-image can actually hinder helping behaviour. Social psychological research on cyberbullying has accelerated in recent years as the unfortunate phenomenon escalates in today's technological societies. When surveyed, many young people recall at least one experience of being bullied or harassed online, and many more have witnessed it (Choi et al., 2019; Livingstone et al., 2011). And unsurprisingly, the anonymous online environment facilitates bystander behaviour. As we've already seen in relation to bystander behaviour, it occurs in situations where responsibility is diffused throughout a group of witnesses. In the online world, we cannot see and do not always know who the other bystanders are, but bystander effects can be the same online as they are offline: we assume someone else will come forward and offer help. There are risks in coming forwards to help. We could risk further abuse being aimed at the victim online, and/or we risk becoming a victim ourselves. Hence our own self-image can be at risk. Of course what online technology affords us is the ability to help someone while remaining private and anonymous. In their study of online users intentions to help someone, Bastiaensens et al. (2015) found that individuals were more likely to intervene in a case of cyberbullying if they could contact the victim privately and anonymously.

Socializing Altruism

If we can learn altruism, then how might we socialize it? Here are five ways (**Figure 10.10**, overleaf).

Teaching Moral Inclusion

Rescuers of Jews in Nazi Europe, leaders of the American anti-slavery movement, Chinese peasants and medical missionaries shared at least one thing in common: they included people who differed from themselves within the human circle to which their moral values and rules of justice applied.

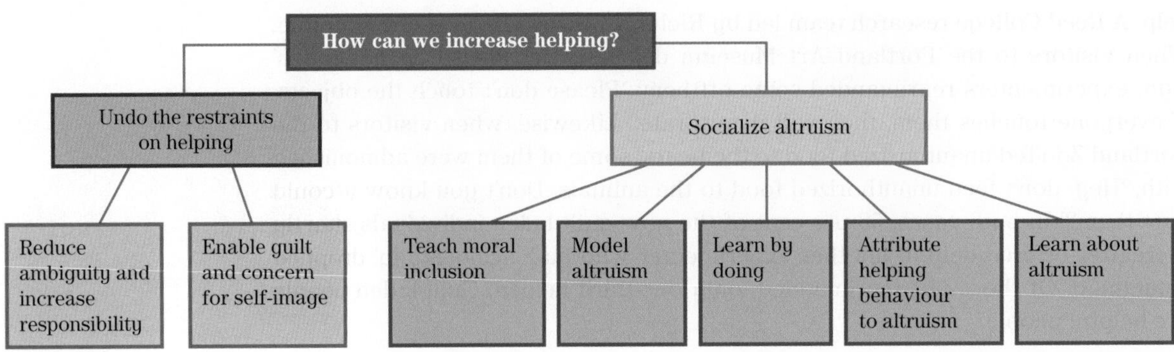

FIGURE 10.10 Practical ways to increase helping

moral exclusion the perception of certain individuals or groups as outside the boundary within which one applies moral values and rules of fairness. Moral inclusion is regarding others as within one's circle of moral concern

For further discussion of ingroup/outgroup behaviour and how this is created, see Chapter 13.

Moral exclusion – omitting certain people (and animals) from one's circle of moral or social concern – has the opposite effect. It justifies all sorts of harm, from discrimination to genocide (Opotow, 1990; Staub, 2006; Tyler & Lind, 1990). Exploitation or cruelty becomes acceptable, even appropriate, towards those people we regard as undeserving or as non-persons (and also towards animals outside one's circle of concern). The Nazis excluded Jews, Gypsies, homosexuals, people with severe mental disorders and the mentally disabled from their moral community by killing them. Anyone who participates in enslavement, death squads or torture practises a similar exclusion. To a lesser extent, moral exclusion describes those of us who concentrate our concerns, favours and financial inheritance upon 'our people' (for example, our children) to the exclusion of others. This extreme social identity, caring only for those belonging to the ingroup, is therefore a dangerous strategy for everybody in the outgroups.

In Chapter 7 on conformity and obedience we reviewed how Stephen Reicher and his colleagues in the UK (Reicher & Haslam, 2004; Haslam & Reicher, 2007, 2014; Reicher et al., 2008) have re-examined the classical social psychological studies on 'banality of evil' and how perpetrators make a virtue out of evil (Staub, 1989). Genocides are perpetrated against others not because of what they have done but because of the groups they belong to. Creating a cohesive ingroup through shared social identification implies the exclusion of specific populations, regarding them as outgroups. By constituting the outgroup as a danger to the existence of the uniquely virtuous ingroup, the defence of the ingroup and the annihilation of the outgroup can be presented as a virtue to be celebrated (Reicher et al., 2008).

To focus on and favour 'our people' also implies restrictions in the public empathy for the human costs of war. Reported war deaths are typically 'our deaths'. To perceive the enemy in a war as important as a human being as the soldier from your own country requires a recategorization and an extension of your social identity. There is nothing 'natural' in grieving only for the dead soldier from your own country and not showing the same sadness when the enemy dies. It depends on who we define as our ingroup.

Inviting advantaged people to put themselves in others' shoes, to imagine how they feel, also helps (Batson & Powell, 2003). To 'do unto others as you would have them do unto you', one must take the others' perspective.

Modelling Altruism

Earlier we noted that seeing unresponsive bystanders makes us less likely to help. People reared by extremely punitive parents, as were many delinquents and chronic criminals, also show much less of the empathy and principled caring that typifies altruists.

If we see or read about someone helping, we are more likely to offer assistance. It's better, find Robert Cialdini and his co-workers (2003a, 2003b), *not* to publicize rampant tax cheating, littering and teen drinking, and instead to emphasize – to define a norm of – people's widespread honesty, cleanliness and abstinence. In one experiment, they asked visitors not to remove petrified wood from along the paths of the Petrified Forest National Park. Some were also told that 'past visitors have removed the petrified wood'. Other people who were told that 'past visitors have left the petrified wood' to preserve the park were much less likely to pick up samples placed along a path.

Modelling effects were also apparent within the families who risked their lives to rescue Jews in the 1930s and 1940s, and of 1950s' civil rights activists. In both cases these exceptional altruists said they had warm and close relationships with at least one parent who was, similarly, a strong 'moralist' or committed to humanitarian causes (Oliner & Oliner, 1988; Rosenhan, 1970). Their families and friends had taught them the norm of helping and caring for others. That 'prosocial value orientation' acquired during socialization led them to include people from other groups in their circle of moral concern and to feel responsible for others' welfare, noted altruism researcher Ervin Staub (1989, 1991, 1992).

Staub (1999) knows of what he speaks:

> As a young Jewish child in Budapest I survived the Holocaust, the destruction of most European Jews by Nazi Germany and its allies. My life was saved by a Christian woman who repeatedly endangered her life to help me and my family, and by Raoul Wallenberg, the Swede who came to Budapest and with courage, brilliance, and complete commitment saved the lives of tens of thousands of Jews destined for the gas chambers. These two heroes were not passive bystanders, and my work is one of the ways for me not to be one.

Learning by Doing

Staub (2005a) has shown that just as immoral behaviour fuels immoral attitudes, so helping increases future helping. Children and adults learn by doing. In a series of studies with children near age 12, Staub and his students found that after children were induced to make toys for hospitalized children or for an art teacher, they became more helpful. So were children after teaching younger children to make puzzles or use first aid.

When children act helpfully, they develop helping-related values, beliefs and skills, notes Staub. Helping also helps satisfy their needs for a positive self-concept. On a larger scale, 'service learning' and volunteer programmes woven into a school curriculum have been shown to increase later citizen involvement, social responsibility, co-operation and leadership (Andersen, 1998; Putnam, 2000). Attitudes follow behaviour. Helpful actions therefore promote the self-perception that one is caring and helpful, which in turn promotes further helping.

Attributing Helpful Behaviour to Altruistic Motives

Another clue to socializing altruism comes from research on what Chapter 4 called the **overjustification effect**: when the justification for an act is more than sufficient, the person may attribute the act to the extrinsic justification rather than to an inner motive. Rewarding people for doing what they would do anyway therefore undermines intrinsic motivation. We can state the principle positively: by providing people with just enough justification to prompt a good deed (weaning them from bribes and threats when possible), we may increase their pleasure in doing such deeds on their own.

overjustification effect the result of bribing people to do what they already like doing; they may then see their actions as externally controlled rather than intrinsically appealing

Batson et al. (1978, 1979) put the overjustification phenomenon to work. In several experiments, they found that students felt most altruistic after they agreed to help someone without payment or implied social pressure. When pay had been offered or social pressures were present, people felt less altruistic after helping.

In another experiment, the researchers led students to attribute a helpful act to compliance ('I guess we really don't have a choice') or to compassion ('The guy really needs help'). Later, when the students were asked to volunteer their time to a local service agency, 25 per cent of those who had been led to perceive their previous helpfulness as mere compliance now volunteered; of those led to see themselves as compassionate, 60 per cent volunteered. The moral? When people wonder, 'Why am I helping?' it's best if the circumstances enable them to answer, 'Because help was needed, and I am a caring, giving, helpful person'.

Inferring that one is a helpful person seems also to have happened when Dolinski (2000) stopped pedestrians on the streets of Wroclaw, Poland, and asked them for directions to a non-existent 'Zubrzyckiego Street' or to an illegible address. Everyone tried unsuccessfully to help. After doing so, about two-thirds (twice the number of those not given the opportunity to try to help) agreed when asked by someone 100 metres farther down the road to watch their heavy bag or bicycle for 5 minutes.

Learning about Altruism

Researchers have found another way to boost altruism, one that provides a happy conclusion to this chapter. Some social psychologists worry that as people become more aware of social psychology's findings, their behaviour may change, thus invalidating the findings (Gergen, 1994). Will learning about the factors that inhibit altruism reduce their influence? Sometimes, such 'enlightenment' is not our problem but one of our goals.

Beaman et al. (1978) revealed that once people understand why the presence of bystanders inhibits helping, they become more likely to help in group situations. The researchers used a lecture to inform some students how bystander inaction can affect the interpretation of an emergency and feelings of responsibility. Other students heard either a different lecture or no lecture at all. Two weeks later, as part of a different experiment in a different location, the participants found themselves walking (with an unresponsive confederate) past someone slumped over or past a person sprawled beneath a bicycle. Of those who had not heard the helping lecture, a quarter paused to offer help; twice as many of those 'enlightened' did so.

Having read this chapter, perhaps you, too, have changed. As you come to understand what influences people's responses, will your attitudes and your behaviour be the same?

Focus on

The Benefits – and The Costs – of Empathy-Induced Altruism

People do most of what they do, including much of what they do for others, for their own benefit, claimed Batson et al. (2004), in their summary of research on altruism among individuals in the West. It may be their results would have been different in other, more collectivistic cultures. But neither in individualistic nor in competitive cultures is egoism the whole story of helping. There is also a genuine altruism rooted in empathy, in feelings of sympathy and compassion for others' welfare. We are supremely social creatures. Consider the following.

Empathy-induced altruism:

- *produces sensitive helping.* Where there is empathy, it's not just the thought that counts, its sympathizing and alleviating the other's suffering.
- *inhibits aggression.* Show Batson someone who feels empathy for a target of potential aggression and he'll show you someone who's unlikely to favour attack, someone who's as likely to forgive as to harbour anger. In general, women in the West report more empathic feelings than men, and they are less likely to support war and other forms of aggression (Jones, 2003). But women in political positions do not differ so much from men. World history gives accounts of women rulers who have acted aggressively and declared war on other countries: Boudica, Katherine the Great, Elizabeth I. The UK Prime Minister Margaret Thatcher's declaration of war against Argentina in 1982 serves as a more recent example. The power of the situation is strong. Women also declare war when they are in the same positions as men.
- *increases co-operation.* In laboratory experiments, Batson and Ahmad (2001) found that people in potential conflict are more trusting and co-operative when they feel empathy for the other. Personalizing an outgroup, by getting to know people in it, helps people understand their perspective.
- *improves attitudes towards stigmatized groups.* Take others' perspective, allow yourself to feel what they feel, and you may become more supportive of others like them (the homeless, those with AIDS, or even convicted criminals).

But empathy-induced altruism comes with liabilities, notes the Batson group:

- It can be harmful. People who risk their lives on behalf of others sometimes lose them. People who seek to do good can also do harm, sometimes by unintentionally humiliating or demotivating the recipient. Eagerness to help can also cause increased physical harm to victims. Consider the example of traffic accident victims where enthusiastic helpers may actually do more damage than good by moving them.
- It can't address all needs. It's easier to feel empathy for a needy individual than, say, for Mother Earth, whose environment is being stripped and warmed at the peril of our descendants.
- It burns out. Feeling others' pain is painful, which may cause us to avoid situations that evoke our empathy, or to experience 'burnout' or 'compassion fatigue'.
- It can feed favouritism, injustice and indifference to the larger common good. Empathy, being particular, produces partiality – towards a single child or family or pet. Moral principles, being universal, produce concern for unseen others as well.

Empathy-based estate planning bequeaths inheritances to particular loved ones, whereas morality-based estate planning is more inclusive. When their empathy for someone is aroused, people will violate their own standards of fairness and justice by giving that person favoured treatment (Batson et al., 1997b). Ironically, note Batson et al. (1999a), empathy-induced altruism can therefore 'pose a powerful threat to the common good [by leading] me to narrow my focus of concern to those for whom I especially care – the needing friend – and in so doing to lose sight of the bleeding crowd'. No wonder charity so often stays close to home.

Consider suicide bombers. Could suicide bombing be looked upon as an altruistic act? The suicide bombers kill themselves because they believe they contribute to a better life for their ingroup and also their family. They sacrifice their life for the welfare of others. The question is not if they really contribute to a better world or not, but what the suicide bombers believe in and their motivation for killing themselves.

In 2008, Batson had a rethink of his position on empathy-induced altruism. Perhaps it wasn't so bad after all, and perhaps it was possible to offer help without self-benefit. Reflecting on his previous work on empathy and altruism, he stated: 'I assumed that everything we humans do, no matter how beneficial to others, is really directed toward the ultimate goal of one or more forms of self-benefit. But over the years, I have come to believe this assumption was wrong.' (p. 2). In a fascinating review of empirical studies and real-world events, Batson acknowledges that sometimes people help without thought for themselves, and indeed it's a good job they do so, when we consider the atrocities that occur on a global scale.

In January 2020, bush fires spread rapidly through Australia. Caused by a catastrophic combination of extreme heat, drought and strong winds, these fires burnt vast areas of land, killed people and wildlife, and destroyed homes and livelihoods (Newey, 2020). In response, the rest of the world offered help in the form of voluntary firefighting, refuge, monetary donations, and medical assistance. On losing his home of 50 years to the fire, Australian Brett Cripps' immediate response to spotting two families surrounded by flames, was to offer them escape on his tiny boat (Mazzoni, 2020), as his house burned. It is hard to imagine how this act of altruism, at a time of intense personal tragedy, could be considered self-beneficial. In his lecture, Batson (2008) concludes: 'Looking back, the evidence that empathic concern produces altruistic motivation has certainly changed the way I think about prosocial motives, emotion, and behavior. I suspect it has – or will – change the way you think about them as well.'

Questions

1 Is it possible for us to help others without it being driven by a desire to benefit ourselves in some way?

2 Can you think of a time when you were able to see a set of circumstances through the eyes of an outgroup? Did this change your perception of that group?

3 Can you think of a time when empathizing with someone or a group was harmful either to you or the group or person concerned?

SUMMING UP: HELPING

WHY DO WE HELP?

- *The social-exchange theory* assumes that helping, like other social behaviours, is motivated by a desire to exchange rewards, to be fair and just, to give and receive. The rewards may be external, appreciated by others, or internal, improving personal self-esteem. Thus, after wrongdoing, people often become more willing to offer help. Sad people also tend to be helpful. Finally, there is a striking feel good–do good effect: happy people are helpful people.

- *The reciprocity norm* stimulates us to help those who have helped us.
- *The social-responsibility norm* beckons us to help needy people, even if they cannot reciprocate, so long as they are deserving. Women in crisis, partly because they may be seen as more needy, receive more offers of help than men, especially from men.
- *Evolutionary psychology* proposes two types of helping: devotion to kin and reciprocity. Some evolutionary psychologists, however, believe that the genes of selfish individuals are more likely to survive than the genes of self-sacrificing individuals. Thus, selfishness is our natural tendency and society must therefore teach helping.
- We can evaluate the theories according to the ways in which they characterize prosocial behaviour as based on tit-for-tat exchange and/or unconditional helpfulness. Each can be criticized for using speculative or after-the-fact reasoning, but they do provide a coherent scheme for summarizing observations of prosocial behaviour.
- In addition to helping that is motivated by external and internal rewards, and the evading of punishment or distress, there appears also to be a genuine, empathy-based altruism. With their empathy aroused, many people are motivated to assist others in need or distress, even when their helping is anonymous or their own mood will be unaffected.

WHEN WILL WE HELP?

- Several situational influences work to inhibit or to encourage altruism. As the number of bystanders at an emergency increases, any given bystander is (1) less likely to notice the incident, (2) less likely to interpret it as an emergency, and (3) less likely to assume responsibility. Experiments on helping behaviour pose an ethical dilemma but fulfil the researcher's mandate to enhance human life by discovering important influences on behaviour.
- When are people most likely to help? One circumstance that promotes helping is having at least a little spare time; those in a hurry are less likely to help. Another is feeling a sense of similarity with the person needing the help.
- We tend to help those whom we perceive as being close to us, our family or people we categorize as belonging to our ingroup. To help ingroup members strengthens our social identity and group cohesion, and boosts our self-image.

WHO WILL HELP?

- In contrast to altruism's potent situational and mood determinants, personality test scores have served as only modest predictors of helping.
- Social psychological research on whether religious people are more likely to be helpful is mixed, with supporting evidence in both directions. Overall, though, it seems having some religious faith does tend to facilitate helping behaviour such as helping strangers and donating to charity.
- People in societies where few believe in a god help to the same degree as in other societies.

HOW CAN WE INCREASE HELPING?

Research suggests that we can enhance helpfulness in three ways.

- First, we can reverse those factors that inhibit helping. We can take steps to reduce the ambiguity of an emergency to make a personal appeal, and to increase feelings of responsibility.

- Second, we can even use reprimands or evoke guilt feelings or a concern for self-image. However, in the case of cyberbullying, it is sometimes the ability to remain anonymous that facilitates helping.
- Third, we can teach altruism. Children who view helpful behaviour tend to act helpfully. If we want to promote altruistic behaviour, we should remember the overjustification effect: when we coerce good deeds, intrinsic love of the activity often diminishes. If we provide people with enough justification for them to decide to do good, but not much more, they will attribute their behaviour to their own altruistic motivation and henceforth be more willing to help. Learning about altruism, as you have just done, can also prepare people to perceive and respond to others' needs.

Critical Questions

1. How has social psychology defined altruism?
2. Would you expect the same motivation for helping in all cultures? Explain.
3. Which arguments can be used in favour of and against genuine altruism?
4. What limitations does social psychological research, including experiments and real-world studies, have when trying to understand the conditions under which we will, and will not, help someone?
5. What is the criticism against Darley and Latané's study of the bystander effect?
6. In what way is empathy important for helping?
7. To what extent do you think helping behaviour has 'evolved' in human societies?

Recommended Reading

Classic Papers

Batson, D. C., Batson, J. G., Slingsby, J. K., Harrell, K. L., Peekna, H. M., & Todd, M. R. (1991). Empathic joy and the empathy-altruism hypothesis. *Journal of Personality & Social Psychology, 61*(3), 413–426.

Dawkins, R. (2006). *The selfish gene.* Oxford University Press.

Latané, B., & Darley, J. M. (1968). Bystander intervention in emergencies: Diffusion of responsibility. *Journal of Personality and Social Psychology, 8*(4), 377–383.

Trivers, R. L. (1971). The evolution of reciprocal altruism. *Quarterly Review of Biology, 46*(1), 35–57.

Contemporary Papers

Batson, C. D. (2014). *The altruism question: Toward a social-psychological answer.* Psychology Press.

Fischer, P., Krueger, J. I., Greitemeyer, T., Vogrincic, C., Kästenmüller, A., Frey, D., Heene, M., Wicher, M., & Kainbacher, M. (2011). The bystander effect: A meta-analytic review on bystander intervention in dangerous and non-dangerous emergencies. *Psychological Bulletin, 137*(4), 517–537.

Levine, M., & Manning, R. (2013). Social identity, group processes, and helping in emergencies. *European Review of Social Psychology, 24*(1), 225–251.

11 SMALL GROUP PROCESSES

'Never doubt that a small group of thoughtful, committed citizens can change the world.'
Anthropologist Margaret Mead

In Chapter 7 we considered how people's actions and behaviour can be influenced to conform to, or obey, those around us. In this chapter we examine how we are influenced when we are part of a small group. Can small and minority groups be just as influential as majority ones?

For the purposes of this chapter the term 'group', used throughout, is an inference to a 'social group' as opposed to a mere assemblage of persons or objects gathered or located together. A social group shares some form of connectedness or unity. At almost every turn, we are involved in small groups – couples having dinner, housemates hanging out, students in a seminar discussion group, workers for a company, soldiers plotting strategy. How do these groups influence individuals' behaviour, values, attitudes and beliefs?

Group interactions often have dramatic effects. Intellectual college students hang out with other intellectuals, and they strengthen one another's intellectual interests. Deviant youths may hang out with other deviant youths, amplifying one another's antisocial tendencies. Online gamers take part in massively multiplayer online role-playing games (MMORPGs), meet like-minded people and strengthen their creative and reasoning skills. But how do these groups affect the attitudes of the people in the group? And what influences lead groups to good and bad decisions?

Individuals influence their groups. As the 1957 classic film *12 Angry Men* opens, 12 wary murder trial jurors file into the jury room. It is a hot day. The tired jurors are close to agreement and eager for a quick verdict convicting a teenage boy of knifing his father. But one maverick, played by Henry Fonda, refuses to vote guilty. As the heated deliberation proceeds, the jurors one by one change their minds until they reach a unanimous verdict: 'Not guilty'. In real trials, a lone individual seldom sways the entire group. Yet history is made by minorities that sway majorities. What helps make a minority – or a leader – persuasive?

We will examine these intriguing phenomena of group influence one at a time. But first things first: what is a group and why do groups exist?

What Is a Group?

The answer to this question seems self-evident – until several people compare their definitions. Are jogging partners a group? Are airplane passengers a group? Is a group a set of people who identify with one another, who sense they belong together? Is a group those who share common goals and rely on one another? Does a group form when individuals become organized? Do their relationships with one another continue over time? These are questions and definitions that have exercised the mind of social psychologists for some time!

So does a collection of co-present individuals in a situation constitute a 'group'? Not according to group dynamics expert Marvin Shaw (1981), who argues that all groups have one thing in common: their members interact with one another. Therefore, he defines a **group** as two or more people who interact and influence one another. This would allow for online interactions between people to be thought of as 'groups'. Prominent social psychologist John Turner (1987) argues that group members do not need to interact in order to feel being a 'group'. They don't need to

group two or more people who interact with and influence one another and perceive one another as 'us' be in one another's presence but group members simply have to identify as a group and perceive themselves as 'us' in contrast to 'them'. As such, an individual can act and think as a group member even when they're alone (see Chapters 12 and 13 for further discussion).

In the 1957 film *12 Angry Men*, one lone juror goes against his fellow jurors and refuses to vote 'guilty'. Slowly but surely he influences the other 11 jurors to also conclude 'not guilty'. History tells of minorities who sway majorities into changing their minds.

SOURCE: ©Silver Screen Collection/Getty Images

Groups may exist for a number of reasons – to meet a need to belong, to provide information, to supply rewards, to accomplish goals. Throughout this chapter we shall explore social psychological research that has started with varying understandings of what a 'group' is. At its simplest, people who are merely in one another's presence do sometimes influence one another. At a football game, they may perceive themselves as 'us' fans in contrast with 'them' who root for the other team. In this chapter we consider the structure and composition of groups, followed by three examples of collective influence: *social facilitation, social loafing* and *deindividuation*. These three phenomena can occur with minimal interaction (in what we call 'minimal group situations'). Then we consider three examples of social influence in interacting groups: *group polarization, groupthink* and *minority influence*.

The Structure and Composition of Groups

What Holds a Group Together?

Group cohesiveness is what holds a group together. A sense of team spirit and 'we-ness' rather than simply 'I'. Cohesion is about perceiving things in common with other group members. Social psychologists have understood group cohesiveness as being attraction to the group as a whole, rather than simply liking some individuals within it (Lott & Lott, 1965). The more cohesive the group, the more likely it is to remain together. Badea et al. (2012) observed that it also seems to be associated with success. When participants were presented with successful teams of fashion designers and architects, they regarded the groups as highly homogenous, and therefore highly cohesive. But can cohesiveness get in the way of performance? Hogg and Hains (1998) found that very cohesive groups, built on strong identification and attraction to the group, tended to make poorer decisions than those groups based on friendship and interpersonal attraction. As we shall see later in the chapter, being too similar can be detrimental to the group.

So what is it that group members find so attractive? What are they conforming to? In Chapter 4, we examine how cultural and societal norms guide our perceptions, judgements and behaviour. Norms can be formal with legal recognition (e.g. do not commit murder), but can also be informal and implicit. Groups have their own sets of norms that differentiate them from others. These norms not only describe beliefs about the way the world is, but also regulate individual members' behaviour. In Chapter 7 we examine the formation of norms in Sherif's (1935, 1937) experiments on the autokinetic phenomenon. As the perceptual illusion made reality ambiguous, individuals turned to one another for the right answer about how far a pinpoint of light had moved in an otherwise dark room. These group judgements persisted even when individuals were asked to give a private judgement. We return to group norms in Chapter 12, but for now we can say that the more a member identifies with the group, the more likely they are to adhere to the group's norms (Livingstone et al., 2011). And violating a group norm may well result in that member being rejected by the rest of the group. The likelihood of being shunned by the group depends on that individual's role and status within the group.

While norms characterize the whole group, individuals occupy different roles in groups. These may be based on abilities and qualities, and/or their relationships with other members of the group. Whatever the role, they should improve the group in some way. The role one occupies in a group can offer a sense of identity and purpose, as well as a guide on what behaviour is expected of that person (see Chapters 3 and 13). Roles may be recognized formally (e.g. in the workplace) or informally (e.g. amongst a group of friends). Of course, conflict can arise as a consequence of these roles. Individuals with different roles may clash as they try to fulfil them (e.g. a headmaster and a teacher), or they may experience role conflict as they occupy different roles across different groups (e.g. a mother, teacher, wife). The danger of a role is that individuals may lose sight of themselves in acting it out.

We see evidence of individuals losing sight of themselves in Zimbardo's prison study, discussed in detail in Chapter 7.

But of course not all roles are equal, and people hold very different statuses within a group. Status can have consequences for how individuals identify and behave in relation to the group. Fischer et al. (2007) found that low-status employees in a workplace displayed least cohesion to the group, had low identification with the group, and were most opposed to proposed changes to merge their workforce with another. Täuber and van Leeuwen (2012) observed that low-status members were more likely to offer help to outgroup members than high-status members. The leader of a group usually has the highest status as he or she is the most influential member, often with the power to change the structure and composition, and sometimes even the norms, of a group. Status is not a fixed entity but can change over time and space. We shall consider the role of leaders later in this chapter.

Formal and informal communication networks describe the paths along which individuals within a group interact. As people occupy different roles within a group, they will need to communicate to some individuals and not others. Communication networks have been most commonly examined in professional organizations where employers and employees recognize quite formal structures in their communications with each other. Within a small group, each individual member may be able to communicate directly with every other member, meaning a leader can discuss decisions with everyone. Boggs et al. (2005) report research that shows 'all-channel communication' networks are typically associated with high levels of group morale and performance. 'Wheel' communication networks describe the leader as the central medium through which all group members interact. Balkundi et al. (2011) found that workplace leaders who interacted with lower-status group members were perceived as charismatic and enhanced group performance. However, in large groups such structures are not always sustainable. Those who make the decisions may not be able to discuss them with everyone. If you think of big organizations such as universities, it would become a very cumbersome experience if all ideas and decisions were discussed with every member of staff before they were carried out. As such, there will be patterns of communication, such as 'chains' of command, which dictate who communicates with whom, and information is fed back to the decision-maker by means of a few select people rather than everyone. Of course this quest for efficiency and productivity can come at the cost of group satisfaction. The more input group members feel they've had over a decision the happier and more satisfied they are. So the roles we occupy will afford some people with the responsibility of making decisions on behalf of other members.

Social Facilitation: How Are We Affected by the Presence of Others?

Let's explore social psychology's most elementary question: are we affected by the mere presence of another person? 'Mere presence' means people are not competing, do not reward or punish, and in fact do nothing except be present as a passive audience or as **co-actors**. Would the mere presence of others affect a person's jogging, eating, typing or examination performance? The search for the answer is a scientific mystery story.

co-actors co-participants working individually on a noncompetitive activity

The Mere Presence of Others

In Chapter 1 we considered one of social psychology's first experiments that took place more than a century ago. Norman Triplett (1898), a psychologist interested in bicycle racing, noticed that cyclists' times were faster when they raced together than when each one raced alone against the clock. Before he peddled his hunch (that others' presence boosts performance), Triplett asked children to wind string on a fishing reel as rapidly as possible. They wound faster when they worked with co-actors than when they worked alone.

Ensuing experiments found that others' presence improves the speed with which people do simple multiplication problems and cross out designated letters. It also improves the accuracy with which people perform simple motor tasks, such as keeping a metal stick in contact with a dime-sized disc on a moving turntable (Allport, 1920; Dashiell, 1930; Travis, 1925). This **social facilitation** effect also occurs with animals. In some classic early work, in the presence of others of their species, ants excavate more sand, chickens eat more grain and sexually active rat pairs mate more often (Bayer, 1929; Chen, 1937; Larsson, 1956).

social facilitation (1) original meaning: the tendency of people to perform simple or well-learned tasks better when others are present (2) current meaning: the strengthening of dominant (prevalent, likely) responses in the presence of others

But wait: other early studies revealed that on some tasks the presence of others *hinders* performance. In the presence of others, cockroaches, parakeets and green finches learn mazes more slowly (Allee & Masure, 1936; Gates & Allee, 1933; Klopfer, 1958). This disruptive effect also occurs with people. Others' presence diminishes efficiency at learning nonsense syllables, completing a maze and performing complex multiplication problems (Dashiell, 1930; Pessin, 1933; Pessin & Husband, 1933). It can even interfere with passing your driving test, as Rosenbloom et al. (2007) found when they compared learner drivers tested in pairs with those tested alone. It also seems that the presence of virtual others can hinder performance. Park and Catrambone (2007) discovered that while the presence of virtual humans facilitated their participants in achieving simple tasks, it hindered them in the accomplishment of complex tasks.

Saying that the presence of others sometimes facilitates performance and sometimes hinders it is about as satisfying as the typical Scottish weather forecast – predicting that it might be sunny but then again it might rain. By 1940 research activity in this area had ground to a halt, and it lay dormant for 25 years until awakened by the touch of a new idea.

Research close-up

An Experiment on the Social Facilitation of Gambling Behaviour

Source: *Rockloff, M. J., & Dyer, V. (2007).* An experiment on the social facilitation of gambling behavior. *Journal of Gambling Studies, 23,* 1–12.

Introduction

Behaviours can be socially facilitated by the presence of others. This study investigated whether gambling would also be prone to social facilitation if it was done in the presence of other gamblers. Do gamblers gamble more frequently and intensively when surrounded by other gamblers? Does the desire to appear skilful to others, and the lights and bells signalling a 'win' on the machine, facilitate gambling behaviour? Or perhaps the presence of other gamblers might inhibit gambling behaviour if she or he fears appearing like an actual loser? An experiment was conducted to find out.

Method

A total of 116 participants (50 male, 66 female, aged 18–67) who were gamblers based in Queensland, Australia took part. They were all given $5 for agreeing to take part, and told they would be invited to gamble on an electronic gambling machine (EGM). They could, if they chose, use their $5 participation fee as a stake, but any other money gambled would be their own. All participants agreed to this and their $5 was taken from them. All participants were led to a room on their own containing an EGM, where they took part. Players were informed it was possible to win up to $50 on a game. Their time ended when they either ran out of money or chose to quit. Unknown to the participants, half of them were given faked information via the sound of bells that a player in the room next to them had won, and half were not. Furthermore, half the participants witnessed flashing banners on their screen, which indicated a player in an adjacent room had won, and again half were not. The study was interested in the final payout each participant received from the EGM before they stopped playing (which would indicate how much they had lost), the number of games they played, the average amount they bet, and how quickly they played.

Results

Those participants who had received fake information through sound (bell) and sight (banner) gambled the most amount of money. They left the experiment with no money left. This was a significant difference from those participants who received either no fake information, or sound only, or sight only.

Bet size did not differ between the participants regardless of which condition they were in.

Those participants subjected to both the sound of the bell and the flashing banner played more games than participants in either the bell only, the banner only, or no fake information conditions. The sound and sight participants also played more slowly than the other gamblers.

Discussion

This experiment presents social facilitation effects on gambling behaviour when the presence of other 'winning' gamblers is implied. It increases gambling behaviour, the amount of money lost, and the speed of play. These findings have implications for gambling venues. The larger the venue and the more players there are, the greater the amount of gambling will be due to social facilitation effects.

Critical Reflections

This study does seem to offer some convincing evidence that social facilitation effects occur in gambling. Gamblers gamble more in terms of frequency and amount, in the presence of other gamblers.

But before we get carried away, some caution is needed before arriving at this conclusion. This study only considers 'implied' presence of others. The sounds of bells and the seeing of banners represents 'fake' gamblers. It does not show what gamblers do when in the physical (or online) presence of other gamblers. Nor does it examine why social facilitation effects occur. The authors note that further work is needed in gambling venues to test the conclusions produced by their experiment. In particular, since this study was conducted, social psychological research has taken into account online gambling and gaming behaviour, to consider the effect others have on behaviour.

Social psychologist Robert Zajonc wondered whether these seemingly contradictory findings could be reconciled. As often happens at creative moments in science, Zajonc (1965) used one field of research to illuminate another. In this case the illumination came from a well-established principle in experimental psychology: arousal enhances whatever response tendency is dominant. Increased arousal enhances performance on easy tasks for which the most likely – 'dominant' – response is the correct one. People solve easy anagrams, such as *akec*, fastest when they are aroused. On complex tasks, for which the correct answer is not dominant, increased arousal promotes *incorrect* responding. On harder anagrams, such as *theloacco*, people do worse when anxious.

Could this principle solve the mystery of social facilitation? It seemed reasonable to assume that others' presence will arouse or energize people (Mullen et al., 1997); most of us can recall feeling tense or excited in front of an audience. If social arousal facilitates dominant responses, it should *boost performance on easy tasks* and *hurt performance on difficult tasks*.

With that explanation, the confusing results made sense. Winding fishing reels, doing simple multiplication problems, and eating were all easy tasks for which the responses were well learned or naturally dominant. Sure enough, having others around boosted performance. Learning new material, doing a maze and solving complex mathematics problems were more difficult tasks for which the correct responses were initially less probable. In these cases, the presence of others increased the number of *incorrect* responses on these tasks. The same general rule – *arousal facilitates dominant responses* – worked in both cases (see **Figure 11.1**). Suddenly, what had looked like contradictory results no longer seemed contradictory.

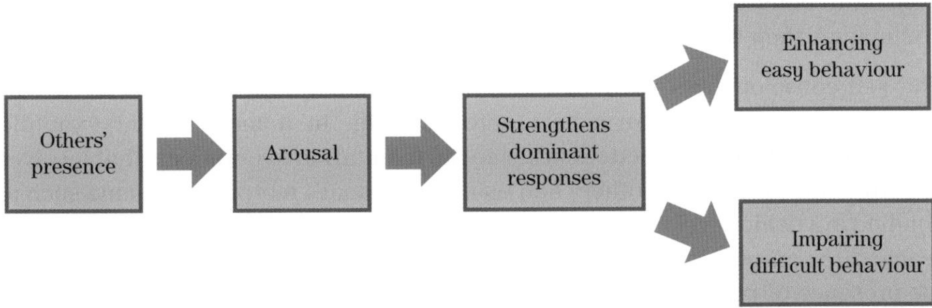

FIGURE 11.1 The effects of social arousal
Robert Zajonc (1965) reconciled apparently conflicting findings by proposing that arousal from others' presence strengthens dominant responses (the correct responses only on easy or well-learned tasks).

Zajonc's solution, so simple and elegant, left other social psychologists thinking what Thomas H. Huxley thought after first reading Darwin's *On the Origin of Species:* 'How extremely stupid not to have thought of that!' It seemed obvious – once Zajonc had pointed it out. Perhaps, however, the pieces fit so neatly only through the spectacles of hindsight. Would the solution survive direct experimental tests?

After hundreds of studies and thousands of volunteers, the solution has survived: social arousal facilitates dominant responses, whether right or wrong. For example, Hunt and Hillery (1973) found that in others' presence, students took less time to learn a simple maze and more time to learn a complex one (just as the cockroaches do!). And Michaels et al. (1982) found that good pool players in a student union (who had made 71 per cent of their shots while being unobtrusively observed) did even better (80 per cent) when four observers came up to watch them play. Poor shooters (who had previously averaged 36 per cent) did even worse (25 per cent) when closely observed. Skip forwards a few decades and Bowman et al. (2013) observe the same process in the performance of online gamers. Skilled gamers excel in the physical presence of others. Unskilled ones get worse!

But what about people who are used to being in crowded contexts with lots of people around them? In the big cities and in collective cultures like India and China, we might wonder if people are influenced by the presence of others to the same degree as people in more sparsely populated areas and independent cultures. Presumably not. We get used to the presence of others as well as everything else in a culture. So crowding and the presence of others may not have a similar impact in all cultures.

Why Are We Aroused in the Presence of Others?

What you do well, you will be energized to do best in front of others (unless you become hyper-aroused and self-conscious). What you find difficult may seem impossible in the same circumstances. What is it about other people that creates arousal? There is evidence to support at least three possible factors (Aiello & Douthitt, 2001): evaluation apprehension, distraction and mere presence.

Evaluation Apprehension

evaluation apprehension concern for how others are evaluating us

Nickolas Cottrell (1968) surmised that observers make us apprehensive because we wonder how they are evaluating us. To test whether **evaluation apprehension** exists, Meglino (1976) recruited 40 college students who were tested for dominance. They found that those who were highly dominant became even more dominant when evaluated by someone else. However, for those low in dominance, they became less dominant while being evaluated.

The self-consciousness we feel when being evaluated can also interfere with behaviours that we perform best automatically. In a more recent example, Fantoni et al. (2016) returned to earlier social facilitation experiments that involved the effect the presence of others had on an individual's motor movements such as winding in a fishing reel (Triplett, 1898). In their experiment, male adult participants reached for an object and moved it from one place to another. They found that the presence of others affected the speed and accuracy of this motor movement. When in the presence of a high status person, the participant was quicker in carrying out the task, but at the expense of accuracy. In the presence of a low status attendee, they were slower but more accurate. The researchers suggest that the high-status condition creates a competitive environment which propels motor movement to speed. However in the low-status condition, a more cooperative environment is created, which facilitates accuracy. Evaluation apprehension affects the most simple of tasks such as reaching for an object and moving it!

Mere Presence

Zajonc (1965), however, believes that the mere presence of others produces some arousal even without evaluation apprehension or arousing distraction. For example, most runners are energized when running with someone else, even one who neither competes nor evaluates.

This is a good time to remind ourselves that a good theory is a scientific shorthand: it simplifies and summarizes a variety of observations (see Chapter 2). **Social facilitation theory** does this well. It is a simple summary of many research findings. A good theory also offers clear predictions that (1) help confirm or modify the theory, (2) guide new exploration, and (3) suggest practical applications. Social facilitation theory has definitely generated the first two types of prediction: (1) the basics of the theory (that the presence of others is arousing and that this social arousal enhances dominant responses) have been confirmed, and (2) the theory has brought new life to a long-dormant field of research.

social facilitation theory (1) original meaning: the tendency of people to perform simple or well-learned tasks better when others are present (2) current meaning: the strengthening of dominant (prevalent, likely) responses in the presence of others

Are there (3) some practical applications? We can make some educated guesses. As **Figure 11.2** shows, many new office buildings have replaced private offices with large, open areas divided by low partitions. Open-plan offices are now commonplace, which you might have witnessed in your university. Might the resulting awareness of others' presence help boost the performance of well-learned tasks but disrupt creative thinking on complex tasks? Can you think of other possible applications?

Absent Friends

Of course, online groups do not involve the physical presence of others. People can be part of groups and communities without ever having physically met any of their fellow members. The rise in the use of Internet chat rooms, self-help groups and large forums such as Facebook, Instagram and Twitter has seen groups of people formed online, sharing stories, swapping experiences and motivating one another to achieve goals.

Beffa-Negrini et al. (2002) point out that there are extra challenges in facilitating online groups. Without the physical presence of people who can show emotions such as empathy and offer immediate feedback, members of online groups can soon feel isolated and misunderstood. The challenge for online groups is to remain good-humoured, provide each other with positive feedback and praise, and to encourage the expression of emotions.

In the 'open-office plan', people work in the presence of others. How might this affect worker efficiency? Can you think of any problems this kind of environment might create which affects performance?

SOURCE: ©Monkey Business Images/Shutterstock

Consider online teaching and learning. As teaching practices move more towards collaborative online environments to deliver information, this poses an interesting challenge to tutors and students. How can you facilitate and motivate a group you can't see? McFadzean and McKenzie (2001) suggest that tutors need to deliver information and encourage students to work collaboratively as a team. De Smet et al. (2009) examined how tutors provide teaching and social support to students using online discussion groups. They found that, as time went on, tutor contributions decreased as students engaged more in peer tutoring. Students help each other to learn, teaching and motivating one another towards their common goal.

So where physical presence is not possible group members still require social facilitation but in a way that can be delivered online. As Beffa-Negrini et al. (2002) argue, this should be in the form of a sense of community, so each member can share their experiences, goals and aspirations.

Social Loafing: Do Individuals Exert Less Effort in a Group?

In a team tug-of-war, will eight people on a side exert as much force as the sum of their best efforts in individual tugs-of-war? If not, why not? What level of individual effort can we expect from members of work groups?

Social facilitation usually occurs when people work towards individual goals and when their efforts, whether winding fishing reels or solving maths problems, can be individually evaluated. These situations parallel some everyday work situations, but not those in which people pool their efforts towards a *common* goal and where individuals are *not* accountable for their efforts. A team tug-of-war provides one such example, so does a class group project on which all students get the same grade. On such 'additive tasks' – tasks where the group's achievement depends on the sum of the individual efforts – will team spirit boost productivity? Will bricklayers lay bricks faster when working as a team than when working alone? One way to attack such questions is with laboratory simulations.

Many Hands Make Light Work

Nearly a century ago, French engineer Max Ringelmann found that the collective effort of tug-of-war teams was but half the sum of the individual efforts (Kravitz & Martin, 1986). That suggests, contrary to the presumption 'in unity there is strength', that group members may actually be *less* motivated when performing additive tasks. Maybe, though, poor performance stemmed from poor co-ordination – people pulling a rope in slightly different directions at slightly different times. A group of Massachusetts researchers led by Alan Ingham (1974) cleverly eliminated that problem by making individuals think others were pulling with them, when in fact they were pulling alone. Blindfolded participants were assigned the first position in the apparatus and told, 'Pull as hard as you can'. They pulled 18 per cent harder when they knew they were pulling alone than when they believed that behind them two to five people were also pulling.

social loafing the tendency for people to exert less effort when they pool their efforts towards a common goal than when they are individually accountable

Latané et al. (1979) and Harkins et al. (1980) kept their ears open for other ways to investigate this phenomenon, which they labelled **social loafing**. They observed that the noise produced by six people shouting or clapping 'as loud as you can' was less than three times that produced by one person alone. Like the tug-of-war task, however, noise-making is vulnerable to group inefficiency. So Latané and his associates followed Ingham's example by leading their participants to believe others were shouting or clapping with them, when in fact they were doing so alone.

Their method was to blindfold six people, seat them in a semicircle and have them put on headphones, over which they were blasted with the sound of people shouting or clapping. People could not hear their own shouting or clapping, much less that of others. On various trials they were instructed to shout or clap either alone or along with the group. People who were told about this experiment guessed the participants would shout louder when with others, because they would be less inhibited (Harkins, 1981). The actual result? Social loafing: when the participants believed five others were also either shouting or clapping, they produced one-third less noise than when they thought themselves alone. Social loafing occurred even when the participants were high school cheerleaders who believed themselves to be cheering together rather than alone (Hardy & Latané, 1986).

Curiously, those who clapped both alone and in groups did not view themselves as loafing; they perceived themselves as clapping equally in both situations. This parallels what happens when students work on group projects for a shared grade. While they all agree loafing occurs – no one admits to doing the loafing.

Social psychological research has found that individuals who see themselves as 'average' tend to be less likely to engage in social loafing than those who consider themselves to be of superior ability (Huguet et al., 1999). This seems to be particularly the case when the collective task is an easy one. **Evaluation apprehension** also plays a role in the occurrence of social loafing. Arterberry et al. (2007) observed that when 5-year-old children were asked to complete an easy and a difficult puzzle with a partner, they displayed social loafing when they believed their individual input was left unevaluated compared to when they believed their efforts were being monitored. However, when asked to complete an easy puzzle with another child with their individual efforts being monitored, the children performed better than when they did the easy puzzle alone. The sense of having your efforts evaluated increases performance.

evaluation apprehension concern for how others are evaluating us

In this and 160 other studies (Karau & Williams, 1993), we see a twist on one of the psychological forces that makes for social facilitation: evaluation apprehension. In the social loafing experiments, individuals believed they were evaluated only when they acted alone. The group situation (rope pulling, shouting, and so forth) *decreased* evaluation apprehension. When people are not accountable and cannot evaluate their own efforts, responsibility is diffused across all group members (Cummings et al., 2013; Harkins & Jackson, 1985; Hoigaard et al., 2013; Kerr & Bruun, 1981; Kidwell & Robie, 2003). By contrast, the social facilitation experiments *increased* exposure to evaluation. When made the centre of attention, people self-consciously monitor their behaviour. So, when being observed *increases* evaluation concerns, social facilitation occurs; when being lost in a crowd *decreases* evaluation concerns, social loafing occurs (**Figure 11.2**, overleaf).

To motivate group members, one strategy is to make individual performance identifiable. Some team sport coaches do this by filming and evaluating each player individually. Whether in a group or not, people exert more effort when their outputs are individually identifiable. Hoigaard and Ingvaldsen (2006) discovered that when individuals were made identifiable in a team sport floorball tournament, not only did social loafing reduce but their individual performance increased.

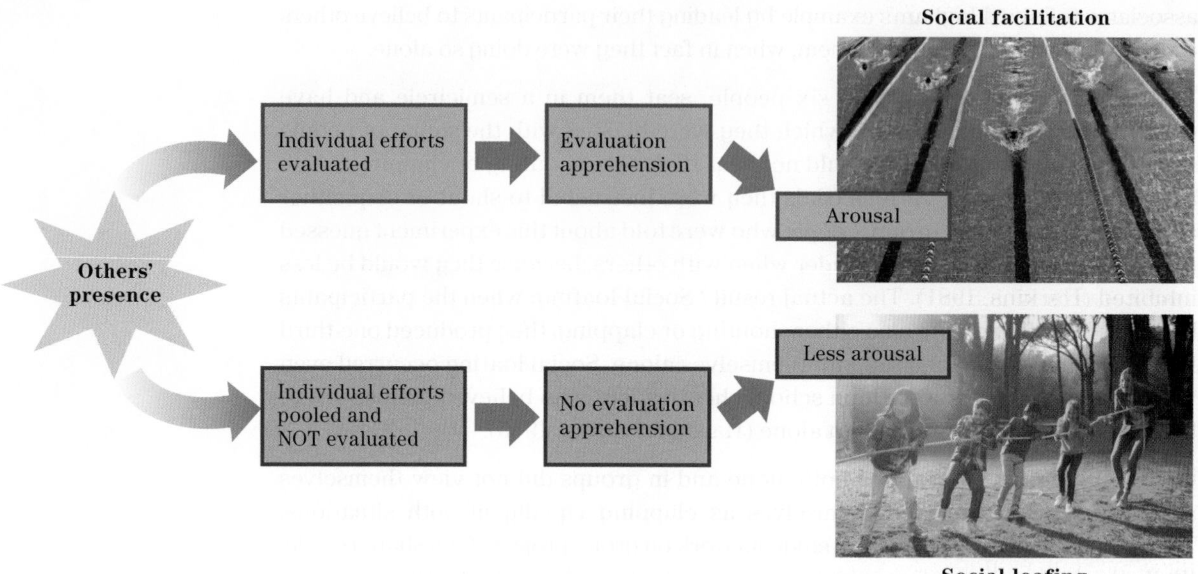

FIGURE 11.2 Social facilitation or social loafing?

When individuals cannot be evaluated or held accountable, loafing becomes more likely. An individual swimmer is evaluated on her ability to win the race. In tug-of-war, no single person on the team is held accountable, so any one member might relax or loaf.

SOURCE: (T) ©Shutterstock/Dean Drobot; (B) ©Robert Daly/Caia Image/Glow Images

Social Loafing in Everyday Life

How widespread is social loafing? In the laboratory the phenomenon occurs not only among people who are pulling ropes, cycling, shouting and clapping, but also among those who are pumping water or air, evaluating poems or editorials, producing ideas, typing and detecting signals. Do these consistent results generalize to everyday worker productivity?

Consider this: a key job in a pickle factory is picking the right size dill pickle halves off the conveyor belt and stuffing them into jars. Unfortunately, workers are tempted to stuff any size pickle in, because their output is not identifiable (the jars go into a common hopper before reaching the quality-control section). In this amusing yet classic study, Williams et al. (1981) note that research on social loafing suggests making individual production identifiable, and raises the question: 'How many pickles could a pickle packer pack if pickle packers were only paid for properly packed pickles?'

Some researchers have focused on perceptions of social loafing rather than its actual occurrence. Perceiving other members of a group as not contributing equally to a group goal can have implications for how that individual is treated by other group members. The tendency to perceive social loafing within a group has been shown to be related to how strongly an individual identifies with the group and its purpose.

In Høigaard et al.'s (2006) study of Norwegian football players, they found that those players who identified strongly with the team norm of competition and winning and regarded the group as cohesive, did not perceive their fellow team members as social loafers. However, those players who joined the team for social reasons rather than to win games, and did not regard the team as a cohesive unit, perceived high levels of social loafing among their fellow team members.

Whether the phenomenon of social loafing is a cross-cultural one, is a matter of debate (Clark & Baker, 2011). Some social psychological research has revealed that people in collectivist cultures do exhibit less social loafing than do people in individualist cultures (Karau & Williams, 1993; Kugihara, 1999). Loyalty to family and work groups runs strong in collectivist cultures. Earley (1989) has argued that those cultures which rest on collectivist beliefs rather than individualistic ones show less occurrence of social loafing. In his comparison of managerial trainees in the USA and China, he found that social loafing was much less prevalent among the Chinese workers. This view has received more recent empirical support from Hong et al. (2008) who also found that Chinese participants engaged in less social loafing than North Americans. However, this view has been challenged, in particular by researchers who examine the occurrence and perceptions of social loafing levels in domestic and international students' performance in higher education. For example, Clark and Barker (2011) compared the perceptions of social loafing between Chinese and New Zealand students studying at New Zealand higher education colleges. They found no difference between the two cultural groups in what social loafing was, both considered it to be a negative phenomenon that occurs in groups and something to be avoided where possible. Despite this, both New Zealand and Chinese students admitted to engaging in social loafing in assessed groupwork.

While this made them feel guilty, it could reward them with higher grades. Hence the collectivist background of the Chinese students did not seem to influence their attitudes to social loafing nor their behaviour. Conversely, it has been argued that international students have been influenced by the country in which they are studying, and therefore do not truly reflect how most Chinese (for example) feel about social loafing and groupwork (Parker et al., 2009). Perhaps more cross-cultural work is needed to examine social loafing at school, college and the workplace, in the broadly termed collectivistic countries themselves.

There is another possible explanation of social loafing. When rewards are divided equally, regardless of how much one contributes to the group, any individual gets more reward per unit of effort by free-riding in the group. So people may be motivated to slack off when their efforts are not individually monitored and rewarded. Situations that welcome **free-riders** can therefore be highly advantageous for those who exploit the opportunity (Jones, 2013). For example, see the Research Close-Up: The Frustrating Experience of Free-riders in Group Work.

free-riders people benefiting from the group but giving little in return

But surely collective effort does not always lead to slacking off. Sometimes the goal is so compelling and maximum output from everyone is so essential that team spirit maintains or intensifies effort. In an Olympic crew race, will the individual rowers in an eight-person crew pull their oars with less effort than those in a one- or two-person crew?

The evidence assures us they will not. People in groups loaf less when the task is *challenging, appealing* or *involving* (Karau & Williams, 1993; Simms & Nichols, 2014). On challenging tasks, people may perceive their efforts as indispensable. When people see others in their group as unreliable or as unable to contribute much, they work

Social loafing occurs when people work in groups but without individual accountability – unless the task is challenging, appealing or involving and the group members are friends.
SOURCE: ©Juice Images/Alamy Stock Photo

harder (Plaks & Higgins, 2000; Williams & Karau, 1991). Adding incentives or challenging a group to strive for certain standards also promotes collective effort (Ferrante et al., 2006; Harkins & Szymanski, 1989). Group members will work hard when convinced that high effort will bring rewards (Harcum & Badura, 2001; Shepperd & Taylor, 1999).

Groups also loaf less when their members are *friends* or identified with their group, rather than strangers (Davis & Greenlees, 1992; Karau & Williams, 1997; Worchel et al., 1998). Even just expecting to interact with someone again serves to increase effort on team projects (Groenenboom et al., 2001). Collaborate on a class project with others whom you will be seeing often and you will probably feel more motivated than you would if you never expect to see them again.

Research close-up

The Frustrating Experience of Free-Riders in Group Work

Source: Hall, D., & Buzwell, S. (2013). The problem of free-riding in group projects: Looking beyond social loafing as a reason for non-contribution. *Active Learning in Higher Education, 14*(1), 37–49.

Introduction

Group work is increasingly being used as a form of assessment in higher education. Group work activities can facilitate students' mastery of transferable team skills which can prove valuable in the workplace. Consequently the benefits of this type of assessment include the fact that it provides students with relevant experience for their future careers, it allows students to be active agents in their learning, and it reduces teachers' administrative load (such as time spent marking). However, students are not always convinced by the benefits of group work. Groups can be dysfunctional, and the presence of 'free-riders' can make the experience unpleasant. Free-riders put in little effort to the group's productivity, yet reap the rewards of everyone else's efforts. The reasons for free-riding are complex and diverse, ranging from poor communication skills, laziness, feelings of inadequacy and lack of understanding of the group task. They can be voluntary or involuntary. Sometimes other group members facilitate an individual's free-riding when they feel that particular member may be an obstacle to the group's success. Hence the group is superficially inclusive of that participant, but exclusive in terms of executing the task. Free-riding is difficult for teachers to detect, and results in group members feeling frustrated when a free-rider is awarded a grade that does not reflect their lack of effort in the group.

This study was interested in students' own perceptions of free-riding. What causes did they attribute to this phenomenon? What impact does it have on others? Is free-riding more frequent in some academic disciplines than others?

Method

The participants were 205 students, aged 18–30 years old (the majority aged 18–24 years), from across all faculties at an Australian university, including natural and social sciences, humanities, engineering and IT. Of the sample, 65.2 per cent were male students, and 34.8 per cent were female, which reflects the gender composition of the university.

The participants were asked to reflect on their experience of group work, and consider: how those groups were formed, the allocation of roles within them, and whether there was a designated group leader. On a 5-point **Likert scale**, students were asked to rate: their knowledge of the task concerned, their enjoyment of taking part in the group work, and their overall experience of taking part. They were also asked an open-question asking how group work could be improved and allowing them to elaborate on the answers provided in the Likert survey.

Likert scale typically used in attitudinal research, this is a rating scale consisting of a number of items (or statements) against which participants rate how they feel about them. The scale typically has a neutral midpoint (e.g. neither agree or disagree)

The Likert scale data was analysed quantitatively, and the open-ended question data was analysed qualitatively using thematic textual analysis.

Results

The Likert scale data revealed that overall, students rated their group work experience as average (mean = 3.06, SD = 1.268); 44 per cent rated their experience as 'good' or 'excellent', and 32 per cent rated their experience as 'poor' or 'very poor'. No differences were found between the various academic disciplines.

The thematic analysis of the open-ended data showed that the major concern students had about group work was the occurrence of free-riding and marks not reflecting the efforts of individuals. For example, one student noted that:

> Group projects in an ideal situation, where work is divided up evenly and all participants are enthused about the project, would ultimately benefit each individual member. Realistically though, this is not the case. Generally one or two people do the majority of the work, and [other] group members prove to be apathetic, willing only to do the bare minimum, or lack the initiative to take on work unless directed, which is not only frustrating but also unfair. (p. 43)

Other reasons for the occurrence of free-riding included different working styles, with some students perceived to have a more laissez-faire approach to work. Dispositional reasons were also offered with free-riders being depicted as lazy, unreliable and unknowledgeable. Consequently students reported having to put in more effort to compensate for the free-riders, such that the group as a whole did not suffer,

Discussion

Students generally had a positive view and experience of group work. However, there were some clear concerns about the presence of free-riders in group work and the impact they have on the rest of the group, for all disciplines. Feelings of frustration were common throughout the sample, as students reported the lack of fairness when those perceived as free-riders received higher marks than they deserved. The reasons for free-riding were typically situated within the free-rider: it was their incompetence, their poor working style, their laziness and so on. Moreover, those who didn't free-ride worked harder to compensate. However, this assumes that free-riding is a voluntary decision: the student chooses not to participate equally in the group. But free-riding may be involuntary. They may prefer to work alone and find group work difficult to cope with. Personal circumstances may influence their poor contribution, such as illness or a bereavement. Being unable to communicate effectively in a group (e.g. due to a language barrier), feelings of low-status and/or low-esteem may also contribute to perceived free-riding.

It is not the role of the students to identify free-riders and the cause of their free-riding, because as this paper shows, they typically assume it is voluntary. Instead, it is the role of the educational establishment to set assessments that catch free-riding early on in the process, and identify the cause. This will enable group work to function more effectively and enjoyably for all concerned.

Critical Reflections

This research offers some important insights into how free-riding can occasionally be (mis)interpreted by group members, risking unfair treatment of those perceived to be guilty of behaving in this way. However, as with all research there's always some value in reflecting on how it was carried out and the conclusions arrived at. For example, consider that the participants were asked about their most recent experience of group work. Hence this is not reflective of their general experience of group work. Furthermore, not all group work is the same. It would be worth knowing something about the types of group work being considered, as the presence of free-riding may be more or less present or detectable, and also impact more or less on others, depending on what it is that the group is being asked to do.

Group Polarization: Do Groups Intensify our Opinions?

Many conflicts grow as people on both sides talk mostly with like-minded others. Does interaction with like-minded people amplify pre-existing attitudes? If so, why?

Studies of people in small groups have produced a principle that helps explain both bad and good outcomes: group discussion often strengthens members' initial inclinations. The unfolding of this research on **group polarization** illustrates the process of enquiry – how an interesting discovery often leads researchers to hasty and erroneous conclusions, which ultimately are replaced with more accurate conclusions.

group polarization group-produced enhancement of members' pre-existing tendencies. When a rather homogenous group discusses a topic, the opinion of the group members often merges into a more extreme one, strengthening the members' average tendency

The Case of the 'Risky Shift'

A research literature of more than 300 studies began with a surprising finding by Stoner (1961), then an MIT graduate student. For his master's thesis in industrial management, Stoner tested the commonly held belief that groups are more cautious than individuals. He posed decision dilemmas in which the participant's task was to advise imagined characters how much risk to take. Put yourself in the participant's shoes: what advice would you give the character in this situation?

Helen is a writer who is said to have considerable creative talent but who so far has been earning a comfortable living by writing cheap westerns. Recently she has come up with an idea for a potentially significant novel. If it could be written and accepted, it might have considerable literary impact and be a big boost to her career. On the other hand, if she cannot work out her idea, or if the novel is a flop, she will have expended considerable time and energy without remuneration.

Imagine that you are advising Helen. Please check the *lowest* probability that you would consider acceptable for Helen to attempt to write the novel.

Helen should attempt to write the novel if the chances that the novel will be a success are at least:

___ 1 in 10
___ 2 in 10

___ 3 in 10
___ 4 in 10
___ 5 in 10
___ 6 in 10
___ 7 in 10
___ 8 in 10
___ 9 in 10
___ 10 in 10 (Place a check here if you think Helen should attempt the novel only if it is certain that the novel will be a success.)

After making your decision, guess what this book's average reader would advise. Having marked their advice on a dozen such items, five or so individuals would then discuss and reach agreement on each item. How do you think the group decisions compared with the average decision before the discussions? Would the groups be likely to take greater risks, be more cautious, or stay the same?

To everyone's amazement, the group decisions were usually riskier. Dubbed the 'risky shift phenomenon', this finding set off a wave of group risk-taking studies. These revealed that risky shift occurs not only when a group decides by consensus; after a brief discussion, individuals, too, will alter their decisions. What is more, researchers successfully repeated Stoner's finding with people of varying ages and occupations in a dozen nations.

During discussion, opinions converged. Curiously, however, the point towards which they converged was usually a lower (riskier) number than their initial average. Here was a delightful puzzle. The small risky shift effect was reliable, unexpected and without any immediately obvious explanation. What group influences produce such an effect? And how widespread is it? Do discussions in juries, business committees and military organizations also promote risk taking? Does this explain why teenage reckless driving, as measured by death rates, nearly doubles when a 16- or 17-year-old driver has two teenage passengers rather than none (Chen et al., 2000)?

However, the risky shift was not universal. There were decision dilemmas on which people became more *cautious* after discussion. One of these featured 'Roger', a young married man with two school-age children and a secure but low-paying job. Roger can afford life's necessities but few of its luxuries. He hears that the stock of a relatively unknown company may soon triple in value if its new product is favourably received or decline considerably if it does not sell. Roger has no savings. To invest in the company, he is considering selling his life insurance policy.

Can you see a general principle that predicts both the tendency to give riskier advice after discussing Helen's situation and more cautious advice after discussing Roger's? If you are like most people, you would advise Helen to take a greater risk than Roger, even before talking with others. It turns out there is a strong tendency for discussion to accentuate these initial leanings; groups discussing the 'Roger' dilemma became more risk-averse than they were before discussion.

So there seem to be other concerns that influence our risky or cautious decisions. Hensley (1977) has argued that one of the factors in making a risky decision is age. From his studies on the risky shift, he found that participants who were teenagers made riskier decisions than older participants. Abrams et al. (2006) found that contrary to what you might think when people drink alcohol together as a group, they actually regulate each other's behaviour. Therefore, sometimes, being part of a group may lead to safer decisions and behaviour rather than riskier ones. Finney (1978) observed that the desire to engage in risky behaviour may, to some extent, be understood by the culture the participant is from. He points out that many risky shift studies take place using North American participants, where the values of success, status and risk are held in high esteem. Hence, to encourage someone to take further risks may reflect North American cultural values rather than just be a feature of small group decisions.

Do Groups Intensify Opinions?

Realizing that this group phenomenon was not a consistent shift towards increased risk, the phenomenon became reconceived as a tendency for group discussion to *enhance* group members' initial leanings. This idea led investigators to propose what Moscovici and Zavalloni (1969) called group polarization: *discussion typically strengthens the average inclination of group members.*

Group Polarization Experiments

This new view of the changes induced by group discussion prompted experimenters to have people discuss attitude statements that most of them favoured or most of them opposed. Would talking in groups enhance their shared initial inclinations as it did with the decision dilemmas? In groups, would risk takers take bigger risks, bigots become despisers, and givers become more philanthropic? That's what the group polarization hypothesis predicts (**Figure 11.3**).

Dozens of classic and contemporary studies confirm group polarization. Moscovici and Zavalloni (1969) observed that discussion enhanced French students' initially positive attitude towards their president and negative attitude towards Americans. Brauer et al. (2001) found that French students' dislike for certain other people was exacerbated after discussing their shared negative impressions. Palmer and Loveland (2008) observed that when interview panel members discussed interviewees post-interview it led to a polarized evaluation of candidates' performance as 'good' or 'bad', and individual pre-interview ratings became less accurate assessments.

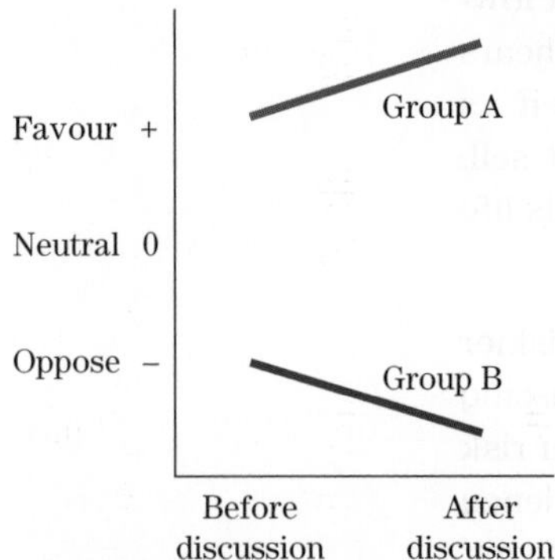

FIGURE 11.3 Group polarization
The group polarization hypothesis predicts that discussion will strengthen an attitude shared by group members.

Social psychological experiments like those outlined above neatly demonstrate a robust phenomenon: group polarization. However, perhaps what they cannot convey are the serious, and sometimes devastating, consequences group polarization can have. Take, for example, the increased focus on group polarization within online communities. As observed with physical groups, online groups are also prone to group polarization (Tsikerdekis, 2013). We are now able to communicate with members of large groups, both online and offline, and in doing so share opinions, ideas and expertise. While on the surface this might seem desirable, some researchers have noted serious implications. For example, within the healthcare profession, health experts can collectively discuss a case online and offline. However, increased collaboration between healthcare professionals can risk poorer medical decisions being made, especially when all members of the group respect and trust one another (Kaba et al., 2016). A glance at the research on group polarization shows that it has been attributed to matters such as consumers being pressured into buying things they don't actually want or need (Breitsohl et al., 2015), through to radicalization of people by terrorist organizations (Post & Panis, 2011; Tsintsadze-Maass & Maass, 2014).

Group Polarization in Everyday Life

In everyday life people associate mostly with others whose attitudes are similar to their own. (See Chapter 5, or just look at your own circle of friends.) Does everyday group interaction with like-minded friends intensify shared attitudes? Do nerds become nerdier?

Group Polarization in Schools

A real-life parallel to the laboratory phenomenon is what education researchers have called the 'accentuation' effect: over time, initial differences among groups of college students become accentuated. If the first-year students at college X are initially more intellectual than the students at college Y, that gap is likely to increase by the time they graduate. This phenomenon has been studied with respect to the controversial practice of teachers' grouping students on the basis of ability, and the impact this 'setting' exercise has on learning (e.g. Abraham, 1989; Boaler et al., 2000; Francis et al., 2017). The gaps between the sets widens, not just educationally but also socially.

Research has also shown that group polarization doesn't just occur in groups of students, but also amongst education staff. One intriguing example comes from an exploration of decision-making processes by school disciplinary panels in Kenya (Aloka & Bojuwoye, 2013). Disciplinary panels are conducted for students who exhibit bad conduct in school in Kenya. These panels can comprise of teachers, practitioners, advisors, counsellors and so forth, depending on the nature of the misconduct. Research by Aloka and Bojuwoye (2013) noted that the decisions individual panel members made prior to the meeting were different after the meeting. Indeed the panel created a polarization of opinions regarding how to deal with the student. The researchers note that individual decisions become influenced in the presence of others they may deem of higher social status, and therefore more credible, than themselves.

Group Polarization in Communities

Polarization also occurs in communities, as people self-segregate. 'Crunchy places . . . attract crunchy types and become crunchier', observes Brooks (2005). 'Conservative places . . . attract conservatives and become more so.' Neighbourhoods become echo chambers, with opinions ricocheting off kindred-spirited friends.

Where you live, and who you live in close proximity to, can influence your beliefs and values.

SOURCE: ©geogif/Shutterstock

People who reside in the same community can become like-minded people, confirming to one another their beliefs and what they value and hold dear. Even if information comes into the group that debunks what they think they know, it makes no difference. The community holds steadfastly onto their false beliefs, and any disconfirming information is not only dismissed but can function to strengthen the group's incorrect view (Bessi et al., 2015; Kennedy & Pronin, 2008). On the basis of this, some studies have suggested that perhaps it is better not to talk at all to a group for fear of creating and strengthening group polarization! For example, Paluck (2010) conducted a field experiment in the Eastern Democratic Republic of the Congo. In her study Paluck tested the impact a weekly aired talk show on the radio would have on the opinions of its listeners about conflict, ethnic minorities and cooperation in the DRC. Paluck worked with the programme makers of a popular radio soap opera titled *Kumbuka Kesho* (Think of Tomorrow). The soap opera is set in a fictional town which experiences high levels of political corruption and conflict between the ethnic groups that live there. Paluck organized for the soap opera to be followed by a 15-minute talk show in which listeners could phone in and discuss matters relating to conflict and cooperation in the DRC. The radio broadcasters ensured that in some towns of the region, the listener would just hear the soap opera as normal, while in other towns they would hear the soap opera followed by the talk show. What she found was that those listeners who called into the talk show presented increasingly hardened intolerant attitudes to other ethnic groups. Their opinions became polarized around a narrative of conflict and prejudice towards ethnic minorities in the DRC. At the end of the year-long experiment Paluck sent out a questionnaire to all listeners, including those who had heard the talk show and those who hadn't, about their views on ethnic minorities, conflict and cooperation. What she found was that those exposed to the talk show (and who had possibly contributed to it) reported far higher levels of prejudice, were less willing to help other ethnic groups, and reported more conflict than those who had not heard the talk show. The talk show had polarized negative attitudes to ethnic minorities. Paluck's startling conclusion was that sometimes it's perhaps better not to talk.

When we think of polarization in communities, we might immediately be tempted to think about communities as in geographical neighbourhoods, and indeed this is what some research has focused on. As researchers have pointed out, space influences social actions. Hence, where we physically live influences who we see and interact with on a regular basis – our neighbours. We see them frequently, and in doing so can build strong relationships with those we are physically close to. The exchange of information, news and gossip spreads quickly in geographical communities with strong ties between its members (Morales et al., 2019). Perhaps one of the most sobering examples is the effect group polarization had on attitudes and behaviours towards Jews across Eastern Europe after World War II. Kopstein and Wittenberg (2011) found that those communities which were characterized by polarization between Jewish and non-Jewish groups, with simmering tensions and hostile attitudes towards Jews, prior to the outbreak of war, were much more likely to erupt into violence once World War II was declared. In contrast, those communities that enjoyed inter-ethnic civil engagement, where groups were assimilated, were not prone to erupting into violent clashes between Jews and non-Jews.

During actual community conflicts, like-minded people associate increasingly with one another, amplifying their shared tendencies. Gang delinquency emerges from a process of mutual reinforcement within neighbourhood gangs, whose members share attributes and hostilities (Bjorgo, 2005; Cartwright, 1975). If 'a second out-of-control 15-year-old moves in [on your block]', surmises Lykken (1997), 'the mischief they get into as a team is likely to be more than merely double what the first would do on his own . . . A gang is more dangerous than the sum of its individual parts.' Indeed, 'unsupervised peer groups' are 'the strongest predictor' of a neighbourhood's crime victimization rate, report Veysey and Messner (1999). Moreover, experimental interventions that take delinquent adolescents and group them with other delinquents, actually – no surprise to any group polarization researcher – increase the rate of problem behaviour (Dishion et al., 1999).

Group Polarization on the Internet

Online groups are another kind of community. E-mail, blogs and social media offer a space for like-minded people to find one another and interact. In Facebook, for example, there are tens of thousands of groups of kindred spirits discussing religion, politics, hobbies, cars, music, you name it. The Internet's countless virtual groups enable peacemakers and neo-Nazis, geeks and goths, conspiracy theorists and cancer survivors to chat with like-minded others and find support for their shared concerns, interests and suspicions. Freedom of communication, lack of censorship and anonymity means the Internet offers a perfect medium for expressing views, both positive and negative (Wang et al., 2018). Without the non-verbal nuances of face-to-face contact, will such discussions produce group polarization? Sia et al. (2002) think so. Their experiments on the effects of computer-mediated communication (CMC) found that the lack of visual cues and the increase in anonymity led to raised group polarization. They suggest that people are more likely to generate novel arguments and engage in a game of one-upmanship when individuals' social presence is reduced. E-mail, Google and chat rooms 'make it much easier for small groups to rally like-minded people, crystallize diffuse hatreds and mobilize lethal force', observes Wright (2003).

Wang et al. (2018) examined how Internet communities can contribute to the spread of rumours and 'fake news'. Our recent history reveals an array of such occurrences over the Internet, which you may have seen (and even unwittingly participated in). Famous people have been reported dead, while still very much alive! Candidates running for election have found themselves smeared over the Internet with false rumours about their behaviour. Commercial companies have also come under attack with false claims such as KFC accused of using mutated chickens in its food. Wang et al. (2018) note that the likelihood of a rumour being spread across the Internet is high if the rumour is considered to be believable, has come from a credible source, is of interest, and is repeated by others – especially those individuals who belong to our 'network clusters'. We discuss strategies of persuasion in Chapter 6 and the conditions under which we find a message convincing. And this is what Wang et al. (2018) found when they asked Chinese participants how likely they would be to spread an untrue rumour concerning a paper manufacturing company going bankrupt. Seeing a believable and interesting rumour spread by their online peers, enhanced the likelihood that they themselves would spread it. Furthermore, discussing a rumour with our online friends, leads to group polarization. The group's opinions gain strength and credibility. If our peers believe it, then the chances are we will also, and we will all believe it, fervently. Convinced by the rumour's truth, people spread it rapidly throughout their networks and into those of other people.

Explaining Polarization

Why do groups adopt stances that are more exaggerated than that of their average individual member? Researchers hoped that solving the mystery of group polarization might provide some insights into group influence. Solving small puzzles sometimes provides clues for solving larger ones.

Detailed discussion of social identity, self-categorization and group identity can be found in Chapters 12 and 13.

Among several proposed theories of group polarization, three are presented here. One deals with the arguments presented during a discussion, the second with how members of a group view themselves vis-à-vis the other members, and the third considers how a group's identity influences the decisions it makes. The first idea is an example of what Chapter 7 calls *informational influence* (influence that results from accepting evidence about reality). The second is an example of *normative influence* (influence based on a person's desire to be accepted or admired by others). The third looks at *group identity* and takes a social identity and self-categorization theoretical approach.

Informational Influence

informational influence conformity occurring when people accept evidence about reality provided by other people

Deutsch and Gerard (1955) consider **informational influence** as the willingness to accept information offered by someone else as accurate evidence of the truth. This creates a shift in attitude as we become persuaded by the information presented to us, by someone we consider to be a credible and reliable source. In a group situation, discussion elicits a pooling of ideas, which will favour a dominant viewpoint (Myers & Lamm, 1976). Some discussed ideas are common knowledge to group members (De Dreu et al., 2008; Gigone & Hastie, 1993; Larson et al., 1994; Stasser, 1991). Other ideas may include persuasive arguments that some group members had not previously considered. *Arguments,* in and of themselves, matter.

Active participation in discussion produces more attitude change than does passive listening. Participants and observers hear the same ideas, but when participants express them in their own words, the verbal commitment magnifies the impact. The more group members repeat one another's ideas, the more they rehearse and validate them (Brauer et al., 1995).

Bornstein and Greene (2011) invite us to consider the example of a jury. Juries are made up of ordinary people required to offer a verdict, usually about someone's guilt or innocence, in an extraordinary set of circumstances – a court of law. Jurors do not have special qualifications to do so. In fact they are chosen because they do not have any special qualifications. As ordinary people like you and me they must sift through the information and evidence presented to them to reach a verdict. As a group, they discuss what has been revealed in the trial in order to agree on a verdict. Social psychological research is replete with examples of jurors being subject to cognitive biases, such as only remembering that information which is consistent with their beliefs or own experiences (Carlson & Russo, 2001). But perhaps what is most intriguing of all, is that whatever pre-deliberation decision the majority of jurors make before the trial begins, is 90 per cent of the time the same decision the entire jury arrives at after the trial (Bornstein & Greene, 2011). The minority who disagreed at the start, become convinced through deliberation of the information by the majority. Informational influence is at work. This is especially the case for a trial that requires a unanimous verdict from the jury.

Other research invites us to consider the role of informational influence when engaging in online buying (e.g. Lee et al., 2011; Pavlou & Fygenson, 2006). Imagine you're looking to buy a new laptop. Short on time, and short on computer knowledge, you look to online suppliers to see what laptops are available for your budget. What helps you to decide? Well apart from the obvious financial constraints, customers look to the information provided by the supplier, but also that offered by other customers who bought that particular laptop. What features did they find useful, not-so-useful, what worked, what didn't work, is it value for money and so on. The information from people just like us, who bought them, can be a major contributor to our decision to buy.

Normative Influence

As we consider in Chapter 7, normative influence occurs when we conform to the expectations of others. We do what we 'ought' to do. Then norms of the group shape our behaviour. We allow ourselves to be led by the group for positive rewards such as social acceptance and approval. This process happens when we believe the group is monitoring our behaviour and has the power to punish or reward us (look at the explanation of Asch's line study in Chapter 7).

As Festinger (1954) argued in his influential theory of **social comparison**, 'we humans want to evaluate our opinions and abilities, something we can do by comparing our views with others'. We are most persuaded by people in our 'reference groups' – groups we identify with (Abrams et al., 1986, 2005; Hogg et al., 1990). Moreover, wanting people to like us, we may express stronger opinions after discovering that others share our views.

social comparison evaluating one's opinions and abilities by comparing oneself to others

Neighbors et al. (2008) examined the role family and friends have on the drinking behaviour of college students in their first year of study. The team asked 811 students, aged 17–21 years, to report on their alcohol drinking in a typical week. Using a Likert scale, they were also asked about the approval by friends, family, typical students, same-sex students, and their own approval, of their drinking behaviour. This was a measure of the **injunctive norms** which guide behaviour. The study discovered a **positive correlation** between how much participants drank, and how positively they thought their friends, family and themselves approved of the behaviour (injunctive norms). Their drinking behaviour was influenced by what parents and families were thought to endorse. This behaviour was not influenced by the perceived approval of others the student didn't know. The team suggest that if we are to tackle high levels of drinking in college students, we need to target the injunctive norms which steer the behaviour. Thus, it is our nearest and dearest who shape our behaviour.

injunctive norms perception of the approval of a behaviour by others

positive correlation when two variables both increase, or both decrease

Merely learning others' choices contributes to the bandwagon effect that creates blockbuster songs, books and movies. Salganik et al. (2006) experimented with the phenomenon by engaging 14,341 Internet participants in listening to and, if they wished, downloading previously unknown songs. The researchers randomly assigned some participants to a condition that disclosed previous participants' download choices. Among those given that information, popular songs became more popular and unpopular songs became less popular.

Group polarization research illustrates the complexity of social psychological inquiry. Much as we like our explanations of a phenomenon to be simple, one explanation seldom accounts for all the data. Because people are complex, more than one factor frequently influences an outcome. In group discussions, persuasive arguments predominate on issues that have a factual element ('Is she guilty of the crime?'). Social comparison sways responses on value-laden judgements ('How long a sentence should she serve?') (Kaplan, 1989). On the many issues that have both factual and value-laden aspects, the two factors work together.

Discovering that others share one's feelings (social comparison) unleashes arguments (informational influence) supporting what everyone secretly favours. In recent times, the informational and normative influences on group polarization and decisions has gained considerable currency in the psychology of consumerism, including online purchasing. Understanding how to pitch products to online groups through mediums such as Facebook, has drawn heavily upon social psychological knowledge about group processes (e.g. Kuan et al., 2014; Lord et al., 2001). Group polarization has also found a place in environmental psychology, where researchers have examined the role injunctive norms (what I think I should do) and descriptive norms (what I think others like me do), play in facilitating pro-environmental action (e.g. Smith et al., 2012). Workplace and environmental psychology are discussed in more detail in Chapter 15.

Group Identity

Some social psychologists, in particular social identity theorists (SITs) and self-categorization theorists (SCTs), have argued that the social groups to which we belong go some way to explaining why group polarization occurs (Turner, 1991; Turner et al., 1987). Recall John Turner's position about what constitutes a 'group' at the beginning of this chapter. A group does not necessarily have to constitute physically present individuals interacting with one another. Simply feeling and perceiving oneself to be a member of a group is sufficient to think and act as one. The groups to which we belong in society provide us with a 'social identity'. This identity means feeling psychologically attached to a group and having things in common with our fellow members (ingroup members), and thinking of ourselves as quite different from other social groups (outgroup members) in relevant ways. In distinguishing one group from another, group members may converge on a position in a debate that clearly marks them out from other groups. Turner (1991) argues that they achieve consensus around the group's prototypical position, 'that best defines what the group has in common compared to other relevant outgroups' (pp. 76–77).

To illustrate what this means let's consider a classic experimental study by Hogg et al. (1990). They asked their participants to individually offer advice, choosing between a range of risky and cautious options, on a choice dilemma (as we've seen in the risky shift studies). Participants were then told they would be put in a group of people whose views on the dilemma best matched their own. They were shown photographs of their, supposed, ingroup engaged in debate, and listened to them using headphones. These discussions were of a group making a risky, a cautious or a neutral decision to a series of dilemmas. The participants were also given information about debates made by groups other than their own (outgroups). What Hogg and his colleagues wanted to know was what the effect of these group discussions would be on the participants' own decisions. What they found was that when participants believed they were members of a group that made risky decisions, when exposed to outgroups making cautious decisions the individual participant also made extremely risky choices. As social identity theory and self-categorization theory would predict, the participant was conforming to an ingroup norm (of risk) and exaggerating their decision to maximize the difference between their ingroup and the outgroup. Likewise, if a participant believed s/he belonged to a cautious group, when shown evidence of risky outgroups, the individual made very cautious decisions. As Hogg et al. suggest, 'an ingroup confronted by a risky outgroup will polarize towards caution, an ingroup confronted by a cautious outgroup will polarize towards risk' (1990, p. 77).

This explanation of behaviour in groups is something we explore in Chapters 12 and 13 where we consider broader intergroup relations.

Groupthink: Do Groups Hinder or Assist Good Decisions?

When do group influences hinder good decisions? When do groups promote good decisions, and how can we lead groups to make optimal decisions?

Do the social psychological phenomena we have been considering occur in sophisticated groups such as corporate boards or the president's cabinet? Is there likely to be self-justification, self-serving bias, a cohesive 'we feeling' promoting conformity and stifling dissent? Public commitment producing resistance to change? Group polarization? Social psychologist Irving Janis (1971, 1982) wondered whether such phenomena might help explain good and bad group decisions made by some twentieth-century American presidents and their advisers. To find out, he analysed the decision-making procedures that led to several major fiascos.

- *Pearl Harbor.* In the weeks preceding the December 1941 Pearl Harbor attack that put the USA into the Second World War, military commanders in Hawaii received a steady stream of information about Japan's preparations for an attack on the USA somewhere in the Pacific. Then military intelligence lost radio contact with Japanese aircraft carriers, which had begun moving straight for Hawaii. Air reconnaissance could have spotted the carriers or at least provided a few minutes' warning. But complacent commanders decided against such precautions. The result: no alert was sounded until the attack on a virtually defenceless base was under way. The loss: 18 ships, 170 planes and 2,400 lives.
- *The Bay of Pigs invasion.* In 1961, US President John Kennedy and his advisers tried to overthrow Fidel Castro by invading Cuba with 1,400 CIA-trained Cuban exiles. Nearly all the invaders were soon killed or captured, the USA was humiliated and Cuba allied itself more closely with the former USSR. After learning the outcome, Kennedy wondered aloud, 'How could we have been so stupid?'
- *The Vietnam War.* From 1964 to 1967, US President Lyndon Johnson and his 'Tuesday lunch group' of policy advisers escalated the war in Vietnam on the assumption that US aerial bombardment, defoliation and search-and-destroy missions would bring North Vietnam to the peace table with the appreciative support of the South Vietnamese populace. They continued the escalation despite warnings from government intelligence experts and nearly all US allies. The resulting disaster cost more than 58,000 American and 1 million Vietnamese lives, polarized Americans, drove the president from office and created huge budget deficits that helped fuel inflation in the 1970s.

groupthink 'the mode of thinking that persons engage in when concurrence-seeking becomes so dominant in a cohesive in-group that it tends to override realistic appraisal of alternative courses of action' (Janis, 1971)

Janis (1971) believed those blunders were bred by the tendency of decision-making groups to suppress dissent in the interests of group harmony, a phenomenon he called **groupthink**. In work groups, camaraderie boosts productivity (Mullen & Copper, 1994; Nohria et al., 2008). It can also boost reputation. For example, Wuchty et al. (2007) observed that team-work in academia seems to pay off. Science papers written by groups of authors were twice as likely to be read and cited by other authors than those papers written by individuals. Moreover, team spirit is good for morale. But when making decisions, close-knit groups may pay a price. Redding (2012) argues that social psychology scholars are guilty of groupthink. He claims that social psychology departments tend to discourage conservative academics from applying for a job, and that the generation of knowledge, research and thought in the discipline is therefore not as 'ideologically diverse' (p. 513) as it should be. Janis (1971) believed that the soil from which groupthink sprouts includes:

- an amiable, *cohesive* group
- relative *isolation* of the group from dissenting viewpoints
- a *directive leader* who signals what decision he or she favours.

When planning the ill-fated Bay of Pigs invasion, the newly elected President Kennedy and his advisers enjoyed a strong *esprit de corps*. Arguments critical of the plan were suppressed or excluded, and the president soon endorsed the invasion.

Symptoms of Groupthink

From historical records and the memoirs of participants and observers, Janis (1971) identified eight groupthink symptoms. These symptoms are a collective form of dissonance reduction that surface as group members try to maintain their positive group feeling when facing a threat (McKimmie et al., 2003; Turner et al., 1992).

The first two groupthink symptoms lead group members to *overestimate their group's might and right.*

- *An illusion of invulnerability.* The groups Janis studied all developed an excessive optimism that blinded them to warnings of danger. Told that his forces had lost radio contact with the Japanese carriers, Admiral Kimmel, the chief naval officer at Pearl Harbor, joked that maybe the Japanese were about to round Honolulu's Diamond Head. They actually were, but Kimmel's laughing at the idea dismissed the very possibility of its being true.

- *Unquestioned belief in the group's morality.* Group members assume the inherent morality of their group and ignore ethical and moral issues. The Kennedy group knew that adviser Arthur Schlesinger, Jr, and Senator J. William Fulbright had moral reservations about invading a small, neighbouring country. But the group never entertained or discussed those moral qualms.

Group members also become *closed minded.*

- *Rationalization.* The groups discount challenges by collectively justifying their decisions. President Johnson's Tuesday lunch group spent far more time rationalizing (explaining and justifying) than reflecting upon and rethinking prior decisions to escalate. Each initiative became an action to defend and justify.

- *Stereotyped view of opponent.* Participants in these groupthink tanks consider their enemies too evil to negotiate with or too weak and unintelligent to defend themselves against the planned initiative. The Kennedy group convinced itself that Castro's military was so weak and his popular support so shallow that a single brigade could easily overturn his regime.

Finally, the group suffers from pressures towards *uniformity*.

- *Conformity pressure.* Group members rebuffed those who raised doubts about the group's assumption and plans, at times not by argument but by personal sarcasm. Once, when President Johnson's assistant Bill Moyers arrived at a meeting, the president derided him with, 'Well, here comes Mr. Stop-the-Bombing'. Faced with such ridicule, most people fall into line.
- *Self-censorship.* Since disagreements were often uncomfortable and the groups seemed to be in consensus, members withheld or discounted their misgivings. In the months following the Bay of Pigs invasion, Schlesinger (1965, p. 255) reproached himself 'for having kept so silent during those crucial discussions in the Cabinet Room, though my feelings of guilt were tempered by the knowledge that a course of objection would have accomplished little save to gain me a name as a nuisance'.
- *Illusion of unanimity.* Self-censorship and pressure not to puncture the consensus create an illusion of unanimity. What is more, the apparent consensus confirms the group's decision. This appearance of consensus was evident in these three fiascos and in other fiascos before and since. Speer (1971), an adviser to Adolf Hitler, described the atmosphere around Hitler as one where pressure to conform suppressed all deviation. The absence of dissent created an illusion of unanimity.

  > *In normal circumstances people who turn their backs on reality are soon set straight by the mockery and criticism of those around them, which makes them aware they have lost credibility. In the Third Reich there were no such correctives, especially for those who belonged to the upper stratum. On the contrary, every self-deception was multiplied as in a hall of distorting mirrors, becoming a repeatedly confirmed picture of a fantastical dream world which no longer bore any relationship to the grim outside world. In those mirrors I could see nothing but my own face reproduced many times over. No external factors disturbed the uniformity of hundreds of unchanging faces, all mine.* (Speer, 1971, p. 379).

- *Mindguards.* Some members protect the group from information that would call into question the effectiveness or morality of its decisions. Before the Bay of Pigs invasion, Robert Kennedy took Schlesinger aside and told him, 'Don't push it any further'. Secretary of State Dean Rusk withheld diplomatic and intelligence experts' warnings against the invasion. They thus served as the president's 'mindguards', protecting him from disagreeable facts rather than physical harm.

Groupthink symptoms can produce a failure to seek and discuss contrary information and alternative possibilities (**Figure 11.4**, overleaf). Some journalists, and political and financial commentators, have pondered the extent to which groupthink was a factor in the global economic crisis. Did banks and businesses fail to listen to critical voices from lone individuals and people outside of their institutions warning of a financial crisis if expansion and money-lending continued? According to a report published by the International Monetary Fund's Independent

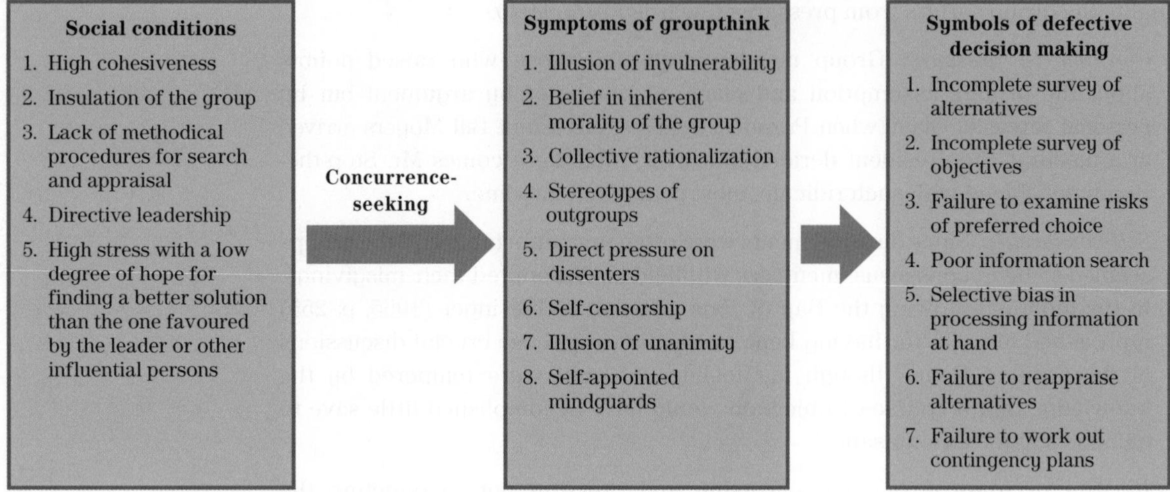

FIGURE 11.4 Theoretical analysis of groupthink

SOURCE: Janis and Mann (1977, p. 132).

Evaluation Office, yes (IMF, 2011). The report found that despite concerns raised by board members and one staff member, who even wrote a paper detailing the path that the crisis would take, these apprehensions were not followed up on. Added to this, some of the IMF's staff felt that they could not voice their worries, for fear that it would negatively influence their career.

Groupthink has also been used to explain lack of action over climate change. Booker (2018) notes the role of political leaders in squashing debate, offering false promises and directing attention on other issues, while the world continues to heat up with devastating consequences including drought, floods and wildfire. In her TedX speech well-known teenage climate activist Greta Thunberg (2018) noted the importance of bringing dissenting voices into the discussion: 'I often talk to people who say, "No, we have to be hopeful and to inspire each other, and we can't tell [people] too many negative things" . . . But, no — we have to tell it like it is. Because if there are no positive things to tell, then what should we do, should we spread false hope? We can't do that, we have to tell the truth.'

There is also some cross-cultural evidence for the occurrence of groupthink. Ko (2005) found that groupthink occurred in focus groups in Hong Kong when the group contained members who were recognized to be of high status. He suggests this reflects cultural rules about trusting those who are recognized as having high status.

Greta Thunberg: A dissenting voice that has challenged groupthink and facilitated action to tackle climate change.

SOURCE: ©Sean Gallup/Getty Images

British psychologists Ben Newell and David Lagnado (2003) believe groupthink symptoms may have also contributed to the Iraq War. They and others (e.g. Badie, 2010) contended that both Saddam Hussein and George W. Bush surrounded themselves with like-minded advisers and intimidated opposing voices into silence. Moreover, they each received filtered information that mostly supported their assumptions – Iraq's expressed assumption that the invading force could be resisted, and the

USA's assumption that Iraq had weapons of mass destruction, that its people would welcome invading soldiers as liberators and that a short, peaceful occupation would soon lead to a thriving democracy.

Critiquing the Concept of Groupthink

Although Janis's ideas and observations have received enormous attention, some researchers were sceptical (Fuller & Aldag, 1998; Hart, 1998; Kramer, 1998). The evidence was retrospective, so Janis could pick supporting cases. Follow-up experiments suggested that:

- directive leadership is indeed associated with poorer decisions, because subordinates sometimes feel too weak or insecure to speak up (McCauley, 2001)
- groups do prefer supporting over challenging information (Schulz-Hardt et al., 2000)
- when members look to a group for acceptance, approval and social identity, they may suppress disagreeable thoughts (Hogg & Hains, 1998; Turner & Pratkanis, 1997).

Yet friendships need not breed groupthink (Esser, 1998; Mullen et al., 1994). Secure, highly cohesive groups (say, a family) can provide members with freedom to disagree. Packer (2009) argues that we shouldn't assume individuals in groups are always reluctant to express private concerns. In fact those individuals who identify strongly with the group are willing to point out the flaws in a group's reasoning if s/he believes it will improve the group in some way. This seems to be enhanced when group members physically bump into one another all the time. The American entrepreneur Steve Jobs, founder of Apple Inc and Pixar Animation Studios, used this phenomenon to his advantage. Planning Pixar's headquarters, he ensured the building was structured in such a way that everyone who worked there would be forced into running into one another albeit working, going to the canteen, or even the bathroom (Lehrer, 2012). Jobs knew that accidental meetings with colleagues led to teamwork, resulting in creativity, debate and high-quality productivity. The norms of a cohesive group can favour either consensus, which can lead to groupthink, or critical analysis, which prevents it (Postmes et al., 2001). When academic colleagues in a close-knit department share their draft manuscripts with one another, they *want* critique: 'Do what you can to save me from my own mistakes.' In a free-spirited atmosphere, cohesion can enhance effective teamwork, too.

'Truth springs from argument amongst friends.'

Philosopher David Hume, 1711–76

Reflecting on the critiques of groupthink, Paulus (1998) reminds us of Leon Festinger's observation that the only unchanging theory is an untestable one. 'If a theory is at all testable, it will not remain unchanged. It has to change. All theories are wrong.' Thus, said Festinger, we shouldn't ask whether a theory is right or wrong but, rather, 'how much of the empirical realm can it handle and how must it be modified'. Irving Janis, having tested and modified his own theory before his death in 1990, would surely have welcomed others continuing to reshape it. In science, that is how we grope our way towards truth, by testing our ideas against reality, revising them and then testing them some more.

Preventing Groupthink

Flawed group dynamics help explain many failed decisions; sometimes too many cooks spoil the broth. However, given open leadership, a cohesive team spirit can improve decisions. Sometimes two or more heads are better than one.

In search of conditions that breed good decisions, Janis also analysed two seemingly successful ventures: the Truman administration's formulation of the Marshall Plan for getting Europe back on its feet after the Second World War, and the Kennedy administration's handling of the former USSR's attempts to install missile bases in Cuba in 1962. Janis's (1982) recommendations for preventing groupthink incorporate many of the effective group procedures used in both cases.

- Be impartial – do not endorse any position.
- Encourage critical evaluation; assign a 'devil's advocate'. Better yet, welcome the input of a genuine dissenter, which does even more to stimulate original thinking and to open a group to opposing views, report Nemeth et al. (2001a, 2001b).
- Occasionally subdivide the group, then reunite to air differences.
- Welcome critiques from outside experts and associates.
- Before implementing, call a 'second-chance' meeting to air any lingering doubts.

When such steps are taken, group decisions may take longer to make, yet ultimately prove less defective and more effective.

Group Problem Solving

Not every group decision is flawed by groupthink. As Ahlfinger and Esser (2001) have shown, when a group is led by someone who promotes their own solutions, they tend to fall into the trap of groupthink, making poor decisions. However, when their leader is a non-promotional one, ready to discuss a range of solutions, groupthink is much less likely to occur. Postmes et al. (2001) have made the point that it depends what norms a group is based on as to whether it will display groupthink. They observed that those groups whose norms mean that new information from outside the group is not valued, are much more likely to fall prey to groupthink than those whose norms permit the sharing of extra information.

So, under some conditions, two or more heads really are better than one. Laughlin and Adamopoulos (1980), Laughlin (1996) and Laughlin et al. (2003) have shown this with various intellectual tasks. Consider one of their analogy problems:

Assertion is to disproved as action is to

a. hindered

b. opposed

c. illegal

d. precipitate

e. thwarted.

Most college students miss this question when answering alone, but answer correctly (thwarted) after discussion. Moreover, Laughlin finds that if just two members of a six-person group are initially correct, two-thirds of the time they convince all the others. If only one person is correct, this 'minority of one' almost three-quarters of the time fails to convince the group. And when given tricky logic problems, three, four or five heads are better than two (Laughlin et al., 2006).

Warnick and Sanders (1980) and Hinsz (1990) confirmed that several heads can be better than one when they studied the accuracy of eyewitness reports of a videotaped crime or job interview. Interacting groups of eyewitnesses gave accounts that were much more accurate than those provided by the average isolated individual. Several heads critiquing one another can also allow the group to avoid some forms of cognitive bias and produce some higher-quality ideas (McGlynn et al., 1995; Wright et al., 1990).

Brainstorming with computer communication allows creative ideas to flow freely (Gallupe et al., 1994). But contrary to the popular idea that face-to-face brainstorming generates more creative ideas than do the same people working alone, researchers agree it isn't so (Paulus et al., 1995, 1997, 2000; Paulus, 1998; Stroebe & Diehl, 1994). And contrary to the popular idea that brainstorming is most productive when the brainstormers are admonished 'not to criticize', encouraging people to debate ideas appears to stimulate ideas and to extend creative thinking beyond the brainstorming session (Nemeth et al., 2004).

People *feel* more productive when generating ideas in groups (partly because people disproportionately credit themselves for the ideas that come out). But time and again researchers have found that people working alone usually will generate *more* good ideas than will the same people in a group (Rietzschel et al., 2006). Large brainstorming groups are especially inefficient. In accord with social loafing theory, large groups cause some individuals to free-ride on others' efforts. In accord with normative influence theory, they cause others to feel apprehensive about voicing oddball ideas. And they cause 'production blocking' – losing one's ideas while awaiting a turn to speak (Nijstad et al., 2003). As John Watson and Francis Crick demonstrated in discovering DNA, challenging two-person conversations can more effectively engage creative thinking. Watson later recalled that he and Crick benefited from *not* being the most brilliant people seeking to crack the genetic code. The most brilliant researcher 'was so intelligent that she rarely sought advice' (quoted by Cialdini, 2005). If you are (and regard yourself as) the most gifted person, why seek others' input? Like Watson and Crick, psychologists Daniel Kahneman and the late Amos Tversky similarly collaborated in their exploration of intuition and its influence on economic decision making. (See Chapter 4.)

However, Brown and Paulus (2002) have identified three ways to enhance group brainstorming.

1 *Combine group and solitary brainstorming.* Their data suggest using group brainstorming followed by solo brainstorming rather than the reverse order or either alone. With new categories primed by the group brainstorming, individuals' ideas can continue flowing without being impeded by the group context that allows only one person to speak at a time.

2 *Have group members interact by writing.* Another way to take advantage of group priming, without being impeded by the one-at-a-time rule, is to have group members write and read, rather than speak and listen. Brown and Paulus describe this process of passing notes and adding ideas, which has everyone active at once, as 'brainwriting'.

3 *Incorporate electronic brainstorming.* There is a potentially more efficient way to avoid the verbal traffic jams of traditional group brainstorming in larger groups: let individuals produce and read ideas on networked computers.

So, when group members freely combine their creative ideas and varied insights, the frequent result is not groupthink but group problem solving. The wisdom of groups is evident in everyday life as well as in the laboratory.

- *Game shows.* For a befuddled contestant on *Who Wants to Be a Millionaire?*, a valuable lifeline was to 'ask the audience', which usually offered wisdom superior to the contestant's intuition.
- *Google.* Google has become a dominant search engine by harnessing what Surowiecki (2004) calls *The Wisdom of Crowds.* Google interprets a link to page X as a vote for page X, and weights most heavily links from pages that are themselves highly ranked. Harnessing the democratic character of the Web, Google often takes less than one-tenth of a second to lead you right to what you want.

Thus, we can conclude that when information from many diverse people is combined, all of us together can become smarter than almost any of us alone. We're in some ways like a flock of geese, not one of which has a perfect navigational sense. Nevertheless, by staying close to one another, a group of geese can navigate accurately. The flock is smarter than the bird.

How Do Minorities Influence the Group?

Groups influence individuals. But when – and how – do individuals and minority groups influence more powerful groups?

Each chapter in this social influence unit concludes with a reminder of our power as individuals. We have seen that cultural situations mould us, but we also help create and choose these situations; pressures to conform sometimes overwhelm our better judgement, but blatant pressure motivates us to assert our individuality and freedom; persuasive forces are powerful, but we can resist persuasion by making public commitments and by anticipating persuasive appeals.

At the beginning of this chapter, we considered the film *12 Angry Men,* in which a lone juror eventually wins 11 others over to his view. Although that may be a rare occurrence in a jury room, in most social movements a small minority will sway, and then eventually become, the majority. 'All history', wrote Ralph Waldo Emerson, 'is a record of the power of minorities, and of minorities of one'. Think of Copernicus and Galileo, of Martin Luther King, Jr, of Nelson Mandela, and Greta Thunberg. The abolition of apartheid in South Africa and the move towards equality for Blacks and Whites is attributed to the influence of Nelson Mandela and those few who shared his vision for a peaceful transformation of the country. The conscious awakening of what is happening to our climate is thanks to young activists like Greta Thunberg who shout above the crowd, refusing to be gagged by the powerful elite. Indeed, if minority viewpoints never prevailed, history would be static and nothing would ever change.

What makes a minority persuasive? Experiments initiated by Serge Moscovici in Paris have identified several determinants of minority influence: *consistency, self-confidence* and *defection*. Throughout our discussion of minority influence, keep in mind that 'minority influence' refers to minority *opinions*, not to ethnic minorities.

Consistency

More influential than a minority that wavers is a minority that sticks to its position. Moscovici developed his theory of social influence on the social psychological observation that people do not like inconsistency, conflict and disagreement. In fact, they are motivated to reduce it. When a minority tries to influence a majority they capitalize on this by creating uncertainty and anxiety among majority group members. As we know from the studies of social influence we discussed in Chapter 7, majority influence is based on preservation of dominant norms among the majority and the preservation of the status quo. But Moscovici argued that what distinguished minority influence was that it challenged these dominant norms, disrupted the status quo and could be revolutionary as it promoted social change. He claimed that many of the social psychological studies of majority influence were actually demonstrations of minority influence. Consider: Solomon Asch's line study displayed one true participant being influenced by a few stooges.

Moscovici argued that what was happening was a single participant was being influenced away from what everyone else would see in similar circumstances to what the stooges claimed to see. It was the power of consistency between minority members that caused a majority to rethink their ideas and be influenced. Moscovici et al. (1969) developed the blue–green studies, which were a variation on Asch's earlier line studies. In the study four participants and two confederates of the experimenter were seated in a room and shown a series of slides. The slides were coloured blue. The participants were then asked to say out loud what colour they thought the slides were. In those trials where the two stooges consistently said 'green', the real participants became influenced. However, in those trials where the two stooges were inconsistent in their answers, influence did not occur. Moscovici et al. concluded that minority influence occurs because it has particular effects on the majority: it creates doubt and offers a possible alternative way of looking at things. The only way to restore certainty and consistency is for the majority to shift to the viewpoint of the minority.

Experiments show – and experience confirms – that non-conformity, especially persistent non-conformity, is often painful, and that being a minority in an online or an offline group can be unpleasant (Bazarova et al., 2012; Levine, 1989; Lücken & Simon, 2005). That helps explain a *minority slowness effect* – a tendency for people with minority views to express them less quickly than do people in the majority (Bassili, 2003). People may attribute your dissent to psychological peculiarities (Papastamou & Mugny, 1990).

Nevertheless, a minority may stimulate creative thinking. For example, Kenworthy et al. (2008) found that participants placed in numerically minority groups generated more original arguments to strengthen their position on a debate than those placed within majority groups. Mucchi-Faina and Pagliaro (2008) observed how the presence of a minority produces ambivalence among the majority, and under these circumstances the minority is likely to have influence. They suggest that the reason for this is that the state of ambivalence causes a state of **cognitive dissonance** (as we discuss in Chapter 4) and people are motivated to reduce the

cognitive dissonance
tension that arises when one is simultaneously aware of two inconsistent cognitions. For example, dissonance may occur when we realize that we have, with little justification, acted contrary to our attitudes. This inconsistency is unpleasant, and people use different methods to combat the dissonance. Concept coined by Leon Festinger (1957)

uncomfortable feelings this creates. Martin et al. (2008) note that those arguments produced as a consequence of minority influence are much more resistant to counter-persuasion than those formed by a majority group. University students who have racially diverse friends, or who are exposed to racial diversity in discussion groups, display less simplistic thinking (Antonio et al., 2004). With dissent from within one's own group, people take in more information, think about it in new ways, and often make better decisions.

'We dislike arguments of any kind; they are always vulgar, and often convincing.'
Oscar Wilde (1895)

Some successful companies have recognized the creativity and innovation sometimes stimulated by minority perspectives, which may contribute new ideas and stimulate colleagues to think in fresh ways. 3M, which has been famed for valuing 'respect for individual initiative', has welcomed employees spending time on wild ideas. Many organizations now actively encourage their employees to engage in blue sky thinking to get the creative juices flowing and break away from traditional ways of thinking, to solve problems, invent new products, come up with new ideas and so on (e.g. Evans, 2012). However, a word of caution is offered by psychologists, who warn there should be some direction to this creativity if decisions are ever to be made and outcomes arrived at (Plucker et al., 2004).

Self-confidence

Consistency and persistence convey self-confidence (Gardikiotis, 2011). Nemeth and Wachtler (1974) reported that any behaviour by a minority that conveys self-confidence – for example, taking the head seat at the table – tends to raise self-doubts among the majority. By being firm and forceful, the minority's apparent self-assurance may prompt the majority to reconsider its position. This is especially so on matters of opinion rather than fact. Based on their research at Italy's University of Padova, Maass et al. (1996) report that minorities are less persuasive when answering a question of fact ('From which country does Italy import most of its raw oil?') than attitude ('From which country should Italy import most of its raw oil?').

Defections from the Majority

In 1904, Mark Twain wrote: 'Whenever you find yourself on the side of the majority, it's time to pause and reflect' (Paine, 2006). As we've seen, simply going along with the group may not always be the wisest thing to do. Alternative opinions are silenced, when in fact questioning the status quo may be worthwhile. A persistent minority punctures any illusion of unanimity. When a minority consistently doubts the majority wisdom, majority members become freer to express their own doubts and may even switch to the minority position. But what about a lone defector, someone who initially agreed with the majority but then reconsidered and dissented? In their jury-simulation experiments, Nemeth and Wachtler (1974) found that – not unlike the *12 Angry Men* scenario – once one defection occurs, others often soon follow, initiating a snowball effect.

Are these factors that strengthen minority influence unique to minorities? Wolf and Latané (1985; Wolf, 1987) and Clark (1995) believe not. They argue that the same social forces work for both majorities and minorities. Informational influence (via persuasive arguments) and normative influence (via social comparison) fuel both group polarization and minority influence. And if consistency, self-confidence and defections from the other side strengthen the minority, such variables also strengthen a majority. The social impact of any position, majority or minority, depends on the strength, immediacy and number of those who support it.

Martin and Hewstone (2008) agree with Moscovici, however, that minorities are more likely than majorities to convert people to *accepting* their views. And from their analyses of how groups evolve over time, Levine and Moreland (1985) conclude that new recruits to a group exert a different type of minority influence than do long-time members. Newcomers exert influence through the attention they receive and the group awareness they trigger in the old-timers. Established members feel freer to dissent and to exert leadership.

There is a delightful irony in this new emphasis on how individuals can influence the group. Historically, the idea that the minority could sway the majority was itself a minority view in social psychology. Nevertheless, by arguing consistently and forcefully, Moscovici and others have convinced the majority of group influence researchers that minority influence is a phenomenon worthy of study. And the way that several of these minority influence researchers came by their interests should, perhaps, not surprise us. Maass (1998) became interested in how minorities could effect social change after growing up in post-war Germany and hearing her grandmother's personal accounts of fascism. Nemeth (1999) developed her interest while she was a visiting professor in Europe 'working with Henri Tajfel and Serge Moscovici. The three of us were "outsiders" – I an American Roman Catholic female in Europe, they having survived World War II as Eastern European Jews. Sensitivity to the value and the struggles of the minority perspective came to dominate our work.'

Of course, the power of a minority over a majority may not always be positive. Factor and colleagues (2011) argue that minority groups have a tendency to exhibit risky behaviours. This was certainly the case during the London riots of August 2011. The story of a 29-year-old man from Tottenham in London who was killed by police officers, led to widespread riots in the UK. Protest riots that began in the Tottenham area of London quickly spread to other parts of London and UK cities including Liverpool, Manchester and Birmingham. Bohannon (2012) reports on the role of Twitter and other social media in spreading the news and opinions of what had happened to millions of people. Chaos ensued as incitements to riot were co-ordinated across social media. The riots evolved into large-scale protests against the economic downturn, a disaffected youth, and the state. People died as a result of the mayhem. Salmivalli (2010) examined the influence of a minority on bullying behaviour in school. She observed how bullies who target victims become socially reinforced by the majority group. They come to be regarded as powerful, of high status, and the majority group accepts the behaviour. She argues that when we tackle bullying the focus should not simply be on the bully but on the influence exerted upon the whole group, which allows and encourages the behaviour. Being persuaded by a minority may not always be for the greater good.

See Chapters 9 and 13 for further discussion on aggression and the influence on crowd behaviour.

Focus on

Have Small Group Processes such as Risky Shift and Groupthink Contributed to Cyber-Bullying?

The invention of the Internet has changed our world. It has made information on most topics you can think of readily available to us. The Internet has shaped the way we communicate with one another, and how we form friendships. The presence of sites such as Facebook, Twitter and Reddit has made us accessible to one another without too much effort. The invention is so good that many schools, colleges and universities integrate online learning with face-to-face learning, and study and support groups are set up online. However, has the invention of the Internet also led to increased opportunities for small groups (such as an online study group) to engage in bullying? The statistics for bullying suggest it has. Moreover, cyber-bullying tends to occur within social groups (Mishna et al., 2009, 2012).

Being famous does not make you immune to being the victim of online abuse. Gorton and Garde-Hansen (2013) look at the trolling of US singer Madonna which occurred around the time of the launch of her *Hard Candy* album in 2009. The trolls posted outtake promotion photographs for the album, with offensive comments regarding her ageing body on Facebook. Madonna was 50 years old at the time. Other posters joined in, making mostly abusive comments about her body. The posts and the photographs were eventually removed from Facebook.

Remember the lessons from this chapter and also have a look at Chapters 7 and 8, that make the case that individuals often do things when they're in a group, which they wouldn't do on their own. Sometimes this is explained as a feature of anonymity and being lost in a crowd, but often online group members do know one another. They are not anonymous. In fact, it is precisely this knowing who somebody is that may explain why someone is singled out from a group and bullied online. Chaffin (2008) points out that adolescents and teenagers who are recognized as being outsiders to the group offline, may find those divisions reinforced online, as they become excluded from discussions, name-called, and therefore bullied. If the group is cohesive and maintains a norm of punishing those individuals it considers 'outsiders', some members may find themselves subject to harassment from the rest of the group. The small group processes of risky shift and groupthink can occur, such that risky decisions and negative forms of actions are collectively agreed on, and those members considered deviants find themselves severely harassed as a consequence. Chaffin observes that individuals desperate to 'fit in' with a group may engage in cyber-bullying to show themselves as true members and identify (and punish) those regarded as deviants and outsiders.

The occurrence of cyber-bullying is now taken so seriously that many agencies and websites have been set up to tackle the specific problem.

Questions

1 Are there any other reasons you can think of which might explain why cyber-bullying is on the increase?

2 How might we begin to tackle cyber-bullying and Internet trolling?

3 Do you think online learning groups are as effective as face-to-face ones?

SUMMING UP: SMALL GROUP PROCESSES

WHAT IS A GROUP?

- Social psychologists have differing definitions of a group, but what they agree on is that a group defines a collection of people who share a sense of 'we-ness'. They identify themselves as a group.
- But what holds groups together? Group cohesion is based on attraction to the group. The more cohesive the group, the greater the likelihood of its members sticking together as a group. Group cohesion is associated with group success but also failure.
- Groups are based on norms that describe their beliefs and regulate group members' behaviour.
- Individuals in groups occupy different roles that offer them a sense of identity and purpose. However, members may experience role clash or conflict.
- Different roles are associated with status, which has consequences for how much an individual identifies with the group and their behaviour within it. Group leaders have the highest status providing him or her with the means to change the group's norms, structure and composition if required.
- Communication networks are the formal and informal paths through which group members interact. The group's morale and productivity is often associated with the network that is in place. While direct access to the leader in order to influence decisions may be ideal, it is not always possible or desirable.

SOCIAL FACILITATION: HOW ARE WE AFFECTED BY THE PRESENCE OF OTHERS?

- Social psychology's most elementary issue concerns the mere presence of others. Some early experiments on this question found that performance improved with observers or co-actors present. Others found that the presence of others can hurt performance. Robert Zajonc reconciled those findings by applying a well-known principle from experimental psychology: arousal facilitates dominant responses. Because the presence of others is arousing, the presence of observers or co-actors boosts performance on easy tasks (for which the correct response is dominant) and hinders performance on difficult tasks (for which incorrect responses are dominant).
- But why are we aroused by others' presence? Experiments suggest that the arousal stems partly from evaluation apprehension and partly from distraction – a conflict between paying attention to others and concentrating on the task. Other experiments suggest that the presence of others can be arousing even when we are not evaluated or distracted.
- In online groups, physical presence is not always possible. Instead, social facilitation needs to be developed by other means, such as creating a sense of community through shared experiences, goals and aspirations.

SOCIAL LOAFING: DO INDIVIDUALS EXERT LESS EFFORT IN A GROUP?

- Social facilitation researchers study people's performance on tasks where they can be evaluated individually. However, in many work situations, people pool their efforts and work towards a common goal without individual accountability.
- Group members often work less hard when performing such 'additive tasks'. This finding parallels everyday situations where diffused responsibility tempts individual group members to free-ride on the group's effort.
- People may, however, put forth even more effort in a group when the goal is important, rewards are significant, intragroup communication occurs and team spirit exists.
- Social loafing predominantly exists in cultures where an independent self is endorsed.
- Social loafing is much less prevalent in those cultures where an interdependent sense of self exists.

GROUP POLARIZATION: DO GROUPS INTENSIFY OUR OPINIONS?

- Potentially positive and negative results arise from group discussion. While trying to understand the curious finding that group discussion enhanced risk taking, investigators discovered that discussion actually tends to strengthen whatever is the initially dominant point of view, whether risky or cautious.
- In everyday situations, too, group interaction tends to intensify opinions. This *group polarization* phenomenon provided a window through which researchers could observe group influence.
- Three explanations of group influence are: *informational, normative* and *group identity.*

GROUPTHINK: DO GROUPS HINDER OR ASSIST GOOD DECISIONS?

- Analysis of several international fiascos indicates that group cohesion can override realistic appraisal of a situation. This is especially true when group members strongly desire unity, when they are isolated from opposing ideas, and when the leader signals what he or she wants from the group.
- Symptomatic of this overriding concern for harmony, labelled groupthink, are (1) an illusion of invulnerability, (2) rationalization, (3) unquestioned belief in the group's morality, (4) stereotyped views of the opposition, (5) pressure to conform, (6) self-censorship of misgivings, (7) an illusion of unanimity, and (8) 'mindguards' who protect the group from unpleasant information. Critics have noted that some aspects of Janis's groupthink model (such as directive leadership) seem more implicated in flawed decisions than others (such as cohesiveness).
- Both in experiments and in actual history, however, groups sometimes decide wisely. These cases suggest ways to prevent groupthink: upholding impartiality, encouraging 'devil's advocate' positions, subdividing and then reuniting to discuss a decision, seeking outside input, and having a 'second-chance' meeting before implementing a decision.
- Research on group problem solving suggests that groups can be more accurate than individuals; groups also generate more and better ideas if the group is small or if, in a large group, individual brainstorming follows the group session.

HOW DO MINORITIES INFLUENCE THE GROUP?

- Although a majority opinion often prevails, sometimes a minority can influence and even overturn a majority position. Even if the majority does not adopt the minority's views, the minority's speaking up can increase the majority's self-doubts and prompt it to consider other alternatives, often leading to better, more creative decisions.
- In experiments, a minority is most influential when it is consistent and persistent in its views, when its actions convey self-confidence and after it begins to elicit some defections from the majority.

Critical Questions

1. What are some of the influences a small group can have on its members?
2. Under what conditions might social loafing occur in a group?
3. What explanations have been given for group polarization?
4. Do you think social psychology is guilty of groupthink? What evidence can you present to illustrate?
5. To what extent is the risky shift a cultural phenomenon?
6. How is minority influence different to majority influence?

Recommended Reading

Here are some recommended classic and contemporary readings on small group processes, covering some of the issues we've outlined in this chapter.

Classic Papers

Fiedler, F. E. (1966). The effect of leadership and cultural heterogeneity on group performance: A test of the contingency model. *Journal of Experimental Social Psychology, 2*(3), 237–264.

Janis, I. L. (1973). Groupthink and group dynamics: A social psychological analysis of defective policy decisions. *Policy Studies Journal,* 2(1), 19–25.

Moscovici, S., Lage, E., & Naffrechoux, M. (1969). Influence of a consistent minority on the responses of a majority in a color perception task. *Sociometry, 32*(4), 365–380.

Stoner, J. (1968). Risky and cautious shifts in group decisions: The influence of widely held values. *Journal of Experimental Social Psychology, 4,* 442–459.

Turner, M. E., & Pratkanis, A. R. (1998). Twenty-five years of groupthink theory and research: Lessons from the evaluation of a theory. *Organizational Behavior and Human Decision Processes, 73*(2–3), 105–115.

Contemporary Papers

Abrams, D., Hopthrow, T., Hulbert, L., & Frings, D. (2006). 'Groupdrink'? The effect of alcohol on risk attraction among groups versus individuals. *Journal of Studies on Alcohol, 67*(4), 628–636.

Packer, D. J. (2009). Avoiding groupthink: Whereas weakly identified members remain silent, strongly identified members' dissent about collective problems. *Psychological Science, 20*(5), 546–548.

Redding, R. E. (2012). Likes attract: The sociopolitical groupthink of (social) psychologists. *Perspectives on Psychological Science, 7*(5), 512–515.

12 SOCIAL CATEGORIZATION AND SOCIAL IDENTITY

'Integrity simply means not violating one's own identity.'
Erich Fromm, sociologist and psychoanalyst

Human beings live in a complex social environment. Our social world is filled up with countless people. People we see when walking in the street or sitting on a train; people we interact with at work, or in a shop, or through social media; people we see on television or read about in a newspaper. How do we navigate in this maze? How do we simplify, order and structure our social environment? How do we make sense of the people who cross our path in the multiplicity of social situations we are constantly involved in? What kind of strategies do we use in order to turn a potentially chaotic and unpredictable social reality into something that is understandable, manageable and predictable?

A Categorized Social World

social categorization the cognitive partitioning of the social world into relatively discrete categories of individuals

One of the main psychological tools that we use when trying to understand and make sense of people is **social categorization** (see Chapter 4 for a discussion of the various ways in which we make sense of social reality). I may not personally know the person who has just stepped onto the bus where I am sitting, or the one who is checking my blood pressure in the hospital, or the one who is reading the morning news on the television channel I am watching. However, I can assign them to social categories. The person on the bus is 'elderly'; the one who is dealing with my blood pressure is a 'nurse'; the one who is reading the news is a 'journalist'. By putting these people into 'pigeonholes', I am able to interpret their behaviour and to respond to it appropriately.

Consider, however, that for social categorization to be really useful and to guide me through the social environment, the categories that I choose have to be relevant to the context I am dealing with. For instance, categorizing the person on the bus as elderly makes it possible for me to offer them my seat. Categorizing him or her as a 'blue-eyed' person, or more generally as a 'man' or 'woman', would be irrelevant in that circumstance, and would prevent me from behaving in the most appropriate way. Consistent with this important caveat, the social psychologist Henri Tajfel defined the process of social categorization as 'the ordering of social environment in terms of groupings of persons in a manner which makes sense to the individual' (1978, p. 61). See 'Focus On: The Group in the Mind' at the end of the chapter.

Level of Category Inclusiveness

Social categories stand in hierarchical relationships, as they may have different levels of inclusiveness. For instance, the categories Tuscan and Sicilian are included in the category Italian, which in turn is included in the category European (Cantor & Mischel, 1979). Cognitive psychologists have found that, as far as non-social categories are concerned, basic-level categories tend to be used more often than either very inclusive or very exclusive categories (**Figure 12.1**). It is more common to identify an animal as a 'dog' (basic level) than as either a 'German shepherd' (lowest level) or as a 'mammal' (highest level). Rosh et al. (1976) argue that basic-level categories are the first to be learned, and the natural level at which objects are named. This, however, does not apply to social categories. As will become clearer later in the chapter, the categories we select to make sense of the social reality strongly depend on contextual, cultural and motivational factors.

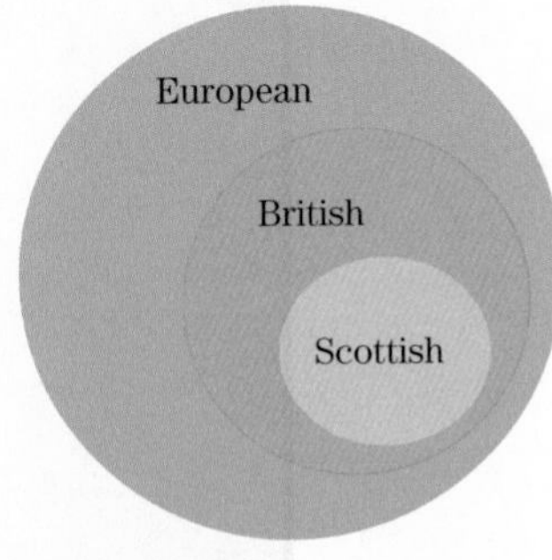

FIGURE 12.1 The inclusiveness of social categories
Social categories vary in degree of inclusiveness. The category Scottish is included in that of British, which is included in the category European.

Category Prototypes and Exemplars

On which basis are people assigned to categories? Do they have to possess a fixed number of characteristics in order to be seen as a category member? Social psychologists believe that this is not the case. Instead, people must possess some degree of resemblance to the category **prototype**. This is a category member that possesses a list of features that are seen as typical of the social category. Although the prototype may be represented by a specific and concrete individual, this is often not a true person but an abstraction, an ideal embodiment of the essence of the category (e.g. Cantor & Mischel, 1977; Rosh, 1978). Members of social categories differ in terms of how prototypical of the category they are seen to be. The closer one is to the prototype, the more prototypical he or she is considered to be. For instance, an Italian who is passionate, romantic and artistic minded will probably be seen as closer to the prototype of an Italian than one who is rather cold, controlled and technically minded.

Beyoncé: a worldwide famous exemplar of the category of 'pop singers'.
SOURCE: ©Tinseltown/Shutterstock

It is also possible to assign people to a social category on the basis of how similar they are to some category exemplar (Smith & Zárate, 1992). Instead of being abstractions, exemplars are category members that one has encountered. Ariana Grande, Taylor Swift and Beyoncé could be seen as exemplars of the category of 'pop singers'. As a consequence, if we see a person whose way of singing and performing is in some ways similar to one of these popular characters, we are likely to assign this person to the category of 'pop singers'.

prototype a social category member who is believed to possess the typical features of the social category

The Accentuation Effect

When we assign a person to a social category, not only do we rely on some fundamental similarities between the categorized person and either a prototype or a category exemplar, but we also take into account relevant differences between this person and those who belong to other categories. If we ascribe, say, John to the category of 'scientists', we are both establishing that John shares some characteristics in common with other scientists (a certain type of knowledge, an enquiring mind) and that he is different from 'lay people' or from 'artists'. The reason why social categorization is based on patterns of similarity and difference is that the best way to simplify and organize the social world is to make a clear distinction between those who belong and those who do not belong to a certain group.

However, category boundaries are not always clear-cut. Consider, for instance, the 'Black' and 'White' people categories. While some individuals perfectly fit our notion of either a 'Black' or a 'White' person, others fall somewhere between what we tend to recognize as 'Black' and what we tend to see as 'White'. How, then, do we deal with this? How can a clear categorical distinction be created? If we act in a context where skin colour is not relevant at all, making clear distinctions in terms of the Black–White dichotomy may simply not be necessary. However, when skin colour is important, as in some social and political contexts, our mind will tend to perceive those who lean slightly towards the black colour as more black than they really are, and those who lean towards white as whiter than they are. This phenomenon is known as the **accentuation effect** (Tajfel & Wilkes, 1963; Tajfel et al., 1964). Basically, both the differences between members of different categories and the

accentuation effect a tendency to exaggerate similarities within categories and differences between categories similarities among members of the same categories are exaggerated. Through this cognitive accentuation, categories become unambiguous and the context becomes clear and intelligible. Obviously, accentuating the similarities among members of a category means to perceive all of them as more resemblant to the category prototype than we would normally do.

A classic demonstration of the accentuation effect was offered by Tajfel and Wilkes (1963). These researchers asked the participants in the experiment to judge the length of a set of individual lines from a continuous series. However, the four shorter lines were labelled as 'A' and the four longer ones as 'B'. They found that participants exaggerated the difference in length between lines belonging to the A type and lines pertaining to the B type (**Figure 12.2**).

outgroup homogeneity a tendency to perceive and cognitively represent the members of an outgroup as very similar to one another, as being 'all the same'

Clearly, this is only an indirect form of evidence for social categorization, as the stimuli used in the experiment are physical rather than social. However, social psychologists have provided plenty of evidence for the accentuation effect in the perception of people too. For instance, in an experiment run at the University of Geneva (Doise et al., 1978), a group of participants were asked to judge the members of three different social groups, by rating them in terms of characteristic traits. Some participants judged members of the three Swiss linguistic groups (Italian Swiss, French Swiss and German Swiss), while other participants judged members of two Swiss linguistic groups and members of a foreign national group (for instance, Italian Swiss, French Swiss and Germans). It was found that the members of the different Swiss linguistic groups were perceived as more similar to one another when judged in the context of a foreign group. Clearly, this is because in such a context the two Swiss groups were seen as part of an overall category, the Swiss, which was contrasted with the foreign group.

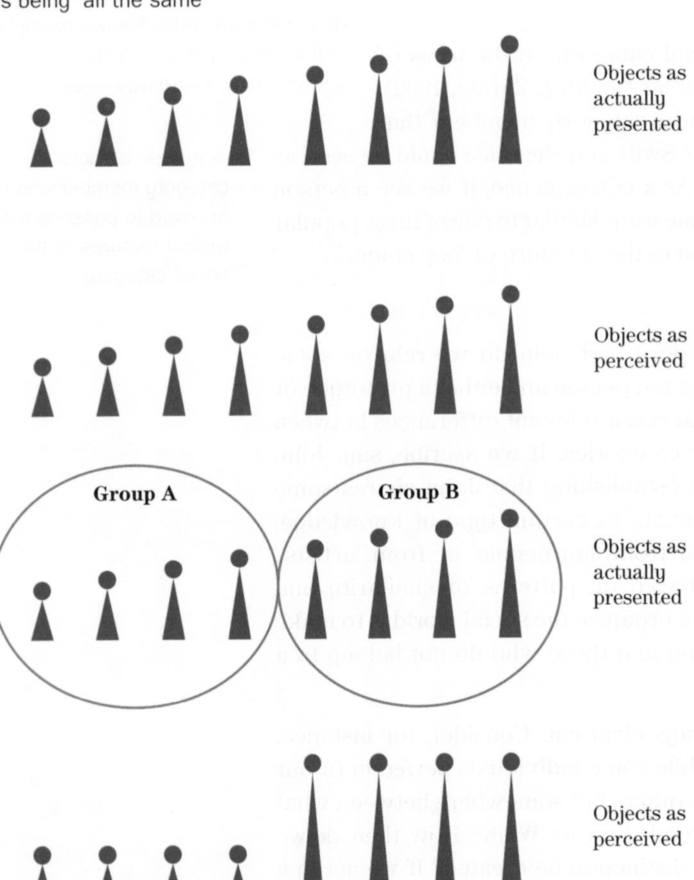

FIGURE 12.2 The accentuation effect
If objects in a set are not assigned to categories, people's perception of the objects' height will be relatively accurate. However, when objects are assigned to distinct categories, people will exaggerate differences between categories and similarities within categories, especially if categories are important to the perceivers. This effect applies not only to the physical world, but to the social world as well

Because it is prone to the accentuation effect, social categorization is at the basis of a phenomenon that has been widely investigated by social psychologists: group homogeneity (Tajfel, 1978). This means that members of a group are seen as being 'all the same'. This is believed to be particularly true when one has to describe and judge groups that are in conflict with a group of which one is a member. This specific type of perception is defined as **outgroup homogeneity**.

Social Categories and Stereotypes

Because social categorization exaggerates intra-category similarities, social psychologists see it as the basis of stereotype formation. A stereotype is a generalization about a social group, in the sense that similar characteristics are ascribed to virtually all group members (Allport, 1954). For example, in many societies 'women' are seen as emotional and volatile, 'Gypsies' are perceived as inclined to theft, 'Germans' are considered inflexible and efficient, and 'pop stars' seem spoiled and capricious. Obvious variations among the members of a social category are often ignored.

Stereotypes tend to be culturally transmitted and are therefore widespread within society (Macrae et al., 1996; Tajfel & Forgas, 1981). According to Allport (1954), stereotypes obey the 'law of least effort'. They spare people from forming differentiated judgements about others by providing shortcuts for understanding others, in the form of sketchy representations and ready-to-use beliefs (Fiske, 1989b).

The Selection of Social Categories

The social situations that we face often include people belonging to a variety of social categories. How do we decide which categories are relevant in each specific social situation?

Suppose I am attending a football match between Manchester United and Real Madrid (an English and a Spanish team respectively). Presumably, on the stands there will be individuals pertaining to all sorts of groups: 'men' and 'women', 'youngsters' and 'older' people, 'White' and 'Black' people. Probably, there will also be 'taxi drivers', 'shop assistants', 'members of the Labour Party', and more or less numerous representatives of many other groups. Which categories will capture my attention? Which ones will I select and use? I will almost certainly focus my attention on 'Man. United supporters' and 'Real Madrid supporters'. I will look at the colour of the shirts and scarfs, and I will listen to the chants of the two groups of supporters. The reason why I will focus on these two categories and virtually ignore all others is obvious: these two are the categories that, in this situation, include the highest number of members and are more relevant and meaningful. That is, these are the categories that best 'fit' the situation (Bruner, 1957; Oakes et al., 1994).

Each individual in this picture can be seen as either a 'business person', or in terms of gender ('man' or 'woman'), or in racial terms ('White', 'Black', 'Asian'). The social categories we focus upon will depend on how well these categories fit the situation and on how psychologically accessible they are.

SOURCE: ©Hryshchyshen Serhii/Shutterstock

But fit is not the only factor at play when selecting social categories. First, we bring our own preconceptions and expectations into social situations. When I attend a psychology class at university, I am likely to see many 'psychology students' and one 'lecturer' (students and lecturers being the categories that best fit the situation). This is because these are the categories that I expect to be represented during a university class. If there are some students' parents in attendance, I might overlook them simply because I do not expect them to be there. Second, we bring our desires, motivations and interests into social situations, and these may also determine the social categories that we use. If I am interested in finding a romantic partner, I might categorize the people around me in terms of gender. Or, if I was a person who is very sensitive to religious issues, I could immediately define the members of a social situation as 'Christians' and 'Muslims'. This means that, when trying to make sense of a social situation, the social categories that have special relevance and importance to a person – or, as social psychologists tend to put it, the social categories that are more cognitively 'accessible' – are more likely to be employed.

It is important to note, however, that decisions about which categories are relevant within a given context, and which characteristics those categories have (i.e. their content, their prototypical members) are rarely made in isolation. In most situations, we discuss, debate and argue with other people about the nature of social contexts and social categories. This occurs through an incessant process of communication and negotiation (Billig, 1987). Our view of social categories, like our view of the social world in general, is inherently and inescapably social.

The Fluidity of Social Categories and Stereotypes

The fact that social categories that are used to make sense of a social situation are selected on the basis of their fit with social context and their cognitive accessibility means that they are flexible and malleable psychological tools. If this was not the case, social categorization would not help people to represent an ever-changing, fluid and kaleidoscopic social reality. All aspects of social categories and social categorization are variable.

- Changes in the situation may shift the level of inclusiveness of the social categories we select. The experiment conducted by Doise and colleagues (1978) shows that in one context the Italian Swiss, the French Swiss and the German Swiss can be seen as three different social categories, but as soon as German Swiss are replaced by the social category of Germans, the Italian Swiss and the French Swiss are collapsed into a single, over-inclusive social category: that of Swiss people.
- The same social category may have different prototypes as the general frame changes. As a consequence, the stereotype content of a given social category will also change with the general frame (Ford & Stangor, 1992). Haslam et al. (1992) studied the way in which Australians perceived Americans during the first Gulf War, in 1991. It was found that participants who were asked to judge both Americans and Russians perceived the Americans as more 'aggressive' than participants who judged Americans alone. Clearly, because Russians did not approve of the American invasion of Iraq, bringing them into the context increased the perceived aggressiveness of Americans.

See Chapter 3 for a full treatment of how people think and feel about their own self, as well as how they go about understanding it.

The Social Categorization of the Self

So far we have focused on the way we position other people into social categories. But the social world does not include just others. Importantly, the self tends to be part of the world we try to understand. In other words, in most circumstances we are part of the social context that we try to structure and make sense of. In those circumstances we therefore assign ourselves to a psychologically relevant category; that is, we engage in self-categorization.

'We live in a social environment which is in constant flux. Much of what happens to us is related to the activities of groups to which we do or do not belong.'

Tajfel (1981)

Cognitive Aspects of Self-categories

From a cognitive perspective, self-categories are like other social categories.

- Self-categories have different degrees of inclusiveness. So, I can see myself as Flemish, a Belgian and a European.
- Self-categories have their prototypes and exemplars. If I am a Spanish socialist, I will have an idea of what the 'typical', 'true' socialist should be like (say, somebody with a strong belief in equality and solid anti-fascist values), and will consider Pedro Sánchez (the Secretary-General of the Spanish Socialist Workers' Party and current Prime Minister of Spain) as an exemplar of my category. Also, how typical of the socialist group I perceive myself to be, will depend on how similar to the prototype of a socialist and to Sánchez, I see myself.
- The similarities among the members of a self-category, including the self, and the differences between the members of a self-category and the members of another relevant category, are exaggerated. If I am a Roman Catholic and discuss religion with a Protestant, I may become acutely aware of the many similarities I have with other Roman Catholics, and of my differences from Protestants, as far as religious issues are concerned.
- The accentuation of similarities between myself and other members of my category will lead to self-stereotyping, that is, to self-perception in terms of some general features that are seen as applicable to virtually all members of my category.

Contextual Variability in Self-categorization and Self-stereotyping

Self-categories are also similar to other social categories in terms of their contextual flexibility and variability. This means that the type of social categories to which I ascribe myself, and the stereotypical content of these categories, shift from one context to another.

To start, I can categorize myself as a member of totally unrelated categories depending on the situation. I will be a 'Buddhist' when I recite my mantras in the early morning, a 'student' when I attend a university class in the afternoon, and a 'golf player' when I enjoy a game of golf in the evening. Also, the self-categories I use in different contexts may have varying levels of inclusiveness. I can see myself as 'Scottish' during the Six Nations rugby tournament, as 'British' when watching the Olympic Games, and as a 'European' when I am visiting the USA.

But the context does not only affect the type of self-category to which I ascribe; it also affects the way I perceive myself as a category member. For instance, suppose that I am a psychologist and I am discussing the importance of the scientific approach with a believer in magic. In this situation I may feel a highly prototypical member of the category of 'scientists'. However, if a physicist joins the debate, I may feel a bit less prototypical of the category. Even the content of the same self-category, that is my self-stereotype, may change depending on the comparative context. Hopkins et al. (1997) investigated the way in which Scottish people stereotyped their own national group members in different contexts. When the participants in the study were asked to describe the Scottish and the Greeks, the Scottish were seen as aloof, hardworking, organized and not particularly warm. But when participants described the Scottish and the English, the Scottish were portrayed as warm and not so aloof. Sani et al. (2003; see also Sani & Bennett, 2001) found a similar phenomenon in an investigation of children's gender stereotypes. For instance, the study revealed that 5- to 7-year-old male children perceived themselves ('boys') as especially big, brave, strong and tough when judgements were made after judging the group of 'girls', but when the judgement was made after judging 'grown-up men' they saw themselves as mainly 'loud' and 'talkative'. In both studies mentioned above, the traits that are emphasized in the different contexts are those that maximize the differences between the self-category and the other category that is salient in the context.

How Do Social Categories Become Self-categories?

Although self-categories are more or less psychologically relevant depending on context, and their content and meaning are fluid and changeable, people do belong to a number of social categories in a stable fashion, and some of them may be particularly central to self and chronically salient, meaning they are psychologically prominent and important across many contexts. How do specific social categories become self-categories? Broadly speaking, there are two ways in which social categories are applied to self.

First, there are social categories we are socialized into from birth. For instance, apart from very rare cases, we are born as either a male or a female. Since cultures have strong expectations about appropriate male and female behaviours, attitudes and emotions, we very quickly learn that we are either male or female, and absorb the norms that apply to our category (see Chapter 14 for a fuller discussion of the social psychological implications of gender categories). Similarly, we grow up within specific families, social classes, ethnic groups and nations. These groups have their own beliefs, values, attitudes, mentalities and habits, which are transmitted to their members through a process of socialization and acculturation. As with gender, we soon learn that we are members of specific families, social classes, ethnic and national groups, and we internalize the values and norms of those groups. Obviously, at some stage in life we may reject certain groups and decide we do not belong to them, but for most people these categories – or some of them at least – are the most important categories, and are therefore central to their sense of self.

Second, there are groups and categories that we choose to join at some point in life. We may join a social club, become supporters of a sports team, become members of a university, ascribe to a political party, join a band or affiliate to a religious organization. Some of these memberships may not be of special relevance to us, while others may become really important. Some football supporters, for instance, see their loyalty to the team as one of the most defining aspects of self (a phenomenon that is fairly common in Europe and South America). They travel all over the world to see their team play, avidly read all the news about their team, participate in Internet forums dedicated to their teams, and hang around in specific places to chat, conceive new songs and chants, and prepare banners and flags.

Social Identity

Although, from a purely cognitive perspective, self-categories are like other social categories, they are in many ways special. Self-categorization allows us to know where we stand in the social world, to distinguish between 'us' and 'them', to know who we are. Therefore, the social categorization of the self gives us an identity, more specifically a **social identity**. Note that self-categorization and social identity are separate (although related) ideas. Self-categorization allows us to categorize ourselves and others into social groups by deciding who is like us (a fellow member of our group, or an ingroup member) and who is not like us (a non-member of our group, or an outgroup member). Who we perceive to be ingroup members and outgroup members changes with the context we find ourselves in, and depends upon which of our many social group memberships is currently **salient**, or psychologically prominent and important. For instance, if I (as a woman) were to attend a women's group meeting, I would categorize myself and others in terms of gender, with women as ingroup members and men as outgroup members. However, if I was then to attend a football match, I would categorize myself and others in terms of team allegiance, with supporters of my team as ingroup members, and supporters of the rival team as outgroup members. This means I perceived women who support my rival football team as ingroup members when I was in the women's group and as outgroup members when I was at the football match, while I perceived men who support my football team as outgroup members when I was in the women's group and as ingroup members when I was at the football match. Meanwhile, we develop our social identity from the groups we categorize ourselves as being members of (e.g. 'I am a woman', 'I am a football fan'). Social psychologists distinguish social (or group) identity from our **personal (or individual) identity**, which is to do with our unique, peculiar, idiosyncratic features, those aspects that are unrelated to membership of a group.

The notion of social identity is used in several disciplines, including sociology, anthropology, political science and, even, archaeology. However, in social psychology this concept is one of the pillars of **social identity theory** (Tajfel & Turner, 1986) and **self-categorization theory** (Turner et al., 1987), which have been conceived and systematized during the 1970s and 1980s. Together, they form the **social identity approach**.

Henri Tajfel defined social identity as 'that part of an individual's self-concept which derives from his knowledge of his membership of a social group (or groups) together with the value and emotional significance attached to that membership' (Tajfel, 1978, p. 63). This definition makes it clear that being a member of a category is not sufficient to confer a social identity. For instance, the fact that I pay annual fees for membership of the association for the safeguarding of local monuments does not automatically imply that this membership is psychologically important to me. I may pay the fees out of habit, or simply because I feel some sort of civic or moral obligation to sustain the association, without necessarily feeling that membership of the association truly matters to the kind of person I am. To be identified with a category means to feel somehow attached to this category, to invest emotionally in this membership, to consider this category as important for my self-definition. If I feel attached to New Zealand, and being a New Zealander

social identity that part of our self-definition that derives from our membership of social groups

salient when a social group becomes psychologically important or prominent to a person in a specific context, leading to them categorizing themselves and others on the basis of their membership or non-membership of that social group

personal identity that part of our self-definition that derives from our unique, peculiar, idiosyncratic characteristics

social identity theory a theory accredited to Tajfel and Turner, which is based on the assumption that people belong to social groups and derive a social identity from these groups. According to the theory we derive much of our self-esteem from our social identity, and when social identity is not satisfactory we may pursue a number of strategies to improve it

self-categorization theory a theory about the ways in which people come to identify with groups and about the consequences of group (or social) identification, especially in terms of how people think and feel about their fellow ingroup members and the way people behave within the group

social identity approach an umbrella term used to describe the over-arching principles of social identity theory and self-categorization theory matters to me, this means that this is part of my self-definition and that I am identified with New Zealand.

As we anticipated above, the most important self-categories, and therefore the categories with which people tend to identify strongly, are often those we are born into, such as gender, family or ethnic self-categories. However, self-categories based on groups that we join later in life may also become important social identities. For instance, I may become involved in, or even be a funder of, a local bird-watching club, and devote many hours every week to the maintenance of the club and the promotion of its activities. This membership may become a crucial expression of what I like and what I do, and inform my sense of who I am. I may, that is, feel strongly identified with a local bird-watching club.

Social identity has very important implications for our relationships with other group members and for our relations with members of other groups too. In this chapter we will focus on the implications of social identity for processes within the group, leaving the discussion of social identity's consequences for processes between groups to the next chapter. First, we will discuss the implications of social identity for influence processes within groups.

In Chapter 7 we discussed how people facing a unanimous group may feel pressure to conform to the majority, even when the majority position is manifestly wrong. We saw that social psychologists have explained conformity as resulting from two types of influence. These are normative influence, based on people's need to avoid ridicule and isolation, and informational influence, derived from a need to be correct in tandem with an assumption that the unanimous majority must be correct. But does any majority influence people by virtue of being a majority, or does the influence depend largely on how the majority is perceived in relation to self?

People Conform to Majorities Categorized as Ingroup

Available evidence suggests that the extent to which people conform to a majority depends on the relationship between the self and the majority. The majority position will lead to conformity only when the members of the majority are seen as sharing a social identity with the self (Balaam & Haslam, 1998). Therefore, a left-winger who gets involved in a discussion about the rights of immigrants with members of a neo-fascist group will hardly be persuaded by the arguments put forward by the discussants, regardless of how united and unanimous they are. On the contrary, the same person might find the arguments that emerge from a discussion with other left-wingers to be very persuasive, even if he or she was initially a bit sceptical about those arguments. This phenomenon was demonstrated by Dominic Abrams and his colleagues (Abrams et al., 1986). They created a situation that was exactly like the one used by Asch in his classic studies of conformity. Basically, participants in the experiment had to judge which one of a set of three lines was similar to a standard line. However, only one participant produced spontaneous judgements, while, unbeknown to him/her, all the other participants had been instructed by the experimenter to make a wrong judgement. Results showed that the naive participant tended to conform to the unanimous (and wrong!) majority only when the members of that majority were designated as ingroup members (psychology students). When the confederates were presented as outgroup members (students of ancient history), the naive participant made independent, and correct, judgements.

For a detailed overview of the Asch conformity studies and their experimental situations, see Chapter 7.

We should keep in mind, however, that people may have different levels of identification with an ingroup, and that this has implications for their strength of loyalty to the group. Researchers have found that stronger levels of group identification enhance group members' willingness to comply with the group's norms (Barreto & Ellemers, 2000).

People Convert to Minorities seen as Ingroup

The importance of shared social identity is not confined to conformity (i.e. situations in which a minority is influenced by a majority). As David and Turner (1996, 1999) repeatedly demonstrated, as long as they are perceived as an ingroup source of information, a minority of people are perfectly capable of exerting influence on a majority up to the point of converting the majority members to the position of the minority. For instance, environmentalists exerted a very modest impact as long as they were seen as an outgroup made up of odd, bizarre and unconventional people. However, as it became obvious that they were speaking for 'us', and were therefore part of an ingroup, their campaigns were taken much more seriously and their ideas quickly absorbed by mainstream society.

Why Are Ingroup Members Especially Influential?

According to the self-categorization theory (Turner et al., 1987), the reason why members of an ingroup are especially influential is twofold. First, group members see one another as qualified to offer valid information about the correct beliefs and values (McGarty et al., 1993). Second, a collection of individuals sharing a social identity in common feel part of a social entity that transcends their own individual self, and that should maintain a level of cohesion and unity if it wants to exist as such. As a result, group members assume that there should be consensus on the group norms (values, beliefs, attitudes) (Haslam, 2004). After all, without some degree of consensus on group norms, a group could hardly be defined as a group at all.

In sum, shared social identity (1) turns group members into reliable sources of information on the norms that should be consensually agreed, and (2) creates an expectation of agreement (**Figure 12.3**). This leads group members to give special consideration to each other's positions, and to be open to reciprocal influence, so that they gradually move towards an integrated and common position (Postmes, 2003).

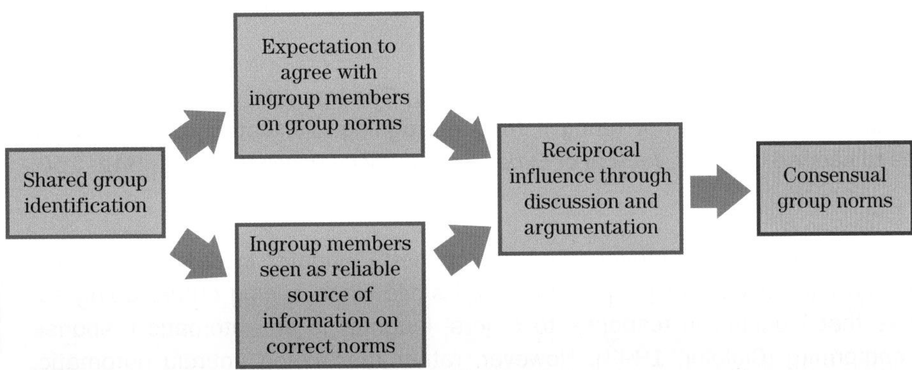

FIGURE 12.3 From shared group identification to group consensus

Will members of this group be able to reach consensus? Their shared social identity will foster reciprocal trust and raise expectations of agreement, thereby facilitating the achievement of consensus.
SOURCE: ©Rawpixel.com/Shutterstock

On the contrary, group members will expect to disagree with members of relevant outgroups. As a consequence, they will tend to distance themselves from the position of outgroup members, in order to emphasize and mark out the differences between the ingroup and the outgroup. (See Chapter 11 for the implications of these mechanisms for group polarization.)

This process was empirically demonstrated in an experiment conducted by Postmes et al. (2000). These researchers showed that when different groups of students were encouraged to communicate via e-mail, each group gradually converged towards both a common type of email content (i.e. the type of humour they used) and a similar stylistic form (i.e. punctuation and capitalization) of their messages. This shows that once a collection of individuals share a common identification, reciprocal influence leads to the creation of consensual norms that distinguish the ingroup from outgroups.

Note, however, that while shared social identity tends to *facilitate* the achievement of consensus, the content of social identity is not something that people accept automatically. People engage in an ongoing discussion in which the content of the group identity, the boundaries of the group and the group prototype are argued over and negotiated, often through sophisticated linguistic and rhetorical strategies (Antaki & Widdicombe, 1998) (see Chapter 13 for more on the role played by language in the way we relate to the world). This implies that sometimes the process of communication that is meant to create consensus actually ends up in disagreement. As we will see later in this chapter, ingroup disagreement may, on occasions, give rise to factionalism and schism.

Research close-up

Laughing: The Influence of the Ingroup

Source: Platow, M. J., Haslam, S. A., Both, A., Chew, I., Cuddon, M., Goharpey, N., Maurer, J., Rosini, S., Tsekouras, A., & Grace, D. (2005). It's not funny if *they're* laughing: Self-categorization, social influence, and responses to canned laughter. *Journal of Experimental Social Psychology, 41,* 542–550.

Introduction

Some television programmes make use of pre-recorded (or 'canned') laughter in order to produce audience laughter, based on knowledge that people laugh and smile when seeing others doing so. Some researchers believe that laughing in response to others' laughter is an automatic response based on non-thinking conformity (Cialdini, 1993). However, rather than being entirely automatic, responses to canned laughter might be partly determined by *who* is laughing. Based on the self-categorization theory's assumption that social influence is largely a group process, and that people are more easily influenced by an ingroup rather than outgroup source, this study tests the hypothesis that canned laughter believed to originate from an ingroup will produce stronger laughter than canned laughter believed to come from an outgroup.

Method

The experiment involved undergraduate students from La Trobe University in Australia. They sat individually at a desk facing a two-way mirror and listened to an audiotape of a man reciting a stand-up comedy routine, where various jokes were made. However, half of participants were told that the recording was made with a La Trobe University student audience (ingroup), while the other half were told that the recording was made with a One National Party audience (outgroup). Also, half of participants in either the ingroup or outgroup audience situation heard recorded laughter at the end of each joke, while half of participants did not hear any laughter. Therefore, this experiment included four conditions: ingroup audience laughing; ingroup audience not laughing; outgroup audience laughing; outgroup audience not laughing. After listening to the audiotape, participants were asked to rate the comedian in terms of how humorous and entertaining he was, using a 1 to 7-point scale (1 = not at all humorous/entertaining; 7 = extremely humorous/entertaining). In addition, the frequency with which participants smiled and laughed, as well as the total amount of time they spent laughing (calculated in seconds), were recorded by researchers placed behind the two-way mirror.

Results

As one might expect, an audiotape including canned laughter prompted longer laughter than an audiotape without canned laughter. Concerning the nature of the audience (i.e. whether it was ingroup or outgroup), this had virtually no effects when the audiotape was without canned laughter, but had large and statistically significant effects when the audiotape included canned laughter. Specifically, participants rated the comedian as much more humorous and entertaining when the audience was believed to be made up of ingroup members than when it was believed to be formed by outgroup members. In addition, an ingroup audience led to three times as frequent smiling and laughing, and to four times longer laughter than an outgroup audience (see **Figure 12.4**).

Discussion

These results suggest that people find jokes particularly funny and laugh a lot when they hear fellow ingroup members laughing. Hearing outgroup members laughing produces much cooler reactions. This appears to confirm that ingroup members are the people we rely upon for information about the social world, and who therefore have the ability to influence us. It should be noted, however, that the outgroup used in this experiment (a political party that is known to be generally disliked by participants) was rather extreme. Future research should explore this process using different inter-group contexts. Also, studies should assess people's reaction when the group membership of a laughing audience is not known. In this case, it is possible that people's reaction is based on their guessed similarity with the audience.

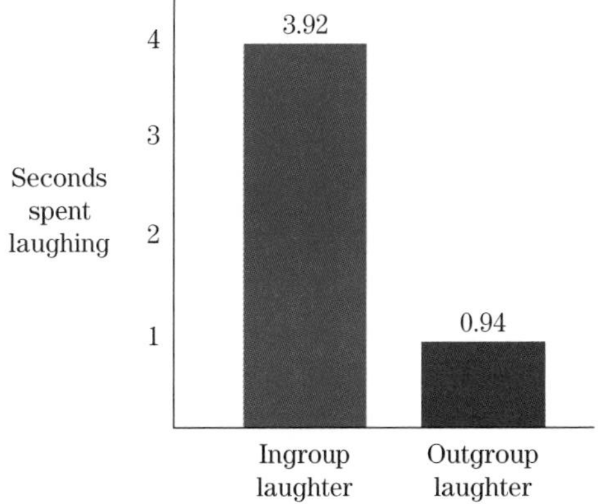

FIGURE 12.4 Recorded average time laughing (in seconds) for participants hearing either an ingroup or an outgroup audience laughter

SOURCE: Based on Platow et al. (2005).

Critical Reflections

This study involves a clever manipulation of the perceived source of the laughter that participants heard. Moreover, the results provide novel support to the social identity approach to social influence. However, we could argue that there might be problems with the **ecological validity** of the study. Comedy and humour are forms of entertainment we tend to consume in an everyday relaxed state, such as with the family at home, or with friends at the cinema. To what extent does asking participants to listen to an audiotape of a stand-up comic in a laboratory reproduce this experience? Might it be useful for the authors to attempt to replicate the study in a more naturalistic environment? It might also be interesting to explore whether manipulation of the perceived source of laughter affects whether people are more or less likely to laugh at 'off-colour' jokes that could be interpreted as racist, sexist or homophobic.

ecological validity the extent to which findings observed in a study reflect what actually occurs in natural settings. Psychological laboratory research has been criticized for its low ecological validity

Leaders as 'Entrepreneurs of Social Identity'

What does it take to be a leader? In Chapter 11 we noted that the group has the capacity to shape the characteristics of its leader. Hollander (1995), for instance, was very clear about the fact that a wanting-to-be group leader must take into consideration the needs and aspirations of the group members.

Researchers in the field of social identity have elaborated on this assumption, and have proposed that leadership is essentially a group phenomenon, and that the notion of social identity is central to a proper understanding of leadership (Hogg et al., 1998; Haslam et al., 2011). Social identity has two important implications for leadership.

1. The ideal leader is expected to be a quintessential representation of the group identity. This means that the leader's ideas and behaviours are evaluated in terms of how closely they match the group prototype. A group member will be recognized as a true leader to the extent that he or she is seen as an incarnation of the group prototype. However, being recognized as the prototypical member of a social group, and therefore being accepted as group leader, doesn't just happen. Individuals who aspire to become leaders have to convince the group that they are true group prototypes.
2. A highly prototypical leader will be able to exert a strong influence on the other group members. This is because this type of leader will be seen as especially qualified to indicate the correct group norms. A prototypical leader will therefore be in a position to define and shape the group identity (Von Cranach, 1986). However, in order to transform and renew the group identity, a leader must persuade the group members that the new norms and values that he or she is proposing are consistent with the group identity.

In summary, either wanting-to-be leaders or actual leaders must use an array of linguistic and rhetorical strategies in order to construe (1) themselves as congruent with the group prototype, and (2) their proposed course of action as consistent with the group identity. Reicher and Hopkins (1996) – two British social psychologists who study the social construction of social categories and identities – have defined leaders as 'entrepreneurs of social identity'.

Silvio Berlusconi became the political leader of the centre-right in Italy by promoting the image of the prototypical entrepreneurial and anti-communist Italian. Once recognized as leader, Berlusconi was able to dictate the agenda of his political group.

SOURCE: ©Alexandros Michailidis/Shutterstock

To illustrate the process of becoming prototypical of a social category, and of using prototypicality to shape social identity, we can reflect on the emergence of Silvio Berlusconi as political leader in Italy, in 1994. In the years preceding the 1994 Italian political elections, the old centrist political establishment had lost credibility because of the incrimination of several prominent politicians for corruption. As a consequence, the majority of Italians became political 'orphans' in search of a new referent. Berlusconi cleverly tried to fill this void by presenting himself as the incarnation of all the values that those Italians embraced, such as economic freedom and anti-communism. The fact that he was a very rich and successful businessman made his candidature credible. As a result, he was quickly recognized as the prototypical member of this social group. After becoming the leader of the centre-right political group, Berlusconi was able to turn his electorate against the judges who were investigating political corruption, because he himself was not on good terms with these judges. He presented them as rigid and authoritarian prosecutors, who were insensitive to the rights that people should be granted in democratic countries, and who aligned with the political adversaries of the centre-right, the 'communists'. In sum, before the elections Berlusconi modelled his programme and image on the expectations of the social group he aspired to represent, and once he was recognized as the group prototype he used his role to instil new beliefs in the group members, in accordance with his own agenda.

Reicher and Hopkins' (1996) analysis of the speeches of two political leaders of the 1980s, Neil Kinnock (leader of the Labour Party) and Margaret Thatcher (leader of the Conservative Party), concerning the 1984–85 British miners' strike, constitutes another interesting example of how leaders try to shape identities (**Figure 12.5**). In their analysis, Reicher and Hopkins found that each leader described the context of the strike in terms of two social

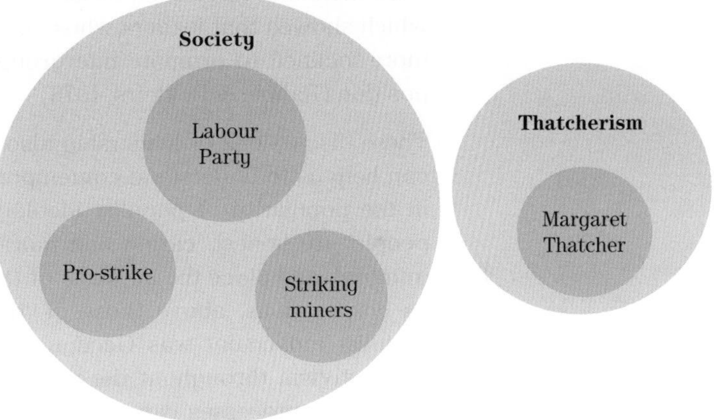

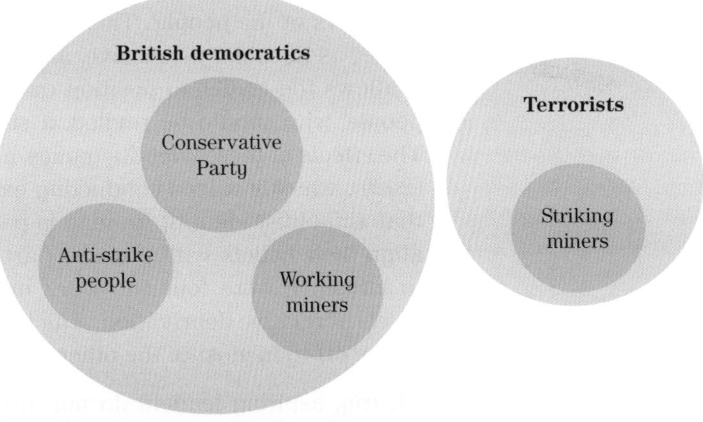

FIGURE 12.5 Linguistic construction of social categories involved in the strike

categories: a large and positively depicted social category, of which he or she was the prototypical representative, and a very small social category, which was identified as the enemy. As Reicher and Hopkins explain, 'Thatcher constructs a frame of "democracy against terrorism" wherein the inclusive category is British, is anti-strike, is represented by the Conservatives and the working miners and is defending itself against an exclusive category of the NUM [National Union of Mineworkers] executive. Kinnock constructs a frame of "Thatcherism against society" wherein the inclusive category is the people, is pro-strike, is represented by the Labour Party and the striking miners and is defending itself against an exclusive category of Margaret Thatcher' (1996, p. 369). In summary, Reicher and Hopkins show that, in this case, the aim of the speakers is to present themselves as the prototype of the national society, in order to back up either the aspiration to become the national leader (Kinnock) or the legitimization of an actual leadership (Thatcher).

Individuals who want to be seen as group prototypes may use ruthless and irresponsible strategies in order to achieve their aim. For instance, a leader who is struggling to be recognized as prototype, may use the 'us' versus 'them' rhetoric and show outgroup hostility in order to reinforce his or her position (Haslam, 2004). Such instances have been observed even in a controlled laboratory experiment, which showed that leaders whose position within their group was unstable were more inclined to promote intergroup conflict than leaders with a more secure position (Rabbie & Bekkers, 1978).

These discussions of leadership also highlight how the social identity approach can help us to understand contemporary political issues, such as the recent rise in the popularity of populist ideologies. Populism involves the belief that 'the people' are honest, caring and moral, while 'the elite' are corrupt, selfish and immoral, and place the interests of themselves and groups they care about, such as corporations, above those of 'the people'. Perhaps the best-known recent populist movement was Occupy, whose members carried out acts of protest and activism throughout the world in 2011–2012. Social identity research into leadership processes can help to shed light on what makes populist ideologies appealing to potential members. For instance, it is often noted that populist parties and movements tend to be fronted by charismatic leaders who make good use of rhetorical strategies which help them to position themselves as ingroup, or 'members of the people'. This ingroup categorization makes people perceive the leader as likeable, persuasive, and as someone they should follow. Additionally, it allows the leader to position outgroups, such as the elite, as 'enemies of the people' who should be reviled: a strategy known as populist identity framing. The effects of these 'identity games' are powerful: research by Bos and colleagues (2020), which involved conducting experiments in 15 different countries, showed that anti-elitist identity framing is particularly effective at persuading people to align their beliefs with populist parties. Perhaps unsurprisingly, these attempts to influence were found to work most effectively on people experiencing high levels of relative deprivation, which is when a person feels that they are generally worse off than most of the other people in their society.

Clearly, aspiring leaders do not always promote hatred and division; in some situations they may endorse positive change and renovation. This might seem to contradict the idea that, if they want to be accepted by their prospective followers, aspiring leaders need to be seen as group prototypes. However, aspiring leaders who preach change and innovation do so in line with the 'group Zeitgeist', and by arguing that change is needed to reinforce, strengthen or be faithful to the true group identity. Consider, for instance, Barack Obama's first speech after being elected as US president for the first time, in 2008. Here, he explained why, in his opinion, the American people had voted for him. He stated: 'I believed that Democrats and Republicans and Americans of every political stripe were hungry for new ideas, new leadership, and a new kind of politics – one that favours common sense over ideology; one that focuses on those values and ideals we hold in common as Americans.' Basically, Obama said that he won because he proposed a change that would realign the Americans with their own true values and beliefs. In stating this, Obama was presenting himself as a genuine incarnation (a prototypical instance) of the American identity.

Social Identity and Respect

People like to feel valued and respected. Positive evaluation from others is normally welcome. But is our desire to feel wanted and liked unconditional? Do we welcome recognition and appreciation from anybody, without distinction? Clearly this is not the case. As observed by Ellemers et al. (2004), we can probably remember situations in which the appreciation of others was not so important, such as when we remained indifferent to positive judgements from parents or teachers because these judgements were simply irrelevant. We might also remember instances in which the appreciation of others was even unwelcome, such as when 'someone we defined as less desirable (a nerd, a geek, or a no-no) latched onto us like a limpet, even worshipped us, but was just seen as a source of acute embarrassment in front of our "true" friends' (Ellemers et al., 2004, p. 155). When does appreciation and respect from others induce positive emotions, and when does it lead to indifference, or even embarrassment and disgust?

According to Ellemers et al. (2004; see also Spears et al., 2005), the way people respond to appreciation and respect from others depends on how the self and the appreciative others are defined and categorized. As we have already pointed out, people seek validation of their beliefs from others who are categorized as ingroup members. As a consequence, appreciation and positive evaluation coming from an ingroup source is welcome, reassuring and flattering. On the contrary, people do not see outgroup members as a source of validation, and so their judgements have hardly any relevance to self. In fact, when differentiating between ingroup and outgroup is especially important, appreciation from outgroup members may be unwelcome, if not deeply embarrassing and displeasing. Ellemers and her colleagues offer the example of a male pop group that fashions itself as a 'heavy-metal band from hell'. If it was discovered that the biggest fans of this band are teenyboppers and pensioners, the members of the band would probably be displeased.

To support their hypothesis, Ellemers et al. (2004) recruited students from the University of Amsterdam, and presented them with a vignette. Each participant had to imagine a situation in which he or she sits on a tram and, on seeing a young boy pushing an old lady away from the last available seat, comments that

Positive judgements are especially appreciated when they come from ingroup members.

SOURCE: ©Hongqi Zhang/Michaeljung/123RF

the old lady wanted to sit there. At this point, the participant had to imagine that a group of student bystanders respond favourably to the protagonist's behaviour and express their disapproval for the boy's behaviour. However, some participants in the experiment were told to imagine that the group of student bystanders are from the University of Amsterdam (the ingroup), while other participants were told to imagine that the bystanders are from the Free University (a rival university in Amsterdam, and therefore an outgroup). When, subsequently, participants were asked to rate how much collective self-esteem they would feel as members of the University of Amsterdam, those who had imagined that the bystanders were ingroup members produced higher collective self-esteem ratings than those who had imagined that the bystanders were outgroup members. These results are in line with a social identity approach to respect: positive feedback from an ingroup source will raise one's group-related self-regard more than appreciation from an outgroup source.

Social Identity and Help

In the Research Close-Up: Identity and Emergency Intervention in Chapter 10 we discussed the experiment conducted by Levine et al. (2005), in which it was found that an injured stranger wearing an ingroup team shirt is more likely to receive help than when wearing a rival team shirt or an unbranded sports shirt. This is a clear demonstration that social identity may play a crucial part in helping behaviour and support; people will help to the extent that they share the same social identity with the person who needs help.

This assumption has been confirmed in other studies conducted by Levine and his colleagues. In one study, Levine and Thompson (2004) asked a sample of British students to specify the likelihood that they would offer financial help (money donations, giving old clothes) and political help (signing petitions, joining action groups) following a natural disaster in Europe. Results showed that students were more likely to help when their European identity was made psychologically salient (by displaying a large colour European Union flag on the cover of the questionnaire) than when the British identity was made salient (by displaying a colour reproduction of a large British Union flag). Intriguingly, these findings imply that identification with the whole world community might increase one's willingness to endorse global cooperation and policies aiming at increasing global public good. This found confirmation in a cross-national questionnaire study involving participants from the United States, Italy, Russia, Argentina, South Africa and Iran, conducted by Buchan et al. (2011). Participants with higher scores on a scale measuring identification with 'the world as a whole' appeared to be more concerned with global issues such as climate change or the growing gap between people living in wealth and poverty around the world.

There are cases, however, in which helping members of an outgroup may be a means to advance a group's interest. For instance, Hopkins et al. (2007) found that after being reminded that the English stereotype the Scottish as 'mean', Scottish students were much more likely to give money to an outgroup (a Welsh charity) than when such a reminder did not take place. Importantly, whether or not they were reminded of their supposed meanness did not make any difference to how much money they would donate to the ingroup (a Scottish charity). Clearly, these students were particularly concerned with challenging a negative stereotype attached to the national ingroup, and used outgroup helping as a strategy to improve the image of the ingroup. This strategic tendency has been explored more widely by Nadler (2016) in his intergroup helping as status relations model, where he argues that powerful groups may give help to weaker groups as a way to maintain their dominance and control.

Although there are reasons why we may help outgroup members, we are generally more likely to help fellow ingroup members, as Levine et al.'s (2005) football fan study shows. Perhaps this tendency to be particularly helpful to ingroup members is somehow related to a more general tendency to be especially self-involved in the emotional experiences of other members of an ingroup. For example, people show greater levels of arousal, empathy and attention when observing the pleasure and displeasure of others who belong to the same group as the self than when the observed others belong to an outgroup (Brown et al., 2006). Furthermore, people interpret facial expressions of emotion much more accurately when looking at ingroup members than when looking at outgroup members (Young & Hugenberg, 2010).

Group Identity Norms, Deviance and Schism

Although shared group identification tends to accentuate the similarities among group members, and therefore their relative prototypicality, intragroup differences in prototypicality remain. While the more prototypical members are seen as core members, the less prototypical ones are considered to be marginal and peripheral. These less prototypical members may be perceived as a serious threat to the integrity of the group. The values and beliefs held by group deviants deny social identity, because these values and beliefs undermine shared consensus and reciprocal validation within the group. So, how are marginal members treated by core members? How do mainstream members cope with threats to social identity coming from deviants?

The Black Sheep Effect

A common reaction is to dislike ingroup deviants more than outsiders. After all, disagreement with outgroup members is not problematic and does not endanger the ingroup's worldviews. Outgroup members are different from 'us' by definition, and, as we have already seen, ingroup members do not expect nor want to be in agreement with them. Serious disagreement with ingroup members can, on the contrary, be profoundly destabilizing. How can we be sure that we are correct if even people who are meant to be like us contradict our position? In line with this, Marques and Yzerbyt (1988) found that law students rated a good performance of another law student more favourably than an equally good performance of a philosophy student, but rated a poor performance by another law student less favourably than an equally poor performance by a philosophy student.

Another study asked a sample of Belgian students to evaluate attractive and unattractive Belgian and North African students on a set of personality adjectives. It was found that while attractive Belgian students were evaluated more positively than attractive North African students, unattractive Belgian students were evaluated more negatively than unattractive North African students (Marques et al., 1988).

Unsurprisingly, deviants are often expelled from the group. The political and religious domains offer countless examples of members who are forced to leave the group because they are against the orthodoxy and are considered as traitors. However, getting rid of deviants is perhaps not the most important measure taken by the group establishment and majority. The existence of deviants may actually constitute an opportunity to reinforce the virtue of group identity. By punishing deviant behaviour harshly, the group establishment will be able to emphasize what is and is not normative and accepted behaviour within the group. As observed by Forsyth (2009), norms often appear as such only when they are violated and violation is sanctioned. Deviance can therefore help to define more precisely the normative criteria for group membership, and be seen as functional for social identity. The tendency to derogate ingroup deviant members in order to reinforce ingroup boundaries and stress normative and counter-normative behaviour is known as the **black sheep effect** (**Figure 12.6**) (Marques & Yzerbyt, 1988).

black sheep effect the tendency to criticize and derogate more harshly than members of an outgroup the members of an ingroup who deviate from the group norms

When Deviance and Criticism from the Inside Are Accepted

Consider, however, that if group members who do not align completely with the group's norms were systematically marginalized and rejected, all groups would be condemned to become very rigid entities that are unable to change and develop. However, this is not the case. In some cases group members who criticize the group do not prompt defensive and aggressive reactions from mainstream group members. Hornsey (2005) listed two circumstances in which criticism directed to the group coming from other group members is seen as legitimate and valuable.

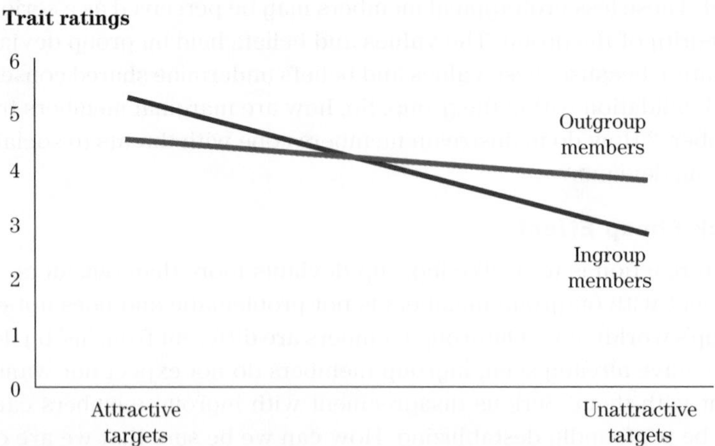

FIGURE 12.6 The black sheep effect
When asked to rate target individuals by using trait adjectives, people give higher ratings to mainstream ingroup members than to mainstream outgroup members. However, concerning black sheep members (i.e. those members who do not conform to the group's normative expectations), people assign lower ratings to ingroup black sheep than to outgroup black sheep.

First, people will accept criticism coming from ingroup members when the critics are seen as genuinely aiming to improve the group. If those who criticize appear to be invested in the group and to care for it, then criticism will be seen as constructive and therefore legitimate (Hornsey et al., 2004). Second, internal criticism will be accepted when it is perceived as timely and as delivered in an appropriate manner.

There are also situations in which punishing deviants may simply not be a good idea from a strategic point of view. For instance, if the positions of a political party are unpopular with the voting public, stressing group norms may widen the gap between the party line and the voting public. Therefore, party members may strategically decide to give more support to deviants in order to enhance the group's chances of success. This has been demonstrated by Morton et al. (2007). These researchers found that supporters of the Conservative Party in the UK gave more support to a potential leader who proposed to abandon ingroup norms and pursue radical change (i.e. a deviant leader) when public support for the party was perceived to be decreasing, compared to when it was perceived to be increasing.

The extent to which deviants are rejected may also vary depending on the group's cultural background. Groups endorsing a collectivistic ethos value relationships, harmony and the idea of 'sticking with the group', even when this implies a high personal cost. Because they are strongly concerned with group uniformity and oneness, these groups see deviance as a threat. On the contrary, individualistically orientated groups are socialized to value independence, autonomy and individual expression. As a consequence, individualistic groups may see deviance as a manifestation of self-expression, and therefore they may accept it to a higher degree. This was demonstrated in an experiment about the attitude of collectivist and individualist people towards either deviant or mainstream members of the ingroup (Hornsey et al., 2006). Results showed that deviant opinions were evaluated less negatively when the group had an individualistic rather than collectivistic ethos. There is, however, a paradox here, in that valuing independence and an ability to stand out is in itself a norm to which members of groups with an individualistic ethos *conform* (Jetten et al., 2002). So, in some cases, people may conform to independence! See Research Close-Up: Evaluating Deviants in Individualistic and in Collectivistic Cultures.

Research close-up

Evaluating Deviants in Individualistic and in Collectivistic Cultures

Source: *Hornsey, M. J., Jetten, J., McAuliffe, B. J., & Hogg, M. A. (2006).* The impact of individualist and collectivist group norms on evaluations of dissenting group members. *Journal of Experimental Social Psychology, 42,* 57–68.

Introduction

Deviants are seen as a problem by mainstream group members. This is because those who challenge the group norms break the unity and cohesion of the group, and question the nature of the group identity. As a consequence, deviants tend to be disliked and sanctioned. But are deviants evaluated negatively in all types of groups? It is hypothesized that the extent to which deviants are disliked will depend on whether the group holds an individualistic or a collectivistic ethos. Groups that have an individualistic ethos place importance on independence, and value people who are able to elaborate and express their own opinions in spite of possible pressures from other group members. Therefore, as Jetten et al. (2002) showed, groups with an individualistic ethos have a norm that prescribes challenging the norms! On the other hand, groups holding a collectivistic ethos value group cohesion and harmony, as well as the pursuit of collective goals and objectives. As a consequence, these groups tend to value members who avoid conflict and criticism, and who make an effort to fit in.

Method

This experiment had two conditions. In one condition, participants read a document emphasizing the collectivist orientation of students at the University of Queensland, while in the other condition participants read a document stressing the individualistic ethos of the students. At this point, the Australian government's proposal to introduce upfront fees was presented to all participants, who were subsequently told that the vast majority of University of Queensland students opposed this proposal. Finally, participants were asked to consider the opinion of an anonymous student about upfront fees, and evaluate this specific student by specifying how positively they saw him or her, on a scale ranging from 1 to 9, where higher ratings indicated more positive attitudes. However, half of the participants were told that this anonymous student was against upfront fees (and was therefore 'concordant' with the group majority), while the other half were told that the anonymous student was in favour of upfront fees (and was therefore a 'deviant').

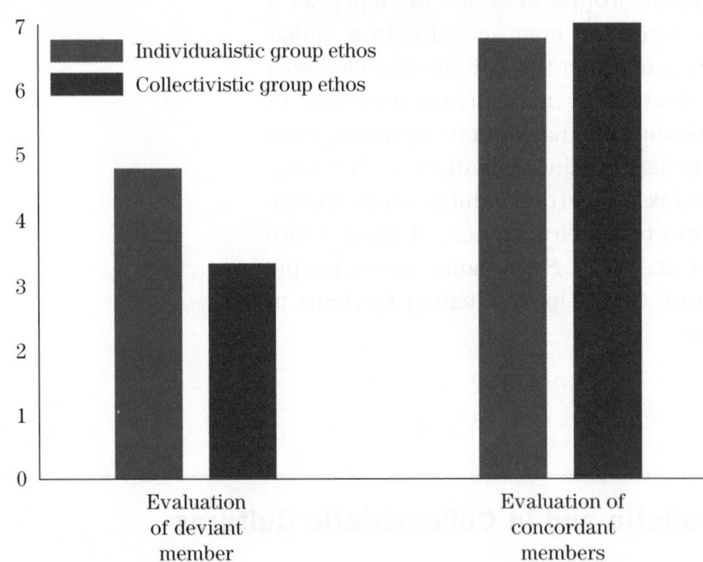

FIGURE 12.7 Evaluation of deviant and concordant members in individualistic and collectivistic groups
Members of the University of Queensland student group who endorsed an individualistic group ethos evaluated ingroup members who deviated from the majority position more positively than members who endorsed a collectivistic group ethos. However, the favoured cultural ethos had no effects on the evaluations of concordant members
SOURCE: Data from Hornsey et al. (2006).

Results

As shown in **Figure 12.7**, students who had been primed with an individualistic ethos evaluated the deviant more positively than students who had been primed with a collectivistic ethos (mean ratings were 4.62 and 3.14 respectively for each condition). This indicated clearly that the group holding an individualistic ethos accepted dissent and disagreement more than the group with a collectivistic ethos. Concerning the concordant student, participants in the collectivistic group gave slightly better evaluations than participants in the individualistic group, but differences were not statistically significant (means were 6.66 and 6.92 respectively).

Discussion

This study demonstrates that group deviants are perceived and treated differently depending on the group cultural ethos. Individualistic groups will see deviants in a less negative light than collectivistic groups, due to the fact that individualistic cultures place greater emphasis on values such as independence and uniqueness. It should be noted, however, that the group ethos is not necessarily static. In fact, the group ethos may change at different stages of group development. For instance, Worchel (1998) suggested that collectivist norms are more commonly observed early in the life of a group, when the group needs clear, well-defined norms and goals, and that more individualistic norms may develop later in a group's life, once the group is well established.

Critical Reflections

As interesting as this study's results are in highlighting the importance of a group's cultural ethos, it should be noted that some social psychological studies involving priming have come under fire in recent years as part of the replication crisis, which has involved researchers finding that many psychological effects that were well established in previous studies are difficult or impossible to replicate in modern times (see the Focus On in Chapter 2 for more information about the importance of replication). Understandably, this has called the validity and reliability of these previous studies into question. Work by authors such as Doyen et al. (2012) has called priming studies into question, either showing that priming effects cannot be replicated, or that they do occur, but are unlikely to be caused by the mechanisms proposed in the original studies. It is therefore important for us to appraise social psychological studies such as this one critically, and to explore whether their effects can be replicated.

Peripheral Group Members

Although, as discussed above, there may be group members who consciously decide to criticize the group and therefore accept to be seen, at least temporarily, as peripheral (non-prototypical) group members, there are also group members who are seen as peripheral against their will. These group members tend to feel more anxious and less confident than core (prototypical) group members (Louis, 1980; Moreland, 1985). What are the consequences of this emotionally aversive state? How do peripheral group members try to resolve this unpleasant situation? Researchers have investigated this issue, and found that peripheral group members employ a variety of strategies in order to feel more prototypical, and to be seen by other ingroup members as such. This is especially the case with members who value the group and strongly identify with it. Individuals for whom group membership is irrelevant will not be so concerned about their group prototypicality (Schmitt & Branscombe, 2002).

'Alienation from others is thus a deprivation of social being, for it is within our bonds that the self is forged and maintained.'
Robert F. Murphy, *The Body Silent* (1990)

Increased Conformity to Ingroup Standards

One very common strategy adopted by marginal group members who invest psychologically in the group is to increase their conformity with ingroup standards. This is exactly what Wicklund and Braun (1987) demonstrated in an experimental study: participants who were strongly committed to a social group but were not yet accomplished group members were more likely to describe themselves in terms of the group features than core members. In this study, it was also found that participants' conformity to the standards of a valued social group increased when their sense of accomplishment was threatened.

Increased Derogation of Non-prototypical Members and Praise of Prototypical Members

Threats to group prototypicality also affect the extent to which a highly identified group member will use prototypical group features as a standard when judging other group members. Schmitt and Branscombe (2002) argue that individuals whose prototypicality is questioned are induced to feel 'bad' group members, because they damage the distinctiveness of the group as well as its cohesion and homogeneity. As a consequence, these individuals will seek to be 'good' group members by vigorously endorsing and defending group identity. Schmitt and Branscombe suggest that a way of protecting group identity is evaluating group members in terms of their fit to the ingroup prototype. Consistent with this suggestion, these researchers found that men who highly identified with their gender group were much more derogatory towards non-prototypical men, and much more favourable towards prototypical men, when they were led to believe that they were non-prototypical, compared to when they were told that they were highly prototypical. Intriguingly, these findings are nicely illustrated by a character from the 1999 Oscar-awarded movie *American Beauty:* the Colonel of the US Marine Corps, Frank Fitts, played by Chris Cooper. Fitts overtly hates homosexuals, and reacts violently to behaviours he dislikes. At one point in the movie, however, Fitts tries to kiss a neighbour who happens to be a male, thereby revealing the meaning of his constant effort to present himself in public as a quintessential 'man'.

Increased Derogation of Outgroup Members

High group identifiers who do not feel secure about their group prototypicality are also more prone to derogate members of relevant outgroups. Breakwell (1979) ran an experiment in which people were ostensibly tested in order to see if they could join a desirable 'good-anagram-solvers' group. However, some participants were given an opportunity to cheat on the scoring of an anagram test. Subsequently, these illegitimate members of the good-anagram-solvers groups displayed more extreme outgroup derogation than participants who felt legitimate members of the group. Breakwell, as well as other social psychologists (e.g. Tajfel, 1978), believe that group members who feel illegitimate derogate outgroups in order to justify their group membership to themselves, because no one else knows about their illegitimate membership. According to Noel et al. (1995), however, illegitimate group members derogate the outgroup in order to present themselves as non-peripheral and legitimate group members in the eyes of other group members, so as to be accepted and improve their status and prototypicality within the group (**Figure 12.8**).

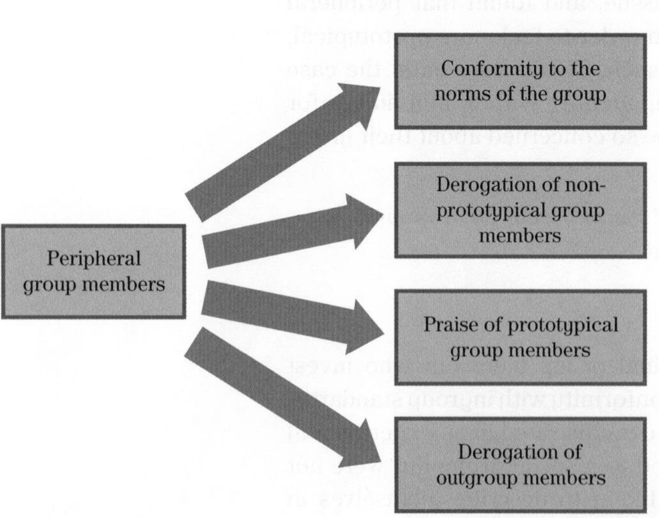

FIGURE 12.8 Strategies used by peripheral group members in order to enhance their position within the group

Contested Identities and Schism

Who is a marginal and who is a core group member is not always consensually agreed within a group. In some cases, group members that are accused of denying and betraying the group identity may refute this accusation. They may claim that their beliefs and behaviours are consistent with the group identity, and that it is actually those blaming them who are the heretics. This is far from unusual, and it is one of the possible consequences of shared social identity.

The group norms that define the group's identity are not set in stone. On the contrary, group members are involved in an ongoing process of negotiation about the nature of such norms. As a consequence, existing norms are constantly refined, adjusted, modified and, in some circumstances, dropped and replaced with entirely new norms. The aim of this process is to define the group identity in a clear and unambiguous way, thereby achieving consensus and unity. But sometimes consensus fails! The crystallization of relatively homogeneous factions, each holding different views about what should and should not be the group identity, can result in conflict and tension within groups. This may eventually result in **schism**.

schism the partition of a social group into separate factions and the ultimate secession of at least one faction from the group

Fabio Sani and his colleagues have investigated the processes that underlie schisms in social groups in a series of studies involving real groups (see Sani, 2008, for a summary of research). The major study within this research programme concerned the schism within the Church of England over the issue of the ordination of women to the priesthood (Sani, 2005; Sani & Reicher, 1999, 2000; Sani & Todman, 2002).

In March 1994 the first 32 women were ordained priests at Bristol Cathedral. Over the following years a group formed by hundreds of clergymen and thousands of lay people left the Church of England because of women priesthood. Why did so many members of the Church of England leave their beloved church over this specific issue? Sani and colleagues studied this schism longitudinally using interviews and questionnaires completed by members of the Church of England who either accepted or rejected the new legislation. The data analysis revealed that for some members the Church of England's decision to ordain women to the priesthood signified a radical departure from its doctrine and creed, which implied a complete denial of its nature and identity. According to these members, the ordination of women was turning the Church of England into a different church, something that was completely different from what it used to be. As one interviewee declared, by ordaining women priests the Church of England had 'chucked up scripture, overcome authority, kicked tradition in the teeth, and decided it's a protestant sect' (Sani & Reicher, 1999). As a consequence of this position, many of these members seceded from the Church of England. Those members who supported the legislation had, however, a completely different view. In their opinion, the legislation was totally consistent with the history of the Church of England and its group identity. What is more, the supporters of women priesthood argued that the legislation allowed the Church to accomplish more fully its true identity. The then-Archbishop of Canterbury put it plainly: 'We are not departing from a traditional concept of ministry, we are talking about an extension of the same ministry to include women . . . Christianity is all about God liberating, renewing and drawing out what has been there implicitly from the beginning.'

These analyses show that the schism resulted from a debate concerning the relationship between a specific norm (the legislation on women priests) and the group identity as a whole (the identity of the Church of England). Members perceived the norm either as fully consistent with the group identity, in which case they endorsed the norm and happily stayed in the group, or as overthrowing the group identity, in which case they strenuously opposed the norm and seriously considered joining the schism. Sani (2005) found that the main reasons why those who perceived the group's identity as being overthrown ultimately developed schismatic intentions were that they experienced aversive emotions (especially dejection and agitation) and lost their identification with the group. Sani also found that the likelihood of unhappy members joining a schism depended ultimately on their perceived ability to voice their dissent within the group. The lower the perceived voice the higher the chances of leaving the group. Put differently, opponents wondered what might happen to them in the future, as group members. If they foresaw ostracism, discrimination and isolation, they generally opted for a schism (**Figure 12.9**). On the other hand, if they believed that they would be respected and would retain an active role in the group, they were more inclined to stay.

Sani and Pugliese (2008) replicated these findings in a study of a schism that took place within an Italian right-wing political party, Alleanza Nazionale, in 2001. Alleanza Nazionale (AN) was founded in 1994, and constituted a renewed version of a party that was created after the end of the Second World War, which claimed the legitimacy of the fascist experience. Since the creation of Alleanza Nazionale the party secretary, Gianfranco Fini, had made it clear that the party fully accepted democratic values. However, when in 2003 Fini visited Israel and publicly described fascism as the *male assoluto* ('ultimate evil') of the twentieth century, some party members who still had a sense of respect for Mussolini and nostalgia for the fascist regime rebelled. This group, led by Mussolini's niece, Alessandra Mussolini, decided to secede from AN, and founded a new breakaway party. Sani and Pugliese found that those group members who left the party saw Fini's speech as a rupture with the historical continuity of the party and as a denial of the group identity, and also feared that they would end up being marginalized within the party. On the contrary, the majority that endorsed Fini believed that the speech was a necessary development in line with the group identity.

Social Identity Motives

Why do people identify with groups? Is social identification driven by some psychological motives? Obviously, there may be many motives, including

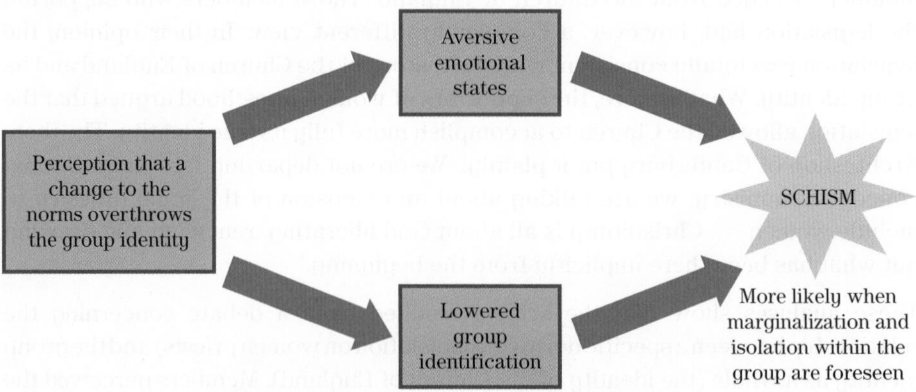

FIGURE 12.9 The schismatic process
How a faction within a group may decide to join a schism and leave the group.

instrumental and practical ones. However, social psychologists believe that some specific psychological motives are deeply ingrained in the human mind and are therefore widespread. Vignoles et al. (2006) have demonstrated that social identities which satisfy important psychological motives are seen by people as especially central to their self-definition. Below we briefly discuss five social identity motives that have been explored at length by social psychologists, some of which were also included in the list of motives studied by Vignoles et al.'s (2006) studies.

The Self-Esteem Motive

Social psychologists agree that a core motive for social identification is the one for self-esteem. As we discussed in Chapter 3, we strive for a positive evaluation of ourselves, and when our self-esteem is threatened we use a variety of strategies to restore or enhance self-esteem (Hoyle et al., 1999).

Being a member of a group may enhance two different, yet related types of self-esteem. First, a positively valued ingroup can be a source of **collective self-esteem** (Luhtanen & Crocker, 1992), that is, positive regard for the ingroup as a whole. Collective self-esteem is especially pursued in collectivistic cultures, which place special emphasis on the importance of interconnectedness among individuals and on group goals and life. Researchers have found that collective self-esteem is higher among allocentric individuals – that is, people who have been socialized into collectivistic cultures – than among idiocentric individuals – that is, people who have been raised into individualistic cultures (Crocker et al., 1994). Second, a positively valued ingroup can be a source of personal self-esteem, that is, positive regard for the individual self. Personal self-esteem is especially sought in individualistic societies, where people are socialized to focus their attention and invest their energies on the enhancement of the individual self.

collective self-esteem positive regard for a group of which one is a member

Because highly regarded groups may satisfy both forms of self-esteem, people generally want to belong to groups that have high status and prestige (Tajfel & Turner, 1986). In order to assess the group status, group members compare the ingroup with relevant outgroups. This is a specific form of social comparison (a concept we have discussed in Chapter 3), in the sense that rather than comparing the individual self with other individuals, people compare their own group with other groups.

The Distinctiveness Motive

Various social psychologists have observed that humans have a pervasive need for uniqueness and distinctiveness (Breakwell, 1986; Brewer, 1991). This is because highlighting the differences between self and others is an important aspect of self-definition, particularly in the West. How could a single individual know who he or she is without establishing the way in which he or she differs from others? Importantly, the need for distinctiveness does not apply exclusively to the personal self; it is just as much concerned with the collective self, that is social identity (Tajfel et al., 1971; Vignoles et al., 2000). As we have repeatedly observed, identifying with a social category implies recognition that we are similar to some people and different from others and the accentuation of these intragroup similarities and intergroup differences. This marks out the boundaries between 'us' and 'them', thereby providing group members with a sense of distinctiveness. Countless types of identity markers (e.g. flags, clothing, body painting, linguistic

See Chapter 9 on attraction and intimacy for a more extended discussion of the need to relate to others to become and remain a human being.

jargon, tastes) can be used to emphasize differences between groups and to maintain group distinctiveness (Sani & Thomson, 2001).

Berger and Heath (2008) argue that members of a group may even abandon tastes and habits that have been adopted for a long time, if this allows distinction from an outgroup. These researchers found that a group of students stopped wearing a particular wristband after discovering that other students, from the 'geeky' academically focused dormitory next door, also began wearing that type of wristband.

The Motive to Belong

Another need that social psychologists believe to be fundamental and universal is the need to belong, or to relate to others, to become and remain a human being. Social identity provides a reassuring sense of inclusion, and therefore it constitutes a potent means for the satisfaction of the need to belong. Knowles and Gardner (2008) conducted an experiment in which they asked a group of participants to think and write about a time in which they felt intensely rejected in some way, and another group to think and write about a time in which they felt very accepted in some way. Then, participants were asked to rate the perceived cohesiveness and importance of their ingroups. It was found that participants who thought about rejection saw their groups as much more cohesive and united than participants who thought about acceptance. Clearly, people primed with social rejection were motivated to be part of a meaningful and solid group. Interestingly, fear of rejection seems to have an effect on the size of groups that are sought out. Pickett et al. (2002) have shown that if people's belongingness is threatened, as when they are told that they belong to a very rare personality category, they will seek out identification with larger and more inclusive groups.

The Motive to Achieve Symbolic Immortality

Through group identification people may become parts of collective entities that seem immune to the corrosion of time. The sense of belonging to something that transcends my mere individual existence may provide me with a sense of **symbolic immortality**; a sense that, while I may be physically mortal, a part of me (my values, beliefs and deeds) will survive through my group. This means that social identity protects people from the terror engendered by fear of death, which according to terror management theory (see Chapter 13 for more on this theory) is a fundamental, inescapable dimension of the human condition (Pyszczynski et al., 2000). Social psychologists have reasoned that, if it is true that social identification may protect against the terror prompted by the idea that we must ultimately die, then if people are reminded of their own mortality they should increase their identification with relevant groups. This proposition has been tested and confirmed by researchers. For instance, it has been found that after thinking and writing about the prospect of their own death, people exhibit an enhanced ingroup favouritism and identification (Castano et al., 2002), and endorse harsher punishment for group deviants (Rosenblatt et al., 1989). These findings have been confirmed by Sani et al. (2009), who showed that fear of death enhances social identity to the extent that the values and beliefs of the group with which one identifies are perceived to endure through time.

symbolic immortality
a form of immortality that is not based on escaping physical death but on the symbolic continuation of the self across time (e.g. through offspring or the transmission of one's cultural values to the new generations)

There can be a negative side to these enhanced feelings of social identity, however. For instance, it has been shown that the desire to uphold and protect the norms and values of one's group in the context of mortality salience can, in some cases, motivate acts of suicide terrorism and endorsement of ingroup military brutality (Hirschberger & Ein-Dor, 2006; Pyszczynski et al., 2006). It seems strangely ironic that the fear of death can motivate behaviour which may lead to the loss of thousands of innocent lives, but knowledge of this could perhaps help to prevent future atrocities of this nature.

The Motive for Uncertainty Reduction

As many social psychologists have pointed out, people tend to have low tolerance for uncertainty about social reality and their own place within it (Festinger, 1950). According to Hogg et al. (2008), 'group membership is a very effective way to resolve epistemic uncertainty. This is because groups prescribe who we are and how we should behave. Groups also provide consensual validation for our perceptions, feelings, attitudes, and behaviors' (p. 1270). These social psychologists also state that groups that are perceived as having high **entitativity** – that is, groups that are seen as being very homogeneous and cohesive, thereby looking like single and bounded entities (Campbell, 1958; Hamilton & Sherman, 1996) – are better suited for uncertainty reduction.

entitativity the extent to which a collection of individuals is perceived as forming a single, unified and cohesive entity

This is because entitative groups provide people with clear norms and unambiguous social identities. To demonstrate this assumption, Michael Hogg and his colleagues (Hogg et al., 2007) asked members of either the Labour or the Liberal Party in Australia to rate the perceived entitativity of their own political party. Then participants were instructed to think about those aspects of their life that made them feel uncertain about themselves, their life and their future. Finally, participants' identification with their political party was assessed. Results show that people whose self-uncertainty was primed identified more strongly with their political group when this was seen as high in entitativity.

It is important to note, however, that people will not be happy just with any version of what the group is like and where it comes from. The sense of being a cohesive entity with a clear trajectory and well-defined values and standards is important, but even more important is to claim for the group the desired history, values and standards. That means that 'who we are' and 'where we come from' are issues that are actively constructed by the members of a group – especially the group establishment and leaders – through language (Potter & Wetherell, 1987).

Social Identity and Health

Our social identity affects not only our social behaviours and thoughts, but also our health and the way we feel physically. Researchers exploring this area call it the social identity approach to health, or 'the social cure' (Haslam et al., 2018; Wakefield et al., 2019). There are three main ways in which social identity and health are connected.

1 Social identity influences our perception of, and response to, symptoms. For instance, concerning perception of symptoms, a soldier involved in a military campaign is likely to find a bone fracture less painful than an ordinary person, in line with values related to strength of character that are typical of a soldier identity. Regarding response to symptoms, refusal to see oneself as a 'cardiovascular problem sufferer' might lead to downplaying early symptoms of a heart attack and failure to seek prompt medical attention.

2 Social identity has implications for health behaviour. Whether or not one engages in health-promoting behaviour may depend on the degree to which such behaviour is consistent with the norms of the social group with which one identifies. For example, identification with the group of 'athletes' is likely to restrain me from drinking; on the other hand, if I identify with the group of 'university students' I may indulge in binge drinking.

3 Social identity impacts upon our biology. When I identify with a group, I feel confident that ingroup members will offer help and support in case of difficulties. This is likely to increase my perceived ability to cope with tasks, thereby reducing the physiological stress I experience. For instance, if I identify strongly with my workplace I will tend to see my colleagues as reliable sources of support. This will enhance my perceived ability to cope with work-related tasks, and as a consequence will reduce stress and enhance well-being.

In this section we explore research on these three forms of interplay between social identity and health, in some detail.

Social Identity and Symptom Perception

The relationship between the biological aspects of an illness and the perception of the relevant symptoms is not straightforward. For instance, the same injury can produce substantially different degrees of pain in different people, and even in the same person on different occasions (Melzack & Wall, 1988). That means that in many circumstances symptom perception may have more to do with psychology than biology. Social psychologists contend an important way in which our psychology affects symptom perception is through our social identity (St. Claire & Clucas, 2012). Researchers have found that social identity may impact upon symptom perception in at least two important ways.

First, social identity may influence the perceived severity of symptoms when one is ill. St. Claire and He (2009) asked older people about their levels of hearing after emphasizing either their membership in the 'group of older people' or their unique, individual characteristics. Participants who thought about themselves as older people reported more hearing-related problems than those who thought about themselves in terms of their individual traits. These results confirm that a person who suffers from an illness will likely identify with the group of people suffering from that specific illness and, as a consequence, will conform to symptoms that are believed to be normative of that illness group membership.

The second way in which social identity may impact upon symptom perception is by influencing how serious and distressing specific symptoms are perceived to be. For instance, symptoms may be perceived as especially serious when they constitute a threat to identity, as demonstrated by R. M. Levine (1999). This researcher primed a sample of female secretaries with either a 'secretary' or a 'female' identity, and then asked them to evaluate the seriousness of a number of different illnesses or injuries. Results revealed that judgements depended on the identity that had been primed. Participants who defined themselves in terms of their gender identity appeared to be especially worried by illnesses and injuries that threatened physical attractiveness (e.g. facial scar, a broken nose). On the other hand, those who saw themselves in terms of their professional identity (secretaries) emphasized the seriousness of illnesses and injuries that had negative implications for their work (e.g. painful hands, high fever).

Social Identity and Health Behaviour

In her opening to the 2002 World Health Report, the then director-general of the World Health Organization, Gro Harlem Brundtland, stated that 'too many of us are living dangerously – whether we are aware of that or not' (Brundtland, 2002, p. 3). This report intensified debate and research into health behaviour – broadly defined as behaviour that is somehow associated with one's health status, irrespective of current health or motivations (Morrison & Bennett, 2006). Why do people engage in risky behaviours, and how can we promote healthier behaviours?

The theory of reasoned action (TRA; Fishbein, 1979) and its extension, the theory of planned behaviour (TPB; Ajzen, 1985; Hunter et al., (2003) found that subjective norms were not predictive of women's intention to see a doctor in relation to breast cancer symptoms. Social identity researchers argue that, rather than focusing on subjective norms, we should focus on social identity-based norms when considering health behaviour. Consistent with that, Terry and Hogg (1996) found that, as long as a given health behaviour is relevant to an ingroup and that the person in question has a relatively high level of identification with that ingroup, the ingroup's norms will predict their behavioural intentions. Specifically, these researchers found that identification with the group 'friends and peers at university' positively influenced intentions to engage in regular exercise and in sun-protective behaviour among those who identified strongly with the group, as these behaviours were seen to be normative of the group. Ajzen & Madden (1986) have produced an ample volume of research on these themes (see Chapter 5 for a detailed description of TRA and TPB). Both theories assume that actual health behaviour is predicted by behavioural intention, which in turn is predicted by attitude toward the behaviour and by subjective norms. TPB also postulates the existence of a third predictor of behavioural intention: perceived behavioural control. In general, these theories are well supported by evidence.

For instance, Stewart-Knox et al. (2005) conducted a 3-year longitudinal interview study to investigate the reasons for taking up smoking among pre-adolescents from various economically deprived areas in Northern Ireland. Analysis of data revealed that the peer group influenced smoking uptake, but that this did not normally happen through direct persuasion, but rather because of children striving to conform to the normative behaviour of the peer group with which they identified. In a study involving a large sample of Danes aged 16–24 years, Verkooijen et al. (2007) found that risks of substance use were higher for participants who identified with pop, skate/hip-hop, techno and hippie groups than for participants who identified with sporty, quiet and religious groups. These effects were found to be positively mediated by the degree to which participants saw substance use as normative of the group. Additionally, a study involving university students in the UK, for whom heavy drinking is normative, revealed that greater identification with the group of UK university students was associated with stronger drinking intentions (Livingstone et al., 2011).

The fact that different social contexts may prompt the salience of different social identities implies that one's normative attitudes toward health behaviour may shift across contexts. In other words, attitudes towards health behaviour may vary in accordance with the different social identities that form the basis for self-definition from situation to situation (Tarrant et al., 2012). Consistent with this principle, Tarrant and Butler (2011) found that university students expressed much lower intentions of engaging in health-promoting behaviour when their student identity was made salient than when their national identity was emphasized.

Health behaviours can be further enhanced by identifying with multiple groups. Sani and colleagues (2015) found that the more groups participants identified with, the more likely they were to exercise regularly, eat healthily, drink moderately, and not to smoke. Similarly, Miller et al. (2016) explored group identification and health behaviour in adolescents. The authors found that while identification with the family and the school both predicted reduced odds of smoking, binge drinking and cannabis use, identification with friends increased the odds of engaging in these behaviours (unsurprising, given what we learnt earlier regarding group norms and health behaviour). However, the authors found that when family, school and friend identification were investigated simultaneously, adolescents who identified with all three groups were less likely to smoke, binge drink and use cannabis than those who identified with none, one, or two of these groups. From these results the authors concluded that 'more group identifications increase the likelihood of individuals identifying with a group with healthy norms, which will help protect against negative behaviour. Indeed, in the current study, it is only identification with the friend group that predicts unhealthy behaviour, so it is likely that identification with the family and school group protect against the negative norms encouraged by identification with the friend group' (p. 301).

Intriguingly, in some circumstances group identification and the consequent compliance with group norms may have positive implications not only for ingroup members but also for people coming into contact with them. In a study involving a sample of Swiss nurses, Falomir-Pichastor et al. (2009) found that higher identification with the professional group of nurses was linked to a higher likelihood of getting a 'flu vaccination, a behaviour prescribed by the nurses' group norms. Because the vaccination of healthcare workers appears to be effective in reducing morbidity and mortality in residential care settings and long-term care hospitals (Carman et al., 2000), we can infer that the extent to which nurses identify with their professional group may have very important implications for patients' health.

Social Identity, Positive Physiological Processes and Health

Group identification has been found to promote positive physiological outcomes and to reduce feelings of stress. Platow et al. (2007) found that people undertaking a physically painful activity (i.e. immersing a hand into a bath of ice water) not only reported feeling less pain, but also had lower levels of physiological stress when they received support from an ingroup (i.e. a member of the same faculty) than when support was received from a member of an outgroup (i.e. a member of another faculty). Reicher and Haslam (2006) conducted a study where participants played the role of either prisoners or guards within a purpose-built environment. It was found that prisoners teamed up to challenge the guards, which increased group identification. In turn, this led to lower physiological stress (measured through levels of cortisol in saliva). On the contrary, because they felt uncomfortable with the exercise of power, guards failed to identify with their group. This produced increased levels of physiological stress (see Chapter 13 for a more detailed discussion of this study). Wegge et al. (2012) conducted an experiment involving call centre agents, in which it was found that organizational identification functioned as a buffer against physiological stress – measured by assessing immunoglobulin A (IgA) concentration in participants' saliva – caused by unfriendly customers.

In line with the fact that group identification facilitates positive physiological processes, group identification has also been found to have positive effects on various dimensions of both physical and mental health. Tewari et al. (2012) studied pilgrims' participation in a month-long Hindu religious festival. They found that, in spite of enduring hardship due to very low temperature, unsanitary conditions, severe cold and very high levels of noise, pilgrims' health and well-being increased during the festival. As the researchers explain, following their religious beliefs and enacting religious rituals allowed the pilgrims to affirm their social identity, which in turn benefited health. More specifically concerning mental health, a study of people with multiple sclerosis attending support groups revealed that patients who identified strongly with the support group had markedly lower levels of depression than patients who had lower identification with the support group (Wakefield et al., 2013). Latrofa et al. (2009) studied a sample of southern Italians, a group who suffers from a historical social stigma within Italy. Knowledge that they were the target of prejudice was a negative predictor of psychological well-being of participants in this study. However, increased identification with the group of southern Italians positively predicted psychological well-being, thereby compensating for the detrimental effects of perceived prejudice.

A long duration mass gathering, such as the Indian pilgrimage event known as the Magh Mela, may attract millions of people. In spite of exposure to various health risks, as the event unfolds participants report improved levels of well-being, resulting from enactment of a valued social identity (Tewari et al., 2012).

SOURCE: ©prabhat kumar verma/Shutterstock

Importantly, researchers have demonstrated that the positive impact of social identification on health is, at least in part, mediated by social support. In a study of theatre production teams during a production, Haslam et al. (2009) found that higher team identification at the outset predicted lower likelihood to experience burnout during the most demanding phases of a production (i.e. dress rehearsal and performance), primarily because team identification facilitated reciprocal social support among team members. The interplay between social identity, mutual support and well-being has also been investigated by researchers of crowd behaviour in mass emergencies. Drury (2012) argues that the experience of common threat that characterizes mass emergencies and disasters leads to a temporary breakdown in social class, ethnic group, and other hierarchical status distinctions among survivors, which in turn creates a sense of 'we-ness', a shared social identity. This enhances reciprocal helping, routine civility, and expectations of support, which in turn have positive consequences for well-being.

Knowledge of these processes have been used to develop the Groups4Health (G4H) intervention, which provides education and support to people experiencing mental ill health and loneliness, so that they can join new groups and reconnect with old ones. G4H has been shown to improve social connectedness and mental health by increasing social identification (Haslam et al., 2016), and to reduce loneliness and frequency of doctor appointments (Haslam et al., 2019). Since Cruwys and colleagues (2018) have shown that lack of social connection predicts increases in healthcare appointments, G4H represents an effective way to address the unmet social needs of frequent healthcare attenders, which in turn will help to lessen the burden on overstretched healthcare services. Indeed, as Kellezi and colleagues (2019) note, there is a pressing need for health professionals to address the psychosocial issues of their patients in order to maximize the efficiency and efficacy of healthcare services. The social cure perspective represents an important step towards this.

The Development of Social Categorization and Social Identity

The tendency to structure the social world in terms of social categories, and to identify with certain categories, which is typical of adults, is not something people are born with. Developmental social psychologists have investigated which social categories are of paramount importance to children, when self-categorization emerges, and some central social identity processes in children (Barrett, 2007; Bennett & Sani, 2004, 2008).

Social Categorization in Children

Developmental and social psychologists have assumed that gender and ethnicity are the two most important and psychologically consequential categories among children. The ability to structure the social world in terms of gender and in terms of racial and ethnic categories emerges in early childhood (see Ruble et al., 2004, for an excellent review). Concerning gender, studies have revealed that many children start labelling the sexes shortly after their second birthdays, and that by 3 years of age all children can use gender as a criterion to sort photographs (Leinbach & Fagot, 1993). The ability to label people in accordance with their ethnicity emerges a bit later, after 3 years of age (Katz & Kofkin, 1997). However, awareness of ethnic categories develops rapidly after 4 years of age (Aboud & Amato, 2001).

The features of category members upon which children appear to focus have been found to change across the years (Sani et al., 2000). Prior to the age of 7–8 years, children seem to pay attention mainly to overt physical features and other external characteristics (skin colour, clothing, hairstyle), as well as traits and dispositions (nice, nasty). It is only later, at around 10 years of age, that children start conceiving of category members in terms of their shared beliefs and values.

By a very early age, children are able to categorize people in accordance with their ethnicity.

SOURCE: ©Peera_stockfoto/Shutterstock

The Beginnings of Self-Categorization

The development of self-categorization occurs in parallel with the development of social categorization. As children become able to order the environment in terms of relevant social categories, they also become able to assign the self to one category. In the second year of life children can allocate a picture of themselves to a set of pictures of other same-sex children (Ruble & Martin, 1998). With regard to race and ethnicity, Katz and Kofkin (1997) found that by 3 years of age, more than two-thirds of Euro-American children could attach ethnic labels to themselves, but that only one-third of

African-American children could do so. These findings show that the emergence of ethnic self-categorization may depend, at least in part, on the comparative value that society attaches to different ethnic groups. Children from disadvantaged and low-status groups find race self-labelling more problematic than children from higher-status groups.

What are the factors that facilitate the emergence of social categorization and self-categorization? According to Ruble et al. (2004) both cognitive and social factors are at play. From a cognitive point of view, the ability to see and partition the world in terms of social categories and the ability to categorize the self as a member of specific categories depends very much on children's appreciation of category constancy (Ruble et al., 2004). Children must be able to understand that certain social categories, such as gender and race, may have fixed properties, and that their members cannot switch from one category to another. As far as the role of society is concerned, it is obvious that a child's cultural and social background has a large role to play in determining which categories are known first, and when they are first known. For instance, children living in a very homogeneous cultural group may form an idea of ethnic categories later in their lives than children living in a multi-ethnic cultural group, or in a group characterized by inter-ethnic tension.

From Self-Categorization to Social Identity

When does mere self-labelling ('I am French', 'I am a girl') turn into social identity? When does a child begin giving importance to being a member of one group rather than another? Quintana (1998) suggests that it is only at about 10 years of age that children start appreciating the implications that social categories have for society and for the self. At this age, self-categories become meaningful and central aspects of the self-concept, and a clear sense of being part of a group, a sense of 'we', accompanied by a clear sense of the value attached to the group, emerges.

However, other researchers contend that younger children may be more sophisticated than we imagine. In a year-long field study based on observation and interviews with children attending a multi-ethnic, inner-city primary school in England, Connolly (1998) found that children as young as 5 are perfectly capable of discussing and negotiating their gender, race and other group identities, in a fairly sophisticated fashion. In line with this, Ruble et al. (2004) suggest that incorporation of social category memberships into the self-concept may take place gradually during the school years, as this is the period when 'children's sense of self becomes more complex as they are exposed to a new social environment outside the family' (p. 34).

Sani and Bennett (2009) have used an experimental approach to explore the genesis of group identification in children aged 5 to 11. Following the principles of self-categorization theory, they conceive group identification as the ability to perceive the self in terms of the stereotypes attached to the self-category. Consistent with such conceptualization of group identification, Sani and Bennett presented children with sets of cards identifying particular trait adjectives (e.g. nice, friendly, shy, loud) and asked them to rate the extent to which the traits applied to the self, to the ingroup, and to the outgroup. After a distraction task, children were asked to remember for whom (self, ingroup or outgroup) each trait had been rated. Results showed that traits rated for the self were confused more frequently with traits rated for the ingroup than with traits rated for the outgroup.

This was the case for all children, including the 5 year olds, and for all the ingroups that were considered, that is, the gender, age and family ingroup. Therefore, this study revealed that, at least from the age of 5 years, psychologically relevant ingroups become integral parts of children's self-system.

Social Identity and Derogation of Ingroup Deviants

Recognizing that group norm deviance constitutes a departure from group norms, and that, therefore, deviant members may threaten social identity and its distinctiveness, is an important step into children's developing sense of 'we'. Abrams et al. (2003) argue that an understanding of the implications of atypicality and the importance of group loyalty imply a fairly sophisticated way of thinking, and therefore they appear later than group identification and group preference. Once children start appreciating the implications of group deviance, they engage in evaluative intragroup differentiation. That is, they compare ingroup members with one another and judge them on the basis of their adherence to the group norms. At this point, in line with the black sheep effect, children will dislike anti-normative ingroup members more than anti-normative outgroup members.

In a study involving children aged 6 and 11, Abrams et al. (2003) collected data confirming their prediction. Children who were participating in a summer school were presented with statements ostensibly made by other children – who were either attending the same summer school (ingroup members) or a different one (outgroup members) – concerning the comparative quality of the two summer schools. The 'typical' summer school attendees declared that their own summer school was better than the other (normative position), while 'deviants' stated that the two summer schools were equally enjoyable (anti-normative position). Results revealed that all children liked typical ingroup members more than typical outgroup members. However, in addition to this, the older children disliked ingroup deviants more than outgroup deviants.

Focus on

The Group in the Mind

Social psychologists studying group behaviour before the advent of the social identity approach tended to conceive a social group as a collection of individuals interacting and relating to one another merely in terms of their individual identities and characteristics. For instance, specifically concerning the nature of group cohesion, Lott and Lott (1961) argued that this emerges when interaction between different people allows achievement of goals or is rewarding in some other way. It did not occur to these researchers that – as contended by the social identity approach – group cohesion may actually result from an active effort to achieve unity made by people who have a sense of sharing the same group membership and identification.

The social identity approach to group processes started as a rebellion against the individualistic approach to group behaviour. According to a social identity perspective, people do not understand the social world merely as a collection of individuals interacting with one another *as individuals.* On the contrary, people see the social world as made of human aggregates standing in power and status relationships with one another, and see the self as being included in some of these categories and excluded from others. This, as we have seen in this chapter, has important consequences for our social conduct. To the extent that others are seen as members of an ingroup, we are more prone to be influenced by them, more willing to help them, and particularly flattered and pleased when they show admiration and respect towards us. Also, individuals who, despite their nominal membership in an ingroup, appear to deviate from the group norms, are especially disliked and derogated. In addition, identification with specific groups may affect our health in various ways. Last but not least, seeing others as members of an outgroup creates the preconditions for prejudice, bias, confrontation and aggression (as you will see in the next chapter).

The fact that *the group is in the mind* is important not only for an understanding of how people relate to fellow ingroup members and to members of relevant outgroups, it is also crucial for making sense of social change. It is because people form representations of the social structure and their own place within it that they are able to conceive different structures and act upon the world in order to change the way things are. Had South African black people been unable to represent their social environment in terms of a hegemonic white group and an oppressed black group, they would have never conceived of an alternative reality, nor fought for the achievement of that alternative reality. Therefore, a social psychology that did not focus on people's representation of social reality in terms of ingroup and outgroup would be incapable of explaining the social psychological side of the radical changes that have occurred in racial relations in South Africa over recent decades.

In summary, individuals live in groups, but the groups are, in turn, in the mind of individuals. As Turner and Oakes (1997) put it, *the mind is socially structured;* it has evolved to understand the world in terms of group relations, and to act upon the world in order to either maintain or change the nature of these relations. Appreciating this crucial assumption is a precondition for a full understanding of how people relate to one another.

Although this chapter has explored the social identity approach's ability to explain many facets of human behaviour, this approach has not been without its critics. Perhaps most famously, Rabbie and colleagues (1989) argued that participants' apparent ingroup favouritism can be better explained by a Behavioural Interaction Model, which involves the idea that group members act with the aim of maximizing their personal gain, rather than working with the rest of the group towards developing a positive social identity. This is known as the interdependence theory of group processes, because it suggests that groups are comprised of interdependent people who each want to maximize their personal gains. Unsurprisingly, this view has been criticized by social identity theorists (Turner & Bourhis, 1996), who have argued that interdependence theorists misunderstand the social identity approach, and that interdependence theory actually involves the assumption that social categorization processes occur in groups. However, this debate encourages us to remember that any theory is one possible explanation for some real-world phenomenon/phenomena, and that we can never 'prove' theory to be 'correct', because other researchers can come along at any time and present evidence which challenges our own. Thus, while the social identity approach is highly popular within European social psychology, we must remember that it is not accepted and supported by all.

Questions

1. Think about a social group (family, friends, sport team, etc.) to which you are strongly attached. Would you say that you relate to each single group member as an individual, independent from shared group membership, or that the fact of belonging to the same group adds a special flavour to the relationship with each group member?
2. Can you think of any example from either past or contemporary history where awareness of sharing membership in a social group has led to important socio-political transformations?

SUMMING UP: SOCIAL CATEGORIZATION AND SOCIAL IDENTITY

A CATEGORIZED SOCIAL WORLD

- Social categories may be more or less inclusive. For instance, the social category 'European' is more inclusive than 'Italian', which in turn is more inclusive than 'Tuscan'.
- People are assigned to social categories on the basis of their resemblance to (1) the category prototype (an abstract idea representing the essence of the category), and (2) some category exemplar (a category member that one has encountered).
- The similarities among members of a social category are exaggerated in order to mark out differences between groups. This cognitive phenomenon is known as the 'accentuation effect'.
- The accentuation effect is the basis of stereotype formation. A stereotype is a generalization about a social group, in that similar characteristics are attributed to virtually all group members.
- The social categories that are used to make sense of a given situation are those that best 'fit' the situation and that are more 'accessible' to the perceiver.
- Social categories are flexible mental tools. The level of inclusiveness, the nature of prototype and exemplars, and the stereotypical content of a social category vary from situation to situation.
- The cognitive principles that characterize social categories also apply to self-categories, that is, social categories to which one assigns oneself. This also implies that self-categories are contextually fluid, like any other social category.
- Social categories become self-categories either because we are socialized into them from birth, or from a very early stage in life (this is the case, for instance, with gender and ethnic categories), or because we intentionally join them at some point in life (this is, for instance, the case with social clubs and political parties).

SOCIAL IDENTITY

- Social identity has important implications for social influence, in that (1) conformity to a majority is more likely when the majority is seen as sharing the same social identity with the target of influence, and (2) conversion to a minority is facilitated when the minority is seen as sharing the same social identity with the target of influence. Sources perceived as ingroup are more influential because they are seen as reliable and competent, and because people expect to agree with similar others.
- The group leader is expected to be as close as possible to the group prototype. At the same time, a leader that meets this requirement will exert a strong influence on group members and will therefore be able to define and shape the group identity. Group members wanting to be leaders will devise strategies to present themselves as group prototypes, and actual leaders will devise strategies to persuade followers about the necessity of given actions. Aspirant leaders and actual leaders can therefore be seen as 'entrepreneurs of identity'.
- People like to feel valued and respected, but their desire is not unconditional. Individuals seek respect from ingroup members, but tend to remain indifferent to, or even be annoyed and embarrassed by, respect coming from an outgroup source, because this may disconfirm and weaken their desire to incarnate ingroup values and norms, and to be different from the outgroup.
- People are more inclined to help others when they are categorized as ingroup, rather than outgroup. On occasion people may be particularly helpful to outgroup members in order to enhance the image of the ingroup.

GROUP IDENTITY NORMS, DEVIANCE AND SCHISM

- Ingroup deviants are disliked and derogated more than outgroup members, because they threaten group unity and social identity. Sanctioning deviants is an opportunity for the majority to emphasize what is normative and what is counter-normative.
- Peripheral group members fear rejection and, as a consequence, employ strategies to increase their felt and perceived prototypicality. In particular, they may (1) increase conformity to ingroup standards, (2) vigorously derogate non-prototypical members and praise prototypical ones, and (3) publicly derogate outgroup members.
- The content of the group identity, as well as the degree of prototypicality of group members, is often debated and contested within a group. In some circumstances a minority may believe that the group as a whole has adopted norms that deny the group identity, and may not recognize the group leaders as truly prototypical. This may cause a schism, as the minority members may leave the group in order to join either a breakaway group or an already existing group.

SOCIAL IDENTITY MOTIVES

- There are several motives that lead people to identify with social groups. One is a motive for individual and collective self-esteem. Valuing our group positively is a source of self-esteem.
- Social identity marks out the differences between 'us' and 'them', between ingroup and outgroup. This enhances the feeling of distinctiveness.
- The need to belong is widely considered as a necessity and characteristic of *Homo sapiens*. Social identity provides a source of affiliation and inclusion, thereby satisfying the need for belonging.
- Death is probably the major psychological threat in human experience. As a consequence, humans strive to achieve symbolic immortality. A way to achieve symbolic immortality is through social identity, because groups – especially kin, national and ethnic ones – tend to be perceived as long-lasting and quasi-eternal entities.
- Groups prescribe people who they are and how they should behave. Groups also provide consensual validation for people's perceptions and beliefs. As such, they contribute to reduce uncertainty about self and social reality.

SOCIAL IDENTITY AND HEALTH

- As well as affecting our social behaviour and thoughts, social identity may impact upon our mental and physical health: this is known as the social cure.
- Social identity determines how severe a symptom is perceived to be. For instance, identifying with the group of 'older people' may increase one's sense of having hearing problems. Social identity may also influence the perceived seriousness of a symptom. A broken nose may raise greater worries among women identified with their gender group than among women identified with their professional group.
- Whether people engage or not in healthy behaviour will largely depend on group norms. If a given health behaviour is relevant to the norms of an ingroup (e.g. abstinence from drinking alcohol as a rule for members of a religious group), members of such ingroup are likely to comply with the behaviour. Compliance will be greater among members with strong levels of group identification.
- Group identification implies that social support received from a member of an ingroup is perceived as more genuine and disinterested, and produces more positive physiological outcomes, than support offered by a member of an outgroup. As a consequence, group identification may pave the way toward better mental and physical health.

- This knowledge has been applied to create the Groups4Health intervention, which encourages people to enhance their health and social connectivity by joining new groups and reconnecting with old ones.

THE DEVELOPMENT OF SOCIAL CATEGORIZATION AND SOCIAL IDENTITY

- To date, research has shown that children can label people in terms of their gender by the age of 3, and in terms of their ethnic group by the age of 4. Also, the criteria for the assignment of individuals to social categories appears to change across development. Younger children focus exclusively on physical and other external characteristics, while older children are able to point to belief systems as well.
- The development of self-categorization goes in parallel with that of social categorization. However, ethnic self-categorization may appear later in children from minority groups than in children from majority groups. The emergence of self-categorization is based on both cognitive factors (e.g. the appreciation that social categories may be immutable) and social factors (e.g. ingroup status, relevance of a given category-system in society).
- The ability to identify with a social category, understood as stereotyping the self in terms of the group norms, probably emerges before the age of 5. From the age of 5 children also show an ability to discuss and negotiate gender, race and other identities. However, it is probably not until 10 years of age that children fully appreciate the deep meaning and the wider social implications of their social identities.
- Very soon after the beginnings of self-categorization and the first manifestations of social identification, children become sensitive to issues of group typicality and deviance. At approximately 8 years of age children already tend to derogate ingroup counter-normative behaviour, as a means to protect ingroup distinctiveness and identity.

Critical Questions

1. Do you agree that in some circumstances we behave in terms of the norms of a relevant ingroup? Can you think of any example from your own experience?
2. How important is it, in your opinion, that a wanting-to-be group leader present him/herself as a prototypical representative of the group?
3. Why do mainstream group members see group deviants as a threat?
4. Why is the 'accentuation effect' so important?
5. Is any of the social identity motives discussed in this chapter more important than the others?
6. Might there be instances where group memberships could be bad for our health, rather than good for it?

Recommended Reading

Classic Studies

Tajfel, H. (1981). *Human groups and social categories: Studies in social psychology.* Cambridge University Press.

Turner, J. C., Hogg, M. A., Oakes, P. J., Reicher, S. D., & Wetherell, M. S. (1987). *Rediscovering the social group: A self-categorisation theory.* Basil Blackwell.

Contemporary Studies

Ellemers, N. (2012). The group self. *Science, 336,* 848–852.

Haslam, S. A. (2004). *Psychology in organizations: The social identity approach* (2nd ed.). Sage.

Haslam, S. A., O'Brien, A., Jetten, J., Vormedal, K., & Penna, S. (2005). Taking the strain: Social identity, social support, and the experience of stress. *British Journal of Social Psychology, 44,* 355–370.

Hornsey, M. J. (2008). Social identity theory and self-categorization theory: A historical review. *Social and Personality Psychology Compass, 2*(1), 204–222.

Leach, C. W., van Zomeren, M., Zebel, S., Vliek, M. L. W., Pennekamp, S. F., Doosje, B., & Spears, R. (2008). Group-level self-definition and self-investment: A hierarchical (multicomponent) model of in group identification. *Journal of Personality & Social Psychology, 95,* 144–165.

Wakefield, J. R., Bowe, M., Kellezi, B., McNamara, N., & Stevenson, C. (2019). When groups help and when groups harm: Origins, developments, and future directions of the 'social cure' perspective of group dynamics. *Social and Personality Psychology Compass, 13*(3), e12440.

13 PREJUDICE, INTERGROUP RELATIONS AND CONFLICT

'Why is it that people prefer to be addressed in groups, rather than individually?'
Soren Kierkegaard

Following the annual Apprentice Boys' march in August 1969 a three-day riot broke out in Derry between both sides of the city's sectarian divide. The rioting spread to many areas across Northern Ireland where the escalating violence caused serious injury and deaths. Tensions between Catholic nationalists and Protestant loyalists continued until the peace process began in 1998 and an end to the Troubles was reached in 2007. In May 1985, the Heysel Stadium disaster saw 39 Juventus football fans crushed to death when a fence separating them from the Liverpool fans collapsed during a football game after fighting broke out between the rival club supporters. All English football clubs were banned from all European competitions for five years. In Oldham, a small town in the north-west of England, some of the worst racially motivated riots seen in recent times occurred between 26 and 28 May 2001. In a town with an Asian population of 11 per cent, underlying interracial tensions between Whites and Asian-Muslims in the area exploded into riots. This sparked race riots in other northern areas of England. In May 2008, newspapers reported attacks on Mozambique citizens in South Africa, which had caused them to flee the country. In 2020, American members of the Black Lives Matter movement protested the deaths of numerous Black people by police officers.

prejudice a preconceived negative judgement of a group and its individual members

In our examples above, something they have in common is collective feelings of **prejudice**. Prejudice towards people of a different race or ethnicity. Prejudice towards people of a different religion. Prejudice towards people who support a different football team. Is what we're witnessing, then, simply a collection of highly prejudiced individuals who come together with malicious intent, or is there something about the relations between groups that shapes our behaviour in particular ways?

intergroup relations when two or more groups interact

The above are also examples of very negative intergroup relations. **Intergroup relations** are when two or more distinct groups interact. But of course relations between groups do not always involve violence and injury. We experience intergroup relations in our everyday lives. They include such things as political negotiations between parties, management and union talks, employer and employee relations, competitions between sports teams, international agreements between nations, and so on.

Social psychologists have a long-standing interest in intergroup relations as they affect our behaviour in profound ways. People often behave very differently when they're in a group than they would do on their own. You have probably experienced behaving differently when you're in an intergroup situation (e.g. a student protest) than you would do alone. So there seems to be something about intergroup relations that changes what we do and who we are. This chapter aims to explore the relationship between individuals, groups and prejudice, and explores social psychological suggestions for resolving intergroup conflict.

Understanding Prejudice

Prejudice is one of the major topics of interest in social psychology. Key questions include: how do we define prejudice? When do intergroup relations and conflict result in acts of prejudice? Do some people have prejudiced personalities? Is it possible for people to be implicitly prejudiced? What social conditions foster prejudice? Is prejudice inevitable or can it be reduced? These are challenges social psychologists try to meet in understanding the causes of prejudice.

What Is Prejudice?

To be prejudiced towards someone is to 'prejudge' them. Prejudice is an *attitude* about a group, or a member of a group based on their membership of it. In Chapter 5 on Attitudes and Behaviour we considered how an attitude is a distinct combination of feelings, inclinations to act, and beliefs. It can be easily remembered as the ABCs of attitudes: *a*ffect (feelings), *b*ehaviour tendency (inclination to act) and *c*ognition (beliefs). A prejudiced person may *dislike* those different from self and *behave* in a discriminatory manner, *believing* them to be ignorant and dangerous. Like many attitudes, prejudice is complex. For example, it may include a component of patronizing affection that serves to keep the victim disadvantaged.

Within social psychology the study of prejudice really came into being in the 1920s when the focus was on 'race' and 'racism'. In his classic book *The Nature of Prejudice*, Gordon Allport (1954) offered a famous definition of ethnic prejudice when he suggested it 'is ill thinking of others without sufficient warrant' (p. 6) and 'is an antipathy based on a faulty and inflexible generalization' (p. 9). Other groups face profound prejudice and discrimination too. For instance, overweight people may face slim prospects in modern Western societies when they seek employment or a romantic partner. In correlational studies conducted in the West, overweight people marry less often, gain entry into less desirable jobs, and make less money. In experiments where some people are made to appear overweight, they are perceived as less attractive, intelligent, happy, self-disciplined and successful (Gortmaker et al., 1993; Hebl & Heatherton, 1998; Pingitore et al., 1994). Weight discrimination seems to occur at every employment stage in Western and developed societies – hiring, placement, promotion, compensation, discipline and redundancy (Roehling, 2000).

Let's distinguish prejudice from discrimination. While *prejudice* is a negative *attitude*, **discrimination** is negative *behaviour*. Discriminatory behaviour often has its source in prejudicial attitudes (Dovidio et al., 1996). As Chapter 5 emphasized, however, attitudes and behaviour are often loosely linked. Prejudiced attitudes need not breed hostile acts, nor does all oppression spring from prejudice. **Racism** and **sexism** are institutional practices that discriminate, sometimes even when there is no prejudicial intent. If word-of-mouth hiring practices in an all-white business have the effect of excluding potential non-white employees, the practice could be called racist – even if an employer intended no discrimination.

discrimination unjustified negative behaviour towards a group or its members

racism (1) an individual's prejudicial attitudes and discriminatory behaviour towards people of a given race, or (2) institutional practices (even if not motivated by prejudice) that subordinate people of a given race

sexism (1) an individual's prejudicial attitudes and discriminatory behaviour towards people of a given sex, or (2) institutional practices (even if not motivated by prejudice) that subordinate people of a given sex

Prejudice pervades all areas of social life, but some people seem to express prejudice towards certain groups regardless of the situation. Their acts of prejudice are severe. Do some people have prejudiced personalities?

Explanations for Prejudice

The Prejudiced Personality

After the events of the Second World War, social psychologists began to ask some searching questions about the nature of prejudice. The kinds of questions they asked were:

- Why are some people drawn to fascist ideologies and practices while others are not?
- Why are some people extremely prejudiced and racist?
- Why do some people carry out unspeakable acts of racism and prejudice, or obey orders from other people to do so?

In the 1940s, University of California, Berkeley researchers – two of whom had fled Nazi Germany – set out on an urgent research mission: to uncover the psychological roots of an anti-Semitism so poisonous that it caused the slaughter of millions of Jews, and turned many millions of Europeans into indifferent spectators. Else Frenkel-Brunswik, Daniel Levinson and Nevitt Sanford were psychologists involved in personality research from a Freudian perspective. Theodor Adorno provided a political and sociological perspective. Together, they wrote their most famous book, *The Authoritarian Personality* (1950, abridged version reprinted 1982). Although his name heads the alphabetical list of authors, Adorno made a relatively small contribution. His name is credited in only 5 of the 23 chapters in the book.

The Berkeley researchers discovered that hostility towards Jews often coexisted with hostility towards other minorities. In those who were strongly prejudiced, prejudice appeared to not be specific to one group, but reflected an entire way of thinking about those who are 'different'. Moreover, these judgemental, **ethnocentric** people shared certain tendencies with each other: an intolerance for weakness, a punitive attitude and a submissive respect for their ingroup's authorities, as reflected in their agreement with such statements as 'Obedience and respect for authority are the most important virtues children should learn'. From those findings, Adorno et al. (1950) theorized an **authoritarian personality** that is particularly prone to engage in prejudice and stereotyping.

ethnocentric believing in the superiority of one's own ethnic and cultural group, and having a corresponding disdain for all other groups

authoritarian personality a personality that is disposed to favour obedience to authority and intolerance for outgroups and those of lower status

They did not regard the cause of prejudice as a consequence of social conditions (e.g. conforming to a particular ideology), but instead argued that it was rooted within the individual's personality. A particular personality type was predisposed to prejudice. The authoritarian personality was characterized by the possession of particular traits, including:

- high levels of prejudice towards minority groups
- the holding of positive sentiments about authority, and being submissive to those considered to hold authority over oneself
- very harsh behaviour towards those considered inferior to oneself
- a strong belief in power, dominance and discipline
- an obsession with rank and status
- an inability to tolerate ambiguity or uncertainty, and the need for a rigidly defined world
- have problems achieving intimacy, yet may have a preoccupation with sex
- a tendency to displace anger and resentment onto weaker others
- a high level of superstitious belief.

The original authoritarian personality research was based on what the authors hoped was as diverse a sample as possible: 2,000 adult white Californians. They were all given questionnaires that measured their attitudes towards prejudice, anti-Semitism, ethnocentrism (racism), political preferences, economic conservatism and fascism. This became known as the F-Scale, which measured the strength of a person's anti-democratic personality. The hypothesis was that the factors contained within the F-Scale would correlate highly for those people who have a prejudiced personality. Or, in other words, people who are highly prejudiced are also politically right-wing or 'conventionalists' and highly authoritarian. The F-Scale contains 77 items in total. Here are a few examples.

- If people would talk less and work more, everybody would be better off.
- Some day it will probably be shown that astrology can explain a lot of things.
- Sex crimes, such as rape and attacks on children, deserve more than mere imprisonment; such criminals ought to be publicly whipped, or worse.
- Homosexuals are hardly better than criminals and ought to be severely punished.
- No insult to our honour should ever go unpunished.
- No matter how they act on the surface, men are interested in women for only one reason.
- Nobody ever learned anything really important except through suffering (taken from Adorno et al., 1982, pp. 184–186).

Adorno and his colleagues argued that people who agreed with the above items were displaying an authoritarian personality. But how did this personality arise? To find out, they conducted clinical interviews with some of the participants to gain more factual material on their responses from the questionnaire, but also to allow them freedom to express what they felt about their own situation and their relationships with others. The schedule for these interviews included questions on their childhood, sex, politics, education and social relationships. One of the most cited findings of these interviews and questionnaires is consistently reported experiences of being dominated by excessively stern disciplinarian parents. Adopting a psychoanalytic stance, Adorno and his colleagues argued that while the child must repress his/her hostility towards their overpowering parents, they project it onto apparently weaker others. The researchers proposed that these 'others' were typically ethnic minority groups that are often marginalized within society. These groups were perceived as dangerous elements within the world, which thus needed to be disciplined and controlled. An authoritarian personality seemed to be the result of this strict upbringing.

Sigmund Freud's (1856–1939) work on psychoanalysis influenced Adorno's understanding of the nature of prejudice.
SOURCE: ©Everett Historical/ Shutterstock

Although you might think recollections of childhood experiences with strict parents might be characterized by feelings of hatred, when individuals were interviewed about their upbringing they usually offered glorified accounts of their parents. However, these accounts tended to be based on their physical appearance rather than their personalities. Other patterns were apparent too. Highly prejudiced women gave stories of being victimized by their parents, including being unjustly punished and picked on. Highly prejudiced men tended to display the highest levels of submission to parental authority and often magnified the status of their family.

Since this original study took place, some distinct problems have been found with the F-Scale. The scale item wording is quite leading, and it is scored in such a way that people's tendency to agree to items would produce artificial correlations. Some social psychologists have raised the point that if researchers know what the experimental hypotheses are when they set out to do the research, they may well interpret the data in a way that supports them. In other words, they find what they set out to find: a phenomenon known as **confirmation bias**. Also, as the authors themselves admit, while the sample is representative of 'non-Jewish, white, native-born, middle-class Americans' (Adorno et al., 1982, p. 23), it is difficult to generalize beyond that. In addition, how accurate are adults' recollections of their childhood?

confirmation bias a tendency to search for information that confirms one's preconceptions, rather than considering opposing information

Prejudiced Thinking

Rokeach (1960) agreed with the concept of a prejudiced personality, but wondered if it was more to do with a particular rigid style of thinking. Dogmatic and closed-minded thinking meant that such people were resistant to change their beliefs even in the light of new information. See **Figure 13.1** for an example of one of Rokeach's tests for dogmatic and closed-minded thinking.

Despite these misgivings about the F-Scale, many subsequent studies have shown that people who do have authoritarian sentiments also tend to have other things in common, such as right-wing political ideas, idealization of parents, strong beliefs in strict parenting and a submissive acceptance of authority. The F-Scale has been subject to revisions in recent years and continues to be used in social psychology to measure levels of authoritarianism.

Groups tend to enhance the pre-existing tendencies of members. See more extensive treatment of group polarization in Chapter 11, with specific reference to its impact in and on groups.

One major problem with these personality explanations of prejudice is that they tend to under-emphasize situational and cultural influences. The environment in which people live shapes their attitudes and behaviour and, as research has found, their prejudices.

For example, Siegel and Siegel (1957) conducted a field experiment on two groups of American students. While one group lived in housing that was positioned in a 'conservative' area, others resided in housing that was in an area characterized by more liberal attitudes. Levels of authoritarianism were recorded over 12 months using the F-Scale. Increases in levels of authoritarianism were observed in the group in the conservative housing over the 12 months, whereas those in the liberal housing decreased. Siegel and Siegel argue this demonstrates the impact our surroundings have on prejudiced attitudes. But an alternative explanation for these findings, however, might be that they reflect the phenomenon of 'group polarization'.

Clearly there's more to prejudice than just parental practices, so let's turn our attention to some explanations of prejudice that examine the influence of the situation and social environment or context.

social dominance orientation a motivation to have one's group dominate other social groups

In what way are any or all of the following concepts interrelated?

Buddhism, Capitalism, Catholicism, Christianity, Communism, Democracy, Fascism, Judaism, Protestantism, Socialism

FIGURE 13.1 An example of one of the tests Rokeach devised to illustrate the relationship between cognitive style and prejudice. He suggested that a flexible thinker would notice that all the concepts are related as they define a set of beliefs or worldviews. A more rigid thinker might group the religions separately from the political beliefs.

The Social Context of Prejudice

Social Dominance Theory

Social dominance theory (SDT) assumes that some social groups are positioned higher in society than others, and as a result have access to more power and resources, and are valued more positively than those lower down. How people respond to this social hierarchy depends on their social dominance orientation. Studies based on SDT, in cultures where equality is the norm, predict that those high in **social dominance orientation** will have a preoccupation with ensuring their own social group's high status and will seek to achieve high-status professional careers. Pratto et al. (1994) argue that this desire to be on top can result in prejudiced attitudes and behaviour as people at the top seek to maintain an unequal status quo, supporting practices that maintain the current ideological climate that keeps them there. The authors argue that this desire to be on top can result in prejudiced attitudes and behaviour, as people at the top seek to maintain an unequal status quo, supporting practices that maintain the current ideological climate that keeps them there.

In some cultures, for instance East Asia, social hierarchies have a long tradition and are more accepted than in the West. Everybody has their place on the social ladder, and it is regarded as natural that some people are leaders who hold dominant positions and are obeyed by those occupying lower rungs of the ladder. Hofstede (1980) characterized such societies as those with a large power distance. In most European societies and the USA, the power distance is much less, and the goal is for equal rights among citizens.

Particularly striking are people high in social dominance orientation and authoritarian personality. For example, Stones (2006) found that anti-gay prejudice was predicted in men who were high in right-wing authoritarianism and social-dominance orientation. Carter et al. (2006) observed that people who held authoritarian attitudes and were high in social dominance were much more likely to rely on stereotypical information about other social and cultural groups.

Although right-wing authoritarianism and social dominance seem to be important features in prejudice, identifying as belonging to a social group is also significant. For example, Nickerson and Louis (2008) reported that attitudes towards asylum seekers in Australia are predicted by right-wing authoritarianism, social dominance and social identification as Australian. Those who perceived themselves as Australian expressed much less welcoming attitudes to asylum seekers than those who self-identified as human.

Terror Management Theory

Terror management theory (TMT) asserts that human beings are painfully aware of their own mortality, and this remains an anxiety throughout life. We are the only species that know one day we will die. However, being a member of a culture serves as a buffer to such stress as it makes people feel as though they are valuable and meaningful contributors to a society, increasing their sense of positive self-esteem (also see Chapter 12 for further discussion of TMT). The work of Rosenblatt et al. (1989) has proposed that culture provides a sense of protection to individuals, giving them a sense of a 'just world' (recall Lerner's just world hypothesis from Chapter 4) and immortality through their contribution to a cultural community. Terror management theory claims that 'people will respond positively to those who bolster their cultural-anxiety-buffers and negatively to those who threaten their cultural-anxiety-buffers' (Rosenblatt et al., 1989, p. 682). For example, Greenberg and colleagues (1990) found that when participants' Christian religious background was made salient, they gave very positive evaluations of other Christians and negative evaluations of Jews. Perhaps this is unsurprising, but what they also found was very strong positive reactions to someone who praised their cultural worldview, and extremely negative reactions to those who opposed it. Interestingly, but perhaps not surprisingly, participants with high levels of authoritarianism were also very negative towards those whose attitudes were dissimilar to their own.

In study after study, thinking about your own mortality – by writing a short essay on dying and the emotions aroused by thinking about death – provokes enough insecurity to intensify ingroup favouritism and outgroup prejudice (Greenberg et al., 1990). One study found that, among whites in the West, thinking about death can even promote liking for racists who argue for white superiority. With death on their minds, people exhibit **terror management**. They shield themselves from the threat of their own death by derogating those who challenge their worldviews (and thus further arouse their anxiety). When people are already feeling vulnerable about their mortality, prejudice helps them to bolster a threatened belief system. Thinking about death can also, however, lead people to pursue communal feelings and behaviours, such as togetherness and altruism (McGregor et al., 2001).

terror management according to 'terror management theory', people are motivated to subdue the terror stemming from human awareness of mortality. Based on the notion that people would be restricted by the fear of their own death if they could not 'deal with this', the theory suggests that people adhere more strongly to their cultural worldviews and beliefs, and subscribe self-esteem from these, to suppress death-related thoughts

As we touched on in Chapter 12, reminding people of their death can also affect support for important public policies. Before the 2004 US presidential election, giving people cues related to death – including asking them to recall their emotions related to the 9/11 attack or subliminally exposing them to 9/11-related pictures – increased support for President George W. Bush Jr and his anti-terrorism policies (Landau et al., 2004). In Iran, reminders of death increased college students' support for suicide attacks against the USA (Pyszczynski et al., 2006).

An Arizona State University research team argues that the nature of an outgroup threat influences perceptions of the outgroup (Cottrell & Neuberg, 2005; Maner et al., 2005). For example, when the safety of one's ingroup is threatened, people will be vigilant for signs of outgroup anger. When the researchers activated self-protection concerns (for example, by having participants view scary movie clips), they found that white people perceived greater anger in African American male and Arab faces.

Despised outgroups can also serve to strengthen the ingroup. The perception of a common enemy unites a group. School spirit is seldom so strong as when the football game is with the arch-rival. The sense of comradeship among workers is often highest when they all feel a common antagonism towards management. When the need to belong is met, people become more accepting of outgroups, report Mikulincer and Shaver (2001). They subliminally primed some Israeli students with words that fostered a sense of belonging (*love, support, hug*) and primed others with neutral words. The students then read an essay that was supposedly written by a fellow Jewish student, and another essay supposedly written by an Arab student. When primed with neutral words, the Israeli students evaluated the supposed Israeli student's essay as superior to the supposed Arab student's essay. When the participants were primed with a sense of belonging, that bias disappeared.

However, TMT tends to assume that all humans are motivated to avoid thinking about their own death. Thinking about death in this way tends to be more prevalent in independent and individualistic cultures with low population density than in interdependent and collectivistic cultures with high population density. In independent cultures each individual's focus is more on him/herself as being someone unique and essential, whereas in interdependent and collectivistic cultures where people do not stand out and instead surrender to the family, kin or nation, each individual accepts death as an inevitable part of the group's development. Furthermore, we cannot assume what 'cultural' values or norms an individual will identify with and conform to. For example, Jessop and Wade (2008) found that making binge-drinkers and non-binge drinkers aware of the mortality risks of drinking actually increased binge-drinking in both samples! The authors found that participants drank more in order to bolster their self-esteem after it was threatened by the mortality prime. Participants were thus conforming to cultural norms other than those desired by the researchers. Jonas et al. (2008) also note that cultures differ widely from one another, offering contradictory norms for behaviour. To understand how (or if) threats to mortality will influence behaviour, we need to examine the cultural norms that the group or individual is attending to at the time.

Prejudice and Stereotyping

Chapter 12 discussed how stereotypes form as simplified representations of social groups. Many social psychologists have argued that these mental representations have a strong link to prejudice. The negative evaluations that mark prejudice are often supported by negative stereotypes. As we've already noted, to stereotype is to generalize. To simplify the world, we generalize: the British are reserved; Americans are outgoing; professors are absent-minded. Here are some widely shared stereotypes uncovered in recent research:

- During the 1980s, women who assumed the title of 'Ms' were seen as more assertive and ambitious than those who called themselves 'Miss' or 'Mrs' (Dion, 1987; Dion & Cota, 1991; Dion & Schuller, 1991). Now that 'Ms' is the standard female title, the stereotype has shifted. It's married women who keep their own surnames that are seen as assertive and ambitious (Crawford et al., 1998; Etaugh et al., 1999).
- Public opinion surveys reveal that Europeans have definite ideas about other Europeans. They see the Germans as relatively hard-working, the French as pleasure-loving, the British as cool and unexcitable, the Italians as amorous and the Dutch as reliable (one expects these findings to be reliable, considering that they come from Willem Koomen and Michiel Bähler, 1996, at the University of Amsterdam).
- Europeans also view southern Europeans as more emotional and less efficient than northern Europeans (Linssen & Hagendoorn, 1994). The stereotype of the southerner as more expressive even holds within countries: Pennebaker et al. (1996) report that across 20 northern hemisphere countries (but not in six southern hemisphere countries), southerners within a country are perceived as more expressive than northerners.

Familiar stereotypes:

'Heaven is a place with an American house, Chinese food, British police, a German car, and French art. Hell is a place with a Japanese house, Chinese police, British food, German art, and a French car.'

Anonymous, as reported by Yueh-Ting Lee (Bower, 1996)

Such generalizations can be more or less true (and are not always negative). Teachers' stereotypes of achievement differences in students from different gender, ethnic and class backgrounds tend to mirror reality (Madon et al., 1998).

Basking in reflected glory. Mesut Özil, a German footballer with Turkish heritage who played for Germany in the 2018 FIFA World Cup, noted how the German media described him as a fellow German as the excitement of a potential German victory grew before the tournament, but described him as a Turkish immigrant after Germany did badly in the tournament.
SOURCE: ©MDI/Shutterstock

'Stereotypes', note Jussim et al. (1995), 'may be positive or negative, accurate or inaccurate.' An accurate stereotype may even be desirable. We call it 'sensitivity to diversity' or 'cultural awareness in a multicultural world'. To stereotype the British as more concerned about punctuality than Mexicans is to understand what to expect and how to get along with people from each culture.

Zanna (1993) suggests that prejudice arises as a consequence of holding negative stereotypes about a group, but also when we feel a group has blocked our own group's access to a valued goal or contradicts our 'norms' and 'values'. Prejudice may also be caused by having negative past experiences with members of a group, or arises as a consequence of having negative feelings towards a group. Devine (1989) argues that stereotyping is an inevitable consequence of cognition and directly linked to prejudice. She notes the example of white Americans, who have been exposed to a racist culture that denigrates African Americans. Through such conditioning, white Americans hold negative stereotypes of African Americans.

Stereotyping of social groups has also been shown to affect how we 'see' them. Fiske (1998) found that prejudice biases the way people perceive the facial appearance of outgroup members. In a study that examined how Moroccan faces were seen by participants in the Netherlands, she found that the negative stereotyped traits participants held of Moroccans as being criminal were perceived as actually being visible in their faces.

meta-stereotype the stereotype that we believe a specific outgroup holds about our ingroup

Stereotypes do not just affect how we see outgroups but also how we perceive ourselves. **Meta-stereotypes** are the stereotypes we believe a specific outgroup holds about our ingroup, and are often perceived by ingroup members as unfair and unwarranted. Meta-stereotypes (regardless of whether or not they are accurate depictions of how the outgroup in question actually stereotypes the ingroup) can affect ingroup members' perceptions of, and interactions with, the outgroup. Vorauer et al. (1998; Vorauer & Sakamoto, 2008) found that white Canadians' perceptions of being negatively stereotyped by Aboriginal Canadians led to negative emotions about intergroup interaction and decreases in self-esteem. Moreover, highly prejudiced white Canadians felt stereotyped by Aboriginal Canadians even when they were not, and this affected their subsequent interactions with them. Ingroup members may also attempt to challenge the veracity of meta-stereotypes through their behaviour, such as by being helpful when they believe that the outgroup stereotypes them as mean (Hopkins et al., 2007), or refusing to ask for needed help when they believe that the outgroup stereotypes them as dependent (Wakefield et al., 2012).

How else might we go about challenging stereotypes and the discrimination that may result from them? Devine (1989) argues that only deliberate and conscious acts intended to break the habit of prejudice will stop stereotype-related discrimination. More specifically, Gawronski et al. (2008) have found that negative stereotypes can be inhibited if participants are given training in affirming positive counter-stereotypes of social groups. Interestingly, they found that participants who are given training in order to help them disconfirm negative stereotypes actually experienced *enhanced* activation of those stereotypes.

Social Identity Theory and Self-categorization Theory

In Chapter 12 we outlined the processes of categorization, identification with social groups, social comparison and stereotyping as fundamental features of SIT and SCT. Both theories point out that individuals are motivated to seek positive identity from their group memberships. Time after time, studies show that people highlight their connection with someone successful with whom they share a common identity. More interesting is that this process can occur even when the person has had no involvement in the successful individual's success. This phenomenon of **basking in reflected glory** (BIRG) has been most prominently investigated in relation to football fans and their association with the team they support. Boen et al. (2002) showed that football supporters sought private contact with their team's players when the team had won. Cialdini et al. (1976) noted changes in students' language when their school football team won. Suddenly 'we' had won, rather than just the team! Furthermore, students wore more school-identifying clothes when the team had won as opposed to when it had lost. BIRGing isn't just limited to football support, but has been observed in people's friendships with socially popular others. Dijkstra et al. (2010) found that people who associated with popular peers did so to achieve high status and popularity for themselves by basking in their reflected glory. The flip-side of BIRGing, **cutting off reflected failure** (CORF) has also been identified, as individuals try to distance themselves from unsuccessful individuals they would normally associate with. Boen and his team found fans of unsuccessful teams did not seek out contact with team players when they lost a match. Miller (2009) discovered that after a US presidential campaign, signs in gardens and windows endorsing the successful Democrat candidate, Barack Obama, were displayed much longer than those supporting the Republican candidate, John McCain. So BIRGing and CORFing seem to be forms of impression management as we strive to maintain our positive identity. However, it seems that self-esteem is also involved, as those who are high in self-esteem seem to be less prone to CORFing than those with low self-esteem (Cialdini et al., 1976; Miller, 2009).

basking in reflected glory (BIRG) to associate with a successful individual or group, despite having no direct involvement in their success

cutting off reflected failure (CORF) to distance self from an individual or group you would usually identify with, when that individual or group fails

Because of our social identifications, we conform to group norms (see Chapter 11). We sacrifice ourselves for team, family and even our nation. And the more important our social identity and the more strongly attached we feel to a group, the more we react prejudicially to threats from another group (Crocker & Luhtanen, 1990; Hinkle et al., 1996). Israeli historian and former Jerusalem deputy mayor Benvenisti (1988) reported that among Jerusalem's Jews and Arabs, social identity has been so central to self-concept that it constantly reminds them of who they are not. Thus, on the integrated street where he lived, his own children – to his dismay – 'have not acquired a single Arab friend'.

However, these processes of ingroup identification and ingroup bias do not necessarily translate into prejudice against others: they are about achieving positive intergroup differentiation rather than outgroup derogation. So positive feelings towards our own groups need not be mirrored by equally strong negative feelings for outgroups. Where prejudice may occur is when intergroup comparison threatens the ingroup's positive identity. When such threats are regarded as illegitimate acts on the part of low-status outgroups to challenge the position of the higher-status ingroup, and group boundaries are perceived to be **impermeable**, intergroup prejudice is likely. For example, the migration of Polish workers into

impermeable when a group cannot be exited by ingroup members or entered by outgroup members. The opposite is permeable the British labour market has led to explicit and implicit prejudice aimed at the Polish outgroup. Such intergroup prejudice is based on perceptions of threat felt by some British workers in terms of their competence to carry out jobs given to Polish workers, as well as the competition for work. To understand prejudice, we need some understanding of the concerns of group members, and the social context in which groups and the relationships between them are understood.

Prejudiced attitudes towards other groups not only influence how we behave towards them, but also shape the way we judge their behaviour. An example of how we may attribute guilt based on stereotypes of social group membership is provided by Dixon et al. (2002). They found that White British participants thought a suspect was more likely to be guilty of a crime when he had a Birmingham accent (rather than standard pronunciation), was presented as Black (rather than White) and was accused of the blue-collar crime of armed robbery (rather than the white-collar crime of cheque fraud). You can imagine how such prejudiced attitudes might have real-world consequences for the groups involved.

You may remember that in Chapter 4 we considered the fundamental attribution error: we attribute so much of other people's behaviour to their inner dispositions that we discount important situational forces. The error occurs partly because our attention focuses on the person, not the situation. A person's ethnicity, race or sex gets vivid attention; the situational forces working upon that person are less visible. Until recently, because gender-role constraints were hard to see, we attributed men and women's behaviour solely to their innate dispositions. Pettigrew's (1979) concept of the ultimate attribution error (UAE) proposes that groups account for ingroup members' behaviour in fundamentally different ways than they do the behaviour of other groups, especially when there is a history of conflict and tension between them. Positive behaviour by outgroup members is more often dismissed. It may be seen as a 'special case' ('He is certainly bright and hardworking – not at all like other . . .'), as owing to luck or some special advantage ('She probably passed her driving test because the test centre needed to fill its quota of female drivers'), as demanded by the situation ('Under the circumstances the mean Scot had to pay the bill'), or as attributable to extra effort ('Asian students get better grades because they're so compulsive'). Disadvantaged groups and groups that stress modesty (such as the Chinese) exhibit less of this **group-serving bias** (Fletcher & Ward, 1989; Heine & Lehman, 1997; Jackson et al., 1993).

group-serving bias explaining away outgroup members' positive behaviours; also attributing negative behaviours to their dispositions (while excusing such behaviour by one's own group)

Such attributions often serve to apparently warrant the stereotypes held about groups. A classic example comes from Taylor and Jaggi (1974), who found that Hindus in India explained the positive and negative behaviour of other Hindus and Muslims in ways predicted by the UAE.

The group-serving bias can subtly colour our language. A team of University of Padua (Italy) researchers led by Anne Maass (Maass, 1999; Maass et al., 1995) has found that positive behaviours by another ingroup member are often described as being evidence of general dispositions (for example, 'Karen is helpful'). When performed by an outgroup member, the same behaviour is often described as a specific, isolated act ('Carmen opened the door for the man with the cane'). With negative behaviour, the specificity reverses: 'Eric shoved her' (an isolated act by an ingroup member) but 'Enrique was aggressive' (an outgroup member's general disposition). Maass calls this group-serving bias the *linguistic intergroup bias*

(LIB). Furthermore, this effect is greater when a group is threatened by another, as Maass et al. (1996) discovered. Studying opposed groups of hunters and environmentalists in northern Italy, the researchers found that when hunters were presented with hostile messages about them from the environmentalists, the LIB effect was stronger than when they received positive messages from this group. The same effect was found when environmentalists were presented with either negative or positive messages about themselves from the hunters. The LIB effect has also been associated with implicit prejudice. Von Hippel et al. (1997) reported those Caucasian participants who displayed implicit prejudice towards African Americans by means of an IAT (implicit association test) reflected this bias in their linguistic reactions to the group. For bi- and multicultural individuals, it seems that they can reflect their identification with whichever culture is most salient to them at the time, by means of the LIB. Hsu (2011) found that bicultural Asian American participants were able to switch their language to higher or lower abstraction towards ethnic Asians or European Americans, depending on which culture they were primed with, and their identification with that group at the time. It seems that this ability to describe your talk about members of your own group in abstract positive ways, and dismiss ingroup members' negative incidents in isolated terms, is a marker of being a good group member (Assilaméhou & Testé, 2013).

IAT (implicit association test) is covered later in this chapter with regard to prejudice and also in Chapter 5 with regard to attitudes; these sections help provide a more comprehensive overview of this measure.

However, intergroup attributions are not simply a matter of ingroup favouritism as suggested by Pettigrew, but tend to reflect wider societal norms and values. Hewstone and Ward (1985) replicated Taylor and Jaggi's study in Malaysia, and found that while Malay participants explained their own behaviour and that of the Chinese in ways predicted by the UAE, the Chinese participants also favoured the Malays, displaying outgroup favouritism. The researchers argue that this reflects the perceived legitimate lower social status of the Chinese in Malaysian society.

The important point is that prejudiced attitudes can affect group attributions. Hegarty and Golden (2008) found that participants who held prejudiced attitudes about stigmatized groups, such as gay men, lesbians and alcoholics, gave attributions for their behaviour that supported their prejudices and maintained their undesirable group position.

Prejudice and discrimination depend on the social climate and how acceptable it is to express prejudice within a society. It seems as if tolerance for derogatory utterances and discrimination is higher in some time periods than others. As such, some social psychologists have looked at how prejudice is produced in language, and what this tells us about the social context in which it occurs.

The Language of Prejudice

Discursive Psychology and Prejudice

Discursive psychologists have focused on prejudiced language. You may recall from Chapter 5 that discursive psychologists propose that attitudes are evaluations made in discourse rather than underlying mental entities that drive behaviour. This has consequences for how they study prejudice. Not as an attitude, but as language.

Categorization as a Discursive Process

The social identity approach (SIT and SCT) assumes the cognitive process of categorization is crucial in explaining prejudice. Discursive psychologists challenge this, arguing instead that social groups, their meaning, membership and differences between them, are produced in language. So instead of trying to uncover the inner cognitive motives that drive the expression of prejudice, discursive theorists treat its expression in language as the act of prejudice itself.

One of the forerunners of this model of prejudice is Michael Billig, based on his early work with Henri Tajfel. Billig (1985) points out that for us to categorize the social world, we must also be able to particularize it so that instances can be placed into a category. We must also be able to make judgements about which category, or social group, to use under a certain set of circumstances. So are we just bureaucrats doomed to an eternity of categorizing the world in the same way, forever filing papers into the same folders, or are we creative about how we organize our filing cabinet? Sometimes, we may not categorize at all. Billig argues that we are more creative than cognitive explanations of prejudice suggest. We often treat people as individuals rather than members of social groups, perhaps even arguing against their inclusion into a social group. This creativity, or flexibility in categorization and particularization, is a feature of language. We have available to us an infinite number of ways of describing the world. How we do it depends on what we're trying to do at a particular time. We have equal capacity to be prejudiced or tolerant in our language and in our thinking.

The Ideology of Prejudice

Billig notes that Tajfel never applied his own social identity theory to the event that concerned him the most – his experiences as a European Jew during the Holocaust. Perhaps Tajfel couldn't explain away the Holocaust as a simple process of categorization. Did Germans really murder Jews simply to enhance their ingroup self-esteem? Does depersonalization of people into a common outgroup really mean the same as their dehumanization? Tajfel recognized the role of ideology in how social groups were perceived, but had little clue on how this might be analysed. There is clearly a difference between prejudice and bigotry. Stereotypes of Germans who reserve the sun-loungers with their beach towels are hardly comparable with Nazi German stereotypes of Jews as parasites who deserve to be killed. Billig suggests we need to understand the ideological assumptions produced in the language of prejudice and hatred and the point at which prejudice develops into bigotry and murder.

Reicher and Hopkins (2001) call this the 'politics of category construction'. How social groups are understood discursively can justify discriminatory practices that disadvantage particular groups. For example, Every and Augoustinos (2008) observe that asylum seekers in Australia are commonly referred to as 'illegal immigrants' by the media and government. This supports government policies that continue to marginalize and disadvantage asylum seekers in Australia by presenting them as deviant and criminal. In their study of interviews with White South Africans post-apartheid, Durrheim and Dixon (2001) found they still portrayed Blacks as polluting the beaches with their uncivil behaviour. The researchers examined how this is reflected in Whites and Blacks continuing to engage in racial segregation by populating different areas of beaches.

Ideology also influences the way we talk about sexuality. In Korobov's (2004) interviews with heterosexual men, he found that they were often caught on the horns of an ideological dilemma. On the one hand, they do not want to appear homophobic or prejudiced, yet on the other, they wish to preserve traditional forms of masculinity that promote heterosexuality and debunk political correctness.

The 'Taboo' of Prejudice

The studies we've just described use qualitative methods. Bonilla-Silva and Forman (2000) argue prejudiced views are captured in interviews and focus groups in ways that survey methods would miss. Ask someone directly if they are prejudiced or racist and they will probably tell you 'No'. Why? Participants are concerned with social desirability, wanting to appear tolerant and unprejudiced. So how much can we rely on questionnaires and surveys to find out about prejudice (see Chapter 2 for a discussion on methods)?

Augoustinos and Every (2007a, 2007b) point to agreement across most social scientific disciplines that explicit forms of prejudice and 'old-fashioned racism' are taboo. But we should be wary of assuming this means people are now less prejudiced than they used to be. Barker (1981) proposes that explicit forms of racism ('**old racism**') have been replaced with '**new racism**'. Openly expressing racist or ethnocentric sentiments is taboo, but subtle prejudice or racism can work to present the speaker (or writer) as 'reasonable' while at the same time enabling him/her to engage in prejudice.

old racism explicit, blatant forms and practices of racism

new racism implicit, subtle often disguised forms and practices of racism

Of course, one strategy to avoid a charge of being prejudiced is to deny it. Van Dijk (1992, 1993) notes how people often use disclaimers such as: 'I'm not racist but . . .', and 'I'm not sexist but . . .'. This overt expression of cultural tolerance inoculates against the prejudiced remark which follows it.

Edwards (2003) suggests people 'do' prejudice by describing 'them' in ways that justify the negative views held of them. Consider the example below that comes from the work of Cristian Tileaga:

382	*Chris*	*To what extent do you think Romanies are to blame for these*
383		*conflicts and violences?*
384	*Sandra*	*Cos' they don't (.) cos' they don't work (.) they don't*
385		*like to work (.) They are not happy with (.)*
386	*Chris*	*How would you characterize them?*
387	*Sandra*	*Unadaptable (.) these ones are unadaptable (.) they cannot integrate*
388		*in (.) in fact, even in the other countries (.) have their gypsies*
389		*adapted? (.) No (.) Only that, it is the Romanians gypsies that*
390		*Europe talks about, you have just these ones (.) it is only our*
391		*gypsies that are the biggest thieves and bandits who strike (.) But*
392		*Romanians have tried to integrate them, we made them schools (.)*
393		*they have tv shows in the gypsy (.) language*

(taken from Tileaga, 2006, p. 27)

Sandra and Chris characterize the behaviour of 'the Romanies' in ways that are used to justify their prejudice against Romany people.

deracialization the justification of the racial marginalization of groups on the basis of non-racial features

A common finding in discursive work is that people can justify racial prejudice towards other groups on non-racial grounds. Reeves (1983) calls this **deracialization**. Augoustinos et al. (1999) noted how racist comments directed at indigenous Australians were considered to be 'justifiable anger' on the basis that such groups received privileges from the government owing to their minority-group status. Figgou and Condor (2006) observed how Greek participants justified their prejudice against Albanian immigrants on the basis of their belief that the immigrants posed a risk to the Greeks, leading to feelings of fear.

Minority groups can be presented in both positive and negative terms. Lynn and Lea (2003) examined media representations of asylum seekers in Britain as being either 'genuine' or 'bogus'. While 'we' will be hospitable to the 'genuine' ones, 'we' shall not be tolerant to the 'bogus' ones.

Jokes and humour may be used to disguise the seriousness of a prejudiced remark (Guerin, 2003). Billig (2001) reports the use of jokes and humour to minimize the seriousness of extremely racist discourse on the Internet websites of the Ku Klux Klan. On the other hand, Dobai and Hopkins (2019) showed how minority group members may use humour as a way to negotiate interactions with prejudiced members of the majority group.

But who determines what is prejudiced? Edwards (2003) warns that social psychologists should try to refrain from imposing their own judgements and instead listen to what their participants regard as prejudiced language. For example, Condor et al. (2006) found that when people do recognize prejudice or racism in conversation, they may try to protect the 'face' of those who produced it. Consider an extract from her work:

1	*Jack*	*[. . .] let's face it, it's not as if they're wanted here. We have enough low-*
2		*life here already without importing [other people's.*
3	*Hilda*	*[Jack! ((to Susan)) I'm sorry about*
4		*that. He's not xenophobic. It's it' not=*
5	*Jack*	*=it's not racist, no. We've never been racist, have we Hilda?*
6	*Hilda*	*No. We've got nothing against=*
7	*Jack*	*=nothing against the refugees. I have every sympathy for them. But*
8		*you'd be mad not to ask, why are they all coming here?*

(taken from Condor et al., 2006, p. 452)

Language does not have to be blatantly racist for it to discriminate and oppress others.

Subtle and Implicit Prejudice

Discursive theorists alert us to how prejudice might be communicated subtly through language. Aware of the social taboo of prejudice, people develop strategies for concealing prejudiced remarks. But are people sometimes simply unaware of their prejudices? How do we measure prejudice that people are unaware of, or do so in a way that doesn't cause participants to behave in a socially desirable manner? Social psychologists have developed methods for measuring subtle and implicit prejudice.

Let's look at some used to measure racial and ethnic prejudice.

Racial and Ethnic Prejudice

In the context of the world, every race and ethnic group is a minority. Non-Hispanic Whites, for example, are only one-fifth of the world's people and will be one-eighth within another half-century. Thanks to mobility and migration over the past two centuries, the world's races and ethnic groups now intermingle, in relations that are sometimes hostile, sometimes amiable.

To a molecular biologist, skin colour is a trivial human characteristic, one controlled by a minuscule genetic difference. Moreover, nature doesn't cluster races in neatly defined categories. It is people, not nature, who sometimes label Tiger Woods 'African American' (his ancestry is 25 per cent African) or 'Asian American' (he is also 25 per cent Thai and 25 per cent Chinese) – or even as Native American or Dutch (he is one-eighth each).

Today, blatant prejudice based on biological criteria has nearly disappeared. Previously such prejudice was upheld in the institutional practices of many societies. Until the 1970s many banks routinely denied mortgages to unmarried women and to minority applicants, with the result that most homeowners were White men or White heterosexual married couples. Films and television programmes have also reinforced prevailing cultural attitudes. The muddleheaded, wide-eyed African American butlers and maids in 1930s movies helped perpetuate the stereotypes they reflected. Today, many people find such images offensive, and they are a far cry from movies such as Jordan Peele's *Get Out* (2017), where intelligent and complex Black characters call attention to the far more subtle forms of racism which occur in modern society. We have seen the abolition of the regime of apartheid in South Africa, and the election of the USA's first Black president, Barack Obama. Considering what a thin slice of history is covered by the years since slavery was practised, the changes are dramatic.

Shall we conclude, then, that racial and ethnic prejudice is extinct in the Western world? Not if we consider the 8,496 bias-related offences that took place in the USA in 2018 (FBI, 2020), or the small proportion of Whites who, as **Figure 13.2** shows (overleaf), would not vote for a Black presidential candidate.

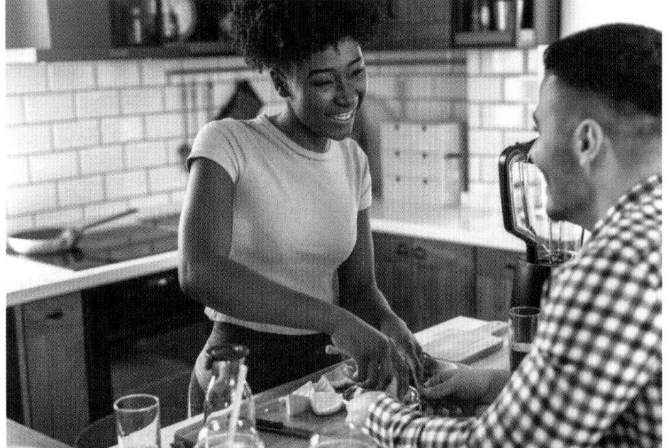

Although prejudice dies last in socially intimate contacts, interracial marriage has increased in most countries (Pew, 2006).
SOURCE: ©Lordn/Shutterstock

While the blatant expressions of prejudice may be on a sharp decline, and no longer receive the same kinds of institutional support they once did, more subtle forms of prejudice are still rife.

Subtle Forms of Prejudice

So, prejudiced attitudes and discriminatory behaviour surface when they can hide behind the screen of some other motive. In Western countries blatant prejudice is being replaced by subtle

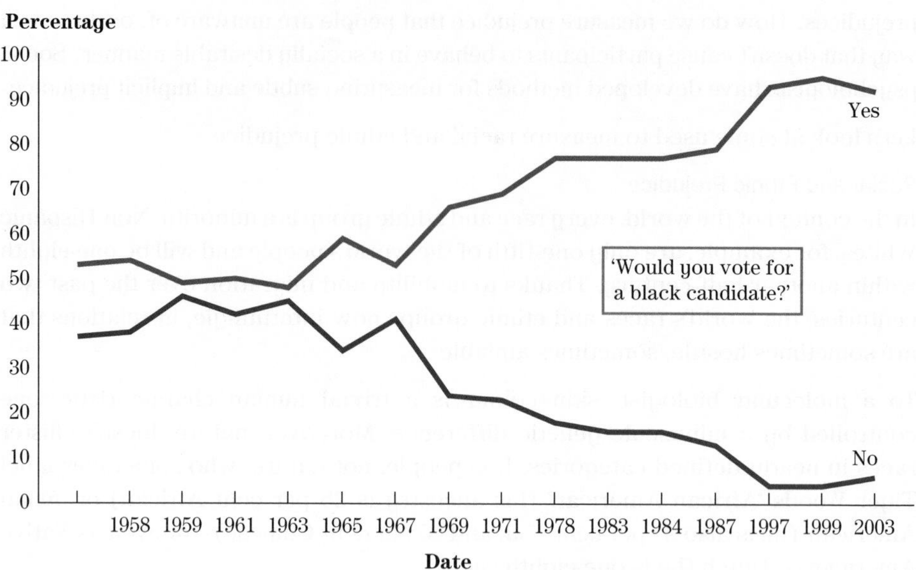

FIGURE 13.2 Changing racial attitudes of White Americans from 1958 to 2003
SOURCE: Data from Gallup polls (gallup.com).

prejudice (exaggerating ethnic differences, feeling less admiration and affection for immigrant minorities, rejecting them for supposedly non-racial reasons) (Pedersen & Walker, 1997; Tropp & Pettigrew, 2005a). Modern prejudice often appears subtly, in our preferences for what is familiar, similar and comfortable (Dovidio et al., 1992; Esses et al., 1993; Gaertner & Dovidio, 2005).

Modern prejudice even appears as a sensitivity that leads to exaggerated reactions to isolated minority persons – both over-praising their accomplishments and over-criticizing their mistakes (Fiske, 1989a; Hart & Morry, 1997; Hass et al., 1991). It also appears as patronization. For example, Harber (1998) gave White students at Stanford University a poorly written essay to evaluate. When the students thought the writer was Black, they rated it *higher* than when they were led to think the author was White, and they rarely offered harsh criticisms. The evaluators, perhaps wanting to avoid the appearance of bias, patronized the essayists with lower standards. Such 'inflated praise and insufficient criticism' may hinder minority student achievement, Harber noted.

Katz and Hass (1988) argue that people tend to not be against a group per se, but will have both positive and negative feelings towards them. This has been defined as ambivalent racism. Gaertner and Dovidio (2000) distinguish the ambivalent racist from the aversive racist. The aversive racist will actively avoid interracial encounters because of the guilt they feel about their negative thoughts about Blacks. When such an encounter cannot be avoided, the aversive racist will promote egalitarian values, yet if their prejudice can be justified on non-racial grounds, they may then discriminate against them. See **Table 13.1** for a summary.

Implicit Prejudice

A raft of experiments (Banaji, 2004; Bargh & Chartrand, 1999; Devine, 1989, 2005; Fazio et al., 1995; Greenwald et al., 2000; Wittenbrink et al., 1997) suggest that prejudiced and stereotypic evaluations can occur outside people's awareness. We've considered

TABLE 13.1 Types of subtle racism

Name	Primary citations	Description of main features
Symbolic racism	Henry & Sears (2002) McConahay & Hough (1976) Sears (1988)	Symbolic racists reject old-style racism but still express prejudice indirectly (e.g. as opposition to policies that help racial minorities)
Ambivalent racism	Katz (1981) Katz & Hass (1988) Katz et al. (1986)	Ambivalent racists experience an emotional conflict between positive and negative feelings towards stigmatized racial groups
Modern racism	McConahay (1986)	Modern racists see racism as wrong but view racial minorities as making unfair demands or receiving too many resources
Aversive racism	Dovidio & Gaertner (1986)	Aversive racists believe in egalitarian principles such as racial inequality but have a personal aversion towards racial minorities

SOURCE: Plous (2008).

the implicit association test (IAT) with respect to the measurement of attitudes (Chapter 5) and persuasion (Chapter 6). Implicit association tests measure reaction times to see how quickly people associate concepts, indicating their implicit attitudes. Some social psychological studies briefly flash words or faces that 'prime' (automatically activate) group stereotypes. Participants are unaware that their activated stereotypes may then bias their behaviour. For example, Niens et al. (2004) found that Northern Ireland students revealed more sectarian attitudes which favoured their Protestant (or Catholic) ingroup and were biased against the respective Catholic (or Protestant) outgroup, as compared to explicit measures of prejudice.

So, how widespread are automatic prejudiced reactions to African Americans? Experiments have used the IAT to show such reactions in varied contexts. For example, in experiments by Greenwald et al. (1998, 2000), 9 in 10 White people took longer to identify pleasant words (such as *peace* and *paradise*) as 'good' when associated with Black rather than White faces. The participants consciously expressed little or no prejudice; their bias was unconscious and unintended. Moreover, Hugenberg and Bodenhausen (2003) report that the more strongly people exhibit such implicit prejudice, the readier they are to perceive anger in Black faces (**Figure 13.3**, overleaf).

In separate experiments, Correll et al. (2002, 2006) and Greenwald et al. (2003b) invited people to press buttons quickly to 'shoot' or 'not shoot' men who suddenly appeared on-screen holding either a gun or a harmless object such as a flashlight or a bottle. The participants (both Blacks and Whites, in one of the studies) more often mistakenly shot harmless targets who were Black. In a related series of studies, Payne (2001) and Judd et al. (2004) found that when primed with a Black rather than a White face, people think guns: they more quickly recognize a gun and they more often mistake a tool, such as a wrench, for a gun. In a related study, Eberhardt et al. (2004) demonstrated that the reverse effect can occur. Exposing people to weapons makes them pay more attention to faces of African Americans and even makes police officers more likely to judge stereotypical-looking African Americans as criminals.

It also appears that different brain regions are involved in automatic and consciously controlled stereotyping (Correll et al., 2006; Cunningham et al., 2004;

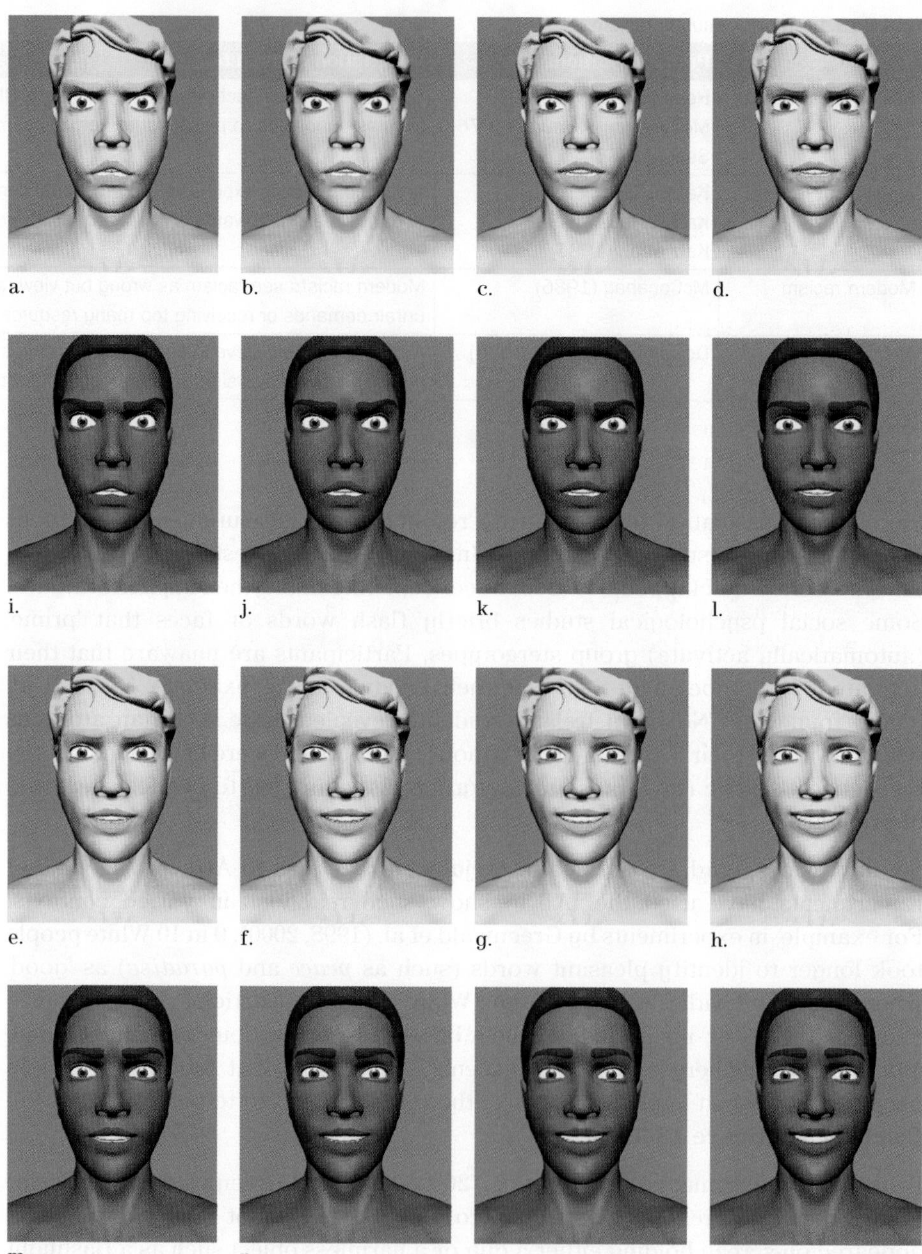

FIGURE 13.3 Facing prejudice

Where does the anger disappear? Kurt Hugenberg and Galen Bodenhausen showed university students a movie of faces morphing from angry to happy. Those who had scored as most prejudiced (on an implicit racial attitudes test) perceived anger lingering more in ambiguous Black than White faces.

Eberhardt, 2005). Pictures of members of outgroups that motivate feelings of disgust (such as drug addicts and the homeless) elicit more amygdala activity than frontal cortex activity (Harris & Fiske, 2006). This suggests that automatic prejudices involve primitive regions of the brain associated with fear, such as the amygdala, whereas controlled processing is more closely associated with the frontal cortex, which enables conscious thinking.

Even the social scientists who study prejudice seem vulnerable to it, note Greenwald and Schuh (1994). They analysed biases in authors' citations of social science articles by people with selected non-Jewish names (Erickson, McBride, etc.) and Jewish names (Goldstein, Siegel, etc.). Their analysis of nearly 30,000 citations, including 17,000 citations of prejudice research, found something remarkable: compared with Jewish authors, non-Jewish authors had 40 per cent higher odds of citing non-Jewish names. (Greenwald and Schuh could not determine whether Jewish authors were over-citing their Jewish colleagues or whether non-Jewish authors were over-citing their non-Jewish colleagues, or both.)

Implicit prejudice. When Joshua Correll and his colleagues invited people to react quickly to people holding either a gun or a harmless object, race influenced perceptions and reactions.

SOURCE: ©Ingram Publishing/Alamy

As we considered in Chapter 5, the use of IATs to measure implicit prejudice has not been without its critics. The creators of the IAT, Mahzarin Banaji and Anthony Greenwald, note that the findings of the IAT should be treated with caution, but it nevertheless measures implicit prejudice. Some social psychologists have contended that features of individual participants, such as their age, may be reflected in their performance on the IAT. For example, Stewart et al. (2009) consider their finding that older White adults demonstrate more racial prejudice on the IAT than younger ones. Is it that older people are more prejudiced than younger ones? Stewart and his colleagues claim that what's being measured here is how much control participants have over suppressing prejudiced associations. With age, deficits occur in inhibitory ability.

Gender Prejudice

How pervasive is prejudice against women? In Israel the high court reconsidered a ruling on orthodox buses that segregate men from women. Previously women had been required to sit at the back of the bus so that they remain separated from men in public. The women challenging the bus system argued this was a form of gender prejudice. Here we consider gender stereotypes.

Gender Stereotypes

Two research conclusions are indisputable: strong gender stereotypes exist, and members of the stereotyped group accept the stereotypes. Men and women agree that you *can* judge the book by its sexual cover. In one survey, Jackman and Senter (1981) found that gender stereotypes were much stronger than racial stereotypes. For example, only 22 per cent of men thought the two sexes equally 'emotional'. Of the remaining 78 per cent, those who believed females were more emotional outnumbered those who thought males were by 15 to 1. And what did the women believe? To within 1 percentage point, their responses were identical.

Remember that stereotypes are generalizations about a group of people and may be true, false or overgeneralized from a kernel of truth. Sometimes stereotypes exaggerate differences. But not always, observed Swim (1994). She found that Pennsylvania State University students' stereotypes of men's and women's restlessness, non-verbal sensitivity, aggressiveness, and so forth were reasonable approximations of actual gender differences. Moreover, such stereotypes have persisted across time and culture. Averaging data from 27 countries, Williams et al. (1999, 2000) found that people everywhere perceive women as more agreeable, and men as more outgoing.

Stereotypes (beliefs) are not prejudices (attitudes). Stereotypes may support prejudice. One might believe, without prejudice, that men and women are 'different yet equal'. Let us see how researchers probe for gender prejudice.

Sexism: Benevolent and Hostile

Eagly et al. (1991) and Haddock and Zanna (1994) report that people don't respond to women with gut-level negative emotions as they do to certain other groups. Most people like women more than men. They perceive women as more understanding, kind and helpful. A *favourable* stereotype, which Eagly (1994) dubs the *women-are-wonderful effect,* results in a favourable attitude.

> *'Women are wonderful primarily because they are [perceived as] so nice. [Men are] perceived as superior to women in agentic [competitive, dominant] attributes that are viewed as equipping people for success in paid work, especially in male-dominated occupations.'*
>
> Eagly (1994)

But gender attitudes often are ambivalent, report Glick and Fiske (1996, 2001) and their colleagues (Glick et al., 2000) from their surveys of 15,000 people in 19 nations. While they note that blatant *hostile sexism* (e.g. 'Once a man commits, she puts him on a tight leash') has generally waned over time in Western nations, the more insidious *benevolent sexism* is still common. This involves the idea that women are beautiful and delicate creatures, who should thus be put on a pedestal and looked after by men. Although benevolent sexism may seem less troubling than hostile sexism, endorsement of benevolent sexist views correlates with many more problematic opinions, such as attributing less blame to rapists (Abrams et al., 2003).

Stereotypes about men also come in contrasting pairs. Glick et al. (2004) report ambivalent sexism towards men with *benevolent* attitudes of men as powerful and *hostile* attitudes that characterize men as immoral. People who endorse benevolent sexism towards women also tend to endorse benevolent sexism towards men. These complementary ambivalent sexist views of men and women may serve to justify the status quo in gender relations (Jost & Kay, 2005).

Gender Discrimination

One heavily publicized finding of discrimination against women came from a 1968 study in which Philip Goldberg gave women students at Connecticut College several short articles and asked them to judge the value of each. Sometimes a given article was attributed to a male author (for example, John T. McKay) and sometimes to a female author (for example, Joan T. McKay). In general, the articles received lower ratings when attributed to a female. That's right: women discriminated against women.

David Myers obtained Goldberg's materials in 1980 and repeated the experiment with his own students. They (women and men) showed no such tendency to deprecate women's work. The most common result across 104 studies involving almost 20,000 people was *no difference*. On most comparisons, judgement of someone's work was unaffected by whether the work was attributed to a female or a male. Summarizing other studies of people's evaluations of women and men as leaders, professors, and so forth, Eagly (1994) concluded, 'Experiments have *not* demonstrated any *overall* tendency to devalue women's work'.

Is gender bias fast becoming extinct in Western countries? Has the women's movement nearly completed its work? As with racial prejudice, both blatant gender prejudice and subtle remain present in society.

One such bias can be seen in analysis of birth announcements (Gonzalez & Koestner, 2005). Parents announce the birth of their baby boys with more pride than the birth of their baby girls. In contrast, they announce the birth of their baby girls with more happiness than the birth of their baby boys. It seems that even at birth, parents are already describing their boys in terms of status and their girls in terms of relationships.

In the world beyond democratic Western countries, gender discrimination looms even larger. Two-thirds of the world's unschooled children are girls (United Nations, 1991). Around the world, people tend to prefer having baby boys. In the USA in 1941, 38 per cent of expectant parents said they preferred a boy if they could have only one child; 24 per cent preferred a girl; and 23 per cent said they had no preference. In 2003 the answers were virtually unchanged, with 38 per cent still preferring a boy (Lyons, 2003; Simmons, 2000). With the widespread use of ultrasound to determine the sex of a foetus and the growing availability of abortion, these preferences are affecting the number of boys and girls. The net result is tens of millions of 'missing women'. This is compounded by issues such as forced marriages of young girls and female genital mutilation, both of which are still commonplace in many non-Western cultures.

To conclude, overt prejudice against people of colour and against women is far less common today than it was in the mid-twentieth century. The same is true of prejudice against homosexual people. Nevertheless, techniques that are sensitive to subtle prejudice still detect widespread bias. And in parts of the world, gender prejudice makes for misery. Therefore, we need to look carefully and closely at the social, emotional and cognitive sources of prejudice.

Intergroup Conflict

People's identification with a social group can lead to conflict with other groups. The occurrence of intergroup conflict has been widely studied by social psychologists. Why does conflict between groups occur? Can social psychologists explain this conflict?

Intergroup behaviour is behaviour based on the perception that individuals belong to distinct social groups.

intergroup behaviour
behaviour that is based on the perception that individuals belong to distinct social groups

Almost every nation claims concern not only for peace but, mistrusting other nations, arms itself in self-defence. The result is a world that has been spending in excess of $2 billion per day on arms and armies, while hundreds of millions die of malnutrition and untreated disease.

conflict a perceived incompatibility of actions, goals or values between two or more parties

The elements of **conflict** are similar at many levels, whether we examine conflict between nations in an arms race, trying to control oil resources, religious factions disputing points of doctrine, or corporate executives and workers disputing salaries. Whether their perceptions are accurate or inaccurate, people in conflict sense that one side's gain is the other's loss. Often the result is that everybody loses!

A relationship or an organization without conflict is possibly apathetic. Conflict signifies involvement, commitment and caring. If conflict is understood and recognized, it can end oppression and stimulate renewed and improved human relations. Without conflict, people seldom face and resolve their problems. Conflicts are necessary for development and change. Conflict in itself is not the evil. The problem is the means and weapons often used to solve or reduce that conflict.

Let's consider some social psychological explanations for intergroup conflict.

Realistic Conflict Theory

One explanation comes from Sherif and Sherif (1953, 1964; Sherif et al., 1961), who offer an environmental explanation for conflict between groups. Rather than conflict being the outcome of a dysfunction in individuals' psychological states, it is factors in the social situation that are thought to be to blame. Sherif and Sherif argue that it is competition for scarce resources that leads to intergroup conflict.

realistic conflict theory negative relations between social groups are based on real competition for scarce resources

Sherif and Sherif thought the perceived differences in resources between groups became manifest as psychological states of the group members. This became the basis of their **realistic conflict theory**, illustrated in their series of boys' camp studies (see Research Close-Up: The Robbers Cave Experiment).

Sherif and Sherif illustrated that conflict between groups is not simply down to the personalities of a few individuals, but a consequence of the environment, which can lead to displays of aggression, ingroup solidarity, stereotyping and prejudice.

Of course, not all intergroup conflict is characterized by competition over lack of scarce resources. Is simply feeling psychologically attached to a group sufficient to cause conflict and prejudice?

Categorization, Stereotyping and Social Groups

Henri Tajfel was fascinated by the work of the Sherifs, but what had really caught his attention was the boys' identification with a group to which they had been randomly assigned. It seemed as though something psychological happened to people when they were put in a group (see Chapter 12).

ingroup 'us' – a group of people who share a sense of belonging, a feeling of common identity (often contrasted with outgroup)

outgroup 'them' – a group that people perceive as distinctively different from or apart from their ingroup

In a group situation we stereotype ourselves and others on the basis of group membership. Lippmann (1922) argued such mental shortcuts are mostly works of fiction. They are exaggerated generalizations that are partial, biased and contain evaluations, and in an intergroup situation used to perceive the outgroup as inferior and the ingroup as superior.

Tajfel wanted to see if people would favour their **ingroup** and be hostile to the **outgroup** even when there was no reward for doing so. In other words he wanted to know if the 'competition' between groups was simply about scarce resources, or if it was actually about being able to distinguish one's group favourably in comparison to another.

Research close-up

The Robbers Cave Experiment

Source: Sherif, M. (1958). Superordinate goals in the reduction of intergroup conflict. *American Journal of Sociology, 63*(4), 349–356.

Introduction

Muzafer Sherif noted that social scientists had not really effectively reduced intergroup conflict. Attempts to do so, which included contact between groups, appeals to fairness and morality, and addressing stereotypes, had in his opinion failed to understand and address intergroup conflict generally. Sherif began with the idea that it is conflict over resources that underlies prejudice between groups. To demonstrate this, a series of studies were conducted to show how intergroup conflict could be induced through competition over scarce resources. What Sherif wanted to know was, if competition was the basis for intergroup conflict, could it be reduced by bringing the groups together to work co-operatively for shared resources? To do this they conducted three boys' camp studies that ran in 1949, 1953 and 1954 at Robbers Cave State Park in Oklahoma.

Method

The studies involved a two-week summer camp for 11- to 12-year-old White middle-class North American boys to engage in a series of activities during the summer holidays. Sherif notes that they were 'healthy, normal boys' and 'well adjusted in school and neighbourhood, and academically successful' with a mean IQ 'above average' (p. 353). Researchers, including Muzafer Sherif, acted as camp counsellors and activity leaders recording the behaviour of the boys throughout the two weeks. Across all three studies a pattern of stages in the experiment was implemented. The first was an initial milling period where the boys were free to form their own friendships. The second stage involved splitting the boys into two groups. Existing friendships that had formed in the initial milling period were split across the two groups. The two groups were kept separate from each other, and engaged in group-specific activities. During this time firm friendships formed within the groups as they developed a sense of group cohesion. In the third stage competitions were organized between the groups such that one group could only gain resources at the expense of the other group. In the later studies the researchers introduced a fourth stage that meant both groups had to work collaboratively in order to bring a positive reward for everyone. Collaborative activities included fixing the water supply for camp. These were goals that could not be achieved through the efforts of one group alone, but required both groups working together.

Results

Sherif reports that across all of the studies, once competition between the two groups began, hostility arose. Negative stereotypes and attitudes were formed about members of the opposing group. They engaged in name-calling, cruel chanting, fights and raids of the other group's cabins. Furthermore, both groups expressed a desire to be as physically distant from one another as possible. However, ingroup solidarity and co-operation intensified, as the boys bonded within their groups more closely in the face of competition from the other group. Blatant bragging of their own group's superiority emerged. Sherif also witnessed rearrangements of power and status within each group, as the boys developed new norms and values to fit with the hostile situation they found themselves in.

As the groups were brought together through the introduction of superordinate goals, requiring they work together, Sherif observed that acts such as derogatory name-calling ceased. When asked to rate stereotypes about the opposing group, these became favourable. Friendships slowly began to form across the two groups. The blatant bragging stopped. The groups worked together to achieve collective goals.

Discussion

Sherif concluded that this study showed that not only must groups communicate with one another in order to reduce conflict, but they should also work together to achieve goals that are beneficial for all concerned. So mere contact is insufficient on its own to dispel intergroup conflict. When pulling together for the good of everyone, groups learn about one another; negative stereotypes previously held about other groups are seen to be untrue. Sherif argued that this series of studies not only showed how conflict could be created between people and groups in terms of competing for scarce resources, but also shed light on how it could be resolved, by creating superordinate goals which required groups to work together in order to achieve them.

Critical Reflections

Sherif's Robbers Cave studies have been very influential within social psychology, and have taught us much about how intergroup conflict may arise. But is it the case that all intergroup conflict is based on competition over scarce or desired resources? Sherif seems to be able to explain some causes of conflict. Tensions can break out between groups when unemployment is high and available jobs and housing are scarce. But what about the conflict that exists between football fans, rival gangs, groups of children in the playground? Scarce resources are not the basis for all intergroup conflict.

Competition kindles conflict.

SOURCE: Courtesy of The Drs. Nicholas and Dorothy Cummings Center for the History of Psychology, University of Akron

Criticisms can also be levelled at Sherif's choice of sample and the artificial conditions under which the experiments were carried out. All of the sample were White middle-class boys. The creation of the groups was artificial. How well does this reflect everyday intergroup conflict? This calls the **ecological validity** of the research into question. Furthermore, if the groups had failed to achieve the superordinate goals, would the cross-group friendships have continued, or would the original rivalry between the two groups have re-emerged? These shortcomings limit our ability to draw conclusions from Sherif's research.

ecological validity the extent to which findings observed in a study reflect what actually occurs in natural settings. Psychological laboratory research has been criticized for its low ecological validity

The experiment we discussed in Chapter 12, by Henri Tajfel and Michael Billig, demonstrated how little it takes to provoke favouritism towards 'us' and unfairness towards 'them'. The mere experience of being formed into groups may promote **ingroup bias**. Ask children, 'Which are the better, the children in your school or the children at [another school nearby]?' They will probably say their own school has better children. Abrams et al. (2003) found that children as young as 5 years old display ingroup favouritism.

ingroup bias the tendency to favour one's own group

Tajfel suggested that these groups resulted in perceptual illusions, as individuals saw members of their own group and those of others, as more homogeneous than they really are. As we discussed in Chapter 12, in an intergroup context, we experience accentuation effects.

Social Comparison

But why do we engage in this ingroup favouritism? We evaluate ourselves partly by our group memberships. Having a sense of 'we-ness' strengthens our self-concepts. It *feels* good. We seek not only *respect* for ourselves but also *pride* in our groups (Smith & Tyler, 1997). Seeing our groups as superior helps us feel even better. It's as if we all think, 'I am an X [name your group]. X is good. Therefore, I am good.' As much of our lives are tied up with social group membership we are concerned with maintaining the positive image and evaluation of our group. One way of doing this is to compare your group with others in favourable terms. To do this, the group needs to compare itself with others on dimensions that are favourable for the ingroup.

Some social psychologists have argued that the motivation behind group comparisons isn't so much about self-esteem as about achieving optimal distinctiveness (Brewer, 1991) or reducing the uncertainty of social reality. Whatever the motivation, social psychologists who adopt a social identity theory (SIT) or self-categorization theory (SCT) perspective agree that the process of social comparison seems to be one that groups engage in to make their own group membership meaningful, and they strive to do so in ways that make their own group appear favourable.

Let's consider an example. Benjamin et al. (2003) conducted an ethnographic small-scale study of two English primary schools that promote educational inclusion, accepting children from a variety of backgrounds. However, they found that despite the spirit of inclusion the children understood each other as belonging to distinct social groups based on social class. To mark the boundaries between these groups, those children from middle-class backgrounds defined their 'success' based on their academic abilities, appearing superior to the working-class children. Those children from the working-class areas often sabotaged their academic abilities, instead preferring to define their 'success' on the basis of their street knowledge and non-academic activities. So the dimension for social comparison moves so that the ingroup can regard itself as superior to the outgroup.

Devos et al. (2002) note a wide range of emotions that can occur in various intergroup relations. A powerful outgroup can instil fear. One that threatens or blocks the goals of an ingroup can result in anger and frustration. In extreme cases, an outgroup whose moral standards don't quite match our own may evoke disgust. Leach et al. (2003) investigated the feeling of 'schadenfreude' among Dutch football supporters. Schadenfreude is 'malicious pleasure' at the misfortune of someone else (also see Chapter 3). They found that Dutch football supporters experienced high levels of schadenfreude when the German football team lost to another international side in a football tournament.

Lacking a positive personal identity, people may seek self-esteem by identifying with a group. Many disadvantaged youths find pride, power and identity in gang affiliations. Many superpatriots define themselves by their national identities

(Staub, 1997a, 2005b). And many people at a loose end find identity in their associations with new religious movements, self-help groups or fraternity clubs (**Figure 13.4**).

'There is a tendency to define one's own group positively in order to evaluate oneself positively.'
J. C. Turner (1984)

Crowds

The early social explanations of aggressive behaviour in groups focused particularly on the crowd, and tried to answer the question why people behaved violently when surrounded by others.

The Group Mind

Gustave Le Bon (1841–1931) was one of the most influential writers on crowd behaviour (see Chapter 1). Writing during a time of political and social unrest in France he observed the revolutionary crowds in his country and tried to understand their behaviour. However, this was not really an objective exploration of the crowd. Le Bon, himself coming from a solidly bourgeois family, greatly mistrusted the uprising and revolutionary crowd, and was appalled by what he perceived as their savage behaviour. In his book *The Crowd* (1895) Le Bon argued that: 'By the mere fact that he forms part of an organised crowd, a man descends several rungs on the ladder of civilisation. Isolated he may be a cultivated individual; in a crowd he is a barbarian – that is a creature acting by instinct.' (p. 32).

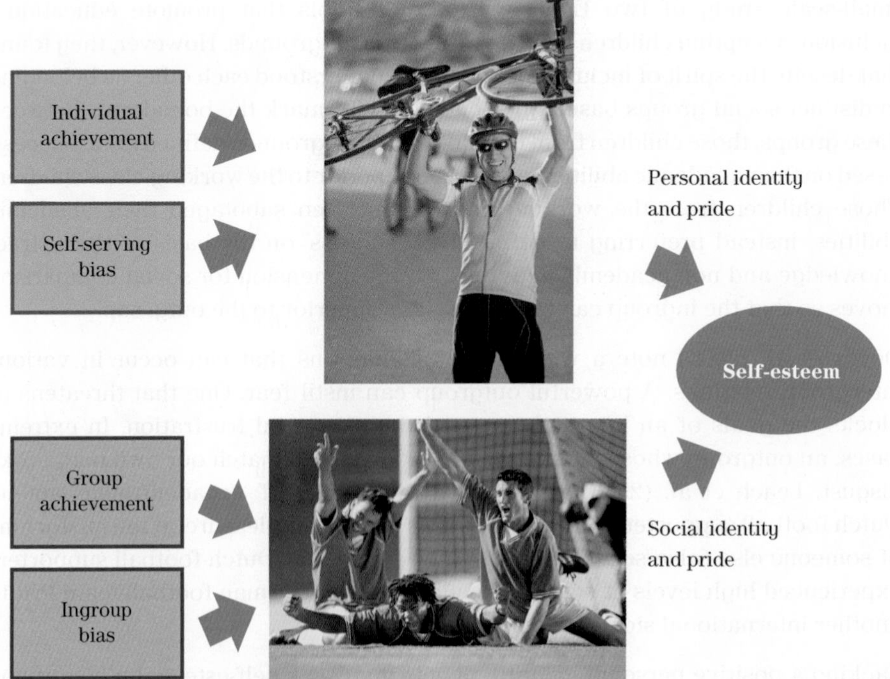

FIGURE 13.4 Personal identity and social identity together feed self-esteem
SOURCE: (T) ©Terry Vine/Blend Images LLC (B) ©Digital Vision/Punchstock

Gustave Le Bon (1841–1931) was one of the most influential writers on crowd behaviour. He believed that people behaved like barbarians in crowds due to a loss of conscious rationality.
SOURCE: ©Bettmann/Getty

In Chapter 8 we briefly considered how Le Bon's ideas had been used to explain aggression. Le Bon thought that when individuals become immersed in a crowd they lose their conscious rationality and more primitive instincts take over, causing barbaric behaviour. Individuals lose control of their minds in a crowd. As the 'racial unconscious' takes over, crowds behave aggressively. Losing individual responsibility for their actions, crowd members feel invisible. Le Bon believed that aggressive impulses were transmitted to members of the crowd unconsciously by contagion. In this almost hypnotic state individuals follow others in acts that they would never usually do.

Sigmund Freud (1921) claimed that, within the crowd, the superego which contains society's norms and values that constrained primitive urges, was replaced by the primitive 'id', a bundle of uncontrolled and irrational impulses. These ideas clearly influenced Le Bon.

'Crowds are somewhat like the sphinx of ancient fable: It is necessary to arrive at a solution of the problems offered by their psychology or to resign ourselves to being devoured by them.'
Le Bon (1908)

Le Bon's work was highly influential. It gave people a good excuse not to engage with the opinions and actions of the crowd. It also offered a way of controlling crowds at a time when people lived in fear of the collapse of the social order. Even the fascist dictator Mussolini noted his gratitude to Le Bon for such illumination on the matter. But subsequent social psychological theories have pointed out particular problems with Le Bon's theory:

1. Le Bon was describing the revolutionary crowds of France, yet they don't get a mention in his work. Are all crowds the same? Do they arise for the same reasons? What are they reacting against? The crowd is removed from the circumstances under which it arose.
2. It assumes crowds have a fixed set of behaviours that are released. But surely there is diversity within the crowd as well as between crowds.
3. It gives no indication of 'who' will be affected. By using the concepts of suggestion and contagion, surely everyone should join in. But this isn't the case. The police rarely join in with a rioting crowd. We might be a bit surprised if they did! So there must be some basis on which people identify with a crowd in order for them to join one.
4. It assumes crowd members are anonymous and irrational. Crowd members may be anonymous to those outside of the crowd, but they are often known to others within the crowd. So do they really lose their sense of self? What may seem irrational to an outsider may not be regarded as irrational to those within the crowd.

These concerns have been addressed in subsequent social psychological theories of the crowd. Let's begin by turning to one of Le Bon's claims which did inform a later theory on crowd behaviour: the idea that people become anonymous within the crowd.

Deindividuation

Leon Festinger (Festinger et al., 1952) coined the term '**deindividuation**' to explain what happens when people become anonymous within a crowd or group.

deindividuation loss of self-awareness and evaluation apprehension; occurs in group situations where responsiveness to positive or negative group norms is fostered, or where anonymity is increased

Under these conditions, people's sense of individual identity and responsibility for their actions becomes lost as individuals become anonymous within the crowd. Studies that have tried to demonstrate the effects of deindividuation have tended not to focus on crowds, but on small and large groups. Remember that in Chapter 11 we saw how deindividuation led to social loafing, as people reduced their individual effort within the anonymity of the group.

Festinger et al. (1952) found that when their group of participants were made unidentifiable by dressing in laboratory coats they were much more controversial, and some might say bold, in their discussions about their feelings towards their parents.

In one study that does examine crowds, Mann (1981) observed baiting when a person threatened to commit suicide by jumping off a bridge or building. In his study of 21 cases, Mann found that in 10 of them the crowd started to bait and jeer at the person threatening to kill themselves. Mann suggests that deindividuation is partly responsible for this crowd behaviour, including the large size of the group, whether the attempt occurred at night-time and the physical distance between the crowd and victim. During the time of apartheid in South Africa, Colman (1991) reported how South African courts actually took deindividuation and the loss of responsibility into account when sentencing murderers. The Truth and Reconciliation Committees in South Africa maintain a defence that offences which took place during apartheid can be blamed on deindividuation within a political system, and as such the perpetrator can be forgiven on the basis s/he was serving that system. In one case, the court accepted extenuating circumstances for four out of eight railway worker defendants accused of murdering eight strike breakers. In another, the death sentences of five defendants who killed a young woman via 'necklacing' (involving placing a burning tyre around the victim's torso) were reduced to 20 months' imprisonment. As Colman warns, such psychological explanations for crowd behaviour have practical and ethical implications for society.

The work of Philip Zimbardo has offered some of the most revealing work in the area. In a study reminiscent of Milgram's electric shock experiment, Zimbardo (1970) dressed female participants in hoods and robes to deindividuate them. He paired them with a female confederate and asked the participant to assess how well the confederate did on a paired-associate learning task by administering electric shocks to them. He found that those dressed in hoods and robes gave much higher electric shocks than those participants who were not. Zimbardo argued that this had occurred because there had been a diffusion of responsibility across the hooded participants, causing a 'weakening of controls based on guilt, shame, fear and commitment'.

Zimbardo's Stanford Prison Experiment took place in 1971, and illustrated how people's behaviour is affected when they become deindividuated playing a particular role. In response to an advert for people to take part in a study based at Stanford University, 24 White middle-class male volunteers were randomly assigned on the toss of a coin to the role of 'prison guard' or 'prisoner'. They were then dressed in the appropriate uniform and lived in a mock-up of a prison camp based at the university. Although the study was planned to last two weeks, it was stopped after only six days. The participants quickly internalized their roles and began to behave accordingly. The guards became aggressive and brutal, subjecting their prisoners to inhumane conditions and acts of physical and verbal abuse. Those who had been assigned to the role of prisoner simply accepted the abuse. As the conditions of the prison deteriorated and the brutality of the guards escalated, the experiment was stopped. Was it the lack of self-awareness and feelings of deindividuation that led to such a shocking conclusion? As we shall see later in this chapter, Steve Reicher and Alex Haslam have challenged Zimbardo's conclusions.

Although the Stanford Prison Experiment is a fascinating, if somewhat disturbing, insight into how deindividuation affects people's behaviour, it was Diener (1980) who used the principles of deindividuation to developed a model of crowd behaviour. He felt that when in a large group or crowd, individuals drifted towards an extreme lack of self-awareness. Under these conditions people do not self-monitor, are unable to retrieve standards and norms of behaviour from memory, do not plan their actions, become driven by immediate cues, and feel little or no responsibility for their behaviour. Usual self-regulation of behaviour is blocked (see **Figure 13.5**, overleaf).

Although proposed as a model of crowd behaviour, Diener's study remained at the level of small groups. With his colleagues, Diener's study of Halloween trick-or-treaters (Diener et al., 1976) explored whether children being anonymous in a group would lead to them 'stealing' sweets from houses they visited on Halloween. More stealing occurred when the children were anonymous and in a group. Diener then told one child, who was anonymous due to their costume, that they were the leader of the group, making them responsible for the actions of the other group members. Diener found that if the leader stole sweets then incidences of stealing committed by other group members increased. Diener suggested that what was going on here was a modelling effect. The children copied their leader, especially when their leader was anonymous to those they stole from.

But does the crowd always behave aggressively? This seems to be a legacy that has come from Le Bon's particular political stance on the revolutionary crowds of France. Does deindividuation always result in negative behaviour? If so, why didn't the prisoners in the Zimbardo study also behave aggressively? It's the role of 'prisoner' or 'guard' that guides behaviour. Do people blindly accept the roles that are given to them and behave accordingly? Recent research suggests not. See Research Close-Up: The Psychology of Tyranny for a contemporary reinterpretation of Zimbardo's prison experiment, carried out by Steve Reicher and Alex Haslam.

Emergent Norm Theory

Turner and Killian (1972) say that the crowd is just an extreme form of a group. The only distinction between a crowd and a group is that groups usually have some history or tradition associated with them, whereas crowds are often spontaneous gatherings of people. **Emergent norm theory** was proposed to explain how this occurred. When potential crowd members first meet, an initial period of 'milling' occurs as members meet each other. Certain individuals become more prominent than others. Through 'keynoting activities' it is the behaviour of these prominent individuals that become characteristic of the crowd as a whole. So rather than

emergent norms those norms that 'emerge' within a group or crowd that influence the behaviour of those involved

I. Many or most everyday activities (not self-aware and not self-regulating)

A. Habitual behavioural sequences
B. Scripted behaviours
C. Well-learned reactions to stimuli
D. Outward focus of attention
E. Well-planned sequences

II. Self-awareness and self-regulation initiated by:

A. Novel situations
B. Evaluation by others
C. Behaviour produces unexpected outcomes
D. Self-focusing stimuli
E. Behaviour clearly related to one's morals or standards

III. Self-awareness and self-regulation:

A. Self-monitoring
B. Retrieval of personal and social standards and comparison of own behaviour to standards
C. Self-reinforcement
D. Planning and foresight
E. Behaviour often inhibited by fear of punishment

IV. Deindividuation caused by (self-awareness and individual self-conception blocked):

A . Perceptual immersion in the group
B. Outcome attribution immersion
C. Action and other factors using conscious processing capacity
D. Outward focus of attention
E. Conceiving the group as a united whole

V. Self-regulatory capacities lost when deindividuated:

A. Can't easily monitor own behaviour or perceive products of own actions
B. Social and personal standards can't be retrieved and can't compare behaviour to own standards
C. Can't generate self-reinforcement
D. Can't use planning or foresight
E. Lack of ego inhibitions regarding future punishment
F. Person becomes more reactive to immediate cues, emotions and motivations

FIGURE 13.5 Self-awareness and self-regulation versus deindividuation
Individuals alternate between I, II and III all the time. When the self-regulatory feedback loop is blocked in stage IV (such as in a crowd), the individual enters stage V (deindividuation).
SOURCE: Diener (1980).

individuals' identity being lost in a crowd it is maintained and becomes the basis for the formation of group norms. The crowd acts as one on the basis of norms which emerge during the initial milling process, and each individual being surveyed by other crowd members.

Some problems with this concept of crowd behaviour have been noted:

- How are these norms spread so rapidly across the group?
- Many crowds do have a history, such as a Black Lives Matter protest crowd to name just one example, so these norms do not always emerge spontaneously. So what is the difference between a group and a crowd?
- It seems as though the 'norms' of the group are actually determined by a few powerful individual personalities (keynoting activities), but why do other people follow them blindly?
- Is our behaviour in a group or crowd simply the result of being surveyed by others? Perhaps we behave in a particular way because we feel we should.

Emergent norm theory is an individualistic account of crowd behaviour reducing the explanation to a few individuals. Some social psychologists have argued that any theory of crowds needs to look not only at the individuals involved, but also at the crowd's norms. These norms reflect a particular ideological understanding of the world and the group's place within it.

The theories we've considered so far try to explain a crowd in terms of what happens to the individuals who compose it. Put simply, what's missing so far is some consideration of the context in which crowds form. They don't just occur, but occur for a reason.

Social Identity Theory and Crowds

Members of a crowd are usually bound together in a common cause. This might be in direct opposition to another crowd (as in a riot) or to make a collective statement about a political, religious or social cause, or even to raise awareness about a social problem.

Using a social identity theory (SIT) approach Reicher (1984) focused on the riots that occurred in the St Paul's area of Bristol in England. On 2 April 1980, the police raided the Black and White café situated on Grosvenor Road in the St Paul's area. This was the start of a period of rioting where people were injured and arrested. Although the escalation of the riot was quick, those participating had a shared history and identity as the St Paul's community. Regarding the raid as another sign of being treated unfairly by the police, the residents reacted. Reicher observed the crowd behaving in a way that was consistent with the social identity of being 'St Paul's community'. Legitimate targets (the police) were distinguished from illegitimate targets (innocent bystanders). Twenty-one police vehicles were damaged and 22 police officers injured. Ordinary civilians were not attacked. Offices and shops that were regarded as representative of the 'establishment' were damaged (e.g. banks, post offices, Department of Health and Social Security buildings). There were also geographical limits to the crowd's behaviour. The police were chased out of the St Paul's area but not beyond its limits. This study raises some interesting challenges to the theories of crowd behaviour noted earlier. This is not an out-of-control crowd. Nor is there an absence of personal identity, but an increase in a shared social identity. This is the basis for a crowd that acts as one. Not everyone catches 'crowd fever'! Only those for whom 'St Paul's' is a meaningful identity, participate.

More recently, Stott and Reicher (2011) explored the 2011 English riots from a social identity theory perspective. Paralleling Reicher's observations from the

St Paul's riot, they argued that the rioting was not evidence of mass immorality, but instead was a symptom of citizens' deeply held grievances with the police, which were brought to a head by events such as the murder of Mark Duggan by police officers (Stott et al., 2017). As with the St Paul's riot, Stott and Reicher argue that the 2011 riots gave disenfranchised people a sense of collective empowerment, and a feeling that they at last were able to get their point across and to be heard. This conceptualization is a far cry from the 'mad mob' that was discussed in the media (and by politicians) at the time.

Research close-up

The Psychology of Tyranny

Source: Haslam, S.A., & Reicher, S. (2012). When prisoners take over the prison: A social psychology of resistance. *Personality and Social Psychology Review, 16*(2), 154–179.

Introduction

Phillip Zimbardo's classic Stanford Prison Experiment, conducted in 1971, had shown that simply asking people to fulfil a role (as a prisoner or guard) changed their thinking and their behaviour. Not only that, but this change could result in acts which that same individual would otherwise consider to be unacceptable and cruel. In December 2001, Steve Reicher and Alex Haslam partially replicated Zimbardo's classic Stanford Prison Experiment. Broadcast on the BBC for a period of 8 days, 15 men put into the roles of prisoner or guard were watched by the researchers and the public. Would they observe the same results and reach the same conclusions in the UK as Zimbardo had 30 years earlier in the US?

Method

Ensuring sample diversity across both roles, the researchers divided their participants into 5 guards and 10 prisoners. Those assigned to the role of guard were given uniforms and details of tasks the prisoners needed to do in order for the institution to run smoothly. Guards were given ways of enforcing their authority, including keys to lockable prison cells, 'treats' (such as sweets and cigarettes), and putting prisoners on a bread and water diet. The researchers carried out daily psychometric and physiological tests on the men, and the viewing public saw an edited hour of observational data as the men went about conducting their lives in accordance with the role they had been assigned to.

Results

Reicher and Haslam found in their study that the guards did not take on their role easily. They reported being troubled with their authoritative role over the prisoners. Disagreeing on how to carry out their role, they failed to bond as a team.

The prisoners also failed to respond as a group, rejecting their low standard of living. They were given restricted living space, a poor diet and no privileges. The prisoners adopted their own strategies for dealing with this. Some accepted their lot while others tried to improve their conditions. But this all changed when a new prisoner, a trade union official, was included. This led to greater cohesion between the prisoners and by Day 4 they began to challenge the guards. Unlike what was experienced in Zimbardo's original study, here the prisoners mocked the guards, undermining their authority. On Day 6, some of the prisoners managed to break into and occupy the guards' area, and refused to leave.

The roles of prisoner and guard consequently collapsed and a new structure was developed creating greater equality between prisoners and guards. The prisoners were glad to have more access to resources and the guards were relieved to relinquish the power that had made them feel so uncomfortable. Indication of their relief is found in the increases in positive mental health at this time. The collapse of the prisoner–guard hierarchy led to a single self-governing commune. But those prisoners who had been very active in challenging the old regime sabotaged the new commune. Now feeling marginalized by the new 'equal' system, they tried to challenge it.

Some of the prisoners and guards decided to try and re-establish the original prisoner–guard structure. They would run the prison, and reinforce the parameters of prisoners (e.g. cramped living conditions, poor diet) and guards (good food, freedom). They met with researchers to request this structure, arguing for a structure of inequality for themselves. As the threat of tyranny loomed, the programme was ended prematurely, in a move that mirrored the early end to Zimbardo's original study. While Zimbardo's study was ended when the original guards became too tyrannical, in Haslam and Reicher's experiment, it was brought to a close when some of the original guards and prisoners, dissatisfied with the commune that had emerged, eventually took on the identity of 'guard' and sought to impose a tyrannical regime.

Discussion

Reicher and Haslam concluded that social identity is the basis for tyranny. People may behave in tyrannical ways when they accept a particular role or identity that seems to require it. In Zimbardo's original study, this is what had happened. The 'guards' had internalized their identity and acted accordingly, forcing the early close to the experiment. In Haslam and Reicher's study it was the failure to accept guard and prisoner identities that led to a shared social identity and the emergence of the commune. Tyranny was proposed when some of the prisoners and guards resisted this new shared social identity, and demanded a reinstatement of the old regime but under their control. It is the desire for an identity, or the wish to resist one, that can form the basis for tyranny.

Critical Reflections

Reicher and Haslam's BBC Prison Study represents an important turning-point in modern social psychology. By actively questioning the findings of Zimbardo's Stanford Prison Experiment, these researchers challenged much of the received knowledge on intergroup relations and how social roles affect behaviour. More recent revelations (Jarrett, 2018) that Zimbardo may have caused much of the guard brutality by telling the guards to behave violently have only added to the criticisms levelled at the Stanford Prison Experiment.

The BBC Prison Study has not been without its own controversies, however: Zimbardo has criticized the study, noting that because it was televised, it wasn't a faithful replication of the prison conditions he had created at Stanford. However, as Haslam and Reicher point out, neither their study nor Zimbardo's could claim to replicate a true prison experience. People do not usually volunteer to go to prison, nor are they free to leave, as was the case for participants in both studies. Rather, the aim was to find out how people respond to roles given to them, their readiness to identify with them, and the behavioural consequences of living in an environment where inequality is initially established between them.

Similar findings have been obtained in research with football crowds, which again emphasizes the role of social identity in guiding behaviour. Stott and colleagues (2001) compared the experiences and actions of England and Scotland football hooligans. While the England fans have a historical tradition of aggressive behaviour,

England football fans.
SOURCE: ©Luke Broughton/Shutterstock

Scotland fans do not. This has an impact on how they are perceived and treated by other groups, including the police. During the France 1998 World Cup, Scotland fans were not expected to behave badly. The level of policing was minimal and the fans displayed a carnival atmosphere. In contrast, the England fans, who were expected to behave aggressively, experienced extreme levels of policing. Stott makes the point that where this level of policing exceeds the potential threat posed by England fans, rioting behaviour is likely. From their observations and interviews conducted with supporters, they reported that England fans felt other groups treated them unfairly and often violently, as they assumed that they would inevitably be met with hooliganism.

Intergroup Harmony

So far we've focused on different types of intergroup conflict and prejudice, and examined them from a range of theoretical perspectives. But can we reduce intergroup conflict and prejudice? Let's consider some of the strategies social psychologists have proposed for improving intergroup relations.

Contact

Might putting two conflicting individuals or groups into close contact enable them to know and like each other?

meta-analysis an analysis where researchers synthesise data from a number of independent studies on the same topic so that they can look for overall patterns and trends in the data

In a painstakingly complete **meta-analysis**, Tropp and Pettigrew (2005a; Pettigrew & Tropp, 2006) assembled data from 516 studies of 250,555 people in 38 nations. In 94 per cent of studies, *increased contact predicted decreased prejudice.* This is especially so for majority group attitudes towards minorities (Tropp & Pettigrew, 2005b).

Why? Gordon Allport is credited with formulating the 'contact hypothesis'. This proposes that prejudice and conflict are often based on groups simply being ignorant of each other. As they lack knowledge of other groups' values and beliefs, they fear them and fail to notice when groups may have things in common with their own group. However, for Allport it wasn't simply that any contact would improve intergroup relations. Indeed, contact can fuel conflict and prejudice as negative expectations of outgroup members bias judgements of them and create self-fulfilling prophecies. Rather, contact should be done under a series of 'optimal conditions'. These are as follows:

1 Contact is frequent and prolonged.
2 Contact is with stereotypical members of the group.
3 Contact is done with a genuine aspiration for improving relations.
4 Contact occurs between individuals of equal status.
5 Contact is free from competition.

6 Contact is supported by formal structures (e.g. education, government policy).

7 Contact is organized around the achievement of superordinate goals.

With such a long list you might wonder if contact under these conditions is really possible!

There is the further problem: the theory involves the assumption that prejudice is based on ignorance. The danger of course is that conflict is based on conflicts of interest. Such contact may only highlight the differences between groups rather than serve to dissolve them. It is because of issues such as this that authors such as McKeown and Dixon (2017) have highlighted the need for researchers to explore the phenomenon of intergroup contact in a critical manner.

Contact, and Allport's 'contact hypothesis' in particular, have been used in social psychological studies that test improvement in intergroup relations. This has been researched in the area of ethnic conflict and prejudice towards minority groups seeking asylum in European countries. Another very prevalent area of research is that of racial conflict and prejudice.

Does Desegregation Improve Racial Attitudes?

School desegregation has produced measurable benefits, such as leading more Blacks to attend and succeed in college (Stephan, 1988). On the surface this of course meets one of Allport's 'optimal conditions' for contact in terms of the contact receiving institutional support. But does desegregation of schools, neighbourhoods and workplaces also produce favourable social results? The evidence is mixed.

On the one hand, many studies conducted during and shortly after mid-twentieth-century desegregation initiatives found Whites' attitudes towards Blacks improving markedly. Whether the people were department store clerks and customers, merchant marines, government workers, police officers, neighbours or students, racial contact led to diminished prejudice (Amir, 1969; Pettigrew, 1969). When Deutsch and Collins (1951) took advantage of a made-to-order natural experiment, they observed similar results. In accord with state law, New York City desegregated its public housing units; it assigned families to apartments without regard to race. In a similar development across the river in Newark, New Jersey, Blacks and Whites were assigned to separate buildings. When surveyed, White women in the desegregated development were far more likely to favour interracial housing and to say their attitudes towards Blacks had improved. Exaggerated stereotypes had wilted in the face of reality. As one woman put it, 'I've really come to like it. I see they're just as human as we are.'

Findings such as these have influenced broader policy decisions such as the desegregation of schools in the USA and South Africa. Yet studies of the effects of school desegregation have been less encouraging. After reviewing all the available studies, Stephan (1986) concluded that racial attitudes had been little affected by desegregation. For Blacks, the noticeable consequence of desegregated schooling was less on Whites' attitudes than on their increased likelihood of attending integrated (or predominantly White) colleges, living in integrated neighbourhoods and working in integrated settings. Attitudes hadn't really changed.

Likewise, many student exchange programmes have disappointingly poor effects on student attitudes towards their host countries. For example, when eager

American students study in France, often living with other Americans as they do so, their stereotypes of the French tend not to improve (Stroebe et al., 1988). Contact also failed to allay the loathing of Rwandan Tutsis by their Hutu neighbours, or to eliminate the sexism of many men living and working in constant contact with women. People may more easily despise the homosexuals or immigrants whom they have never knowingly met, but they can also scorn people they see often.

Thus, we can see that sometimes desegregation improves racial attitudes; and sometimes – especially when there is anxiety or perceived threat (Pettigrew, 2004) – it doesn't. Such disagreements excite the scientist's detective spirit. What explains the difference? So far, we've been lumping all kinds of desegregation together. Actual desegregation occurs in many ways and under vastly different conditions.

When Does Desegregation Improve Racial Attitudes?

Let's consider another of Allport's optimal conditions – frequent and prolonged contact. Might the frequency of interracial contact be a factor? Indeed it seems to be. Researchers have gone into dozens of desegregated schools and observed with whom children of a given race eat, talk and loiter. Race influences contact. Whites disproportionately associate with Whites, Blacks with Blacks (Schofield, 1982, 1986). In one study of Dartmouth University e-mail exchanges, Black students, though only 7 per cent of students, sent 44 per cent of their e-mails to other Black students (Sacerdote & Marmaros, 2005).

The same self-imposed segregation was evident in a South African desegregated beach, as Dixon and Durrheim (2003) discovered when they recorded the location of Black, White and Indian beach-goers one midsummer (30 December) afternoon (**Figure 13.6**). Even in areas where segregation had never been a policy, desegregated neighbourhoods, cafeterias and restaurants, too, may fail to produce integrated interactions (Clack et al., 2005; Dixon et al., 2005a, 2005b).

Efforts to facilitate contact sometimes help, but sometimes fall flat. 'We had one day when some of the Protestant schools came over,' explained one Catholic youngster after a Northern Ireland school exchange (Cairns & Hewstone, 2002). 'It was supposed to be like . . . mixing, but there was very little mixing. It wasn't because we didn't want to; it was just really awkward.' The lack of mixing stems partly from 'pluralistic ignorance': many Whites and Blacks say they would like more contact but misperceive that the other does not reciprocate their feelings.

Friendship

In contrast, the more encouraging older studies of store clerks, soldiers and housing project neighbours involved considerable interracial contact, more than enough to reduce the anxiety that marks initial intergroup contact. Other studies involving prolonged, personal contact – between Black and White prison inmates, between Black and White girls in an interracial summer camp, between Black and White university room-mates, and between Black, Coloured (mixed-race) and White South Africans – show similar benefits (Clore et al., 1978; Foley, 1976; Holtman et al., 2005; Van Laar et al., 2005). Among American students who have studied in Germany or in Britain, the greater their contact with host country people, the more positive their attitudes (Stangor et al., 1996). A range of studies suggest that those who form *friendships* with outgroup members develop more positive attitudes towards the outgroup (Pettigrew & Tropp, 2000; Wright & Bougie, 2007). For example, Page-Gould et al. (2008) found that cross-group

FIGURE 13.6 Desegregation needn't mean contact
After this Scottburgh, South Africa, beach became 'open' and desegregated in the new South Africa, Blacks (represented by green dots), Whites (yellow dots) and Indians (blue dots) tended to cluster with their own race.
SOURCE: Adapted from Dixon and Durrheim (2003).

friendships between Latinos and Whites reduced intergroup anxiety and improved liking for the outgroup. Turner et al. (2007) reported similar findings for White school children who make friends who are South Asian. This isn't just reported in research on race but also in studies that consider prejudices on the basis of sexual orientation. For example, Vonofakou et al. (2007) noted how heterosexual men's attitudes towards gay men became much more positive when they made a gay friend. It's not just head knowledge of other people that matters; it's also the *emotional* ties that form with intimate friendships and that serve to reduce anxiety (Hewstone, 2003; Pettigrew & Tropp, 2000).

But 'group salience' also helps bridge divides between people. If you forever think of that friend solely as an individual, your affective ties may not generalize to other members of the friend's group (Miller, 2002). Ideally, then, we should form trusting friendships across group lines but also recognize that the friend represents those in another group – with whom we turn out to have much in common.

We will be most likely to befriend people who differ from us if their outgroup identity is initially minimized – if we see them as essentially like us rather than feeling threatened by their being different. If our liking for our new friends is to generalize to others, their group identity must at some point become salient. So, to reduce prejudice and conflict, we had best initially minimize group diversity, then acknowledge it, then transcend it.

Surveys of nearly 4,000 Europeans reveal that friendship is a key to successful contact: if you have a minority group friend, you become much more likely to express sympathy and support for the friend's group, and even somewhat more support for immigration by that group. It's true of West Germans' attitudes towards Turks, French people's attitudes towards Asians and North Africans, Netherlanders' attitudes towards Surinamers and Turks, Britons' attitudes towards West Indians and Asians, and Northern Ireland Protestants' and Catholics' attitudes towards each other (Brown et al., 1999; Hamberger & Hewstone, 1997; Paolini et al., 2007; Pettigrew, 1997). Likewise, anti-gay feeling is lower among people who know gays personally (Herek, 1993; Kaiser Family Foundation, 2001). Additional studies of attitudes towards the elderly, the mentally ill, HIV/AIDS patients and those with disabilities confirm that contact and especially friendship often predicts positive attitudes (Hewstone, 2003).

equal-status contact the principle that to reduce prejudice between people these should have close contact, in a setting where equal status can be assured, while they work on shared goals requiring co-operation. In addition such initiatives should be supported and encouraged by a broader network

Equal-status Contact

Social psychologists who advocated desegregation never claimed that all contact would improve attitudes. They expected poor results when contacts were competitive, unsupported by authorities, and unequal (Pettigrew, 1988; Stephan, 1987). Before 1954 many prejudiced Whites had frequent contact with Blacks – as shoeshine men and domestic workers. Such unequal contact can breed attitudes that merely justify the continuation of inequality. So it's important that the contact be **equal-status contact**, like that between the store clerks, the soldiers, the neighbours, the prisoners and the summer campers.

Shared predicaments trigger co-operation, as these people on climate strike in Germany demonstrate.
SOURCE: ©Timo Nausch/Shutterstock

Co-operation

Although equal-status contact can help, it is sometimes not enough. It didn't help when Muzafer Sherif stopped the competition at the summer camp and brought the two groups together for non-competitive activities such as watching films, eating and setting off fireworks. By that time the competition between the two groups was so strong that mere contact only provided opportunities for taunts and attacks. Desegregating the two groups promoted their social interaction. Another remedy had to be found. Co-operation was required to unite the two groups in working together to achieve a common goal. Think back to the successful and the unsuccessful desegregation efforts. The army's racial mixing of rifle companies not only brought Blacks and Whites into equal-status contact but also made them interdependent. Together, they were striving towards a shared goal.

So does competitive contact divide and *co-operative* contact unite? Consider what happens to people who together face a common predicament. In conflicts at all levels, from couples to rival teams to nations, shared threats and common goals breed unity.

Common External Threats Build Cohesiveness

Together with others, have you ever been caught in a blizzard, punished by a teacher, or persecuted and ridiculed because of your social, ethnic, racial or religious identity? If so, you may recall feeling close to those with whom you shared the predicament. Perhaps previous social barriers were dropped as you helped one another dig out of the snow or struggled to cope with your common enemy.

Such friendliness is common among those who experience a shared threat. Lanzetta (1955) observed this when he put four-man groups of naval Reserve Officers' Training Corps cadets to work on problem-solving tasks and then began informing them over a loudspeaker that their answers were wrong, their productivity inexcusably low, their thinking stupid. Other groups did not receive this harassment. Lanzetta observed that the group members under duress became friendlier to one another, more co-operative, less argumentative, less competitive. They were in it together. And the result was a cohesive spirit.

Having a common enemy unified the groups of competing boys in Sherif's camping experiments – and in many subsequent experiments (Dion, 1979). Times of interracial strife similarly heighten group pride. For Chinese university students in Toronto, facing discrimination has heightened a sense of kinship with other Chinese (Pak et al., 1991). Just being reminded of an outgroup (say, a rival school) heightens people's responsiveness to their own group (Wilder & Shapiro, 1984). When keenly conscious of who 'they' are, we also know who 'we' are.

Leaders may even create a threatening external enemy as a technique for building group cohesiveness. For the group, the nation, the world, having a common enemy is powerfully unifying. For example, Palestinian suicide bombers in Israel rallied partisan Jews behind the Prime Minister Ariel Sharon and his government, while the Israeli Defence Force killing of Palestinians and the destruction of their property united Muslim factions in their animosity towards Sharon (Pettigrew, 2003). And, after the USA attacked Iraq, Pew Research Centre (2003) polls of Indonesian and Jordanian Muslims found rising anti-Americanism. The 53 per cent of Jordanians who expressed a positive view of Americans in the summer of 2002 plummeted to 18 per cent shortly after the war. 'Before the war, I would have said that if Osama [Bin Laden] was responsible for the two towers, we would not be proud of it,' said one Syrian 21-year-old Islamic law student. 'But if he did it now we would be proud of him' (Rubin, 2003).

Superordinate Goals Foster Co-operation

superordinate goal a shared goal that necessitates co-operative effort; a goal that overrides people's differences from one another

Closely related to the unifying power of an external threat is the unifying power of **superordinate goals**, goals that unite all in a group and require co-operative effort. To promote harmony among his warring campers, Sherif introduced such goals. He created a problem with the camp water supply, necessitating both groups' co-operation to restore the water. Given an opportunity to rent a movie, one expensive enough to require the joint resources of the two groups, they again co-operated. When a truck 'broke down' on a camp excursion, a staff member casually left the tug-of-war rope nearby, prompting one boy to suggest that they all pull the truck to get it started. When it started, a backslapping celebration ensued over their victorious 'tug-of-war against the truck'.

After working together to achieve such superordinate goals, the boys ate together and enjoyed themselves around a campfire. Friendships sprouted across group lines. Hostilities plummeted (**Figure 13.7**). On the last day, the boys decided to travel home together on one bus. During the trip they no longer sat by groups. As the bus approached Oklahoma City and home, they, as one, spontaneously sang 'Oklahoma' and then bade their friends farewell. With isolation and competition, Sherif made strangers into bitter enemies. With superordinate goals, he made enemies into friends.

Group identity feeds, and is fed by, competition. *The Xenophobe's Guide to the Scots* makes the observation that Scots divide non-Scots 'into two main groups: (1) The English; (2) The Rest'. As rabid Chicago Cubs fans are happy if either the Cubs win or the White Sox lose, so rabid fans of Scottish soccer rejoice in either a Scotland victory or an England defeat. 'Phew! They Lost,' rejoiced one Scottish tabloid front-page headline after England's 1996 Euro Cup defeat – by Germany, no less.
SOURCE: ©Edinburghcitymom/Shutterstock

Are Sherif's experiments mere child's play? Or can pulling together to achieve superordinate goals be similarly beneficial with adults in conflict? Blake and Mouton (1979) wondered. So in a series of two-week experiments involving more than 1,000 executives in 150 different groups, they re-created the essential features of the situation experienced by the two boys groups in the summer camp. Each group first engaged in activities by itself, then competed with another group, and then co-operated with the other group in working towards jointly chosen superordinate goals. Their results provided 'unequivocal evidence that adult reactions parallel those of Sherif's younger subjects'.

The co-operative efforts by boys at Sherif's summer camp ended in success. Would the same harmony have emerged if the water had remained off, the movie unaffordable, the truck still stalled? Probably not. Worchel et al. (1977, 1978; Worchel & Norvell, 1980) confirmed that *successful* co-operation between two groups boosts their attraction for each other. If previously conflicting groups *fail* in a co-operative effort, however, and if conditions allow them to attribute their failure to each other, the conflict may worsen. Sherif's groups were already feeling hostile to each other. Thus, failure to raise sufficient funds for the movie might have been attributed to one group's 'stinginess' and 'selfishness'. That would have exacerbated rather than alleviated their conflict.

Should we have 'known it all along'? Gordon Allport spoke for many social psychologists in predicting, 'Prejudice . . . may be reduced by equal status contact between majority and minority groups in the pursuit of common goals' (1954, p. 281). Co-operative learning experiments confirmed Allport's insight, making Slavin (1985) and his colleagues (Slavin et al., 2003) optimistic: 'Thirty years after Allport laid out the basic principles operationalised in cooperative learning methods, we finally have practical, proven methods for implementing contact theory in the desegregated classroom . . . Research on cooperative learning is one of the greatest success stories in the history of educational research.'

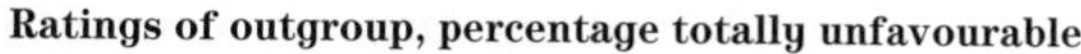
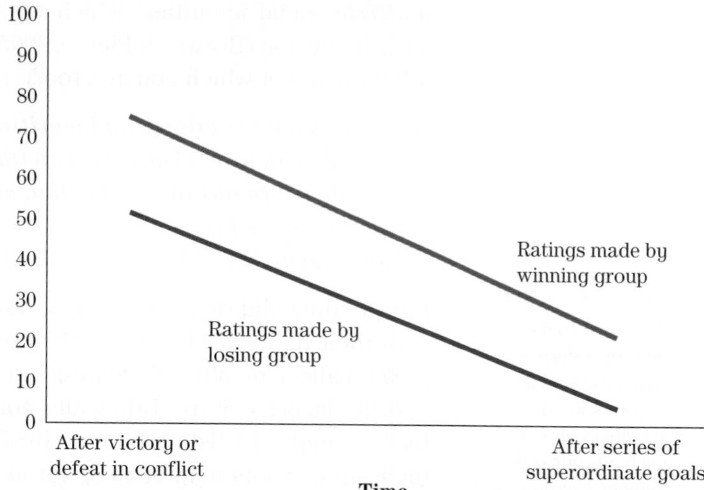

FIGURE 13.7 After competition, the groups of the Eagles and the Rattlers rated each other unfavourably. After they worked co-operatively to achieve superordinate goals, hostility dropped sharply.

SOURCE: Data from Sherif (1966, p. 84).

So, co-operative, equal-status contacts exert a positive influence on boy campers, industrial executives, college students and schoolchildren. Does the principle extend to all levels of human relations? Are families unified by pulling together to farm the land, restore an old house or sail a sloop? Are communal identities forged by barn raisings, group singing or cheering on the football team? Is international understanding bred by international collaboration in science and space, by joint efforts to feed the world and conserve resources, by friendly personal contacts between people of different nations? Indications are that the answer to all those questions is yes (Brewer & Miller, 1988; Desforges et al., 1991, 1997; Deutsch, 1985, 1994). Thus, an important challenge facing our divided world is to identify and agree on our superordinate goals and to structure co-operative efforts to achieve them.

Promoting 'common ingroup identity'. The banning of gang colours and the common European practice of school uniform aim to change 'us' and 'them' to 'we'.

SOURCE: ©Shutterstock/wavebreakmedia

Groups and Superordinate Identities

In everyday life, we often reconcile multiple identities (Gaertner et al., 2000, 2001; Hewstone & Greenland, 2000; Huo et al., 1996). We acknowledge our subgroup identity (as parent or child) and then transcend it (sensing our superordinate identity as a family). Blended families and corporate mergers leave us mindful of who we were, and who we are. Pride in our ethnic heritage can complement our larger communal or national identity. Being mindful of our *multiple* social identities, which we partially share with anyone else, enables social cohesion (Brewer & Pierce, 2005; Crisp & Hewstone, 1999, 2000). 'I am many things, some of which you are, too.'

'Most of us have overlapping identities which unite us with very different groups. We can love what we are, without hating what – and who – we are not. We can thrive in our own tradition, even as we learn from others, and come to respect their teachings.'
Kofi Annan, Nobel Peace Prize Lecture, 2001

Our own social identity is derived from the social groups we are members of and this feeds our self-esteem. Chapter 12 offers extensive coverage of social identity and how we evaluate ourselves in relation to this.

But in ethnically diverse cultures, how do people balance their ethnic identities with their national identities? They may have what identity researcher Phinney (1990) calls a 'bicultural' identity, one that identifies with both the ethnic culture and the larger culture. Ethnically conscious Asians living in England may also feel strongly British (Hutnik, 1985). French Canadians who identify with their ethnic roots may or may not also feel strongly Canadian (Driedger, 1975). Hispanic Americans who retain a strong sense of their 'Cubanness' (or of their Mexican or Puerto Rican heritage) may feel strongly American (Roger et al., 1991). As DuBois (1903, p. 17) explained in *The Souls of Black Folk*, 'The American Negro [longs] . . . to be both a Negro and an American'.

Researchers have wondered whether pride in one's group competes with identification with the larger culture. We evaluate ourselves partly in terms of our group memberships. Seeing our own group (our school, our employer, our family, our race, our nation) as good helps us feel good about ourselves. A positive ethnic identity can therefore contribute to positive self-esteem; so can a positive mainstream culture identity. 'Marginal' people, who have neither a strong ethnic nor a strong mainstream cultural identity (**Table 13.2**), often have low self-esteem. Bicultural people, who affirm both identities, typically have a strongly positive self-concept (Phinney, 1990). Often, they alternate between their two cultures, adapting their language and behaviour to whichever group they are with (LaFromboise et al., 1993).

pluralism respect for differences between cultures within a prevailing culture

assimilation meshing different cultural values and habits into the prevailing culture

Debate continues over the ideals of multiculturalism, or **pluralism** (celebrating differences), versus **assimilation** (meshing one's values and habits with the prevailing culture). On one side are those who believe, as the Department of Canadian Heritage (2006) has declared, that 'multiculturalism ensures that all citizens can keep their identities, can take pride in their ancestry and have a sense of belonging. Acceptance gives Canadians a feeling of security and self-confidence, making them open to and accepting of diverse cultures.' On the other side are those who concur with Britain's former Commission for Racial Equality chair, Trevor Phillips (2004), in worrying that multiculturalism separates people rather than encouraging common values, a view that inspired the Rwandan

TABLE 13.2 Ethnic and cultural identity

Identification with majority group	Identification with ethnic group	
	Strong	**Weak**
Strong	Bicultural	Assimilated
Weak	Separated	Marginal

government to adopt the official view that 'there is no ethnicity here. We are all Rwandan.' In the aftermath of Rwanda's ethnic bloodbath, government documents and government-controlled radio and newspapers have ceased mentioning Hutu and Tutsi (Lacey, 2004). In the space between multiculturalism and assimilation lies 'diversity within unity', a perspective advocated by sociologist Amitai Etzioni (2005). 'It presumes that all members of a given society will fully respect and adhere to those basic values and institutions that are considered part of the basic shared framework of the society. At the same time, every group in society is free to maintain its distinct subculture – those policies, habits, and institutions that do not conflict with the shared core.'

By forging unifying ideals, immigrant countries such as the USA, Canada and Australia have avoided ethnic wars. In these countries, Irish and Italians, Swedes and Scots, Asians and Africans seldom kill in defence of their ethnic identities. Nevertheless, even the immigrant nations struggle between separation and wholeness, between people's pride in their distinct heritage and unity as one nation, between acknowledging the reality of diversity and questing for shared values.

How good relations between groups can be fostered has received much attention from SCT theorists. Miller and Brewer (1984) suggest that forms of intergroup contact can highlight group boundaries, so they propose a '**de-categorization**' (or personalization) model where personal rather than group identity and contact is the focus. However, Samuel Gaertner suggests such avoidances of group boundaries are simply not possible in the real-world and offers the '**common ingroup identity model**', where members of different groups are encouraged to 're-categorize' themselves as belonging to a common ingroup sharing a superordinate identity. Gaertner et al. (1993, 2000) report that working co-operatively leads people to define a new, inclusive group that dissolves their former subgroups. They define this as '**re-categorization**'. Old feelings of bias against another group diminish when members of the two groups sit alternately around a table (rather than on opposite sides), give their new group a single name, and then work together under conditions that foster a good mood. 'Us' and 'them' become 'we'. This has been demonstrated by Lam et al. (2006), who found that when Hong Kong adolescents were asked to read a newspaper article that suggested Hong Kong would be disadvantaged if China joined the World Trade Organization (WTO), they displayed negative attitudes towards Chinese mainlanders, especially when such judgements were made under time pressure. However, when they read a

de-categorization where intergroup contact is facilitated by 'de-categorizing' group members through an emphasis on individual personal characteristics rather than group identity

common ingroup identity model when members of different social groups re-categorize themselves into one group

re-categorization where intergroup contact is facilitated by 're-categorizing' group members under an inclusive common ingroup focusing on a superordinate identity

Marching together for Scottish independence. During the run-up to the Scottish Independence Referendum in 2014, people from diverse ethnic and social backgrounds joined together to celebrate their shared feelings of Scottishness and to highlight their desire for an independent Scotland.
SOURCE: ©Mo and Paul/Shutterstock

newspaper article that suggested the Chinese were facing an economic threat from Japan if China joined the WTO, they re-categorized themselves as Chinese and displayed negative evaluations of the Japanese.

dual identities where group individuals hold superordinate and subordinate identities

More recently the idea of '**dual identities**' has been proposed, which suggests that minority group members might adopt a strategy of holding both superordinate and subordinate identities, in order to fit into mainstream society. Glasford and Dovidio (2011) remark that a common ingroup identity can encourage positive intergroup attitudes and reduce tension. But, the values upon which this common identity is often based, 'favours advantaged groups'. So pure assimilation into the majority group may not be ideal for minority group members. In contrast, a dual identity not only promotes a common superordinate identity but also draws attention to, and respect for, distinct subordinate identities. Recognition of dual identities can help foster values that enable a multicultural society to respect both similarities and differences between groups. Where dual identity exists, minority group members are motivated to establish contact with the majority group to enhance greater intergroup harmony (Glasford & Dovidio, 2011). However, some researchers have argued that having a dual identity can be a double-edged sword. For it to work, the majority group must accept the superordinate identity claims of minority group members, and welcome the subordinate identity. Baysu et al. (2011) looked at the high school experiences of Turkish Belgian young adults. They compared the different strategies that second-generation Turkish participants adopted to fit into high school in Belgium. They found that those who used a separated strategy, emphasizing their different ethnic Turkish identity, were very resilient in the face of discrimination and intergroup hostility. They performed well at school as they tried to overcome the negative stereotypes Belgians had of this group. Other students adopted an assimilation strategy, becoming acculturated into Belgian life and national identity. They upheld Belgian norms and values, and as such performed well when their own ethnic group was threatened. By distancing themselves from the Turkish ethnic group, they could affirm their commitment to the Belgian national group and display this through good academic performance. Finally, those students who had adopted a dual identity approach had a more difficult time. In Belgium, recognition and tolerance of other ethnic identities is poor. As such, those participants who adopted a dual identity found themselves unaccepted in terms of a common national (superordinate) Belgian identity, or an ethnic (Turkish) one. Baysu et al. (2011) point out that dual identity strategies do not seem to work in environments where a minority group is subject to high levels of threat. When the level of threat is low, and society is more accepting of diverse ethnic cultures, dual identifiers actually perform much better in school than those who adopt a separated or assimilated strategy.

Communication

To resolve a social dilemma, people must communicate. In the laboratory, as in real life, group communication sometimes degenerates into threats and name-calling (Deutsch & Krauss, 1960). More often, communication enables people to co-operate (Bornstein & Rapoport, 1988; Bornstein et al., 1989). Discussing the dilemma forges a group identity which enhances concern for everyone's welfare. It devises group norms and consensus expectations and puts pressure on members to follow them. Particularly when people are face to face it enables them to commit themselves to co-operation (Bouas & Komorita, 1996; Drolet & Morris, 2000; Kerr & Kaufman-Gilliland, 1994; Kerr et al., 1997; Pruitt, 1998).

Conflicting parties have other ways to resolve their differences. Andersen et al. (2008) note that how communication is conducted between groups can be extremely important for resolution of intergroup conflict. When we convey warmth, respect and co-operation, peace is more likely.

When husband and wife, or labour and management, or nation X and nation Y disagree, they can **bargain** with each other directly. They can ask a third party to **mediate** by making suggestions and facilitating their negotiations. Or they can **arbitrate** by submitting their disagreement to someone who will study the issues and impose a settlement.

bargaining seek resolution to a conflict through direct negotiation between parties

mediate an attempt by a neutral third party to resolve a conflict by facilitating communication and offering suggestions

arbitrate resolution of a conflict by a neutral third party who studies both sides and imposes a settlement

Bargaining

If you want to buy or sell a new car, are you better off adopting a tough bargaining stance – opening with an extreme offer so that splitting the difference will yield a favourable result? Or are you better off beginning with a sincere 'good-faith' offer?

Experiments suggest no simple answer. Tough bargaining may lower the other party's expectations, making the other side willing to settle for less (Yukl, 1974). But toughness can sometimes backfire. Being tough is a potential lose–lose scenario. If the other party responds with an equally tough stance, both may be locked into positions from which neither can back down without losing face. In the weeks before the 1991 Persian Gulf War, the first President Bush threatened, in the full glare of publicity, to 'kick Saddam's ass'. Saddam Hussein, no less macho, threatened to make 'infidel' Americans 'swim in their own blood'. After such belligerent statements, it was difficult for each side to evade war and save face.

Mediation

A third-party mediator may offer suggestions that enable conflicting parties to make concessions and still save face (Pruitt, 1998). If my concession can be attributed to a mediator, who is gaining an equal concession from my antagonist, then neither of us will be viewed as weakly caving in to the other's demands.

Turning Win-Lose into Win-Win

Mediators also help resolve conflicts by facilitating constructive communication. Their first task is to help the parties rethink the conflict and gain information about others' interests (Thompson, 1998). Typically, people on both sides have a competitive 'win–lose' orientation: they are successful if their opponent is unhappy with the result, and unsuccessful if their opponent is pleased (Thompson et al., 1995). The mediator aims to replace this win–lose orientation with a co-operative 'win–win' orientation, by prodding both sides to set aside their conflicting demands and instead to think about each other's underlying needs, interests and goals. In experiments, Thompson (1990a, 1990b) found that, with experience, negotiators become better able to make mutually beneficial trade-offs and thus to achieve win–win resolutions.

Unravelling Misperceptions with Controlled Communications

Communication often helps reduce self-fulfilling misperceptions. Perhaps you can recall experiences similar to that of this college student:

Often, after a prolonged period of little communication, I perceive Mary's silence as a sign of her dislike for me. She, in turn, thinks that my quietness is a result of my being mad at her. My silence induces her silence, which makes me even more silent . . . until this snowballing effect is broken by some occurrence that makes it necessary for us to interact. And the communication then unravels all the misinterpretations we had made about one another.

The outcome of such conflicts often depends on *how* people communicate their feelings to one another. Programmes train couples and children how to manage conflicts constructively (Horowitz & Boardman, 1994). If managed constructively, conflict provides opportunities for reconciliation and more genuine harmony. Psychologists Ian Gotlib and Catherine Colby (1988) offer advice on how to avoid destructive quarrels and how to have good quarrels.

Conflict researchers report that a key factor is *trust* (Ross & Ward, 1995). If you believe the other person is well intentioned, you are then more likely to divulge your needs and concerns. Lacking trust, you may fear that being open will give the other party information that might be used against you.

When the two parties mistrust each other and communicate unproductively, a third-party mediator – a marriage counsellor, a labour mediator, a diplomat – sometimes helps. Often the mediator is someone trusted by both sides. In the 1980s it took an Algerian Muslim to mediate the conflict between Iran and Iraq, and the Pope to resolve a geographical dispute between Argentina and Chile (Carnevale & Choi, 2000).

After coaxing the conflicting parties to rethink their perceived win–lose conflict, the mediator often has each party identify and rank its goals. When goals are compatible, the ranking procedure makes it easier for each to concede on less important goals so that both achieve their chief goals (Erickson et al., 1974; Schulz & Pruitt, 1978). South Africa achieved internal peace when Black and White South Africans granted each other's top priorities – replacing apartheid with majority rule and safeguarding the security, welfare and rights of Whites (Kelman, 1998).

The mediator will often structure the encounter to help each party understand and feel understood by the other. The mediator may ask the conflicting parties to restrict their arguments to statements of fact, including statements of how they feel and how they respond when the other acts in a given way. Also, the mediator may ask people to reverse roles and argue the other's position, or to imagine and explain what the other person is experiencing.

These peace-making principles – based partly on laboratory experiments, partly on practical experience – have helped mediate both international and industrial conflicts (Blake & Mouton, 1962, 1979; Fisher, 1994; Wehr, 1979). One small team of Arab and Jewish Americans, led by social psychologist Herbert Kelman (1997), has conducted workshops bringing together influential Arabs and Israelis. Another social psychologist team, led by Ervin Staub and Laurie Ann Pearlman (2005, 2006; Staub et al., 2005), worked in Rwanda between 1999 and 2003 training facilitators and journalists to understand and write about Rwanda's trauma in ways that promote healing and reconciliation. Using methods such as those we've considered, Kelman and colleagues counter misperceptions and have participants seek creative solutions for their common good. Isolated, the participants are free to speak directly to their adversaries without fear that their constituents are second-guessing what they are saying. The result? Those from both sides typically come to understand the other's perspective and how the other side responds to their own group's actions.

Arbitration

Some conflicts are so intractable, the underlying interests so divergent, that a mutually satisfactory resolution is unattainable. In Bosnia and Kosovo, both Serbs and Muslims could not have jurisdiction over the same homeland. In this and many other cases, a third-party mediator may – or may not – help resolve the conflict.

If not, the parties may turn to *arbitration* by having the mediator or another third party *impose* a settlement. Disputants usually prefer to settle their differences without arbitration so that they retain control over the outcome. McGillicuddy et al. (1987) observed this preference in an experiment involving disputants coming to a dispute settlement centre. When people knew they would face an arbitrated settlement if mediation failed, they tried harder to resolve the problem, exhibited less hostility and thus were more likely to reach agreement.

Typically, however, the final offer is not as reasonable as it would be if each party, free of self-serving bias, saw its own proposal through others' eyes. Negotiation researchers report that most disputants are made stubborn by 'optimistic overconfidence' (Kahneman & Tversky, 1995). Successful mediation is hindered when, as often happens, both parties believe they have a two-thirds chance of winning a final-offer arbitration (Bazerman, 1986, 1990).

Conciliation

Sometimes tension and suspicion run so high that even communication, let alone resolution, becomes all but impossible. Each party may threaten, coerce or retaliate against the other. Unfortunately, such acts tend to be reciprocated, escalating the conflict. So, would a strategy of appeasing the other party by being unconditionally co-operative produce a satisfying result? Often not. In laboratory games, those who are 100 per cent co-operative often are exploited. Politically, a one-sided pacifism is usually out of the question.

Social psychologist Charles Osgood (1962, 1980) advocated a third option, one that is conciliatory yet strong enough to discourage exploitation. Osgood called it 'graduated and reciprocated initiatives in tension reduction'. He nicknamed it **GRIT**, a label that suggests the determination it requires. GRIT aims to reverse the 'conflict spiral' by triggering reciprocal de-escalation. To do so, it draws upon social psychological concepts, such as the norm of reciprocity and the attribution of motives.

GRIT acronym for 'graduated and reciprocated initiatives in tension reduction' – a strategy designed to de-escalate international tensions

GRIT requires one side to initiate a few small de-escalatory actions, after *announcing a conciliatory intent.* The initiator states its desire to reduce tension, declares each conciliatory act before making it and invites the adversary to reciprocate. Such announcements create a framework that helps the adversary correctly interpret what otherwise might be seen as weak or tricky actions. They also bring public pressure to bear on the adversary to follow the reciprocity norm.

Next, the initiator establishes credibility and genuineness by carrying out, exactly as announced, several verifiable *conciliatory acts.* This intensifies the pressure to reciprocate. Making conciliatory acts diverse – perhaps offering medical help, closing a military base and lifting a trade ban – keeps the initiator from making a significant sacrifice in any one area and leaves the adversary freer to choose its own means of reciprocation. If the adversary reciprocates voluntarily, its own conciliatory behaviour may soften its attitudes. Deutsch (1993) captured the spirit of GRIT in advising negotiators to be '"firm, fair, and friendly": *firm* in resisting intimidation, exploitation, and dirty tricks; *fair* in holding to one's moral principles and not reciprocating the other's immoral behaviour despite his or her provocations; and *friendly* in the sense that one is willing to initiate and reciprocate cooperation'.

Does GRIT really work? In laboratory dilemma games a successful strategy has proved to be simple 'tit-for-tat', which similarly begins with a co-operative opening play and thereafter matches the other party's last response (Axelrod & Dion, 1988; Parks & Rumble, 2001; Van Lange & Visser, 1999). Although it begins co-operatively, tit-for-tat immediately punishes non-co-operation and also immediately forgives hostile opponents as soon as they make a co-operative move. In a lengthy series of experiments Svenn Lindskold and his associates found 'strong support for the various steps in the GRIT proposal' (see, e.g. Lindskold et al., 1976; Lindskold & Han, 1988). In laboratory games, announcing co-operative intent *does* boost co-operation. Repeated conciliatory acts *do* breed greater trust (although self-serving biases often make one's own acts seem more conciliatory and less hostile than those of the adversary). Maintaining an equality of power *does* protect against exploitation.

Lindskold was not contending that the world of the laboratory experiment mirrors the more complex world of everyday life. Rather, experiments enable us to formulate and verify powerful theoretical principles, such as the reciprocity norm and the self-serving bias. As Lindskold (1981) noted, 'It is the theories, not the individual experiments that are used to interpret the world'.

Real-world Applications

GRIT-like strategies have occasionally been tried outside the laboratory, with promising results. During the Berlin crisis of the early 1960s, US and Russian tanks faced each other barrel to barrel. The crisis was defused when the Americans pulled back their tanks step by step. At each step, the Russians reciprocated. Similarly, in the 1970s small concessions by Israel and Egypt (for example, Israel allowing Egypt to open up the Suez Canal, Egypt allowing ships bound for Israel to pass through) helped reduce tension to a point where the negotiations became possible (Rubin, 1981).

Focus on

Is Prejudice All in our Heads?

Developments in the field of social neuroscience have influenced social psychologists interested in prejudice. As our ability to see neural processes in the brain increases with the advancement of brain-imaging techniques, does this mean we can observe neural reactions that might be responsible for our prejudices? Certainly there is evidence that some activity goes on in our brains which seems to be associated with racist attitudes. For example, Phelps et al. (2000) found that when White participants saw African American faces (black), there was greater amygdala activation than when they were shown European American faces (white). But is it the brain causing the prejudice, or the prejudice causing the activity in the brain?

Remember our discussion of schemas in Chapter 4? There we considered work that noted how schemas help us to perceive the world around us. We are very quick to recognize what we 'expect' to see. Gaertner and McLaughlin (1983), for example, found that participants were much quicker to recognize positive words when they were preceded by a white face than when preceded by a black face. Why? Well, that's because they fit our schemas, argue the researchers. So regardless of whether these participants think they are prejudiced or not, these racial stereotypes exist in their minds (Fiske & Taylor, 1991).

Todorov et al. (2006) suggest that while we can see these processes in the brain, what they reflect is social and cultural learning, norms and values. They have been acquired in a particular social context, and tend to occur when we are asked to compare unfamiliar people on a salient group characteristic such as race. As social psychological work on categorization has emphasized, people are motivated to enhance their own group, and seek out information that maximizes differences between 'us' and 'them'. So when comparing black faces with white ones we see the neural processes associated with doing so.

It is observations such as these that led to the development of social neuroscience, which attempts to explore biological processes within social contexts. As Amodio and Keysers (2018) note, social neuroscience has much to say about intergroup relations, and how we might go about reducing prejudice. For instance, Mattan et al. (2018) have shown that different brain networks are associated with race-based judgements and status-based judgements of individuals, with race-based judgements involving purely perceptual networks, and status-based judgements involving perceptual and/or knowledge-based networks.

This has implications for how we might go about developing effective prejudice-reduction interventions. For instance, it suggests that racial prejudice is best addressed by attempting to attenuate superficial perceptual-based reactions to black versus white faces. Various fMRI studies have shown this to be successfully achieved through processes such as individuation, which is when a participant is encouraged to see a target as a unique individual, rather than just 'a Black person', for example (Freeman et al., 2010). Freeman and colleagues found that while superficial judgements of a target based on their race activated the amygdala (which is the main brain area involved in processing emotions such as anger and fear), individualized judgements of a target activated a brain network that is believed to play a role in theory of mind: the ability to appreciate that others hold different views and perspectives to our own. This increases the likelihood of the target being treated as a fellow human being who should be respected, rather than an outgroup member who should be feared.

There are other ways in which we can override our tendency to make negatively biased assumptions about another group. In Chapter 10, we considered how people are quick to help people they perceive to be fellow ingroup members. They feel empathy towards them. EEG studies back this up, showing that when White participants watch another White person perform an action, they 'mentally resonate' with them, exhibiting high levels of motor activity in their cortex (Gutsell & Inzlicht, 2012). However, when they see Black people perform the same activity, this neural activity is absent. Inzlicht et al. (2012) propose that if racial prejudice is culturally learned, such that we do not 'mentally resonate' with other races, then it should be possible to override it, and reduce prejudice. In their study, some of their White participants were asked to mimic the actions of a Black actor when he reached for a glass of water. When these participants were then measured for implicit racism, they showed reduced implicit racism unlike those White participants who had simply observed the Black actor, but hadn't mimicked him. The researchers conclude that putting yourself in the shoes of a member of an outgroup can reduce prejudice, and kick-start those brain processes that underlie 'mentally resonating' with them.

Maister et al. (2013) took this further by using the 'rubber hand illusion', which involves hiding one of the participant's hands from their view with a mirror, and showing them the reflection of a rubber hand in the mirror. When the rubber hand and the participant's hidden hand are stroked simultaneously, the participant usually begins to feel as if the rubber hand belong to them. By using a black rubber hand, the researcher gave White participants the experience of owning a black body. The researchers found that the more intensely the participants experienced ownership of the hand, the more their implicit racial biases reduced. The researchers describe this as evidence of perceived self-other body overlap playing an important role in prejudice reduction.

Questions

1. Is it possible to 'unlearn' prejudice?
2. To what extent do you think implicit measures of prejudice capture what is going on in our heads? Are they a faithful reflection of activity in the brain?

SUMMING UP: PREJUDICE, INTERGROUP RELATIONS AND CONFLICT

UNDERSTANDING PREJUDICE

- Social psychological explanations of prejudice have ranged from the study of personality characteristics, prejudiced attitudes, the demands of social cognition, its relationship to social context and its expression in language.
- Personality explanations have emphasized the role of authoritarianism, rigid thinking and political preferences in highly prejudiced individuals.
- Social cognition explanations have considered the role of categorization and the formation of stereotypes to ingroups and outgroups in prejudice.
- Some social psychologists have examined the social hierarchies of social groups within a society and considered how individuals' beliefs about the existence of inequalities are related to levels of prejudice.
- A threat to one's cultural worldview may cause even further faith in that worldview and prejudice towards those who challenge it.
- Discursive psychologists have investigated how prejudice is constructed in talk and text, producing and reproducing common-sense ways of understanding 'them' and 'us'.
- Prejudice exists in subtle and unconscious guises as well as overt, conscious forms. Researchers have devised subtle survey questions and indirect methods for assessing people's attitudes and behaviour to detect unconscious prejudice.
- Racial prejudice has become far less overtly prevalent, but it still exists in subtle forms.
- Similarly, prejudice against women has lessened in recent decades. Nevertheless, strong gender stereotypes and a fair amount of gender bias are still found. Though less obvious, prejudice lurks.

INTERGROUP CONFLICT

- Intergroup conflict defines negative behaviour that occurs between distinct social groups on the basis of membership of that group. Social psychologists have been particularly concerned with the conditions under which conflict will occur.

- Realistic conflict theory suggests that conflict is likely between groups when there is a battle for scarce resources.
- Social identity theory and self-categorization theory argue that conflict will occur even in the absence of competition for scarce resources. Individuals identify with groups and stereotype the characteristics of their group and others in socially relevant and meaningful ways. Groups will engage in conflict when they perceive the existence of an outgroup as a threat to the identity and values of the ingroup.

CROWDS

- Social psychologists have examined the behaviour of crowds as visible demonstrations of negative intergroup relations.
- Some theorists have suggested that being in a crowd causes a psychological change within the individuals who constitute the crowd. Le Bon's 'group mind' emphasizes the irrationality of the crowd as individuals become submerged as the 'racial unconscious' takes over their usual psychological functioning.
- Deindividuation theorists have argued that people in crowds lose their sense of identity and responsibility. This decrease in self-monitoring leads to aggressive behaviour as individuals experience anonymity within the crowd.
- Emergent norm theorists have argued that, rather than losing identity, what happens in a crowd situation is that certain individuals engage in 'keynoting activities', which leads to the formation of emergent norms and values, collectively shared and expressed by the group as a whole.
- Social identity theorists have focused on the social context in which crowd behaviour occurs. The crowd distinguishes itself in meaningful ways from 'others', forming a social identity which guides appropriate and meaningful behaviour.

INTERGROUP HARMONY

- *Contact, co-operation, communication* and *conciliation* can transform hostility into harmony; when contact encourages emotional ties with individuals identified with an outgroup and when it is structured to convey *equal status*, hostilities often lessen.
- Contacts are especially beneficial when people work together to overcome a common threat or to achieve a superordinate goal. Taking their cue from experiments on *co-operative contact*, several research teams have replaced competitive classroom learning situations with opportunities for co-operative learning, with heartening results.
- Conflicting parties often have difficulty communicating. A *third-party mediator* can promote communication by prodding the antagonists to replace their competitive win–lose view of their conflict with a more co-operative win–win orientation. Mediators can also structure communications that will peel away misperceptions and increase mutual understanding and trust. When a negotiated settlement is not reached, the conflicting parties may defer the outcome to an *arbitrator*, who either dictates a settlement or selects one of the two final offers.
- Sometimes tensions run so high that genuine communication is impossible. In such cases, small conciliatory gestures by one party may elicit reciprocal conciliatory acts by the other party. One such conciliatory strategy, GRIT (graduated and reciprocated initiatives in tension reduction), aims to alleviate tense international situations.

Critical Questions

1. Is crowd behaviour irrational?
2. What explanations have social psychologists offered for negative relations between groups?
3. What are the possible limitations of a personality explanation of prejudice?
4. How can the insights of social psychology be applied to tackling prejudice in the real world?

Recommended Reading

Listed below are some classic and contemporary readings in social psychology on intergroup relations, conflict and prejudice.

Classic Sources

Adorno, T. W., Frenkel-Brunswik, E., Levenson, D. J., & Sanford, R. N. (1950). *The authoritarian personality*. Harper and Row.

Allport, G. W. (1954). *The nature of prejudice*. Perseus Books.

Reicher, S. D. (1984). The St Paul's riot: An explanation of the limits of crowd action in terms of a social identity model. *European Journal of Social Psychology, 14*, 1–21.

Contemporary Sources

Condor, S., Abell, J., Figgou, L., Gibson, S., & Stevenson, C. (2006). 'They're not racist': Prejudice denial, mitigation and suppression in dialogue. *British Journal of Social Psychology, 45*, 441–462.

Durrheim, K., & Dixon, J. A. (2001). The role of place and metaphor in racial exclusion: South Africa's beaches as sites of shifting racialisation. *Ethnic and Racial Studies, 24*, 433–450.

Glasford, D. E., & Dovidio, J. F. (2011). E pluribus unum: Dual identity and minority group members' motivation to engage in contact, as well as change. *Journal of Experimental Social Psychology, 47*(5), 1021–1024.

McKeown, S., & Dixon, J. (2017). The 'contact hypothesis': Critical reflections and future directions. *Social and Personality Psychology Compass, 11*(1), e12295.

Stott, C., & Reicher, S. (2011). *Mad mobs and Englishmen? Myths and realities of the 2011 riots.* Constable & Robinson.

14 BIOLOGY, CULTURE AND GENDER

"By birth, the same; by custom, different."
The Analects

In this chapter, we shall explore in more detail biological, social and cultural influences that shape our lives and underlie psychological explanations. How much of our thinking and behaviour is down to our biology, and how much is shaped by socialization from our environment? As we shall see, the invisible strings that shape our behaviour cannot be illuminated easily with just a biological or social and cultural explanation. You are probably familiar with the 'nature versus nurture' argument to explain our thinking and behaviour. This argument assumes that biological and social and cultural forces are at opposite ends of a metaphorical tug-of-war showdown to reveal the stronger force in shaping our lives. But as we shall see, the nature versus nurture debate is not terribly helpful or correct in understanding thinking and behaviour. Rather it is a complex interaction of these forces that drives our experiences. To offer a more accurate metaphor, biology, sociality and culture are in a co-dependent relationship with one another.

Imagine just for a moment, approaching Earth from light-years away, alien scientists are assigned to study the species *Homo sapiens*. Their plan: to observe two randomly sampled humans. Their first subject, Jill, is a verbally combative trial lawyer who grew up in the northern English city of Manchester but moved south seeking the 'London lifestyle'. After an affair and a divorce, Jill is enjoying a second marriage. Friends describe Jill as an independent thinker who is self-confident, competitive and somewhat domineering.

Their second subject, Pietro, lives with a spouse and their two children in Sicily. Pietro is proud of being a good child, a loyal spouse and a protective parent. Friends describe Pietro as kind, gentle, respectful, sensitive and supportive of extended family.

From their small sample of these two people, what might our alien scientists conclude about human nature? Would they wonder whether the two are from different subspecies? Or would they be struck by deeper similarities beneath the surface differences?

The questions faced by our alien scientists are those faced by today's earthbound scientists: How do we humans differ? How are we alike? Are there differences between men and women? Those questions are central to a world where social and cultural diversity has become obvious for everybody. In a world struggling with social and cultural differences, can we learn to accept our diversity, value all identities and recognize the extent of our human kinship? Sure we can. To see why, let's consider the evolutionary, cultural and social roots of our humanity, and examine in what ways we are similar and how we are different.

How Are We Influenced by Human Nature and Cultural Diversity?

Throughout its history, social psychology has grappled with biological and cultural explanations of human behaviour. This discussion is sometimes, rather misguidedly, referred to as the nature nurture debate. But are nature and nurture really two distinct perspectives?

biological outfit the biological processes, including genetic heritage, that shape living organisms

The relationship between biology and culture is complex but fascinating. How does the **biological outfit** of a newborn baby prepare it for development to adulthood within a particular culture? How do biology and culture interact to create a mature person with a mind, language and other psychological functions? There are no hard and fast answers. We cannot ignore the influence our biology has on human development and socialization. But neither can we explain away our attitudes, values, norms, motivation, cognitions, emotions and behaviour as simply a matter of biology. Social psychology engages with biological, social and cultural influences to understand how human beings develop, and are influenced, throughout their lives.

Most people – and not least students of social psychology – have wondered how much of themselves stems from their parents and family, from their inherited genes, and how much is due to their upbringing, socialization and environment. Sometimes we recognize characteristics of our parents in our self and we see similarities in ways of talking, walking and even attitudes. Looking at our physical attributes we are definitely aware of inherited traits, for instance hair and eye colour, shape of face and height. But what about psychological characteristics? Do we inherit from our parents how to think, feel and behave as well? Yes, most of us have to admit there are similarities between the psychological traits of children and their parents. But are these inherited in the same way as the physical marks? Are they something handed over from our ancestors through our genetic outfit, or is it a social and cultural heritage? Our fascination with our family tree has been further fuelled by the Internet and advances in genetic testing. It is now relatively straightforward for many of us to search for our ancestry, which we hope might reveal some answers to 'who' we are (Smolenyak Smolenyak & Turner, 2004). Do we become similar to our family, parents and siblings because we learn to think, feel and behave like them through the socialization process? What about the case of adopted children? Such children are genetically dissimilar to their adoptive parents, but do they become similar to them through socialization processes? Questions like these have been topics in psychology for many years. Today most social psychologists agree that nature and nurture interact. Human biology and culture both contribute and in many ways influence each other. But *how* do they contribute and relate to each other?

Here we examine how our genes, instincts and inborn qualities interact with social and cultural influences and experiences. We will explore how higher psychological functions such as emotions, memory, motivation, attitudes and values develop in humans on the basis of inherited genes and elementary instinctive drives representing nature. But with the development of thinking and language in humans, we are not slaves to these instinctive drives. We can question, judge and rationalize our behaviour and that of others. We can create rules to facilitate a civil society, making some social acts and thoughts permissible and others prohibited. Our ways of perceiving, thinking and language are produced in a particular culture with its social rules, values and norms about what is desirable and what is not. To understand the development and creation of human psychology in this way makes it possible to explain why people are similar but also different.

Therefore, we need to consider both the genetic outfit and the cultural impact to understand human beings: our genes and inborn qualities and instincts enable an adaptive and developing human brain – a cerebral structure that receives cultural impact due to its **plasticity**.

brain plasticity the changes that occur in the organization and structure of the brain as a result of experience and individual physical or psychological activity

However, many body functions are also dependent on the environment. Production of the hormones adrenaline and noradrenaline will be influenced by how stressful we regard a social situation to be. Other hormones and physiological processes also react to the environment. The brain adjusts to the social situation and our psychological reactions. It develops new capacity as a result of our physical and mental activity and how we cope with the situation. It stores what happens and creates new ways of thinking, feeling and behaving. This physical and mental activity produces structural changes in the brain due to the brain plasticity in humans (Kolb & Gibb, 2011).

Historically, the brain was looked upon as anatomically hardwired at birth (Fiske & Taylor, 2013). However, an enormous amount of modern-day research has revealed that the brain never stops changing and adjusting (e.g. Ambady & Bharucha, 2009; Cai et al., 2014; Gergen, 2010; Klimecki, 2015). So it is not really legitimate any longer to regard the brain as a fixed collection of wired-up neurons like the hardware in a personal computer. The interconnections between neurons are changing all the time and brain structure is more like software; it becomes updated through cultural and social experience. This explains the importance of social and cultural influences since experiences are internalized and stored both in mind and brain. Doidge (2007) stated that neuroplasticity is 'one of the most extraordinary discoveries of the twentieth century'.

Genes, Evolution and Behaviour

The universal behaviours that define human nature arise from our biological similarity. Anthropologists have told us that if we could trace our ancestors back 100,000 or more years, we would see that geographically we are all from land that we now call Africa (Shipman, 2003). In response to climate change and the availability of food, those early hominids migrated across Africa into Asia, Europe, the Australian subcontinent and, eventually, the Americas. As they adapted to their new environments, early humans developed differences that, measured on anthropological scales, are relatively recent and superficial. For example, those who stayed in Africa had darker skin pigment – what Harvard psychologist Steven Pinker (2002) calls 'sunscreen for the tropics' – and those who went far north of the equator evolved lighter skins capable of synthesizing vitamin D in less direct sunlight.

We were Africans so recently that 'there has not been much time to accumulate many new versions of the genes', notes Pinker (2002, p. 143). And, indeed, biologists who study our genes have found that we humans – even humans as seemingly different as Jill and Pietro – are strikingly similar in their genes, like members of one tribe. We may be more numerous than chimpanzees, but chimps are more genetically varied than humans. We also share the majority of our genes with other species – for instance, mice.

To explain how *Homo sapiens,* and all species, developed, the British naturalist Charles Darwin (1859) proposed an evolutionary process. Darwin's idea, to which philosopher Daniel Dennett (2005) would give 'the gold medal for the best idea anybody ever had', was that **natural selection** enables evolution.

natural selection the evolutionary process by which heritable traits that best enable organisms to survive and reproduce in particular environments are passed to ensuing generations

The idea behind natural selection, simplified, is as follows.

- Organisms have many and varied offspring (usually many more than humans).
- Those offspring compete for survival in their environment.
- Certain biological and behavioural variations increase their chances of reproduction and survival in that natural environment.

- Those offspring that do survive are more likely to pass their genes to ensuing generations.
- Thus, over time, population characteristics may change.

The exciting thing about evolution is not that our understanding is perfect or complete but that it is the foundation stone for the rest of biology.
Donald Kennedy, Editor-in-Chief, *Science*, 2005

Natural selection implies that certain genes – those which predisposed traits that increased the odds of surviving long enough to reproduce and nurture descendants – became more abundant. In the snowy Arctic environment, for example, genes programming a thick coat of camouflaging white fur have won the genetic competition in polar bears. In hot, desert environments, genes programming estivation (the summer equivalent of hibernation) predominate in a number of species. So perhaps it is simply our selfish genes assuring their reproduction, which drive our behaviour and the way in which we experience the world around us.

Biologically speaking, one major purpose of life is to produce offspring. But biology does not have a conscious purpose. It does what it has to do without any intent. Different from other species, men and women can decide whether they want offspring or not. To produce children is, psychologically speaking, not always the purpose for humans, and there are huge variations between cultures or countries in the degree to which people consider children to be an important part of their lives.

Our social situation also influences our decisions about how many children we have, and whether we have any at all (see **Figure 14.1** overleaf). In this way the biological evolutionary principle does not govern humans' behaviour in the same way as in other species. When women of the European Union and United States who are mothers were asked how many children they would like, most wanted more than they currently have (Livingston, 2014). Yet this desire occurs against a falling birth rate. Social and economic pressures mean these women have fewer children than they actually want. Challenges such as the cost of raising children, and women leaving it longer until they have children, means fewer children.

It also seems that an increasing number of women, and men, are voluntarily choosing to be child-free. According to the Office for National Statistics (2019) for the UK, 25 per cent of women who have a university education are still childless at 40 years of age. A survey of US women found that 1 in 5 women now enter menopause having never borne a child. This is a marked increase from 1 in 10 post-menopause women not having a child in the 1970s (Livingston & Cohn, 2010). In Europe, Italy and Spain are examples of an increasing trend towards childlessness. Japan has seen a sharp rise in childless women over the last decade (*The Economist*, 2017).

So what is making childlessness attractive? Research has offered a range of explanations. In some countries, such as Germany and Sweden, highly educated women, but also men who have little or no education, are choosing to remain childless. Why? Well, it seems that childless women invest their time in their careers rather than raising children. Career-focused women often discover that taking time out to have a child can be detrimental to their career. A Pew Survey

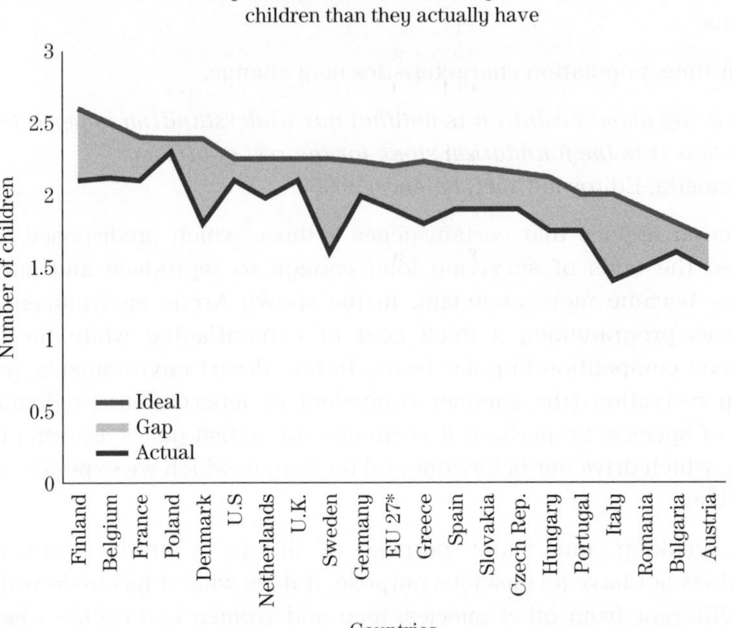

**Mean for all 27 nations who were members of the European Union in 2011*

Only countries with a population of over 5 million are shown. Actual fertility in Europe is based on biological children only. European ideal fertility based on responses to: "And for you personally, what would be the ideal number of children you would like to have or would have liked to have had?" U.S. ideal fertility based on responses to: "What do you think is the ideal number of children for a family to have?" Respondents providing non-numerical answers were excluded from the analysis.
Sources: European data from 2011 Eurobarometer, U.S. data from 2006 and 2008 General Social Survey.

FIGURE 14.1 You can't always have what you want?
SOURCE: Livingston (2014)

found that working mothers are the ones who have to compromise their careers to raise children (Parker, 2015). So whilst women may have negotiated their way into the workplace, they have yet to negotiate the flexibility needed to juggle careers with a family (*The Economist*, 2017). However, for childless men it is more likely that they have not found a suitable partner and/or it is the lack of a reliable job and income that renders them childless. Concerns about the detrimental impact human population has on the environment is also a factor in voluntary childlessness, as well as changing attitudes towards remaining child-free. The stigma of not having children has mostly disappeared from developed countries. It is those countries that value individualism with the highest rates of childlessness (Miettinen et al., 2015; Livingston & Cohn, 2010; Petter, 2017; *The Economist*, 2017).

Natural Selection and Evolutionary Psychology

Since Darwin wrote about evolution of the species and the theory of natural selection more than 150 years ago, there have been competing explanations of how the selection process actually happens. Today we realize that the forces behind evolution are more complex than Darwin thought. Simply the survival of the fittest and natural selection does not fully explain how human beings develop and acquire their abilities and how they forward them to the next generation. Due to cultural impact, the way humans do this is different from how it is done in other animal species. For example, we consider the impact that the forces of natural selection have on human behaviours relating to aggression (Chapter 8), attraction (Chapter 9), and helping (Chapter 11). In all of these cases, those forces do not simply drive the behaviour but function to a greater or lesser extent as part of a complex interaction with societal and cultural influences.

In the freezing temperatures of the Arctic, the polar bear has developed a thick white fur coat that not only maintains body heat, but also offers camouflage to aid hunting.
SOURCE: ©Paul Cameron Allen/Shutterstock

Natural selection, Darwin's principle for evolution of biological characteristics, has gained popularity with social psychologists. *Evolutionary psychology* studies how natural selection predisposes not just physical traits – polar bears' coats, bats' sonar, humans' colour vision – but psychological traits and social behaviours that enhance the preservation of one's genes (Buss, 2005). Confer et al. (2010) note the goal of evolutionary psychology is 'to study human behaviour as the product of evolved psychological mechanisms that depend on internal and environmental input for their development, activation, and expression in manifest behaviour' (p. 11).

For an introduction to evolutionary psychology and its influence on social psychology, see Chapter 1.

According to evolutionary psychologists any distinction between nature and nurture, or biological and cultural, is meaningless and redundant. Our environment shapes physiological and psychological mechanisms, and likewise our physiological and psychological mechanisms shape our environment. The bottom-line though, is that for evolutionary psychologists, these processes are shaped and adapted to increase our chances of survival and reproduction (Confer et al., 2010; Lewis et al., 2017). See "The Social Construction of Sex and Gender".

Neurobiology and Culture

In earlier chapters of this book we consider research that has looked for a genetic explanation for social behaviours. For example, we look at the 'silver fox' in Chapter 8, which shows how aggression can be genetically 'bred out' of a species and increase domestication. Genes make up the structure and immediate function of the brain at birth, but the environment exerts heavy influence on the brain. Every day the newborn's brain is flooded with new information through the sensory organs. The neurons, or brain cells, are responsible for sending that information to the part of the brain best equipped to handle it. This requires that each neuron 'knows' the proper pathways. The genes have, at birth, laid down the mental road map **neurons** must follow and built its major 'highways' between the basic areas of the brain. Environmental influence plays the key role in forging a denser and more complex network of interconnections. These smaller avenues and side roads make the transfer of information between neurons more efficient and rich with situation-specific detail. At birth, each neuron has approximately 2,500 **synapses** or connections. By the time we have reached 2–3 years of age, sensory stimulation and environmental experience have taken full advantage of the brain's plasticity; each neuron now boasts around 15,000 synapses (Kolb & Gibb, 2011).

neurons brain cells

synapse the connection between neurons

Remember Jill and Pietro at the start of this chapter? They are different and similar at the same time. As members of one great family, *Homo sapiens,* they share a common biology, behavioural tendencies, instincts and basic needs. Each of them sleeps and wakes, feels hunger and thirst, and develops language through identical mechanisms. As babies they both needed to be cared for by someone, and through their development from children to adults, they have acquired their specific cultural languages, norms and values, through identical mechanisms and without even being aware of it. The cultural context in which we live influences our behaviour so we have to be sure to take this into account when studying social phenomena.

Everybody is therefore born into a specific, but dynamic culture that *cultivates* (the Latin word for culture) every human being. But what is culture? And in what way is culture different from a society or social forces?

Culture is a term that has been given many meanings. More than 50 years ago Alfred Kroeber and Clyde Kluckhohn (1952) presented no fewer than 164 definitions. More recently, Spencer-Oatey and Franklin (2012) observed that culture is 'a notoriously difficult term to define' (p. 1). In her review of how culture has been understood across time and disciplines, she reveals some agreement in defining the concept. It is multi-layered and exists in observable artifacts (e.g. dress, physical spaces, manners), values (why we behave and think in the way we do), and underlying assumptions (what we assume about the world and relationships within it). In social psychology, culture is most commonly applied as the term for the patterns of knowledge, beliefs and behaviour, or the set of shared attitudes, norms, values, goals and practices that characterize a group. Language and culture have both emerged as means of using symbols to construct **social identity**. Children acquire language in the same way as they acquire basic cultural norms and values – through interaction with older members of their cultural group. Understood in this way we can see how culture influences our behaviour and the way we interpret others behaviour (see Chapter 4 for more on attribution processes). This is why we observe fascinating differences between people of different cultures, ranging from what they eat to how they dress, how to behave when someone dies, marriage, pregnancy and birth, and what our bodies look like. And as we are beginning to hint at here, culture also shapes, and is shaped by, our biology. Or as Walsh and Yun (2016) state: 'Genes and culture are both information transmission devices; the former laying the foundation for the latter, and the latter then influencing the former' (p. 2).

social identity that part of our self-definition that derives from our membership of social groups

Very helpfully, evolutionary psychologists have offered two understandings of how culture can emerge: *evoked culture (or evocation)* and *transmitted culture (or transmission)* (Confer et al., 2010). Let's start with the simpler one to understand; transmitted culture. Transmitted culture refers to the ideas, practices, values, representations that at least two people share. These are 'transmitted' across a group through interaction. Dawkins (2016) uses the term '**meme**' to refer to the cultural information which we hold in our minds and transmit to others through social learning. An example of transmitted culture might be what we think happens after we die. Evoked culture describes the differences that exist between groups of people as a consequence of the social and environmental conditions in which they live. In their review of examples of evoked culture in relation to mate preferences, Gangestad et al. (2006) offer us some interesting cases to illustrate the concept. Consider those who reside in places with high levels of parasites. Parasites are detrimental to our health. Their presence on our bodies is observable from open-sores, weeping eyes, and a degradation in physical appearance. In such places, *physical* attractiveness is highly valued. Why? Because it is an indicator

meme a unit of information stored in the mind and transmitted to others through social learning that a potential mate is healthy and does not suffer from a high parasite-load – hence they are more likely to reproduce, survive, and take care of their offspring. In societies where resources are unevenly distributed, risk-taking behaviour is apparent and desirable. Why? Because we respond to the need to grab whatever resources we can to avoid being left with nothing. In countries where food is scarce, plumper body sizes are considered more attractive than slimmer ones (Forbes et al., 2007). Where food is abundant, we have preferences for thinner body shapes as it displays wealth, status and self-control (Ember et al., 2005; Sugiyama, 2005, Tovee et al., 2006; also see Chapter 9 for further discussion on attraction). Fundamentally evoked culture nods to ultimate human truths (e.g. we need to reproduce to survive as a species, we need resources) but looks at how our behaviour in response to those truths is adapted as a consequence of social and environmental conditions.

So, Jill and Pietro – and all of us everywhere – are cultural, social and biological creatures. We join groups, conform and recognize distinctions of social status. We return favours, punish offences and grieve a child's death. Confronted by those with dissimilar attitudes or attributes, perhaps belonging to '**outgroups**', we react warily or negatively. Our alien scientists could drop in anywhere and find humans conversing and arguing, laughing and crying, feasting and dancing, singing and worshipping. Everywhere, humans prefer living with others – in families and communal groups – to living alone. Everywhere, the family dramas that entertain us – from Greek tragedies to Chinese fiction to Mexican soap operas – portray similar plots (Dutton, 2006). Similarly, adventure stories in which strong and courageous men, supported by wise old people, overcome evil to the delight of beautiful women or threatened children. Such commonalities define our shared human nature founded on our biological and genetic similarity.

outgroup 'them' – a group that people perceive as distinctively different from or apart from their ingroup

As social psychologist Roy Baumeister (2005b, p. 29) observes, 'Evolution made us for culture'. Biology and culture work together. Humans, more than any other animal, harness the power of culture to make life better. 'Culture is a better way of being social', Baumeister writes. We have culture to thank for our communication through language, our driving safely on one side of the road, our eating fruit in winter, and our use of money to pay for our cars and fruit. Culture facilitates our survival and reproduction, and nature has blessed us with a brain that, like no other, enables culture. Other animals show the rudiments of culture, thinking and language. Our biology, and especially our brain, developed through evolution and made thinking and language appropriation possible. We come prepared to learn language and to bond and cooperate with others in securing food, caring for young and protecting ourselves. People's 'natures are alike', said Confucius; 'it is their habits that carry them far apart'. So we share similarities, but there are also vast differences between individuals as a result of cultural and social forces. Despite increasing education, 'we are not moving toward a uniform global culture: cultural convergence is not taking place. A society's cultural heritage is remarkably enduring' (Baumeister, 2005b, p. 46).

Cultural Diversity

Cultural diversity surrounds us and we become aware of different customs, lifestyles, ways of thinking and behaviour. Confronting another culture is sometimes a startling experience. A German student, accustomed to speaking to

'Herr Professor' only on rare occasions, considers it strange that at universities in other countries most faculty office doors are open and students stop by freely. An Iranian student on her first visit to a McDonald's restaurant fumbles around in her paper bag looking for the eating utensils until she sees other customers eating their french fries with, of all things, their hands. Foreigners visiting Japan often struggle to master the rules of the social game – when to take their shoes off, how to pour the tea, when to give and open gifts, how to act towards someone higher or lower in the social hierarchy.

In the modern world, where international travel is relatively easy, cultural diversity has flourished. Our careers, our studies and our relationships may take us to another country. Whether we move to another country out of choice or necessity, the result is bringing cultures together. Migration and refugee evacuations are mixing cultures more than ever. 'East is East and West is West, and never the twain shall meet', wrote the nineteenth-century British author Rudyard Kipling in his poem 'The Ballad of East and West' (1889). But today, East and West, and North and South, meet all the time. Italy is home to many Albanians, Germany to Turks, UK to Pakistanis, and the result is both friendship and conflict.

Switzerland has the highest immigrant population of any European country with 30 per cent of its 8.6 million residents being foreign-born. Between 2015 and 2016, Sweden, Hungary, Austria and Norway all saw their immigrant population status rise by at least 1 per cent. This survey, conducted by the Pew Research Center (Connor & Krogstad, 2016), reports this increase is significant when we consider that the US immigration status has only risen by 1 per cent in the last 10 years. The United Arab Emirates has the highest population of immigrants in the world, where 80 per cent of its 9.6 million residents were born elsewhere, including places as diverse from one another as the Philippines, Iran, India, and the UK.

And of course, contact with people from other cultures needn't be in physical proximity, face-to-face. It can be achieved remotely. As a result of the increase in online communication, we have more intercultural contact with people than in the past. It's not face-to-face, but it still brings us into dialogue with others. It could be argued that as we mix more and more, either online or offline, the differences between us are being ironed out. Indeed the idea that the forces of globalization, made possible through advancements in technology, are diluting and even dissolving cultural differences is a hotly contested and complex topic. One aspect of that debate is whether the Internet decreases the perceived cultural differences between us, smoothing out our peculiarities as we discover common ground, or whether it sharpens those differences, making us more aware of them. To offer some insight into the topic, Marcoccia (2012) examined two online discussion forums for French and Moroccan web users. Both forums were for the open discussion of current and social affairs and neither was moderated nor regulated. Marcoccia observed some standardization of culture insofar as English is the 'cyberlingua franca' of the Internet. To give some background context on this, long before the Internet was invented, international business was predominantly conducted in English – sometimes referred to as a 'universal language'. Consequently English has been taught in schools all over the world. We have a rich history of using English for international communication. Hence it is little surprise to discover that English has become the cyberlingua-franca of the Internet.

To be understood beyond your own speech community, you may need to communicate in English. The reduction in social information (such as smiling and nodding the head), means interaction is more constrained. As such, computer-mediated communication (CMC) cultural norms seem to have arisen which govern online intercultural-communications, such as 'netiquette' and emoticons, which we broadly share. That said, Marcoccia noted cultural differences between the French and Moroccan web users in how messages were framed, phrased, and what content was considered important. It seems some standardization is required so that global dialogue is possible. This then becomes the platform for sharing our cultural peculiarities with an international audience.

As we work, play and live with people from diverse cultural backgrounds, it helps to understand how our cultures influence us and how our cultures differ. In a conflict-laden world, achieving peace requires a genuine appreciation and understanding for differences as well as similarities (see Chapter 13).

Norms: Expected Behaviour

As etiquette rules illustrate, all cultures have their accepted ideas about appropriate behaviour. We often view these social expectations, or **norms**, as a negative force that imprisons people in a blind effort to perpetuate tradition. For example, in Chapter 7 on conformity and obedience we explored studies that illustrate how norms are established in a group, and discussed our tendency to follow group norms even when we personally dissociate ourselves from them. Cultural norms do restrain and control us – so successfully and so subtly that we hardly sense their existence. Like fish in the ocean, we are all so immersed in our cultures that we must leap out of them to understand their influence. 'When we see other Dutch people behaving in what foreigners would call a Dutch way', note Dutch psychologists Willem Koomen and Anton Dijker (1997), 'we often do not realize that the behaviour is typically Dutch'. We understand our motherland only by experience of a foreign country.

norms standards for accepted, typical and expected behaviour. Norms prescribe 'proper' behaviour. (In a different sense of the word, norms also describe what most others do – what is normal)

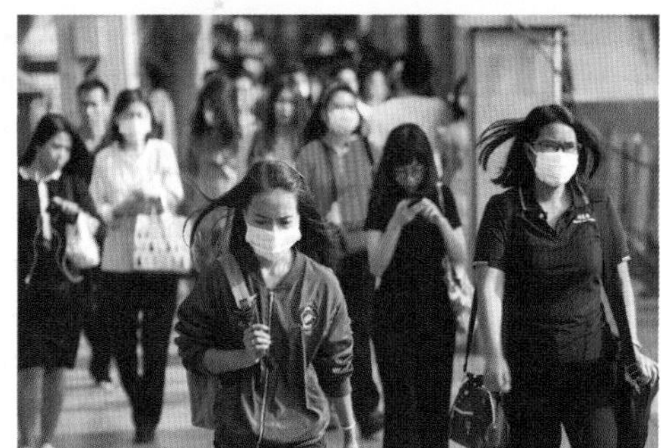

To many in the Western world, the Asian mouth mask may seem strange. To those wearing it, it is protection against pollution, and also a courtesy to others when the wearer is physically sick and concerned with infecting others.

SOURCE: ©2p2play/Shutterstock

There is no better way to learn the norms of our culture than to visit or study another culture and see that its members do things *that* way, whereas we do them *this* way.

Social norms play an important role in all societies and groups. They make social relations more predictable and less perilous. Just as a stage play moves smoothly when the actors know their lines, social behaviour occurs smoothly when people know what to expect. Norms grease the social machinery. In unfamiliar situations, when the norms may be unclear, we monitor others' behaviour and adjust our own accordingly.

Many people, social psychologists included, do not have any experience of East Asian cultures. Sometimes the textbooks mention that the Chinese are more 'collectivist' and less 'individualist' than people in the West (see Chapter 3). But the Chinese, and the rest of people living in Asia, or Africa, were typically absent from social psychological textbooks. The focus was on the people living in the West, especially in North America. The Americans' and the Europeans' ways of thinking, feeling and behaving, and their psychological make-up were generalized to all people in the world (see also Chapter 1).

Today we know this is not correct. People in all cultures have certainly the same abilities and psychological make-up to some degree, but they are at the same time very different. The blend of components that make us a person differs from culture to culture, but the biological elements which make us a human being are the same. In all cultures there exists individualism and collectivism (Hofstede, 2001; Hofstede & Hofstede, 2005), and people acquire independent and interdependent ways of thinking in all cultures and societies. But the specific mixture of individualism and collectivism in a specific culture is unique (Kolstad & Horpestad, 2009).

Cultural Similarity

Beneath the veneer of cultural differences, some cross-cultural psychologists look for 'an essential universality' (Lonner, 1980; Stahl & Elbeltagi, 2004). As members of one species, we find that the processes that underlie our differing behaviours are much the same everywhere. At ages 4 to 5, children across the world begin to exhibit a '**theory of mind**' that enables them to infer what others in their culture are thinking (Frith & Frith, 2005; Norenzayan & Heine, 2005). No matter what culture they belong to, if one child sees a toy being moved while another child isn't looking, they are able to infer that the other child will still think the toy is in the same place, and will understand the child's surprise when they discover it has moved. They can see the world from someone else's point of view. Achieving a theory of mind and understanding false beliefs, is a cognitive developmental milestone in a child's life, no matter where they live. Furthermore, it's not just some cognitive processes that transcend cultures but also norms about our interactions with others.

theory of mind the ability to attribute mental states to others and oneself. To be able to see the world from someone else's point of view

Universal Friendship Norms

People everywhere have some common norms for friendship. From a study that looked at norms underlying friendships for European-Americans and Hindu-Indians, Miller et al. (2014) found different emphases upon *communal* and *exchange* norms between the two groups. Whereas communal norms refer to friendships based on offering help when needed with no expectation of receiving anything in return, exchange norms assume we will – so helping someone is based on the assumption they will help us at a later date. Both communal and exchange norms define friendships for European-Americans and Hindu-Indians. However, Hindu-Indians place more importance on communal norms, whereas for European-Americans it is exchange norms that define good friendships.

Some research has found differences in friendship between men and women. While communal characteristics including loyalty and trust are the hallmarks of friendship for both men and women, women consider their friendships to be a more important part of their lives than men do (Hall, 2011). And do you tend to think it's women who gossip? Well, research suggests that it is men! A study by Watson (2012) found that gossip was a feature of good friendships for men, but not for women.

Universal Social Belief Dimensions

Another common norm that can be seen across cultures lies in social belief dimensions. Hong Kong social psychologists Kwok Leung and Michael Harris Bond (2004, 2009), state there are five universal dimensions to social beliefs. Leung et al. (2002) define social beliefs as a variety of social behaviours across contexts, actors, people and time periods. In short, they are statements about 'how the world functions' (Leung et al., 2002, p. 289). Their Social Axioms Survey (SAS)

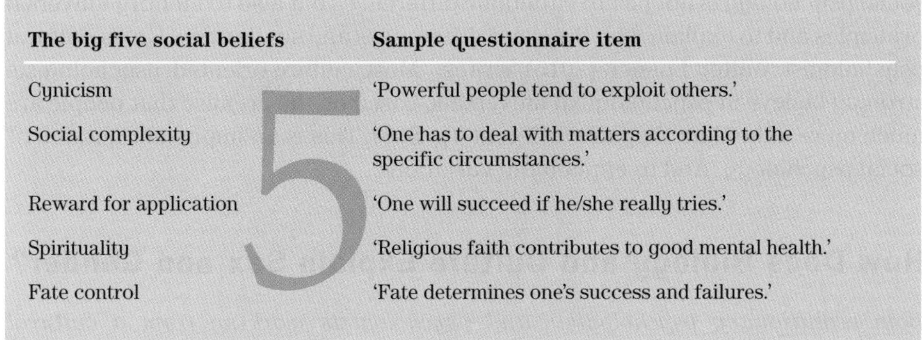

The big five social beliefs	Sample questionnaire item
Cynicism	'Powerful people tend to exploit others.'
Social complexity	'One has to deal with matters according to the specific circumstances.'
Reward for application	'One will succeed if he/she really tries.'
Spirituality	'Religious faith contributes to good mental health.'
Fate control	'Fate determines one's success and failures.'

FIGURE 14.2 Leung and Bond's universal social belief dimensions

is a measure of these beliefs. More than 40 national groups are studied and in each country people vary in the extent to which they endorse and apply these five social understandings in their daily lives: cynicism, social complexity, reward for application, spirituality and fate control (**Figure 14.2**). People's adherence to these social beliefs appears to guide their living. Those who espouse cynicism express lower life satisfaction and favour assertive influence tactics and right-wing politics. Those who espouse reward for application are inclined to invest themselves in study, planning and competing (Bond et al., 2004).

Differences in the endorsement of social beliefs between religious groups have also been noted. Some social beliefs about the world seem to be useful defence mechanisms, protecting people against anxieties about death. Higher levels of belief in fate control, and lower levels of religiosity, predicted greater death anxiety (Hui et al., 2007). Others, such as the universal taboo against incest, serve the function of preventing inbreeding depressions. However, the strength of this taboo has been found to differ between men and women, and cultures (Thornhill, 1991). Evolutionary psychologists have explained these gender differences as a result of parental investment. As women invest more than men in pregnancy and childcare, they are more cautious in ensuring the health and survival of that child (Antfolk et al., 2012). With respect to culture, Thornhill (1991) observes the incest taboo is held more strongly in patrilocal cultures, where married heterosexual couples live with the man's relatives, than in matrilocal cultures where they live with the woman's relatives. Why? Because men want to be sure their offspring, to whom they leave their wealth, are actually theirs.

Cultures mixing. As these schoolchildren illustrate, immigration and globalization are bringing once-distant cultures together.

SOURCE: ©Robert Kneschke/Shutterstock

Some norms are culture-specific, others are universal. The force of culture appears in varying norms, whereas it is largely our human nature – the characteristics of *Homo sapiens* – that accounts for the universality of some norms. Thus, we might think of nature as universal and nurture as culture-specific. We are born the same and become different.

So far in this chapter, we have affirmed our biological kinship as members of one human family. We have acknowledged our cultural diversity. And we have noted how norms vary within and across cultures. Remember that our quest in social psychology is not just to catalogue differences but also to identify universal principles and to explain why there are differences and similarities. Cross-cultural psychologist Walter Lonner (2015) writes, 'Most culture-oriented psychologists strongly believe in psychological universals, based on the premise that people are much more alike than they are different' (p. 808). This is an important mission of social psychology. And to explain the variations.

How Does Biology and Culture Explain Sex and Gender?

Both evolutionary psychologists and psychologists working from a cultural perspective have sought to explain and differentiate sex and gender in humans. Before considering their views, let's look at some basic issues: Are we alike? Do we differ? And why?

So far we have considered the influence biology and culture has over the way we think and behave. Here we will consider this relationship with a specific example, that of **gender**, to illustrate how these similarities and differences between us have been studied by social psychologists.

gender the characteristics, whether biological or socially influenced, by which people define male and female

Before we do it is useful to define what we mean by the terms '**sex**' and 'gender'. Sex and gender are not the same. Sex refers to biological and reproductive characteristics and is usually assigned at birth. We are usually born a member of the male sex or the female sex. Gender is a pattern of behaviours recognized as 'feminine' or 'masculine', and as such **gender roles** are established. Gender is socially constructed and used to refer to those ways in which a culture elaborates upon nature.

sex the biological characteristics, including hormones, genes and physiology, that determines whether an individual is understood to be male or female

gender role the set of social expectations based on gender stereotypes of how a person should act, think and feel based on their actual or perceived sex

Perhaps you have noticed that social psychological studies often look for sex differences in their design. They note how many men (or boys) and how many women (or girls) took part. Is this because we assume there might be fundamental differences between the sexes in their thoughts and behaviour?

Sex and Gender Similarities and Differences

There are many obvious dimensions of human diversity – height, weight, hair colour, to name just a few. When babies are born, usually the first thing people want to know is, 'Is it a boy or a girl?' When a hermaphrodite child is born with a combination of male and female sex organs, physicians and family have traditionally felt compelled to assign the child a gender and to diminish the ambiguity surgically. The term '**intersex**' appears in medical language to refer to the appearance of hormones, chromosomes and/or sexual organs which do not conform to what we expect male and female bodies to look like (Jenkins & Short, 2017). It is typically regarded as a medical condition, or disorder, requiring treatment. The message seems to be simple: everyone *must* be assigned a sex.

intersex the appearance of sex characteristics including hormones, chromosomes, and sexual organs, in an individual which do not conform to traditional definitions of 'male' or 'female'

But between male and female there is, biologically and socially speaking, essentially nothing, at least not at birth. Genetically speaking, 'of the 46 chromosomes in the human genome, 45 are unisex', notes Harris (1998). Females and males are therefore similar in many physical traits and developmental milestones, such as the age of sitting up, teething and walking. They are also alike in many psychological traits, such as overall vocabulary, creativity, intelligence, self-esteem and happiness.

Indeed, notes Hyde (2005) from her review of 46 meta-analyses (each a statistical digest of dozens of studies), the common result for most variables studied is *similarity*.

Sam Smith defines as non-binary, rejecting being categorized as either male or female.

SOURCE: ©Featureflash Photo Agency/Shutterstock

queer an umbrella term to refer to individuals who do not identify as heterosexual, and who may not recognize any sex and gender categories

Despite this genetic basis, most societies categorize people into male and female. McCredie (2011) gives the mundane but revealing example of public toilets. Biological sex, she argues, is a very convenient, if misguided and unnecessary, method of organizing and categorizing people. We even segregate where we go to the toilet, which can be an issue if you don't identify with either 'male' or 'female', or trans-individual and find yourself wondering which toilet door to go through. The word '**queer**' has been adopted as something of an umbrella term by individuals who do not identify themselves in the binary language of heterosexuality. To identify as queer is to stand against the categorization of your sexual identity and to reject the assumption that gender and sexuality are intertwined (Carr et al., 2017). People may identify as lesbian, gay, bisexual, transgender, non-binary, pansexual and nonsexual. For example, the UK singer Sam Smith defines himself as non-binary. In an interview with the *New York Post*, he states that 'I feel just as much a woman as I am man' (*New York Post*, 2017). His sentiments have contributed to recent decisions to remove gendered awards from television and music award ceremonies (e.g. Best Female Solo Artist), such as MTV. When asked for your gender to register your Facebook profile, you now have 71 options to choose from, including 'Gender Fluid', 'Pangender' and 'Genderqueer' (Williams, 2014).

Some research suggests that there are differences, and it is these differences, not the many similarities, that capture attention and make news. Take as an example Marin et al.'s (2012) study that revealed women remember bad news better than men do. It was also claimed that women were more stressed out by these news events. Interesting? Yes. Newsworthy? Yes, if we consider that this study was subsequently reported in online news forums. Accurate? Well, that's more tricky to answer. Its critics point to its small sample size (just 28 men and 28 women) and its calculation of the statistics (Willis, 2012). More recently, research has focused on debunking some of these stereotypical sex and gender differences. For example, Swedish research has rebuked the commonly held notion that women are better at multitasking than men (Mäntylä, 2013). Similarly, work by Carothers and Reis (2013) refutes the view that men and women have distinctive traits. In the past, some researchers have argued there was a tendency to publish studies that reveal sex and gender differences, and this is an example of **confirmation bias**, where we believe (and publish) what we expect to be the case. Journal editors are arguably more keen to publish studies that show significant differences between the sexes than those which do not. Contemporary research now questions many of these assumptions.

The South African runner Caster Semenya was ordered to take a gender identity test when she blew everyone away in the women's 800-metre race at the World Championships in Berlin in September 2009. The tests revealed her to have three times the level of testosterone than expected in a woman. In 2019 she was banned from defending her 800-metre world record by the Swiss Supreme Court, as she refused to take testosterone-reducing drugs. The case has sparked an ongoing debate about how to define 'men' and 'women' in international athletics.

SOURCE: ©CP DC Press/Shutterstock

Social psychology is littered with examples of differences found between men and women on a variety of topics. Sometimes these differences reflect West European stereotypes about men and women. Sometimes the differences found directly challenge such views. Before we get into a discussion about whether we should be looking for differences at all, let's compare men's and

confirmation bias a tendency to search for information that confirms one's preconceptions, rather than considering opposing information

women's social connection, moral reasoning and dominance, and then consider how biology and culture might explain them. Do gender differences reflect biological differences or are they solely culturally constructed – a reflection of the roles that men and women often play and the situations in which they act? Or do genes and culture both play a role? Can we bend the genders?

Independence Versus Connectedness

Gender differences have been uncovered in social psychological studies on independence and connectedness (e.g. Bekker & Assen, 2008; Guimond et al., 2006). Individual men display outlooks and behaviour that vary from fierce competitiveness to caring nurturance. So do individual women. Without denying that, some researchers in classic work, such as Chodorow (1978, 1989), Gilligan (1982) and her colleagues (1990), and more recently Felmlee and her team (2012) have contended that women more than men give priority to close, intimate relationships.

Where gender differences have been found, women have often been portrayed as lacking or deficient in some way. Consider the work of Kohlberg (1958) on moral reasoning as a case in point. Testing his theory that there are six stages to moral development by asking male participants to resolve moral dilemmas involving male characters, he concluded that achieving stage six (universal ethical principles) was a reflection of superior moral development. When he tested his theory on women, using the same moral dilemmas, he found that they failed to achieve stage six. His conclusion was that women are unable to develop the same high levels of moral reasoning as men. Somewhat perturbed, Gilligan (1982) focused on the moral outlook of American women and men. She had spotted that, in Kohlberg's analysis, high levels of moral reasoning were assumed to involve the implementation of abstract principles, whereas inferior levels were thought to include consideration of the local situation in which the dilemma had occurred. In her own study, Gilligan also found consistent differences between men and women in how they engaged in moral reasoning. When asked what it means to say something is morally right or wrong, men mentioned abstract ideals of duty, justice and individual freedom, while women raised the theme of helping others. This was not a case of inferior reasoning on the part of women, she argued, but simply reflected gender differences in how we do it. In a similar vein, Horn (2003) found that adolescent boys gave social regulatory and personal justifications for excluding someone from their peer group. Adolescent girls on the other hand, tended to give moral reasons such as breaking friendship norms (e.g. spreading gossip) within the group.

Gilligan's work has met with some criticism, including finding differences where none might exist. Skoe et al. (2002) at the Norwegian University of Science and Technology asked men and women to rate the importance of a range of moral dilemmas. They concluded that the observed differences between women and men were a function of gender-role identity rather than biological sex. Participants high in femininity showed more empathic concern for other people, and androgynous people reported more helpful behaviours than did all others.

In general it has been argued in social psychological work that women more than men give priority to helping others (Konrad et al., 2000). We discussed in Chapter 11 how these forms of helping had become feminized. In most of the care-giving professions, such as social worker, teacher and nurse, women outnumber men. The reasons for this, however, are not obvious. Is it because women actually care more or is it because women are more likely to be successful in being offered these kinds of jobs than men are? Or perhaps it is because women are fulfilling a stereotype that they *should* care more – and therefore find it easier to enter these professions more often than men do? Research by Ming Te Wang and colleagues (2013) found that although women perform just as well as men in science and maths subjects, they are much less likely to enter a STEM (science, technology, engineering and maths) career. In the UK, of the 32.5 million people in the workforce, only one million of them are women in STEM-related occupations (Wise Campaign, 2019). Why? Biological explanations have located the cause in men's superior spatial and mathematical ability over women, and suggested that with appropriate training women can perform equally well (Baron-Cohen, 2003; Reilly et al., 2017). Contrarily, other research has found that these differences between the sexes do not exist in those cultures where the cultural gender-gap does not exist, such as Sweden (Guiso et al., 2008). Wang et al. (2013) hypothesize that the answer may lie in the values children are being socialized into and their self-perceptions of what they're good at. If women are led to believe they are natural carers and must balance work and family, then perhaps it is no surprise to see them in different careers to men. In this view, the differences between men and women are not biologically determined but are socially constructed. Whether women are now receiving correct training to redress their biological differences from men, or whether cultural values are now shifting, or its the result of both processes, women studying and entering STEM careers in countries such as the UK, are on the rise (Wise Campaign, 2019).

Social psychologists still disagree as to why gender differences occur. Research is ongoing but as yet no definitive conclusions can be drawn on this. Given the complexity of this area, it is likely that the results may show a combination of factors are behind these differences, but we still await research confirmation.

SOURCE: ©CP DC Press/Shutterstock

Social Dominance

From Asia to Africa and Europe to Australia, people rate men as more dominant, driven and aggressive. Moreover, studies of nearly 80,000 people across 70 countries show that men more than women rate power and achievement as important (Schwartz & Rubel, 2005). That said, gender differences are shrinking in many industrialized societies as women assume more managerial and leadership positions. Yet on a global scale, consider the following.

- In a survey of how many women occupied seats in 193 national parliaments, they only accounted for 50 per cent or more at the lower level of that parliament in three countries: Rwanda (61 per cent), Cuba (53 per cent) and Bolivia (53 per cent). Women hold less than 50 per cent of seats in any national parliament at the higher level or senate (IPU, 2019).
- Women own less than 20 per cent of the world's land, due to having no property rights in many parts of the world (Villa, 2017).
- There is a gender pay gap between men and women in Europe. In 2017, women's gross earnings were on average 16 per cent lower than men's. The largest gender pay gaps were reported in Estonia (25.6 per cent) and the lowest in Romania (3.5 per cent) (Eurostat, 2019).

Men's style of communicating arguably undergirds their social power. In writing, some research has shown that women tend to use more communal prepositions ('with'), fewer quantitative words and more present tense (Mulac et al., 2001; Mulac & Lundell, 1994). One computer program, which taught itself to recognize gender differences in word usage and sentence structure, successfully identified the author's gender in 80 per cent of 920 British fiction and non-fiction works (Koppel et al., 2002).

Perhaps you have noticed that men and women not only talk about different topics but also use language and articulate words differently, at least in English? Trudgill's (1974) work has been particularly helpful in revealing gender differences in spoken language. His classic studies, conducted in many countries inside and outside Europe, found that when you control for factors such as social class, ethnicity and age, women consistently use prestigious forms of language. In other words, female speakers use linguistic forms that are considered to be more correct than those used by male speakers. Women and girls also become more flexible in their pronunciation. So informal forms of language are not just associated with working-class speech but with other aspects of working-class culture such as masculinity. This may lead men to adopt more non-standard linguistic forms than women.

So perhaps then, in conversation, men's style reflects their concern for independence, women's for connectedness. Men are more likely to act as powerful people often do – talking assertively, interrupting intrusively, touching with the hand, staring more, smiling less. Conversely, women's influence style tends to be more indirect – less interruptive, more sensitive, more polite, less cocky. However, the question remains, if these differences do exist, what is responsible for them and why do they exist?

Research close-up

Don't Stand So Close to Me? The Influence of Sex and Gender on Interpersonal Distance

Source: Uzzell, D., & Horne, N. (2006). The influence of biological sex, sexuality and gender role on interpersonal distance. *British Journal of Social Psychology, 45*, 579–597.

Introduction

Personal space is considered a marker of type and intensity of relationships. Romantic couples tend to be physically closer to one another in public than acquaintances. When a stranger 'invades' our personal space, we feel uncomfortable. Since 1983 there has been a marked decline in published psychological research on personal space. The reasons for this include problems in methodology. Projective experiments have asked participants to imagine how far into their personal space they would allow another person, indicating their response with a drawing or using dolls. This technique demands complex cognitive skills such as memory and drawing (to scale!), which may prove inaccurate. Laboratory-based experiments have typically used 'stop-distance' methods. A participant approaches another participant and states 'stop' at the point at which the space between them is uncomfortable. Issues of accurate measurement and ecological validity have troubled such studies. Naturalistic observations of people interacting with one another have high ecological validity, but have proved difficult to accurately and reliably measure and control. Personal space research has tended ►

to focus on sex differences, typically revealing that men tend to maintain bigger distances between one another than women do. This was explained as a consequence of women inevitably having more affiliative (feminine) characteristics than men do. However, this past research assumed that biological sex determines gender-role characteristics (femininity and masculinity), and ignored social and cultural influences on gender as well as sexuality.

The current study investigates the extent to which interpersonal distance (IPD) between men and women are influenced by sex, gender role and sexuality. Three hypotheses are tested:

1 Gender role (masculine/feminine) will account for more variability in IPD than biological sex (male/female).
2 The IPD of masculine/masculine pairs will be greater than feminine/feminine pairs.
3 The IPD of intermediate/intermediate pairs will be different from masculine/masculine or feminine/feminine pairs.

Method

A sample of 72 Sussex University, UK, students were recruited. University students were deliberately chosen to ensure representation of differing gender roles and sexualities within the sample. Only white students were approached to ensure race was controlled as a possible influencing variable. Students were randomly recruited either directly through the university's LGBT society or outside the Student Union building. Of the sample, 34 were male, 38 female, and ages ranged from 17 to 31 years, with a mean age of 21.2 years. Of the females, 33 self-reported as heterosexual, 4 as lesbian, and 1 as bisexual. Of the male students 25 were heterosexual, 8 were gay, and 1 was bisexual. Most were from the UK. They were told they were participating in a memory experiment.

To ascertain the gender role of participants, the researchers asked them to complete Bem's Sex Role Inventory (BSRI) (Bem, 1974). This comprises of 60 adjectives. Twenty adjectives reflect masculine characteristics (e.g. competitive), 20 reflect feminine characteristics (e.g. caring), and 20 are neutral (e.g. adaptable). Participants rate on a 7-point Likert scale how well each item describes them (1 = never true, 7 = always true). The resulting score positions participants on a scale that runs from very masculine to very feminine. Participants were categorized as 'masculine', 'feminine', or 'intermediate' based on their BSRI score. Participants were also asked to report their age, sex, nationality and sexuality.

Participants were then randomly placed into groups of six. Each group should therefore contain a mix of gender role (as identified by the BSRI), biological sex and sexuality. Participants were taken to a laboratory and told the aim of the study was to talk to the other five people in their group and then remember facts about them. The laboratory was split into three stations, labelled A, B and C. At each station was a mat that enabled an accurate measurement of the distance between the two participants as they interacted with one another.

Participants were told to chat to each person in their group in turn, for 2 minutes, at the indicated station (A, B or C). Posters displayed questions they could ask each other (e.g. what did you have for breakfast?). Video cameras were positioned at each station to record the interaction. At the end of the 2 minutes, they were asked to move to another station and speak to a different person in their group. This procedure continued until each participant had chatted to every other person in their group for 2 minutes. Once this was completed, participants were debriefed regarding the true nature of the study.

No significant differences in IPD were found between those students who knew each other prior to the study, and those who didn't.

Results

Scores from the BSRI classified 75 per cent of the males as 'masculine' and 75 per cent of the females as 'feminine'. Hence, 25 per cent of men and 25 per cent of women displayed a gender role that was incongruent with their biological sex. A two-way ANOVA showed a main effect of sex on BSRI scores $F(1,70) = 14.70$, $p < .01$.

Hypothesis 1 predicted gender role (masculine, feminine) would account for more variability in IPD than biological sex. This was supported by a two-way ANOVA on the data which revealed a significant effect for gender role, $F = 4.3$ df $= 2,71$ $p < .18$. Looking at the mean IPD for *masculinity* (mean = 25.7, *SD* = 2.4) and *femininity* (mean = 22.4, *SD* = 2.7), participants who identified as masculine (from the BSRI), had greater IPD than those who identify as feminine, regardless of their biological sex. The *intermediate participants* mean (mean = 24.2, *SD* = 2.7) was significantly different from that of the *femininity* participants' mean ($F = 9.6$ $p < .000$), but not the masculinity mean. Biological sex did not account for any variation in IPD between participants.

Hypothesis 2 predicted that the IPD of *masculine/masculine* pairs would be significantly greater than those of *feminine/feminine* pairs. A factorial ANOVA supports this prediction: $F(5, 163) = 3.92$ $p < .05$. A post-hoc analysis revealed that heterosexual female pairs differed significantly in IPD from heterosexual male/lesbian pairings and also heterosexual male/heterosexual female pairings.

Hypothesis 3 predicted that *intermediate/intermediate* pairs would significantly differ in IPD from *masculine/masculine* pairs or *feminine/feminine* pairs. This hypothesis was not supported.

Discussion

Gender role (as assessed on the BSRI) accounts for IPD rather than biological sex or sexuality. This suggests that cultural and social influences which shape gender role contribute to personal space. However, biological sex does correlate with gender roles (males are more likely to be classified as masculine on the BSRI, and women as feminine). This suggests biological sex exerts considerable influence on which gender roles we identify with, which may then influence other spheres of our lives such as occupation choice. Furthermore it suggests that 'masculine' and 'feminine' are constructions participants readily identify with. Pairings that involved a masculine person (e.g. *masculine/feminine*) were significantly different to pairings that did not involve a masculine person (e.g. *feminine/intermediate*). This means masculine participants are more influential in spatial interactions as their preference for greater personal space is adhered to.

In summary, this study makes two important contributions to the social psychological research on personal space. Firstly it shows how advances in technology, such as the measuring stations (A, B, C), can help ensure more accurate reports on spatial interactions. Secondly, it provides evidence that it is the social and cultural constructions of gender which shape behaviour rather than biological sex.

Critical Reflections

The researchers point out some limitations with their work. The **ecological validity** of the study is not as high as a naturalistic observation. However, the researchers note this is a trade-off to ensure accurate measurement. Moreover, it is, they argue, more ecologically valid than a typical laboratory-experiment using techniques such as 'stop-distance'. They suggest digitally configuring the measuring-mat technique for use in a natural setting.

ecological validity the extent to which findings observed in a study reflect what actually occurs in natural settings. Psychological laboratory research has been criticized for its low ecological validity

There are other aspects of this study we can critically reflect upon. Have another look at the sample size and the representation of differing gender, sex and sexualities. The sample is perhaps not as diverse nor as representative as we might wish, especially if we want to make claims about sex, sexuality and gender. As we explore in this chapter, ways of understanding gender, sex and sexuality are more numerous and varied than what is captured and studied in this experiment. In terms of ethics, were the researchers right to deliberately misguide their participants as to the true nature of their study? Once debriefed as to the true nature of the study, Uzzell and Horne note that no participants withdrew their data from the study.

Untangling sex and gender is complex. In the study, the researchers found that whilst biological sex didn't influence IPD, it did influence gender-role. Men are masculine, women are feminine. Some of this might be driven by the small sample size. But we can also ask questions about the reliability, validity and the relevance of the BSRI in contemporary society. The BSRI has been widely criticized on these grounds (e.g. Hoffman & Borders, 2001). Does it measure what it sets out to measure? Are femininity and masculinity relevant concepts in today's world? Does it take cultural differences into account? If we revisit the nature vs nurture debate, we might be tempted to try and answer questions such as: is it biological sex driving the gender role and behaviour, or is the gender role driving biological sex and behaviour? Rather than focusing on the direction of the influential force, it is the exploration of the inter-relationship between biology and social and cultural influences that reveal critical insights into our behaviour.

Much of the style we attribute to men is typical of people (men and women) in positions of status and power (Hall et al., 2006). For example, students nod more when speaking with professors than when speaking with peers, and women nod more than men (Helweg-Larsen et al., 2004). Men – and people in high-status roles – tend to talk more loudly and to interrupt more (Hall et al., 2005). Moreover, individuals vary; some men are characteristically hesitant and deferential, some women direct and assertive.

Genes, Culture and Gender: Doing What Comes Naturally?

In explaining gender differences, inquiry has focused on two influences: biology and culture.

'Anatomy is destiny' proclaimed Sigmund Freud (1924, p. 274). Really? There are, of course, certain salient biological sex differences. We also find them in most other species and the difference is important for many reasons. But do these natural distinctions in physical attributes, women with breasts and wide hips, men with more muscle mass and wide shoulders, also influence psychological characteristics and behaviour? To some extent. The biology, genes and hormones make psychological functions possible and they also can influence some different behaviour for the two sexes. For example, the fact that women give birth and can breastfeed their babies for months means most cultures expect women to play a nurturing role towards their children more often than men do. Therefore we will find in most cultures that women take care of children. This fact is therefore partly a result of biology and partly a consequence of ascribed gender roles.

Gender and Hormones

If genes predispose gender-related traits, they do so by their effect on our bodies. In male embryos, the genes direct the formation of testes, which begin to secrete testosterone, the male sex hormone that influences masculine appearance. Studies indicate that girls who were exposed to excess testosterone during foetal development tend to exhibit more tomboyish play behaviour than other girls (Hines, 2004). Other case studies have followed males who, having been born without penises, are reared as girls (Reiner & Gearhart, 2004).

In their account of sex and gender in psychology, Denmark et al. (2004) give an example of a well-documented case of sex reassignment. The case concerns a set of twins born in Canada in 1965. At 7 months of age, the boy John experienced a genital condition which eventually resulted in the removal of his penis. On the basis of expert advice from sex-researcher Dr Money, John became Joan and her sex was reassigned through surgery. Maintaining a record of Joan's progress, Money upheld the case as evidence that sexual identity was something that was learnt rather than dictated by biology. Being raised as female had, Money claimed, successfully overwritten the genetic coding as male. However, other researchers who also monitored Joan found that by the time she was a teenager, she was rebelling against her feminine identity. John was experiencing what we now know to be **gender dysphoria**. Her gait was described as 'masculine'. Her interest was in 'male' occupations and hobbies. Her sex was surgically reassigned to male at the age of 14 years, and at the age of 25 years, John married a heterosexual woman but his bitterness over the initial sex reassignment blighted the rest of his life. Depressed and unemployed, John committed suicide in 2004. See Colapinto (1997) for a fascinating interview carried out with John.

gender dysphoria describes the feeling that one's gender identity does not match their biological sex (also known as gender identity disorder)

The John/Joan case has been widely cited to support both nature and nurture arguments about gender. Whilst some argue this is a clear case of the power of biological determinism, others argue that it is firm evidence for the environmental features which shaped John and Joan's gender identity. But perhaps what this case tells us is that this dichotomy is really a complex inter-relationship. We can see biology and culture operating their forces in this particular scenario, and it is not clear that one is driving the other. For example, some evidence suggests foetal exposure to hormones shapes early brain and sex-gene development which has a bearing on sexual identity at birth. But that exposure can be a result of the environmental conditions the mother is experiencing, such as poor nutrition and stress (e.g. Kim et al, 2017; de Rooij et al., 2016). So, yes, some sexual determinism seems evident but so does the cultural and social environment in which we are raised. As Denmark et al. (2004) propose, the appearance of sexual genitalia is not sufficient to determine sexual or gender identity.

Culture and Gender

Earlier in this chapter we noted different understandings of what is meant by the concept of culture. Gender is an interesting illustration of how cultural processes work to shape how we should behave, and the anticipated disapproval and possible repercussions when those expectations are violated (Kite, 2001). For example, in many developing countries, girls are expected to marry before the age of 18 years. The issue of child brides has been widely investigated, along with the inescapable consequences of non-consensual sex and high-rates of HIV in young married girls and women with little control over their own lives (Best, 2005).

Where and when cultural values shift, so do expectations. Take the concept of 'fathering' says Sullivan (2010). Across Europe and Northern America, our expectations of what being a good father involves have changed. As more women, and especially mothers, return to full-time work after giving birth, possibly earning more money than the father of their child, expectations about childcare have started to shift. Sullivan observes that the time spent on childcare is now more equal in families where the father is educated above the age of 16 years. In some countries, such as the UK, changes in the law regarding maternity and paternity paid leave from work, have facilitated this shift in childcare responsibilities.

That said, these shifts can be slow and even in contemporary dual-career relationships old habits die hard; men still do most of the household repairs and women arrange the childcare (Bianchi et al., 2000). Dixon and Wetherell (2004) found an interesting paradox: when asked how in principle housework should be divided, most heterosexual couples endorsed a principle of equality. In practice, however, the same couples were not only engaged in an unequal allocation of labour in their homes, but also considered it as fair. Viala (2011) studied the lives of first-time parents resident in Denmark. Who would be caring for their children? What did they think the role of parent involved? The parents she interviewed noted a duty of joint parental responsibilities. Parenting was a new challenge to be met equally by both parents. However, Viala found that participants also upheld traditional gender stereotypes to resolve childcare dilemmas. It was women who were expected to take leave from work to care for their children on the grounds that her job was less demanding than the father's. As Viala concludes, despite the visible appearance of equality within our societies, traditional gendered stereotypes still influence day-to-day parenting practices. And research by Katz-Wise and her team (2010) offers similar conclusions. They found that the onset of parenthood sparks traditional gender-role attitudes and behaviours in both parents, but especially women.

Barrett (2015) writes that even in the modern-day Western world, the heterosexual nuclear family remains the norm. This norm is reflected in the way we spatially organize our homes with a master bedroom and smaller rooms for children, which has cultural meanings and values embedded within it (Johnson & Longhurst, 2010). In her interviews with lesbian and gay couples, some of whom have children, Barrett (2015) explores how domestic labour and childcare are divided in these households. Here are two examples of what she finds. The first is taken from an interview with Justin, a police officer, who lives with his male partner. The second is from Dale, a gay man who lives with his partner Hal and their children:

> Justin: 'I don't think there's any expectations in a gay couple of how you should keep the house. There is more in a heterosexual relationship.' (p. 201)
>
> Dale: 'In some respects I'll do the more traditionally masculine things like taking the car for the brakes [i.e. getting the brakes repaired] . . . But then, I'll do the dusting and vacuuming and laundry . . . So we have a division of labor, but fifty percent of my chores are masculinized and fifty percent are feminized, and same for Hal.' (p. 202)

These extracts from Barrett reflect knowledge of cultural values about traditional gender roles with respect to housework, but also their subversion. Whilst Justin

Challenging traditional ideas about sex and gender.
SOURCE: ©Monkey Business Images/Shutterstock

refers to a lack of expectations for how gay couples distribute housework compared to heterosexual relationships, Dale notes how he and Hal engage in both traditionally male and female domestic duties.

Dixon and Wetherell (2004) argue traditional gender roles in domestic life may be reproduced in a cultural language which regards these practices as fair. Drawing on recent developments in discursive psychology (see Chapter 1 for an overview of discursive psychology), they argue that an adequate social psychology of domestic life and gender requires attention to, and a perspective on, everyday language. Investigations of gender inequalities and negotiations over 'fair shares' can benefit from directions provided by **social constructionism** and the more complex views of subjectivity and social relations present in psychology (Dixon & Wetherell, 2004).

social constructionism
an approach to how our understanding of reality is formed and structured, which argues that all cognitive functions originate in social interaction, and must therefore be explained as products of social interactions

The Social Construction of Sex and Gender

Rather than asking if there are biological and/or cultural differences between the sexes or genders, social constructionists consider the *performance* of gender (Speer & Stokoe, 2011). This body of research is particularly interested in how gender roles, and masculinity and femininity, are *constructed* in a society, and *assigned* certain traits, attributes, meanings and values. Gender differs between societies and across the social, ethnic and cultural groups within those societies. Even for a single individual, gender behaviours change over time and within different social contexts. From birth onwards, both sexes are conditioned by parental and other adult responses to behave, think, act and interact in gender-specific role manifestations.

Simply living in our world exposes us to myriad images and ideas about desirable masculine and feminine identities. Interestingly, recent research suggests that with increasing access to other cultural ideals, the differences between us are becoming less apparent as we form a global culture (Hudson, 2011; Shaw & Tan, 2014; Tan et al., 2013). We receive messages from the day we are born about what is appropriate for a boy and girl, man and woman. Advertising, toys, clothing and popular media further disseminate and reinforce notions of what is 'right' for girls and women; what is 'desirable' for men and boys. So our tendency to conform and to accept what seems 'natural' makes us easy targets for all marketing departments. This in turn influences our behaviour. Shopping for toys for your young son's birthday, what you buy will almost certainly be influenced by gender-toy-marketing strategies. Consequently you are more likely to come away from the shop having purchased a train set rather than a doll's house for his birthday.

A little girl playing with a doll.
SOURCE: ©Aaron Amat/Shutterstock

Social psychologists influenced by constructionism have challenged gender difference research, questioning the extent to which researchers can use gender (and biological sex) as an analytic category. To do so, they argue, is to assume that gender is a fixed 'trait' that resides within individuals and that all women share the same psychology of 'woman-ness' and men, 'man-ness'.

The argument is that this kind of research simply reproduces the male–female dichotomy and results in an exaggeration of sex differences. If we go looking for gender differences, then we may surely find them.

In Chapter 1 of her influential landmark book *Gender Trouble* (1990), Judith Butler claims that the apparent coherence of the categories of sex, gender and sexuality (such as masculine heterosexual male) is culturally constructed and reinforced through the exhibition and repetition of such gendered and sexualized behaviour publicly. Or in other words, we 'perform' gender. These acts establish the appearance of an essential 'core' gender and sex. But actually, gender and sex is a social construct.

Some researchers have examined if and how people use 'gender' in their everyday interactions, and what they consider these gender identities to be and involve. Stokoe (2000, 2004) argues that the 'doing' of gender in a society is constituted in people's everyday communication. Focusing on these daily interactions can tell us a lot about how gender is culturally acquired and used. Rather than comparing what men and women say and do, we should look at when and how people themselves refer to their sex or gender in communication, and why. Let's illustrate with an example from Stokoe's work. Below is an extract taken from a discussion between a group of university students on how to complete a task that's been set them:

> Ben: Is someone scribing, who's writing it?
> Nick: Oh yeah
> Mark: Well you can't read my writing [points to Kay] she wants to do it
> Kay: Eh?
> Nick: Well, secretary, female
> Kay: Well, secretary female, eh heh heh heh, I'm wearing glasses, I must be the secretary
>
> (Stokoe, 2004)

As we can see, the discussion immediately turns to the business of writing down an account of the decisions they make as a group. Stokoe directs us towards how the task of secretary is assigned to Kay by Nick on the basis of her gender. Here we can see how gender stereotypes are produced and reproduced in communication. Kay doesn't reject her assigned role, but she accepts it on the basis of her wearing glasses rather than being female. Qualitative research such as this, that focuses on when and how gender is mentioned by people, tells us something about how this identity is understood by people themselves, and what differences *they* construct between men and women (rather than the researcher).

Let's consider another example, this time from the healthcare profession. In the US, obtaining access to cosmetic surgery is usually about what you are willing to pay. Body enhancements such as rhinoplasty, botox, lip-fillers, dermal-fillers, liposuction and breast augmentation have become commonplace. However, points out Whitehead et al. (2012), if you want a sex change, you are going to need approval from a trained psychologist or equivalent professional before it can be done. Whitehead and her colleagues interviewed US healthcare professionals who advertised their services as being 'trans-positive' or 'trans-friendly'. Their interest was in how healthcare professionals' definitions of gender influenced decisions to approve or reject sex modification surgery. Some practitioners interviewed held biological essentialist views of gender, whilst others favoured a more spiritual view, noting that gender was not just ingrained in the brain but also the psyche, or the soul. For both biological and spiritual views, gender is binary: you're one thing or the other, male or female. Other practitioners, however, held more fluid understandings of gender, noting that whilst your biological sex is determined at birth, your gender is how you behave, which can change day to day and is not necessarily binary. You can perhaps see how these differing understandings of gender might be used to support or reject sex-reassignment surgery. So how we construct gender can have some very profound implications not just for our own lives but also others.

evolutionary psychology a field of study that looks at the role of evolutionary processes and principles of natural selection in shaping cognition and behaviour

natural selection the evolutionary process by which heritable traits that best enable organisms to survive and reproduce in particular environments are passed to ensuing generations

sexual selection those characteristics (adaptations) which arise as a result of successful reproduction, and are based on intrasexual and intersexual competition

How Does Evolutionary Psychology Explain Gender?

We have considered how biology and culture have been understood as explanations for sex and gender. We could view these as opposing forces: one force pushes us towards a rather essentialist biological approach that places sex and gender firmly within our DNA. Another force pulls us towards the role our social environment and culture play in forming and shaping our sex and gender. But as we've seen, to define this as a 'one or the other' battle, in which we declare either biology or culture as more important, is to over-simplify what is rather a complex relationship between them. Here, we'll consider in a little more detail how **evolutionary psychology** has approached the topics of sex and gender. In doing so, we examine one way in which this complex relationship has been studied and illustrated in social psychology.

Evolutionary Psychology and the Evolved Mind

The human brain is approximately 1,350 cubic centimeters in size and extraordinarily complex. Trying to understand why and how it is designed and functions in the way that it does, and how the environment shapes and is shaped by it, is the business of evolutionary psychology. 'At its broadest, evolutionary psychology is the study of the evolved mind', writes Jeffares and Sterelny (2012, p. 1). Based on Charles Darwin's (1859) theories of **natural** and **sexual selection**, the human mind or brain is designed to ensure we survive and continue as a species in an ever-changing and highly variable world. For evolutionary psychologists, how we think and behave can be explained as adaptations that solve problems which threaten our survival and reproduction. Underlying the presumptions is a principle: *nature selects traits that help send one's genes into the future.*

Charles Darwin's theories of natural and sexual selection combine the forces of biology and culture to explain human behaviour.
SOURCE: ©ShutterStockStudio/Shutterstock

However, evolutionary explanations of human behaviour and cognition have been met with resistance, usually due to a misrepresentation of the discipline. And this resistance is particularly evident when it comes to the topic of sex and gender (e.g. Winegard et al., 2014). This misrepresentation arguably falls into the nature versus nurture dichotomy. Evolutionary approaches are assumed to be biological (nature), with either no consideration of culture (nurture) or to be competing with culture. Yet, evolutionary psychology rejects genetic determinism and 'invokes the role of the environment at every step of the causal process' (Confer et al., 2010, p. 120). So let's consider the topics of sex and gender to identify how nature and nurture are entwined within this approach.

Evolutionary Paradoxes?

According to evolutionary psychologists, heterosexual men tend to feel attracted to women who are younger than them, and whose physical features, such as youthful faces and forms, suggest fertility. Moreover, the older the man, the greater the age difference he prefers when selecting a mate. In their twenties, men prefer, and marry, women only slightly younger. In their sixties, men prefer, and marry, women averaging about 10 years younger (Kenrick & Keefe, 1992; Schwarz & Hassebrauck, 2012). Women of all ages sometimes prefer men just slightly older than themselves and feel attracted to men whose wealth, power and ambition promise resources for protecting and nurturing offspring. Once again, say the evolutionary psychologists, we see that natural selection predisposes men to feel attracted to female features associated with fertility (Buss, 1989; also see Chapter 9). But how do evolutionary psychologists explain topics such as voluntary childlessness and homosexuality, where the reproduction of our genes through offspring is either undesired or unlikely?

Voluntary Childlessness

Not everyone wants, or can have, children. In fact there is a rise in people choosing not to have children in developed countries. In a survey of voluntary childlessness in 38 countries, including Belgium, India, Ireland and Latvia, Hudde (2018) asked why. He discovered that couples who hold different attitudes about parenting and responsibilities are increasingly choosing to remain childless. Indeed as gender roles become more fluid, long-held assumptions about roles in a relationship, for example who will do the childcare, who will earn the money, and so on, may dissolve. Conversely, those couples who share similar attitudes to gender roles are more likely to have children (Arpino et al., 2015). To put this into context a little, research on childlessness in sub-Saharan Africa, have focused on the challenges infertile women face in countries that are **pronatalist**, such as Nigeria. Women who cannot have children can encounter social ostracism, rejection from their husband, and have their land and possessions taken away from them. To be childless is to not be a grown woman but to remain a child, possibly even stereotyped as a witch (Dimka & Dein, 2013). Childlessness is not voluntary in such cultures as the consequences of not having children can be devastating, particularly for women. Different cultures hold very different ideas and values about gender and children. Social norms regulate what is preferred and they can develop independent of any genetic selection.

pronatalist the belief that child-bearing is important and desirable for humans, which is often reinforced in cultural practices and policies

Aarsson and Altman (2006) offer an intriguing evolutionary explanation for voluntary childlessness in developed countries. They suggest that the desire to 'leave something of oneself' after our death, may not just refer to the genes in our offspring but our cultural influence on others. If we recall evolutionary psychologists' description of *transmitted culture* and Richard Dawkins' concept of meme described earlier in this chapter, we can figure out how this might work. If we are evolved to ensure our survival and continuation in the world, this desire to leave a legacy may not be genetic, but could be a meme. This could be music, film or literature we've written, a family firm which becomes culturally

The author Jane Austen (1775–1817) did not have children, but she did leave behind a large body of literature which has influenced modern-day popular culture.
SOURCE: ©Pictorial Press Ltd/ Alamy Stock Photo

important, our charitable works, and so on. The point is, that by not having children, we invest our time and energies into *meme-transmission,* which endures beyond our death. Our legacy of music might influence others. Our written words could have a huge impact on people and society after our death. If we turn to Chapter 1 of this book, we can see some examples of meme-transmission in the form of philosophers and theorists who have shaped social psychology, and we will also notice that most of them are men. As Aarsson and Altman conclude, in those cultures where women can exercise power over their fertility, they are investing their resources into meme-transmission to redefine a previously male-dominated world – including social psychology!

Homosexuality

Sometimes referred to as Darwin's paradox, homosexuality seems to defy the basic principles of evolutionary theory (Adriaens & De Block, 2006). Same-sex relationships do not usually result in reproduction. Evolutionary psychologists themselves note this limitation of the theory (e.g. Barrett et al., 2002; Confer et al., 2010). That said, explanations have been proposed. One is the **kin altruism theory**, first put forward by E.O. Wilson (1975). This theory suggests some individuals do not reproduce. Instead they invest their energies into helping their genetic relatives raise their offspring. However, empirical research in support of this has been mixed. Some has found no evidence that gay men in England (Rahman & Hull, 2005), the USA (Bobrow & Bailey, 2001), and Canada (Abild et al., 2014), invest more time with their nieces and nephews than heterosexual men. However other work has observed that in some countries such as Samoa, they do (Vasey & VanderLaan, 2010, 2011). Explanations for these cross-cultural differences include geographical proximity to nieces and nephews and cultural acceptance of homosexuality (Abild et al., 2013, 2014).

kin altruism theory describes the situation where a person does not have children themselves, but instead invests their energies and resources into helping their immediate relatives raise children

Adriaens and De Block (2006) offer an explanation that incorporates both evolutionary psychology and social constructionism. They note that male same-sex relationships have a long global history. The men themselves were sometimes married, sometimes single. These relationships could bring benefits such as access to resources and valuable contacts. The researchers propose that such behaviour became categorized as homosexuality with the rise of formal religions. Christianity, for example, preached the virtues of heterosexuality and the perils of homosexuality. Consequently men had a choice – one or the other. Those who chose homosexuality were considered deviant and often subject to homophobia. The point being made here is that sexuality is not a fixed trait. Rather it can be chosen as an adaptive strategy for navigating benefits which aid our survival in a rather complex world. As indeed can heterosexuality.

But what of lesbianism? On the surface this also offers something of a problem for evolutionary psychologists. However, evolutionary psychologists have put forward some intriguing explanations for lesbianism that combine genes and culture. Firstly, it is noted that many women, regardless of sexual orientation, feel sexually attracted to other women at some point in their lives (Chivers et al., 2014). Yet, it is a minority that engage in homosexual relationships. If we revisit kin selection theory we can follow its argument that homosexual women invest their energies into helping raise the offspring of their genetic relatives. However, there is no empirical evidence to support this (Apostolou et al., 2017). It has also been suggested that female sexual identities are fluid, and lesbianism is a historical way for women to pool resources for childcare when there is a lack of available men (Kuhle & Radtke, 2013). But this begs the question regarding why a sexual relationship is required when a platonic friendship would achieve the same objective (Apostolou et al., 2017)? Other studies have tried to define lesbian 'types' and ascribe characteristics to them. For example, Bassett et al. (2001) differentiate between 'butch' and 'femme' lesbians. Butch lesbians are attributed with masculine traits such as dominance and assertiveness, whereas femme lesbians are feminine, displaying sensitivity, kindness and happiness. According to Bassett et al., femme lesbians display jealousy over physically attractive rivals. Butch lesbians get jealous over wealthier ones.

Other studies have focused on motivations for lesbian relationships that include evolution as an explanatory tool. For example, Harrison et al. (2008) surveyed 131 LGBT psychology students about their sexual experiences and relationships. They discovered that those who identified as lesbian women were more likely to have suffered sexual abuse from men, as a child and/or adult, than heterosexual women. The researchers suggest that choosing a lesbian relationship in some circumstances, such as these, can be a strategy for ensuring your own survival and those of any offspring you may have. This is not to say all lesbians have suffered sexual abuse from men. Similarly, Crane-Seeber and Crane (2010) look at the social, historical and political context in which sexual identities, notably heterosexuality and lesbianism, have been defined and valued. Gendered roles have been fulfilled in line with what society expects. One consequence of this has been the suppression of female sexuality and power. Our thinking, our bodies and our (sexual) behaviour is shaped through our relationships with others, and lesbianism can be a powerful challenge to the subordination of women. Ultimately, the claim is that lesbianism can be understood as an evolutionary adaptation in response to patriarchal relations which historically have proven detrimental to women's survival and reproduction (Muscarella, 2000).

These are just some of the psychological approaches that have been taken in understanding homosexuality. It is certainly not exhaustive of a fascinating, and sometimes controversial body of work on sex, gender and sexuality.

What Can We Conclude About Genes and Culture?

Biology and culture play out in the context of each other. Rather than thinking of them as opposing forces, we can understand them as working in tandem, to help us navigate our way through the world.

Genes and Culture

What we've outlined in this chapter is a view that doesn't see genes and culture as competitors. Cultural norms subtly but powerfully affect our attitudes and behaviour, but they don't do so independently of biology. Taking gender as an example, this chapter has examined how this interaction works in shaping our thinking and behaviour.

Advances in neurobiology and neuropsychology indicate how experience and activity change the brain and establish new connections between neurons (Quartz & Sejnowski, 2002). Our brain develops and increases its capacity due to its plasticity. Visual experience activates genes that develop the brain's visual area. Parental touch activates genes that help offspring cope with future stressful events. The brain is not hardware, a given structure, set in stone, but is instead an ever-adapting piece of software.

The Power of The Situation and The Person

'There are trivial truths and great truths', declared the physicist Niels Bohr (cited in Banaji, 2004). 'The opposite of a trivial truth is plainly false. The opposite of a great truth is also true.' Social psychology teaches us a great truth: *the power of the situation*. This great truth about the power of external pressures would explain our behaviour if we were passive, like tumbleweeds. But, unlike tumbleweeds, we are not just blown here and there by the situations in which we find ourselves. We act; we react. We respond; we get responses.

Perhaps emphasizing the power of culture leaves you somewhat uncomfortable. Most of us resent any suggestion that external forces determine our behaviour; we see ourselves as free beings, as the originators of our actions (well, at least of our good actions). We worry that assuming cultural reasons for our actions might lead to what philosopher Jean-Paul Sartre called 'bad faith' – evading responsibility by blaming something or someone for one's fate.

Social situations do profoundly influence individuals. But individuals also influence social situations. The two *interact*. Every individual is not only influenced by culture – we also create and change culture by acting on it.

interaction a relationship in which the effect of one factor (such as biology) depends on another factor (such as environment)

The **interaction** occurs in at least three ways:

1 *A given social situation often affects different people differently*. Because our minds do not see reality identically or objectively, we respond to a situation as we construe it.

2 *People often choose their situations*. Given a choice, sociable people elect situations that evoke social interaction. When you chose your university or place to live, you were also choosing to expose yourself to a specific set of social influences.

3 *People often create their situations*. Our preconceptions can be self-fulfilling: if we expect someone to be extraverted, hostile, intelligent or sexy, our actions towards the person may induce the very behaviour we expect.

The reciprocal causation between situations and persons allows us to see people as either *reacting to* or *acting upon* their environment. Each perspective is correct, for we are both the products and the architects of our culture and the social world.

Thus, power resides both in persons and in situations. We create and are created by our cultural worlds.

Focus on

Mind the Gap: From Sexed Brains to Gendered Behaviour

As we've seen in this chapter, there is a tendency for researchers to emphasize any differences between the genders. Arguably guilty of confirmation bias, journals have been keen to publish those results that confirm what we believe about men and women. This can also be termed a 'publication bias', as journals have traditionally published positive findings that reveal sex and gender differences. And what we often believe is that they are different – socially, physiologically and psychologically. Books like John Gray's *Men Are from Mars, Women Are from Venus* have sold millions of copies. However, as we've also seen in this chapter, there is an increasing body of work that questions gender differences reported by earlier studies. One area that has been brought to task is that of neuroscience and its findings that men and women have different brains.

Fine (2010) remarks that historically women have been thought to have smaller and lighter brains than men, and this was held responsible for their intellectual inferiority compared to men. Recent advances in neuroscience have meant that we can now see those differences, if they exist, in the structure and functioning of the brain (e.g. Baron-Cohen, 2004). But they are not without criticism. For example, some neuroscientists claim there are sex differences in functional cerebral asymmetry (FCAs). One key illustration of this is that men use the left hemisphere for language and the right for visual processing. Women, on the other hand, use both hemispheres for language and visual processing (e.g. Hausmann et al., 1998). Biological differences such as these have influenced some misguided gendered perceptions about the sexes. This leads many to (mis)perceive that men are better at visual processing and spatial awareness (and parking the car!) and women are better at language (and not at parking the car!). Men are better at science, because they focus on detail and can integrate information, and women are better at empathy. As Fine notes, the apparent 'facts' of neuroscience have become 'a springboard for scientifically unwarranted claims about men's and women's different psychological abilities' (2010, p. 282). But these 'facts' may not be quite so factual as they appear.

Fine points out that neuroscience results are often based on very small sample sizes (the technology is extremely expensive to use!), and the conclusions drawn are not always representative of what the neuroimaging shows. Researchers are keen to ignore similarities found between men and women and focus on any sex differences – no matter how small that difference may be (recall our earlier mention of confirmation and publication biases!). And the impressive technology may mean we're keen to accord any results it produces with more credibility than we should. Hausmann (2017) reports the complexity in trying to confirm sex differences in FCAs based not only on methodological issues (such as small sample sizes, marginal significance levels, and what participants are asked to do in the tests), but also the array of other factors, that are not gender, which may contribute to the results. These include age of participants, individual differences, and the presence of sex hormones (e.g. where a woman is in her menstrual cycle) which may influence brain functioning at the time of the test. In short, researchers interested in sex and gender might be guilty of what Fine calls 'neuro-realism'.

As we discussed earlier in this chapter, the brain is a piece of software, not hardware. Sex differences found in the brain might be a consequence of cultural impact rather than physiologically determined differences.

Questions

1 How much weight should social psychologists give to the findings of **neuroscience** in explaining differences between men and women?

2 Why do you think we tend to treat the results and conclusions from neuroscience as factual?

3 Should we pursue neuroscientific techniques to better understand sex and gender?

neuroscience describes the study of the brain and nervous system in human and non-human animals

SUMMING UP: BIOLOGY, CULTURE AND GENDER

HOW ARE WE INFLUENCED BY HUMAN NATURE AND CULTURAL DIVERSITY?

- Social psychology has historically grappled with nature and nurture explanations for human behaviour.
- Nowadays, most social psychologists recognize the need to study biology and culture as a co-dependent relationship rather than competing forces.
- Modern research into the brain has revealed its plasticity. The brain is not hardwired as previously thought, but is software, shaping and being shaped by our environment.
- Evolutionary psychologists examine how human nature is adapted to increase the likelihood of our survival and continuation. This adaptation is the result of biological and cultural forces to optimize our chances of success.
- There are many definitions of culture, including the distinction between evoked and transmitted culture.
- Modern-day travel and technology means we are exposed to cultural diversity more than ever before in our ancestral past.
- Cultural norms provide guidelines for how to think and behave appropriately in our current surroundings. Some norms seem to be universally shared, whilst others are culture-specific.

HOW DOES BIOLOGY AND CULTURE EXPLAIN SEX AND GENDER?

- Social psychological research has typically embedded assumptions about sex and gender into the design of the studies (e.g. experiments).
- Sex refers to biological characteristics, whereas gender denotes the patterns of behaviour recognized as feminine or masculine.
- At birth, sex is usually assigned to an individual, including medical correction if deemed necessary.
- The dichotomy of male and female may be over-simplistic, failing to capture those individuals who do not identify as either.
- Social psychological research has focused on gender differences on a range of topics, including independence vs connectedness, and social dominance.

GENES, CULTURE AND GENDER: DOING WHAT COMES NATURALLY?

- Biological differences between the sexes influences psychological characteristics and behaviour to some extent.
- Culture also influences our psychological characteristics and behaviour to some extent. As cultural values shift across time and space, we adapt.

- Cultural expectation of nuclear families based on heterosexual couples holds norms about gender roles, especially with respect to domestic labour and childcare. Modern-day relationships that are not heteronormative pose a challenge to these assumptions.
- Social constructionists argue gender is performed by individuals in language. So dichotomies between male and female are not fixed traits but are defined and reproduced through the way we talk and interact with one another.

HOW DOES EVOLUTIONARY PSYCHOLOGY EXPLAIN GENDER?

- Evolutionary psychologists study the evolved mind – or brain – based on Charles Darwin's theories of natural and sexual selection.
- Evolutionary psychology has been misrepresented as an essentialist biological approach, which views sex and gender as biologically determined. Rather, evolutionary psychology incorporates the role of the environment in its explanations of human nature and behaviour.
- Some paradoxes have been suggested for evolution-based explanations. Two examples are voluntary childlessness and homosexuality. Both defy the desire to reproduce one's genes into the future in the form of offspring.
- Evolutionary psychologists offer explanations for these paradoxes, which include the role of the environment. Some researchers note that our desire to 'leave oneself behind' after death may not necessarily be genetic, but can be in the form of a cultural legacy (or meme).

WHAT CAN WE CONCLUDE ABOUT GENES AND CULTURE ?

- Biological and cultural explanations need not be contradictory. Indeed, they interact. Biological factors operate within a cultural context, and culture builds on a biological foundation.
- Advances in research and technology have given us a better understanding of the complex relationship between biology and culture, which underlies human behaviour.
- The great truth about the power of social influence is but half the truth if separated from its complementary truth: the power of the person. Persons and situations interact in at least three ways. First, individuals vary in how they interpret and react to a given situation. Second, people choose many of the situations that influence them. Third, people help create their social situations.

Critical Questions

1. What contribution do you think evolutionary psychology has made to social psychological understandings of human behaviour?
2. To what extent do you think evolutionary psychology has successfully explained 'paradoxes' to its underlying assumptions about human nature?
3. Biology and culture interact, but is one force more dominant in this relationship?
4. What do we mean by 'plasticity of the brain' and why is it important for social psychological phenomena?
5. Should social psychology continue to differentiate between males and females in its research designs?
6. Is social psychology right to examine sex and gender differences?
7. Are sex and gender just constructions of language?

Recommended Reading

Here are some readings you might want to follow up to continue your exploration of the influence of biology and culture on human behaviour, including gender.

Classic Readings

Darwin, C. (2009). *Origin of species.* Penguin Classics.

Eagly, A. H. & Wood, W. (1999). The origins of sex differences in human behavior. *American Psychologist, 54*(6), 408–423.

Gilligan, C. (1982). *In a different voice: Psychological theory and women's development.* Harvard University Press.

Wilson, E. O. (1978). *On human nature.* Harvard University Press.

Contemporary Readings

Butler, J. (2004). *Undoing gender.* Routledge.

Colapinto, J. (1997, December 11). The true story of John/Joan. *The Rolling Stone:* https://www.healthyplace.com/gender/inside-intersexuality/the-true-story-of-john-joan

Confer, J. C., Easton, J. A., Fleischman, D. S., Goetz, C. D., Lewis, D. M. G., Perilloux, C., & Buss, D. M. (2010). Evolutionary psychology: Controversies, questions, prospects, and limitations. *American Psychologist, 65*(2), 110–126.

Fine, C. (2010). From scanner to sound bite: Issues in interpreting and reporting sex differences in the brain. *Current Directions in Psychological Science, 19*(5), 280–283.

Hopcroft, R. L. (2016). *Evolution and gender: Why it matters for contemporary life.* Routledge.

Petersen, J. L., & Hyde, J. S. (2011). Gender differences in sexual attitudes and behaviors: A review of meta-analytic results and large datasets. *Journal of Sex Research, 48*(2–3), 149–165.

15 APPLIED SOCIAL PSYCHOLOGY

'The purpose of psychology is to give us a completely different idea of the things we know best.'
Paul Valery

Throughout this textbook, we note some real-world applications of social psychological research. These examples are not just to show the discipline's relevance and impact on our everyday lives, but also offer practical testing grounds for our theories, methods and ideas. Social psychological research can, and has been, successfully applied to many topics, including physical and mental health, workplace and leadership matters, and environmental issues. In fact many of the studies we have considered in this textbook have not only been published in social psychology journals, but span a range of disciplines and interests including health, politics, economics, history, geography, biology, and so on. However, as a relatively new science as compared to disciplines such as physics, chemistry, and geography, social psychology is still finding its feet. That said, it would be wise not to underestimate the impact that it has already made, and continues to make, in our everyday lives. In this final chapter we focus on these three specific areas in which social psychology has proved to be extremely valuable:

1. 'Social Psychology in the Workplace' examines the role of social psychological processes in our working lives.
2. 'Social Psychology, Health and Illness' applies social psychology to promoting mental and physical health, and tackling illness.
3. 'Social Psychology, the Environment and the Sustainable Future' explores how social psychological principles might help avert the ecological crisis that arguably threatens to engulf us as a result of increasing consumption, global warming and environmental disasters.

Social Psychology in the Workplace

Most of us will spend much of our adult lives in a work environment of some kind or another. You may be studying social psychology with the aim of obtaining skills and knowledge that will equip you for future working life. Yet the workplace is more complex than simply a means of earning money. Some people even enjoy it! For many people, it is a positive experience and is a key feature in defining their sense of self and identity. This is probably because most of us spend around a third of our lives at work. According to EU data of working hours within the European Union, on average we spend 40.3 hours a week at work (Smith, 2018). Across his or her lifetime, the average British worker is at work for 3,507 days (Bailey, 2018). The rewards are not simply material, but psychological. In our modern world, the workplace is a constantly changing environment. With the advent of technology and increasing leaps forward in virtual communication, the workplace has become a place requiring a multitude of diverse skills. Not only must you learn the skills and abilities to do the job, but you need to communicate effectively with your colleagues in the immediate vicinity, as well as those separated by geographical distance, using remote means such as e-mail and videoconferencing. Many workplaces are international communities. Whether your workplace is a formal or informal organisation, a local, national or international one, what they all have in common is that they constitute a community of people engaged in social interaction for a shared purpose. Social psychology has proved very useful in providing insights into, and explanations of, how people behave in organizational environments, and how to maximize their work performance whilst also improving their well-being.

The disciplines of organizational behaviour and social psychology are brought together to constitute what is known as '**organizational psychology**'.

organizational psychology the disciplines of organizational behaviour and social psychology, examining social processes within the workplace and other organizations

Motivating People to Work

Organizational psychology has used insights from social psychology to offer answers to the following questions.

- What motivates people to work and how is it related to performance?
- How can we identify and tackle stress and maintain well-being in the workplace?
- What makes someone a good leader at work, and what effect does it have on employee performance and relationships?
- How effective is teamwork?

'Laziness may appear attractive, but work gives satisfaction.'
Anne Frank

How and Why Are People Motivated to Work?

What motivates people to pursue work-related goals and often dedicate their adult lives to the cause? To what extent is motivation related to performance? Personal and social explanations have been offered to understand the role of motivation in the workplace.

Motivation can be defined as a choice about where to direct your energy, how persistently, and how much effort to put in to achieve a goal. Of course you are probably more motivated to achieve some goals than others. Organizational psychology is interested in the role of motivation in the workplace and its relationship to work-related goals and performance.

An assembly line in China. How do you increase motivation, reduce tedium and offer job satisfaction in such working environments?
SOURCE: ©plavevski/Shutterstock

Although initial explorations of motivation were based in monotonous workplaces that characterized a lot of early industry, today the workplace is a much more diverse place for many of us, which has meant a change in how researchers and employers understand motivation. This has led to an array of psychological theories that focus both within and beyond the individual to examine the role of motivation in the workplace.

Theories of Motivation

Early investigations into motivation mostly concerned the inner workings of the individual. Landy and Conte (2007) outline Abraham Maslow's 'need theory' (Maslow, 1943), which proposes that all human beings have five basic sets of needs, arranged as a 'hierarchy of needs', that they seek to satisfy (see **Figure 15.1**). The theory proposes that once one set of needs has been mastered, attention then turns to the next, higher, level of needs.

The five needs are as follows.

1. Physiological needs. These are basic biological needs such as food, drink, sleep, sex.
2. Security/safety needs. This refers to the need to have a secure and safe environment (e.g. a home).

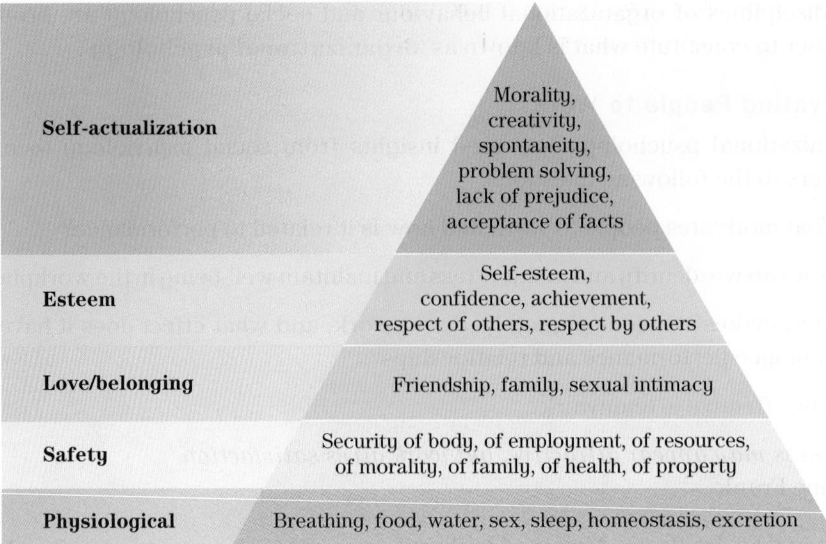

FIGURE 15.1 Maslow's hierarchy of needs
SOURCE: Adapted from Finkelstein (2006).

3 Social belonging needs. These concern forming interpersonal relationships and social bonds and attachments with others. They also include a need to be accepted by others.

4 Esteem needs. These define the need to be recognized and respected by self and others.

5 Self-actualization needs. This describes an individual's need to fulfil their potential. Maslow felt few people ever achieve this need and most were always striving towards it.

Applied to the workplace, we can see how these five needs apply to our daily working practices and how these needs can be addressed by organizations. Consider the following examples:

1 Physiological needs. Working for financial gain enables us to put food on the table and to keep a roof over our heads. Our working conditions – such as temperature, lighting, furniture, hours, should be optimal to ensure we are comfortable in the workplace, hence maximizing our performance potential.

2 Security/safety needs. Our working environment should protect us from risk or harm. Workplace risk and safety assessments are typically carried out to ensure this. We need to feel our selves and our possessions are safe and secure at work.

3 Social belonging needs. The workplace should be a place that fosters friendships and social cohesiveness, encouraging a shared sense of belonging and identity amongst its employees. Many workplaces have 'away days' to facilitate networks and consolidate friendships and teamwork in a neutral setting. Company sports teams, quiz teams, and social events also function to increase social belonging to the organization and to each other.

4 Esteem needs. Our work performance should be recognized and rewarded by others. It is important that we know we are carrying out our job well through

approval from others. Company recognition of our efforts, such as incentive schemes, appraisals and promotion, are just a few examples of how our esteem can be boosted in the workplace.

5 Self-actualization needs. Translated into the workplace this is the need for employees to feel fulfilled. Individuals want to confirm that they are achieving their full potential within the organization. The employee should be empowered, creative, and passionate about their work.

Supporters of Maslow's theory recommend that the norms and values which form the corporate culture of the workplace, should be aligned with meeting these needs. The result of doing so is a highly productive, engaged, committed, and happy workforce (Jerome, 2013).

However, as Landy and Conte (2007) point out, if all humans have these five sets of needs within the workplace then we can safely assume that all workers will be operating at different levels of the hierarchy. Some people may be working simply to pay the bills whereas others want to challenge themselves in some way. This gives a manager or supervisor a tricky problem: to satisfy everyone they require tailor-made attention to the needs of every individual employee. As attractive as this sounds, it isn't terribly practical, especially in a large organization with hundreds, possibly thousands, of employees.

Challenges to Maslow's theory include those that come from Rouse (2004), who argues it has limited applicability in the modern workplace. Firstly, these five needs do not really fall into the neat levels suggested by Maslow. Instead they are complex and inter-related. Secondly, it is assumed that all employees will work through the hierarchy of needs in the same order – which they may not. And thirdly, there are more needs to be met than the five outlined by Maslow, such as finding the work stimulating and feeling unstressed. We can also add that to locate needs and motivation within the biology of the person is to ignore the social influences on people's own perception and construction of what they need.

Further criticisms of Maslow's hierarchy of needs model are based on the cultural assumptions upon which it rests. Gambrel and Cianci (2003) invite us to think about the context in which Maslow developed the theory. It was based on middle-class US managers in the 1940s and arguably promotes the ideals of the American Dream. The American Dream reflects the values and principles of an **individualistic society** such as the need to be self-ambitious, to stand out from the crowd, to achieve financial success and prosper, to climb the social ladder, and so on. It assumes we want to get ahead, that we have freedom of speech and movement, and that we believe we control our own destiny. Understood in this context, we start to see how a corporate culture that aligns itself with meeting Maslow's hierarchy of needs, supports the goals of individualism. But what about the workplace in more collectivist cultures such as China? **Collectivist societies**, or cultures, have some differences from individualistic ones. The concern is not with the individual but with the group – usually your immediate family. Opinions and values are group-held ones. Standing out from the crowd, pursuing your own ambitions and aspirations, are frowned upon. What matters is family, fairness and the nation – not the self. Consequently the hierarchy of needs requires some rethinking as well as restructuring when applied to the Chinese workplace. Citing the work of Nevis (1983), Gambrel and Cianci outline an attempt to do so.

individualism or independence a cultural orientation where the individual is more important than the group. People in such cultures commonly give priority to one's own goals over group goals, and define one's identity in terms of personal attributes rather than group identifications (compare to collectivism)

collectivism a cultural orientation where the group is more important than the individual. People in such cultures commonly give priority to the goals of their group and define their identity accordingly (the opposite of individualism)

In Nevis's proposal, esteem is removed from the hierarchy of needs, self-actualization is redefined as service to others, individualism is removed, and the order is changed. The first need to be mastered is social belonging. Following from this are physiological needs, then safety, and finally self-actualization.

Thus, whilst Maslow's hierarchy of needs model remains a relevant and useful motivational theory for today's workforce, caution is recommended in applying it. It promotes an ideal-case scenario for a specific cultural context. The messy, diverse and complex everyday reality of our working lives does not easily fit into a model such as this.

The work of B. F. Skinner and his behaviourist theory is evident throughout the many topics of social psychology, and it appears in many chapters of this book. In Chapter 1 we observe that Skinner argued the environment has a real impact on people's behaviour. This certainly is a move away from the biological focus of motivation theories. The work of Skinner informs modern-day behaviourist approaches to workplace motivation and performance. An outline of such an approach is provided by McGee and Johnson (2015). Starting from the point of recruitment, McGee and Johnson describe how a behaviourist approach emphasizes analysing the job role to be filled. A note is taken of what skills, abilities and knowledge it requires to successfully execute the role. Lessons are learned from the past of previous occupiers of that role. What worked, and what didn't. The search for the new recruit can then begin. However, this search is not based on traits an individual has which might be desirable for the workplace generally, such as intelligence and ambition, but rather on the specific skills, abilities and knowledge they have. The preferred candidate for the job is the one who most closely matches those skills, abilities and knowledge ascertained from the employer's scrutiny of the role. Once in the role, motivation to perform well in it can be manipulated using intrinsic and extrinsic rewards. As an example of an extrinsic reward, we can imagine that the reward of increased pay from the employer might motivate increased work performance from the employee. An intrinsic reward might be job satisfaction, feelings of empowerment, and opportunities to be creative. Alternatively, poor performance can be sanctioned (e.g. a formal warning) or addressed through training, depending on its cause.

We previously noted the importance of integrating Maslow's hierarchy of needs into a workplace's corporate culture. The same argument has been made for behaviourist principles. However, *how* and *what* workplace behaviour is reinforced is complex, especially in today's busy working environments. Bushardt et al. (2007) outline different levels at which rewards can be offered. At the *system* level, they are part and parcel of being an employee of a particular organization. This can include private healthcare, childcare vouchers, gym membership, discounts on shopping and so forth. Everyone gets these as a reward for continued service to the employer. In terms of motivation, they may not be especially effective at the individual level. Employees might do 'just enough' to avoid being fired or sanctioned in some other way. *Individual* rewards have better potential for motivating and reinforcing work performance. These include promotion, awards and pay increases. Bushardt and his colleagues suggest that whilst these kinds of rewards might motivate individuals more effectively than system rewards, they often fail to encourage employees to reach their full potential.

They put this down to how performance is measured – which may not be an accurate indicator of someone's actual performance – and when these rewards are made available (e.g. at a particular point in the working calendar). Annual appraisal processes are common ways of assessing and rewarding performance in the workplace. Consequently if an individual feels their efforts are not being recognized, the rewards will not reinforce their productivity levels. Likewise, if efforts are not rewarded (and reinforced) at the time they are being exerted, there is little motivation to continue. Furthermore, bearing in mind the hectic pace of the modern-day workplace, managers responsible for measuring performance and delivering rewards (and sanctions) may not have the time nor the energy to spend with each individual employee to obtain a full and accurate picture of their performance and productivity and reward (or sanction) it appropriately. Instead, Bushardt et al. recommend that rewards and sanctions become an embedded part of organizational culture that are continuously recognized and endorsed privately and publicly by all. They are part of the workplace's organizational learning and history. Favourable practices are publicly acknowledged as a workplace norm that uphold a commonly shared workplace value. Deviances are also publicly recognized and sanctioned at the time of their occurrence. By focusing on the workplace culture rather than the individuals, Bushardt and his team argue managers can motivate their workforce to enhance their performance and secure the adoption of excellent working practices.

Behaviourist approaches to workplace motivation are not without their critics. Landy and Conte warn that a fundamental criticism of Skinner's work is that it can offer something of a passive image of the person. There is no role for active decision-making on the part of the employee. He or she simply responds to the rewards and sanctions that are put before him or her. But as individuals we clearly do make decisions and judgements about which rewards we want to pursue and which we do not.

With this criticism in mind, let's consider a theory of workplace motivation based on behaviourist principles, but which includes the role of cognition and consciousness more fully.

Victor Vroom's **VIE theory** (1964) suggests that motivation can be understood as a response to expectancy, valence, and instrumentality (sometimes expressed as $M = V \times I \times E$), and adopts a metaphor of the individual as an active scientist as they work out where to direct their energy. What Vroom means by valence, instrumentality and expectancy is described below.

VIE theory (valence–instrumentality–expectancy theory) Vroom's theory suggests motivation is a combination of valence, instrumentality and expectancy. Our behaviour thus results from people's conscious choices, which are shaped by their expectations of various outcomes

- *Valence.* This refers to the notion that some aspects of the workplace and working life are more attractive (e.g. being paid) than others (e.g. long hours). The task of the employer is to work out what employees find attractive and want more of, in order to motivate them.
- *Instrumentality.* This describes the relationship between performance, reward and cost. For example, if I put energy into getting a promotion (performance) it will mean more pay (reward), but may also mean longer hours and loss of weekends (cost). In deciding whether to increase my performance for the reward an employee must do a cost-benefit analysis. The employer should ensure that these rewards are available, visible and attainable for the employee.

- *Expectancy*. This concerns the employee's beliefs that increasing effort will result in successful performance to obtain the reward. The employee asks him/herself if s/he can actually perform the task. The responsibility of the employer is to ensure workers have the training and supervision they need to perform successfully, and have the opportunity to receive the reward as a result.

Although Vroom's VIE theory was formulated over 50 years ago, it remains highly influential in the fields of social and organizational psychology. Suciu et al. (2013) documented the importance of the appraisal process for increasing motivation levels of Romanian civil servants. Whilst appraisal of their job performance is a legal requirement for civil servants, Suciu and colleagues claim that when it is done properly it raises motivation levels. These appraisal processes are crucial for influencing civil servants' expectancy levels (building confidence and skills), establishing instrumentality (e.g. 'If I achieve these objectives, of which I'm capable, I will be rewarded') and identifying valence (what that reward will be) which will then motivate the worker – in this case the civil servant. Vroom and his proponents advise that employers need to engage their employees in the process of goal-setting. By offering employees some choice in their working goals, employers ensure their workforce are motivated by those aspects of the workplace they find attractive, and performance is enhanced to achieve those goals and rewards. Feeling in control of your working life is essential in motivating and engaging people in the workplace (Deci & Ryan, 2014; Vroom & Jago, 1988).

This is arguably a little different from Skinner's conception of the individual who simply responds to rewards, or Maslow's view of the individual who seeks to satisfy particular needs. Within Vroom's theory, both internal and external factors are involved in motivation. The task of the employer, who seeks increased motivation, is to clearly outline the benefits of increased performance and encourage the employee's capabilities of achieving this.

Coaching in the Workplace

Psychologists have recently turned their attention to the practice of coaching to motivate and inspire employees into increasing their performance and well-being in the workplace (for some good examples see Aoun et al., 2011; Kombarakaran et al., 2008; Theeboom et al., 2014; Wentz et al., 2012). The rise in coaching schools and regulatory bodies such as the International Coaching Federation (www.coachfederation.org) and the Association for Coaching (AC) (www.associationforcoaching.com) is testament to this surge in interest. Across workplaces (including universities), the use of internal and external coaches to motivate employees has proved popular. Coaches motivate and encourage their coachees to be proactive in their pursuit of rewards and goals within their work. They aim to facilitate coachees to overcome challenges in their job, increase their performance and productivity, and adapt to an ever-changing and complex workplace environment. Interestingly, it is the coachee who drives the session, rather than the coach. The coach facilitates the critical and creative thinking (Bell & Kozlowski, 2008). In the early days of workplace coaching, coaches tended to be a boss or line manager and sessions took place face-to-face. However, it is now becoming increasingly common for coaches to be a suitably trained peer or external agent, and for sessions to not only be carried face-to-face but also remotely using the telephone or Internet. Whoever the coach is, their role is to help the coachee set attainable goals, identify obstacles, develop resilience, adapt, and create change for success. When done properly, its advocates state that success should be seen at an individual level as well as an organizational one. A happy and productive workforce is in the interests of the organization as well as the individual.

The role of a coach is different to that of a mentor. A mentor is usually someone with more experience than the mentee in their area of work, whereas the coach typically is not. The role of the mentor is to impart knowledge and advice based on that advanced experience of working in the field. This can be valuable information in the workplace for a colleague who is less experienced and wishes to progress their career or overcome a challenge. In other words, we can think of the mentor as a 'teacher' (Bresser & Wilson, 2016). The coach however, is not a teacher. The coach is a facilitator. Whilst the starting point for the mentor is that the mentor has the answers, the coach's starting point is that it is the coachee who has the answers. The role therefore of the coach is to help their coachee (re)discover their own skills and knowledge (including self-knowledge) to find the answers and progress forwards. This is done through insightful constructive questioning and active listening to the coachee. The coach often has coaching tools at their disposal, such as the 'performance wheel', which coachees can engage with to map out and reflect on those skills, abilities and knowledge they have, and identify gaps. Whilst coaching tends to be a short-term strategy, mentoring is usually longer term. Although different in their approach, both coaching and mentoring can be extremely effective in attaining benefits for the individual and the institution.

From the picture we've painted so far, it seems coaching can create a win-win situation for everyone concerned. And it seems the psychological research supports its success in enhancing the performance, productivity and well-being of those who take part. Employees improve on standard measures such as skill development, attitudes to the workplace, relationships with co-workers, and management of, and reduction in, stress levels through coaching (Fischer & Beimers, 2009; Theebom et al., 2014). However, some psychologists have been more sceptical. Challenges to the practice of coaching include how its effectiveness is measured, what it is that we should be measuring to evaluate its effectiveness (Grant et al., 2010), how to align individual goals with organizational ones, and a general lack of consistency in how coaching is practised and delivered (Jones et al., 2016). Furthermore, as coaching focuses on the employee's ability to become resilient in the face of challenges, it means responsibility falls to the employee rather than the employer. But what if the employer is failing their employees in some way? Poor working conditions, unfair practices, and morally dubious codes of conduct might be the reality of someone's working environment. Overcoming these obstacles is not the employees' responsibility but the organisation's. That said, the research does seem to show an overall benefit from coaching in the workplace to motivate the workforce, especially when it's done by an internal coach.

Fairness and Goals

People are motivated to work when they feel they're being treated fairly in comparison with others. John Stacey Adams's **equity theory** deals with the processes people go through in deciding if their relationship is fair or unfair. Equity theory proposes that people view the world in terms of inputs and outputs. We are concerned with what investments we've made (e.g. time, effort, money) and what we get out as a result (e.g. friendship, pay, affection). Where the input matches the output, people feel satisfied. We also compare our inputs and outputs

equity theory seeks to explain motivation in terms of perceptions of fairness. Where an individual believes he/she is being treated fairly he/she will be more motivated to engage in a task with those of others. If we apply this to the context of the workplace then we can imagine a situation where each employee considers the amount of effort they have put into a task and what they receive as a reward, and compares this with their fellow co-workers to check they're being treated the same. Where no discrepancy exists, tension should not exist either. People feel they are being treated fairly in their work. However, where discrepancy is perceived to exist, say your colleague has received more time off work than you for their efforts, then motivation will diminish, tension will arise and you may well take action to try to sort things out so that they are more fair. We can frame this as a matter of **distributive** and **procedural justice** (Colquitt et al., 2001; Tyler & De Cremer, 2005; Van Dijke et al., 2015). Employees should feel that they are being treated fairly. Rewards should be 'deserved', based on effort and merit (distributive justice). Moreover, the processes that underlie those decisions concerning the allocation of rewards should be transparent and fair (procedural justice).

distributive justice where the distribution of rewards are fair and perceived to be based on merit

procedural justice where the processes by which decisions are made are perceived to be fair

Unsurprisingly, our sense of motivation diminishes if we feel our needs are not being met by our employer. **Relative deprivation theory** (Stouffer et al., 1949; Smith & Pettigrew, 2015) describes the experience of not receiving those rewards which we feel we deserve. Or in other words, what we got is not what we expected. It affects our emotions, our behaviour and our thinking. Cheng et al. (2018) found that civil servants who thought they were overqualified for the job they were doing, spent more time cyber-loafing than those who felt appropriately qualified. Their investment in training was not being recognized and met, and so feeling rather angry, frustrated and undervalued, they wasted time surfing the Internet. Arnold et al. (1998) emphasize how changes in the modern workplace, such as 'downsizing', 'restructuring' and 'cutbacks', may mean employees feel unfairly treated and devalued, especially if their role becomes redefined or the threat of redundancy looms. Consequently motivation levels may plummet, along with performance and well-being.

relative deprivation the experience of not receiving the positive outcomes we feel we have deserved

People of course, are also motivated to achieve 'goals'. Locke and Latham's **goal-setting theory** (2002) considers how our ability to achieve them is shaped by incentives, self-perceptions, desirability and the accessibility of the goal. But we often have many goals to achieve and limited time and resources to do this in. Louro et al. (2007) found that previous success in moving closer to a desired goal motivates people to continue moving towards it even if that goal still seems far away. However, once the goal is within reach, the individual can relax, enjoy their success in getting so far, and divert their attention towards other goals. Pieters and Zeelenberg suggest that this is one strategy that people use to juggle multiple goals when there are time constraints. People are motivated to strive for goals as long as they accept the goal is worthwhile and achievable. If a goal is of no value to you, then you're not likely to be motivated to strive to attain it.

goal-setting theory that motivation is linked to the setting of desirable, challenging and achievable goals

Identity and Motivation

How might our own identity influence our motivation in the workplace? Brown (2001) outlines four types of identity we experience within the workplace: individual (our personal sense of self), group (collective identification with our colleagues within the workplace), organizational (identification with the workplace itself) and cultural (identification with wider society). As we note in Chapters 12 and 13, social identity theory and self-categorization theory are motivational theories of behaviour born in social psychology. They assume people are motivated to maintain positive self-image and self-esteem. They do so by positively comparing the groups to which they belong, with groups to which they do not belong (outgroups). Cornelissen et al. (2007) observe that when people categorize at a personal level they are motivated to do things that promote their personal identity, but when categorized at social level they become motivated to do things that promote group membership and group identity. Hence, part of our motivation to work can be understood to be tied in with our motivation to present a positive personal and/or social/group identity. We are motivated to agree with those we consider our fellow group members. Therefore, identification with the organization as a whole and the groups within it, cognitively shapes our own norms, values and behaviour and those of the workplace itself.

Haslam (2001) revisits equity theory to illustrate the importance of identity in motivation. He suggests that equity theory tends to assume that workers live in a 'cosy world' where boundaries between groups at work are permeable, and everyone believes that upward mobility is possible for anyone. Under these circumstances equity theory is plausible. But what if workers do not feel they are treated fairly for their efforts? What if the boundaries are not permeable within the workplace? What if promotion is impossible? What if we don't identify with the organization as a whole? Under these circumstances an 'us' (workers) and 'them' (management) situation may emerge within the workplace. If workers perceive their working environment to be unfair they may transgress workplace rules to obtain better outcomes (e.g. frequent and prolonged absenteeism, extended tea breaks, pilfering of company stock) and 'get one over' the management.

Doing too much too quickly. Working long hours at a frantic pace is one of the physical causes of stress.

SOURCE: ©Diego Cervo/Shutterstock

Stress and Well-Being in the Workplace

Modern understandings of stress consider the interaction between the individual and the environment. Psychologists have examined heightening stress levels within academia in some countries, as workloads increase and resources become depleted against a backdrop of economic austerity. This can have a negative impact on academics' research, productivity and work outcomes (Jacobs et al., 2007). Stress contributes to absenteeism, physical and mental health problems, accidents, conflict and litigation (Landy & Conte, 2008). In her report 'Pressure Vessels', psychologist Liz Morrish (2019) documents deteriorating mental health across university staff in the UK as a result of increased stress levels. She notes rises of over 50 per cent in referrals to occupational health and counselling services to address mental health problems. In their study of a merger between two US universities – one of high status focused on research, and the other of lower status focused on teaching – Slade et al. (2016) found very high levels of stress amongst the staff of both institutions post-merger. Whilst this exercise may have cut costs for the universities, it had negative implications for their staff, causing high stress levels. If we consider this through a social identity theory and self-categorization theory lens, we can imagine how mergers such as this can have consequences for employees' personal and workplace identities (see Chapter 12 for an explanation of social identity and self-categorization). The merger represented a threat to staff university identity. In short, stress affects the physiological and psychological well-being of people.

The European Foundation for the Improvement of Living and Working Conditions (https://www.eurofound.europa.eu/) distinguishes between two kinds of stress: physical stress (such as long hours, harsh lighting, frantic pace) and psychological stress (such as relationships with colleagues, demands of the role, conflict between home and working life).

Of course occupational stress has its consequences, ranging from heart problems (Byrne & Espnes, 2008; Collins, 2001) to depression (Nieuwenhuijsen et al., 2003; Tennant, 2001), to alcoholism (Smith et al., 2005), substance abuse (Lourel et al., 2008) and even death (Privitera et al., 2014; Stanley et al., 2018), or what the Japanese call 'karoshi', which literally means overworked to death (Kanai, 2009)! However, we need to exercise some caution here. We don't all find the same things stressful. Also, what causes us stress in one situation may not cause us stress in another. And sometimes, a little stress might be considered 'good stress' as it can motivate us (Ongori & Agolla, 2008; Stevenson & Harper, 2006).

If we return to social identity theory, Haslam (2004) considers how our working identity (a collective feeling of 'we-ness' with our colleagues) and our routine working practices can define what we consider to be stressful. Let's consider an example from Haslam et al. (2005). What would you find more stressful: working in a bar or disposing of bombs? The answer lies in what you consider to be a 'normal' part of your job. In their sample of bar workers and bomb disposal experts, they found that membership of these occupational groups led to different expectations of stress. While the bomb disposal experts reported that they would consider working behind a noisy bar more stressful than disposing of bombs, the bar workers thought bomb-disposal was much more stressful than serving drinks to customers behind a bar. Similarly the discovery of a live bomb was not regarded as stressful to the bomb disposal expert but was very stressful for the bar worker. Haslam and his team make a further suggestion regarding whether we feel stressed or not at work. They propose that the more we identify with the occupational group to which we belong (such as bomb-disposal expert), the less stress we feel. It's who 'we' are and it's what 'we' do. Any feelings of stress are reduced by the support we expect from our colleagues – our fellow ingroup members. This study is a good example of how our membership into a particular group offers us norms of what to expect from the job and our colleagues, which then influences how we perceive potential stressors. What is deviant from what we expect may be stressful.

Workplace Bullying

One particular form of aggression in the workplace is bullying. We examine bullying behaviour in Chapter 8. Workplace bullying is thought to be widespread. Hauge et al. (2010) discovered from their study of employees in Norway, that workplace bullying is a significant predictor of anxiety, depression and employment dissatisfaction. Similar findings are apparent in Finchilescu et al.'s (2019) research into the bullying of nurses in Zimbabwe. They found that bullying became rife when hospital resources were low and staff were over-stretched in terms of workload. These working environments were characterized with nurses perceiving themselves to be powerless against an authoritarian management style. Unable to control these poor working conditions led to feelings of anger and frustration. Unable to direct these feelings at management, nurses projected their feelings onto their fellow nurses. Again, perhaps unsurprisingly, nurses being bullied showed poor job satisfaction and expressed the desire to leave.

However, as we note in Chapter 8, how we define bullying has implications for its recognition (Parzefall & Salin 2010). Many official reports of workplace bullying only recognize it if it has occurred for six months or more. If we take into account bullying that has occurred for less than six months, then we might expect workplace bullying to be even more prevalent than reports suggest.

In some cases the intervention of a third party to alleviate the problem works. However, this usually occurs only if victim and bully can be separated within the workplace. Sadly, however, often the intervention of a third party can cause the problem to escalate, if this separation can't be obtained. Some theorists suggest that sometimes the only effective way to deal with bullying is to leave the organization altogether. Finchilescu et al. (2019) found the provision of social and emotional support for victims of bullying can improve mental health but doesn't really impact positively on job satisfaction or desire to leave.

Recently, European research into workplace bullying has centred on the role of leadership in either perpetrating the behaviour or allowing it to continue. This makes sense when we consider that most instances of workplace bullying are perpetrated by a boss (or manager, supervisor) over her or his workers (Neilsen et al., 2005). Autocratic and laissez-faire styles of leadership seem to be particular culprits. Whilst the autocratic leader in the workplace intimidates, criticizes and closes down complaints about their inappropriate behaviour (Warszewska-Makuch et al., 2015), the laissez-faire leader is indifferent, ineffective, and allows bullying to go unchallenged (Dussault & Frenette, 2015). However, a workplace boss who is seemingly transparent, authentic, supportive, emotionally stable and self-confident can effectively negate bullying by building an organization based on mutual trust (Warszewska-Makuch et al., 2015).

Whistleblowing

A whistleblower is typically defined as someone who is an 'insider' in possession of private knowledge, observes inappropriate/illegal/unethical or otherwise immoral acts, and exposes them publicly to an external agency who can intervene, and/or the general public if deemed to be in the public's best interests. Or in other words, to whistleblow is to expose the standards, norms and values a group 'should' be upholding and the violation of them.

Perhaps two of the most notable whistleblowers in recent times is the founder of WikiLeaks Julian Assange and US activist and soldier Chelsea Manning. Assange published material 'leaked' to him by Manning regarding atrocities allegedly carried out by the US military during the Iraq (2003–2011) and Afghanistan (2001–present day) wars. These documents became known as the Iraq War Logs and the Afghan War Logs respectively. In her role with the military, Manning had access to classified information, which she smuggled to Assange in 2010. Manning was convicted on the grounds of espionage and fraud in 2010. Assange has also been convicted and is currently detained in a UK prison. Whether they were right to blow the whistle is a hotly debated topic.

Chelsea Manning, a notable whistleblower on the US military.

SOURCE: ©Jstone/Shutterstock

Clearly whistleblowing carries some risks for the individual and the organization. Blow the whistle in the workplace and you may lose your job, your reputation, your friends, and even your freedom. To try and mitigate some of this, in 2019 the EU passed legislation that permits anonymous whistleblowing, meaning the individual does not have to report breaches and/or violations of working practices internally. They can report directly to an external agency without their employer's knowledge. Furthermore, EU law protects whistleblowers from being demoted, dismissed or retaliated against by the organization they are reporting on (Kayali, 2019).

But why would someone want to blow the whistle on the organization they work for? Anvari et al. (2019) offer a social identity explanation. Imagine for a moment that you see wrongdoing by your team within the company you work for. Perhaps you observe some illegal trading, workplace bullying, or the illicit receiving of goods. What do you do? Anvari et al. suggest some options. You could say nothing and be complicit in the wrongdoing. You could leave the organization. You could try to challenge the behaviour through company processes such as at a staff meeting, try reasoning with those causing the problem, or lodge a complaint through internal reporting procedures. Or you can blow the whistle and expose the wrongdoing to an external body. Which will you choose? Your first decision is whether you're going to take action or not. From a social identity perspective, it is suggested that this decision will be based on how strongly you identify with the group committing the wrongdoing, which might be a team within the organization, or the organization itself. Having a strong sense of psychological belonging and attachment to this group, sharing its values and norms, means that you will feel responsible – and possibly ashamed – when those values and norms are breached by your fellow ingroup members. Hence, you are motivated to put things right. Whistleblowing could harm the group to which you belong and feel a sense of loyalty towards. The motivation, therefore, is to address this within the group itself. There is also another level of identification – that of a superordinate group. This is not the group that committed the wrongdoing but another broader and relevant group with whom you may strongly identify yourself as a member. This could be the organization, the profession (e.g. psychologists) or even a professional body that upholds standards and codes of conduct for your profession (e.g. the British Psychological Society). If the norms and values of a superordinate group which you strongly identify with have been transgressed as a consequence of the wrongdoing, you will be motivated to act.

Okay, motivated to act, but what do you do? This, claims Anvari et al. (2019) depends on your perception of power. If you believe you have sufficient power, processes and support to challenge wrongdoings and norm violations within the group – what Anvari et al. call 'intragroup power' – then you are likely to attempt to rectify the problems through internal mechanisms. If, however, you feel you do not have the power needed to deal with the matter internally, but believe that an external body (such as another organization or the public) does – called 'vicarious intergroup power' – then you might whistleblow. You still have to weigh up the risks of doing so though (such as possibly losing your job, social ostracism, etc.). The decision to stay silent is typically based on weak identification with the immediate ingroup and the superordinate group, or strong identification with the ingroup and/or superordinate group but a feeling of powerlessness. Neither internal nor external strategies to address the problem are perceived to be of benefit. The exit strategy is often taken by those who do not strongly identify with the group (or individual) committing the wrongdoing, but do strongly identify with the superordinate group (e.g. the profession). Again, weighing up the costs of leaving a job (such as can I afford to?) come into play here when making these decisions.

Leaders and Leadership

In our chapters on conformity and obedience (Chapter 7), persuasion (Chapter 6), small group processes (Chapter 10), and social categorization and identity (Chapter 12) we consider the role of leaders. Leadership is the process of influence that facilitates followers to reach goals. However, defining leadership and understanding its relationship to the behaviour of followers is a tricky business. This issue has been of central importance in the workplace for fairly obvious reasons. Most workplaces are characterized by some kind of hierarchical structure such that one person, or a body of people are the leaders. There may be one overall leader, or several leaders with different levels of authority. However, what they all have in common is the exercise of power over their subordinates.

'It is better to lead from behind and to put others in front, especially when you celebrate victory when nice things occur. You take the front line when there is danger. Then people will appreciate your leadership.'
Nelson Mandela

We've already seen in this chapter the negative impact leaders can have on the mental well-being of workers. Theories of leadership began with trying to identify the traits of leaders. Known as the **trait approach**, this theory aims to predict leaders on the basis of physical characteristics such as intelligence, height, extroversion, dominance, and so on. Although intriguing work searching for how various traits influence the attainment of leadership roles continues, it was clear that the trait approach could only bring the field so far. One contemporary example of a trait approach to leadership is the work of Danish psychologists Lasse Laustsen and Michael Peterson. Their investigations on our perception of physical facial features and our assumptions about what kind of leader they will be offers support to the principles upon which **evolutionary psychology** is based (see Chapters 1 and 14 for more on evolutionary psychology). They highlight that during times of international and/or civil struggle and conflict, people have a preference for political leaders with dominant masculine facial features, such as a pronounced jawline, bushy eyebrows, small eyes, and a square face, as well as low-pitched voice (Laustsen et al., 2015). Such physical and audible features are considered reliable cues as to what traits that person possesses – that is, a dominant face and a low voice represents high levels of testosterone, resulting in a strong, dominant and forceful character, capable of dealing with threats to the nation with aggression if necessary (Laustsen & Petersen, 2015, 2017; Zilioli et al., 2015). However, there is a cost to having such a leader – they might exploit their own nation for their own ends. Consequently during times of peace, people prefer leaders with a less dominant face and a higher pitched voice; one that conveys kindness, cooperation and harmony. The key point here is that contemporary trait theories of leaders and leadership emphasize the social context in which effective leaders are chosen. What traits we want from our leaders depends on the social and political context in which we find ourselves.

trait approach this approach to leadership regards certain physical characteristics, such as height and intelligence, as predictors of leadership

evolutionary psychology a field of study that looks at the role of evolutionary processes and principles of natural selection in shaping cognition and behaviour

Alternative approaches to leadership have considered the relationship between the leader and those they lead. Fiedler's (1967) **contingency approach** proposed that 'who' is the leader, and what kind of leader they will be, is contingent upon the situation.

contingency approach this claims that the style of leadership adopted should be contingent upon the environmental circumstances

Fiedler argued that the style of leadership adopted will depend on how much control the leader has in the environment. Where they have little control or their power is ambiguous, they may well adopt a more authoritative style of leadership. Similarly a leader may adapt their style to suit the requirements of their staff. If an employee is suffering a crisis in confidence a more supportive leadership style may be taken to try to address the problem.

A potential problem with these theories is that they risk over-simplifying leadership to a process of matching the leadership style to the situation. Perhaps something more complex is going on. Vroom and Jago (2007) warn that: 'Viewing leadership in purely dispositional or purely situational terms is to miss a major portion of the phenomenon . . . leadership is a process of motivating others to work together collaboratively to accomplish things' (p. 23).

These kinds of contingency approaches do beg the question 'who is following who?' Without willing followers, there isn't a successful leader. And if the leader is constantly changing the style of leadership to fit the worker, then it may make you wonder who's in charge?

Who Is Following Who?

transactional leadership emphasizes the quality of the interaction between leader and follower in achieving a successful relationship

Transactional leadership describes the role of the leader in transforming the behaviour of a worker so that they can then achieve a mutually desired goal. The focus is not on the qualities of the leader, but on the quality of the relations that exist between leader and follower. The measure of success for such a relationship is whether it produces benefits for both the leader and the follower.

Researchers into leadership have considered the role of *charisma* on leadership. Some of this work has emphasized the charisma factor of world leaders such as Martin Luther King, Silvio Berlusconi, Nelson Mandela, Winston Churchill and, arguably, Donald Trump (see Chapter 10). Charismatic leaders seem to share some personal characteristics such as self-confidence and common appeal, which makes them attractive to their audience (see some of the main features of persuasion outlined in Chapter 6).

It is not just their audience for whom they are attractive. Balmas and Sheafer (2013) argue that Western media has become increasingly focused on charismatic leaders. Consequently news coverage sometimes gives more exposure to a charismatic foreign leader than a less charismatic national one. Furthermore, charismatic leaders are also able to enhance the self-esteem and self-image of their followers to redefine their objectives (e.g. House & Shamir, 1993; Sheafer, 2001, 2008). That said, there is of course a rather dark side to charisma. Charisma and an autocratic style can pave the way for bullying, indoctrination, extremism and terrorism (e.g. Beevor, 2016; Hofmann & Dawson, 2014; Ingram, 2016; Samnani & Singh, 2013).

Rather than seeing charisma as an attribute of leaders, it has been suggested that it is an attribution (Joose, 2014). In a social constructionist account of leadership, Hansbrough (2012) argues that these leaders do not actually possess charismatic traits. Rather, their followers read charisma into their behaviour by virtue of their role as leaders.

Female Leaders

Let's return to our list of examples of charismatic leaders: Martin Luther King, Silvio Berlusconi, Nelson Mandela, Winston Churchill, Donald Trump. As well as being (arguably!) charismatic, they are also men. So where are the women leaders? You'd be forgiven if the name of a female leader doesn't come to mind as easily because they're simply not well-represented at this level or indeed any level. Eagly and Carli (2007) observe that of the 50 largest corporations within the European Union, women constitute just 11 per cent of top executives and 4 per cent are CEOs or heads of a board. Cooper (2016) cites survey data of the largest 350 corporations in Europe, of which women CEOs are found in just 18 of them. And it is not just women who are under-represented at leadership level. Eagly and Chin (2010) note that minority ethnic, racial and sexual identity groups are still struggling to get into these positions (see Focus On: Diversity and Leadership).

In the past, researchers including psychologists have pointed at the 'glass ceiling' which seems to preclude women from reaching the highest levels within an organization. More recently, Eagly and Carli (2007) suggest replacing the notion of a glass ceiling with a 'leadership labyrinth' that women must navigate in order to make it to top executive level. If it was a glass ceiling, no woman would ever make it to the top – yet a handful do. The labyrinth depicts a challenging journey that includes effective career networking and strategizing (also referred to as building *social capital*) whilst managing family commitments, and stereotypical assumptions about female traits and leadership. The traditional caring friendly female traits do not sit too well with the assertive and aggressive masculine traits that are assumed to depict effective leadership (McDonagh & Paris, 2012). Consequently women who lead in a traditionally male way can find themselves disliked by both men and women (Phelan et al., 2012).

The concept of the 'glass cliff' coined by Ryan and Haslam (2005) describes women who do make it to leadership levels, but are appointed when the organisation over which they preside is in trouble. Strife within the workplace, and economic constraints and downturns can be the reality for many women leaders. In other words, women leaders can be set up to fail. Consequently they are blamed for negative events, which were often set in motion before their leadership appointment. In their review of research into the glass cliff a decade later, Ryan, Haslam and their colleagues conclude that the phenomena remains as true now as it did then. They suggest that instead of focusing on why women are put into precarious leadership positions, we should now shift to examining why and how men are put into advantageous leadership positions – or as the authors term this, being facilitated to sit on the 'glass cushion' (Ryan et al., 2016).

In efforts to overcome the clash in perceptions of favourable feminine traits and desirable leadership qualities, a female leadership style seems to have emerged. Eagly and Carli (2007) look to examples of successful female leaders who adopt a mix of a **transactional** and **transformational leadership** style. What they found was that the emphasis is on collaboration, support and rewarding effort, which in the long run, argue researchers, is actually a more effective leadership style. In fact social psychological research suggests that women can be put off aspiring to the executive levels of their organization by the presence of an elite female leader who appears unapproachable (Hoyt & Simon, 2011). Rather than inspiring their female followers, they can intimidate them and have a negative impact on their self-perceptions. To inspire and motivate, as well as successfully

transactional leadership emphasizes the quality of the interaction between leader and follower in achieving a successful relationship

transformational leadership leadership that, enabled by a leader's vision and inspiration, exerts significant influence lead an organization, the leader, regardless of sex, needs to empower, reward and identify with their workers. Furthermore, changes are needed in organizational activities and expectations, such as a rethinking of recruitment strategies, networking, performance evaluation, hours spent at the office, and achieving female critical mass at top levels to avoid tokenistic gestures. Or in other words, a disruption to the organization which challenges traditional gender and workplace norms and stereotypes.

Focus on

Diversity and Leadership

Social psychology has contributed a wealth of knowledge on leadership. We've outlined some of this work in Chapters 10 and 12, as well as in this current chapter. Furthermore, the discipline has researched women's leadership in considerable detail (Eagly & Chin, 2010). That work has examined the challenges women face in getting into leadership roles, and how to behave once they're there. But what about access to leadership for people from other racial, ethnic and sexual minority groups? This, state Eagly and Chin, has received much less attention. Why? Well some of the answers to that question involve pointing an accusatory finger at social psychology.

In their report, Eagly and Chin (2010) review some of the work that has been carried out on diversity identity and leadership. That research describes some of the pressure felt by leaders from diverse groups to behave like the stereotypical white male leader – such as being authoritative and domineering. But of course people from other groups bring their own cultural style. Moreover, they have often overcome some incredibly difficult challenges and experiences to get to that position, which can mean they are extremely competent and adept problem-solvers. So yes, they may differ quite remarkably from 'a white man' leader stereotype, but surely, argue Eagly and Chin, that is precisely what can make them very good leaders. They know what exclusion feels like. Consequently they can be very creative, flexible, inclusive and open to change. Those are qualities that are very much needed in a world where different identity groups are increasingly interconnected, and the issues we face are complex and require alternative problem-solving approaches.

So why might we point the finger at social psychology? The lack of research done on diversity and leadership is clearly one area that needs addressing. Take another look at the leadership theories. Do you spot a North American bias? That is what Eagly and Chin think. This is perhaps not surprising when we consider the historical North American influence upon social psychology (see Chapter 1). Eagly and Chin argue that the values upheld by those theories are characteristic of North America, dominated by the politics of capitalism. They urge leadership scholars to think about how leadership theories can examine and address diversity, and acknowledge then challenge stereotypical assumptions about 'who' and 'what' makes a good leader. This process has started in social psychology, but much more needs to be done.

Questions

1 Do you agree that leadership theories are culturally and politically biased? What examples can you think of to evidence your answer?

2 Why might leaders from ethnic, racial, and sexual minority groups be beneficial in the workplace?

3 What are the main characteristics you would want to see in your line manager at work?

Leadership and Ingroup Prototypicality

Social identity theory and self-categorization theory approaches to leadership have argued that it's very difficult to consider leaders and leadership without an analysis of the group they represent. If a group is to perform effectively, it must work as a collective unit and the leader must be recognized as representative of it. The proposal here is that leaders are *prototypical ingroup* members (see Chapter 12). They define and are defined by the group they represent. This means they must not only change as the group's objectives and identity change, but must also be accepted by all as the legitimate leader. De Cremer et al. (2008) report that a leader who is recognized as truly representative of the group is also perceived as fair, which in turn motivates their followers to cooperate with him or her. So the ability to lead is not a property of the individual but the property to legitimately represent the group. Working together as a group seems to be a recipe for success. That said, some word of caution seems wise here. Where there is some doubt over the group's aims or goals, which in turn casts doubt over the leader, research suggests that followers may prefer a less prototypical leader who nevertheless provides direction (Rast et al., 2012).

Ursula Von der Leyen, president of the European Commission. She is the first woman to hold this post.
SOURCE: ©Alexandros Michailidis/Shutterstock

Charismatic leadership. The former leader of the African National Congress, ex-president of South Africa and anti-apartheid activist, Nelson Mandela.
SOURCE: © Alessia Pierdomenico/Shutterstock

Teamwork and Group Decisions

Something we have noted so far in the social psychology of an organization is the importance of making workers feel part of the decision-making processes and organizational identity. This facilitates motivation and feelings of well-being, and allows for greater worker satisfaction and productivity.

However, there are some words of warning from social psychology that concern the effectiveness of group decisions and teamwork. In Chapter 10 we consider the phenomena of **risky shift**, **groupthink**, **group polarization** and **social loafing** which occur in groups, such as those in the workplace or organization. Stoner's (1961) concept of risky shift reports the tendency of small groups to make riskier decisions than the individuals would have done on their own. Janis's (1972) concept of groupthink proposes that decisions made in groups tend to be bad ones. Moscovici and Zavalloni's (1969) concept of group polarization suggests that when in groups, individuals become more extreme in their attitudes. Latané et al.'s (1979) principle of social loafing observes that when in groups, as individual effort becomes less identifiable, there is a tendency for individuals to social loaf and put in less effort than they would do if given the task to perform by themselves.

risky shift describes the phenomena that occurs when a group makes a riskier decision than the individuals would

groupthink 'The mode of thinking that persons engage in when concurrence-seeking becomes so dominant in a cohesive in-groupthat it tends to override realistic appraisal of alternative courses of action' (Irving Janis, 1971)

These concepts seem to more than hint that individuals think and behave irrationally when in a group situation. Something odd happens to their thinking such that bad decisions are made in groups. But perhaps these phenomena are the rational response to processes of group identification (Haslam, 2004)? As individuals form a group for a common purpose, they develop a group identity. As such they form group norms that characterize the meaning of the group and its group polarization group-produced enhancement of members' pre-existing tendencies. When a rather homogenous group discusses a topic, the opinion of the group members often merges into a more extreme one, strengthening the members' average tendency

social loafing the tendency for people to exert less effort when they pool their efforts towards a common goal than when they are individually accountable

members. The tendency to make risky and extreme decisions is understood to be a reflection of ingroup distinctiveness and identification.

Haslam outlines Vroom and Yetton's (1973) proposed model to guide managers when involving others in work decisions. They suggest a leader must decide if:

1 they need a high quality decision
2 they could make the decision on their own
3 they need the acceptance of subordinates
4 the problem is a structured one
5 workers only accept the decision if they're involved
6 workers share the same goals as the leader and the organization
7 workers are likely to disagree with the solution.

As Haslam points out, group participation in decision-making has become increasingly fashionable in recent years in the workplace. In the likely event that a group decision is thought to be needed, then some measures should be in place to avoid extreme, risky or just plain daft decisions being made.

The application of social psychology has been extremely useful in organizational psychology to understand everyday working life. The concepts of social psychology have been used to offer insights into the role of motivation, leadership, stress and teamwork in accomplishing a happy and efficient workforce.

Social Psychology, Health and Illness

'The mind has great influence over the body, and maladies often have their origin there.'

Jean Baptiste Molière, 1622–1673

Among the many thriving areas of applied social psychology is one that relates social psychology's concepts to problems such as loneliness, anxiety, depression, mood swings and physical illness, as well as to happiness, excitement and well-being. This bridge-building research between social psychology, health and illness seeks answers to five main questions important for **clinical psychology** and **health psychology**.

clinical psychology the study, assessment, and treatment of people with psychological difficulties

health psychology the study of the psychological and behavioural roots of health and illness, giving behavioural medicine input on prevention and treatment of illness

1 How do the ways in which we think about self and others fuel problems such as depression, loneliness, anxiety and ill health as well as optimism, energy and good health?
2 As laypeople or as psychologists, how can we improve our judgements and predictions about others?
3 How might people reverse maladaptive thought patterns and promote positive ones?
4 Is it possible to 'nudge' people's behaviour towards adopting healthy lifestyles?
5 What part do close, supportive relationships play in health and happiness?

What Social and Cognitive Processes Accompany Psychological Problems?

One of psychology's most intriguing research frontiers concerns the social and cognitive processes that accompany psychological disorders. What are the memories, attributions and expectations of depressed, lonely, shy or illness-prone people, and how are they shaped by experience and relationships in the social world?

Distortion or Realism?

Are all sad and depressed people unrealistically negative? The **negativity hypothesis** suggests they are. Those who feel depressed tend to be overly self-critical and pessimistic (Dunn et al., 2007). However, there is another view, which is that those who are depressed are expressing **depressive realism** (Crocker et al., 1988) – also known as the 'sadder-but-wiser effect'. To find out which view is more accurate, Szu-Ting Fu et al. (2012) compared people clinically diagnosed with major depression, those suffering chronic fatigue syndrome, and 'healthy' (non-depressed) controls. The researchers adopted trait-items from a previous study which comprised of 36 adjectives reflecting a depressed and/or anxious state of mind (e.g. gloomy) and another 36 adjectives which were not associated with depression or anxiety (e.g. optimistic). The participants were shown 18 of the adjectives related to depression and/or anxiety and 18 of the adjectives not related to depression or anxiety. A total of 36 of the 72 adjectives were shown to the participant. Presented with the adjectives one at a time, participants were asked to answer Yes or No as to whether they applied to their self, the world or their future. Participants were then shown all 72 adjectives and asked to indicate which ones they had seen before, and rate their confidence in their answer. The results proved intriguing. The healthy and the chronic-fatigue syndrome participants were equally accurate in the recognition task. However, the major depressed participants were significantly less accurate. Hence there was little support for the 'depressive realism' hypothesis. However, where the groups differed was in the confidence of their answer. Whereas both healthy and chronic-fatigue syndrome participants were neither over- nor under-confident, the clinically major depressed participants expressed low confidence. This, argues the researchers, suggests support for the 'negativity hypothesis'. Whether recognition of trait items is a good indicator of depressive realism and the negativity hypothesis is of course, a matter of critical discussion.

negativity hypothesis depressed people are overly critical and pessimistic in their views of self, the world, and others

depressive realism the tendency of mildly depressed people to make accurate rather than self-serving judgements, attributions and predictions

Moore and Fresco (2012) conducted a review of all psychological publications conducted on depressive realism, and concluded that on the whole it seems that this hypothesis is the most supported by research. However, they also advise caution. Their review of published work revealed a range of methods and measures to define and evaluate depressive realism. This means that there is a lack of consensus over what depressive realism is and how to measure it.

Underlying the thinking of depressed people are their attributions of responsibility. In Chapter 4 we explore how people's attributional style reflects their view of life. In some classic work, Abramson et al. (1978) noted that depressed people tend to exhibit a negative **explanatory style**. As shown in **Figure 15.2**, this explanatory style attributes failure and setbacks to causes that are *stable* ('It's going to last for ever'), *global* ('It's going to affect everything I do') and *internal* ('It's all my fault').

explanatory style one's habitual way of explaining life events. A negative, pessimistic, depressive explanatory style attributes failure to stable, global and internal causes

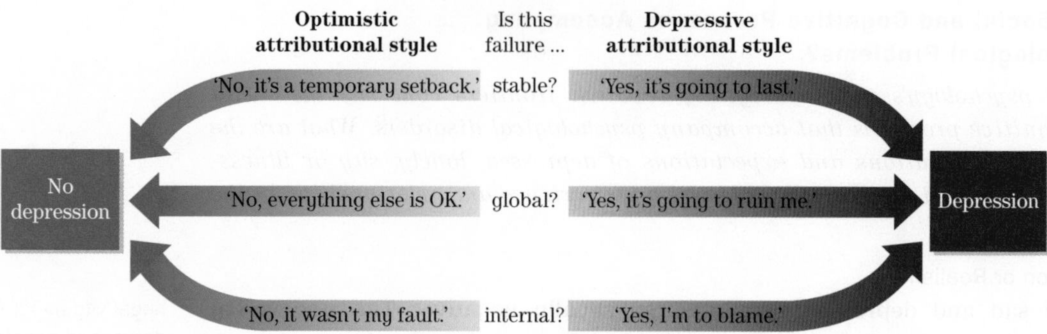

FIGURE 15.2 Depressive explanatory style
Depression is linked with a negative, pessimistic way of explaining and interpreting failures.

The result of this pessimistic, over-generalized, self-blaming thinking, say Abramson et al. (1978), is a sense of hopelessness.

Sadness can also be linked to how we view our 'self'. Higgins's (1989) self-discrepancy theory notes that differences between our 'actual self' (who we are) 'ideal self' (who we'd like to be) and our 'ought self' (who we should be) can lead to feelings of anxiety, disappointment and hopelessness (as we see in Chapter 3). These discrepancies have been widely studied in relation to eating disorders. Sawdon et al. (2007) have argued that it is a discrepancy between the actual self and our future and potential self that is related to eating disorders and depression. In their study of male body builders, Devrim et al. (2018) report a relationship between eating disorders and muscle dysmorphia (the belief that your body is too thin and/or without enough muscle). This study shows how feeling disturbed and dissatisfied with the perception of one's body and sense of self (actual self) may not only make bodybuilders head to the gym, but this striving towards an ideal potential self also negatively impacts upon their quality of life. In some cases this can lead to eating disorders, depression, over-exercising, drug abuse, and even suicide (e.g. Angelakis et al., 2016).

Unhappy Moods Cause Negative Thinking

As we see in Chapter 4, our moods colour our thinking. When we *feel* happy, we *think* happy. We see and recall a good world. But let our mood turn gloomy, and our thoughts switch to a different track. Off come the rose-tinted glasses; on go the dark glasses. Our relationships seem to sour, our self-images tarnish, our hopes for the future dim, people's behaviour seems more sinister.

'To the man who is enthusiastic and optimistic, if what is to come should be pleasant, it seems both likely to come about and likely to be good, while to the indifferent or depressed man it seems the opposite.'
Aristotle, *The Art of Rhetoric*

Sadness may also be contagious and trigger reciprocal sadness in others. Emotional contagion theory (Hatfield et al., 1994) describes how witnessing the emotional expressions of others may lead to emotional mimicry of not only the expression but also the emotion itself. This effect has been well documented in face-to-face encounters. For example, college students who have roommates who are down in the dumps tend to become a little downcast themselves (Burchill & Stiles, 1988; Joiner, 1994; Sanislow et al., 1989). In dating couples, too, sadness and happiness are often contagious (Katz et al., 1999). More recently attention has turned to emotional contagion across online social networks. This research reveals that emotions are contagious across networks such as Twitter and Facebook (Rosenquist et al., 2011). Positive and negative posts by your friends influence your mood (Chmeil et al., 2011; Coviello et al., 2014). In a very large study of over 689,000 Facebook users, Kramer et al. (2014) discovered that our positive and negative status updates influence our friends' subsequent posts. This is a landmark study which offers some very compelling evidence that emotions are contagious in the absence of face-to-face contact and non-verbal cues. That said, it is also a controversial one as the participants were unaware of their participation. Randomly selected, their status updates were manipulated for their friends' viewing. The question of ethics is something we come across time and again in social psychology (see Chapter 2 for more on this). Do the ends justify the means? What this study tells us is that just being exposed to an emotion is sufficient for contagion. In evolutionary terms this is perhaps unsurprising. Expressing our emotions is a way of affirming social bonds and seeking out help and support (Coviello et al., 2014). Bearing in mind the global reach of social networks, our moods have more outward impact than ever before.

We can see, then, that being unhappy, down and depressed has cognitive and behavioural effects not just on ourselves, but others too. Does it also work the other way around: do sadness and depression have cognitive *origins?*

Negative Thinking Encourages Low Mood

To be sad and down is natural when experiencing severe stress – losing a job, getting divorced or rejected, or suffering any experience that disrupts our sense of who we are and why we are worthy human beings (Amato & Kane, 2011; Daly & Delaney, 2013). The brooding that comes with this short-term sadness can be adaptive. Insights gained during times of inactivity may later result in better strategies for interacting with the world.

Why are some people so affected by *minor* stresses? Evidence suggests that when stress-induced rumination is filtered through a negative explanatory style, the frequent outcome is sadness and depression (Hankin et al., 2007; Nolen-Hoeksema, 2000). Sanjuan and Magallares (2008) found that the link between negative explanatory style and depression is found in people who attribute uncontrollable causes for bad events. It is our perceived inability to prevent the bad things from happening that feeds the depression.

Despite a wealth of studies that confirm the link between attributional style and sadness or depression in the experimental laboratory, we can reasonably ask how well they stand up to scrutiny in the real world. Studies of attributional style have typically been measured using questionnaires in response to a hypothetical case-study. In an attempt to offer a more realistic study of attributional style and depression, Habermas et al. (2007) examined the life narratives of depressed patients with non-depressed controls in Germany. Participants were interviewed for an hour and asked about their life story and memories. The researchers found that the depressed patients tended to deviate from a linear telling of their life and instead focused on the past. In contrast the non-depressed life narratives were more based in the present and future. Furthermore, the depressed tended to use a negative explanatory style as they accounted for events within their lives.

The non-depressed were much more self-enhancing in their evaluations of their life events.

Seligman (1991, 1998, 2002) believes that self-focus and self-blame help explain the high prevalence of depression in the Western world today. He believes that the decline of religion and family, plus the growth of individualism, breeds hopelessness and self-blame when things don't go well. Failed courses, careers and relationships produce despair when we stand alone, with nothing and no one to fall back on. Whether we seek professional help can be as much a matter of culture as well as a personal decision and finances. Andersson and her team (2013) looked at rates of depression among people aged 18–40 years in South Africa. Over 31 per cent of their sample of 977 people suffered from depression, yet the majority did not seek any help – especially those aged 18–29 years and those with a low income. Andersson and her team found that as well as practical barriers to getting help, such as financial cost and accessing the care, there were also cultural and social barriers including social stigma, misperceptions and misbeliefs about depression, and a failure to recognize it (what Andersson et al., term 'health literacy'). Hence we need to also consider how cultural norms influence definition, cause and understanding of psychological states. We shall return to this later in the chapter.

These insights into the thinking style and social conditions linked with depression have prompted social psychologists to study thinking patterns associated with other problems. How do those who are plagued with excessive loneliness, shyness or substance abuse view themselves? How well do they recall their successes and their failures? To what do they attribute their ups and downs? Where is their attention focused – on themselves or on others?

Loneliness

Loneliness, whether chronic or temporary, is a painful awareness that our social relationships are less numerous or meaningful than we desire. Our social network does not function. Do you remember how you felt when you first started at university? Did you feel lonely at any time? Cruwys et al. (2018) found that young people who were just starting university, tended to see their GP on a frequent basis for moral support. Hashim and Khodarahimi (2012) considered the loneliness felt by first-year university students in Malaysia. Four weeks into their first year and the students felt a little lonely. Friendships were still being developed. At 14 weeks into their first year, the students reported feeling even more lonely. Why? Well, the researchers suggest that when students begin university they tend to focus on the number of friendships, making friends with whoever they come into contact with – a room-mate or a class-mate, for example. But as we integrate ourselves more into university life, that number decreases as we become increasingly discerning about our friendships. Now the focus is on quality rather than quantity of those friendships. But there is a cost to this, which is loneliness whilst we sort through our friendships to develop sustainable ones that will see us through our university years and possibly beyond.

Happily most of us overcome feelings of loneliness during our time at university, as we make friends. But there are more serious aspects to loneliness. As we get older our networks tend to decrease. We give more credence to a few meaningful relationships over lots of peripheral connections. Inevitably though, as we age, we can lose those close to us either as a result of their mortality, ill-health, or simply by not being able to access those friendships any more. And social isolation is closely related to poor mental and physical health (e.g. Cacioppo et al., 2010; Chen & Feeley, 2014; Segrin & Domschke, 2011). In their longitudinal study of 6,105 Irish people aged 50 years and over Santini and colleagues (2016) found that poor quantity and quality of social networks led to feelings of social isolation and loneliness, which in turn led to depression for men and women. Kearns et al. (2015) studied rates of loneliness in deprived communities based in Glasgow. Deprived communities can suffer especially high levels of social isolation due to lack of money, fear of crime, and neighbours with whom they do not wish to associate. Kearns' study found that those people who reported the strongest feelings of loneliness had infrequent contact with their families, neighbours, and little or no emotional support. Moreover, those with depression also suffered from more mental health problems including anxiety and depression. Loneliness can also increase our risk for high blood pressure and heart disease (Hawkley et al., 2006). So our friends really are good for us. Feelings of loneliness can be adaptive. The path of loneliness signals people to seek social connections, which facilitate survival (Cacioppo et al., 2014).

Feeling lonely can lead to mental health problems, including depression

SOURCE: ©Ingram Publishing

Perceiving Others Negatively

Chronically lonely people seem caught in a vicious circle of self-defeating social cognitions and social behaviours. They perceive their interactions as making a poor impression, blame themselves for their poor social relationships and see most things as beyond their control. Moreover, they perceive others in negative ways (e.g. Gilbert & Irons, 2010; Nasser et al., 2011).

Being slow to self-disclose (see Chapter 9), lonely people disdain those who disclose too much too soon (Kahn & Garrison, 2009). This dislike of self-disclosure has not only been seen in face-to-face communications but also in computer-mediated-communication. The more lonely the person, the less they seem to want to disclose, but what they do share is often dishonest and negative (Leung, 2002).

Anxiety and Shyness

Shyness is a form of social anxiety characterized by self-consciousness and worry about what others think (Schmidt & Buss, 2010). It can make us feel socially awkward, uncomfortable and unhappy. Some sceptics have argued that shyness is a normal behaviour, but in recent times it has been recognized as a mental disorder (Scott, 2006). This has fuelled the commercial activities of medicine and mental health agencies (Lane, 2007). One look at the 'cures' offered for shyness reveals a bewildering array of self-help books, therapy and medication, to alleviate our shyness. The sceptics might be forgiven for their scepticism. On the contrary, others have argued that the reason shyness is relevant to the mental health industry is because we now understand it better than we did (Crozier & Alden, 2003). We also know that some people feel shy and anxious in almost any situation in which they may feel they are being evaluated, such as having a casual lunch with a co-worker. For these people, shyness and anxiety is more a trait

When a person is eager to impress important people, social anxiety is natural.

SOURCE: ©fizkes/Shutterstock

than a temporary state. It can contribute to what psychologists and clinicians call social anxiety disorder (SAD). This is not to be confused with Seasonal Affective Disorder, which is also known as SAD.

Modern research has increasingly examined the relationship between shyness, social anxiety, and the use of computer-mediated communication. Responding to someone using text rather than phoning avoids a social situation a shy person might feel awkward in (Reid & Reid, 2007). Likewise, virtual friends on Facebook might be easier to communicate with than the offline ones we see face-to-face (Bardi & Brady, 2010; Chiou et al., 2014). And the people using instant messaging services and Facebook the most frequently, are often the shyest (Orr et al., 2009). Whilst this activity might give the shy and anxious person a sense of social connectedness, it can also impinge on their capacity to make friends in the real world (Guo et al., 2018).

But what causes shyness? In a review of shyness and social anxiety disorder, Bögels and her team (2010) review a plethora of possible causes, ranging from genetics to socialization to past experiences. They argue that it is difficult to give any exact cause as social fears about different things (e.g. public speaking, interacting with others) suggest different causes. Moreover, the criteria for diagnosing SAD by the DSM is not all-encompassing. The wide variety of measures to capture shyness and social anxiety reveal a lack of consistency over its definition and expression (Leary, 2013). So any theory is going to be just that, a theory. For example, Schlenker and Leary (1982, 1985; also Leary & Kowalski, 1995) answer questions of causes of shyness and social anxiety by applying self-presentation theory. As we see in Chapters 3 and 5, self-presentation theory assumes that we are eager to present ourselves in ways that make a good impression. The implications for social anxiety are straightforward: *we feel anxious when we are motivated to impress others but we doubt our ability to do so.* This simple principle helps explain a variety of research findings, each of which may ring true in your own experience. We seem to feel most anxious when we are:

- with powerful, high-status people – people whose impressions of us matter, such as at a job interview or an important meeting
- in an evaluative context, such as when making a first impression on the parents of one's fiancé
- self-conscious (as shy people often are) and our attention is focused on ourselves and how we are coming across – such as public speaking
- focused on something central to our self-image, as when a college professor presents ideas before peers at a professional convention
- in novel or unstructured situations, such as a first school dance or first formal dinner, where we are unsure of the social rules.

For most people, the tendency in all such situations is to be cautiously self-protective: to talk less; to avoid topics that reveal one's ignorance; to be guarded about oneself; to be unassertive, agreeable and smiling. But for the chronically shy and anxious, this can be a very unpleasant experience. To illustrate how self-presentation theory understands shyness, let's consider a research example from Australia. Stritzke et al. (2004) compared shy and non-shy Internet users on four aspects of shyness as depicted by self-presentation theory: fear of rejection, reluctance to initiate relationships, avoidance of self-disclosure, and unwillingness to provide support and/or advice. They found that when they compared shy and non-shy participants on these aspects of shyness with respect to their offline behaviour, big differences were evident between them. However, when they looked at their online behaviour, these differences were very much reduced. The researchers offer this as support for a self-presentation theory of shyness, noting that when we are online, auditory and visual cues about ourselves and others are absent from the interaction, so our fear of being rejected is diminished. It is less threatening to present a positive self-image online than offline. Furthermore, rather than presenting a negative view of computer-mediated-interaction (CMC) for shy people, Stritzke and colleagues argue that it can be a very useful tool for initiating and developing friendships, tackling shyness, and mastering social competency.

To reduce social anxiety in the short term some people turn to alcohol. Alcohol lowers anxiety as it reduces self-consciousness (Young et al., 2015). Cox et al. (2006) distinguish between positive and negative motives for drinking behaviour amongst secondary school and university students. Positive motives include approval from peers, trying to 'fit in' and to reduce inhibitions. Negative motives include 'drowning your sorrows' and to cope with a difficult situation. Thus, chronically self-conscious people are especially likely to drink following a failure or when struggling to cope with a social situation they feel anxious about. Cox et al. (2006) found that it is the negative motives for drinking alcohol which predict long-term drinking problems.

Beliefs about Health and Illness

Most clinicians recognize that treatment for illness must take into account patients' beliefs about their own health. In the 1950s, the Health Belief Model (Rosenstock, 1974) was formulated to guide explanations as to why patients varied in their willingness to engage with treatment. The model is based on the principles of stimulus-response as outlined in Skinner's Behaviourist theory (see Chapter 1) and cognitive theory. Whilst Skinner maintained that behaviour would occur if it was reinforced in some way and associated with positive consequences, cognitive theory suggested that behaviour is facilitated by the value placed upon it and the expectation that it will produce a positive outcome (Champion & Skinner, 2008). Within a clinical context, the Health Belief Model rests on four pillars against which people decide whether to engage with treatment for their illness. These are: *Perceived Susceptibility* – the extent to which we think we are likely to suffer from the illness; *Perceived Severity* – how serious we consider the illness to be; *Perceived Benefits* – what benefits we think we will obtain as a result of treatment; *Perceived Barriers* – any barriers that may prevent us from obtaining treatment such as cost and access.

The Health Belief Model has been applied to understand the lack of uptake of treatment for diabetes. Ağralı and Akyar (2014) found that negative health beliefs explained the lack of engagement with treatment for type 2 diabetes among adults aged 65 years and above. This was particularly pronounced for women, people aged 70 years and older, and those of a low educational and economic status. The researchers note that for these people, the perceived barriers to treatment were high, the benefits considered low, and the severity of diabetes and susceptibility under-estimated. Consequently, Ağralı and Akyar advise that diabetes intervention programmes must include some element of training that takes into account these beliefs and tries to address them, if we are to encourage people to seek the help they need.

This need for training is also encouraged in the work of Hjelm et al. (2011) who looked at cases of diagnosed gestational diabetes in pregnant Swedish and African women living in Sweden. Upon diagnosis they found that Swedish women were active in combating diabetes, making relevant changes to their diet, took sick-leave from work, avoided stressful environments, changed their diet, researched the illness, and followed a variety of recommended healthcare interventions. They understood the causes to be hormonal and hereditary. In contrast the African women did not know the cause, and took a more passive healthcare approach, following prescriptions, watching and waiting, falsely believing the diabetes would disappear once the child was born. Hjelm and her team argue that real-world studies such as this, reveal that better training is required in maternity care to ensure correct information is given, and to address the health beliefs their patients hold. Hjelm has also conducted work looking at health beliefs of diabetes in Zimbabwean women (Hjelm & Mufunda, 2010), sufferers of diabetic foot ulcers in Uganda (Hjelm & Beebwa, 2013) and diabetic athletes in Latin America (Hjelm & Bard, 2013). Again, what distinguishes those who take up treatment options from those who do not, is what they believe about their condition. Ge et al. (2016) found that some sufferers of diabetes in China did not seek treatment because they believed in 'letting nature takes its course'. Others sought help from folk-healers, used home remedies and/or sought appropriate professional help.

Meyer (2015) emphasizes the importance of understanding the concept of resilience in developing health interventions. He defines resilience as 'being able to survive and thrive in the face of adversity' (p. 210). Focusing on LGBT people, Meyers argues that minority groups such as LGBT face specific stressors that can negatively impact upon health. These include discrimination, stigma, negative social attitudes and rejection. In response, minority group members can develop resilience through social support and coping. Identifying strongly as a minority group member can serve as a buffer to stress as it can offer a source of support and strength from other members. Poor health can be the result of a lack of resilience. For example, strong minority group identification can also serve to make us more vulnerable to stressors such as prejudice. In tackling health issues faced by LGBT people, Meyers suggests that interventions should address the individual's personal resilience, but also community resilience – which can be at the level of the LGBT group or even the nation. Understanding the individual in their social context is key to tackling health issues.

What is revealing about all of these studies is that not only are our individual beliefs about health highly influential when it comes to obtaining treatment, or failure to do so, but also how our social, including culture, influences those beliefs. We consider the powerful force of culture upon our lives in Chapter 15.

Socially Constructed Disorders

As we emphasize in this book, the cultural discursive labels we attach to things influence how we perceive, evaluate and respond to them. How physical psychological disorders are defined and understood is influenced by the cultural and social context in which people live and the language they use to communicate their norms and values. For example, Faraone et al. (2003) report the USA as having the highest prevalence of attention deficit hyperactivity disorder (ADHD) in the world, affecting 1 in 20 American children. However, this does not mean it is an American disorder. The symptoms recognized as indicative of ADHD are as prevalent throughout the rest of the world as they are in the USA. The difference is in if, and how, the behaviour disorder is diagnosed by medical professionals outside the USA. If ADHD is not diagnosed, it means many children with ADHD do not receive the support and medical interventions they need.

Consider the medical condition of myalgic encephalomyelitis (ME). As Horton-Salway (2002) notes, ME has been given many different labels within the medical profession (e.g. chronic-fatigue syndrome, post-viral fatigue syndrome), which reflect its many definitions and assumptions about symptoms, cause and how seriously it should be taken as an illness. There is a debate within the medical profession as to whether these different labels actually describe different disorders and no clear consensus exists as to *what* ME actually is and *how* it should be treated. As Horton-Salway points out, it is only relatively recently that the World Health Organization accepted ME as a 'real illness'. In everyday language it has been labelled as 'yuppie flu'. The origins of this derogatory term for ME come from the demographic of people who sought medical help for chronic fatigue in the 1980s; high income earners with high educational backgrounds. This has unfortunately undermined the seriousness with which ME has been regarded; dismissing the condition as being 'all in the mind'. In her work on the illness, Horton-Salway (2002, 2004, 2007) has examined how both doctors and those suffering from ME distinguish between the genuine sufferer and those who 'jump on the bandwagon' seeking sympathy or an excuse for other psychological problems. Claiming to have an illness isn't straightforward. Nor is reaching diagnosis and obtaining treatment from the doctor. These processes require both patient and doctor to negotiate their way around cultural understandings of what it means to have the illness and justify the attachment of a particular medical label. As Horton-Salway states, for ME sufferers this requires some tricky footwork in avoiding accusations of being a fake. For doctors trying to identify an illness clouded by many definitions and understandings, and confronted with the possibility that a patient's claim may be illegitimate, they must construct the mental and physical identity and well-being of the patient in order to make a diagnosis.

The identification, labelling and evaluation of physical and psychological medical conditions (such as ME) are a complex feature of the social world in which we find ourselves. It's something that requires social construction and discursive defence if we are to treat them as legitimate and real claims about our state of health.

What Influences Clinical Judgements?

Do the influences on our social judgement (discussed in Chapters 3 to 5) also affect clinicians' judgements of clients? If so, what biases should clinicians and their clients be wary of?

A parole board talks with a convicted rapist and ponders whether to release him. A clinical psychologist ponders whether her patient is seriously suicidal. A physician notes a patient's symptoms and decides whether to recommend an invasive test. A school social worker ponders whether a child's overheard threat was a macho joke, a single outburst or a signal indicating a potential school assassin.

Such judgements are also *social* judgements and thus vulnerable to cultural and cognitive biases, such as illusory correlations, overconfidence bred by hindsight, and self-confirming diagnoses (Garb, 2005). Let's see why alerting mental health workers to how people form impressions (and mis-impressions) might help avert serious misjudgements (McFall, 2000).

Illusory Correlations

As we note in Chapter 4, it is tempting to see correlations where none exists. Clinicians, like all of us, may perceive illusory correlations. If expecting particular responses or a particular association we all have a tendency to *perceive* it, regardless of whether the data are supportive.

Hindsight and Overconfidence

Rosenhan (1973) provided an early example of potential error in after-the-fact explanations. To test mental health workers' clinical insights, they each made an appointment with a different mental hospital admissions office and complained of 'hearing voices'. Apart from giving false names and vocations, they reported their life histories and emotional states honestly and exhibited no further symptoms. Most were diagnosed as schizophrenic and remained hospitalized for two to three weeks. Hospital clinicians then searched for early incidents in the pseudo-patients' life histories and hospital behaviour that 'confirmed' and 'explained' the diagnosis. Rosenhan tells of one pseudo-patient who truthfully explained to the interviewer that he had a close relationship with his mother but was rather remote from his father during his early childhood. During adolescence and beyond, however, his father became a close friend while his relationship with his mother had broken down. His present relationship with his wife was characteristically close and warm. Apart from occasional angry exchanges, friction was minimal.

The interviewer, inaccurately believing the person suffered from schizophrenia, explained the problem this way:

> This white 39-year-old male . . . manifests a long history of considerable ambivalence in close relationships, which begins in early childhood. A warm relationship with his mother cools during his adolescence. A distant relationship to his father is described as becoming very intense. Affective stability is absent. His attempts to control emotionality with his wife and children are punctuated by angry outbursts and, in the case of the children, spankings. And while he says that he has several good friends, one senses considerable ambivalence embedded in those relationships also.

Rosenhan later told some staff members (who had heard about his controversial experiment but doubted such mistakes could occur in their hospital) that during the next three months one or more pseudo-patients would seek admission to their hospital. After the three months, he asked the staff to guess which of the 193 patients admitted during that time were really pseudo-patients. Of the 193 new patients, 41 were accused by at least one staff member of being pseudo-patients. Actually, the study had already finished and no more pseudo-patients had been admitted. Hence, the 41 patients thought to be fake were genuine mental health patients.

Self-confirming Diagnoses

So far we've seen that mental health clinicians sometimes perceive illusory correlations and that hindsight explanations can err. A third problem with clinical judgement is that the patients themselves may also supply information that fulfils clinicians' expectations (Nardone & Portelli, 2005).

A body of social psychological work spear-headed by Snyder (1984), in collaboration with Swann and others (e.g. see Synder & Stukes, 1999; Synder & Swann, 1978), examined how behavioural expectancies guided both clinicians and patients in therapeutic encounters. Swayed by first impressions and sometimes brief case notes, clinicians can search for confirming information of what they expect the diagnosis to be. Patients guided by the 'expertise' of the therapist, may unwittingly exhibit symptoms of the diagnosis as it is being decided upon. More recently, Tandos and Stukas (2010) found further evidence of this. They asked 38 postgraduate therapy student trainees to assess 72 undergraduate student clients in counselling sessions. The researchers found that if the trainee therapists were given false information that suggested their client was depressed, they found evidence of it as the client expressed depressed behaviours. This is a good example of the **confirmation bias** (see Chapter 4). The clients were not depressed, but both therapist and client fulfilled the expectation that they were. Our assumptions and expectations about another help create the kind of person we see.

confirmation bias a tendency to search for information that confirms one's preconceptions, rather than considering opposing information

One final example of self-confirming diagnoses is one many of us will be familiar with. Feeling poorly, a little under-the-weather, or concerned about what appears to be an ongoing medical problem, you might be tempted to conduct an Internet search to self-diagnose your condition. Having done so, you may well reach the diagnosis you expected. However, Greving and Sassenberg (2015) offer some food for thought before taking those self-diagnoses too seriously. In their studies they found that your emotions and fears of threat about your health influence the search items you enter into an Internet trawl, and the outcomes (diagnosis) of that search which you pay attention to and remember. In short, we find what we expected to find.

What are Some Social Psychological Approaches to Treatment?

We have considered patterns of thinking that are linked with problems in living, ranging from sadness and depression to extreme shyness to physical illness. We now turn to explore various treatments, evidenced by research, to alleviate these maladaptive thought patterns.

Therapy is a social encounter, and social psychologists have suggested how their principles might be integrated into existing treatment techniques. Let's consider three approaches.

Inducing Internal Change through External Behaviour

In Chapter 5 we review a broad range of evidence for a simple but powerful principle: our actions affect our attitudes. The roles we play, the things we say and do, and the decisions we make influence who we are.

Consistent with this attitudes-follow-behaviour principle, several psychotherapy techniques prescribe action.

- Behaviour therapists try to shape behaviour on the theory that the client's inner disposition will also change after the behaviour changes.
- In assertiveness training, the individual may first role-play assertiveness in a supportive context, then gradually implement assertive behaviours in everyday life.
- Rational-emotive therapy (Ellis, 1962) assumes that we generate our own emotions; clients receive 'homework' assignments to talk and act in new ways that will generate new emotions: challenge that overbearing relative. Stop telling yourself you're an unattractive person and ask someone out.
- Self-help groups subtly induce participants to behave in new ways in front of the group – to express anger, cry, act with high self-esteem, express positive feelings.

All these techniques share a common assumption: if we cannot directly control our cognitions and feelings by sheer willpower, we can influence them indirectly through our behaviour.

Cognitive behavioural therapy (CBT) has proved increasingly popular in treating mental health issues, including obsessive compulsive disorders, depression and social phobias. CBT aims to break clients' negative ways of thought and action through a series of meetings between therapist and client, which may take place in the form of one-to-one or group therapy (NHS, 2016). In a series of meetings, clients are given scenarios in order to practise behaviours that they would otherwise find challenging. An example comes from McManus et al. (2010) who conducted a phenomenological study on eight clients suffering from social phobias, receiving CBT at the Maudsley Hospital in London. In their detailed thematic analysis of interviews with the clients, the researchers found that among other things, being encouraged to try out new behaviours, often ones they found scary, were helpful in readjusting patterns of thinking. A trusting relationship with the therapist was also crucial, as was acceptance of anxiety as a state of being. What changed as a result of the therapy was how the client thought about things. Rather than focusing on the self, feeling anxious, and engaging in safety behaviours (such as avoiding social interaction), clients focused on the world around them and acknowledged other people feel anxious too as they engaged in social behaviours. CBT has increasingly been delivered over the Internet in attempts to make the treatment more accessible and relieve pressure off mental health practitioners. However, CBT both offline and online is not without its critics. It is time consuming, can be expensive, doesn't last long enough, and the scenarios that clients work through during therapy may not transfer beyond this setting (e.g. Berg et al., 2008; Halmetoja et al., 2014; Johnson & Friborg, 2015).

Intervention mapping (IM) describes a 6-step framework for identifying and addressing health problems through behaviour. It has been adopted as an intervention programme for a wide range of health conditions, such as cancer (Besharati et al., 2017), obesity (Pittson & Wallace, 2011), HIV (Merlin et al., 2018) and asthma (Mesters et al., 2018). The six steps are as follows:

1. Needs assessment – identify the problem and for 'who' it is a problem.
2. State change objectives – what the behavioural outcome of the intervention will be, and the influences over that behaviour which need to be targeted.

3 Design the program – this should be theory and evidence-based, and offer practical solutions for delivering the desired change.

4 Produce the program – refine the intervention program to suit the desired audience and problem, write all the materials, pilot the program, produce the final version.

5 Plan the implementation of the program – identify who will use it and how the program will be implemented.

6 Evaluation – develop protocols to evaluate the program, for example assessment questions, feedback.

Let's consider a successful example of the adoption of IM from Ghana. Like many other developing countries, children under the age of 5 years experience high mortality from fevers, including malaria and pneumonia. Lack of immediate access to appropriate healthcare facilities, financial and geographical barriers, and poor healthcare knowledge mean many families do not receive the help needed. To address this problem in an area of Ghana, Abbey and her team (2017) used IM to develop a strategy for tackling the behaviours of individuals, healthcare workers, and the community. Following the six-step protocol the authors began by assessing the needs and identifying the problem (Step 1). Using a mix of qualitative and quantitative methods, the current behaviours and attitudes of families, healthcare workers and the community more generally were explored in understanding how fevers such as malaria and pneumonia were (mis)understood and (not)acted upon. This step revealed some startling problems. Lack of knowledge for correct diagnosis, poor access to medication, over-reliance on traditional medicines, and suspicion over the healthcare profession, were just some of the problems identified. This gave the researchers clear indications as to what the change objectives (Step 2) of their programme should be. These included: ensuring caregivers seek prompt healthcare assistance when a child has a fever; belief that the drug will cure the child; community understands a good parent is one who acts quickly; the service is free of charge; healthcare workers are friendly and helpful, and so on. To achieve these objectives, an intervention programme was designed and produced (Steps 3 and 4) that would speak to families/caregivers, healthcare community workers, the healthcare profession, and the community. Borrowing concepts from psychology such as **modelling** (see Chapters 4 and 11 for examples of this concept), the researchers presented a range of methods including educational videos, drama, and stories involving role models whom families, healthcare workers and the community identified with and could copy. Adopters and implementers of the programme (e.g. community healthcare workers and health professionals) were identified (Step 5) and trained on how to deliver it. Furthermore, where existing skill sets and knowledge needed updating, this was carried out. Finally evaluation of the programme (Step 6) was considered in terms of working out what the indicators would be to measure its effectiveness. The reported results are impressive. Healthcare workers and professionals embraced the programme and their knowledge and skills improved. Crucially, it was also accepted by the community and consequently mortality rates in children who developed a fever dropped by 30–44 per cent during the trial phase of the programme (30 months). Not only had the IM changed people's external behaviour, but also their beliefs and attitudes about this particular healthcare issue.

modelling the acquisition of behaviour on the basis of observing that of others (models) nudge theory proposes that desired behaviour can be 'nudged' through small changes made to the environment

From the field of behavioural economics, **nudge theory** has become increasingly popular in psychology (Thaler & Sunstein, 2008). Nudge theory proposes that a desired behaviour can be achieved by making a small but significant change to someone's environment. A fascinating example comes from Dreibelbis et al. (2016), who wanted to encourage more hygienic hand-washing behaviour in two rural schools in Bangladesh. In deprived rural areas, matters of hygiene are perhaps understandably not always a priority. This of course becomes a recipe for the spreading of infection and disease across a community. Basic hand-washing after using the toilet, using soap, would go far in mitigating the problem. Both schools in the study had a designated latrine area and hand-washing station. But prior to any nudging, only 4 per cent of children across the two schools (4 out of 114) were observed to wash their hands with soap after using the toilet. That's a lot of dirty hands! The nudge was then introduced. The toilets and the hand-washing station had something of a makeover. They were made highly visible using paint. Furthermore, a set of footprints and handprints were brightly painted onto the pathway connecting the toilet to the hand-washing station, where the soap was placed. Did this work? Yes it did. Observers watched the children as they left the toilet to see if they would go to the hand-washing station and use the soap. At the time the nudge was introduced, 68 per cent of children (108 out of 158) were now washing their hands properly. Six weeks after the nudge had been introduced, 74 per cent (164 out of 222) were now washing their hands after a trip to the toilet. This technique has since been adapted and applied to 25 schools in Zambia, where the 'nudge' has been soap-on-a-rope hanging in the classroom (Naluonde et al., 2018). As a student goes to the toilet, they take the soap-on-a-rope with them and hand it back to the teacher on their return. Again, a very simple technique induced behavioural change. But was it temporary? The team identified what they called a 'stickiness' problem. Three months after the intervention, hand-washing with the soap began to wane. They suggest that nudge techniques need to be evaluated and reinforced over a longer period of time so that the behaviour change becomes habitual.

How Do Social Relationships Support Health and Well-Being?

Our relationships are fraught with stress. 'Hell is others,' wrote Jean-Paul Sartre. And stress also aggravates health problems such as coronary heart disease, hypertension and suppression of our disease-fighting immune system.

Still, on balance, close relationships contribute less to illness than to health and happiness. Close relationships provide our greatest heartaches, but also our greatest joys.

Close Relationships and Health

Eight extensive investigations, each interviewing thousands of people across several years, have reached a common conclusion: close relationships predict health (Berkman, 1995; Ross et al., 2019; Ryff & Singer, 2000). Health risks are greater among lonely people, who often experience more stress and sleep less well (Cacioppio et al., 2002a, 2002b, 2003). Compared with those with few social ties, those who have close relationships with friends, kin or other members of close-knit religious or community organizations are less likely to die prematurely. Feeling connected to others and having someone to share the trials and tribulations of life, really does help to mitigate against mental and physical illness (Berkman & Syme, 1979; Holt-Lunstadt et al., 2010).

Let's consider a fascinating example. In 1882 a group of eleven Italians from Roseto Valfortore (a small town in south-east Italy) found jobs in Bangor (Pennsylvania). The Rosetans created a new town on a rocky hillside near Bangor. They named the town Roseto. They built a church, schools, a park, a convent, and a cemetery. Up to the early 1960s, people in Roseto maintained close family ties and cohesive community relationships. In the late 1950s, a physician called Stewart Wolf casually discovered that for Rosetans under the age of 65 years, it was very rare to have heart disease. As a result, from 1962 Roseto became the object of a long inquiry, and the health of its people was compared mainly with the adjacent community of Bangor (which was served by the same water supply, physicians, and hospital facilities as Roseto). It was found that Rosetans were much less likely to die from myocardial infarction than the people in Bangor. For instance, during the period 1935–1944, the mortality rates per 1,000 were 39.7 per cent and 23.0 per cent respectively for men in Bangor and for men in Roseto. Similarly, the mortality rate in this age group was 23.5 per cent and 12.5 per cent for women in Bangor and in Roseto. In the mid-1960s the young Rosetans started living a less community-oriented life, in line with mainstream American lifestyle. Gradually, the difference between Rosetan and people from Bangor in terms of myocardial infarction disappeared (Egolf et al., 1992). It is perhaps unclear whether genetic and/or diet influences were partly responsible for this decline in health. They almost certainly were. However, it does seem to suggest that our close social ties also have a positive impact on our lives.

Furthermore, research suggests that outgoing, affectionate, relationship-orientated people are also less susceptible to cold viruses administered to them by an experimenter.

The research on the positive impact our close relationships have on our well-being is impressive. In one five-year study of 423 elderly married couples, those who *gave* the most social support (from lifts and errands for friends and neighbours to emotional support of their spouse) enjoyed greater longevity, even after controlling for age, sex, initial health and economic status (Brown et al., 2003). Especially among women, suggests a Finnish study that tracked more than 700 people's illnesses, it is better to give than only to receive (Väänänen et al., 2005).

Moreover, losing social ties heightens the symptoms as well as the risk of disease.

- A study of 235 irritable bowel syndrome (IBS) sufferers found that those who reported the most debilitating symptoms were those with negative social relationships, characterized with conflict (Lackner et al., 2013).
- A 7-year longitudinal Swedish study reveals that women who suffer perinatal loss and receive little support from their partner, are more likely to suffer long-term depression and relationship breakdown than women who are supported by their partner during this time (Turton et al., 2009).
- A study of 30,000 men revealed that when a marriage ends, men drink and smoke more and eat fewer vegetables and more fried foods (Eng et al., 2001).

Confiding and Health

'Friendship is a sovereign antidote against all calamities.'

Seneca, 5 BC–AD 65

So there is a link between social support and health. Why? Perhaps those who enjoy close relationships eat better, exercise more, and smoke and drink less. Perhaps friends and family help bolster our self-esteem. Perhaps a supportive network helps us evaluate and overcome stressful events. When we are wounded by someone's dislike or the loss of a job, a friend's advice, help and reassurance may indeed be good medicine. Even when the problem isn't mentioned, friends provide us with distraction and a sense that, come what may, we're accepted, liked and respected.

Social psychological experiments confirm the benefits of engaging with stressful experiences. In one, Lepore et al. (2000) had students view a stressful slide show and video on the Holocaust and either talk about it immediately afterwards or not. Two days later, those who talked were experiencing less stress and fewer intrusive thoughts. Even mentally revisiting a recent problem that was still 'stressing you out' – vividly recalling the incident and associated feelings – served to boost active coping and mood (Rivkin & Taylor, 1999).

In an impressive array of studies, James Pennebaker has observed how expressing our emotions, being ready to forgive and confessing our fears, hopes, anxieties and dreams can be good for our physiological health, reducing blood pressure, improving our immune system and even helping to overcome insomnia. But we should be careful in assuming a one-way relationship. Rather it seems that our health, physiology and social relations are involved in a complex relationship, each influencing and shaping the other. Pennebaker et al. (2004) found that high levels of testosterone were correlated with a lack of social connections in natural language. Pennebaker and Stone (2003) have also examined how the specific words we use reveal our emotional and cognitive state, as well as serve as markers of our identity and how we view the world. The identification of these patterns in language suggests that those suffering from mental health problems such as mania, depression and suicide idealization tend to be preoccupied with their 'self' to the exclusion of those around them who could, potentially, offer help and support.

Poverty, Inequality and Health We have seen connections between health and the feelings of control that accompany a positive explanatory style. And we have seen connections between health and social support. Feelings of control and support together with healthcare and nutrition factors help explain why economic status correlates with longevity (Rambotti, 2015).

Bad health isn't good for one's income. But most evidence indicates that the strongest arrow runs from poverty towards ill health (Sapolsky, 2005). So how *does* poverty 'get under the skin'? The answers include (1) reduced access to quality health care (in countries where there is no public and free health care on equal terms for everybody, as it is in many European countries), (2) unhealthier lifestyles (smoking is much more common among less educated and lower-income people), and, to a striking extent, (3) increased stress. To be poor is to be at risk for increased stress, negative emotions and a toxic environment (Adler & Snibbe, 2003; Chen, 2004; Gallo & Matthews, 2003). To be poor is to be sleep deprived after working a second job, earning pay cheques that don't cover the bills, commuting on crowded public transport, living in a high-pollution area and doing hard labour that's controlled by someone else.

Poverty and its associated stresses help explain the lower life expectancy of disadvantaged minorities. In Israel, for example, the minority group of Arab-Palestinians have a lower life expectancy, as a consequence of infectious and chronic diseases, than the Jewish majority. The difference can be explained as an outcome of social inequality between the two groups, which includes access to healthcare (Saabneh, 2016). People also die younger in regions with great income inequality (e.g. Messias, 2003).

Is inequality merely an indicator of poverty? The mixed evidence indicates that poverty matters but that inequality matters, too. Lynch et al. (1998, 2000) report that people at every income level are at greater risk of early death if they live in a community with great income inequality. It's not just being poor, it's also *feeling* poor, relative to one's surroundings, that proves toxic. And that, Sapolsky (2005) suggests, helps explain why the USA, which has the greatest income inequality of Westernized nations, simultaneously ranks number 1 in the world on healthcare expenditures and number 29 on life expectancy.

Close Relationships and Happiness

Confiding painful feelings is good not only for the body but for the soul as well. That's the conclusion of studies showing that people are happier when supported by a network of friends and family.

Some studies, summarized in Chapter 3, compare people in a competitive, individualistic culture, such as the USA, Canada and Australia, with those in collectivist cultures, such as China and many developing countries. Individualistic cultures offer independence, privacy and pride in personal achievements. Collectivist cultures, with their tighter social bonds, offer protection from loneliness, alienation, divorce and stress-related diseases. Indeed it seems collectivist cultures have much to teach us about happiness. Zhang and Veenhoven (2008) suggest that the Chinese philosophy of Confucianism, with its emphasis on compassion, social relations and concern for others, offers extremely apt advice for ensuring happiness in the modern Western world.

Being attached to friends with whom we can share intimate thoughts has two effects, observed the seventeenth-century philosopher Francis Bacon. 'It redoubleth joys, and cutteth griefs in half.'

Across the lifespan, friendships foster self-esteem and well-being (Hartup & Stevens, 1999). Here are some examples.

- Friendships are very important for young children as they help to develop self-confidence, self-esteem, a sense of security, and are a platform for learning (Ladd, 2009).
- In a 10-year longitudinal study conducted with 1,477 people aged 70 years and above living in residential care in Adelaide, Australia, it was found that those who had maintained lots of close friendships lived longer than those who had fewer friends (Giles et al., 2005).
- Having a close friend nearby makes us less susceptible to physical illness when we experience stress (Fonagy, 2003).
- Rejection by friends can lower self-esteem and increase materialism, in an attempt to self-comfort but also buy back friendship (Jiang et al., 2015).

Social Psychology, the Environment and the Sustainable Future

'Being in touch with the natural world is crucial.'
Sir David Attenborough – Natural Historian

Of course, life is good for many of us. We enjoy luxuries unknown even to royalty in centuries past: hot showers, flush toilets, central air-conditioning, microwave ovens, jet travel, wintertime fresh fruit, big-screen digital television, Internet and Post-it notes. But on the horizon, beyond the sunny skies of comfort and convenience, dark clouds of an environmental disaster are gathering pace. The Earth's temperature has risen to unprecedented heights in the last century, mostly as a result of human behaviour (IPCC, 2007). The Global Report on Internal Displacement (IDMC, 2019) notes that since 2009, one person every second has been displaced by a weather-related hazard or disaster. Flooding has accounted for 8.6 million displacements, and storms for 7.5 million since 2008. The worst affected countries are China, the Philippines, Cuba and the US. Extreme rainfall has led to an escalation of deadly landslides across the globe (Haque et al., 2019). The UN Refugee Agency warns that climate-related disasters will push more and more vulnerable people into poverty, with an escalation in conflict as a result for basic human resources.

How well is social psychology placed to address these looming environmental issues and help foster a sustainable future? Very well placed, argues Kazdin (2009). Indeed, considering psychology's concerns with social issues and the contributions it has already made to society, he goes even further, to suggest we have a duty to get involved. Yet the scale of the problem to be tackled is large and complex (see **Table 15.1**). This is why Kazdin views environmental concerns as an example of a 'wicked problem'. So how should we be involved?

Kazdin warns that many of psychology's suggestions may be temporary sticking-plasters rather than permanent solutions, but even so we have much to offer on the road of ensuring long-term personal, social and environmental well-being. For example, social psychological knowledge about persuasion and the framing

TABLE 15.1 Salient characteristics of wicked problems

There is no single, definitive or simple formulation of the problem
The problem is not likely to be the result of an event (e.g. tsunami, hurricane) but rather a set of intersecting trends that co-occur and co-influence each other
The problem has embedded in it, other problems
There is no one solution, no single one-shot effort that will eliminate the problem
The problem is never likely to be solved
Multiple stakeholders are likely to be involved, and this fact leads to multiple formulations of what 'really' is the problem and therefore what are legitimate or appropriate solutions
Values, culture, politics and economics are likely to be involved in the problem and in possible strategies to address the problem
Information as a basis for action will be incomplete because of the uniqueness of the problem and the complexities of its interrelations with other problems
The problem is likely to be unique and therefore does not easily lend itself to previously tried strategies

SOURCE: Taken from Kazdin (2009).

of messages (Chapters 5 and 6) can help in influencing people's attitudes and behaviour. Let's consider a couple of examples.

The consumption of bottled water has increased globally, with many people believing that bottled water is healthier than tap water (Niccolucci et al., 2011). As billions of bottles of water are consumed, think how much plastic is used to package it; the fuel required to ship the bottles to stores nationally and internationally; the energy used in refrigerating the bottles once they're in the stores. If we can influence a reduction in the consumption of bottled water, we increase savings in plastic, fuel and energy.

In Chapter 5 we discuss how changing people's behaviour requires an appeal to their attitudes. Similarly, if you've been in a hotel you may have come across a message asking you to reuse your towels if possible, thus saving on energy required in washing them. Goldstein et al. (2008) found that people were more likely to reuse their towels if they were appealed to using a socially normative message (e.g. 'Most of our guests reuse their towels') rather than a general message about the environment (e.g. 'Help save the environment'). This appeal to 'what other people do' has been the basis of successful nudge theory approaches to encouraging environmentally sustainable behaviour change. Ayres et al. (2013) discovered that if households received reports of their neighbours' energy consumption, as well as their own from the electricity and gas supplier, this peer-comparison nudged them to decrease the amount of energy they used. This proved particularly effective when this peer-comparison was accompanied with personalized energy-saving tips and emoticons to express current 'good' or 'bad' energy use. As we see in Chapter 6, how we frame a message has implications for how people respond to and act upon it.

In the rest of this chapter, we'll consider some pressing environmental concerns and how social psychology has been put to use in addressing them.

An Environmental Call to Action

In 1950 the Earth carried 2.5 billion people and 50 million cars. Today it has 7.7 billion people and 1.42 billion cars, and economic growth in developing countries is putting millions more cars on the road. In addition to being a waste-disposal problem, cars burn fuel. This combustion, along with the burning of coal and oil to generate electricity and heat buildings, produces an excess of carbon dioxide, which – along with other greenhouse gases from agricultural and industrial sources – contributes to global warming. This has sparked a surge in some countries in the manufacture and sale of 'environmentally friendly' vehicles, which as we will see later in this chapter, is not without controversy.

In April 2018, Patricia Espinosa, Executive Secretary of the United Nations Framework Convention on Climate Change, told the world's press that:

> *We are witnessing the severe impacts of climate change throughout the world. Every credible scientific source is telling us that these impacts will only get worse if we do not address climate change and it also tells us that our window of time for addressing it is closing very soon... We need to dramatically increase our ambitions.*
>
> UN News (2018)

Amur (Siberian) tigers reside in the forested areas of the Russian Far East. Their need for vast hunting territories to ensure survival brings them into conflict with humans, and has brought tigers such as these to the brink of extinction. Conservation groups work hard to sustain a relationship in which tigers and humans can live side by side.

SOURCE: ©Conny Sjostrom/Shutterstock

Global warming is causing not only climate change itself but also environmental destruction. Plants and animals are gradually migrating towards the poles and towards higher elevations, interfering with polar and alpine ecosystems. Semi-arid agricultural and grazing lands, notably those in sub-Saharan Africa, are gradually turning into desert.

In addition to these global warming-linked effects, ecosystems around the world are in danger because of human exploitation. As the Earth's population increases, the demand increases for resources to produce basic human necessities (food, clothing, shelter) as well as luxuries. Most of the world's original forest cover has been taken down, and what remains in the tropics is being cleared for agriculture, livestock grazing, logging and settlements. With deforestation comes soil erosion, diminished absorption of greenhouse gases, and greater extremes of rainfall and temperature, resulting in periodic floods and droughts, and the devastation of many animal species. A growing population's appetite for fish, together with ecosystem destruction, has also led to major depletion in fish stocks, including wild salmon, Atlantic cod, haddock, herring and other species (for some fairly recent examples see Karavellas, 2000; Lukin, 2013; Inogwabini, 2014; McGinn, 1998; Morton, 2005).

While environmental experts unsurprisingly possess the most knowledge about climate change, as compared to journalists, politicians and laypeople, Sundblad et al. (2009) found that, across the board, more is known about what is causing climate change rather than the current climatic state and its future consequences.

Enabling Sustainable Living

'One day fairly soon we will all go belly up like guppies in a neglected fishbowl. I suggest an epitaph for the whole planet: . . . "We could have saved it, but we were too darn cheap and lazy".'

Kurt Vonnegut, 'Notes from My Bed of Gloom', 1990

Those optimistic about the future see two routes to sustainable lifestyles: (1) increasing technological efficiency and agricultural productivity; and (2) moderating consumption and decreasing population. Let's explore social psychology's role in facilitating the success of these approaches.

New Technologies

One component in a sustainable future is improved eco-technologies (Giannetti et al., 2004). For example, in recent times hybrid cars, which conserve fuel by using an electric power cell, have become more commonplace in developed countries, as have flex-fuel cars, which can run on ethanol produced from a variety of vegetable sources such as soybeans, or on a mixture of ethanol and petrol.

However, the public often requires some persuading to adapt to and adopt new technologies. Moreover, new technologies are rarely without caution and criticism. Terwel et al. (2009) consider the example of CSS (carbon dioxide capture and storage) technology, which is important in managing climate change. They observe that 'public acceptance is essential for successful implementation of this technology'. However, their research shows public suspicion of industrial organizations that provide this service. They are attributed with self-serving motives (such as increasing their image and profile as well as profits), and as such are not trusted to be providing the public with a service that is in their best interests. On the other hand, when the work is carried out by an environmental organization, they are thought to be providing a public service and are trusted to carry out the work.

social representations socially shared beliefs – widely held ideas and values, including our assumptions and cultural ideologies. Our social representations help us to make sense of our world

Devine-Wright and Devine-Wright (2009) examined how the public think about renewable energy sources to generate electricity in England and Scotland. The implementation of renewable energy sources has been backed in government policy as the UK seeks to meet its targets in reducing greenhouse gas emissions. Using **Social Representations Theory** (see Chapter 4), participants were invited to discuss, and visually represent by means of drawings, what they understood by traditional methods of generating electricity (the National Grid) and renewable energy sources (such as wind turbines). What they found was that participants held complex and contradictory understandings. While traditional methods of electricity generation could be represented in terms of big ugly A-frame pylons, they could also be regarded as impressive and dramatic symbols of an organized civilized society. Likewise renewable energy sources such as wind turbines could be represented as positive steps towards environmental change, but also as destroyers of the countryside imposed by government forces – especially if their local area was a possible site for new energy technologies. Devine-Wright and Devine-Wright (2009) argue that if the government is to pursue this technology change with the support of the public, it needs to engage them in debate in order to address the sense that this is an unnecessary imposition in their back yard over which they have no control.

Positive steps towards environmental change and sustainability, or an imposition on the countryside? Changing the way we live needs to involve the public in the wider debate about a sustainable future.

SOURCE: ©Thinkstock Images/Getty Images

In 2018, the council of the West Midlands city of Coventry in the UK, installed free electric charging points for electric vehicles throughout its streets. Why? To encourage people to switch from petrol and diesel cars to hybrids and electric vehicles. How? By making it very easy, and free, to charge those vehicles. If we think about this intervention through the lens of the **Theory of Planned Behaviour** (see Chapter 5), being able to carry out an action (perceived self-efficacy) is an important factor in changing behaviours and attitudes. In this example, perceived barriers of cost and inaccessibility are removed. Does it work? Well, that's a question we should be able to answer soon. However, research carried out in France suggests we should be hopeful. Patt et al. (2019) found that Paris residents with private driveways who could readily access their own electric charging point, said they would be willing to purchase an electric car – especially if installation of the electric charging point was free. Those who parked on the street or in a communal space where access would be less easy, were not quite so willing – *unless* they were told installation of electric chargers on the streets and in communal areas would be free. Then they were as willing to purchase an electric vehicle as those with the private driveway.

theory of planned behaviour (TPB) as TRA, but with the addition that people's behaviour is shaped by their confidence in being able to perform it, or having it under their control

Whilst the creation of new eco-technologies is to be applauded, what is crucial is convincing people to adopt them, as well as more sustainable lifestyles generally.

Otto et al. (2014) analysed World Bank data on global energy consumption per person. As we shall see in the next section of this chapter, the data is not promising. Despite these technologies, energy consumption is, at best, levelling off rather than falling. Otto and his team argue that companies have targeted extrinsic motivations to encourage people to adopt eco-technologies, such as focusing on lower-costs, using public transport rather than their car, and receiving discounts in tax, claims to save you time, and so on. Whilst that might change behaviour for the short term, we really need to tackle intrinsic motivations for long-term change – or what Otto and his colleagues call, a request to behave irrationally for the good of everyone. And by irrational they mean acceptance that a sustainable lifestyle may cost you more in time and money, could result in less overseas holidays and mean less clothes in the wardrobe. To achieve that, the benefits of protecting the natural world must be felt *within* individuals and driven by a concern and a connection with that world and each other as a collectivity (Brugger et al., 2011; Clayton & Myers, 2015; Kaiser & Byrka, 2011).

Reducing Consumption

The second component of a sustainable future is the control of consumption. Since 2009, China has been the country with the largest energy consumption in the world. A sharp acceleration in consumption is attributed to the growth in transport fuel. In contrast, the European Union has seen its energy consumption decrease, especially in Germany. Why? Milder winters as well as the creation of more efficient energy is the cause (Enerdata, 2019). Unless we argue that today's less-developed countries are somehow less deserving of an improved standard of living, we must anticipate that their consumption will increase. But the challenge is to ensure this increase is done in a sustainable way. As it does, developed countries must consume less. The decline in energy consumption across the EU offers promise for the future (York, 2007).

The world's population growth rate has decelerated, especially in developed nations. Even in less-developed countries, when food and social security has improved and women have become educated and empowered, birth rates have fallen. This has been attributed to a causal relationship between education and fertility in women, where the investment of time and energy has gone into building a career rather than raising a family, consequently motherhood is put on hold until later in life, if at all (Cygan-Rehm & Maeder, 2013; Samir & Lutz, 2017). In the most populated country in the world, China's controversial one-child policy, which was in place from 1979 to 2015, arguably contributed to falling population rates. But if birth rates everywhere instantly fell to a replacement level of 2.1 children per woman, the lingering momentum of population growth, fuelled by the bulge of people living longer, would continue for years to come.

Our material appetites continue to swell – more people seek personal computers, air-conditioning, jet travel. But why? Two principles drive this psychology of consumption.

Our Human Capacity for Adaptation

adaptation-level phenomenon the tendency to adapt to a given level of stimulation and thus to notice and react to changes starting from that level

The **adaptation-level phenomenon** is our tendency to judge our experience (for example, of sounds, temperatures or income) relative to a neutral level defined by our prior experience. We adjust our neutral levels – the points at which sounds seem neither loud nor soft, temperatures neither hot nor cold, events neither pleasant nor unpleasant – on the basis of our experience. We then notice and react to up or down changes from those levels.

Thus, as our achievements rise above past levels, we feel successful and satisfied. As our social prestige, income or in-home technology improves, we feel pleasure. Before long, however, we adapt. What once felt good comes to register as neutral, and what formerly was neutral now feels like deprivation.

To be sure, adaptation to some events, such as the death of a spouse, may be incomplete, as the sense of loss lingers (Diener et al., 2006). Yet, we generally underestimate our adaptive capacity. People have difficulty predicting the intensity and duration of their future positive and negative emotions, a phenomenon called 'impact bias'. The elation from getting what we want – riches, top examination scores, Italy winning the World Cup – evaporates more rapidly than we expect. We also sometimes 'miswant'. When first-year university students predicted their satisfaction with various housing possibilities shortly before entering their school's housing lottery, they focused on physical features. When contacted a year later, it was the social features, such as a sense of community, that predicted happiness, report Dunn et al. (2003). Likewise, Van Boven and Gilovich (2003) observe from their surveys and experiments that positive *experiences* (often social experiences) leave us happier. The best things in life are not things.

Our Wanting to Compare

Happiness is relative to our comparisons with others, especially with others within our own groups (Lyubomirsky, 2001; Zagefka & Brown, 2005). Whether we feel good or bad depends on whom we're comparing ourselves with. We are slow-witted or clumsy only when others are smart or agile.

Further feeding our luxury fever is the tendency to compare upwards: as we climb the ladder of success or affluence, we mostly compare ourselves with peers who are at or above our current level, not with those who have less. People living in communities where a few residents are very wealthy tend to feel less satisfied as they compare upwards.

The adaptation-level and social comparison phenomena give us pause for thought. They imply that the quest for happiness through material achievement requires continually expanding affluence. But the good news is that adaptation to simpler lives can also happen. If we shrink our consumption by choice or by necessity, we will initially feel a pinch, but it will pass. Indeed, thanks to our capacity to adapt and to adjust comparisons, the emotional impact of significant life events – losing a job or even a disabling accident – dissipates sooner than most people suppose.

So, what can be done to moderate consumption by those who can afford to over-consume?

How we travel is one of the most important decisions we can make when it comes to thinking about the environment (Collins & Chambers, 2005). Wall et al. (2007) examined how staff and students at DeMontfort University in the UK explained their intention to change or maintain their car use in travelling to and from work. Adopting Ajzen's theory of planned behaviour (see Chapter 5) and Schwartz's **norm-activation theory (NAT)**, which was developed to explain altruistic behaviour, Wall et al. examined what factors were important to people in making decisions about travel. What they found was that the intention to reduce car use

norm-activation theory (NAT) seeks to explain behaviour that is performed for the benefit of others rather than self was better explained by altruistic motives rather than personal ones. A sense of personal obligation, the perceived consequences of one's actions and a sense of control were important factors in choosing alternative and more environmentally friendly modes of travel to work. So appealing to one's personal moral obligations to the environment seems to be important when trying to change people's habits, especially when a change in habits may mean less convenience and flexibility for the individual.

Perhaps social psychology can help point the way to greater well-being, by documenting *materialism,* by informing people that *economic growth does not automatically improve human morale,* and by helping people understand *why materialism and money fail to satisfy.* As Kahneman and Deaton (2010) point out, earning a lot of money and buying things might give you a sense of satisfaction with your life, but it does not buy happiness or emotional well-being. That said, it perhaps depends on what you spend your money on. Dunn et al. (2011) note some of the things we can spend our money on which will make us happier. This includes life experiences. Experiences, they argue, usually last longer than material goods. Your memory of a hot-air balloon-ride over the Serengeti will probably last longer than the brand new car you have parked in your driveway. Dunn and colleagues also note that we feel happier when we spend our money in ways that benefit others rather than ourselves. As we explore throughout this book, but particularly in Chapters 11 and 12 of this book, connecting with others is a fundamental part of feeling satisfied with our own lives. We are, after all, social animals, and paying attention to the quality of our relationships with others is extremely beneficial in securing happiness. Similarly, Dunn et al. advise paying 'close attention' to the happiness of others. It is a good predictor of what we will also find joy in. Have a look at the world happiness report (www.worldhappiness.report) for some cross-cultural surveys on what makes us happy.

Close, supportive relationships are a key element in well-being.

SOURCE: ©Mint Images Limited/Alamy Stock Photo

Environmental and Conservation Psychology: Responses and Resilience to Disasters

What might social psychology contribute to our responses to environmental disasters and resilience to future ones?

In recent times we have seen an escalation in global environmental disasters. Some are outlined in Chapter 4. In the grip of a heatwave across Europe in 2019 we have seen wildfires tear through Spain, storms destroy crops in France, tornados in Croatia injuring many people, high winds and floods causing chaos in Italy, and record temperatures in Poland leading to a surge in energy consumption as people switched on the air conditioning. Further afield, during 2019 we have seen landslides in China, hurricanes and earthquakes in the US, wildfires in Hawaii, flooding in Bangladesh, Malaysia, Mexico and India displacing millions of people, and cyclones in Mozambique. This is just a few of the many environmental disasters that have affected us on a global scale in 2019. Alarmingly, the United Nations claims that we experience at least one environmental disaster caused by climate change every week (Harvey, 2019). Many don't make it to the headlines and go unreported. So what can we do as social psychologists?

Environmental and Conservation Psychology

Environmental psychology came about in the 1950s, mainly in response to environmental degradation, human population increases, and the depletion of natural resources. However, as psychologists have been quick to point out, the roots of this field are much older than this. Humans have long been interested in the relationship they have to the earth (Spencer et al., 2009). The discipline is primarily focused on the physical environment but has three main strands of work that cut across other fields. The first is a concern with human behaviour within a physical space – which might be the lab, the football stadium, the forest, university, and so on. The second is an interest in the two-way interaction between space and people. So whilst your physical environment might lead you to behave in particular ways (e.g. be quiet in church, chant at a football match), we are also able to change the physical spaces we occupy. Thirdly, to purposefully engage with other disciplines – such as biology, architecture, history – to share knowledge and improve our understanding of the relationship between people and their environment (Clayton, 2012). As environmental psychologist, Robert Gifford, so neatly puts it: 'Wherever you go, there you are and it matters . . . We are always embedded in a place' (2014, p. 543).

environmental psychology a discipline of psychology that focuses on the relationship between people and their environment

As environmental climate-related disasters become increasingly common and severe, a shift in emphasis has arguably occurred within environmental psychology to focus on 'green' issues such as conservation, consumption, sustainable behaviour, and the relationship we have with the natural world. In their review of environmental psychological studies of pro-environmental behaviour change, Kormos and Gifford (2014) examined the relationship between self-report measures of pro-environmental behaviour (e.g. questionnaires) and objective measures of the behaviour (e.g. observation). Kormos and Gifford reveal some statistical concerns in these studies which suggest that what people say they do, is not necessarily what they actually do. As we discuss in Chapter 2, self-report measures can be biased as a result of a range of problems including **social desirability** and poor memory recall. However, the pros of self-report measures, such as how quickly and cheaply they can be administered, have tended to outweigh the cons and they have arguably become the 'go to' method of environmental scientists (Gifford et al., 2011; Kormos & Gifford, 2014). More specifically, Gifford et al., (2011) question the usefulness of attitudinal studies to assess behaviour. They invite us to consider the following comparison: a high-income person who cares a lot for the environment and lives in the suburbs, with a low-income person who does not care at all for the environment and lives in a downtown area. Whose behaviour is more likely to be environmentally friendly? Let's fill in a little more detail. The poorer person doesn't drive, lives in a small apartment requiring little heat, and doesn't go abroad on holiday. The wealthier person drives a hybrid car, lives in a spacious house with green-energy appliances, buys organic food, and holidays overseas. If we just look at their attitudes, it might appear as though the higher-income earner has the greener lifestyle, but if we look at behaviour, it is the low-income earner who has less of a detrimental impact on the environment. The gap between our attitudes and behaviours is discussed in Chapter 5.

social desirability refers to the tendency of participants to respond in a way that will be viewed favourably by others, including the researcher

In the 1990s the field of **conservation psychology** was defined, which brought together not only environmental psychologists, but all psychologists with an

conservation psychology a field of psychology that focuses on the relationship between people and the natural world

Biophilic buildings, such as One Central Park in Sydney, are an example of trying to connect people with nature, even in some of the most urban and heavily built-up areas.

SOURCE: ©Katharina13/Shutterstock

interest in addressing matters of environmental sustainability and resilience. In their landmark book, *Conservation Psychology: Understanding and Promoting Human Care for Nature,* Clayton and Myers (2015) make a bold claim; that before humans will do anything to protect and restore the natural world, they have to care about it. This includes facilitating good attitudes *and* sustainable behaviours towards the natural world – key concepts in social psychology for long-term change.

'We shape our buildings, and afterwards our buildings shape us.'

Winston Churchill – British Prime Minister, 1940–1945

As a result of these fields of enquiry and the sharing of knowledge across disciplines and sub-disciplines, social psychology has become well placed to encourage sustainable behaviour and help people mitigate against environmental disasters; forging resilience against crises that do occur. Indeed to understand how people think and react to environmental disasters we need insights into human social cognition and its many quirks (see Chapter 4). As such, social psychology becomes crucial to understanding how people (mis)perceive and respond to environmental risks.

availability heuristic a rule of thumb that judges the likelihood of things based on their availability in memory. If something comes readily to mind, we presume it to be commonplace

Perception of Risk

Risk perception here refers to our subjective evaluation of the likelihood of an environmental disaster happening and what its characteristics will be. We know from a wealth of social psychological work that people are not perfect at identifying or evaluating environmental risk. They often under- or over-estimate the likelihood and the severity (Slovic, 1992). As we see in Chapter 4, people use heuristics when they try to understand the world around them. Let's take the example of climate change; an undeniably highly complex issue. Unless you're a scientist with a specific interest in it and in possession of the relevant knowledge, you're probably going to make judgements about it based on heuristical thinking. The **availability heuristic** affects our estimates of likelihood. If we can bring an environmental disaster to mind easily, we tend to assume that's because its commonplace. For example, Mase et al. (2015) found that agricultural advisors who perceived variations in weather change, believed climate change was occurring in response to human activities, and that agricultural practices needed to be revised accordingly. And it is not just advisors who are influenced by the weather. Research shows that the rest of us are too. Experiencing a spate of warm weather, or even the presence of dead plants, can ratchet up how commonplace and serious we believe global warming to be (e.g. Guéguen, 2012). However, what we can bring to mind easily is not just what we've experienced, but also what we see in the media. The slow creep of biodiversity loss is less easily imagined, and certainly under-reported, but arguably poses more threat to all of us than the polar-bear clinging to the ice-cap that is so readily available in our minds.

Climate change is happening elsewhere? We can bring vivid images of climate change to mind easily, but the gradual environmental changes that affect us all are less easily imagined.

SOURCE: ©Richard Wear/ Design Pics

In a study trying to understand why people in Dhaka City, Bangladesh, were so woefully under-prepared for earthquakes, Paul and Bhuiyan (2010) asked 444 residents who lived there. Bangladesh has a history of major earthquakes which has had a significant impact upon its people and its infrastructure. So why not prepare for the likelihood it will happen again? Paul and Bhuiyan's survey found that whilst their participants acknowledged an earthquake was likely, and that it would result in death and injury, they did not believe it would affect them personally. Displaying the **optimism bias**, Paul's participants did not believe it would affect them or their families, or their possessions. This is also an example of *psychological distancing* where the negative effects of an environmental disaster are pushed away from the individual and onto others. Impacts can also be distanced through time (it will happen in the future) and space (not here). Yet if we address this, then change can occur. Arnocky et al. (2014) discovered that if students were primed to imagine themselves 4 years into the future, they expressed more concern for the environment and willingness to take pro-social action about environmental degradation, than if they were primed to consider themselves as they are today. Minimizing the psychological distance between the individual and the 'problem' seems to help motivate attitudes and actions towards environmental sustainability.

optimism bias the belief that negative events will not happen to one's self

Responding and Resilience

When an environmental disaster strikes, we respond. Often our response is too late, and we react to the event as it happens or afterwards. So, why are we so slow to prepare for disasters, even when we know they're likely to happen?

A body of work by Robert Gifford, including broadcasts for the BBC, offers some answers. Many of these answers lie in the biases and heuristics that define human cognition – some of which we've already discussed here and in Chapter 4. These include optimism bias, **confirmation bias**, **judgemental discounting**, **illusion of control** and so on. These all offer some explanation as to why we fail to act in good time. But interestingly, Gifford offers an evolutionary and neuroscientific explanation for these quirks in our cognition: our *ancient brain*. He points out that according to neuro-scientists, the human brain has not physically changed much over the past 30,000 years, but our environment has. Thirty thousand years ago we were living off the land, wandering around looking for food and shelter, primed to deal with immediate threats to our basic requirements to survive. Long-term thinking about the future was not necessary. It was the here and now that mattered simply to survive the day. However, environmental degradation, climate change and disasters require future planning, of which we're capable but it's not our default position. We're still programmed to deal with immediate threats.

confirmation bias a tendency to search for information that confirms one's preconceptions, rather than considering opposing information

judgemental discounting describes the dismissing or under-estimation of risk when the prospect of it happening is uncertain, remote, or unlikely to affect us personally

illusion of control perception of uncontrollable events as subject to one's control or as more controllable than they are

But there is good news. Research has documented collective community action to respond and be resilient to environmental disasters (e.g. Gow & Paton, 2008). *Community resilience* refers to 'the capacity or ability of a community to anticipate, prepare for, respond to, and recover quickly from impacts of disasters' (Mayunga, 2007, p. 2). This goes beyond the formal top-down responses we would expect from the police, fire brigade, politicians and so on to a disaster, but instead examines bottom-up responses, where local people pool their resources to support one another. The social scientists call such resources 'social capital'; or, as LaLone (2012) terms it, 'neighbours helping neighbours'. Resources pooled could be financial, to fund flood defences for homes, for example, or could be food and shelter should disaster strike. In her study of resilience amongst the rural Pulaski community, affected by tornadoes in the Appalachian area in 2011, LaLone looks at this community's resilience in the immediate aftermath of the tornadoes and beyond. Shared community identity, as well as social norms of reciprocity amongst neighbours, resulted in aid being organized and distributed very quickly. Neighbours and friends helped with clean-up operations whilst looking for anyone trapped under the rubble. Moreover, in the following weeks, as the formal agencies withdrew their services, the Pulaski community continued to raise money and embark on an agreed plan of resilience against future disasters. So it seems social psychological understandings of identity and the relationship to pro-social behaviour are vital to not just understanding resilience, but also offer a way forward in tackling environmental disasters before they happen.

'All our wants, beyond those which a very moderate income will supply, are purely imaginary.'
Henry St John, Letter to Swift, 1719

Research close-up

Nudging Ourselves Towards Sustainable Behaviour

Source: Torma, G., Aschemann-Witzel, J., & Thógersen, J. (2018). I nudge myself: Exploring 'self-nudging' strategies to drive sustainable consumption behaviour. *International Journal of Consumer Studies, 42*(1), 141–154.

Introduction

When we visit the shops to buy our groceries we are not rational consumers. We tend to rely on shortcuts such as what we've bought before and are tempted by 'offers' and 'deals'. We might also be in a rush, on a budget, dealing with a crying toddler, and all manner of other circumstances that affect how we shop. This means that for most of us, our consumer habits are not environmentally friendly. We don't want to take the effort to read labels to check if a product is 'green'. We're reluctant to pay the extra money to purchase an ecologically friendly onion, and so on. Engaging in environmentally friendly behaviour usually requires more effort. But if we have environmentally friendly intentions (or attitudes) is it possible that we might 'nudge' ourselves into behaviour that fits with those intentions? This study aimed to find out if self-nudging was a strategy used by people who considered themselves as having an environmentally friendly identity with 'green' intentions.

Method

Employees of a Danish university were asked to suggest possible participants for the study. Ten participants were recruited as a result. They were seven women and three men, aged 25–70 years, from a range of occupational backgrounds but predominantly jobs requiring a fairly advanced level of educational training (e.g. academic staff, biologist). All ten had signed up to an 'organic box' delivery of food independently of the study. This entailed a weekly delivery of organic fruit and vegetables sufficient to feed four people for 3–4 days. Participants were interviewed at a location of their choice for between 60 and 90 minutes. The recordings were transcribed verbatim. The semi-structured interviews began with questions asked about their shopping and eating habits before signing up to the organic box scheme and afterwards. Problem-centred interviewing (PCI) was then used to gain insights into participants' motivations and reflections on their decision to sign up to an organic box. Interviews were transcribed using thematic textual analysis.

Findings

Participants reported dissatisfaction with their former shopping habits. They reflected on the way they made choices about products. Choices were often governed by situational factors such as being in a rush, or not finding the product you wanted to rushing to grab something else. They also noted mindless shopping. For example, one interview stated that:

> 'I would go to the supermarket and I would put the list in my pocket, and I'll try and remember what's on the list, but then I will see an offer and I will buy it, you know, I'll see, so I buy with my eyes, I'll see the strawberries, and get the strawberries, I love good food, so I will just buy what I see: I see a good offer on steak, and, you know, I'll buy the steak. It'll be, it will be too expensive. (. . .) So it's a perfect thing that (I) don't have to shop.'

Participants also noted how their intention to buy organic was often thwarted by that product being unavailable in the shop, or too expensive, or didn't look very appetizing. Consequently, signing up to the organic box resolved those issues (it is a fixed price box), and provided a long-term commitment to behaving in a sustainable way with respect to food choices.

Since receiving the boxes, participants reported a change in their eating habits. One participant claimed that:

> 'So you know, we should all – we should all try to eat less, have healthier diet, eat less meat and then we may be able to get to the situations where we have sustainable farming (. . .). The box is quite a nice reminder of what you are trying to – we all need reminders sometimes of, yeah, that we want to live more sustainably, or it is just a reminder about, trying to. . . have a healthier diet, yeah, I guess have a healthier diet in that case.'

Discussion

This study has explored how people 'nudge' themselves to resolve the intention (or attitude)–behaviour gap. They can be 'at peace' with their pro-environmentally friendly identity. Some initial cognitive effort (signing up) resolves a longer-term problem which requires little further effort. The box arrives every week. Participants like the organic box service as it forces them into engaging in sustainable behaviour. For long-term behavioural change, self-nudging is important as it involves commitment and resolves an internal dilemma. Therefore studies into nudging behaviour should further consider the role of self-nudging as well as nudges provided by researchers.

Critical Reflections

The researchers themselves acknowledge some limitations of their study. Social desirability bias may have influenced interviewee responses. Moreover the study took place in one country and therefore does not take cross-cultural comparisons into account. We could add to this list that the study only considered participant behaviour with respect to particular eating habits. It tells us nothing about their other environmentally friendly behaviour (or lack of it!). There are other issues to be mindful of here when considering this study. Ten participants is quite a small sample. Might we have found more diverse views from a larger and more diverse sample? Related to this, these participants already have pro-environmental attitudes. Understanding how and why they nudged themselves is not too challenging. What is more challenging is how self-nudging might occur in people who do not have pro-environmental intentions. Is this at all possible?

SUMMING UP: APPLIED SOCIAL PSYCHOLOGY

- Social psychology seeks to understand real-world issues and offer insights that will ensure we live happier and healthier lives. Three examples of areas in which social psychology has been applied are the workplace, health and illness, and the environment.
- Motivation to work comes from a range of factors including the satisfaction of personal and professional needs and goals, perceptions of fairness, self-esteem and the development of a positive self and social identity.
- To understand and tackle stress in the workplace we need to pay attention to physiological and psychological contributors. These range from immediate situational problems in our working environment to our relationships with others.
- Effective leadership in the workplace requires the adaptation of a style that is appropriate to the organization and fosters harmonious and positive relationships with others.
- Research into leadership would benefit from closer scrutiny of processes that hinder diversity at the most senior levels of management. Leadership research has the potential to encourage and facilitate better representation across all cultural, ethnic, racial, sexual and gender groups in positions of leadership.
- Teamwork helps to increase motivation, efficiency, accomplishment of goals and well-being within the workplace. However, the downsides of teamwork mean that decisions made can be unnecessarily extreme and risky.
- Clinical judgements can be influenced by a range of cognitive, social and cultural biases.
- Behaviour problems such as depression and loneliness can be understood by examining cognitive processes such as attributional style, and also social relations that exist within a particular situation and/or in a culture.
- Changes in external behaviour can be nudged, and may lead to internal change in cognitions and emotions.
- Health and happiness are influenced by social relations such as close supportive relationships.
- Concepts in social psychology can help humanity prepare against environmental disasters and create a sustainable future by increasing energy-saving technology and attending to our own behaviour.
- To build a sustainable and satisfying future, we can individually seek and, as a society, promote close relationships, social networks based on belief, positive thinking habits and engaging activity.

Critical Questions

1. What insights have social psychologists offered to help managers motivate their employees in the workplace?
2. What can we learn from social psychology about health and well-being?
3. How might cultural norms and values influence our understandings of health and illness?
4. How can social psychology help address the problem of over-consumption?
5. What role can social psychology play in encouraging environmentally sustainable behaviours such as recycling, food-shopping, etc?
6. How can social psychology foster resilience to environmental disasters?

Recommended Reading

Listed below are some classic and contemporary readings in applied social psychology in the workplace, health and illness, and the environment and sustainable future.

Classic Readings

Abramson, L. Y., Seligman, M. E. P., & Teasdale, J. D. (1978). Learned helplessness in humans: Critique and reformulation. *Journal of Abnormal Psychology, 87,* 49–74.

Fiedler, F. E. (1967). *A theory of leadership effectiveness.* McGraw-Hill.

Ittelson, W. H., Proshansky, H., Rivlin, L., & Winkel, G. (1974). *An introduction to environmental psychology.* Holt, Rinehart &Winston.

Maslow, A. H. (1943). A theory of human motivation. *Psychological Review, 50*(4), 370–396.

Contemporary Readings

Clayton, S., & Myers, G. (2015). *Conservation psychology: Understanding and promoting human care for nature.* John Wiley & Sons.

Gifford, R., Kormos, C., & McIntyre, A. (2011). Behavioral dimensions of climate change: Drivers, responses, barriers, and interventions. *Wiley Interdisciplinary Reviews: Climate Change, 2*(6), 801–827.

Landy, F., & Conte, J. (2007). *Work in the 21st century: An introduction to industrial and organizational psychology.* Blackwell.

Laustsen, L., Petersen, M. B., & Klofstad, C. A. (2015). Vote choice, ideology, and social dominance orientation influence preferences for lower pitched voices in political candidates. *Evolutionary Psychology, 13*(3), 1–13.

Meyer, I. H. (2015). Resilience in the study of minority stress and health of sexual and gender minorities. *Psychology of Sexual Orientation and Gender Diversity, 2*(3), 209–213.

Ryan, M. K., Haslam, S. A., Morgenroth, T., Rink, F., Stoker, J., & Peters, K. (2016). Getting on top of the glass cliff: Reviewing a decade of evidence, explanations, and impact. *The Leadership Quarterly, 27*(3), 446–455.

Epilogue

A knowledge of social psychology, we believe, has the power to restrain intuition with critical thinking, illusion with understanding, and judgementalism with compassion. In these 15 chapters, we have assembled social psychology's insights into belief and persuasion, love and hate, conformity, intergroup relations, prejudice and independence. We have glimpsed incomplete answers to intriguing questions: how do our attitudes feed and get fed by our actions? What leads people sometimes to hurt and sometimes to help one another? What kindles social conflict, and how can we transform closed fists into helping hands? Answering such questions expands our minds. Such has been our experience, and hopefully yours too. We hope you enjoy your journey into social psychology and all that it has to offer.

References

A

Aarssen, L. W. and Altman, S. T. (2006). Explaining below-replacement fertility and increasing childlessness in wealthy countries: Legacy drive and the 'Transmission Competition' hypothesis. *Evolutionary Psychology,* **4**(1), 290–302. https://doi.org/10.1177/147470490600400125.

Abay, K.A., Blalock, G., & Berhane, G. (2017). Locus of control and technology adoption in developing country agriculture: Evidence from Ethiopia. *Journal of Economic Behavior and Organization,* **143,** 98–115.

Abbey, A. (1987). Misperceptions of friendly behavior as sexual interest: A survey of naturally occurring incidents. *Psychology of Women Quarterly,* **11,** 173–194.

Abbey, A. (1991). Misperception as an antecedent of acquaintance rape: A consequence of ambiguity in communication between women and men. In A. Parrot (Ed.), *Acquaintance rape.* John Wiley.

Abbey, A., McAuslan, P., & Ross, L. T. (1998). Sexual assault perpetration by college men: The role of alcohol, misperception of sexual intent, and sexual beliefs and experiences. *Journal of Social and Clinical Psychology,* **17,** 167–195.

Abbey, M., Bartholomew, K. L., Chinbuah, M. A., Gyapong, M., Gyapong, J. O., & van Den Borne, B. (2017). Development of a theory and evidence-based program to promote community treatment of fevers in children under five in a rural district in southern Ghana: An intervention mapping approach. *BMC Public Health,* **17**(1), 1–11. https://doi.org/10.1186/s12889-016-3957-1

ABC News (2004, 28 December). Whistleblower revealed abuse at Abu Ghraib prison. ABCNEWS.go.com.

Abell, J. (2012). Volunteering to help conserve endangered species: An identity approach to human-animal relationships. *Journal of Community and Applied Social Psychology,* **23,** 157–170.

Abell, J., & Stokoe, E. H. (2001). Broadcasting the royal role: Constructing culturally situated identities in the Princess Diana Panorama interview. *British Journal of Social Psychology,* **40,** 417–435.

Abelson, R. P. (1972). Are attitudes necessary? In B. T. King & E. McGinness (Eds.), *Attitudes, conflict and social change.* Academic Press.

Abild, M., Vanderlaan, D., & Vasey, P. (2013). No evidence for treating friends' children like kin in Canadian androphilic men. *Journal of Sex Research,* **50**(7), 697–703.

Abild, M. L., VanderLaan, D. P., & Vasey, P. L. (2014). Does geographic proximity influence the expression of avuncular tendencies in Canadian androphilic males?*Journal of Cognition and Culture,* **14**(1–2), 41–63.

Aboud, F. E., & Amato, M. (2001). Developmental and socialization influences on intergroup bias. In R. Brown & S. Gaertner (Eds.), *Blackwell handbook of social psychology: Intergroup processes* (Vol. 4). Blackwell.

Abraham, J. (1989). Testing Hargreaves' and Lacey's differentiation-polarisation theory in a setted comprehensive. *British Journal of Sociology,* **40**(1), 46–81.

Abrams, D., Hogg, M. A., Hinkle, S., & Often, S. (2005). The social identity perspective on small groups. In M. S. Poole & A. B. Hollingshead (Eds.), *Theories of small groups: Interdisciplinary perspectives* (pp. 99–137). Sage Publications. https://doi.org/10.4135/9781483328935.n4

Abrams, D., Hopthrow, T., Hulbert, L. G., & Frings, D. (2006). Groupdrink? The effect of alcohol on risk attraction among groups versus individuals. *Journal of Studies on Alcohol,* **67**(4), 628–636.

Abrams, D., Rutland, A., & Cameron, L. (2003). The development of subjective group dynamics: Children's judgements of normative and deviant in-group and out-group individuals. *Child Development,* **74**(6), 1840–1856.

Abrams, D., Viki, G. T., Masser, B., & Bohner, G. (2003). Perceptions of stranger and acquaintance rape: The role of benevolent and hostile sexism in victim blame and rape proclivity. *Journal of Personality and Social Psychology,* **84**(1), 111–125.

Abrams, D., Wetherell, M., Cochrane, S., Hogg, M. A., & Turner, J. C. (1986). Knowing what to think by knowing who you are: Self-categorization and the nature of norm formation, conformity and group polarization. *British Journal of Social Psychology,* **29,** 97–119.

Abramson, L. Y., Seligman, M. E. P., & Teasdale, J. D. (1978). Learned helplessness in humans: Critique and reformulation. *Journal of Abnormal Psychology,* **87,** 49–74.

Acevedo, B. P., & Aron, A. (2009). Does a long-term relationship kill romantic love?*Review of General Psychology,* **13**(1), 59–65.

Addis, M. E., & Mahalik, J. R. (2003). Men, masculinity, and the contexts of help seeking. *American Psychologist,* **58,** 5–4.

Addison, S. J., & Thorpe, S. J. (2004). Factors involved in the formation of attitudes towards those who are mentally ill. *Social Psychiatry and Psychiatric Epidemiology,* **39,** 228–234.

Adler, N. E., & Snibbe, A. C. (2003). The role of psychosocial processes in explaining the gradient between socioeconomic status and health. *Current Directions in Psychological Science,* **12,** 119–123.

Adorno, T., Frenkel-Brunswik, E., Levinson, D., & Sanford, R. N. (1950). *The authoritarian personality.* Harper.

Adorno, T. W., Frenkel-Brunswik, E., Levinson, D. J., & Sanford, R. N. (1982). *The authoritarian personality* (abridged ed.). Norton.

Adriaens, P. R., & De Block, A. (2006). The evolution of a social construction: The case of male homosexuality. *Perspectives in Biology and Medicine,* **49**(4), 570–585.

Ağralı, H., & Akyar, ï. (2014). Older diabetic patients' attitudes and beliefs about health and illness. *Journal of Clinical Nursing,* **23**(21–22), 3077–3086. https://doi.org/10.1111/jocn.12540

Ahlfinger, N. R., & Esser, J. K. (2001). Testing the groupthink model: Effects of promotional leadership and conformity predisposition. *Social Behavior and Personality,* **29**(1), 31–41.

Ahluwalia, R. (2000). Examination of psychological processes underlying resistance to persuasion. *Journal of Consumer Research,* **27**(2), 217–232. https://doi.org/10.1086/314321

Aiello, J. R., & Douthitt, E. Z. (2001). Social facilitation from Triplett to electronic performance monitoring. *Group Dynamics: Theory, Research, and Practice,* **5,** 163–180.

Aikman, S. N., Min, K. E., & Graham, D. (2006). Food attitudes, eating behaviour and the information underlying food attitudes. *Appetite,* **47,** 111–114.

Ainsworth, M. D. S. (1973). The development of infant–mother attachment. In B. Caldwell & H. Ricciuti (Eds.), *Review of child development research* (Vol. 3). University of Chicago Press.

Ainsworth, M. D. S. (1979). Infant–mother attachment. *American Psychologist,* **34,** 932–937.

Ajzen, I. (1985). From intentions to actions: A theory of planned behaviour. In J. Kuhl & J. Beckmann (Eds.), *Action control: From cognition to behaviour* (pp. 11–39). Springer Verlag.

Ajzen, I., & Fishbein, M. (1977). Attitude–behavior relations: A theoretical analysis and review of empirical research. *Psychological Bulletin,* **84,** 888–918.

Ajzen, I., & Fishbein, M. (2005). The influence of attitudes on behavior. In D. Albarracin, B. T. Johnson, & M. P. Zanna (Eds.), *The handbook of attitudes.* Erlbaum.

Ajzen, I., & Madden, T. J. (1986). Prediction of goal-directed behavior: Attitudes, intentions, and perceived behavioral control. *Journal of Experimental Social Psychology,* **22,** 453–474.

Akin, A. (2012). Self-handicapping and burnout. *Psychological Reports,* **110**(1), 187–196.

Aknin, L. B., Van de Vondervoort, J. W., & Hamlin, J. K. (2018). Positive feelings reward and promote prosocial behavior. *Current Opinion in Psychology,* **20,** 55–59. https://doi.org/10.1016/j.copsyc.2017.08.017

Aknin, L. B., Whillans, A. V., Norton, M. I., & Dunn, E. W. (2019). Happiness and proscoial behaviour: An evaluation of the evidence. In J. Helliwell, R. Layard, & J. Sachs (Eds.), *World happiness report 2019.* Sustainable Development Solutions Network. https://worldhappiness.report/ed/2019/happiness-and-prosocial-behavior-an-evaluation-of-the-evidence/

Aksoy, A., & Robins, K. (2002). Banal transnationalism: The difference that television makes. University of Oxford Transnational Communities Programme Working Paper Series. http://www.transcomm.ac.uk/wp/02,

Albarracin, D., Gillette, J. C., Ho, M-H., Earl, A. N., Glasman, L. R., & Durantini, M. R. (2005). A test of major assumptions about behavior change: A comprehensive look at the effects of passive and active HIV-prevention interventions since the beginning of the epidemic. *Psychological Bulletin,* **131**, 856–897.

Albarracin, D., McNatt, P. S., Klein, C. T. F., Ho, R. M., Mitchell, A. L., & Kumkale, G. T. (2003). Persuasive communications to change actions: An analysis of behavioral and cognitive impact in HIV prevention. *Health Psychology,* **22**, 166–177.

Albouy, J., & Decaudin, J. M. (2018). Age differences in responsiveness to shocking prosocial campaigns. *Journal of Consumer Marketing,* **35**(3), 328–339. https://doi.org/10.1108/JCM-02-2016-1713

Alfred, C. (2015, 20 March). 20 years ago, a shadowy cult poisoned the Tokyo subway. *Huffington Post.* https://www.huffingtonpost.co.uk/2015/03/20/tokyo-subway-sarin-attack_n_6896754.html

Alhabash, S., & Wise, K. (2012). PeaceMaker: Changing students' attitudes toward Palestinians and Israelis through video game play (Report). *International Journal of Communication (Online).* University of Southern California, Annenberg School for Communication & Journalism, Annenberg Press.

Allee, W. C., & Masure, R. M. (1936). A comparison of maze behavior in paired and isolated shell-parakeets (*Melopsittacus undulatus Shaw*) in a two-alley problem box. *Journal of Comparative Psychology,* **22**, 131–155.

Allemand, M., Amberg, I., Zimprich, D., & Fincham, F. D. (2007). The role of trait forgiveness and relationship satisfaction in episodic forgiveness. *Journal of Social and Clinical Psychology,* **26**, 199–217.

Allen, V. L., & Levine, J. M. (1969). Consensus and conformity. *Journal of Experimental Social Psychology,* **5**, 389–399.

Allison, S. T., Jordan, M. R., & Yeatts, C. E. (1992). A cluster-analytic approach toward identifying the structure and content of human decision making. *Human Relations,* **45**, 49–72.

Allport, F. (1920). The influence of the group upon association and thought. *Journal of Experimental Psychology,* **3**, 159–182.

Allport, F. (1924). *Social psychology.* Houghton Mifflin.

Allport, G. W. (1935). Attitudes. In C. M. Murchinson (Ed.), *Handbook of social psychology* (pp. 789–844). Clark University Press.

Allport, G. W. (1954). *The nature of prejudice.* Perseus Books.

Aloka, P. J. O., & Bojuwoye, O. (2013). Group polarization effects on decisions by selected Kenyan secondary school disciplinary panels. *Journal of Psychology in Africa,* **23**(2), 275–282. https://doi.org/10.1080/14330237.2013.10820624

Altman, I., & Taylor, D. A. (1973). *Social penetration: The development of interpersonal relationships.* Holt, Rinehart & Winston.

Amato, P. R., & Kane, J. B. (2011). Parents' marital distress, divorce, and remarriage: Links with daughters' early family formation transitions. *Journal of Family Issues,* **32**(8), 1073–1103. https://doi.org/10.1177/0192513X11404363

Ambady, N., & Bharucha, J. (2009). Culture and the brain. *Current Directions in Psychological Science,* **18**(6), 342–345. https://doi.org/10.1111/j.1467-8721.2009.01664.x

American Society for Aesthetic Plastic Surgery, The (2018). Procedural statistics 2018. https://www.surgery.org/media/statistics

American Society of Plastic Surgeons (2019, June 12). *More men undergo plastic surgery as the daddy-do-over trend rises in popularity.* https://www.plasticsurgery.org/news/press-releases/more-men-undergo-plastic-surgery-as-the-daddy-do-over-trend-rises-in-popularity

Ames, D. R. (2004). Strategies for social inference: A similarity contingency model of projection and stereotyping in attitude prevalence estimates. *Journal of Personality and Social Psychology,* **87**, 573–585.

Amichai-Hamburger, Y., McKenna, K. Y., & Tal, S. A. (2008). E-empowerment: Empowerment by the Internet. *Computers in Human Behavior,* **24**(5), 1776–1789.

Amir, Y. (1969). Contact hypothesis in ethnic relations. *Psychological Bulletin,* **71**, 319–342.

Amodio, D. M., & Keysers, C. (2018). Editorial overview: New advances in social neuroscience: from neural computations to social structures. *Current Opinion in Psychology,* **24**, iv–vi.

Amodio, D. M., & Ratner, K. G. (2011). A memory systems model of implicit social cognition. *Current Directions in Psychological Science,* **20**, 143–148.

Andersen, S. M. (1998). *Service learning: A national strategy for youth development. A position paper issued by the Task Force on Education Policy.* Institute for Communitarian Policy Studies, George Washington University.

Andersen, S. M., & Chen, S. (2002). The relational self: An interpersonal social-cognitive theory. *Psychological Review,* **109**, 619–645.

Andersen, S. M., Saribay, S. A., & Thorpe, J. S. (2008). Simple kindness can go a long way: Relationships, social identity and engagement. *Social Psychology,* **39**(1), 59–69.

Anderson, C. A. (1999). Attributional style, depression, and loneliness: A cross-cultural comparison of American and Chinese students. *Personality and Social Psychology Bulletin,* **25**, 482–499.

Anderson, C. A. (2001). Heat and violence. *Current Directions in Psychological Science,* **10**(1), 33–38.

Anderson, C. A. (2003). Video games and aggressive behavior. In D. Ravitch and J. P. Viteritti (Eds.), *Kids stuff: Marking violence and vulgarity in the popular culture.* Johns Hopkins University Press.

Anderson, C. A. (2004). An update on the effects of violent video games. *Journal of Adolescence,* **27**, 113–122.

Anderson, C. A., & Bushman, B. J. (1997). External validity of 'trivial' experiments: The case of laboratory aggression. *Review of General Psychology,* **1**, 19–41.

Anderson, C. A., & Bushman, B. J. (2002). Human aggression. *Annual Review of Psychology,* **53**, 27–51.

Anderson, C. A., Berkowitz, L., Donnerstein, E., Huesmann, L. R., Johnson, J. D., Linz, D., Malamuth, N. M., & Wartella, E. (2003). The influence of media violence on youth. *Psychological Science in the Public Interest,* **4**(3), 81–110.

Anderson, C. A., Bushman, B. J., Donnerstein, E., Hummer, T. A., & Warburton, W. (2015). SPssI research summary on media violence. *Analyses of Social Issues and Public Policy,* **15**(1), 4–19.

Anderson, C. A., Carnagey, N. L., & Eubanks, J. (2003). Exposure to violent media: The effects of songs with violent lyrics on aggressive thoughts and feelings. *Journal of Personality and Social Psychology,* **84**(5), 960–971.

Anderson, C. A., Carnagey, N. L., Flanagan, M., Benjamin, A. J. Jr., Eubanks, J., & Valentine, J. C. (2004). Violent video games: Specific effects of violent content on aggressive thoughts and behavior. *Advances in Experimental Social Psychology,* **36**, 199–249.

Anderson, C. A., Deuser, W. E., & DeNeve, K. M. (1995). Hot temperatures, hostile affect, hostile cognition, and arousal: Tests of a general model of affective aggression. *Personality and Social Psychology Bulletin,* **21**, 434–448.

Anderson, C. A., Lepper, M. R., & Ross, L. (1980). Perseverance of social theories: The role of explanation in the persistence of discredited information. *Journal of Personality and Social Psychology,* **39**, 1037–1049.

Anderson, C. A., Shibuya, A., Ihori, N., Swing, E. L., Bushman, B. J., Sakamoto, A., Rothstein, H. R., & Saleem, M. (2010). Violent video game effects on aggression, empathy, and prosocial behavior in Eastern and Western countries: A meta-analytic review. *Psychological Bulletin,* **136**, 151–173.

Anderson, C., Keltner, D., & John, O. P. (2003). Emotional convergence between people over time. *Journal of Personality and Social Psychology,* **84**, 1054–1068.

Andersson, G., Noack, T., Seierstad, A., & Weedon-Fekjær, H. (2006). The demographics of same-sex marriages in Norway and Sweden. *Demography,* **43**, 79–98.

Andersson, L. M. C., Schierenbeck, I., Strumpher, J., Krantz, G., Topper, K., Backman, G., Ricks, E., & van Rooyen, D. (2013). Help-seeking behaviour, barriers to care and experiences of care amongst persons with depression in Eastern Cape, South Africa. *Journal of Affective Disorders,* **151**, 439–448.

Andreas, J. B., & Watson, M. W. (2009). Moderating effects of family environment on the association between children's aggressive beliefs and their aggression trajectories from childhood to adolescence. *Development and Psychopathology,* **21**, 189–205.

Andreoni, J., & Petrie, R. (2008). Beauty, gender

and stereotypes: Evidence from laboratory experiments. *Journal of Economic Psychology*, **29**(1), 73–93.

Andrews, P. W., & Thomson, J. A., Jr (2009). The bright side of being blue: Depression as an adaptation for analyzing complex problems. *Psychological Review*, **116**(3), 620–654.

Ang, R. P., & Goh, D. H. (2010). Cyberbullying among adolescents: the role of affective and cognitive empathy, and gender. *Child Psychiatry and Human Development*, **41,** 387–310.

Ängarne-Lindberg, T. (2009). Fifteen years after parental divorce: Mental health and experienced life-events. *Nordic Journal of Psychiatry*, **61,** 32–43.

Angelakis, I., Gooding, P. A., & Panagioti, M. (2016). Suicidality in body dysmorphic disorder (BDD): A systematic review with meta-analysis. *Clinical Psychology Review*, **49,** 55–66. https://dx.doi.org/10.1016/j.cpr.2016.08.002

Anker, A. E., Akey, J. E., & Feeley, T. H. (2013). Providing social support in a persuasive context: Forms of social support reported by organ procurement coordinators. *Health Communication*, **28**(8), 835–845. https://doi.org/10.1080/10410236.2012.728468

Antaki, C., & Widdicombe, S. (1998). *Identities in talk*. Sage.

Antfolk, J., Karlsson, M., Bäckström, A., & Santtila, P. (2012). Disgust elicited by third-party incest: The roles of biological relatedness, co-residence, and family relationship. *Evolution and Human Behavior*, **33**(3), 217–223. https://doi.org/10.1016/j.evolhumbehav.2011.09.005

Antonio, A. L., Chang, M. J., Hakuta, K., Kenny, D. A., Levin, S., & Milem, J. F. (2004). Effects of racial diversity on complex thinking in college students. *Psychological Science*, **15,** 507–510.

Antonucci, T., Akiyama, H., & Takahashi, K. (2004). Attachment and close relationships across the life span. *Attachment and Human Development*, **6**(4), 353–370.

Anvari, F., Wenzel, M., Woodyatt, L., & Haslam, S. A. (2019). The social psychology of whistleblowing: An integrated model. *Organizational Psychology Review*, **9**(1), 41–67. https://doi.org/10.1177/204138661984908

Aoun, S., Osseiran-Moisson, R., Shahid, S., Howat, P., & O'Connor, M. (2011). Telephone lifestyle coaching: Is it feasible as a behavioural change intervention for men?*Journal of Health Psychology*, **17**(2), 227–236. https://doi.org/10.1177/1359105311413480

Apostolou, M., Shialos, M., Khalil, M., & Paschali, V. (2017). The evolution of female same-sex attraction: The male choice hypothesis. *Personality and Individual Differences*, **116,** 372–378. https://doi.org/10.1016/j.paid.2017.05.020

Archer, J. (1991). The influence of testosterone on human aggression. *British Journal of Psychology*, **82,** 1–28.

Arendt, H. (1963/1994). *Eichmann in Jerusalem: A report on the banality of evil*. Viking Press, Penguin.

Arkin, R. M., Lake, E. A., & Baumgardner, A. H. (1986). Shyness and self-presentation. In W. H. Jones, J. M. Cheek, & S. R. Briggs (Eds.), *Shyness: Perspectives on research and treatment*. Plenum.

Armor, D. A., & Taylor, S. E. (1996). Situated optimism: Specific outcome expectancies and self-regulation. In M. P. Zanna (Ed.), *Advances in experimental social psychology* (Vol. 30). Academic Press.

Arnett, J. J. (2010). Oh, grow up! Generational grumbling and the new life stage of emerging adulthood – Commentary on Trzesniewski & Donnellan (2010). *Perspectives on Psychological Science*, **5,** 89–92.

Arnocky, S., Milfont, T., & Nicol, J. (2014). Time perspective and sustainable behavior: Evidence for the distinction between consideration of immediate and future consequences. *Environment and Behavior*, **46**(5), 556–582.

Arnold, J., Cooper, C. L., & Robertson, I. T. (1998). *Work psychology: Understanding human behaviour in the workplace*. Prentice-Hall.

Aron, A., & Aron, E. (1989). *The heart of social psychology* (2nd ed.). Lexington Books.

Aron, A., Aron, E. N., & Norman, C. (2001). The self expansion model of motivation and cognition in close relationships and beyond. In M. Clark & G. Fletcher (Eds.), *Blackwell handbook in social psychology:* Vol. 2. *Interpersonal processes* (pp. 478–501). Blackwell.

Aron, A., Fisher, H., Mashek, D. J., Strong, G., Li, H., & Brown, L. L. (2005). Reward, motivation, and emotion systems associated with early-stage intense romantic love. *Journal of Neurophysiology*, **94,** 327–337.

Aron, A., Lewandowski, G. W. Jr, Mashek, D., & Aron, E. N. (2013). The self-expansion model of motivation and cognition in close relationships. In J. Simpson & L. Campbell (Eds.), *The Oxford handbook of close relationships* (pp.90–115). Oxford University Press.

Aron, A., Norman, C. C., Aron, E. N., McKenna, C., & Heyman, R. E. (2000). Couples' shared participation in novel and arousing activities and experienced relationship quality. *Journal of Personality and Social Psychology*, **78,** 273–284.

Aron, A., Steele, J. L., Kashdan, T. B., & Perez, M. (2006). When similars do not attract: Tests of a prediction from the self-expansion model. *Personal Relationships*, **13**(4), 387–396.

Aronson, E., & Linder, D. (1965). Gain and loss of esteem as determinants of interpersonal attractiveness. *Journal of Experimental Social Psychology*, **1,** 156–171.

Arora, R. (2005). China's 'Gen Y' bucks tradition. Gallup Poll, http://www.gallup.com/poll/15934/Chinas-Gen-Bucks-Tradition.aspx (accessed 27 August 2013).

Arpan, L. M. (2002). When in Rome? The effects of spokesperson ethnicity on audience evaluation of crisis communication. *Journal of Business Communication*, **39**(3), 314–339. https://doi.org/10.1177/002194360203900302

Arpino, B., Esping-Andersen, G., & Pessin, L. (2015). How do changes in gender role attitudes towards female employment influence fertility? A macro-level analysis. *European Sociological Review*, **31**(3), 370–382. https://doi.org/10.1093/esr/jcv002

Arterberry, M. E., Cain, K. M., & Chopko, S. A. (2007). Collaborative problem solving in five-year-old children: Evidence of social facilitation and social loafing. *Educational Psychology*, **27**(5), 577–596.

Asch, S. E. (1946). Forming impressions of personality. *Journal of Abnormal and Social Psychology*, **41,** 258–290.

Asch, S. E. (1952). *Social psychology*. Prentice-Hall.

Asch, S. E. (1955, November). Opinions and social pressure. *Scientific American*, pp. 31–35.

Asch, S. E., & Zukier, H. (1984). Thinking about persons. *Journal of Personality and Social Psychology*, **46,** 1230–1240.

Assilaméhou, Y., & Testé, B. (2013). How you describe a group shows how biased you are: Language abstraction and inferences about a speaker's communicative intentions and attitudes toward a group. *Journal of Language and Social Psychology*, **32**(2), 202–211.

Assouline, S. G., Colangelo, N., Ihrig, D., & Forstadt, L. (2006). Attributional choice for academic success and failure by intellectually gifted student. *Gifted Child Quarterly*, **50**(4), 283–294.

Atherton, O. E., Tackett, J. L., Ferrer, E., & Robins, R. W. (2017). Bidirectional pathways between relational aggression and temperament from late childhood to adolescence. *Journal of Research in Personality*, **67,** 75–84. https://doi.org/10.1016/j.jrp.2016.04.005

Augoustinos, M., & Every, D. (2007a). The language of 'race' and prejudice: A discourse of denial, reason, and liberal-practical politics. *Journal of Language and Social Psychology*, **26**(2), 123–141.

Augoustinos, M., & Every, D. (2007b). The language of contemporary racism. *Journal of Language and Social Psychology*, **26**(2), 123–141.

Augoustinos, M., Tuffin, K., & Sale, L. (1999). Race talk. *Australian Journal of Psychology*, **51,** 90–97.

Augoustinos, M., Walker, I., & Donaghue, N. (2006). *Social cognition: An integrated introduction*. Sage.

Axelrod, R., & Dion, D. (1988). The further evolution of cooperation. *Science*, **242,** 1385–1390.

Ayres, I., Raseman, S., & Shih, A. (2013). Evidence from two large field experiments that peer comparison feedback can reduce residential energy usage. *Journal of Law, Economics, and Organization*, **29**(5), 992–1022. https://doi.org/10.1093/jleo/ews020

Ayres, R., Ingram, J., Rees, A., Neale, J., Beattie, A., & Telfer, M. (2014). Enhancing motivation within a rapid opioid substitution treatment feasibility RCT: A nested qualitative study. *Substance Abuse Treatment, Prevention and Policy*, **9**(1), 44. https://doi.org/10.1186/1747-597X-9-44

Azar, B. (2008). IAT: Fad or fabulous. *Monitor on Psychology*, **39**(7), 44. https://www.apa.org/monitor/2008/07-08/psychometric

Azrin, N. H. (1967, May). Pain and aggression. *Psychology Today,* pp. 27–33.

B

Baars, B. J., & McGovern, K. (1996). Cognitive views of consciousness: What are the facts? How can we explain them? In M. Velmans (Ed.), *The science of consciousness: Psychological, neuropsychological, and clinical reviews.* Routledge.

Babad, E., Bernieri, F., & Rosenthal, R. (1991). Students as judges of teachers' verbal and nonverbal behavior. *American Educational Research Journal,* **28**, 211–234.

Back, M. D., Stopfer, J. M., Vazire, S., Gaddis, S., Schmukle, S. C., Egloff, B., & Gosling, S. D. (2010). Facebook profiles reflect actual personality, not self-idealization. *Psychological Science,* **21**, 372–374.

Backåberg, S., Gummesson, C., Brunt, D., & Rask, M. (2015). 'Is that really my movement?' Students' experiences of a video-supported interactive learning model for movement awareness. *International Journal of Qualitative Studies on Health and Well-Being,* **10**(1), 1–11. https://doi.org/10.3402/qhw.v10.28474

Badahdah, A. M. (2005). Attribution and helping behavior: Testing the attribution-affect-help judgment model in a Saudi sample. *Psychological Reports,* **97**(2), 538–544. https://doi.org/10.2466/pr0.97.2.538-544

Badea, C., Brauer, M., & Rubin, M. (2012). The effects of winning and losing on perceived group variability. *Journal of Experimental Social Psychology,* **48**(5), 1094–1099.

Badie, D. (2010). Groupthink, Iraq, and the war on terror: Explaining US policy shift toward Iraq. *Foreign Policy Analysis,* **6**(4), 277–296.

Bail, K., Cook, R., Gardner, A., & Grealish, L. (2009). Writing ourselves into a web of obedience: A nursing policy analysis. *International Journal of Nursing Studies,* **46**(11), 1457-1466.

Bailenson, J. N., & Yee, N. (2006). A longitudinal study of task performance, head movements, subjective report, simulator sickness, and transformed social interaction in collaborative virtual environments. *PRESENCE: Teleoperators and Virtual Environments,* **15**(6).

Bailey, G. (2018, 26 September). British people will work for an average of 3507 days over a lifetime, survey says. *The Independent.* https://www.independent.co.uk/life-style/british-people-work-days-life-time-overtime-quit-job-survey-study-a8556146.html

Balaam, B. J., & Haslam, S. A. (1998). A closer look at the role of social influence in the development of attitudes to eating. *Journal of Community and Applied Social Psychology,* **8**, 195–212.

Baldwin, M. W., Keelan, J. P. R., Fehr, B., Enns, V., & Koh-Rangarajoo, E. (1996). Social-cognitive conceptualization of attachment working models: Availability and accessibility effects. *Journal of Personality and Social Psychology,* **71**, 94–109.

Bali, A. (2015). Psychological factors affecting sports performance. *International Journal of Physical Education, Sports and Health,* **1**(6), 92–95.

Balkundi, P., Kilduff, M., & Harrison, D. A. (2011). Centrality and charisma: Comparing how leader networks and attributions affect team performance. *Journal of Applied Psychology,* **96**(6), 1209.

Balmas, M., & Sheafer, T. (2014). Charismatic leaders and mediated personalization in the international arena. *Communication Research,* **41**(7), 991–1015. https://doi.org/10.1177/0093650213510936

Balsamo, B., Geil, M.D., Ellis, R., & Wu, J. (2018). Confirmation bias affects user perception of knee braces. *Journal of Biomechanics,* **75**, 164–170, https://doi.org/10.1016/j.jbiomech.2018.04.028

Banaji, M. R. (2004). The opposite of a great truth is also true: Homage of Koan #7. In J. T. Jost, M. R. Banaji, & D. A. Prentice (Eds.), *Perspectivism in social psychology: The yin and yang of scientific progress.* American Psychological Association.

Banaji, M. R. (2004). The opposite of a great truth is also true: Homage to Koan #7. https://sites.fas.harvard.edu/~mrbworks/articles/manuscripts/McGuire.pdf

Bandawe, C. (2010). A brief history of social psychology and its contribution to health in Malawi. *Malawi Medical Journal,* **22**(2), 34–37.

Bandura, A. (1973). *Aggression: A social learning analysis.* Prentice-Hall.

Bandura, A. (1979). The social learning perspective: Mechanisms of aggression. In H. Toch (Ed.), *Psychology of crime and criminal justice.* Holt, Rinehart & Winston.

Bandura, A. (1997). *Self-efficacy: The exercise of control.* Freeman.

Bandura, A. (2000). Social cognitive theory: An agentic perspective. *Annual Review of Psychology,* **52**, 1–26.

Bandura, A., & Walters, R. H. (1959). *Adolescent aggression.* Ronald Press.

Bandura, A., & Walters, R. H. (1963). *Social learning and personality development.* Holt, Rinehart and Winston.

Bandura, A., Pastorelli, C., Barbaranelli, C., & Caprara, G. V. (1999). Self-efficacy pathways to childhood depression. *Journal of Personality and Social Psychology,* **76**, 258–269.

Bandura, A., Ross, D., & Ross, S. A. (1961). Transmission of aggression through imitation of aggressive models. *Journal of Abnormal and Social Psychology,* **63**, 575–582.

Banks, S. M., Salovey, P., Greener, S., Rothman, A. J., Moyer, A., Beauvais, J., & Epel, E. (1995). The effects of message framing on mammography utilization. *Health Psychology,* **14**, 178–184.

Barak, A., & Gluck-Ofri, O. (2007). Degree and reciprocity of self-disclosure in online forums. *CyberPsychology & Behavior,* **10**(3), 407–417.

Barash, D. (1979). *The whisperings within.* Harper & Row.

Barata, R., Castro, P., & Martins-Loução, M. (2017). How to promote conservation behaviours: The combined role of environmental education and commitment. *Environmental Education Research,* **23**(9), 1322–1334.

Barber, B. M., & Odean, T. (2001). Boys will be boys: Gender, overconfidence and common stock investment. *Quarterly Journal of Economics,* **116**, 261–292.

Barber, N. (1995). The evolutionary psychology of physical attractiveness: Sexual selection and human morphology. *Ethology and Sociobiology,* **16**, 395–424.

Barclay, P. (2010). Altruism as a courtship display: Some effects of third-party generosity on audience perceptions. *British Journal of Psychology,* **101**, 123–135.

Bardi, C. A., & Brady, M. F. (2010). Why shy people use instant messaging: Loneliness and other motives. *Computers in Human Behavior,* **26**(6), 1722-1726.

Barelds, D. P. H., & Barelds-Dijkstra, P. (2007). Love at first sight or friends first? Ties among partner personality trait similarity, relationship onset, relationship quality, and love. *Journal of Social and Personal Relationships,* **24**(4), 479–496.

Bargh, J. A. (2018). It was social consistency that mattered all along. *Psychological Inquiry,* **29**(2), 60–62. https://doi.org/10.1080/1047840X.2018.1480586

Bargh, J. A., & Chartrand, T. L. (1999). The unbearable automaticity of being. *American Psychologist,* **54**, 462–479.

Bargh, J., & Morsella, E. (2008). The unconscious mind. *Perspectives on Psychological Science,* **3**(1), 73–79.

Bargh, J. A., Chen, M., & Burrows, L. (1996). Automaticity of social behavior: Direct effects of trait construct and stereotype activation on action. *Journal of Personality and Social Psychology,* **71**(2), 230–244.

Bargh, J. A., McKenna, K. Y. A., & Fitzsimons, G. M. (2002). Can you see the real me? Activation and expression of the 'true self' on the Internet. *Journal of Social Issues,* **58**, 33–48.

Bargh, J., Schwader, K., Hailey, S., Dyer, R., & Boothby, E. (2012). Automaticity in social-cognitive processes. *Trends in Cognitive Sciences,* **16**(12), 593–605.

Barker, M. (1981). *The new racism: Conservatives and the ideology of the tribe.* Junction Books.

Barker, R., Dembo, T. & Lewin, K. (1941). Frustration and aggression: An experiment with young children, *University of Iowa Studies in Child Welfare,* **18**, 1–314.

Barnett, M. D., Moore, J. M., & Harp, A. R. (2017). Who we are and how we feel: Self-discrepancy theory and specific affective states. *Personality and Individual Differences,* **111**, 232–237.

Baron, R. A. (1977). *Human aggression.* Plenum Press.

Baron, R. A., & Richardson, D. R. (2007). *Human aggression.* Plenum Press.

Baron, R. S., Kerr, N. L., & Miller, N. (1992). *Group process, group decision, group action.* Brooks/Cole.

Baron-Cohen, S. (2003). *The essential difference: Men, women, and the extreme male brain.* Allen-Lane.

Baron-Cohen, S. (2004). *The essential difference.* Penguin Books.

Barreto, M., & Ellemers, N. (2000). The impact of respect versus neglect of self-identities on identification and group loyalty. *Personality and Social Psychology Bulletin,* **28,** 629–639.

Barrett, C. (2015). Queering the home. *Home Cultures,* **12**(2), 193–211.

Barrett, L., Dunbar, R., & Lycett, J. (2002). *Human evolutionary psychology.* Palgrave.

Barrett, M. (Ed.) (2007). *Children's knowledge, beliefs and feelings about nations and national groups.* Psychology Press.

Bartels, A., & Zeki, S. (2000, 27 November). The neural basis of romantic love. *Neuroreport,* **11,** 3829–3834.

Bartels, A., & Zeki, S. (2004). The neural correlates of maternal and romantic love. *Neuroimage,* **21,** 1155–1166.

Bartholomew, K., & Horowitz, L. (1991). Attachment styles among young adults: A test of a four-category model. *Journal of Personality and Social Psychology,* **61,** 226–244.

Bartholow, B. D., & Heinz, A. (2006). Alcohol and aggression without consumption: Alcohol cues, aggressive thoughts, and hostile perception bias. *Psychological Science,* **17,** 30–37.

Bartholow, B. D., Anderson, C. A., Carnagey, N. L., & Benjamin, A. J., Jr. (2004). Interactive effects of life experience and situational cues on aggression: The weapons priming effect in hunters and nonhunters. *Journal of Experimental Social Psychology,* **41,** 48–60.

Bartholow, B. D., Bushman, B. J., & Sestir, M. A. (2006). Chronic violent video game exposure and desensitization to violence: Behavioral and event-related brain potential data. *Journal of Experimental Social Psychology,* **42**(4), 532–539.

Bártová, K., Štěrbová, Z., Martinec Nováková, L., Binter, J., Varella, M., & Valentova, A. (2017). Homogamy in masculinity–femininity is positively linked to relationship quality in gay male couples from the Czech Republic. *Archives of Sexual Behavior,* **46**(5), 1349–1359.

Bartsch, A., & Kloß, A. (2019). Personalized charity advertising. Can personalized prosocial messages promote empathy, attitude change, and helping intentions toward stigmatized social groups? *International Journal of Advertising,* **38**(3), 345-363.

Bassett, J., Pearcey, S., & Dabbs, J. M., Jr. (2001). Jealousy and partner preference among butch and femme lesbians. *Psychology, Evolution and Gender,* **3,** 155–165. https://doi.org/10.1080/14616660110067375.

Bassili, J. N. (2003). The minority slowness effect: Subtle inhibitions in the expression of views not shared by others. *Journal of Personality and Social Psychology,* **84,** 261–276.

Bastiaensens, S., Vandebosch, H., Poels, K., Kvan Cleemput, K., DeSmet, A. & De Bourdeaudhuij, I. (2015). 'Can I afford to help?' How affordances of communication modalities guide bystanders' helping intentions towards harassment on social network sites. *Behaviour and Information Technology,* **34**(4), 425–435. https://doi.org/10.1080/01449 29X.2014.983979

Bastian, B., & Haslam, N. (2006). Psychological essentialism and stereotype endorsement. *Journal of Experimental Social Psychology,* **42,** 228–235.

Bastounis, M., & Minibas-Poussard, J. (2012). Causal attributions of work-place gender equality, just world belief, and the self/other distinction. *Social Behaviour and Personality,* **40,** 433–452.

Batson, C. D. (2001). Addressing the altruism question experimentally. In S. G. Post, L. B. Underwood, J. P. Schloss, & W. B. Hurlbut (Eds.), *Altruism and altruistic love: Science, philosophy, and religion in dialogue.* Oxford University Press.

Batson, C. D. (2008). Empathy-induced altruistic motivation. In P. R. Shaver & M. Mikulincer (Eds.), *Prosocial motives, emotions, and behavior.* Washington, DC: American Psychological Association.

Batson, C. D. (2014). *The altruism question: Toward a social-psychological answer.* Psychology Press.

Batson, C. D., & Ahmad, N. (2001). Empathy-induced altruism in a prisoner's dilemma II: What if the target of empathy has defected? *European Journal of Social Psychology,* **31**(1), 25–36.

Batson, C. D., & Powell, A. A. (2003). Altruism and prosocial behavior. In T. Millon & M. J. Lerner (Eds.), *Handbook of psychology: Personality and social psychology* (Vol. 5). Wiley.

Batson, C. D., & Thompson, E. R. (2001). Why don't moral people act morally? Motivational considerations. *Current Directions in Psychological Science,* **10,** 54–57.

Batson, C. D., & Weeks, J. L. (1996). Mood effects of unsuccessful helping: Another test of the empathy-altruism hypothesis. *Personality and Social Psychology Bulletin,* **22,** 148–157.

Batson, C. D., Ahmad, N., & Stocks, E. L. (2004). Benefits and liabilities of empathy-induced altruism. In A. G. Miller (Ed.), *The social psychology of good and evil.* Guilford Press.

Batson, C. D., Ahmad, N., Yin, J., Bedell, S. J., Johnson, J. W., & Templin, C. M. (1999). Two threats to the common good: Self-interested egoism and empathy-induced altruism. *Personality and Social Psychology Bulletin,* **25**(1), 3-16.

Batson, C. D., Batson, J. G., Slingsby, J. K., Harrell, K. L., Peekna, H. M., & Todd, M. R. (1991). Empathic joy and the empathy-altruism hypothesis. *Journal of Personality and Social Psychology,* **61**(3), 413–426.

Batson, C. D., Coke, J. S., Jasnoski, M. L., & Hanson, M. (1978). Buying kindness: Effect of an extrinsic incentive for helping on perceived altruism. *Personality and Social Psychology Bulletin,* **4,** 86–91.

Batson, C. D., Duncan, B. D., Ackerman, P., Buckley, T., & Birch, K. (1981). Is empathic emotion a source of altruistic motivation? *Journal of Personality and Social Psychology,* **40,** 290–302.

Batson, C. D., Fultz, J., & Schoenrade, P. A. (1987). Distress and empathy: Two qualitatively distinct vicarious emotions with different motivational consequences. *Journal of Personality,* **55,** 19–40.

Batson, C. D., Harris, A. C., McCaul, K. D., Davis, M., & Schmidt, T. (1979). Compassion or compliance: Alternative dispositional attributions for one's helping behavior. *Social Psychology Quarterly,* **42,** 405–409.

Batson, C. D., Kobrynowicz, D., Dinnerstein, J. L., Kampf, H. C., & Wilson, A. D. (1997a). In a very different voice: Unmasking moral hypocrisy. *Journal of Personality and Social Psychology,* **72,** 1335–1348.

Batson, C. D., Sager, K., Garst, E., Kang, M., Rubchinsky, K., & Dawson, K. (1997b). Is empathy-induced helping due to self-other merging? *Journal of Personality and Social Psychology,* **73,** 495–509.

Batson, C. D., Thompson, E. R., & Chen, H. (2002). Moral hypocrisy: Addressing some alternatives. *Journal of Personality and Social Psychology,* **83,** 330–339.

Baumeister, R. F. (1996). Should schools try to boost self-esteem? Beware the dark side. *American Educator,* **20,** 14–19, 43.

Baumeister, R. F. (Ed.) (1999). *The self in social psychology.* Psychology Press (Taylor & Francis).

Baumeister, R. F. (2005a). Rejected and alone. *The Psychologist,* **18,** 732–735.

Baumeister, R. F. (2005b). *The cultural animal: Human nature, meaning, and social life.* Oxford University Press.

Baumeister, R. F., & Exline, J. J. (2000). Self-control, morality, and human strength. *Journal of Social and Clinical Psychology,* **19,** 29–42.

Baumeister, R. F., & Ilko, S. A. (1995). Shallow gratitude: Public and private acknowledgement of external help in accounts of success. *Basic and Applied Social Psychology,* **16,** 191–209.

Baumeister, R. F., & Leary, M. R. (1995). The need to belong: Desire for interpersonal attachment as a fundamental human motivation. *Psychological Bulletin,* **117,** 497–529.

Baumeister, R. F., & Scher, S. J. (1988). Self-defeating behavior patterns among normal individuals: Review and analysis of common self-destructive tendencies. *Psychological Bulletin,* **104**(1), 3–22.

Baumeister, R. F., Muraven, M., & Tice, D. M. (2000). Ego depletion: A resource model of volition, self-regulation, and controlled processing. *Social Cognition,* **18,** 130–150.

Baumgardner, A. H., Kaufman, C. M., & Levy, P. E. (1989). Regulating affect interpersonally: When low esteem leads to greater enhancement. *Journal of Personality and Social Psychology,* **56,** 907–921.

Baumrind, D. (2013). Is Milgram's deceptive research ethically acceptable?*Theoretical & Applied Ethics,* **2**(2), 18. https://www.muse.jhu.edu/article/536091.

Bayer, E. (1929). Beitrage zur zeikomponenten theorie des hungers. *Zeitschrift fur Psychologie,* **112,** 1–54.

Baysu, G., Phalet, K., & Brown, R. (2011). Dual identity as a two-edged sword identity threat and minority school performance. *Social Psychology Quarterly,* **74**(2), 121–143.

Bazarova, N. N., Walther, J. B., & McLeod, P. L. (2012). Minority influence in virtual groups: A comparison of four theories of minority influence. *Communication Research*, **39**(3), 295–316.

Bazerman, M. H. (1986, June). Why negotiations go wrong. *Psychology Today*, pp. 54–58.

Bazerman, M. H. (1990). *Judgment in managerial decision making* (2nd ed.). Wiley.

Beals, K. P., Impett, E. A., & Peplau, L. A. (2002). Lesbians in love: Why some relationships endure and others end. *Journal of Lesbian Studies*, **6**(1), 53–63.

Beaman, A. L., Barnes, P. J., Klentz, B., & McQuirk, B. (1978). Increasing helping rates through information dissemination: Teaching pays. *Personality and Social Psychology Bulletin*, **4**, 406–411.

Beames, S. (2005). Expeditions and the social construction of the self. *Australian Journal of Outdoor Education*, **9**(1), 4. http://link.galegroup.com/apps/doc/A146935728/AONE?u=tou&sid=AONE&xid=7cb19784.

Becker, S. W., & Eagly, A. H. (2004). The heroism of women and men. *American Psychologist*, **59**, 163–178.

Beersma, B., & Van Kleef, G. A. (2011). How the grapevine keeps you in line: Gossip increases contributions to the group. *Social Psychological & Personality Science*, **2**(6), 642–649.

Beevor, E. (2016). Coercive radicalization: Charismatic authority and the internal strategies of ISIS and the Lord's Resistance Army. *Studies in Conflict and Terrorism*, **40**(6), 496–521. https://doi.org/10.1080/1057610X.2016.1221256

Beffa-Negrini, P. A., Cohen, N. L., & Miller, B. (2002). Strategies to motivate students in online learning environments. *Journal of Nutrition Education and Behavior*, **34**(6), 334–340.

Bekker, M. H., & van Assen, M. A. (2008). Autonomy-connectedness and gender. *Sex Roles*, **59**(7–8), 532.

Bekkers, R. (2007). Measuring altruistic behaviour in surveys: The all-or-nothing dictator. *Survey Research Methods*, **1**(3), 139–144.

Bekoff, M., & Bexell, S. M. (2010). Ignoring nature: Why we do it, the dire consequences, and the need for a paradigm shift to save animals, habitats, and ourselves. *Human Ecology Review*, **17**(1), 70-74.

Bell, B. S., & Kozlowski, S. W. J. (2008). Active learning: Effects of core training design elements on self-regulatory processes, learning, and adaptability. *Journal of Applied Psychology*, **93**, 296–316. https://doi.org/10.1037/0021-9010.93.2.296

Bell, P. A. (2005). Reanalysis and perspective in the heat-aggression debate. *Journal of Personality and Social Psychology*, **89**, 71–73.

Belson, W. A. (1978). *Television violence and the adolescent boy.* Saxon House, Teakfield Ltd.

Bem, D. J. (1972). Self-perception theory. *Advances in Experimental Social Psychology*, **6**, 1–62.

Bem, D. J. (2011). Feeling the future: Experimental evidence for anomalous retroactive influences on cognition and affect. *Journal of Personality and Social Psychology*, **100**, 407–425.

Bem, S. L. (1974). The measurement of psychological androgyny. *Journal of Consulting and Clinical Psychology*, **42**, 155–162.

Benavides, A. D., Keyes, L. M., & Pulley, B. (2016). Understanding the recruitment methods and socialization techniques of terror networks by comparing them to youth gangs: Similarities and divergences. In S. Ekici, H. Akdoğan, E. Ragab, A. Ekici, & R. Warnes (Eds.) *Countering terrorist recruitment in the context of armed counter-terrorism operations*, NATO Science for Peace and Security Series (Vol.125, pp. 40–54). IOS Press.

Benjamin, S., Nind, M., Hall, K., Collins, J., & Sheehy, K. (2003). Moments of inclusion and exclusion: Pupils negotiating classroom contexts. *British Journal of Sociology of Education*, **24**(5), 547–558.

Bennett, M., & Sani, F. (Eds.) (2004). *The development of the social self.* Psychology Press.

Bennett, M., & Sani, F. (2008). Children's subjective identification with social groups. In S. R. Levy & M. Killen (Eds.), *Intergroup attitudes and relations in childhood through adulthood.* Oxford University Press.

Bennett, R., & Vijaygopal, R. (2018). An assessment of UK drivers' attitudes regarding the forthcoming ban on the sale of petrol and diesel vehicles. *Transportation Research Part D: Transport and Environment*, **62**, 330–344.

Benoit, W. L. (1997). Hugh Grant's image restoration discourse: An actor apologizes. *Communication Quarterly*, **45**(3), 251–267.

Benozio, A., & Diesendruck, G. (2015). From effort to value: Preschool children's alternative to effort justification. *Psychological Science*, **26**(9), 1423–1429. https://doi.org/10.1177/0956797615589585

Bensley, L., & van Eenwyk, J. (2001). Video games and real-life aggression: Review of the literature. *Journal of Adolescent Health*, **29**, 244–257.

Benvenisti, M. (1988, 16 October). Growing up in Jerusalem. *New York Times Magazine*, pp. 34–37.

Berg, C., Raminani, S., Greer, J., Harwood, M., & Safren, S. (2008). Participants' perspectives on cognitive-behavioral therapy for adherence and depression in HIV. *Psychotherapy Research*, **18**, 271–280.

Berg, J. H., & McQuinn, R. D. (1986). Attraction and exchange in continuing and noncontinuing dating relationships. *Journal of Personality and Social Psychology*, **50**, 942–952.

Berger, J., & Heath, C. (2008). Who drives divergence? Identity signaling, outgroup dissimilarity, and the abandonment of cultural tastes. *Journal of Personality and Social Psychology*, **95**, 593–607.

Berglas, S., & Jones, E. E. (1978). Drug choice as a self-handicapping strategy in response to noncontingent success. *Journal of Personality and Social Psychology*, **36**, 405–417.

Berkman, L. F. (1995). The role of social relations in health promotion. *Psychosomatic Medicine*, **57**, 245–254.

Berkman, L. F. & Syme, S. L. (1979). 'Social networks, host resistance and mortality: A nine-year follow up study of Alameda county residents'. *American Journal of Epidemiology*, **109**, 186-204.

Berkowitz, L. (1968, September). Impulse, aggression and the gun. *Psychology Today*, pp. 18–22.

Berkowitz, L. (1972). Social norms, feelings, and other factors affecting helping and altruism. In L. Berkowitz (Ed.), *Advances in experimental social psychology* (Vol. 6). Academic Press.

Berkowitz, L. (1978). Whatever happened to the frustration–aggression hypothesis? *American Behavioral Scientists*, **21**, 691–708.

Berkowitz, L. (1981, June). How guns control us. *Psychology Today*, pp. 11–12.

Berkowitz, L. (1983). Aversively stimulated aggression: Some parallels and differences in research with animals and humans. *American Psychologist*, **38**, 1135–1144.

Berkowitz, L. (1984). Some effects of thoughts on anti- and prosocial influences of media events: A cognitive–neoasociationistic analysis. *Psychological Bulletin*, **95**(3), 410–427.

Berkowitz, L. (1989). Frustration–aggression hypothesis: Examination and reformulation. *Psychological Bulletin*, **106**, 59–73.

Berkowitz, L. (1995). A career on aggression. In G. G. Brannigan & M. R. Merrens (Eds.), *The social psychologists: Research adventures.* McGraw-Hill.

Berkowitz, L. (1998). Affective aggression: The role of stress, pain, and negative affect. In R. G. Geen & E. Donnerstein (Eds.), *Human aggression: Theories, research, and implications for social policy.* Academic Press.

Berkowitz, L. (2003). Affect, aggression, and antisocial behavior. In R. J. Davidson, K. R. Scherer, & H. H. Goldsmith (Eds.), *Handbook of affective sciences* (pp. 804–823). Oxford University Press.

Berkowitz, L. (2012). A different view of anger: The cognitive-neoassociation conception of the relation of anger to aggression. *Aggressive Behavior*, **38**(4), 322–333.

Berkowitz, L., & Geen, R. G. (1966). Film violence and the cue properties of available targets. *Journal of Personality and Social Psychology*, **3**, 525–530.

Berkowitz, L., & LePage, A. (1967). Weapons as aggression-eliciting stimuli. *Journal of Personality and Social Psychology*, **7**, 202–207.

Bernhardt, P. C., Dabbs, J. M., Jr, Fielden, J. A., & Lutter, C. D. (1998). Testosterone changes during vicarious experiences of winning and losing among fans at sporting events. *Physiology and Behavior*, **65**, 59–62.

Bernhardt, J. M., Mays, D., & Hall, A. K. (2012). Social marketing at the right place and right time with new media. *Journal of Social Marketing* **2**(2), 130–137.

Bernstein, D. M., Erdfelder, E., Meltzoff, A. N., Peria, W., & Loftus, G. R. (2011). Hindsight bias from 3 to 95 years of age. *Journal of Experimental Psychology: Learning, Memory, and Cognition*, **37**(2), 378–391. https://doi-org.libezproxy.open.ac.uk/10.1037/a0021971

Berntson, G. G., & Cacioppo, J. T. (2000). Psychobiology and social psychology: Past present, and future. *Personality and Social Psychology Review,* **4,** 3–15.

Berri, D. J., Simmons, R., Van Gilder, J., & O'Neill, L. (2011). What does it mean to find the face of the franchise? Physical attractiveness and the evaluation of athletic performance. *Economics Letters,* **111**(3), 200–202.

Berscheid, E. (1999). The greening of relationship science. *American Psychologist,* **54,** 260–266.

Berscheid, E., & Hatfield, E. (1969). *Interpersonal attraction* (pp. 46-51). Addison-Wesley.

Berscheid, E., Boye, D., & Walster (Hatfield), E. (1968). Retaliation as a means of restoring equity. *Journal of Personality and Social Psychology,* **10,** 370–376.

Berscheid, E., Dion, K., Walster (Hatfield), E., & Walster, G. W. (1971). Physical attractiveness and dating choice: A test of the matching hypothesis. *Journal of Experimental Social Psychology,* **7,** 173–189.

Bertram, G., & Bodenhausen, G. V. (2005). Accessibility effects on implicit social cognition: The role of knowledge activation and retrieval experiences. *Journal of Personality and Social Psychology,* **89,** 672–685.

Besharati, F., Karimi-Shahanjarini, A., Hazavehei, S. M. M., Bashirian, S., Bagheri, F., & Faradmal, J. (2017). Development of a colorectal cancer screening intervention for Iranian adults: Applying intervention mapping. *Asian Pacific Journal of Cancer Prevention,* **18**(8), 2193–2199. https://doi.org/10.22034/APJCP.2017.18.8.219.

Besser, A., & Priel, B. (2005). The apple does not fall far from the tree: Attachment styles and personality vulnerabilities to depression in three generations of women. *Personality and Social Psychology Bulletin,* **31,** 1052–1073.

Bessi, A., Coletto, M., Davidescu, G. A., Scala, A., Caldarelli, G., & Quattrociocchi, W. (2015). Science vs conspiracy: Collective narratives in the age of misinformation. *PloS One,* **10**(2), e0118093.

Best, K. (2005). Traditions can imprison women. *Network,* **23**(4), 7. http://link.galegroup.com.libezproxy.open.ac.uk/apps/doc/A135337943/AONE?u=tou&sid=AONE&xid=0da2013d

Best, S. (2010). The Leicester School of Football Hooliganism: An evaluation. *Soccer and Society,* **11**(5), 573–587. https://doi.org/10.1080/14660970.2010.497352

Bhatia, A. (2008). Critical discourse analysis of political press conferences. *Discourse & Society,* **17**(2), 173–203.

Bhattacherjee, A., & Sanford, C. (2006). Influence processes for information technology acceptance: An elaboration likelihood model. *MIS Quarterly,* **30**(4), 805–825.

Bianchi, S. M., Milkie, M. A., Sayer, L. C., & Robinson, J. P. (2000). Is anyone doing the housework? Trends in the gender division of household labor. *Social Forces,* **79,** 191–228.

Bickman, L. (1975). Bystander intervention in a crime: The effect of a mass-media campaign. *Journal of Applied Social Psychology,* **5,** 296–302.

Bickman, L. (1979). Interpersonal influence and the reporting of a crime. *Personality and Social Psychology Bulletin,* **5,** 32–35.

Bickman, L., & Green, S. K. (1977). Situational cues and crime reporting: Do signs make a difference? *Journal of Applied Social Psychology,* **7,** 1–18.

Bierhoff, H. W. (2002). *Prosocial behaviour.* Psychology Press.

Bierhoff, H. W., & Rohmann, E. (2004). Altruistic personality in the context of the empathy–altruism hypothesis. *European Journal of Personality,* **18**(4), 351–365.

Bierhoff, H. W., Klein, R., & Kramp, P. (1991). Evidence for the altruistic personality from data on accident research. *Journal of Personality,* **59,** 263–280.

Billig, M. (1985). Prejudice, categorization and particularization: From a perceptual to a rhetorical approach. *European Journal of Social Psychology,* **15,** 79–103.

Billig, M. (1987). *Arguing and thinking: A rhetorical approach to social psychology.* Cambridge University Press.

Billig, M. (1989). The argumentative nature of holding strong views: A case study. *European Journal of Social Psychology,* **19,** 203–223.

Billig, M. (1996). *Arguing and thinking.* Cambridge University Press.

Billig, M. (2001). Humour and hatred: The racist jokes of the Ku Klux Klan. *Discourse and Society,* **12**(3), 267–289.

Bingenheimer, J. B., Brennan, R. T., & Earls, F. J. (2005). Firearm violence exposure and serious violent behavior. *Science,* **308,** 1323–1326.

Bippus, A. M., Boren, J. P., & Worsham, S. (2008). Social exchange orientation and conflict communication in romantic relationships. *Communication Research Reports,* **25**(3), 227–234.

Birger, M., Swartz, M., Cohen, D., Alesh, Y. A., Grishpan, C., & Kotelr, M. (2003). Aggression: the testosterone-serotonin link. *Israel Medical Association Journal,* **5**(9), 653–658.

Birnbaum, G. E., Weisberg, Y. W., & Jeffry A. Simpson, J. A. (2010). Desire under attack: Attachment orientations and the effects of relationship threat on sexual motivations. *Journal of Social and Personal Relationships,* **28**(4), 448–468.

Bivans, A. M. (1991). *Miss America: In pursuit of the crown.* Mastermedia.

Bizman, A., & Yinon, Y. (2002). Social self-discrepancies and group-based emotional distress. In D. M. Mackie & E. R. Smith (Eds.), *From prejudice to intergroup emotions: Differentiated reactions to social groups.* Psychology Press.

Bjòrgo, T. (2005). Conflict processes between youth groups in a Norwegian city: Polarisation and revenge. *European Journal of Crime, Criminal Law and Criminal Justice,* **13**(1), 44–74.

Black, S., & Hausman, A. (2008). Adolescents' views of guns in a high-violence community. *Journal of Adolescent Research,* **23**(5), 592-610.

Blair, C. A., Thompson, L. F., & Wuensch, K. L. (2005). Electronic helping behavior: The virtual presence of others makes a difference. *Basic and Applied Social Psychology,* **27,** 171–178.

Blake, R. R., & Mouton, J. S. (1962). The intergroup dynamics of win–lose conflict and problem-solving collaboration in union-management relations. In M. Sherif (Ed.), *Intergroup relations and leadership.* Wiley.

Blake, R. R., & Mouton, J. S. (1979). Intergroup problem solving in organizations: From theory to practice. In W. G. Austin & S. Worchel (Eds.), *The social psychology of intergroup relations.* Brooks/Cole.

Blanchard, F. A., & Cook, S. W. (1976). Effects of helping a less competent member of a cooperating interracial group on the development of interpersonal attraction. *Journal of Personality and Social Psychology,* **34,** 1245–1255.

Blanchard-Fields, F., Hertzog, C., & Horhotta, M. (2012). Violate my beliefs? Then you're to blame! Belief content as an explanation for causal attribution biases. *Psychology and Aging,* **27,** 324–337.

Blank, H., Fischer, V., & Erdfelder, E. (2003). Hindsight bias in political elections. *Memory,* **11,** 491–504.

Blanton, H., Pelham, B. W., DeHart, T., & Carvallo, M. (2001). Overconfidence as dissonance reduction. *Journal of Experimental Social Psychology,* **37,** 373–385.

Blass, T. (1990). Psychological approaches to the Holocaust: Review and evaluation. Paper presented to the American Psychological Association convention.

Blass, T. (1991). Understanding behavior in the Milgram obedience experiment: The role of personality, situations, and their interactions. *Journal of Personality and Social Psychology,* **60,** 398–413.

Blass, T. (1996). Stanley Milgram: A life of inventiveness and controversy. In G. A. Kimble, C. A. Boneau, & M. Wertheimer (Eds.), *Portraits of pioneers in psychology* (Vol. II). American Psychological Association.

Blass, T. (2000). The Milgram paradigm after 35 years: Some things we now know about obedience to authority. In T. Blass (Ed.), *Obedience to authority: Current perspectives on the Milgram paradigm.* Erlbaum.

Blass, T. (2004). *The man who shocked the world: The life and legacy of Stanley Milgram.* Basic Books.

Bleske-Rechek, A., & Lighthall, M. (2010). Attractiveness and rivalry in women's friendships with other women. *Human Nature,* **21,** 82–97.

Block J., & Funder, D. C. (1986). Social roles and social perception: Individual differences in attribution and error. *Journal of Personality and Social Psychology,* **51,** 1200–1207.

Boaler, J., Wiliam, D., & Brown, M. (2000). Students' experiences of ability grouping-disaffection, polarisation and the construction of failure. *British Educational Research Journal,* **26**(5), 631–648.

Bobrow, D., & Bailey, J. M. (2001). Is male homosexuality maintained via kin selection? *Evolution and Human Behavior, 22,* 361–368. https://doi.org/10.1016=s1090-5138(01)00074-5

Bodenhausen, G. V. (1993). Emotions, arousal, and stereotypic judgments: A heuristic model of affect and stereotyping. In D. M. Mackie & D. L. Hamilton (Eds.), *Affect, cognition, and stereotyping: Interactive processes in group perception*. Academic Press.

Bodenhausen, G. V. (2005). The role of stereotypes in decision-making processes. *Medical Decision Making*, **25**(1), 112–118. https://doi.org/10.1177/0272989X04273800

Bodenhausen, G. V., Sheppard, L. A., & Kramer, G. F. (1994). Negative affect and social judgment: The differential impact of anger and sadness. *European Journal of Social Psychology*, **24**, 45–62.

Boen, F., Vanbeselaere, N., & Feys, J. (2002). Behavioural consequences of fluctuating group success: An internet study of soccer-team fans. *The Journal of Social Psychology*, **142**(6), 769–781.

Bogaert, A. F. (2006). Toward a conceptual understanding of asexuality. *Review of General Psychology*, **10**(3), 241–250.

Bogardus, E. S. (1925). Measuring social distances. *Journal of Applied Sociology*, **9**, 299–308.

Bögels, S. M., Alden, L., Beidel, D. C., Clark, L. A., Pine, D. S., Stein, M. B., & Voncken, M. (2010). Social anxiety disorder: questions and answers for the DSM-V. *Depression and Anxiety*, **27**(2), 168-189.

Boggiano, A. K., & Ruble, D. N. (1985). Children's responses to evaluative feedback. In R. Schwarzer (Ed.), *Self-related cognitions in anxiety and motivation*. Erlbaum.

Boggiano, A. K., Barrett, M., Weiher, A. W., McClelland, G. H., & Lusk, C. M. (1987). Use of the maximaloperant principle to motivate children's intrinsic interest. *Journal of Personality and Social Psychology*, **53**, 866–879.

Boggs, L., Carr, S. C., Fletcher, R. B., & Clarke, D. E. (2005). Pseudoparticipation in communication networks: The social psychology of broken promises. *Journal of Social Psychology*, **145**(5), 621–624.

Bohannon, J. (2012). Tweeting the London riots. *Science*, **336**(18), 831.

Bond, M. H., Leung, K., Au, A., Tong, K.-K., Reimel de Carrasquel, S., Murakami, F., Yamaguchi, S., Bierbrauer, G., Singelis, T. M., Broer, M., Boen, F., Lambert, S. M., Ferreira, M. C., Noels, K. A., van Bayel, J., Safdar, S., Zhang, J., Chen, L., Solcova, I., . . . Lewis, J. R. (2004). Culture-level dimensions of social axioms and their correlates across 41 cultures. *Journal of Cross-Cultural Psychology*, **35**(5), 548–570.

Bond, R., & Smith, P. B. (1996). Culture and conformity: A meta-analysis of studies using Asch's (1952b, 1956) line judgment task. *Psychological Bulletin*, **119**, 111–137.

Bonilla-Silva, E., & Forman, T. (2000). I'm not a racist, but . . .: Mapping white college students' racial ideology in the USA. *Discourse and Society*, **11**(1), 50–85.

Boo, S., & Park, E. (2013). An examination of green intention: The effect of environmental knowledge and educational experiences on meeting planners' implementation of green meeting practices. *Journal of Sustainable Tourism*, **21**(8), 1129–1147.

Book, A. S., Starzyk, K. B., & Quinsey, V. L. (2001). The relationship between testosterone and aggression: A meta-analysis. *Aggression and Violent Behavior*, **6**, 579–599.

Booker, C. (2018). *Global warming: A case study in Groupthink. How science can shed new light on the most important 'non-debate' of our time.* The Global Warming Policy Foundation, 28.

Borge, A. I. H., Rutter, M., Côté, S., & Tremblay, R. E. (2004). Early childcare and physical aggression: Differentiating social selection and social causation. *Journal of Child Psychology and Psychiatry*, **45**(2), 367–376.

Borick, C. P., & Rabe, B. G. (2010). A reason to believe: Examining the factors that determine individual views on global warming. *Social Science Quarterly*, **91**, 777–800.

Bornstein, B. H., & Greene, E. (2011). Jury decision making: Implications for and from psychology. *Current Directions in Psychological Science*, **20**(1), 63–67.

Bornstein, G., & Rapoport, A. (1988). Intergroup competition for the provision of step-level public goods: Effects of preplay communication. *European Journal of Social Psychology*, **18**, 125–142.

Bornstein, G., Rapoport, A., Kerpel, L., & Katz, T. (1989). Within- and between-group communication in intergroup competition for public goods. *Journal of Experimental Social Psychology*, **25**, 422–436.

Bornstein, R. F., & D'Agostino, P. R. (1992). Stimulus recognition and the mere exposure effect. *Journal of Personality and Social Psychology*, **63**, 545–552.

Bornstein, R. F., Galley, D. J., Leone, D. R., & Kale, A. R. (1991). The temporal stability of ratings of parents: Test–retest reliability and influence of parental contact. *Journal of Social Behavior and Personality*, **6**, 641–649.

Borofsky, G. L., Stollak, G. E., & Messé, L. A. (1971). Sex differences in bystander reactions to physical assault. *Journal of Experimental Social Psychology*, **7**, 313–318.

Bos, L., Schemer, C., Corbu, N., Hameleers, M., Andreadis, I., Schulz, A., Schmuck, D., Carsten, R., &Fawnzi, N. (2020). The effects of populism as a social identity frame on persuasion and mobilisation: Evidence from a 15-country experiment. *European Journal of Political Research*, **59**(1), 3–24.

Bösche, W. (2010). Violent video games prime both aggressive and positive cognitions. *Journal of Media Psychology: Theories, Methods, and Applications*, **22**(4), 139–146.

Bossard, J. H. S. (1932). Residential propinquity as a factor in marriage selection. *American Journal of Sociology*, **38**, 219–224.

Bouas, K. S., & Komorita, S. S. (1996). Group discussion and cooperation in social dilemmas. *Personality and Social Psychology Bulletin*, **22**, 1144–1150.

Bouchard, T. J., Jr., & McGue, M. (2003). Genetic and environmental influences on human psychological differences. *Journal of Neurobiology*, **54**(1), 4–45.

Boulton, M. J., Smith, P. K., & Cowie, H. (2010). Short-term longitudinal relationships between children's peer victimization/bullying experiences and self-perceptions: Evidence for reciprocity. *School Psychology International*, **31**, 296–311.

Bourdieu, P. (1977). *Outline of a theory of practice*. Cambridge University Press.

Bower, B. (1996). Fighting stereotype stigma: Studies chart accuracy, usefulness of inferences about social groups. *Science News*, **149**(26), 408.

Bowlby, J. (1980). *Attachment and loss. Vol. 3: Loss, sadness and depression.* Basic Books.

Bowlby, J. (1988). *A secure base: Parent–child attachment and healthy human development.* Basic Books.

Bowlby, J. (1999). *Attachment and loss. Vol. 1: Attachment* (2nd ed.). Basic Books.

Bowles, S. (2012). Warriors, levelers, and the role of conflict in human social evolution. *Science*, **336**, 876–879.

Bowman, N. D., Weber, R., Tamborini, R., & Sherry, J. (2013). Facilitating game play: How others affect performance at and enjoyment of video games. *Media Psychology*, **16**(1), 39–64.

Brand, R. J., Bonatsos, A., D'Orazio, R., & DeShong, H. (2012). What is beautiful is good, even online: Correlations between photo attractiveness and text attractiveness in men's online dating profiles. *Computers in Human Behavior*, **28**(1), 166–170.

Brand, R., Melzer, M., & Hagemann, N. (2011). Towards an implicit association test (IAT) for measuring doping attitudes in sports. Data-based recommendations developed from two recently published tests. *Psychology of Sport and Exercise*, **12**, 250–256.

Brannon, T. N., Markus, H. R., & Taylor, V. J. (2015). 'Two souls, two thoughts,' two self-schemas: Double consciousness can have positive academic consequences for African Americans. *Journal of Personality and Social Psychology*, **108**(4), 586–609.

Brauer, M., Judd, C. M., & Gliner, M. D. (1995). The effects of repeated expressions on attitude polarization during group discussions. *Journal of Personality and Social Psychology*, **68**, 1014–1029.

Brauer, M., Judd, C. M., & Jacquelin, V. (2001). The communication of social stereotypes: The effects of group discussion and information distribution on stereotypic appraisals. *Journal of Personality and Social Psychology*, **81**, 463–475.

Braverman, J. (2005). The effect of mood on detection of covariation. *Personality and Social Psychology Bulletin*, **31**, 1487–1497.

Breakwell, G. (1979). Illegitimate group membership and intergroup differentiation. *British Journal of Social and Clinical Psychology*, **18**, 141–149.

Breakwell, G. (1986). *Coping with threatened identities.* Methuen.

Breen, G. M., & Matusitz, J. (2008). Preventing youths from joining gangs: How to apply inoculation theory. *Journal of Applied Security Research*, **4**(1–2), 109–128. https://doi.org/10.1080/19361610802210285

Brehm, J. (1956). Post-decision changes in the desirability of alternatives. *Journal of Abnormal and Social Psychology,* **52,** 384–389.

Brehm, S., & Brehm, J. W. (1981). *Psychological reactance: A theory of freedom and control.* Academic Press.

Breitsohl, J., Wilcox-Jones, J. I. & Harris, I. (2015). Groupthink 2.0: An empirical analysis of customers' conformity-seeking in online communities. *Journal of Customer Behaviour,* **14**(2), 87–106.

Bresser, F., & Wilson, C. (2016). What is coaching. In J. Passmore (Ed.) *Excellence in coaching: The industry guide.* Kogan Page.

Brewer, M. B. (1991). The social self: On being the same and different at the same time. *Personality and Social Psychology Bulletin,* **17,** 475–482.

Brewer, M. B., & Miller, N. (1988). Contact and cooperation: When do they work? In P. A. Katz & D. Taylor (Eds.), *Towards the elimination of racism: Profiles in controversy.* Plenum.

Brewer, M. B., & Pierce, K. P. (2005). Social identity complexity and outgroup tolerance. *Personality and Social Psychology Bulletin,* **31,** 428–437.

Brewer, N., & Wells, G.L. (2011). Eyewitness identification. *Current Directions in Psychological Science,* **20,** 24–27.

Briggs, P., Burford, B., De Angeli, A., & Lynch, P. (2002). Trust in online advice. *Social Science Computer Review,* **20**(3), 321–332.

Brinol, P., & Petty, R. E. (2003). Overt head movements and persuasion: A self-validation analysis. *Journal of Personality and Social Psychology,* **84**(6), 1123–1139.

Briscoe, C., & Aboud, F. (2012). Behaviour change communication targeting four health behaviours in developing countries: A review of change techniques. *Social Science & Medicine,* **75**(4), 612–621.

British Psychological Society (2018). *BPS code of ethics and conduct.* https://www.bps.org.uk/news-and-policy/bps-code-ethics-and-conduct

Brooks, D. (2005, 10 August). All cultures are not equal. *New York Times.*

Broomhall, A. G., Phillips, W. J., Hine, D. W., & Loi, N. M. (2017). Upward counterfactual thinking and depression: A meta-analysis. *Clinical Psychology Review,* **55,** 56–73.

Browman, A. S., Destin, M., Carswell, K. L., & Svoboda, R. C. (2017). Perceptions of socioeconomic mobility influence academic persistence among low socioeconomic status students. *Journal of Experimental Social Psychology,* **72**(C), 45–52.

Brown, A. D. (2001). Organization studies and identity: Towards a research agenda. *Human Relations,* **54,** 113–121.

Brown, J. D., & Dutton, K. A. (1994). From the top down: Self-esteem and self-evaluation. Unpublished manuscript, University of Washington.

Brown, K. T., Brown, T. N., Jackson, J. S., Sellers, R. M., & Manuel, W. J. (2003). Teammates on and off the field? Contact with Black teammates and the racial attitudes of White student athletes. *Journal of Applied Social Psychology,* **33,** 1379–1403.

Brown, L. M., Bradley, M. M., & Lang, P. J. (2006). Affective reactions to pictures of ingroup and outgroup members. *Biological Psychology,* **71,** 303–311.

Brown, R., Maras, P., Masser, B., Vivian, J., & Hewstone, M. (2001). Life on the ocean wave: Testing some intergroup hypotheses in a naturalistic setting. *Group Processes and Intergroup Relations,* **4,** 81–97.

Brown, R., Vivian, J., & Hewstone, M. (1999). Changing attitudes through intergroup contact: The effects of group membership salience. *European Journal of Social Psychology,* **29,** 741–764.

Brown, T. J., Ham, S. H., & Hughes, M. (2010). Picking up litter: An application of theory-based communication to influence tourist behaviour in protected areas. *Journal of Sustainable Tourism,* **18**(7), 879–900. https://doi.org/10.1080/09669581003721281

Brown, V. R., & Paulus, P. B. (2002). Making group brainstorming more effective: Recommendations from an associative memory perspective. *Current Directions in Psychological Science,* **11,** 208–212.

Brugger, A., Kaiser, F. G., & Roczen, N. (2011). One for all? Connectedness to nature, inclusion of nature, environmental identity, and implicit association with nature. *European Psychologist,* **16,** 324–333. https://doi.org/10.1027/1016-9040/a000032

Brundtland, G. H. (2002). Message from the director-general. In: *The world health report 2002: Reducing risks, promoting healthy life.* World Health Organization.

Brunel, F. F., & Nelson, M. R. (2003, September). Message order effects and gender differences in advertising persuasion. *Journal of Advertising Research,* **43**(3), 330+. http://link.galegroup.com.libezproxy.open.ac.uk/apps/doc/A110222023/AONE?u=tou&sid=AONE&xid=63edf73f

Bruner, J. S. (1957). On perceptual readiness. *Psychological Review,* **64,** 123–152.

Bruner, J. S. (1990). *Acts of meaning.* Harvard University Press.

Buchan, N. R., Brewer, M. B., Grimalda, G., Wilson, R. K., Fatas, E., & Foddy, M. (2011). Global social identity and global cooperation. *Psychological Science,* **22,** 821–828.

Buchan, N. R., Grimalda, G., Wilson, R., Brewer, M., Fatas, E., & Foddy, M. (2009). Globalization and human cooperation. *Proceedings of the National Academy of Sciences, USA,* **106,** 4138–4142. https://doi.org/10.1073/pnas.0809522106

Buehler, R., & Griffin, D. (2003). Planning, personality, and prediction: The role of future focus in optimistic time predictions. *Organizational Behavior and Human Decision Processes,* **92,** 80–90.

Buehler, R., Griffin, D., & Ross, M. (1994). Exploring the 'planning fallacy': When people underestimate their task completion times. *Journal of Personality and Social Psychology,* **67,** 366–381.

Buehler, R., Griffin, D., & Ross, M. (2002). Inside the planning fallacy: The causes and consequences of optimistic time predictions. In T. Gilovich, D. Griffin, & D. Kahneman (Eds.), *Heuristics and biases: The psychology of intuitive judgment.* Cambridge University Press.

Buffardi, L. E., & Campbell, W. K. (2008). Narcissism and social networking websites. *Personality and Social Psychology Bulletin,* **34,** 1303–1314.

Bui, N. H. (2014). I don't believe it! Belief perseverance in attitudes toward celebrities. *Psychology of Popular Media Culture,* **3**(1), 38–48. https://doi-org.libezproxy.open.ac.uk/10.1037/a0034916

Burchill, S. A. L., & Stiles, W. B. (1988). Interactions of depressed college students with their roommates: Not necessarily negative. *Journal of Personality and Social Psychology,* **55,** 410–419.

Burger, J. M. (2009). Replicating Milgram: Would people still obey today? *American Psychologist,* **64**(1), 1–11.

Burger, J. M., & Caldwell, D. F. (2003). The effects of monetary incentives and labeling on the foot-in-the-door effect: Evidence for a self-perception process. *Basic and Applied Social Psychology,* **25,** 235–241.

Burger, J. M., & Pavelich, J. L. (1994). Attributions for presidential elections: The situational shift over time. *Basic and Applied Social Psychology,* **15,** 359–371.

Burger, J. M., Messian, N., Patel, S., del Prade, A., & Anderson, C. (2004). What a coincidence! The effects of incidental similarity on compliance. *Personality and Social Psychology Bulletin,* **30,** 35–43.

Burger, J. M., Soroka, S., Gonzago, K., Murphy, E., & Somervell, E. (2001). The effect of fleeting attraction on compliance to requests. *Personality and Social Psychology Bulletin,* **27,** 1578–1586.

Burgess, R. L., & Huston, T. L. (Eds.) (2013). *Social exchange in developing relationships.* Elsevier.

Burke, R. D., & Sunley, R. (1998). Youth subcultures in contemporary Britain. In K. Hazelhurst & C. Hazlehurst (Eds.), *Gangs and youth subcultures: International explorations.* Transaction.

Burke, S., & Goodman, S. (2012). 'Bring back Hitler's gas chambers': Asylum seeking, Nazis and Facebook – a discursive analysis. *Discourse & Society,* **23**(1), 19–33.

Burkholder, R. (2003, 14 February). Unwilling coalition? Majorities in Britain, Canada oppose military action in Iraq. *Gallup Poll Tuesday Briefing.* www.gallup.com/poll.

Burr, V. (2006). Bystander intervention. In S. Taylor & D. Langdridge (Eds.), *Critical readings in social psychology.* Open University Press.

Burr, W. R. (1973). *Theory construction and the sociology of the family.* Wiley.

Burson, K. A., Larrick, R. P., & Klayman, J. (2006). Skilled or unskilled, but still unaware of it: How perceptions of difficulty drive miscalibration in relative comparisons. *Journal of Personality and Social Psychology,* **90,** 60–77. https://doi.org/10.1037/0022-3514.90.1.60

Bushardt, S. C., Lambert, J., & Duhon, D. L. (2007). Selecting a better carrot: Organizational learning, formal rewards and culture - a behavioral perspective. *Journal of Organizational Culture, Communications & Conflict,* **11**(2), 67-79.

Bushman, B. J. (1998). Priming effects of media violence on the accessibility of aggressive constructs in memory. *Personality and Social Psychology Bulletin,* **24,** 537–545.

Bushman, B. J. (2002). Does venting anger feed or extinguish the flame? Catharsis, rumination, distraction, anger, and aggressive responding. *Personality and Social Psychology Bulletin,* **28,** 724–731.

Bushman, B. J. (2005). Violence and sex in television programs do not sell products in advertisements. *Psychological Science,* **16,** 702–708.

Bushman, B. J., & Anderson, C. A. (1998). Methodology in the study of aggression: Integrating experimental and nonexperimental findings. In R. Geen & E. Donnerstein (Eds.), *Human aggression: Theories, research and implications for policy.* Academic Press.

Bushman, B. J., & Anderson, C. (2001). Media violence and the American public. *American Psychologist,* **56,** 477–489.

Bushman, B. J., & Anderson, C. A. (2002). Violent video games and hostile expectations: A test of the general aggression model. *Personality and Social Psychology Bulletin,* **28,** 1679–1686.

Bushman, B. J., & Anderson, C. A. (2009). Comfortably numb: Desensitizing effects of violent media on helping others. *Psychological Science,* **20,** 273–277.

Bushman, B. J., & Baumeister, R. (1998). Threatened egotism, narcissism, self-esteem, and direct and displaced aggression: Does self-love or self-hate lead to violence? *Journal of Personality and Social Psychology,* **75,** 219–229.

Bushman, B. J., & Bonacci, A. M. (2002). Violence and sex impair memory for television ads. *Journal of Applied Psychology,* **87,** 557–564.

Bushman, B. J., & Huesmann, L. R. (2006). Short-term and long-term effects of violent media on aggression in children and adults. *Archives of Pediatric and Adolescent Medicine,* **160**(4), 348–352. https://doi.org/10.1001/archpedi.160.4.348

Bushman, B. J., Baumeister, R. F., & Phillips, C. M. (2001). Do people aggress to improve their mood? Catharsis beliefs, affect regulation opportunity, and aggressive responding. *Journal of Personality and Social Psychology,* **81,** 17–32.

Bushman, B. J., Baumeister, R. F., Thomaes, S., Ryu, E., Begeer, S., & West, S. G. (2009). Looking again, and harder, for a link between low self-esteem and aggression. *Journal of Personality,* **77,** 427–446.

Bushman, B. J., Bonacci, A. M., Pedersen, W. C., Vasquez, E. A., & Miller, N. (2005a). Chewing on it can chew you up: Effects of rumination on triggered displaced aggression. *Journal of Personality and Social Psychology,* **88,** 969–983.

Bushman, B. J., Wang, M. C., & Anderson, C. A. (2005b). Is the curve relating temperature to aggression linear or curvilinear? Assaults and temperature in Minneapolis reexamined. *Journal of Personality and Social Psychology,* **89,** 62–66.

Bushman, B. J., Wang, M. C., & Anderson, C. A. (2005c). Is the curve relating temperature to aggression linear or curvilinear? A response to Bell (2005) and to Cohn and Rotton (2005). *Journal of Personality and Social Psychology,* **89,** 74–77.

Buss, D. M. (1989). Sex differences in human mate preferences: Evolutionary hypotheses tested in 37 cultures. *Behavioral and Brain Sciences,* **12,** 1–49.

Buss, D. (2016). *The evolution of desire: Strategies of human mating.* Basic Books.

Buss, D. M. (2016). *The evolution of desire: Strategies of human mating.* Basic Books.

Buss, D. M., & Shackelford, T. K. (1997). Human aggression in evolutionary psychological perspective. *Clinical Psychology Review,* **17,** 605–619.

Buss, D. M. (Ed.) (2005). *The handbook of evolutionary psychology.* Wiley.

Buss, D. M., & Shackelford, T. K. (2008). Attractive women want it all: Good genes, economic investment, parenting proclivities, and emotional commitment. *Evolutionary Psychology,* **6,** 134–146.

Buston, P. M., & Emlen, S. T. (2003). Cognitive processes underlying human mate choice: The relationship between self-perception and mate preference in Western society. *Proceedings of the National Academy of Sciences,* **100,** 8805–8810.

Butcher, S. H. (1951). *Aristotle's theory of poetry and fine art.* Dover Publications.

Butler, J. (1990). *Gender trouble: Feminism and the subversion of identity.* Routledge.

Butler, J. (2004). *Undoing gender.* Routledge.

Byrne, D., & Clore, G. L. (1970). A reinforcement model of evaluative responses. *Personality: An International Journal,* **1,** 103–128.

Byrne, D. G., & Espnes, G. A. (2008). Occupational stress and cardiovascular disease. *Stress and Health,* **24,** 231–238.

Bytwerk, R. L. (1976). Julius Streicher and the impact of *Der Stürmer. Wiener Library Bulletin,* **29,** 41–46.

C

Cacioppo, J. T., & Berntson, G. G. (1992). Social psychological contributions to the decade of the brain: Doctrine of multilevel analysis. *American Psychologist,* **47**(8), 1019.

Cacioppo, J. T., & Cacioppo, S. (2013). Social neuroscience. *Perspectives on Psychological Science,* **8**(6), 667–669.

Cacioppo, J. T., & Decety, J. (2011). Social neuroscience: Challenges and opportunities in the study of complex behaviour. *Annals of the New York Academy of Sciences: The Year in Cognitive Neuroscience Issue,* 162–173.

Cacioppo, J. T., & Ortigue, S. (2011). Social neuroscience: How a multidisciplinary field is uncovering the biology of human interactions. *Cerebrum, 17.* Published online 19 December.

Cacioppo, J. T., & Petty, R. E. (1981). Electromyograms as measures of extent and affectivity of information processing. *American Psychologist,* **36,** 441–456.

Cacioppo, J. T., & Petty, R. E. (1986). Social processes. In M. G. H. Coles, E. Donchin, & S. W. Porges (Eds.), *Psychophysiology.* Guilford Press.

Cacioppo, J. T., Berntson, G. G., & Decety, J. (2010). Social neuroscience and its relationship to social psychology. *Social Cognition,* **28**(6), 675–685.

Cacioppo, J. T., Cacioppo, S., & Boomsma, D. I. (2014). Evolutionary mechanisms for loneliness. *Cognition & Emotion,* **28**(1), 3–21.

Cacioppo, J. T., Cacioppo, S., & Petty, R. E. (2018). The neuroscience of persuasion: A review with an emphasis on issues and opportunities. *Social Neuroscience,* **13**(2), 129–172.

Cacioppo, J. T., Crites, S. L., Gardner, W. L., & Berntson, G. G. (1994). Bioelectrical echoes from evaluative categorizations: I. A late positive brain potential that varies as a function of trait negativity and extremity. *Journal of Personality and Social Psychology,* **67,** 115–125.

Cacioppo, J. T., Hawkley, L. C., & Bernstson, G. G. (2003). The anatomy of loneliness. *Current Directions in Psychological Science,* **12,** 71–74.

Cacioppo, J. T., Hawkley, L. C., Bernstson, G. G., Ernst, J. M., Gibbs, A. C., Stickgold, R., & Hobson, J. A. (2002a). Do lonely days invade the nights? Potentialsocial modulation of sleep efficiency. *Psychological Science,* **13,** 384–387.

Cacioppo, J. T., Hawkley, L. C., Crawford, L. E., Ernst, J. M., Burlseon, M. H., Kowalewski, R. B., Malarkey, W. B., Van Cauter, E., & Bernstson, G. G. (2002b). Loneliness and health: Potential mechanisms. *Psychosomatic Medicine,* **64,** 407–417.

Cacioppo, J. T., Hawkley, L. C., & Thisted, R. A. (2010). Perceived social isolation makes me sad: Five year cross-lagged analyses of loneliness and depressive symptomatology in the Chicago Health, Aging, and Social Relations Study. *Psychology of Aging,* **25**(2), 453–463.

Cacioppo, J. T., Petty, R. E., Feinstein, J. A., & Jarvis, W. B. G. (1996). Dispositional differences in cognitive motivation: The life and times of individuals varying in need for cognition. *Psychological Bulletin,* **119,** 197–253.

Caddell, L.S. & Clare, L. (2010). The impact of dementia on self and identity: A systematic review. *Clinical Psychology Review,* **30**(1), 113–126.

Cadwalladr, C. (2009, March 1). How Bridgend was damned by distortion. *The Guardian.* https://www.theguardian.com/lifeandstyle/2009/mar/01/bridgend-wales-youth-suicide-media-ethics

Cai, L., Chan, J. S., Yan, J. H., & Peng, K. (2014). Brain plasticity and motor practice in cognitive aging. *Frontiers in Aging Neuroscience,* **6,** 31. https://www.frontiersin.org/article/10.3389/fnagi.2014.00031

Cairns, E., & Hewstone, M. (2002). The impact of peacemaking in Northern Ireland on intergroup behavior. In S. Gabi & B. Nevo (Eds.), *Peace education: The concept, principles, and practices around the world.* Erlbaum.

Calogero, R. M., Boroughs, M., & Thompson, J. K. (2007). The impact of Western beauty ideals on the lives of women and men: A sociocultural perspective. In

V. Swami & A. Furnham (Eds.), *Body beautiful: Evolutionary and sociocultural perspectives* (pp. 259–298). Palgrave Macmillan.

Calvo-Merrino, B., Glaser, D. E., Grezes, J., Passingham, R. E., & Haggard, P. (2005). Action observation and acquired motor skills. *Cerebral Cortex,* **15**, 1243–1249.

Campbell, A. (2013). The evolutionary psychology of women's aggression. *Philosophical Transactions of the Royal Society, B,* 368: http://doi.org/10.1098/rstb.2013.0078

Campbell, D. T. (1958). Common fate, similarity, and other indices of the status of aggregates of persons as social entities. *Behavioral Science,* **3**, 14–25.

Campbell, D. T. (1975a). The conflict between social and biological evolution and the concept of original sin. *Zygon,* **10**, 234–249.

Campbell, D. T. (1975b). On the conflicts between biological and social evolution and between psychology and oral tradition. *American Psychologist,* **30**, 1103–1126.

Campbell, J. D., & Fairey, P. J. (1989). Informational and normative routes to conformity: The effect of faction size as a function of norm extremity and attention to the stimulus. *Journal of Personality and Social Psychology,* **57**(3), 457.

Campbell, W. K., & Sedikides, C. (1999). Self-threat magnifies the self-serving bias: A meta-analytic integration. *Review of General Psychology,* **3**, 23–43.

Campbell, W. K., Rudich, E., & Sedikides, C. (2002). Narcissism, self-esteem, and the positivity of self-views: Two portraits of self-love. *Personality and Social Psychology Bulletin,* **28**, 358–368.

Canale, N., Griffiths, M.D., Vieno, A., Siciliano, V., & Molinaro, S. (2016). Impact of Internet gambling on problem gambling among adolescents in Italy: Findings from a large-scale nationally representative survey. *Computers in Human Behavior,* **57**, 99–106.

Canary, D. J., & Stafford, L. (2001). Equity in the preservation of personal relationships. In J. Harvey & A. Wenzel (Eds.), *Close romantic relationships: Maintenance and enhancement* (pp. 141–160). Psychology Press.

Cantor, N. & Mischel, W. (1979). Prototypes in person perception. In L. Berkowitz (Ed.), *Advances in experimental social psychology* (Vol. 12). Academic Press.

Cantor, N., & Mischel, W. (1977). Traits as prototypes: Effects on recognition memory. *Journal of Personality & Social Psychology,* **35**, 38–48.

Caputo, D., & Dunning, D. (2005). What you don't know: The role played by errors of omission in imperfect self-assessments. *Journal of Experimental Social Psychology,* **41**, 488–505.

Carducci, B. J., Cosby, P. C., & Ward, D. D. (1978). Sexual arousal and interpersonal evaluations. *Journal of Experimental Social Psychology,* **14**, 449–457.

Carlo, G., PytlikZillig, L. M., Roesch, S. C., & Dienstbier, R. A. (2009). The elusive altruist: The psychological study of the altruistic personality (pp. 271–294). In D. Narvaez & D. K. Lapsley (Eds.), *Personality, identity, and character: Explorations in moral psychology.* Cambridge University Press.

Carlson, J., & Hatfield, E. (1992). *The psychology of emotion.* Holt, Rinehart & Winston.

Carlson, K., & Russo, J. (2001). Biased interpretation of evidence by mock jurors. *Journal of Experimental Psychology: Applied,* **7**(2), 91-103.

Carlston, D. E., & Shovar, N. (1983). Effects of performance attributions on others' perceptions of the attributor. *Journal of Personality and Social Psychology,* **44**, 515–525.

Carlston, D. E., & Skowronski, J. J. (2005). Linking versus thinking: Evidence for the different associative and attributional bases of spontaneous trait transference and spontaneous trait inference. *Journal of Personality and Social Psychology,* **89**, 884–898.

Carman, W. F., Elder, A. G., Wallace, L. A., McAulay, K., Walker, A., Murray, G., & Stott, D. J. (2000). Effects of influenza vaccination of health-care workers on mortality of elderly people in long-term care: A randomised controlled trial. *The Lancet,* **355**, 93–97.

Carnegie, D. (1998). *How to win friends and influence people.* Galahad Books.

Carnevale, P. J., & Choi, D.-W. (2000). Culture in the mediation of international disputes. *International Journal of Psychology,* **35**, 105–110.

Caron, A., Lafontaine, M. F., Bureau, J. F., Levesque, C., & Johnson, S. M. (2012). Comparisons of close relationships: An evaluation of relationship quality and patterns of attachment to parents, friends, and romantic partners in young adults. *Canadian Journal of Behavioural Science/Revue canadienne des sciences du comportement,* **44**(4), 245.

Carothers, B. J., & Reis, H. T. (2013). Men and women are from Earth: Examining the latent structure of gender. *Journal of Personality and Social Psychology,* **104**(2), 385–407. https://doi.org/10.1037/a0030437

Carr, B. B., Hagai, E. B., & Zurbriggen, E. (2017). Queering Bem: Theoretical intersections between Sandra Bem's scholarship and queer theory. *Sex Roles,* **76**(11–12), 655–668. https://doi.org/10.1007/s11199-015-0546-1

Carr, P., Goodman, S., & Jowett, A. (2019). 'I don't think there is any moral basis for taking money away from people': Using discursive psychology to explore the complexity of talk about tax. *Critical Discourse Studies,* **16**(1), 84–95.

Carrasco, M., Barker, E. D., Tremblay, R. E., & Vitaro, F. (2006). Eysenck's personality dimensions as predictors of male adolescent trajectories of physical aggression, theft and vandalism. *Personality and Individual Differences,* **41**(7), 1309–1320.

Carter, E. R., & Murphy, M. C. (2017). Consensus and consistency: Exposure to multiple discrimination claims shapes Whites' intergroup attitudes. *Journal of Experimental Social Psychology,* **73**, 24–33.

Carter, J. D., Hall, J. A., Carney, D. R., & Rosip, J. C. (2006). Individual differences in the acceptance of stereotyping. *Journal of Research in Personality,* **40**, 1103–1118.

Carter, S., & Snow, C. (2004, May). Helping singles enter better marriages using predictive models of marital success. Paper presented to the American Psychological Society convention.

Cartwright, D. S. (1975). The nature of gangs. In D. S. Cartwright, B. Tomson, & H. Schwartz (Eds.), *Gang delinquency.* Brooks/Cole.

Carvallo, M., & Gabriel, S. (2006). No man is an island: The need to belong and dismissing avoidant attachment style. *Personality and Social Psychology Bulletin,* **32**, 697–709.

Carver, C. S. (2003). Self-awareness. In *Handbook of self and identity* (pp. 179–196). Guilford Press.

Carver, C. S., & Scheier, M. F. (1978). Self-focusing effects of dispositional self-consciousness, mirror presence, and audience presence. *Journal of Personality and Social Psychology,* **36**, 324–332.

Carver, C. S., & Scheier, M. F. (1981). *Attention and self-regulation.* Springer-Verlag.

Caspi, A., McClay, J., Moffitt, T., Mill, J., Martin, J., Craig, I. W., Taylor, A., & Poulton, R. (2002). Role of genotype in the cycle of violence in maltreated children. *Science,* **297**, 851–854.

Cassidy, J. (2000). Adult romantic attachments: A developmental perspective on individual differences. *Review of General Psychology Special Issue: Adult attachment,* **4**, 111–131.

Castano, E., Yzerbyt, V., Paladino, M. P., & Sacchi, S. (2002). I belong, therefore, I exist: Ingroup identification, ingroup entitativity, and ingroup bias. *Personality and Social Psychology Bulletin,* **28**, 135–143.

Castelli, L., Macrae, N. C., Zogmaister, C., & Arcuri, L. (2004). A tale of two primes: Contextual limits on stereotype activation. *Social Cognition,* **22**(2), 233–247.

Castro, F. N., & de Araujo Lopes, F. (2011). Romantic preferences in Brazilian undergraduate students: From the short term to the long term. *Journal of Sex Research,* **48**(5), 479–485.

Cauberghe, V., De Pelsmacker, P., Janssens, W., & Dens, N. (2009). Fear, threat and efficacy in threat appeals: Message involvement as a key mediator to message acceptance. *Accident Analysis and Prevention,* **41**(2), 276–285.

Cázares, A. (2010). Proficiency and attitudes toward information technologies' use in psychology undergraduates. *Computers in Human Behavior,* **26**(5), 1004–1008.;//

Cesarani, D. (2004). *Eichmann: His life and crimes.* Heinemann.

Cesario, J., & Higgins, E. T. (2008). Making message recipients 'feel right': How nonverbal cues can increase persuasion. *Psychological Science,* **19**(5), 415–420.

Cha, E. S., Kim, K. H., & Patrick, T. E. (2008). Predictors of intention to practice safer sex among Korean college students. *Archives of Sexual Behavior,* **37**, 641–651.

Chaffin, S. M. (2008). The new playground bullies of cyberspace: Online peer sexual harassment. *Howard Law Journal,* **51**(3), 773–818.

Chaiken, S. (1980). Heuristic versus systematic information processing and the use of source versus message cues in persuasion. *Journal of Personality and Social Psychology,* **39,** 752–766.

Chamie, J., & Mirkin, B. (2011). Same-sex marriage: A new social phenomenon. *Population and Development Review,* **37**(3), 529-551.

Champion, V. L., & Skinner, C. S. (2008). The health belief model. *Health Behavior and Health Education: Theory, Research, and Practice,* **4,** 45–65.

Chang, C. (2014). Guilt regulation: The relative effects of altruistic versus egoistic appeals for charity advertising. *Journal of Advertising,* **43**(3), 211–227.

Chang, C. T., & Lee, Y. K. (2009). Framing charity advertising: Influences of message framing, image valence, and temporal framing on a charitable appeal. *Journal of Applied Social Psychology,* **39**(12), 2910-2935.

Chartrand, T. L., & Bargh, J. A. (1999). The chameleon effect: The perception–behavior link and social interaction. *Journal of Personality and Social Psychology,* **76,** 893–910.

Chasin, C. D. (2011). Theoretical issues in the study of asexuality. *Archives of Sexual Behavior,* **40**(4), 713–723.

Chen, E. (2004). Why socioeconomic status affects the health of children: A psychosocial perspective. *Current Directions in Psychological Science,* **13,** 112–115.

Chen, F. F., & Kenrick, D. T. (2002). Repulsion or attraction? Group membership and assumed attitude similarity. *Journal of Personality and Social Psychology,* **83,** 111–125.

Chen, L.-H., Baker, S. P., Braver, E. R., & Li, G. (2000). Carrying passengers as a risk factor for crashes fatal to 16- and 17-year-old drivers. *Journal of the American Medical Association,* **283,** 1578–1582.

Chen, S. C. (1937). Social modification of the activity of ants in nest-building. *Physiological Zoology,* **10,** 420–436.

Chen, S., Lee-Chai, A. Y., & Bargh, J. A. (2001). Relationship orientation as moderator of the effects of social power. *Journal of Personality and Social Psychology,* **80,** 183–187.

Chen, X., & Silverstein, M. (2000). Intergenerational social support and the psychological well-being of older parents in China. *Research on Aging,* **22**(1), 43–65.

Chen, Y., & Feeley, T. H. (2014). Social support, social strain, loneliness, and well-being among older adults: an analysis of the Health and Retirement Study. *Journal of Social and Personal Relationships,* **31**(2), 141–161.

Cheney, R. (2003, 16 March). Comments on Face the Nation. *CBS News.*

Cheng, B., Zhou, X., Guo, G., & Yang, K. (2018). Perceived overqualification and cyberloafing: A moderated-mediation model based on equity theory. *Journal of Business Ethics,* 1–13. https://doi.org/10.1007/s10551-018-4026-8

Cherry, F. (1995). *The stubborn particulars of social psychology.* Routledge.

Chester, D. S., & DeWall, C. N. (2015). The pleasure of revenge: Retaliatory aggression arises from a neural imbalance toward reward. *Social Cognitive and Affective Neuroscience,* **11**(7), 1173–1182.

Chiang, J. K. H., & Suen, H. Y. (2015). Self-presentation and hiring recommendations in online communities: Lessons from LinkedIn. *Computers in Human Behavior,* **48,** 516-524.

Ching, H., Daffern, M., & Thomas, S. (2012). Appetitive violence: A new phenomenon? *Psychiatry, Psychology and Law,* **19**(5), 745–763.

Chiou, W. B., & Wan, C. S. (2006). Sexual self-disclosure in cyberspace among Taiwanese adolescents: Gender differences and the interplay of cyberspace and real life. *CyberPsychology & Behavior,* **9**(1), 46–53.

Chiou, W. B., Chen, S. W., & Liao, D. C. (2014). Does Facebook promote self-interest? Enactment of indiscriminate one-to-many communication on online social networking sites decreases prosocial behavior. *Cyberpsychology, Behavior, and Social Networking,* **17**(2), 68–73.

Chivers, M. L., Roy, C., Grimbos, T., Cantor, J. M., & Seto, M. C. (2014). Specificity of sexual arousal for sexual activities in men and women with conventional and masochistic sexual interests. *Archives of Sexual Behavior,* **43,** 931–940. http://dx.doi.org/10.1007/s10508-013-0174-1

Chmiel, A., Sienkiewicz, J., Thelwall, M., Paltoglou, G., Buckley, K., Kappas, A., & Hotyst, J. A. (2011). Collective emotions online and their influence on community life. *PloS ONE,* **6**(7), e22207.

Chodorow, N. J. (1978). *The reproduction of mother: Psychoanalysis and the sociology of gender.* University of California Press.

Chodorow, N. J. (1989). *Feminism and psychoanalytic theory.* Yale University Press.

Choi, I., & Choi, Y. (2002). Culture and self-concept flexibility. *Personality and Social Psychology Bulletin,* **28,** 1508–1517.

Choi, I., Nisbett, R. E., & Norenzayan, A. (1999). Causal attribution across cultures: Variation and universality. *Psychological Bulletin,* **125,** 47–63.

Choi, K., Cho, S., & Lee, J. (2019). Impacts of online risky behaviors and cybersecurity management on cyberbullying and traditional bullying victimization among Korean youth: Application of cyber-routine activities theory with latent class analysis. *Computers in Human Behavior,* **100,** 1–10.

Chua, H. F., Boland, J. E., & Nisbett, R. E. (2005a). Cultural variation in eye movements during scene perception. *Proceedings of the National Academy of Sciences,* **102,** 12629–12633.

Chua, H. F., Leu, J., & Nisbett, R. E. (2005b). Culture and diverging views of social events. *Personality and Social Psychology Bulletin,* **31,** 925–934.

Chua-Eoan, H. (1997, 7 April). Imprisoned by his own passions. *Time,* 40–42.

Cialdini, R. B. (2003). Crafting normative messages to protect the environment. *Current Directions in Psychological Science,* **12**(4), 105–109.

Cialdini, R. B., & Goldstein, N. J. (2004). Social influence: Compliance and conformity. *Annual Review of Psychology,* **55,** 591–621.

Cialdini, R. B., & Schroeder, D. A. (1976). Increasing compliance by legitimizing paltry contributions: When even a penny helps. *Journal of Personality and Social Psychology,* **34,** 599–604.

Cialdini, R. B., Borden, R. J., Thorne, A., Walker, M. R., Freeman, S., & Sloan, L. R. (1976). Basking in reflected glory: Three (football) field studies. *Journal of Personality and Social Psychology,* **34**(3), 366.

Cialdini, R. B., Cacioppo, J. T., Bassett, R., & Miller, J. A. (1978). Lowball procedure for producing compliance: Commitment then cost. *Journal of Personality and Social Psychology,* **36,** 463–476.

Cialdini, R. B., Demaine, L. J., Barrett, D. W., Sagarin, B. J., & Rhoads, K. L. V. (2003). The poison parasite defense: A strategy for sapping a stronger opponent's persuasive strength. Unpublished manuscript, Arizona State University.

Cialdini, R. B., Vincent, J. E., Lewis, S. K., Catalan, J., Wheeler, D., & Danby, B. L. (1975). Reciprocal concessions procedure for inducing compliance: The door-in-the-face technique. *Journal of Personality and Social Psychology,* **31,** 206–215.

Cialdini, R. B., Wissler, R. L., & Schweitzer, N. J. (2003). The science of influence: Using six principles of persuasion to negotiate and mediate more effectively. *GP Solo,* **20**(6), 36.

Cialdini, R. B. (2009). *Influence: Science and practice* (5th ed.). Allyn & Bacon.

Cialdini, R. B. (1993). *Social influence: Science and practice* (3rd ed.). Harper & Collins.

Cialdini, R. B. (1995). A full-cycle approach to social psychology. In G. G. Brannigan & M. R. Merrens (Eds.), *The social psychologists: Research adventures.* McGraw-Hill.

Cialdini, R. B. (2001). *Influence: Science and practice* (4th ed.). Allyn & Bacon.

Cialdini, R. B. (2005). Basic social influence is underestimated. *Psychological Inquiry,* **16,** 158–161.

Cinnirella, M., & Green, B. (2007). Does 'cyber-conformity' vary cross-culturally? Exploring the effect of culture and communication medium on social conformity. *Computers in Human Behavior,* **23**(4), 2011–2025. https://doi.org/10.1016/j.chb.2006.02.009

Clack, B., Dixon, J., & Tredoux, C. (2005). Eating together apart: Patterns of segregation in a multi-ethnic cafeteria. *Journal of Community and Applied Social Psychology,* **15,** 1–16.

Claidière, N., Bowler, M., & Whiten, A. (2012). Evidence for weak or linear conformity but not for hyper-conformity in an everyday social learning context. *PLoS one,* **7**(2), e30970.

Clark, J. K., Wegener, D. T., Habashi, M. M., & Evans, A. T. (2012). Source expertise and persuasion: The effects of perceived opposition or support on message scrutiny. *Personality and Social Psychology Bulletin,* **38**(1), 90–100. https://doi.org/10.1177/0146167211420733

Clark, J. L., & Green, M. C. (2018). Self-fulfilling prophecies: Perceived reality of online interaction drives expected outcomes of online communication. *Personality and Individual Differences,* **133,** 73–76.

Clark, J., & Baker, T. (2011). 'It's not fair!' Cultural attitudes to social loafing in ethnically diverse groups. *Intercultural Communication Studies,* **20**(1), 124–140.

Clark, M. S. (1984). Record keeping in two types of relationships. *Journal of Personality and Social Psychology,* **47,** 549–557.

Clark, M. S. (1986). Evidence for the effectiveness of manipulations of desire for communal versus exchange relationships. *Personality and Social Psychology Bulletin,* **12,** 414–425.

Clark, M. S., & Bennett, M. E. (1992). Research on relationships: Implications for mental health. In D. Ruble & P. Costanzo (Eds.), *The social psychology of mental health.* Guilford Press.

Clark, M. S., & Mills, J. (1979). Interpersonal attraction in exchange and communal relationships. *Journal of Personality and Social Psychology,* **37,** 12–24.

Clark, M. S., & Mills, J. (1993). The difference between communal and exchange relationships: What it is and is not. *Personality and Social Psychology Bulletin,* **19,** 684–691.

Clark, M. S., Mills, J., & Corcoran, D. (1989). Keeping track of needs and inputs of friends and strangers. *Personality and Social Psychology Bulletin,* **15,** 533–542.

Clark, M. S., Mills, J., & Powell, M. C. (1986). Keeping track of needs in communal and exchange relationships. *Journal of Personality and Social Psychology,* **51,** 333–338.

Clark, R. D., III (1995). A few parallels between group polarization and minority influence. In S. Moscovici, H. Mucchi-Faina, & A. Maass (Eds.), *Minority influence.* Nelson-Hall.

Clarke, A. C. (1952). An examination of the operation of residual propinquity as a factor in mate selection. *American Sociological Review,* **27,** 17–22.

Clarke, V. A., Lovegrove, H., Williams, A., & Machperson, M. (2000). Unrealistic optimism and the health belief model. *Journal of Behavioral Medicine,* **23**(4), 367–376. https://doi.org/10.1023/A:1005500917875

Clary, E. G., & Snyder, M. (1999). The motivations to volunteer: Theoretical and practical considerations. *Current Directions in Psychological Science,* **8**(5), 156–159.

Clayton, S. (2012). *The Oxford handbook of environmental and conservation psychology.* Oxford University Press.

Clayton, S., & Myers, G. (2015). *Conservation psychology: Understanding and promoting human care for nature.* John Wiley & Sons.

Cline, V. B., Croft, R. G., & Courrier, S. (1973). Desensitization of children to television violence. *Journal of Personality and Social Psychology,* **27,** 360–365.

Clore, G. L., Bray, R. M., Itkin, S. M., & Murphy, P. (1978). Interracial attitudes and behavior at a summer camp. *Journal of Personality and Social Psychology,* **36,** 107–116.

Clore, G. L., Wiggins, N. H., & Itkin, G. (1975). Gain and loss in attraction: Attributions from nonverbal behavior. *Journal of Personality and Social Psychology,* **31,** 706–712.

Cobb-Clark, D. A., Kassenboehmer, S. C., & Sinning, M. G. (2016). Locus of control and savings. *Journal of Banking and Finance,* **73**(C), 113–130.

Coccaro, E. (2017). Testosterone and aggression: More than just biology?*Biological Psychiatry,* **82**(4), 234.

Codol, J. P. (1975). On the so-called superior conformity of the self behavior: Twenty experimental investigations. *European Journal of Social Psychology,* **5,** 457–501.

Cohn, E. G., & Rotton, J. (2005). The curve is still out there: A reply to Bushman, Wang, and Anderson's (2005) 'Is the curve relating temperature to aggression linear or curvilinear?' *Journal of Personality and Social Psychology,* **89,** 67–70.

Colapinto, J. (1997, December 11). The true story of John/Joan. *The Rolling Stone:* https://www.healthyplace.com/gender/inside-intersexuality/the-true-story-of-john-joan

Collins, C. M., & Chambers, S. M. (2005). Psychological and situational influences on commuter-transport mode choice. *Environment and Behavior,* **37**(5), 640–661.

Collins, S. M. (2001). Emerging methods for the physiological assessment of occupational stress. *Work,* **17**(3), 209–219.

Colman, A. (1991). Crowd psychology in South African murder trials. *American Psychologist,* **46**(10), 1071–1079.

Colquitt, J. A., Conlon, D. E., Wesson, M. J., Porter, C. O. L. H., & Yee, K. (2001). Justice at the millennium. A meta-analytic review of 25 years of organizational justice research. *Journal of Applied Psychology,* **86,** 425–445.

Colyn, L. A., & Gordon, A. K. (2013). Schadenfreude as a mate-value-tracking mechanism. *Personal Relationships,* **20,** 524–545.

Condor, S., Figgou, L., Abell, J., Gibson, S., & Stevenson, C. (2006). 'They're not racist . . .' Prejudice denial, mitigation and suppression in dialogue. *British Journal of Social Psychology,* **45,** 441–462.

Confer, J. C., Easton, J. A., Fleischman, D. S., Goetz, C. D., Lewis, D. M. G., Perilloux, C., & Buss, D. M. (2010). Evolutionary psychology: Controversies, questions, prospects, and limitations. *American Psychologist,* **65**(2), 110–126.

Conger, R. D., Cui, M., Bryant, C. M., & Elder, G. H. (2000). Competence in early adult romantic relationships: A developmental perspective on family influences. *Journal of Personality and Social Psychology,* **79,** 224–237.

Congressional Record (1969, November 18–25). *Proceedings and debates of the 91st Congress, First Session,* 115(26), p. 35653.

Conley, T. D., & Moors, A. C. (2014). More oxygen please! How polyamorous relationship strategies might oxygenate marriage. *Psychological Inquiry,* **25**(1), 56–63.

Connolly, P. (1998). *Racism, gender identities and young children: Social relations in a multi-ethnic, inner-city primary school.* Routledge.

Connor, P., & Krogstad, J. M. (2016, June 15). Immigrant share of population jumps in some European countries. *Pew Research Center:*https://www.pewresearch.org/fact-tank/2016/06/15/immigrant-share-of-population-jumps-in-some-european-countries/

Conway, F., & Siegelman, J. (1979). *Snapping: America's epidemic of sudden personality change.* Delta Books.

Conway, J. R., Noe, N., Stulp, G., & Pollett, T. V. (2015). Finding your soulmate: Homosexual and heterosexual age preferences in online dating. *Personal Relationships,* **22**(4), 666–678.

Cooper, J. (2007). *Cognitive dissonance: Fifty years of a classic theory.* Sage https://doi.org/10.4135/9781446214282

Cooper, M. (2016, September). The share of female CEOs in Europe has doubled over the past seven years – to 4%, *Quartz.* https://qz.com/794383/the-share-of-female-ceos-in-europe-has-doubled-over-the-past-seven-years-to-4/

Cornelissen, J. P., Haslam, S. A., & Balmer, J. M. (2007). Social identity, organizational identity and corporate identity: Towards an integrated understanding of processes, patternings and products. *British Journal of Management,* **18,** S1-S16. https://doi.org/10.1111/j.1467-8551.2007.00522.x

Correia, I., Alves, H., Sutton, R., Ramos, M., Gouveia-Pereira, M., & Vala, J. (2012). When do people derogate or psychologically distance themselves from victims? Belief in a just world and ingroup identification. *Personality and Individual Differences,* **53,** 747–752.

Correll, J., Park, B., Judd, C. M., & Wittenbrink, B. (2002). The police officer's dilemma: Using ethnicity to disambiguate potentially threatening individuals. *Journal of Personality and Social Psychology,* **83,** 1314–1329.

Correll, J., Urland, G. R., & Ito, T. A. (2006). Event-related potentials and the decision to shoot: The role of threat perception and cognitive control. *Journal of Experimental Social Psychology,* **42,** 120–128.

Cote, K. A., McCormick, C. M., Geniole, S. N., Renn, R. P., & MacAulay, S. D. (2013). Sleep deprivation lowers reactive aggression and testosterone in men. *Biological Psychology,* **92,** 249–256.

Cote, S. M., Vaillancourt, T., Barker, E. D., Nagin, D. S., & Tremblay, R. E. (2007). Thejoint development of physical and indirect aggression: Predictors of continuityand change during childhood. *Developmental Psychopathology,* **19**(01), 37–55. http://dx.doi.org/10.1017/S0954579407070034

Cottrell, C. A., & Neuberg, S. L. (2005). Different emotional reactions to different groups: A sociofunctional threat-based approach to prejudice. *Journal of Personality and Social Psychology,* **88,** 770–789.

Cottrell, C. A., Neuberg, S. L., & Li, N. P. (2007). What do people desire in others? A sociofunctional perspective on the importance of different valued characteristics. *Journal of Personality and Social Psychology,* **92**(2), 208–231.

Cottrell, N. B. (1968). Performance in the presence of other human beings: Mere presence, audience, and affiliation effects. In E.C. Simmel, R.A. Hoppe, & G.A. Milton (Eds.), *Social facilitation and imitative behavior* (pp. 91–110). Allyn & Bacon.

Cottrell, N. B., Wack, D. L., Sekerak, G. J., & Rittle, R. M. (1968). Social facilitation of dominant responses by the presence of an audience and the mere presence of others. *Journal of Personality and Social Psychology,* **9**, 245–250.

Coviello, L., Sohn, Y., Kramer, A. D. I., Marlow, C., Franceschetti, M., Christakis, N. A., & Fowler, J. H. (2014). Detecting emotional contagion in massive social networks. *PLoS ONE,* **9**(3):e90315. https://doi.org/10.1371/journal.pone.0090315

Cowan, D. E., & Bromley, D. G. (2015). *Cults and new religions : A brief history* (2nd ed.). John Wiley & Sons.

Cox, W. M., Hosier, S. G., Crossley, S., Kendall, B., & Roberts, K. L. (2006). Motives for drinking, alcohol consumption, and alcohol-related problems among British secondary-school and university students. *Addictive Behaviors,* **31**(12), 2147–2157. https://doi.org/10.1016/j.addbeh.2006.02.023

Coyne, S., & Archer, J. (2004). Indirect aggression in the media: A content analysis of British television programs. *Aggressive Behavior,* **30**, 254–271.

Coyne, S. M., Linder, J. R., Nelson, D. A., & Gentile, D. A. (2012). 'Frenemies, fraitors, and mean-em-aitors': Priming effects of viewing physical and relational aggression in the media on women. *Aggressive Behavior,* **38**(2), 141–149.

Crane-Seeber, J., & Crane, B. (2010). Contesting essentialist theories of patriarchal relations: Evolutionary psychology and the denial of history. *Journal of Men's Studies,* **18**(3), 218–237. https://doi.org/10.3149/jms.1803.218

Crawford, M., Stark, A. C., & Renner, C. H. (1998). The meaning of Ms.: Social assimilation of a gender concept. *Psychology of Women Quarterly,* **22**, 197–208.

Crawford, T. J. (1974). Sermons on racial tolerance and the parish neighborhood context. *Journal of Applied Social Psychology,* **4**, 1–23.

Crisp, R. J., & Hewstone, M. (1999). Differential evaluation of crossed category groups: Patterns, processes, and reducing intergroup bias. *Group Processes and Intergroup Relations,* **2**, 307–333.

Crisp, R. J., & Hewstone, M. (2000). Multiple categorization and social identity. In D. Capozza & R. Brown (Eds.), *Social identity theory: Trends in theory and research.* Sage.

Crocker, J. (2002). The costs of seeking self-esteem. *Journal of Social Issues,* **58**, 597–615.

Crocker, J., & Knight, K. M. (2005). Contingencies of self-worth. *Current Directions in Psychological Science,* **14**, 200–203.

Crocker, J., & Luhtanen, R. (1990). Collective self-esteem and ingroup bias. *Journal of Personality and Social Psychology,* **58**, 60–67.

Crocker, J., & Luhtanen, R. (2003). Level of self-esteem and contingencies of self-worth: Unique effects on academic, social, and financial problems in college students. *Personality and Social Psychology Bulletin,* **29**, 701–712.

Crocker, J., & Park, L. E. (2004). The costly pursuit of self-esteem. *Psychological Bulletin,* **130**, 392–414.

Crocker, J., & Wolfe, C. (2001). Contingencies of self-worth. *Psychological Review,* **108**, 593–623.

Crocker, J., Alloy, L. B., & Kayne, N. T. (1988). Attributional style, depression, and perceptions of consensus for event. *Journal of Personality and Social Psychology,* **54**, 840–846.

Crocker, J., Luhtanen, R., Blaine, B., & Broadnax, S. (1994). Collective self-esteem and psychological wellbeing among white, black, and Asian college students. *Personality & Social Psychology Bulletin,* **20**, 503–513.

Crocker, J., Hannah, D. B., & Weber, R. (1983). Person memory and causal attributions. *Journal of Personality and Social Psychology,* **44**, 55–66.

Cropanzano, R., & Mitchell, M. S. (2005). Social exchange theory: An interdisciplinary review. *Journal of Management,* **31**, 874–900.

Cropanzano, R., Stein, J., & Goldman, B. M. (2007). Self-interest. In E. H. Kessler & J. R. Bailey (Eds.), *Handbook of organizational and managerial wisdom* (pp. 181–221). Sage.

Croyle, R. T., & Cooper, J. (1983). Dissonance arousal: Physiological evidence. *Journal of Personality and Social Psychology,* **45**, 782–791.

Crozier, R. W., & Alden, L. E. (2003). *International handbook of social anxiety: Concepts, research and interventions relating to the self and shyness.* Wiley.

Crumlish, N., & Kelly, B. (2009). How psychiatrists think. *Advances in Psychiatric Treatment,* **15**, 72–79.

Cruwys, T., Wakefield, J. R. H., Sani, F., Dingle, G. A., & Jetten, J. (2018). Social isolation predicts frequent attendance in primary care. *Annals of Behavioral Medicine,* **52**(10), 817–829. https://doi.org/10.1093/abm/kax054

Cryer, C., Knox, A., Martin, D., & Barlow, J. (2002). Hip protector compliance among older people living in residential care homes. *Injury Prevention,* **8**(3), 202-206.

Cuddy, A., Rock, M., & Norton, M. (2007). Aid in the aftermath of hurricane Katerina: Inferences of secondary emotions and intergroup helping. *Group Processes and Intergroup Relations,* **10**, 107–118.

Cullen, P., Vaughan, G., Li, Z., Price, J., Yu, D., & Sullivan, E. (2019). Counting dead women in Australia: An in-depth case review of femicide. *Journal of Family Violence,* **34**(1), 1–8.

Cummings, J. N., Kiesler, S., Bosagh Zadeh, R., & Balakrishnan, A. D. (2013). Group heterogeneity increases the risks of large group size: A longitudinal study of productivity in research groups. *Psychological Science,* **24**(6), 880–890.

Cunningham, W. A., Johnson, M. K., Raye, C. L., Gatenby, J. C., Gore, J. C., & Banaji, M. R. (2004). Separable neural components in the processing of black and white faces. *Psychological Science,* **15**, 806–813.

Custers, K., & Van den Bulck, J. (2013). The cultivation of fear of sexual violence in women processes and moderators of the relationship between television and fear. *Communication Research,* **40**(1), 96–124.

Cygan-Rehm, K. & Maeder, M. (2013). The effect of education on fertility: Evidence from a compulsory schooling reform. *Labour Economics,* **25**(C), 35-48.

D

D'Argenbeau, A., Collette, F., Van der Linden, M., Laureys, S., Del Fiore, G., Degueldre, C., Luxen, A., & Salmon, E. (2005). Self-referential reflective activity and its relationship with rest: A PET study. *Neuroimage,* **25**, 616–624.

Dabbs, J. M., Jr, & Janis, I. L. (1965). Why does eating while reading facilitate opinion change? An experimental inquiry. *Journal of Experimental Social Psychology,* **1**, 133–144.

Dabbs, J. M., Jr, & Morris, R. (1990). Testosterone, social class, and antisocial behavior in a sample of 4, 462 men. *Psychological Science,* **1**, 209–211.

Daly, M., & Delaney, L. (2013). The scarring effect of unemployment throughout adulthood on psychological distress at age 50: Estimates controlling for early adulthood distress and childhood psychological factors. *Social Science & Medicine,* **80**(19), 98–105.

Darity, W. (2008). *Social judgment theory.* Macmillan.

Darley, J. M. (1992). Social organization for the production of evil. *Psychological Inquiry,* **3**(2), 199–218. https://doi.org/10.1207/s15327965pli0302_28

Darley, J. M., & Batson, C. D. (1973). From Jerusalem to Jericho: A study of situational and dispositional variables in helping behavior. *Journal of Personality and Social Psychology,* **27**, 100–108.

Darley, J. M., & Berscheid, E. (1967). Increased liking as a result of the anticipation of personal contact. *Human Relations,* **20**, 29–40.

Darley, J. M., & Latané, B. (1968). Bystander intervention in emergencies: Diffusion of responsibility. *Journal of Personality and Social Psychology,* **8**, 377–383.

Darley, S., & Cooper, J. (1972). Cognitive consequences of forced noncompliance. *Journal of Personality and Social Psychology,* **24**, 321–326.

Darwin, C. (1859/1988). *The origin of species.* In P. H. Barrett & R. B. Freeman (Eds.), *The works of Charles Darwin* (Vol. 15). New York University Press.

Darwin, C. (2009). *On the origin of species.* Penguin Classics.

Das, E. H. H. J., de Wit, J. B. F., & Stroebe, W. (2003). Fear appeals motivate acceptance of action recommendations: Evidence for a positive bias in the processing of persuasive messages. *Personality and Social Psychology Bulletin*, **29**, 650–664.

Dashiell, J. F. (1930). An experimental analysis of some group effects. *Journal of Abnormal and Social Psychology*, **25**, 190–199.

Davenport, S. W., Bergman, S. M., Bergman, J. Z., & Fearrington, M.E. (2014). Twitter versus Facebook: Exploring the role of narcissism in the motives and usage of different social media platforms. *Computers in Human Behavior*, **32**, 212–220.

David, B., & Turner, J. C. (1996). Studies in self-categorization and minority conversion: Is being a member of the out-group an advantage? *British Journal of Social Psychology*, **35**, 179–199.

David, B., & Turner, J. C. (1999). Studies in self-categorization and minority conversion: The in-group minority in intragroup and intergroup contexts. *British Journal of Social Psychology*, **38**, 115–134.

Davies, A. P. C., Goetz, A. T., & Shackelford, T. K. (2008). Exploiting the beauty in the eye of the beholder: The use of physical attractiveness as a persuasive tactic. *Personality and Individual Differences*, **45**(4), 302–306. https://doi.org/10.1016/j.paid.2008.04.016

Davies, M. F. (1997). Belief persistence after evidential discrediting: The impact of generated versus provided explanations on the likelihood of discredited outcomes. *Journal of Experimental Social Psychology*, **33**, 561–578.

Davis, C. G., Lehman, D. R., Silver, R. C., Wortman, C. B., & Ellard, J. H. (1996). Self-blame following a traumatic event: The role of perceived avoidability. *Personality and Social Psychology Bulletin*, **22**, 557–567.

Davis, C. G., Lehman, D. R., Wortman, C. B., Silver, R. C., & Thompson, S. C. (1995). The undoing of traumatic life events. *Personality and Social Psychology Bulletin*, **21**, 109–124.

Davis, J. L., & Rusbult, C. E. (2001). Attitude alignment in close relationships. *Journal of Personality and Social Psychology*, **81**, 65–84.

Davis, K. E. (1995). *Reshaping the female body*. Routledge.

Davis, K. E. (2002). A dubious equality: Men, women and cosmetic surgery. *Body Society*, **8**, 49–65.

Davis, K. E., & Jones, E. E. (1960). Changes in interpersonal perception as a means of reducing cognitive dissonance. *Journal of Abnormal and Social Psychology*, **61**, 402–410.

Davis, L., & Greenlees, C. (1992). Social loafing revisited: Factors that mitigate – and reverse – performance loss. Paper presented at the Southwestern Psychological Association convention.

Dawes, R. M. (1990). The potential nonfalsity of the false consensus effect. In R. M. Hogarth (Ed.), *Insights in decision making: A tribute to Hillel J. Einhorn*. University of Chicago Press.

Dawkins, R. (1976). *The selfish gene*. Oxford University Press.

Dawkins, R. (2006). *The selfish gene*. Oxford University Press.

Dawkins, R. (2016). *The selfish gene: 40th anniversary edition*. Oxford University Press.

Day, R. D., Lewis, C., O'Brien, M., & Lamb, M. E. (2005). Fatherhood and father involvement: Emerging constructs and theoretical orientations. In V. L. Bengston, A. C. Acock, K. R. Allen, P. Dillworth-Anderson & D. M. Klein (Eds.), *Sourcebook of family theory and research*. Sage.

de Almeida, R. M., Ferrari, P. F., Parmigiani, S., & Miczek, K. A. (2005). Escalated aggressive behavior: Dopamine, serotonin and GABA. *European Journal of Pharmacology*, **526**(1), 51–64.

De Bruijn, G. J., Kroeze, W., Oenema, A., & Brug, J. (2008). Saturated fat consumption and the theory of planned behaviour: Exploring additive and interactive effects of habit strength. *Appetite*, **51**, 318–323.

De Cremer, D., van Dijke, M., Brebels, L., & Hoogervorst, N. (2008). Motivation to cooperate in organisations: The case of prototypical leadership and procedural fairness. *Psychologica Belgica*, **48**(2-3), 157–175. https://doi.org/10.5334/pb-48-2-3-157

De Dreu, C. K., Nijstad, B. A., & van Knippenberg, D. (2008). Motivated information processing in group judgment and decision making. *Personality and Social Psychology Review*, **12**(1), 22–49.

De Gregorio, F., & Sung, Y. (2010). Understanding attitudes toward and behaviors in response to product placement: A consumer socialization framework. *Journal of Advertising*, **39**(1), 83–96.

De Houwer, J. (2003). The extrinsic affective Simon task. *Experimental Psychology* (formerly *Zeitschrift Für Experimentelle Psychologie*), **50**(2), 77–85.

De Houwer, J., Thomas, S., & Baeyens, F. (2001). Associative learning of likes and dislikes: A review of 25 years of research on human evaluative conditioning. *Psychological Bulletin*, **127**, 853–869.

De Long, G. W. (1883). *The voyage of the Jeannette*. Kegan Paul, Trench.

de Rooij, S. R. Caan, M. W. A., Swaab, D. F., Nederveen, A. J., Majoie, C. B., Schwab, M., Painter, R. C., & Roseboom, T. J. (2016). Prenatal famine exposure has sex-specific effects on brain size. *Brain*, **139**(8), 2136–2142. https://doi-org.libezproxy.open.ac.uk/10.1093/brain/aww132

De Smet, M., Keer, H. V., & Valcke, M. (2009). Cross-age peer tutors in asynchronous discussion groups: A study of the evaluation in tutor support. *Instrumental Science*, **37**, 87–105.

De Wit, J. B. F., Das, E., & Vet, R. (2008). What works best: Objective statistics or a personal testimonial? An assessment of the persuasive effects of different types of message evidence on risk perception. *Health Psychology*, **27**(1), 110–115.

De, S., Gelfand, M. J., Nau, D., & Roos, P. (2015). The inevitability of ethnocentrism revisited: Ethnocentrism diminishes as mobility increases. *Scientific Reports*, **5**, 1–7. https://doi.org/10.1038/srep17963

DeBruine, L. M. (2002). Facial resemblance enhances trust. *Proceedings of the Royal Society of London*, **269**, 1307–1312.

Decety, J., & Sommerville, J. A. (2003). Shared representations between self and other: A social cognitive neuroscience view. *Trends in Cognitive Science*, **7**, 527–533.

Decety, J., Cowell, J. M., Lee, K., Mahasneh, R., Malcolm-Smith, S., Selcuk, B., & Zhou, X. (2015). The negative association between religiousness and children's altruism across the world. *Current Biology*, **25**(22), 2951–2955.

Deci, E. L., & Ryan, R. M. (1985). *Intrinsic motivation and self-determination in human behavior*. Plenum.

Deci, E. L., & Ryan, R. M. (1991). A motivational approach to self: Integration in personality. In R. Dienstbier (Ed.), *Perspectives on motivation* (Vol. 38). Nebraska Symposium on Motivation. University of Nebraska Press.

Deci, E. L., & Ryan, R. M. (1997). Behaviorists in search of the null: Revisiting the undermining of intrinsic motivation by extrinsic rewards. Unpublished manuscript, University of Rochester.

Deci, E. L., & Ryan, R. M. (2014). The importance of universal psychological needs for understanding motivation in the workplace. In M. Gagne (Ed.) *The Oxford handbook of work engagement, motivation, and self-determination theory* (pp. 13–32). Oxford University Press.

Deci, E. L., La Guardia, J. G., Moller, A. C., Scheiner, M. J., & Ryan, R. M. (2006). On the benefits of giving as well as receiving autonomy support: Mutuality in close friendships. *Personality and Social Bulletin*, **32**, 313–327.

DeLisi, M., Vaughn, M. G., Gentile, D. A., Anderson, C. A., & Shook, J. J. (2013). Violent video games, delinquency, and youth violence: New evidence. *Youth Violence and Juvenile Justice*, **11**(2), 132-142.

della Cava, M. R. (2003, 2 April). Iraq gets sympathetic press around the world. *USA Today*: www.usatoday.com.

Demir, M., Şimşek, Ö. F., & Procsal, A. D. (2013). I am so happy 'cause my best friend makes me feel unique: Friendship, personal sense of uniqueness and happiness. *Journal of Happiness Studies*, **14**(4), 1201–1224.

Denmark, F., Rabinowitz, V. C., & Sechzer, J. A. (2004). *Engendering psychology: Women and gender revisited*. Taylor & Francis.

Dennett, D. (2005, 26 December). Spiegel interview with evolution philosopher Daniel Dennett: Darwinism completely refutes intelligent design. *Der Spiegel*: www.service.dspiegel.de.

Densley, J., Cai, T., & Hilal, S. (2014). Social dominance orientation and trust propensity in street gangs. *Group Processes and Intergroup Relations*, **17**(6), 763–779. https://doi.org/10.1177/1368430214533161

Denson, T. F., DeWall, C. N., & Finkel, E. J. (2012). Self-control and aggression. *Current Directions in Psychological Science*, **21**(1), 20–25.

Denson, T. F., O'Dean, S. M., Blake, K. R., & Beames, J. R. (2018). Aggression in women: Behavior, brain and hormones. *Frontiers in Behavioral Neuroscience*, May 2. https://doi.org/10.3389/fnbeh.2018.00081

Denson, T. F., Ronay, R., von Hippel, W., & Schira, M. M. (2013). Endogenous testosterone and cortisol modulate neural responses during induced anger control. *Social Neuroscience,* **8**(2), 165–177.

Denson, T. F., von Hippel, W., Kemp, R., & Teo, L. S. (2010). Glucose consumption decreases impulsive aggression in response to provocation in aggressive individuals. *Journal of Experimental Social Psychology,* **46**(6), 1023–1028.

Department of Canadian Heritage (2006). What is multiculturalism? www.pch.gc.

DePaulo, B. M., Charlton, K., Cooper, H., Lindsay, J. J., & Muhlenbruck, L. (1997). The accuracy–confidence correlation in the detection of deception. *Personality and Social Psychology Review,* **1,** 346–357.

Derlega, V., Metts, S., Petronio, S., & Margulis, S. T. (1993). *Self-disclosure.* Sage.

Dermer, M., & Pyszczynski, T. A. (1978). Effects of erotica upon men's loving and liking responses for women they love. *Journal of Personality and Social Psychology,* **36,** 1302–1309.

Desforges, D. M., Lord, C. G., Pugh, M. A., Sia, T. L., Scarberry, N. C., & Ratcliff, C. D. (1997). Role of group representativeness in the generalization part of the contact hypothesis. *Basic and Applied Social Psychology,* **19,** 183–204.

Desforges, D. M., Lord, C. G., Ramsey, S. L., Mason, J. A., Van Leeuwen, M. D., West, S. C., & Lepper, M. R. (1991). Effects of structured cooperative contact on changing negative attitudes toward stigmatized social groups. *Journal of Personality and Social Psychology,* **60,** 531–544.

Deutsch, M. (1985). *Distributive justice: A social psychological perspective.* Yale University Press.

Deutsch, M. (1993). Educating for a peaceful world. *American Psychologist,* **48,** 510–517.

Deutsch, M. (1994). Constructive conflict resolution: Principles, training, and research. *Journal of Social Issues,* **50,** 13–32.

Deutsch, M., & Collins, M. E. (1951). *Interracial housing: A psychological evaluation of a social experiment.* University of Minnesota Press.

Deutsch, M., & Gerard, H. B. (1955). A study of normative and informational social influence upon individual judgment. *Journal of Abnormal and Social Psychology,* **51,** 629–636.

Deutsch, M., & Krauss, R. M. (1960). The effect of threat upon interpersonal bargaining. *Journal of Abnormal and Social Psychology,* **61,** 181–189.

Devine, P. G. (1989). Stereotypes and prejudice: Their automatic and controlled components. *Journal of Personality and Social Psychology,* **56,** 5–18.

Devine, P. G. (2005). Breaking the prejudice habit: Allport's inner conflict revisited. In J. F. Dovidio, P. Glick, & L. A. Rudman (Eds.), *On the nature of prejudice: Fifty years after Allport.* Blackwell.

Devine-Wright, H., & Devine-Wright, P. (2009). Social representations of electricity network technologies: Exploring processes of anchoring and objectification through the use of visual research methods. *British Journal of Social Psychology,* **48,** 357–373.

Devos, T., Silver, L. A., Mackie, D. M., & Smith, E. R. (2002). Experiencing intergroup emotions. In D. M. Mackie & E. R. Smith (Eds.), *From prejudice to intergroup emotions: Differentiated reactions to social groups.* Psychology Press.

Devrim, A., Bilgic, P., & Hongu, N. (2018). Is there any relationship between body image perception, eating disorders, and muscle dysmorphic disorders in male bodybuilders?*American Journal of Men's Health,* **12**(5), 1746-1758.

DeWall, C. N., & Bushman, B. J. (2009). Hot under the collar in a lukewarm environment: Words associated with hot temperature increase aggressive thoughts and hostile perceptions. *Journal of Experimental Social Psychology,* **45**(4), 1045–1047.

DeWall, C. N., Baumeister, R. F., Stillman, T. F., & Gailliot, M. T. (2007). Violence restrained: Effects of self-regulation and its depletion on aggression. *Journal of Experimental Social Psychology,* **43,** 62–76.

DeWall, C. N., Pond, R. S., Jr, Campbell, W. K., & Twenge, J. M. (2011). Tuning in to psychological change: Linguistic markers of psychological traits and emotions over time in popular U.S. song lyrics. *Psychology of Aesthetics, Creativity, and the Arts,* **5,** 200–207.

Di Falco, S., & Sharma, S. (2018). Investing in climate change adaptation: Motivations and green incentives in the Fiji Islands. *Ecological Economics,* **154,** 394–408.

Diamond, J. (1996, December). The best ways to sell sex. *Discover,* pp. 78–86.

Diamond, L. M. (2003). What does sexual orientation orient? A biobehavioral model distinguishing romantic love and sexual desire. *Psychological Review,* **110,** 173–192. http://dx.doi.org/10.1037/0033-295X.110.1.173

DiDonato, T., Ullrich, J., & Krueger, J. I. (2011). Social perception as induction and inference: An integrative model of intergroup differentiation, ingroup favouritism, and differential accuracy. *Journal of Personality and Social Psychology,* **100,** 66–83.

Diekman, A. B., McDonald, M., & Gardner, W. L. (2000). Love means never having to be careful: The relationship between reading romance novels and safe sex behavior. *Psychology of Women Quarterly,* **24,** 179–188.

Diener, E. (1980). Deindividuation: The absence of self-awareness and self-regulation in group members. In P. B. Paulus (Ed.), *The psychology of group influence.* Erlbaum.

Diener, E., Fraser, S. C., Beaman, A. L., & Kelem, R. T. (1976). Effects of deindividuation variables on stealing among Halloween trick-or-treaters. *Journal of Personality and Social Psychology,* **33,** 178–183.

Diener, E., Lucas, R. E., & Scollon, C. N. (2006). Beyond the hedonic treadmill: Revising the adaptation theory of well-being. *American Psychologist,* **61,** 305–314.

Dijksterhuis, A., Smith, P. K., van Baaren, R. B., & Wigboldus, D. H. J. (2005). The unconscious consumer: Effects of environment on consumer behavior. *Journal of Consumer Psychology,* **15,** 193–202.

Dijkstra, J. K., Cillessen, A. H., Lindenberg, S., & Veenstra, R. (2010). Basking in reflected glory and its limits: Why adolescents hang out with popular peers. *Journal of Research on Adolescence,* **20**(4), 942–958.

Dimberg, U., Thunberg, M., & Grunedal, S. (2002). Facial reactions to emotional stimuli: Automatically controlled emotional responses. *Cognition and Emotion,* **16**(4), 449–472.

Dimka, R. A., & Dein, S. L. (2013). The work of a woman is to give birth to children: Cultural constructions of infertility in Nigeria. *African Journal of Reproductive Health,* **17**(2), 102–117.

Dino, A., Reysen, S., & Branscombe, N. R. (2009). Online interactions between group members who differ in status. *Journal of Language and Social Psychology,* **28**(1), 85–93. https://doi.org/10.1177/0261927X08325916

Dion, K. K., & Dion, K. L. (1991). Psychological individualism and romantic love. *Journal of Social Behavior and Personality,* **6,** 17–33.

Dion, K. K., & Dion, K. L. (1996). Cultural perspectives on romantic love. *Personal Relationships,* **3,** 5–17.

Dion, K. L. (1979). Intergroup conflict and intragroup cohesiveness. In W. G. Austin & S. Worchel (Eds.), *The social psychology of intergroup relations.* Brooks/Cole.

Dion, K. L. (1987). What's in a title? The Ms. stereotype and images of women's titles of address. *Psychology of Women Quarterly,* **11,** 21–36.

Dion, K. L., & Cota, A. A. (1991). The Ms. stereotype: Its domain and the role of explicitness in title preference. *Psychology of Women Quarterly,* **15,** 403–410.

Dion, K. L., & Dion, K. K. (1988). Romantic love: Individual and cultural perspectives. In R. J. Sternberg & M. L. Barnes (Eds.), *The psychology of love.* Yale University Press.

Dion, K. L., & Schuller, R. A. (1991). The Ms. stereotype: Its generality and its relation to managerial and marital status stereotypes. *Canadian Journal of Behavioural Science,* **23,** 25–40.

Dion, K., Berscheid, E., & Walster, E. (1972). What is beautiful is good. *Journal of Personality and Social Psychology,* **24,** 285–290.

Disasters Emergency Committee (2018). *2018 Indonesia Tsunami Appeal Six-month Report.* https://www.dec.org.uk/article/2018-indonesia-tsunami-appeal-six-month-report

Dishion, T. J., McCord, J., & Poulin, F. (1999). When interventions harm: Peer groups and problem behavior. *American Psychologist,* **54,** 755–764.

Dixon, J., & Durrheim, K. (2003). Contact and the ecology of racial division: Some varieties of informal segregation. *British Journal of Social Psychology,* **42,** 1–23.

Dixon, J., & Wetherell, M. (2004). On discourse and dirty nappies: Gender, the division of household labour and the social psychology of distributive justice. *Theory and Psychology*, **14**(2), 167–189.

Dixon, J., Durrheim, K., & Tredoux, C. (2005a). Beyond the optimal contact strategy: A reality check for the contact hypothesis. *American Psychologist*, **60**, 697–711.

Dixon, J., Mahoney, B., & Cocks, R. (2002). Accents of guilt? Effects of regional accent, race, and crime type on attributions of guilt. *Journal of Language and Social Psychology*, **21**(2), 162–168.

Dixon, J., Tredoux, C., & Clack, B. (2005b). On the microecology of racial division: A neglected dimension of segregation. *South African Journal of Psychology*, **35**, 395–411.

Dobai, A., & Hopkins, N. (2019). Humour is serious: Minority group members' use of humour in their encounters with majority group members. *European Journal of Social Psychology*. https://doi.org/10.1002/ejsp.2612

Dodge, M. (2006). Juvenile police informants: Friendship, persuasion, and pretense. *Youth Violence and Juvenile Justice*, **4**(3), 234–246.

Dogra, N., Omigbodum, O., Adedokun, T., Bella, T., Ronzoni, P., & Adesokan, A. (2012). Nigerian secondary school children's knowledge of and attitudes to mental health and illness. *Clinical Child Psychology and Psychiatry*, **17**(3), 336–353.

Doidge, N. (2007). *The brain that changes itself: Stories of personal triumph from the frontiers of brain science*. Penguin Group.

Doise, W., Deschamps, J.-C., & Meyer, G. (1978). The accentuation of intra-category similarities. In H. Tajfel (Ed.), *Differentiation between social groups*. Academic Press.

Dolinski, D. (2000). On inferring one's beliefs from one's attempt and consequences for subsequent compliance. *Journal of Personality and Social Psychology*, **78**(2), 260.

Dolinski, D., & Nawrat, R. (1998). 'Fear-then-relief' procedure for producing compliance: Beware when the danger is over. *Journal of Experimental Social Psychology*, **34**, 27–50.

Dollard, J., Doob, L., Miller, N., Mowrer, O. H., & Sears, R. R. (1939). *Frustration and aggression*. Yale University Press.

Dolnik, L., Case, T. I., & Williams, K. D. (2003). Stealing thunder as a courtroom tactic revisited: Processes and boundaries. *Law and Human Behavior*, **27**, 265–285.

Donnellan, M. B., Larsen-Rife, D., & Conger, R. D. (2005a). Personality, family history, and competence in early adult romantic relationships. *Journal of Personality and Social Psychology*, **88**, 562–576.

Donnellan, M. B., Trzesniewski, K. H., Robins, R. W., Moffitt, T. E., & Caspi, A. (2005b). Low self-esteem is related to aggression, antisocial behaviour, and delinquency. *Psychological Science*, **16**, 328–335.

Dovidio, J. F. (1991). The empathy-altruism hypothesis: Paradigm and promise. *Psychological Inquiry*, **2**, 126–128.

Dovidio, J. F. and Gaertner, S. L. (Eds.) (1986). The aversive form of racism. In J. F. Dovidio & S. L. Gaertner (Eds.), *Prejudice, discrimination and racism* (pp. 61–89). Academic Press.

Dovidio, J. F., Brigham, J. C., Johnson, B. T., & Gaertner, S. L. (1996). Stereotyping, prejudice and discrimination: Another look. In C. N. Macrae, C. Stangor, & M. Hewstone (Eds.), *Stereotypes and stereotyping*. Guilford Press.

Dovidio, J. F., Gaertner, S. L., Anastasio, P. A., & Sanitioso, R. (1992). Cognitive and motivational bases of bias: Implications of aversive racism for attitudes toward Hispanics. In S. Knouse, P. Rosenfeld, & A. Culbertson (Eds.), *Hispanics in the workplace*. Sage.

Doyen, S., Klein, O., Pichon, C. L., & Cleeremans, A. (2012). Behavioral priming: It's all in the mind, but whose mind? *PloS One*, **7**(1), e29081.

Drabman, R. S., & Thomas, M. H. (1974). Does media violence increase children's toleration of real-life aggression? *Developmental Psychology*, **10**, 418–421.

Drabman, R. S., & Thomas, M. H. (1975). Does TV violence breed indifference? *Journal of Communications*, **25**(4), 86–89.

Drabman, R. S., & Thomas, M. H. (1976). Does watching violence on television cause apathy? *Pediatrics*, **57**, 329–331.

Dreibelbis, R., Kroeger, A., Hossain, K., Venkatesh, M., & Ram, P. (2016). Behavior change without behavior change communication: Nudging handwashing among primary school students in Bangladesh. *International Journal of Environmental Research and Public Health*, **13**(1), 129. https://doi.org/10.3390/ijerph13010129

Drescher, A., & Schultheiss, O. C. (2016). Meta-analytic evidence for higher implicit affiliation and intimacy motivation scores in women, compared to men. *Journal of Research in Personality*, **64**, 1–10.

Drewes, A. (2008). Bobo revisited: What the research says. *International Journal of Play Theory*, **17**(1), 52–65.

Driedger, L. (1975). In search of cultural identity factors: A comparison of ethnic students. *Canadian Review of Sociology and Anthropology*, **12**, 150–161.

Driskell, J. E., & Mullen, B. (1990). Status, expectations, and behaviour: A meta-analytic review and test of the theory. *Personality and Social Psychology Bulletin*, **16**(3), 541–553.

Drivdahl, S. B., Zaragoza, M. S., & Learned, D. M. (2009). The role of emotional elaboration in the creation of false memories. *Applied Cognitive Psychology*, **23**, 13–35.

Droba, D. D. (1932). Methods for measuring attitudes. *Psychological Bulletin*, **29**(5), 309–323.

Drolet, A. L., & Morris, M. W. (2000). Rapport in conflict resolution: Accounting for how face-to-face contact fosters mutual cooperation in mixed-motive conflicts. *Journal of Experimental Social Psychology*, **36**, 26–50.

Drury, J. (2012). Collective resilience in mass emergencies and disasters: A social identity model. In J. Jetten, C. Haslam, & S. A. Haslam (Eds.), *The social cure: Identity, health and well-being*. Psychology Press.

Drury, J., Stott, C., & Farsides, T. (2003). The role of police perceptions and practices in the development of 'public disorder'. *Journal of Applied Social Psychology*, **33**(7), 1480–1500.

DuBois, W. E. B. (1903/1961). *The souls of black folk*. Fawcett Books.

Duffy, M. (2003, 9 June). Weapons of mass disappearance. *Time*, pp. 28–33.

Dufner, M., Rauthmann, J. F., Czarna, A. Z., & Denissen, J. J. A. (2013). Are narcissists sexy? Zeroing in on the effect of narcissism on short-term mate appeal. *Personality and Social Psychology Bulletin*, **39**, 870–882.

Duncan, M., & Murdock, B. (2000). Recognition and recall with precuing and postcuing. *Journal of Memory and Language*, **42**(3), 301–313.

Dunham, Y., Newheiser, A. K., Hoosain, L., Merrill, A., & Olson, K. R. (2014). From a different vantage: Intergroup attitudes among children from low-and intermediate-status racial groups. *Social Cognition*, **32**, 1–21.

Dunlap, R. E. (2008). The new environmental paradigm scale: From marginality to worldwide use. *Journal of Environmental Education*, **40**(1), 3–18.

Dunlap, R. E., & Van Liere, K. D. (1978). The 'new ecological paradigm': A proposed measuring instrument and preliminary results. *Journal of Environmental Education*, **9**(4), 10–19.

Dunn, B. D., Dalgleish, T., Lawrence, A. D., & Ogilvie, A. D. (2007). The accuracy of self-monitoring and its relationship to self-focused attention in dysphoria and clinical depression. *Journal of Abnormal Psychology*, **116**, 1–15.

Dunn, E. W., Gilbert, D. T., & Wilson, T. D. (2011). If money doesn't make you happy, then you probably aren't spending it right. *Journal of Consumer Psychology*, **21**, 115–125.

Dunn, E. W., Wilson, T. D., & Gilbert, D. T. (2003). Location, location, location: The misprediction of satisfaction in housing lotteries. *Personality and Social Psychology Bulletin*, **29**, 1421–1432.

Dunn, K. I., Mohr, P. B., Wilson, C. J., & Wittert, G. A. (2008). Beliefs about fast food in Australia: A qualitative analysis. *Appetite*, **51**, 331–334.

Dunn, M., Thomas, J. O., Swift, W., & Burns, L. (2011). Athletes' estimates of the prevalence of illicit drug use: Evidence for the false consensus effect. *Drug and Alcohol Review*, **31**(1), 27–32.

Dunn, R. A., Zhou, S., & Lent, M. (2011). But is a picture worth a thousand people? Effects of pictorial vividness and numeric representation on attitudes toward the China-Tibet issue. *China Media Research*, **7**(2), 57–65. http://link.galegroup.com.libezproxy.open.ac.uk/apps/doc/A256457444/AONE?u=tou&sid=AONE&xid=65dcc824

Dunning, D. (2005). *Self-insight: Roadblocks and detours on the path to knowing thyself* (Essays in social psychology). Psychology Press.

Dunning, D., & Hayes, A. F. (1996). Evidence for egocentric comparison in social judgment. *Journal of Personality and Social Psychology*, **71**, 213–229.

Dunning, D., Griffin, D. W., Milojkovic, J. D., & Ross, L. (1990). The overconfidence effect in social prediction. *Journal of Personality and Social Psychology,* **58,** 568–581.

Dupré, J. (2008). Against maladaptationism: Or what's wrong with evolutionary psychology? In M. Mazzotti (Ed.), *Knowledge as social order: Rethinking the sociology of Barry Barnes* (pp. 165–180). Routledge.

Duriez, B. (2004). Are religious people nicer people? Taking a closer look at the religion–empathy relationship. *Mental Health, Religion & Culture,* **7**(3), 249–254.

Durrheim, K., & Dixon, J. (2001). Geographies of racial exclusion: Beaches as family spaces. *Ethnic and Racial Studies,* **24,** 333–350.

Dussault, M., & Frenette, É. (2015). Supervisors transformational leadership and bullying in the workplace. *Psychological Reports,* **117**(3), 724–733. https://doi.org/10.2466/01.PR0.117c30z2

Dutton, D. (2006, 13 January). Hardwired to seek beauty. *The Australian:* www.theaustralian.news.com.au.

Duval, T. S., & Wicklund, R. A. (1972). *A theory of objective self awareness.* Academic Press.

E

Eagly, A. H. (1994). Are people prejudiced against women? Donald Campbell Award invited address, American Psychological Association convention.

Eagly, A. H., & Carli, L. L. (2007). Women and the labyrinth of leadership. *Harvard Business Review,* **85**(9), 62–71.

Eagly, A. H., & Chaiken, S. (1993). *The psychology of attitudes.* Harcourt Brace Jovanovich.

Eagly, A. H., & Chaiken, S. (1998). Attitude structure and function. In D. Gilbert, S. Fiske, & G. Lindzey (Eds.), *The handbook of social psychology*(4th ed.). McGraw-Hill.

Eagly, A. H., & Chaiken, S. (2005). Attitude research in the 21st century: The current state of knowledge. In D. Albarracín, B. T. Johnson, T. Blair & M. P. Zanna (Eds.), *The handbook of attitudes.* Lawrence Erlbaum.

Eagly, A. H., & Chin, J. L. (2010). Diversity and leadership in a changing world. *The American Psychologist,* **65**(3), 216–224.

Eagly, A. H., & Crowley, M. (1986). Gender and helping behavior: A meta-analytic review of the social psychological literature. *Psychological Bulletin,* **100**(3), 283–308. https://doi.org/10.1037/0033-2909.100.3.283

Eagly, A. H., & Wood, W. (1999). The origins of sex differences in human behavior: Evolved dispositions versus social roles. *American Psychologist,* **54,** 408–423.

Eagly, A. H., Ashmore, R. D., Makhijani, M. G., & Longo, L. C. (1991). What is beautiful is good, but . . .: A metaanalytic review of research on the physical attractiveness stereotype. *Psychological Bulletin,* **110,** 109–128.

Eagly, A. H., Wood, W., & Chaiken, S. (1978). Casual inferences about communicators and their effect on opinion change. *Journal of Personality and Social Psychology,* **36,** 424–435.

Eagly, A. H., Wood, W., & Diekman, A. B. (2000). Social role theory of sex differences and similarities: A current appraisal. In T. Eckes & H. M. Trautner (Eds.), *The developmental social psychology of gender* (pp. 123–174). Lawrence Erlbaum.

Earley, C. P. (1989). Social loafing and collectivism: A comparison of the United States and the People's Republic of China. *Administrative Science Quarterly,* **34,** 565–581.

Eaves, L., Hatemi, P., Prom-Womley, E., & Murrelle, L. (2008). Social and genetic influences on adolescent religious attitudes and practices. *Social Forces,* **86**(4), 1621-1646.

Ebbesen, E. B., Duncan, B., & Konecni, V. J. (1975). Effects of content of verbal aggression on future verbal aggression: A field experiment. *Journal of Experimental Social Psychology,* **11,** 192–204.

Eberhardt, J. L. (2005). Imaging race. *American Psychologist,* **60,** 181–190.

Eberhardt, J. L., Purdie, V. J., Goff, P. A., & Davies, P. G. (2004). Seeing black: Race, crime, and visual processing. *Journal of Personality and Social Psychology,* **87,** 876–893.

Ebneter, D. S., Latner, J. D., & O'Brien, K. S. (2011). Just world beliefs, causal beliefs, and acquaintance: Associations with stigma toward eating disorders and obesity. *Personality and Individual Differences,* **51,** 618–622.

Echterhoff, G., & Higgins, E. T. (2017). Creating shared reality in interpersonal and intergroup communication: The role of epistemic processes and their interplay. *European Review of Social Psychology,* **28,** 175–226.

Echterhoff, G., Kopietz, R., & Higgins, E. T. (2013). Adjusting shared reality: Communicators' memory changes as their connection with their audience changes. *Social Cognition,* **31,** 162–186.

Edelstein, A. (2018). Intimate partner jealousy and femicide among former Ethiopians in Israel. *International Journal of Offender Therapy and Comparative Criminology,* **62**(2), 383–403. https://doi.org/10.1177/0306624X16652453

Edwards, D. (1997). *Discourse and cognition.* Sage.

Edwards, D. (2003). Analysing racial discourse: The discursive psychology of mind-world relationships. In H. Van der Berg, M. Wetherell, & H. Houtkoop-Seenstra (Eds.), *Analysing race talk: Multidisciplinary approaches to the interview.* Cambridge University Press.

Edwards, D. A., & Casto, K. V. (2013). Women's intercollegiate athletic competition: Cortisol, testosterone, and the dual hormone hypothesis as it relates to status among teammates. *Hormones and Behavior,* **64**(1), 153–160.

Edwards, D., & Middleton, D. (1987). Conversation and remembering: Bartlett revisited. *Applied Cognitive Psychology,* **1,** 77–92.

Edwards, D., & Potter, J. (2005). Discursive psychology, mental states and descriptions. In H. te Molder & J. Potter (eds), *Conversation and cognition.* Cambridge University Press.

Egolf, B., Lasker, J., Wolf, S., & Potvin, L. (1992). The Roseto effect: A 50-year comparison of mortality rates. *American Journal of Public Health,* **82,** 1089–1092.

Ehrenberg, M. F., Robertson, M., & Pringle, J. (2012). Attachment style and marital commitment in the context of remarriage. *Journal of Divorce & Remarriage,* **53**(3), 204–219.

Ehrlinger, J., Gilovich, T., & Ross, L. (2005). Peering into the bias blind spot: People's assessments of bias in themselves and others. *Personality and Social Psychology Bulletin,* **31,** 680–692.

Eibach, R. P., Libby, L. K., & Gilovich, T. D. (2003). When change in the self is mistaken for change in the world. *Journal of Personality and Social Psychology,* **84,** 917–931.

Eisenberg, M. E., Ackard, D. M., Resnick, M. D., & Neumark-Sztainer, D. (2009). Casual sex and psychological health among young adults: Is having 'friends with benefits' emotionally damaging? *Perspectives on Sexual and Reproductive Health,* **41**(4), 231–237.

Eisenberg, N., Fabes, R. A., Schaller, M., Miller, P., Carlo, G., Poulin, R., Shea, C., & Shell, R. (1991). Personality and socialization correlates of vicarious emotional responding. *Journal of Personality and Social Psychology,* **61,** 459–470.

Eisenberger, R., & Rhoades, L. (2001). Incremental effects of reward on creativity. *Journal of Personality and Social Psychology,* **81,** 728–741.

Eisenberger, R., & Shanock, L. (2003). Rewards, intrinsic motivation, and creativity: A case study of conceptual and methodological isolation. *Creativity Research Journal,* **15,** 121–130.

Ellemers, N. (2012). The group self. *Science,* **336,** 848–852.

Ellemers, N., Doosje, B., & Spears, R. (2004). Sources of respect: The effects of being liked by ingroups and outgroups. *European Journal of Social Psychology,* **34,** 155–172.

Ellis, A. (1962). *Reason and emotion in psychotherapy: A comprehensive method of treating human disturbances.* Carol Publishing.

Ellis, L. (2005). A theory explaining biological correlates of criminality. *European Journal of Criminology,* 2, 287–315.

Ellis, L. (2011). Evolutionary neuroandrogenic theory and universal gender differences in cognition and behavior. *Sex Roles,* **64,** 707–722.

Ellison, N. B., Heino, R. D., & Gibbs, J. L. (2006). Self-presentation processes in the online dating environment. *Journal of Computer-Mediated Communication,* **11**(2), 415–441.

Elms, A. C. (1995). Obedience in retrospect. *Journal of Social Issues,* **51,** 21–31.

Elms, A. C., & Baumrind, D. (2007). Issue 1: Is deception of human participants ethical? In J. A. Nier (Ed.), *Taking sides: Clashing views in social psychology* (2nd ed.). McGraw-Hill.

Ember, C. R., Ember, M., Korotyaev, A., & De Munck, V. (2005). Valuing thinness or fatness in women: Re-evaluating the effects of resource scarcity. *Evolution and Human Behavior,* **26,** 257–270.

Enerdata (2019). Global Energy Statistical Yearbook 2019. https://yearbook.enerdata.net/

Eng, P. M., Kawachi, I., Fitzmaurice, G., & Rimm, E. B. (2001). Effects of marital transitions on changes in dietary and other health behaviors in men. Paper presented to the American Psychosomatic Society meeting.

Engell, A. D., Haxby, J. V., & Todorov, A. (2007). Implicit trustworthiness decisions: Automatic coding of face properties in the human amygdala. *Journal of Cognitive Neuroscience,* **19,** 1508–1519.

Engemann, K. M., & Owyang, M. T. (2003, April). So much for that merit raise: The link between wages and appearance. *The Regional Economist* (www.stlouisfed.org).

English, D. J., Newton, R. R., Lewis, T. L., Thompson, R., Kotch, J. B., & Weisbart, C. (2009). At-risk and maltreated children exposed to intimate partner aggression/violence. *Child Maltreatment,* **14**(2), 157–171.

Englund, M., Luckner, A., Whaley, G., Egeland, B., & Harris, K. R. (2004). Children's achievement in early elementary school: Longitudinal effects of parental involvement, expectations, and quality of assistance. *Journal of Educational Psychology,* **96**(4), 723–730.

Epley, N., Savitsky, K., & Kachelski, R. A. (1999, September/October). What every skeptic should know about subliminal persuasion. *Skeptical Inquirer,* pp. 40–45.

Epstein, R., Pandit, M., & Thakar, M. (2013). How love emerges in arranged marriages: Two cross-cultural studies. *Journal of Comparative Family Studies,* **44**(3), 341–360.

Epstein, S., & Feist, G. J. (1988). Relation between self and other-acceptance and its moderation by identification. *Journal of Personality and Social Psychology,* **54,** 309–315.

Erickson, B., Holmes, J. G., Frey, R., Walker, L., & Thibaut, J. (1974). Functions of a third party in the resolution of conflict: The role of a judge in pretrial conferences. *Journal of Personality and Social Psychology,* **30,** 296–306.

Erikson, E. H. (1963). *Childhood and society.* Norton.

Erlandsson, K., Jinghede Nordvall, C., Öhman, A., & Häggström-Nordin, E. (2012). Qualitative interviews with adolescents about 'friends-with-benefits' relationships. *Public Health Nursing,* **30**(1), 47–57.

Eron, L. D. (1963). Relationship of TV viewing habits and aggressive behavior in children. *Journal of Abnormal and Social Psychology,* **67**(2), 193–196.

Eron, L., Huesmann, L., Lefkowitz, M., & Walder, L. (1972). Does television violence cause aggression?*American Psychologist,* **27**(4), 253–263.

Escobar-Chaves, S. L., Tortolero, S. R., Markham, C. M., Low, B. J., Eitel, P., & Thickstun, P. (2005). Impact of the media on adolescent sexual attitudes and behaviors. *Pediatrics,* **116,** 303–326.

Esser, J. K. (1998, February–March). Alive and well after 25 years. A review of groupthink research. *Organizational Behavior and Human Decision Processes,* **73,** 116–141.

Esses, V. M., Haddock, G., & Zanna, M. P. (1993). Values, stereotypes, and emotions as determinants of intergroup attitudes. In D. Mackie & D. Hamilton (Eds.), *Affect, cognition and stereotyping: Interactive processes in intergroup perception.* Academic Press.

Etaugh, C. E., Bridges, J. S., Cummings-Hill, M., & Cohen, J. (1999). 'Names can never hurt me': The effects of surname use on perceptions of married women. *Psychology of Women Quarterly,* **23,** 819–823.

Etzioni, A. (2005). *The diversity within unity platform.* The Communitarian Network.

Eurostat (2019). *Gender pay gap statistics.* https://ec.europa.eu/eurostat/statistics-explained/index.php/Gender_pay_gap_statistics#Gender_pay_gap_levels_vary_significantly_across_EU

Evans, N. (2012). Destroying collaboration and knowledge sharing in the workplace: A reverse brainstorming approach. *Knowledge Management Research & Practice,* **10**(2), 175–187.

Everett, J. A. C., & Earp, B. D. (2015). A tragedy of the (academic) commons: Interpreting the replication crisis in psychology as a social dilemma for early-career researchers. *Frontiers in Psychology,* 1152. https://doi.org/10.3389/fpsyg.2015.01152

Every, D., & Augoustinos, M. (2008). Constructions of Australia in pro- and anti-asylum seeker political discourse. *Nations and Nationalism,* **14**(3), 562–580.

Ewert, A., Place, G., & Sibthorp, J. (2005). Early-life outdoor experiences and an individual's environmental attitudes. *Leisure Sciences,* **27,** 225–239.

Exline, J. J., & Lobel, M. (1999). The perils of outperformance: Sensitivity about being the target of a threatening upward comparison. *Psychological Bulletin,* **125,** 307–337.

F

Factor, R., Kawachi, I., & Williams, D. R. (2011). Understanding high-risk behavior among non-dominant minorities: A social resistance framework. *Social Science & Medicine,* **73,** 1292–1301.

Falomir-Pichastor, J. M., Toscani, L., & Huyghues Despointes, S. (2009). Determinants of flu vaccination among nurses: The effects of group identification and professional responsibility. *Applied Psychology,* **58,** 42–58.

Fanelli, D. (2011). Negative results are disappearing from most disciplines and countries. *Scientometrics,* **90,** 891–904.

Fanti, K., & Henrich, C. (2015). Effects of self-esteem and narcissism on bullying and victimization during early adolescence. *Journal of Early Adolescence,* **35**(1), 5–29.

Fantoni, C., Rigutti, S., Piccoli, V., Sommacal, E., & Carnaghi, A. (2016). Faster but less careful prehension in presence of high, rather than low, social status attendees. *PLoS ONE,* **11**(6), E0158095.

Faraone, S. V., Sergeant, J. A., Gillberg, C., & Biederman, J. (2003). The worldwide prevalence of ADHD: Is it an American condition? *World Psychiatry,* **2**(2), 104–113.

Farmer, Y., Bissiere, M., & Benkirane, A. (2018). Impacts of authority and unanimity on social conformity in online chats about climate change. *Canadian Journal of Communication,* **43,** 265–279.

Farr, R. M. (1996). *The roots of modern social psychology.* Blackwell.

Farwell, L., & Weiner, B. (2000). Bleeding hearts and the heartless: Popular perceptions of liberal and conservative ideologies. *Personality and Social Psychology Bulletin,* **26,** 845–852.

Fawcett Society (2017). *Fawcett Society report – Sounds Familiar – reveals hostility, complacency and a blame culture against women.* https://www.fawcettsociety.org.uk/News/fawcett-report-hostility-complacency-blame-culture-against-women

Faye, C. (2012). American social psychology: Examining the contours of the 1970s crisis. *Studies in History and Philosophy of Biological and Biomedical Sciences,* **43,** 514–521.

Fazio, R. H., & Olson, M. A. (2003). Implicit measures in social cognition research: Their meaning and use. *Annual Review of Psychology,* **54**(1), 297–327.

Fazio, R. H., Jackson, J. R., Dunton, B. C., & Williams, C. J. (1995). Variability in automatic activation as an unobtrusive measure of racial attitudes: A bona fide pipeline? *Journal of Personality and Social Psychology,* **69,** 1013–1027.

FBI Uniform Crime Reporting (2018). *2018 Hate crime statistics.* https://ucr.fbi.gov/hate-crime/2018/tables/table-1.xls

Feeney, B. C., & Thrush, R. L. (2010). Relationship influences on exploration in adulthood: The characteristics and function of a secure base. *Journal of Personality and Social Psychology,* **98,** 57–76.

Feeney, B. C., & Van Vleet M. (2010). Growing through attachment: The interplay of attachment and exploration in adulthood. *Journal of Personal and Social Relationships,* **27**(2), 226–234.

Feeney, J., Peterson, C., & Noller, P. (1994). Equity and marital satisfaction over the family life cycle. *Personality Relationships,* **1,** 83–99.

Fehr, B. (1996). *Friendship processes.* Sage.

Fehr, B., & Harasymchuk, C. (2017). A prototype matching model of satisfaction in same-sex friendships. *Personal Relationships,* **24**(3), 683–693.

Fehr, E. & Fischbacher, U. (2003). The nature of human altruism. *Nature,* **425,** 784–791.

Feingold, A. (1992b). Good-looking people are not what we think. *Psychological Bulletin,* **111,** 304–341.

Feldman, R. S., & Prohaska, T. (1979). The student as Pygmalion: Effect of student expectation on the teacher. *Journal of Educational Psychology,* **71,** 485–493.

Feldman, R. S., & Theiss, A. J. (1982). The teacher and student as Pygmalions: Joint effects of teacher and student expectations. *Journal of Educational Psychology,* **74,** 217–223.

Felmlee, D., Orzechowicz, D., & Fortes, C. (2010). Fairy tales: Attraction and stereotypes in same-gender relationships. *Sex Roles,* **62**(3–4), 226–240.

Felmlee, D., Sweet, E., & Sinclair, H. C. (2012). Gender rules: Same- and cross-gender friendships norms. *Sex Roles,* **66**(7–8), 518–529.

Felson, R. B. (1984). The effect of self-appraisals of ability on academic performance. *Journal of Personality and Social Psychology,* **47**, 944–952.

Fenigstein, A., & Carver, C. S. (1978). Self-focusing effects of heartbeat feedback. *Journal of Personality and Social Psychology,* **36**, 1241–1250.

Fennis, B. M., Das, E. H. H. J., & Pruyn, A. T. H. (2004). 'If you can't dazzle them with brilliance, baffle them with nonsense': Extending the impact of the disrupt-then-reframe technique of social influence. *Journal of Consumer Psychology,* **14**(3), 280–290.

Ferguson, C. J. (2010). Blazing angels or resident evil? Can violent video games be a force for good?. *Review of General Psychology,* **14**(2), 68–81.

Ferguson, C. J., & Savage, J. (2012). Have recent studies addressed methodological issues raised by five decades of television violence research? A critical review. *Aggression and Violent Behavior,* **17**(2), 129–139.

Fernández, J., & Bliss, S. (2016). Schizophrenia and the estranged self. *Journal of Evaluation in Clinical Practice,* **22**(4), 615–621.

Fern, E. F., Monroe, K. B., & Avila, R. A. (1986). Effectiveness of multiple request strategies: A synthesis of research results. *Journal of Marketing Research,* **23**, 144–152.

Ferrante, C. J., Green, S. G., & Forster, W. R. (2006). Getting more out of team projects: Incentivizing leadership to enhance performance. *Journal of Management Education,* **30**(6), 788–797.

Feshbach, S., & Singer, R. D. (1971). *Television and aggression: An experimental field study.* Jossey-Bass.

Festinger, L. (1950). Informal social communication. *Psychological Review,* **57**, 271–282.

Festinger, L. (1954). A theory of social comparison processes. *Human Relations,* **7**, 117–140.

Festinger, L. (1957). *A theory of cognitive dissonance.* Stanford University Press.

Festinger, L. (1964a). *Conflict, decision, and dissonance.* Stanford, CA: Stanford University Press.

Festinger, L. (1964b). Behavioral support for opinion change. *Public Opinion Quarterly,* **28**(3), 404–417.

Festinger, L., & Carlsmith, J. M. (1959). Cognitive consequences of forced compliance. *Journal of Abnormal and Social Psychology,* **58**, 203–210.

Festinger, L., Pepitone, A., & Newcomb, T. (1952). Some consequences of deindividuation in a group. *Journal of Abnormal and Social Psychology,* **47**, 382–389.

Festinger, L., Schachter, S., & Back, K. (1950). *Social pressures in informal groups: A study of a housing community.* Stanford University Press.

Feynman, R. (1967). *The character of physical law.* MIT Press.

Fiedler, F. E. (1966). The effect of leadership and cultural heterogeneity on group performance: A test of the contingency model. *Journal of Experimental Social Psychology,* **2**(3), 237–264.

Fiedler, F. (1967). *A theory of leadership effectiveness.* McGraw-Hill.

Fieldler, K., Schenck, W., Watling, M., & Menges, J. (2005). Priming trait inferences through pictures and moving pictures: The impact of open and closed mindsets. *Journal of Personality and Social Psychology,* **88**, 229–244.

Figgou, L., & Condor, S. (2006). Irrational categorization, natural intolerance and reasonable discrimination: Lay representations of prejudice and racism. *British Journal of Social Psychology,* **45**, 219–243.

Finchilescu, G., Bernstein, C., & Chihambakwe, D. (2019). The impact of workplace bullying in the Zimbabwean nursing environment: Is social support a beneficial resource in the bullying–well-being relationship? *South African Journal of Psychology,* **49**(1), 83–96. https://doi.org/10.1177/0081246318761735

Findley, M. J., & Cooper, H. M. (1983). Locus of control and academic achievement: A literature review. *Journal of Personality and Social Psychology,* **44**, 419–427.

Fine, C. (2010). From scanner to sound bite: Issues in interpreting and reporting sex differences in the brain. *Current Directions in Psychological Science,* **19**(5), 280–283.

Finkel, E. J., & Campbell, W. K. (2001). Self-control and accommodation in close relationships: An interdependence analysis. *Journal of Personality and Social Psychology,* **81**, 263–277.

Finkel, E. J., Eastwick, P. W., Karney, B. R., Reis, H. T., & Sprecher, S. (2012). Online dating: A critical analysis from the perspective of psychological science. *Psychological Science in the Public Interest,* **13**(1), 3–66.

Finkenauer, C., Engels, R. C., Branje, S. J., & Meeus, W. (2004). Disclosure and relationship satisfaction in families. *Journal of Marriage and Family,* **66**(1), 195–209.

Finney, P. (1978). Personality traits attributed to risky and conservative decision makers: Culture values more than risk. *Journal of Psychology: Interdisciplinary and Applied,* **99**(2), 187–197.

Fischer, P., Greitemeyer, T., Omay, S. I., & Frey, D. (2007). Mergers and group status: The impact of high, low and equal group status on identification and satisfaction with a company merger, experienced controllability, group identity and group cohesion. *Journal of Community and Applied Social Psychology,* **17**(3), 203–217.

Fischer, P., Krueger, J. I., Greitemeyer, T., Vogrincic, C., Kästenmüller, A., Frey, D., Heene, M., Wicher, M., & Kainbacher, M. (2011). The bystander effect: A meta-analytic review on bystander intervention in dangerous and non-dangerous emergencies. *Psychological Bulletin,* **137**(4), 517–537.

Fischer, R. L., &Beimers, D. (2009). 'Put me in, Coach': A pilot evaluation of executive coaching in the nonprofit sector. *Nonprofit Management and Leadership,* **19**, 507–522. https://doi.org/10.1002/nml.234

Fischhoff, B. (1982). Debiasing. In D. Kahneman, P. Slovic, & A. Tversky (Eds.), *Judgment under uncertainty: Heuristics and biases.* Cambridge University Press.

Fisek, M. H., & Hysom, S. J. (2008). Status characteristics and reward expectations: A test of a theory of justice in two cultures. *Social Science Research,* **37**(3), 769–786.

Fishbein, M. (1979). A theory of reasoned action: Some applications and implications. *Nebraska Symposium on Motivation,* **27**, 65–116.

Fishbein, M., & Ajzen, I. (2011). *Predicting and changing behavior: A reasoned action approach.* Psychology Press.

Fisher, H. (1994, April). The nature of romantic love. *Journal of NIH Research,* **6**(4), 59–64.

Fisher, H. (2004). Dumped! *New Scientist,* **181**, 2434–2441.

Fiske, S. T. (1989a). Interdependence and stereotyping: From the laboratory to the Supreme Court (and back). Invited address, American Psychological Association convention.

Fiske, S. T. (1989b). Examining the role of intent: Toward understanding its role in stereotyping and prejudice. In J. S. Uleman & J. A. Bargh (Eds.), *Unintended thought.* Guilford Press.

Fiske, S. T. (1998). Stereotypes, prejudice, and discrimination, In D. T. Gilbert, S. T. Fiske, & G. Lindzey (Eds.), *Handbook of social psychology* (Vol. 2). McGraw-Hill.

Fiske, S. T. (2004). *Social beings: A core motives approach to social psychology.* Wiley.

Fiske, S. T., & Taylor, S. E. (1991). *Social cognition* (2nd ed.). McGraw-Hill.

Fiske, S. T., & Taylor, S. E. (2007). *Social cognition: From brains to culture.* McGraw-Hill.

Fiske, S. T., & Taylor, S. E. (2013). *Social cognition: From brains to culture.* Sage.

Fiske, S. T., Harris, L. T., & Cuddy, A. J. C. (2004). Why ordinary people torture enemy prisoners. *Science,* **306**, 1482–1483.

Fletcher, A. C., Steinberg, L., & Williams-Wheeler, M. (2004a). Parental influences on adolescent problem behaviour: Revisiting Stattin and Kerr. *Child Development,* **75**(3), 781–796.

Fletcher, G. J. O., & Ward, C. (1989). Attribution theory and processes: A cross-cultural perspective. In M. H. Bond (Ed.), *The cross-cultural challenge to social psychology.* Sage.

Fletcher, G. J. O., Simpson, J. A., Thomas, G., & Giles, L. (1999). Ideals in intimate relationships. *Journal of Personality and Social Psychology,* **76**, 72–89.

Foa, U. G., & Foa, E. B. (1975). *Resource theory of social exchange.* General Learning Press.

Foley, L. A. (1976). Personality and situational influences on changes in prejudice: A replication of Cook's railroad game in a prison setting. *Journal of Personality and Social Psychology,* **34**, 846–856.

Fonagy, P. (2003). The interpersonal interpretive mechanism: The confluence of genetics and attachment theory in development. In V. Green (Ed.),

Emotional development in psychoanalysis, attachment theory and neuroscience (pp. 107–126). Brunner-Routledge.

Fontaine, N., Carbonneau, R., Barker, E. D., Vitaro, F., Hébert, M., Côté, S. M., Nagin, D. S., Zoccolillo, M., & Tremblay, R. E. (2008). Girls' hyperactivity and physical aggression during childhood and adjustment problems in early adulthood. *Archives of General Psychiatry*, **65**(3), 320–328.

Forbes, G. B., Collinsworth, L. L., Jobe, R. L., Braun, K. D., & Wise, L. M. (2007). Sexism, hostility toward women, and endorsement of beauty ideals and practices: Are beauty ideals associated with oppressive beliefs?*Sex Roles*, **56**, 265–273.

Forbes, K. F., & Zampelli, E. M. (2014). Volunteerism: The influences of social, religious, and human capital. *Nonprofit and Voluntary Sector Quarterly*, **43**(2), 227–253.

Ford, T. E., & Stangor, C. (1992). The role of diagnosticity in stereotype formation: Perceiving group means and variances. *Journal of Personality and Social Psychology*, **63**(3), 356.

Forsyth, D. R. (2009). *Group dynamics*. Wadsworth.

Fortune, E., Goodie, A., & Maisto, S. A. (2012). Cognitive distortions as a component and treatment focus of pathological gambling: A review. *Psychology of Addictive Behaviors*, **26**(2), 298–310.

Foster, C. A., Witcher, B. S., Campbell, W. K., & Green, J. D. (1998). Arousal and attraction: Evidence for automatic and controlled processes. *Journal of Personality and Social Psychology*, **74**, 86–101.

Fox, J., & Potocki, B. (2016). Lifetime video game consumption, interpersonal aggression, hostile sexism, and rape myth acceptance: A cultivation perspective. *Journal of Interpersonal Violence*, **31**(10), 1912–1931. https://doi.org/10.1177/0886260515570747

Francis, B., Archer, L., Hodgen, J., Pepper, D., Taylor, B., & Travers, M. C. (2017). Exploring the relative lack of impact of research on 'ability grouping' in England: A discourse analytic account. *Cambridge Journal of Education*, **47**(1), 1–17.

Frank, J. D. (1974). *Persuasion and healing: A comparative study of psychotherapy*. Schocken.

Frank, J. D. (1982). Therapeutic components shared by all psychotherapies. In J. H. Harvey & M. M. Parks (Eds.), *The Master Lecture series: Vol. 1. Psychotherapy research and behavior change*. American Psychological Association.

Frank, M. G., & Gilovich, T. (1989). Effect of memory perspective on retrospective causal attributions. *Journal of Personality and Social Psychology*, **57**, 399–403.

Frank, R. (1999). *Luxury fever: Why money fails to satisfy in an era of excess*. The Free Press.

Frankel, A., & Snyder, M. L. (1987). Egotism among the depressed: When self-protection becomes self-handicapping. Paper presented at the American Psychological Association convention.

Fransen, M. L., Verlegh, P. W. J., Kirmani, A., & Smit, E. G. (2015). A typology of consumer strategies for resisting advertising, and a review of mechanisms for countering them. *International Journal of Advertising*. **34**(1), 1–11. https://doi.org/10.1080/02650487.2014.995284

Franzen, A., Mader, S., & Winter, F. (2018). Contagious yawning, empathy, and their relation to prosocial behavior. *Journal of Experimental Psychology*, **147**(12), 1950–1958. https://doi.org/10.1037/xge0000422.

Fraser, A. M., Padilla-Walker, L. M., Coyne, S. M., Nelson, L. J., & Stockdale, L. A. (2012). Associations between violent video gaming, empathic concern, and prosocial behavior toward strangers, friends, and family members. *Journal of Youth and Adolescence*, **41**(5), 636–649.

Freedman, J. S. (1965). Long-term behavioral effects of cognitive dissonance. *Journal of Experimental Social Psychology*, **1**, 145–155.

Freeman, J. B., Schiller, D., Rule, N. O., & Ambady, N. (2010). The neural origins of superficial and individuated judgements about ingroup and outgroup members. *Human Brain Mapping*, **31**(1), 150–159.

Freud, E. (2017, October 31). What is your biggest regret? Here are people's devastatingly honest answers. *The Guardian*. https://www.theguardian.com/lifeandstyle/2017/oct/31/biggest-regret-devastatingly-honest-twitter-bad-choices

Freud, S. (1921). *Group psychology and the analysis of the ego*. International Psychoanalytic Publishing House.

Freud, S. (1924). The dissolution of the Oedipus complex. In E. Jones (Ed.), *The standard edition of the complete psychological works of Sigmund Freud* (Vol. 19, pp. 172–179). Hogarth.

Freysteinsdóttir, F. J. (2018). Femicide in a small Nordic welfare society. *Journal of Comparative Social Work*, **13**(1), 35–56.

Friedman, T. L. (2003a, 9 April). Hold your applause. *New York Times:* www.nytimes. com.

Friedman, T. L. (2003b, 4 June). Because we could. *New York Times:* www.nytimes. com.

Frith, C., & Frith, U. (2005). Theory of mind. *Current Biology*, **15**(17), R644–646. https://doi.org/10.1016/j.cub.2005.08.041

Fromm, E. (1973). *The anatomy of human destructiveness*. Holt, Rinehart & Winston.

Frosdick, S., & Marsh, P. E. (2005). *Football hooliganism*. Willan.

Fujisawa, K. K., Kutsukake, N., & Hasegawa, T. (2008). Reciprocity of prosocial behavior in Japanese preschool children. *International Journal of Behavioral Development*, **32**(2), 89–97.

Fuller, S. R., & Aldag, R. J. (1998). Organizational Tonypandy: Lessons from a quarter century of the groupthink phenomenon. *Organizational Behavior and Human Decision Processes*, **73**, 163–185.

Furnham, A. (2003). Belief in a just world: Research progress over the past decade. *Personality and Individual Differences*, **34**, 795–817.

G

Gaertner, L., Sedikides, C., & Graetz, K. (1999). In search of self-definition: Motivational primacy of the individual self-, motivational primacy of the collective self-, or contextual primacy? *Journal of Personality and Social Psychology*, **76**, 5–18.

Gaertner, S. L., & Dovidio, J. F. (2000). *Reducing intergroup bias: The common ingroup identity model*. Psychology Press.

Gaertner, S. L., & Dovidio, J. F. (2005). Understanding and addressing contemporary racism: From aversive racism to the Common Ingroup Identity Model. *Journal of Social Issues*, **61**, 615–639.

Gaertner, S. L., & McLaughlin, J. P. (1983). Racial stereotypes: Associations and ascriptions of positive and negative characteristics. *Social Psychology Quarterly*, **46**, 23–40.

Gaertner, S. L., Dovidio, J. F., Anastasio, P. A., Bachman, B. A., & Rust, M. C. (1993). The Common Ingroup Identity Model: Recategorization and the reduction of intergroup bias. In W. Stroebe & M. Hewstone (Eds.), *European Review of Social Psychology* (Vol. 4). Wiley.

Gaertner, S. L., Dovidio, J. F., Nier, J. A., Banker, B. S., Ward, C. M., Houlette, M., & Loux, S. (2000). The common ingroup identity model for reducing intergroup bias: Progress and challenges. In D. Capozza & R. Brown (Eds.), *Social identity processes: Trends in theory and research*. Sage.

Gaertner, S. L., Mann, J., Murrell, A., & Dovidio, J. F. (2001). Reducing intergroup bias: The benefits of recategorization. In M. A. Hogg & D. Abrams (eds), *Intergroup relations: Essential readings*. Philadelphia, PA: Psychology Press.

Gailliot, M. T. (2008). Unlocking the energy dynamics of executive function: Linking executive functioning to brain glycogen. *Perspectives in Psychological Science*, **3**, 245–263.

Gailliot, M. T., & Baumeister, R. F. (2007). Self-regulation and sexual restraint. Dispositionally and temporarily poor self-regulation abilities contribute to failures at restraining sexual behaviour. *Personality and Social Psychology Bulletin*, **33**, 173–186.

Galak, J., LeBoeuf, R. L., Nelson, L. D., & Simmons, J. P. (2012). Correcting the past: Failures to replicate Psi. *Journal of Personality and Social Psychology*, **103**, 933–948.

Gallagher, S., & Gergen, K. (2011). The social construction of self. In S. Gallagher (Ed.), *The Oxford handbook of the self*. Oxford University Press.

Gallo, L. C., & Matthews, K. A. (2003). Understanding the association between socio economic status and physical health: Do negative emotions play a role? *Psychological Bulletin*, **129**, 10–51.

Gallupe, R. B., Cooper, W. H., Grise, M. L., & Bastianutti, L. M. (1994). Blocking electronic brainstorms. *Journal of Applied Psychology*, **79**, 77–86.

Gambrel, P. A., & Cianci, R. (2003). Maslow's hierarchy of needs: Does it apply in a collectivist culture. *Journal of Applied Management and Entrepreneurship*, **8**(2), 143–161.

Gamer, R. (2005). What's in a name? Persuasion perhaps. *Journal of Consumer Psychology,* **15**(2), 108–116.

Gámez-Guadix, M., Almendros, C., Calvete, E., & De Santisteban, P. (2018). Persuasion strategies and sexual solicitations and interactions in online sexual grooming of adolescents: Modeling direct and indirect pathways. *Journal of Adolescence,* **63**, 11–18. https://doi.org/10.1016/j.adolescence.2017.12.002

Gan, G., Sterzer, P., Marxen, M., Zimmermann, U. S., and Smolka, M. N. (2015). Neural and behavioral correlates of alcohol-induced aggression under provocation. *Neuropsychopharmacology,* **40**, 2886–2896.

Gangestad, S. W., & Scheyd, G. J. (2005). The evolution of human physical attractiveness. *Annual Review of Anthropology,* **34**, 523-548.

Gangestad, S. W., & Snyder, M. (2000). Self-monitoring: Appraisal and reappraisal. *Psychological Bulletin,* **126**, 530–555.

Gangestad, S. W., Haselton, M. G., & Buss, D. M. (2006). Evolutionary foundations of cultural variation: Evoked culture and mate preferences. *Psychological Inquiry,* **17**(2), 75–95.

Gangestad, S. W., Simpson, J. A., & Cousins, A. J. (2004). Women's preferences for male behavioral displays change across the menstrual cycle. *Psychological Science,* **15**, 203–207.

Gantt, E. E., & Burton, J. (2013). Egoism, altruism, and the ethical foundations of personhood. *Journal of Humanistic Psychology,* **53**(4), 438-460.

Garb, H. N. (2005). Clinical judgment and decision making. *Annual Review of Clinical Psychology,* **1**, 67–89.

García, H., Soriano, E., & Arriaza, G. (2014). Friends with benefits and psychological wellbeing. *Procedia-Social and Behavioral Sciences,* **132**, 241-247.

Garcia-Marques, T., Mackie, D. M., Claypool, H. M., & Garcia-Marques, L. (2004). Positivity can cue familiarity. *Personality and Social Psychology Bulletin,* **30**, 585–593.

Gardikiotis, A. (2011). Minority influence. *Social and Personality Psychology Compass,* **5**(9), 679–693.

Gardner, M. (1997, July/August). Heaven's gate: The UFO cult of Bo and Peep. *Skeptical Inquirer,* 15–17.

Gardner, M. (2004). Mood states and consumer behaviour: A critical review. *Journal of Consumer Behaviour,* **12**, 281–300.

Garner, D. M, Garfinkel, P. E., Schwartz, D., & Thompson, M. (1980). Cultural expectations of thinness in women. *Psychological Reports,* **47**, 183–191.

Garry, M., Manning, C. G., Loftus, E. F., & Sherman, S. J. (1996). Imagination inflation: Imagining a childhood event inflates confidence that it occurred. *Psychonomic Bulletin & Review,* **3**, 208–214.

Gates, M. F., & Allee, W. C. (1933). Conditioned behavior of isolated and grouped cockroaches on a simple maze. *Journal of Comparative Psychology,* **15**, 331–358.

Gawronski, B. (2004). Theory-based bias correction in dispositional inference: The fundamental attribution error is dead, long live the correspondence bias. *European Review of Social Psychology,* **15**(1), 183–217.

Gawronski, B., Deutsch, R., Mbirkou, S., Seibt, B., & Strack, F. (2008). When 'just say no' is not enough: Affirmation versus negation training and the reduction of automatic stereotype activation. *Journal of Experimental Social Psychology,* **44**, 370–377.

Gayle, D., & Younge, G. (2017). Irresponsible reporting of knife crime 'alienating young people'. *The Guardian,* 28 May.

Ge, L., Albin, B., Hadziabdic, E., Hjelm, K., & Rask, M. (2016). Beliefs about health and illness and health-related behavior among urban women with gestational diabetes mellitus in the south east of China. *Journal of Transcultural Nursing,* **27**(6), 593–602. https://doi.org/10.1177/1043659615594677

Geniole, S. N., Carré, J. M., & McCormick, C. M. (2011). State, not trait, neuroendocrine function predicts costly reactive aggression in men after social exclusion and inclusion. *Biological Psychology,* **87**(1), 137–145.

Geniole, S. N., Denson, T. F., Dixson, B. J., Carré, J. M., & McCormick, C. M. (2015). Evidence from meta-analyses of the facial width-to-height ratio as an evolved cue of threat. *PLoS ONE,* **10**(7), E0132726.

Gentile, D. (2013). Catharsis and media violence: A conceptual analysis. *Societies,* **3**(4), 491–510.

Gentile, D. A., & Anderson, C. A. (2003). Violent video games: The newest media violence hazard. In D. A. Gentile (Ed.), *Media violence and children* (pp. 131–152).Ablex.

Gentile, D. A., Coyne, S., & Walsh, D. A. (2011). Media violence, physical aggression, and relational aggression in school age children: A short-term longitudinal study. *Aggressive Behavior,* **37**(2), 193–206.

Gentile, D. A., Lynch, P. J., Linder, J. R., & Walsh, D. A. (2004). The effects of violent video game habits on adolescent hostility, aggressive behaviors, and school performance. *Journal of Adolescence,* **27**(1), 5–22.

Gerard, H. B., Wilhelmy, R. A., & Conolley, E. S. (1968). Conformity and group size. *Journal of Personality and Social Psychology,* **8**, 79–82.

Gerber, J., Wheeler, L., & Suls, J. (2018). A social comparison theory meta-analysis 60 years on. *Psychological Bulletin,* **144**(2), 177.

Gerbner, G., & Gross, L. (1976). Living with television: The violence profile. *Journal of Communication,* **26**(2), 173–199.

Gergen, K. (2001). *Social construction in context.* Sage.

Gergen, K. J. (1973). Social psychology as history. *Journal of Personality and Social Psychology,* **26**, 309–320.

Gergen, K. J. (1994). *Toward transformation in social knowledge* (2nd ed.). Sage.

Gergen, K. J. (1999). *An invitation to social construction.* Sage.

Gergen, K. J. (2010). The acculturated brain. *Theory & Psychology,* **20**(6), 795–816.

Giannetti, B. F., Bonilla, S. H., & Almeida, C. M. V. B. (2004). Developing eco-technologies: A possibility to minimize environmental impact in southern Brazil. *Journal of Cleaner Production,* **12**(4), 361–368. https://doi.org/10.1016/S0959-6526(03)00033-7

Gibbons, A. (2004). American Association of Physical Anthropologists meeting: Tracking the evolutionary history of a 'warrior' gene. *Science,* **304**, 818–819.

Gibbs, J. L., Ellison, N. B., & Lai, C. H. (2011). First comes love, then comes Google: An investigation of uncertainty reduction strategies and self-disclosure in online dating. *Communication Research,* **38**(1), 70-100.

Gibney, M., Howard-Hassman, R. E., Coicard, J., & Steiner, N. (2008). The age of apology: Facing up to the past. *International Journal of Transactional Justice,* **2**, 429–430.

Gibson, B., & Sachau, D. (2000). Sandbagging as a self-presentational strategy: Claiming to be less than you are. *Personality and Social Psychology Bulletin,* **26**, 56–70.

Gibson, B., & Sanbonmatsu, D. M. (2004). Optimism, pessimism, and gambling: The downside of optimism. *Personality and Social Psychology Bulletin,* **30**, 149–160.

Gibson, S. (2013a). 'The last possible resort': A forgotten prod and the in situ standardization of Stanley Milgram's voice-feedback condition. *History of Psychology,* **16**(3), 177–194.

Gibson, S. (2013b). Milgram's obedience experiments: A rhetorical analysis. *British Journal of Social Psychology,* **52**(2), 290–309.

Gibson, S. (2014). Discourse, defiance, and rationality: 'Knowledge work' in the 'obedience' experiments. *Journal of Social Issues,* **70**(3), 424–438.

Gibson, S. (2017). Developing psychology's archival sensibilities: Revisiting Milgram's 'obedience' experiments. *Qualitative Psychology,* **4**(1), 73–89.

Gibson, S. (2019). Obedience without orders: Expanding social psychology's conception of 'obedience'. *British Journal of Social Psychology,* **58**(1), 241–259.

Gibson, S., Blenkinsopp, G., Johnstone, E., & Marshall, A. (2018). Just following orders? The rhetorical invocation of 'obedience' in Stanley Milgram's post-experiment interviews. *European Journal of Social Psychology,* **48**, 585–599.

Gifford, R. (2014). Environmental psychology matters. *Annual Review of Psychology,* **65**, 541–579.

Gifford, R., Kormos, C., & McIntyre, A. (2011). Behavioral dimensions of climate change: Drivers, responses, barriers, and interventions. *Wiley Interdisciplinary Reviews: Climate Change,* **2**(6), 801–827.

Gigerenzer, G., & Goldstein, D. G. (1996). Mind as computer: Birth of a metaphor. *Creativity Research Journal,* **9**(2&3), 131–144.

Gigerenzer, G., & Todd, P. M. (1999). *Simple heuristics that make us smart.* Oxford University Press.

Gigone, D., & Hastie, R. (1993). The common knowledge

effect: Information sharing and group judgment. *Journal of Personality and Social Psychology,* **65,** 959–974.

Gilbert, D. T., & Ebert, J. E. J. (2002). Decisions and revisions: The affective forecasting of changeable outcomes. *Journal of Personality and Social Psychology,* **82,** 503–514.

Gilbert, D. T., & Jones, E. E. (1986). Perceiver-induced constraint: Interpretations of self-generated reality. *Journal of Personality and Social Psychology,* **50,** 269–280.

Gilbert, D. T., & Malone, P. T. (1995). The correspondence bias. *Psychological Bulletin,* **117**(1), 21–38.

Gilbert, D. T., & Wilson, T. D. (2000). Miswanting: Some problems in the forecasting of future affective states. In J. Forgas (Ed.), *Feeling and thinking: The role of affect in social cognition.* Cambridge University Press.

Gilbert, D. T., Giesler, R. B., & Morris, K. A. (1995). When comparisons arise. *Journal of Personality and Social Psychology,* **69,** 227–236.

Gilbert, D. T., King, G., Pettigrew, S., & Wilson, T. D. (2016). Comment on 'Estimating the reproducibility of psychological science'. *Science,* **351**(6277), 1037.

Gilbert, G. N., & Mulkay, M. (1984). *Opening Pandora's box: A sociological analysis of scientists discourse.* Cambridge University Press.

Gilbert, P., & Irons, C. (2004). A pilot exploration of the use of compassionate images in a group of self-critical people. *Memory,* **12**(4), 507–516. https://doi.org/10.1080/09658210444000115

Giles, L. C., Glonek, G. F. V., Luszcz, M. A., & Andrews, G. R. (2005). Effect of social networks on 10 year survival in very old Australians: The Australian longitudinal study of aging. *Journal of Epidemiology and Community Health,* **59**(7), 574–579. https://doi.org/10.1136/jech.2004.025429

Giles, M., McClenahan, C., Cairns, E., & Mallet, J. (2004). An application of the theory of planned behaviour to blood donation: The importance of self-efficacy. *Health Education Research,* **19**(4), 380–391.

Gilibert, D., & Banovic, I. (2009). Effect of training in psychology on the causal interpretation of a clinical case. *European Journal of Psychology of Education,* **23**(4), 373–385.

Gillies, J., & Neimeyer, R. A. (2006). Loss, grief, and the search for significance: Toward a model of meaning reconstruction in bereavement. *Journal of Constructivist Psychology,* **19**(1), 31–65. https://doi.org/10.1080/10720530500311182

Gilligan, C. (1982). *In a different voice: Psychological theory and women's development.* Harvard University Press.

Gilligan, C., Lyons, N. P., & Hanmer, T. J. (Eds.) (1990). *Making connections: The relational worlds of adolescent girls at Emma Willard School.* Harvard University Press.

Gilovich, T., Kerr, M., & Medvec, V. H. (1993). Effect of temporal perspective on subjective confidence. *Journal of Personality and Social Psychology,* **64,** 552–560.

Gilovich, T., Savitsky, K., & Medvec, V. H. (1998). The illusion of transparency: Biased assessments of others' ability to read one's emotional states. *Journal of Personality and Social Psychology,* **75,** 332–346.

Gintis, H. (2000). Strong reciprocity and human sociality. *Journal of Theoretical Biology,* **206,** 169–179.

Gintis, H. (2003). The hitchhiker's guide to altruism: Gene–culture coevolution, and the internalization of norms. *Journal of Theoretical Biology,* **220,** 407–418.

Giuffrida, A. (2020). Pope Francis apologises after slapping woman's hand. *The Guardian,* 1 Jan:https://www.theguardian.com/world/2020/jan/01/pope-francis-apologises-after-slapping-womans-hand

Glaser, B. G., & Strauss, A. L. (1965). *Awareness of dying.* Aldine.

Glaser, B. G., & Strauss, A. L. (1967). *The discovery of grounded theory: Strategies for qualitative research.* Aldine.

Glasford, D. E., & Dovidio, J. F. (2011). *E Pluribus Unum:* Dual identity and minority group members' motivation to engage in contact, as well as social change. *Journal of Experimental Social Psychology,* **47,** 1021–1024.

Glasford, D. E., Pratto, F., & Dovidio, J. F. (2008). Intragroup dissonance: Responses to ingroup violation of personal values. *Journal of Experimental Social Psychology,* **44,** 1057–1064.

Glass, D. C. (1964). Changes in liking as a means of reducing cognitive discrepancies between self-esteem and aggression. *Journal of Personality,* **32,** 531–549.

Glass, R. I. (2004). Perceived threats and real killers. *Science,* **304,** 927.

Glatz, T., Stattin, H., & Kerr, M. (2012). A test of cognitive dissonance theory to explain parents' reactions to youths' alcohol intoxication. *Family Relations, 61*(4), 629–641. https://doi.org/10.1111/j.1741-3729.2012.00723.x

Gleason, M. E. J., Iida, M., Bolger, N., & Shrout, P. E. (2003). Daily supportive equity in close relationships. *Personality and Social Psychology Bulletin,* **29,** 1036–1045.

Glenn, N. O. (1980). Values, attitudes, and beliefs. In O. G. O'Brim & J.Kagan (Eds.), *Constancy and change in human development.* Harvard University Press.

Glick, P., & Fiske, S. T. (1996). The ambivalent sexism inventory: Differentiating hostile and benevolent sexism. *Journal of Personality and Social Psychology,* **70,** 491–512.

Glick, P., & Fiske, S. T. (2001). An ambivalent alliance: Hostile and benevolent sexism as complementary justifications for gender inequality. *American Psychologist,* **56,** 109–118.

Glick, P., Fiske, S. T. & 29 others (2000). Beyond prejudice as simple antipathy: Hostile and benevolent sexism across cultures. *Journal of Personality and Social Psychology,* **79,** 763–775.

Glick, P., Lameiras, M., Fiske, S., et al. (2004). Bad but bold: Ambivalent attitudes toward men predict gender inequality in 16 nations. *Journal of Personality and Social Psychology,* **86,** 713–728.

Gobodo-Madikizela, P. (2003). *A human being died that night: A South African story of forgiveness.* Houghton Mifflin.

Goethals, G. R., Messick, D. M., & Allison, S. T. (1991). The uniqueness bias: Studies of constructive social comparison. In J. Suls & T. A. Wills (Eds.), *Social comparison: Contemporary theory and research.* Erlbaum.

Goffman, E. (1959). *The presentation of self in everyday life.* Penguin Books.

Goh, J. O., Chee, M. W., Tan, J. C., Venkatraman, V., Hebrank, A., Leshikar, E.D., Jenkins, L., Sutton, B. P., Gutchess, A. H., & Park, D. (2007). Age and culture modulate object processing and object-science binding in the ventral visual area. *Cognitive, Affective and Behavioral Neuroscience,* **7,** 44–52.

Goldberg, A., Smith, J., & Perry-Jenkins, M. (2012). The division of labor in lesbian, gay, and heterosexual new adoptive parents. *Journal of Marriage and Family,* **74**(4), 812–828.

Goldhagen, D. J. (1996). *Hitler's willing executioners.* Knopf.

Goldsmith, C. (2003, 25 March). World media turn wary eye on US. *Wall Street Journal,* p. A12.

Goldsmith, R. E., Clark, R. A., & Lafferty, B. A. (2005). Tendency to conform: A new measure and its relationship to psychological reactance. *Psychological Reports,* **96**(3), 591–594.

Goldstein, A. P., Glick, B., & Gibbs, J. C. (1998). *Aggression replacement training: A comprehensive intervention for aggressive youth* (rev. ed.). Research Press.

Goldstein, D. G., & Gigerenzer, G. (2002). Models of ecological rationality: The recognition heuristic. *Psychological Review,* **109**(1), 75–90.

Goldstein, N. J., Cialdini, R. B., & Griskevicius, V. (2008). A room with a viewpoint: Using social norms to motivate environmental conservation in hotels. *Journal of Consumer Research,* **35**(3), 472–482.

Gonzalez, A. Q., & Koestner, R. (2005). Parental preference for sex of newborn as reflected in positive affect in birth announcements. *Sex Roles,* **52,** 407–411.

Goodhart, D. E. (1986). The effects of positive and negative thinking on performance in an achievement situation. *Journal of Personality and Social Psychology,* **51,** 117–124.

Goodman, S., & Carr, P. (2017). The just world hypothesis as an argumentative resource in debates about unemployment benefits. *Journal of Community and Applied Social Psychology,* **27**(4), 312–323.

Gortmaker, S. L., Must, A., Perrin, J. M., Sobol, A. M., & Dietz, W. H. (1993). Social and economic consequences of overweight in adolescence and young adulthood. *New England Journal of Medicine,* **329,** 1008–1012.

Gorton, K., & Garde-Hansen, J. (2013). From old media whore to new media troll: The online negotiation of Madonna's ageing body. *Feminist Media Studies,* **13**(2), 288–302.

Gotlib, I. H., & Colby, C. A. (1988). How to have a good quarrel. In P. Marsh (Ed.), *Eye to eye: How people interact.* Salem House.

Gott, M., & Hinchliff, S. (2003). How important is sex in later life? The views of older people. *Social Science & Medicine,* **56**(8), 1617–1628.

Gough, B., McFadden, M., & McDonald, M. (2013). *Critical social psychology: An introduction* (2nd ed.). Palgrave Macmillan.

Gould, R., Brounstein, P. J., & Sigall, H. (1977). Attributing ability to an opponent: Public aggrandizement and private denigration. *Sociometry,* **40,** 254–261.

Gouldner, A. W. (1960). The norm of reciprocity: A preliminary statement. *American Sociological Review,* **25,** 161–178.

Gow, K., & Paton, D. (2008). *The phoenix of natural disasters: Community resilience.* Nova Science.

Grönlund, H., Holmes, K., Kang, C., Cnaan, R. A., Handy, F., Brudney, J. L., Haski-Leventhal, D., Hustinx, L., Kassam, M., Meijs, L. C. P. M., Pessi, A. B., Ranade, B., Smith, K. A., Yamauchi, N., & Zrinščak, S. (2011). Cultural values and volunteering: A cross-cultural comparison of students' motivation to volunteer in 13 countries. *Journal of Academic Ethics,* **9**(2), 87–106.

Grand View Research (2017). Cosmetic surgery and procedure market analysis by Type (surgical, nonsurgical), region (North America, Europe, Asia Pacific, Latin America, Middle East & Africa), and segment forecasts, 2018–2025. https://www.grandviewresearch.com/industry-analysis/cosmetic-surgery-procedure-market

Grant, A., & Sonnentag, S. (2010). Doing good buffers against feeling bad: Prosocial impact compensates for negative task and self-evaluations. *Organizational Behavior and Human Decision Processes,* **111**(1), 13–22.

Grant, A. M., Passmore, J., Cavanagh, M. J., &Parker, H. (2010). The state of play in coaching today: A comprehensive review of the field. *International Review of Industrial and Organizational Psychology,* **25,** 125–167. https://doi.org/10.1002/9780470661628

Graziano, W. G., & Bruce, J. W. (2008). Attraction and the initiation of relationships: A review of the empirical literature. In S. Sprecher, A. Wenzel & J. Harvey (Eds.), *Handbook of relationship initiation* (pp. 269–295). Psychology Press.

Graziano, W. G., Jensen-Campbell, L., & Finch, J. F. (1997). The self as a mediator between personality and adjustment. *Journal of Personality and Social Psychology,* **73,** 392–404.

Green, A. (2007). To know it is to love it? A psychological discussion of the mere exposure and satiation effects in music listening. *Psyke & Logos,* **28**(1), 210–227.

Greenberg, J., Pyszczynski, T., Solomon, S., Rosenblatt, A., Veeder, M., Kirkland, S., & Lyon, D. (1990). Evidence for terror management theory II: The effects of mortality salience on reactions to those who threaten or bolster the cultural worldview. *Journal of Personality and Social Psychology,* **58,** 308–318.

Greenberg, J., Solomon, S., & Pyszczynski, T. (1997). Terror management theory of self-esteem and cultural worldviews: Empirical assessments and conceptual refinements. *Advances in Experimental Social Psychology,* **29,** 61–142.

Greene, K., Derlega, V. J., & Mathews, A. (2006). Self-disclosure in personal relationships. In A. L. Vangelisti & D. Perlman (Eds.), *The Cambridge handbook of personal relationships* (pp. 409–427). Cambridge University Press.

Greenwald, A. G. (1975). On the inconclusiveness of crucial cognitive tests of dissonance versus self-perception theories. *Journal of Experimental Social Psychology,* **11,** 490–499.

Greenwald, A. G., & Banaji, M. R. (1995). Implicit social cognition: Attitudes, self-esteem, and stereotypes. *Psychological Review,* **102,** 4–27.

Greenwald, A. G., & Schuh, E. S. (1994). An ethnic bias in scientific citations. *European Journal of Social Psychology,* **24,** 623–639.

Greenwald, A. G., Abrams, R. L., Naccache, L., & Dehaene, S. (2003a). Long-term semantic memory versus contextual memory in unconscious number processing. *Journal of Experimental Psychology,* **29**(2), 235–247.

Greenwald, A. G., Banaji, M. R., Rudman, L. A., Farnham, S. D., Nosek, B. A., & Rosier, M. (2000). Prologue to a unified theory of attitudes, stereotypes, and self-concept. In J. P. Forgas (Ed.), *Feeling and thinking: The role of affect in social cognition and behavior.* Cambridge University Press.

Greenwald, A. G., McGhee, D. E., & Schwartz, J. L. K. (1998). Measuring individual differences in implicit cognition: The implicit association test. *Journal of Personality and Social Psychology,* **74,** 1464–1480.

Greenwald, A. G., Nosek, B. A., & Banaji, M. R. (2003b). Understanding and using the implicit association test: I. An improved scoring algorithm. *Journal of Personality and Social Psychology,* **85,** 197–216.

Greenwald, A. G., Poehlman, T. A., Uhlmann, E. L., & Banaji, M. R. (2009). Understanding and using the implicit association test. III. Meta-analysis of predictive validity. *Journal of Personality and Social Psychology,* **97**(1), 17–41.

Greenwood, J. (2004). *The disappearance of the social in American social psychology.* Cambridge University Press.

Greifeneder, R., Scheibehenne, B., & Kleber, N. (2010). Less may be more when choosing is difficult: Choice complexity and too much choice. *Acta Psychologica,* **133,** 45–50.

Greving, H., & Sassenberg, K. (2015). Counter-regulation online: Threat biases retrieval of information during Internet search. *Computers in Human Behavior,* **50,** 291–298.

Grewal, R., Mehta, R., & Kardes, F. R. (2000). The role of the social-identity function of attitudes in consumer innovativeness and opinion leadership. *Journal of Economic Psychology,* **21,** 233–252.

GRID (2018), Global Report on Internal Displacement. Norwegian Refugee Council:http://www.internal-displacement.org/global-report/grid2018/downloads/2018-GRID.pdf

Griffiths, B., & Pedersen, A. (2009). Prejudice and the function of attitudes relating to Muslim Australians and indigenous Australians. *Australian Journal of Psychology,* **61**(4), 228–238.

Griffiths, M. D. (1994). The role of cognitive bias and skill in fruit machine gambling. *British Journal of Psychology,* **85,** 351–369.

Griffiths, M. D. (1997). Video games and aggression. *The Psychologist,* **10**(9), 397–401.

Griskevicius, V., Goldstein, N. J., Mortensen, C. R., Cialdini, R. B., & Kenrick, D. T. (2006). Going along versus going alone: When fundamental motives facilitate strategic (non)conformity. *Journal of Personality and Social Psychology,* **91**(2), 281–294.

Groenenboom, A., Wilke, H. A. M., & Wit, A. P. (2001). Will we be working together again? The impact of future interdependence on group members' task motivation. *European Journal of Social Psychology,* **31,** 369–378.

Grose, J., & Coplan, R. J. (2015). Longitudinal outcomes of shyness from childhood to emerging adulthood. *Journal of Genetic Psychology,* **176,** 408–413.

Grote, N. K., & Clark, M. S. (2001). Perceiving unfairness in the family: Cause or consequence of marital distress? *Journal of Personality and Social Psychology,* **80,** 281–293.

Grove, J. R., Hanrahan, S. J., & McInman, A. (1991). Success/failure bias in attributions across involvement categories in sport. *Personality and Social Psychology Bulletin,* **17,** 93–97.

Grover, K., & Miller, C. (2012). Does expressed acceptance reflect genuine attitudes? A bogus pipeline study of the effects of mortality salience on acceptance of a person with AIDS. *Journal of Social Psychology,* **152**(2), 131–135.

Guadagno, R.E., Okdie, B. M., Kruse, S. A. (2011). Dating deception: Gender, online dating, and exaggerated self-presentation. *Computers in Human Behavior,* **28**(2), 642–647.

Guéguen, N. (2012). Dead indoor plants strengthen belief in global warming. *Journal of Environmental Psychology,* **32**(2), 173–177.

Guéguen, N., Martin, A., & Meineri, S. (2011). Mimicry and helping behavior: an evaluation of mimicry on explicit helping request. *Journal of Social Psychology,* **151**(1), 1–4.

Guenther, C. L., & Alicke, M. D. (2008). Self-enhancement and belief perseverance. *Journal of Experimental Social Psychology,* **44,** 706–712.

Guerin, B. (2003). Combating prejudice and racism: New interventions from a functional analysis of racist language. *Journal of Community and Applied Social Psychology,* **13,** 29–45.

Guffey, J. E., Larson, J. G., Zimmerman, L., & Shook, B. (2007). The development of a Thurstone scale for identifying desirable police officer traits. *Journal of Police and Criminal Psychology*, **22**(1), 1–9.

Guimond, S., Chatard, A., Martinot, D., Crisp, R. J., & Redersdorff, S. (2006). Social comparison, self-stereotyping, and gender differences in self-construals. *Journal of Personality and Social Psychology*, **90**(2), 221–242. http://dx.doi.org/10.1037/0022-3514.90.2.221

Guiso, L., Monte, F., Sapienza, P., & Zingales, L. (2008). Diversity, culture, gender, and math. *Science*, **320**(5880), 1164–1165. https://doi.org/10.1126/science.1154094

Gundersen, E. (2001, 1 August). MTV is a many splintered thing. *USA Today*, p. 1D.

Güngör, D., Karasawa, M., Boiger, M., Dinçer, D., & Mesquita, B. (2014). Fitting in or sticking together: The prevalence and adaptivity of conformity, relatedness, and autonomy in Japan and Turkey. *Journal of Cross-Cultural Psychology*, **45**(9), 1374–1389. https://doi.org/10.1177/0022022114542977

Guo, Q., Sun, P., & Li, L. (2018). Shyness and online prosocial behavior: A study on multiple mediation mechanisms. *Computers in Human Behavior*, **86**, 1–8. https://doi.org/10.1016/j.chb.2018.04.032

Gupta, N. D., Etcoff, N. L., & Jaeger, M. M. (2016). Beauty in mind: The effects of physical attractiveness on psychological well-being and distress. *Journal of Happiness Studies*, **17**(3), 1313–1325.

Gupta, R., Pillai, V. K., Punetha, D., & Monah, A. (2015). Love experiences of older African Americans: A qualitative study. *Journal of International Women's Studies*, **16**(3), 277–293.

Gurung, R., & Vespia, K. (2007). Looking good, teaching well? Linking liking, looks, and learning. *Teaching of Psychology*, **34**(1), 5–10.

Gutsell, J. N., & Inzlicht, M. (2012). Intergroup differences in the sharing of emotive states: neural evidence of an empathy gap. *Social Cognitive and Affective Neuroscience*, **7**(5), 596–603.

Guyer, J., Fabrigar, L., & Vaughan-Johnston, T. (2019). Speech rate, intonation, and pitch: Investigating the bias and cue effects of vocal confidence on persuasion. *Personality and Social Psychology Bulletin*, **45**(3), 389-405.

H

Ha, T., van den Berg, J. E. M., Engels, R. C. M. E., & Lichtwarck-Aschoff, A. (2012). Effects of attractiveness and status in dating desire in homosexual and heterosexual men and women. *Archives of Sexual Behaviour*, **41**, 673–682.

Haas, B. W., Brook, M., Remillard, L., Ishak, A., Anderson, I. W., & Filkowski, M. M. (2015). I know how you feel: The warm-altruistic personality profile and the empathic brain. *PLoS ONE*, **10**(3): e0120639. https://doi.org/10.1371/journal.pone.0120639

Habermas, T., Ott, L., Schubert, M., Schneider, B., & Pate, A. (2008). Stuck in the past: Negative bias, explanatory style, temporal order, and evaluative perspectives in life narratives of clinically depressed individuals. *Depression and Anxiety*, **25**(11), E121–E132. https://doi.org/10.1002/da.20389

Haddock, G., & Zanna, M. P. (1994). Preferring 'housewives' to 'feminists'. *Psychology of Women Quarterly*, **18**, 25–52.

Haider-Markel, D., & Joslyn, M. (2008). Beliefs about the origins of homosexuality and support for gay rights: An empirical test of attribution theory. *The Public Opinion Quarterly*, **72**(2), 291–310. http://www.jstor.org.libezproxy.open.ac.uk/stable/25167626

Hakokōngäs, E., & Sakki, I. (2016). Visualized collective memories: Social representations of history in images found in Finnish history textbooks. *Journal of Community and Applied Social Psychology*, **26**, 496–517. https://doi.org/10.1002/casp.2276

Hall, D., & Buzwell, S. (2013). The problem of free-riding in group projects: Looking beyond social loafing as a reason for non-contribution. *Active Learning in Higher Education*, **14**(1), 37–49.

Hall, J. A. (2011). Sex differences in friendship expectations: A meta-analysis. *Journal of Social and Personal Relationships*, **28**(6), 723–747.

Hall, J. A., Coats, E. J., & LeBeau, L. S. (2005). Nonverbal behavior and the vertical dimension of social relations: A meta-analysis. *Psychological Bulletin*, **131**, 898–924.

Hall, J. A., Rosip, J. C., LeBeau, L. S., Horgan, T. G., & Carter, J. D. (2006). Attributing the sources of accuracy in unequal-power dyadic communication: Who is better and why? *Journal of Experimental Social Psychology*, **42**, 18–27.

Hall, J., Whalley, H. C., McKirdy, J. W., Sprengelmeyer, R., Santos, I. M., Donaldson, D. I., McGonigle, D. J., Young, A. W., McIntosh, A. M., Johnstone, E. C., & Lawrie, S. M. (2010). A common neural system mediating two different forms of social judgment. *Psychological Medicine*, **40**, 1183–1192.

Hall, K., Goldstein, D. M., & Ingram, M. B. (2016). The hands of Donald Trump: Entertainment, gesture, spectacle. *HAU: Journal of Ethnographic Theory*, **6**(2), 71-100.

Halmetoja, C. O., Malmquist, A., Carlbring, P., & Andersson, G. (2014). Experiences of internet-delivered cognitive behavior therapy for social anxiety disorder four years later: A qualitative study. *Internet Interventions*, **1**(3), 158–163.

Hamamura, T. (2012). Are cultures becoming individualistic? A cross-temporal comparison of individualism–collectivism in the United States and Japan. *Personality and Social Psychology Review*, **16**(1), 3–24. https://doi.org/10.1177/1088868311411587

Hamberger, J., & Hewstone, M. (1997). Inter-ethnic contact as a predictor of blatant and subtle prejudice: Tests of a model in four West European nations. *British Journal of Social Psychology*, **36**, 173–190.

Hamblin, R. L., Buckholdt, D., Bushell, D., Ellis, D., & Feritor, D. (1969, January). Changing the game from get the teacher to learn. *Transaction*, pp. 20–25, 28–31.

Hamermesh, D. S. (2011). *Beauty pays: Why attractive people are more successful*. Princeton University Press.

Hamilton, D. L., & Sherman, S. J. (1996). Perceiving persons and groups. *Psychological Review*, **103**, 336–355.

Hammersley, R. (2011). Pathways through drugs and crime: Desistance, trauma and resilience. *Journal of Criminal Justice*, **39**(3), 268–272. http://dx.doi.org/10.1016/j.jcrimjus.2011.02.006

Hammond, T. B., & Horswill, M. S. (2002). The influence of desire for control on drivers' risk-taking behaviour. *Transportation Research Part F*, **4**, 271–277.

Han, S., & Northoff, G. (2008). Culture-sensitive neural substrates of human cognition: A transcultural neuroimaging approach. *Nature Reviews Neuroscience*, **9**, 646–654.

Haney, C., Banks, C., & Zimbardo, P. (1973). A study of prisoners and guards in a simulated prison. In E. Aronson (Ed.), *Readings about the social animal* (3rd ed.). Freeman.

Hankin, B. L., Lakdawalla, Z., Carter, I. L., Abela, J. R. Z., & Adams, P. (2007). Are neuroticism, cognitive vulnerabilities and self-esteem overlapping or distinct risks for depression? Evidence from exploratory and confirmatory factor analyses. *Journal of Social and Clinical Psychology*, **26**, 29–63. https://doi.org/10.1521/jscp.2007.26.1.29

Hannon, P. A., Rusbult, C. E., Finkel, E. J., & Kasashiro, M. (2010). In the wake of betrayal: Amends, forgiveness, and the resolution of betrayal. *Personal Relationships*, **17**, 253–278.

Hansbrough, T. K. (2012). The construction of a transformational leader: Follower attachment and leadership perceptions. *Journal of Applied Social Psychology*, **42**, 1533–1549. https://doi.org/10.1111/j.1559-1816.2012.00913.x

Hansen, J. & Wänke, M. (2009). Liking what's familiar: The importance of unconscious familiarity in the mere-exposure effect. *Social Cognition*, **27**(2), 161–182.

Haque, U., da Silva, P. F., Devoli, G., Pilz, J., Zhao, B., Khaloua,, A., Wilopo, W., Andersen, P., Lu, P., Lee, J., Yamamoto, T., Keellings, D., Wu, J.-H., & Glass, G. E. (2019). The human cost of global warming: Deadly landslides and their triggers (1995–2014). *Science of The Total Environment*, **682**, 673–684. https://doi.org/10.1016/j.scitotenv.2019.03.415

Harber, K. D. (1998). Feedback to minorities: Evidence of a positive bias. *Journal of Personality and Social Psychology*, **74**, 622–628.

Harcum, E. R., & Badura, L. L. (2001). Social loafing as response to an appraisal of appropriate effort. *Journal of Psychology*, **124**(6), 629–637.

Hardy, C., & Latané, B. (1986). Social loafing on a cheering task. *Social Science*, **71**, 165–172.

Haritos-Fatouros, M. (1988). The official torturer: A learning model for obedience to the authority of violence. *Journal of Applied Social Psychology*, **18**, 1107–1120.

Haritos-Fatouros, M. (2012). *The psychological origins of institutionalized torture.* Routledge.

Harkins, S. G. (1981). Effects of task difficulty and task responsibility on social loafing. Presentation to the First International Conference on Social Processes in Small Groups, Kill Devil Hills, North Carolina.

Harkins, S. G., & Jackson, J. M. (1985). The role of evaluation in eliminating social loafing. *Personality and Social Psychology Bulletin,* **11,** 457–465.

Harkins, S. G., & Szymanski, K. (1989). Social loafing and group evaluation. *Journal of Personality and Social Psychology,* **56,** 934–941.

Harkins, S. G., Latané, B., & Williams, K. (1980). Social loafing: Allocating effort or taking it easy? *Journal of Experimental Social Psychology,* **16,** 457–465.

Harmon-Jones, E., & Allen, J. J. B. (2001). The role of affect in the mere exposure effect: Evidence from psychophysiological and individual differences approaches. *Personality and Social Psychology Bulletin,* **27,** 889–898.

Harrigan, W. and Commons, M., 2015. Replacing Maslow's needs hierarchy with an account based on stage and value. *Behavioral Development Bulletin,* **20**(1), pp.24-31.

Harris, J. R. (1998). *The nurture assumption.* Free Press.

Harris, L. T., & Fiske, S. T. (2006). Dehumanizing the lowest of the low: Neuroimaging responses to extreme outgroups. *Psychological Science,* **17**(10), 847–853.

Harris, M. B. (1974). Mediators between frustration and aggression in a field experiment. *Journal of Experimental Social Psychology,* **10,** 561–571.

Harrison, A. A. (1977). Mere exposure. In L. Berkowitz (Ed.), *Advances in experimental social psychology* (Vol. 10). Academic Press.

Harrison, M. A., Hughes, S. M., Burch, R. L., & Gallup, G. G. (2008). The impact of prior heterosexual experiences on homosexuality in women. *Evolutionary Psychology,* **6**(2). https://doi.org/10.1177/147470490800600208

Hart, A. J., & Morry, M. M. (1997). Trait inferences based on racial and behavioral cues. *Basic and Applied Social Psychology,* **19,** 33–48.

Hart, P. (1998). Preventing groupthink revisited: Evaluating and reforming groups in government. *Organizational Behavior and Human Decision Processes,* **73,** 306–326.

Hartup, W. W., & Stevens, N. (1999). Friendships and adaptation across the life span. *Current Directions in Psychological Science,* **8**(3), 76–79. https://doi.org/10.1111/1467-8721.00018

Harvey, F. (2019, July). One climate crisis disaster happening every week, UN warns. *The Guardian.* https://www.theguardian.com/environment/2019/jul/07/one-climate-crisis-disaster-happening-every-week-un-warns

Hasbrouck, J. (2017). Student-focused coaching. *Theory Into Practice,* **56**(1), 21–28.

Haselhuhn, M. P., Wong, E. M., & Ormiston, M. E. (2013). Self-fulfilling prophecies as a link between men's facial width-to-height ratio and behavior. *PLoS ONE,* **8**(8), E72259.

Hashim, I., & Khodarahimi, S. (2012). Loneliness and the development of social relationships in Malaysian university students. *Social Behavior and Personality,* **40**(2), 227–238. https://doi.org/10.2224/sbp.2012.40.2.227

Haslam, C., Cruwys, T., Chang, M. X. L., Bentley, S. V., Haslam, S. A., Dingle, G. A., & Jetten, J. (2019). GROUPS 4 HEALTH reduces loneliness and social anxiety in adults with psychological distress: Findings from a randomized controlled trial. *Journal of Consulting and Clinical Psychology,* **87**(9), 787.

Haslam, C., Cruwys, T., Haslam, S. A., Dingle, G., & Chang, M. X. L. (2016). Groups 4 Health: Evidence that a social-identity intervention that builds and strengthens social group membership improves mental health. *Journal of Affective Disorders,* **194,** 188–195.

Haslam, C., Jetten, J., Cruwys, T., Dingle, G., & Haslam, S. A. (2018). *The new psychology of health: Unlocking the social cure.* Routledge.

Haslam, N. (2019). The many roles of dehumanization in genocide. In L. S. Newman (Ed.), *Confronting humanity at its worst: Social psychological perspectives on genocide* (pp. 119–138). Oxford University Press.

Haslam, N., & Loughnan, S. (2014). Dehumanization and infrahumanization. *Annual Review of Psychology,* **65,** 399–423.

Haslam N., Loughnan S., & Perry, G. (2014). Meta-Milgram: An empirical synthesis of the obedience experiments. *PLoS ONE,* **9**(4): e93927. https://doi.org/10.1371/journal.pone.0093927

Haslam, N., Loughnan, S., & Sun, P. (2011). Beastly: What makes animal metaphors offensive? *Journal of Language and Social Psychology,* **30,** 311–325. https://doi.org/10.1177/0261927X11407168

Haslam, S. A. (2001). *Psychology in organizations: The social identity approach.* Sage.

Haslam, S. A. (2004). *Psychology in organizations: The social identity approach,* 2nd edn. London: Sage.

Haslam, S. A. (2004). *Psychology in organizations: The social identity approach* (2nd ed.). Sage.

Haslam, S., & Reicher, S. (2007). Beyond the banality of evil: Three dynamics of an interactionist social psychology of tyranny. *Personality and Social Psychology Bulletin,* **33**(5), 615–622.

Haslam, S., & Reicher, S. (2014). Just obeying orders?*New Scientist,* **223**(2986), 28–31.

Haslam, S. A., Jetten, J., & Waghorn, C. (2009). Social identification, stress and citizenship in teams: A five-phase longitudinal study. *Stress and Health,* **25,** 21–30.

Haslam, S. A., O'Brien, A., Jetten, J., Vormedal, K., & Penna, S. (2005). Taking the strain: Social identity, social support, and the experience of stress. *British Journal of Social Psychology,* **44**(3), 355-370.

Haslam, S. A., Reicher, S. D., & Birney, M. E. (2014). Nothing by mere authority: Evidence that in an experimental analogue of the Milgram paradigm participants are motivated not by orders but by appeals to science. *Journal of Social Issues,* **70**(3), 473–488.

Haslam, S. A., Reicher, S. D., Millard, K., & McDonald, R. (2015). 'Happy to have been of service': The Yale archive as a window into the engaged followership of participants in Milgram's 'obedience' experiments. *British Journal of Social Psychology,* **54**(1), 55–83.

Haslam, S. A., Turner, J. C., Oakes, P. J., McGarty, C., & Hayes, B. K. (1992). Context-dependent variation in social stereotyping 1: The effects of intergroup relations as mediated by social change and frame of reference. *European Journal of Social Psychology,* **22,** 3–20.

Hass, R. G., Katz, I., Rizzo, N., Bailey, J., & Eisenstadt, D. (1991). Cross-racial appraisal as related to attitude ambivalence and cognitive complexity. *Personality and Social Psychology Bulletin,* **17,** 83–92.

Hatemi, P., McDermott, R., & Eaves, L. (2015). Genetic and environmental contributions to relationships and divorce attitudes. *Personality and Individual Differences,* **72,** 135–140.

Hatfield, E. (1988). Passionate and compassionate love. In R. J. Sternberg & M. L. Barnes (Eds.), *The psychology of love.* Yale University Press.

Hatfield, E., & Rapson, R. (2006). Passionate love, sexual desire, and mate selection: Cross-cultural and historical perspectives. In P. Noller & J. A. Feeney (Eds.), *Close relationships: Functions, forms and processes.* Psychology Press/ Taylor & Francis.

Hatfield, E., & Rapson, R. L. (2008). Passionate love and sexual desire: Multidisciplinary perspectives. In J. P. Forgas & J. Fitness (Eds.), *Social relationships: Cognitive, affective, and motivational processes* (pp.21–38). Psychology Press.

Hatfield, E., & Rapson, R. L. (2009). The neuropsychology of passionate love. In E. Cuyler and M. Ackhart (Eds.), *Psychology of relationships.* Nova Science.

Hatfield, E., & Rapson, R. L. (2011). Culture and passionate love. In F. Deutsch, M. Boehnke, U. Kühnen, & K. Boehnke (Eds.), *Rendering borders obsolete: Cross-cultural and cultural psychology as an interdisciplinary, multi-method endeavor: Proceedings from the 19th International Congress of the International Association for Cross-Cultural Psychology.* https://scholarworks.gvsu.edu/iaccp_papers/83/

Hatfield, E., Bensman, L., & Rapson, R. L. (2012). A brief history of social scientists' attempts to measure passionate love. *Journal of Social and Personal Relationships,* **29**(2), 143–164.

Hatfield, E., Cacioppo, J., & Rapson, R. (1994). *Emotional contagion.* Cambridge University Press.

Hatfield, E., Rapson, R. L., & Martel, L. D. (2007). Passionate love and sexual desire. In S. Kitayama & D. Cohen (Eds.), *Handbook of cultural psychology.* Guilford Press.

Hatfield (was Walster), E., Walster, G. W., & Berscheid, E. (1978). *Equity: Theory and research.* Allyn and Bacon.

Hauge, L. J., Skogstad, A., & Einarsen, S. (2010). The relative impact of workplace bullying as a social stressor at work. *Scandinavian Journal of Psychology*, **51**(5), 426–433. https://doi.org/10.1111/j.1467-9450.2010.00813.x

Hauser, D. (2005, 30 June). Five years of abstinence-only-until-marriage education: Assessing the impact. *Advocates for Youth:* www.advocatesforyouth.org.

Hausmann, L. R. M., Levine, J. M., & Higgins, T. E. (2008). Communication and group perception: Extending the 'saying-is-believing' effect. *Group Processes and Intergroup Relations*, **11**(4), 539–554.

Hausmann, M. (2017). Why sex hormones matter for neuroscience: A very short review on sex, sex hormones, and functional brain asymmetries. *Journal of Neuroscience Research*, **95**(1–2), 40–49.

Hausmann, M., Behrendt-Körbitz, S., Kautz, H., Lamm, C., Radelt, F., & Güntürkün, O. (1998). Sex differences in oral asymmetries during word repetition. *Neuropsychologia*, **36**, 1397–1402.

Hawkley, L. C., Masi, C. M., Berry, J. D., & Cacioppo, J. T. (2006). Loneliness is a unique predictor of age-related differences in systolic blood pressure. *Psychology and Aging*, **21**(1), 152–164.

Hayes, S. C., Rincover, A., & Volosin, D. (1980). Variables influencing the acquisition and maintenance of aggressive behavior: Modeling versus sensory reinforcement. *Journal of Abnormal Psychology*, **89**(2), 254–262.

Hazan, C., Gur-Yaish, N., & Campa, M. (2004). What does it mean to be attached? In W. S. Rholes and J. A. Simpson (Eds.), *Adult attachment: Theory, research, and clinical implications*. Guilford Press.

Heatherton, T. F., & Vohs, K. D. (2000). Interpersonal evaluations following threats to self: Role of self-esteem. *Journal of Personality and Social Psychology*, **78**, 725–736.

Heatherton, T. F., Macrae, C. N., & Kelley, W. M. (2004). What the social brain sciences can tell us about the self. *Current Directions in Psychological Science*, **13**, 190–193.

Hebl, M. R., & Heatherton, T. F. (1998). The stigma of obesity in women: The difference is black and white. *Personality and Social Psychology Bulletin*, **24**, 417–426.

Hebl, M. R., & King, E. B. (2004). You are what you wear: An interactive demonstration of the self-fulfilling prophecy. *Teaching of Psychology*, **31**(4), 260–262.

Hegarty, P., & Golden, A. M. (2008). Attributional beliefs about the controllability of stigmatized traits: Antecedents or justifications of prejudice? *Journal of Applied Social Psychology*, **38**(4), 1023–1044.

Heider, F. (1946). Attitudes and cognitive organization. *Journal of Psychology*, **21**, 107–112.

Heider, F. (1958). *The psychology of interpersonal relations*. Wiley.

Heine, S. J. (2005). Constructing good selves in Japan and North America. In R. Sorrentino, D. Cohen, J. M. Olson, & M. P. Zanna (Eds.), *Culture and social behavior: The Ontario symposium* (Vol. 10, pp. 95–116). Erlbaum.

Heine, S. J., & Lehman, D. R. (1997). The cultural construction of self-enhancement: An examination of group-serving biases. *Journal of Personality and Social Psychology*, **72**, 1268–1283.

Heine, S. J., Kitayama, S., Lehman, D. R., Takata, T., Ide, E., Leung, C., & Matsumoto, H. (2001). Divergent consequences of success and failure in Japan and North America: An investigation of self-improving motivations and malleable selves. *Journal of Personality and Social Psychology*, **81**, 599–615.

Heine, S. J., Lehman, D. R., Markus, H. R., & Kitayama, S. (1999). Is there a universal need for positive self-regard? *Psychological Review*, **106**, 766–794.

Heisenberg, W. (1958). *Physics and philosophy: The revolution in modern science*. Prometheus.

Helliwell, J., Huang, H., & Wang, S. (2019). Changing world happiness. In J. Helliwell, R. Layard, & J. Sachs (Eds.), *World happiness report 2019*. Sustainable Development Solutions Network. https://worldhappiness.report/ed/2019/changing-world-happiness/

Helweg-Larsen, M., Cunningham, S. J., Carrico, A., & Pergram, A. M. (2004). To nod or not to nod: An observational study of nonverbal communication and status in female and male college students. *Psychology of Women Quarterly*, **28**, 358–361.

Hemsley, G. D., & Doob, A. N. (1978). The effect of looking behavior on perceptions of a communicator's credibility. *Journal of Applied Social Psychology*, **8**, 136–144.

Hendrick, C., & Hendrick, S. S. (2009). Love. In S. J. Lopez & C. R. Snyder (Eds.), *Oxford handbook of positive psychology* (2nd ed.). Oxford University Press.

Hendrick, S. S., & Hendrick, C. (2008). Satisfaction, love, and respect in the initiation of romantic relationships. In S. Sprecher, A. Wenzel, & J. Harvey (Eds.), *Handbook of relationship initiation*. Psychology Press.

Henry, P. J., & Sears, D. O. (2002). The symbolic racism 2000 scale. *Political Psychology*, **23**, 253–283.

Hensley, W. E. (1977). Probability, personality, age, and risk taking. *Journal of Psychology*, **95**(1), 139–145.

Hepach, R., Vaish, A., & Tomasello, M. (2012). Young children are intrinsically motivated to see others helped. *Psychological Science*, **23**(9), 967–972.

Herbert, J. (2015). *Testosterone: Sex, power, and the will to win*. https://ebookcentral.proquest.com

Herek, G. M. (1987). Can functions be measured? A new perspective on the functional approach to attitudes. *Social Psychology Quarterly*, **50**, 285–303.

Herek, G. M. (1993). Interpersonal contact and heterosexuals' attitudes toward gay men: Results from a national survey. *Journal of Sex Research*, **30**, 239–244.

Hern, E., Glazebrook, W., & Beckett, M. (2005). Reducing knife crime. *British Medical Journal*, **330**, 1221. https://doi.org/10.1136/bmj.330.7502.1221

Hertbert, J. (2015). *Testosterone: Sex, power, and the will to win*. https://ebookcentral.proquest.com

Herzlich, C. (1973). *Health and illness: A social psychological analysis*. Academic Press.

Hewstone, M. (2003). Intergroup contact: Panacea for prejudice? *The Psychologist*, **16**, 352–355.

Hewstone, M., & Fincham, F. (1996). Attribution theory and research: Basic issues and applications. In M. Hewstone, W. Stroebe, & G. M. Stephenson (Eds.), *Introduction to social psychology: A European perspective*. Blackwell.

Hewstone, M., & Greenland, K. (2000). Intergroup conflict. Unpublished manuscript, Cardiff University.

Hewstone, M., & Ward, C. (1985). Ethnocentrism and causal attribution in Southeast Asia. *Journal of Personality and Social Psychology*, **48**, 614–623.

Hibbert, S. A., Hogg, G., & Quinn, T. (2002). Consumer response to social entrepreneurship: The case of the Big Issue in Scotland. *International Journal of Nonprofit and Voluntary Sector Marketing*, **7**(3), 288–301.

Higgins, E. T. (1987). Self-discrepancy: A theory relating self and affect. *Psychological Review*, **94**(3), 319–340.

Higgins, E. T. (1989). Self-discrepancy theory: What patterns of self-beliefs cause people to suffer? In *Advances in experimental social psychology* (Vol. 22, pp. 93–136). Academic Press.

Higgins, E. T., & Bargh, J. A. (1987). Social cognition and social perception. *Annual Review of Psychology*, **38**, 369–425.

Higgins, E. T., & McCann, C. D. (1984). Social encoding and subsequent attitudes, impressions and memory: 'Context-driven' and motivational aspects of processing. *Journal of Personality and Social Psychology*, **47**, 26–39.

Higgins, E. T., & Rholes, W. S. (1978). Saying is believing: Effects of message modification on memory and liking for the person described. *Journal of Experimental Social Psychology*, **14**, 363–378.

Highfield, R. (2005, November 2). Attractive women are more than just a pretty face. *The Telegraph:* https://www.telegraph.co.uk/news/uknews/1502002/Attractive-women-are-more-than-just-a-pretty-face.html

Hilmert, C. J., Kulik, J. A., & Christenfeld, N. J. S. (2006). Positive and negative opinion modeling: The influence of another's similarity and dissimilarity. *Journal of Personality and Social Psychology*, **90**, 440–452.

Hilton, D. (2007). Causal explanation: From social perception to knowledge-based causal attribution. In A. W. Kruglanski & E. T. Higgins (Eds.), *Social psychology: Handbook of basic principles* (pp. 232–253). Guilford Press.

Hines, M. (2004). *Brain gender*. Oxford University Press.

Hinkle, S., Fox-Cardamone, L., Haseleu, J. A., Brown, R., & Irwin, L. M. (1996). Grassroots political action as an intergroup phenomenon. *Journal of Social Issues*, **52**(1), 39–51.

Hinsz, V. B. (1990). Cognitive and consensus processes in group recognition memory performance. *Journal of Personality and Social Psychology*, **59**, 705–718.

Hirschberger, G., & Ein-Dor, T. (2006). Defenders of a lost cause: Terror management and violent resistance to the disengagement plan. *Personality and Social Psychology Bulletin,* **32**(6), 761–769.

Hitsch, G. J., Hortaçsu, A., & Ariely, D. (2010). What makes you click? Mate preferences in online dating. *Quantitative Marketing and Economics,* **8**(4), 393–427.

Hjelm, K., & Bard, K. (2013). Beliefs about health and illness in Latin-American migrants with diabetes living in Sweden. *The Open Nursing Journal,* **7**, 57–65. https://doi.org/10.2174/1874434601307010057

Hjelm, K., & Beebwa, E. (2013). The influence of beliefs about health and illness on foot care in Ugandan persons with diabetic foot ulcers. *The Open Nursing Journal,* **7**(1), 123–132. https://doi.org/10.2174/1874434601307010123

Hjelm, K., & Mufunda, E. (2010). Zimbabwean diabetics' beliefs about health and illness: An interview study. *BMC International Health and Human Rights,* **10**(1), 7. https://doi.org/10.1186/1472-698X-10-7

Hjelm, K., Berntorp, K., & Apelqvist, J. (2012). Beliefs about health and illness in Swedish and African-born women with gestational diabetes living in Sweden. *Journal of Clinical Nursing,* **21**(9–10), 1374–1386. https://doi.org/10.1111/j.1365-2702.2011.03834.x

Hoaken, P. N. S., Hamill, V. L., Ross, E. H., Hancock, M., Lau, M. J., & Tapscott, J. L. (2012). Drug use and abuse and human aggressive behavior. In J. Verster, K. Brady, M. Galanter, & P. Conrod (Eds.), *Drug abuse and addiction in medical illness.* Springer.

Hoaken, P. N., & Stewart, S. H. (2003). Drugs of abuse and the elicitation of human aggressive behavior. *Addictive Behaviors,* **28**(9), 1533–1554.

Hodges, B. H., & Geyer, A. L. (2006). A nonconformist account of the Asch experiments: Values, pragmatics, and moral dilemmas. *Personality and Social Psychology Review,* **10**(1), 2–19.

Hoffman, R. M., & Borders, L. D. (2001). Twenty-five years after the Bem Sex-Role Inventory: A reassessment and new issues regarding classification variability. *Measurement and Evaluation in Counseling and Development,* **34**, 39–55.

Hofling, C. K., Brotzman, E., Dalrymple, S., Graves, N., & Pierce, C. M. (1966). An experimental study in nurse-physician relationships. *Journal of Nervous and Mental Disease,* **143**(2), 171–180.

Hofmann, D. C., & Dawson, L. L. (2014). The neglected role of charismatic authority in the study of terrorist groups and radicalization. *Studies in Conflict and Terrorism,* **37**(4), 348–368. https://doi.org/10.1080/1057610X.2014.879436

Hofstede, G. (1980). *Culture's consequences: International differences in work-related values.* Sage.

Hofstede, G. (2001). *Culture's consequences, comparing values, behaviors, institutions, and organizations across nations.* Sage.

Hofstede, G., & Hofstede, G. J. (2005). *Cultures and organizations: Software of the mind* (rev. and expanded 2nd ed.). McGraw-Hill.

Hogg, M. A., & Hains, S. C. (1998). Friendship and group identification: A new look at the role of cohesiveness in groupthink. *European Journal of Social Psychology,* **28**, 323–341.

Hogg, M. A., & Smith, J. R. (2007). Attitudes in social context: A social identity perspective. *European Review of Social Psychology,* **18**(1), 89-131.

Hogg, M. A., Hains, S. C., & Mason, I. (1998). Identification and leadership in small groups: Salience, frame of reference, and leader stereotypicality effects on leader evaluations. *Journal of Personality and Social Psychology,* **75**, 1248–1263.

Hogg, M. A., Hohman, Z. P., & Rivera, J. E. (2008). Why do people join groups? Three motivational accounts from social psychology. *Social and Personality Psychology Compass,* **2**, 1269–1280.

Hogg, M. A., Sherman, D. K., Dierselhuis, J., Maitner, A. T., & Moffitt, G. (2007). Uncertainty, entitativity, and group identification. *Journal of Experimental Social Psychology,* **43**, 135–142.

Hogg, M. A., Turner, J. C., & Davidson, B. (1990). Polarized norms and social frames of reference: A test of the self-categorization theory of group polarization. *Basic and Applied Social Psychology,* **11**, 77–100.

Hõigaard, R., & Ingvaldsen, R. P. (2006). Social loafing in interactive groups: The effects of identifiability on effort and individual performance in floorball. *Athletic Insight,* **8**(2), 52–63.

Hõigaard, R., Boen, F., De Cuyper, B., & Peters, D. M. (2013). Team identification reduces social loafing and promotes social laboring in cycling. *International Journal of Applied Sports Science,* **25**(1), 33–40.

Hõigaard, R., Säfvenbom, R., & Tònnessen, F. E. (2006). The relationship between group cohesion, group norms and perceived social loafing in soccer teams. *Small Group Research,* **37**(3), 217–232.

Holland, R. W., Hendriks, M., & Aarts, H. (2005). Smells like clean spirit: Nonconscious effect of scent on cognition and behavior. *Psychological Science,* **16**, 689–693.

Hollander, E. P. (1958). Conformity, status, and idiosyncrasy credit. *Psychological Review,* **65**, 117–127.

Hollander, E. P. (1995). Organizational leadership and followership. In P. Collett & A. Furnham (Eds.), *Social psychology at work: Essays in honour of Michael Argyle.* Routledge.

Holmberg, D., & Holmes, J. G. (1994). Reconstruction of relationship memories: A mental models approach. In N. Schwarz & S. Sudman (Eds.), *Autobiographical memory and the validity of retrospective reports.* Springer-Verlag.

Holtgraves, T. (1997). Styles of language use: Individual and cultural variability in conversational indirectness. *Journal of Personality and Social Psychology,* **73**, 624–637.

Holt-Lunstad, J., Smith, T. B., & Layton, J. B. (2010). Social relationships and mortality risk: A meta-analytic review. *PLoS Med* **7**(7): e1000316. https://doi.org/10.1371/journal.pmed.1000316

Holtman, Z., Louw, J., Tredoux, C., & Carney, T. (2005). Prejudice and social contact in South Africa: A study of integrated schools ten years after apartheid. *South African Journal of Psychology,* **35**, 473–493.

Honeynet Project (2004). http://www.honeynet.org.uk

Hong, Y., Li, X., Mao, R., & Stanton, B. (2007). Internet use among Chinese college students: Implications for sex education and HIV prevention. *Cyber Psychology and Behavior,* **10**(2), 161–169.

Hong, Y., Wyer, R. Jr, & Fong, C. (2008). Chinese working in groups: Effort dispensability versus normative influence. *Asian Journal of Social Psychology,* **11**(3), 187–195.

Hood, K. B., & Shook, N. J. (2013). Conceptualizing women's attitudes toward condom use with the tripartite model. *Women and Health,* **53**(4), 349–368.

Hoorens, V., & Nuttin, J. M. (1993). Overvaluation of own attributes: Mere ownership or subjective frequency? *Social Cognition,* **11**, 177–200.

Hoorens, V., Nuttin, J. M., Herman, I. E., & Pavakanun, U. (1990). Mastery pleasure versus mere ownership: A quasi-experimental cross-cultural and cross-alphabetical test of the name letter effect. *European Journal of Social Psychology,* **20**, 181–205.

Hopcroft, R. L. (2016). *Evolution and gender: Why it matters for contemporary life.* Routledge.

Hopkins, M., & Treadwell, J. (2014). *Football hooliganism, fan behaviour and crime : Contemporary issues.* Palgrave Macmillan. https://doi.org/10.1057/9781137347978

Hopkins, N., Regan, M., & Abell, J. (1997). On the context dependence of national stereotypes: Some Scottish data. *British Journal of Social Psychology,* **36**, 553–563.

Hopkins, N., Reicher, S., Harrison, K., Cassidy, C., Bull, R., & Levine, M. (2007). Helping to improve the group stereotype: On the strategic dimension of prosocial behavior. *Personality & Social Psychology Bulletin,* **33**, 776–788.

Horn, S. S. (2003). Adolescents' reasoning about exclusion from social groups. *Developmental Psychology,* **39**(1), 71.

Hornsey, M. J. (2005). Why being right is not enough: Predicting defensiveness in the face of group criticism. *European Review of Social Psychology,* **16**, 301–334.

Hornsey, M. J. (2008). Social identity theory and self-categorization theory: A historical review. *Social and Personality Psychology Compass,* **2**(1), 204–222.

Hornsey, M. J., Jetten, J., McAuliffe, B. J., & Hogg, M. A. (2006). The impact of individualist and collectivist group norms on evaluations of dissenting group members. *Journal of Experimental Social Psychology,* **42**, 57–68.

Hornsey, M. J., Trembath, M., & Gunthorpe, S. (2004). 'You can criticize because you care': Identity attachment, constructiveness, and the intergroup sensitivity effect. *European Journal of Social Psychology*, **34**, 499–518.

Hornstein, H. (1976). *Cruelty and kindness*. Prentice-Hall.

Horowitz, S. V., & Boardman, S. K. (1994). Managing conflict: Policy and research implications. *Journal of Social Issues*, **50**, 197–211.

Horton-Salway, M. (2002). Bio-psycho-social reasoning in GPs' case narratives: The discursive construction of ME patients' identities. *Health: An Interdisciplinary Journalfor the Social Study of Health, Illness and Medicine*, **6**(4), 401–421.

Horton-Salway, M. (2004). The local production of knowledge:disease labels, identities and category entitlements in ME support group talk. *Health: An Interdisciplinary Journal for the Social Study of Health, Illness and Medicine*, **8**(3), 351–371.

Horton-Salway, M. (2007). The ME bandwagon and other labels: Constructing the genuine case in talk about a controversial illness. *British Journal of Social Psychology*, **46**, 895–914.

Hoshino-Browne, E., Zanna, A. S., Spencer, S. J., & Zanna, M. P. (2004). Investigating attitudes cross-culturally: A case of cognitive dissonance among East Asians and North Americans. In G. Haddock & G. R. Maio (Eds.), *Contemporary perspectives on the psychology of attitudes*. Psychology Press.

House, R. J., & Shamir, B. (1993). Toward the integration of transformational, charismatic and visionary theories. In M. M. Chemers & R. Ayman (Eds.), *Leadership theory and research: Perspectives and directions*. Academic Press.

Hovland, C. I., Janis, I. L., & Kelley, H. H. (1953). *Communication and persuasion*. Yale University Press.

Hovland, C. I., Lumsdaine, A. A., & Sheffield, F. D. (1949). *Experiments on mass communication. Studies in social psychology in World War II* (Vol. III). Princeton University Press.

Howard, D. J., & Kerin, R. A. (2011). The effects of name similarity on message processing and persuasion. *Journal of Experimental Social Psychology*, **47**(1), 63–71.

Howitt, D., & Cramer, D. (2016). *Research methods in psychology*. Pearson Education.

Hoyle, R. H., Kernis, M. H., Baldwin, M. W., & Leary, M. R. (1999). *Selfhood: Identity, esteem, regulation*. Westview Press.

Hoyt, C. L., & Simon, S. (2011). Female leaders: Injurious or inspiring role models for women?*Psychology of Women Quarterly*, **35**(1), 143–157. https://doi.org/10.1177/0361684310385216

Hsee, C. K., & Hastie, R. (2006). Decision and experience: Why don't we choose what makes us happy? *Trends in Cognitive Sciences*, **10**, 31–37.

Hsu, L. H. (2011). Linguistic intergroup bias tells ingroup/outgroup orientation of bicultural Asian Americans. *International Journal of Intercultural Relations*, **35**(6), 853–866.

Huang, W. (2005). An Asian perspective on relationship and marriage education. *Family Process*, **44**(2), 161–173.

Hudde, A. (2018). Societal agreement on gender role attitudes and childlessness in 38 countries. *European Journal of Population*, **34**, 745–767.

Hudson, C. (2011). From rugged individual to Dishy Dad: Reinventing masculinity in Singapore. *Genders, 54*. https://www.colorado.edu/gendersarchive1998-2013/2011/10/01/rugged-individual-dishy-dad-reinventing-masculinity-singapore

Huesmann, L. R., Moise-Titus, J., Podolski, C.-L., & Eron, L. D. (2003). Longitudinal relations between children's exposure to TV violence and their aggressive and violent behavior in young adulthood: 1977–1992. *Developmental Psychology*, **39**, 201–222.

Hugenberg, K., & Bodenhausen, G. V. (2003). Facing prejudice: Implicit prejudice and the perception of facial threat. *Psychological Science*, **14**, 640–643.

Huguet, P., Charbonnier, E., & Monteil, J. M. (1999). Productivity loss in performance groups: People who see themselves as average do not engage in social loafing. *Group Dynamics: Theory, Research, and Practice*, **3**(2), 118–131.

Hui, V. K.-Y., Bond, M. H., & Ng, T. S. W. (2007). General beliefs about the world as defensive mechanisms against death anxiety. *Omega: Journal of Death and Dying*, **54**(3), 199–214.

Hume, D. (1739/1911). *A treatise on human nature* (2 vols.). Dent.

Hummert, M. L., Garstka, T. A., Greenwald, A. G., Mellott, D. S., & O'Brien, L. T. (2002). Using the implicit association test to measure age differences in implicit social cognitions. *Psychology and Aging*, **17**(3), 482–495.

Hunt, H. R., & Gross, A. M. (2009). Prediction of exercise in patients across various stages of bariatric surgery: A comparison of the merits of the Theory of Reasoned Action versus the Theory of Planned Behavior. *Behavior Modification*, **33**(6), 795–817. https://doi.org/10.1177/0145445509348055

Hunt, M. (1993). *The story of psychology*. Doubleday.

Hunt, P. J., & Hillery, J. M. (1973). Social facilitation in a location setting: An examination of the effects over learning trials. *Journal of Experimental Social Psychology*, **9**, 563–571.

Hunter, J. D. (2002, 21–22 June). To change the world. Paper presented to the Board of Directors of the Trinity Forum, Denver, CO.

Hunter, M. S., Gruenfeld, E. A., & Ramirez, A. J. (2003). Help-seeking intentions for breast-cancer symptoms: A comparison of the self-regulation model and the theory of planned behaviour. *British Journal of Health Psychology*, **8**, 319–333.

Huo, Y. J., Smith, H. J., Tyler, T. R., & Lind, E. A. (1996). Superordinate identification, subgroup identification, and justice concerns: Is separatism the problem; is assimilation the answer? *Psychological Science*, **7**, 40–45.

Huq, N. L., & Chowdhury, M. E. (2012). Assessment of the utilization of HIV interventions by sex workers in selected brothels in Bangladesh: An exploratory study. *The Qualitative Report*. Nova Southeastern University, Inc. http://link.galegroup.com.libezproxy.open.ac.uk/apps/doc/A351608854/AONE?u=tou&sid=AONE&xid=d4390cd9

Huston, T. L., Niehuis, S., & Smith, S. E. (2001). The early marital roots of conjugal distress and divorce. *Current Directions in Psychological Science*, **10**, 116–119.

Hutnik, N. (1985). Aspects of identity in a multi-ethnic society. *New Community*, **12**, 298–309.

Hyde, J. S. (2005). The gender similarities hypothesis. *American Psychologist*, **60**, 581–592.

I

Ickes, B. (1980). On disconfirming our perceptions of others. Paper presented at the American Psychological Association convention.

IMF (2011, September 13). IEO annual report 2011. https://www.imf.org/en/Publications/Independent-Evaluation-Office-Reports/Issues/2016/12/31/IEO-Annual-Report-2011-24901

Ingham, A. G., Levinger, G., Graves, J., & Peckham, V. (1974). The Ringelmann effect: Studies of group size and group performance. *Journal of Experimental Social Psychology*, **10**, 371–384.

Inglehart, M. R., Markus, H., & Brown, D. R. (1989). The effects of possible selves on academic achievement – a panel study. In J. P. Forgas & J. M. Innes (Eds.), *Recent advances in social psychology: An international perspective*. Elsevier Science.

Ingram, H. J. (2016). *The charismatic leadership phenomenon in radical and militant Islamism*. Routledge.

Inogwabini, B. I. (2014). Bushmeat, over-fishing and covariates explaining fish abundance declines in the Central Congo Basin. *Environmental Biology of Fishes*, **97**(7), 787–796. https://doi.org/10.1007/s10641-013-0179-6

Intergovernmental Panel on Climate Change (IPCC). (2007). *Summary for policymakers. Climate change 2007: The physical science basis. Contribution of Working Group I to the Fourth Assessment Report of the Intergovernmental Panel on Climate Change*. Cambridge University Press.

Internal Displacement Monitoring Centre (IDMC) (2019). Global Report on Internal Displacement 2019. http://www.internal-displacement.org/global-report/grid2019/

Inzlicht, M., Gutsell, J. N., & Legault, L. (2012). Mimicry reduces prejudice. *Journal of Experimental Social Psychology*, **48**, 361–365.

Ioannidis, J. P. A. (2005). Why most published research findings are false. *PLoS Medicine*, **2**(8): e124. https://doi.org/10.1371/journal.pmed.0020124.

IPU (Inter-Parliamentary Union) (2019). *Women in national parliaments: Situation as of 1st February 2019*. http://archive.ipu.org/wmn-e/classif.htm

Ireland, T. O., & Smith, C. A. (2009). Living in partner-violent families: Developmental links to antisocial behavior and relationship violence. *Journal of Youth Adolescence*, **38**, 323–339.

Ito, T. A., Miller, N., & Pollock, V. E. (1996). Alcohol and aggression: A meta-analysis on the moderating effects of inhibitory cues, triggering events, and self-focused attention. *Psychological Bulletin,* **120,** 60–82.

Ittelson, W. H., Proshansky, H., Rivlin, L., & Winkel, G. (1974). *An introduction to environmental psychology.* Holt, Rinehart & Winston.

Iyengar, S. S., & Lepper, M. R. (2000). When choice is demotivating: Can one desire too much of a good thing? *Journal of Personality and Social Psychology,* **79,** 995–1006.

Izuma, K., Matsumoto, M., Murayama, K., Samejima, K., Sadato, N., Matsumoto, K., & Smith, E. E. (2010). Neural correlates of cognitive dissonance and choice-induced preference change. *Proceedings of the National Academy of Sciences,* **107**(51), 22014–22019. https://doi.org/10.1073/pnas.1011879108

J

Jackman, M. R., & Senter, M. S. (1981). Beliefs about race, gender, and social class different, therefore unequal: Beliefs about trait differences between groups of unequal status. In D. J. Treiman & R. V. Robinson (Eds.), *Research in stratification and mobility* (Vol. 2). JAI Press.

Jackson, J. W., Kirby, D., Barnes, L., & Shepard, L. (1993). Institutional racism and pluralistic ignorance: A cross-national comparison. In M. Wievorka (Ed.), *Racisme et modernite.* Editions la Décourverte.

Jackson, L. A., Hunter, J. E., & Hodge, C. N. (1995). Physical attractiveness and intellectual competence: A meta-analytic review. *Social Psychology Quarterly,* **58,** 108–123.

Jacobs, P. A., Tytherleigh, M. Y., Webb, C., & Cooper, C. L. (2007). Predictors of work performance among higher education employees: An examination using the AssET Model of Stress. *International Journal of Stress Management,* **14**(2), 199–210.

Jacobs, R. C., & Campbell, D. T. (1961). The perpetuation of an arbitrary tradition through several generations of a laboratory microculture. *Journal of Abnormal and Social Psychology,* **62,** 649–658.

Jahoda, G. (2007). *A history of social psychology: From the eighteenth-century enlightenment to the Second World War.* Cambridge University Press.

James, W. (1890, reprinted 1950). *The principles of psychology* (2 vols.). Dover Publications.

Jamieson, D. W., Lydon, J. E., Stewart, G., & Zanna, M. P. (1987). Pygmalion revisited: New evidence for student expectancy effects in the classroom. *Journal of Educational Psychology,* **79,** 461–466.

Janes, L. M., & Olson, J. M. (2000). Jeer pressure: The behavioral effects of observing ridicule of others. *Personality and Social Psychology Bulletin,* **26,** 474–485.

Janis, I. L. (1971, November). Groupthink. *Psychology Today,* 43–46.

Janis, I. L. (1973). Groupthink and group dynamics: A social psychological analysis of defective policy decisions. *Policy Studies Journal,* **2**(1), 19–25.

Janis, I. L. (1982). Counteracting the adverse effects of concurrence-seeking in policy-planning groups: Theory and research perspectives. In H. Brandstatter, J. H. Davis, & G. Stocker-Kreichgauer (Eds.), *Group decision making.* Academic Press.

Janis, I. L., & Mann, L. (1977). *Decision-making: A psychological analysis of conflict, choice and commitment.* Free Press.

Janis, I. L., Kaye, D., & Kirschner, P. (1965). Facilitating effects of eating while reading on responsiveness to persuasive communications. *Journal of Personality and Social Psychology,* **1,** 181–186.

Janis, I.L. (1972). *Victims of groupthink.* Houghton Mifflin.

Janiszewski, C., & Uy, D. (2008). Precision of the anchor influences the amount of adjustment. *Psychological Science,* **19**(2), 121–127.

Jankowiak, W. R., & Fischer, E. F. (1992). A cross-cultural perspective on romantic love. *Ethnology,* **31,** 149–155.

Janssen, L., Fennis, B. M., & Pruyn, A. T. H. (2010). Forewarned is forearmed: Conserving self-control strength to resist social influence. *Journal of Experimental Social Psychology,* **46**(6), 911–921. https://doi.org/10.1016/j.jesp.2010.06.008.

Jaremka, L. M., Bunyan, D. P., Collins, N. L., & Sherman, D. K. (2011). Defensive distancing: Self-affirmation and risk regulation in response to relationship threats. *Journal of Experimental Social Psychology,* **47**(1), 264–268.

Jarrett, C. (2018). Newly analysed recording challenges Zimbardo's account of his infamous prison experiment. BPS Research Digest website: https://digest.bps.org.uk/2018/07/03/newly-analysed-recording-challenges-zimbardos-account-of-his-infamous-prison-experiment/

Jearey-Graham, N., & Macleod, C. I. (2017). Gender, dialogue and discursive psychology: A plot sexuality intervention with South African high-school learners. *Sex Education: Sexuality, Society and Learning,* **17**(5), 555–576.

Jeffares, B., & Sterelny, K. (2012). Evolutionary psychology. In E. Margolis, R. Samuels, & S. P. Stich (Eds.), *The Oxford handbook of philosophy of cognitive science.* Oxford University Press. https://doi.org/10.1093/oxfordhb/9780195309799.013.0020

Jelalian, E., & Miller, A. G. (1984). The perseverance of beliefs: Conceptual perspectives and research developments. *Journal of Social and Clinical Psychology,* **2,** 25–56.

Jenkins, T. M., & Short, S. E. (2017). Negotiating intersex: A case for revising the theory of social diagnosis. *Social Science & Medicine,* **175,** 91–98. https://doi.org/10.1016/j.socscimed.2016.12.047

Jerome, N. (2013). Application of the Maslow's hierarchy of need theory; impacts and implications on organizational culture, human resource and employee's performance. *International Journal of Business and Management Invention,* **2**(3), 39-45.

Jessop, D. C., & Wade, J. (2008). Fear appeals and binge drinking: A terror management theory perspective. *British Journal of Health Psychology,* **13,** 773–788.

Jetten, J., Hornsey, M. J., & Adarves-Yorno, I. (2006). When group members admit to being conformist: The role of relative intragroup status in conformity self-reports. *Personality and Social Psychology Bulletin,* **32,** 162–173.

Jetten, J., Postmes, T., & McAuliffe, B. J. (2002). We're *all* individuals: Group norms of individualism and collectivism, levels of identification and identity threat. *European Journal of Social Psychology,* **32,** 189–207.

Jiang, J., Zhang, Y., Ke, Y., Hawk, S. T., & Qiu, H. (2015). Can't buy me friendship? Peer rejection and adolescent materialism: Implicit self-esteem as a mediator. *Journal of Experimental Social Psychology,* **58,** 48–55.

Jiang, L. C., Bazarova, N. N., & Hancock, J. T. (2013). From perception to behavior: Disclosure reciprocity and the intensification of intimacy in computer-mediated communication. *Communication Research,* **40**(1), 125–143.

Jin, S. V., & Ryu, E. (2018). 'The paradox of Narcissus and Echoin the instagram pond' in light of the selfie culture from Freudian evolutionary psychology: Self-loving and confident but lonely. *Journal of Broadcasting & Electronic Media,* **62**(4), 554–577. https://doi.org/10.1080/08838151.2018.1474881

Jingree, T. (2017). Using critical discursive psychology to examine carer discourses about facilitating independence for people with learning disabilities in UK services. *SAGE Research Methods Cases Part 2.* https://dx.doi.org/10.4135/9781526414007

Johnson, C. B., Stockdale, M. S., & Saal, F. E. (1991). Persistence of men's misperceptions of friendly cues across a variety of interpersonal encounters. *Psychology of Women Quarterly,* **15,** 463–475.

Johnson, G., Lewis, R. A., & Reiley, D. (2016). Location, location, location: repetition and proximity increase advertising effectiveness. Available at ssRN 2268215.

Johnson, T. J., & Friborg, O. (2015). The effects of cognitive behavioral therapy as an anti-depressive treatment is falling: A meta-analysis. *Psychological Bulletin,* **141,** 747–768.

Johnston, L., & Longhurst, R. (2010). *Space, place and sex: Geographies of sexualities.* Rowman & Littlefield.

Joiner, T. E., Jr. (1994). Contagious depression: Existence, specificity to depressed symptoms, and the role of reassurance seeking. *Journal of Personality and Social Psychology,* **67,** 287–296.

Jonas, E., Martens, A., Kayser, D. N., Fritsche, I., Sullivan, D., & Greenberg, J. (2008). Focus theory of normative conduct and terror-management theory: The interactive impact of mortality salience and norm salience on social judgement. *Journal of Personality and Social Psychology,* **95**(6), 1239–1251.

Jones, E. E. (1976). How do people perceive the causes of behavior? *American Scientist,* **64,** 300–305.

Jones, E. E., & Davis, K. E. (1965). A theory of correspondent inferences: From acts to dispositions. *Advances in Experimental Social Psychology,* **2,** 219–266.

Jones, E. E., & Harris, V. A. (1967). The attribution of attitudes. *Journal of Experimental Social Psychology,* **3,** 2–24.

Jones, E. E., & Nisbett, R. E. (1971). *The actor and the observer: Divergent perceptions of the cases of behavior.* General Learning Press.

Jones, E. E., Rock, L., Shaver, K. G., Goethals, G. R., & Ward, L. M. (1968). Pattern of performance and ability attribution: An unexpected primacy effect. *Journal of Personality and Social Psychology,* **10,** 317–340.

Jones, J. M. (1988). Racism in black and white: A bicultural model of reaction and evolution. In P. A. Katz and D. A. Taylor (Eds.), *Eliminating racism: Profiles in controversy.* Plenum Press.

Jones, J. M. (2003). TRIOS: A psychological theory of the African legacy in American culture. *Journal of Social Issues,* **59,** 217–242.

Jones, J. M. (2004). Whites are from Mars, OJ is from planet Hollywood: Blacks don't support OJ and whites just don't get it. In M. Fine, L. Weis, L. P. Pruitt, & A. Burns (Eds.), *Off white: Readings on power, privilege and resistance* (pp. 89–97). Routledge.

Jones, J. T., & Cunningham, J. D. (1996). Attachment styles and other predictors of relationship satisfaction in dating couples. *Personal Relationships,* **3,** 387–399.

Jones, J. T., Pelham, B. W., Mirenberg, M. C., & Hetts, J. J. (2002). Name letter preferences are not merely mere exposure: Implicit egotism as self-regulation. *Journal of Experimental Social Psychology,* **38**(2), 170–177.

Jones, K. (2013). Discouraging social loafing during team-based assessments. *Teaching Innovation Projects,* **3**(1), Article 13: http://ir.lib.uwo.ca/tips/vol3/iss1/13

Jones, R. A., & Brehm, J. W. (1970). Persuasiveness of one- and two-sided communications as a function of awareness there are two sides. *Journal of Experimental Social Psychology,* **6,** 47–56.

Jones, R. J., Woods, S. A., & Guillaume, Y. R. (2016). The effectiveness of workplace coaching: A meta-analysis of learning and performance outcomes from coaching. *Journal of Occupational and Organizational Psychology,* **89,** 249–277. https://doi.org/10.1111/joop.12119

Jones, S. C., & Magee, C. A. (2011). Exposure to alcohol advertising and alcohol consumption among Australian adolescents. *Alcohol and Alcoholism,* **46**(5), 630–637. https://doi.org/10.1093/alcalc/agr080

Jones, S. C., & Owen, N. (2006). Using fear appeals to promote cancer screening—are we scaring the wrong people?. *International Journal of Nonprofit and Voluntary Sector Marketing,* **11**(2), 93–103.

Joose, P. (2014). Becoming a God: Max Weber and the social construction of charisma. *Journal of Classical Sociology,* **14**(3), 266–283. https://doi.org/10.1177/1468795X14536652

Jordan, C. H., Spencer, S. J., Zanna, M. P., Hoshino-Browne, E., & Correll, J. (2003). Secure and defensive high self-esteem. *Journal of Personality and Social Psychology,* **85,** 969–978.

Joslyn, M. R., & Haider-Markel, D. P. (2017). Gun ownership and self-serving attributions for mass shooting tragedies. *Social Science Quarterly,* **98**(2), 429–442.

Jost, J. T., & Kay, A. C. (2005). Exposure to benevolent sexism and complementary gender stereotypes: Consequences for specific and diffuse forms of system justification. *Journal of Personality and Social Psychology,* **88,** 498–509.

Jourard, S. M. (1964). *The transparent self.* Van Nostrand.

Judd, C. M., Blair, I. V., & Chapleau, K. M. (2004). Automatic stereotypes vs. automatic prejudice: Sorting out the possibilities in the Payne (2001) weapon paradigm. *Journal of Experimental Social Psychology,* **40,** 75–81.

Jussim, L. (2005). Accuracy in social perception: Criticisms, controversies, criteria, components and cognitive processes. *Advances in Experimental Social Psychology,* **37,** 1–93.

Jussim, L. (2017). Précis of *Social perception and social reality: Why accuracy dominates bias and self-fulfilling prophecy. Behavioral and Brain Sciences,* **40,** e1.

Jussim, L., & Harber, K. D. (2005). Teacher expectations and self-fulfilling prophecies: Knowns and unknowns, resolved and unresolved controversies. *Personality and Social Psychology Review,* **9**(2), 131–155.

Jussim, L., & Harber, K. (2005). Teacher expectations and self-fulfilling prophecies: Knowns and unknowns, resolved and unresolved controversies. *Personality and Social Psychology Review,* **9**(2), 131–155.

Jussim, L., McCauley, C. R., & Lee, Y.-T. (1995). Introduction: Why study stereotype accuracy and inaccuracy? In Y. T. Lee, L. Jussim, & C. R. McCauley (Eds.), *Stereotypes accuracy: Toward appreciating group differences.* American Psychological Association.

K

Kaba, A., Wishart, I., Fraser, K., Coderre, S., & McLaughlin, K. (2016). Are we at risk of groupthink in our approach to teamwork interventions in health care? *Medical Education,* **50**(4), 400–408.

Kadir, H. A. (2012). School gangs of Yogyakarta: Mass fighting strategies and masculine charisma in the city of students. *Asia Pacific Journal of Anthropology,* **13**(4), 352–365. https://doi.org/10.1080/14442213.2012.697188

Kahle, L. R., & Berman, J. (1979). Attitudes cause behaviors: A cross-lagged panel analysis. *Journal of Personality and Social Psychology,* **37,** 315–321.

Kahlor, L. A., & Eastin, M. S. (2011). Television's role in the culture of violence toward women: A study of television viewing and the cultivation of RMA in the United States. *Journal of Broadcasting & Electronic Media,* **55,** 215–231. https://doi.org/10.1080/08838151.2011.566085

Kahn, J. H., & Garrison, A. M. (2009). Emotional self-disclosure and emotional avoidance: Relations with symptoms of depression and anxiety. *Journal of Counseling Psychology,* **56,** 573–584.

Kahneman, D., & Deaton, A. (2010). High income improves evaluation of life but not emotional well-being. *Proceedings of the National Academy of Sciences of the United States of America,* **107**(38), 16489–16493. http://www.jstor.org.libezproxy.open.ac.uk/stable/20779694

Kahneman, D., & Snell, J. (1992). Predicting a changing taste: Do people know what they will like? *Journal of Behavioral Decision Making,* **5**(3), 187–200.

Kahneman, D., & Tversky, A. (1979). Intuitive prediction: Biases and corrective procedures. *Management Science,* **12,** 313–327.

Kahneman, D., & Tversky, A. (1995). Conflict resolution: A cognitive perspective. In K. Arrow, R. Mnookin, L. Ross, A. Tversky, & R. Wilson (Eds.), *Barriers to the negotiated resolution of conflict.* Norton.

Kaiser Family Foundation (2001, November 13). National survey. Most gays and lesbians see greater acceptance. News release: www.kff.org.

Kaiser, F. G., & Byrka, K. (2011). Environmentalism as a trait:Gauging people's prosocial personality in terms of environmental engagement. *International Journal of Psychology,* **46,** 71–79.

Kalla, J. L., & Broockman, D. E. (2018). The minimal persuasive effects of campaign contact in general elections: Evidence from 49 field experiments. *American Political Science Review,* **112**(1), 148–166. https://doi.iorg/10.1017/S0003055417000363

Kanagaretnam, K., Lobo, G. J., & Mohammad, E. (2008). Determinants and consequences of large CEO pay. *International Journal of Accounting and Finance,* **1,** 61–82.

Kanagawa, C., Cross, S. E., & Markus, H. R. (2001). 'Who am I?' The cultural psychology of the conceptual self. *Personality and Social Psychology Bulletin,* **27,** 90–103.

Kanai, A. (2009). Karoshi ('work to death') in Japan. *Journal of Business Ethics,* **84,** 209–216.

Kanazawa, S., & Kovar, J. L. (2004). Why beautiful people are more intelligent. *Intelligence,* **32,** 227–243.

Kaplan, M. F. (1989). Task, situational, and personal determinants of influence processes in group decision making. In E. J. Lawler (Ed.), *Advances in group processes* (Vol. 6). JAI Press.

Karau, S. J., & Williams, K. D. (1993). Social loafing: A meta-analytic review and theoretical integration. *Journal of Personality and Social Psychology,* **65,** 681–706.

Karau, S. J., & Williams, K. D. (1997). The effects of group cohesiveness on social loafing and compensation. *Group Dynamics: Theory, Research, and Practice,* **1,** 156–168.

Karavellas, D. (2000). Sustainable consumption and fisheries. In B. Heap and J. Kent (Eds.), *Towards sustainable consumption: A European perspective.* The Royal Society.

Karney, B. R., & Bradbury, T. N. (1997). Neuroticism, marital interaction, and the trajectory of marital satisfaction. *Journal of Personality and Social Psychology,* **72**, 1075–1092.

Kashima, E. S., & Kashima, Y. (1998). Culture and language: The case of cultural dimensions and personal pronoun use. *Journal of Cross-Cultural Psychology,* **29**, 461–486.

Kashima, Y., & Kashima, E. S. (2003). Individualism, GNP, climate, and pronoun drop: Is individualism determined by affluence and climate, or does language use play a role? *Journal of Cross-Cultural Psychology,* **34**(1), 125–134. https://doi.org/10.1177/0022022102239159

Kasket, E. (2012). Continuing bonds in the age of social networking: Facebook as a modern-day medium. *Bereavement Care,* **31**(2),https://doi.org/10.1080/02682621.2012.710493

Kassin, S. M., Goldstein, C. C., & Savitsky, K. (2003). Behavioral confirmation in the interrogation room: On the dangers of presuming guilt. *Law and Human Behavior,* **27**, 187–203.

Katz, D. (1960). The functional approach to the study of attitudes. *Public Opinion Quarterly,* **6**, 248–268.

Katz, E. (1957). The two-step flow of communication: An up-to-date report on a hypothesis. *Public Opinion Quarterly,* **21**, 61–78.

Katz, I. (1981). *Stigma: A social psychological analysis.* Erlbaum.

Katz, I., & Hass, R. G. (1988). Racial ambivalence and American value conflict: Correlational and priming studies of dual cognitive structures. *Journal of Personality and Social Psychology,* **55**, 893–905.

Katz, I., Wackenhut, J., & Hass, R. G. (1986). Racial ambivalence, value duality, and behavior. In J. Dovidio & S. L. Gaertner (Eds.), *Prejudice discrimination and racism: Theory and research.* Academic Press.

Katz, J., Beach, S. R. H., & Joiner, T. E., Jr. (1999). Contagious depression in dating couples. *Journal of Social and Clinical Psychology,* **18**, 1–13.

Katz, P. A., & Kofkin, J. A. (1997). Race, gender, and young children. In S. S. Luthar, J. A. Burack, D. Cicchetti, & J. Weisz (Eds.), *Developmental psychopathology: Perspectives on adjustment, risk, and disorder.* Cambridge University Press.

Katzev, R., & Wang, T. (1994). Can commitment change behavior? A case study of environmental actions. *Journal of Social Behavior and Personality,* **9**, 13–26.

Katzev, R., Edelsack, L., Steinmetz, G., & Walker, T. (1978). The effect of reprimanding transgressions on subsequent helping behavior: Two field experiments. *Personality and Social Psychology Bulletin,* **4**, 126–129.

Katz-Wise, S. L., Priess, H. A., & Hyde, J. S. (2010). Gender-role attitudes and behavior across the transition to parenthood. *Developmental Psychology,* **46**(1), 18–28.

Kayali, L. (2019, 12 March). Europe agrees on protection rules for whistleblowers. *Politico.* https://www.politico.eu/article/europe-agrees-on-protection-rules-for-whistleblowers/

Kazdin, A. (2009). Psychological science's contribution to a sustainable environment: Extending our reach to a grand challenge of society. *American Psychologist,* **64**(5), 339–356.

Kearns, A., Whitley, E., Tannahill, C., & Ellaway, A. (2015). Loneliness, social relations and health and well-being in deprived communities. *Psychology, Health & Medicine,* **20**(3), 332–344.

Kelemen, W. L., Winningham, R. G., & Weaver, C. A., III (2007). Repeated testing sessions and scholastic aptitude in college students' metacognitive accuracy. *European Journal of Cognitive Psychology,* **19**, 689–717. https://doi.org/10.1080/09541440701326170

Keller, E. B., & Berry, B. (2003). *The influentials: One American in ten tells the other nine how to vote, where to eat, and what to buy.* The Free Press.

Kelley, H. H. (1973). The processes of causal attribution. *American Psychologist,* **28**(2), 107.

Kelley, H. H., & Thibault, J. W. (1978). *Interpersonal relationships: A theory of interdependence.* John Wiley.

Kellezi, B., Wakefield, J. R. H., Stevenson, C., McNamara, N., Mair, E., Bowe, M., Wilson, I., & Halder, M. M. (2019). The social cure of social prescribing: A mixed-methods study on the benefits of social connectedness on quality and effectiveness of care provision. *BMJ Open,* **9**(11), e033137.

Kelly, B., Halford, J. C. G., Boyland, E. J., Chapman, K., Bautista-Castaño, I., Berg, C., Caroli, M., Cook, B., Coutinho, J. G., Effertz, T., Grammatikaki, E., Keller, K., Leung, R., Manios, Y., Monteiro, R., Pedley, C., Prell, H., Raine, K., Recine, E., . . . Summerbell, C. (2010). Television food advertising to children: A global perspective. *American Journal of Public Health,* **100**(9), 1730–1736. https://doi.org/10.2105/AJPH.2009.179267.

Kelman, H. C. (1997). Group processes in the resolution of international conflicts: Experiences from the Israeli–Palestinian case. *American Psychologist,* **52**, 212–220.

Kelman, H. C. (1998). Building a sustainable peace: The limits of pragmatism in the Israeli–Palestinian negotiations. Address to the American Psychological Association convention.

Kennedy, K., & Pronin, E. (2008). When disagreement gets ugly:Perceptions of bias and the escalation of conflict. *Personality and Social Psychology Bulletin,* **34**, 833–848.

Kenny, D. A. (1994). *Interpersonal perception: A social relations analysis.* Guilford Press.

Kenny, D. A., & Acitelli, L. K. (2001). Accuracy and bias in the perception of the partner in a close relationship. *Journal of Personality and Social Psychology,* **80**, 439–448.

Kenrick, D. T., & Keefe, R. C. (1992). Age preferences in mates reflect sex differences in reproductive strategies. *Behavioral and Brain Sciences,* **15**, 75–133.

Kenworthy, J. B., Hewstone, M., Levine, J. M., Martin, R., & Willis, H. (2008). The phenomenology of minority–majority status: Effects on innovation in argument generation. *European Journal of Social Psychology,* **38**, 624–636.

Keren, G., & Schul, Y. (2009). Two is not always better than one: A critical evaluation of two-system theories. *Perspectives on Psychological Science,* **4**(6), 533–550.

Kernis, M. H. (2003). High self-esteem: A differentiated perspective. In E. C. Chang & L. J. Sanna (Eds.), *Virtue, vice, and personality: The complexity of behavior.* APA Books.

Kerr, M., & Stattin, H. (2000). What parents know, how they know it, and several forms of adolescent adjustment: Further evidence for a reinterpretation of monitoring. *Developmental Psychology,* **36**, 366–380.

Kerr, N. L., & Bruun, S. E. (1981). Ringelmann revisited: Alternative explanations for the social loafing effect. *Personality and Social Psychology Bulletin,* **7**, 224–231.

Kerr, N. L., & Kaufman-Gilliland, C. M. (1994). Communication, commitment, and cooperation in social dilemma. *Journal of Personality and Social Psychology,* **66**(3), 513.

Kerr, N. L., Garst, J., Lewandowski, D. A., & Harris, S. E. (1997). That still, small voice: Commitment to cooperate as an internalized versus a social norm. *Personality and Social Psychology Bulletin,* **23**, 1300–1311.

Kesebir, S., & Oishi, S. (2010). A spontaneous self-reference effect in memory: Why some birthdays are harder to remember than others. *Psychological Science,* **21**(10), 1525–1531.

Khan, S., & Pedersen, A. (2010). Black African immigrants to Australia: Prejudice and the function of attitudes. *Journal of Pacific Rim Psychology,* **4**(2), 116–129.

Kidder, C., White, K., Hinojos, M., Sandoval, M., & Crites, S. (2018). Sequential stereotype priming: A meta-analysis. *Personality and Social Psychology Review,* **22**(3), 199–227.

Kidwell Jr., R. E., &Robie, C. (2003). Withholding effort in organizations: Toward development and validation of a measure. *Journal of Business and Psychology,* **17**, 537–561. https//doi.org/10.1023/A:1023456319134

Kiesler, C. A. (1971). *The psychology of commitment: Experiments linking behavior to belief.* Academic Press.

Kihlstrom, J. F., & Cantor, N. (1984). Mental representations of the self. In L. Berkowitz (Ed.), *Advances in experimental social psychology* (Vol. 17). Academic Press.

Kilgour, P. W., Reynaud, D., Northcote, M. T., & Shields, M. (2015). Role-playing as a tool to facilitate learning, self-reflection and social awareness in teacher education. *International Journal of Innovative Interdisciplinary Research,* **2**, 8–20.

Kim, D. J., Davis, E. P., Sandman, C. A., Sporns, O., O'Donnell, B. F., Buss, C., & Hetrick, W. P. (2017).

Prenatal maternal cortisol has sex-specific associations with child brain network properties. *Cerebral Cortex*, **27**(11), 5230–5241. https://doi.org/10.1093/cercor/bhw303

Kim, H., & Cabeza, R. (2007). Trusting our memories: Dissociating the neural correlates of confidence in veridical versus illusory memories. *Journal of Neuroscience*, **27**(45), 12190–12197.

Kim, H., & Markus, H. R. (1999). Deviance of uniqueness, harmony or conformity? A cultural analysis. *Journal of Personality and Social Psychology*, **77**, 785–800.

Kim, J., & Hatfield, E. (2004). Love types and subjective well-being: A cross cultural study. *Social Behavior and Personality*, **32**(2), 173–182.

Kim, Y. I., & Jang, S. J. (2017). Religious service attendance and volunteering: A growth curve analysis. *Nonprofit and Voluntary Sector Quarterly*, **46**(2), 395–418.

Kimura, A., Wada, Y., Goto, S., Tsuzuki, D., Cai, D., Oka, T., & Ippeita, D. (2009). Implicit gender-based food stereotypes: Semantic priming experiments on young Japanese. *Appetite*, **52**(2), 521–524.

Kirkham, J. A., Smith, J. A., & Havsteen-Franklin, D. (2015). Painting pain: An interpretative phenomenological analysis of representations of living with chronic pain. *Health Psychology*, **34**(4), 398–406.

Kirsh, S. J., Olczak, P. V., & Mounts, J. R. W. (2005). Violent video games induce an affect processing bias. *Media Psychology*, **7**, 239–250.

Kitayama, S. (2000). Collective construction of the self and social relationships: A rejoinder and some extensions. *Child Development*, **71**(5), 1143–1146.

Kitayama, S., & Karasawa, M. (1997). Implicit self-esteem in Japan: Name letters and birthday numbers. *Personality and Social Psychology Bulletin*, **23**, 736–742.

Kitayama, S., & Markus, H. R. (1995). Culture and self: Implications for internationalizing psychology. In N. R. Godlberger & J. B. Veroff (Eds.), *The culture and psychology reader*. New York University Press.

Kite, M. E. (2001). Changing times, changing gender roles: Who do we want women and men to be? In R. K. Unger (Ed.), *Handbook of the psychology of women and gender*. Wiley.

Kjaer, T. W., Nowak, M., & Lou, H. C. (2002). Reflective self-awareness and conscious states: PET evidence for a common midline parietofrontal core. *Neuroimage*, **17**, 1080–1086.

Klein, I., & Snyder, M. (2003). Stereotypes and behavioral confirmation: From interpersonal to intergroup perspectives. *Advances in Experimental Social Psychology*, **35**, 153–235.

Klein, O., Snyder, M., & Livingston, R. W. (2004). Prejudice on the stage: Self-monitoring and the public expression of group attitudes. *British Journal of Social Psychology*, **43**, 299–314.

Klein, W. M., & Kunda, Z. (1992). Motivated person perception: Constructing justifications for desired beliefs. *Journal of Experimental Social Psychology*, **28**, 145–168.

Kleinke, C. L., Peterson, T. R., & Rutledge, R. R. (1998). Effects of self-generated facial expressions on mood. *Journal of Personality and Social Psychology*, **74**, 272–279.

Klempka, A., & Stimson, A. (2014). Anonymous communication on the internet and trolling. *Concordia Journal of Communication Research*, **1**(2). https://digitalcommons.csp.edu/comjournal/vol1/iss1/2

Klimecki, O. M. (2015). The plasticity of social emotions. *Social Neuroscience*, **10**(5), 466–473.

Klinesmith, J., Kasser, T., & McAndrew, F. T. (2006). Guns, testosterone, and aggression. *Psychological Science*, **17**(7), 568–571.

Klopfer, P. H. (1958). Influence of social interaction on learning rates in birds. *Science*, **128**, 903.

Knee, C. R., Lonsbary, C., Canevello, A., & Patrick, H. (2005). Self-determination and conflict in romantic relationships. *Journal of Personality and Social Psychology*, **89**(6), 997–1009.

Kniffin, K. M., & Wilson, D. S. (2004). The effect of nonphysical traits on the perception of physical attractiveness: Three naturalistic studies. *Evolution and Human Behavior*, **25**(2), 88–101.

Knowles, M. L., & Gardner, W. L. (2008). Benefits of membership: The activation and amplification of group identities in response to social rejection. *Personality and Social Psychology Bulletin*, **34**, 1200–1213.

Knox, R. E., & Inkster, J. A. (1968). Postdecision dissonance at post-time. *Journal of Personality and Social Psychology*, **8**, 319–323.

Ko, A. S. O. (2005). Organizational communications in Hong Kong: A cultural approach to groupthink. *Corporate Communications*, **10**(4), 351–357.

Kogut, T., & Ritov, I. (2007). 'One of us': Outstanding willingness to help save a single identified compatriot. *Organizational Behavior and Human Decision Processes*, **104**(2), 150–157.

Kohlberg, L. (1958). The development of modes of thinking and choices in Years 10 to 16 (PhD dissertation). University of Chicago.

Kolb, B., & Gibb, R. (2011). Brain plasticity and behaviour in the developing brain. *Journal of the Canadian Academy of Child and Adolescent Psychiatry*, **20**(4), 265–276.

Kolstad, A., & Horpestad, S. (2009). Self-construal in Chile and Norway. Implications for cultural differences in individualism and collectivism. *Journal of Cross-Cultural Psychology*, **40**(2), 275–281.

Kombarakaran, F. A., Yang, J. A., Baker, M. N., & Fernandes, P. B. (2008). Executive coaching: It works! *Consulting Psychology Journal: Practice and Research*, **60**, 78–90. https://doi.org/10.1037/1065-9293.60.1.78

Konrad, A. M., Ritchie, J. E., Jr, Lieb, P., & Corrigall, E. (2000). Sex differences and similarities in job attribute preferences: A meta-analysis. *Psychological Bulletin*, **126**, 593–641.

Koomen, W., & Bahler, M. (1996). National stereotypes: Common representations and ingroup favouritism. *European Journal of Social Psychology*, **26**, 325–331.

Koomen, W., & Dijker, A. J. (1997). Ingroup and outgroup stereotypes and selective processing. *European Journal of Social Psychology*, **27**, 589–601.

Koonz, C. (2003). *The Nazi conscience*. Belknap Press.

Koop, C. E. (1987). Report of the Surgeon General's workshop on pornography and public health. *American Psychologist*, **42**, 944–945.

Koppel, M., Argamon, S., & Shimoni, A. R. (2002). Automatically categorizing written texts by author gender. *Literary and Linguistic Computing*, **17**, 401–412.

Kopstein, J. S., & Wittenberg, J. (2011). Deadly communities: Local political milieus and the persecution of Jews in Occupied Poland. *Comparative Political Studies*, **44**(3), 259–283. https://doi.org/10.1177/0010414010384370

Koriat, A., Lichtenstein, S., & Fischhoff, B. (1980). Reasons for confidence. *Journal of Experimental Social Psychology: Human Learning and Memory*, **6**, 107–118.

Kormos, C., & Gifford, R. (2014). The validity of self-report measures of proenvironmental behavior: A meta-analytic review. *Journal of Environmental Psychology*, **40**, 359–371.

Korobov, N. (2004). Inoculating against prejudice: A discursive approach to homophobia and sexism in adolescent male talk. *Psychology of Men and Masculinity*, **5**(2), 178–189.

Koval, P., Laham, S. M., Haslam, N., Bastian, B., & Whelan, J. A. (2012). Our flaws are more human than yours: Ingroup bias in humanising negative characteristics. *Personality and Social Psychology Bulletin*, **38**, 283–295. https://doi.org/10.1177/0146167211423777

Koydemir, S., Şimşek, Ö. F., & Demir, M. (2014). Pathways from personality to happiness: Sense of uniqueness as a mediator. *Journal of Humanistic Psychology*, **54**(3), 314–335.

Krahé, B., & Busching, R. (2013). Charging neutral cues with aggressive meaning through violent video game play. *Societies*, **3**(4), 445–456.

Kramer, A. D. I., Guillory, J. E., & Hancock, J. T. (2014). Emotional contagion through social networks. *Proceedings of the National Academy of Sciences*, **111**(24), 8788–8790.

Kramer, R. M. (1998). Revisiting the Bay of Pigs and Vietnam decisions 25 years later: How well has the groupthink hypothesis stood the test of time? *Organizational Behavior and Human Decision Processes*, **73**(2–3), 236–271.

Kraus, S. J. (1995). Attitudes and the prediction of behavior: A meta-analysis of the empirical literature. *Personality and Social Psychology Bulletin*, **21**, 58–75.

Kraut, R. E., & Lewis, S. H. (1982). Person perception and self-awareness: Knowledge of influences on one's own judgments. *Journal of Personality and Social Psychology*, **42**, 448–460.

Kravitz, D. A., & Martin, B. (1986). Ringelmann rediscovered: The original article. *Journal of Personality and Social Psychology*, **50**, 936–941.

Krebs, D. L. (1970). Altruism – An examination of the concept and a review of the literature. *Psychological Bulletin,* **73,** 258–302.

Krebs, D. L. (1975). Empathy and altruism. *Journal of Personality and Social Psychology,* **32,** 1134–1146.

Krebs, D. L. (1998). The evolution of moral behaviors. In C. Crawford & D. L. Krebs (Eds.), *Handbook of evolutionary psychology: Ideas, issues and applications.* Lawrence Erlbaum.

Krisberg, K. (2004). Successful truth – antismoking campaign in funding jeopardy: New commission works to save campaign. *Medscape:* www.medscape.com.

Kristiansson, M., Sorman, K., Tekwe, C., & Calderon-Garciduenas, L. (2015). Urban air pollution, poverty, violence and health: Neurological and immunological aspects as mediating factors. *Environmental Research,* **140,** 511.

Kroeber, A. L., & Kluckhohn, C. (1952). Culture: A critical review of concepts and definitions. *Papers, Peabody Museum of Archaeology & Ethnology, Harvard University,* **47**(1), viii, 223.

Krosnick, J. A., & Schuman, H. (1988). Attitude intensity, importance, and certainty and susceptibility to response effects. *Journal of Personality and Social Psychology,* **54,** 940–952.

Krueger, J., & Clement, R. W. (1994). The truly false consensus effect: An ineradicable and egocentric bias in social perception. *Journal of Personality and Social Psychology,* **67,** 596–610.

Krueger, J. I., & Funder, D. C. (2004a). Towards a balanced social psychology: Causes, consequences and cures for the problem-seeking approach to social behavior and cognition. *Behavioral and Brain Sciences,* **27**(3), 313–327.

Krueger, J. I., & Funder, D. C. (2004b). Social psychology: A field in search of a center. *Behavioral and Brain Sciences,* **27**(3), 361–367.

Krueger, R. F., Hicks, B. M., & McGue, M. (2001). Altruism and antisocial behavior: Independent tendencies, unique personality correlates, distinct etiologies. *Psychological Science,* **12,** 397–402.

Kruger, J., & Dunning, D. (1999). Unskilled and unaware of it: How difficulties in recognizing one's own incompetence lead to inflated self-assessments. *Journal of Personality and Social Psychology,* **77,** 1121–1134.

Kruger, J., & Evans, M. (2004). If you don't want to be late, enumerate: Unpacking reduces the planning fallacy. *Journal of Experimental Social Psychology,* **40,** 586–598.

Kruger, J., Wirtz, D., & Miller, D. T. (2005). Counterfactual thinking and the first instinct fallacy. *Journal of Personality and Social Psychology,* **88,** 725–735.

Kruglanski, A. W., & Golec de Zavala, A. (2005). Individual motivations, the group process and organizational strategies in suicide terrorism. In E. M. Meyersson Milgrom (Ed.), *Suicide missions and the market for martyrs: A multidisciplinary approach.* Princeton University Press.

Kruglanski, A. W., & Thompson, E. P. (1999). Persuasion by a single route: A view from the unimodel. *Psychological Inquiry,* **10**(2), 83–109.

Krugman, P. (2003, 18 February). Behind the great divide. *New York Times:* www.nytimes.com.

Krull, D. S., Loy, M. H.-M., Lin, J., Wang, C.-F., Chen, S., & Zhao, X. (1999). The fundamental attribution error: Correspondence bias in individualist and collectivist cultures. *Personality and Social Psychology Bulletin,* **25,** 1208–1219.

Kuan, K. K., Zhong, Y., & Chau, P. Y. (2014). Informational and normative social influence in group-buying: Evidence from self-reported and EEG data. *Journal of Management Information Systems,* **30**(4), 151–178.

Kubacka, K. E., Finkenauer, C., Rusbult, C. E., & Keijsers, L. (2011). Maintaining close relationships: Gratitude as a motivator and a detector of maintenance behavior. *Personality and Social Psychology Bulletin,* **37**(10), 1362–1375.

Kubany, E. S., Bauer, G. B., Pangilinan, M. E., Muroka, M. Y., & Enriquez, V. G. (1995). Impact of labeled anger and blame in intimate relationships. *Journal of Cross-Cultural Psychology,* **26,** 65–83.

Kugihara, N. (1999). Gender and social loafing in Japan. *Journal of Social Psychology,* **139,** 516–526.

Kuhle, B. X., & Radtke, S. (2013). Born both ways: The alloparenting hypothesis for sexual fluidity in women. *Evolutionary Psychology,* **11,** 304–323. http://dx.doi.org/10.1177/147470491301100202

Kuhn, M., & McPartland, T. S. (1954). An empirical investigation of self-attitudes. *American Sociological Review,* **19,** 68–76.

Kuiper, N. A. (1981). Convergent evidence for the self as a prototype: The 'inverted-URT effect' for self and other judgments. *Personality and Social Psychology Bulletin,* **7**(3), 438–443.

Kuiper, N. A., & Rogers, T. B. (1979). Encoding of personal information: Self-other differences. *Journal of Personality and Social Psychology,* **37,** 499–514.

Kulik, J. A. (1983). Confirmatory attributions and the perpetuation of social beliefs. *Journal of Personality and Social Psychology,* **44,** 1171–1181.

Kumkale, G. T., & Albarracín, D. (2004). The sleeper effect in persuasion: A meta-analytic review. *Psychological Bulletin,* **130**(1), 143.

Kundera, M. (1990). *Immortality.* Grove Press.

Kunkel, D., Cope-Farrar, K., Biely, E., Maynard-Farinola, W. J., & Donnerstein, E. (2001). *Sex on TV 2.* The Henry J. Kaiser Family Foundation.

Kunst, J. R., Bailey, A., Prendergast, C., & Gundersen, A. (2019). Sexism, rape myths and feminist identification explain gender differences in attitudes toward the# metoo social media campaign in two countries. *Media Psychology,* **22**(5), 818–843.

Kunst-Wilson, W. R., & Zajonc, R. B. (1980). Affective discrimination of stimuli that cannot be recognized. *Science,* **207,** 557–558.

Kurdek, L. A. (1991). Correlates of relationship satisfaction in cohabiting gay and lesbian couples:Integration of contextual, investment, and problem-solving models. *Journal of Personality and Social Psychology,* **61,** 910–922.

Kurdek, L. A. (1994). Areas of conflict for gay, lesbian, and heterosexual couples: What couples argue about influences relationship satisfaction. *Journal of Marriage and the Family,* **56,** 923–934.

Kurdek, L. A. (1995). Assessing multiple determinants of relationship commitment in cohabiting gay, cohabiting lesbian, dating heterosexual, and married heterosexual couples. *Family Relations,* **44,** 261–266.

Kurdek, L. A. (2004). Are gay and lesbian cohabiting couples *really* different from heterosexual married couples? *Journal of Marriage and the Family,* **66,** 880–900.

Kurdek, L. A. (2005). What do we know about gay and lesbian couples? *Current Directions in Psychological Science,* **14,** 251–254.

Kurdek, L. A. (2006). Differences between partners from heterosexual, gay, and lesbian couples. *Journal of Marriage and Family,* **68,** 509–528.

Kurdek, L. A. (2008). A general model of relationship commitment: Evidence from same-sex partners. *Personal Relationships,* **15**(3), 391–405.

L

La Rochefoucauld, F. (1665). *Maxims.*

La Torre, G., Saulle, R., Unim, B., Angelillo, I. F., Baldo, V., Bergomi, M., Cacciari, P., Castaldi, S., Del Corno, G., Di Stanislao, F., Pana, A., Gregorio, P., Grillo, O.C., Gross, P., La Rosa, F., Nante, N., Pavia, M., Pelissero, G., Quarto, M., Ricciardi, W., Romano, G., . . . Boccia, A. (2014). Knowledge, attitudes, and smoking behaviours among physicians specializing in public health: A multicentre study. *BioMed Research International,* **2014,** 516734.

Lacey, M. (2004, 9 April). A decade after massacres, Rwanda outlaws ethnicity. *New York Times:* www.nytimes.com.

Lackner, J. M., Gudleski, G. D., Firth, R., Keefer, L., Brenner, D. M., Guy, K., Simonetti, C., Radziwon, C., Quinton, S., Krasner, S. S., Katz, L., Garbarino, G., Iacobucci, G., & Sitrin, M. D. (2013). Negative aspects of close relationships are more strongly associated than supportive personal relationships with illness burden of irritable bowel syndrome. *Journal of Psychosomatic Research,* **74**(6), 493–500. https://doi.org/10.1016/j.jpsychores.2013.03.009

Ladd, G. W. (2009). Trends, travails, and turning points in early researchon children's peer relationships: Legacies and lessons for our time? In K. H. Rubin, W. M. Bukowski, & B. Laursen (Eds.), *Handbook of peer interactions, relationships, and groups.* Guilford Press.

LaFromboise, T., Coleman, H. L. K., & Gerton, J. (1993). Psychological impact of biculturalism: Evidence and theory. *Psychological Bulletin,* **114,** 395–412.

Laird, J. D. (1974). Self-attribution of emotion: The effects of expressive behavior on the quality of emotional experience. *Journal of Personality and Social Psychology,* **29,** 475–486.

Laird, J. D. (1984). The real role of facial response in the experience of emotion: A reply to Tourangeau and Ellsworth, and others. *Journal of Personality and Social Psychology,* **47,** 909–917.

Lakin, J. L., & Chartrand, T. L. (2003). Using nonconscious behavioral mimicry to create affiliation and rapport. *Psychological Science,* **14,** 334–339.

Lakin, J. L., & Chartrand, T. L. (2003). Using nonconscious behavioral mimicry to create affiliation and rapport. *Psychological Science,* **14**(4), 334–339.

Lalancette, M.-F., & Standing, L. (1990). Asch fails again. *Social Behavior and Personality,* **18,** 7–12.

Lalonde, R. N. (1992). The dynamics of group differentiation in the face of defeat. *Personality and Social Psychology Bulletin,* **18,** 336–342.

LaLone, M. B. (2012). Neighbors helping neighbors: An examination of the social capital mobilization process for community resilience to environmental disasters. *Journal of Applied Social Science,* **6**(2), 209–237. https://doi.org/10.1177/1936724412458483

Lam, S., Chiu, C., Lau, I. Y., Chan, W., & Yim, P. (2006). Managing intergroup attitudes among Hong Kong adolescents: Effects of social category inclusiveness and time pressure. *Asian Journal of Social Psychology,* **9,** 1–11.

Lamal, P. A. (1979). College students' common beliefs about psychology. *Teaching of Psychology,* **6**(3), 155–158.

Lammers, J., & Stapel, D. A. (2011). Power increases dehumanization. *Group Processes and Intergroup Relations,* **14**(1), 113–126.

Lammers, J., Stapel, D. A., & Galinksy, A. D. (2010). Power increases hypocrisy: Moralizing in reasoning, immorality in behaviour. *Psychological Science,* **21**(5), 737–744.

Landau, M. J., Meier, B. P., & Keefer, L. A. (2010). A metaphor-enriched social cognition. *Psychological Bulletin,* **136,** 1045–1067.

Landau, M. J., Solomon, S., Greenberg, J., Cohen, F., Pyszczynski, T., Arndt, J., Miller, C. H., Ogilvie, D. M., & Cook, A. (2004). Deliver us from evil: The effects of mortality salience and reminders of 9/11 on support for President George W. Bush. *Personality and Social Psychology Bulletin,* **30,** 1136–1150.

Landy, F., & Conte, J. (2007). *Work in the 21st century: An introduction to industrial and organizational psychology.* Blackwell.

Lane, C. (2007). *Shyness: How normal behavior became a sickness.* Yale University Press.

Lane, E. R. (2000). *The loss of happiness in market democracies.* Yale University Press.

Langbein, H. (1994). *Against all hope.* Paragon House.

Langdridge, D. (2007). *Phenomenological psychology: Theory, research and method.* Pearson Education.

Langdridge, D. (2008). Phenomenology and critical social psychology: Directions and debates in theory and research. *Social and Personality Psychology Compass,* **2**(3), 1126–1142.

Langer, E. J. (1977). The psychology of chance. *Journal for the Theory of Social Behavior,* **7,** 185–208.

Langer, E. J., & Roth, J. (1975). Heads I win, tails it's chance: The illusion of control as a function of the sequence of outcomes in a purely chance task. *Journal of Personality and Social Psychology,* **32,** 951–955.

Langlois, J. H., Kalakanis, L., Rubenstein, A. J., Larson, A., Hallam, M., & Smoot, M. (2000). Maxims or myths of beauty? A meta-analytic and theoretical review. *Psychological Bulletin,* **126**(3), 390–423.

Lannin, D. G., Guyll, M., Vogel, D. L., & Madon, S. T. (2013). Reducing the stigma associated with seeking psychotherapy through self-affirmation. *Journal of Counseling Psychology,* **60**(4), 508–519. https://doi.org/10.1037/a0033789

Lanzetta, J. T. (1955). Group behavior under stress. *Human Relations,* **8,** 29–53.

LaPiere, R. T. (1934). Attitudes versus actions. *Social Forces,* **13**(2), 230–237.

Larsen, K. S. (1974). Conformity in the Asch experiment. *Journal of Social Psychology,* **94,** 303–304.

Larsen, K. S. (1990). The Asch conformity experiment: Replication and transhistorical comparisons. *Journal of Social Behavior and Personality,* **5**(4), 163–168.

Larsen, S. E., & Fitzgerald, L. F. (2011). PTSD symptoms and sexual harassment: The role of attributions and perceived control. *Journal of Interpersonal Violence,* **26**(13), 2555–2567.

Larson, J. R., Jr, Foster-Fishman, P. G., & Keys, C. B. (1994). Discussion of shared and unshared information in decision-making groups. *Journal of Personality and Social Psychology,* **67,** 446–461.

Larsson, K. (1956). *Conditioning and sexual behavior in the male albino rat.* Almqvist & Wiksell.

Lash, C. (1979). *The culture of narcissism: American life in an age of diminishing expectations.* Norton & Company.

Lassiter, G. D., & Dudley, K. A. (1991). The a priori value of basic research: The case of videotaped confessions. *Journal of Social Behavior and Personality,* **6,** 7–16.

Lassiter, G. D., & Irvine, A. A. (1986). Videotaped confessions: The impact of camera point of view on judgements of coercion. *Journal of Applied Social Psychology,* **16,** 268–276.

Lassiter, G. D., Geers, A. L., Handley, I. M., Weiland, P. E., & Munhall, P. J. (2002). Videotaped interrogations and confessions: A simple change in camera perspective alters verdicts in simulated trials. *Journal of Applied Psychology,* **87,** 867–874.

Lassiter, G. D., Munhall, P. J., Berger, I. P., Weiland, P. E., Handley, I. M., & Geers, A. L. (2005). Attributional complexity and the camera perspective bias in videotaped confessions. *Basic and Applied Social Psychology,* **27,** 27–35.

Lasswell, H. D. (1948). The structure and function of communication in society. *The Communication of Ideas,* **37,** 215–228.

Latané, B. (1981). The psychology of social impact. *American Psychologist,* **36**(4), 343–356.

Latané, B., & Dabbs, J. M., Jr (1975). Sex, group size and helping in three cities. *Sociometry,* **38,** 180–194.

Latané, B., & Darley, J. M. (1968a). Bystander intervention in emergencies: Diffusion of responsibility. *Journal of Personality and Social Psychology,* **8**(4), 377–383.

Latané, B., & Darley, J. M. (1968b). Group inhibition of bystander intervention in emergencies. *Journal of Personality and Social Psychology,* **10,** 215–221.

Latané, B., & Darley, J. M. (1970). *The unresponsive bystander: Why doesn't he help?* Appleton-Century-Crofts.

Latané, B., & Nida, S. (1981). Ten years of research on group size and helping. *Psychological Bulletin,* **89,** 308–324.

Latané, B., & Rodin, J. (1969). A lady in distress: Inhibiting effects of friends and strangers on bystander intervention. *Journal of Experimental Social Psychology,* **5,** 189–202.

Latané, B., Williams, K., & Harkins, S. (1979). Many hands make light the work: The causes and consequences of social loafing. *Journal of Personality and Social Psychology,* **37,** 822–832.

Latané, B., Williams, K., & Harkins, S. (1979). Many hands make light the work: The causes and consequences of social loafing. *Journal of Personality and Social Psychology,* **37**(6), 822–832.

Latrofa, M., Vaes, J., Pastore, M., & Cadinu, M. (2009). 'United we stand, divided we fall'! The protective function of self-stereotyping for stigmatised members' psychological well-being. *Applied Psychology,* **58,** 84–104.

Lau-Gesk, L., & Drolet, A. (2008). The publicly self-conscious consumer. Prepared to be embarrassed. *Journal of Consumer Psychology,* **18,** 127–136.

Laughlin, P. R. (1996). Group decision making and collective induction. In E. H. Witte & J. H. Davis (Eds.), *Understanding group behavior: Consensual action by small groups.* Erlbaum.

Laughlin, P. R., & Adamopoulos, J. (1980). Social combination processes and individual learning for six-person cooperative groups on an intellective task. *Journal of Personality and Social Psychology,* **38,** 941–947.

Laughlin, P. R., Hatch, E. C., Silver, J. S., & Boh, L. (2006). Groups perform better than the best individuals on letters-to-numbers problems: Effects of group size. *Journal of Personality and Social Psychology,* **90,** 644–651.

Laughlin, P. R., Zander, M. L., Knievel, E. M., & Tan, T. K. (2003). Groups perform better than the best individuals on letters-to-numbers problems: Informative equations and effective strategies. *Journal of Personality and Social Psychology,* **85,** 684–694.

Laustsen, L., & Petersen, M. B. (2015). Does a competent leader make a good friend? Conflict, ideology and the psychologies of friendship and followership. *Evolution and Human Behavior,* **36**(4), 286-293.

Laustsen, L., & Petersen, M. B. (2017). Perceived conflict and leader dominance: Individual and contextual factors behind preferences for dominant leaders. *Political Psychology,* **38**(6), 1083-1101.

Laustsen, L., Petersen, M. B., & Klofstad, C. A. (2015). Vote choice, ideology, and social dominance orientation influence preferences for lower pitched voices in political candidates. *Evolutionary Psychology,* **13**(3). https://doi.org/10.1177/1474704915600576

Lazare, A. (2004). *On apology.* Oxford University Press.

Le Bon, G. (1895). *Psychologie des foules.* University of France Press.

Le, B., & Agnew, C. R. (2003). Commitment and its theorized determinants: A meta-analysis of the Investment Model. *Personal Relationships,* **10**(1), 37–57.

Leach, C. W., & Spears, R. (2008). 'A vengefulness of the impotent': The pain of in-group inferiority and schadenfreude toward successful out-groups. *Journal of Personality and Social Psychology,* **95,** 1383–1396.

Leach, C. W., & Spears, R. (2009). Dejection at in-group defeat and schadenfreude toward second- and third-party out-groups. *Emotion,* **9,** 659–665.

Leach, C. W., Spears, R., Branscombe, N. R., & Doosje, B. (2003). Malicious pleasure: Schadenfreude at the suffering of another group. *Journal of Personality and Social Psychology,* **84**(5), 932–943.

Leach, C. W., van Zomeren, M., Zebel, S., Vliek, M. L. W., Pennekamp, S. F., Doosje, B., & Spears, R. (2008). Group-level self-definition and self-investment: A hierarchical (multicomponent) model of in-group identification. *Journal of Personality and Social Psychology,* **95,** 144–165.

Leary, M. R., Nezlek, J. B., Radford-Davenport, D., Martin, J., & McMullen, A. (1994). Self-presentation in everyday interactions: Effects of target familiarity and gender composition. *Journal of Personality and Social Psychology,* **67,** 664–673.

Leary, M. R., & Kowalski, R. M. (1995). *Social anxiety.* Guilford Press.

Leary, M. R. (1998). The social and psychological importance of self-esteem. In R. M. Kowalski & M. R. Leary (Eds.), *The social psychology of emotional and behavioral problems.* American Psychological Association.

Leary, M. R. (2003). Interpersonal aspects of optimal self-esteem and the authentic self. *Psychological Inquiry,* **14,** 52–54.

Leary, M. R. (2004). *The curse of the self: Self-awareness, egotism, and the quality of human life.* Oxford University Press.

Leary, M. R. (2007). Motivational and emotional aspects of the self. *Annual Review of Psychology,* **58,** 317–344.

Leary, M. R. (2013). Social anxiety, shyness, and related constructs. In J. P. Robinson, P. R. Shaver, & L. S. Wrightsman (Eds.), *Measures of personality and social psychological attitudes*(pp. 161–176). Academic Press.

Lee, A. Y., & Aaker, J. L. (2004). Bringing the frame into focus: The influence of regulatory fit on processing fluency and persuasion. *Journal of Personality and Social Psychology,* **86,** 205–218.

Lee, F., Hallahan, M., & Herzog, T. (1996). Explaining real-life events: How culture and domain shape attributions. *Personality and Social Psychology Bulletin,* **22,** 732–741.

Lee, J. A. (1998). Ideologies of lovestyle and sexstyle. In V. C. de Munck (Ed.), *Romantic love and sexual behavior: Perspectives from the social sciences.* Praeger/Greenwood.

Lee, M. K. O., Shi, N., Cheung, C. M. K., Lim, K. H., & Sia, C.L. (2011). Consumer's decision to shop online: The moderating-role of positive informational social influence. *Information & Management,* **48**(6), 185–191.

Lee, Y-S., & Waite, L. (2005). Husband's and wife's time spent on housework: A comparison of measures. *Journal of Marriage and Family,* **67,** 328–336.

Lefcourt, H. M. (1982). *Locus of control: Current trends in theory and research.* Erlbaum.

Lehmiller, J. J., VanderDrift, L. E., & Kelly, J. R. (2011). Sex differences in approaching friends with benefits relationships. *Journal of Sex Research,* **48**(2–3), 275–284. https://doi.org/10.1080/00224491003721694

Lehrer, J. (2012). *Imagine: How creativity works.* Houghton Mifflin Harcourt.

Lei, H., Chiu, M., Cui, Y., Zhou, W., & Li, S. (2018). Parenting style and aggression: A meta-analysis of Mainland Chinese children and youth. *Children and Youth Services Review,* **94,** 446–455.

Leinbach, M. D., & Fagot, B. I. (1993). Categorical habituation to male and female faces: Gender schematic processes in infancy. *Infant Behavior and Development,* **16,** 317–332.

Lemay, E., Clark, M., & Greenberg, A. (2010). What is beautiful is good because what is beautiful is desired: Physical attractiveness stereotyping as projection of interpersonal goals. Personality and Social Psychology Bulletin, 36(3), 339–353.

L'Engle, M. (1973). *A wind in the door.* Bantam, Doubleday, Dell.

Lennon, A., & Watson, B. (2011). 'Teaching them a lesson?' A qualitative exploration of underlying motivations for driver aggression. *Accident Analysis and Prevention,* **43**(6), 2200–2208.

Lepore, S. J., Ragan, J. D., & Jones, S. (2000). Talking facilitates cognitive-emotional processes of adaptation toan acute stressor. *Journal of Personality and Social Psychology,* **78,** 499–508.

Lepper, M. R., & Greene, D. (Eds.) (1979). *The hidden costs of reward.* Erlbaum.

Lerner, M. J. (1980). *The belief in a just world: A fundamental delusion.* Plenum.

Lerner, M. J., & Miller, D. T. (1978). Just world research and the attribution process: Looking back and ahead. *Psychological Bulletin,* **85,** 1030–1051.

Lerouge, D., & Smeesters, D. (2008). Knowledge activation after information encoding: Implications of trait priming on person judgement. *Journal of Experimental Social Psychology,* **44,** 429–436.

Lester, J. N., Wong, J. Y., O'Reilly, M., & Kiyimba, N. (2018). Discursive psychology: Implications for counseling psychology. *The Counseling Psychologist,* **46**(5), 576–607.

Leung, K., & Bond, M. H. (2004). Social axioms: A model of social beliefs in multicultural perspective. *Advances in Experimental Social Psychology,* **36,** 119–197.

Leung, K., & Bond, M. H. (Eds.) (2009). *Psychological aspects of social axioms: Understanding global belief systems.* International and cultural psychology series. Springer Science + Business Media.

Leung, K., Bond, M. H., Reimel de Carrasquel, S., Muñoz, C., Hernández, M., Murakami, F., Yamaguchi, S., Bierbrauer, G., & Singelis, T. M. (2002). Social axioms: The search for universal dimensions of general beliefs about how the world functions. *Journal of Cross-Cultural Psychology,* **33,** 286–302.

Leung, L. (2002). Loneliness, self-disclosure, and ICQ ('I seek you') use: The impact of the Internet, multimedia and virtual reality on behavior and society. *Cyberpsychology and Behavior,* **5**(3), 241–251. https://doi.org/10.1089/109493102760147240.

Leventhal, H. (1970). Findings and theory in the study of fear communications. In L. Berkowitz (Ed.), *Advances in experimental social psychology* (Vol. 5). Academic Press.

Levine, J. M. (1989). Reaction to opinion deviance in small groups. In P. Paulus (Ed.), *Psychology of group influence: New perspectives.* Erlbaum.

Levine, J. M., & Moreland, R. L. (1985). Innovation and socialization in small groups. In S. Moscovici, G. Mugny, & E. Van Avermaet (Eds.), *Perspectives on minority influence.* Cambridge University Press.

Levine, M. (1999). Rethinking bystander non-intervention: Social categorization and the evidence of witnesses at the James Bulger Murder trial. *Human Relations,* **52**(9), 1133–1155.

Levine, M., & Manning, R. (2013). Social identity, group processes, and helping in emergencies. *European Review of Social Psychology,* **24**(1), 225–251.

Levine, M., & Thompson, K. (2004). Identity, place, and bystander intervention: social categories and helping after natural disasters. *Journal of Social Psychology,* **144,** 229–245.

Levine, M., Prosser, A., Evans, D., & Reicher, S. (2005). Identity and emergency intervention: How social group membership and inclusiveness of group boundaries shape helping behavior. *Personality and Social Psychology Bulletin,* **31**(4), 443–453.

Levine, R. M. (1999). Identity and illness: The effects of identity salience and frame of reference on evaluation of illness and injury. *British Journal of Health Psychology,* **4,** 63–80.

Levine, R. V. (2001). Cross-cultural differences in helping strangers. *Journal of Cross-Cultural Psychology,* **32,** 543–560.

Levine, R. V. (2003). The kindness of strangers. *American Scientist,* **91,** 226–233.

Levine, R. V., Martinez, T. S., Brase, G., & Sorenson, K. (1994). Helping in 36 US cities. *Journal of Personality and Social Psychology,* **67,** 69–82.

Levitan, L. C., & Visser, P. S. (2007). The impact of the social context on resistance to persuasion: Effortful versus effortless responses to counter-attitudinal information. *Journal of Experimental Social Psychology,* **44,** 640–649.

Levine, M. (2012). Helping in emergencies: Revisiting Latané and Darley's bystander studies. In J. R. Smith & S. A. Haslam (Eds.), *Social psychology: Revisiting the classic studies*(pp. 192–208). Sage.

Levitt, M. (2013). Genes, environment and responsibility for violent behavior: 'Whatever genes one has it is preferable that you are prevented from going around stabbing people'. *New Genetics and Society,* **32**(1), 4–17.

Lew, A., Mann, T., Myers, H., Taylor, S., & Bower, J. (2007). Thin-ideal media and women's body dissatisfaction: Prevention using downward social comparisons on non-appearance dimensions. *Sex Roles,* **57**(7), 543–556.

Lewandowsky, S., Stritzke, W. G. K., Oberauer, K., & Morales, M. (2005). Memory for fact, fiction, and misinformation: The Iraq War 2003. *Psychological Science,* **16,** 190–195.

Lewin, K. (1936). *A dynamic theory of personality.* McGraw-Hill.

Lewis, C. S. (1952). *Mere Christianity.* Macmillan.

Lewis, C., & Lamb, M. E. (2006). Father–child relationships and children's development: A key to durable solutions? In Rt Hon. Lord Justice Thorpe & R. Budden (Eds.), *Durable solutions.* Family Law/Jordans.

Lewis, D. M. G., Al-Shawaf, L., Conroy-Beam, D., Asao, K., & Buss, D. M. (2017). Evolutionary psychology: A how-to guide. *American Psychologist,* **72**(4), 353–373.

Lewis, D., & Mills, G. Riley. (2012). *The pin drop principle: Captivate, influence, and communicate better using the time-tested methods of professional performers*(1st ed.). Jossey-Bass.

Lewis, I., Watson, B., Tay, R., & White, K. M. (2007). The role of fear appeals in improving driver safety: A review of the effectiveness of fear-arousing (threat) appeals in road safety advertising. *International Journal of Behavioural Consultation and Therapy,* **3**(2), 203–222.

Lewis, R. S., Goto, S. G., & King, L. L. (2008). Culture and context: East Asian American and European American differences in P3 event-related potentials and self-construal. *Personality and Social Psychology Bulletin,* **34,** 623–634.

Leyens, J. P., Paladino, M. P., Rodriguez, R. T., Vaes, J., Demoulin, S., Rodriguez, A. P., & Gaunt, R. (2000). The emotional side of prejudice: The attribution of secondary emotions to ingroups and outgroups. *Personality and Social Psychology Review,* **4,** 186–197.

Leyens, J.-P., Camino, L., Parke, R. D., & Berkowitz, L. (1975). Effects of movie violence on aggression in a field setting as a function of group dominance and cohesion. *Journal of Personality and Social Psychology,* **32,** 346–360.

Li, E. P. H., Min, H. J., Belk, R. W., Kimura, J., & Bahl, S. (2008). Skin lightening and beauty in four Asian cultures. *Advances in Consumer Research,* **35,** 444–449.

Li, N. P., Bailey, J. M., Kenrick, D. T., & Linsenmeier, J. A. (2002). The necessities and luxuries of mate preferences: Testing the tradeoffs. *Journal of Personality and Social Psychology,* **82**(6), 947.

Li, W. Q., Li, L. M. W., & Li, M. (2019). Residential mobility reduces ingroup favouritism in prosocial behaviour. *Asian Journal of Social Psychology,* **22**(1), 3–17.

Liberman, B.E., Block, C.J., & Koch, S.M. (2011). Diversity trainer preconceptions: The effects of trainer race and gender on perceptions of diversity trainer effectiveness. *Basic and Applied Social Psychology,* **33**(3), 279–293.

Lichtenstein, S., & Fischhoff, B. (1980). Training for calibration. *Organizational Behavior and Human Performance,* **26,** 149–171.

Lieberman, D., & Hatfield, E. (2018). Passionate love: Cross-cultural and evolutionary perspectives. In R. J. Sternberg & K. Sternberg (Eds.), *The new psychology of love.* Cambridge University Press.

Lieberman, M. D. (2007). The X- and C-Systems: The neural basis of automatic and controlled social cognition. In E. Harmon-Jones & P. Winkielman (Eds.), *Social neuroscience: Integrating biological and psychological explanations of social behavior.* Guilford Press.

Likert, R. (1932). A technique for the measurement of attitudes. *Archives of Psychology,* **140,** 1–55.

Likowski, K. U., Mühlberger, A., Seibt, B., Pauli, P., & Weyers, P. (2008). Modulation of facial mimicry by attitudes. *Journal of Experimental Social Psychology,* **44**(4), 1065–1072. https://doi.org/10.1016/j.jesp.2007.10.007.

Lilienfeld, S. O. (2012). Public skepticism of psychology: Why many people perceive the study of human behavior as unscientific. *American Psychologist,* **67**(2), 111–129.

Lim, L. (2009). A two-factor model of defensive pessimism and its relations with achievement motives. *Journal of Psychology,* **143**(3), 318–336.

Limanowski, J., & Hect, H. (2011). Where do we stand on locating the self? *Psychology,* **2**(4), 312–317.

Linden-Andersen, S., Markiewicz, D., & Dole, A.-B. (2009). Perceived similarity among adolescent friends: The role of reciprocity, friendship quality, and gender. *Journal of Early Adolescence,* **29**(5), 617–637.

Linder, J. R., & Gentile, D. A. (2009). Is the television rating system valid? Indirect, verbal, and physical aggression in programs viewed by fifth grade girls and associations with behavior. *Journal of Applied Developmental Psychology,* **30,** 286–297.

Lindsay, D. S., Hagen, L., Read, J. D., Wade, K. A., & Garry, M. (2004). True photographs and false memories. *Psychological Science,* **15,** 149–154.

Lindskold, S. (1981). The laboratory evaluation of GRIT: Trust, cooperation, aversion to using conciliation. Paper presented at the American Association for the Advancement of Science convention.

Lindskold, S., & Han, G. (1988). GRIT as a foundation for integrative bargaining. *Personality and Social Psychology Bulletin,* **14**(2), 335–345.

Lindskold, S., Bennett, R., & Wayner, M. (1976). Retaliation level as a foundation for subsequent conciliation. *Behavioral Science,* **21**(1), 13–18.

Lines, R. (2005). The structure and function of attitudes toward organizational change. *Human Resource Development Review,* **4**(1), 8–32.

Linssen, H., & Hagendoorn, L. (1994). Social and geographical factors in the explanation of the content of European nationality stereotypes. *British Journal of Social Psychology,* **33,** 165–182.

Lippa, R. A. (2007). The preferred traits of mates in a cross-national study of heterosexual and homosexual men and women: An examination of biological and cultural influences. *Archives of Sexual Behaviour,* **36,** 193–208.

Lippmann, W. (1922). *Public opinion.* Harcourt and Brace.

Little, A. C., Jones, B. C., DeBruine, L. M., & Feinberg, D. R. (2008). Symmetry and sexual dimorphism in human faces: Interrelated preferences suggest both signal quality. *Behavioral Ecology,* **19**(4), 902–908.

Livingston, G. (2014, April 11). Birth rates lag in Europe and the U.S., but the desire for kids does not. Pew Research Center: https://www.pewresearch.org/fact-tank/2014/04/11/birth-rates-lag-in-europe-and-the-u-s-but-the-desire-for-kids-does-not/

Livingston, G., & Cohn, D. (2010, June 25). Childlessness up among all women: Down among women with advanced degrees. Pew Research Center: https://www.pewsocialtrends.org/2010/06/25/childlessness-up-among-all-women-down-among-women-with-advanced-degrees/

Livingston, R. W. (2001). What you see is what you get: Systematic variability in perceptual-based social judgment. *Personality and Social Psychology Bulletin,* **27,** 1086–1096.

Livingstone, A. G., Young, H., & Manstead, A. S. R. (2011). 'We drink, therefore we are': The role of group identification and norms in sustaining and challenging heavy drinking 'culture'. *Group Processes and Intergroup Relations,* **14,** 637–649.

Livingstone, S. (2005). Assessing the research base for the policy debate over the effects of foodadvertising to children. *International Journal of Advertising,* **24**(3), 273–296.

Livingstone, S., Haddon, L., Görzig, A., & Olafsson, K. (2011). *Risks and safety on the Internet: The perspective of European children: Full findings and policy implications from the EU Kids Online Survey of 9–16 year olds and their parents in 25 countries.* LSE London: EU Kids Online.

Lo Presti, L., Chang, P., & Taylor, M. (2014). Young Australian adults' reactions to viewing personalised UV photoaged photographs. *The Australasian Medical Journal,* **7**(11), 454-461.

Locke, A., & Yarwood, G. (2017). Exploring the depths of gender, parenting and 'work': Critical discursive psychology and the 'missing voices' of involved fatherhood. *Community, Work & Family,* **20**(1), 4–18.

Locke, E. A., & Latham, G. P. (2002). Building a practically-useful theory of goal setting and task motivation: A35-year odyssey. *American Psychologist,* **57,** 701–717.

Lockwood, P., Dolderman, D., Sadler, P., & Gerchak, E. (2004). Feeling better about doing worse: Social comparisons within romantic relationships. *Journal of Personality and Social Psychology,* **87,** 80–95.

Loewenstein, J., Raghunathan, R., & Heath, C. (2011). The repetition-break plot structure makes effective television advertisements. *Journal of Marketing,* **75**(5), 105-119.

Loftus, E. F. (2003). Make-believe memories. *American Psychologist,* **58,** 867–873.

Loftus, E. F., & Bernstein, D. M. (2005). Rich false memories: The royal road to success. In A. F. Healy (Ed.), *Experimental cognitive psychology and its applications.* American Psychological Association.

Loftus, E. F., & Klinger, M. R. (1992). Is the unconscious smart or dumb? *American Psychologist,* **47,** 761–765.

Long, S., Mollen, D., & Smith, N. (2012). College women's attitudes towards sex workers. *Sex Roles,* **66**(1), 117–127.

Lonner, W. J. (1980). The search for psychological universals. In H. C. Triandis & W. W. Lambert (Eds.), *Handbook of cross-cultural psychology* (Vol. 1). Allyn and Bacon.

Lonner, W. J. (2015). Half a century of cross-cultural psychology: A grateful coda. *American Psychological Association,* **70**(8), 804–814.

Lonsdale, A. J., & North, A. C. (2012). Musical taste and the representativeness heuristic. *Psychology of Music,* **40**(2), 131–142.

Lord, C. G., Lepper, M. R., & Preston, E. (1984). Considering the opposite: A corrective strategy for social judgment. *Journal of Personality and Social Psychology,* **47,** 1231–1243.

Lord, K. R., Lee, M. S., & Choong, P. (2001). Differences in normative and informational social influence. *ACR North American Advances,* **28,** 280–285.

Losch, M. E., & Cacioppo, J. T. (1990). Cognitive dissonance may enhance sympathetic focus, but attitudes are changed to reduce negative affect rather than arousal. *Journal of Experimental Social Psychology,* **26,** 289–304.

Lott, A. J., & Lott, B. E. (1961). Group cohesiveness as interpersonal attraction: A review of relationships with antecedent and consequent variables. *Psychological Bulletin,* **64,** 259–309.

Lott, A. J., & Lott, B. E. (1965). Group cohesiveness as interpersonal attraction: A review of relationships with antecedent and consequent variables. *Psychological Bulletin,* **64**(4), 259.

Lott, A. J., & Lott, B. E. (1974). The role of reward in the formation of positive interpersonal attitudes. In T. Huston (Ed.), *Foundations of interpersonal attraction.* Academic Press.

Louis, M. R. (1980). Surprise and sense making: What newcomers experience in entering unfamiliar organizational settings. *Administrative Science Quarterly,* **25,** 226–251.

Lourel, M., Abdellaoui, S., Chevaleyre, S., Paltrier, M., & Gana, K. (2008). Relationships between psychological job demands, job control and burnout among firefighters. *North American Journal of Psychology,* **10,** 489–449.

Louro, M., Pieters, R., & Zeelenberg, M. (2007). Dynamics of multiple-goal pursuit. *Journal of Personality and Social Psychology,* **93,** 174–193.

Lowenstein, D. (2000, 20 May). Interview. *The World Today:* www.cnn.com/TRANSCRIPTS/0005/20/stc.00.html.

Lu, L. (2003). Defining the self-other relation: The emergence of a composite self. *Indigenous Psychological Research in Chinese Societies,* **20,** 139–207.

Lu, L., & Yang, K.-S. (2006). Emergence and composition of the traditional-modern bicultural self of people in contemporary Taiwanese societies. *Asian Journal of Social Psychology,* **9**(3), 167–175.

Lücken, M., & Simon, B. (2005). Cognitive and affective experiences of minority and majority members: The role of group size, status, and power. *Journal of Experimental Social Psychology,* **41,** 396–413.

Luhtanen, R., & Crocker, J. (1992). A collective self-esteem scale: Self-evaluation of one's social identity. *Personality & Social Psychology Bulletin,* **18,** 302–318.

Lukin, A. (2013). The present state of an Arctic charr (Salvelinus alpinus L.) population in Lake Imandra subjected to overfishing. *Journal of Ichthyology,* **53**(10), 804–808. https://doi.org/10.1134/S0032945213100056

Lumsdaine, A. A., & Janis, I. L. (1953). Resistance to 'counterpropaganda' produced by one-sided and two-sided 'propaganda' presentations. *Public Opinion Quarterly,* **17,** 311–318.

Lumsden, A., Zanna, M. P., & Darley, J. M. (1980). When a newscaster presents counter-additional information: Education or propaganda? Paper presented to the Canadian Psychological Association annual convention.

Luo, S., & Klohnen, E. C. (2005). Assortative mating and marital quality in newlyweds: A couple-centered approach. *Journal of Personality and Social Psychology,* **88,** 304–326.

Luo, S., & Zhang, G. (2009). What leads to romantic attraction: Similarity, reciprocity, security, or beauty? Evidence from a speed-dating study. *Journal of Personality,* **77**(4), 933–964.

Lykken, D. T. (1997). The American crime factory. *Psychological Inquiry,* **8,** 261–270.

Lynch, J. W., Kaplan, G. A., Pamuk, E. R., Cohen, R. D., Heck, K. E., Balfour, J. L., & Yen, I. H. (1998). Income inequality and mortality in metropolitan areas of the United States. *American Journal of Public Health,* **88,** 1074–1080.

Lynch, J. W., Smith, G. D., Kaplan, G. A., & House, J. S. (2000). Income inequality and health: A neo-material interpretation. *British Medical Journal,* **320,** 1200–1204.

Lynn, N., & Lea, S. J. (2003). A phantom menace and the new Apartheid: The social construction of asylum seekers in the United Kingdom. *Discourse and Society,* **14**(4), 425–452.

Lyons, L. (2003, September 23). Oh, boy: Americans still prefer sons. *Gallup Poll Tuesday Briefing:* www.gallup.com.

Lyubomirsky, S. (2001). Why are some people happier than others? The role of cognitive and motivational processes in well-being. *American Psychologist,* **56,** 239–249.

M

Ma, V., & Schoeneman, T. J. (1997). Individualism versus collectivism: A comparison of Kenyan and American self-concepts. *Basic and Applied Social Psychology,* **19,** 261–273.

Maass, A. (1998). Personal communication from Universita degli Studi di Padova.

Maass, A. (1999). Linguistic intergroup bias: Stereotype perpetuation through language. In M. P. Zanna (Ed.), *Advances in experimental social psychology,* **31,** 79–121.

Maass, A., Milesi, A., Zabbini, S., & Stahlberg, D. (1995). Linguistic intergroup bias: Differential expectancies or in-group protection? *Journal of Personality and Social Psychology,* **68,** 116–126.

Maass, A., Volparo, C., & Mucchi-Faina, A. (1996). Social influence and the verifiability of the issue under discussion: Attitudinal versus objective items. *British Journal of Social Psychology,* **35,** 15–26.

MacDonald, G., Zanna, M. P., & Holmes, J. G. (2000). An experimental test of the role of alcohol in relationship conflict. *Journal of Experimental Social Psychology,* **36,** 182–193.

MacDonald, T. K., & Ross, M. (1997). Assessing the accuracy of predictions about dating relationships: How and why do lovers' predictions differ from those made by observers? Unpublished manuscript, University of Lethbridge.

MacLeod, G. (2018). The Grenfell Tower atrocity. *City,* **22**(4), 460–489. https://doi.org/10.1080/13604813.2018.1507099

Macrae, C. N., & Bodenhausen, G. V. (2000). Social cognition: Thinking categorically about others. *Annual Review of Psychology,* **51,** 93–120.

Macrae, C. N., & Johnston, L. (1998). Help, I need somebody: Automatic action and inaction. *Social Cognition,* **16,** 400–417.

Macrae, C. N., & Martin, D. (2007). A boy primed Sue: Feature-based processing and person construal. *European Journal of Social Psychology,* **37,** 793–805.

Macrae, C. N., Alnwick, M. A., Milne, A. B., & Schloerscheidt, A. M. (2002). Person perception across the menstrual cycle: Hormonal influences on social cognitive functioning. *Psychological Science,* **13,** 532–536.

Macrae, C. N., Stangor, C., & Hewstone, M. (1996). *Stereotypes and stereotyping.* Guilford Press.

Maddux, J. E., & Gosselin, J. T. (2003). Self-efficacy. In M. R. Leary & J. P. Tangney (Eds.),

Handbook of self and identity. Guilford Press.

Madjar, N., Shklar, N., & Moshe, L. (2016). The role of parental attitudes in children's motivation toward homework assignments. *Psychology in the Schools*, **53**(2), 173–188. https://doi.org/10.1002/pits.21890

Madon, S., Jussim, L., Keiper, S., Eccles, J., Smith, A., & Palumbo, P. (1998). The accuracy and power of sex, social class, and ethnic stereotypes: A naturalistic study in person perception. *Personality and Social Psychology Bulletin*, **24**, 1304–1318.

Mae, L., Carlston, D. E., & Skowronski, J. J. (1999). Spontaneous trait transference to familiar communicators: Is a little knowledge a dangerous thing? *Journal of Personality and Social Psychology*, **77**(2), 233–246.

Maestripieri, D., Henry, A., & Nickels, N. (2017). Explaining financial and prosocial biases in favor of attractive people: Interdisciplinary perspectives from economics, social psychology, and evolutionary psychology. *Behavioral and Brain Sciences*, **40**, E19. https://doi.org/10.1017/S0140525X16000340, e19

Mähöen, T. A., Jasinskaja-Lahti, I., & Liebkind, K. (2011). The impact of perceived social norms, gender, and intergroup anxiety on the relationship between intergroup contact and ethnic attitudes of adolescents. *Journal of Applied Social Psychology*, **41**(8), 1877–1899.

Maio, G. R., & Haddock, G. (2007). Attitude change. In E. T. Higgins & A. W. Kruglanski (Eds.), *Social psychology: A handbook of basic principles*(pp. 565–586). Guilford Press.

Maister, L., Sebanz, N., Knoblich, G., & Tsakiris, M. (2013). Experiencing ownership over a dark-skinned body reduces implicit racial bias. *Cognition*, **128**(2), 170–178.

Malle, B. F. (2006). The actor–observer asymmetry in causal attribution: A (surprising) meta analysis. *Psychological Bulletin*, **132**, 895–919.

Malle, B. (2008). Fritz Heider's legacy: Celebrated insights, many of them misunderstood. *Social Psychology*, **39**(3), 163–173.

Malle, B. F., & Holbrook, J. (2012). Is there a hierarchy of social inferences? The likelihood and speed of inferring intentionality, mind, and personality. *Journal of Personality and Social Psychology*, **102**, 661–684.

Manago, A. M., Graham, M. B., Greenfield, P. M., & Salimkhan, G. (2008). Self-presentation and gender on MySpace. *Journal of Applied Developmental Psychology*, **29**, 446–458.

Maner, J. K., Kenrick, D. T., Becker, V., Robertson, T. E., Hofer, B., Neuberg, S. L., Delton, A. W., Butner, J., & Schaller, M. (2005). Functional projection: How fundamental social motives can bias interpersonal perception. *Journal of Personality and Social Psychology*, **88**, 63–78.

Manley, M. H., Diamond, L. M., & van Anders, S. M. (2015). Polyamory, monoamory, and sexual fluidity: A longitudinal study of identity and sexual trajectories. *Psychology of Sexual Orientation and Gender Diversity*, **2**(2), 168–180.

Mann, L. (1981). The baiting crowd in episodes of threatened suicide. *Journal of Personality and Social Psychology*, **41**(4), 703–709.

Mannarini, T., Roccato, M., & Russo, S. (2015). The false consensus effect: A trigger of radicalization in locally unwanted land uses conflicts? *Journal of Environmental Psychology*, **42**, 76–81.

Manning, R., Levine, M., & Collins, A. (2007). The Kitty Genovese murder and the social psychology of helping: The parable of the 38 witnesses. *American Psychologist*, **62**(6), 555–562.

Manning, R., Levine, M., & Collins, A. (2008). The legacy of the 38 witnesses and the importance of getting history right. *American Psychologist*, September, 562.

Mäntylä, T. (2013). Gender differences in multitasking reflect spatial ability. *Psychological Science*, **24**(4), 514–520.

Manuck, S. B., Flory, J. D., Ferrell, R. E., & Muldoon, M. F. (2004). Socio-economic status covaries with central nervous system serotonergic responsitivity as a function of allelic variation in the serotonin transporter gene-linked polymorphic region. *Psychoneuroendocrinology*, **21**(1), 20–25.

Marcoccia, M. (2012). The internet, intercultural communication and cultural variation. *Language and Intercultural Communication*, **12**(4), 353–368. https://doi.org/10.1080/14708477.2012.722101.

Marcus, S. (1974, January 13). Review of *Obedience to authority*. *New York Times Book Review*, pp. 1–2.

Marcus-Newhall, A., Pedersen, W. C., Carlson, M., & Miller, N. (2000). Displaced aggression is alive and well: A meta-analytic review. *Journal of Personality and Social Psychology*, **78**, 670–689.

Maree, J. E. (2010). 'No condom, no sex': Easy to say, but not possible for all South African women. *Health SA Gesondheid: Journal of Interdisciplinary Health Sciences*, **15**(1). http://link.galegroup.com.libezproxy.open.ac.uk/apps/doc/A249797521/AONE?u=tou&sid=AONE&xid=32773224

Margolin, G., Vickerman, K. A., Ramos, M. C., Duman Serrano, S., Gordis, E. B., Iturralde, E., Oliver, P. H., & Spies, L. A. (2009). Youth exposed to violence: Stability, co-occurrence and context. *Clinical Child and Family Psychology Review*, **12**, 39–54.

Marin, M. F., Morin-Major, J. K., Schramek, T. E., Beaupré, A., Perna, A., Juster, R. P., & Lupien, S. J. (2012). There is no news like bad news: Women are more remembering and stress reactive after reading real negative news than men. *PloS One*, **7**(10), e47189.

Markey, P. M. (2000). Bystander intervention in computer-mediated communication. *Computers in Human Behavior*, **16**(2), 183–188.

Markowitz, E. M., & Shariff, A. F. (2012). Climate change and moral judgement. *Nature Climate Change*, **2**(4), 243–247. https://doi.org/10.1038/nclimate1378

Marks, G., & Miller, N. (1987). Ten years of research on the false-consensus effect: An empirical and theoretical review. *Psychological Bulletin*, **102**, 72–90.

Markus, H. R. (2001, 7 October). Culture and the good life. Address to the Positive Psychology Summit conference, Washington, DC.

Markus, H. R. (2005). Telling less than we can know: The too tacit wisdom of social psychology. *Psychological Inquiry*, **16**(4), 180–184.

Markus, H. R., & Kitayama, S. (1991). Culture and the self: Implications for cognition, emotion, and motivation. *Psychological Review*, **98**, 224–253.

Markus, H. R., & Kitayama, S. (1991). Culture and the self: Implications for cognition, emotion, and motivation. *Psychological Review*, **98**(2), 224.

Markus, H. R., & Nurius, P. (1986). Possible selves. *American Psychologist*, **41**, 954–969.

Markus, H. R., & Wurf, E. (1987). The dynamic self-concept: A social psychological perspective. *Annual Review of Psychology*, **38**, 299–337.

Marques, J. M., Yzerbyt, V. Y., & Leyens, J. P. (1988). The "black sheep effect": Extremity of judgements towards in-group members as a function of group identification. *European Journal of Social Psychology*, **18**, 1–16.

Marsden, P., & Attia, S. (2005). A deadly contagion? *The Psychologist*, **18**, 152–155.

Marsh, H. W., & O'Mara, A. (2008). Reciprocal effects between academic self-concept, self-esteem, achievement, and attainment over seven adolescent years. Unidimensional and multidimensional perspectives of self-concept. *Personality and Social Psychology Bulletin*, **34**, 542–552.

Marsh, H. W., & Young, A. S. (1997). Causal effects of academic self-concept on academic achievement: Structural equation models of longitudinal data. *Journal of Educational Psychology*, **89**, 41–54.

Marsh, H. W., Kong, C.-K., & Hau, K.-T. (2000). Longitudinal multilevel models of the big-fish-little-pond effect on academic self-concept: Counterbalancing contrast and reflected-glory effects in Hong Kong schools. *Journal of Personality and Social Psychology*, **78**, 337–349.

Marshall, J. (2014). Mirror neurons. *Proceedings of the National Academy of Sciences of the United States of America*, **111**(18), 6531; https://doi.org/10.1073/pnas.1404652111

Martin, B. A., & Dula, C. S. (2010). More than skin deep: Perceptions of, and stigma against, tattoos. *College Student Journal*, **44**(1), 200–206. http://link.galegroup.com.libezproxy.open.ac.uk/apps/doc/A221092151/AONE?u=tou&sid=AONE&xid=92ba709f

Martin, J., & Sugarman, J. (2009). Does interpretation in psychology differ from interpretation in natural science? *Journal for the Theory of Social Behaviour*, **39**, 19–37.

Martin, L. L., & Erber, R. (2005). The wisdom of social psychology: Five commonalities and one concern. *Psychological Inquiry,* **16,** 194–202.

Martin, R., & Hewstone, M. (2008). Majority versus minority influence, message processing and attitude change: The source-context-elaboration model. *Advances in Experimental Social Psychology,* **40,** 237–326.

Martin, R., Hewstone, M., & Martin, P. Y. (2008). Majority versus minority: The role of message processing in determining resistance to counter-persuasion. *European Journal of Social Psychology,* **38,** 16–34.

Martino, S. C., Collins, R. L., Kanouse, D. E., Elliott, M., & Berry, S. H. (2005). Social cognitive processes mediating the relationship between exposure to television's sexual content and adolescents' sexual behavior. *Journal of Personality and Social Psychology,* **89,** 914–924.

Mase, A.S., Cho, H., & Prokopy, L.S.. (2015). Enhancing the Social Amplification of Risk Framework (SARF) by exploring trust, the availability heuristic, and agricultural advisors' belief in climate change. *Journal of Environmental Psychology,* **41,** 166–176.

Maslow, A. H. (1943). A theory of human motivation, *Psychological Review,* **50**(4), 370–396.

Masuda, T., & Kitayama, S. (2004). Perceiver-induced constraint and attitude attribution in Japan and the US: A case for the cultural dependence of the correspondence bias. *Journal of Experimental Social Psychology,* **40,** 409–416.

Matheson, K., Cole, B., & Majka, K. (2003). Dissidence from within: Examining the effects of intergroup context on group members' reactions to attitudinal opposition. *Journal of Experimental Social Psychology,* **39,** 161–169.

Matsick, J. L., Conley, T. D., Ziegler, A., Moors, A. C., & Rubin, J. D. (2014). Love and sex: Polyamorous relationships are perceived more favourably than swinging and open relationships. *Psychology & Sexuality,* 5(4), 339–348.

Matsumoto, D., & Juang, L. (2016). *Culture and psychology.* Cengage Learning.

Mattan, B. D., Wei, K. Y., Cloutier, J., & Kubota, J. T. (2018). The social neuroscience of race-based and status-based prejudice. *Current Opinion in Psychology,* **24,** 27–34.

Maxwell, G. M. (1985). Behaviour of lovers: Measuring the closeness of relationships. *Journal of Personality and Social Psychology,* **2,** 215–238.

Maxwell, R., Trotter, C., Verne, J., Brown, P., & Gunnell, D. (2007). Trends in admissions to hospital involving an assault using a knife or other sharp instrument, England, 1997–2005. *Journal of Public Health,* **29**(2), 186–190.

Mayunga, J. S. (2007). Understanding and applying the concept of community disaster resilience: A capital-based approach. Paper prepared for the Summer Academy for Social Vulnerability and Resilience Building, 22–28 July, Munich, Germany. http://www.ehs.unu.edu/file/get/3761.

Mazur, A., & Booth, A. (1998). Testosterone and dominance in men. *Behavioral and Brain Sciences,* **21,** 353–363.

Mazzoni, A. (2020, January 2). Local hero saves two families who were almost killed by bushfires in his tinny moments after watching his own house burn down. *Daily Mail Australia:* https://www.dailymail.co.uk/news/article-7845389/Local-hero-saves-dozen-tourists-tinny-watching-house-burn-down.html

Mazzuca, J. (2002, 20 August). Teens shrug off movie sex and violence. *Gallup Tuesday Briefing:* www.gallup.com.

Mbeng, L. O., Probert, J., Phillips, P. S., & Fairweather, R. (2009). Assessing public attitudes and behaviour to household waste management in Cameroon to drive strategy development: A Q methodological approach. *Sustainability,* **1**(3), 556–572.

McAndrew, F. T. (1981). Pattern of performance and attributions of ability and gender. *Journal of Personality and Social Psychology,* **7,** 583–587.

McAndrew, F. T. (2002). New evolutionary perspectives on altruism: Multilevel-selection and costly-signaling theories. *Current Directions in Psychological Science,* **11,** 79–82.

McArthur, L. A. (1972). The how and what of why: Some determinants of consequences of causal attributions. *Journal of Personality and Social Psychology,* **22,** 171–193.

McCann, C. D., & Hancock, R. D. (1983). Self-monitoring in communicative interactions: Social cognitive consequences of goal-directed message modification. *Journal of Experimental Social Psychology,* **19,** 109–121.

McCauley, C. D. (2001). Leader training and development. In S. J. Zaccaro & R. J. Klimoski (Eds.), *The nature of organizational leadership: Understanding the performance imperatives confronting today's leaders.* Jossey Bass.

McClure, J. (1998). Discounting causes of behavior: Are two reasons better than one? *Journal of Personality and Social Psychology,* **74,** 7–20.

McConahay, J. B. (1986). Modern racism, ambivalence, and the modern racism scale. In J. F. Dovidio and S. L. Gaertner (Eds.), *Prejudice, discrimination and racism.* Academic Press.

McConahay, J. B., & Hough, J. C., Jr (1976). Symbolic racism. *Journal of Social Issues,* **32,** 23–45.

McCormack, A., & Griffiths, M. D. (2012). Motivating and inhibiting factors in online gambling behaviour: A grounded theory study, *International Journal of Mental Health and Addiction,* **10**(1), 39–53. https://doi-org.libezproxy.open.ac.uk/10.1007/s11469-010-9300-7

McCredie, J. (2011). *Making girls and boys : Inside the science of sex.* University of New South Wales Press.

McDermott, R., Tingley, D., Cowden, J., Frazzetto, G., & Johnson, D. D. (2009). Monoamine oxidase A gene (MAOA) predicts behavioral aggression following provocation. *Proceedings of the National Academy of Sciences,* **106**(7), 2118–2123.

McDermott, T. (2005). *Perfect soldiers: The hijackers: Who they were, why they did it.* HarperCollins.

McDonagh, K. J., & Paris, N. M. (2012). The leadership labyrinth: Career advancement for women. *Frontiers of Health Services Management,* **28**(4), 22–28. https://doi.org/10.1097/01974520-201204000-00004

McDougall, W. (1908). *An introduction to social psychology.* Methuen.

McDowell, D. J., & Parke, R. D. (2009). Parental correlates of children's peer relations: An empirical test of a tripartite model. *Developmental Psychology,* **45,** 224–235. https://doi.org/10.1037/a0014305

McFadzean, E., & McKenzie, J. (2001). Facilitating virtual learning groups: A practical approach. *Journal of Management Development,* **20**(6), 470–494.

McFall, R. M. (2000). Elaborate reflections on a simple manifesto. *Applied and Preventive Psychology,* **9,** 5–21.

McFarland, C., & Ross, M. (1985). The relation between current impressions and memories of self and dating partners. Unpublished manuscript, University of Waterloo.

McGannon, K.R., & Smith, B. (2015). Centralizing culture in cultural sport psychology research: The potential of narrative inquiry and discursive psychology. *Psychology of Sport & Exercise,* **17,** 79–87.

McGarty, C., Turner, J. C., Oakes, P. J., & Haslam, S. A. (1993). The creation of uncertainty in the influence process: The roles of stimulus information and disagreement with similar others. *European Journal of Social Psychology,* **23,** 17–38.

McGee, H., & Johnson, D. (2015). Performance motivation as the behaviorist views it. *Performance Improvement,* **54**(4), 15-21.

McGillicuddy, N. B., Welton, G. L., & Pruitt, D. G. (1987). Third-party intervention: A field experiment comparing three different models. *Journal of Personality and Social Psychology,* **53,** 104–112.

McGinn, A. P. (1998, 20 June). Hidden forces mask crisis in world fisheries. *Worldwatch Institute:* www.worldwatch.org.

McGinty, K., Knox, D., & Zusman, M. E. (2007). Friends with benefits: Women want 'friends,' men want 'benefits'. *College Student Journal,* **41**(4), 1128–1131.

McGlone, M. S., & Tofighbakhsh, J. (2000). Birds of a feather flock conjointly (?): Rhyme as reason in aphorisms. *Psychological Science,* **11,** 424–428.

McGlothlin, H., & Killen, M. (2005). Children's perceptions of intergroup and intragroup similarity and the role of social experience. *Journal of Applied Developmental Psychology,* **26**(6), 680–698.

McGlynn, R. P., Tubbs, D. D., & Holzhausen, K. G. (1995). Hypothesis generation in groups constrained by evidence. *Journal of Experimental Social Psychology,* **31,** 64–81.

McGraw, A. P., Mellers, B. A., & Tetlock, P. E. (2005). Expectations and emotions of Olympic athletes. *Journal *of Experimental Social Psychology,* **41,** 438–446.

McGregor, I., Zanna, M. P., Holmes, J. G., & Spencer, S. J. (2001). Conviction in the face of uncertainty: Going to extremes and being oneself. *Journal of Personality and Social Psychology,* **80,** 472–478.

McGuckin, C., & Lewis, C. A. (2003). A cross-national perspective on school bullying in Northern Ireland: A supplement to Smith et al. (1999). *Psychological Reports,* **93,** 279–287.

McGuckin, C., & Lewis, C. A. (2008). Management of bullying in Northern Ireland schools: A prelegislative survey. *Educational Research,* **50**(1), 9–23.

McGuire, W. J. (1964). Inducing resistance to persuasion: Some contemporary approaches. In L. Berkowitz (Ed.), *Advances in experimental social psychology* (Vol. 1). Academic Press.

McGuire, W. J. (1985). Attitudes and attitude change. In G. Lindzey and E. Aronson (Eds.), *The handbook of social psychology* (Vol. 2). Random House.

McGuire, W. J., & Padawer-Singer, A. (1978). Trait salience in the spontaneous self-concept. *Journal of Personality and Social Psychology,* **33,** 743–754.

McGuire, W. J., McGuire, C. V., & Winton, W. (1979). Effects of household sex composition on the salience of one's gender in the spontaneous self-concept. *Journal of Experimental Social Psychology,* **15,** 77–90.

McKay-Nesbitt, J., Manchanda, R. V., Smith, M. C., & Huhmann, B. A. (2011). Effects of age, need for cognition, and affective intensity on advertising effectiveness. *Journal of Business Research,* **64**(1), 12–17.

McKenna, K. Y. A., & Bargh, J. A. (2000). Plan 9 from cyberspace: The implications of the Internet for personality and social psychology. *Personality and Social Psychology Review,* **4,** 57–75.

McKenna, K. Y. A., Green, A. S., & Gleason, M. E. J. (2002). Relationship formation on the Internet: What's the big attraction? *Journal of Social Issues,* **58,** 9–31.

McKeown, S., & Dixon, J. (2017). The 'contact hypothesis': Critical reflections and future directions. *Social and Personality Psychology Compass,* **11**(1), e12295.

McKimmie, B. M., Terry, D. J., Hogg, M. A., Manstead, A. S., Spears, R., & Doosje, B. (2003). I'm a hypocrite, but so is everyone else: Group support and the reduction of cognitive dissonance. *Group Dynamics: Theory, Research, and Practice,* **7**(3), 214–224.

McManus, F., Peerbhoy, D., Larkin, M., & Clark, D.M. (2010). Learning to change a way of being: An interpretative phenomenological perspective on cognitive therapy for social phobia. *Journal of Anxiety Disorders,* **24**(6), 581–589. https://doi.org/10.1016/j.janxdis.2010.03.018

McMillen, D. L., & Austin, J. B. (1971). Effect of positive feedback on compliance following transgression. *Psychonomic Science,* **24,** 59–61.

McPherson, M., Smith-Lovin, L., & Cook, J. M. (2001). Birds of a feature: Homophily in social networks. *Annual Review of Sociology,* **27,** 415–444.

McVie, S. (2010). *Gang membership and knife-carrying: Findings from the Edinburgh study of youth transitions and crime.* Scottish Government Social Research.

Mead, G. H. (1934). *Mind, self, and society.* University of Chicago Press.

Medvec, V. H., & Savitsky, K. (1997). When doing better means feeling worse: The effects of categorical cutoff points on counterfactual thinking and satisfaction. *Journal of Personality and Social Psychology,* **72,** 1284–1296.

Medvec, V. H., Madey, S. F., & Gilovich, T. (1995). When less is more: Counterfactual thinking and satisfaction among Olympic medalists. *Journal of Personality and Social Psychology,* **69,** 603–610.

Meek, R. (2011). The possible selves of young fathers in prison. *Journal of Adolescence,* **34**(5), 941–949.

Meglino, B. M. (1976). The effect of evaluation on dominance characteristics: An extension of social facilitation theory. *Journal of Psychology,* **92**(2), 167–172. https://doi.org/10.1080/00223980.1976.9921351

Mehl, M. R., & Pennebaker, J. W. (2003). The sounds of social life: A psychometric analysis of students' daily social environments and natural conversations. *Journal of Personality and Social Psychology,* **84,** 857–870.

Meier, B. P., & Wilkowski, B. M. (2013). Reducing the tendency to aggress: Insights from social and personality psychology. *Social and Personality Psychology Compass,* **7**(6), 343-354.

Meijer, M. M., de Bakker, F. G., Smit, J. H., & Schuyt, T. (2006). Corporate giving in the Netherlands 1995–2003: Exploring the amounts involved and the motivations for donating. *International Journal of Nonprofit and Voluntary Sector Marketing,* **11**(1), 13–28.

Mellers, B., Hertwig, R., & Kahneman, D. (2001). Do frequency representations eliminate conjunction effects: An exercise in adversarial collaboration. *Psychological Science,* **12,** 269–275.

Melzack, R., & Wall, P. D. (1988). *The challenge of pain.* Penguin Books.

Menec, V. H., & Weiner, B. (2000). Observer's reactions to genetic testing: The role of hindsight bias and judgements of responsibility. *Journal of Applied Social Psychology,* **30**(8), 1670–1690.

Merikle, P. M., Smilek, D., & Eastwood, J. D. (2001). Perception without awareness: Perspectives from cognitive psychology. *Cognition,* **79,** 115–134.

Merlin, J. S., Young, S. R., Johnson, M. O., Saag, M., Demonte, W., Kerns, R., Bair, M. J., Kertesz, S., Turan, J. M., Kilgore, M., Clay, O. J., Pekmezi, D., & Davies, S. (2018). Intervention mapping to develop a social cognitive theory-based intervention for chronic pain tailored to individuals with HIV. *Contemporary Clinical Trials Communications,* **10,** 9–16. https://doi.org/10.1016/j.conctc.2018.02.004

Merton, R. K. (1948). The self-fulfilling prophecy. *Antioch Review,* **8,** 193–210.

Messias, E. (2003). Income inequality, illiteracy rate, and life expectancy in Brazil. *American Journal of Public Health,* **93**(8), 1294-1296.

Messner, M., Reinhard, M., & Sporer, S. L. (2008). Compliance through direct persuasive appeals: The moderating role of communicator's attractiveness in interpersonal persuasion. *Social Influence,* **3**(2), 67–83. https://doi.org/10.1080/15534510802045261

Mesters, I., Gijsbers, B., & Bartholomew, L. K. (2018). Promoting sustained breastfeeding of infants at risk for asthma: Explaining the 'active ingredients' of an effective program using intervention mapping. *Frontiers in Public Health.* 6, p. 87. https://doi.org/10.3389/fpubh.2018.00087

Meston, C. M., & Frohlich, P. F. (2003). Love at first fright: Partner salience moderates roller-coaster-induced excitation transfer. *Archives of Sexual Behavior,* **32**(6), 537–544.

Mettee, D. R., &Aronson(1974). Affective reactions to appraisal from others. In T. L. Huston (Ed.), *Foundations of interpersonal attraction* (pp. 236–284). Academic Press.

Meyer, I. H. (2015). Resilience in the study of minority stress and health of sexual and gender minorities. *Psychology of Sexual Orientation and Gender Diversity,* **2**(3), 209–213.

Mezulis, A. H., Abramson, L. Y., Hyde, J. S., & Hankin, B. L. (2004). Is there a universal positivity bias in attributions? A meta-analytic review of individual, developmental, and cultural differences in the self-serving attributional bias. *Psychological Bulletin,* **130,** 711–747.

Michaels, J. W., Blommel, J. M., Brocato, R. M., Linkous, R. A., & Rowe, J. S. (1982). Social facilitation and inhibition in a natural setting. *Replications in Social Psychology,* **2,** 21–24.

Michie, S., Lester, K., Pinto, J., & Marteau, T. M. (2005). Communicating risk information in genetic counseling: An observational study. *Health Education & Behavior,* **32**(5), 589–598.

Mickelson, K. D., Kessler, R. C., & Shaver, P. R. (1997). Adult attachment in a nationally representative sample. *Journal of Personality and Social Psychology,* **73,** 1092–1106.

Miettinen, A., Rotkirch, A., Szalma, I., Donno, A., & Tanturri, M.L. (2015). Increasing childlessness in Europe: Time trends and country differences. Families and Societies Working Paper Series, 33:http://www.familiesandsocieties.eu/wp-content/uploads/2015/03/WP33MiettinenEtAl2015.pdf

Mikulincer, M., & Shaver, P. R. (2001). Attachment theory and intergroup bias: Evidence that priming the secure base schema attenuates negative reactions to outgroups. *Journal of Personality and Social Psychology,* **81,** 97–115.

Mikulincer, M., Florian, V., & Hirschberger, G. (2003). The existential function of close relationships: Introducing death into the science of love. *Personality and Social Psychology Review,* **7,** 20–40.

Mikulincer, M., Shaver, P. R., Gillath, O., & Nitzberg, R. A. (2005). Attachment, caregiving, and altruism: Boosting attachment security increases compassion and helping. *Journal of Personality and Social Psychology,* **89,** 817–839.

Milgram, A. (2000). My personal view of Stanley Milgram. In T. Blass (Ed.), *Obedience to authority: Current perspectives on the Milgram paradigm.* Erlbaum.

Milgram, S. (1961, December). Nationality and conformity. *Scientific American*, pp. 45–51.

Milgram, S. (1963). Behavioral study of obedience. *Journal of Abnormal and Social Psychology,* **67,** 371–378.

Milgram, S. (1965). Some conditions of obedience and disobedience to authority. *Human Relations,* **18,** 57–76.

Milgram, S. (1974). *Obedience to authority: An experimental view.* Harper & Row.

Milgram, S., Bickman, L., & Berkowitz, L. (1969). Note on the drawing power of crowds of different size. *Journal of Personality and Social Psychology,* **13,** 79–82.

Miller, A. G. (2004). What can the Milgram obedience experiments tell us about the Holocaust? Generalizing from the social psychological laboratory. In A. G. Miller (Ed.), *The social psychology of good and evil.* Guilford Press.

Miller, A. G. (2006). Exonerating harmdoers: Some problematic implications of social-psychological explanations. Paper presented to the Society of Personality and Social Psychology convention.

Miller, C. (2010). Guilt and helping. *International Journal of Ethics,* **6**(2–3), 231–252.

Miller, C. B. (2009). Yes we did! Basking in reflected glory and cutting off reflected failure in the 2008 Presidential Election. *Analyses of Social Issues and Public Policy,* **9**(1), 283–296.

Miller, C. E., & Anderson, P. D. (1979). Group decision rules and the rejection of deviates. *Social Psychology Quarterly,* **42,** 354–363.

Miller, J. G., Bland, C., Källberg-Shroff, M., Tseng, C. Y., Montes-George, J., Ryan, K., Das, R., & Chakravarthy, S. (2014). Culture and the role of exchange vs. communal norms in friendship. *Journal of Experimental Social Psychology,* **53,** 79–93. https://doi.org/10.1016/j.jesp.2014.02.006

Miller, K., Wakefield, J. R., & Sani, F. (2016). Greater number of group identifications is associated with healthier behaviour in adolescents. *British Journal of Developmental Psychology,* **34**(2), 291–305.

Miller, L. C., Berg, J. H., & Archer, R. L. (1983). Openers: Individuals who elicit intimate self-disclosure. *Journal of Personality and Social Psychology,* **44,** 1234–1244.

Miller, L. E., & Grush, J. E. (1986). Individual differences in attitudinal versus normative determination of behavior. *Journal of Experimental Social Psychology,* **22,** 190–202.

Miller, L. E., Grabell, A., Thomas, A., Bermann, E., & Graham-Bermann, S. A. (2012). The associations between community violence, television violence, intimate partner violence, parent–child aggression, and aggression in sibling relationships of a sample of preschoolers. *Psychology of Violence,* **2**(2), 165–178.

Miller, N. & Brewer, M. B. (Eds.) (1984). *Groups in contact: The psychology of desegregation.* Academic Press.

Miller, N. (2002). Personalization and the promise of contact theory. *Journal of Social Issues,* **58,** 387–410.

Miller, N. E. (1941). The frustration–aggression hypothesis. *Psychological Review,* **48,** 337–342.

Miller, N., Maruyama, G., Beaber, R. J., & Valone, K. (1976). Speed of speech and persuasion. *Journal of Personality and Social Psychology,* **34,** 615–624.

Miller, N., Pedersen, W. C., Earleywine, M., & Pollock, V. E. (2003). A theoretical model of triggered displaced aggression. *Personality and Social Psychology Review,* **7,** 75–97.

Miller, P. A., Kozu, J., & Davis, A. C. (2001). Social influence, empathy, and prosocial behavior in cross-cultural perspective. In W. Wosinska, R. B. Cialdini, D. W. Barrett & J. Reykowski (Eds.), *The practice of social influence in multiple cultures.* Erlbaum.

Miller, P. J. E., & Rempel, J. K. (2004). Trust and partner enhancing attributions in close relationships. *Personality and Social Psychology Bulletin,* **30,** 695–705.

Miller, R. S., & Schlenker, B. R. (1985). Egotism in group members: Public and private attributions of responsibility for group performance. *Social Psychology Quarterly,* **48,** 85–89.

Miller, R., & Lammas, N. (2010). Social media and its implications for viral marketing. *Asia Pacific Public Relations Journal,* **11**(1), 1-9.

Mims, P. R., Hartnett, J. J., & Nay, W. R. (1975). Interpersonal attraction and help volunteering as a function of physical attractiveness. *Journal of Psychology,* **89,** 125–131.

Mischel, W. (1968). *Personality and assessment.* Wiley.

Mishna, F., Khoury-Kassabri, M., Gadalla, T., & Daciuk, J. (2012). Risk factors for involvement in cyber bullying: Victims, bullies and bully-victims. *Children and Youth Services,* **34**(1), 63–70.

Mishna, F., Saini, M., & Solomon, S. (2009). Ongoing and online: Children and youth's perceptions of cyber bullying. *Children and Youth Services Review,* **31**(12), 1222–1228.

Mita, T. H., Dermer, M., & Knight, J. (1977). Reversed facial images and the mere-exposure hypothesis. *Journal of Personality and Social Psychology,* **35,** 597–601.

Mitchell, G. (2012). Revisiting truth or triviality: The external validity of research in the psychological laboratory. *Perspectives on Psychological Science,* **7**(2), 109–117.

Mitchell, M. S., Cropanzano, R. S., & Quisenberry, D. M. (2012). Social exchange theory, exchange resources, and interpersonal relationships: A modest resolution of theoretical difficulties. In *Handbook of social resource theory* (pp. 99–118). Springer.

Mitchell, T. L., Haw, R. M., Pfeifer, J. E., & Meissner, C. A. (2005). Racial bias in mock juror decision-making: A meta-analytic review of defendant treatment. *Law and Human Behavior,* **29,** 621–637.

Mitchell, T. R., & Thompson, L. (1994). A theory of temporal adjustments of the evaluation of events: Rosy prospection and rosy retrospection. In C. Stubbart, J. Porac, & J. Meindl (Eds.), *Advances in managerial cognition and organizational information processing.* JAI Press.

Mitchell, T. R., Thompson, L., Peterson, E., & Cronk, R. (1997). Temporal adjustments in the evaluation of events: The 'rosy view'. *Journal of Experimental Social Psychology,* **33,** 421–448.

Moeller, F. G., Dougherty, D. M., Swann, A. C., Collins, D., Davis, C. M., & Cherek, D. R. (1996). Tryptophan depletion and aggressive responding in healthy males. *Psychopharmacology,* **126**(2), 97–103.

Moffitt, T. E., Arseneault, L., Belsky, D., Dickson, N., Hancox, R. J., Harrington, H., Houts, R., Poulton, R., Roberts, B. W., Ross, S., Sears, M. R., Thomson, M. W., & Caspi, A. (2011). A gradient of childhood self-control predicts health, wealth, and public safety. *Proceedings of the National Academy of Sciences,* **108**(7), 2693–2698.

Moffitt, T., Caspi, A., Sugden, K., Taylor, A., Craig, I. W., Harrington, H., McClay, J., Mill, J., Martin, J., Braithwaite, A., & Poulton, R. (2003). Influence of life stress on depression: Moderation by a polymorphism in the 5-HTT gene. *Science,* **301,** 386–389.

Mojtahedi, D., Ioannous, M., & Hammond, L. (2018). Group size, misinformation and unanimity influences on co-witness judgements. *Journal of Forensic Psychiatry & Psychology,* **29**(5), 844–865.

Molloy, M. (2013). Dozens of commuters help free woman trapped under train in Japan. *Metro,* 23 July:https://metro.co.uk/2013/07/23/dozens-of-commuters-help-free-woman-trapped-under-train-in-japan-3894738/

Mongeau, P. A. (2013). Fear appeals. In J. P. Dillard & L. Shen (Eds.), *The handbook of persuasion* (2nd ed., pp. 184–199). Sage.

Mongeau, P. A., Knight, K., Williams, J., Eden J., & Shaw, C. (2013). Identifying and explicating variation among friends with benefits relationships. *Journal of Sex Research,* **50**(1), 37–47. https://doi.org/10.1080/00224499.2011.623797

Monin, B., & Norton, M. I. (2003). Perceptions of a fluid consensus: Uniqueness bias, false consensus, false polarization, and pluralistic ignorance in a water conservation crisis. *Personality and Social Psychology,* **29,** 559–567.

Montag, C. (2018). Cross-cultural research projects as an effective solution for the replication crisis in psychology and psychiatry. *Asian Journal of Psychiatry,* **38,** 31–32.

Montoya, R. M., & Horton, R. S. (2004). On the importance of cognitive evaluation as a determinant of interpersonal attraction. *Journal of Personality and Social Psychology,* **86,** 696–712.

Montoya, R. M., & Horton, R. S. (2014). A two-dimensional model for the study of interpersonal attraction. *Personality and Social Psychology Review,* **18**(1), 59–86. https://doi.org/10.1177/1088868313501887

Moons, W. G., Mackie D. M., & Garcia-Marques,

T. (2009). The impact of repetition-induced familiarity on agreement with weak and strong arguments. *Journal of Personality and Social Psychology,* **96**(1), 32–44.

Moore, D. A., & Healy, P. J. (2008). The trouble with overconfidence. *Psychological Review,* **115**, 502–517. https://doi.org/10.1037/0033-295X.115.2.502

Moore, D. W. (2003, 18 March). Public approves of Bush ultimatum by more than 2-to-1 margin. *Gallup News Service:* www.gallup.com.

Moore, D. W. (2004, 20 April). Ballot order: Who benefits? *Gallup Poll Tuesday Briefing:* www.gallup.com.

Moore, M. T., & Fresco, D. M. (2012). Depressive realism: A meta-analytic review. *Clinical Psychology Review,* **32**(6), 496–509.

Moorhouse, J. C., & Wanner, B. (2006). Does gun control reduce crime or does crime increase gun control. *Cato Journal,* **26**(1), 103–124.

Morales, A. J., Dong, X., Bar-Yam, Y., & 'Sandy' Pentland, A. (2019). Segregation and polarization in urban areas. *Royal Society Open Science,* **6**(10), 190573. https://doi.org/10.1098/rsif.2016.1048.

Moreland, R. L. (1985). Social categorization and the assimilation of 'new' group members. *Journal of Personality and Social Psychology,* **48**, 1173–1190.

Moreland, R. L., & Zajonc, R. B. (1977). Is stimulus recognition a necessary condition for the occurrence of exposure effects? *Journal of Personality and Social Psychology,* **35**, 191–199.

Morgan, E. M., Richards, T. C., & VanNess, E. M. (2010). Comparing narratives of personal and preferred partner characteristics in online dating advertisements. *Computers in Human Behavior,* **26**(5), 883–888.

Mori, K., Ito-Koyama, A., Arai, M., & Hanayama, A. (2014). Boys, be independent! Conformity development of Japanese children in the Asch experiment without using confederates. *Psychology,* **5**(7), 617–623.

Morin, A. (2017). The self-reflective function of inner speech: Twelve years later. *Inner Speech Anthology.*

Morin, A., & Everett, J. (1990). Inner speech as a mediator of self-awareness, self-consciousness, and self-knowledge: An hypothesis. *New Ideas in Psychology,* **8**(3), 337-356.

Morris, W. N., & Miller, R. S. (1975). The effects of consensus-breaking and consensus-preempting partners on reduction of conformity. *Journal of Experimental Social Psychology,* **11**, 215–223.

Morrish, L. (2019). Pressure vessels: The epidemic of poor mental health among higher education staff. *HEPI Occcasional Paper, 20.* https://www.hepi.ac.uk/wp-content/uploads/2019/05/HEPI-Pressure-Vessels-Occasional-Paper-20.pdf

Morrison, M., Gan, S., Dubelaar, C., & OppewalIn, H. (2011). In-store music and aroma influences on shopper behaviour and satisfaction. *Journal of Business Research,* **64**(6), 558–564.

Morrison, T. G., Beaulieu, D., Brockman, M., & Beaglaoich, C. Ó. (2013). A comparison of polyamorous and monoamorous persons: Are there differences in indices of relationship well-being and sociosexuality? *Psychology & Sexuality,* **4**(1), 75–91.

Morrison, V., & Bennett, P. (2006). *An introduction to health psychology.* Pearson-Prentice Hall.

Morry, M. M. (2004, June). A test of the attraction–similarity hypothesis among same-sex friends. Talk presented at the 65th Canadian Psychology Association Annual Convention, St John's, NF, Canada.

Morry, M. M. (2005). Relationship satisfaction as a predictor of similarity ratings: A test of the attraction-similarity hypothesis. *Journal of Social and Personal Relationships,* **22**(4), 561–584.

Morry, M. M., Kito, M. I. E., & Ortiz, L. (2011). The attraction–similarity model and dating couples: Projection, perceived similarity, and psychological benefits. *Personal Relationships,* **18**(1), 125-143.

Morton, B. (2005). Over fishing: Hong Kong's fishing crisis finally arrives. *Marine Pollution Bulletin,* **50**(10), 1031–1035.

Morton, T. A., Postmes, T., & Jetten, J. (2007). Playing the game: When group success is more important than downgrading deviants. *European Journal of Social Psychology,* **37**, 599–616.

Moscovici, S. (1985). Social influence and conformity. In G. Lindzey & E. Aronson (Eds.), *The handbook of social psychology* (3rd ed.). Erlbaum.

Moscovici, S. (1988). Notes towards a description of social representations. *European Journal of Social Psychology,* **18**, 211–250.

Moscovici, S., & Zavalloni, M. (1969). The group as a polarizer of attitudes. *Journal of Personality and Social Psychology,* **12**(2), 125–135.

Moscovici, S., Lage, E., & Naffrechoux, M. (1969). Influence of a consistent minority on the responses of a majority in a color perception task. *Sociometry,* **32**(4), 365-380.

Mosquera, P. M. R., Manstead, A. S. R., & Fischer, A. H. (2002). The role of honour concerns in emotional reactions to offences. *Cognition and Emotion,* **16**(1), 143–163.

Moston, S., Engelberg, T., & Skinner, J. (2015). Self-fulfilling prophecy and the future of doping. *Psychology of Sport and Exercise,* **16**(2), 201–207.

Motherhood Project (2001, 2 May). Watch out for children: A mothers' statement to advertisers. Institute for American Values: www.watchoutforchildren.org.

Moyaho, A., Rivas-Zamudio, X., Ugarte, A., Eguibar, J. R., & Valencia, J. (2014). Smell facilitates auditory contagious yawning in stranger rats. *Animal Cognition,* **18**, 279–290.

Mucchi-Faina, A., & Pagliaro, S. (2008). Minority influence: The role of ambivalence toward the source. *European Journal of Social Psychology,* **38**(4), 612–623.

Mulac, A., & Lundell, T. L. (1994). Effects of gender-linked language differences in adults' written discourse: Multivariate tests of language effects. *Language and Communication,* **14**(3), 299–309.

Mulac, A., Bradac, J. J., & Gibbons, P. (2001). Empirical support for the gender-as-culture hypothesis: An intercultural analysis of male/female language differences. *Human Communication Research,* **27**(1), 121–152.

Mulder, R., Pouwelse, M., Lodewijkx, H., & Bolman, C. (2014). Workplace mobbing and bystanders' helping behaviour towards victims: The role of gender, perceived responsibility and anticipated stigma by association. *International Journal of Psychology,* **49**(4), 304–312.

Mullen, B., & Copper, C. (1994). The relation between group cohesiveness and performance: An integration. *Psychological Bulletin,* **115**, 210–227.

Mullen, B., & Goethals, G. R. (1990). Social projection, actual consensus and valence. *British Journal of Social Psychology,* **29**, 279–282.

Mullen, B., & Riordan, C. A. (1988). Self-serving attributions for performance in naturalistic settings: A metaanalytic review. *Journal of Applied Social Psychology,* **18**, 3–22.

Mullen, B., Anthony, T., Salas, E., & Driskell, J. E. (1994). Group cohesiveness and quality of decision making: An integration of tests of the groupthink hypothesis. *Small Group Research,* **25**, 189–204.

Mullen, B., Bryant, B., & Driskell, J. E. (1997). Presence of others and arousal: An integration. *Group Dynamics: Theory, Research, and Practice,* **1**, 52–64.

Muncer, S., Campbell, A., Jervis, V., & Lewis, R. (2001). Ladettes, social representations and aggression. *Sex Roles,* **44**, 33–44.

Muralidharan, S., Dillistone, K., & Shin, J. H. (2011). The Gulf Coast oil spill: Extending the theory of image restoration discourse to the realm of social media and beyond petroleum. *Public Relations Review,* **37**(3), 226–232.

Muraven, M., Tice, D. M., & Baumeister, R. F. (1998). Self-control as a limited resource: Regulatory depletion patterns. *Journal of Personality and Social Psychology,* **74**, 774–790.

Murphy, R. F. (1990). *The body silent.* Norton.

Murray, S. L., & Holmes, J. G. (1997). A leap of faith? Positive illusions in romantic relationships. *Personality and Social Psychology Bulletin,* **23**, 586–604.

Murray, S. L., Holmes, J. G., & Collins, N. J. (2006). Optimizing assurance: The risk regulation system in relationships. *Psychological Bulletin,* **5**, 641–666.

Murray, S. L., Holmes, J. G., & Griffin, D. W. (1996a). The self-fulfilling nature of positive illusions in romantic relationships: Love is not blind, but prescient. *Journal of Personality and Social Psychology,* **71**, 1155–1180.

Murray, S. L., Holmes, J. G., & Griffin, D. W. (1996b). The benefits of positive illusions: Idealization and the construction of satisfaction in close relationships. *Journal of Personality and Social Psychology,* **70**, 79–98.

Murray, S. L., Holmes, J. G., & Griffin, D. W. (2000). Self-esteem and the quest for felt security: How perceived regard regulates attachment processes. *Journal of Personality and Social Psychology,* **78,** 478–498.

Murray, S. L., Holmes, J. G., Gellavia, G., Griffin, D. W., & Dolderman, D. (2002). Kindred spirits? The benefits of egocentrism in close relationships. *Journal of Personality and Social Psychology,* **82,** 563–581.

Muscarella, F. (2000). The evolution of homoerotic behavior in humans. *Journal of Homosexuality,* **40**(1), 51–77.

Musher-Eizenman, D., Holub, S., Miller, A., Goldstein, S., & Edwards-Leeper, L. (2004). Body size stigmatization in preschool children: The role of control attributions. *Journal of Pediatric Psychology,* **29**(8), 613–620.

Muson, G. (1978, March). Teenage violence and the telly. *Psychology Today,* pp. 50–54.

Myers, D. G. (1993). *The pursuit of happiness.* Avon.

Myers, D. G. (2004). The secret to happiness. *Yes!*, Summer, 13–16.

Myers, D. G., & Lamm, H. (1976). The group polarization phenomenon. *Psychological Bulletin,* **83**(4), 602.

Myers, J. E., Madathil, J., & Tingle, L. R. (2005). Marriage satisfaction and wellness in India and the United States: A preliminary comparison of arranged marriages and marriages of choice. *Journal of Counseling & Development,* **83**(2), 183–190.

N

Nadler, A. (2016). Intergroup helping relations. *Current Opinion in Psychology,* **11,** 64–68.

Naidu, T., Sliep, Y., & Dageid, W. (2012). The social construction of identity in HIV/AIDS home-based care volunteers in rural KwaZulu-Natal, South Africa. *Journal of Social Aspects,* **9**(2), 113–126.

Naik, G. (2011, 2 December). Scientists' elusive goal: Reproducing study results. *The Wall Street Journal.*

Nail, P. R., MacDonald, G., & Levy, D. A. (2000). Proposal of a four-dimensional model of social response. *Psychological Bulletin,* **126,** 454–470.

Naluonde, T., Wakefield, C., Markle, L., Martin, A., Tresphor, C., Abdullah, R. & Larsen, D. A. (2018, October). A disruptive cue improves handwashing in school children in Zambia. *Health Promotion International.* https://doi-org.libezproxy.open.ac.uk/10.1093/heapro/day080

Nardone, G., & Portelli, C. (2005). When the diagnosis 'invents' the illness. *Kybernetes,* **34**(3/4), 365–372. https://doi.org/10.1108/03684920510581549

Nasser, R., Doumit, J., & Carifio, J. (2011). Well-being and belief in a just world among rest home residents. *Social Behavior and Personality: An International Journal,* **39**(5), 655–670. http://link.galegroup.com.libezproxy.open.ac.uk/apps/doc/A260874320/AONE?u=tou&sid=AONE&xid=7a33b1b0

National Research Council (2002). *Youth, pornography, and the Internet.* National Academy Press.

Nawrat, R., & Dolinski, D. (2007). 'Seesaw of emotions' and compliance: Beyond the fear-then-relief rule. *Journal of Social Psychology,* **147**(5), 556–571.

Neighbors, C., O'Connor, R. M., Lewis, M. A., Chawla, N., Lee, C. M., & Fossos, N. (2008). The relative impact of injunctive norms on college student drinking: The role of reference group. *Psychology of Addictive Behaviors,* **22**(4), 576.

Nelson, L. D., & Morrison, E. L. (2005). The symptoms of resource scarcity: Judgments of food and finances influence preferences for potential partners. *Psychological Science,* **16,** 167–173.

Nelwati,, N., Abdullah, K.L., & Chan, C.M. (2018). A systematic review of qualitative studies exploring peer learning experiences of undergraduate nursing students. *Nurse Education Today,* **71,** 185–192. https://doi.org/10.1016/j.nedt.2018.09.018

Nemeth, C. J. (1999). Behind the scenes. In D. G. Myers (Ed.), *Social psychology* (6th ed.). McGraw-Hill.

Nemeth, C. J., Brown, K., & Rogers, J. (2001a). Devil's advocate versus authentic dissent: Stimulating quantity and quality. *European Journal of Social Psychology,* **31**(6), 707–720.

Nemeth, C. J., Connell, J. B., Rogers, J. D., & Brown, K. S. (2001b). Improving decision making by means of dissent. *Journal of Applied Social Psychology,* **31**(1), 48–58.

Nemeth, C. J., Personnaz, B., Personnaz, M., & Goncalo, J. A. (2004). The liberating role of conflict in group creativity: A study in two countries. *European Journal of Social Psychology,* **34,** 365–374.

Nemeth, C. J., & Wachtler, J. (1974). Creating the perceptions of consistency and confidence: A necessary condition for minority influence. *Sociometry,* **37,** 529–540.

Neumann, R., & Strack, F. (2000). Approach and avoidance: The influence of proprioceptive and exteroceptive cues on encoding of affective information. *Journal of Personality and Social Psychology,* **79,** 39–48.

Nemeth, C. J., & Wachtler, J. (1974). Creating the perceptions of consistency and confidence: A necessary condition for minority influence. *Sociometry,* **37,** 529–540.

Nevis, E. C. (1983). Using an American perspective in understanding another culture: Towards a hierarchy of needs for the People's Republic of China. *Journal of Applied Behavioral Science,* **19**(3), 249–264.

New York Post (2017). I feel just as much a woman as I am man. *New York Post,* 24th October:https://www.news.com.au/entertainment/celebrity-life/sam-smith-i-feel-just-as-much-a-woman-as-i-am-man/news-story/1ffc1d95c5d053b246c89d80bd3887b5

Newall, N., Chipperfield, J., Clifton, R., Perry, R., Swift, A., & Ruthig, J. (2009). Causal beliefs, social participation, and loneliness among older adults: A longitudinal study. *Journal of Social and Personal Relationships,* **26**(2–3), 273–290.

Newell, B. R., & Shanks, D. R. (2007). Recognising what you like: Examining the relation between the mere-exposure effect and recognition. *European Journal of Cognitive Psychology,* **19**(1), 103–118.

Newell, B. R., & Shanks, D.R. (2007). Recognising whatyou like: Examining the relationbetween the mere-exposureeffect and recognition. *European Journal of CognitivePsychology,* **19**(1), 103–118.

Newey, S. (2020, January 7). Australia is burning – but why are the bushfires so bad and is climate change to blame? *The Telegraph:* https://www.telegraph.co.uk/global-health/climate-and-people/australia-burning-bushfires-bad/

Newman, L. S. (1993). How individualists interpret behavior: Idiocentrism and spontaneous trait inference. *Social Cognition,* **11,** 243–269.

Newport, F., Moore, D. W., Jones, J. M., & Saad, L. (2003, 21 March). Special release: American opinion on the war. *Gallup Poll Tuesday Briefing.* www.gallup.com/poll/tb/goverpubli/s0030325.asp.

Ng-Mak, D. S., Salzinger, S., Feldman, R. S., & Stueve, C. A. (2004). Pathologic adaptation to community violence among inner-city youth. *American Journal of Orthopsychiatry,* **74,** 196–208.

Nguyen, H., & Wodon, Q. (2018). Faith affiliation, religiosity, and altruistic behaviors: An analysis of Gallup World Poll data. *Review of Faith and International Affairs,* **16**(2), 15–22.

NHS (2016). Overview: Cognitive behavioural therapy. https://www.nhs.uk/conditions/cognitive-behavioural-therapy-cbt/#

NHS Digital (2018, 3 July). Around 1.6 million fewer adult smokers in England in six years. https://digital.nhs.uk/news-and-events/latest-news/around-1.6-million-fewer-adult-smokers-in-england-in-six-years

Niccolucci, V., Botto, S., Rugani, B., Nicolardi, V., Bastianoni, S., & Gaggi, C. (2011). The real water consumption behind drinking water: The case of Italy. *Journal of Environmental Management,* **92**(10), 2611–2618. https://doi.org/10.1016/j.jenvman.2011.05.033.

Nicholson, N., Cole, S. G., & Rocklin, T. (1985). Conformity in the Asch situation: A comparison between contemporary British and US university students. *British Journal of Social Psychology,* **24,** 59–63.

Nickerson, A. M., & Louis, W. R. (2008). Nationality versus humanity? Personality, identity, and norms in relation to attitudes toward asylum seekers. *Journal of Applied Social Psychology,* **38**(3), 796–817.

Nickerson, R. S. (1998). Confirmation bias: A ubiquitous phenomenon in many guises. *Review of General Psychology,* **2,** 175–220.

Nielsen, M. B., Matthiesen, S. B., & Einarsen, S. (2005). Leadership and interpersonal conflicts: Symptoms of posttraumatic stress among targets of bullying from supervisors. *Nord Psykol,* **57,** 391–415. https://doi.org/10.1080/00291463.2005.10637381

Niens, U., Cairns, E., & Bishop, S. (2004). Prejudiced or not? Hidden sectarianism among students in Northern Ireland. *Journal of Social Psychology,* **144**(2), 163–180.

Nieuwenhuijsen, K., De Boer, A. G. E. M., Verbeek, J. H. A. M., Blonk, R. W. B., & Van Dijk, F. J. H. (2003). The Depression Anxiety Stress Scales (DASS): Detecting anxiety disorder and depression in employees absent from work because of mental health problems. *Occupational and Environmental Medicine,* **60**(suppl 1), i77–i82.

Nigg, J. T. (2003). Response inhibition and disruptive behaviors. *Annals of the New York Academy of Sciences,* **1008**(1), 170–182.

Nijstad, B. A., Stroebe, W., & Lodewijkx, H. F. M. (2003). Production blocking and idea generation: Does blocking interfere with cognitive processes? *Journal of Experimental Social Psychology,* **39,** 531–548.

Nisbett, R. E. (2003). *The geography of thought: How Asians and Westerners think differently . . . and why.* Free Press.

Nisbett, R. E., & Masuda, T. (2003). Culture and point of view. *Proceedings of the National Academy of Sciences,* **100,** 11163–11170.

Nisbett, R. E., & Ross, L. (1980). *Human inference: Strategies and shortcomings of social judgment.* Prentice-Hall.

Nisbett, R. E., Caputo, C., Legant, P., & Marecek, J. (1973). Behavior as seen by the actor and as seen by the observer. *Journal of Personality and Social Psychology,* **27**(2), 154–164.

Noel, J. G., Wann, D. L., & Branscombe, N. R. (1995). Peripheral ingroup membership status and public negativity toward outgroups. *Journal of Personality and Social Psychology,* **68,** 127–137.

Nohria, N., Groysberg, B., & Lee, L. (2008). Employee motivation: A powerful new model. *Harvard Business Review,* **86**(7/8), 78.

Nolan, S. A., Flynn, C., & Garber, J. (2003). Prospective relations between rejection and depression in young adolescents. *Journal of Personality and Social Psychology,* **85,** 745–755.

Nolen-Hoeksema, S. (2000). The role of rumination in depressive disorders and mixed anxiety/depressive symptoms. *Journal of Abnormal Psychology,* **109,** 504–511. https://doi.org/10.1037/0021-843X.109.3.504

Norem, J. K. (2000). Defensive pessimism, optimism, and pessimism. In E. C. Chang (Ed.), *Optimism and pessimism.* APA Books.

Norem, J. K., & Cantor, N. (1986). Defensive pessimism: Harnessing anxiety as motivation. *Journal of Personality and Social Psychology,* **51,** 1208–1217.

Norenzayan, A., & Heine, S. J. (2005). Psychological universals: What are they and how can we know? *Psychological Bulletin,* **131,** 763–784.

Nosek, B. A., & Banaji, M. R. (2001). The go/no-go association task. *Social Cognition,* **19**(6), 625–666.

Nosek, B. A., Aarts, A. A., Anderson, C. J., Anderson, J. E., Kappes, H. B., & Open Science Collaboration. (2015). Estimating the reproducibility of psychological science. *Science,* **349**(6251), aac4716-aac4716

Notarius, C., & Markman, H. J. (1993). *We can work it out.* Putnam.

Nowak, M. A., & Sigmund, K. (2005). Evolution of indirect reciprocity. *Nature,* **437**(7063), 1291.

Nussbaum, D. (2012). The role of conceptual replication. *The Psychologist,* **25,** 350.

Nuttin, J. M. Jr. (1984). What's in a name? Opening lecture of the 7th General Meeting of the European Association of Experimental Social Psychology, Tilburg.

Nuttin, J. M., Jr (1987). Affective consequences of mere ownership: The name letter effect in twelve European languages. *European Journal of Social Psychology,* **17,** 318–402.

O

O'Carroll, L. (2018, November 18). UK running out of food warehouse space as no-deal Brexit fears rise. *The Guardian.* https://www.theguardian.com/politics/2018/nov/18/uk-running-out-of-food-warehouse-space-as-no-deal-brexit-fears-rise

O'Connor, A. (2004, 14 May). Pressure to go along with abuse is strong, but some soldiers find strength to refuse. *New York Times:* www.nytimes.com.

O'Fallon, M. J., & Butterfield, K. D. (2012). The influence of unethical peer behaviour on observers' unethical behaviour: A social cognitive perspective. *Journal of Business Ethics,* **109,** 117–131.

O'Reilly, M., Kiyimba, N., & Lester, J. N. (2018). Discursive psychology as a method of analysis for the study of couple and family therapy. *Journal of Marital and Family Therapy,* **44**(3), 409–425.

O'Sullivan, T. (2007) 'Get MediaSmart®': A critical discourse analysis of controversy around advertising to children in the UK. *Consumption Markets & Culture,* **10**(3), 293–314. https://doi.org/10.1080/10253860701365397

Oakes, J. P., Haslam, S. A., & Turner, J. C. (1994). *Stereotyping and social reality.* Blackwell.

Oaten, M., & Cheng, K. (2006). Improved self-control: The benefits of a regular program of academic study. *Basic and Applied Social Psychology,* **28,** 1–16.

Oberholzer-Gee, F. (2007). The helping hand – a brief anatomy. Economics and psychology: A promising new cross-disciplinary field. In B. S. Frey & A. Stutzer (Eds.), *Economics and psychology: A promising new cross-disciplinary field. CESifo seminar series.* MIT Press.

Ochsner, K. N., & Lieberman, M. D. (2001). The emergence of social cognitive neuroscience. *American Psychologist,* **56,** 717–734.

Ochsner, K. N., Beer, J. S., Robertson, E. R., Cooper, J. C., Gabrieli, J. D. E., Kihsltrom, J. F., & D'Esposito, M. (2005). The neural correlates of direct and reflected self-knowledge. *Neuroimage,* **28,** 797–814.

Oddone-Paolucci, E., Genuis, M., & Violato, C. (2000). A meta-analysis of the published research on the effects of pornography. In C. Violato (Ed.), *The changing family and child development.* Ashgate.

Odgers, C. L., Moffitt, T. E., Tach, L. M., Simpson, R. J., Taylor, A., Matthews, C. L., & Caspi, A. (2009). The protective effects of neighborhood collective efficacy on British children growing up in deprivation: A developmental analysis. *Developmental Psychology,* **45**(4), 942–957.

Office for National Statistics (2017). Adult drinking habits in Great Britain: 2005 to 2016. https://www.ons.gov.uk/peoplepopulationandcommunity/healthandsocialcare/drugusealcoholandsmoking/bulletins/opinionsandlifestylesurveyadultdrinkinghabitsingreatbritain/2005to2016

Office for National Statistics (2019, December 4). Childbearing for women born in different years, England and Wales: 2018. https://www.ons.gov.uk/peoplepopulationandcommunity/birthsdeathsandmarriages/conceptionandfertilityrates/bulletins/childbearingforwomenbornindifferentyearsenglandandwales/2018

Ogihara, Y. (2017). Temporal changes in individualism and their ramification in Japan: Rising individualism and conflicts with persisting collectivism. *Frontiers in Psychology,* **8,** 695. https://doi.org/10.3389/fpsyg.2017.00695

Okoro, S. (2014). Plastic surgery is on the rise in Africa: 13 questions to ask before choosing your surgeon. *Radiant, Health & Culture.* https://www.radianthealthmag.com/health-wellness/plastic-surgery-africa-nigeria-beyond/

Oliner, S., and Oliner, P. (1988). *The altruistic personality: Rescuers of Jews in Nazi Europe.* The Free Press.

Olson, I. R., & Marshuetz, C. (2005). Facial attractiveness is appraised in a glance. *Emotion,* **5,** 498–502.

Olson, J. M., Roese, N. J., & Zanna, M. P. (1996). Expectancies. In E. T. Higgins & A. W. Kruglanski (Eds.), *Social psychology: Handbook of basic principles.* Guilford Press.

Olweus, D. (1978). *Aggression in the schools: Bullies and whipping boys.* Hemisphere.

Olweus, D. (1991). Bully/victim problems among schoolchildren: Basic facts andeffects of a school based intervention program. In D. J. Pepler & K. H.Rubin (Eds.), *The development and treatment of childhood aggression* (pp. 411–448). Erlbaum.

Olweus, D. (1993a). *Bullying at school: What we know and what we can do.* Blackwell.

Olweus, D. (1993b). Victimization by peers: Antecedents and long-term outcomes. In K. H. Rubin & J. H. Asendorf (Eds.), *Social withdrawal, inhibition, and shyness* (pp. 315–341). Erlbaum.

Olweus, D. (2001a). Peer harassment: A critical analysis and some important issues. In J. Juvonen & S. Graham (Eds.), *Peer harassment in school* (pp. 3–20). Guilford Press.

Olweus, D., & Limber, S. P. (2010a). The Olweus Bullying Prevention Program:Implementation and evaluation over two decades. In S. R. Jimerson, S. M.Swearer, & D. L. Espelage (Eds.), *The handbook of school bullying: Aninternational perspective* (pp. 377–402). Routledge.

Olweus, D., & Limber, S. P. (2010b). Bullying in school: Evaluation and dissemination of the Olweus Bullying Prevention Program. *American Journal of Orthopsychiatry,* **80**(1), 124–134. http://dx.doi.org/10.1111/j.1939-0025.2010.01015.x

Ongori, H., & Agolla, J. E. (2008). Occupational stress in organizations and its effects on organizational performance. *Journal of Management Research,* **8**(3), 123.

Open Secrets (2005). 2004 election overview: Winning vs spending. www.opensecrets.org.

Opotow, S. (1990). Moral exclusion and injustice: An introduction. *Journal of Social Issues,* **46**, 1–20.

Orne, M. T. (1962). On the social psychology of the psychological experiment: With particular reference to demand characteristics and their implications. *American Psychologist,* **17**(11), 776.

Ornstein, R. (1991). *The evolution of consciousness: Of Darwin, Freud, and cranial fire: The origins of the way we think.* Prentice-Hall.

Orr, E. S., Sisic, M., Ross, C., Simmering, M. G., Arseneault, J. M., & Orr, R. R. (2009). The influence of shyness on the use of Facebook in an undergraduate sample. *Cyberpsychology, Behavior, and Social Networking,* **12**, 337–340.

Osberg, T. M., & Shrauger, J. S. (1986). Self-prediction: Exploring the parameters of accuracy. *Journal of Personality and Social Psychology,* **51**, 1044–1057.

Osberg, T. M., & Shrauger, J. S. (1990). The role of self-prediction in psychological assessment. In J. N. Butcher & C. D. Spielberger (Eds.), *Advances in personality assessment* (Vol. 8). Erlbaum.

Osgood, C. E. (1962). *An alternative to war or surrender.* University of Illinois Press.

Osgood, C. E. (1980). GRIT: A strategy for survival in mankind's nuclear age? Paper presented at the Pugwash Conference on New Directions in Disarmament, Racine, WI.

Osofsky, M. J., Bandura, A., & Zimbardo, P. G. (2005). The role of moral disengagement in the execution process. *Law and Human Behavior,* **29**, 371–393.

Ostrowsky, M. K. (2010). Are violent people more likely to have low self-esteem or high self-esteem? *Aggression and Violent Behavior,* **15**, 69–75.

Oswald, F. L., Mitchell, G., Blanton, H., Jaccard, J., & Tetlock, P. E. (2015). Using the IAT to predict ethnic and racial discrimination: Small effect sizes of unknown societal significance. *Journal of Personality and Social Psychology,* **108**(4), 562–571.

Oswald, F., Mitchell, G., Blanton, H., Jaccard, J., Tetlock, P., & Smith, E. R. (2013). Predicting ethnic and racial discrimination: A meta-analysis of IAT criterion studies. *Journal of Personality and Social Psychology,* **105**(2), 171–192.

Otto, S., Kaiser, F. G., & Arnold, O. (2014). The critical-challenge of climate change for psychology: Preventingrebound and promoting more individual irrationality. *European Psychologist,* **19**, 96–109. https://doi.org/10.1027/1016-9040/a000182

Owens, L., Shute, R., & Slee, P. (2000a). 'Guess what I just heard!': Indirect aggression among teenage girls in Australia. *Aggressive Behavior,* **26**, 67–83.

Owens, L., Slee, P., & Shute, R. (2000b). 'It hurts a hell of a lot . . .': The effects of indirect aggression on teenage girls. *School Psychology International,* **21**(4), 359–376.

Owolabi, A. B. (2009). Effect of consumers mood on advertising effectiveness. *Europe's Journal of Psychology,* **5**(4), 118-127.

Oyserman, D., Coon, H. M., & Kemmelmeier, M. (2002). Rethinking individualism and collectivism: Evaluation of theoretical assumptions and meta-analyses. *Psychological Bulletin,* **128**, 3–72.

Ozer, E. M., & Bandura, A. (1990). Mechanisms governing empowerment effects: A self-efficacy analysis. *Journal of Personality and Social Psychology,* **58**, 472–486.

P

Paciello, M., Fida, R., Cerniglia, L., Tramontano, C., & Cole, E. (2012). High cost helping scenario: The role of empathy, prosocial reasoning and moral disengagement on helping behavior. *Personality and Individual Differences,* **55**(1), 3–7.

Packer, D. J. (2008). On being both with us and against us: A normative conflict model of dissent in social groups. *Personality and Social Psychology Review,* **12**(1), 50–72. https://doi.org/10.1177/1088868307309606

Packer, D. J. (2009). Avoiding groupthink whereas weakly identified members remain silent, strongly identified members dissent about collective problems. *Psychological Science,* **20**(5), 546–548.

Page-Gould, E., Mendoza-Denton, R., & Tropp, L. R. (2008). With a little help from my cross-group friend: Reducing anxiety in intergroup contexts through cross-group friendship. *Journal of Personality and Social Psychology,* **95**(5), 1080–1094.

Paine, A. (2006). *Mark Twain's Notebooks.* Hesperides Press.

Pak, A. W., Dion, K. L., & Dion, K. K. (1991). Social psychological correlates of experienced discrimination: Test of the double jeopardy hypothesis. *International Journal of Intercultural Relations,* **15**, 243–254.

Palasinski, M. (2012). The roles of monitoring and cyberbystanders in reducing sexual abuse. *Computers in Human Behavior,* **28**, 2014–2022.

Pallak, M. S., Mueller, M., Dollar, K., & Pallak, J. (1972). Effect of commitment on responsiveness to an extreme consonant communication. *Journal of Personality and Social Psychology,* **23**, 429–436.

Palmer, J. K., & Loveland, J. M. (2008). The influence of group discussion on performance judgments: Rating accuracy, contrast effects, and halo. *Journal of Psychology: Interdisciplinary and Applied,* **142**(2), 117–130.

Paluck, E. L. (2010). Is it better not to talk? Group polarization, extended contact, and perspective taking in eastern Democratic Republic of Congo. *Personality and Social Psychology Bulletin,* **36**(9), 1170–1185.

Paolini, S., Hewstone, M., & Cairns, E. (2007). Direct and indirect intergroup friendship effects: Testing the moderating role of the affective-cognitive bases of prejudice. *PSPB,* **33**(10), 1406–1420.

Papastamou, S., & Mugny, G. (1990). Synchronic consistency and psychologization in minority influence. *European Journal of Social Psychology,* **20**, 85–98.

Park, D., & Muller, J. (2014). The challenge that Confucian filial piety poses for Korean churches. *HTS Teologiese Studies,* **70**(2), 1–8. http://dx.doi.org.libezproxy.open.ac.uk/10.4102/hts.v70i2.1959

Park, H. S., Levine, T. R., Westerman, C. K., Orfgen, T., &Foregger, S. (2007). The effects of argument quality an involvement type on attitude formation and attitude change: A test of dual-process and social judgment predictions. *Human Communication Research,* **33**, 81–102. https://doi.org/10.1111/j.1468-2958.2007.00290.x

Park, S., & Catrambone, R. (2007). Social facilitation effects of virtual humans. *Human Factors,* **49**(6), 1054–1060.

Parke, J., Griffiths, M. D., & Parke, A. (2007). Positive thinking among slot machine gamblers: A case of maladaptive coping? *International Journal Mental Health Addiction,* **5**, 39–52.

Parke, R. D., Berkowitz, L., Leyens, J. P., West, S. G., & Sebastian, J. (1977). Some effects of violent and nonviolent movies on the behavior of juvenile delinquents. In L. Berkowitz (Ed.), *Advances in experimental social psychology* (Vol. 10). Academic Press.

Parker, I. (1989). *The crisis in modern social psychology, and how to end it.* Routledge.

Parker, I. (1992). *Discourse dynamics: Critical analysis for social and individual psychology.* Routledge.

Parker, I. (2002). *Critical discursive psychology.* Palgrave.

Parker, K. (2015, October). Women more than men adjust their careers for family life. *Pew Research Center:*http://pewrsr.ch/1O5OM6r

Parker, R. S., Haytko, D. L., & Hermans, C. M. (2009). Individualism and collectivism: Reconsidering old assumptions. *Journal of International Business Research,* **8**(1), 127–139.

Parks, C. D., & Rumble, A. C. (2001). Elements of reciprocity and social value orientation. *Personality and Social Psychology Bulletin,* **27**(10), 1301–1309.

Parra Osorio, J. C., Joseph, G., & Wodon, Q. (2016). Religion and social cooperation: Results from an experiment in Ghana. *Review of Faith and International Affairs,* **14**(3), 65–72. https://doi.org/10.1080/15570274.2016.1215845

Parzefall, M.-R., & Salin, D. M. (2010). Perceptions of and reactions to workplace bullying: A social exchange perspective. *Human Relations,* **63**(6), 761–780. https://doi.org/10.1177/0018726709345043

Pashupati, K. (2003). 'I know this brand, but did I like the ad?' An investigation of the familiarity-based sleeper effect. *Psychology & Marketing,* **20**(11), 1017–1043.

Patt, A., Aplyn, D., Weyrich, P., & van Vliet, O. (2019). Availability of private charging infrastructure influences readiness to buy electric cars. *Transportation Research Part A,* **125,** 1–7. https://doi.org/10.1016/j.tra.2019.05.004

Patterson, D. (1996). *When learned men murder.* Phi Delta Kappa Educational Foundation.

Patterson, G. R., Chamberlain, P., & Reid, J. B. (1982). A comparative evaluation of parent training procedures. *Behavior Therapy,* **13,** 638–650.

Patterson, G. R., Littman, R. A., & Bricker, W. (1967). Assertive behavior in children: A step toward a theory of aggression. *Monographs of the Society of Research in Child Development* (Serial No. 113), **32,** 5.

Patterson, T. E. (1980). The role of the mass media in presidential campaigns: The lessons of the 1976 election. *Items,* **34,** 25–30.

Paul, B., & Bhuiyan, R. (2010). Urban earthquake hazard: Perceived seismic risk and preparedness in Dhaka City, Bangladesh. *Disasters,* **34**(2), 337-359.

Paulhus, D. L., & Lim, D. T. K. (1994). Arousal and evaluative extremity in social judgments: A dynamic complexity model. *European Journal of Social Psychology,* **24,** 89–99.

Paulus, P. B. (1998). Developing consensus about groupthink after all these years. *Organizational Behavior and Human Decision Processes,* **73,** 362–375.

Paulus, P. B., Brown, V., & Ortega, A. H. (1997). Group creativity. In R. E. Purser & A. Montuori (Eds.), *Social creativity* (Vol. 2). Hampton Press.

Paulus, P. B., Larey, T. S., & Dzindolet, M. T. (2000). Creativity in groups and teams. In M. Turner (Ed.), *Groups at work: Advances in theory and research.* Hampton.

Paulus, P. B., Larey, T. S., & Ortega, A. H. (1995). Performance and perceptions of brainstormers in an organizational setting. *Basic and Applied Social Psychology,* **17,** 249–265.

Paunonen, S. (2006). You are honest, therefore I like you and find you attractive. *Journal of Research in Personality,* **40**(3), 237–249.

Pavlou, P. A. & Fygenson, M. (2006). Understanding and predicting electronic commerce adoption: An extension of the theoryof planned behavior. *MIS Quarterly,* **30**(1), 115–143.

Payne, B. K. (2001). Prejudice and perception: The role of automatic and controlled processes in misperceiving a weapon. *Journal of Personality and Social Psychology,* **81,** 181–192.

Pedersen, A., & Walker, I. (1997). Prejudice against Australian Aborigines: Old-fashioned and modern forms. *European Journal of Social Psychology,* **27,** 561–587.

Pedersen, E. R., LaBrie, J. W., & Lac, A. (2008). Assessment of perceived and actual alcohol norms in varying contexts: Exploring social impact theory among college students. *Addictive Behaviors,* **33,** 552–564.

Pedersen, W. C., Gonzales, C., & Miller, N. (2000). The moderating effect of trivial triggering provocation on displaced aggression. *Journal of Personality and Social Psychology,* **78,** 913–927.

Pegalis, L. J., Shaffer, D. R., Bazzini, D. G., & Greenier, K. (1994). On the ability to elicit self-disclosure: Are there gender-based and contextual limitations on the opener effect? *Personality and Social Psychology Bulletin,* **20,** 412–420.

Pelham, B. W. (2003, January). On the nature of implicit self-esteem: The case of the name letter effect. In *Motivated social perception: The Ontario symposium* (Vol. 9, p. 93). Psychology Press.

Pelham, B., & Crabtree, S. (2008, October 8). Worldwide, highly religious more likely to help others. *World Gallup.* https://news.gallup.com/poll/111013/worldwide-highly-religious-more-likely-help-others.aspx

Pennebaker, J., & Stone, L. D. (2003). Words of wisdom: Language use over the life span. *Journal of Personality and Social Psychology,* **85**(2), 291–301.

Pennebaker, J. W., Rimé, B., & Sproul, G. (1996). Stereotypes of emotional expressiveness of northerners and southerners: A cross-cultural test of Montesquieu's hypotheses. *Journal of Personality and Social Psychology,* **70,** 372–380.

Pennebaker, J., Groom, C., Loew, D., & Dabbs, D. (2004). Testosterone as a social inhibitor: Two case studies of the effect of testosterone treatment on language. *Journal of Abnormal Psychology,* **113**(1), 172–175.

Penner, L. A., Dertke, M. C., & Achenbach, C. J. (1973). The 'flash' system: A field study of altruism. *Journal of Applied Social Psychology,* **3,** 362–370.

Peplau, L., & Fingerhut, A. (2007). The close relationships of lesbians and gay men. *Annual Review of Psychology,* **58**(1), 405–424.

Pericas, J., González, S., Bennasar, M., De Pedro, J., Aguiló, A., & Bauzá, L. (2009). Cognitive dissonance towards the smoking habit among nursing and physiotherapy students at the University of Balearic Islands in Spain. *International Nursing Review,* **56**(1), 95–101. https://doi.org/10.1111/j.1466-7657.2008.00669.x

Perkins, A., Forehand, M., Greenwald, A., & Maison, D. (2008). Measuring the nonconscious: Implicit social cognition in consumer behaviour. In C. P. Haugtvedt, P. M. Herr, & F. R. Kardes (Eds.), *Handbook of consumer psychology.* Psychology Press.

Perrin, S., & Spencer, C. (1981). Independence or conformity in the Asch experiment as a reflection of cultural or situational factors. *British Journal of Social Psychology,* **20,** 205–209.

Persico, N., Postlewaite, A., & Silverman, D. (2004). The effect of adolescent experience on labor market outcomes: The case of height. *Journal of Political Economy,* **112,** 1019–1053.

Pessiglione, M., Petrovic, P., Daunizeau, J., Palminteri, S., Dolan, R. J., & Frith, C. D. (2008). Subliminal instrumental conditioning demonstrated in the human brain. *Neuron,* **59**(4), 561–567.

Pessin, J. (1933). The comparative effects of social and mechanical stimulation on memorizing. *American Journal of Psychology,* **45,** 263–270.

Pessin, J., & Husband, R. W. (1933). Effects of social stimulation on human maze learning. *Journal of Abnormal and Social Psychology,* **28,** 148–154.

Peter, J., Valkenburg, P. M., & Schouten, A. P. (2005). Developing a model of adolescent friendship formation on the Internet. *CyberPsychology & Behavior,* **8**(5), 423–430.

Petersen, J. L., & Hyde, J. S. (2011). Gender differences in sexual attitudes and behaviors: A review of meta-analytic results and large datasets. *Journal of Sex Research,* **48**(2–3), 149–165.

Petter, O. (2017, August 8). Childless women are on the rise, latest study reveals. *The Independent:* https://www.independent.co.uk/life-style/childless-women-on-rise-more-than-ever-before-fertility-crisis-menopause-career-study-reveals-a7882496.html

Pettigrew, T. F. (1969). Racially separate or together? *Journal of Social Issues,* **2,** 43–69.

Pettigrew, T. F. (1979). The ultimate attribution error: Extending Allport's cognitive analysis of prejudice. *Personality and Social Psychology Bulletin,* **55,** 461–476.

Pettigrew, T. F. (1988). Advancing racial justice: Past lessons for future use. Paper for the University of Alabama Conference: Opening Doors: An Appraisal of Race Relations in America.

Pettigrew, T. F. (1997). Generalized intergroup contact effects on prejudice. *Personality and Social Psychology Bulletin,* **23,** 173–185.

Pettigrew, T. F. (2003). Peoples under threat: Americans, Arabs, and Israelis. *Peace and Conflict,* **9,** 69–90.

Pettigrew, T. F. (2004). Intergroup contact: Theory, research, and new perspectives. In J. A. Banks & C. A. McGee Banks (Eds.), *Handbook of research on multicultural education.* Jossey-Bass.

Pettigrew, T. F., & Tropp, L. R. (2000). Does intergroup contact reduce prejudice: Recent meta-analytic findings. In S. Oskamp (Ed.), *Reducing prejudice and discrimination.* Lawrence Erlbaum.

Pettigrew, T. F., & Tropp, L. R. (2006). A meta-analytic test of intergroup contact theory. *Journal of Personality and Social Psychology,* **90,** 751–783.

Petty, R. E., & Cacioppo, J. T. (1979). Effects of forewarning of persuasive intent and involvement on cognitive response and persuasion. *Personality and Social Psychology Bulletin,* **5,** 173–176.

Petty, R. E., & Cacioppo, J. T. (1986). *Communication and persuasion: Central and peripheral routes to attitude change.* Springer-Verlag.

Petty, R. E., & Krosnick, J. A. (Eds.) (1995). *Attitude strength: Antecedents and consequences.* Erlbaum.

Petty, R. E., & Wegener, D. T. (1999). The elaboration likelihood model: Current status and controversies. In S. Chaiken & Y. Trope (Eds.), *Dual-process theories in social psychology.* Guilford Press.

Petty, R. E., Briñol, P., & Tormala, Z. L. (2002). Thought confidence as a determinant of persuasion: The self-validation hypothesis. *Journal of Personality and Social Psychology,* **82,** 722–741.

Petty, R. E., Cacioppo, J. T., & Goldman, R. (1981). Personal involvement as a determinant of argument-based persuasion. *Journal of Personality and Social Psychology,* **41,** 847–855.

Petty, R. E., Haugtvedt, C. P., & Smith, S. M. (1995). Elaboration as a determinant of attitude strength: Creating attitudes that are persistent, resistant, and predictive of behavior. In R. E. Petty & J. A. Krosnick (Eds.), *Attitude strength: Antecedents and consequences. Ohio State University Series on Attitudes and Persuasion* (Vol. 4, pp. 93–130). Lawrence Erlbaum.

Petty, R. E., Schumann, D. W., Richman, S. A., & Strathman, A. J. (1993). Positive mood and persuasion: Different roles for affect under high and low elaboration conditions. *Journal of Personality and Social Psychology,* **64,** 5–20.

Pew (2003). *Views of a changing world 2003. The Pew Global Attitudes Project.* Pew Research Center for the People and the Press: http://people-press.org/reports/pdf/185.pdf.

Pew (2006, 14 March). Guess who's coming to dinner. Pew Research Center (pewresearch.org).

Pew Research Center (2019, 30 May). Where Europe stands on gay marriage and civil unions. https://www.pewresearch.org/fact-tank/2019/05/30/where-europe-stands-on-gay-marriage-and-civil-unions/

Pfeiffer, T., Rutte, C., Killingback, T., Taborsky, M., & Bonhoeffer, S. (2005). Evolution of cooperation by generalized reciprocity. *Proceedings. Biological Sciences,* **272**(1568), 1115–1120. https://doi.org/10.1098/rspb.2004.2988

Phelan, J. E., Moss-Racusin, C. A., & Rudman, L. (2008). Competent yet out in the cold: Shifting criteria for hiring reflect backlash toward agentic women. *Psychology of Women Quarterly,* **32,** 406–413.

Phelps, E. A., O'Connor, K. J., Cunningham, W. A., Funayama, E. S., Gatenby, J. C., Gore, G. C., & Banaji, M. A. (2000). Performance on indirect measures of race evaluation predicts amygdala activation. *Journal of Cognitive Neuroscience,* **12,** 729–738.

Phillips, D. P. (1985). Natural experiments on the effects of mass media violence on fatal aggression: Strengths and weaknesses of a new approach. In L. Berkowitz (Ed.), *Advances in experimental social psychology* (Vol. 19). Academic Press.

Phillips, D. P., Carstensen, L. L., & Paight, D. J. (1989). Effects of mass media news stories on suicide, with new evidence on the role of story content. In D. R. Pfeffer (Ed.), *Suicide among youth: Perspectives on risk and prevention.* American Psychiatric Press.

Phillips, T. (2004, 3 April). Quoted by T. Baldwin & D. Rozenberg in: Britain must scrap multiculturalism. *The Times,* p. A1.

Philpot, R., Liebst, L. S., Levine, M., Bernasco, W., & Lindegaard, M. R. (2019). Would I be helped? Cross-national CCTV footage shows that intervention is the norm in public conflicts. *American Psychologist,* **75**(1), 66–75. https://doi.org/10.1037/amp0000469

Phinney, J. S. (1990). Ethnic identity in adolescents and adults: Review of research. *Psychological Bulletin,* **108,** 499–514.

Pickett, C. L., Silver, M. D., & Brewer, M. B. (2002). The impact of assimilation and differentiation needs on perceived group importance and judgments of ingroup size. *Personality and Social Psychology Bulletin,* **28,** 546–558.

Piliavin, J. A. (2003). Doing well by doing good: Benefits for the benefactor. In C. L. M. Keyes & J. Haidt (Eds.), *Flourishing: Positive psychology and the life well-lived.* American Psychological Association.

Piliavin, J. A., Evans, D. E., & Callero, P. (1982). Learning to 'Give to unnamed strangers': The process of commitment to regular blood donation. In E. Staub, D. Bar-Tal, J. Karylowski, & J. Reykawski (Eds.), *The development and maintenance of prosocial behavior: International perspectives.* Plenum.

Pinel, E. C. (2002). Stigma consciousness in intergroup contexts: The power of conviction. *Journal of Experimental Social Psychology,* **38,** 178–185.

Pingitore, R., Dugoni, B. L., Tindale, R. S., & Spring, B. (1994). Bias against overweight job applicants in a simulated employment interview. *Journal of Applied Psychology,* **79,** 909–917.

Pinker, S. (2002). *The blank slate.* Viking.

Pitner, R. O., Yu, M., & Brown, E. (2011). Exploring the dynamics of middle-aged and older adult residents' perceptions of neighborhood safety. *Journal of Gerontological Social Work,* **54,** 511–527.

Pittson, H., & Wallace, L. (2011). Using intervention mapping to develop a family-based childhood weight management programme. *Journal of Health Services Research & Policy,* **16**(suppl 1), 2–7.

Pizzutti, C., Basso, K., & Goncalves, M. (2016). The effect of the discounted attribute importance in two-sided messages. *European Journal of Marketing,* **50**(9-10), 1703-1725.

Plötner, M., Over, H., Carpenter, M., & Tomasello, M. (2015). Young children show the bystander effect in helping situations. *Psychological Science,* **26**(4), 499–506.

Plaks, J. E., & Higgins, E. T. (2000). Pragmatic use of stereotyping in teamwork: Social loafing and compensation as a function of inferred partner–situation fit. *Journal of Personality and Social Psychology,* **79,** 962–974.

Platow, M. J., Haslam, S. A., Both, A., Chew, I., Cuddon, M., Goharpey, N., Måurer, J., Rosini, S., Tsekouras, A., & Grace, D. M. (2005). It's not funny if *they're* laughing: Self-categorization, social influence, and responses to canned laughter. *Journal of Experimental Social Psychology,* **41,** 542–550.

Platow, M. J., Voudouris, N. J., Coulson, M., Gilford, N., Jamieson, R., Najdovski, L., Papaleo, N. Pollard, C., & Terry, L. (2007). In-group reassurance in a pain setting produces lower levels of physiological arousal: Direct support for a self-categorization analysis of social influence. *European Journal of Social Psychology,* **37,** 649–660.

Plous, S. (2008). The psychology of prejudice, stereotyping and discrimination: An overview. www.understandingPrejudice.org.

Plucker, J. A., Beghetto, R. A., & Dow, G. T. (2004). Why isn't creativity more important to educational psychologists? Potentials, pitfalls, and future directions in creativity research. *Educational Psychologist,* **39**(2), 83–96.

Pohl, R. F., Bayen, U. J., & Martin, C. (2010). A multi-process account of hindsight bias in children. *Developmental Psychology,* **46**(5), 1268–1282. https://doi.org/10.1037/a0020209

Polizzi, C., Fontana, V., Carollo, A., Bono, A., Burgio, S., & Perricone, G. (2016). Sibship and self-esteem in children with asthma. *Pediatric Reports,* **8**(2). https://doi.org/10.4081/pr.2016.6370

Pomazal, R. J., & Clore, G. L. (1973). Helping on the highway: The effects of dependency and sex. *Journal of Applied Social Psychology,* **3,** 150–164.

Pomerantz, A. (1978). Compliment responses. Notes on the cooperation of multiple constraints. In J. Schenkein (Ed.), *Studies in the organisation of conversational interaction.* Academic Press.

Poniewozik, J. (2003, 24 November). All the news that fits your reality. *Time,* 90.

Poobalan, A. S., Aucott, L. S., Clarke, A., Smith, W., & Cairns, S. (2012). Physical activity attitudes, intentions and behaviours among 18–25 year olds: A mixed methods study. *BMC Public Health,* **12**(1), 640–649.

Poortinga, W., Steg, L. & Vlek, C. (2004). Values, environmental concern, and environmental behaviour: A study into household energy use. *Environment and Behavior,* **36**(1), 70–93.

Popper, K. (1963). *Conjectures and refutations: The growth of scientific knowledge.* Routledge.

Post, J. M., & Panis, L. K. (2011). Crimes of obedience: 'Groupthink' at Abu Ghraib, *International Journal of Group Psychotherapy,* **61**(1), 48–66. https://doi.org/10.1521/ijgp.2011.61.1.48

Postmes, T. (2003). A social identity approach to communication in organizations. In S. A. Haslam, D. van Knippenberg, M. J. Platow, & N. Ellemers (Eds.), *Social identity at work: Developing theory for organizational practice.* Psychology Press.

Postmes, T., Spears, R., & Cihangir, S. (2001). Quality of decision making and group norms. *Journal of Personality and Social Psychology,* **80,** 918–930.

Postmes, T., Spears, R., & Lea, M. (2000). The formation of group norms in computer-mediated communication. *Human Communication Research*, **26**, 341–371.

Potârcă, G., Mills, M., & Neberich, W. (2015). Relationship preferences among gay and lesbian online daters: Individual and contextual influences. *Journal of Marriage and Family*, **77**(2), 523–541.

Potter, J. (1996). *Representing reality: Discourse, rhetoric and social construction.* Sage.

Potter, J., & Wetherell, M. (1987). *Discourse and social psychology: Beyond attitudes and behaviour.* Sage.

Poulter, J. (2018). The discursive reconstruction of memory and national identity: The anti-war memorial the Island of Ireland Peace Park. *Memory Studies*, **11**(2), 191–208.

Pratkanis, A. R., Greenwald, A. G., Leippe, M. R., & Baumgardner, M. H. (1988). In search of reliable persuasion effects: III. The sleeper effect is dead. Long live the sleeper effect. *Journal of Personality and Social Psychology*, **54**, 203–218.

Pratto, F., Sidanius, J., Stallworth, L. M., & Malle, B. F. (1994). Social dominance orientation: A personality variable predicting social and political attitudes. *Journal of Personality and Social Psychology*, **67**, 741–763.

Praxmarer, S., & Rossiter, J. (2011). How does the presenter's physical attractiveness persuade? A test of alternative explanations. Working Paper, University of Wollongong.

Privitera, M. R., Rosenstein, A. H., Plessow, F., & LoCastro, T. (2015). Physician burnout and occupational stress: An inconvenient truth with unintended consequences. *Journal of Hospital Administration*, **4**(1), 27–35.

Pronin, E., Lin, D. Y., & Ross, L. (2002). The bias blind spot: Perceptions of bias in self versus others. *Personality and Social Psychology Bulletin*, **28**, 369–381.

Provine, R. R. (2005). Yawning. *American Scientist*, **93**, 532–539.

Provine, R. R. (2012). *Curious behavior: Yawning, laughing, hiccuping and beyond.* Belknap Press of Harvard University Press. https://ebookcentral.proquest.com/lib/open/reader.action?docID=3301119&ppg=23

Pruitt, D. G. (1998). Social conflict. In D. Gilbert, S. T. Fiske, & G. Lindzey (Eds.), *Handbook of social psychology* (4th ed.). McGraw-Hill.

Pryor, J. B., DeSouza, E. R., Fitness, J., Hutz, C., Kumpf, M., Lubbert, K., Pesonen, O., & Erber, M. W. (1997). Gender differences in the interpretation of social-sexual behavior: A cross-cultural perspective on sexual harassment. *Journal of Cross-Cultural Psychology*, **28**, 509–534.

Puentes, J., Knox, D., & Zusman, M. E. (2008). Participants in 'friends with benefits' relationships. *College Student Journal*, **42**(1), 176–180.

Putnam, R. (2000). *Bowling alone: The collapse and revival of American community.* Simon & Schuster.

Pyszczynski, T., Abdollahi, A., Solomon, S., Greenberg, J., Cohen, F., & Weise, D. (2006). Mortality salience, martyrdom, and military might: The great Satan versus the axis of evil. *Personality and Social Psychology Bulletin*, **32**, 525–537.

Pyszczynski, T., Greenberg, J., & Solomon, S. (2000). Why do we need what we need? A terror management perspective on the roots of human social motivation. In E. T. Higgins & A. W. Kruglanski (Eds.), *Motivational science: Social and personality perspectives.* Psychology Press.

Q

Qiu, C., & Yeung, C. (2008). Mood and comparative judgment: Does mood influence everything and finally nothing? *Journal of Consumer Research*, **34**(5), 657–669.

Quadflieg, S., & Macrae, N. (2011). Stereotypes and stereotyping: What's the brain got to do with it? *European Review of Social Psychology*, **22**, 215–273.

Quam, J., & Ryshina-Pankova, M. (2016). 'Let me tell you. . .': Audience engagement strategies in the campaign speeches of Trump, Clinton, and Sanders. *Russian Journal of Linguistics*, **20**(4), 140–160.

Quam, J. K., Whitford, G. S., Dziengel, L. E., & Knochel, K. A. (2010). Exploring the nature of same-sex relationships. *Journal of Gerontological Social Work*, **53**(8), 702–722.

Quartz, S. R., & Sejnowski, T. J. (2002). *Liars, lovers, and heroes: What the new brain science reveals about how we become who we are.* Morrow.

Quintana, S. M. (1998). Development of children's understanding of ethnicity and race. *Applied & Preventive Psychology*, **7**, 27–45.

R

Rabbie, J. M., & Bekkers, F. (1978). Threatened leadership and intergroup competition. *European Journal of Social Psychology*, **8**, 9–20.

Rabbie, J. M., Schot, J.C., & Visser, L. (1989). Social identity theory: A conceptual and empirical critique from the perspective of a behavioural interaction model. *European Journal of Social Psychology*, **19**(3), 171–202.

Rae, J. R., & Olson, K. R. (2018). Test-retest reliability and predictive validity of the implicit association test in children. *Developmental Psychology*, **54**(2), 308–330.

Rahman, Q., & Hull, M. S. (2005). An empirical test of the kin selection hypothesis of male homosexuality. *Archives of Sexual Behavior*, **34**, 461–467.

Rai, R., Mitchell, P., & Faelling, J. (2012). The illusion-of-transparency: Are people egocentric or do people think that lies are easy to detect? *Psychological Studies*, **57**(1), 58–66.

Rambotti, S. (2015). Recalibrating the spirit level: An analysis of the interaction of income inequality and poverty and its effect on health. *Social Science and Medicine*, **139**, 123–131.

Ramirez, J. M., Bonniot-Cabanac, M.-C., & Cabanac, M. (2005). Can aggression provide pleasure? *European Psychologist*, **10**, 136–145.

Rand, J. W. (2000). The demeanor gap: Race, lie detection, and the jury. *Connecticut Law Review*, **33**, 1–14.

Rasmussen, J. (2015). 'Should each of us take over the role as watcher?' Attitudes on Twitter towards the 2014 Norwegian terror alert. *Journal of Multicultural Discourses*, **10**(2), 1–17. https://doi.org/10.1080/17447143.2015.1042882

Rast, D. E., Gaffney, A. M., Hogg, M. A., & Crisp, R. J. (2012). Leadership under uncertainty: When leaders who are non-prototypical group members can gain support. *Journal of Experimental Social Psychology*, **48**(3), 646–653. https://doi.org/10.1016/j.jesp.2011.12.013

Rattan, S. (2011). Self, culture, and anxious experiences. *Journal of Adult Development*, **18**(1), 28–36.

Redding, R. E. (2012). Likes attract: The sociopolitical groupthink of (social) psychologists. *Perspectives on Psychological Science*, **7**(5), 512–515.

Reeves, F. (1983). *British racial discourse.* Cambridge University Press.

Regan, D., & Morrison, T. G. (2011). Development and validation of a scale measuring attitudes toward non-drinkers. *Substance Use and Misuse*, **46**, 580–590.

Regan, P. C., Lakhanpal, S., & Anguiano, C. (2012). Relationship outcomes in Indian-American love-based and arranged marriages. *Psychological Reports*, **110**(3), 915–924. https://doi.org/10.2466/21.02.07.PR0.110.3.915-924

Reichelt, J., Sievert, J., & Jacob, F. (2014). How credibility affects eWOM reading: The influences of expertise, trustworthiness, and similarity on utilitarian and social functions. *Journal of Marketing Communications*, **20**(1-2), 65–81. https://doi.org/10.1080/13527266.2013.797758

Reicher, S. D. (1984). The St Paul's riot: An explanation of the limits of crowd action in terms of a social identity model. *European Journal of Social Psychology*, **14**, 1–21.

Reicher, S., & Haslam, A. (2004). Commentary: The banality of evil. *Anthropology News*, **45**(6), 14–15.

Reicher, S., & Haslam, S. A. (2006). Rethinking the psychology of tyranny: The BBC prison study. *British Journal of Social Psychology*, **45**, 1–40.

Reicher, S., & Haslam, S. A. (2011). After shock? Towards a social identity explanation of the Milgram 'obedience' studies. *British Journal of Social Psychology*, **50**(1), 163–169.

Reicher, S., & Hopkins, N. (1996). Self-category constructions in political rhetoric; an analysis of Thatcher's and Kinnock's speeches concerning the British miners' strike (1984–5). *European Journal of Social Psychology*, **26**, 353–371.

Reicher, S., & Hopkins, N. (2001). *Self and nation.* Sage.

Reicher, S., Haslam, S. A., & Rath, R. (2008). Making a virtue of evil: A five-step social identity model of the development of collective hate. *Social and Personality Psychology Compass,* 2(3), 1313–1344.

Reicher, S. D., Haslam, S. A., & Smith, J. R. (2012). Working toward the experimenter: Reconceptualizing obedience within the Milgram paradigm as identification-based followership. *Perspectives on Psychological Science,* **7,** 315–324.

Reicher, S., Stott, C., Cronin, P., & Adang, O. (2004). An integrated approach to crowd psychology and public order policing. *Policing,* **27**(4), 558–572.

Reid, D. J., & Reid, F. J. M. (2007). Text or talk? Social anxiety, loneliness, and divergent preferences for cell phone use. *Cyber Psychology and Behavior,* **10**(3), 424–435.

Reidy, D. E., Shelley-Tremblay, J. F., & Lilienfeld, S. O. (2011). Psychopathy, reactive aggression, and precarious proclamations: A review of behavioral, cognitive, and biological research. *Aggression and Violent Behavior,* **16**(6), 512–524.

Reidy, D. E., Shirk, S. D., Sloan, C. A., & Zeichner, A. (2009). Men who aggress against women: Effects of feminine gender role violation on physical aggression in hypermasculine men. *Psychology of Men & Masculinity,* **10**(1), 1–12.

Reilly, D., Neumann, D. L., & Andrews, G. (2017). Gender differences in spatial ability: Implications for STEM education and approaches to reducing the gender gap for parents and educators. In M. Khine (Ed.), *Visual-spatial ability in STEM education.* Springer.

Reiner, W. G., & Gearhart, J. P. (2004). Discordant sexual identity in some genetic males with cloacal exstrophy assigned to female sex at birth. *New England Journal of Medicine,* **350,** 333–341.

Reis, H., Maniaci, M., Caprariello, P., Eastwick, P., & Finkel, E. (2011). Familiarity does indeed promote attraction in live interaction. *Journal of Personality and Social Psychology,* **101**(3), 557–570.

Rempel, J. K., Ross, M., & Holmes, J. G. (2001). Trust and communicated attributions in close relationships. *Journal of Personality and Social Psychology,* **81**(1), 57–64.

Reynolds, J., & Wetherell, M. (2003). The discursive climate of singleness: The consequences for women's negotiation of a single identity. *Feminism and Psychology,* **13**(4), 489–510.

Reysen, S., & Levine, R. (2014). People, culture, and place: How place predicts helping toward strangers. In P. J. Rentfrow (Ed.), *Geographical psychology: Exploring the interaction of environment and behavior* (pp. 241–260). American Psychological Association. https://doi.org/10.1037/14272-013

Reza Jalilvand, M., & Samiei, N. (2012). The effect of electronic word of mouth on brand image and purchase intention. *Marketing Intelligence & Planning,* **30**(4), 460–476.

Rhodes, G. (2006). The evolutionary psychology of facial beauty. *Annual Review of Psychology,* **57,** 199–226.

Rhodes, G., Chan, J., Zebrowitz, L. A., & Simmons, L. W. (2003). Does sexual dimorphism in human faces signal health? *Proceedings of the Royal Society, London, B (Suppl),* **270,** S93–S95. https://doi.org/10.1098/rsbl.2003.0023

Rhodewalt, F. (1987). Is self-handicapping an effective self-protective attributional strategy? Paper presented at the American Psychological Association convention.

Rholes, W. S., Newman, L. S., & Ruble, D. N. (1990). Understanding self and other: Developmental and motivational aspects of perceiving persons in terms of invariant dispositions. In E. T. Higgins & R. M. Sorrentino (Eds.), *Handbook of motivation and cognition: Foundations of social behavior* (Vol. 2). Guilford Press.

Rich, F. (2001, 20 May). Naked capitalists: There's no business like porn business. *New York Times:* www.nytimes.com.

Ridge, R. D., & Reber, J. S. (2002). 'I think she's attracted to me': The effect of men's beliefs on women's behavior in a job interview scenario. *Basic and Applied Social Psychology,* **24,** 1–14.

Rietzschel, E. F., Nijstad, B. A., & Stroebe, W. (2006). Productivity is not enough: A comparison of interactive and nominal brainstorming groups on idea generation and selection. *Journal of Experimental Social Psychology,* **42,** 244–251.

Riley, T., & Ungerleider, C. (2012). Self-fulfilling prophecy: How teachers' attributions, expectations, and stereotypes influence the learning opportunities afforded aboriginal students. *Canadian Journal of Education,* **35**(2), 303.

Rinck, M., & Becker, E.S. (2005). A comparison of attentional biases and memory biases in women with social phobia and major depression. *Journal of Abnormal Psychology,* **114,** 62–74.

Risen, J. L., & Gilovich, T. (2007). Target and observer differences in the acceptance of questionable apologies. *Journal of Personality and Social Psychology,* **92**(3), 418–433.

Risen, J. L., Gilovich, T., & Dunning, D. (2007). One-shot illusory correlations and stereotype formation. *Personality and Social Psychology Bulletin,* **33**(11), 1492–1502.

Rist, R. (2000). HER classic reprint-student social class and teacher expectations: The self-fulfilling prophecy in ghetto education. *Harvard Educational Review,* **70**(3), 257–302.

Ritchie, S. J., Wiseman, R., & French, C. C. (2012). Failing the future: Three unsuccessful replications of Bem's 'retroactive facilitation of recall' effect. *PLoS ONE,* **7**(3): e33423. https://doi.org/10.1371/journal.pone.0033423

Rivkin, I. D., & Taylor, S. E. (1999). The effects of mental stimulation on coping with controllable stressful events. *Personality and Social Psychology Bulletin,* **25,** 1451–1462.

Rizzoli, V., Castro, P., Tuzzi, A., & Contarello, A. (2019). Probing the history of social psychology, exploring diversity and views of the social: Publication trends in the European Journal of Social Psychology from 1971 to 2016. *European Journal of Social Psychology,* **49**(4), 671–687. https://doi.org.libezproxy.open.ac.uk/10.1002/ejsp.2528

Roach, M. (1998, December). Why men kill. *Discover,* 100–108.

Robberson, M. R., & Rogers, R. W. (1988). Beyond fear appeals: Negative and positive persuasive appeals to health and self-esteem. *Journal of Applied Social Psychology,* **18,** 277–287.

Roberts, B. W., Edmonds, G., & Grijalva, E. (2010). It is developmental me, not generation me: Developmental changes are more important than generational changes in narcissism – Commentary on Trzesniewski & Donnellan (2010). *Perspectives on Psychological Science,* **5,** 97–102.

Robins, R. W., Caspi, A., & Moffitt, T. E. (2002). It's not just who you're with, it's who you are: Personality and relationship experiences across multiple relationships. *Journal of Personality,* **70,** 925–964. https://doi.org/10.1111/1467-6494.05028

Robins, R. W., Mendelsohn, G. A., Connell, J. B., & Kwan, V. S. Y. (2004). Do people agree about the causes of behavior? A social relations analysis of behavior ratings and causal attributions. *Journal of Personality and Social Psychology,* **86,** 334–344.

Robinson, M. D., & Ryff, C. D. (1999). The role of self-deception in perceptions of past, present, and future happiness. *Personality and Social Psychology Bulletin,* **25,** 595–606.

Robinson, S.B., & Leonard, F. (2018). *Designing quality survey questions.* Sage.

Robinson, T. N., Wilde, M. L., Navracruz, L. C., Haydel, F., & Varady, A. (2001). Effects of reducing children's television and video game use on aggressive behavior. *Archives of Pediatric and Adolescent Medicine,* **155,** 17–23.

Rochat, F. (1993). How did they resist authority? Protecting refugees in Le Chambon during World War II. Paper presented at the American Psychological Association convention.

Rochat, F., & Modigliani, A. (1995). The ordinary quality of resistance: From Milgram's laboratory to the village of Le Chambon. *Journal of Social Issues,* **51,** 195–210.

Rockloff, M. J., & Dyer, V. (2007). An experiment on the social facilitation of gambling behavior. *Journal of Gambling Studies,* **23,** 1–12.

Roediger, H. L., III, & Geraci, L. (2007). Aging and the misinformation effect: A neuropsychological analysis. *Journal of Experimental Psychology: Learning, Memory, and Cognition,* **33**(2), 321–334. https://doi-org.libezproxy.open.ac.uk/10.1037/0278-7393.33.2.321

Roehling, M. V. (2000). Weight-based discrimination in employment: psychological and legal aspects. *Personnel Psychology,* **52,** 969–1016.

Roese, N. J., & Hur, T. (1997). Affective determinants of counterfactual thinking. *Social Cognition,* **15,** 274–290.

Roger, L. H., Cortes, D. E., & Malgady, R. B. (1991). Acculturation and mental health status among Hispanics: Convergence and new directions for research. *American Psychologist,* **46,** 585–597.

Rogers, C. R. (1980). *A way of being.* Houghton Mifflin.

Roggenbuck, J. (1992). Use of persuasion to reduce resource impacts and visitor conflicts. In M. Manfredo (Ed.), *Influencing human behavior: Theory and applications in recreation, tourism and natural resources management.* Sagamore.

Rohrer, J. H., Baron, S. H., Hoffman, E. L., & Swander, D. V. (1954). The stability of autokinetic judgments. *Journal of Abnormal and Social Psychology,* **49,** 595.

Rojahn, J., Komelasky, K. G., & Man, M. (2008). Opposite-sex peers with physical disabilities. *Journal of Developmental and Physical Disabilities,* **20**(4), 389–397.

Rokeach, M. (1960). *The open and closed mind: Investigations into the nature of belief systems and personality systems.* Basic Books.

Roman, C. P. (2006). A worker's personal grief and its impact on processing a group's termination. *Social Work with Groups,* **29**(2–3), 235–242. https://doi.org/10.1300/J009v29n02_15

Rosander, M., & Eriksson, O. (2012). Conformity on the Internet: The role of task difficulty and gender differences. *Computers in Human Behavior,* **28**(5), 1587–1595.

Rosch, E. (1975). Cognitive representations of semantic categories. *Journal of Experimental Psychology,* **104**(3), 192–233.

Rosenberg, L. A. (1961). Group size, prior experience and conformity. *Journal of Abnormal and Social Psychology,* **63,** 436–437.

Rosenblatt, A., Greenberg, J., Solomon, S., Pyszczynski, T., & Lyon, D. L. (1989). Evidence for terror management theory: I. The effects of mortality salience on reactions to those who violate or uphold cultural values. *Journal of Personality and Social Psychology,* **57**(4), 681–690.

Rosenbloom, S. (2008, 3 January). Putting your best cyberface forward. *New York Times,* Style section.

Rosenbloom, T., Shahar, A., Perlman, A., Estreich, D., & Kirzner, E. (2007). Success on a practical driver's licence test with and without the presence of another testee. *Accident Analysis and Prevention,* **39,** 1296–1301.

Rosenhan, D. L. (1970). The natural socialization of altruistic autonomy. In J. Macauley & L. Berkowitz (Eds.), *Altruism and helping behavior.* Academic Press.

Rosenhan, D. L. (1973). On being sane in insane places. *Science,* **179,** 250–258.

Rosenquist, J. N., Fowler, J. H., & Christakis, N. A. (2011). Social network determinants of depression. *Molecular Psychiatry,* **16**(3), 273–281.

Rosenstock, I. (1974). Historical origins of the health belief model. *Health Education & Behavior,* **2**(4), 328–335.

Rosenthal, R. (1985). From unconscious experimenter bias to teacher expectancy effects. In J. B. Dusek, V. C. Hall, & W. J. Meyer (Eds.), *Teacher expectancies.* Erlbaum.

Rosenthal, R. (1991). Teacher expectancy effects: A brief update 25 years after the Pygmalion experiment. *Journal of Research in Education,* **1,** 3–12.

Rosenthal, R. (2002). Covert communication in classrooms, clinics, courtrooms, and cubicles. *American Psychologist,* **57,** 839–849.

Rosenthal, R. (2003). Covert communication in laboratories, classrooms, and the truly real world. *Current Directions in Psychological Science,* **12,** 151–154.

Rosenthal, R., & Jacobson, L. (1968). *Pygmalion in the classroom: Teacher expectation and pupils' intellectual development.* Holt, Rinehart & Winston.

Rosh, E. (1978). Principles of categorization. In E. Rosh and B. B. Lloyd (Eds.), *Cognition and categorization.* Erlbaum.

Rosh, E., Mervis, C. G., Gray, W. D., Johnson, D. M., & Bayes Braem, P. (1976). Basic objects in natural categories. *Cognitive Psychology,* **8,** 382–439.

Ross, E. A. (1908). *Social psychology.* Macmillan.

Ross, K. M., Rook, K., Winczewski, L., Collins, N., & Dunkel Schetter, C. (2019). Close relationships and health: The interactive effect of positive and negative aspects. *Social and Personality Psychology Compass,* **13**(6). https://doi.org/10.1111/spc3.12468

Ross, L. (1977). The intuitive psychologist and his shortcomings: Distortions in the attribution process. In L. Berkowitz (Ed.), *Advances in experimental social psychology* (Vol. 10). Academic Press.

Ross, L. (1981). The 'intuitive scientist' formulation and its developmental implications. In J. H. Havell & L. Ross (Eds.), *Social cognitive development: Frontiers and possible futures.* Cambridge University Press.

Ross, L. (1988). Situationist perspectives on the obedience experiments. Review of A. G. Miller's *The obedience experiments. Contemporary Psychology,* **33,** 101–104.

Ross, L., & Lepper, M. R. (1980). The perseverance of beliefs: Empirical and normative considerations. In R. A. Shweder (Ed.), *New directions for methodology of behavioral science: Fallible judgment in behavioral research.* Jossey-Bass.

Ross, L., & Ward, A. (1995). Psychological barriers to dispute resolution. In M. P. Zanna (Ed.), *Advances in experimental social psychology* (Vol. 27). Academic Press.

Ross, L., Amabile, T. M., & Steinmetz, J. L. (1977). Social roles, social control, and biases in social-perception processes. *Journal of Personality and Social Psychology,* **35,** 485–494.

Ross, L., Lepper, M. R., & Hubbard, M. (1975). Perseverance in self-perception and social perception: Bias attributional processes in the debriefing paradigm. *Journal of Personality and Social Psychology,* **32,** 880–892. https://doi.org/10.1037/0022-3514.32.5.880

Rotenberg, K. J., Gruman, J. A., & Ariganello, M. (2002). Behavioral confirmation of the loneliness stereotype. *Basic and Applied Social Psychology,* **24,** 81–89.

Rothbart, M. K. (2011). *Becoming who we are: Temperament and personality in development.* Guilford Press.

Rothbart, M., & Birrell, P. (1977). Attitude and perception of faces. *Journal of Research Personality,* **11,** 209–215.

Rothbart, M., & Taylor, M. (1992). Social categories and social reality. In G. R. Semin & K. Fielder (Eds.), *Language, interaction and social cognition.* Sage.

Rotter, J. (1973). Internal-external locus of control scale. In J. P. Robinson & R. P. Shaver (Eds.), *Measure of social psychological attitudes.* Institute for Social Research.

Rouse, K. A. G. (2004). Beyond Maslow's hierarchy of needs what do people strive for? *Performance Improvement,* **43**(10), 27–31. https://doi.org/10.1002/pfi.4140431008

Rousseau, J. J. (2016). *The social contract and discourses.* Devoted Publishing.

Ruback, R. B., & Singh, P. (2007). Ingroup bias, intergroup contact and the attribution of blame for riots. *Psychology and Developing Societies,* **19**(2), 249–265.

Rubin, A. (2003, 16 April). War fans young Arabs' anger. *Los Angeles Times:* www.latimes.com.

Rubin, J. Z. (1986). Can we negotiate with terrorists: Some answers from psychology. Paper presented at the American Psychological Association convention.

Rubin, R. B. (1981). Ideal traits and terms of address for male and female college professors. *Journal of Personality and Social Psychology,* **41,** 966–974.

Ruble, D. N., & Martin, C. L. (1998). Gender development. In D. W. Damon (Ed.), *Handbook of child psychology* (Vol. 3, 5th ed.). Holt, Rinehart & Winston.

Ruble, D., Alvarez, J., Bachman, M., Cameron, J., Fuligni, A., Garcia Coll, C., & Rhee, E. (2004). The development of a sense of 'we': The emergence and implications of children's collective identity. In M. Bennett & F. Sani (Eds.), *The development of the social self.* Psychology Press.

Ruby, P., & Decety, J. (2004). How would you feel versus how do you think she would feel? A neuroimaging study of perspective-taking with social emotions. *Journal of Cognitive Neuroscience,* **16,** 988–999.

Rudman, L. A., & Glick, P. (2008). *The social psychology of gender: How power and intimacy shape gender relations.* Guilford Press.

Rudolph, U., Roesch, S. C., Greitenmeyer, T., & Weiner, B. (2004). A meta-analytic review of help giving and aggression from an attributional perspective: Contributions to a general theory of motivation. *Cognition and Emotion,* **18,** 815–848.

Ruiter, R. A. C., Abraham, C., & Kok, G. (2001). Scary warnings and rational precautions: A review of the psychology of fear appeals. *Psychology and Health,* **16,** 613–630.

Rumbelow, H. (2014, January 16). How did this woman combat sex attacks in India? She formed a Fight Club; India's first female Olympic boxer is teaching women self-defence. She tells why. *The Times,* p. 46.

Runciman, W. G. (1966). *Relative deprivation and social justice.* Routledge.

Rusbult, C. E. (1980). Commitment and satisfaction in romantic associations: A test of the investment model. *Journal of Experimental Social Psychology,* **16,** 172–186.

Rusbult, C. E., Johnson, D. J., & Morrow, G. D. (1986). Impact of couple patterns of problem solving on distress and nondistress in dating relationships. *Journal of Personality and Social Psychology,* **50,** 744–753.

Rusbult, C. E., Martz, J. M., & Agnew, C. R. (1998). The investment model scale: Measuring commitment level, satisfaction level, quality of alternatives, and investment size. *Personal Relationships,* **5,** 357–391.

Rusbult, C. E., Morrow, G. D., & Johnson, D. J. (1987). Self-esteem and problem-solving behaviour in close relationships. *British Journal of Social Psychology,* **26,** 293–303.

Rusbult, C. E., Olsen, N., Davis, J. L., & Hannon, P. A. (2001). Commitment and relationship maintenance mechanisms. In J. Harvey & A. Wenzel (Eds.), *Close romantic relationships: Maintenance and enhancement.* Erlbaum.

Russell, N. J. C. (2011). Milgram's obedience to authority experiments: Origins and early evolution. *British Journal of Social Psychology,* **50**(1), 140–162.

Russell, N. J. C., & Gregory, R. J. (2005). Making the undoable doable: Milgram, the Holocaust, and modern government. *American Review of Public Administration,* **35,** 327–349.

Rutherford, A., Vaughn-Blount, K., & Ball, L. C. (2010). Responsible opposition, disruptive voices: Science, social change, and the history of feminist psychology. *Psychology of Women Quarterly,* **34**(4), 460–473. https://doi.org/10.1111/j.1471-6402.2010.01596.x

Ruvolo, A., & Markus, H. (1992). Possible selves and performance: The power of self-relevant imagery. *Social Cognition,* **9,** 95–124.

Ryan, M. K., & Haslam, S. A. (2005). The glass cliff: Evidence that women are over-represented in precarious leadership positions. *British Journal of Management,* **16,** 81–90.

Ryan, M. K., Haslam, S. A., Morgenroth, T., Rink, F., Stoker, J., & Peters, K. (2016). Getting on top of the glass cliff: Reviewing a decade of evidence, explanations, and impact. *The Leadership Quarterly,* **27**(3), 446–455.

Ryan, R. M., & Deci, E. L. (2000). Self-determination theory and the facilitation of intrinsic motivation, social development, and well-being. *American Psychologist,* **55**(1), 68.

Ryff, C. D., & Singer, B. (2000). Interpersonal flourishing: A positive health agenda for the new millennium. *Personality and Social Psychology Review,* **4,** 30–44.

S

Saabneh, A. M. (2016). Arab-Jewish gap in life expectancy in Israel. *European Journal of Public Health,* **26**(3), 433–438. https://doi.org/10.1093/eurpub/ckv211

Saal, F. E., Johnson, C. B., & Weber, N. (1989). Friendly or sexy? It may depend on whom you ask. *Psychology of Women Quarterly,* **13,** 263–276.

Sacerdote, B., & Marmaros, D. (2005). How do friendships form? NBER Working Paper No. 11530: www.nber.org/papers/W11530

Sacks, H. (1992). *Lectures on conversation* (2 vols. Ed. G. Jefferson, with an introduction by E. A. Schegloff). Blackwell.

Sagarin, B. J., Cialdini, R. B., Rice, W. E., & Serna, S. B. (2002). Dispelling the illusion of invulnerability: The motivations and mechanisms of resistance to persuasion. *Journal of Personality and Social Psychology,* **83,** 526–541.

Salganik, M. J., Dodds, P. S., & Watts, D. J. (2006). Experimental study of inequality and unpredictability in an artificial cultural market. *Science,* **311,** 854–856.

Salmivalli, C. (2010). Bullying and the peer group: A review. *Aggression and Violent Behavior,* **15,** 112–120.

Saltzstein, H. D., & Sandberg, L. (1979). Indirect social influence: Change in judgmental processor anticipatory conformity. *Journal of Experimental Social Psychology,* **15,** 209–216.

Samir, K. C., & Lutz, W. (2017). The human core of the shared socioeconomic pathways: Population scenarios by age, sex and level of education for all countries to 2100. *Global Environmental Change,* **42,** 181–192.

Samnani, A.-K., & Singh, P. (2013). When leaders victimize: The role of charismatic leaders in facilitating group pressures. *The Leadership Quarterly,* **24**(1), 189–202. https://doi.org/10.1016/j.leaqua.2012.10.006

Sandfield, A., & Percy, C. (2003). Accounting for single status: Heterosexism and ageism in heterosexual women's talk about marriage. *Feminism & Psychology,* **13**(4), 475–488.

Sani, F. (2005). When subgroups secede: Extending and refining the social psychological model of schisms in groups. *Personality and Social Psychology Bulletin,* **31,** 1074–1086.

Sani, F. (2008). Schism in groups: A social psychological account. *Social and Personality Psychology Compass,* **2,** 718–732.

Sani, F., & Bennett, M. (2001). Contextual variability in young children's gender ingroup stereotype. *Social Development,* **10,** 221–229.

Sani, F., & Bennett, M. (2009). Children's inclusion of the group in the self: evidence from a self-ingroup confusion paradigm. *Developmental Psychology,* **45,** 503–510.

Sani, F., & Pugliese A. C. (2008). In the name of Mussolini: Explaining the schism in an Italian right-wing political party. *Group Dynamics: Theory, Research, and Practice,* **12,** 242–253.

Sani, F., & Reicher, S. (1999). Identity, argument and schism: two longitudinal studies of the split in the Church of England over the ordination of women to the priesthood. *Group Processes & Intergroup Relations,* **2,** 279–300.

Sani, F., & Reicher, S. (2000). Contested identities and schisms in groups: Opposing the ordination of women as priests in the Church of England. *British Journal of Social Psychology,* **39,** 95–112.

Sani, F., & Thomson, L. (2001). We are what we wear: The emergence of consensus in stereotypes of students and managers' dressing style. *Social Behaviour and Personality,* **29,** 695–700.

Sani, F., & Todman, J. (2002). Should we stay or should we go? A social psychological model of schisms within groups. *Personality and Social Psychology Bulletin,* **28,** 1647–1655.

Sani, F., & Todman, J. (2006). *Experimental design and statistics for psychology: A first course.* Blackwell.

Sani, F., Bennett, M., Agostini, L., Malucchi, L., & Ferguson, N. (2000). Children's conception of characteristic features of category members. *Journal of Social Psychology,* **140,** 227–239.

Sani, F., Bennett, M., Mullally, S., & McPherson, J. (2003). On the assumption of fixity in children's stereotypes: A reappraisal. *British Journal of Developmental Psychology,* **21,** 113–124.

Sani, F., Herrera, M., & Bowe, M. (2009). Perceived collective continuity and ingroup identification as defence against death awareness. *Journal of Experimental Social Psychology,* **45,** 242–245.

Sani, F., Madhok, V., Norbury, M., Dugard, P., & Wakefield, J. R. (2015). Greater number of group identifications is associated with healthier behaviour: Evidence from a Scottish community sample. *British Journal of Health Psychology,* **20**(3), 466–481.

Sanislow, C. A., III, Perkins, D. V., & Balogh, D. W. (1989). Mood induction, interpersonal perceptions, and rejection in the roommates of depressed, nondepressed, disturbed, and normal college students. *Journal of Social and Clinical Psychology,* **8,** 345–358.

Sanjuán, P., & Magallares, A. (2008). Coping strategies as link between optimistic explanatory styles and well-being. In T.Freire (Ed.), *Understanding positive life: Research and practice on positive psychology* (pp. 169–182). Climepsi Editores.

Sanna, L. J., Parks, C. D., Meier, S., Chang, E. C., Kassin, B. R., Lechter, J. L., Turley-Ames, K. J., & Miyake, T. M. (2003). A game of inches: Spontaneous use of counterfactuals by broadcasters during major league baseball playoffs. *Journal of Applied Social Psychology,* **33,** 455–475.

Santini, Z. I., Fiori, K. L., Feeney, J., Tyrovolas, S., Haro, J. M., & Koyanagi, A. (2016). Social relationships, loneliness, and mental health among older men and women in Ireland: A prospective community-based study. *Journal of Affective Disorders,* **204,** 59–69. https://doi.org/10.1016/j.jad.2016.06.032

Santos, H., Varnum, M., & Grossmann, I. (2017). Global increases in individualism. *Psychological Science,* **28**(9), 1228–1239.

Sapolsky, B. S., & Tabarlet, J. O. (1991). Sex in prime time television: 1979 versus 1989.

Journal of Broadcasting and Electronic Media, **35**, 505–516.

Sapolsky, R. (2005, December). Sick of poverty. *Scientific American*, 93–99.

Sargent, J. D., Heatherton, T. F., & Ahrens, M. B. (2002). Adolescent exposure to extremely violent movies. *Journal of Adolescent Health*, **31**, 449–454.

Saucier, D. A., & Miller, C. T. (2003). The persuasiveness of racial arguments as a subtle measure of racism. *Personality and Social Psychology Bulletin*, **29**, 1303–1315.

Savage, J. (2004). Does viewing violent media really cause criminal violence? A methodological review. *Aggression and Violent Behavior*, **10**(1), 99–128.

Savage, J. (2008). The role of exposure to media violence in the etiology of violent behavior: A criminologist weighs in. *American Behavioral Scientist*, **51**(8), 1123–1136. https://doi.org/10.1177/0002764207312016

Savage, J., & Yancey, C. (2008). The effects of media violence exposure on criminal aggression: A meta-analysis. *Criminal Justice and Behavior*, **35**(6), 772–791.

Savitsky, K., Epley, N., & Gilovich, T. (2001). Do others judge us as harshly as we think? Overestimating the impact of our failures, shortcomings, and mishaps. *Journal of Personality and Social Psychology*, **81**, 44–56.

Sawdon, A. M., Cooper, M., & Seabrook, R. (2007). The relationship between self-discrepancies, eating disorder and depressive symptoms in women. *European Eating Disorders Review*, **15**, 207–212.

Scanlon, L. J., & Kull, C. A. (2009). Untangling the links between wildlife benefits and community-based conservation at Torra Conservancy, Namibia. *Development Southern Africa*, **26**(1), 75–93.

Schachter, S. (1951). Deviation, rejection and communication. *Journal of Abnormal and Social Psychology*, **46**, 190–207.

Schachter, S. (1959). *The psychology of affiliation*. Stanford University Press.

Schachter, S. (1964). The integration of cognitive and physiological determinants of emotional state. In L. Berkowitz (Ed.), *Advances in experimental social psychology* (Vol. 1). Academic Press.

Schachter, S., & Singer, J. E. (1962). Cognitive, social and physiological determinants of emotional state. *Psychological Review*, **69**(5), 379–399.

Schaffner, P. E., Wandersman, A., & Stang, D. (1981). Candidate name exposure and voting: Two field studies. *Basic and Applied Social Psychology*, **2**, 195–203.

Schaller, M., & Cialdini, R. B. (1988). The economics of empathic helping: Support for a mood management motive. *Journal of Experimental Social Psychology*, **24**, 163–181.

Schatz, P., & Dzvimbo, K. P. (2001). The adolescent sexual world and AIDS prevention: A democratic approach to programme design in Zimbabwe. *Health Promotion International*, **16**(2), 127–136. https://doi.org/10.1093/heapro/16.2.127

Scherrer, K. S. (2008). Coming to an asexual identity: Negotiating identity, negotiating desire. *Sexualities*, **11**(5), 621–641. https://doi.org/10.1177/1363460708094269

Schimel, J., Arndt, J., Pyszczynski, T., & Greenberg, J. (2001). Being accepted for who we are: Evidence that social validation of the intrinsic self reduces general defensiveness. *Journal of Personality and Social Psychology*, **80**, 35–52.

Schkade, D. A., & Kahneman, D. (1998). Does living in California make people happy? A focusing illusion in judgments of life satisfaction. *Psychological Science*, **9**, 340–346.

Schlegel, R. J., Hicks, J. A., King, L. A., & Arndt, J. (2011). Feeling like you know who you are: Perceived true self-knowledge and meaning in life. *Personality and Social Psychology Bulletin*, **37**(6), 745–756. https://doi.org/10.1177/0146167211400424

Schlenker, B. R. (1976). Egocentric perceptions in cooperative groups: A conceptualization and research review. Final Report, Office of Naval Research Grant NR 170–797.

Schlenker, B. R., & Leary, M. R. (1982). Social anxiety and self-presentation: A conceptualization and model. *Psychological Bulletin*, **92**, 641–669.

Schlenker, B. R., & Leary, M. R. (1985). Social anxiety and communication about the self. *Journal of Language and Social Psychology*, **4**, 171–192.

Schlenker, B. R., & Miller, R. S. (1977a). Group cohesiveness as a determinant of egocentric perceptions in cooperative groups. *Human Relations*, **30**, 1039–1055.

Schlenker, B. R., & Miller, R. S. (1977b). Egocentrism in groups: Self-serving biases or logical information processing? *Journal of Personality and Social Psychology*, **35**, 755–764.

Schlenker, B. R., & Weigold, M. F. (1992). Interpersonal processes involving impression regulation and management. *Annual Review of Psychology*, **43**, 133–168.

Schlesinger, A. M., Jr (1965). ***A thousand days.*** *Houghton Mifflin. Cited by I. L. Janis* (1972). *Victims of groupthink*. Houghton Mifflin.

Schlosser, E. (2003, 10 March). Empire of the obscene. *New Yorker*, 61–71.

Schmidt, L. A., & Buss, A. H. (2010). Understanding shyness: Four questions and four decades of research. In K. Rubin & R. Coplan (Eds.), *The development of shyness and social withdrawal* (pp. 23–41). Guilford Press.

Schmidt, M. F. H., Rakoczy, H., Mietzsch, T., & Tomasello, M. (2016). Young children understand the role of agreement in establishing arbitrary norms – but unanimity is key. *Child Development*, **87**(2), 612–626.

Schmitt, D. P., & Pilcher, J. J. (2004). Evaluating evidence of psychological adaptation: How do we know one when we see one? *Psychological Science*, **15**, 643–649.

Schmitt, D. P., Alcalay, L., Allensworth, M., Allik, J., Ault, L., Austers, I., Bennett, K. L., Bianchi, G., Boholst, F., Borg Cunen, M. A., Braeckman, J., Brainerd, E. G. Jr., Caral, L. G. A., Caron, G., Casullo, M. M., Cunningham, M., Daibo, I., De Backer, C., De Souza, E., . . . Zupanèiè, A. (2004). Patterns and universals of adult romantic attachment across 62 cultural regions are models of self and of other pancultural constructs? *Journal of Cross-Cultural Psychology*, **35**(4), 367–402.

Schmitt, M., Maes, J., & Widaman, K. (2010). Longitudinal effects of egoistic and fraternal relative deprivation on well-being and protest. *International Journal of Psychology*, **45**, 122–130. https://doi.org/10.1080/00207590903165067

Schmitt, M. T., & Branscombe, N. R. (2002). The meaning and consequences of perceived discrimination in disadvantaged and privileged social groups. *European Review of Social Psychology*, **12**, 167–199.

Schnall, S., & Laird, J. D. (2003). Keep smiling: Enduring effects of facial expressions and postures on emotional experience and memory. *Cognition and Emotion*, **17**, 787–797.

Schofield, J. (1982). *Black and white in school: Trust, tension, or tolerance?* Praeger.

Schofield, J. W. (1986). Causes and consequences of the colorblind perspective. In J. F. Dovidio & S. L. Gaertner (Eds.), *Prejudice, discrimination, and racism*. Academic Press.

Schot, J., Littvay, L., Turchin, P., Brams, S. J., & Gachter, S. (2016). Lessons from Brexit. *Nature*, **535**, 487–489. https://doi.org/10.1038/535487a

Schug, J., Yuki, M., Horikawa, H., & Takemura, K. (2009). Similarity attraction and actually selecting similar others: How cross-societal differences in relational mobility affect interpersonal similarity in Japan and the USA. *Asian Journal of Social Psychology*, **12**(2), 95–103.

Schulkin, J. (2011). *Adaptation and well-being: Social allostasis*. Cambridge University Press.

Schulz, J. W., & Pruitt, D. G. (1978). The effects of mutual concern on joint welfare. *Journal of Experimental Social Psychology*, **14**, 480–492.

Schulz-Hardt, S., Frey, D., Luthgens, C., & Moscovici, S. (2000). Biased information search in group decision making. *Journal of Personality and Social Psychology*, **78**, 655–669.

Schumann, K. (2012). Does love mean never having to say you're sorry? Associations between relationship satisfaction, perceived apology sincerity, and forgiveness. *Journal of Social and Personal Relationships*, **29**(7), 997–1010.

Schwartz, B. (2000). Self-determination: The tyranny of freedom. *American Psychologist*, **55**, 79–88.

Schwartz, B. (2004). *The tyranny of choice*. Ecco/HarperCollins.

Schwartz, C. E., Keyl, P. M., Marcum, J. P., & Bode, R. (2009). Helping others shows differential benefits on health and well-being for male and female teens. *Journal of Happiness Studies*, **10**(4), 431–448.

Schwartz, C. R., & Graf, N. L. (2009). Assortative matching among same-sex and different-sex couples in the United States, 1990–2000. *Demographic Research*, **21**, 843–878. https://doi.org/10.4054/demres.2009.21.28

Schwartz, S. H. (1975). The justice of need and the activation of humanitarian norms. *Journal of Social Issues,* **31**(3), 111–136.

Schwartz, S. H., & Gottlieb, A. (1981). Participants' postexperimental reactions and the ethics of bystander research. *Journal of Experimental Social Psychology,* **17**, 396–407.

Schwartz, S. H., & Rubel, T. (2005). Sex differences in value priorities: Cross-cultural and multimethod studies. *Journal of Personality and Social Psychology,* **89**, 1010–1028.

Schwarz, N., Bless, H., & Bohner, G. (1991). Mood and persuasion: Affective states influence the processing of persuasive communications. In M. Zanna (Ed.), *Advances in experimental social psychology* (Vol. 24). Academic Press.

Schwarz, S., & Hassebrauck, M. (2012). Sex and age differences in mate-selection preferences. *Human Nature,* **23**, 447–466.

Schweitzer, R., Perkoulidis, S., Krome, S., Ludlow, C., & Ryan, M. (2005). Attitudes towards refugees: The dark side of prejudice in Australia. *Australian Journal of Psychology,* **57**(3), 170–179.

Schwinger, M., Wirthwein, L., Lemmer, G., & Steinmayr, R. (2014). Academic self-handicapping and achievement: A meta-analysis. *Journal of Educational Psychology,* **106**(3), 744–761. https://doi-org.libezproxy.open.ac.uk/10.1037/a0035832

Scott, S. (2006). The medicalisation of shyness: From social misfits to social fitness. *Sociology of Health and Illness,* **28**(2), 133–153.

Scottish Government (2017). *Homicide in Scotland 2016–17.* https://www2.gov.scot/Resource/0052/00525786.pdf

Scottish Government (2019). *Scottish Crime and Justice Survey 2017–2018: Main findings.* https://www.gov.scot/publications/scottish-crime-justice-survey-2017-18-main-findings/

Scudder, V., Scudder, K., & Rosenfeld, K. (2012). *World class communication: How great CEOs win with the public, shareholders, employees, and the media.* John Wiley & Sons.

Seabrook, R., Ward, L., & Giaccardi, S. (2019). Less than human? Media use, objectification of women, and men's acceptance of sexual aggression. *Psychology of Violence,* **9**(5), 536–545.

Sears, D. O. (1981). Life stage effects on attitude change, especially among the elderly. In S. B. Kiesler, J. N. Morgan, & V. K. Oppenheimer (Eds.), *Aging: Social change* (pp. 183–204). Academic Press.

Sears, D. O. (1988). Symbolic racism. In P. A. Katz and D. A. Taylor (Eds.), *Eliminating racism: Profiles in controversy.* Plenum.

Sedikides, C., Rudich, E. A., Gregg, A. P., Kumashiro, M., & Rusbult, C. (2004). Are normal narcissists psychologically healthy? Self-esteem matters. *Journal of Personality and Social Psychology,* **87**(3), 400–416.

Segerstrom, S. C. (2001). Optimism and attentional bias for negative and positive stimuli. *Personality and Social Psychology Bulletin,* **27**, 1334–1343.

Segrin, C., & Domschke, T. (2011). Social support, loneliness, recuperative processes, and their direct and indirect effects on health. *Health Communication,* **26**(3), 221–232.

Seidel, E-M., Eickhoff, S. B., Kellermann, T., Schneider, F., Gur, R. C., Habel, U., & Derntl, B. (2010). Who is to blame? Neural correlates of causal attribution in social situations. *Social Neuroscience,* **5**, 335–350.

Seiter, J. S., & Hatch, S. (2005). Effect of tattoos on perceptions of credibility and attractiveness. *Psychological Reports,* **96**(3), 1113–1120.

Selfhout, M. H., Branje, S. J., & Meeus, W. H. (2007). Similarity in adolescent best friendships: The role of gender. *Netherlands Journal of Psychology,* **63**(2), 42–48.

Selfhout, M., Denissen, J., Branje, S., & Meeus, W. (2009). In the eye of the beholder: Perceived, actual, and peer-rated similarity in personality, communication, and friendship intensity during the acquaintanceship process. *Journal of Personality and Social Psychology,* **96**(6), 1152–1165.

Seligman, M. E. P. (1975). *Helplessness: On depression, development and death.* W. H. Freeman.

Seligman, M. E. P. (1991). *Learned optimism.* Knopf.

Seligman, M. E. P. (1998). The prediction and prevention of depression. In D. K. Routh & R. J. DeRubeis (Eds.), *The science of clinical psychology: Accomplishments and future directions.* American Psychological Association.

Seligman, M. E. P. (2002). *Authentic happiness: Using the new positive psychology to realize your potential for lasting fulfillment.* The Free Press.

Shaffer, D. R., Pegalis, L. J., & Bazzini, D. G. (1996). When boy meets girls (revisited): Gender, gender-role orientation, and prospect of future interaction as determinants of self-disclosure among same- and opposite-sex acquaintances. *Personality and Social Psychology Bulletin,* **22**, 495–506.

Shapiro, S., & Leopold, L. (2012). A critical role for role-playing pedagogy. *TESL Canada Journal,* **29**, 120–130.

Sharma, V., & Kaur, I. (1996). Interpersonal attraction in relation to the loss-gain hypothesis. *Journal of Social Psychology,* **136**(5), 635–638.

Shaw Taylor, L., Fiore, A. T., Mendelsohn, G. A., & Cheshire, C. (2011). 'Out of my league': A real-world test of the matching hypothesis. *Personality and Social Psychology Bulletin,* **37**(7), 942–954.

Shaw, M. E. (1981). *Group dynamics: The psychology of small group behavior.* McGraw-Hill.

Shaw, P., & Tan, Y. (2014). Race and masculinity: A comparison of Asian and Western models in men's lifestyle magazine advertisements. *Journalism & Mass Communication Quarterly,* **91**(1), 118–138. https://doi.org/10.1177/1077699013514410

Sheafer, T. (2001). Charismatic skill and media legitimacy: An actor-centered approach to understanding the political communication competition. *Communication Research,* **28**, 711–736.

Sheafer, T. (2008). Charismatic communication skill, media legitimacy and electoral success. *Journal of Political Marketing,* **7**, 1–24.

Shechory, M., & Ziv, R. (2007). Relationships between gender role attitudes, role division, and perception of equity among heterosexual, gay and lesbian couples. *Sex Roles,* **56**(9–10), 629–638.

Sheese, B. E., & Graziano, W. G. (2005). Deciding to defect: The effects of videogame violence on cooperative behavior. *Psychological Science,* **16**, 354–357.

Shen, L. (2017). Putting the fear back again (and within individuals): Revisiting the role of fear in persuasion. *Health Communication,* **32**(11), 1331–1341. https://doi.org/10.1080/10410236.2016.1220043

Shepperd, J. A. (2003). Interpreting comparative risk judgments: Are people personally optimistic or interpersonally pessimistic? Unpublished manuscript, University of Florida.

Shepperd, J. A., & Taylor, K. M. (1999). Ascribing advantages to social comparison targets. *Basic and Applied Social Psychology,* **21**, 103–117.

Shepperd, J. A., Grace, J., Cole, L. J., & Klein, C. (2005). Anxiety and outcome predictions. *Personality and Social Psychology Bulletin,* **31**, 267–275.

Sherif, M. (1935). A study of some social factors in perception. *Archives of Psychology, 187.*

Sherif, M. (1937). An experimental approach to the study of attitudes. *Sociometry,* **1**, 90–98.

Sherif, M. (1958). Superordinate goals in the reduction of intergroup conflict. *American Journal of Sociology,* **63**(4), 349–356.

Sherif, M. (1966). *In common predicament: Social psychology of intergroup conflict and cooperation.* Houghton Mifflin.

Sherif, C. W., Sherif, M., & Nebergall, R. E. (1965). *Attitude and attitude change: The social judgment-involvement approach.* Greenwood Press. http://dx.doi.org.libezproxy.open.ac.uk/10.2307/2090931

Sherif, M., & Sherif, C. W. (1953). *Groups in harmony and tension: An integration of studies in intergroup behavior.* Harper & Row.

Sherif, M., & Sherif, C. W. (1964). *Reference groups.* Harper & Row.

Sherif, M., & Sherif, C. W. (1969). *Social psychology.* Harper & Row.

Sherif, M., Harvey, O. J., White, B. J., Hood, W., & Sherif, C. W. (1961). *Intergroup conflict and cooperation: The Robbers Cave experiment.* University of Oklahoma Institute of Intergroup Relations.

Sherry, J. L. (2001). The effects of violent video games on aggression: A meta-analysis. *Human Communication Research,* **27**(3), 409–431.

Shipman, P. (2003). We are all Africans. *American Scientist,* **91**, 496–499.

Shostak, M. (1981). *Nisa: The life and words of a !Kung woman.* Harvard University Press.

Shotland, R. L., & Straw, M. K. (1976). Bystander response to an assault: When a man attacks a woman. *Journal of Personality and Social Psychology,* **34,** 990–999.

Shotter, J. (1993). *The cultural politics of everyday life.* Open University Press.

Showers, C., & Ruben, C. (1987). Distinguishing pessimism from depression: Negative expectations and positive coping mechanisms. Paper presented at the American Psychological Association convention.

Sia, C. L., Tan, B. C. Y., & Wei, K. K. (2002). Group polarization and computer-mediated communication: Effects of communication cues, social presence, and anonymity. *Information Systems Research,* **13**(1), 70–90.

Sieff, E. M., Dawes, R. M., & Loewenstein, G. F. (1999). Anticipated versus actual responses to HIV test results. *American Journal of Psychology,* **112,** 297–311.

Siegel, A. E., & Siegel, S. (1957). Reference groups, membership groups and attitude change. *Journal of Abnormal and Social Psychology,* **55,** 360–364.

Siegel, E. F., Dougherty, M. R. & Huber, D. E. (2012). Manipulating the role of cognitive control while taking the implicit association test. *Journal of Experimental Social Psychology,* **48,** 1057–1068.

Siegfried, N., Pienaar, D. C., Ataguba, J. E., Volmink, J., Kredo, T., Jere, M., & Parry, C. D. H. (2014). Restricting or banning alcohol advertising to reduce alcohol consumption in adults and adolescents. *The Cochrane Database of Systematic Reviews, 11.* https://doi.org/10.1002/14651858.CD010704.pub2

Sillars, A., Smith, T., & Koerner, A. (2010). Misattributions contributing to empathic (in)accuracy during parent-adolescent conflict discussions. *Journal of Social and Personal Relationships,* **27**(6), 727–747.

Sillience, E., Briggs, P., Harris, P., & Fishwick, L. (2007). Going online for health advice: Changes in usage and trust practices over the last five years. *Interacting with Computers,* **19**(3), 397–406.

Silva, K., Bessa, J., & de Sousa, L. (2012). Auditory contagious yawning in domestic dogs (Canis familiaris): First evidence for social modulation. *Animal Cognition,* **15**(4), 721–724. https://doi.org/10.1007/s10071-012-0473-2

Silvia, P. J., & Duval, T. S. (2001). Objective self-awareness theory: Recent progress and enduring problems. *Personality and Social Psychology Review,* **5,** 230–241.

Silvia, P. J., & Phillips, A. G. (2013). Self-awareness without awareness? Implicit self-focused attention and behavioral self-regulation. *Self and Identity,* **12**(2), 114–127.

Simmons, J. P., Nelson, L. D., & Simonsohn, U. (2011). False-positive psychology undisclosed flexibility in data collection and analysis allows presenting anything as significant. *Psychological Science,* **22,** 1359–1366.

Simmons, W. W. (2000, December). When it comes to having children, Americans still prefer boys. *The Gallup Poll Monthly,* 63–64.

Simms, A., & Nichols, T. (2014). Social loafing: A review of the literature. *Journal of Management Policy and Practice,* **15**(1), 58–67.

Simon, H. A. (1957). *Models of man: Social and rational.* Wiley.

Simon, P. (1996, 17 April). American provincials. *Christian Century,* 421–422.

Simpson, J. A., Rholes, W. S., & Phillips, D. (1996). Conflict in close relationships: An attachment perspective. *Journal of Personality and Social Psychology,* **71,** 899–914.

Singh, D. (1993). Adaptive significance of female physical attractiveness: Role of waist-to-hip ratio. *Journal of Personality and Social Psychology,* **65,** 293–307.

Singh, D. (2004). Mating strategies of young women: Role of physical attractiveness. *Journal of Sex Research,* **41,** 43–54.

Singh, D., & Young, R. K. (1995). Body weight, waist-to-hip ratio, breasts, and hips: Role in judgments of female attractiveness and desirability for relationships. *Ethology and Sociobiology,* **16,** 483–507.

Singh, R., & Ho, S. J. (2000). Attitudes and attraction: A new test of the attraction, repulsion and similarity-dissimilarity asymmetry hypotheses. *British Journal of Social Psychology,* **39,** 197–211.

Singh, R., & Teoh, J. B. P. (1999). Attitudes and attraction: A test of two hypotheses for the similarity–dissimilarity asymmetry. *British Journal of Social Psychology,* **38,** 427–443.

Siu, A. M., Shek, D. T., & Law, B. (2012). Prosocial norms as a positive youth development construct: A conceptual review. *Scientific World Journal,* 832026. https://doi.org/10.1100/2012/832026

Sivarajasingam, V., Moore, S., & Shepherd, J. P. (2005). Winning, losing, and violence. *Injury Prevention,* **11,** 69–70.

Skinner, B. F. (1963). Operant behavior. *American Psychologist,* **18,** 503–515.

Skitka, L. J., Bauyman, C. W., & Sargis, E. G. (2005). Moral conviction: Another contributor to attitude strength or something more? *Journal of Personality and Social Psychology,* **88,** 895–917.

Skoe, E. E. A., Cumberland, A., Eisenberg, N., Hansen, K., & Perry, J. (2002). The influences of sex and gender role identity on moral cognition and prosocial personality traits. *Sex Roles,* **46**(9–10), 295–309.

Skurnik, I., Yoon, C., Park, D. C., & Schwarz, N. (2005). How warnings about false claims become recommendations. *Journal of Consumer Research,* **31,** 713–724.

Slade, C., Ribando, P., & Fortner, S. (2016). Faculty research following merger: A job stress and social identity theory perspective. *Scientometrics,* **107**(1), 71–89. https://doi.org/10.1007/s11192-016-1881-x

Slater, M., Antley, M., Davison, A., Swapp, D., Guger, C., Barker, C., Pistrang, N., & Sanchez-Vives, M. V. (2006). A virtual reprise of the Stanley Milgram obedience experiments. *PLoS ONE,* **1**(1), e39. https://doi.org/10.1371/journal.pone.0000039 (open access)

Slavin, R. E. (1985). Cooperative learning: Applying contact theory in desegregated schools. *Journal of Social Issues,* **41**(3), 45–62.

Slavin, R. E., Hurley, E. A., & Chamberlain, A. (2003). Cooperative learning and achievement: Theory and research. In W. M. Reynolds & G. E. Miller (Eds.), *Handbook of psychology: Educational psychology* (Vol. 7). Wiley.

Slovic, P. (1972). From Shakespeare to Simon: Speculations – and some evidence – about man's ability to process information. *Oregon Research Institute Research Bulletin,* **12**(2).

Slovic, P. (1992). Perception of risk: Reflections on the psychometric paradigm. In S. Krimsky & D. Golding (Eds.), *Social theories of risk* (pp. 117–152). Praeger.

Smallman, R., Ramos, A., Dickey, K., Dowd, S., & Fields, S. (2018). If only I wasn't so impulsive: Counterfactual thinking and delay-discounting, *Personality and Individual Differences,* **135,** 212–215.

Smirles, K. (2004). Attributions of responsibility in cases of sexual harassment: The person and the situation. *Journal of Applied Social Psychology,* **34**(2), 342–365.

Smith, A. (1759). *The theory of moral sentiments.* A. Millar.

Smith, C. A., & Stillman, S. (2002). What do women want? The effects of gender and sexual orientation on the desirability of physical attributes in the personal ads of women. *Sex Roles,* **46,** 337–341.

Smith, D. R., Devine, S. U. E., Leggat, P. A., & Ishitake, T. (2005). Alcohol and tobacco consumption among police officers. *The Kurume Medical Journal,* **52**(1+2), 63–65.

Smith, E. R., & Zarate, M. A. (1992). Exemplar-based model of social judgment. *Psychological Review,* **99,** 3–21.

Smith, H., & Pettigrew, J. (2015). Advances in relative deprivation theory and research. *Social Justice Research,* **28**(1), 1–6.

Smith, H. J., & Tyler, T. R. (1997). Choosing the right pond: The impact of group membership on self-esteem and group-oriented behavior. *Journal of Experimental Social Psychology,* **33,** 146–170.

Smith, J. R., Louis, W. R., Terry, D. J., Greenaway, K. H., Clarke, M. R., & Cheng, X. (2012). Congruent or conflicted? The impact of injunctive and descriptive norms on environmental intentions. *Journal of Environmental Psychology,* **32**(4), 353–361.

Smith, J., Tran, G. Q., & Thompson, R. D. (2008). Can the theory of planned behavior help explain men's psychological help-seeking? Evidence for a mediation effect and clinical implications. *Psychology of Men and Masculinity,* **9**(3), 179–192.

Smith, K., Alford, J., Hatemi, P., Eaves, L., Funk, C., & Hibbing, J. (2012). Biology, ideology, and epistemology: How do we know political attitudes are inherited and why should we care? *American Journal of Political Science,* **56**(1), 17–33. http://www.jstor.org.libezproxy.open.ac.uk/stable/23075141

Smith, L., Gilhooly, K., & Walker, A. (2003). Factors influencing prescribing decisions in the treatment of depression: A social judgement theory approach. *Applied Cognitive Psychology,* **17,** 51–63.

Smith, M. B. (1978). Psychology and values. *Journal of Social Issues,* **34,** 181–199.

Smith, P. B. (2005). Is there an indigenous European social psychology? *International Journal of Psychology,* **40,** 254–262.

Smith, R. (2018, 20 February). This country works the longest hours in Europe. *World Economic Forum.* https://www.weforum.org/agenda/2018/02/greeks-work-longest-hours-in-europe/

Smith, S. W., Atkin, C. K., Martell, D., Allen, R., & Hembroff, L. (2006). A social judgment theory approach to conducting formative research in a social norms campaign. *Communications Theory,* **16,** 141–152.

Smolenyak Smolenyak, M., & Turner, A. (2004). *Trace your roots with DNA: Using genetic tests to explore your family tree.* Rodale.

Snagowski, J., Wegmann, E., Pekal, J., Laier, C. & Brand, M. (2015). Implicit associations in cybersex addiction: Adaption of an Implicit Association Test with pornographic pictures. *Addictive Behaviors,* **49,** 7-12.

Snyder, C. R., & Fromkin, H. L. (1980). *Uniqueness: The human pursuit of difference.* Plenum Press.

Snyder, C. R., & Fromkin, H. L. (1980). *Uniqueness: The human pursuit of difference.* Plenum.

Snyder, C. R., & Higgins, R. L. (1988). Excuses: Their effective role in the negotiation of reality. *Psychological Bulletin,* **104,** 23–35.

Snyder, M. (1984). When belief creates reality. In L. Berkowitz (Ed.), *Advances in experimental social psychology* (Vol. 18). Academic Press.

Snyder, M. (1984). When belief creates reality. In L.Berkowitz (Ed.), *Advances in experimental social psychology* (Vol. 18). Academic Press.

Snyder, M. (1987). *Public appearances/private realities: The psychology of self-monitoring.* Freeman.

Snyder, M., Grether, J., & Keller, K. (1974). Staring and compliance: A field experiment on hitch-hiking. *Journal of Applied Social Psychology,* **4,** 165–170.

Snyder, M., Tanke, E. D., & Berscheid, E. (1977). Social perception and interpersonal behavior: On the self-fulfilling nature of social stereotypes. *Journal of Personality and Social Psychology,* **35,** 656–666.

Snyder, M., & Stukas, A. A. (1999). Interpersonal processes: The interplay of cognitive, motivational, and behavioral activities in social interaction. *Annual Review of Psychology,* **50,** 273–303.

Snyder, M., & Swann, W. B. Jr. (1978). Behavioral confirmation in social interaction: From social perception to social reality. *Journal of Experimental Social Psychology,* **14,** 148–162.

Sober, E., & Wilson, D. S. (1998). *Unto others: The evolution and psychology of unselfish behavior.* Harvard University Press.

Solomon, H., & Solomon, L. Z. (1978). Effects of anonymity on helping in emergency situations. Paper presented at the Eastern Psychological Association convention.

Solomon, H., Solomon, L. Z., Arnone, M. M., Maur, B. J., Reda, R. M., & Rother, E. O. (1981). Anonymity and helping. *Journal of Social Psychology,* **113,** 37–43.

Sorhagen, N. (2013). Early teacher expectations disproportionately affect poor children's high school performance. *Journal of Educational Psychology,* **105**(2), 465–477.

Sowden, S., Koletsi, S., Lymberopoulos, E., Militaru, E., Catmur, C., & Bird, G. (2018). Quantifying compliance and acceptance through public and private social conformity. *Consciousness and Cognition,* **65,** 359–367.

Spears, R., & Leach, C. W. (2004). Intergroup schadenfreude: Conditions and consequences. In L. Z. Tiedens & C. W. Leach (Eds.), *The social life of emotions: Studies in emotion and social interaction.* Cambridge University Press.

Spears, R., Ellemers, N., & Doosje, B. (2005). Let me count the ways in which I respect thee: Does competence compensate or compromise lack of liking from the group? *European Journal of Social Psychology,* **35,** 263–279.

Speer, A. (1971). *Inside the Third Reich: Memoirs* (P. Winston & C. Winston trans.). Avon Books.

Speer, A. (1971). *Inside the Third Reich: Memoirs* (P. Winston & C. Winston. trans.). New York: Avon Books.

Speer, S. A., & Stokoe, E. (2011). *Conversation and gender.* Cambridge University Press.

Spencer, C., Gee, K., & Sutton, J. (2009). The roots and branches of environmental psychology. *The Psychologist,* **22,** 180–183.

Spencer-Oatey, H., & Franklin, P. (2012). What is culture. *A Compilation of Quotations. GlobalPAD Core Concepts,* 1–22.

Spiegel, H. W. (1971). *The growth of economic thought.* Duke University Press.

Spitz, H. H. (1999). Beleaguered *Pygmalion:* A history of the controversy over claims that teacher expectancy raises intelligence. *Intelligence,* **27,** 199–234.

Spotts, E. L., Neiderhiser, J. M., Towers, H., Hansson, K., Lichtenstein, P., Cederblad, M., Pedersen, N. L., & Reiss, D. (2004). Genetic and environmental influences on marital relationships. *Journal of Family Psychology,* **18**(1), 107–119.

Sprecher, S. (2001). Equity and social exchange in dating couples: Associations with satisfaction, commitment, and stability. *Journal of Marriage and Family,* **63**(3), 599–613.

Sprecher, S., & Hendrick, S. S. (2004). Self-disclosure in intimate relationships: Associations with individual and relationship characteristics over time. *Journal of Social and Clinical Psychology,* **23**(6), 857–877.

Sprecher, S., & Toro-Morn, M. (2002). A study of men and women from different sides of Earth to determine if men are from Mars and women are from Venus in their beliefs about love and romantic relationships. *Sex Roles,* **46,** 131–147.

Sprecher, S., Sullivan, Q., & Hatfield, E. (1994b). Mate selection preferences: Gender differences examined in a national sample. *Journal of Personality and Social Psychology,* **66,** 1074–1080.

Spunt, R. P., & Lieberman, M. D. (2013). The busy social brain: Evidence for automaticity and control in the neural systems supporting social cognition and action understanding. *Psychological Science,* **24,** 80–86.

Squires, P. (2009). The knife crime 'epidemic' and British politics. *British Politics,* **4**(1), 127–157.

St. Claire, L., & Clucas, C. (2012). In sickness and in health: Influences of social categorizations on health-related outcomes. In J. Jetten, C. Haslam, & S. A. Haslam (Eds.), *The social cure: Identity, health and well-being.* Psychology Press.

St. Claire, L., & He, Y. (2009). How do I know if I need a hearing aid? Further support for the self-categorisation approach to symptom perception. *Applied Psychology,* **58,** 24–41.

Staats, A. W., & Staats, C. K. (1958). Attitudes established by classical conditioning. *Journal of Abnormal and Social Psychology,* **57**(1), 37–40.

Stahl, B. C., & Elbeltagi, I. (2004). Cultural universality versus particularity in CMC. *Journal of Global Information Technology Management,* **7**(4), 47–65.

Stangor, C., Jonas, K., Stroebe, W., & Hewstone, M. (1996). Influence of student exchange on national stereotypes, attitudes and perceived group variability. *European Journal of Social Psychology,* **26,** 663–675.

Stanley, I. H., Boffa, J. W., Smith, L. J., Tran, J. K., Schmidt, N. B., Joiner, T. E., & Vujanovic, A. A. (2018). Occupational stress and suicidality among firefighters: Examining the buffering role of distress tolerance. *Psychiatry Research,* **266,** 90–96.

Stanley, S., Edwards, V., Ibinarriaga-Soltero, B., & Krause, G. (2018). Awakening psychology: Investigating everyday life with social mindfulness. *Sage Research Methods Cases Part 2.* https://dx.doi.org/10.4135/9781526440853

Stark, R., & Bainbridge, W. S. (1980). Networks of faith: Interpersonal bonds and recruitment of cults and sects. *American Journal of Sociology,* **85,** 1376–1395.

Stasser, G. (1991). Pooling of unshared information during group discussion. In S. Worchel, W. Wood, & J. Simpson (Eds.), *Group process and productivity.* Sage.

Stattin, H., & Kerr, M. (2000). Parental monitoring: A reinterpretation. *Child Development,* **71,** 1070–1083.

Staub, E. (1989). *The roots of evil: The origins of genocide and other group violence.* Cambridge University Press.

Staub, E. (1991). Altruistic and moral motivations for helping and their translation into action. *Psychological Inquiry,* **2,** 150–153.

Staub, E. (1992). The origins of caring, helping and nonaggression: Parental socialization, the family system, schools, and cultural influence. In S. Oliner & P. Oliner (Eds.), *Embracing the other: Philosophical, psychological, and theological perspectives on altruism.* New York University Press.

Staub, E. (1996). Altruism and aggression in children and youth: Origins and cures. In R. Feldman (Ed.), *The psychology of adversity.* University of Massachusetts Press.

Staub, E. (1997). Blind versus constructive patriotism: Moving from embeddedness in the group to critical loyalty and action. In D. Bar-Tal and E. Staub (Eds.), *Patriotism in the lives of individuals and nations.* Nelson-Hall.

Staub, E. (1999). Behind the scenes. In D. G. Myers (Ed.), *Social psychology*(6th ed.). McGraw-Hill.

Staub, E. (2003). *The psychology of good and evil: Why children, adults, and groups help and harm others.* Cambridge University Press.

Staub, E. (2005a). The origins and evolution of hate, with notes on prevention. In R. J. Sternberg (Ed.), *The psychology of hate.* American Psychological Association.

Staub, E. (2005b). The roots of goodness: The fulfillment of basic human needs and the development of caring, helping and nonaggression, inclusive caring, moral courage, active bystandership, and altruism born of suffering. In G. Carlo & C. P. Edwards (Eds.), *Moral motivation through the life span: Theory, research, applications. Nebraska Symposium on Motivation, 51.* University of Nebraska Press.

Staub, E. (2006). Reconciliation after genocide, mass killing, or intractable conflict: Understanding the roots of violence, psychological recovery, and steps toward a general theory. *Political Psychology,* **27**(6), 867–894.

Staub, E., & Pearlman, L. A. (2005). Psychological recovery and reconciliation after the genocide in Rwanda and in other post-conflict settings. In R. Sternberg & L. Barbanel (Eds.), *Psychological interventions in times of crisis.* Springer-Verlag.

Staub, E., & Pearlman, L. A. (2006). Advancing healing and reconciliation. In R. Sternberg & L. Barbanel (Eds.), *Psychological interventions in times of crisis.* Springer.

Staub, E., Pearlman, L. A., Gubin, A., & Hagengimana, A. (2005). Healing, reconciliation, forgiving and the prevention of violence after genocide or mass killing: An intervention and its experimental evaluation in Rwanda. *Journal of Social and Clinical Psychology,* **24,** 297–334.

Steele, C. M. (1988). The psychology of self-affirmation: Sustaining the integrity of the self. In L. Berkowitz (Ed.), *Advances in experimental social psychology* (Vol. 21). Academic Press.

Steele, C. M., Southwick, L. L., & Critchlow, B. (1981). Dissonance and alcohol: Drinking your troubles away. *Journal of Personality and Social Psychology,* **41,** 831–846.

Stephan, W. G. (1986). The effects of school desegregation: An evaluation 30 years after *Brown.* In R. Kidd, L. Saxe, & M. Saks (Eds.), *Advances in applied social psychology.* Erlbaum.

Stephan, W. G. (1987). The contact hypothesis in intergroup relations. In C. Hendrick (Ed.), *Group processes and intergroup relations.* Sage.

Stephan, W. G. (1988). School desegregation: Short-term and long-term effects. Paper presented at the national conference 'Opening doors: An appraisal of race relations in America', University of Alabama.

Stephan, W. G., Berscheid, E., & Walster, E. (1971). Sexual arousal and heterosexual perception. *Journal of Personality and Social Psychology,* **20,** 93–101.

Stephens, A. N., & Ohtsuka, K. (2014). Cognitive biases in aggressive drivers: Does illusion of control drive us off the road? *Personality and Individual Differences,* **68,** 124–129.

Sternberg, R. J. (1988). Triangulating love. In R. J. Sternberg & M. L. Barnes (Eds.), *The psychology of love.* Yale University Press.

Sternberg, R. J. (1998). *Love is a story: A new theory of relationships.* Oxford University Press.

Sternberg, R. J. (2004). A triangular theory of love. In H. T. Reis & C. E. Rusbult (Eds.), *Close relationships: Key readings.* Taylor & Francis.

Sternberg, R. J. (2006). A duplex theory of love. In R. J. Sternberg & K. Weis (Eds.), *The new psychology of love.* Yale University Press.

Sternberg, R. J., & Grajek, S. (1984). The nature of love. *Journal of Personality and Social Psychology,* **47,** 312–329.

Stevenson, A., & Harper, S. (2006). Work stress and student learning experience. *Journal of Quality Assurance in Education,* **14**(2), 167–178.

Stewart, B. D., von Hippel, W., & Radvansky, G. A. (2009). Age, race, and implicit prejudice: Using process dissociation to separate the underlying components. Research Report, *Psychological Science,* **20**(2), 164–168.

Stewart-Knox, B. J., Sittlington, J., Rugkåsa, J., Harrisson, S., Treacy, M., & Abaunza, P. S. (2005). Smoking and peer groups: Results from a longitudinal qualitative study of young people in Northern Ireland. *British Journal of Social Psychology,* **44**(3), 397–414.

Stock, N. M., Whale, K., Jenkinson, E., Rumsey, N., & Fox, F. (2013). Young people's perceptions of visible difference. *Diversity and Equality in Health and Care,* **10,** 41–51.

Stocks, E. L., Lishner, D. A., & Decker, S. K. (2009). Altruism or psychological escape: Why does empathy promote prosocial behavior? *European Journal of Social Psychology,* **39**(5), 649–665.

Stokoe, E. H. (2000). Toward a conversation analytic approach to gender and discourse. *Feminism Psychology,* **10,** 552–563.

Stokoe, E. H. (2004). Gender and discourse, gender and categorization: Current developments in language and gender research. *Qualitative Research in Psychology,* **1**(2), 107–129.

Stone, A., & Wright, T. (2012). Evaluations of people depicted with facial disfigurement compared to those with mobility impairment. *Basic and Applied Psychology,* **34,** 212–225.

Stoner, J. (1968). Risky and cautious shifts in group decisions: The influence of widely held values. *Journal of Experimental Social Psychology,* **4,** 442–459.

Stoner, J. A. F. (1961). A comparison of individual and group decisions involving risk. Unpublished master's thesis, Massachusetts Institute of Technology, 1961. Cited by D. G. Marquis (1962). Individual responsibility and group decisions involving risk. *Industrial Management Review,* **3,** 8–23.

Stoner, J. A. F. (1961). *A comparison of individual and group decisions involving risk* (Doctoral dissertation, Massachusetts Institute of Technology). https://dspace.mit.edu/bitstream/handle/1721.1/11330/33120544-MIT.pdf

Stones, C. R. (2006). Antigay prejudice among heterosexual males: right-wing authoritarianism as a stronger predictor than social-dominance orientation and heterosexual identity. *Social Behavior and Personality,* **34**(9), 1137–1150.

Stopher, P. (2012). *Collecting, managing and assessing data in sample surveys.* Cambridge University Press. https://ebookcentral.proquest.com/lib/open/detail.action?docID=833420

Storms, M. D. (1973). Videotape and the attribution process: Reversing actors' and observers' points of view. *Journal of Personality and Social Psychology,* **27,** 165–175.

Storms, M. D. (1980). Theories of sexual orientation. *Journal of Personality and Social Psychology,* **38,** 783–792.

Storms, M. D. (1980). Theories of sexual orientation. *Journal of Personality and Social Psychology,* **38**(5), 783–792.

Story, P., & Forsyth, D. (2008). Watershed conservation and preservation: Environmental engagement as helping behavior. *Journal of Environmental Psychology,* **28**(4), 305–317.

Stott, C., & Reicher, S. (2011). *Mad mobs and Englishmen? Myths and realities of the 2011 riots.* Constable & Robinson.

Stott, C., Drury, J., & Reicher, S. (2017). On the role of a social identity analysis in articulating structure and collective action: The 2011 riots in Tottenham and Hackney. *British Journal of Criminology,* **57**(4), 964–981.

Stott, C., Hutchison, P., & Drury, J. (2001). 'Hooligans abroad?': Inter-group dynamics, social identity and participation in collective 'disorder' at the 1998 World Cup finals. *British Journal of Social Psychology,* **40**(3), 359–384.

Stotzer, R. L., & Hossellman, E. (2012). Hate crimes on campus racial/ethnic diversity and campus safety. *Journal of Interpersonal Violence,* **27**(4), 644–661.

Stouffer, S. A., Suchman, E. A., DeVinney, L. C., Star, S. A., & Williams, R. M. (1949). *The American soldier: Adjustment during army life* (Vol. 1). Princeton University Press.

Strack, F., & Deutsch, R. (2004). Reflective and impulsive determinants of social behavior. *Personality and Social Psychology Review,* **8**(3), 220–247.

Strassberg, D. S., & Holty, S. (2003). An experimental study of women's Internet personal ads. *Archives of Sexual Behaviour,* **32**(3), 253–260.

Straus, M. A., & Gelles, R. J. (1980). *Behind closed doors: Violence in the American family*. Anchor, Doubleday.

Streeter, S. A., & McBurney, D. H. (2003). Waist–hip ratio and attractiveness: New evidence and a critique of 'a critical test'. *Evolution and Human Behavior,* **24,** 88–98.

Stritzke, W. G. K., Nguyen, A., & Durkin, K. (2004). Shyness and computer-mediated communication: A self-presentational theory perspective. *Media Psychology,* **6**(1), 1–22. https://doi.org/10.1207/s1532785xmep0601_1

Stroebe, W., & Diehl, M. (1994). Productivity loss in idea-generating groups. In W. Stroebe & M. Hewstone (Eds.), *European review of social psychology* (Vol. 5). Wiley.

Stroebe, W., Lenkert, A., & Jonas, K. (1988). Familiarity may breed contempt: The impact of student exchange on national stereotypes and attitudes. In W. Stroebe & A. W. Kruglanski (Eds.), *The social psychology of intergroup conflict*. Springer-Verlag.

Strömwall, L. A., Alfredsson, H., & Landström, S. (2013). Rape victim and perpetrator blame and the just world hypothesis: The influence of victim gender and age. *Journal of Sexual Aggression,* **19,** 207–217.

Strong, S. R. (1978). Social psychological approach to psychotherapy research. In S. L. Garfield & A. E. Bergin (Eds.), *Handbook of psychotherapy and behavior change* (2nd ed.). Wiley.

Stroufe, B., Chaikin, A., Cook, R., & Freeman, V. (1977). The effects of physical attractiveness on honesty: A socially desirable response. *Personality and Social Psychology,* **3,** 59–62.

Subramani, M. R., & Rajagopalan, B. (2003). Knowledge-sharing and influence in online social networks via viral marketing. *Communications of the ACM,* **46**(12), 300–307.

Suciu, L. E., Mortan, M., & Lazar, L. (2013). Vroom's expectancy theory. An empirical study: Civil servant's performance appraisal influencing expectancy. *Transylvanian Review of Administrative Sciences,* **9**(39), 180–200.

Sugiyama, L. S. (2005). Physical attractiveness in adaptationist perspective. In D. M. Buss (Ed.), *The handbook of evolutionary psychology* (pp. 292–343). Wiley.

Sui, J., & Liu, C. H. (2009). Can beauty be ignored? Effects of facial attractiveness on covert attention. *Psychonomic Bulletin & Review,* **16,** 276–281.

Sullivan, D., Landau, M., Young, I., Stewart, S., & Smith, E. R. (2014). The dramaturgical perspective in relation to self and culture. *Journal of Personality and Social Psychology,* **107**(5), 767–790.

Sullivan, O. (2010). Changing differences by educational attainment in fathers' domestic labour and child care. *Sociology,* **44**(4), 716–733.

Suls, J., Wan, C. K., & Sanders, G. S. (1988). False consensus and false uniqueness in estimating the prevalence of health-protective behaviors. *Journal of Applied Social Psychology,* **18,** 66–79.

Sundblad, E.-L., Biel, A., & Gärling, T. (2009). Knowledge and confidence in knowledge about climate change among experts, journalists, politicians, and laypersons. *Environment and Behavior,* **41**(2), 281–302. https://doi.org/10.1177/0013916508314998

Surowiecki, J. (2004). *The wisdom of crowds*. Doubleday.

Svensson, A. (2011). Facebook – the social newspaper that never sleeps: A study of Facebook eWOM's persuasiveness on the receivers. MSc thesis. University of Gothenburg, https://gupea.ub.gu.se/bitstream/2077/26249/1/gupea_2077_26249_1.pdf

Swami, V., & Tovée, M. J. (2006). The influence of body mass index on the physical attractiveness preferences of feminist and nonfeminist heterosexual women and lesbians. *Psychology of Women Quarterly,* **30**(3), 252–257. https://doi.org/10.1111/j.1471-6402.2006.00293.x

Swann, W. B., Jr, & Gill, M. J. (1997). Confidence and accuracy in person perception: Do we know what we think we know about our relationship partners? *Journal of Personality and Social Psychology,* **73,** 747–757.

Swann, W. B., Jr, & Read, S. J. (1981). Acquiring self-knowledge: The search for feedback that fits. *Journal of Personality and Social Psychology,* **41,** 1119–1128.

Swann, W. B., Jr, Rentfrow, P. J., & Gosling, S. D. (2003). The precarious couple effect: Verbally inhibited men + critical, disinhibited women = bad chemistry. *Journal of Personality and Social Psychology,* **85,** 1095–1106.

Swann, W. B., Jr, Sellers, J. G., & McClarty, K. L. (2006). Tempting today, troubling tomorrow: The roots of the precarious couple effect. *Personality and Social Psychology Bulletin,* **32,** 93–103.

Swann, W. B., Jr, Stein-Seroussi, A., & Giesler, R. B. (1992a). Why people self-verify. *Journal of Personality and Social Psychology,* **62,** 392–401.

Swann, W. B., Jr, Stein-Seroussi, A., & McNulty, S. E. (1992b). Outcasts in a white lie society. The enigmatic worlds of people with negative self-conceptions. *Journal of Personality and Social Psychology,* **62,** 618–624.

Swann, W. B., Jr, Wenzlaff, R. M., Krull, D. S., & Pelham, B. W. (1991). Seeking truth, reaping despair: Depression, self-verification and selection of relationship partners. *Journal of Abnormal Psychology,* **101,** 293–306.

Swim, J. K. (1994). Perceived versus meta-analytic effect sizes: An assessment of the accuracy of gender stereotypes. *Journal of Personality and Social Psychology,* **66,** 21–36.

Symons, C. S., & Johnson, B. T. (1997). The self-reference effect in memory: A meta-analysis. *Psychological Bulletin,* **121,** 371–394.

Szu-Ting Fu, T., Koutstaal, W., Poon, L., & Cleare, A. J. (2012). Confidence judgment in depression and dysphoria: The depressive realism vs. negativity hypotheses. *Journal of Behavior Therapy and Experimental Psychiatry,* **43**(2), 699–704.

T

Tafarodi, R. W., Shaughnessy, S. C., Yamaguchi, S., & Murakoshi, A. (2011). The reporting of self-esteem in Japan and Canada. *Journal of Cross-Cultural Psychology,* **42**(1), 155–164. https://doi.org/10.1177/0022022110386373

Tahir, M. A. (2012). Determinants of psychological well-being and self-esteem in married and unmarried women. *Pakistan Journal of Clinical Psychology,* **11**(2). http://link.galegroup.com.libezproxy.open.ac.uk/apps/doc/A311675500/AONE?u=tou&sid=AONE&xid=d40f22aa

Tajfel, H. (1981). *Human groups and social categories: Studies in social psychology*. Cambridge University Press.

Tajfel, H. (1974). Social identity and intergroup behaviour. *Social Science Information,* **13**(2), 65–93.

Tajfel, H. (1978). *Differentiation between social groups*. Academic Press.

Tajfel, H. (1981). *Human groups and social categories: Studies in social psychology*. London: Cambridge University Press.

Tajfel, H., & Forgas, J. P. (1981). Social categorization: Cognitions, values, and groups. In J. P. Forgas (Ed.), *Social cognition: Perspectives on everyday understanding*. Academic Press.

Tajfel, H., & Turner, J. C. (1986). The social identity theory of intergroup behaviour. In S. Worchel & W. G. Austin (Eds.), *Psychology of intergroup relations* (2nd ed.). Nelson-Hall.

Tajfel, H., & Wilkes, A. L. (1963). Classification and quantitative judgment. *British Journal of Psychology,* **54,** 101–114.

Tajfel, H., Flament, C., Billig, M. G., & Bundy, R. F. (1971). Social categorization and intergroup behaviour. *European Journal of Social Psychology,* **1,** 149–177.

Tajfel, H., Sheikh, A. A., & Gardner, R. C. (1964). Content of stereotypes and the inference of similarity between members of stereotyped groups. *Acta Psychologica,* **22,** 191–201.

Takano, Y., & Sogon, S. (2008). Are Japanese more collectivistic than Americans? Examining conformity in in-groups and the reference-group effect. *Journal of Cross-Cultural Psychology,* **39**(3), 237–250.

Talbert, B. (1997, 2 February). Bob Talbert's quote bag. *Detroit Free Press,* p. 5E, quoting *Allure* magazine.

Tan, Y., Shaw, P., Cheng, H., & Kwangmi, K. (2013). The construction of masculinity: A cross-cultural analysis of men's lifestyle magazine advertisements. *Sex Roles,* **69**(5), 237–249. https://doi.org/10.1007/s11199-013-0300-5

Tandos, J., & Stukas, A. A. (2010). Identity negotiation in psychotherapy: The influence of diagnostic and rapport-building strategies on the effects of clinical expectations. *Self and Identity,* **9**(3), 241–256. https://doi.org/10.1080/15298860902979331

Tang, A., Van Lieshout, R., Lahat, A., Duku, E., Boyle, M., Saigal, S., & Schmidt, L. (2017). Shyness trajectories across the first four decades predict mental health outcomes. *Journal of Abnormal Child Psychology.* **45**(8), 1621–1633. doi: 10.1007/s10802-017-0265-x

Tang, S. H., & Hall, V. C. (1995). The overjustification effect: A meta-analysis. *Applied Cognitive Psychology,* **9**(5), 365–404.

Tarabah, A., Badr, L. K., Usta, J., & Doyle, J. (2016). Exposure to violence and children's desensitization attitudes in Lebanon. *Journal of Interpersonal Violence,* **31**(18), 3017–3038. https://doi.org/10.1177/0886260515584337

Tarrant, M., & Butler, K. (2011). Effects of self-categorization on orientation towards health. *British Journal of Social Psychology,* **50,** 121–139.

Tarrant, M., Hagger, M. S., & Farrow, C. V. (2012). Promoting positive orientation towards health through social identity. In J. Jetten, C. Haslam, & S. A. Haslam (Eds.), *The social cure: Identity, health and well-being.* Psychology Press.

Täuber, S., & van Leeuwen, E. (2012). When high group status becomes a burden. *Social Psychology,* **43**(2), 98–107.

Taylor, D. M., & Jaggi, V. (1974). Ethnocentrism and causal attribution in a South Indian context. *Journal of Cross-Cultural Psychology,* **5,** 162–171.

Taylor, S. E. (1983). Adjusting to threatening events: A theory of cognitive adaptation. *American Psychologist,* **38,** 1161–1173.

Taylor, S. E. (1989). *Positive illusions: Creative self-deception and the healthy mind.* Basic Books.

Taylor, S. E., & Brown, J. D. (1988). Illusion and well-being: A social psychological perspective on mental health. *Psychological Bulletin,* **103**(2), 193.

Taylor, S. E., Lerner, J. S., Sherman, D. K., Sage, R. M., & McDowell, N. K. (2003). Are self-enhancing cognitions associated with healthy or unhealthy biological profiles? *Journal of Personality and Social Psychology,* **85,** 605–615.

Taylor, S. P., & Chermack, S. T. (1993). Alcohol, drugs and human physical aggression. *Journal of Studies on Alcohol,* Supplement No. 11, 78–88.

Teigen, K. H., Evensen, P. C., Samoilow, D. K., & Vatne, K. B. (1999). Good luck and bad luck: How to tell the difference. *European Journal of Social Psychology,* **29,** 981–1010.

Tennant, C. (2001). Work-related stress and depressive disorders. *Journal of Psychosomatic Research,* **51**(5), 697–704.

Terry, D. J., & Hogg, M. A. (1996). Group norms and the attitude-behavior relationship: A role for group identification. *Personality and Social Psychology Bulletin,* **22,** 776–793.

Terwel, B. W., Harinck, F., Ellemers, N., & Daamen, D. D. L. (2009). How organizational motives and communications affect public trust in organizations: the case of carbon dioxide capture and storage. *Journal of Environmental Psychology,* **29,** 290–299.

Tesser, A. (1988). Toward a self-evaluation maintenance model of social behavior. In L. Berkowitz (Ed.), *Advances in experimental social psychology* (Vol. 21). Academic Press.

Testa, M. (2002). The impact of men's alcohol consumption on perpetration of sexual aggression. *Clinical Psychology Review,* **22,** 1239–1263.

Tetlock, P. E. (1998). Close-call counterfactuals and beliefsystem defenses: I was not almost wrong but I was almost right. *Journal of Personality and Social Psychology,* **75,** 639–652.

Tetlock, P. E. (1999). Theory-driven reasoning about plausible pasts and probable futures in world politics: Are we prisoners of our preconceptions? *American Journal of Political Science,* **43,** 335–366.

Tewari, S., Khan, S., Hopkins, N., Srinivasan, N., & Reichers, S. (2012). Participation in mass gatherings can benefit well-being: Longitudinal and control data from a North Indian Hindu pilgrimage event. *PLoS One,* **7,** e47291.

Teymoori, A., & Trappes, R. (2017). A revolution in thinking. *The Psychologist,* **30,** 92–95. https://thepsychologist.bps.org.uk/volume-30/july-2017/revolution-thinking

Thaler, R. H., & Sunstein, C. B. (2008). *Nudge: Improving decisions about health, wealth and happiness.* Yale University Press.

The Economist (2017, July 27). The rise of childlessness. https://www.economist.com/international/2017/07/27/the-rise-of-childlessness

Theeboom, T., Beersma, B., &van Vianen, A. E. M. (2014). Does coaching work? A meta-analysis on the effects of coaching on individual level outcomes in an organizational context. *Journal of Positive Psychology,* 9, 1–18. https://doi.org/10.1080/17439760.2013.837499

Theurer, K., & Wister, A. (2010). Altruistic behaviour and social capital as predictors of well-being among older Canadians. *Ageing and Society,* **30,** 157–181.

Thi, M. D. A., Brickley, D. B., Vinh, D. T. N., Colby, D. J., Sohn, A. H., Trung, N. Q., Giang le, T., & Mandel, J. S. (2008). A qualitative study of stigma and discrimination against people living with HIV in Ho Chi Minh City, Vietnam. *AIDS Behaviour,* **12,** 63–70.

Thøgersen, J. (2014). Unsustainable consumption: Basic causes and implications for policy. *European Psychologist,* **19,** 84–95. doi: 10.1027/1016-9040/a000176

Thompson, L. (1990a). An examination of naive and experienced negotiators. *Journal of Personality and Social Psychology,* **59,** 82–90.

Thompson, L. (1990b). The influence of experience on negotiation performance. *Journal of Experimental Social Psychology,* **26,** 528–544.

Thompson, L. (1998). *The mind and heart of the negotiator.* Prentice-Hall.

Thompson, L., Valley, K. L., & Kramer, R. M. (1995). The bittersweet feeling of success: An examination of social perception in negotiation. *Journal of Experimental Social Psychology,* **31,** 467–492.

Thompson, R., Olsen, Y., Mitchell, R., Davis, A., Rowland, S. & John, A. (2004). Lost at sea: Where is all the plastic? *Science,* **304,** 838.

Thornhill, N. W. (1991). An evolutionary analysis of rules regulating human inbreeding and marriage. *Behavioral and Brain Sciences,* **14**(2), 247–261. https://doi.org/10.1017/S0140525X00066449

Thorpe, R., Fileborn, B., Hawkes, G., Pitts, M., & Minichiello, V. (2015). Old and desirable: Older women's accounts of ageing bodies in intimate relationships. *Sexual and Relationship Therapy,* **30**(1), 156–166.

Thunberg, G. (2018, November). The disarming case to act right now on climate change. https://www.ted.com/talks/greta_thunberg_the_disarming_case_to_act_right_now_on_climate_change.

Thurstone, L. L. (1928a). Attitudes can be measured. *American Journal of Sociology,* **33,** 529–554.

Thurstone, L. L. (1928b). An experimental study of nationality preferences. *Journal of General Psychology,* **1,** 405–425.

Tice, D. M., Butler, J. L., Muraven, M. B., & Stillwell, A. M. (1995). When modesty prevails: Differential favorability of self-presentation to friends and strangers. *Journal of Personality and Social Psychology,* **69,** 1120–1138.

Tileaga, C. (2006). Representing the 'other': A discursive analysis of prejudice and moral exclusion in talk about Romanies. *Journal of Community and Applied Social Psychology,* **16,** 19–41.

Timmermans, A., Boer, C., & Werf, H. (2016). An investigation of the relationship between teachers' expectations and teachers' perceptions of student attributes. *Social Psychology of Education,* **19**(2), 217–240.

Tinkler, P., & Jackson, C. (2007). 'Ladettes' and 'modern girls': 'Troublesome' young femininities. *The Sociological Review,* **55**(2), 251–272.

Todd, A. R., Molden, D. C., Ham, J., & Vonk, R. (2011). The automatic and co-occurring activation of multiple social inferences. *Journal of Experimental Social Psychology,* **47,** 37–49.

Todorov, A., Harris, L. T., & Fiske, S. T. (2006). Toward socially inspired social neuroscience. *Brain Research,* **1079**(1), 76–85.

Tolich, M. (2014). What can Milgram and Zimbardo teach ethics committees and qualitative researchers about minimizing harm? *Research Ethics,* **10**(2), 86–96. https://doi.org/10.1177/1747016114523771

Toma, C. L., & Hancock, J. T. (2010). Looks and lies: The role of physical attractiveness in online dating self-presentation and deception. *Communication Research,* **37**(3), 335–351.

Tomlinson, M. F., Brown, M., & Hoaken, P. N. (2016). Recreational drug use and human aggressive behavior: A comprehensive review since 2003. *Aggression and Violent Behavior,* **27,** 9–29. https://doi.org.10.1016/j.avb.2016.02.004

Tomorrow, T. (2003, 30 April). Passive tense verbs deployed before large audience; stories remain unclear. www.240.pair.com/tomtom/pages/ja/ja_fr.html

Torma, G., Aschemann-Witzel, J., & Thøgersen, J. (2018). I nudge myself: Exploring 'self-nudging' strategies to drive sustainable consumption behaviour. *International Journal of Consumer Studies,* **42**(1), 141–154.

Tosun Altınöz, Ş., Altınöz, A. E., Utku, Ç., Eşsizoğlu, A., & Candansayar, S. (2018). Femicide: Psychosocial characteristics of the perpetrators in Turkey. *International Journal of Offender Therapy and Comparative Criminology,* **62**(13), 4174–4186. https://doi.org/10.1177/0306624X18763765

Totterdell, P., Kellett, S., Teuchmann, K., & Briner, R. B. (1998). Evidence of mood linkage in work groups. *Journal of Personality and Social Psychology,* **74**(6), 1504.

Tovée, M. J., Swami, V., Furnham, A., & Mangalparsad, R. (2006). Changing patterns of attractiveness as observers are exposed to a different culture. *Evolution and Human Behavior,* **27**, 443–456.

Traut-Mattausch, E., Schulz-Hardt, S., Greitemeyer, T., & Frey, D. (2004). Expectancy confirmation in spite of disconfirming evidence: The case of price increases due to the introduction of the Euro. *European Journal of Social Psychology,* **34**, 739–760.

Travis, L. E. (1925). The effect of a small audience upon eye–hand coordination. *Journal of Abnormal and Social Psychology,* **20**, 142–146.

Trewin, D. (2001). *Australian social trends 2001.* Australian Bureau of Statistics.

Triandis, H. C. (1982). Incongruence between intentions and behavior: A review. Paper presented at the American Psychological Association convention.

Triandis, H. C., Bontempo, R., Villareal, M. J., Asai, M., & Lucca, N. (1988). Individualism and collectivism: Cross-cultural perspectives on self-ingroup relationships. *Journal of Personality and Social Psychology,* **54**, 323–338.

Triplett, N. (1898). The dynamogenic factors in pacemaking and competition. *American Journal of Psychology,* **9**, 507–533.

Trivers, R. L. (1971). The evolution of reciprocal altruism. *Quarterly Review of Biology,* **46**(1), 35–57.

Trivers, R. (2006). Reciprocal altruism: 30 years later. In P. M. Kappeler & C. P. van Schaik (Eds.), *Cooperation in primates and humans.* Springer.

Tromholt, M. (2016). The Facebook experiment: Quitting Facebook leads to higher levels of well-being. *Cyberpsychology, Behavior and Social Networking,* **19**(11), 661–666.

Tropp, L. R., & Pettigrew, T. F. (2005a). Differential relationships between intergroup contact and affective and cognitive dimensions of prejudice. *Personality and Social Psychology Bulletin,* **31**, 1145–1158.

Tropp, L. R., & Pettigrew, T. F. (2005b). Relationships between intergroup contact and prejudice among minority and majority status groups. *Psychological Science,* **16**, 951–957.

Trudgill, P. (1974). *Sociolinguistics: An introduction to language and society.* Penguin Books.

Trusov, M., Bucklin, R. E., & Pauwels, K. (2009). Effects of word-of-mouth versus traditional marketing: findings from an internet social networking site. *Journal of Marketing,* **73**(5), 90–102.

Trut, L., Oskina, I., & Kharlamova, A. (2009). Animal evolution during domestication: The domesticated fox as a model. *Biological Essays,* **31**, 349–360.

Trzesniewski, K. H., & Donnellan, M. B. (2010). Rethinking 'generation me': A study of cohort effects from 1976–2006. *Perspectives on Psychological Science,* **5**, 58–75.

Trzesniewski, K. H., & Donnellan, M. B. (2009). Reevaluating the evidence for increasingly positive self-views among high school students: More evidence for consistency across generations (1976–2006). *Psychological Science,* **20**, 920–922.

Tsai, C.-C., & Chang, C.-H. (2007). The effect of physical attractiveness of models on advertising effectiveness for male and female adolescents. *Adolescence,* **42**, 827–836.

Tsai, W. C., Huang, T. C., & Yu, H. H. (2012). Investigating the unique predictability and boundary conditions of applicant physical attractiveness and non-verbal behaviours on interviewer evaluations in job interviews. *Journal of Occupational and Organizational Psychology,* **85**(1), 60–79.

Tsang, J.-A. (2002). Moral rationalization and the integration of situational factors and psychological processes in immoral behavior. *Review of General Psychology,* **6**, 25–50.

Tse, A. C. B., & Lee, R. P. W. (2001). Zapping behavior during commercial breaks. *Journal of Advertising Research,* **41**(3), 25–29.

Tsikerdekis, M. (2013). The effects of perceived anonymity and anonymity states on conformity and groupthink in online communities: A Wikipedia study. *Journal of the American Society for Information Science and Technology,* **64**(5), 1001–1015.

Tsintsadze-Maass, E., & Maass, R. (2014). Groupthink and terrorist radicalization. *Terrorism and Political Violence,* **26**(5), 735–758.

Turanovic, J. J., Pratt, T. C., & Piquero, A. R. (2017). Exposure to fetal testosterone, aggression, and violent behavior: A meta-analysis of the 2D:4D digit ratio. *Aggression and Violent Behavior,* **33**, 51–61. https://doi.org/10.1016/j.avb.2017.01.008.

Turner, J. C. (1984). Social identification and psychological group formation. In H. Tajfel (Ed.), *The social dimensions: European developments in social psychology* (Vol. 2). Cambridge University Press.

Turner, J. C. (1987). *Rediscovering the social group: A self-categorization theory.* Basil Blackwell.

Turner, J. C. (1991). *Social influence.* Brooks/Cole.

Turner, J. C. & Bourhis, R. Y. (1996). Social identity, interdependence and the social group: A reply to Rabbie et al. In W. P. Robinson (Ed.), *Social groups and identities: Developing the legacy of Henri Tajfel* (pp. 25–63). Butterworth-Heinemann.

Turner, J. C., & Oakes, P. J. (1997). The socially structured mind. In C. McGarty & S. A. Haslam (Eds.), *The message of social psychology.* Blackwell.

Turner, J. C., Hogg, M. A., Oakes, P. J., Reicher, S. D., & Wetherell, M. (1987). *Rediscovering the social group: A self-categorisation theory.* Blackwell.

Turner, M. E., & Pratkanis, A. R. (1997). Mitigating groupthink by stimulating constructive conflict. In C. K. W. De Dreu & E. Van de Vliert (Eds.), *Using conflict in organizations.* Sage.

Turner, M. E., & Pratkanis, A. R. (1998). Twenty-five years of groupthink theory and research: Lessons from the evaluation of a theory. *Organizational Behavior and Human Decision Processes,* **73**(2–3), 105–115.

Turner, M. E., Pratkanis, A. R., Probasco, P., & Leve, C. (1992). Threat cohesion and group effectiveness: Testing a social identity maintenance perspective on groupthink. *Journal of Personality and Social Psychology,* **63**, 781–796.

Turner, R. H., & Killian, L. M. (1972). *Collective behaviour.* Prentice-Hall.

Turner, R. N., Hewstone, M., & Voci, A. (2007). Reducing explicit and implicit outgroup prejudice via direct and extended contact: The mediating role of self-disclosure and intergroup anxiety. *Journal of Personality and Social Psychology,* **93**(3), 369–388.

Turton, P., Evans, C., & Hughes, P. (2009). Long-term psychosocial sequelae of stillbirth: Phase II of a nested case-control cohort study. *Archives of Women's Mental Health,* **12**(1), 35–41. https://doi.org/10.1007/s00737-008-0040-7.

Tversky, A., & Kahneman, D. (1974). Judgment under uncertainty: Heuristics and biases. *Science, New Series,* **185**(4157), 1124–1131.

Tversky, A., & Kahneman, D. (1983). Extensional versus intuitive reasoning: The conjunction fallacy in probability judgment. *Psychological Review,* **90**, 293–315.

Twenge, J. M. (2006). *Generation me.* Free Press.

Twenge, J. M., & Campbell, W. K. (2009). *The narcissism epidemic: Living in an age of entitlement.* The Free Press.

Twenge, J. M., & Campbell, W. K. (2010). Birth cohort differences in the monitoring the future dataset and elsewhere: Further evidence for generation me – Commentary on Trzesniewski & Donnellan (2010). *Perspectives on Psychological Science,* **5**, 81–88.

Twenge, J. M., & Campbell, W. K. (2013). *The narcissism epidemic: Living in the age of entitlement.* Atria.

Twenge, J. M., Catanese, K. R., & Baumeister, R. F. (2003). Social exclusion and the deconstructed state: Time perception, meaninglessness, lethargy, lack of emotion, and self-awareness. *Journal of Personality and Social Psychology,* **85**, 409–423.

Twenge, J. M., Konrath, S., Foster, J. D., Campbell, W. K., & Bushman, B. J. (2008). Egos inflating over time: A cross-temporal meta-analysis of the Narcissistic Personality Inventory. *Journal of Personality,* **76**, 875–901.

Tyler, T. R., & De Cremer, D. (2005). Process-based leadership: Fair procedures and reactions to organizational change. *The Leadership Quarterly,* **16**(4), 529–545.

Tyler, T. R., & Lind, E. A. (1990). Intrinsic versus community-based justice models: When does group membership matter? *Journal of Social Issues,* **46,** 83–94.

U

Uleman, J. S. (1989). A framework for thinking intentionally about unintended thoughts. In J. S. Uleman & J. A. Bargh (Eds.), *Unintended thought: The limits of awareness, intention, and control.* Guilford Press.

UN News (2018, 30 April). Nations begin drafting 'operating manual' for climate action at UN conference in Bonn. https://news.un.org/en/story/2018/04/1008572

UN Office on Drugs and Crime. (2019). *Global study on homicide.* https://www.unodc.org/gsh/

Unger, R. K. (1985). Epistemological consistency and its scientific implications. *American Psychologist,* **40,** 1413–1414.

United Nations (1991). *The world's women 1970–1990: Trends and statistics.* United Nations.

United Nations Office on Drugs and Crime (UNODC) (2018). *Global study on homicide: Gender-related killing of women and girls.* https://www.unodc.org/documents/data-and-analysis/GSH2018/GSH18_Gender-related_killing_of_women_and_girls.pdf

Uphold-Carrier, H., & Utz, R. (2012). Parental divorce among young and adult children: A long-term quantitative analysis of mental health and family solidarity. *Journal of Divorce & Remarriage,* **53**(4), 247–266.

Urbaniak, G. C., & Kilmann, P. R. (2006). Niceness and dating success: A further test of the nice guy stereotype. *Sex Roles,* **55**(3–4), 209–224.

Uzzell, D., & Horne, N. (2006). The influence of biological sex, sexuality and gender role on interpersonal distance. *British Journal of Social Psychology,* **45,** 579–597.

V

Väänänen, A., Buunk, B. P., Kivimäki, M., Pentti, J., &Vahtera, J. (2005). When it is better to give than to receive: Long-term health effects of perceived reciprocity in support exchange. *Journal of Personality and Social Psychology,* **89,** 176–193.

Vaillancourt, T. (2012). Students aggress against professors in reaction to receiving poor grades: An effect moderated by student narcissism and self-esteem. *Aggressive Behavior,* **39,** 71–84.

Valkenburg, P. M., & Peter, J. (2007). Who visits online dating sites? Exploring some characteristics of online daters. *CyberPsychology & Behavior,* **10**(6), 849–852.

Vallone R. P., Griffin, D. W., Lin, S., & Ross, L. (1990). Overconfident prediction of future actions and outcomes by self and others. *Journal of Personality and Social Psychology,* **58**(4), 582.

Van Aelst, P., Maddens, B., Noppe, J., & Fiers, S. (2008). Politicians in the news: Media or party logic? Media attention and electoral success in the Belgian election campaign of 2003. *European Journal of Communication,* **23**(2), 193–210.

van Baaren, R. B., Holland, R. W., Karremans, R. W., & van Knippenberg, A. (2003a). Mimicry and interpersonal closeness. Unpublished manuscript, University of Nijmegen.

Van Baaren, R. B., Holland, R. W., Kawakami, K., & van Knippenberg, A. (2004). Mimicry and prosocial behavior. *Psychological Science,* **15,** 71–74.

van Baaren, R. B., Holland, R. W., Steenaert, B., & van Knippenberg, A. (2003b). Mimicry for money: Behavioral consequences of imitation. *Journal of Experimental Social Psychology,* **39,** 393–398.

van Bommel, M., van Prooijen, J. W., Elffers, H., & van Lange, P. A. (2016). Booze, bars, and bystander behavior: People who consumed alcohol help faster in the presence of others. *Frontiers in Psychology,* **7,** 128. https://doi.org/10.3389/fpsyg.2016.00128

Van Boven, L., & Gilovich, T. (2003). To do or to have? That is the question. *Journal of Personality and Social Psychology,* **85,** 1193–1202.

Van Boven, L., & Loewenstein, G. (2003). Social projection of transient drive states. *Personality and Social Psychology Bulletin,* **29,** 1159–1168.

Van Dijke, M., De Cremer, D., Brebels, L., & Van Quaquebeke, N. (2015). Willing and able: Action-state orientation and the relation between procedural justice and employee cooperation. *Journal of Management,* **41**(7), 1982–2003.

Van Dijk, T. A. (1992). Discourse and the denial of racism. *Discourse and Society,* **3,** 87–118.

Van Dijk, T. A. (1993). *Elite discourses and racism.* Sage.

Van Kleef, G. A., Van den Berg, H., & Heerdink, M. W. (2015). The persuasive power of emotions: Effects of emotional expressions on attitude formation and change. *Journal of Applied Psychology,* **100**(4), 1124–1142.

Van Laar, C., Levin, S., Sinclair, S., & Sidanius, J. (2005). The effect of university roommate contact on ethnic attitudes and behavior. *Journal of Experimental Social Psychology,* **41,** 329–345.

Van Lange, P. A., & Visser, K. (1999). Locomotion in social dilemmas: How people adapt to cooperative, tit-for-tat, and noncooperative partners. *Journal of Personality and Social Psychology,* **77**(4), 762.

Van Leeuwen, E., & Täuber, S. (2011). Demonstrating knowledge: The effects of group status on outgroup helping. *Journal of Experimental Social Psychology,* **47,** 147–156.

Van Norel, Nienke D., Kommers, Piet A.M., Van Hoof, Joris J., & Verhoeven, Joost W.M. (2014). Damaged corporate reputation: Can celebrity Tweets repair it?*Computers in Human Behavior,* **36,** 308–315.

Van Zoonen, K., Kleiboer, A., Cuijpers, P., Smit, J., Penninx, B., Verhaak, P., & Beekman, A. (2016). Determinants of attitudes towards professional mental health care, informal help and self-reliance in people with subclinical depression. *International Journal of Social Psychiatry,* **62**(1), 84-93.

Vandello, J. A., & Cohen, D. (2003). Male honor and female fidelity: Implicit cultural scripts that perpetuate domestic violence. *Journal of Personality and Social Psychology,* **84**(5), 997–1010.

VanderLaan, D. P., & Vasey, P. L. (2011). Relationship status and elevated avuncularity in Samoan fa'afafine. *Personal Relationships,* **19,** 326–339. https://doi.org/10.1111=j.1475-6811.2011.01364.x

Vares, T. (2009). Reading the 'sexy oldie': Gender, age(ing) and embodiment. *Sexualities,* **12**(4), 503–524.

Vasey, P. L., & VanderLaan, D. P. (2010). Avuncular tendencies in Samoan fa'afafine and the evolution of male androphilia. *Archives of Sexual Behavior,* **39,** 821–830. https://doi.org/10.1007=S10508-008-9404-3

Vazire, S., & Carlson, E. N. (2010). Self-knowledge of personality: Do people know themselves? *Social and Personality Psychology Compass,* **4,** 605–620.

Vazire, S., & Gosling, S. D. (2004). e-Perceptions: Personality impressions based on personal websites. *Journal of Personality and Social Psychology,* **87,** 123–132.

Vazire, S., & Wilson, T. D. (2012). *Handbook of self-knowledge.* Guilford Press.

Verbakel, E., & Kalmijn, M. (2014). Assortative mating among Dutch married and cohabiting same-sex and different-sex couples. *Journal of Marriage and Family,* **76**(1), 1–12.

Verhoeven, A., Adriaanse, M., De Vet, E., Fennis, B., & De Ridder, D. (2014). Identifying the 'if' for 'if-then' plans: Combining implementation intentions with cue-monitoring targeting unhealthy snacking behaviour. *Psychology & Health,* **29**(12), 1–33.

Verkooijen, K. T., de Vries, N. K., & Nielsen, G. A. (2007). Youth crowds and substance use: The impact of perceived group norm and multiple group identification. *Psychology of Addictive Behaviors,* **21,** 55–61.

Verkooijen, K., Stok, F., & Mollen, S. (2015). The power of regression to the mean: A social norm study revisited. *European Journal of Social Psychology,* **45**(4), 417–425.

Verplanken, B. (1991). Persuasive communication of risk information: A test of cue versus message processing effects in a field experiment. *Personality and Social Psychology Bulletin,* **17,** 188–193.

Verrastro, V., Petruccelli, I., Diotaiuti, P., Petruccelli, F., Dentale, F., & Barbaranelli, C. (2016). Self-serving bias in the implicit and explicit evaluation of partners and exes as parents: A pilot study. *Psychological Reports,* **118**(1), 251–265.

Veysey, B. M., & Messner, S. F. (1999). Further testing of social disorganization theory: An elaboration of Sampson and Groves's 'Community structure and crime'. *Journal of Research in Crime and Delinquency,* **36,** 156–174.

Viala, E. S. (2011). Contemporary family life: A joint venture with contradictions. *Nordic Psychology,* **63**(2), 68–87.

Vignoles, V. L., Chryssochoou, X., & Breakwell, G. M. (2000). The distinctiveness principle: Identity, meaning, and the bounds of cultural relativity. *Personality and Social Psychology Review,* **4,** 337–354.

Vignoles, V. L., Regalia, C., Manzi, C., Golledge, J., & Scabini, E. (2006). Beyond self-esteem: Influence of multiple motives on identity construction. *Journal of Personality and Social Psychology,* **90,** 308–333.

Villa, M. (2017, January 11). Women own less than 20% of the world's land: It's time to give them equal property rights. *World Economic Forum:* https://www.weforum.org/agenda/2017/01/women-own-less-than-20-of-the-worlds-land-its-time-to-give-them-equal-property-rights

Villanueva, L. S. (2017). Interpersonal closeness, self-disclosure and attachment styles of university students in the Philippines. *Journal of Education and Social Sciences,* **6**(2). https://www.jesoc.com/wp-content/uploads/2017/04/KC6_28.pdf

Vincent, W., Parrott, D. J., & Peterson, J. L. (2011). Combined effects of masculine gender–role stress and sexual prejudice on anger and aggression toward gay men. *Journal of Applied Social Psychology,* **41**(5), 1237–1257.

Visser, P. S., & Krosnick, J. A. (1998). Development of attitude strength over the life cycle: Surge and decline. *Journal of Personality and Social Psychology,* **75,** 1389 –1410.

Visser, P. S., & Mirabile, R. R. (2004). Attitudes in the social context: The impact of social network composition on individual-level attitude strength. *Journal of Personality and Social Psychology,* **87,** 779–795.

Vollum, S., & Buffington-Vollum, J. (2010). An examination of social-psychological factors and support for the death penalty: Attribution, moral disengagement, and the value-expressive function of attitudes. *American Journal of Criminal Justice,* **35,** 15–36.

Von Cranach, M. (1986). Leadership as a function of group action. In C. F. Graumann & S. Moscovici (Eds.), *Changing conceptions of leadership.* Springer-Verlag.

Von Hippel, W., Sekaquaptewa, D., & Vargas, P. (1997). The linguistic intergroup bias as an implicit indicator of prejudice. *The Journal of Experimental and Social Psychology,* **33,** 490–509.

Vonofakou, C., Hewstone, M., & Voci, A. (2007). Contact with out-group friends as a predictor of meta-attitudinal strength and accessibility of attitudes towards gay men. *Journal of Personality and Social Psychology,* **92**(5), 804–820.

Vorauer, J. D., & Sakamoto, Y. (2008). Who cares what the outgroup thinks? Testing an information search model of the importance individuals accord to an outgroup member's view of them during intergroup interaction. *Journal of Personality and Social Psychology,* **95,** 1467–1480.

Vorauer, J. D., Main, K. J., & O'Connell, G. B. (1998). How do individuals expect to be viewed by members of lower status groups? Content and implications of meta-stereotypes. *Journal of Personality and Social Psychology,* **75**(4), 917.

Vroom, V. (1964). *Work and motivation.* Wiley & Sons.

Vroom, V. H., & Jago, A. G. (1988). *The new leadership: Managing participation in organizations.* Prentice-Hall.

Vroom, V. H., & Jago, A. G. (2007). The role of the situation in leadership. *American Psychologist,* **62**(1), 17–24.

Vroom, V. H., & Yetton, P. W. (1973). *Leadership and decision-making.* University of Pittsburgh Press.

W

Wagenaar, W. A. (1988). *Paradoxes of gambling behaviour.* Lawrence Erlbaum.

Wagner, J., Hoppmann, C., Ram, N., & Gerstorf, D. (2015). Self-esteem is relatively stable late in late life: The role of resources in the health, self-regulation, and social domains. *Developmental Psychology,* **51**(1), 136–149.

Wagner, J., Voelkle, M. C., Hoppmann, C. A., Luszcz, M. A., & Gerstorf, D. (2018). We are in this together: Dyadic patterns of self-esteem change in late-life couples. *International Journal of Behavioral Development,* **42**(1), 34–42. https://doi.org/10.1177/0165025416679742

Wakefield, J. R. H., Bickley, S., & Sani, F. (2013). The effects of identification with a support group on the mental health of people with multiple sclerosis. *Journal of Psychosomatic Research,* **74,** 420–426.

Wakefield, J. R., Bowe, M., Kellezi, B., McNamara, N., & Stevenson, C. (2019). When groups help and when groups harm: Origins, developments, and future directions of the 'Social Cure' perspective of group dynamics. *Social and Personality Psychology Compass,* **13**(3), e12440.

Wakefield, J. R., Hopkins, N., & Greenwood, R. M. (2012). Thanks, but no thanks: Women's avoidance of help-seeking in the context of a dependency-related stereotype. *Psychology of Women Quarterly,* **36**(4), 423–431.

Walker, R. (2004, 5 December). The hidden (in plain sight) persuaders. *New York Times Magazine:* www.nytimes.com.

Wall, R., Devine-Wright, P., & Mill, G. A. (2007). Comparing and combining theories to explain proenvironmental intentions: The case of commuting-mode choice. *Environment and Behavior,* **39**(6), 731–753.

Walla, P., Brenner, G., & Koller, M. (2011). Objective measures of emotion related to brand attitude: A new way to quantify emotion-related aspects relevant to marketing. *PloS One,* **6**(11), e26782.

Wallace, B. (2013). *Getting Darwin wrong: Why evolutionary psychology won't work.* Andrews UK Limited.

Waller, J. (2002). *Becoming evil: How ordinary people commit genocide and mass killing.* Oxford.

Waller, T., Lampman, C., & Lupfer-Johnson, G. (2012). Assessing bias against overweight individuals among nursing and psychology students: An implicit association test. *Journal of Clinical Nursing,* **21**(23-24), 3504–3512.

Walsh, A., & Yun, I. (2016). Evoked culture and evoked nature: The promise of gene-culture co-evolution theory for sociology, *Frontiers in Sociology,* **1,** 1–8. https://doi.org/10.3389/fsoc.2016.00008

Walster (Hatfield), E. (1965). The effect of self-esteem on romantic liking. *Journal of Experimental Social Psychology,* **1,** 184–197.

Walster (Hatfield), E., & Festinger, L. (1962). The effectiveness of 'overheard' persuasive communications. *Journal of Abnormal and Social Psychology,* **65,** 395–402.

Walster, E., Aronson, V., Abrahams, D., & Rottman, L. (1966). Importance of physical attractiveness in dating behavior. *Journal of Personality and Social Psychology,* **4,** 508-516

Walther, J. B. (2007). Selective self-presentation in computer-mediated communication: Hyperpersonal dimensions of technology, language and cognition, *Computers in Human Behavior,* **23,** 2538-2557.

Walther, J. B., van der Heide, B., Kim, S-Y., Westerman, D., & Tong, S. T. (2008). The role of friends' appearance and behaviour on evaluations of individuals on Facebook: Are we known by the company we keep? *Human Communication Research,* **34,** 28–49.

Wang, M., & Chen, Y. (2006). Age differences in attitude change: Influences of cognitive resources and motivation on responses to argument quantity. *Psychology and Aging,* **21**(3), 581–589. https://doi.org/10.1037/0882-7974.21.3.581

Wang, M. T., Eccles, J. S., & Kenny, S. (2013). Not lack of ability but more choice individual and gender differences in choice of careers in science, technology, engineering, and mathematics. *Psychological Science,* **24**(5), 770–775.

Wang, Q., Yang, X., & Xi, W. (2018). Effects of group arguments on rumor belief and transmission in online communities: An information cascade and group polarization perspective. *Information & Management,* **55**(4), 441–449.

Wang, X., Pipes, L., Trut, L. N., Herbeck, Y., Vladimirova, A. V., Gulevich, R. G., Kharlamova, A. V., Johnsond, J. L., Aclande, G. M., Kukekova, A. V., & Clark, A. G. (2018). Genomic responses to selection for tame/aggressive behaviors in the silver fox (*Vulpes vulpes*). *Proceedings of the National Academy of Sciences,* **115**(41), 10398–10403.

Ward, W. C., & Jenkins, H. M. (1965). The display of information and the judgment of contingency. *Canadian Journal of Psychology,* **19,** 231–241.

Ware, L. J., Lassiter, G. D., Patterson, S. M., & Ransom, M. R. (2008). Camera perspective bias in videotaped confessions: Evidence that visual attention is a mediator. *Journal of Experimental Psychology: Applied,* **14**(2), 192–200.

Warneken, F., & Tomasello, M. (2006). Altruistic helping in human infants and young chimpanzees. *Science,* **311,** 1301–1303.

Warneken, F., & Tomasello, M. (2008). Extrinsic rewards undermine altruistic tendencies in 20-month-olds. *Developmental Psychology,* **44**(6), 1785–1788.

Warneken, F., & Tomasello, M. (2014). Extrinsic rewards undermine altruistic tendencies in 20-month-olds. *Motivation Science,* **1,** 43–48. https://doi.org/10.1037/2333-8113.1.S.43.

Warnick, D. H., & Sanders, G. S. (1980). The effects of group discussion on eyewitness accuracy. *Journal of Applied Social Psychology,* **10**, 249–259.

Warren, N. C. (2005, March 4). Personal correspondence from founder of eHarmony.com.

Warszewska-Makuch, M., Bedyńska, S., & Żołnierczyk-Zreda, D. (2015). Authentic leadership, social support and their role in workplace bullying and its mental health consequences. *International Journal of Occupational Safety and Ergonomics,* **21**(2), 128–140. https://doi.org/10.1080/10803548.2015.1028230

Wason, P. C. (1960). On the failure to eliminate hypotheses in a conceptual task. *Quarterly Journal of Experimental Psychology,* **12**, 129–140.

Watson, D. (1982, November). The actor and the observer: How are their perceptions of causality divergent? *Psychological Bulletin,* **92**, 682–700.

Watson, D. C. (2012). Gender differences in gossip and friendship. *Sex Roles, 67*(9–10), 494–502.

Watson, D., Klohnen, E. C., Casillas, A., Nus Simms, E., Haig, J., & Berry, D. S. (2004). Match makers and deal breakers: Analyses of assortative mating in newlywed couples. *Journal of Personality,* **72**, 1029–1068.

Weatherall, A., & Holland, M. M. (2018). Using discursive psychology and conversation analysis to study 'obedience' and 'defiance' in Milgram's experiments. *SAGE Research Methods Cases Part 2.* https://dx.doi.org/10.4135/9781526449160

Weaver, A. D., MacKeigan, K. L., & MacDonald, H. A. (2011). Experiences and perceptions of young adults in friends with benefits relationships: A qualitative study. *Canadian Journal of Sexuality,* **20**(1), 41–53.

Weaver, J., Filson Moses, J., & Snyder, M. (2016). Self-fulfilling prophecies in ability settings. *Journal of Social Psychology,* **156**(2), 179–189.

Webb, T. L., & Sheeran, P. (2006). Does changing behavioral intentions engender behavior change? A meta-analysis of the experimental evidence. *Psychological Bulletin,* **132**, 249–268.

Wegge, J., Schuh, S. C., & van Dick, R. (2012). 'I feel bad', 'we feel good'? Emotions as a driver for personal and organizational identity and organizational identification as a resource for serving unfriendly customers. *Stress and Health,* **28**, 123–136.

Wegner, D. M. (2002). *The illusion of conscious will.* MIT Press.

Wegner, D. M., Sparrow, B., & Winerman, L. (2004). Vicarious agency: Experiencing control over the movements of others. *Journal of Personality and Social Psychology,* **86**, 838–848.

Wehr, P. (1979). *Conflict regulation.* Westview Press.

Wei, R., Lo, V.-H., & Wu, H. (2010). Internet pornography and teen sexual attitudes and behavior. (Report). *China Media Research,* **6**(3), 66.

Weiner, B. (1980). A cognitive (attribution)-emotion-action model of motivated behavior: An analysis of judgments of help-giving. *Journal of Personality and Social Psychology,* **39**, 186–200.

Weiner, B. (1986). *An attribution theory of motivation and emotion.* Springer.

Weiner, B. (1995). *Judgments of responsibility: A foundation for a theory of social conduct.* Guilford Press.

Weiner, B. (2006). *Social motivation, justice, and the moral emotions. An attributional approach.* Lawrence Erlbaum.

Weinstein, N. D. (1980). Unrealistic optimism about future life events. *Journal of Personality and Social Psychology,* **39**, 806–820.

Weinstein, N. D. (1982). Unrealistic optimism about susceptibility to health problems. *Journal of Behavioral Medicine,* **5**, 441–460.

Weitzman, A., Cowan, S., & Walsh, K. (2017). Bystander interventions on behalf of sexual assault and intimate partner violence victims. *Journal of Interpersonal Violence,* 1–25. https://doi.org/10.1177/0886260517696873

Wells, G. L., & Petty, R. E. (1980). The effects of overt head movements on persuasion: Compatibility and incompatibility of responses. *Basic and Applied Social Psychology,* **1**, 219–230.

Wells, S., Graham, K., Speechley, M., & Koval, J. (2005). Drinking patterns, drinking contexts and alcohol-related aggression among late adolescent and young adult drinkers. *Addiction,* **100**, 933–944. https://doi.org/10.1111/j.1360-0443.2005.001121.x

Wentz, E., Nyden, A., & Krevers, B. (2012). Development of an internet-based support and coaching model for adolescents and young adults with ADHD and autism spectrum disorders: A pilot study. *European Child Adolescent Psychiatry,* **21**, 611–622. https://doi.org/10.1007/s00787-012-0297-2

Werner, C. M., Stoll, R., Birch, P., & White, P. H. (2002). Clinical validation and cognitive elaboration: Signs that encourage sustained recycling. *Basic and Applied Social Psychology,* **24**, 185–203.

Werner, K., & Dickson, G. (2018). Coworker knowledge sharing and peer learning among elite footballers: Insights from German Bundesliga players. *Sport Management Review,* **21**(5), 596–611. https://doi.org/10.1016/j.smr.2018.02.001

West, S. G., & Brown, T. J. (1975). Physical attractiveness, the severity of the emergency and helping: A field experiment and interpersonal simulation. *Journal of Experimental Social Psychology,* **11**, 531–538.

West, S. G., Whitney, G., & Schnedler, R. (1975). Helping a motorist in distress: The effects of sex, race, and neighborhood. *Journal of Personality and Social Psychology,* **31**, 691–698.

Westrup, U., & Planader, A. (2013). Role-play as a pedagogical method to prepare students for practice: The students' voice. *Higher Education,* **3**, 199–210.

Wetherell, M., & Maybin, J. (1996). The distributed self: A social constructionist perspective. In R. Stevens (Ed.), *Understanding the self* (1). Sage.

Wetherell, M., & Potter, J. (1992). *Mapping the language of racism: Discourse and the legitimation of exploitation.* Harvester Wheatsheaf.

White, J. W., & Kowalski, R. M. (1994). Deconstructing the myth of the nonaggressive woman: A feminist analysis. *Psychology of Women Quarterly,* **18**, 487–508.

White, K., & Lehman, D. R. (2005). Culture and social comparison seeking: The role of self-motives. *Personality and Social Psychology Bulletin,* **31**, 232–242.

Whitehead, A.N. (1911). *An introduction to mathematics.* Henry Holt & Co.

Whitehead, J., Thomas, J., Forkner, B., & Lamonica, D. (2012). Reluctant gatekeepers: 'Trans-positive' practitioners and the social construction of sex and gender. *Journal of Gender Studies,* **21**(4), 387–400.

Whittaker, J. O., & Meade, R. D. (1967). Social pressure in the modification and distortion of judgment: A crosscultural study. *International Journal of Psychology,* **2**, 109–113.

Whitty, M. T. (2008). Revealing the 'real' me, searching for the 'actual' you: Presentations of self on an Internet dating site. *Computers in Human Behavior,* **24**, 1707–1723.

Whitty, M. T., & Young, G. (2016). *Cyberpsychology:The study of individuals, society and digital technologies.* John Wiley & Sons.

Wicker, A. W. (1969). Attitudes versus actions: The relationship of verbal and overt behavioral responses to attitude objects. *Journal of Social Issues,* **25**, 41–78.

Wicklund, R. A., & Braun, O. L. (1987). Incompetence and the concern with human categories. *Journal of Personality & Social Psychology,* **53**, 373–382.

Wiemer, J., & Pauli, P. (2016). Fear-relevant illusory correlations in different fears and anxiety disorders: A review of the literature. *Journal of Anxiety Disorders,* **42**, 113–128.

Wieselquist, J., Rusbult, C. E., Foster, C. A., & Agnew, C. R. (1999). Commitment, pro-relationship behavior, and trust in close relationships. *Journal of Personality and Social Psychology,* **77**, 942–966.

Wilde, O.F.O.W. (1895). *The importance of being earnest,* Act III.

Wilder, D. A., & Shapiro, P. N. (1984). Role of out-group cues in determining social identity. *Journal of Personality and Social Psychology,* **47**, 342–348.

Williams, J. E., Satterwhite, R. C., & Best, D. L. (1999). Pancultural gender stereotypes revisited: The Five Factor model. *Sex Roles,* **40**, 513–525.

Williams, J. E., Satterwhite, R. C., & Best, D. L. (2000). Five-factor gender stereotypes in 27 countries. Paper presented at the XV Congress of the International Association for Cross-Cultural Psychology, Pultusk, Poland.

Williams, K. D., & Karau, S. J. (1991). Social loafing and social compensation: The effects of expectations of coworker performance. *Journal of Personality and Social Psychology,* **61**, 570–581.

Williams, K., Harkins, S. G., & Latané, B. (1981). Identifiability as a deterrant to social loafing: Two cheering experiments. *Journal of Personality and Social Psychology,* **40**(2), 303.

Williams, R. (2014). Facebook's 71 gender options come to UK users. *The Telegraph*, 27 June:https://www.telegraph.co.uk/technology/facebook/10930654/Facebooks-71-gender-options-come-to-UK-users.html

Willis, M. (2012, October 15). Forgettable study sparks sexist headlines about women remembering. *The Conversation:* http://theconversation.com/forgettable-study-sparks-sexist-headlines-about-women-remembering-10112

Wills, T. A. (1981). Downward comparison principles in social psychology. *Psychological Bulletin,* **90,** 245–271. http://dx.doi.org/10.1037/0033-2909.90.2.245

Wilson, A. E., Allen, J. W., Strahan, E. J., & Ethier, N. (2008). Getting involved: Testing the effectiveness of a volunteering intervention on young adolescents' future intentions. *Journal of Community and Applied Social Psychology,* **18**(6), 630–637.

Wilson, E. O. (1975). *Sociobiology: The new synthesis.* Harvard University Press.

Wilson, E. O. (1978). *On human nature.* Harvard University Press.

Wilson, J. Q., & Kelling, G. L. (1982). Broken windows. *Atlantic Monthly,* **249**(3), 29–38.

Wilson, T. D., & Gilbert, D. T. (2005). Affective forecasting: Knowing what to want. *Current Directions in Psychological Science,* **14,** 131–134.

Wilson, W. R. (1979). Feeling more than we can know: Exposure effects without learning. *Journal of Personality and Social Psychology,* **37,** 811–821.

Winch, R. F. (1958). *Mate selection: A study of complementary needs.* Harper & Row.

Winegard, B. M., Winegard, B. M., & Deaner, R. O. (2014). Misrepresentations of evolutionary psychology in sex and gender textbooks. *Evolutionary Psychology.* https://doi.org/10.1177/147470491401200301

Wines, M. (2005, 23 September). Crime in South Africa grows more vicious. *New York Times:* www.nytimes.com.

Winstone, W., & Gervis, M. (2006). Countertransference and the self-aware sport psychologist: Attitudes and patterns of professional practice. *The Sport Psychologist,* **20**(4), 495–511. https://doi.org/10.1123/tsp.20.4.495

Wise Campaign (2019). Statistics: Latest stats on women and girls' participation in STEM in the UK. https://www.wisecampaign.org.uk/statistics/

Wisman, A., & Koole, S. L. (2003). Hiding in the crowd: Can mortality salience promote affiliation with others who oppose one's worldviews? *Journal of Personality and Social Psychology,* **84,** 511–526.

Wittenbrink, B., Judd, C. M., & Park, B. (1997). Evidence for racial prejudice at the implicit level and its relationship with questionnaire measures. *Journal of Personality and Social Psychology,* **72,** 262–274.

Wodak, R. (2009). *The discourse of politics in action: Politics as usual.* Palgrave Macmillan.

Wodak, R., & Meyer, M. (2009). *Methods for critical discourse analysis.* Sage.

Wohl, M. J. A., & Enzle, M. E. (2002). The deployment of personal luck: Sympathetic magic and illusory control in games of pure chance. *Personality and Social Psychology Bulletin,* **28,** 1388–1397.

Wohl, M. J. A., Salmon, M. A., Hollingshead, S. J., & Kim, H. S. (2017). An examination of the relationship between social casino gaming and gambling: The bad, the ugly and the good. *Journal of Gambling Issues,* **35,** 1–23.

Wolf, S. (1987). Majority and minority influence: A social impact analysis. In M. P. Zanna, J. M. Olson, & C. P. Herman (Eds.), *Social influence: The Ontario symposium on personality and social psychology* (Vol. 5). Erlbaum.

Wolf, S., & Latané, B. (1985). Conformity, innovation and the psycho-social law. In S. Moscovici, G. Mugny & E. Van Avermaet (Eds.), *Perspectives on minority influence.* Cambridge University Press.

Wolfradt, U., & Dalbert, C. (2003). Personality, values and belief in a just world. *Personality and Individual Differences,* **35,** 1911–1918.

Wong, C. L., Harris, J. A., & Gallate, J. E. (2012). Evidence for a social function of the anterior temporal lobes: Low-frequency rTMS reduces implicit gender stereotypes. *Social Neuroscience,* **7,** 90–104.

Wood, J. V., Heimpel, S. A., & Michela, J. L. (2003). Savoring versus dampening: Self-esteem differences in regulating positive affect. *Journal of Personality and Social Psychology,* **85,** 566–580.

Wood, R. T. A., & Griffiths, M. D. (2004). Adolescent lottery and scratchcard players: Do their attitudes influence their gambling behaviour? *Journal of Adolescence,* **27,** 467–475.

Woodzicka, J. A., & LaFrance, M. (2001). Real versus imagined gender harassment. *Journal of Social Issues,* **57**(1), 15–30.

Worchel, S. (1998). A developmental view of the search for group identity. In S. Worchel, J. F. Morales, D. Páez, & J.-C. Deschamps (Eds.), *Social identity: International perspectives.* Sage.

Worchel, S., & Norvell, N. (1980). Effect of perceived environmental conditions during cooperation on intergroup attraction. *Journal of Personality and Social Psychology,* **38,** 764–772.

Worchel, S., Andreoli, V. A., & Folger, R. (1977). Intergroup cooperation and intergroup attraction: The effect of previous interaction and outcome of combined effort. *Journal of Experimental Social Psychology,* **13,** 131–140.

Worchel, S., Axsom, D., Ferris, F., Samah, G., & Schweitzer, S. (1978). Deterrents of the effect of intergroup cooperation on intergroup attraction. *Journal of Conflict Resolution,* **22,** 429–439.

Workman, M. (2010). A behaviourist perspective on corporate harassment online: Validation of a theoretical model of psychological motives. *Computers & Security,* **29,** 831–839.

World Health Organization (2012). Femicide: Understanding and addressing violence against women. https://www.who.int/reproductivehealth/publications/violence/rhr12_38/en/

Wright, E. F., Lüüs, C. A., & Christie, S. D. (1990). Does group discussion facilitate the use of consensus information in making causal attributions? *Journal of Personality and Social Psychology,* **59,** 261–269.

Wright, R. (2003, June 29). Quoted by Thomas L. Friedman, 'Is Google God?' *New York Times:* www.nytimes.com.

Wright, S. C., & Bougie, E. (2007). Intergroup contact and minority-language education: Reducing language-based discrimination and its negative impact. *Journal of Language and Social Psychology,* **26**(2), 157–181.

Wu, K., Garcia, S., & Kopelman, S. (2018). Frogs, ponds, and culture: Variations in entry decisions. *Social Psychological and Personality Science,* **9**(1), 99–106.

Wuchty, S., Jones, B. F., & Uzzi, B. (2007). The increasing dominance of teams in production of knowledge. *Science,* **316,** 1036–1039.

Wundt, W. (1916). *Elements of folk psychology: Outlines of a psychological history of the development of mankind.* Allen & Unwin (German original 1912).

Wyland, C., & Forgas, J. (2010). Here's looking at you kid: Mood effects on processing eye gaze as a heuristic cue. *Social Cognition,* **28**(1), 133-144.

Y

Yan, Y., & Bissell, K. (2014). The globalization of beauty: How is ideal beauty influenced by globally published fashion and beauty magazines? *Journal of Intercultural Communication Research,* **43**(3), 194–214.

Yang, H., Ramasubramanian, S., & Oliver, M. B. (2008). Cultivation effects on quality of life indicators: Exploring the effects of American television consumption on feelings of relative deprivation in South Korea and India. *Journal of Broadcasting & Electronic Media,* **52**(2), 247–267.

Yanowitch, R., & Coccaro, E. F. (2011). The neurochemistry of human aggression. *Advances in Genetics* A, *75,* 151–169. http://doi.org/10.1016/B978-0-12-380858-5.00005-8

Yonezawa, T., Sato, K., Uchida, M., Matsuki, N., & Yamazaki, A. (2016). Presence of contagious yawning in sheep. *Animal Science Journal,* **88**(1), 195–200. https://doi.org/10.1111/asj.12681

Yong, E. (2012). Bad copy. *Nature,* **485,** 298–300.

York, R. (2007). Demographic trends and energy consumption in European Union Nations, 1960–2025. *Social Science Research,* **36**(3), 855-872.

Young, C. M., DiBello, A. M., Traylor, Z. K., Zvolensky, M. J., & Neighbors, C. (2015). A longitudinal examination of the associations between shyness, drinking motives, alcohol use, and alcohol-related problems. *Alcoholism, Clinical and Experimental Research,* **39**(9), 1749–1755. https://doi.org/10.1111/acer.12799

Young, R., Sweeting, H., & West, P. (2007). A longitudinal study of alcohol use and antisocial behaviour in young people. *Alcohol and Alcoholism,* 30 October, 1–11. https://doi.org/10.1093/alcalc/agm147

Young, S. G., & Hugenberg, K. (2010). Mere social categorization modulates identification of facial expressions of emotion.

Journal of Personality and Social Psychology, **99**, 964–977.

Yousif, Y., & Korte, C. (1995). Urbanization, culture, and helpfulness. *Journal of Cross-Cultural Psychology*, **26**, 474–489.

Yovetich, N. A., & Rusbult, C. E. (1994). Accommodative behavior in close relationships: Exploring transformation of motivation. *Journal of Experimental Social Psychology*, **30**, 138–164.

Yukl, G. (1974). Effects of the opponent's initial offer, concession magnitude, and concession frequency on bargaining behavior. *Journal of Personality and Social Psychology*, **30**, 323–335.

Z

Zagefka, H., & Brown, R. (2005). Comparisons and perceived-deprivation in ethnic minority settings. *Personality and Social Psychology Bulletin*, **31**, 467–482.

Zagefka, H., Noor, M., Brown, R., de Moura, G. R., & Hopthrow, T. (2011). Donating to disaster victims: Responses to natural and humanly caused events. *European Journal of Social Psychology*, **41**(3), 353–363.

Zajonc, R. B. (1965). Social facilitation. *Science*, **149**, 269–274.

Zajonc, R. B. (1968). Attitudinal effects of mere exposure. *Journal of Personality and Social Psychology*, **9**(2), 1–27.

Zajonc, R. B. (1970, February). Brainwash: Familiarity breeds comfort. *Psychology Today*, **3**, 32–35, 60–62.

Zajonc, R. B. (1980). Feeling and thinking: Preferences need no inferences. *American Psychologist*, **35**, 151–175.

Zajonc, R. B. (1998). Emotions. In D. Gilbert, S. T. Fiske & G. Lindzey (Eds.), *Handbook of social psychology* (4th ed.). McGraw-Hill.

Zajonc, R. B. (2000). Massacres: Mass murders in the name of moral imperatives. Unpublished manuscript, Stanford University.

Zajonc, R. B., Reimer, D. J., & Hausser, D. (1973). Imprinting and the development of object preference in chicks by mere repeated exposure. *Journal of Comparative and Physiological Psychology*, **83**, 434–440.

Zamboanga, B. L., Ham, L. S., Tomaso, C. C., Audley, S., & Pole, N. (2016). 'Try walking in our shoes': Teaching acculturation and related cultural adjustment processes through role-play. *Teaching of Psychology*, **43**(3), 243–249. https://doi.org/10.1177/0098628316649484

Zanna, M. P. (1993). Message receptivity: A new look at the old problem of open- vs closed-mindedness. In A. Mitchell (Ed.), *Advertising: Exposure, memory and choice*. Erlbaum.

Zanna, M. P., & Olson, J. M. (1982). Individual differences in attitudinal relations. In M. P. Zanna, E. T. Higgins, & C. P. Herman (Eds.), *Consistency in social behavior: The Ontario symposium* (Vol. 2). Erlbaum.

Zanna, M. P., & Rempel, J. K. (1988). Attitudes: A new look at an old concept. In D. Bar-Tal and A. Kruglanski (Eds.), *The social psychology of knowledge*. Cambridge University Press.

Zebrowitz, L. A., & Montepare, J. A. (2008). Social psychological face perception: Why appearance matters. *Social and Personality Psychology Compass*, **2**(3), 1497–1517.

Zebrowitz-McArthur, L. (1988). Person perception in cross-cultural perspective. In M. H. Bond (Ed.), *The cross-cultural challenge to social psychology*. Sage.

Zhang, G., & Veenhoven, R. (2008). Ancient Chinese philosophical advice: Can it help us find happiness today? *Journal of Happiness Studies*, **9**, 425–443.

Zhao, J., Hahn, U., &Osherson, D. (2014). Perception and identification of random events. *Journal of Experimental Psychology: Human Perception and Performance*, **40**, 1358–1371.

Zilioli, S., Sell, A. N., Stirrat, M., Jagore, J., Vickerman, W., & Watson, N. V. (2015). Face of a fighter: Bizygomatic width as a cue of formidability. *Aggressive Behavior*, **41**(4), 322-330.

Zillman, D. (1979). *Hostility and aggression*. Erlbaum.

Zillmann, D. (1989b). Effects of prolonged consumption of pornography. In D. Zillmann & J. Bryant (Eds.), *Pornography: Research advances and policy considerations*. Erlbaum.

Zillmann, D., & Bryant, J. (1974). Effect of residual excitation on the emotional response to provocation and delayed aggressive behavior. *Journal of Personality and Social Psychology*, **30**(6), 782–791.

Zillmann, D., & Weaver, J. B., III (1999). Effects of prolonged exposure to gratuitous media violence on provoked and unprovoked hostile behavior. *Journal of Applied Social Psychology*, **29**, 145–165.

Zillmer, E. A., Harrower, M., Ritzler, B., & Archer, R. P. (1995). *The quest for the Nazi personality: A psychological investigation of Nazi war criminals*. Erlbaum..

Zimbardo, P. G. (1970). The human choice: Individuation, reason, and order versus deindividuation, impulse, and chaos. In W. J. Arnold & D. Levine (Eds.), *Nebraska symposium on motivation, 1969*. University of Nebraska Press.

Zimbardo, P. G. (2007). *The Lucifer effect: Understanding how good people turn evil*. Random House

Zimmer, C. (2005, November). The neurobiology of the self. *Scientific American*, 93–101.

Zollo, F., & Quattrociocchi, W. (2018). Misinformation spreading on Facebook. In S. Lehmann and Y. Y. Ahen (Eds.), *Complex spreading phenomena in social systems: Influence and contagion in real-world social networks* (pp. 177–196). Springer.

Zuckerman, E. W., & Jost, J. T. (2001). What makes you think you're so popular? Self-evaluation maintenance and the subjective side of the 'friendship paradox'. *Social Psychology Quarterly*, **64**, 207–223.

Name Index

B

D

E

F

G

H

I

J

K

L

N

O

P

Q

R

S

T

U

V

Y

Z

Subject Index

A

D

G

H

I

J

Q

R